THE OXFORD HANDBOOK OF

GLOBAL STUDIES

THE OXFORD HANDBOOK OF

GLOBAL STUDIES

Edited by

MARK JUERGENSMEYER
SASKIA SASSEN
MANFRED B. STEGER

Managing Editor

VICTOR FAESSEL

OXFORD
UNIVERSITY PRESS

OXFORD
UNIVERSITY PRESS

Oxford University Press is a department of the University of Oxford. It furthers
the University's objective of excellence in research, scholarship, and education
by publishing worldwide. Oxford is a registered trade mark of Oxford University
Press in the UK and certain other countries.

Published in the United States of America by Oxford University Press
198 Madison Avenue, New York, NY 10016, United States of America.

© Oxford University Press 2019

Library of Congress Cataloging-in-Publication Data
Names: Juergensmeyer, Mark, editor. | Sassen, Saskia, editor. |
Steger, Manfred, editor. | Faessel, Victor, editor.
Title: The Oxford handbook of global studies / edited by Mark Juergensmeyer,
Saskia Sassen, Manfred B Steger, Victor Faessel.
Description: New York : Oxford University Press, [2018]
Identifiers: LCCN 2018008310 | ISBN 9780190630577 (Hard Cover) |
ISBN 9780190630584 (updf) | ISBN 9780190630591 (epub)
Subjects: LCSH: Globalization—Study and teaching.
Classification: LCC JZ1318 .O96 2018 | DDC 303.48/2—dc23
LC record available at https://lccn.loc.gov/2018008310

Contents

PART III GLOBAL CONCERNS: ISSUES AND THEMES AT THE CORE OF GLOBAL RESEARCH AND TEACHING

PART IV GLOBAL CITIZENSHIP: IDEAS AND INSTITUTIONS FOR AN EMERGING GLOBAL WORLD

PREFACE

THE emergence of a new field of studies is both an exciting and daunting venture, and the *Oxford Handbook of Global Studies* has been crafted to respond to both of these aspects—to show the significance of the field and to explore some of the issues that are related to its development. Since the end of the Cold War, globalization has been reshaping the modern world. New technologies facilitate the movement of people, goods, services, money, ideas, and culture across political borders more easily and quickly than ever before. Despite the growing mountain of digitalized information readily accessible in real-time to billions around the world, globalization has unsettled people's familiar frames of reference. New sources of insecurity and disruption are reflected in a public discourse that increasingly revolves around global issues such as transnational migration, global terrorism, pandemics, global financial crises, the planetary climate crisis, and the widening North-South inequality gap. Increasingly anti-globalism has become a global phenomenon, manifested by protest movements against immigration and international trade. And these are but the most prominent entries in a long list of global challenges that reach deeply into every aspect of daily life.

Responding to these global issues effectively requires the generation and implementation of new ideas that go beyond the traditional academic framework of the twentieth century. In particular, a better understanding is needed regarding how the local has become entangled with the global in the myriad ways that have profoundly shaped how daily lives are conducted in the twenty-first century. This imperative to grasp these complex global dynamics stands at the very center of a new transdisciplinary effort—global studies—to reorder human knowledge and create innovative learning environments. Indeed, demand for individual courses and for curricula designed for undergraduate and graduate degrees in global studies has dramatically risen in academic centers around the world. Increasingly, the terms "global" or "globalization" are included in course titles, textbooks, academic job postings, and extracurricular activities. Moreover, an array of new scholarship has risen to make sense of it in its various transnational manifestations—including economic, social, cultural, ideological, technological, environmental, and in new communications. These topics have been studied through traditional and novel approaches, and the *Handbook* will explore the various aspects of this emerging field.

This means there is a lot to cover in a single volume, beginning with the question of what global studies actually is. Several essays focus on this question, how the field developed, and what are its historical antecedents. Other essays explore analytic and conceptual approaches to teaching and research in global studies, and the largest section deals with the subject matter of global studies, challenges from migration and new media to the global city and the emergence of a transnational capitalist class. The final sections look at aspects of the new global society—the ideas and institutions that have appeared to provide the elements of a worldwide civil order in the global era.

This *Handbook* focuses on global studies more than on the phenomenon of globalization itself, though the various aspects of globalization are central to understanding how the field is currently being shaped. Indeed, global studies both embraces and exudes a certain *mentalité* that might be called the "global imaginary." Giving its objective and subjective aspects equal consideration, global studies suggests that enhanced interconnectivity does not merely happen in the world "out there" but also operates through our consciousness "in here." To recognize the significance of global consciousness, however, does not support premature proclamations of the death of the nation-state. Conventional national and local frameworks have retained significant power. Although the nation-state is not disappearing, it is true that it has been forced by globalization to seek sometimes rather uneasy accommodations with a slowly evolving architecture of global governance—an embryonic form of global society that can no longer be derided as a utopian pipedream.

For these reasons, the topics listed in the section on *global concerns* should not be taken to be an exhaustive list of what global studies is about, but rather an attempt to highlight some of the issues that are central to the research and teaching programs of the global studies field. Many of these topics are embraced by other disciplines, from economics to history and cultural studies, and appropriately so. The term "global studies" demarcates not only programs and departments that bear that name, but to the many efforts to globalize existing disciplines in courses and programs that focus on global sociology, for example, or global history. This *Handbook* will provide a resource for these disciplines as well as for the many new programs that are specifically called "global studies."

Throughout the essays in this *Handbook* are attempts to think globally about global studies. By that are meant efforts to look at global phenomena with varied lenses—to "decolonialize global studies," as one author put it—and not privilege any particular geographic, ideological, political, or gendered point of view. This diversity will be found throughout the volume, though critical perspectives on global studies are highlighted in essays that focus on the view of globalization from the global South, for example, and from a feminist perspective.

Then there is the matter of diversity of approaches to the study of topics in the field. Though most authors in this volume—among the most distinguished scholars in the field— agree with the main contours of what global studies is, as outlined in the opening essays in the volume, there are still subtle differences in interpretation. Is global studies only the study of globalization, for example? This depends, in part, on what one means by globalization, but it also reflects some differences in how one conceives of the field.

This diversity becomes enlarged when one considers the many methodological and theoretical approaches to analyzing global phenomena. The section on *global thinking*, for example, offers examples of some that are particularly relevant to developing innovative research strategies. The concluding section on *global citizenship* also seeks to illuminate the reasons and dynamics behind the growing interest in transnational education initiatives, and embraces the pedagogical mission of fostering global citizenship as defined in the United Nations Secretary General's 2012 "Global Education First Initiative" and many other cosmopolitan visions anchored in universal values of justice, diversity, and solidarity. This section also explores the rise of embedded cosmopolitan visions that link the global to the local and in return, the local to the global.

But the sharp reader will notice that not all of our authors agree on everything. And this may be a good thing—a new field is nourished by the diversity of methodological approaches. Thus, no attempt has been made to homogenize the essays in this volume and pretend as if there were a few analytic approaches that dominate the field. Fortunately, global studies is far too young to be ossified in any rigid analytic formulations. Rather, we can think of it as a "space of tension" framed by multiple disagreements *and* agreements in which the very problematic of the global is being continuously produced and contested.

Hence, what this *Handbook* offers is the chronicle of fresh new ways of thinking about global phenomena and dynamics that are emerging to shape our changing world. Its contributors have sought to pay tribute to the growing significance of the field as an unorthodox academic "space of tension" linking the arts, sciences, and humanities. Animated by an ethical imperative to globalize knowledge, such transdisciplinary efforts have the potential to reconfigure our discipline-oriented academic infrastructure. In this sense, the chapters of this volume constitute not only a *Handbook* about a new field of studies, but also an engaged guide to an even more interconnected global future.

Contributors

Paul Amar
University of California, Santa Barbara

Helmut K. Anheier
Hertie School of Governance

Richard P. Appelbaum
University of California, Santa Barbara

Mohammed A. Bamyeh
University of Pittsburgh

Paul Battersby
RMIT University

Upendra Baxi
University of Warwick

Walden Bello
State University of New York at Binghamton

Patrick Bond
Wits School of Governance, University of the Witwatersrand

Karen Buckley
University of Manchester

Sucheng Chan
University of California, Santa Barbara

Sara R. Curran
Jackson School of International Studies, University of Washington

Simon Dalby
Balsillie School of International Affairs, Wilfrid Laurier University

Eve Darian-Smith
University of California, Irvine

Donatella della Porta
European University Institute, Florence

Allard Duursma
London School of Economics

Hilal Elver
University of California, Santa Barbara

Daniel E. Esser
School of International Service, American University

Richard Falk
University of California, Santa Barbara

Michael Forman
University of Washington-Tacoma

Richard Giulianotti
Loughborough University

Jairus Victor Grove
University of Hawai'i at Manoa

Clive Hamilton
Charles Sturt University, Canberra

Jeffrey Haynes
London Metropolitan University

Kathryn H. Jacobsen
George Mason University

Paul James
Western Sydney University

Habibul Haque Khondker
Zayed University

Tania Lewis
RMIT University

Jack Lule
Lehigh University

Katherine Marshall
School of Foreign Service, Georgetown University

James H. Mittelman
School of International Service, American University

Valentine M. Moghadam
Loughborough University

Manoranjan Mohanty
Council for Social Development, New Delhi

Tuija Parikka
St. Johns University

Roland Robertson
University of Pittsburgh and University of Aberdeen

William I. Robinson
University of California, Santa Barbara

Ravi K. Roy
Southern Utah University

Dominic Sachsenmaier
Georg-August-University Göttingen

Hans Schattle
Yonsei University, Korea

Jan Aart Scholte
University of Gothenburg

Nandita Sharma
University of Hawai'i at Manoa

Mona Kanwal Sheikh
Danish Institute for International Studies

Jeb Sprague
University of California, Santa Barbara

Peter J. Taylor
Northumbria University

Monica Duffy Toft
The Fletcher School, Tufts University, and Peace Research Institute, Oslo

Thomas D. Willett
Claremont Graduate University

Linda Williams
RMIT University

THE OXFORD HANDBOOK OF

GLOBAL STUDIES

PART I

GLOBAL STUDIES

The Emergence of a New Academic Field

CHAPTER 1

....

WHAT IS GLOBAL STUDIES?

....

MANFRED B. STEGER

ALTHOUGH scholars within the field of global studies (GS) debate over how to define the term, most agree that it has emerged in the twenty-first century as a multidisciplinary and transdisciplinary field of inquiry dedicated to the exploration of the many dimensions of globalization and other transnational phenomena. Perhaps the most important keyword of our time, "globalization" remains a contested and open-ended concept, especially with respect to its normative implications. Although the phenomenon has been extensively studied in sociology, economics, anthropology, geography, history, political science, and other fields, it falls outside the established disciplinary framework. After all, "globalization" is only of secondary concern in these traditional fields organized around different master concepts: "society" in sociology, "resources" and "scarcity" in economics, "culture" in anthropology, "space" in geography, "the past" in history, "power" and "governance" in political science, and so on. By contrast, GS has placed the keyword without a firm disciplinary home at the core of its intellectual enterprise. The rise of GS, therefore, not only represents a clear sign of the proper recognition of new kinds of social interdependence and enhanced forms of mobility but also demonstrates that the nineteenth-century realities that gave birth to the conventional disciplinary architecture are no longer ours (Jameson 1998: xi). At the same time, however, GS is not hermetic, for it welcomes various approaches and methods that contribute to a transnational analysis of the world as a single interactive system.

The field of GS is sometimes compared to the disciplines of international relations (IR) and international studies (IS). Still, their differences clearly outweigh their similarities. Mainstream IR considers the state as the principal mover of world politics and thus *the* central unit of analysis. This means that the actions of states—especially with regard to security issues—are foregrounded at the expense of other crucial areas, such as economics and culture. By contrast, GS researchers consider the state as but one actor in today's fluid web of material and ideational interdependencies that includes proliferating non-state entities, nongovernmental organizations, transnational social movements, and other social and political forces "beyond the state."[1] This multicentric and multidimensional understanding of our globalizing world makes GS a porous field with strong "applied" interests in public policy. GS scholars frequently seize upon issues that are often excluded from IR—for example, issues connected to gender, poverty, global media, public health, migration, and ecology. This problem-centered focus of GS encourages the forging of strong links among the worlds of academia, political organizations, nongovernmental organizations, and social movements.

Most important, GS both embraces and exudes a certain *mentalité*, which I have called the "global imaginary" (Steger 2008; Steger and James 2013). It refers to a sense of the social whole that frames our age as one shaped by the intensifying forces of globalization. Giving its objective and subjective aspects equal consideration, GS suggests that enhanced interconnectivity does not merely happen in the world "out there" but also operates through our consciousness "in here." To recognize the significance of global consciousness, however, does not support premature proclamations of the "death of the nation-state." Conventional national and local frameworks have retained significant power as well as reconfigured those central functions. Although the nation-state is not dying, globalization has forced it to accommodate an incipient and slowly evolving architecture of "global governance." Hence, it is not surprising that GS researchers show great interest in transnational educational initiatives centered on the promotion of "global citizenship" and other "embedded" cosmopolitan visions that link the local to the global and vice versa.

In the roughly two decades of its existence, GS has attracted scores of unorthodox faculty and unconventional students who share its sincere commitment to studying transnational processes, interactions, and flows from multiple and transdisciplinary perspectives. Still, there are large sections of the academic community that have either not heard of GS at all or are still unclear about its scope and methods. So what, exactly, is GS and what does it entail? Responding to these persistent demands for clarification, this chapter seeks to provide a general overview of the main contours and central features of GS.[2] Although scores of globalization scholars still quarrel over what themes and approaches their field should or should not encompass, it would be a mistake to close one's eyes to existing agreements and common approaches that have become substantial enough to identify four central "pillars" or "framings" of GS: globalization, transdisciplinarity, space and time, and critical thinking. But before presenting the new field's conceptual and thematic framework in more detail, let us start by considering some important institutional developments that have aided its rapid growth.

THE INSTITUTIONAL GROWTH OF GLOBAL STUDIES

Creating a special academic context for the study of globalization, GS has become gradually institutionalized in the academy. Yet, GS does not view itself as just another cog in the disciplinary machine of contemporary higher education. Despite today's trendy talk about "globalizing knowledge" and "systematic internationalization"—which is often more about the neoliberal reinvention of the academy as "big business" than about creating new spaces of epistemological diversity—the traditional Western academic framework of knowledge specialization has survived largely intact into the twenty-first century. Often forced to make compromises and find less than desirable accommodations with the dominant academic order, GS challenges a fractured, Eurocentric mindset that encourages the division of knowledge into sharply demarcated areas populated by disciplinary "insiders." Although it seeks to blaze new trails of social inquiry, GS is not afraid of presenting itself as a fluid and porous intellectual terrain rather than a novel, well-defined item on the dominant disciplinary menu. To use Fredric Jameson's (1998: xvi) felicitous term, the new field inhabits an academic "space of tension" framed by multiple disagreements *and* agreements in which the very problematic of globalization itself is being continuously produced and contested.

The educational imperative to grasp the complex spatial and social dynamics of globalization animates the transdisciplinary efforts of GS to reorder human knowledge and create innovate learning environments. Relying on conceptual and analytic perspectives that are not anchored in a single discipline, the new field expands innovative interdisciplinary approaches pioneered in the 1970s and 1980s, such as world-systems analysis, postcolonial studies, cultural studies, environmental and sustainability studies, and women's studies. The power of the rising global imaginary and its affiliated new ideologies of "market globalism," justice globalism, and religious globalisms goes a long way in explaining why GS programs, departments, research institutes, and professional organizations have sprung up in major universities throughout the world, including in the Global South (Steger 2013). Recognizing this trend, many existing IS programs have been renamed "global studies." Demand for courses and undergraduate and postgraduate degrees in GS has dramatically risen. Increasingly, we see the inclusion of the terms "global" or "globalization" in course titles, textbooks, academic job postings, and extracurricular activities. Universities and colleges in the United States have supported the creation of new GS initiatives that are often funded by major government institutions and philanthropists. For example, Northwestern University recently announced a donation of $100 million—the largest single gift in its history—from the sister of the prominent investor Warren Buffett for the establishment of the Roberta Buffett Institute for Global Studies.

Drawing on thematic and methodological resources from the social sciences and humanities, GS now encompasses approximately 300 undergraduate and graduate programs in the United States alone.[3] Some pioneering universities, such as the University of California, Santa Barbara or the University of North Carolina at Chapel Hill, house programs that serve nearly 1,000 GS undergraduate majors. The Division of Global Affairs at Rutgers University–Newark and RMIT University's (Melbourne, Australia) School of Global, Urban, and Social Studies accommodate hundreds of master's and doctoral students. In 2015, the University of California, Santa Barbara launched the first doctoral program in GS at a tier 1 research university in the United States. In addition to the creation of these successful degree-granting programs, there has been a phenomenal growth of scholarly literature on globalization. New journals, book series, textbooks, academic conferences, and professional associations such as the international Global Studies Consortium or the Global Studies Association have embraced the novel umbrella designation of "global studies."

Clearly, the fledgling field and its associated global imaginary have come a long way in a relatively short period of time. However, its success also depended to a significant extent on the redirection of funding by US government and philanthropic organizations from established IS and area studies programs to the newcomer "global studies." Indeed, this reorientation toward GS occurred in the ideological context of the rise of "neoliberalism," an economistic doctrine at the core of a comprehensive worldview I have called "market globalism" (Steger and Roy 2010). As Isaac Kamola's (2010) pioneering work on the subject has demonstrated, starting in the mid-1990s, a number of important funders announced plans to replace "area" structures with a "global" framework. For example, the Social Science Research Council recommended defunding "discrete and separated area committees" that were reluctant to support scholars interested in "global" developments and policy-relevant "global issues." When conventional area studies experts realized that traditional sources of funding were quickly drying up, many joined the newly emerging GS cohort of scholars centered on the study of "globalization." Major universities, too, reduced the level of support for area studies teaching and research programs while developing new investment schemes and strategic plans that provided for the creation of new "global studies" or "global affairs" programs and centers. Major professional organizations such as the National Association of State Universities and Land Grant Colleges and the American Association of Colleges and Universities eagerly joined these instrumental efforts to synchronize the initiatives of "globalizing the curriculum" and "recalibrating college learning" to the shifting economic landscape of the "new global century" (Kamola 2010).

Convinced that GS programs will earn a more prominent place within the quickly changing twenty-first-century landscape of higher education characterized by shrinking budgets and new modes of instruction, a growing number of academics—loosely referred to in this chapter as "global studies scholars"—have begun to synthesize various common theoretical perspectives and problem-oriented approaches. Their efforts have contributed to the necessary mapping exercise without falling prey to the fetish of disciplinary boundary making. Building on these efforts, I contend in this chapter that it is now possible to present GS as a reasonably holistic transdisciplinary project dedicated to exploring processes of globalization with the aim of engaging the complex global problems the world is facing in the twenty-first century (McCarty 2014). To this purpose, the next four sections of this chapter offer a general overview of the four major conceptual framings that give coherence to the field.

The First Pillar of Global Studies: Globalization

Globalization is the principal subject of GS and thus constitutes the first pillar of the emerging field. At the same time, the global also serves as the conceptual framework through which GS scholars investigate the contemporary and historical dynamics of thickening interdependence. The birth and rising fortunes of GS are inextricably linked to the emergence of globalization as a prominent theme in late twentieth-century public discourse. But the buzzword was not invented ex nihilo during the neoliberal Roaring Nineties as shorthand for the liberalization and worldwide integration of markets. In fact, it had been used as early as the 1930s in academic fields as varied as education and psychology, society and culture, politics and IR, and economics and business (Steger and James 2015). At the same time, the powerful ideological and political dynamics of the 1990s served as crucial catalysts for the cross-fertilization of public and academic discourses on the subject. These raging globalization debates of the past decades attest to enormous interest in the academic study of globalization as a multidimensional phenomenon.

Attempts to develop objective, quantifiable assessments of the causes, contents, and consequences of globalization have become a key issue for contemporary social science research and social policy. Researchers have sought to develop empirical measures of globalization based on various indicators. These efforts led to the rapid proliferation of major globalization indices such as the KOF Index of Globalization.[4] Today, readers interested in globalization can select among thousands and thousands of pertinent books, articles, and encyclopedia entries. In our digital age, these writings can be tracked down with unprecedented speed and precision through new technologies such as the search engine Ngram, Google's mammoth database collated from more than 5 million digitized books available free to the public for online searches. In 2015, the exceptionally rich Factiva database listed 355,838 publications referencing the term "globalization." The Expanded Academic ASAP database produced 7,737 results with "globalization" in the title, including 5,976 journal articles, 1,404 magazine articles, and 355 news items. The ISI Web of Knowledge listed a total of 8,970 references with "globalization," the EBSCO Host Database yielded 17,188 results, and the Proquest Newspaper Database showed 25,056 articles.

Despite continuing disagreements regarding how to define globalization, GS scholars have put forward various definitions and collected them in comprehensive classification tables (Al-Rodhan and Stoudmann 2006). One major obstacle in the way of producing useful definitions of globalization is that the term has been variously used in both academic literature and the popular press to describe a process, a condition, a system, a force, and an age. Given that these concepts have very different meanings, their indiscriminate usage is often obscure and invites confusion. For example, a sloppy conflation of process and condition encourages circular definitions that explain little. The familiar truism that globalization (the process) leads to more globalization (the condition) does not allow us to draw meaningful analytical distinctions between causes and effects. Hence, we ought to adopt the term *globality* to signify a *social condition* characterized by extremely tight global economic, political, cultural, and environmental interconnections across national borders and civilizational boundaries. The term *globalization*, by contrast, applies not to a condition but a multidimensional set of *social processes* pushing toward globality.

GS scholars exploring the dynamics of globalization are particularly keen on pursuing research questions related to themes of social change, which connect the human and natural sciences. How does globalization proceed? What is driving it? Is it one cause or a combination of factors? Is globalization a continuation of modernity or is it a radical break? Does it create new forms of inequality and hierarchy or is it lifting millions of people out of poverty? Is it producing cultural homogeneity or diversity? What is the role of new technologies in accelerating and intensifying global processes? Note that the conceptualization of globalization as a dynamic process rather than as a static condition also highlights the fact that it is an uneven process: People living in various parts of the world are affected very differently by the transformation of social structures and cultural zones.

The principal voices in the academic globalization debates can be divided into four distinct intellectual camps: globalizers, rejectionists, skeptics, and modifiers. Most GS scholars fall into the category of *globalizers*, who argue that globalization is a profoundly transformative set of social processes that is moving human societies toward unprecedented levels of interconnectivity (Held and McGrew 2002; Mittelman 2000; Scholte 2005). While committed to a big picture approach, globalizers nonetheless tend to focus their research efforts on one of the principal dimensions of globalization: economics, politics, culture, or ecology. By contrast, *rejectionists* contend that most of the accounts offered by globalizers are incorrect, imprecise, or exaggerated. Arguing that such generalizations often amount to little more than "globaloney," they dismiss the utility of globalization for scientific academic discourse (Veseth 2010). Their contention that just about everything that can be linked to some transnational process is often cited as evidence for globalization and its growing influence. The third camp in the contemporary globalization debates consists of *skeptics* who acknowledge some forms and manifestations of globalization while also emphasizing its limited nature (Hirst et al. 2009; Rugman 2001). Usually focusing on the economic aspects of the phenomenon, skeptics claim that the world economy is not truly global but, rather, a regional dynamic centered on Europe, East Asia, Australia, and North America. The fourth camp in these academic debates consists of *modifiers* who acknowledge the power of globalization but dispute its novelty and thus the innovate character of social theories focused on the phenomenon. They seek to modify and assimilate globalization theories to traditional approaches in IS, world-systems theory, or other related fields, claiming that a new conceptual paradigm is unwarranted (Wallerstein 2004).

In recent years, it has become increasingly evident that neither modifiers nor rejectionists have offered convincing arguments for their respective views. Although objections to the overuse of the term have forced the participants in the globalization debates to hone their analytic skills, the wholesale rejection of globalization as a "vacuous concept" has often served as a convenient excuse to avoid dealing with the actual phenomenon itself. Rather than constructing overly ambitious "grand narratives" of globalization, many GS researchers in the globalizers and skeptics camps have instead wisely opted for more modest approaches that employ mixed methodologies designed to provide explanations of particular manifestations of the process.

The Second Pillar of Global Studies: Transdisciplinarity

The profound changes affecting social life in the global age require examinations of the growing forms of complexity and reflexivity (Giddens 1990). This means that the global dynamics of interconnectivity can no longer be approached from a single academic discipline or area of knowledge. Emphasizing the analysis of global complexity and reflexivity commits GS scholars to the development of more comprehensive explanations of globalization, which highlight the complex intersection between a multiplicity of driving forces, embracing economic, technological, cultural, and political change (Held et al. 1999). Hence, the conceptual frameworks of influential GS researchers explore these growing forms of interdependence through "domains," "dimensions," "networks," "flows," "fluids," and "hybrids"—the key terms behind their transdisciplinary attempts to globalize the social science research imagination (Castells 2010; Kenway and Fahey 2008; Urry 2003). Recognizing the importance of increasing complexity for their systematic inquiries, they consciously embrace transdisciplinarity in their efforts to understand the shifting dynamics of interconnectedness. Thus, their exploration of complex forms of global interdependence not only combats knowledge fragmentation and scientific reductionism but also facilitates an understanding of the "big picture," which is indispensable for stimulating the political commitment needed to tackle the pressing global problems of our time. Multidimensional processes of globalization and their associated global challenges, such as climate change, pandemics, terrorism, digital technologies, marketization, migration, urbanization, and human rights, represent examples of transnational issues that both cut across and reach beyond conventional disciplinary boundaries.

Although university administrators in the United States and elsewhere have warmed up to interdisciplinarity, most instructional activities in today's institutions of higher education still occur within an overarching framework of the disciplinary divisions. The same holds true for academic research in the social sciences and humanities, where scholars continue to produce specialized problems to which solutions can be found primarily within their own disciplinary orientations.[5] Critical of this tendency to compartmentalize the complexity of social existence into discrete spheres of activity, GS has evolved as a self-consciously transdisciplinary field committed to the engagement and integration of multiple knowledge systems and research methodologies. Typically hailing from traditional disciplinary backgrounds, faculty members are often attracted to GS because they are deeply critical of the entrenched conventions of disciplinary specialization inherent in the Eurocentric academic framework. Appreciative of a more flexible intellectual environment that allows for the bundling of otherwise disparate conceptual fields and geographical areas into a single object of study, GS scholars seek to overcome such forms of disciplinary "silo thinking."

The concept of "transdisciplinarity" is configured around the Latin prefix "trans" ("across" or "beyond"). It signifies the systemic and holistic integration of diverse forms of knowledge by cutting *across* and through existing disciplinary boundaries and paradigms in ways that reach *beyond* each individual discipline. If interdisciplinarity can be characterized by the mixing of disciplinary perspectives involving little or moderate integration, then transdisciplinarity should be thought of as a deep fusion of disciplinary knowledge that produces new understandings capable of transforming or restructuring existing disciplinary paradigms (Alvargonzalez 2011; Repko 2012). But the transdisciplinary imperative to challenge, go beyond, transgress, and unify separate orientations does not ignore the importance of attracting scholars with specific disciplinary backgrounds. Moreover, transdisciplinarians put complex real-world problems at the heart of their intellectual efforts. The formulation of possible resolutions of these problems requires the deep integration of a broad range of perspectives from multiple disciplinary backgrounds (Pohl 2010: 69; Pohl and Hadorn 2008: 112).

Yet, full transdisciplinarity—understood as activities that transcend, recombine, and integrate separate disciplinary paradigms—remains an elusive goal for most academics. This includes GS scholars associated with currently existing academic programs in the field. Some have achieved a high degree of transdisciplinary integration, whereas others rely more on multi- and interdisciplinary activities that benefit students and faculty alike. For GS, the task is to expand its foothold in the dominant academic landscape while at the same time continuing its work against the prevailing disciplinary order. To satisfy these seemingly contradictory imperatives, GS has retained its ambition to project globalization across the conventional disciplinary matrix while at the same time accepting with equal determination the pragmatic task of finding some accommodation within the very disciplinary structure it seeks to transform. Such necessary attempts to reconcile these diverging impulses force scholars to play at least one, and preferably more, of three distinct roles—depending on the concrete institutional opportunities and constraints they encounter in their academic home environment.

First, GS scholars often assume the role of *intrepid mavericks* willing to establish GS as a separate discipline—as a first but necessary step toward the more holistic goal of comprehensive integration. To be sure, mavericks possess a certain spirit of adventure that makes it easier for them to leave their original disciplinary setting behind to cover new ground. But being a maverick also carries the considerable risk of failure. Second, a number of GS scholars have embraced the role of *radical insurgents* seeking to globalize established disciplines from within. This means working toward the goal of carving out a GS dimension or status for specific disciplines such as political science or sociology. Finally, some GS faculty have slipped into the role of *tireless nomads* traveling perpetually across and beyond disciplines in order to reconfigure existing and new knowledge around concrete globalization research questions and projects. The nomadic role, in particular, demands that academics familiarize themselves with vast literatures on pertinent subjects that are usually studied in isolation from each other. Indeed, one of the most formidable intellectual challenges lies in the integration and synthesis of multiple strands of knowledge in a way that does justice to the complexity and fluidity of our globalizing world.

The Third Pillar of Global Studies: Space and Time

The development of GS has been crucially framed by new conceptions of space and time. After all, globalization manifests in volatile dynamics of spatial integration and differentiation. These give rise to new temporal frameworks dominated by notions of instantaneity and simultaneity, which assume ever-greater significance in academic investigations into globalization. Thus deeply resonating with spatio-temporal meanings, the keyword unites two semantic parts: "global" and "ization." The primary emphasis is on "global," which reflects people's growing awareness of the increasing significance of global-scale phenomena such as global economic institutions, transnational corporations, global civil society, the World Wide Web, global climate change, and so on. Indeed, the principal reason the term was coined in the first place had to do with people's recognition of intensifying spatio-temporal dynamics. Globalization processes create incessantly new geographies and complex spatial arrangements. This is especially true for the latest spatial frontier in human history: cyberspace. The dynamics of digital connectivity have shown themselves to be quite capable of pushing human interaction deep into the "virtual reality" of a world in which geography is no longer a factor.

Several GS pioneers developed approaches to globalization that put matters of time and space at the very core of their research projects. Consider, for example, Roland Robertson's (1992: 6–7) snappy definition of globalization as "the compression of the world into a single place." It underpinned his efforts to develop a spatially sophisticated concept of "glocalization" capable of counteracting the relative inattention paid to spatiality in the social sciences. Commenting on the remarkable fluidity of spatial scales in a globalizing world, Robertson focused on those complex and uneven processes "in which the constraints of geography on social and cultural arrangements recede and in which people become increasingly aware that they are receding" (Robertson 2005). Similarly, Arjun Appadurai (1996: 188) developed subtle insights into what he called the "global production of locality"—a new spatial dynamic that was occurring more frequently in "a world that has become deterritorialized, diasporic, and transnational." Or consider David Harvey's (1989: 137, 265, 270–273) influential inquiry into the spatial origins of contemporary cultural change centered on the uneven geographic development of capitalism. His innovative account generated new concepts such as "time–space compression" or "the implosion of space and time," which affirmed the centrality of spatio-temporal changes at the heart of neoliberal globalization and its associated postmodern cultural sensibilities.

GS scholars have explored a number of crucial spatio-temporal themes, such as the ongoing debate concerning whether globalization represents the consequence of modernity or a postmodern break, the changing role of the nation-state, the changing relationship between territory and sovereignty, the growing significance of global cities, the increasing fluidity of spatial scales, new periodization efforts around time and space, and the emergence of global history as a transdisciplinary endeavor. Let us consider, for example, the crucial dynamics of "deterritorialization." "Territoriality" refers to the use of territory for political, social, and economic ends. In modernity, the term has been associated with a largely successful strategy for establishing the exclusive jurisdiction implied by state "sovereignty" (Agnew 2009: 6). State control of bounded "national" terrain promised citizens living on the "inside" the benefits of relative security and unity in exchange for their exclusive loyalty and allegiance to the nation-state. By the second half of the twentieth century, social existence in such relatively fixed spatial containers had gone on for such a long time that it struck most people as the universal mode of communal life in the world. However, the latest wave of globalization gathering momentum in the 1980s and 1990s exposed the artificiality of territoriality as a social construct and its historical role as a specific human technique for managing space and time in the interests of modern state power.

The impact of globalization on conventional forms of territoriality and the related changing nature of the "international system" have raised major questions concerning the significance of the nation-state and the relevance of conventional notions of "territory" and "sovereignty" in analyzing the new spatial practices associated with globalization. This new spatial agenda also involves an important subset of issues pertaining to the proliferation and growing impact of non-state actors; the emergence of a "global civil society" no longer confined within the borders of the territorial state; the prospects for global governance understood as the norms and institutions that define and mediate relations between citizens, societies, markets, and states on a global scale; and the pluralization and hybridization of individual and collective identities. Various commentators have pointed to a growing gap between global space, where new problems arise, and national space, which proves increasingly inadequate for managing these transnational issues (Castells 2008; Thakur and Weiss 2011). These mounting spatial incompatibilities combine with the increasing power of neoliberalism and the absence of effective institutions of global governance to produce interrelated crises of state legitimacy and economic equity that undermine democratic politics.

Although there is virtual agreement among GS scholars that today's respatialization dynamics are profound and accelerating, there remain significant differences between a small band of thinkers comfortable with advancing an extreme thesis of "absolute" deterritorialization and a much larger group holding more moderate, "relativist" views. Absolutist views rose to prominence during the 1990s when spectacular neoliberal market reforms diminished the role of the state in the economy. Politics anchored in conventional forms of territoriality was seen as losing out to the transnational practices of global capitalism in which the state's survival in diminished form depended on its satisfactory performance of its new role as a handmaiden to global free-market forces (Ohmae 1996).

While acknowledging the growing significance of deterritorialization dynamics in a globalizing world, relativists argued for the continued relevance of sub-global territorial units, albeit in reconfigured forms. The increasing inability of nation-states to manage the globalization processes forced them to change into what Manuel Castells (2008: 88) calls the "network state," characterized by shared sovereignty and responsibility, flexibility of procedures of governance, and greater diversity in the relationships between governments and citizens in terms of time and space. Similarly, Saskia Sassen (2007) and Neil Brenner (1999) suggest that globalization involves not only the growth of supraterritoriality but also crucial processes and practices of "down-scaling" that occur deep inside the local, national, and regional. Perhaps the most critical of these spatial restructuring processes facilitated by states involves the localization of the control and command centers of global capitalism in "global cities" that assume great significance as pivotal places of spatial dispersal and global integration located at the intersection of multiple global circuits and flows involving migrants, ideas, commodities, and money (Sassen 2001).

As our discussion of the third pillar of GS has shown, the field owes much to the efforts of innovative human geographers and urban studies experts to develop new theoretical approaches that help us understand the changing spatial dynamics of our time. But GS is equally indebted to the intellectual initiatives of sociologists and historians willing to re-think the conceptual frameworks governing the temporal record of human activity. The emergent field of global history, for example, is based on the central premise that processes of globalization require more systematic historical treatments and, therefore, that the study of globalization deserves a more prominent place on the agenda of historical research (Clarence-Smith, Pomeranz, and Vries 2006; Hopkins 2002; Mazlish 2006; Mazlish and Iriye 2005). Parting with narratives centered on the development of nations or Eurocentric "world histories," global historians investigate the emergence of our globalized world as the result of exchanges, flows, and interactions involving many different cultures and societies—past and present. Recognizing the historical role of powerful drivers of globalization, many GS scholars have integrated historical schemes in their study of intensifying human interactions across geographical, conceptual, and disciplinary boundaries.

THE FOURTH PILLAR OF GLOBAL STUDIES: CRITICAL THINKING

Few GS scholars would object to the proposition that their field is significantly framed by "critical thinking." After all, GS constitutes an academic space of tension that generates critical investigations into our age as one shaped by the intensifying forces of globalization. Going beyond the purely cognitive understanding of "critical thinking" as "balanced reasoning" propagated by leading Anglo-American educators during the second half of the twentieth century, this fourth pillar reflects the field's receptivity to the activity of social criticism that problematizes unequal power relations and engages in ongoing social struggles to bring about a more just global society.

Advancing various critical perspectives, GS scholars from throughout the world draw on different currents and methods of "critical theory"—an umbrella term for modes of thought committed to the reduction of exploitation, commodification, violence, and alienation. Such a "critical global studies" (CGS) calls for methodological skepticism regarding positivistic dogmas and "objective facts"; the recognition that some facts are socially constructed and serve particular power interests; the public contestation of uncritical mainstream stories spun by corporate media; the decolonization of the Western imagination; and an understanding of the global as a multipolar dynamic reflecting the concerns of the marginalized Global South even more than those of the privileged North. Taking sides with the interest of social justice, CGS thinkers exercise what William Robinson (2005: 14) calls a "preferential option for the subordinate majority of global society."

There is much empirical evidence to suggest that dominant neoliberal modes of globalization have produced growing disparities in wealth and well-being within and among societies. They have also led to an acceleration of ecological degradation, new forms of militarism and digitized surveillance, previously unthinkable levels of inequality, and a chilling advance of consumerism and cultural commodification. The negative consequences of such a corporate-led "globalization-from-above" became subject to democratic contestation in the 1990s and impacted the evolution of critical theory in at least two major ways. First, they created fertile conditions for the emergence of powerful social movements advocating a people-led "globalization-from-below." These transnational activist networks, in turn, served as catalysts for the proliferation of new critical theories developing within the novel framework of globalization.

Many CGS thinkers were inspired by local forms of social resistance to neoliberalism, such as the 1994 Zapatista uprising in Chiapas, Mexico; the 1995 strikes in France and other areas of Europe; and the powerful series of protests in major cities throughout the world following in the wake of the iconic 1999 anti-World Trade Organization demonstration in Seattle. Critical intellectuals interacted with the participants of these alter-globalization movements at these large-scale protest events or at the massive meetings of the newly founded World Social Forum in the 2000s. They developed and advanced their critiques of market globalism in tandem with constructive visions for alternative global futures. Because the struggles over the meanings and manifestations of globalization occurred in interlinked local settings throughout the world, they signified a significant alteration in the geography of critical thinking. As French sociologist Razmig Keucheyan (2013: 3) has emphasized, the academic center of gravity of these new forms of critical thinking was shifting from the traditional centers of learning located in Old Europe to the top universities of the New World. The United States, in particular, served as a powerful economic magnet for job-seeking academics from throughout the world while also posing as the obvious hegemonic target of their criticisms.

Indeed, during the past quarter century, America has managed to attract a large number of talented postcolonial critical theorists to its highly reputed and well-paying universities and colleges. A significant number of these politically progressive recruits, in turn, promptly put their newly acquired positions of academic privilege into the service of their socially engaged ideologies, which resulted in a vastly more effective production and worldwide dissemination of their critical publications. Moreover, the global struggle against neoliberalism that heated up in the 1990s and 2000s also contributed significantly to the heightened international exposure of cutting-edge critical theorists located in the vast terrains of Asia,

Latin America, and Africa. In particular, the permanent digital communication revolution centered on the World Wide Web and the new social media made it easier for these voices of the Global South to be heard in the dominant North. In fact, the "globalization of critical thinking" culminated in the formation of a "world republic of critical theories" (Keucheyan 2013: 21, 73). Although this global community of critical thinkers is far from homogeneous in its perspectives and continues to be subjected to considerable geographic and social inequalities, it has had a profound influence on the evolution of GS.

Still, we need to be careful not to exaggerate the extent to which such CGS perspectives pervade the field. Our discussion of the developing links between the global justice movement and CGS scholars should not seduce us into assuming that *all* academics affiliated with GS programs support radical or even moderate socially engaged perspectives on what constitutes their field and what it should accomplish. After all, global thinking is not inherently "critical" in the socially engaged use of the term. An informal perusal of influential globalization literature produced during the past fifteen years suggests that nearly all authors express some appreciation for critical thinking understood as a cognitive ability to "see multiple sides of an issue" (in this case, the issue is "globalization"). But only approximately two-thirds of well-published globalization scholars take their understanding of "critical" beyond the social-scientific ideal of "balanced objectivity" and "value-free research" and thus challenge in writing the dominant social arrangements of our time and/or promote emancipatory social change (Steger 2009). This locates the remaining one-third of globalization authors within a conceptual framework that transnational sociologist William Robinson (2005: 12) has provocatively characterized as "noncritical globalization studies." Obviously, GS scholars relegated to this category would object to Robinson's classification on the basis of their differing understanding of what "critical thinking" entails.

CGS scholars seek to produce globalization theory that is useful to emancipatory global social movements, and this is what animates their "global activist thinking." Most of them could be characterized as "rooted cosmopolitans" who remain embedded in local environments while at the same time cultivating a global consciousness as a result of their vastly enhanced contacts to like-minded academics and social organizations across national borders. Stimulated by the vitality of emergent global civil society, CGS scholar–activists have thought of new ways of making their intellectual activities in the ivory tower relevant to the happenings in the global public sphere. These novel permutations of global activist thinking manifested themselves in the educational project of cultivating what is increasingly referred to as "global citizenship." The teaching of these new civic values in GS has also been linked to the production of emancipatory knowledge that can be used directly in the ongoing struggle of the global justice movement against the dominant forces of globalization-from-above.

Concluding Remarks: Critiques of Global Studies

Having presented the new field's conceptual and thematic framework, we might want to close this chapter by considering GS's capacity for self-criticism. The critical thinking framing of GS creates a special obligation for all scholars working in the field to listen to and take seriously internal and external criticisms with the intention of correcting existing shortcomings, illuminating blind spots, and avoiding theoretical pitfalls and dead ends. As is the case for any newcomer bold enough to enter today's crowded and competitive arena of academia, GS, too, has been subjected to a wide range of criticisms ranging from constructive interventions to ferocious attacks.

One influential criticism concerns the limited scope and status of "actual global studies as it is researched and taught at universities around the world" (Pieterse 2013: 504). For such critics, the crux of the problem lies with the field's intellectual immaturity and lack of focus. They allege that currently existing GS programs and conferences are still relatively rare and haphazard; they resemble "scaffolding without a roof." Finally, they bemoan the supposed dearth of intellectual innovators willing and able to provide necessary "programmatic perspectives on global studies" framed by those that are "multicentered and multilevel thinking," and, therefore, capable of "adding value" to the field (Pieterse 2013: 505).

Such criticism resonates with the often shocking discrepancy between the rich conceptual promise of the field and the poor design and execution of "actual global studies as it is researched and taught at universities around the world." There is some truth to complaints that a good number of GS programs lack focus and specificity, which makes the field appear to be a rather nebulous study of "everything global." Like most of the other interdisciplinary efforts originating in the 1990s, GS programs sometimes invite the impression of a rather confusing combination of wildly different approaches reifying the global level of analysis. Another troubling development in recent years has been the use of "global studies" as a convenient catchphrase by academic entrepreneurs eager to cash in on its popularity with students. Thus, a desirable label has become attached to a growing number of conventional area studies curricula, IS offerings, and diplomacy and foreign affairs programs—primarily for the purpose of boosting their market appeal without having to make substantive changes to the traditional teaching and research agenda attached to such programs. Although some of these programs have in fact become more global over time, in other cases these instrumental appropriations of the GS label have not only caused much damage to the existing GS "brand" but also cast an ominous shadow on the future of the field.

Despite its obvious insights, however, Pieterse's (2013) account of "actually existing global studies" strikes this writer as unbalanced and somewhat exaggerated. Much of the available empirical data show that there are promising pedagogical and research efforts underway in the field. These initiatives suggest that the instructive pessimism of the critics must be matched by cautious optimism. To be sure, an empirically based examination of the field shows GS as a project that is still very much in the making. Yet, the field's tender age and relative inexperience should not deter globalization scholars from acknowledging the field's considerable intellectual achievements and growing institutional infrastructure. GS "as it actually exists" has come a long way from its rather modest and eclectic origins in the 1990s. The regular meetings of the Global Studies Associations (United Kingdom and North America) and the annual convention of the Global Studies Consortium provide ample networking opportunities for globalization scholars from throughout the world. Moreover, GS scholars are developing serious initiatives to recenter the social sciences toward global systemic dynamics and incorporate multilevel analyses. They are rethinking existing analytical frameworks that expand critical reflexivity and methodologies unafraid of mixing various research strategies.

Another important criticism of GS comes from postcolonial thinkers located both within and without the field of GS. As Robert Young (2003) explains, postcolonial theory is a related set of perspectives and principles that involves a conceptual reorientation toward the perspectives of knowledges developed outside the West—in Asia, Africa, Oceania, and Latin America. By seeking to insert alternative knowledges into the dominant power structures of the West as well as the non-West, postcolonial theorists attempt to "change the way people think, the way they behave, to produce a more just and equitable relation between the different people of the world" (p. 7). Emphasizing the connection between theory and practice, postcolonial intellectuals consider themselves critical thinkers challenging the alleged superiority of Western cultures, racism and other forms of ethnic bias, economic inequality separating the Global North from the South, and the persistence of "Orientalism"—a discriminatory, Europe-derived mindset so brilliantly dissected by late postcolonial theorist Edward Said (1979).

A number of postcolonial and indigenous theorists have examined the connections between globalization and postcolonialism (Krishna 2009). While most have expressed both their appreciation and their affinity for much of what GS stands for, they have also offered incisive critiques of what they view as the field's troubling geographic, ethnic, and epistemic location within the hegemonic Western framework. The noted ethnic studies scholar Ramón Grosfoguel (2005: 284), for example, offers a clear and comprehensive summary of such postcolonial concerns: "Globalization studies, with a few exceptions, have not derived the epistemological and theoretical implications of the epistemic critique coming from subaltern locations in the colonial divide and . . . continue to produce a knowledge from the Western man 'point zero' god's-eye view."

Such postcolonial criticisms of GS provide an invaluable service by highlighting some remaining conceptual parochialisms behind its allegedly "global" theoretical and practical concerns. Indeed, their intervention suggests that GS thinkers have not paid enough attention to the postcolonial imperative of contesting the dominant Western ways of seeing and knowing. Thus, they force scholars working in the field to confront crucial questions that are often relegated to the margins of intellectual inquiry. Is critical theory sufficiently global to represent the diverse voices of the multitude and speak to the diverse experiences of disempowered people throughout the world? What sort of new and innovative ideas have been produced by public intellectuals who do not necessarily travel along the theoretical and geographical paths frequented by Western critical thinkers? Are there pressing issues and promising intellectual approaches that have been neglected in CGS? These questions also relate to the central role of the English language in GS. With English expanding its status as the academic lingua franca, thinkers embedded in Western universities still hold the monopoly on the production of critical theories. Important contributions from the Global South in languages other than English often fall through the cracks or only register in translated form on the radar of the supposedly "global" academic publishing network years after their original publication.

As noted in the previous discussion of the fourth pillar of GS, however, it is essential to acknowledge the progress that has been made in GS to expand its "space of tension" by welcoming and incorporating Global South perspectives. As early as 2005, for example, a quarter of the contributions featured in Appelbaum and Robinson's (2005) *Critical Globalization Studies* anthology came from authors located in Africa, Asia, and Latin America. Since then, pertinent criticisms from within that demanded the inclusion of multiple voices and perspectives from throughout the world have proliferated. Consider, for example, Eve Darian-Smith's (2015) recent critique of taken-for-granted assumptions on the part of Western scholars to speak for others in the Global South. Moreover, scores of public intellectuals hailing from the Global South have not only produced influential studies on globalization but also stood in solidarity with movement activists struggling against the forces of globalization-from-above.[6] As demonstrated by the diversity of views and perspectives represented in this volume, many GS scholars are paying attention to these important postcolonial interventions. Still, there is still plenty of room for further improvement.

Let me end this chapter with a bit of speculation about the future of GS. Perhaps its most pressing task for the next decade is to keep chipping away at the disciplinary walls that still divide the academic landscape Animated by an ethical imperative to globalize knowledge, such transdisciplinary efforts have the potential to reconfigure our discipline-oriented academic infrastructure around issues of global public responsibility (Kennedy 2015: xv). This integrative endeavor must be undertaken steadily and tirelessly—but also carefully and with the proper understanding that diverse and multiple forms of knowledge are sorely needed to educate a global public. The necessary appreciation for the interplay between specialists and generalists must contain a proper respect for the crucial contributions of the conventional disciplines to our growing understanding of globalization. But the time has come to take the next step.

NOTES

1. Thus, GS is closer to social constructivism in IR, which deconstructs the unitary actor model of the state in favor of a more complex conception that emphasizes an amalgam of interests, identities, and contingency.
2. For a book-length treatment of this question, see Steger and Wahlrab (2016). This chapter contains the principal arguments of the book in compressed form.
3. For a listing of these colleges and universities, see https://bigfuture.collegeboard.org/college-search.
4. For a recent discussion of "objective" measurements of globalization with a view toward advancing the construction of new globalization indices, see Martens et al. (2015).
5. In this chapter, I employ a very broad definition of "science" that extends to the humanities. The discussion of what does and what does not constitute science is certainly germane with respect to transdisciplinarity, but it extends well beyond the scope of this chapter.
6. See, for example, Zeleza (2003), Mendieta (2008), Krishna (2009), Nassar (2010), Singh (2013), and Amin (2014).

REFERENCES

Agnew, John A. 2009. *Globalization and Sovereignty*. Lanham, MD: Rowman & Littlefield.
Al-Rodhan, Nayef R. F., and Gerard Stoudmann. 2006, June 19. "Definition of Globalization: A Comprehensive Overview and a Proposed Definition." In *Program on*

the Geopolitical Implication of Globalization and Transnational Security, GCSP Policy Brief Series.

Alvargonzalez, David. 2011. "Multidisciplinarity, Interdisciplinarity, Transdisciplinarity, and the Sciences." *International Studies in the Philosophy of Science* 25 (4): 387–403.

Amin, Samir. 2014. *Capitalism in the Age of Globalization: The Management of Contemporary Society*. London: Zed Books.

Appadurai, Arjun. 1996. *Modernity at Large: Cultural Dimensions of Globalization*. Minneapolis: University of Minnesota Press.

Appelbaum, Richard P., and William I. Robinson, eds. 2005. *Critical Globalization Studies*. New York: Routledge.

Brenner, Neil. 1999. "Beyond State-Centrism? Space, Territoriality, and Geographical Scale in Globalization Studies." *Theory and Society* 28 (1): 39–78.

Castells, Manuel. 2008. "The New Public Sphere: Global Civil Society, Communication Networks, and Global Governance." *Annals of the American Academy of Political and Social Science* 616: 78–93.

Castells, Manuel. 2010. *The Rise of the Network Society: The Information Age: Economy, Society and Culture*. 2nd ed. Hoboken, NJ: Wiley-Blackwell.

Clarence-Smith, William Gervase, Kenneth Pomeranz, and Peer Vries. 2006. "Editorial." *Journal of Global History* 1 (1): 1–2.

Darian-Smith, Eve. 2015. "Global Studies—The Handmaiden of Neoliberalism?" *Globalizations* 12 (2): 164–168.

Giddens, Anthony. 1990. *The Consequences of Modernity*. Stanford, CA: Stanford University Press.

Grosfoguel, Ramón. 2005. "The Implications of Subaltern Epistemologies for Global Capitalism: Transmodernity, Border Thinking, and Global Coloniality." In *Critical Globalization Studies*, edited by R. Appelbaum and W. I. Robinson, 283–292. New York: Routledge.

Harvey, David. 1989. *The Condition of Postmodernity: An Enquiry into the Origins of Cultural Change*. Cambridge, UK: Blackwell.

Held, David, and Anthony McGrew. 2002. *Globalization/Anti-Globalization*. Stanford, CA: Stanford University Press.

Held, David, Anthony McGrew, David Goldblatt, and Jonathan Perraton. 1999. *Global Transformations: Politics, Economics and Culture*. Cambridge, UK: Polity.

Hirst, Paul, Grahame Thompson, and Simon Bromley. 2009. *Globalization in Question: The International Economy and the Possibilities of Governance*. 3rd ed. Cambridge, UK: Polity.

Hopkins, A. G., ed. 2002. *Globalization in World History*. New York: Norton.

Jameson, Fredric. 1998. "Preface." In *The Cultures of Globalization*, edited by F. Jameson and M. Miyoshi, xi–xvii. Durham, NC: Duke University Press.

Kamola, Isaac. 2010. "Producing the Global Imaginary: Academic Knowledge, Globalization, and the Making of the World." PhD dissertation, University of Minnesota, Chapter 4.

Kennedy, Michael. 2015. *Globalizing Knowledge: Intellectuals, Publics, and Universities in Transition*. Stanford, CA: Stanford University Press.

Kenway, Jane, and Johannah Fahey, eds. 2008. *Globalizing the Research Imagination*. New York: Routledge.

Keucheyan, Razmig. 2013. *Left Hemisphere: Mapping Critical Theory Today*. London: Verso.

Krishna, Sankaran. 2009. *Globalization and Postcolonialism: Hegemony and Resistance in the Twenty-First Century*. Lanham, MD: Rowman & Littlefield.

Martens, Pim, Marco Caselli, Philippe de Lombarde, Lukas Figge, and Jan Aart Scholte. 2015. "New Directions in Globalization Indices." *Globalizations* 12 (2): 217–228.

Mazlish, Bruce. 2006. *The New Global History*. London: Routledge.

Mazlish, Bruce, and Akira Iriye, eds. 2005. *The Global History Reader*. New York: Routledge.

McCarty, Philip C. 2014. "Communicating Global Perspectives." *Basel Papers in European Global Studies*, 105. https://europa.unibas.ch/fileadmin/user_upload/europa/PDFs_Basel_Papers/BS105.pdf.

Mendieta, Eduardo. 2008. *Global Fragments: Globalizations, Latinamericanisms, and Critical Theory*. Albany: State University of New York Press.

Mittelman, James H. 2000. *The Globalization Syndrome*. Princeton, NJ: Princeton University Press, 2000.

Nassar, Jamal R. 2010. *Globalization and Terrorism: The Migration of Dreams and Nightmares*. 2nd ed. Lanham, MD: Rowman & Littlefield.

Ohmae, Kenichi. 1996. *The End of the Nation-State: The Rise of Regional Economies*. New York: Free Press.

Pieterse, Jan Nederveen. 2013. "What Is Global Studies?" *Globalizations* 10 (4): 499–514.

Pohl, Christian. 2010. "From Transdisciplinarity to Transdisciplinary Research." *Transdisciplinary Journal of Engineering & Science* 1 (1): 65–73.

Pohl, Christian, and Gertrude Hirsch Hadorn. 2008. "Methodological Challenges of Transdisciplinary Research." *Natures Sciences Sociétés*, 16 (2): 111–121.

Repko, Allen F. 2012. *Interdisciplinary Research: Process and Theory*. 2nd ed. Thousand Oaks, CA: Sage.

Robertson, Roland. 1992. *Globalization: Social Theory and Global Culture*. London: Sage.

Robertson, Roland. 2005. "The Conceptual Promise of Glocalization: Commonality and Diversity." *Art-e-Fact* (4): http://artefact.mi2.hr/_a04/lang_en/theory_robertson_en.htm.

Robinson, William I. 2005. "Critical Globalization Studies." In *Critical Globalization Studies*, edited by R. Appelbaum and W. I. Robinson, 11–18. New York: Routledge.

Rugman, Alan. 2001. *The End of Globalization*. New York: Random House.

Said, Edward. 1979. *Orientalism*. New York: Vintage.

Sassen, Saskia. 2001. *The Global City: New York, London, Tokyo*. 2nd ed. Princeton, NJ: Princeton University Press.

Sassen, Saskia. 2007. "The Places and Spaces of the Global: An Expanded Analytic Terrain." In *Globalization Theory: Approaches and Controversies*, edited by D. Held and A. G. McGrew, 79–105. Cambridge, UK: Polity.

Scholte, Jan Aart. 2005. *Globalization: A Critical Introduction*. 2nd ed. Houndmills, UK: Palgrave Macmillan.

Singh, Supriya. 2013. *Globalization and Money: A Global South Perspective*. Lanham, MD: Rowman & Littlefield.

Steger, Manfred B. 2008. *The Rise of the Global Imaginary: Political Ideologies from the French Revolution to the Global War on Terror*. New York: Oxford University Press.

Steger, Manfred B. 2009. *Globalisms: The Great Ideological Struggle of the Twenty-First Century*. 3rd ed. Lanham, MD: Rowman & Littlefield.

Steger, Manfred B. 2013. *Globalization: A Very Short Introduction*. 3rd ed. Oxford, UK: Oxford University Press.

Steger, Manfred B., and Paul James. 2013. "Levels of Subjective Globalization: Ideologies, Imaginaries, Ontologies." *Perspectives on Global Development and Technology* 12 (1–2): 17–40.

Steger, Manfred B., and Ravi K. Roy. 2010. *Neoliberalism: A Very Short Introduction*. Oxford, UK: Oxford University Press.

Steger, Manfred B., and Amentahru Wahlrab. 2016. *What Is Global Studies? Theory & Practice*. New York: Routledge.

Thakur, Ramesh, and Thomas G. Weiss. 2011. *Thinking About Global Governance: Why People and Ideas Matter*. New York: Routledge.

Urry, John. 2003. *Global Complexity*. Cambridge, UK: Polity.

Veseth, Michael. 2010. *Globaloney 2.0: The Crash of 2008 and the Future of Globalization*. Lanham, MD: Rowman & Littlefield.

Wallerstein, Immanuel. 2004. *World-Systems Analysis: An Introduction*. Durham, NC: Duke University Press.

Young, Robert J. C. 2003. *Postcolonialism: A Very Short Introduction*. Oxford, UK: Oxford University Press.

Zeleza, Paul Tiyambe. 2003. *Rethinking Africa's Globalization*. Trenton, NJ: Africa World Press.

FURTHER READING

Anheier, Helmut K., and Mark Juergensmeyer, editors. 2012. *Encyclopedia of Global Studies*. 4 vols. London: Sage.

Campbell, Patricia J., Aran MacKinnon, and Christy R. Stevens. 2010. *Introduction to Global Studies*. Hoboken, NJ: Wiley-Blackwell.

Juergensmeyer, Mark, ed. 2014. *Thinking Globally: A Global Studies Reader*. Berkeley: University of California Press.

Smallman, Shawn C., and Kimberely Brown. 2015. *Introduction to International and Global Studies*. 2nd ed. Raleigh: University of North Carolina Press.

Steger, Manfred B., ed. 2014. *The Global Studies Reader*. 2nd ed. New York: Oxford University Press.

Steger, Manfred B., and Paul James, ed. 2015. *Globalization: The Career of a Concept*. London and New York: Routledge.

Steger, Manfred B., and Amentahru Wahlrab. 2016. *What Is Global Studies? Theory & Practice*. New York: Routledge.

CHAPTER 2

....

THE EVOLUTION OF GLOBAL STUDIES

....

MARK JUERGENSMEYER

IN one sense, it is easy to date the beginning of the academic field of global studies. In fact, one can almost precisely put a date on it. The year was 1995. It was then that California State University at Monterey began a global studies undergraduate program. It was also the year that the University of California at Santa Barbara created an academic unit that led to an undergraduate major two years later and then to graduate programs on both the MA and PhD levels. The first MA program in global studies was established in 1997 at Hitotsubashi University in Tokyo, and by the end of the first decade of the twenty-first century there were hundreds of undergraduate majors called global studies and dozens of graduate programs throughout the world, including Shanghai, Melbourne, Moscow, Leipzig, Cairo, London, Los Angeles, and New York City.

In another sense, however, global studies has been around seemingly forever, if one means by that term the study of human activity on a broad conceptual scale, and generalizations about that activity that are deemed to be universally applicable. In this sense, Plato's Republic was an innovation in global studies. And so were the Analects of Kung Fu Tse and the Arthashastra of Kautilya. The towering figures in the birth of the social sciences, Max Weber (1864–1920) and Émile Durkheim (1858–1917), were also pioneers in global studies. Weber tried to make sense of what was distinctive and what was similar among the cultural patterns of India, China, Judaism, and Protestant Christianity. He also showed that rational–legal authority and its associated bureaucratization was a globalizing process. Durkheim analyzed from a global perspective the rise of organic solidarity, based on functional interdependence. The great social theorist, Karl Marx (1818–1883), likewise assumed that his theories were universal, arguing that capitalism was a globalizing force, one in which both production systems and markets would eventually expand to encompass the entire world.

Scholarship in the twentieth century was at times similarly sweeping in its scope. In the humanities, historians such as Arnold Toynbee surveyed the world's civilizations, and William McNeill placed "the rise of the West" in global context. The Harvard pioneer in comparative religion, Wilfred Cantwell Smith, understood religion as a changing feature of the world's cultural interactions. Edward Said showed how colonial mentalities infected the perspective of Western scholarship on non-Western subjects. In the social sciences, Talcott Parsons showed the relevance of culture to social structures, and his disciple, Robert Bellah, explored the significance of these implications from Tokugawa-era Japan to Muslim societies and modern America. Immanuel Wallerstein, in examining what he called world systems of economic and political interdependence, foreshadowed the development of the field of global political economy.

By the end of the twentieth century, the scholarly world was prepared for the next great challenge—understanding the era of globalization. Roland Robertson was one of the first sociologists to talk about globalization and its specific manifestations, glocalization. Arjun Appadurai turned an anthropological attention from geographic landscapes to a variety of social "scapes," culturally shaped understandings of the world. David Held pioneered in the field of global politics, and Mary Kaldor examined an emerging global civil society. Kwame Anthony Appiah and Ulrich Beck described what appeared to be a cosmopolitan strand of public civility in the new global order. Saskia Sassen observed the rise of the global city; Dominic Sachsenmaier, A. G. Hopkins, and Pamela Kyle Crossley explored new ways of thinking about global history; Thomas Pogge and Giles Gunn explored the possibility of a global ethics; Manfred Steger considered the implications of the "global imaginary"; and Jan Nederveen Pieterse showed how hybridity theory was essential for understanding the cultural aspects of globalization.

EMERGENCE OF A NEW FIELD

Individual scholarship is not quite a field, however, and the way that these varied interests in globalization and the global dimension of societies and cultures have coalesced into teaching and research programs is an interesting story (Steger and Wahlrab 2017). For that, we have to return to the late 1990s and the first decade in the twenty-first century when in universities and colleges throughout the world, scholars and teachers were coming together to consider ways of conceiving global studies as a field to be taught and an arena in which to do credible research. They were convinced that globalization was one of the critical features of their time, and to study it was to focus on the central feature of life in the twenty-first century. But how does one go about doing this? Is it really possible to study the whole world? Doesn't this mean studying almost everything? And if so, where does one begin?

These were the questions in the minds of a group of scholars who met in Tokyo in 2008. They had met the year before in Santa Barbara, California, with the idea of exploring the creation of a new international organization for representatives of graduate programs called global studies that were just then emerging in various universities throughout the world. In the first decade of the twenty-first century, scholars were creating global studies programs in dozens of universities in Asia, Europe, and North America, including Japan, South Korea, China, India, Germany, Denmark, Russia, the United Kingdom, Australia, Canada, and the United States. When the scholars came together in Tokyo in 2008, their first task was to answer the question of what global studies was and to define the major features of the field.

They came expecting to disagree. After all, each of these programs had developed independently from the others. One would think that the field of global studies would be defined vastly differently in Tokyo, Leipzig, and Melbourne. But as it turned out, this was not the case. There was a great deal of agreement at the outset regarding what the field of global studies contained and how to go about studying it. The main characteristics of global studies that they agreed on at that founding meeting of the international Global Studies Consortium in Tokyo are similar to what Manfred Steger, in Chapter 1 of this volume, calls the central pillars of the field of global studies. They include the following features:

Transnationality: The Global Studies Consortium's founding members agreed that the field of global studies is broader than the nation-state. In its broadest sense, it focuses on globalization—the events, activities, ideas, trends, processes, and phenomena that appear across national boundaries and cultural regions and touch on all regions of the world. These include activities such as economic distribution systems and ideologies such as nationalism or religious beliefs. Global studies also includes the study of transnational activities and processes that may not affect everyone on the planet but have a significant impact beyond a single nation or cultural region. The use of the internet, for instance, has not yet caught on in every undeveloped corner of the world but is a transnational phenomenon on a far-reaching scale. Certain pandemics, for example, may affect primarily one region of the world but have the potential of becoming global. Hence, global studies examines transnational activities and processes that expand beyond particular nations and cultural regions. The scholars in global studies use the term "cultural regions" as well as nations because these kinds of global flows of activity and ideas transcend the limitations of regions even when they are not the same as national boundaries. Historically, much of the activity that we call transnational might more properly be called transregional because it occurred before the concept of nation was applied to states.

Interdisciplinarity: Because transnational phenomena are complex, they are examined from many disciplinary points of view. In general, global studies does not keep strict disciplinary divisions among, for instance, sociological, historical, political, literary, or other academic fields. Rather, it takes a problem-focused approach, examining situations such as global warming or the rise of new religio-political ideologies as specific cases. Each of these problem areas requires multiple perspectives to make sense of them—perspectives that may be economic, political, social, cultural, religious, ideological, or environmental. Scholars involved in global studies often work in interdisciplinary teams or freely borrow from one field to another. They come from all fields of the social sciences (especially from sociology, economics, political science, geography, and anthropology). And many are also related to the humanities, including particularly the fields of history, literature, religious studies, and the arts. Some have expertise in areas of science, such as environmental studies and public health, or in professional fields such as law, public policy, and medicine. At the innovative edge of interdisciplinarity is thinking that is transdisciplinary. These are attempts to develop theoretical models and conceptual tools to explore aspects of transnational and global phenomena that do not rely on any specific disciplinary field. Although in its infancy, these attempts to theoretically examine global "scapes," "flows," and "processes" may be important aspects of future attempts to ground the research agenda of the field of global studies.

Trans-temporality: Simply stated, this aspect of global studies means taking seriously historical precedents for global phenomena as well as their contemporary and timeless manifestations. Globalization has a history. Although the pace and intensity of globalization have increased enormously in the post-Cold War period of the twentieth century and even more so in the twenty-first century, transnational activities have had historical antecedents. There are moments in history—such as the development of the Silk Road between East Asia and the Middle East during the Han Dynasty in the third century BCE and the rich culture of the ancient Mediterranean world during the Roman and Greek Empires that was developing at the same time—when there was a great deal of transnational activity and interchange on economic, cultural, and political levels. The global reach of the Mongol Empire in the thirteenth and fourteenth centuries and that of European colonialism from the sixteenth century to the twentieth century provide other examples of the global strata of culture, education, technology, and economic activity upon which are based many aspects of the globalization of the twenty-first century. Thus, to understand fully the patterns of globalization today, it is necessary to probe their historical precedents. It also means moving beyond the limitations of space and time to consider, as Roland Robertson has said, the compression of the world in a single space or, as Manfred Steger has put it, the transcendence of space and time in a globalized world. Perhaps nothing illustrates this space–time transcendence more than the internet, which has become one of the primary means of communicating and accessing knowledge. The internet resides in cyberspace rather than physical space, and its information storage is timeless. These aspects of the digital age require new ways of considering space–time dimensions and the phenomena of trans-temporality.

Critical perspectives: The dominant American and European views of globalization are not the only ones. Although many aspects of contemporary globalization are based on European colonial precedents, most global studies scholars do not accept uncritically the notion that people in the West should be the only ones to benefit from economic, political, and cultural globalization. Some global studies scholars avoid using the term "globalization" to describe their subject of study because the term sometimes is interpreted to imply the promotion of a Western-dominated hegemonic project aimed at spreading the acceptance of laissez-faire liberal economics throughout the world. Rather, they may say that they study transnational or global issues. Other scholars use the term "globalization" but qualify it; they describe their approach as "critical globalization studies," implying that their examination of globalization is not intended to promote or privilege Western economic models of globalization but, rather, to understand it. Behind this hesitation to uncritically adopt the term "globalization" is the notion that one should not uncritically analyze any of the global phenomena. Rather, the scholar is required to view them from many cultural perspectives and from perspectives that may be outside the mainstream in scholarly fields. Scholars of global studies acknowledge that globalization and other global issues, activities, and trends can be viewed differently from different areas of the world and from different racial, gendered, and socioeconomic positions within each locality. For that reason, scholars of global studies sometimes speak of "many globalizations" or "multiple perspectives on global studies." This position acknowledges that there is no dominant paradigm or perspective in global studies that is valued over others.

These four features of global studies—transnationality, interdisciplinarity, trans-temporality, and critical perspectives—are principles embraced by representatives of all the founding programs in the international Global Studies Consortium that met at that fateful occasion at Sophia University in Tokyo in 2008. But to one degree or another, these elements are found in most programs of study and research that call themselves global studies wherever they have been established throughout the world. What is remarkable is how consistent these principles are even within far-flung places that have developed global studies on their own without using any other program as a model. Curiously, from Cairo to Copenhagen, from Melbourne to Leipzig, and from Shanghai to Santa Barbara, the field of global studies has developed with these four principles as prominent features of their programs.

There are differences among the programs, however. The difference in emphasis and organization is in part due to whether the academic unit that embraces global studies is primarily an existing department that incorporates the global dimensions of its study as a subfield, an interdisciplinary teaching program for undergraduate majors, a career-oriented master's program for graduate students, or a doctoral program for graduates and postgraduates to pursue research agenda in the study of global phenomena. In the following sections, these are discussed in turn.

GLOBAL SUBFIELDS OF EXISTING DEPARTMENTS

As globalization became a significant aspect of the world's society at the turn of the twenty-first century, many departments began to incorporate the global dimension of their studies as a subfield of the discipline. Global history, global sociology, and global politics, for instance, have become prominent areas of study within the disciplines of history, sociology, and political science, respectively. In some cases, students can major in one of these subfields, both at the undergraduate level and at the graduate level. Some degrees in global studies are offered by traditional departments, such as the global education master's degree at the University of Illinois, the global economic history degree offered by the economic history department at the London School of Economics and Political Science (LSE), or the global politics graduate degree also offered at LSE. Other departments allow students to specialize in the global aspects of their discipline (e.g., global sociology, global history, or global anthropology) even though their degree is not demarcated as being global studies-related. Some specialized global studies programs are interdisciplinary, such as the Global Metropolitan Studies PhD emphasis at the University of California, Berkeley.

Although these departmental global studies subfields are not interdisciplinary, they focus on transnational phenomena and are often critical and trans-temporal in their methodological approaches. In many cases, they reach beyond disciplinary boundaries to work with other departments in setting up undergraduate- and graduate-level interdisciplinary global studies programs. At some universities, interdisciplinary committees provide a global studies emphasis or minor for students who are pursuing a graduate degree in a particular discipline. This allows a student who is a sociologist, for example, to meet in interdepartmental seminars with graduate students from other departments, take courses outside the student's discipline, and receive a credential for doing so. At some universities, their diplomas read "with an emphasis in global studies" under their proclamation of having received a PhD in a particular department.

Global Studies as a Teaching Field in Undergraduate Programs

Most undergraduate teaching programs in global studies began as interdisciplinary majors, usually under the jurisdiction of a coordinating committee of faculty representing a variety of departments. Often, existing programs in international and area studies were renamed as global studies programs. In some cases, all that was changed was the name. In other cases, as in the program in transnational studies at the University of Aarhus in Denmark, the programs were redesigned to focus on transnational processes and patterns and to address global problems.

When the undergraduate teaching programs have been created anew or redesigned, they usually follow the four principles that the Global Studies Consortium has identified as characteristic of the field of global studies. Undergraduate programs typically focus more on contemporary issues than on historical ones, however, particularly issues of the global economy, global inequalities and fair labor practices, environmental protection, global governance, security and the rise of terrorism, and human rights concerns throughout the world. It is common practice for at least a few of the courses to be designed specifically for global studies. Typically, one or two courses will be taught as introductions or surveys to the field of global studies, and then students will be allowed to choose from a list of existing courses that cover one or more of the contemporary issues that are regarded as germane to the field. They will also be allowed to take courses that relate to global history and to cultural areas, especially in non-Western regions.

In many cases, students will be expected to study abroad for one or more terms during their undergraduate studies and to become linguistically competent in a non-English language. Most undergraduate majors in global studies have an area studies component, but this raises the issue of how the global studies programs are related to area studies fields. This question is particularly acute at universities that are large enough to have established programs in East Asia Studies, South Asia Studies, Middle Eastern Studies, Latin American Studies, and the like. Often, the faculty related to these area studies programs will be wary of global studies, just as they have been wary of the field of international studies in the past, viewing these broader programs as competitive and offering watered-down versions of the expertise that they provide in particular regions of the world. On the other hand, when global studies students are required to take area-focused and foreign language courses, this provides a larger audience for these courses. And in some cases, funding is more likely to be available for area-related courses if they are part of a wider international or global studies curriculum. So it is an ambivalent relationship.

It should also be noted that some of the interdisciplinary programs in global studies were established by faculty who were motivated by high ideals, to help train the global citizens of the future. This has sometimes been listed as an additional feature to the four principles of global studies identified by the Global Studies Consortium, and it is an ideal that is especially prominent in the goals of faculty who have volunteered their time and energy to create and sustain programs in global studies: They have been motivated by a desire to make the world a better place in which to live. By focusing on global problems, they imply that they want to help solve those problems. They also hope to foster a sense of global citizenship among their students. They like to think that they are helping create "global literacy"—the ability of students to function in an increasingly globalized world—by helping students understand both the specific aspects of diverse cultures and traditions and the commonly experienced global trends and patterns. Other teachers assert that they are providing training in "global leadership," giving potential leaders of transnational organizations and movements the understanding and skills that will help them solve problems and deal with issues on a global scale.

CAREER-ORIENTED GLOBAL STUDIES GRADUATE PROGRAMS

Some of the first graduate programs in global studies also focused on global issues and problem-solving approaches. Some programs, such as University of California, Santa Barbara's MA program in global studies and the degree programs of the School of Global Affairs at the American University in Cairo, were consciously designed along the model of the well-established programs in international policy at such institutions as the Johns Hopkins School of Advanced International Studies in Washington, DC, the Woodrow Wilson School of Public and International Affairs at Princeton University, and Columbia University's School of International and Public Affairs. These are programs that offer a two-year degree aimed at providing a high-level understanding of the international milieu and managerial skills that prepare future leaders in business, journalism, government agencies, and international nonprofit organizations. The global studies master's programs were similarly designed, but with a focus on transnational rather than international issues and aimed at students seeking careers in the nonprofit world of international nongovernment humanitarian and social service agencies rather than in business and government.

The master's degree in global studies at the University of North Carolina at Chapel Hill is described as a two-year "applied research" degree program aimed at preparing students for leadership positions in transnational organizations. At RMIT University in Melbourne, Australia, an existing graduate program in development studies was brought under the umbrella of a new School of Global, Urban, and Social Studies and redirected toward the study of the relationship between the development of local economies and societies and the contexts of economic and cultural globalization that affect the local situations. At Roskilde University in Denmark, students are given the option of a two-year degree in global studies or one that combines global studies with such practical fields as business, communications, and development. The European Union's Global Studies consortium based at Leipzig University in Germany has placed the graduates of its two-year master's program in a variety of governmental and social service agencies throughout the world.

RESEARCH-ORIENTED GLOBAL STUDIES
GRADUATE PROGRAMS

In addition to these discipline-focused, interdisciplinary, and problem-oriented programs of global studies, there is an increasing number of graduate programs that are research oriented and focus on the theoretical issues of globalization. Almost all of the PhD programs in global studies fall into this category, and many of the MA programs are designed to be research oriented as well as career oriented. These are programs in which concepts of globalization are central, and all four principles of global studies apply: They are transnational, interdisciplinary, trans-temporal, and critical in their research agenda. These programs are usually supported by faculty who are solely dedicated to the field of global studies and belong to a department, program, or school that usually has "global studies" as part of its name. At Wilfred Laurier University in Canada, for instance, global studies-dedicated faculty teach exclusively in the global studies program. Global studies units that are designated as "programs" usually offer bachelor's but not graduate degrees, although at the University of California, Santa Barbara and elsewhere, MA graduate degrees have been offered by a global studies program that functions as an embryonic department.

As mentioned previously, the first graduate program in global studies was established in 1997 at Hitotsubashi University in Japan, which has its own dedicated faculty in the Global Issues Division of the Graduate School of Social Sciences. The division has become the degree-granting Institute of Global Issues. Its website proclaims that its global studies graduate programs offer "an issue-focused methodology, solution-oriented analysis and de-Eurocentric thinking." Nearby at Sophia University, also in Tokyo, the Graduate School of Global Studies was established in 2006 with its own faculty that support both MA and PhD programs in English language medium. RMIT Melbourne has graduate degree programs in global studies in its School of Global, Urban, and Social Studies. Its website describes its global studies degree programs as "interdisciplinary and comprehensive." Some of the first graduate global studies programs in Europe were established at Leipzig, Freiburg, Roskilde, Aarhus, and LSE. In the United States, the first graduate global studies programs were based at the University of California, Santa Barbara, Arizona State University, and Rutgers University. By 2010, more than sixty graduate programs—primarily at the master's degree level—were functioning in East Asia, Europe, and North America. Graduate degree programs were also established in India, Egypt, and China.

Some of the most interesting degree programs in global studies have been cooperative ventures between several universities. In 2001, the first joint global studies MA was created, based at Albert-Ludwigs-Universität in Freiburg, Germany, along with partner universities in Argentina, India, and South Africa. The first consortium MA program in global studies was sponsored by the European Union's Erasmus Mundus Program in 2005, based at the Universities of Leipzig, Vienna, Wroclaw, and LSE. PhD programs in global studies developed later. In 2014, Humboldt University in Berlin offered a PhD in global studies in conjunction with five other universities: Chulalongkorn University, Jawaharlal Nehru University, FLACSO Argentina, Università di Bologna, and Universidade Federal Fluminense. Students are expected to spend at least one year at each of two of the universities. By 2006, several universities had established PhD graduate programs in global studies, including Sophia University in Tokyo and RMIT University in Melbourne. The first PhD in global studies in the United States was the one in Global Affairs created at Rutgers University in Newark in 2006.

Most of these degree programs have been housed in interdisciplinary programs, departments, divisions, or schools labeled "global studies." The program in Global and International Studies at the University of California, Santa Barbara became established as the Department of Global Studies after the approval of its PhD program in global studies in 2015. Arizona State University created a School of Global Studies in 1996. Later, a department of Society and Globalization was created at Roskilde University in Denmark and a School of Global, Urban, and Social Studies was established at RMIT University in Melbourne. A School of Global Studies was also created at Sikkim University in India, a graduate School of Global Affairs was established at American University in Cairo, and Indiana University created a graduate School of Global and International Studies based on the largest assembly of area studies centers and programs of any university in the United States.

RESEARCH CENTERS, ASSOCIATIONS, AND PUBLICATION OUTLETS

As a research field, global studies touches on many scholars outside the lists of those faculty involved in teaching programs or subfields of disciplines. A variety of research centers, journals, publication series, and academic associations have been created since the turn of the twenty-first century in response to the proliferation of global studies-related research and to facilitate interdisciplinary cooperation.

One of the first research centers in the field was the Centre for Global Governance that was launched at LSE in 1992. In 2001, Yale University established the Center for the Study of Globalization, which began publishing an online journal, *Yale Global OnLine*. The Orfalea Center for Global and International Studies was established at the University of California, Santa Barbara in 2006; and in 2015, Northwestern University received $100 million to launch the Buffet Institute of International Studies. Similar institutes have been established throughout the world.

One of the reasons why these centers and academic programs arose so quickly in the decades around the turn of the twenty-first century is that money was available to create them. In some cases, as the family names of Orfalea, Buffet, and others indicate, individuals and private family foundations have understood the importance of dealing with such global issues as environmental protection, human rights, and worldwide inequalities. They have been persuaded that providing funds for scholars to work collectively on these projects would be a contribution to helping solve the world's problems. In other cases, institutions such as Indiana University have seen the importance of this growing field within the academic community and want to marshal their own existing resources in a way that would give prominence to their institutions by providing the funds to develop the field. In yet other cases, governmental funding has been available. In Europe, the Erasmus Mundus Consortium in Global Studies, based at Leipzig University, has been successful in applying for grants from the European Union, which has supported the consortium and provided generous grants to participating students from throughout the world.

In the United States, several consortia of universities have taken advantage of federal funding to create joint research centers. Since 2006, centers in global studies have been funded by the National Resource Centers (NRC) program of the US Department of Education. The funds for these centers are also known as Title VI grants due to the fact that the NRC program was formally established in Title VI, Part A, § 602 of the US Congress's Higher Education Act of 1965. The funding program was established for the purpose of providing grants to American universities to establish, strengthen, and operate language and area or international studies centers. The grants are given every four years on a competitive basis, usually amounting to approximately $200,000 per year. Global studies centers funded by this program include the Indiana University Center for the Study of Global Change, the Center for Global Studies at the University of Illinois at Urbana–Champaign, the University of Minnesota Center for Global Initiatives at the Institute for Global Studies, the University of North Carolina at Chapel Hill, the Center for Global Studies at the University of Washington, and the Center for Global Studies at the University of Wisconsin–Madison.

In addition to these research and programmatic centers that deal with global studies as a whole, many centers have been established to focus on one aspect of global studies or a particular disciplinary perspective. For instance, Duke University has established the Center for Global Studies and the Humanities, Trinity College has created the Center for Urban and Global Studies, and the University of California medical campus at San Francisco has created the Center for Global Health. Perhaps 200 or more centers for global studies have been established throughout the world with varying degrees of institutional support.

To meet the need for publication outlets of these proliferating centers for research, a spate of new journals and publication series have been established. One of the first journals to be established in the field of global studies was *Global Networks: A Journal of Transnational Affairs*, launched in the United Kingdom in 2001 and sponsored by the Global Studies Association, which held its first meeting in Manchester in 2000. Also associated with the Global Studies Association is the quarterly journal published by Routledge, *Globalizations*, established in 2003, which is often cited as the leading journal in the field, and the *Journal of Critical Globalization Studies*, also based in the United Kingdom. Another offshoot of conferences of individual scholars in global studies is *The Global Studies Journal*, associated with the yearly Global Studies Conference, which holds meetings for individual scholars at locales throughout the world. *Global Policy*, launched in 2010, offers academic and general-interest essays in an internet magazine format. It was originally based in London but then moved to Durham University with support from other institutions, including LSE and the Hertie School of Governance in Berlin. A group of scholars in Russia provided the impetus behind *The Journal of Globalization Studies*, which was launched in 2010 with the mission of taking the perspective of developing as well as developed countries into account.

Perhaps the best known online feature magazine related to the field of global studies is *Yale Global OnLine*, a professionally edited journal of brief essays on contemporary issues that was launched in 2002 and is sponsored by Yale University's Center for the Study of Globalization. *Global-e* is oriented toward the academic community rather than the general public, and it provides brief articles related to the field of global studies. It was inaugurated in 2006 and has been sponsored by centers of global studies at the University of Wisconsin–Madison, the University of Washington, the University of Illinois, the University of

North Carolina at Chapel Hill, and the University of California, Santa Barbara. Editorial responsibilities have rotated among the sponsoring centers.

The first online peer-reviewed journal in global studies was the Canada-based journal *Globalization*, established in 2001. *New Global Studies*, founded in 2006 and published on-line by Berkeley Electronic Press, is associated with the Global History Project based at Harvard University and Massachusetts Institute of Technology; its scope is broader than history, however, encompassing contemporary social, political, and economic aspects of globalization. The *Asia Journal of Global Studies* is an offshoot of the Asian Global Studies Association and is published online yearly. *Globality Studies Journal: Global History, Society, Civilization* was established in 2006 by the Center for Global and Local History at Stony Brook University, New York. *Exploring Globalization* is an online journal published by the Office of Global Learning at Fairleigh Dickinson University; it primarily publishes reviews and brief essays.

There are also journals relating to particular aspects of global society and culture, such as the *Journal of Global Ethics, Journal of Global History, Journal of Global Legal Studies, Global Economy Journal, Global Finance Journal, Global News Journal, Journal of Global Business, Journal of Global Marketing, Journal of Global Health Sciences,* and *Global Media Journal.* In addition, there are the *Journal of Global Buddhism* and the *Journal of Global Drug Policy and Practice.*

Several book publishers are committed to making global studies one of their areas of specialization. Routledge has published a series of books on "Foundations of Global Studies," and it also has a series on "Global Institutions," "Global Cooperation," and "Global Political Economy." The University of California Press has developed a list of textbooks and monographs related to global studies and is launching an online journal on global studies. In addition, there are series related to the global aspects of particular fields. The University of Chicago Press has a series on "Global History," for instance, and Routledge has one on "Global Health" and another on "Global Ethics."

EMERGING TRENDS IN GLOBAL STUDIES

All of the busy research activity and program building in global studies throughout the world gives the impression of a field that has arrived. But no academic field has really "arrived," in the sense of reaching a point of stasis and forever staying the same. No doubt that the subject matter of global studies will change considerably from year to year as new developments appear on the scene that deserve attention. The social and political repercussions of global warming, for instance, are bound to require a whole new arena of inquiry as the environmental situation deteriorates and vast numbers of people are uprooted from their habitats.

There will also be changes in the way that global studies is conducted as an academic enterprise. During the initial years in which programs of global studies were being developed, the scholars involved in them usually had a high degree of unanimity of purpose and a strong collegial spirit that masked any internal differences in the way they conceptualized the field and its role within the larger academic community. However, as time has passed and programs have ripened into maturity, fissures have sometimes developed, and differences of opinion have led to creative tensions. I call these tensions "creative" because I think that it is unlikely that they will cause programs to dissolve or break apart, and they will likely produce creative attempts to resolve the differences in agreeable ways, either as syntheses or as compatible accommodations. Until they are resolved, however, they will continue to be points of difference and dispute among scholars involved in helping develop and sustain the emerging field. The following tensions are among the most critical.

Global as Theme Versus Primary Focus

When many programs of global studies began, they were promoted by scholars who viewed the global aspect of their work as one theme in their commitment to a discipline. The European Union Consortium based in Leipzig, for instance, was established by scholars who were historians and dedicated to developing global history as a credible subfield within that discipline. As the program has developed, however, increasingly students and other faculty involved have pressured the program to expand to a wide range of topics and methodologies in global studies, which the program has done. Still, it took some growing pains.

At the University of California, Santa Barbara, the core faculty in the global studies program initially retained at least half of their positions in the departments from which they came, including sociology, history, religious studies, and literature. It was thought that the global studies program would service the whole of the liberal arts with introductory courses that students from any major could take and that all of the faculty would retain partial membership in their original departments. As the program developed and the number of undergraduate majors rose to nearly 1,000 and new graduate programs were created, courses became restricted to global studies majors, and new faculty were tied exclusively to global studies as their academic home. Debates emerged within the department about the degree to which it should be concerned about helping develop the global dimension of other departments versus strengthening the core faculty and curriculum of its own department.

The stories from Leipzig and Santa Barbara can be replicated in many other places throughout the world where global studies has become institutionalized. In these places, the demands of servicing undergraduate and graduate students who identify solely with the field have challenged the idea that the mission of global studies should be to "globalize the whole curriculum" of the university, as one of the early mission statements of a global studies program put it. There is virtue to both approaches, and something is lost either way. If global studies only serves its own students and faculty, it fails to serve the wider academic community. And if it devotes too much energy to the broader mission of globalizing the liberal arts, it may fail to develop a substantial core faculty and curriculum at a crucial moment of development for an embryonic field.

Global Theory Versus Practice

Within departments of global studies there is another tension emerging that relates in part to what the intellectual core of the field should be about and in part to the matter of what its mission should be. One way of describing this tension is theory versus practice. Many global studies programs have had a practical, problem-solving side from the beginning, including the School of Global, Urban and Social Studies at RMIT in Melbourne, where an existing master's program in development was incorporated into the school. At the American University in Cairo, where the president of the university had formerly been the dean of international affairs at Columbia University, the idea of the School of Global Affairs was to create practical, career-oriented curricula to prepare students for leadership roles in international and transnational organizations. Its mission was clear.

In other universities, however, the matter was less certain. At Shanghai University and the universities associated with the consortia based at Freiburg, Humboldt, and Leipzig Universities in Germany, the approach to global studies has tended to be much more theoretical. The emphasis has been on historical antecedents to, and social theories about, the emergence of globalization in the twenty-first century. Many of the students taking the courses may plan on professional non-academic careers after graduation, but the curricula definitely have a theoretical, non-issue-oriented tenor to them.

The global studies graduate programs at Roskilde University in Denmark and at Sophia University in Japan, however, try to strike a balance. Many of the courses are indeed historical and theoretical, but some are not, and students are encouraged to work on real-world themes and problems rather than strictly academic topics. At Roskilde, students are allowed to pair their global studies graduate programs with practical graduate fields such as business or public health. At Santa Barbara, when the master's program in global and international studies was first conceived, there was a debate about whether it should offer a Master of Global Affairs, in the manner of the Master in International Affairs degree given by other professional schools for international career training, signaling that the curriculum was providing professional training. The other option was to offer an MA—a Master of Arts degree similar to any other MA in the liberal arts. The MA won, with the understanding that the program would provide academic preparation that would meet the needs of both kinds of students—those who were planning on further academic work and those who were planning for a professional career in a transnational organization. The debate continues, however, whether the program should be more practical or theoretical on the MA level. On the PhD level, there is agreement that the training should be more theoretical and academic.

Global Scholar as Academic Insider Versus Outsider

To some extent, the "theoretical versus practical" tension is parallel to another, one that relates to the institutional stance of the field. Should global studies strive to take its role as a standard field of studies in lockstep with other disciplines in the university? Or should it stay partially as an outsider, a gadfly raising critical issues at the edge of academia's establishment? In some ways, this dilemma is one that is faced by other newly created fields, such as ethnic studies, feminist studies, and queer studies, in which many of the founders were scholars who viewed the role of their intellectual activity to be one that challenged the established norms rather than fitting comfortably in them.

Scholars in global studies who see it playing a prophetic role are those who are most in favor of the principle of "taking a critical perspective," a position with which most global studies scholars agree. The question is how far to take that critical posture. Those who take a "critical globalization" approach to global studies are sometimes accused of adopting an anti-business leftist agenda. Those who adopt a more conservative approach are also accused of bias, of favoring the status quo and abandoning a central principle of the field—to see globalization from multiple perspectives. Often, these internal debates about the stance of global studies carry a political edge to them, and sometimes the tone is one of the Global South versus the established West.

Most scholars of global studies welcome this conversation, however, because it strikes at the heart of what global studies is as an intellectual enterprise. Many of those scholars who have been attracted to global studies have been so for just this reason—they appreciate the conceptual challenges of trying to view the world as a whole, not just from one perspective on the planet but, rather, from multiple perspectives. They want to be challenged by the points of view of different regions, different voices, different races, and different genders and sexualities. They want to take seriously the perspectives of both the established hegemonic core and the aggrieved alternative outliers. For this reason, global studies as a field is likely to be enhanced by the vitality of the conversation related to this tension between insider and outsider, as it will with the other tensions. All of them are bound to increasingly engage the adherents of global studies in intellectually productive ways as the field develops in the future.

REFERENCE

Steger, Manfred B., and Amentahru Wahlrab. 2017. *What Is Global Studies? Theory and Practice*. New York: Routledge.

FURTHER READING

Anheier, Helmut K., and Mark Juergensmeyer, eds. 2012. *Encyclopedia of Global Studies*. 4 vols. London: Sage.

Appadurai, Arjun. 1996. *Modernity at Large: Cultural Dimensions of Globalization*. Minneapolis: University of Minnesota Press.

Appelbaum, Richard P., and William Robinson, eds. 2005. *Critical Globalization Studies*. New York: Routledge.

Appiah, Kwame Anthony. 2006. *Cosmopolitanism: Ethics in a World of Strangers*. New York: Norton.

Bhagwati, Jagdish. 2004. *In Defense of Globalization*. New York: Oxford University Press.

Brysk, Alison, ed. 2002. *Globalization and Human Rights*. Berkeley: University of California Press.

Campbell, Patricia J., Aran MacKinnon, and Christy R. Stevens. 2010. *Introduction to Global Studies*. Hoboken, NJ: Wiley-Blackwell.

Chanda, Nayan. 2007. *Bound Together: How Traders, Preachers, Adventurers, and Warriors Shaped Globalization*. New Haven, CT: Yale University Press.

Gunn, Giles. 2001. *Beyond Solidarity: Pragmatism and Difference in a Globalized World*. Chicago: University of Chicago Press.

Held, David, and Anthony McGrew. 2007. *Globalization/Anti-Globalization: Beyond the Great Divide*. London: Polity.

Juergensmeyer, Mark, ed. 2008. *The Oxford Handbook of Global Religion*. New York: Oxford University Press.

Juergensmeyer, Mark, ed. 2014. *Thinking Globally: A Global Studies Reader*. Berkeley: University of California Press.

Kaldor, Mary. 2003. *Global Civil Society: An Answer to War*. London: Polity.

Nederveen Pieterse, Jan, ed. 2000. *Global Futures: Shaping Globalization*. New York: Zed Books.

Robertson, Roland. 1992. *Globalization: Social Theory and Global Culture*. London: Sage.

Sassen, Saskia. 1996. *Losing Control? Sovereignty in a Global Age*. New York: Columbia University Press.

Steger, Manfred B., ed. 2014. *The Global Studies Reader*. 2nd ed. New York: Oxford University Press.

CHAPTER 3

....

HISTORICAL ANTECEDENTS
OF THE FIELD

....

ROLAND ROBERTSON

ANY substantive examination of the historical antecedents of the growing transdisciplinary field of global studies requires much sensitivity to a holistic longue durée framework of social and intellectual development. It is not good enough to trace the field to the latest phase of globalization after World War II or even to go back to the beginnings of the modern social sciences in the nineteenth century. For instance, in *Life Beyond Earth*, Coustenis and Encrenaz (2013: 1) cogently maintain that the search for life in the universe has never ceased to intrigue and amaze human beings: "After the first ideas had arisen on cosmology (the structure of the cosmos) and cosmogony (its creation), early civilizations and philosophers turned their minds towards living beings and how they came to be." They argue that once the first "scientific" minds gained some degree of autonomy in different areas of the world, innovative ideas were initiated in Egypt, the Indies, the Americas, China, and Europe. In Greece, for example, Aristarchus (310–230 BC) conceived the idea of what we now call the heliocentric solar system. Eratosthenes (276–194 BC) demonstrated that the earth was spherical and also demonstrated the distance to the moon, while Anaximander (610–546 BC) had worked out a structure for the whole universe.

This longue durée way of thinking could well be regarded as the very earliest beginning of what is now called "global studies" (Robertson 2016; Steger and Wahlrab 2017). Any serious discussion of the latter necessitates an exploration of how one goes about discovering the origins or antecedents of the field. In turn, this must also involve what is meant by not merely the term "global studies" but also—even more specifically—the term "globalization." In addition to emphasizing the importance of longue durée thinking, this chapter traces the antecedents of global studies up to the period of the great explorations and innovations of the fifteenth and sixteenth centuries, including the "discovery" of East Asia, on the one hand, and the Americas, on the other hand. This was also the period of the invention of the printing press and movable type, facilitating, inter alia, the Renaissance, the Reformation, and the Enlightenment. Each of these has until recently been thought of as a European development, but it must be noted that the purely European origins of the Renaissance in particular have been persuasively challenged (Jardine and Brotton 2000). Meanwhile, a number of societies outside of Europe have had their own enlightenments, emulated from yet other societies.

The theme of globalization is not only the master narrative of the global studies field but also one of the more prominent topics in intellectual and journalistic discourse of the present. There should be little doubt that it is one of the most significant issues of our time. However, in the process of obtaining this status as "buzzword" in both public and academic discourse, the concept of globalization has become grossly distorted, at least with regard to its use since the early years of the present century. Especially in the public discourse, the dominant meaning of globalization amounts to "free trade" and virtually nothing else, although this meaning goes paradoxically in tandem with the reality of increasing nationalism. Moreover, in acquiring this narrower meaning, globalization has become a highly pejorative term, particularly during the virtually global furor surrounding the rise of national populism reflected in the so-called Brexit (the attempt on the part of the UK government to leave the European Union) and the related phenomenon of "Trumpism" that culminated in the stunning 2016 election victory of the highly controversial national populist Donald Trump. It is important to state here that in its stricter and more sophisticated meaning—particularly since the mid-1980s and early 1990s—globalization as word and concept has been much richer than its present-day sloganistic meaning. Despite its fairly recent distortion, the meaning of globalization (and of "glocalization") must be intellectually revived for there to be a ground for the field of global studies. In other words, the this chapter attempts to avoid the distortion of what was once and may yet again become a vital concept, even if there was never a *fully* settled, stable, meaning of the concept of globalization. Along these lines, the concept of globalization has by now also been supplemented by that of glocalization (Robertson 1992, 1994, 1995).

The immediate origins of what has become known as global studies, including the "tighter" theme of globalization, are largely to be found in intellectual work accomplished by late eighteenth-century and nineteenth-century sociologists, geographers, anthropologists, historians, and others (Robertson 2012). We are presently at a crucial point in the crystallization of global studies into what might be called a "metadiscipline" or "transdiscipline" (Robertson 1996a), the latter term having rapidly developed in tandem with more recent attempts to demarcate the field. In this sense, the task of this chapter is to historically and geographically identify and locate the domain of what we now regard as comprising global studies. Doing this will involve calling to mind numerous people and places whose academic significance, strictly speaking, may not be immediately apparent, but it is emphatically stressed that these phenomena need to be included among the antecedents of the field of global studies. This is very well demonstrated in Nayan Chanda's (2007) comprehensive book. Chanda writes about traders, preachers, adventurers, and warriors who have been involved in what he calls the shaping of globalization. Similarly, a large amount of this chapter includes what might be called "pre-academic" developments.

To this should be added that the manner and degree to which historical and geographical phenomena were excluded as well as included in the record of what might constitute antecedents for global studies has to be recognized. In this particular respect, it will be seen that, for example, the "invention" of Eurasia and, more specifically, the development of the so-called Silk Road have been historically crucial to the way in which we now refer to the globe as a whole, although these are certainly not the only factors or "inventions" of importance to the crystallization of the idea of *the global*. It is conventional to think of the

Silk Road as having been built during the Chinese Han dynasty, during the period 207 BC through 220 AD. However, recent scholarship considers the Silk Road as having a much longer time span than this. Indeed, the vital book on the subject, *The Silk Roads* (Frankopan 2015), bears the subtitle, *A New History of the World.*

China has made many claims as to it being the oldest civilization in the world—hence the phrase "the Middle Kingdom." Irrespective of this claim, there can be no doubt as to the global–historical significance of China. Originally known as *Zhongguo* and historically without any fixed boundaries, China has been what Nathan and Scobell (2012: 19) refer to as "an uneasy amalgam of lands and peoples created by history." In fact, the phrase "Middle Kingdom" came much later and is more or less equivalent to what we now mean by the word China; the first unified Chinese state, the Qin (221–206 BC), was spread over an area only approximately one-fourth of the size of present-day China. The Chinese do not view themselves historically as a nation-state, or even as an empire. Rather, they have seen themselves as constituting the center of civilization. From a Chinese standpoint, other kingdoms and tribes were less or more civilized depending on whether they were culturally close to what were regarded as the indigenous Han people. Of course, China has long been recognized for numerous innovations, such as the compass, gunpowder, and paper, and to this extent could well be regarded as one of the original centers for the development of global studies. Its scholarship and sense of the sacred are very important in this respect, to the extent that China could be regarded as one of the most important centers of the development of what we now call theology. Although many scholars do not recognize Confucianism as a "genuine" religion, this position has been convincingly disputed by Sun (2013), among others, in her book, *Confucianism as a World Religion.*

Although the Silk Road is not usually considered to be as historically fundamental as a number of other civilizational developments, notably those of Ancient Greece and Ancient Rome, it is mentioned here because its current prominence in academic discussion draws our attention to many topics that bear directly on the antecedents of global studies. In his important volume, *The Silk Roads*, Frankopan (2015) rewrites, as it were, the history of the world, dealing with numerous features that bear on our current concerns, including such phenomena as the development, spread, and expansion of the major religious faiths, the invention of the idea of heaven (and hell), and other spatial constructs that we now think of as integral to global studies—all of these quite independently of the more material aspects of world creation and interconnection.

Although we must be careful not to be too involved in purely semantic issues, these cannot be avoided. The use of phrases or words such as planet Earth, the globe, the world, the universe(s), and so on, rather than a simple semantic indulgence, has often turned out to be crucial to the development of a sense of the wider world, as is well demonstrated in Gluck and Tsing's *Words in Motion* (2009).

Even though the Silk Road has become crucial to the way in which the world is imagined and its significance cannot be overestimated, continents and regions (including seas and oceans) other than those linked by the Silk Road(s) are extremely important in any attempt to demarcate or locate the global arena. Antarctica and the Arctic, as well as bays, oceans, and seas, must be considered as integral to what is usually called globality. An excellent contribution to the global–historical significance of seas is David Abulafia's *The Great Sea* (2012), in which it is emphasized that the Mediterranean, the main subject of the book, has in fact possessed many names, including Our Sea, the White Sea, the Great Sea, the Middle

Sea, the Great Green, the Inner Sea, the Encircled Sea, the Friendly Sea, the Faithful Sea, and the Bitter Sea. On the other hand, Sunil Amrith (2013) has argued that the Bay of Bengal has perhaps been of greater significance with respect to the linking of regions and the development of diasporas, and illustrates what he describes as artificial distinctions between various aspects of the human condition. The Bay of Bengal has certainly figured in the linking of East and West, particularly with respect to massive migrations connecting various areas of the world. It was, Amrith argues, "once a region at the heart of global history. It was forgotten in the second half of the twentieth century, carved up by the boundaries of nation-states, its shared past divided into the separate compartments of national histories" (p. 1). He goes on to point out that by the beginning of the present century, the Bay of Bengal had regained its importance to international politics.

Maps and the Relativization of Space

Issues pertaining to extraterrestrial phenomena and the exploration thereof have had a strong bearing on the contemporary preoccupation with planet Earth. This focus has contributed vastly to the *relativization* of the planet. It is here maintained that the processes of relativization are crucial to the formation of the transdiscipline of global studies. Of course, such relativization was more than anticipated by such scholars as Galileo and Copernicus.

Two crucial aspects of relativization are the phenomena of space and spatiality, as well as that of territory (Elden 2013). These are greatly facilitated by maps. Moreover, the discipline of geography, which largely involves the study and use of maps, is closely bound up with the issue of history, as is well illustrated in Jerry Brotton's book, *A History of the World in Twelve Maps* (2012). The intellectual consideration of maps often goes under the rubric of cartography, which was largely brought into being through the work of Ptolemy (Garfield 2012), whose rules of cartography, recorded in the second century, derived from the prior study of astronomy. It was Ptolemy (100–168 AD) who pictured the world in map, or cartographic, form. He deduced the tropic lines and equator by noting the places where the planets passed directly overhead, "making his best guess of East–West distances by the light of a lunar eclipse" (Garfield 2012: 12). Moreover, Ptolemy placed the North at the top of the map, the position where the pole pointed to a lone star and held still through the night. It was in such terms that the language of maps was subsequently developed. The Babylonian world map (c. 600 BC) is frequently thought of as the first known whole world map, although the earliest examples of prehistoric art (i.e., what subsequently became known as art) predated the maps of the Babylonians by more than 25,000 years.

The relationship between geography and "religion" has, relatively speaking, been ignored by students of the global. It might be more appropriate to speak of the connection between mythology and geography, insofar as both maps and myths provide worldviews, orientations to the world. Diana Eck (2012), in her book *India: A Sacred Geography*, comments insightfully on the ways in which this occurs and the manner in which myths and maps converge. She notes that one finds such convergence in various regions extending back to ancient Greece. In fact, it was Eratosthenes in the third-century BC who was the first to coin the very word "geography." In the Jewish tradition, or in Israel-oriented history, land and location were or are intimately connected. The same is true of China's relationship to Beijing, which was the center of the cultural life of the Middle Kingdom together with its associated conception of the Mandate of Heaven.

Indeed, the "discovery" of heaven was worldwide, having been present in numerous civilizations—the Babylonian, the Chinese, the Indian, the Mayan, and the Andean. As Francis Robinson (2016: 138) states, in Ancient Greece "it gained a form of scientific basis as it became linked to advances in mathematics in particular the work of Ptolemy of Alexandria . . . whose *Almagest* gave a mathematical account of the movement of the heavenly bodies." This work continued to be orthodox until the time of Copernicus in the sixteenth century. Note that this Greek and Roman achievement was later inherited by Muslims, who brought to it a more definitely scientific meaning that was later to be introduced into medieval Europe.

What I have just called the discovery of heaven enables me to introduce the highly topical themes of axiality and transcendence. It is important to point out initially that conceptions of the mundane and the extra-mundane should be regarded as basically theological, this being particularly but not exclusively true of the Christian Church. The notion of axiality was brought into prominence mainly by Karl Jaspers, whose most well-known work, in its German version, was *The Origin and Goal of German History* (1953). In a lengthy edited volume, *The Axial Age and Its Consequences* (2012), dedicated to the memory of Jaspers, sociologists Robert Bellah and Hans Joas reference the approach of Charles Taylor (2012) in maintaining that the Axial revolution involved a new tension between the transcendental and mundane orders. Leaving aside Taylor's reservations about this formulation, the volume explores in great detail the ideas of axiality and transcendence. The basic idea of an Axial age, or Axial revolution, is that the so-called great world religions each started during approximately the same period, spanning the years 800–200 BC. Even though Jaspers himself did not actually invent the term "Axial age," he is nevertheless usually given the credit for it. Since the mid-twentieth century, the Israeli sociologist and polymath Shmuel Eisenstadt has been the leader in this field. Central to this research program has been the theme of transcendence, in the particular sense of new ways of thinking that go beyond the world as it has been known. Regardless of the problems associated with the relationships between these different breakthroughs across the world, these phenomena taken as a whole certainly involve the restructuring of everyday life, and to that extent they had a profound effect on global relations and understandings generally.

What Eck (2012: 52) calls the more ecumenical traditions, such as Buddhism, Christianity, and Islam, have traveled across vast cultural regions and have developed multiple cultural forms, thereby engaging in, as she calls it, the composition and recomposition of more universal maps of the entire world. Eck states that while "these traditions may have centerpoints, like Rome and Mecca, they have also developed a global spiritual life, a worldwide church or a universal *ummah*" (p. 52). Eck maps with considerable sophistication what she calls a "sacred geography of an imagined landscape" (p. 52). Her leading proposition is that the whole of India is a large network of pilgrimage places—"referential, inter-referential, ancient and modern, complex and ever-changing" (p. 2)—a phrase she also uses for her definition of sacred geography. In producing a vast exploration of Indian sacred geography, she draws attention to the ways in which the world or even the cosmos as a whole is to be found in *particular and specific* places.

Of course, pilgrimages have played a crucial role in the linking of religion and geography in many areas of the world. Eck (2012: 16) references the work of Edney (1997: 1), who argues that "imperialism and mapmaking intersect in the most basic manner." Here, both Edney and Eck are particularly concerned with India, where the intimacy between mapping and religion is highly evident. But the point is more generally applicable: Although pilgrimage is for the most part a religious phenomenon, it clearly has a strong influence on the making of the world generally.

This claim raises again the issue of the relationship between consciousness and culture, on the one hand, and connectivity, on the other hand. Stated simply, one cannot reasonably envisage connections being made other than in tandem with images that transcend connections. In other words, in the last instance, it is images or imaginaries that are the more significant factor. The importance of pilgrimages is indicated by their significance in Buddhism, Christianity, and notably Islam, in which individual Muslims are expected to undertake a pilgrimage, or *hajj*, at least once in their lifetime if healthy and financially capable enough to make the journey to Mecca. The hajj is particularly important because it symbolizes the equality and solidarity of all Muslims. Like other pilgrimages, the hajj enhances the sense of the world outside one's usual place of residence, hence its relevance as an antecedent of global studies.

Pilgrimages have for ages been undertaken all over the world. Yet there can be no clear dividing line between such pilgrimages and other types of "sacred" journey. Inasmuch as sacredness in the looser sense encompasses other culturally significant places and geographies, this category would certainly encompass Compostela, Lourdes, Walsingham, Fatima, Mount Fuji, the Ganges, Guadeloupe, and many others, including those of first nation peoples such as Australian Aborigines and North American tribes.

A related kind of significance applies to the notion of the *diaspora*. The term originates from the Greek word for dispersion, but it gained special historical purchase in reference to the fact that many Jewish communities were located far from Israel. This idea of diaspora started in 586 BC when many Jews were forcibly removed to Babylonia to work as slave labor (Dufoix 2003). Here, it is crucial to emphasize again that words, concepts, and ideas continuously change over time and across space—a theme that has become increasingly important in studies of the world as a whole. An excellent example of this thesis is conveyed by the very title of Gluck and Tsing's (2009) already referenced book, *Words in Motion: Toward a Global Lexicon* (see also Bilgrami 2016). Also, it is clear that conceptions of the relationship between the local and the global vary considerably from place to place (Sachsenmaier 2011). This point is crucial in any discussion of the historical antecedents or foundations of global studies, in the sense that the relationship between the local and the global has become essential to contemporary discussions of globalization and, specifically, glocalization.

GLOBAL HISTORY AND GLOBAL STUDIES

Given the significance of the topic of global history in the early 2000s, together with the globalization of numerous aspects of human life, it is most appropriate to tackle the issue of the antecedents of the field of global studies in terms of the intimate relationship between globalization and global studies. As I have previously noted, it should be borne in mind that the study of planet Earth is increasingly related to astrophysical and astronomical research, necessitating the *relativization* of the place and status of Earth in the universe. It should be emphasized, however, that the matter of relativization is also bound up with theological and mythological ideas. Although processes of relativization have clearly intensified and consolidated our sense of the world as a single, territorial place (Geyer and Bright 1995), it is important to stress that theology, in the broadest sense, was in many respects the first "discipline" to become involved in what we now know as global studies. Limitations of space preclude full consideration here of the earliest theologians and metaphysicians.

In their delineation of the growing field of global studies, Steger and Wahlrab (2017) briefly explore the subject of global history and what they call the crucial matter of periodization. In so doing, among recent authors they mention such people as Bruce Mazlish, Nayan Chanda, Jürgen Osterhammel, A. G. Hopkins, and others. Although I do not in any way disagree with this list, I nonetheless draw attention to the fact that global history had begun by no later than the late 1980s, notably in the work of Charles Bright and Michael Geyer (1987), who revamped their critique in 1995. Both of these contributions were extensively critiqued by Robertson (1996b). Note that at the beginning of the twentieth century, the study of world, as opposed to global, history was in vogue, but this fashion went into sharp decline during the 1930s.

Although not normally considered as connected to the general field of global studies, questions concerning the origins of the world as a whole and those that dwell upon it are an integral part of the tracing of antecedents. In other words, and more specifically, the general problem of what is often called first principles is vital. Moreover, the problem of first principles is also associated with the theme of time travel and related tropes (Evans 2014). Questions about beginnings, creation, and creation narratives generally form much of the basis for the works of classical philosophers, notably those of ancient Greece and Rome. Needless to say, however, even while these works have been prominent in Western life generally, recent years have witnessed the increasing recognition of the writings of intellectuals from other civilizations or civilizational complexes, as suggested by the previous example of the Silk Road and Eurasia. In fact, during approximately the past 150 years, the study of civilizations has become increasingly significant in writings of scholars throughout the world (Cowen 2001; Robertson 1992, 2014).

One striking example of this is John Darwin's book, *After Tamerlane* (2007). This volume is particularly important because he rejects attempts to trace the origins of modern globalization back to the history of Europe. Instead, Darwin maintains that the shape of world history has been much more intermittent and complex—not to say competitively empire-building—driven by forces outside Europe, particularly within Asia. In reviewing what she characterizes as a magnificent contribution to modern scholarship, Maya Jasanoff (2007) argues that *Tamerlane* "overturns smug Eurocentric teleologies to present a compelling new perspective on intellectual history" (p. 35). Broadly speaking, Darwin's book can be regarded as a significant part of the general tendency to provincialize Europe and its history. This tendency is a prominent feature of modern scholarship, and Jasanoff herself has written in the same vein about imperial ventures in East Asia along roughly the same lines (Jasanoff 2005).

Although the prominence of the Silk Road, Eurasia in general, and China specifically have been particularly conspicuous in recent scholarship, attention to other spheres of study is expanding as well. The ways in which Greek and Indian developments were historically linked, and the manner in which much of ancient Greek philosophy and historiography was greatly influenced by intellectual developments in North Africa, are currently undergoing serious reconsideration (Bernal 1987). Relevant here is an older work by Teggart (1939), whose book on Rome and China insisted that the study of the past can only be accomplished effectively when it is fully understood that all peoples have their own histories and that these run concurrently and in the same world. The act of comparing them, according to John Darwin (2007), was the beginning of knowledge. It might well be added that comparison and the ability and proclivity to compare civilizations and regions constitute the epistemological foundation of what we now call global studies.

I argue that this emphasis on comparison and relativization is at least as important as the more commonly heralded notion of reflexivity. It should be emphasized that the chief features of what is nowadays referred to as "global history" are the qualitative density and quantitative increase of connections of what has over a long period of history been kept more or less apart (Manjapra 2014). However, I stress that the issue of connections—more precisely, connectivity—has been seriously overemphasized in much of the work on globalization and related matters (Robertson 2011). James and Steger (2016: 21) have appropriately referred to "a changing world of connectivity fetishism."

Connectivity fetishism is well illustrated in a book chapter by John Hutchinson (2011) titled "Globalisation and Nation Formation in the *Longue Durée*." In a considerable number of examples across many centuries—from Alexander the Great, Attila, Genghis Khan, and Tamerlane through Greek–Oriental syncretism to the first of what Hutchinson calls global civilizations—he consistently refers to globalization in terms of its involving networks and connectivity. Yet Hutchinson's extensive piece makes no mention of culture, imaginaries, or like phenomena. Although religion is occasionally mentioned, it is in no way central to his analysis. Hutchinson's work is singled out here only because of its illustrative significance; similar examples are numerous.

One significant complication in this context is posed by the recent special focus on what has been called global intellectual history (Moyn and Sartori 2013). Specifically, one has to bear in mind the overlap between the history of ideas per se and the empirical circumstances to which they ostensibly refer. The problem of the analytic relationship between comparative and global studies is something that certainly cannot be avoided in any attempt to interrogate the historical antecedents of global studies as a field. In fact, it may well be that this transdisciplinary field has arisen around this very issue.

In light of the foregoing, it is necessary to consider the manner in which parts of the world have been analytically connected. The emphasis on connectivity has in large part arisen from an early twenty-first century concern with spatiality, both globe-wide and worldwide and even, as previously discussed, extending to the cosmic level (Dickens and Ormrod 2007).

A significant and very early proponent of what has come to be called global studies was the ancient Greek historian and political theorist Polybius (219–167 BC). Polybius is of particular importance in the present context in large part because of the relatively recent attention that has been paid to his work, but it is worth noting that his work was well known among intellectuals of both ancient Greek and ancient Rome in the centuries after his death (Inglis and Robertson 2004, 2005). Among the ways in which Polybius influenced subsequent authors were his far-reaching conceptions of empire, which are of obvious relevance to the idea of globalization, as is his anticipation of the concept of the global imaginary. His interest in the latter and his conception of universal historiography contrasted considerably with the works of Plato (427–347 BC) and Aristotle (385–323 BC), for whom the city-state was of much more direct concern. Admittedly, Polybius viewed the world as a kind of extension of the Roman Republic, but nonetheless there are well-developed ideas in his writings on world history that clearly anticipate much of what we would now call the global condition. The considerable relevance of this difference between ancient Greece and ancient Rome has been discussed probingly and at length in *The Ancient City* (Coulanges 1980). In their list of significant early contributors to universal, world, and "big history," Steger and Wahlrab (2017) specify, in addition to Polybius, the Greek philosopher Herodotus (484–425 BC), the Chinese historian Sima Qian (145–90 BC), the Persian chronicler Al-Tabari (839–923 AD), and the North African historian and sociologist Ibn Khaldun (1332–1406 AD). Each of these antecedents preceded any definite discipline, at least in the conventional modern sense, and most certainly did not confine themselves to national frameworks (simply because the latter did not then exist).

It is at this juncture that it is appropriate to return to the already discussed phenomenon of the Silk Road(s). Clearly, the widening of the horizons and experiences facilitated by the building of the Silk Road(s), which linked what became known as Asia and Europe, was essential in the development of ideas concerning global history. Here, it is important to state that the issue of the relationship between connectivity and "culture" is of obvious importance, in the sense that the Silk Road(s) could not have been built without some kind of "image" of its possibility and/or desirability—which makes very clear why connectivity and consciousness go hand in hand. As discussed previously, the linking of so-called East and West, or Orient and Occident, has been the most salient factor involved in establishing a sense of the world as a whole, thereby making possible the very idea of global history. As an aside, it might be said in turn that science fiction was also made popular in the same manner—indeed, in a sense there is now little apparent difference between science fiction and "real science."

Most so-called histories of the world often neglect much, if not all, of the southern hemisphere. However, note that world or global history is as "well known" to so-called primal people as it is to the more "civilized" or advanced. What is now known as global anthropology has made this very clear. In this regard, the writings of Anna Tsing have been particularly relevant, beginning with her *In the Realm of the Diamond Queen* (1993). The dominant thrust of Tsing's argument is that even though a place may be geographically isolated and outside "others" not distinctly known, the *imagination* of the other is highly salient in the lives of the indigenous people. This recognition is prevalent among an increasingly large number of contemporary anthropologists.

It is appropriate here to bring into sharp focus the issue of the ways in which early modern science considered life beyond Earth, particularly Galileo (Sobel 2000) and Copernicus (Kuhn 1957). Although many thinkers had considered the problem well before either, it is undoubtedly true that these two authors have had the most forceful impact on writings on this topic during the past few centuries, at least with respect to the theme of antecedents of global studies (Finocchiaro 1997; Gingerich 1993). As previously remarked, considering life beyond Earth has been and still is crucial in our comprehension of the globe, more specifically and relevantly global studies. It should be clear from the foregoing that the theme of global studies is broad as well as deep. Furthermore, it is more than worth considering the question as to why global studies gains in prominence at the present time. Any satisfactory answer to this question would have to delve into a vast range of so-called disciplines and their mutations—to some extent the project undertaken by Dickens and Ormrod (2007) in their book, *Cosmic Society: Towards a Sociology of the Universe*. However, the latter overemphasizes the significance of space exploration and tourism in the modes of colonialism and imperialism. A greater concern with mythological issues and the dimension of the social imaginary would have greatly enhanced the significance of this project. (Indeed, in mentioning mythology, it should be borne in mind that much of science fiction is indeed mythological.) This is not to say, however, that the latter interest is totally absent from the book, and in fact the opening chapters of this volume are wide ranging and innovative, ranging from ancient Greek philosophers such as Aristotle and Plato to subsequent Western scientists including Newton, Galileo, and Copernicus. Also included in their brief survey are contemporary mysticism, mathematics, and physics.

An excellent example of the mixing of science fiction, "real" science, and mythology, not to speak of the advent of modernity, is Banerjee's *We Modern People* (2012). Banerjee persuasively connects large-scale and revolutionary twentieth-century projects such as the Trans-Siberian Railroad and the highly innovative campaign to transform the Russian/ Soviet imagination. Perhaps the most crucial aspect of Banerjee's project is her treatment of science fiction as a form of apprehending and comprehending the world and cosmos as a whole. Despite her "modernity," Banerjee may fruitfully be quoted here:

> The gradual elision of the Trans-Siberian railroad with first Siberia, then the nation, and ultimately the entire planet, or the airplane and spaceship, which became the lifelines of universal brotherhood and a vast cosmic organism, challenged the very foundations of Enlightenment conception of space.(p. 33)

What makes this observation relevant is precisely that it brings together and coordinates the "ancient" and the "modern."

Sebastian Conrad (2016) concludes his impressive book, *What Is Global History?* with the question as to whether we should abandon the vocabulary of the global altogether. He answers that we certainly should not do so. At the very least, we need what he calls a catchword—"a catchword that allows us to discuss seemingly different pasts in one frame, and to look into connections that earlier paradigms rendered invisible" (p. 234). He concludes his volume with the claim that the slow disappearance of the discourse of the global will then, paradoxically, indicate the triumph of global history as a paradigm.

Even if this chapter has not been specifically concerned with global history as such, undoubtedly Conrad's (2016) contribution casts light on our topic of historical antecedents and thus justifies this brief, concluding discussion of global history. The trend in the direction of the latter has been excellently discussed by Linda Colley (2013), who poses the question— or, more accurately, provides a description—as to why North American global history is more cosmopolitan than global histories emerging from other regions of the world. In one sense, Conrad himself responds to this question by stating that world or global history is as old as historiography itself, beginning with Herodotus and Polybius. Conrad's overriding argument is that until relatively recently, world—or global—history has been conducted as a way of "othering." In other words, the study of the global—in global studies as well as global history—might in itself constitute a form of boundary making that is not sufficiently inclusive to warrant the label "global." The degree to which this is entirely accurate has not been explored in this chapter, but there is little doubt as to the persuasiveness of this thesis.

Conclusion

It should be emphasized that much of what is presented in this chapter corresponds to my intuition that the real historical antecedents of global studies are modes of thinking, reorientations of space, fluid mapping exercises, and innovative historical explorations rather than specific events or instances that should be considered as markers of the "global." Although I am committed to a longue durée historical framework, my exposition has both relied and commented on the writings of recent, or relatively recent, authors. But this apparent paradox can be resolved in a relatively simple way. I have integrated these authors into my discussion of the longue durée historical antecedents of global studies because they enable us to consider the ways in which antecedents must be interrogated through "global" modes of thinking that are sensitive to both the unavoidable necessity of focusing on the "objective" past and the desirability of finding new ways of understanding the crucial subjective dimensions of globalization. The future of global studies as a new academic project depends on such holistic and longue durée approaches to the past.

References

Abulafia, D. 2012. *The Great Sea: A Human History of the Mediterranean*. London: Penguin.

Amrith, S. S. 2013. *The Crossing of the Bay of Bengal: The Furies of Nature and the Fortunes of Migrants*. Cambridge, MA: Harvard University Press.

Banerjee, A. 2012. *We Modern People: Science Fiction and the Making of Russian Modernity*. Middletown, CT: Wesleyan University Press.

Bellah, R. N. and H. Joas, eds. 2012. *The Axial Age and Its Consequences*. Cambridge, MA: Harvard University Press.

Bernal, M. 1987. *Black Athena: The Afroasiatic Routes of Classical Civilization. Vol. 1: The Fabrication of Ancient Greece, 1785–1985*. London: Vintage.

Bilgrami, A., ed. 2016. *Beyond the Secular West*. New York: Columbia University Press.

Bright, P., and M. Geyer. 1987. "For a Unified History of the World in the Twentieth Century." *Radical History Review* 39: 69–91.

Brotton, J. 2012. *A History of the World in Twelve Maps*. London: Lane.

Chanda, N. 2007. *Bound Together: How Traders, Preachers, Adventurers and Warriors Shaped Globalization*. New Haven, CT: Yale University Press.

Colley, L. 2013. "Wide-Angled." *London Review of Books* 35 (18): 18–19.

Conrad, S. 2016. *What Is Global History?* Princeton NJ: Princeton University Press.

Coulanges, N. D. F. de. 1980. *The Ancient City*. Baltimore, MD: Johns Hopkins University Press.

Coustenis, A., and T. Encrenaz. 2013. *Life Beyond Earth: The Search for Habitable Worlds in the Universe*. Cambridge, UK: Cambridge University Press.

Cowen, N. 2001. *Global History: A Short Overview*. Cambridge, UK: Polity.

Darwin, J. 2007. *After Tamerlane: The Global History of Empire*. London: Lane.

Dickens, P., and J. S. Ormrod. 2007. *Cosmic Society: Towards a Sociology of the Universe*. London: Routledge.

Dufoix, S. 2003. *Diasporas*. Berkeley: University of California Press.

Eck, D. L. 2012. *India: A Sacred Geography*. New York: Random House.

Edney, M. 1997. *Mapping an Empire: The Geographical Construction of British India 1765–1843.* Chicago: University of Chicago Press.

Elden, S. 2013. *The Birth of Territory.* Chicago: University of Chicago Press.

Evans, G. R. 2014. *First Light: A History of Creation Myths from Gilgamesh to the God Particle.* London: Tauris.

Finocchiaro, M. A. 1997. *Galileo on the World Systems.* Berkeley: University of California Press.

Frankopan, P. 2015. *The Silk Roads: A New History of the World.* London: Bloomsbury.

Garfield, S. 2012. *On the Map: Why the World Looks the Way It Does.* London: Profile Books.

Geyer, M., and C. Bright. 1995. "World History in a Global Age." *American Historical Review* 100 (4): 1034–1060.

Gingerich, O. 1993. *The Eye of Heaven: Ptolemy, Copernicus, Kepler.* New York: American Institute of Physics.

Gluck, C., and A. L. Tsing, eds. 2009. *Words in Motion: Toward a Global Lexicon.* Durham, NC: Duke University Press.

Hutchinson, J. 2011. "Globalisation and Nation Formation in the *Longue Durée.*" In *Nationalism and Globalisation: Conflicting or Complementary?* edited by D. Halikiopoulou and S. Vasilopoulou, 84–99. New York: Routledge.

Inglis, D., and R. Robertson. 2004. "Beyond the Gates of the Polis: Reworking the Classical Routes of Classical Sociology." *Journal of Classical Sociology* 4 (2): 165–189.

Inglis, D., and R. Robertson. 2005. "The Ecumenical Analytic: 'Globalization,' Reflexivity and Revolution in Greek Historiography." *European Journal of Social Theory* 8 (2): 99–122.

James, P., and M. Steger. 2016. "Globalization and Global Consciousness: Levels of Connectivity." In *Global Culture: Consciousness and Connectivity*, edited by R. Robertson and D. Buhari-Gulmez, pp. 21–40. Farnham, UK: Ashgate.

Jardine, L., and J. Brotton. 2000. *Global Interests: Renaissance Art Between East and West.* London: Reaktion.

Jasanoff, M. 2005. *Edge of Empire: Lives, Culture and Conquest in the East, 1750–1850.* New York: Knopf/Fourth Estate.

Jasanoff, M. 2007. "Review of *After Tamerlane: The Global History of Empire*, London: Allen Lane." *The Guardian*, May 12: 3/5–4/5.

Jaspers, K. 1953. *The Origin and Goal of History.* London: Routledge.

Kuhn, T. S. 1957. *The Copernican Revolution.* Cambridge, MA: Harvard University Press.

Manjapra, K. 2014. *Age of Entanglement: German and Indian Intellectuals Across Empire.* Cambridge, MA: Harvard University Press.

Moyn, S., and A. Sartori. 2013. *Global Intellectual History.* New York: Columbia University Press.

Nathan, A. J., and A. Scobell. 2012. *China's Search for Security.* New York: Columbia University Press.

Robertson, R. 1992. *Globalization: Social Theory and Global Culture.* London: Sage.

Robertson, R. 1994. "Globalisation or Glocalisation?" *Journal of International Communication* 1: 33–52.

Robertson, R. 1995. "Glocalization: Time–Space and Homogeneity–Heterogeneity." In *Global Modernities*, edited M. Featherstone, S. Lash, and R. Robertson, 458–471. London: Sage.

Robertson, R. 1996a. "Globality, Globalization and Transdisciplinarity." *Theory, Culture & Society* 13 (4): 127–132.

Robertson, R. 1996b. *The New Global History: A Sociological Assessment.* Sao Paulo, Brazil: Instituto de Estudos Avancados, Colecao Documentos Serie Teoria Politica 17.

Robertson, R. 2011. "Global Connectivity and Global Consciousness." *American Behavioral Scientist* 55 (10): 1336–1345.

Robertson, R. 2012. "Global Studies, Early Academic Approaches." In *Encyclopedia of Global Studies*, edited by H. K. Anheier and M. Juergensmeyer, 741–743. Thousand Oaks, CA: Sage.

Robertson, R. 2014. "Civilization(s), Ethnoracism, Antisemitism, Sociology." In *Antisemitism and the Constitution of Sociology*, edited by M. Stoetzler, pp. 216–245. Lincoln: University of Nebraska Press.

Robertson, R. 2016. "Considerations on Global Studies." In *The Art and Science of Sociology: Essays in Honor of Edward A. Tiryakian*, edited by R. Robertson and J. Simpson, 131–148. London: Anthem Press.

Robinson, F. 2016. "Global History from an Islamic Angle." In *The Prospect of Global History*, edited by J. Belich, J. Darwin, M. Frenz, and C. Wickam, 127–145. Oxford, UK: Oxford University Press.

Sachsenmaier, D. 2011. *Global Perspectives on Global History: Theories and Approaches in a Connected World*. Cambridge, UK: Cambridge University Press.

Sobel, D. 2000. *Galileo's Daughter: A Historical Memoir of Science, Faith and Love*. London: Penguin.

Steger, M. B., and A. Wahlrab. 2017. *What Is Global Studies? Theory and Practice*. New York: Routledge.

Sun, A. 2013. *Confucianism as a World Religion: Contested Histories and Contemporary Realities*. Princeton, NJ: Princeton University Press.

Taylor, C. 2012. "What Was the Axial Revolution?" In *The Axial Age and Its Consequences*, edited by R. H. Bellah and H. Joas, 30–46. Cambridge, MA: Harvard University Press.

Teggart, F. 1939. *Rome and China*. Berkeley: University of California Press.

Tsing, A. L. 1993. *In the Realm of the Diamond Queen: Marginality in an out of the Way Place*. Princeton, NJ: Princeton University Press.

CHAPTER 4

··

MAJOR FIGURES IN THE FIELD OF GLOBAL STUDIES

PAUL JAMES

THE field of globalization studies flowered in the 1990s.[1] This springtime of attention could have happened earlier, and there is nothing special about the 1990s that suggested the inevitability of such efflorescence. However, after a series of tentative forays into the question of globalization beginning in the 1950s, and some extraordinary changes in both the form of globalization and the sense of a global imaginary across the second half of the twentieth century, it was 1990 that marked the beginning of the first period of sustained attention to globalization. In fact, as most writers now understand, processes of globalization had been going on for centuries, but it was across the year 1990 that the first ongoing scholarly dialogue began about what this process means.

A path-breaking anthology was published in that year by Sage Publications, concurrently developed through the important originating journal, *Theory, Culture & Society*, also published by Sage. The volume brought together a series of authors who were to become some of the most important writers in the field of globalization studies and, more broadly, global studies: Arjun Appadurai, Zygmunt Bauman, Peter Beyer, Ulf Hannerz, Jonathan Friedman, Anthony King, Roland Robertson, Bryan Turner, and Immanuel Wallerstein. All went on to write on globalization in depth, the last—Wallerstein—despite his initial disavowal of the usefulness of the term. The anthology was called *Global Culture: Nationalism, Globalization and Modernity* (1990) and was edited by Mike Featherstone, who was to become a pivotal figure in the formation of the field, well published, massively cited, but without himself writing anything that contributed systematically to any of its major theoretical or empirical breakthroughs. Globalization studies as a subject-based field is full of idiosyncrasies like that—as is global studies, the broader, more encompassing field of enquiry that emerged from it.

These early beginnings show how important editing and publishing was to both the rise of globalization studies and global studies. Editors at Sage Publications in the 1990s, including Stephen Barr, Chris Rojek, and then later the editors at Polity Press, including David Held, Anthony Giddens, and John Thomson, should be recognized as early makers of the fields, just as Mike Featherstone is rightly recognized along with the other contributors to the 1990 anthology as one of many important progenitors.

Globalization studies can be defined as a field that coalesces around a constellation of themes: processes and subjectivities of globalization, conditions of globality, and ideologies of globalism. These themes are also subjects of global studies. However, as the broader transdisciplinary field, global studies includes and goes beyond those subject orientations to questions of what it means to live in a globalizing world, including questions of changing spatiality and temporality (Steger and Wahlrab 2017).[2] The patterns of theoretical contribution to global studies in relation to understanding globalization are difficult to fathom. None of the major early figures in the field—Appadurai, Robertson, Sassen, Scholte, Steger, and Tomlinson—became major systematizing theorists, and none of the systematizing theorists who contributed to the field—Beck, Bourdieu, Castells, Giddens, Harvey, and Wallerstein—added more than the occasional insight to manifold contributions made by other writers. None of the writers on globalization persisted in developing an encompassing theory for a phenomenon that all described as increasingly encompassing. And nearly all of these writers developed their own definitions of the process of globalization, usually without reference to each other.

Surveying the field leaves one initially perplexed. It does not lend itself to the usual well-defined textbook parade of canons. Puzzling examples of mixed and contradictory contributions abound. Wallerstein begins by rejecting the generalizing force of the concept of globalization, and then later as the concept took the world by storm, he incorporates it into his schema as a lower level background term, apparently comfortable that his approach is already comprehensive enough to subsume it. What others called "globalization," he said is just the epiphenomenon of a contemporary transition period (Wallerstein 2000). His categories of analysis brooked no major intrusion, and his approach suffered accordingly by being fixed into an awkward form of structuralism. Nevertheless, his world systems' categories forced others to respond—scholars from Jan Aart Scholte to Roland Robertson, whose work across the 1980s and 1990s was acutely piqued by world systems theory, sought other ways of understanding the world as a social whole. For a field to come into dialogical existence, it needs its critics.

By comparison, Saskia Sassen is a mobile conceptual conjurer, moving on without taking prior conceptual schemas with her. One schema or conceptual array serves its purpose for one deep empirical analysis, and then another is developed for the next. She is well known for her important formative analysis of the global city (1991), along with Anthony King's *Global Cities* (1990), published the year before. However, she rarely uses the term "globalization" or writes directly about it—*A Sociology of Globalization* (2007) is an exception. A path-breaking book titled *Globalization and Its Discontents* (1999) marked her place in the field, but that text tends to talk about globalization indirectly. The title was not her idea, she acknowledges, but rather her editor's (Sassen 2015).

Very different again, Roland Robertson was always deeply self-conscious about using the concept of globalization. He continues to use it often and carefully. He is the first scholar to lay out a periodization of the long history of globalization. However, initially at least, he knew so little of the history of others using the concept before him that he assumed that he had conjured it out of his own mind (Robertson 2015). And perhaps in one way he was right. For there was no single, clear, originating insight that brought the concept of globalization into existence. And there were dozens of uses of the concept before it had any dialogical purchase on a community of scholarly writing necessary to form a field—hence the opening inference of this chapter that it was a series of edited collections, beginning with

Global Culture, which initiated the critical dialogues that began to make the field of global studies.

From the 1950s until the 1980s, the concept emerged in numerous isolated articles, created out of the minds of very different writers—only to go nowhere—and then, by the end of the 1990s, it was suddenly everywhere. This chapter seeks to work out how and why this happened. The many figures of global studies—the entrepreneurial editor, the structuralist disavower, the mobile conjuror, and the self-conscious conceptualizer—all made major contributions to the field along with dozens of other equally important writers, but not one carried through in a systematic way to develop a generalizing or explanatory theory of globalization. This chapter asks why. It seeks to track the emergence of the focused field of globalization studies through a discussion of some selected major figures—Roland Robertson, Arjun Appadurai, David Held, Anthony McGrew, Anthony Giddens, Manfred Steger, and so on—as well as two figures who have now been largely forgotten, Paul Meadows and George Modelski (Figure 4.1). The chapter also seeks to map the originating force of the field as a whole and to understand what gave rise to such a paradoxically fragmented singularity. It is to this question that the first part of the chapter turns.[3]

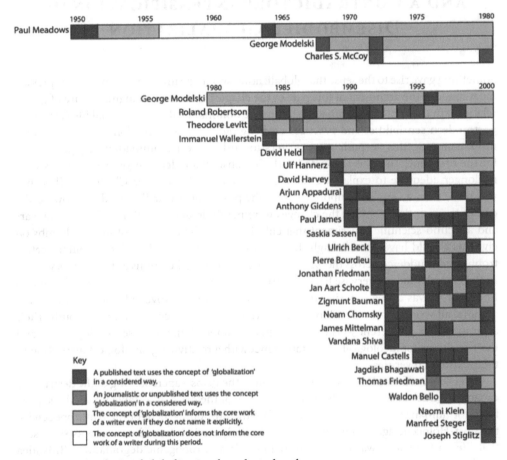

FIGURE 4.1 Analysis of globalization by selected authors, 1950–2000.

Understanding the intermediate-term context for the explosion of attention to the question of globalization is an important part of understanding the nature of the writing on globalization itself. Two key clusters of social change stand out. The first is the changing nature of globalization across the middle to late twentieth century linked to uneven challenges to the assumed dominance of modernization. The second is the paradigm shift in social enquiry and intellectual practice, particularly in the ways of understanding theory. These clusters—the first of practice and the second of theory—rebounded on each other, affecting the nature of the field in vital ways. Together, they brought questions of globalization to the fore, and at the same time they mitigated the possibility of developing general *explanatory* theories of globalization. In summary, my argument in this chapter is that across the 1980s and 1990s, scholars of globalization became increasingly convinced of the importance of understanding the phenomenon of globalization, as simultaneously they deferred questions concerning the "why" of globalization to concentrate on issues concerning "how" and "what"—mostly "what."

Cluster 1: Changing Social Relations and a Contradictory Intensification of Disembodied Globalization

Something gave rise to the sense that globalization should be investigated in itself. Expressed most broadly, the argument of this part of the chapter is that the changing nature of global relations, in the context of a broader shift in the dominant valences of social life (emergent postmodern sensibilities and practices challenging the continuing dominance of modernity), came together to push some writers toward a direct examination of globalization for the first time. This was associated with the sense that older categories of analysis were no longer adequate to explaining the complexity of social life (see Cluster 2). This shift was more than a simple disruption. Across the post–World War II period and toward the end of the twentieth century, the changes were manifold and redoubling. Two global wars and a techno-scientific experiment that culminated in the dropping of nuclear bombs on civilians should have been enough. In the case of World War II, a global military catastrophe had shuddered across the whole world, causing reverberations as far away as villages in the Global South, otherwise barely aware that a war was in progress. But this did not do it. Rather, it was changes during the peace-time years that provoked a series of different authors, all writing from the Global North even if they had been born in the South. Their aspirations for a different world, their dismay at intensifying adverse developments, and their concerns for ideological contestation met with a relativizing ontological disruption to their existential verities.

Older senses of the planet came under assault. The 1950s' supercharging of the destructive capacity of nuclear weaponry destroyed the sense of the earth as a stable unassailable platform for humans to flourish. And, long before the pronouncement of the Anthropocene—the post-Holocene age of human impact—the early environmental movements suggested that life on the planet was threatened by multiple anthropogenic degradations. This idea of planet Earth as vulnerable was redoubled by an ontological jolt that hit the world's populations as photographs of the earth taken from outer space circulated around the globe. The 1968 photos showed a small, vulnerable, blue planet floating in a vast sea of black, with the moon in the foreground providing a destabilizing horizon of reference. This relativizing of the place of planet Earth in relation to the universe had a profound impact, confirming the "obviousness" of an emerging global imaginary. The image was called "earthrise." Fifteen months later, the first Earth Day was celebrated, which some claim was a confirmation of an increasing global consciousness (Poole 2008). Coupled with other developments across the twentieth century, such as the fragmenting of religious certainty (Taylor 2007), these changes contributed to an existential relativizing of older certainties about being human in relation to others and to nature.

This unsettling of social life came together with a number of further changes directly impinging on ways of understanding. Older forms of globalization—named as colonization and territorial imperialism—gave way to more abstract extensions of power: economic, political, and cultural. For example, powerful institutions of globalization, particularly global corporations, were palpably present in some local situations, but at the same time their extensive and deterritorializing power spread across the world in a way that could increasingly only be understood by embarking upon the political economy of abstract numbers—slow painstaking research into global financial transactions (Sassen 1999). Similarly, communications technologies had physically entered people's homes in the form of television; however, when in 1960 the world's first artificial communications satellite went into orbit above the planet, understanding how it would impact globalizing communications had become the stuff of experts (Tomlinson 1999). At the same time, decolonization across the 1940s to 1960s, the development of new forms of transnational localized violence, and a globalizing Cold War all confirmed that globalization could not hide beneath other names that had been used to describe earlier global extensions of power: colonization, imperialism, and capitalism. This is not to suggest that those long-run complex phenomena could ever be reduced to manifestations of globalization, but it is to argue that through these changes globalization came out of hiding. And this occurred just as globalization had begun to consolidate its reach across time and space in new ways.

My argument here is that lifted out of the immediacies of locality and caught up in the upheaval of relativizing change, the early writers on globalization were "forced," in Marx's terms, to confront the conditions of their existence. It is true that Marx's words are both dated by the gender specific pronouns and exaggeratedly prophetic: "All that is solid melts into air, all that is holy is profaned, and man is at last forced to face with sober senses, his real conditions of life, and his relations with his kind" (Marx and Engels 1848: 17). Nevertheless, they foretold of a period when reflexivity about existence would become generalized beyond a few philosophers. Much later, the Marxist David Harvey (1989) called this shift "the condition of postmodernity," brilliantly insightful but again overstating its epochal singularity.

This did not mean that a veil was lifted away completely and that everybody now understood that processes of globalization were key processes to be analyzed in depth. In *The Condition of Postmodernity*, for example, Harvey (1989) only uses the concept of "globalization" once in passing (p. 137). And most writers turned their work to understanding other cognate processes of the human condition rather than globalization. Theorists in the Frankfurt School focused on the totalizing conditions of mass consumption. The world systems theorists focused on the comprehensive upheavals of capitalism. Writers on postcolonialism took a very different, often postmodern, path to attempt to understand the continuing configurations of abstracted power. Nevertheless, almost without exception, these scholars shared with the emerging writers on globalization a sense that something new was happening. We were entering an age in which we needed new vantage points and new ways of seeing to understand global horizons.

All of these changes combined in an assault on the assumed dominance of the modern. In a rant of theoretical exuberance, one writer even went so far as argue that humanity was moving from the age of modernity to the age of globality (Albrow 1996). This argument does not work for a number of reasons. It makes a singular epochal claim, assuming the singularity of the global imaginary (perhaps because it presents itself as such), and it leaves out the tensions and contradictions that ensue in the overlaying of ontological formations. Second, it involves a category mistake, treating a spatial concept that describes the set of processes extending social relations across world space—globalization—as if it is an ontological condition or formation in the same way that "the modern" or "the post-modern" might be described. However, Albrow's work did point to the momentousness of the changes and the issue that modern ways of living and knowing were no longer so comfortably dominant, even in the West.[4]

Cluster 2: A Paradigm Shift in Social Enquiry and Intellectual Practice

The second contextual cluster of changes concerns the way in which theory came to be approached during the development of the field and into the present. During the period of the middle to late twentieth century, there was a fracturing of confidence in generalizing theory and an almost conclusive break with Grand Theory. This was also an ideological contest over the nature of meaning. The fracturing had comprehensive consequences for the field. Paradoxically, at the very time that scholars were seeking to understand globalization as a generalizing phenomenon—and during a period of its unprecedented intensity and scale—generalizing theory was on the wane. Some tried to develop general theories, but all faltered—or did badly.

The implication here is not that there should have been more high theory. Rather, it is to argue that there were no equivalent generalizing scholars in this field to Benedict Anderson, Ernest Gellner, and Anthony Smith in nationalism studies. Writing nearly a decade prior to *Global Culture* (Featherstone 1990), none of these scholars were high theorists. But all three were confident in their *explanatory* reach, each seeking to consolidate major theses on the formation of nations and nationalism. By comparison, writers on globalization went on occasional theoretical adventures and scouting raids, usually falling back to social mapping and elaborate descriptions of particular dimensions of the field. It is telling in terms of our concern here to understand the contextualizing moment for addressing globalization directly that after the high points of the 1980s in nationalism studies with books such as *Imagined Communities* (Anderson 1983), that field went in the same direction as global studies. In global studies, this took the form of conducting surveys, elaborating examples, and making theoretical pronouncements without having recourse to a generalizing theory or an integrated methodology. This occurred as a series of connected processes, with different writers working variously in accordance with one or more of the trends discussed next.

- Direct lineages of classic social theory are broken, segmented, or refocused.

Although a minority of writers on globalization sought to develop their approaches in the light of earlier classical theorists—writers such as Marx, Durkheim, and Weber—these lineages no longer had the same force. One response took the form of focusing efforts on a particular dimension of globalization rather than attempting to explain its interconnections. For example, the Argentinian Marxist, Ronnie Munck, reoriented his work around Karl Polanyi and spent considerable energy rebutting what he argued was an ideologically charged argument put forward by writers such as Castells that while capital was globalizing, the labor movement was in retreat (Munck 2002). He then sought to document other countermovements to globalization (Munck 2007). Other writers, in the neo-Marxist lineage—Christopher Chase-Dunn, Paul Hirst, Anthony McGrew, Ronnie Munck, Mark Rupert, William Robinson, and Leslie Sklair—all went in different variously productive directions. Paul Hirst and Grahame Thompson (1999) went down a strange rabbit hole, arguing that rather than contemporary "globalization," we were actually witnessing just another wave of "internationalization." This argument was true for trade and the movement of commodities, but not much else. The British Trotskyist Justin Rosenberg (2000) made some effective points of critique against three major figures in contemporary globalization theory—Jan Aart Scholte (2000), Rob Walker (1993), and Anthony Giddens (1999)—but quickly reverted to the older concept of capitalist "uneven development" as the key to understanding contemporary globalizing forces. Of these Marxists, only Anthony McGrew attempted to systematize a general approach to globalization. However, in the end, he with his colleagues embarked upon the path of *empirical generalization*, with occasional theoretical recursions—the next response in these series of ambivalences about *explanatory* theory—rather than developing a general explanatory approach to globalization.

- Generalizing analyses tend to either take a direct path of empirical generalization, mapping the phenomenon in great detail, or, when they do move between differently abstracted levels of analysis, these levels are left unconnected.

The volume *Global Transformations* (1999) by David Held, a political philosopher, Anthony McGrew, an international relations theorist, David Goldblatt, a theorist of environmental politics, and Jonathan Perraton, an economist, is a landmark example of the first tendency. It takes the path of empirical generalization rather than linking its impressive detailed empirical work to an overarching approach that explored the determinations of globalizing connectivity and subjectivity and its consequences. The volume was one of the most important early renderings of globalization. It worked across the broad domains of economy, ecology, politics, and culture (see Figure 4.3)—a very useful way of qualifying the mainstream emphasis on economic globalization. However, it remains an example of how generalizing approaches tended to stay at the level of an empirical mapping of the phenomenon. David Harvey's work is an example of the second tendency. The *Condition of Postmodernity* (Harvey 1989) is written in two halves. The first half is a fairly conventional political economy of the transformation from Fordism to post-Fordism, and the second half is a path-breaking but unresolved analysis of the transformations of ontological bases of time and space given the emergence of postmodernity. The methodologies and insights of these two parts are never brought together in more than a rub-against-each-other kind of way.

Anthony Giddens is also an instructive example here. Throughout the 1980s and 1990s, he had been working on a grand theoretical approach called structuration theory. However, by the time he wrote in a focused way on globalization in *Runaway World* (1999), his approach had become less theoretically integrated and more descriptive. His major point in that brief booklet became that globalization is complex, shapes the way that we live, and is linked to the expansive dynamic of late modernity. In an earlier text, *The Consequences of Modernity* (1990), Giddens had an opportunity to do something much more. For example, his work on time–space distanciation and the structuration of power lent itself beautifully to discussing the complexities of a spatial phenomenon such as globalization. He writes,

> In the modern era, the level of time–space distanciation is much higher than in any previous period, and the relations between local and distant social forms and events become correspondingly "stretched." Globalisation refers essentially to that stretching process, in so far as the modes of connection between different social contexts or regions become networked across the earth's surface as a whole. (p. 64)

And there, with those intriguing words, his analysis of the changing nature of globalizing spatiality effectively stops.

- Approaches to global interrelationality become increasingly wary of grand narratives and singular embracing theories.

Across the late twentieth century, the suspicion of any generalizing theoretical explanations of particular phenomena intensified. This suspicion was paralleled by a claim made by some that the postmodern condition could be characterized by the end of grand narratives (ideologies) of all kinds: nationalism, socialism, liberalism, and, by implication, globalism. This was coupled with a clanging critique of Grand Theory. Metaphors of flux, hybridity, and constant change prevailed, overlaying late-modern metaphors of plurality. For example, Arjun Appadurai (1996) and Zygmunt Bauman (1998) turned to concepts of "fluidity" and "liquidity," respectively. This was the case not just for the explicit post-structuralists. When Chamsy el-Ojeili and Patrick Hayden wrote their book *Critical Theories of Globalization* (2006), looking back on more than a decade of developing approaches to globalization, they found themselves describing a critical pluralism of "theories" rather than developing their own approach. Nothing had changed when Barrie Axford came to write his impressive *Theories of Globalization* (2013).

In all of these cases, there was no attempt to develop a theory of globalization as such. Rather, these and other related writers—writers as diverse as Ulf Hannerz, James Mittelman, Heikki Patomaki, George Ritzer, and Jan Aart Scholte—sought to explore the complexity of globalization across different domains or areas of interest. Scholte (2000), for example, used the domains of production, governance, identity, and knowledge, but he made no special theoretical claim for these domains. They are treated as just useful analytical categories in which to order information and develop an eclectic synthesis. As Scholte describes it, Stephen Kennedy, an editor at Macmillan Publishers, influenced the form of that book significantly, pulling it back from being too abstract and too focused on methodology (Scholte 2015). One brave soul who did attempt a comprehensive and systematic theory of globalization came out of the Weberian tradition—Malcolm Waters (2001)—but his approach was full of definitional and structural problems. Having been a pioneer of the field, he did not write another significant article or book on globalization after 2001. It was if he had made his mark and moved on.

- A globalizing publishing industry encouraged extensive exploration of themes in globalization, but only so long as they sold well in the new setting of academic capitalism and mass tertiary education.

Shifts in the forms of enquiry—including in publishing, teaching, and learning—can be explained in part through layering of practice beyond "print capitalism" (Anderson 1983). Relevant to global studies, it encouraged a culture of compilation. The first shift is the rise of textbooks. From the 1960s to 2000, the number of university students in the United States doing an undergraduate four-year degree, for example, doubled to over 9 million, with mass teaching in large early year courses requiring textbooks (Thompson 2005). Admittedly among the many ordinary survey books, there were four magnificent textbooks in the area of global studies: Peter Dicken's *Global Shift* (1992), which focused on economic issues; David Held et al.'s *Global Transformations* (1999), a remarkable coverage of the politics, economics, culture, and ecology of globalization (discussed previously); Jan Aart Scholte's *Globalization* (2000), a sophisticated volume, reworked and marketed as a textbook by adding the subtitle "A Critical Introduction" (also previously mentioned); and Robin Cohen and Paul Kennedy's gentle but compelling coverage of themes in transnational social life, *Global Sociology* (2000). But none of these writers went on to develop their own theories of globalization, even though on reading their textbooks the acuity and sophistication of the writing suggest that these authors could have, in different circumstances, productively headed in that direction.

The second shift is the move to anthologies, handbooks, and subject-area encyclopedias. Many writers in the field gave significant energy and time to bringing together singular shorter pieces into compendiums where the possibility of integrated theoretical attempts to develop an understanding of the social whole gave way to creative mosaics of editorial construction.[5]

The third shift is the massive shift in academic emphasis in scholarly publishing toward articles in journals, especially those with high-impact citation records. This is coupled with the fourth shift: the bourgeoning of field-specific—as opposed to discipline-based—journals. Here, journals such as *Globalizations, Global Society, Global Environmental Politics, Journal of Global Ethics*, and *Globalization and Health* are important examples among the myriad of emerging journals. This meant that an overwhelming amount of writing was published in the globalization space, much of it with theoretical elements, but it did not lend itself to having the structure and integrated direction of classical monograph writing. Just as articles began to take on a life on their own, sold separately from the journals through global publishing platforms, theoretical pronouncements and excitations floated free from integrated theories.

This takes us to the fifth issue. Most of the prominent monographs that were written were more compilations of essays than dedicated monographs. Roland Robertson's influential *Globalization* (1992) was stitched together from earlier articles. Both books that Mike Featherstone wrote on globalization were roughly connected collections of previously published articles, as were volumes such as Arjun Appadurai's very influential *Modernity at Large: Cultural Dimensions of Globalization* (1996), Jonathan Friedman's provocative *Cultural Identity and Global Process* (1994), and James Mittelman's series of surveys of the field, including *Whither Globalization* (2004).

The sixth shift is the move to constrained subject-focused descriptive books. The key example here is the "Globalization" series published by Rowman & Littlefield, edited by Manfred Steger and Terrell Carver. Characteristically, however, instead of developing a theory of war in the context of globalization, Tarak Barkawi wrote a wonderful evocative primer called *Globalization and War* (2006). Thereafter, he maintained a research focus on war but did not return to the question of globalization. The phenomenon of subject-focused books is related to the development of the short-book series, for example, as published by Oxford University Press. Manfred Steger's elegant long essay, *Globalization* (2003), is exemplary here. It is theoretically sophisticated and empirically astute, without having the space to do more than cover the basic issues. Thomas Hylland Eriksen's wonderful short book, *Globalization* (2007), in the Berg key concepts series is comparable. Astounding insights are buried in an introductory text and left in a form that cries out for integrating into a life's work. As Eriksen wrote in that book, "In the thirteenth century a Thomas Aquinas could spend an entire life-time trying to reconcile two important sets of texts" (p. 17)—now a globalizing world combined with the speed of academic life disembeds such dedicated work. In effect proving his own point, Eriksen's only return to the field in a generalizing way was to bring out a second edition of the same primer seven years later.

Having given some context to the many contributions to understanding globalization—a bourgeoning that never sees the fruits of theory ripen—the chapter now turns to discuss some generative figures, writers who represent different ways of approaching globalization. Each case provides an opportunity to expand upon our contextualizing discussion. Although the output of these very different writers suggests multiple pathways, the argument of the chapter about the difficulty of developing a broad, systematic, and adaptable methodology appears to be confirmed.

GLOBALIZATION AS UNSETTLEMENT: PAUL MEADOWS AND GEORGE MODELSKI

Two writers who do not normally get cited as progenitors of the field, Paul Meadows and George Modelski, began using the concept of globalization in the contemporary sense of the word long before others now most commonly associated with breakthroughs in understanding globalization. Both of them were modest men, attempting to understand a world in upheaval. There was no connection between them, although they were not alone. Others using the concept of globalization in different settings across the 1950s to 1970s included Richard Snyder, Michael Brecher, Inis L. Claude, Jr., François Perroux, and Alfred E. Eckes, Jr. All of these writers acutely felt the sense of discontinuity and change, supporting the argument that it was the double process of being lifted out of taken-for-granted verities and feeling the intensity of upheaval that gave rise to the possibility of addressing globalization directly and in itself.

The first key figure, Paul Meadows, was a passionate American sociologist and originally a Methodist clergyman. This religious sensibility is more than incidentally important to my overall argument, and I return to it later. He was driven to understand the nature of the rapidly industrializing world in the post-World War II period. *The Culture of Industrial Man* (1950) describes a world of "vast unsettlement" characterized by tensions and dilemmas: military destruction through nuclear weapons and civil wars, political cleaving through ideological clashes and national competition, and cultural fragmentation caused by technological fetishism and what Meadows calls "massive retreats from reality" (p. 1). These globalizing torsions, twisted into being by an industrial civilization, he argued, have produced problems that are far more compelling than those described by Cold War propaganda. The problems of our age accumulate around one question that is urgent for everybody, he says: "How can an industrial civilization persist?" It shadows every conversation and every private moment:

> Before the globalization of industrial aggressions and panics, there was seldom any occasion for widespread or persisting doubt. For the myth guiding the destinies of the West, the myth of infinite progress, was satisfying and self-corroborative, as most myths are. But our myth began to lose its grip at the very point where its salesmanship has been most persuasive: the pragmatic test of results. Our loudly vaunted mastery of the human environment has begun to slip, and neither the ingenuity nor the enthusiasm of a wartime industrialism nor of a postwar reconstruction can permanently reassure us. Something is on trial: neither capitalism, nor communism, nor science, nor religion. In this upheaval of our private worlds it is industrial culture which stands in question. (pp. 2–3)

In summary, a global crisis of industrialism has become normalized, he argued. A year later, in 1951, Meadows contributed an extraordinary piece of writing to the prominent academic journal, *Annals of the American Academy of Political and Social Science*, that has rarely been cited since:

> The culture of any society is always unique, a fact which is dramatically described in Sumner's concept of ethos: "the sum of the characteristic usages, ideas, standards and codes by which a group is differentiated and individualized in character from other groups." With the advent of industrial technology, however, this tendency toward cultural localization has been counteracted by a stronger tendency towards cultural universalization. With industrialism, a new cultural system has evolved in one national society after another; its global spread is incipient and cuts across every local ethos. Replacing the central mythos of the medieval Church, this new culture pattern is in a process of "globalization," after a period of formation and formulation covering some three or four hundred years of westernization. (p. 11)

A number of important things are happening in this article: First, globalization is defined for the first time in terms that contemporary authors would recognize as continuous with current definitions; second, globalization is located in a conductive relation to processes of localization, universalization, and Westernization; and, third, globalization is seen as emerging slowly across history. Beyond these points, the key issue that I draw attention to here is that globalization-in-itself emerged from the shadows for writers who in the aftermath of a world war were trying the universality and intensity of change and upheaval.

The second major figure in globalization studies, George Modelski, was a scholar of international relations. He wrote an essay in 1968 that defined "globalization" in a way that prefigured many later discussions. He begins with a normative argument based on a layering methodology: "A condition for the emergence of a multiple-autonomy form of world politics arguably is the development of a global layer of interaction substantial enough to support continuous and diversified institutionalization" (p. 389). This is linked to a definition that recalls Paul Meadows' more optimistic moments:

> We may define this process as globalization; it is the result of the increasing size, complexity and sophistication of world society. Growth and consolidation of global interdependence and the emergent necessities of devising ways and means of handling the problems arising therefrom support an increasingly elaborate network of organizations. World order in such a system would be the product of the interplay of these organizations, and world politics an effort to regulate these interactions. (p. 389)

This passage and the article in general reveal a remarkably sophisticated rendition of the complex processes of political globalization. His writing does not have the passion of Meadows, and it does not attribute the upheaval to global processes themselves, but he is very aware of the epochal change sweeping across the world. National wars and global inequalities, he argues, dominate the landscape, and globalization offers new alternatives (Modelski 1972). Again, it is the challenges of upheaval that motivate his writing.

Despite the force of the arguments by Modelski and Meadows, for more than two decades, few citations appeared that linked their work to the theme of globalization, and there is little or no evidence of their approach to globalization having a direct influence on those who came after.

Globalization Signaled by Global Consciousness: McCoy and Robertson

The phrase "globalization of culture" appears repeatedly throughout Charles S. McCoy's book, *When Gods Change: Hope for Theology* (1980), including the title of Part One, "Plural Gods and Globalization of Culture." The theme is listed in the index as "Global, globalization" followed by twenty-eight citations. Despite this work, McCoy is also largely forgotten as a figure in global studies.

McCoy's understanding of globalization is bound up with the concept of pluralism (a key term in my argument about changing and contested ontological valences that become attached to processes of globalization). He believes that pluralism "permeates the entire fabric of contemporary living" (1980: 45). Pluralism, according to McCoy, manifested itself as social diversity that shifts the boundaries of awareness. Diversity comes from increased exchange and encounters within and between nation-states and regions, between religious and linguistic communities, and as a result of heightened ethnic and sexual consciousness (pp. 44–45). McCoy believes that such cross-cultural exchanges are necessary for people to transcend their own limitations, and he views this as part of the divine architecture (Rolnick 1997: 19). In a phrase that prefigures the notion of globalization as space–time compression, McCoy states that "communication and travel has reduced the size of the globe" (1980: 75).

Like Meadows before him, McCoy was a United Methodist minister. Their sense of existential unsettlement is strong. Theological transformation is necessary, McCoy argues, because existing cultures are breaking out of their isolation and a new culture on a global scale is emerging. The horizons of human communities are not long limited to a specific geographical area or ideological group. A common realm of meaning and communication is extending across old boundaries and throughout the world. Through radio, television, and film, through travel and cultural exchange, the horizons of young and old are being widened. Blue jeans are worn and rock music is heard in Hamburg, Tokyo, and Berkeley. World news is reported in London, Buenos Aires, and Cairo. The language is different, the emphasis varied, but the events and meanings are increasingly similar. Human culture is becoming global in scope. During the past century, the emerging globalization of culture has placed increasing pressure on the Constantinian theological paradigm of the West (McCoy 1980: 30).

Roland Robertson took up the same theme of cultural extension, again out of an interest in the changing nature of religion. Here, the number of major figures in globalization whose primary field began in religious studies is, at least as I would argue, no coincidence: Meadows, McCoy, and Robertson (1992), but also Bryan Turner (1994) and Mark Juergensmeyer (2000, 2008), as well as Peter Beyer, Olivier Roy, and Assaf Moghadam.

The strengths of Robertson's work are many. Very early on, he recognized the long-term and changing history of globalization. Second, unlike the dominant trend that for a time defined globalization in terms of the demise of the nation-state—perhaps most prominently surfacing in the writings of, for example, Arjun Appadurai and Ulrich Beck—Robertson recognized the complex intersection and layering of nationally and globally constituted social relations. Third, he showed how, across its long uneven history, globalization contributed to a relativization of social meaning and social practice, including the notion of a "world system," developed by Wallerstein.

Writing five years before the pivotal text *Global Culture: Nationalism, Globalization and Modernity* (Featherstone 1990), Roland Robertson and JoAnn Chirico (1985) talked of a broad cultural recognition of global interconnection in the mainstream: "To speak of the modern global circumstance as 'a single place' has, in other words, become so common as to make it virtually uncontroversial' (p. 220). The generalizing force of this recognition is overstated, but it certainly was the case that discussions of globalization had entered the mainstream through popularizers of economic globalization such as Clyde Farnsworth (1981) and Theodore Levitt (1983) writing in the *New York Times* and *Harvard Business Review*, respectively. The burgeoning business discourses of the first wave of popular journalistic attention tended to be thin on analysis and thick on hyperbole. Most suggested that globalization was a completely new phenomenon symbolized by the triumph of the capitalist market. Levitt's writing signaled the rise of the global corporation carried by a worldwide communications revolution. However, this was not the first period in which the emerging force of the global corporation had come to the fore. It goes back to the same time as Meadows and then Modelski were writing. Richard Barnet and Ronald E. Muller published a detailed critical book called *Global Reach: The Power of Multinational Corporations* (1974) on the destructive world dominance of what, despite the book's subtitle, they called "global corporations." And as far back as the 1950s, Sigmund Timberg (1952) had described what he called the third phase of the corporation. Beginning with religious institutionalizing in the thirteenth century and merchant-based imperial extension in the

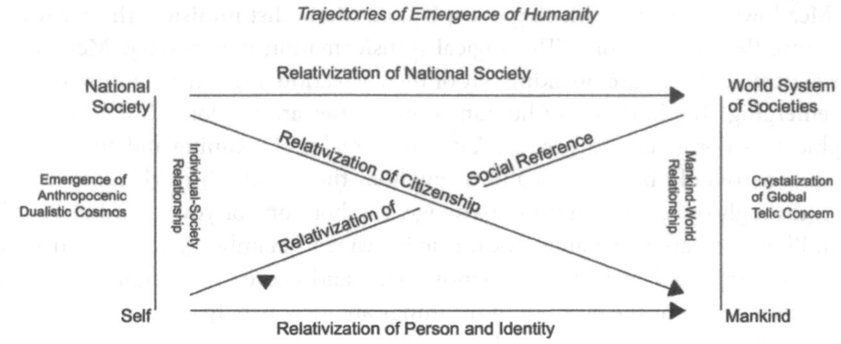

Trajectories of Emergence of Humanity

FIGURE 4.2 Robertson's conception of the global human condition.

Source: Reproduced with permission from Robertson, R., and J. Chirico. 1985. "Humanity, Globalization, and Worldwide Religious Resurgence: A Theoretical Exploration." *Sociological Analysis* 46 (3): 219–242.

seventeenth century, the third phase was the most "inclusive" and international: "more than a happenstance globalization" (p. 477).

Robertson was sensitive both to the force of this movement toward epochal claims— economically *and* culturally—and to the career of the concept of "globalization." He moved his career to take account of both. However, for all of the ferocity of his intellectual commitment, he was not able to develop a systematic theory of globalization. In his early article, he set out what he claimed were the basic four components of a global taxonomy: individual selves, national societies, a system of national societies, and a category to which selves belong—humanity (Figure 4.2; Robertson and Chirico 1985: 222).

However, the model does not fit with his own historical schema, which suggests that forms of globalization occur long before the consolidation of the nation-state as a defining feature of the global system (Robertson 1992). In *Globalization* (1992), Robertson comes to recognize some of the problems with the model, suggesting that it primarily works for twentieth-century developments, but this does not lead to any theoretical refinement, and I cannot find any reference to it after 1992. Neither does he theoretically take forward his own historical schema of the ages of globalization. Later work with David Inglis (Inglis and Robertson 2006), for example, takes the emergence of a global sensibility back to the ancient Greeks, and this provided a wonderful possibility for rethinking systematically, but it was not done.

GLOBALIZATION AS FLOWS OR LAYERS: APPADURAI AND STEGER

Arjun Appadurai takes an explicitly cultural turn, as Roland Robertson did before him and Manfred Steger after. However, instead of taking a critical modernist position to explore the changing order of things, Appadurai heads down the post-structuralist path to emphasize fluidity. This is both his strength and his weakness. It allowed him to see globalization not just as a horizon of connection but as unevenly constitutive of both the local and the far distant. His first and only monograph on the subject, *Modernity at Large: Cultural Dimensions of Globalization* (1996), subsequently had a massive impact and rightly so. It was a scintillating series of essays bringing the global and local together through stories, anecdotes, and personal experience. The book had a wonderful analytical sensibility. It was written by an acute observer of the patterns of social life, but it could do no more than develop some pointers toward a method. The key methodological development was his thin notion of global "scapes," unstructured formations with no boundaries or regularities. Appadurai distinguished different formations of what he called ethnoscapes, mediascapes, technoscapes, financescapes, and ideoscapes. This approach was avidly used for a period as a guide to social mapping, before it lost its standing as different writers realized that apart from the categories of ethnoscapes and perhaps ideoscapes, his global landscape focused too narrowly on the cultural present and the recent past. It faced the same problem of historical stricture as Roland Robertson's model (see Figure 4.2). Broader, more dialectical categories of analysis were needed to understand the unevenness of social continuity and discontinuity, consolidation and fragmentation, across long history. Appadurai never wrote another major text on globalization, and even *Modernity at Large* was only partly focused on globalization, with chapters heading off to discuss the decolonization of Indian cricket and Indian colonial bureaucracy.

Other writers took up the theme of the flows of globalization, but it did not fare any better in later explorations. Zygmunt Bauman turned to the concept of "liquidity" after writing a short essay/book on globalization (Bauman 1998). But consistent with the pattern of ambivalence toward globalization theory argued for in this chapter, globalization in itself becomes only a residual concern in his subsequent writing and is barely mentioned in *Liquid Modernity* (2000). Manuel Castells (1996–1998) oversaw a heroic documenting of the materiality of the space of flows, but his metaphor of "the network" had its own limitations. John Urry (2003) stepped in to elaborate upon the meaning of fluidity by adding his own postmodern inflections. However, adding multiplying and conflicting metaphors to describe complexity in the abstract, for me at least, is singularly unhelpful. This was not necessarily how others in the field responded. For a much more positive take on Urry's work it is worth reading the other writer that I now want to turn to—Manfred Steger (Steger and Wahlrab, 2017: 105–108).

By comparison with Arjun Appadurai, Manfred Steger is a more systematic historian and methodical compiler, while maintaining the storytelling style. This makes him an uncharacteristic figure in the story that I have been elaborating. Unusually, since 2000, his work has been devoted to the theme of globalization, slowly and incrementally pulling different parts together. This has allowed him to slowly build a consistent analytical standpoint, even though he is not by inclination oriented toward theory.

Steger's entry into the field began as a penetrating critique of the dominant ideologies of globalization, giving empirical and analytical body to the notion of "globalism." In this earlier writing, he treated globalism *as* neoliberalism, giving the impression of the singularity of the cultural–political expression (Steger 2002). However, as his analysis developed, he came to distinguish different kinds of globalism, including market globalism, justice globalism, imperial globalism, and religious globalism. Watching the subtitles of *Globalism* (2002) change from the first to the third edition gives a strong sense of the developing nuances of this approach to ideological complexity. By returning to this work in successive editions, he helped us understand that globalism is therefore much more than the ideology associated with the contemporary dominant variant of globalism—market globalism and ideas of a borderless world. It is complex and it is changing. At this empirical level, Steger uses the same four-domain model of social life first developed for globalization mapping in David Held et al.'s *Global Transformations* (1999), except that he layers the analysis with three levels of entry: ideologies, imaginaries, and ontologies (Figure 4.3).

Tracking the way that a global imaginary came to overlay a prior national imaginary, and to frame changing ideologies, required a long-term, detailed empirical and historical research task. Rather than the more common (and wrong) "globalization equals the end of the nation-state" thesis, *The Rise of the Global Imaginary* (Steger 2009) documented a process of ideological change showing how different and contesting ideologies coalesced in a swirling *global imaginary*. This imaginary assumed dominance in the middle to late twentieth century—the same period that provides the context for the rise of the field of globalization studies.

More recently, a third dimension of analysis appeared in Steger's writing. He has begun to examine the ontologies of globalization, particularly questions of spatiality and temporality (Steger and Wahlrab 2017: Chap. 4). In effect, across nearly a two-decade process of

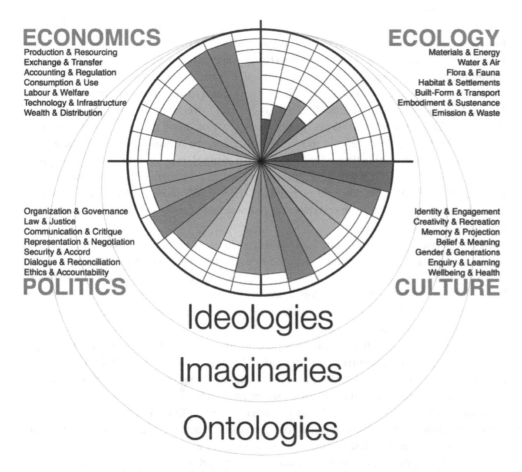

FIGURE 4.3 Steger's domains of globalization in relation to dimensions of analysis.

interconnected writing, three levels of analysis emerged in Steger's writing that help us to understand the complexity of globalization, particularly subjective globalization: ideologies, imaginaries, and ontologies. The first is an analysis of ideologies: coalescing, being contested, and with their proponents seeking to have them become taken for granted as the common sense of the age. The second is an analysis of the social imaginary of globality, not in the sense that the world can be characterized as fully globalized but, rather, in the sense that even as people assert their localized and particularized identities, even as they contest different ideologies, *the global* provides the patterned convocation of the social whole through which people tend to imagine their existence. And the third is analysis of the tensions between ontological formations, understood as the way in which people live basic categories of existence—time, space, embodiment, and knowledge (Steger and James 2013).

As a coda, and a way of drawing this discussion to a close, I note that it is Steger's three-level approach (see Figure 4.3) that has been implicitly used throughout this chapter to structure the analysis of the major figures in the field. (It is perhaps more obvious on re-reading the chapter than the first time through.) One of the key tensions that the chapter describes in exploring the field of enquiry is between the still-current ontology of modernist constructivism and the challenge to this valence by an emerging ontology of postmodern relativism. This tension informs the field in subtle but comprehensive ways. Continuing modernism is expressed methodologically in the realm of social science as the belief that humans construct their worlds and that the role of social enquiry is to expose this process of fabrication. Postmodernism, beyond its harder-edged ideological expressions, is expressed as a gentle suspicion of systematic claims to explanation. What has been argued is that for those writers constituted in this intersection of ontologies—in this argument, all of the major current figures in the field—the method of enquiry that is most comfortable is social mapping with occasional theoretical forays into theory as metaphor. Writers caught in this tension tend to eschew any meta-claims to explanation or determination. They move between concepts of modern pluralism and postmodern fluidity, suspicious of those who would seek to do otherwise.

CONCLUSION

As I have previously argued, now, after more than three decades of debating globalization, we have made some extraordinary gains in understanding. The empirical patterns of the historically changing and uneven nature of globalization are now generally understood. In the various scholarly approaches, much of the hyperbole has tended to drop away, and the normative assessment of globalization has become more sober and qualified. Scholarly approaches have tended to move away from essentializing the phenomenon as necessarily good or bad. Similarly, at least in the scholarly arena, there has been a significant move beyond the reductive tendency to treat globalization only in terms of economic domain.

However, on the other side of the ledger, our central weakness of understanding, at least as I would argue, goes back to the central paradox of globalization studies and global studies—the emergence of an aversion to generalizing theory at a time when the importance of a generalizing category of relations came to the fore. Globalization may simply be the name given to a matrix of processes that extend social relations across world space, but the way in which people live those relations is incredibly complex, changing, and difficult to explain. Thus, we remain in search of generalizing methodologies (not a singular grand theory) that can sensitize us to those empirical complexities while enabling us to abstract patterns of change and continuity. These same methodologies should simultaneously be able to contextualize and explain the nature of the very enquiry that goes into this task—including the task of this chapter.

NOTES

1. With thanks to Timothy Ström for his detailed and extensive research support on the developments of the field of globalization studies. This chapter is based on the research done during a long-term globalization project with Manfred Steger seeking to understand the rise of globalization studies and then global studies as fields of enquiry.
2. From now on in this chapter, I use "global studies" as the encompassing term for both fields, except when I am referring to globalization studies specifically.
3. As an aside, I am not arguing even implicitly for a return to Grand Theory but, rather, for the development of consistent, useful, and systematizing methodologies that enable good empirical work to sustain bold theoretical and normative conclusions.
4. Ironically, it also should be noted that the clash of ontologies came from many directions, not just postmodern relativizing of the relative certainties of modern epistemology. In this period of intensifying globalization, a neo-traditional assault on the modern came from both a distorted Islamism and a politicized Christian fundamentalism. But that is another story.
5. For example, it is characteristic of the general trend that I was lost for a few years editing a 16-volume series of anthologies on globalization (James 2006–2014). The final set comprised 3.5 million words of keynote texts that attempted to document the entire field. The 10,000-word introductions to each volume were intended systematically to break new ground, but it is also typical that I have not had time to bring them together into a single integrated argument about the changing dominant nature of globalization and its determinants.

REFERENCES

Albrow, M. 1996. *The Global Age: State and Society Beyond Modernity*. Cambridge, UK: Polity.
Anderson, B. 1983. *Imagined Communities: Reflections on the Origins and Spread of Nationalism*. London: Verso.
Appadurai, A. 1996. *Modernity at Large: Cultural Dimensions of Globalization*. Minneapolis: University of Minnesota Press.
Axford, B. 2013. *Theories of Globalization*. Cambridge, UK: Polity.
Barnet, R., and R. E. Muller. 1974. *Global Reach: The Power of Multinational Corporations*. New York: Simon & Schuster.
Bauman, Z. 1998. *Globalization: The Human Consequences*. New York: Columbia University Press.
Bauman, Z. 2000. *Liquid Modernity*. Cambridge, UK: Polity.
Castells, M. 1996–1998. *The Rise of the Network Society*. Vols. 1–3. Oxford, UK: Blackwell.

Chase-Dunn, C. 1989. *Global Formation: Structures of the World Economy*. Oxford, UK: Blackwell.

Claude, I. L., Jr. 1965. "Implications and Questions for the Future." *International Organization* 19 (3): 835–846.

Cohen, R., and Paul Kennedy. 2000. *Global Sociology*. Basingstoke, UK: Palgrave Macmillan.

Dicken, P. 2011. *Global Shift: Mapping the Changing Contours of the World Economy*. 6th ed. London: Sage. (Original work published 1992)

el-Ojeili, C., and P. Hayden. 2006. *Critical Theories of Globalization*. Basingstoke, UK: Palgrave Macmillan.

Eriksen, T. H. 2007. *Globalization: The Key Concepts*. Oxford, UK: Berg.

Farnsworth, C. H. 1981. Outlook: Toughening Attitudes on World Trade. *New York Times*, February 8.

Featherstone, M., ed. 1990. *Global Culture: Nationalism, Globalization and Modernity*. London: Sage.

Friedman, J. 1994. *Cultural Identity and Global Process*. London: Sage.

Giddens, A. 1990. *The Consequences of Modernity*. Cambridge, UK: Polity.

Giddens, A. 1999. *Runaway World: How Globalisation is Reshaping Our Lives*. London: Profile.

Harvey, D. 1989. *The Condition of Postmodernity: An Enquiry into the Origins of Cultural Change*. London: Basil Blackwell.

Held, D., A. McGrew, D. Goldblatt, and J. Perraton. 1999. *Global Transformations*. Cambridge, UK: Polity Press.

Hirst, P., and G. Thompson. 1999. *Globalization in Question*. Cambridge, UK: Polity.

Inglis, David, and Roland Robertson. 2006. "From Republican Virtue to Global Imaginary: Changing Visions of the Historian Polybius. *History of the Human Sciences* 19 (1): 1–18.

James, P. 2006–2014. Central Currents in Globalization series, comprising *Globalization and Violence*, vols. 1–4. London: Sage, 2006; *Globalization and Economy*, vols. 1–4. London: Sage, 2007; *Globalization and Culture*, vols. 1–4. London: Sage, 2010; and *Globalization and Politics*, vols. 1–4. London: Sage, 2014.

Juergensmeyer, M. 2000. *Terror in the Mind of God: The Global Rise of Religious Violence*. Berkeley: University of California Press.

Juergensmeyer, M. 2008. *Global Rebellion: Religious Challenges to the Secular State, from Christian Militias to Al Qaeda*. Berkeley: University of California Press.

King, A. D. 1991. *Global Cities*. New York: Routledge.

Levitt, T. 1983. "Globalization of Markets." *Harvard Business Review* 61 (3): 92–102.

Marx, K., and F. Engels. 1848, centenary edn. 1948. *The Communist Manifesto*. London: Lawrence & Wishart.

McCoy, C. S. 1980. *When Gods Change: Hope for Theology*. Nashville, TN: Abingdon.

Meadows, P. 1950. *The Culture of Industrial Man*. Lincoln: University of Nebraska Press.

Meadows, P. 1951. "Culture and Industrial Analysis." *Annals of the American Academy of Political and Social Science* 274: 9–16.

Mittelman, J. H. 2004. *Whither Globalization? The Vortex of Knowledge and Ideology*. London: Routledge.

Modelski, G. 1968. "Communism and the Globalization of Politics." *International Studies Quarterly* 12 (4): 380–393.

Modelski, G. 1972. "Multinational Business: A Global Perspective." *International Studies Quarterly* 16 (4): 407–432.

Munck, R. 2002. *Globalisation and Labour: The New "Great Transformation."* London: Zed Books.

Munck, R. 2007. *Globalization and Contestation: The New Great Counter Movement.* London: Routledge.

Poole, R. 2008. *Earthrise: How Man First Saw the Earth.* New Haven, CT: Yale University Press.

Robertson, R. 1992. *Globalization: Social Theory and Global Culture.* London: Sage.

Robertson, R. 2015. "Interview: Roland Robertson." In *Globalization: The Career of a Concept,* edited by Manfred B. Steger and Paul James, pp. 31–43. Abingdon, UK: Routledge.

Robertson, R., and J. Chirico. 1985. "Humanity, Globalization, and Worldwide Religious Resurgence: A Theoretical Exploration." *Sociological Analysis* 46 (3): 219–242.

Rolnick, P. A. 1997. "The Innovating Covenant: Exploring the Work of Charles S. McCoy." *Tradition & Discovery* 24 (3): 15–28.

Rosenberg, J. 2000. *The Follies of Globalization Theory.* London: Verso.

Sassen, S. 1991. *The Global City: London, Paris, New York.* Princeton, NJ: Princeton University Press.

Sassen, S. 1999. *Globalization and Its Discontents.* New York: Free Press.

Sassen, S. 2007. *A Sociology of Globalization.* New York: Norton.

Sassen, S. 2015. "Interview: Saski Sassen." In *Globalization: The Career of a Concept,* edited by Manfred B. Steger and Paul James, pp. 44–54. Abingdon, UK: Routledge.

Scholte, J. A. 2000. *Globalization: A Critical Introduction.* Basingstoke, UK: Palgrave Macmillan.

Scholte, J. A. 2015. "Interview: Jan Aart Scholte." In *Globalization: The Career of a Concept,* edited by Manfred B. Steger and Paul James, pp. 83–93. Abingdon, UK: Routledge.

Steger, M. B. 2002. *Globalism: The New Market Ideology.* Lanham, MD: Rowman and Littlefield.

Steger, M. B. 2003. *Globalization: A Very Short Introduction.* Oxford, UK: Oxford University Press.

Steger, M. B. 2009. *The Rise of the Global Imaginary: Political Ideologies from the French Revolution to the Global War on Terror.* Oxford, UK: Oxford University Press.

Steger, M. B., and P. James. 2013. "Levels of Subjective Globalization: Ideologies, Imaginaries, Ontologies." *Perspectives on Global Development and Technology* 12 (1–2): 17–40.

Steger, M. B., and A. Wahlrab. 2017. *What is Global Studies? Theory and Practice.* London: Routledge.

Taylor, C. 2007. *A Secular Age.* Cambridge, MA: Harvard University Press.

Thompson, J. S. 2005. *Books in the Digital Age.* Cambridge, UK: Polity.

Timberg, S. 1952. "The Corporation as a Technique of International Administration." *University of Chicago Law Review* 19 (4): 739–758.

Tomlinson, J. 1999. *Globalization and Culture.* Cambridge, UK: Polity.

Turner, B. S. 1994. *Orientalism, Postmodernism and Globalism.* London: Routledge.

Urry, J. 2003. *Global Complexity.* Cambridge, UK: Polity.

Walker, R. B. J. 1993. *Inside/Outside: International Relations as Political Theory.* Cambridge, UK: Cambridge University Press.

Wallerstein, I. 1976. *The Modern World-System: Capitalist Agriculture and the Origins of European World-Economy in the Sixteenth Century.* New York: Academic Press.

Wallerstein, I. 2000. "Globalization or the Age of Transition? A Long-Term View of the Trajectory of the World-System." *International Sociology* 15 (2): 249–265.

Waters, M. 2001. *Globalization.* 2nd ed. London: Routledge.

PART II

GLOBAL THINKING
Analytical Approaches and Conceptual Considerations

CHAPTER 5

··

RESEARCHING THE LOCALIZATIONS OF THE GLOBAL

··

SASKIA SASSEN

THE most widely accepted definitions of globalization emphasize the growing interdependence of the world and the formation of global institutions. One key, often implicit, assumption in this type of definition is that the global and the national are two mutually exclusive domains. Terms such as global studies point to conditions that function at global scales.

Yet at least some of these global conditions also need to be understood as emerging from local settings and dynamics. And while some of these localizations of the global are familiar—for example, the buildings of an international financial center—many others are rarely recognized as such and thus do not get coded as having anything to do with the global. Often, they are far less talked about or recognized than are the broad, overarching macro-level global processes that entail highly visible state-to-state formalized ties and the vast emergent operational space enjoyed by global firms. Both of these very diverse global-level spaces capture the new forms of power and their impressive new technologies. And they completely overshadow the far less visible local instantiations of the global.

The focus of this chapter is on these less visible local instances of the global—the making of global spaces and global actors that inhabit *national* institutional and territorial framings. The organizing proposition of this branch of global studies is that much of what we call globalization is constructed, or emerges from, inside the national. Furthermore, it is often coded and experienced as national. Multiple implications flow from this, including the question of how much of what was historically constructed as the national is still national in the historical (Western) sense of the term. And even if it is no longer national, we cannot assume that it is necessarily global. In fact, many of the transformations we call global are actually often better described as a denationalizing of what was historically constructed as national, as I have explicated at length elsewhere (Sassen 1988, 2008). Some of this can eventually become global, but much of it might simply no longer be national, yet not necessarily global.

This chapter uses the case of major cities as one of the spaces where diverse global processes and projects are constituted. Because the global is so often understood as a condition that transcends the national, capturing the global as it gets constituted at local levels requires specific modes of analysis and interpretation. This also means that the pertinent scholarship covers an enormously broad range of objects of study—from whole cities to sub-urban elements and trans-urban elements. That scholarship also shows the ways in which the urban is a core vector for global studies research focused on micro levels of analysis. The data generated by this type of work are quite different from those generated by research focused on the major global actors—for example, global corporations and the broad range of global governance institutions (see Chapters 1 and 2, this volume).

When this embedding of the global in national settings is left out or overlooked, it easily leads to the notion that what the global gains, the national loses, and vice versa. That, in turn, implies a strong correspondence of national territory with the national; that is, if a process or condition is located in a national institution or in national territory, it must be national. And this will tend to set up a contest between the global and the national: It can easily signal that what is good for the global is not necessarily good for the national. Although this is often the case, as I have shown elsewhere (1991, 2014), we must recognize that the national is increasingly a partial condition and that globalization goes well beyond self-evidently visible global institutions.

Recognizing that the global also dresses itself in the clothing of the local, reshaping the national from inside, opens up a vast research agenda. It means that studying globalization needs to include detailed local research—notably ethnographies—of multiple conditions and dynamics that are the global or are shaped by it but function inside the national and are mostly experienced as national. Cities and neighborhoods, rather than national territory as such, are major sites for such entities; and this further adds to the local appearance of it all.

There is a rich body of research on local instantiations of the global. This work is often less known and has received less attention from the mainstream discussion on globalization focused on self-evidently *global* flows and formations. Anthropologists, geographers, political scientists, sociologists, musicologists, historians, urban planners, architects, environmentalists, filmmakers, artists, and others have generated knowledge about such local instantiations of the global. This amounts to a vast, multifaceted body of knowledge, published in a very broad spectrum of venues—mainstream, alternative, and obscure specialized venues. This chapter focuses on the social sciences very broadly understood.

The first section of this chapter examines how certain types of cities enable micro-level global studies. The second section discusses specifics, notably the making of a global multinodal operational space whose actors range from immigrants to corporations. The third section examines people's networks and the micro global politics they generate. The fourth section examines the state as a kind of in-between space, which is one way to understand its role in subnational global settings. The fifth and final section returns to all the major issues raised via an examination of the destabilizing of older hierarchies of scale.

CITIES: ENABLING MICRO RESEARCH
ON THE GLOBAL

Globalization and digitization have contributed to produce a space for the urban that pivots on both familiar, thick territorial locations and de-territorialized cross-border networks. Such territorial locations can range from spaces of poverty to those with massive concentrations of resources.

Although the technologies are specific to our period, cross-border networks have long been part of the life of major cities. Cities, rather than the kingdoms within which they existed, were the key to the rise, the need, and the making of those networks. Across the centuries, cities have been at the intersection of processes with supra-urban and even intercontinental scaling. Ancient Athens and Rome, the cities of the Hanseatic League, Genoa, Venice, Baghdad, Cairo, Istanbul, Shanghai, and many more were all at the crossroads of major dynamics in their time (Abu-Lughod 1981; Braudel 1984; P. Hall 1966; Stuart Hall 1997; King 1990; Santos et al. 1993; Santos, Souza, and Silveira 1994; Sassen 1988; Sassen-Koob 1982; Stuart 1991). And texts not focused on cities pointed to other networks that contributed to a situated understanding of the global, some quite old (Palloix 1975; Pijl 1998; Sayad 1999; Sklair 1995) and others more recent (Datz 2014; Fraser 2009; Gutman 2016; Prasad and Aneesh 2017; Sassen 2018b; Sommers 2008; Stiglitz and Kaldor 2013; Touraine 2006; Zaloom 2010).

It was the Modern period in the West, marked by the rising power of nation-states, which brought about the strengthening of national borders, an increasingly inward orientation, and a weakened role for cities. This held true even for the powerful nation-states that controlled large empires outside their national sovereign territory. For much of this period, major cities were in many ways far more subordinate to the power of the sovereign than such cities are today, and this held even—and often especially—for the most powerful city in a given country.

That began to change in the 1980s, when deregulation, privatization, and globalization increased. A marking difference in this new period is the rise of direct city-to-city interactions, which were enabled by deregulation and privatization. This eventually gave rise to an accelerated multiplication of networks and a rapid growth in the intensity, complexity, and global span of these networks. Another marking feature of the contemporary period, especially with regard to the economy, is the extent to which significant portions of economies were increasingly becoming dematerialized and digitized, and hence able to move at great speeds through these networks.

These new trends of the 1980s and 1990s generated a significant first body of (mostly) critical scholarship on the new emergent global era (Arrighi 1994; Castells 1989; Cohen, Ruble, et al. 1996; Giddens 1991; Harvey 1985; Held et al. 1999; Hirst and Thompson 1996; Portes and Walton 1981; Robertson 1992; Sassen 1988, 1991; Michael Smith and Feagin 1987; Sousa Santos 2006; Sweet, Fligstein, and Sandholz 2001; Wellman 1999). It is worth noting that the specifics of place are often the factor that enables the critical dimension present in these early texts, an issue I have examined in detail elsewhere (Sassen 2007). In this regard, this scholarship diverges sharply from the more romanticized descriptions of the global that were being published by authors focused on the interests of specific sectors, such as finance and major corporations (Knorr Cetina and Preda 2012). There is also an important new scholarship focused on the theorizing of these epochal transformations, including a focus on coloniality and "de-coloniality," among which a notable scholarship on Latin America (Mendieta 2008; Mignolo 2007; Quijano 2000; Santos et al. 1993; Sousa Santos 2006).

The type of urban space produced in the 1980s and 1990s is partial in a double sense. It accounts for only part of what happens in cities and what cities are about. And, importantly, it inhabits only part of what we might think of as the space of the city, understood in terms as diverse as a city's administrative boundaries or the public life of a city's people. Generally overlooked at the time was that this emergent globalizing of urban space in the 1980s and 1990s left out a vast mix of spaces in these cities: the spaces of inhabitants and businesses that were not part of these novel types of activities and enablements. They ranged from the neighborhoods of the working classes and modest middle classes to those of people and firms engaged in traditional, including often high-income, economies. This underlines the extent to which it is only some parts or elements of a city that might be engaged in those novel cross-border networks; and these, in turn, connected to similarly partial elements of cities throughout the world. Although partial, it did nonetheless lead to major transformations in cities, notably the ways in which cities became part of the live infrastructure of new types of global formations already in the 1980s and 1990s—ranging from financial centers to global civil society. (For this phase, see generally Abu-Lughod 1999; Burdett and Sudjic 2007; Bacqué et al. 2015; Cohen, Carrizosa, et al. 2016; Cohen, Ruble, et al. 1996; Donk et al. 2004; Glasius, Kaldor, and Anheier 2002; King 1996; Sassen 2013; Sayad 1999; Sklair 2017; Smith 2004; Smith and Timberlake 2001; Michael Smith and Favell 2006; Wellman 1999.)

A New Phase: The Making of a Global Multinodal Space

The participation of cities in global networks has continued to expand and has incorporated an increasingly diverse range of urban places, issues, and people (Alderson and Beckfield 2004; Cohen and Simet 2016; Gutman 2015; Kourtit et al. 2014; Liu and Lin 2014; Lloyd 2010; Orr et al. 2016; Sassen 2018a; Parnreiter 2015; Ribas-Mateos 2015; Sassen 2016; Shatkin 2014, 2017; Smith and Kirkpatrick 2015; Xu and Yeh 2010). The core, strategic, and multinodal space is that constituted by the worldwide grid of global cities—now numbering up to 100 cities. This is a space with new economic and political potentials. It is, perhaps, also one of the most strategic spaces for the formation of transnational identities and communities. It is both place centered, in that it is embedded in particular and strategic cities, and trans-territorial, in that it connects sites that are not geographically proximate yet are intensely engaged with each other (via finance, cultural exchanges, specialized lawyering and accounting, etc.).

It is not only the transmigration of capital that takes place in this global grid but also that of people, both rich and poor, from the new "transnational professional workforce" to low-income "migrant workers" (Braverman 1974; Faist 2018; Suzanne Hall 2012; Hillmann and Spaan 2017; Koval et al. 2006; Li et al. 2009; Liu-Farrer 2007, 2011; Portes 2016; Savage 2015; Swiaczny and Hillmann 2017; Sommeiller et al. 2016; Venkatesh 2013; Watson and Bridge 2011). It is also a space for the transmigration of cultural forms—for instance, the re-territorialization of "local" subcultures in sites throughout the world, often far away from their original site (Buechler 2014; Lash 2010; Liu-Farrer 2007, 2011; Nashashibi 2007; US Customs and Border Protection 2016; Watson 2016). It can involve low-income actors such as migrants, minoritized groups, or displaced people (Buechler 2014; Desmond 2016; Movimiento Migrante Mesoamericano 2014; Nashashibi 2007; Sassen 2016; Weinstein

2014a, 2014b; White 2013; Wolford et al. 2013). Or it can involve the new type of young, highly paid professional class that moves around the world but can live and work in similar types of built-environment and subcultures across a growing number of global cities (Fisher and Downey 2006; Parnreiter 2015; Sassen and Dotan 2011; Zaloom 2006, 2010).

Also new is the growing use of digital networks by a broad range of actors, including resource-poor organizations engaged in a variety of cross-border initiatives (see generally Dean et al. 2006; Leistert and Röhle 2011; Malecki 2014; Riemens and Lovink 2002; Rose et al. 2014; Sassen 2016). All of this has increased the number of cities that are part of cross-border networks operating on often vast geographic scales (The Mori Memorial Foundation 2015).

One major, often overlooked marker of these transformations is that whereas the Imperial actors of the past aimed at controlling the full expanse of a conquered territory, today's control modes function through strategic nodes (Sassen 1991, 2018a). This makes them less visible than the old imperial modes of being present. Under such conditions, much of what we experience and represent as the local turns out to be a micro-scale with global span. And the main beneficiaries until now have been major economic actors. But today, even modest actors, including the poor and persecuted, are increasingly using network tools (Sassen 2016).

An important question is whether the worldwide grid of global cities is also a space for a new politics, one going beyond the politics of national culture and identity, even if likely to remain at least partly embedded in it. Among the most radical shifts today in the linkage of people to territory is the loosening of identities away from their traditional sources, such as the nation or the village. Such an unmooring in the process of identity formation engenders new notions of community, membership, and entitlement. This can lead to multiple outcomes, from positive identity mixes within a city to new types of professional elitisms that recur across global cities.

Immigration is one major process through which such transnationalisms can get shaped and have long done so (Ehrenreich and Hochschild 2002; Suzanne Hall et al. 2016; Ribas-Mateos 2005; Sassen 1982, 1988, 2017). Modest local economies are one key vector where such transnational engagements can take place (Brotherton and Kretsedemas 2008; Buechler 2014). Women often play a key role in these neighborhood economies that are part of transnational networks; indeed, in increasingly more cities, this parallel trading circuit is in the hands of immigrant women in the urban economy. But they are also actors in major global processes (Aneesh 2006; Body-Gendrot et al. 2009; Bordes-Benayoun and Schnapper 2006; Moghadam 2005; Naples and Desai 2002; Sassen 2016). Although often not recognized or represented as such in mainstream accounts of the global economy, migration is one of the constitutive processes of globalization today.

Two Very Different Global Circuits

Global firms and immigrants are two major instances of transnationalized actors. Each is marked by cross-border practices. But they belong to very different circuits. These two circuits rarely intersect, and they rarely find themselves in direct economic conflicts with each other inside cities. But both are core constitutive elements of the global within cities. The leading sectors of corporate capital are now global in their organization and material operations. Yet they have very specific territorial insertions guided increasingly by powerful extractive logics (Sassen 2014, 2018a). And many of the disadvantaged workers in global cities are women, immigrants, people of color, and racialized minorities who are making modest local economies.

Each of these very diverse worlds contains men and women whose sense of membership is not necessarily adequately captured in terms of the national but often more in terms of the city in which they live and work (Hagedorn 2007; Jacobson 2013; Krause and Petro 2003; Moghadan 2005; Naples and Desai 2002; Sica and Turner 2005; Michael Smith and Favell 2006; Taylor et al. 2007; Weinstein 2014a). Both of these also often evince cross-border solidarities around issues of substance—for the new global professional workforce, it could be the quality of life in a particular city, whereas for immigrants it might be ongoing links to place of origin. Yet both of these types of very diverse actors find in the global city a strategic site for their economic and political operations.

Large cities in both the Global South and the Global North are the terrain where multiple globalization processes take concrete and localized forms. The rapidly growing and very diverse scholarship focused on these issues as they take shape in cities allows us to capture not only the upper but also the lower circuits of globalization. These localized forms are, in good part, what globalization is about. Furthermore, the thickening transactions that bind cities across borders signal the possibility of a new politics of traditionally disadvantaged actors operating in this new transnational economic geography. This is a politics that arises out of actual participation by workers in the global economy, although under conditions of disadvantage and a lack of recognition, whether as factory workers in export-processing zones or as cleaners on Wall Street (Sassen 2016).

People's Networks: Micropolitics for Global Civil Society

Detecting the presence of globalizing dynamics in thick and often very localized social environments is not always easy. We can use many of the existing research techniques and data sets developed with the national in mind. But the results need to be analyzed through new conceptual and interpretive frameworks—frameworks that recognize the subnational can be one of the sites for the global. These tools can vary enormously. They might include surveys of factories that are part of global commodity chains, in-depth interviews that decipher individual imaginaries about globality, ethnographies of local instantiations of the global, and so on. These tools can all expand the analytic terrain for understanding global processes.

We need both a focus on global-level interdependence and a focus on how the global gets constituted inside the national. Both are a necessary part of the larger effort to theorize and research globalization. The focus on the global as interdependence has dominated discussion and interpretation. This has often made it difficult for locality-focused research to be considered part of the literature on globalization, although this is now changing rapidly. The focus on the nation-state and analytic closure at that level tends to be present in just about all the social sciences. In many social science disciplines, some of the most influential data sets are at the national level, and some of the most advanced methods and data sets require closure of the unit of analysis—that is, the nation-state. Critical to much social science methodological and theoretical developments has been the reliance on the nation-state in order to establish elaborate data sets requiring closure for the most sophisticated technical methods. In the international field, this has led to comparative studies; the most extreme version is the comparison of nation-states, which de facto leaves out precisely those conditions examined in this chapter.

The result of such research practices is a tendency to examine and to interpret issues from the perspective of the nation-state and/or the national state, as has been extensively critiqued by scholars such as Beck and Sznaider (2006) and Taylor (2000), and more recently by Juergensmeyer (2014) and Steger (2014). I add a twist to the discussion about methodological nationalism through my insistence that the national—whether as national territory or national institutions—can become partly denationalized (Sassen 2008: Chaps. 1, 8, and 9). Crucial to the critique of methodological nationalism is that the "nation as container" category is inadequate given the proliferation of transnational dynamics and formations. I share this view, but I add another element: The nation-state as "container" is also undermined by the multiple structurations of the global inside the national, which I view as a process that denationalizes what was historically constructed as national. This allows me to use many of the data sets, methods, and concepts of the social sciences, albeit by positioning them in a different conceptual architecture. Furthermore, I posit that because the national is thick and highly institutionalized, it is not always easy to detect these often partial or highly specialized denationalizations. Mine, then, is a critique of methodological nationalism not exclusively predicated on the fact of transnationalism but, rather, on the possibility of internal denationalization (Sassen 2008).

When we consider the global as partly structured inside the national, we open up analytic terrain for a social science approach to the study of globalization that can also encompass minor instances of the global situated inside the national. A key proposition, then, is that existing social science studies, which may not have been concerned with globalization at all, can in fact contribute to the study of globalization. This helps in overriding a key assumption in the social sciences: the implied correspondence of national territory and national institutions with the national—that is, that if a process or condition is located in a national institution or in national territory, it must be national. This assumption describes conditions that have held, albeit never fully, throughout much of the history of the modern state, especially since First World War I, and to some extent continue to do so today. But these conditions are now partly and actively being unbundled. Different also is the scope of this unbundling.

We might reformulate this proposition as a research project. The fact that a process or entity is located within the territory of a sovereign state does not necessarily mean it is a national process or entity; it might be a localization of the global. Although most such entities and processes are likely to be national, there is an increasing need for empirical research to understand the growing range of localizations of the global. Much of what we continue to code as national today may in fact be such a localization and contain little of the national (as traditionally understood). Developing the theoretical and empirical specifications that allow us to accommodate such conditions is a difficult and collective effort.

The In-Between Space of the State

Given the effort in this chapter to expand the analytic terrain within which to map the question of globalization, the larger research and theorization agenda needs to address aspects of globalization and the state that are lost in dualized accounts. Although there are indeed many components of each of the national and the global that are mutually exclusive, there is a growing, often specific set of components that are not. This is seen, for instance, in critical aspects of the work of ministries of finance, central banks, and specialized technical regulatory agencies, such as those concerned with telecommunications, competition policy, and the war on terrorism.

This in-between domain is not usually part of the research and theorization agenda on globalization. There has long been research on various dimensions of the state's participation in global processes (Datz 2007; Dezalay and Garth 1996; Evans 1997; Fligstein 2001). In many ways, today's era continues a long history of changes that have not altered the fundamental fact of state primacy (Mann 1986, 1993). Both the "strong" and the "weak" versions of neo-Weberian state theory (Evans et al. 1985) share certain aspects of this view. While acknowledging that the primacy of the state may vary given different structural conditions between state and society, these authors tend to understand state power as basically denoting the same conditions throughout history: the ability successfully to implement explicitly formulated policies.

Although this scholarship is not focused on globalization and the state, much in their work can help illuminate critical aspects of this subject. For instance, if we find that the state is one of the strategic institutional domains in which critical work for developing globalization takes place, then we can posit that globalization does not necessarily produce the decline of the state as a whole but neither does it keep the state going as usual or produce merely adaptations to the new conditions. The state becomes the site for foundational transformations in the relation between the private and the public domains, in the state's internal balance of power, and in the larger field of both national and global forces within which the state now has to function (Gill 2015; Sassen 2008: Chaps. 4 and 5).

Tilly's (1990) distinction of the national state from "the state" as such is helpful in this regard. Whereas states are "coercion-wielding organizations that are distinct from households and kinship groups and exercise clear priority in some respects over all other organizations within substantial territories," national states are distinguished by "governing multiple contiguous regions and their cities by means of centralized, differentiated, and autonomous structures" (1–2). The centralized national state acts as an interface between national and supranational forces. Delimiting the national state as one particular form of state allows more analytic freedom in conceptualizing these processes.

Recovering the State's Participation in Global Operations

A first step is to recover the ways in which the state participates in governing the global economy in a context increasingly dominated by deregulation, privatization, and the growing authority of non-state actors. The global economy is a good example to use for illustrating empirical and theoretical issues. But, clearly, the debate regarding globalization and state participation includes a broad range of formations that goes beyond the economy. Importantly, a number of scholars have examined the possibility of a global civil society (Albrow et al. 2008; Alexander 2006; Beck and Sznaider 2006) and transnationalized forms of the social (Itzigsohn et al. 1999; Komlosy et al. 1997; Parnreiter 1995; Pries 2008). One major effort in this scholarship is to examine and theorize potential advantages of transcending nationally oriented state authority and instituting world-level institutional orders.

The work of building a global studies scholarship focused on micro levels inside the nation-state and inside the state apparatus itself is enabled by the notion of a denationalizing of particular, often highly specialized institutional orders inside the state. Nearly all definitions of the state from Weber on emphasize a territorial dimension of state power. Even Mann (1986: 26–27), who is otherwise enormously sensitive to the multiple spaces for the exercise of power in social life, defines the state largely as an organization exercising political power and enforcing cooperation within a bounded territory.

This territorial dimension means that as states have participated in the implementation of the global economic system, they have, in many cases, undergone significant transformations (Sassen, 2008: Parts 2 and 3; 2017). The accommodation of the interests of foreign firms and investors entails a negotiation. At the heart of this negotiation is the development inside national states—through legislative acts, court rulings, and executive orders—of the mechanisms necessary for the reconstitution of certain components of national capital into "global capital." Also necessary is the need to accommodate new types of rights/entitlements for foreign capital in what are still national territories in principle under the exclusive authority of their states. The state here can be conceived of as representing a technical administrative capacity enabling the implementation of a corporate global economy. It is a capacity that cannot quite be replicated at this time by any other institutional arrangement. The background condition is that the state remains as the ultimate guarantor of the "rights" of global capital—that is, the protection of contracts and property rights—and, more generally, a major legitimator of claims rather than a major enabler of the social question (Sassen 2014).

Such an approach is one way of expanding the analytic terrain for mapping globalization—it extends that terrain deep into highly specialized components of the national state. These particular transformations inside the state are partial and incipient but strategic. For instance, such transformations can weaken or alter the organizational architecture for the implementation of international law insofar as the latter depends on the institutional apparatus of national states. Furthermore, they have also created the conditions whereby some parts of national states actually gain relative power (Sassen, 2008: Chap. 4) as a result of that participation in the development of a global economy. Some state agencies become more powerful due to their functional importance for the global economy. This must be distinguished from Skocpol's emphasis on the structural independence of state agencies and their internal rationalization (Skocpol et al. 1985); it also differs from a world-system perspective that would treat "state power" as monolithic, determined by placement in the world system.

These trends toward greater interactions of national and global dynamics are not unidirectional. There have been times when they may have been as strong in some aspects as they are today—for example, the global capital market at the turn of the twentieth century (Hirst and Thompson 1996). Furthermore, state sovereignty was never absolute but, rather, always subject to significant fluctuations. Thus, Arrighi and Silver (1999) argue that historically "each reaffirmation and expansion of legal sovereignty was nonetheless accompanied by a curtailment of the factual sovereignty that rested on the balance of power" (p. 93) and that "the crisis of national sovereignty is no novelty of our time. Rather, it is an aspect of the stepwise destruction of the balance of power that originally guaranteed the sovereign equality of the members of the Westphalian system of states" (p. 94).

A second articulation of the state and globalization pivots on unequal power among states. The world-system scholarship (Wallerstein 1974) has made some of the most important contributions here, as has a strong Marxist and neo-Marxist scholarship (Amin 1970; Robinson 2004). It is in fact some states, particularly the United States and the United Kingdom, that at the beginning of this phase of the 1980s were key actors producing the design for the new standards and legalities needed to ensure protections and guarantees for global firms and markets. One way of putting it is the following: "Denationalized State Agendas and Privatized Norm-Making" (Sassen 2008: Chap. 5).

But often overlooked in analyses of the unequal power of states is the fact that legislative items, executive orders, adherence to new technical standards, and so on will have to be produced through the particular institutional and political structures of each state. The often imposed consensus in the community of states to further globalization is not merely a political decision: It entails specific types of work by a large number of distinct state institutions in each country (Sassen 2008: Chaps. 4 and 5). In terms of research and theorization, this is a vast uncharted terrain: It would mean examining how that production takes place and gets legitimated in different countries. This signals the possibility of cross-national variations (which then would need to be established, measured, and interpreted). To some extent, we may describe this as the production of instances of "institutional isomorphism" (see the essays in Powell and DiMaggio 1991). While Powell and DiMaggio's book analyzes the structural causes for the emergence of formal similarities among organizations across widely separated areas, and the mechanisms of power and legitimation underlying these causes, it tends to assume that organizations already exist within a shared structural field. Once these organizations become mutually relevant, structural forces can act on each to shape them to a common mold. In the situations under analysis here, it is not immediately clear that the various relevant organizations exist within the same organizational fields, and much of the work performed is oriented specifically toward making them co-present with a common (global) field/space.

The Destabilizing of Older Scalar Hierarchies

Where the state is an ambiguous space for the structuring of global processes, the domains briefly described next are more easily recognized as global. Unlike the sociological scholarship on the state, research and theorization on these three domains mostly constitutes a new generation of scholarship far more centrally placed in one or another globalization framing. One organizing proposition that encompasses the diversity of these domains is that each represents a distinct type of multiscalar dynamics.

Global dynamics can destabilize older hierarchies of scale constituted through the practices and power projects of past eras, with the national scale eventually the pre-eminent scale. Today, we see what resembles a return to older imperial spatialities for the economic operations of the most powerful actors: the formation of a global market for capital, a global trade regime, and the internationalization of manufacturing production (Robinson 2014). It is, of course, not simply a return to older forms; it is crucial to recognize the specificity of today's practices and the capabilities enabling these practices. This specificity partly consists of the fact that today's transboundary spaces had to be produced in a context in which most territory is encased in a thick and highly formalized national framework marked by the exclusive authority of the national state. This is, in my reading (Sassen 2008: Chaps. 1, 4, and 5), one of the key features differentiating the current from older phases of globalization.

The global project of powerful firms, the new technical capabilities associated with information and communication technologies, and some components of the work of states have together constituted strategic scales other than the national scale (Castells 1996; Gereffi et al. 2005; Pijl 1998, 2015; Robinson 2004; Sassen 1988, 2008; see generally Applebaum and Robinson 2005; Ren 2011). Most especially among these are subnational scales such as the global city (discussed previously in this chapter) and supranational scales such as global markets (Badie and Vidal 2009; Chen 2005). But there is also a multiplication of horizontal civic global networks and projects (Bordes-Benayoun and Schnapper 2006; Jacobson and Ruffer 2006; Moghadam 2005; Naples and Desai 2002).

These processes and practices—economic, political, and civic—destabilize the scale hierarchies that expressed the power relations and political economy of an earlier period (Aneesh 2006, 2015; Bonilla et al. 1998; Calhoun et al. 2002; Silver 2003). These were, and to a good extent continue to be, organized in terms of institutional size and territorial scope: from the international down to the national, the regional, the urban, and the local, with the national functioning as the articulator of this particular configuration. Notwithstanding multiple different temporal frames, the history of the modern state can be read as the work of rendering national just about all crucial features of society: authority, identity, territory, security, law, and capital accumulation.

Such instances serve to illustrate some of the conceptual, methodological, and empirical issues in this type of research and theorization. One concerns the role of place in a global world. A focus on places helps disaggregate globalization in terms of the multiple specialized cross-border circuits on which different types of places are located. Among the most complex spaces are global cities. These are subnational places where multiple global circuits intersect and thereby position these cities on diverse structured cross-border geographies, each typically with distinct scopes and constituted in terms of distinct practices and actors. For instance, at least some of the circuits connecting São Paulo to global dynamics are different from those of Frankfurt, Johannesburg, or Bombay. Furthermore, distinct sets of overlapping circuits assemble into distinctly structured cross-border geographies. This multiplication of cities and circuits has also intensified older hegemonic geographies: For instance, Madrid has partly reactivated an older geography that reconnects it to Latin America now largely via investment and immigration.

The new interactive technologies reposition the local and invite us to a critical reconceptualizing of the local (Sassen 2012, 2015). Through these new technologies, a financial services firm becomes a microenvironment with continuous global span. But so do resource-poor organizations or households that are part of global activist networks. This begins to destabilize both the notion of context, typically associated with locality, and the notion of physical proximity as a necessary trait of locality. In brief, local scales are not inevitably part of nested scalar hierarchies running from the local to the regional, the national, and the international. Scaling takes on specific contents when the practices and dynamics involved are global but take place at what has been historically constructed as the scale of the national or the local.

Today's rescaling dynamics cut across institutional size and across the institutional encasements of territory produced by the formation of national states. This does not mean that the old hierarchies disappear but, rather, that novel rescalings emerge alongside the old ones and that the former can often trump the latter. Existing theory is not enough to map today's multiplication of practices and actors constitutive of these rescalings.

CONCLUSION

This chapter has focused especially on how the global can get structured inside the national. Such a perspective expands the analytic terrain within which to understand the global in ways that allow us to use methods, concepts, and data of the social sciences even when these were not designed to address the global.

I identified at least three ways in which we can design objects of study that make the subnational one of the terrains for the global. One consists of the endogenizing or the localizing of global dynamics in the national. A second consists of formations that, although global, are articulated with particular actors, cultures, or projects, producing an object of study that requires negotiating a global and a local scale, such as global markets and global networks of activists working in specific localities. A third consists of the denationalizing of what had historically been constructed as national and may still continue to be experienced, represented, and coded as such. This produces an object of study that is contained within national frames but needs to be decoded, such as state institutions that are key producers of instruments needed by global economic actors.

These three types of instances capture distinct social entities and have diverse origins. However, they are not necessarily mutually exclusive. They may well come together in some of the conditions or processes we might want to construct as objects of study.

A focus on such subnationally based processes and dynamics of globalization requires methodologies and theorizations that engage not only global scalings but also subnational scalings *as* components of *global* processes. Studying global processes and conditions that get constituted subnationally has some advantages over studies of globally scaled dynamics, but it also poses specific challenges. It does make possible the use of long-standing research techniques, from quantitative to qualitative, in the study of globalization. It also gives us a bridge for using the wealth of national and subnational data sets as well as specialized scholarships such as area studies. However, all need to be situated in conceptual architectures that are not quite those held by the researchers who generated these research techniques and data sets, as their efforts mostly had little to do with globalization.

REFERENCES

Abu-Lughod, Janet L. 1981. *Rabat: Urban Apartheid in Morocco.* Princeton, NJ: Princeton University Press.

Abu-Lughod, Janet L. 1999. *New York, Chicago, Los Angeles: America's Global Cities.* Minneapolis: University of Minnesota Press.

Albrow, Martin, Helmut Anheier, Marlies Glasius, and Mary Kaldor. 2008. *Global Civil Society 2007/8: Communicative Power and Democracy.* Thousand Oaks, CA: Sage.

Alderson, Arthur S., and Jason Beckfield. 2004. "Power and Position in the World City System." *American Journal of Sociology* 109, no. 4: 811–851.

Alexander, Jeffrey C. 2006. "Global Civil Society." *Theory, Culture, and Society* 23 (2 3): 521 524.

Amin, Samir. 1970. *L'Accumulation a l'échelle mondiale.* Paris: Anthropos.

Aneesh, A. 2006. *Virtual Migration: The Programming of Globalization.* Durham, NC: Duke University Press.

Aneesh, A. 2015. *Neutral Accent: How Language, Labor, and Life Become Global.* Durham, NC: Duke University Press.

Applebaum, R. P., and Robinson, W. I., eds. 2005. *Critical Globalization Studies.* New York: Routledge.

Arrighi, Giovanni. 1994. *The Long Twentieth Century: Money, Power, and the Origins of Our Times.* London: Verso.

Arrighi, Giovanni, and Beverly J. Silver. 1999. *Chaos and Governance in the Modern System.* Minneapolis: University of Minnesota Press.

Bacqué, Marie-Hélène, G. Bridge, M. Benson, T. Butler, E. Charmes, Y. Fijalkow, E. Jackson, L. Launay, and S. Vermeersch. 2015. *The Middle Classes and the City: A Study of Paris and London.* London: Palgrave Macmillan.

Badie, B., and D. Vidal, eds. 2009. *L'Etat du monde 2010.* Paris: La Découverte.

Beck, Ulrich, and Natan Sznaider. 2006. "Unpacking Cosmopolitanism for the Social Sciences: A Research Agenda." *British Journal of Sociology* 57 (1): 2–23.

Body-Gendrot, Sophie, Marisol García Cabeza, and Enzo Mingione. 2009. "Comparative Social Transformations in Urban Regimes." In *Sociology Today: Social Transformations in a Globalizing World,* 359–378. Thousand Oaks, CA: Sage.

Bonilla, F., E. Melendez, R. Morales, and M. Torres de los Angeles. 1998. *Borderless Borders.* Philadelphia, PA: Temple University Press.

Bordes-Benayoun, Chantal, and Dominique Schnapper. 2006. *Diasporas et Nations.* Paris: Odile Jacob.

Braudel, Fernand. 1984. *Civilization and Capitalism, 15th–18th Century.* Translated by Siân Reynolds. New York: Harper & Row.

Braverman, Harry. 1974. *Labor and Monopoly Capital: The Degradation of Work in the Twentieth Century.* New York: Monthly Review Press.

Brotherton, David C., and Philip Kretsedemas, eds. 2008. *Keeping out the Other: A Critical Introduction to Immigration Enforcement Today.* New York: Columbia University Press.

Buechler, Simone Judith. 2014. *Labor in a Globalizing City: Economic Restructuring in São Paulo, Brazil.* Bern, Switzerland: Springer.

Burdett, Richard, and Deyan Sudjic. 2007. *The Endless City: An Authoritative and Visually Rich Survey of the Contemporary City.* London: Phaidon Press.

Calhoun, Craig, Ashley Timmer, and Paul Price. 2002. *Understanding September 11.* New York: New Press.

Castells, Manuel. 1989. *The Informational City*. Oxford, UK: Blackwell.

Castells, Manuel. 1996. *The Rise of the Network Society*. Cambridge, MA: Blackwell.

Chen, X. 2005. *As Borders Bend: Transnational Spaces on the Pacific Rim*. Oxford, UK: Rowman & Littlefield.

Cohen, Michael, Maria Carrizosa, and Margarita Gutman, eds. 2016. *Hábitat en Deuda: Veinte Años de Políticas Urbanas en América Latina*. Buenos Aires, Argentina: Café de las Ciudades.

Cohen, Michael, Blair A. Ruble, Joseph S. Tulchin, and Allison M. Garland, eds. 1996. *Preparing for the Urban Future: Global Pressures and Local Forces*. Washington, DC: Woodrow Wilson Press.

Cohen, Michael, and Lena Simet. 2016. "The Global Urban Futures Project at The New School." Paper presented at the Habitat III Conference on Urban Development. Quito, Ecuador: The Ford Foundation.

Datz, Giselle. 2007. "Global–Nation Interactions and Sovereign Debt Restructuring Outcomes." In *Deciphering the Global: Its Scales, Spaces and Subjects*, edited by S. Sassen, 323–342. New York: Routledge.

Datz, Giselle. 2014. "Varieties of Power in Latin American Pension Finance: Pension Fund Capitalism, Developmentalism and Statism." *Cambridge Core Government and Opposition* 43 (3): 483–510.

Dean, Jodi, Jon Anderson, and Geert Lovink, eds. 2006. *Reformatting Politics: Information Technology and Global Civil Society*. New York: Routledge.

Desmond, Matthew. 2016. *Evicted: Property and Profit in the American City*. New York: Crown.

Dezalay, Yves, and Bryant Garth. 1996. "Fussing About the Forum: Categories and Definitions as Stakes in a Professional Competition." *Law & Social Inquiry* 21 (2): 285–312.

Donk, Wim van de, Brian D. Loader, Paul G. Nixon, and Dieter Rucht. 2004. *Cyberprotest: New Media, Citizens and Social Movements*. New York: Routledge.

Ehrenreich, Barbara, and Arlie Russel Hochschild, eds. 2002. *Global Woman: Nannies, Maids, and Sex Workers in the New Economy*. New York: Holt.

Evans, Peter B., Dietrich Rueschemeyer, and Theda Skocpol. 1985. *Bringing the State Back In*. Cambridge: Cambridge University Press.

Evans, Robins. 1997. "Interference." In *Translation from Drawing to Buildings and Other Essays*, 10–33. Cambridge, MA: MIT Press.

Faist, Thomas. 2018. "The Moral Polity of Forced Migration." *Ethnic and Racial Studies* 41 (3): 412–423.

Fisher, Melissa S., and Greg Downey, eds. 2006. *Frontiers of Capital: Ethnographic Reflections on the New Economy*. Durham, NC: Duke University Press.

Fligstein, Neil. 2001. "Institutional Entrepreneurs and Cultural Frames—The Case of the European Union's Single Market Program." *European Societies* 3: 261–287.

Fraser, Nancy. 2009. *Scales of Justice: Reimagining Political Space in a Globalizing World*. New York: Columbia University Press.

Gereffi, Gary, John Humphrey, and Timothy Strugeon. 2005. "The Governance of Global Value Chains." *Review of International Political Economy* 12 (1): 78–104.

Giddens, Anthony. 1991. *The Consequences of Modernity*. Cambridge, UK: Polity.

Gill, Stephen, ed. 2015. *Critical Perspectives on the Crisis of Global Governance: Reimagining the Future*. London: Palgrave Macmillan.

Glasius, Marlies, Mary Kaldor, and Helmut Anheier, eds. 2002. *Global Civil Society 2002*. Oxford, UK: Oxford University Press.

Gutman, Margarita. 2015. "Hidden and Open Faces of Power in Buenos Aires." *International Journal of Urban Sciences* 19 (1): 20–28.

Gutman, Margarita. 2016. "The Fight for the Future." In *The Futures We Want: Global Sociology and the Struggle for a Better World. Selected Writings from the WebForum*, edited by Markus S. Schulz, 228–229. Germany and USA: Initiative for Transnational Futures, International Sociological Association.

Hagedorn, John M., ed. 2007. *Gangs in the Global City: Alternatives to Traditional Criminology.* Chicago: University of Illinois Press.

Hall, Peter. 1966. *The World Cities.* New York: McGraw-Hill.

Hall, Stuart. 1997. "The Local and the Global: Globalization and Ethnicity." In *Culture, Globalization and the World-System: Contemporary Conditions for the Representation of Identity*, edited by A. King, 19–40. Minneapolis: University of Minnesota Press.

Hall, Suzanne. 2012. *City, Street and Citizen: The Measure of the Ordinary.* London: Routledge.

Hall, Suzanne, Julia King, and Robin Finlay. 2016. "Migrant Infrastructure: Transaction Economies in Birmingham and Leicester, UK." *Urban Studies* 54 (6): 1311–1327.

Harvey, David. 1985. *The Urbanization of Capital.* Oxford, UK: Blackwell.

Held, David. Anthony McGrew, David Goldblatt, and Jonathan Perraton. 1999. *Global Transformations: Politics, Economic and Culture.* Cambridge, UK: Polity.

Hillmann, Felicitas, and Ernst Spaan. 2017. "On the Regional Rootedness of Population Mobility and Environmental Change." *Comparative Population Studies* 42: 25–54.

Hirst, Paul, and Grahame Thompson. 1996. *Globalization in Question: The International Economy and the Possibilities of Governance.* Cambridge, UK: Polity.

Itzigsohn, Jose, Carlos Dore Cabral, Esther Hernandez Medina, and Obed Vazquez. 1999. "Mapping Dominican Transnationalism: Narrow and Broad Transnational Practices." *Ethnic and Racial Studies* 22: 316–339.

Jacobson, David. 2013. *Of Virgins and Martyrs: Women and Sexuality in Global Conflict.* Baltimore, MD: Johns Hopkins University Press.

Jacobson, David, and G. B. Ruffer. 2006. "Scope: Global or National? Social Relations on a Global Scale." In *Dialogues on Migration Policies*, edited by Passy M. Giugni, 25–44. Lexington, MA: Lexington Books.

Juergensmeyer, Mark, ed. 2014. *Thinking Globally: A Global Studies Reader.* Berkeley: University of California Press.

King, Anthony D. 1990. *Urbanism, Colonialism, and the World Economy: Cultural and Spatial Foundations of the World Urban System.* London: Routledge.

King, Anthony D., ed. 1996. *Re-presenting the City. Ethnicity, Capital and Culture in the 21st Century Metropolis.* London: Macmillan.

Knorr Cetina, Karin, and Alex Preda, eds. 2012. *The Oxford Handbook of the Sociology of Finance.* Oxford, UK: Oxford University Press.

Komlosy, A., C. Parnreiter, I. Stacher, and S. Zimmerman, eds. 1997. *Ungeregelt und Untebezahlt: Der Informelle Sektor in der Weltwirstschaft.* Frankfurt, Germany: Brandes & Apsel/Sudwind.

Kourtit, Karima, Cathy Macharis, and Peter Nijkamp. 2014. "A Multi-Actor Multi-Criteria Analysis of the Performance of Global Cities." *Applied Geography* 49: 24–36.

Koval, John P., Larry Bennett, Michael I. J. Bennett, Fassil Demissie, Roberta Garner, and Kiljoong Kim, eds. 2006. *The New Chicago: A Social and Cultural Analysis.* Philadelphia, PA: Temple University Press.

Krause, Linda, and Patrice Petro, eds. 2003. *Global Cities: Cinema, Architecture, and Urbanism in a Digital Age*. New Brunswick, NJ: Rutgers University Press.

Lash, Scott. 2010. *Intensive Culture: Social Theory, Religion, & Contemporary Capitalism*. London: Sage.

Leistert, Oliver, and Theo Röhle. 2011. *Generation Facebook: Über das Leben im Social Net*. Dortmund, Germany: Verlag.

Li, Zhigang, Laurence J. C. Ma, and Desheng Xue. 2009. "An African Enclave in China: The Making of a New Transnational Urban Space." *Eurasian Geography and Economics* 50 (6): 699–719.

Liu, Tao, and George C. S. Lin. 2014. "New Geography of Land Commodification in Chines Cities: Uneven Landscape of Urban Land Development Under Market Reforms and Globalization." *Applied Geography* 51: 118–130.

Liu-Farrer, Gracia. 2007. "Producing Global Economies from Below: Chinese Immigrant Transnational Entrepreneurship in Japan." In *Deciphering the Global: Its Spaces, Scales and Subjects*, edited by S. Sassen, 179–199. New York: Routledge.

Liu-Farrer, Gracia. 2011. *Labour Migration from China to Japan: International Students, Transnational Migrants*. London: Routledge.

Lloyd, Richard. 2010. *Neo-Bohemia: Art and Commerce in the Postindustrial City*. New York: Routledge.

Malecki, Edward J. 2014. "Connecting the Fragments: Looking at the Connected City in 2050." *Applied Geography* 49: 12–17.

Mann, Michael. 1986. *The Sources of Social Power*. Cambridge, UK: Cambridge University Press.

Mann, Michael. 1993. "National-States in Europe and Other Continents: Diversifying, Not Dying." *Daedalus* 122 (3): 115–140.

Mendieta, Eduardo. 2008. *Global Fragments: Globalizations, Latinamericanisms, and Critical Theory*. Albany: State University of New York Press.

Mignolo, Walter. 2007. "Delinking: The Rhetoric of Modernity, the Logic of Coloniality, and the Grammar of De-Coloniality." *Cultural Studies* 21 (2): 449–514.

Moghadam, Valentine M. 2005. *Globalizing Women: Transnational Feminist Networks*. Baltimore, MD: Johns Hopkins University Press.

Movimiento Migrante Mesoamericano. 2014. "Caravana de Madres Centroamericanas: 'Una Década de Lucha y Esperanza.'" November 18, 2014. https://movimientomigrantemesoamericano.org/2014/11/18/caravana-de-madres-centroamericanas-una-decada-de-lucha-y-esperanza.

Naples, Nancy A., and Manisha Desai, eds. 2002. *Women's Activism and Globalization: Linking Local Struggles and Transnational Politics*. New York: Routledge.

Nashashibi, Rami. 2007. "Ghetto Cosmopolitanism: Making Theory at the Margins." In *Deciphering the Global: Its Scales, Spaces and Subjects*, edited by S. Sassen, 243–264. New York: Routledge.

Orr, Bart, Michael Cohen, and Lena Simet. 2016. *The Habitat Commitment Project: Assessing the Past for a Better Urban Future*. New York: Global Urban Futures Project.

Palloix, Christian. 1975. *L'Internationalisation du Capital: Éléments Critiques*. Paris: Maspero.

Parnreiter, Christof. 1995. "Uprooting, Globalization, and Migration: Selected Questions." *Journal fur Entwicklungspolitik* 11 (3): 245–260.

Parnreiter, Christof. 2015. "Las Ciudades Latinoamericanas en la Economía Mundial: La Geografía de Centralidad Económica y sus Transformaciones Recientes." *Economía UNAM* 12 (35): 3–22.

Pijl, Kees van der. 1998. *Transnational Classes and International Relations*. London: Routledge.

Pijl, Kees van der, ed. 2015. *Handbook of the International Political Economy of Production*. Cheltenham, UK: Elgar.

Prasad, Amit, and Aneesh Aneesh, eds. 2017. *Special Issue: Global Assemblages of Technoscience* 22 (1): 1–164.

Pries, L. 2008. "Transnational Actors and World Politics." In *Handbook of International Relations*, edited by W. Carlsnaes, T. Risse, and B. A. Simmons, 426–452. London: Sage.

Portes, Alejandro. 2016. "International Migration and National Development: From Orthodox Equilibrium to Transnationalism." *Sociology of Development* 2 (2): 73–92.

Portes, Alejandro, and John Walton. 1981. *Labor, Class and the International System*. New York: Academic Press.

Powell, W. W., and DiMaggio, P. J., eds. 1991. *The New Institutionalism in Organizational Analysis*. Vol. 17. Chicago: University of Chicago Press.

Quijano, Anibal. 2000. "Coloniality of Power, Eurocentrism and Latin America." *Nepantla: Views from the South* 1 (3): 533–580.

Ren, Xuefei. 2011. *Building Globalization: Transnational Architecture Production in Urban China*. Chicago: University of Chicago Press.

Ribas-Mateos, Natalia. 2005. *The Mediterranean in the Age of Globalisation: Migration, Welfare and Borders*. New Brunswick, NJ: Transaction Publishers.

Ribas-Mateos, Natalia. 2015. *Border Shifts: New Mobilities in Europe and Beyond*. New York: Palgrave Macmillan.

Riemens, Patrice, and Geert Lovink. 2002. "Local Networks: Digital City Amsterdam." In *Global Network, Linked Cities*, edited by S. Sassen, 327–346. New York: Routledge.

Robertson, Roland. 1992. *Globalization: Social Theory and Global Culture*. London: Sage.

Robinson, William I. 2004. *A Theory of Global Capitalism: Production, Class, and State in a Transnational World*. Baltimore, MD: Johns Hopkins University Press.

Robinson, William I. 2014. *Global Capitalism and the Crisis of Humanity*. New York: Cambridge University Press.

Rose, Gillian, Monica Degen, and Clare Melhuish. 2014. "Networks, Interfaces, and Computer-Generated Images: Learning from Digital Visualizations of Urban Redevelopment Projects." *Environment and Planning D: Society and Space* 32 (3): 386–403.

Santos, Milton, Maria Adelia de Souza, Mónica Arroyo, and Francisco Capuano Scarlato, eds. 1993. *O Novo Mapa De Mundo: Fim de Seculo e Globalizacao*. São Paulo, Brazil: Hucitec.

Santos, Milton, Maria Adelia de Souza, and Maria Laura Silveira, eds. 1994. *Território: Globalização e Fragmentação*. São Paulo, Brazil: Hucitec.

Sassen, Saskia. 1982. "Recomposition and peripheralization at the core." In *The New Nomads: Immigration and Change in the International Division of Labor*, edited by M. Dixon and S. Jonas, 88–100. San Francisco, CA: Synthesis.

Sassen, Saskia. 1988. *The Mobility of Labor and Capital*. Cambridge, UK: Cambridge University Press.

Sassen, Saskia. 1991. *The Global City: New York, London, and Tokyo*. Princeton, NJ: Princeton University Press.

Sassen, Saskia. 2007. *A Sociology of Globalization*. New York: W.W. Norton & Company, Inc.

Sassen, Saskia. 2008. "Neither Global nor National: Novel Assemblages of Territory, Authority, and Rights." *Ethics & Global Politics* 1: 1–2.

Sassen, Saskia. 2012. "Interactions of the Technical and the Social: Digital Formations of the Powerful and the Powerless." *Information, Communication & Society* 15: 455–478.

Sassen, Saskia. 2013. "Global Finance and Its Institutional Spaces." In *The Oxford Handbook of the Sociology of Finance*, edited by K. Knorr-Cetina and A. Preda, 13–32. Oxford, UK: Oxford University Press.

Sassen, Saskia. 2014. *Expulsions: Brutality and Complexity in the Global Economy.* Cambridge, MA: Belknap.

Sassen, Saskia. 2015. "Digitization and Work: Potentials and Challenges in Low-Wage Labor Markets." Position Paper. New York: Open Society Foundations.

Sassen, Saskia. 2016. "A Massive Loss of Habitat: New Drivers for Migration." *Sociology of Development* 2 (2): 204–233.

Sassen, Saskia. 2018a. "Embedded Borderings: Making New Geographies of Centrality." *Territory, Politics, Governance* 6: 5–15.

Sassen, Saskia. 2018b. *Cities in a World Economy.* 5th ed. Thousand Oaks, CA: Sage.

Sassen-Koob, Saskia. 1982. "Recomposition and Peripheralization at the Core." *Contemporary Marxism* 5: 88–100.

Sassen, Saskia, and Natan Dotan. 2011. "Delegating, not Returning, to the Biosphere: How to Use the Multi-scalar and Ecological Properties of Cities." *Global Environmental Change* 21 (3): 823–834.

Savage, Mike. 2015. *Social Class Sin the 21st Century.* London: Penguin.

Sayad, Abdelmalek. 1999. *La Double Absence: Des Illusions de l'émigré aux Souffrances de l'immigré.* Paris: Seuil.

Shatkin, Gavin. 2014. "Contesting the Indian City: Global Visions and the Politics of the Local." *International Journal of Urban and Regional Research* 38 (1): 1–13.

Shatkin, Gavin. 2017. *Cities for Profit: The Real Estate Turn in Asia's Urban Politics.* Ithaca: Cornell University Press.

Sica, Alan, and Stephen Turner, eds. 2005. *The Disobedient Generation: Social Theorists in the Sixties.* Chicago: University of Chicago Press.

Silver, B. J. 2003. *Forces of Labor: Workers Movements and Globalizations Since 1870.* Cambridge, UK: Cambridge University Press.

Sklair, Leslie. 1995. *Sociology of the Global System.* Baltimore, MD: Johns Hopkins University Press.

Sklair, Leslie. 2017. *The Icon Project: Architecture, Cities and Capitalist Globalization.* New York: Oxford University Press.

Skocpol, T. P. Evans, and D. Rueschemeyer. 1985. *Bringing the State Back In.* New York: Cambridge University Press.

Smith, David. 2004. "Global Cities in East Asia: Empirical and Conceptual Analysis." *International Social Science Journal* 56 (3): 399–412.

Smith, David, and Michael Timberlake. 2001. "World City Networks and Hierarchies, 1977–1997: An Empirical Analysis of Global Air Travel Links." *American Behavioral Scientist* 44 (10): 1656–1679.

Smith, Michael Peter, and Adrian Favell, eds. 2006. *The Human Face of Global Mobility: International Highly Skilled Migration in Europe, North America and the Asian Pacific.* New Brunswick, NJ: Transaction Publishers.

Smith, Michael Peter, and Joe Feagin. 1987. *The Capitalist City: Global Restructuring and Territorial Development.* London: Sage.

Smith, Michael Peter, and Owen L. Kirkpatrick, eds. 2015. *Reinventing Detroit: The Politics of Possibility.* Comparative Urban and Community Research Book Series, Vol. 11. New Brunswick, NJ: Transaction Publishers.

Sommeiller, Estelle, Mark Price, and Ellis Wazeter. 2016. *Income Inequality in the U.S. by State, Metropolitan Area, and Country*. Washington, DC: Economic Policy Institute.

Sommers, Margaret R. 2008. *Geneologies of Citizenship: Markets, Statelessness and the Rights to Have Rights*. Cambridge, UK: Cambridge University Press.

Sousa Santos, Boaventura. 2006. "Globalizations." *Theory, Culture and Society* 23 (2–3): 393–399.

Steger, Manfred B., ed. 2014. *The Global Studies Reader*. 2nd ed. New York: Oxford University Press.

Stiglitz, Joseph, and Mary Kaldor. 2013. *The Quest for Security: Protection Without Protectionism and the Challenge of Global Governance*. New York: Columbia University Press.

Sweet, Alec Stone, Neil Fligstein, and Wayne Sandholtz. 2001. "The Institutionalization of European Space." In *The Institutionalization of Europe*, edited by A. Sweet, W. Sandholtz, and N. Fligstein, 1–28. Oxford, UK: Oxford University Press.

Swiaczny, Frank, and Felicitas Hillmann. 2017. "Migration und Flucht im Globalen Süden" ("Migration and Flight in the Global South"). *Geographische Rundschau* 3: 46–50.

Taylor, Peter J. 2000. "World Cities and Territorial States Under Conditions of Contemporary Globalization." *Political Geography* 19: 5–32.

Taylor, Peter, Ben Derudder, Pieter Saey, and Frank Witlox. 2007. *Cities in Globalization: Practices, Polices and Theories*. London: Routledge.

The Mori Memorial Foundation. 2015. *The Global Power City Index 2015*, edited by N. Yamato, K. Sasaki, Y. Hamada, K. Ito, and Y. Y. Wong; translated by Alex Yeoman. Tokyo: Nikkei Printing.

Tilly, Charles. 1990. *"Future History": Interpreting the Past, Understanding the Present*. London: Palgrave Macmillan.

Touraine, Alain. 2006. *Un Nouveau Paradigme: Pour Comprendre le Monde d'aujourd'hui*. Paris: Fayard.

US Customs and Border Protection. 2016. *Southwest Family Unit Subject and Unaccompanied Alien Children Apprehensions Fiscal Year 2016*. Washington DC: US Department of Homeland Security.

Venkatesh, Sudhir. 2013. *Floating City: A Rouge Sociologist Lost and Found in New York's Underground Economy*. New York: Penguin.

Wallerstein, Immanuel. 1974. *The Modern World System*. New York: Academic Press.

Watson, Sophie. 2016. "Making Multiculturalism." *Ethnic and Racial Studies* 1: 1–18.

Watson, Sophie, and Gary Bridge. 2011. *The New Blackwell Companion to the City*. Oxford, UK: Blackwell.

Weinstein, Liza. 2014a. "'One-Man Handled': Fragmented Power and Political Entrepreneurship in Globalizing Mumbai." *International Journal of Urban and Regional Research* 38 (1): 14–35.

Weinstein, Liza. 2014b. *The Durable Slum: Dharavi and the Right to Stay Put in Globalizing Mumbai*. Minneapolis: University of Minnesota Press.

Wellman, Barry, ed. 1999. *Networks in the Global Village: Life in Contemporary Communities*. Oxford, UK: Westview.

White, Anne. 2013. "Double Return Migration: Failed Returns to Poland Leading to Settlement Abroad and New Transnational Strategies." *International Migration* 52 (6): 72–84.

Wolford, Wendy, Saturnino M. Borras Jr., Ruth Hall, Ian Scoones, and Ben White. 2013. *Governing Global Land Deals: The Role of the State in the Rush for Land*. West Sussex, UK: Wiley.

Xu, Jiang, and Anthony Yeh. 2010. *Governing and Planning of Mega-City Regions: An International Comparative Perspective*. London: Routledge.

Zaloom, Caitlin. 2006. *Out of the Pits: Traders and Technology from China to London.* Chicago: University of Chicago Press.

Zaloom, Caitlin. 2010. "The City as Value Locus: Markets, Technologies, and the Problem of Worth." In *Urban Assemblages: How Actor-Network Theory Changes Urban Studies*, edited by Ignacio Fabías and Thomas Bender, 253–268. New York: Routledge.

CHAPTER 6

....

GLOCALIZATION

....

HABIBUL HAQUE KHONDKER

THIS chapter has three main sections. The first section seeks to provide a sociology of knowledge perspective on the emergence of the concept glocalization. This section also situates the idea of glocalization in the context of historical processes of intercultural exchanges and borrowings, and it discusses the relationship between glocalization and some of the cognate concepts such as hybridity or intersectionality to underscore the efficacy, if not the comparative advantage, of this concept over some of the competing concepts. It is argued that to understand intercultural interpenetration, glocalization has become a salient concept in the global age while recognizing the continued currency of the related concepts. The second section, the bulk of the chapter, examines how the process of glocalization has shaped and continues to shape various institutional spheres of society in the global age. The examination of a spectrum of spheres ranging from popular culture to laws and religion in society not only provides the evidence of the processes of glocalization at play but also helps sharpen and add rigor to the concept of glocalization. The third and final section of the chapter explores, largely, the role of this concept in global studies. Global studies as a multidisciplinary field of study has gained considerable scholarly attention, and it can be conceived of as studies of the impacts or consequences of the processes of globalization and glocalization. In this section, it is argued that glocalization provides a useful conceptual tool and adds rigor to global studies. The chapter also explores the conceptual and theoretical relationship between globalization and glocalization, often drawing on empirical references to illustrate the discussion. Here, I introduce a distinction between two conceptualizations and, hence, two understandings of globalization—a thin theory and a thick theory of globalization. It is the thick theory of globalization that comes closer to glocalization. In this light, it can be stated, following Roland Robertson (1995, 2003), that globalization leads to glocalization and the two concepts become coterminous; in other words, a nuanced, and thus dense, understanding of globalization is glocalization itself (Khondker 2004). Although glocalization is at the same time both constitutive of and a manifestation of globalization, it may be possible—even desirable—to keep these concepts analytically separate, albeit interrelated. The concept of glocalization, this chapter will demonstrate, may have a great deal of relevance for the field of globalization studies, especially in capturing the nuanced relationships between what is nominally called "global" and what is conceived as "local." In conclusion, the chapter argues that sociological concepts by force of the sheer complexity of the changing empirical realities they seek to handle become complex and abstract. Although some level of abstractness is a necessary aspect of a concept or a theoretical construct, it is also important not to forget that the other goal of a social scientific concept is to illuminate and to add clarity rather than opacity. In this regard, the scholars of global studies can make significant contributions.

ENTER GLOCALIZATION

Some may regard *glocalization* as a faddish term and nothing more than in-house jargon in global studies in general and sociology in particular. Such a charge resonates with the popular image of sociologists, who have often been accused of neologism; in fact, some neologisms, such as Robert Merton's "dysfunction," have over time become an acceptable part of the lexicon and part of the repertoire of everyday language. Glocalization, too, has become part of the social scientific discourse, finding its way into business studies and other disciplines to the extent that a journal[1] dedicated to this subject was introduced in 2013.

The concept glocalization, a synthesis of globalization and localization, owes its origin to Roland Robertson, who first introduced the concept "glocal" in the early 1990s while consolidating his theoretical arguments about globalization (Robertson 1992: 173). He formally articulated and explicated this concept in 1994 and 1995 while defending his concept of globalization and trying to rescue it from the gross simplification in the prevalent social scientific (mainly economic) discourses. Robertson conceptualized globalization abstractly, arguing that "its central *dynamic* [emphasis in original] involves the two-fold processes of the particularization of the universal and the universalization of the particular" (Robertson 1992: 177–178). With hindsight, it can be argued that the idea of glocalization was built into this formulation of globalization. Thus, although the concept glocalization is often thought of separately from globalization, upon reflection it can also be conceived as an aspect of globalization. Since 1992 when the concept was introduced and having been formally articulated in the mid-1990s, other social scientists have contributed to the discussion and have added empirical substance to this concept. Some writers have argued that globalization—the thick globalization—can be viewed in certain senses as glocalization (Beyer 2007; Khondker 2004; Swyngedouw 2004). The idea that a deeper sociological understanding of globalization is but glocalization goes back to Robertson (1992, 1995), the putative originator of this concept. This view is based on the consequences or translation of the processes of globalization at the local, ground level. Some writers viewed globalization primarily as an economic process. Following this line of thought, Swyngedouw (2004) viewed glocalization in terms of scaling of governance to regulate (and perhaps facilitate as well) capitalist production, where the state sits in the middle between the processes of regionalization and localization; both these processes can be subsumed under the rubric of glocalization. As stated by Swyngedouw, glocalization refers to

> (1) the contested restructuring of the institutional level from the national scale both upwards to supra-national or global scales and downwards to the scale of the individual body or the local, urban or regional configurations and (2) the strategies of global localisation of key forms of industrial, service and financial capital. (p. 37)

The notion of glocalization as "rescaling" of institutional forms of capital has implication for governance because "glocalizing" production cannot be separated from "glocalizing" levels of governance (Swyngedouw 1997: 159). Swyngedouw's economic geographic analysis of glocalization dates back to the early 1990s.

The politico-economic context of the emergence of the sociological constructs of globalization and glocalization was the beginning of the neoliberal phase of the global capitalism represented by Prime Minister Margaret Thatcher in Britain, who took office in 1979, and President Ronald Reagan in the United States, who took office in 1980. Both leaders were ideologues and mouthpieces of the "free market" ideology that marginalized society to an extent that sociology as a discipline was at risk. The retreat of the welfare state, the Iranian Revolution of 1979, and the Soviet incursion in Afghanistan in 1980 marked a muscular phase of the Cold War, which later turned out to be the beginning of its end (although not viewed as such at that moment in history). Intellectually, at least, in the studies of social change and development, neo-Marxist dependency theories were maturing into Immanuel Wallerstein's world systems theory, which played a central role in rescuing sociology from methodological nationalism by focusing on the phenomena at the world-systemic level. Robertson and several sociologists were as excited by the world- or globe-centric analysis as they were critical of the supposedly one-sided, economistic analysis in the theory of Wallerstein, who championed a Braudelian version of total history with strong emphasis on material conditions.

Although the post-World War II modernization theory was criticized for its abstract and ahistorical analysis, it gave way to a debate over convergence, divergence, and invariance as a consequence of modernization or large-scale social change, which dominated the imagination of a group of sociologists (Baum 1974, 1977; Robertson and Holzner 1980) who shared a common interest in classical sociology and were influenced by the sociology of Talcott Parsons. A dense intellectual debate often impenetrable to less philosophically inclined sociologists was also influenced by the comparative inter-civilizational analysis of Benjamin Nelson. It was in that intellectual milieu that the ideas of both globalization and glocalization germinated. Roland Robertson, who co-authored a book on international modernization in the late 1960s, was an ardent member of the inter-civilizational analysis group and became the champion of the analytical framework of globalization in the early 1980s.

Robertson (1992) sought to understand the cultural implication of capitalism, a macroglobal process on-the-ground reality: "Global capitalism both promotes and is conditioned by cultural homogeneity and cultural heterogeneity. The production and consolidation of difference and variety is an essential ingredient of contemporary capitalism" (p. 173). Robertson was also one of the pioneers of global studies, with roots in his work on international modernization with J. P. Nettl (1968).

Globalization is "characterized by two distant but closely connected processes. Social actors possess greater senses of 'globality': That is, globalization is marked by increasing subjective consciousness of the world as a whole; or, in other words, it involves heightened awareness of the world as a 'single place'" (Robertson 1992: 6). It is also characterized by a global intensification of social and cultural "connectivity," such as through telecommunications and international travel (cf. Tomlinson 1999; Giulianotti and Robertson 2004: 546). Globalization is also marked culturally by processes of "glocalization," whereby local cultures adapt and redefine any global cultural product to suit their particular needs, beliefs, and customs (Giulianotti and Robertson 2004: 546; Robertson 1992, 1995, 2003; Robertson and White 2004).

Globalization relativizes all particularisms, forcing exponents of specific beliefs or identities to confront and to respond to other, particularistic ideas, identities, and social processes across the universal domain. Thus, although universalism and particularism may appear as categorical antinomies, they are interdependent, fused together in a globe-wide nexus (Robertson 1992: 102). Glocalization captured the interpenetration of the local and the global, and in doing so it goes beyond the dichotomy of the local and the global. To a considerable extent, this conceptual framework accounted for micro-marketing strategies of capitalism. In tourism, one of the largest industries in the world, locale plays a key role. Tourists would loath to travel if every place was the same. Tourists like to see exotic and authentic places. The authenticity of original cultural or architectural features can be preserved, but in some cases, dance and music have to be constructed to suit the tourist gaze. Quoting MacCannell (1989), a pseudo-reconstruction of "authentic otherness" is the general feature of the contemporary phase of the globalization of culture (Robertson 1992: 173). Robertson's framework thus makes important contributions to global studies, which mark out a multidisciplinary, transnational field of study in which the focus is on the empirical processes and the discussion goes beyond national boundaries, reflecting the complex realities of the twenty-first century. In delving into the evolving and complex realities of global studies, the conceptual tools of globalization and glocalization will be of great value.

It is possible to project the ideas of glocalization to understand historical processes of cultural exchanges and diffusion. Human cultures are products of admixtures historically. Sometimes in the processes of cultural adaptation, borrowings took place imperceptibly and unconsciously, sometimes consciously and voluntarily. Despite the cultural nationalists and puritans, historians and cultural anthropologists dispelled the myth of uniqueness of culture long ago. Ralph Linton's (1937) classic essay, "One Hundred Percent American," may be considered a paean to cultural globalization. Historians have provided additional illustrations of intercultural borrowing with profound implication for shaping major cultural episodes. Eurocentric history was a product of its time; new historical research is interrogating and changing many commonly held beliefs about historical sequences, highlighting nonlinearity and exposing Eurocentrism. For example, the writings of Marx and Weber presented an invariant view of history, in which civilizations retained their splendid isolation from each other. It is only modern capitalism, spreading rationality, that promises to result in global convergence. Recent research has shown the influence of Arab Muslim thinkers on the men of ideas responsible for the Renaissance (Hobson 2004: 174–175). The mathematical works of Ibn Al-Haytham may have influenced those of Roger Bacon and other precursors of the Renaissance (Morgan 2008: 104). Bacon, the thirteenth-century Oxford scholar, quoted Ibn al-Haytham; Al-Kindi was another source of inspiration for him (Al-Hassani, Woodcock, and Saoud 2007: 322). About Ibn Al-Haytham's research on optics, the eyeball, and the *camera obscura*, Morgan writes,

> Five hundred years before Leonardo da Vinci, he delves into things that will later be attributed to the great Italian and to Kepler and Descartes, when in fact they, like some Renaissance and post-Renaissance thinkers are really replicating or building on what the great Muslim scientists had established long ago. (p. 104)

Morgan states that it was Muslim history "that had seeded the European Renaissance and enabled many aspects of the modern West and global civilization" (p. xiv). For Jack Goody, culture has always moved both ways: "But earlier the movement was generally from East to West" (Goody, 2004: 14). On the basis of Joseph Needham's research, Goody traces the links between East and West to the Bronze Age in Mesopotamia, not just in the spread of plow and wheel but also in the ideas of astronomy and physiology (Goody 1996: 250).

Renaissance, thus, was more than a linear outcome, a rediscovery of classical Greek and Roman intellectual and artistic heritage. As Greek philosophy once seeded great minds of the Muslim intellectuals between the tenth and twelfth centuries, a phase dubbed as "lost enlightenment," it is now recognized that the intellectual advancements during the golden ages of Muslim civilization "were themselves influenced by the achievements of earlier contributions to human civilization, such as those of ancient China, India and Greece" (Al-Rodhan 2012: 15). A careful history of the circulation of cultural ideas, knowledge, and technology in the world based on methodological cosmopolitanism will reveal a long genealogy of the phenomenon of glocalization.

One of the alleged weaknesses of the concept of glocalization is that it fails to recognize the dimension of power, let alone account for tensions and confrontational politics (Roudometof 2015). Tensions—both political and cultural—arising from contestation of economic and political power are examined later with regard to the conclusion suggesting that glocalization may not be a smooth process. Some of the negative aspects of the world today, such as religious extremism, may be rooted in glocalization and transglocalization. A clarification of the concepts at hand is needed before proceeding to the discussion of the advantages and disadvantages of glocalization. The next section attempts to add some clarity to the conceptual tools.

Concepts such as glocalization (Robertson 1995), "mélange" (Pieterse 1995), "creolization" (Hannerz 1992), disjuncture (Appadurai 1996), and hybridity have been used to describe and analyze the process as well as consequences of the spread of globalization (Turner and Khondker 2010: 69–73). While discussing the processes of glocalization, globalization, or regionalization, it would be useful to keep in mind the methodological construct, "unit of analysis." Depending on the unit of analysis, all these processes can be viewed as taking place at the same time. However, it would be useful for analytical purposes to separate local, national, regional, and global spheres as sui generis despite their interactions and interpenetrations in the present age. People living in a demarcated locality mobilize to put up organized resistance. Global or national movements become localized, just as, sometimes, local movements also become global movements.

We can view all the popular concepts—glocalization, hybridization, creolization, mélange, fusion, and indigenization—either as interchangeable or as context-specific concepts applicable to different contexts; for example, fusion is often used in the context of food or music, and creolization is popularly used with reference to language but also used with regard to food. Hybridization, with roots in botany, is used in popular cultures. However, we can also view them as cognate concepts belonging to a family of concepts. They broadly capture aspects of the intermingling of global and local processes, and the interpenetration of universal and particular. In providing the intellectual context for the rise of glocalization in the sociological discourse, Robertson (2014) claims that it arose in the mid-1990s as globalization was generally perceived—with exceptions—as resulting in homogenization and standardization, and since then it had to encounter "such motifs as polyethnicity; cosmopolitanism, interculturality, synchronicity, hybridity, transculturality, creolization; indigenization; vernacularization; diasporization, and yet others" (Robertson 2013: 1).

Globalization, as a process that leads to new formations, transforms institutions. Glocalization is closely linked to entangled modernity. It evokes an image of fusion, a creative hybridization or syncretization. Whereas hybridization or syncretization evokes a natural progression without conscious choice, glocalization can have both—a semi-natural cultural adaptation and synthesis, almost unwittingly, and a conscious or deliberate choice. An example of the latter is that during the early phase of the Meiji Restoration, one of the over-enthusiastic Japanese leaders—a future education minister—wanted to make English the national language of Japan. And the Meiji constitution of Japan was modeled upon European republics of the time. In Singapore, English was deliberately kept and used as an "official" language—which was consistent with Singapore's export-led growth strategies—and several Western multinational corporations chose Singapore for the disciplined and English-speaking labor force as well as the excellent infrastructure. Although sometimes goals may be set at the global or international level, such as the United Nations' Millennium Development Goals or Sustainable Development Goals, the realization of these goals remains with the state and the local community. Hence, the importance of local- and national-level entities can never be underestimated. And the process of glocalization needs to be understood at both a voluntaristic level and the level of the long, drawn-out process of cultural diffusion and adaptation.

Glocalization has a spatial dimension. Arif Dirlik (2011) notes that globalization, paradoxically, has produced and/or thematized space, especially local space—the production of space in the sense of Henri Lefebvre (1991) can be viewed as a consequence of globalization and an example of glocalization. It may be argued that in most instances, one can demarcate spatially the zones of global, glocal, and local at the same time—sometimes coexisting peacefully and sometimes in tension. Taking, for example, universal law and norms governing gender relations in a populous country such as India, it would be easy to find areas less impacted by the forces of globalization where rules of tradition reign with deleterious consequences.

The impact of global capitalist forces on local communities has to be seen in terms of degrees of intensity. A villager in a remote village of Bangladesh or Nepal can be said to have taken part in the global political economy as a consumer of a global product. Beyond consumption of the industrial commodity, he has very little to do with the globalized economy; hence, his relationship could be defined as passive compared to that of a village woman who, by buying an internet-enabled mobile phone, is actively involved in a global technology-mediated transaction as a worker from the same village laboring in a global metropole—for example, Dubai or Singapore—as a construction worker. The intensity of the impact of the globalization process is varied, and such nuances have implications for the transformation of society. Some of the fissures in many developing societies—but not exclusive to developing societies—can be understood in terms of uneven globalizations.

Robertson's concern was to understand attempts of the "real world" to bring global, in the sense of the macroscopic aspect of contemporary life, into conjunction with the local, in the sense of the microscopic aspect of contemporary life in the late twentieth century. The very formulation, apparently in Japan, of a term such as glocalize (from *dochakuka*, roughly meaning "global localization") is perhaps the best example of this

(Robertson 1992: 174). As Japan became a successful player in the global economy, it had an interest in innovations in all aspects of business, especially marketing its products. This had a direct bearing on "the general problem of the relationship between the universal and the particular" (p. 174).

GLOBALIZATION OF INSTITUTIONS AND EVERYDAY LIFE

There are several institutional spheres in which glocalization is at play. A select number of cases based on the relevance to conceptual clarity are discussed next under seven rubrics. This is by no means an exhaustive list, but it is particularly relevant insofar as twenty-first-century globalization is concerned. All important spheres of life—such as religion, politics, law, education (especially higher education), technology, popular culture and its various components (e.g., food, music, sports, and even social movements, architecture, and museums)—are also affected. Even academic disciplines and curricula are glocalized, sometimes under directives of the state.

Glocalization of Religion

Clifford Geertz (1971) observed interesting differences in Islam as practiced in Java, Indonesia, and Morocco. The same religion in two regions of the world—North Africa and Southeast Asia—takes different forms due to the blending of local indigenous cultures with the universalistic religion. Broadly speaking, Islam in Bangladesh became historically divergent from Islam in Saudi Arabia, despite their common background of Sunni traditions of Islam. Women Living Under Muslim Laws, a transnational organization of Muslim women, highlights the differences of laws and the status of women in Muslim countries. Suffice it to point out that while women in the United Arab Emirates are allowed to fly fighter jets, women in neighboring Saudi Arabia had to wait for the right to drive automobiles until mid 2018. Scholars of Buddhism and Christianity find interesting differences in the practice of the same religion in different areas of the world and trace the changes that transform it in local cultural practices. Sometimes such blending of universal and local can produce unsavory outcomes, such as religious fundamentalism, which is "quintessentially a glocal concept" (Beyer, 2007: 108).

Glocalization of Economy

Bauman (2014) provocatively states, "'Glocalization' means local repair workshops servicing and recycling the output of global factories of problems." Bauman comes to this conclusion by assessing the "localities," especially large cities, as facing the brunt of such globally generated problems as immigration and environmental pollution. The reach of global capital to the remotest peripheries and the consequences have been analyzed ad nauseam.

Apart from the globalization of the economy, a theme well traversed since Adam Smith and Karl Marx, glocalization of the economy has added new dimensions. Glocalization in an economy is manifested in the rise of the informal economy, which covers a whole range of practices from the use of informal space to interactions and other practices. Mohamed Bouazizi in Tunisia was involved in the informal economy, selling products on the streets. One of the growing global trends has been the rise of the informal economy (Neuwirth 2011). Conventional economic thinking links it to lack of economic development and views it as transitional, contending that it will disappear with economic development (La Porta and Shleifer 2014). Although they are attributable to evasion of regulation and the inability of the state to enforce formal rules, informal economies present a vast arena of glocalization. Entrepreneurs armed with a high degree of ingenuity and informal education eke out a living by using global technology creatively, tapping the local conditions. An example is the case of so-called "Phone Ladies" in Bangladesh (Zhao et al. 2015: 49), where rural women sold telephony services by visiting door to door, a scheme pioneered by the Nobel laureate Muhammad Yunus and supported by loans from Grameen Bank. This is a case of innovative application of a universal technology in a particular cultural context. In the sphere of finance, financial inclusion is often organized through micro-finance, which, according to the founder of Grameen Bank, Muhammad Yunus, provides "an ant's perspective to the world." The universalistic ideas of banking blending with the entrepreneurship of rural women are not only changing their economic fortune but also denting the patriarchal culture. The informalization of the economy emanates from the marginalization of certain groups in society, and in the present world, informatization or digitalization plays an important role in the informal economy. Nearly half (49.6%) of the world's 3.6 billion internet users in mid-2016 were in Asia (Internet World Stat 2016). The spread of the internet has also enabled the rise of what may be called formal–informal sectors in the service industries, especially related to the travel industry. Taxi services such as Uber and competitors of hotel services such as Airbnb are examples.

Matusitz (2016) defines glocalization thus: "By and large, 'glocalization' refers to the strategies a multinational corporation employs in order to cater to local idiosyncrasies abroad. The ultimate goal is to gain prominence, appeal and, of course, high annual revenues." Using the example of Wal-Mart in Argentina, Matusitz explains how the company came with preconceived plans and practices that failed, and it became profitable only after it adjusted to the local conditions. In other words, for a global company, glocalization is good for revenue. IKEA, the Swedish furniture company, takes the tack that it "designed for people, not consumers" (IKEA 2017). Globalization and the global marketplace create homogenized consumers; glocal companies target people in the local communities. Redesigning involves local cultural norms, local taste, habits of the people, and other cultural idiosyncrasies.

In the discussion of management, the evidence does not bear out the perception that universal practices drawn from best practices will be valid and useful everywhere, regardless of the cultural contexts. Research determined that management practices are often hybridized, incorporating local practices and beliefs. The re-embedding process in the local cultural milieu is a matter of necessity and acceptability. In terms of the application of this term, business studies played a key role by using it not only as a sociological concept but also as a business strategy. The idea, thus, has been much simplified. Insofar as business strategy is concerned, glocalization means that a company—for example,

Wal-Mart—cannot apply its universal business strategies and methods of operation in another country or culture. One could question how universal those methods are in the first place. There are historical antecedents of this in Fordist policies derived from the assembly-line production of Henry Ford's automobile factory in the United States in the early twentieth century. Later, management gurus introduced the Toyota principles. The Fordist model is, of course, the model of how to rationalize production, or optimize it, to make an organization more productive and improve its service delivery. The focus of the Toyota principles, among others, was how to market the product and improve the services of the shop floor. Glocalization has been used effectively in improving marketing. To do so, one has to take careful note of the local context and the cultural practices. What are the taboos, what are the preferences, and what kind of policies will resonate with local culture? In other words, management cannot just operate with a preconceived set of policies and ideas. It must be open to new ideas and ready to change its policies in light of new information and cultural awareness. When introduced in Germany, Wal-Mart was a failure, but it became successful in Argentina because it succeeded in glocalizing its operations and marketing (Matusitz 2016).

The glocalization of business management and corporatization has a close parallel in government administration or governance. It is often assumed that the ideal governance system can be, in principle, drawn from the best practices found elsewhere. These ideas ignore the constraint or reality of local culture. Dani Rodrik (2008) argues that the best practices need to be adjusted and tamed by the local cultural context. Here, Rodrik places particular emphasis on creativity because there is no end to creative solutions and these will not be an a priori set of policies or practices. There is no such thing as best practices heedless of cultural and geopolitical context. This idea clearly implies the role of glocalization.

Practices such as *Jugaad*, an Indian word for "make do," that localize production and other services to deliver to customers in an affordable way present an example of glocalization of production (Radjou et al. 2012). Rather than the globalizing production of standardized goods and services, such flexible systems change the scale of production, making it more customer-centered using local resources and locally available materials and lowering costs of transportation and centralized modes of production. This model innovative rescaling of production has huge potential, especially for low- and mid-level consumer products.

Globalization of State and Political Discourse

The relationship between the state and the global is complex. Using the template of glocalization, one can examine the interpenetration of global forces in the constitution of the state.

Different states play different roles in the global inter-state system. A state in the Global South is both a trainer and a container of the laboring class to make them available as forces in the global forces of production, and at the same time, it is also a site of global corporate players. The territoriality and stability of state are of immense importance. Overenthusiasm on the part of some writers blinded them to the integrational role of the state in the maintenance of capitalism. As a provider of rules to manage the affairs of the business and discipline the labor force, the state works as a facilitator for capitalist penetration and economic globalization.

Glocalization of Politics

In the political sphere, the relativization of universal concepts such as democracy, the rule of law, and human rights provides exemplars of glocalization. This is best illustrated in the discussions of democracy "with Chinese characteristics" or variants of that discourse. Although the rhetoric of democracy has appeal throughout the world, and the majority of nations have nominally accepted the principles of the United Nations' Universal Declaration of Human Rights, much of the world remains politically unfree, with sluggish penetration of democratic values and institutions. The argument that democracy has to be embedded in or tailored to local traditions and culture is a challenge to the universalistic idea of democracy. Although countries such Japan, India, and Costa Rica have built solid democratic traditions, incorporating and glocalizing the norms with local traditions, for the rest of the world democracy is, at best, a work in progress. In Southeast Asia, some countries have engaged in a good deal of political engineering to make the transition to formal democracy. Because the discourse of democracy has a direct bearing on the contestation of political power, indigenization of political institutions has an ominous ring to it. Glocalization discourse has also dominated the human rights debate with a conservative slant. There are states that welcome the universal standard, and there are others that use the excuse of local traditions that are supposedly antithetical to the universal standard, giving rise to the question, One standard or many standards? Concerns regarding security issues, environmental security, and market freedom also limit political freedom and freedom of expression.

Glocalization of Governance

This introduces a certain degree of flexibility, which leads to flexible governance—that is, governance that is not superimposed from above but is citizen-centered and problem-based. For example, India has a ministry of skill development and entrepreneurship, which is a result of addressing the needs of the country. This is a glocal response to the demands of globalization. There was a time when globalizing pressure from above prompted most countries to create a ministry of environment or of women's affairs. However, how much these ministries have been able to address local issues remains an open question. Glocalization of governance entails fine-tuning and decentralization of administration in order to increase efficiency. The current emphasis on building national and local capacities so as to partake in global processes in a more creative way is an important move toward glocalization.

Glocalization of Culture

Singapore provides a good example of the globalization of and resistance to global culture. Singapore, one of the most globalized places according to the Foreign Policy Index, has been watchful in ensuring that certain aspects of popular culture and independent civil society organizations remain offshore; this was especially the case during its formative years. The authorities promoted what they called "civic society" to fill the space of an autonomous and vociferous civil society during a period of rapid economic and educational globalization. Singapore remains a paradigm of successful globalization and planned glocalization.

Singapore's leadership was pragmatic in retaining English as the lingua franca to more effectively integrate with the global economy, and it nurtured a legalistic, bureaucratic polity that earned global attention and admiration for creating a rule-based political system under a formal democracy. A certain amount of political engineering and innovation took place in the political system, which can be viewed as a conscious attempt at glocalization. The glocal outcome was an illiberal democracy, an open market economy, and an emerging open culture.

This perspective is predicated on not viewing globalization as a gargantuan force obliterating everything in its path but, rather, providing agency to the local conditions in absorbing and adapting global forces to local conditions. A somewhat parallel process was also observed in the past when modernizing elites in many developing societies made a conscious choice of selective borrowings amid heated debates between progressive modernists and conservative traditionalists. Upon closer examination, it was revealed that the so-called traditionalists were also to some extent constructed by the earlier modernist waves. A case in point is gender relations in public. In the Indian subcontinent, some of the so-called "traditional" or "conservative" values owe their origin to English laws instituted by the colonial rulers inspired by Victorian morality. So what appeared to be a traditional Indian value at first blush was, in fact, Victorian moral values dressed up in the cloth of traditionalism. India has been touched by the Valentine's Day fever, in which (heterosexual) lovers hold hands, go to parks, exchange gifts, and sometimes show their mutual affection in public. These "foreign" activities often infuriate conservative Hindus, whose presence in Indian politics is more visible today than two decades ago. These groups often intimidate, beat up, and chase away the lovers from public places in the name of preserving tradition. There are also instances of co-emergence of similar values across cultures. It is the same right-wing Hindu groups that, while remaining vigilant to preserve local traditions, also took an active interest in the politics of distant lands such as the United States, expressing their support for Mr. Donald Trump by organizing a special puja (a religious rite) in 2016.[2] The transcendence of local space to a larger global space is a feature of globalization as well as glocalization. Giddens (1999: 96) defines globalization essentially as "action at distance." In the global age, such action is a two-way process, with no fixed direction.

Glocalization of Popular Culture

Food, music, and movies are important components of popular culture and provide instances for understanding the processes of globalization and glocalization. Robertson put forth the example of CNN and Hollywood, which try to localize (sometimes badly) to the extent that they essentialize cultures. But there are also plenty of examples in which music thrives because of glocalization and globalization. In culinary culture, we see fusion food at one level but also how international food chains accommodate local culture, if often in a symbolic rather than substantial way. Food today is not only structured by both "globalizing" and "localizing" social, political–economic, and cultural forces but also very often figures as a symbol of these forces (Inglis 2010: 493).

McDonald's is a good example of both globalization and glocalization. For example, the Big Mac was invented in Pittsburgh, Pennsylvania, because steel mill workers were not satisfied with the size of McDonald's regular burgers. Similarly, the Filet-o-Fish was added to the menu after a franchisee in Cincinnati, Ohio, found that Catholic customers were not patronizing McDonald's on Fridays because they were avoiding meat products per religious custom (Crothers 2010: 131). The spread of McDonald's in Asia began with Japan, where the first outlet opened in 1971, and since then it has become a part of Japanese culture. The subtle impact of McDonald's on Hong Kong culture was explored by Watson (1997). In Singapore, McDonald's became a favorite reading corner of the studious Singaporean students. In Malaysia during the Ramadan, McDonald's employees wear religious garb because it is a popular place for young Malaysians to break their day-long fast by eating Big Macs and other fare. Fast-food culture has now become glocalized, impacting local food habits and transforming local culture.

Glocalization of Sports and Games

Football (in some places known as soccer) is "the global game" (Giulianotti and Robertson 2004: 546). And football is a glocal game, providing a conceptual bridge between global and local. "Universalization of particularism" entails cultural relativism, which "turns the global game into the 'glocal game'" (p. 547).

In Afghanistan under the Taliban, when a soccer match was in progress, the Taliban police showed up and beat the ball players (male) not so much for playing football but for playing the game wearing shorts in full view of the spectators. This was, surely, an extreme—and perhaps exceptional—case of glocalization. The Taliban interpreted wearing shorts as a violation of Islamic sartorial norms. In other words, a universal game can be adopted, but it has to be adapted in accordance with the local cultural norms as interpreted by the political authority. Similarly, in several Muslim-majority countries, whether girls can play football or participate in swimming events wearing swimming costumes remain sources of controversy. This raises the issue of political power at the heart of glocalization. In the real world, cultural transactions or interpenetrations do not take place outside of the politico-economic contexts. The upshot in this case is not to reject football or swimming, which is an option in some countries, but to accept the global spread of sports while accommodating them in each case to local norms. When the decisions are made by a narrow—but powerful—layer of clerics, there is one set of outcomes; when there is a larger space for public discussion, the outcomes are different.

Cricket, with its global spread through colonial connections, is now also seen outside of the Commonwealth sphere in countries such as the Netherlands, United Arab Emirates, and Afghanistan. The change of the format of the game to accommodate shorter time spans such as limited over games may be seen as an example of "temporal glocalization" to make cricket suit the changing times and locales in high-paced modern society. In becoming a global game rather than a projection of imperial culture, cricket became disembedded from its postcolonial moorings. As mentioned, cricket has been introduced in the Netherlands and the United Arab Emirates, in addition to China—in the latter two cases under state patronage. Cricket, a step in the development of cosmopolitan global culture, also provides a bridge between global and local: "At one level, cricket is about nationalism and ethnic pride, at another level, it is also a metaphor for globalization" (Khondker 2010: 155).

The highly corporatized Indian Premier League (IPL) attracts top cricket players from throughout the world to play for local clubs. The IPL is a spectacle of consumerism and showbiz—some of the cricket teams are owned by Bollywood celebrities. The spectacle has not only introduced a new game format but also added a sideshow of cheerleaders often imported from eastern European countries. The commentators, drawn from mostly English-speaking areas of the Commonwealth, are garbed in traditional Indian dress to add to the spectacle. The music played for the entertainment of the audience and players includes both popular Indian songs and international hits. India has become the mecca of glocalized cricket.

Glocalization of Music

In music, which is the lodestar of popular culture, glocalization has taken place in several formats. First, consider the historical transmigration of musical instruments such as the harmonium, an essential part of "classical" Indian music, or even Pakistani spiritual music, "Qawali," which is inconceivable without harmonium as an accompaniment. The Europeans introduced this portable reed instrument into the Indian subcontinent because carrying an organ of nineteenth-century vintage was a difficult proposition. Missionaries found it useful in spreading the gospel, a practical substitute for a huge sedentary church organ. The harmonium originated in the Nordic world and was probably inspired by a Chinese hand-held reed musical instrument, *sheng*, introduced to Europe by Marco Polo (Gaitonde 2016). Whereas the harmonium's entry to the subcontinental musical repertoire was imperceptible, the tabla, a small percussion instrument, was deliberately adopted in parts of western music to give it an oriental feel. The other classical instrument of Indian music, the sitar, may have roots in Iran.

The other form is contemporary fusion music—for example, the collaboration between Ravi Shankar and George Harrison of the Beatles. Commercial interests have fueled the contemporary blending or fusion because it helps expand the consumer market by appealing to multiple ethnic and national music markets. The spread of certain genres of music worldwide can be seen as an example of thin globalization or Westernization or, more generically, cultural diffusion. The spread of American pop music throughout the world is an example. However, there is also a spread of mixtures or local adaptation—globalization—of the pop genre that has produced Japanese pop (known as J-pop) and Korean pop (K-pop). Moreover, apart from being popular in Korea, K-pop is now making rounds in Europe and the Middle East, attracting large crowds. Even in Asia, K-pop along with Korean televised drama helped create a Pan-Asian popular culture—what one may consider as another illustration of translocalization. There is Arabic hiphop and Hindi or Chinese rap. Singapore, a country most open to a thin version of globalization, had its national and patriotic songs rendered in rap, presumably to court young Singaporeans.

Glocalization of Cinema

In cinema, glocalization has followed the globalization or spread of the technique of moving photography, which originated in France in 1895, moving to the United States—first to New Jersey and then to sunnier Hollywood—in the first decades of the twentieth century.

The first film was made in India in 1913, coincidentally the same year that the Nobel prize was awarded to the first Asian—a Bengali Indian, in fact, named Rabindranath Thakur, or Tagore in Anglicized form. Tagore, a universalist and a humanist, helped build bridges between the East and the West.

In addition to cinema, television shows and serials have been in circulation in the global cultural space. In recent years, Turkish television dramas, dubbed into Spanish and Brazilian Portuguese, have become very popular in South America (Tali 2016). These shows not only play a part in Turkish soft power but also earned $250 billion in 2015. South American viewers find more cultural affinity with the Turkish television shows than they do with American television shows. Turkish dramas are currently watched in 140 countries throughout the world, drawing a viewership of 400 million. In the 1990s, Brazilian television shows were also popular in Malaysia and Indonesia. This is more than just a trade in popular cultures. The very fact that South American viewers could identify more with the Turkish characters than they could with North American ones shows a tendency toward a new sense of identity and individual choices. The themes of migration and modernization are more immediate to the experiences of the audience in South America, as they are in Malaysia. The popularity of Turkish dramas in South America is another example of transglocalization.

Glocalization of Technology

The history of technology reveals that its spread has always been a marker of globalization. Human societies have always borrowed, adapted, and perfected each other's technologies to the extent that except for specialist historians, users do not care about the place of origin of their technologies. To demonstrate a universalizing tendency, an iPhone 6 is an iPhone 6 or a smartphone OS model is the same everywhere and has the same functionality. Yet, there are interesting variations in the usage of the technological device. For example, the use of an iPhone or even an ordinary phone to transfer money has become highly popular in Bangladesh and Kenya, where people feel less secure with other modes of money transfer. Phone transfer is faster and relatively more reliable than other modes. Very few in the advanced societies would even consider this option. The use of a smartphone in telemedicine or to provide health care where the doctor can be connected with a patient in a remote area via Skype and can provide services and transmit health information orally not only speeds up the process but also overcomes the barrier of illiteracy. It creates a new image-centered world from a logocentric world; in this new world, information is presented visually, not textually. As long as people understand oral communication, it works well. In this, we see the world moving to visuality and orality rather than legibility.

In another example of glocalization of technology, young tech-savvy Cameroonians are developing mobile technology-based applications locally at a place called "Silicon Mountain";[3] these applications are now used across many developing countries. This paves the way for transglocalization, in which countries of the Global South are leveraging each other's innovations. Satellite technology and a combination of internet-mediated distribution of news and documentaries have created a far better representation of the local in the global. Stringers and crowdsourcing empower the local in presenting itself to the global arena, as opposed to the global staging the local.

Glocalization of Higher Education

In the field of higher education, one may find interesting changes. Some writers have pointed out the need to embed education in the ethos of the host culture (Patel and Lynch 2013). Patel and Lynch, in an important paper, make a strong case for glocalization in higher education. As experts in higher education, they could see the failure of a modular preconceived package of higher education to be promoted internationally without consideration of the local cultures and constraints. They argued that glocalization was a better alternative to internationalization because glocalization allows retaining local traditions while adopting, incorporating, and embedding the best practices of the norms of international higher education to the local cultural context. For them, "Glocalization empowers and encourages all stakeholders to work harmoniously toward a sustainable future" (p. 223). These writers argued that glocalization not only promotes the linkages of small local communities to a network of communities—thus advancing globalization—but also helps remove ethnocentrism and cultural relativism.

A number of countries in Asia have successfully built world-class universities in a short period of time by reaching out to benchmark universities and thus adopting the strategies of the top universities in the world while also not completely overlooking the local traditions inherited from the colonial days in founding those universities. Some of the most successful universities are glocal universities. Other countries have tried to globalize too fast without realizing what it takes to build a world-class institution. A mere cut-and-paste approach is inherently limited in scope. The National University of Singapore was able to integrate several strands of influence to transform it from a teaching to research and now an entrepreneurial university.

In higher education in particular and education in general, Singapore, Korea, and now China have been successful with regard to blended education, and the university system has grown in tandem with the knowledge production system, especially scientific research. Initial emphasis was to promote research that would have direct relevance to national development. The problem-solving research received a great deal of attention and funding.

An awareness of glocalization points to limitations of both excessive universalism and its opposite, parochialism and ethnocentrism. The indigenization movement emerged as a by-product of nationalism and as a response to mindless universalism that had little time or respect for local traditions.

GLOCALIZATION AND GLOBALIZATION: IMPLICATIONS FOR GLOBAL STUDIES

The previous discussion has illustrated the point that globalization and glocalization are entangled in the empirical world, yet analytically the two concepts are separable. Glocalization, with its conceptual focus of intermingling, has great relevance for the transdisciplinary field of global studies. As scholars of global studies seek to understand the transnational social, cultural, and political processes, they also cannot ignore taking into consideration the local conditions, milieu, and traditions. As they are drawn to exploring how the local interpenetrates with the global, glocalization is poised to provide a useful conceptual framework. The focus of global studies is to understand the relationship among the state, society, and economy, as well as the ideational contexts. The institutional linkages and the emergent complexities (Curran 2008; Urry 2003) can be illustrated by the concept of glocalization. The thin theory of globalization views globalization as the spread of global modernity. Globalization remains indistinguishable from worldwide modernization, with plenty of empirical examples available, including the worldwide spread of mobile phones, the internet, satellite television, family planning, consumer products, and pop music. This thin theory of globalization—globalization *lite*—has found its way into popular imaginations via the works of journalists (Friedman 2005). A thick theory or sociological theory of globalization dates back to the 1980s in the writings of Roland Robertson, John Meyer (1980), and others.

For Beyer (2007), whereas modernization excluded various "others" that were deemed either premodern/traditional or only on the way to modernization, globalization includes us all, even our "others." Beyer's interesting distinction between globalization and modernization that he draws upon Robertson (1995: 27) has bearing on the concept of glocalization. "Modernization," according to Beyer, temporalized its universalism: Eventually, all would/could become modern. Globalization spatializes it: The local has to come to terms with the global. It (re)constitutes itself in the way that it does this. The reverse side of this mutual relation is that the global cannot be global except as plural versions of the local. Hence, globalization is always also glocalization (Robertson 1995)—the global expressed in the local and the local as the particularization of the global (Beyer 2007: 98).

In spatial terms, glocal is separable from global. Glocalization opens up creative possibilities of innovation and value addition from blending and synthesis. It also ushers hope for a multicultural, cosmopolitan world by promoting transglocal cooperation. In this regard, global studies stands to gain from the conceptual innovations of glocalization. The glocal view is of particular importance because it champions innovation and facilitates knowledge sharing and opportunities for learning from each other's experience, and it also incorporates a subaltern view of the world. The subaltern position may be a ballast against the top-down, new liberal globalization, in the future modifying it to a more pluralistic approach.

NOTES

1. *Glocalism: Journal of Culture, Politics and Innovation* (http://www.glocalismjournal.net), with some of the most prominent global intellectuals on its Direction Committee (editorial board), including Amartya Sen, Saskia Sassen, Roland Robertson, Manuel Castells, and Gayatri Spivak.
2. In that sense, the *puja* (Hindu worship) ceremony organized in Delhi by the right-wing, Hindu nationalist group for Donald Trump, in which his image was decorated with vermillion and placed alongside more established Hindu gods, is an example of globalization (Doshi 2016). The group admired the controversial Republican presidential

candidate in 2016 not so much for his piety but for his anti-Muslim stance. The Hindu chauvinists found a kindred soul in Trump in their common hatred of Muslims. This episode can also be seen as an instance of glocalization. Puja, a particularistic religious rite of the Hindu community, has undergone a certain level of glocalization because the ceremony is infused with contemporary themes and global technology.

3. "'Silicon Mountain': Africa's Next Tech Hub." http://www.france24.com/en/observers-direct/20160908-silicon-mountain-africas-next-tech-hub.

REFERENCES

Al-Rodhan, Nayef R. F., ed. 2012. *The Role of the Arab–Islamic World in the Rise of the West: Implications for Contemporary Trans-Cultural Relations.* New York: Palgrave Macmillan.

Appadurai, Arjun. 1996. *Modernity At Large: Cultural Dimesnion of Globalization.* Minneapolis: University of Minnesota Press.

Baum, Rainer C. 1974. "Beyond Convergence: Toward Theoretical Relevance in Quantitative Modernization Research." *Sociological Inquiry* 44 (4): 225–240.

Baum, Rainer C. 1977. "Beyond the 'Iron Cage.'" *Sociology of Religion* 38 (4): 309–330. https://doi.org/10.2307/3710116

Bauman, Zygmunt. 2014. "Glocalization and Hybridity." *Glocalism: Journal of Culture, Politics and Innovation* 14. http://www.glocalismjournal.net/issues/hybridity/articles/glocalization_and_hybridity.kl

Beyer, Peter. 2007. "Globalization and Glocalization." In *Sage Handbook of Sociology of Religion*, edited by James Beckford and N. J. Demerath III, 98–117. Thousand Oaks, CA: Sage.

Crothers, Lane. 2010. *Globalization and American Popular Culture.* Lanham, MD: Rowman & Littlefield.

Curran, Sara R. 2008. "The Global Complexity Framework." *Globalizations* 5 (2): 107–109.

Dirlik, Arif. 2011. "Globalization, Indigenism, Social Movement and the Politics of Place." *Localities* 1: 47–90.

Doshi, Vidhi 2016. "'He's Our Hero': Hindu Nationalists Rally for Donald Trump in India." *The Guardian,* May 3. ttps://www.theguardian.com/us-news/2016/may/13/donald-trump-india-hindu-supporters-new-delhi

Friedman, T. 2005. *The World is Flat.* New York: Farrar, Straus, and Giroux.

Gaitonde, Vishwas R. 2016. "The Birth, Death, and Reincarnation of the Harmonium." *The Mantle,* July 14. http://www.mantlethought.org/arts-and-culture.

Geertz, Clifford. 1971. *Islam Observed: Development in Morocco and Indonesia.* Chicago: University of Chicago Press.

Giddens, Anthony. 1999. *Runaway World: How Globalization is Reshaping Our Lives.* New York: Routledge.

Giulianotti, Richard, and Roland Robertson. 2004. "The Globalization of Football: A Study in the Glocalization of Serious Life." *British Journal of Sociology* 53 (4): 545–568.

Goody, Jack. 1996. *The East in the West.* Cambridge, UK: Cambridge University Press.

Goody, Jack. 2004. *Islam in Europe.* Cambridge, UK: Polity.

Hannerz, U. 1992. *Cultural Complexity.* New York: Columbia University Press.

Hobson, John M. 2004. *The Eastern Origins of Western Civilisation.* Cambridge, UK: Cambridge University Press.

IKEA. 2017. IKEA Catalogue.

Inglis, David. 2010. "Globalization and Food: The Dialectics of Globality and Locality." In *The Routledge International Handbook of Globalization Studies*, edited by Bryan Turner, 492–513. Abingdon, UK: Routledge.

Internet World Stat. 2016. https://www.internetworldstats.com/stats.htm.

Khondker, H. H. 2004. "Glocalization as Globalization: Evolution of a Sociological Concept." *Bangladesh e-Journal of Sociology* 1 (2): 1–9.

Khondker, H. H. 2010. "Globalization, Cricket and National Belonging." In *Cricket and Globalization*, edited by Chris Rumford and Stephen Wagg, 152–171. Newcastle Upon Tyne, UK: Cambridge Scholars Press.

La Porta, Rafael, and Andrei Shleifer. 2014. "Informality and Development." *Journal of Economic Perspectives* 28 (3): 109–126.

Lefebvre, H. 1991. *The Production of Space*. Oxford: Blackwell.

Linton, Ralph. 1937. "One Hundred Percent American." *The American Mercury* 40: 427–429.

MacCannell, D. 1989. *The Tourist: A New Theory of Lesiure Class*. 2nd ed. New York: Schocken.

Matusitz, J. 2016. "A Giant Retailer in Argentina: 'Glocalization' Perspectives." *Portuguese Journal of Social Science* 15 (1): 111–127.

Meyer, John. 1980. "The World Polity and the Authority of the Nation-State." In *Studies of the Modern World-System*, edited by A. Bergesen, 109–137. New York: Academic Press.

Morgan, M. H. 2008. *Lost History: The Enduring Legacy of Muslim Scientists, Thinkers, and Artists*. Basingstoke, UK: Palgrave Macmillan.

Nettl, J. P., and R. Robertson. 1968. *International Systems and Modernization of Societies*. London: Faber & Faber.

Neuwirth, Robert. 2011. *Stealth of Nations: The Global Rise of the Informal Economy*. New York: Pantheon.

Patel, Fay, and H. Lynch. 2013. "Glocalization as an Alternative to Internationalization in Higher Education: Embedding Positive Glocal Learning Perspectives." *International Journal of Teaching and Learning in Higher Education* 25 (2): 223–230.

Pieterse, Jan Nederveen. 1995. "Globalization as Hybridization." In *Global Modernities*, edited by Mike Featherstone, Scott Lash, and Roland Robertson, 45–68. London: Sage.

Radjou, Navi, J. Orabhu, and Simone Ahuja. 2012. *Jugaad Innovation: Think Frugal, Be Flexible, Generate Breakthrough Growth*. San Francisco: Jossey-Bass.

Robertson, Roalnd, and Burkart Holzner, eds. 1980. *Identity and Authority: Explorations in the Theory of Society*. Oxford: Basil Blackwell.

Robertson, Roland. 1992. *Globalization: Social Theory and Global Culture*. London: Sage.

Robertson, Roland. 1995. "Glocalization: Time–Space and Homogeneity–Heterogeneity." In *Global Modernity*, edited by Mike Featherstone, Scott Lash, and Roland Robertson, 25–44. London: Sage.

Robertson, Roland. 2003. "The Conceptual Promise of Glocalization: Commonality and Diversity." *Art-e-Fact*, 4. http://artefact.mi2.hr/_a04/lang_en/theory_robertson_en.htm

Robertson, Roland. 2013. "Coping with Binaries: Bays, Seas, and Oceans." *Glocalism: Journal of Culture, Politics and Innovation* 1: 1–5.

Robertson, Roland, and Kathleen White, eds. 2004. *Globalization: Critical Concepts in Sociology*. London: Routledge.

Rodrik, Dani. 2008. "Getting Governance Right." https://www.project-syndicate.org/commentary/getting-governance-right?barrier=true.

Roudometof, Victor. 2015. "Theorizing Glocalization: Three Interpretations." *European Journal of Social Theory* 19 (3): 391–408.

Swyngedouw, E. 1997. "Neither Global nor Local: 'Glocalization' and the Politics of Scale." In *Spaces of Globalization*, edited by Kevin Cox, pp. 137–166. New York: Guilford.

Swyngedouw, E. 2004. "Globalisation or Clocalisation? Networks, Territories and Rescaling." *Cambridge Review of International Affairs* 17 (10): 25–48.

Tali, Didem. 2016. "An Unlikely Story: Why Do South Americans Love Turkish TV?" BBC, September 8. http://www.bbc.com/news/business-37284938?ocid=socialflow.

Tomlinson, John. 1999. *Globalization and Culture*. Cambridge: Polity.

Turner, Bryan, and H. Khondker. 2010. *Globalization: East and West*. London: Sage.

Urry, J. 2003. *Global Complexity*. Cambridge, UK: Polity.

Watson, James. 1997. *Golden Arches East: McDonald's in East Asia*. Stanford, CA: Stanford University Press.

Zhao, Jungyuan, P. Pablos, and R. Tennyson. 2015. *Organizational Innovation and IT Governance in Emerging Economies*. Hersey, PA: Business Science.

CHAPTER 7

....

GLOBAL HISTORY

....

DOMINIC SACHSENMAIER

THE term "global history" has risen to prominence quickly, and it has done so in different languages and academic systems. Except for a very few authors, hardly anyone used this expression before the 1990s.[1] Today, thousands of publication titles refer to "global history," and new journals have been established in this field—in a variety of languages.[2] Moreover, a prize for global historical scholarship has been established, and several online global history blogs report to a growing international research community.[3] It is quite telling about the growing influence of this field that a good number of monographs and edited volumes have been published that discuss either global historical scholarship at large or single facets thereof (Beckert and Sachsenmaier 2018; Conrad 2016; Olstein 2015; Irirye 2013; Crossley 2008; Mazlish and Iriye 2004).

All this happened despite the fact that historians were rather late to join the global wave in the social sciences and the humanities. During the 1990s, other disciplines in the social sciences and the humanities had been much faster to produce much global scholarly perspectives. During that period, internationally, the most influential works on globalization typically were written by sociologists, anthropologists, or political scientists, and historians initially played only a very minor role in the literature seeking for new, timely ways of thinking globally. At that time, very few joined the debates on globalization flaring up particularly during the first decade after the Cold War.

Various factors made it more difficult for historiography to grow its own branches of global scholarship. First, for a long time, historiography had been particularly closely connected with the institution of the nation state. Many historians had been trained, and subsequently employed, as historians of single nation states. In most countries, history education prioritized national history over transnational historical approaches. Certainly, one or two generations ago, not all historians were mono-national in outlook. Yet for a long time, also the vast majority of historians who have studied more than one nation have typically been experts of single world regions such as Western Europe, Latin America, or East Asia. Second, historiographical methods have long been centered on primary source analysis and archival work. Because historians usually do not work in teams, it seemed hardly possible to cover larger areas of the world through genuine historical research.

For these and other reasons, many influential historians long opined that their colleagues would only be able to think globally when they were writing textbooks or trade books. In countries such as the United States, this indeed had long been the position of world history. During the Cold War era, that field was chiefly taught at small colleges, and with a few exceptions, it was not well represented at research universities. For a long time, world history had a reputation of primarily being a teaching field chiefly drawing upon the already existing secondary literature, without producing much genuine primary source-based research of its own. In the United States and quite a few other countries, world history thus had a rather marginal place within the community of historians.

The differences between the position of world history before the 1990s and global history are striking. Global history is chiefly based at larger, internationally connected universities, and it is widely considered to be a research field. In fact, quite a few internationally leading universities in different world regions have opened research centers in global history. Moreover, there is a growing number of graduate programs in this field, and in many countries, global history tends to be viewed as an innovative center in historical scholarship.

Can this discrepancy between the earlier role of world history and the more recent standing of global historical research be explained by a categorical distinction between these two fields? Particularly during the late 1990s and early 2000s, there have been rather heated debates regarding the relationship between global history and world history. Some historians, such as Bruce Mazlish (1998), maintained that there was a deep divide between the two—that the parameters of both fields were hardly compatible with each other. Others, including Jerry Bentley (1996), took a dissenting view and maintained that world history was undergoing important changes—changes that in large part were compatible with the agenda of global historians. Both sides of that debate agreed that the Eurocentric nineteenth-century Hegelian roots of world history were obsolete and that scholarship needed to develop fresh perspectives as well as new narratives.

In recent years, the debates over the difference between world history and global history have grown calmer. In fact, many individual authors now use both terms, which means there is also no categorical distinction between "world history" and "global history"; also, there are significant overlaps with additional terms such as "transnational history" and "entangled histories." Together, the growing presence of all these expressions in the landscapes of academic historiography shows that the standing of border-crossing thinking and macroscopic historical perspectives has grown significantly stronger. There is now a sizable research community that self-identifies with expressions such as "global history." This research community is no longer chiefly formed by Europeanists going global; rather, global history has become a meeting ground for scholars with different realms of regional expertise. In other words, historians who have been chiefly trained in the history of East Asia, South Asia, Latin America, Western Europe, or other world regions now engage themselves within the framework of global history. Indeed, global history congresses, conferences, and research projects have become important meeting grounds for scholars with different regional emphases. Global history has thus not challenged the importance of regional expertise; it has only placed it into new conceptual and interactive frameworks. Also, on a more general level, it has fostered the growth of interdisciplinary collaboration, including with newly emerging research fields such as global studies. During the Cold War period, world history was able to play roles of that kind only on a far more modest scale.

Contours and Scopes

The field's spectacular rise begs the question of what actually is global history. The definition of this new field is not as apparent as it may seem at first sight: after all, only a tiny fraction of global historical literature is really "global" in the sense of trying to cover the entire world. For instance, if one examines the growing body of journal articles that are labeled as contributions to "global history," one quickly discovers that the vast majority of these operate on much smaller scales. Some of the most influential contributions to the field focus on only two or three world regions—not on the world at large. For instance, in his work *The Great Divergence*, economic historian Kenneth Pomeranz (2001) offers global historical interpretations but bases them on a case study of Europe and China. He particularly focuses on the economic centers of both world regions as well as their relationship with surrounding peripheries and other areas of the world. In that manner, this work not only helps render our understandings of "Europe" and "China" much more complex but also challenges long-dominant master narratives about the exalted role of European history within worldwide contexts. As late as the eighteenth century, Pomeranz argues, European core regions had been by no means more "advanced" than their Chinese counterparts.[4]

Similar to Pomeranz's work, the majority of contributions to global history do not necessarily operate within global frameworks. A wealth of articles, books, and doctoral dissertation projects in global history programs usually do not take the entire world into account but, rather, investigate only a small selection of regions. Quite a few scholars have analyzed single cities from global historical perspectives, and the same has been the case with specific locations such as canals (Huber 2011; Wasserstrom 2009). Other authors have applied the principles of global historical thinking to the history of single countries, regions, or seas (Bender 2002; Bose 2009; Conrad 2010; Duara 2009; Sartori 2008; Tyrell 2007).

Certainly, there are some global historical works that indeed seek to cover the entire globe. This is the case, for instance, with two widely acclaimed depictions of the global nineteenth century: Christopher Alan Bayley's (2004) *The Birth of the Modern World: Global Connections and Comparisons, 1780–1914* and Jürgen Osterhammel's (2014) *The Transformation of the World. A Global History of the Nineteenth Century.* Both monographs offer accounts of the long nineteenth century that decidedly break with the tradition of international perspectives. In other words, both authors do not present the globality of that time period as an addendum of national histories. Although themes such as international diplomacy and nation formation are not ignored by them, they concentrate on wider transformations, connections, and power systems. These can range from the standardization of time to the advent of global consumer patterns and from the spread of ethnic identities to entangled patterns of urbanization.

Although they inevitably mainly rely on secondary literature, works of such a larger scope have grown into landmarks within the landscapes of global historical scholarship. Nevertheless, the latter landscapes are widely characterized by more detailed research projects that are primary-source based. In this specific regard, the contours of global history have grown similar to the patterns of national history. Also here, there are some larger works narrating the history of entire nations. Underneath this level, however, lies a wealth of historical scholarship that contributes to national history but actually operates within much smaller spatial frameworks—for instance, by dealing with single cities or regions that belong to a nation's history but are not tantamount with it.

In that sense, it is certainly safe to say that global historical scholarship has gained acceptance within the historians' guild halls as it has become more like the rest of historiography. There is no radical distinction between the research cultures and methodologies used by global historians and their colleagues active in other fields of historiography. Both appreciate archival work but also respect larger works that are pulling ahead the field by taking the already existing secondary literature as their point of departure. Moreover, despite some corresponding expectations during the 1990s, global history has not become a field mainly characterized by teamwork. Like in the rest of historiography, collective research plays only a marginal role in global historical scholarship: Its protagonists remain scholars who are usually working on single-authored monographs and papers. Certainly, group authorship could greatly expand the range of languages and archives considered in a specific project, but individual authorship cannot be widely replaced in a field such as historiography in which individual narrative choices and an author's choice of concepts greatly matter.

If global history is not radically different from other branches of historiography and if it is not exclusively characterized by genuinely global projects, what else could be the gist of that field? The answer is somehow complex: Global historical scholarship does not necessarily concentrate on the study of one and the same global space; at the same time, however, it is very much spatially defined. Actually, much of global history can be described as a research field experimenting with alternative conceptions of space. Global historians have been among the most vociferous critiques of the idea that single nations constitute quasi-natural containers of the past. For instance, particularly since the 1990s, they have contributed to our understanding of the wealth of cultural transfers across national borders (for more examples, see Sachsenmaier 2014). They have emphasized that the history of global institutions ranging from multinational corporations to intergovernmental organizations cannot be written only from the viewpoints of national history (Mazlish and Chandler 2005; Sluga 2013). In addition, they have argued that also the history of migration is greatly enriched if we leave the parameters of national historiography behind. The latter have studied diasporic communities chiefly as emigrants from—or immigrants to—certain countries, but more recent scholarship is interested in the lasting transnational ties between new and old home countries. In other words, fields such as global history study migrants as networks of people spanning across national borders.[5]

Yet nation-centered thinking is not the only set of spatial concepts from which global historians typically distance themselves. As a field, global history is actually a site of decided critiques of Eurocentric traditions and Western-centric perspectives. Needless to say, the critique of Eurocentrism is by no means unique to global historical thinking; rather, the latter is part of a wider trend that can be observed across much of the humanities and social sciences. In fact, single global historians have been inspired by a variety of other intellectual currents heading in similar directions, including postcolonial historiography (on postcolonial history-writing, see Majumdar 2010).

Global historical efforts to overcome Eurocentric traditions can play out in a variety of ways. First, significant parts of global historical scholarship seek to challenge older world historical narratives centered on the idea of Western exceptionalism. For example, in the aforementioned field of migration history, some studies have shown that nineteenth-century trans-Atlantic migration to North America had sister movements in Asia similar in terms of scale and regional impact (McKeown 2004). Other historians have argued that the European Reformation had striking parallels in different areas of the world, including several South Asian kingdoms, Japan, and China, where, the argument goes, existing state orthodoxies had run into a similar crisis as the Catholic Church in Latin Christendom (McNeill and McNeill 2003).

Second, many historical projects have become more attentive to the history of those people who long tended to be portrayed as rather inactive recipients of European power. This has been the case in colonial history, which as a general trend has come to regard colonial rule as a complex pattern shaped not only by the colonizers but also by many groups on the side of the colonized. Similarly, labor historians have come to write the history of workers under suppressive conditions no longer chiefly as a history of passive victimhood. Heading in different directions, scholars have become interested in topics such as the forms of self-empowerment and self-organization found among workers even within the most oppressive systems (on global labor history, see Lucassen 2006; van der Linden 2008). Going beyond that, fields such as global labor history have witnessed a growing awareness that it is problematic to project European categories and concepts onto other world regions. For example, quite a few labor historians have problematized the idea that certain forms of coerced labor in the history of areas of sub-Saharan African as well as other world regions can be subsumed under a universal concept of "slavery." Applying the latter to all kinds of historical contexts would mean imposing the connotations of a rather specific legal position onto the dissimilar socioeconomic realities of other societies, often boiling down to a great distortion of the overall historical picture (van der Linden and Rodríguez García 2016). The rising levels of caution about terms and concepts used by historians can be seen as a third front on which Eurocentric paradigms are being challenged.

Fourth, quite a few segments of global historical scholarship now run counter to the idea that in the modern age, Western forces were the main shapers of global integration. For instance, some studies have shown that global standardization processes cannot be simply understood as the results of "Westernization." No matter whether it is the globalization of modern prison systems or of the segmentation of time into world time zones, in each case scholars emphasize that innovations of this kind did not simply originate in Europe or the United States and subsequently spread to different areas of the world (Mühlhahn 2009; Ogle 2015). The patterns of diffusions were usually far more complex and multidirectional— which, however, is not to suggest that hegemony and power did not matter in these facets of globalization. A similar message is being conveyed by studies arguing that the notion of universally enforceable human rights originated not only in Europe but also in locations such as Haiti, where they were being employed by rebels against slavery and French colonial rule (Dubois 2004).

Hence, to a certain extent, it is possible to define global history as a countermovement to Eurocentric and nation-centered historiographical traditions. But it is more than that: Global history has grown into an enabling framework for many historians trying out new conceptions of space. Much of global historical scholarship breaks with the ways in which academic historiography has long institutionally separated regional expertise. In global history, experts of Japan study not just Japan, and experts of Eastern Europe focus not just on Eastern Europe. Quite to the contrary, many scholars relate their own expertise with the study of other areas of the world. Moreover, a growing number of scholars have been trained in the history of two or more world regions and are able to read primary sources in a broader variety of languages.

INTERESTS AND FIELDS

As the previously discussed examples indicate, global history did not have a clear epicenter in the landscapes of historical scholarship. It did not originate from a field such as economic history and subsequently spread to other areas of research; at the same time, it had strong links with fields such as global studies. By contrast, interest in transnational and global historical approaches has been on the rise simultaneously in different branches of historiography. Labor history and economic history have witnessed this trend just as cultural and social history have witnessed it. In that sense, there is no clear methodology that could be identified as typical for the practice of global historical scholarship. Actually, in terms of their basic methodological toolboxes, global economic historians are not profoundly different from other economic historians. The same can also be said about other fields. Rather than a set of methodologies, global history is primarily a string of perspectives, and it is characterized by certain types of questions asked about the past.

In general, the study of transfers and connections is now most commonly being associated with the field of global history. For instance, global historians follow the movements of ideologies, fashions, individuals, and masses across different areas of the world (Osterhammel 2006; Service 2010). This is also the case with the global spread of high culture such as classical music; popular culture; and sports, both as a form of state-endorsed exercise and as a form of entertainment (Goldblatt 2016; Kaufmann, Dossin, and Joyeux-Prunel 2015). In addition, many scholars are interested in the spread of diseases just as they want to know more about the internationalization of military technologies and cultures (Engel 2006; Manela 2015). Also, they want to understand better how global movements as well as transnational institutions such as nongovernmental organizations seek to counter the threat of germs and armed conflict (Chaliand 2014; Iriye 2002).

Yet global historical research is not only about connections: it also entails comparisons. The more recent scholarship in the field of historical comparisons differs significantly from the wave of comparative perspectives commonly applied during the 1960s and 1970s (Tilly 1984). The latter had been largely embedded in social scientific traditions, with universal categories as well as quantitative methods playing important roles. By contrast, today's historical comparisons tend to strongly consider historical connections (Steinmetz 2014). In most cases, scholars no longer undertake comparisons in order to deduce an abstract *tertium comparationis*; rather, they do so to better understand a world characterized by interconnections. For instance, this has been the case with scholarship that identifies similarities in pre-nineteenth-century state formation processes in areas of Asia and Europe that may have been partly related to shared factors such as the intensification of long-distance trade (Lieberman 2003, 2009). Other publications apply comparative perspectives to better understand topics such as the persecution of minorities or mass dictatorship as phenomena that can be seen in all areas of the world but that at the same time remain locally specific in terms of their concrete dynamics (Lim, Walker, and Lambert 2013).

This fascination with connections and comparative viewpoints has gone in many different directions. To emphasize again: Global historical research can now be found in most branches of historiography, ranging from global economic history to global intellectual history. For a variety of reasons, intellectual historians were rather late to develop global and transnational platforms for their own field. Yet global intellectual history is growing, and potential research topics in that field are almost countless. This becomes particularly obvious when one recalls that the research questions pursued by scholars in that field have grown much wider than had been the case with the older history of ideas. Rather than focusing on the history of great thinkers in the past, intellectual historians have developed an interest in the wider social, economic, and political changes underlying the transformations of ideas. In order to get a better sense of a society's prevalent discourses and opinion climates, scholars in the field now draw on a much wider spectrum of primary source materials, ranging from pamphlets to newspapers and from official proclamation to administrative documents (Grafton 2006; Megill 2004).

The research agendas of global intellectual history are highly diverse, and they point in fascinating directions (Moyn and Sartori 2013; Sachsenmaier and Sartori 2018). For instance, the spread of the modern intellectual as a social prototype is just beginning to be researched as a global phenomenon (for China, see Cheek 2016). In other words, we do not yet sufficiently understand through what transfers and transformations intellectuals in societies ranging from Chile to Japan emerged over the nineteenth and twentieth centuries—while at the same time they were also rooted in local scholarly traditions. Moreover, the transnational dynamics of Eurocentric thinking still need to be widely researched, as does the global history of anti-Western ideas (Aydin 2007; Mignolo 2000). Similarly, the history of globally circulating concepts ranging from "society" to "modernity" needs to be studied in more detail, particularly with a focus on the history of entanglements across and between languages throughout the world (Liu 1999; Pernau and Sachsenmaier 2016).

Global perspectives have also entered the history of historiography—several monographs offer worldwide accounts of older traditions of historical thinking and of modern academic historiography (Fuchs and Stuchtey 2002; Iggers, Wang, and Mukherjee 2008; Woolf 2011). There are also accounts of world historical thinking and practice that cover different areas of the world (Manning 2003; Sachsenmaier 2016). The global and transnational questions that historians have been asking about their own modern academic field can be roughly grouped into two categories. First, the history of historiography has dealt with the history of discourses, concepts, narratives, as well as the spread of new historiographical schools. For instance, much is known about the origins of fields such as the history of women or the spread of movements such as social history. There is also quite a good understanding of how they spread between institutions and academic systems. A second major area of inquiry has been the development of institutions. Among other research areas, a substantial amount of literature has been investigating a variety of processes leading to the nationalization of the past. In the future, the global and transnational history of historiography will perhaps pay more attention to social and cultural historical perspectives. For example, although we understand quite well the spread of single schools ranging from world systems theory to women's history, we know very little about the networks that link scholars across single universities, countries, and world regions.

In addition to activities in established fields such as intellectual history or economic history, there are other forms of global historical scholarship that do not fit neatly into larger branches of historiography. One case in point is the study of global commodities (Beckert 2014; Dalby 2001; Riello 2013). Taking single commodities ranging from spices to cotton as their starting point, a number of works show how societies, polities, and economies throughout the world were connected with one another through cycles of production, trade, and consumption. For instance, the history of slavery and forced migration was as much a part of the history of cotton as was the emergence of economic systems such as state-sponsored forms of capitalism. Moreover, it becomes clear that cotton was part of the history of global inequalities, power systems, and colonial rule, on the one hand, and the history of mass consumerism as well as other forms of globalization, on the other hand.

Many other areas of historical research that have become more influential over the past generation have been very receptive to global and transnational viewpoints as well. This is the case, for example, with women's history, in which, among other themes, scholars are seeking to explore the spread of certain gender roles across different societies and cultures throughout the world (Gabaccia and Donato 2015; Smith 2004–2005; Weinbaum 2008). Moreover, quite a few scholars have started investigating the presence of women in migration history or the history of transnationally entangled women's movements. This leads to research questions regarding, for example, the exchange dynamics between global movements and grassroots organizations in a wide variety of local settings ranging from Southeast Asia to California.

The list of field-specific global historical research communities could be extended much further. Highly active have been research areas such as global environmental history, global legal history, and global histories of science and technology. All these fields tend to have their own research networks, and each is facing quite specific methodological challenges. For instance, environmental historians often need to work transnationally with data that have been aggregated by nation states and hence are not always comparable or compatible with each other (McNeill 2012; Reilly, Kaufman, and Bodino 2003). By contrast, historians of transnational racist ideologies face a Babylonian world of languages that of course places a heavy constraint on an individual scholar's research possibilities. Hence, it is small wonder that most branches of global historical scholarship have been characterized by their own debates about what global history means to their own field.

Nevertheless, global historians are entangled with each other across the boundaries of specific research fields. There are many organizations, programs, and journals for all kinds of global historical scholarship.[6] Furthermore, there are shared debates about the challenges and problems that global history currently has to face at large.

Challenges and Opportunities

There are various conceptual and institutional problems that global history has to face. As a general trend, global history has been charged with a mobility bias; in other words, its critics have argued that global historians prioritize the history of mobile people, the flows of goods, and the transfer of ideas over other aspects of the human past (Lucassen and Lucassen 2009; Rockefeller 2011). Certainly, as a wider tendency, global historical research has indeed thus far concentrated far more on groups such as migrants, sojourners, travelers, and elite administrators. By implication, the history of social groups such as the peasantry or the urban poor without migration backgrounds has played only a rather peripheral role in the field. Likewise, until recently, global historians tended to primarily study border-crossing networks among intellectuals, artists, and other professionals. Similarly, the history of transnational organizations has received far more attention than that the global entanglements of local ones.

According to some critical observers of global historical thinking, and debates on globalization in general, such research emphases run the risk of constructing a chimera of "boundless connectivity" (Cooper 2001). Certainly, up until the present day, most global historians indeed focused more on the mobile–the interactive aspects of the human past. They have done so since their field in some ways positioned itself as a revisionist movement against national container thinking and a local bias in historical scholarship. In other words, the rise of global and transnational scholarship was supposed to bring to light those aspects of the human past that fell through the cracks of nation-centered or region-centered historiographical traditions. In large part, these aspects indeed have been the flows, connections, and interactions among people, goods, institutions, and ideas across all kinds of boundaries—political, cultural, and geographical.

Yet in the long term, a division of labor between global historians studying flows and transfers and local or national historians focusing on other aspects of the past will hardly be convincing. As the theorists of "glocalization" reminded us a long time ago, there was no detached global dimension in the human past (Robertson 1995); rather, the global constellations and entanglements emerged from a pluriverse of local factors. By implication, this means that especially in more recent centuries, the local in history was not purely local but transnationally connected. In that sense, global historians will continue drawing on local archives and hence also contribute to the study of the local. Going beyond that, it is also quite likely that the field will widen its portfolio and pay more attention to themes that have long played a relatively minor role in global historical scholarship. This is the case, for example, with peasant structures and cultures in many societies that in their own ways were also globally connected. For instance, peasants in many different world regions felt the impact of globally disseminating technologies as well as crops. In this context, one may think, for example, of the spread of New World crops such as the potato, sweet corn, or the tomato, which ended up being widely used from China to Italy. In these societies, the crops had a major influence not only on local cuisines but also on demographic developments as well as several important aspects of local rural life.

Another major challenge, which at the same time is also an opportunity, lies in the current international landscapes of global historical scholarship. After all, border-crossing research has been on the rise in many history departments throughout the world, and the term "global history" is now being used in translation in a wide variety of languages, ranging from Spanish to Mandarin (on the global spread of global historical thinking, see Beckert and Sachsenmaier 2018; Manning 2008). Although global history—like other sectors of the social sciences and humanities—is characterized by transnational collaborations, the concrete interventions of global historical thinking vary among academic systems.

For instance, in China, global history needs to be largely understood as an effort to undo long-established divisions in history departments and to unthink some visions of history emanating from them. For reasons associated with twentieth-century nation-building efforts, the study of Chinese history and world history is institutionally divided rather strictly at most Chinese universities. Moreover, world history—a rather sizable field in China—has for a long time largely focused on the history of industrialized countries, particularly those in North America and Western Europe, in addition to Japan and Russia; other world regions have been quite neglected on the mental maps of Chinese world historians. The growing number of global history institutes in China are thus first dedicated to studying a broader variety of world regions. Second, and most important, they aim to bridge the gap between China experts and other historians in China. In terms of a research agenda, these efforts are connected with the idea of rethinking facets of Chinese history from global and transnational perspectives. They are also linked with efforts to narrate aspects of the global past from Chinese perspectives (on world history in China, see Xu 2007; on global historical research in China, see Wang 2010; Sachsenmaier 2011: Chap. 4).

The trajectories of global historical scholarship in China and in many other areas of the world are not sufficiently recognized among global historians in the West. By contrast, Western scholarship has quite a presence within the communities of global historians of China. All this is indicative of lasting international hierarchies in the field. Such hierarchies are reflected in the geographical distribution of who can afford to ignore whom when theorizing about global constellations. For instance, until recently, a historian in Britain or the United States could become a leading theorist without even acknowledging the existence of works produced in other areas of the world, particularly outside of the West. But a Chinese or Korean scholar, for instance, could not possibly deliver an alleged "global" overview of world history or any other field while only citing Chinese or Korean literature.

Certainly, such influence gaps are conditioned by external factors such as financial resources in the widest sense. Indeed, in many areas of Africa, Central Asia, and the Middle East, there are no well-endowed universities, and there are few functional archives or even libraries that could be considered "up-to date," whatever that may mean in our professional world. Yet Japanese historiography institutionally rests upon excellent (comparatively speaking) working conditions. However, although Japan produces quite remarkable global historical scholarship in terms of both quality and quantity, its presence in international debates is rather limited. This is even the case when Japanese secondary literature becomes available in English translations. Similar things can be said about the literature being produced in a whole range of other academic systems.

If the world in global historical scholarship is becoming a rather interactive place with no clear centers, how does it fit with an academic landscape that in many regards remains centered on the "West"? After all, global thought has become greatly decentered, and the academic consensus on critiquing Eurocentrism has become hardly more than flogging the proverbial dead horse. Although all this marks a great change in disciplinary cultures, the ingrained global hierarchies of professional academic landscapes have not changed. In fact, they largely appear to be centered in the same manner as they were approximately 100 years ago: Historians based in the West are typically much more globally influential than their colleagues based in other areas of the world.

Particularly those historians who are tackling transregional and global research questions should talk more openly about these apparent contradictions between the acclaimed values of global historians as researchers and their lived professional realities. This is not to suggest that increased academic interaction can serve as a panacea. But as an academic field, global history needs to face the question of whether it will ultimately be really convincing to its critics, to other academic fields, and to the general public if there is such a discrepancy between its thinking about history and its lived realities. Can the current critiques of Eurocentric perspectives really be further developed into new, sustainable research landscapes if the humanities' global professional landscapes more closely resemble—in terms of their hierarchies—nineteenth-century facets of world order than twenty-first century world order?

These kinds of problems are not the challenges a field has to face in its initial stages. They are the questions surrounding a rather successful academic field—an area of research that has grown highly visible in different world regions. As such, global history can continue making important interventions—not only in the growing field of global studies and other transdisciplinary academic endeavors but also in a the "real world" of increasing political polarization and rising mobilized prejudice.

Notes

1. Early examples of publications using the expression "global history" are Leften Stavros Stavrianos et al., *A Global History of Man* (Boston: Allyn & Bacon, 1962), and Hans Kohn, *The Age of Nationalism: The First Era of Global History* (New York: Harper, 1962). After the 1960s, "global history" fell out of use for approximately two decades. See Dominic Sachsenmaier, *Global Perspectives on Global History. Theories and Approaches in a Connected World* (Cambridge, UK: Cambridge University Press, 2011), Chapter 2.
2. Examples of journals are the *Journal of Global History*, published by Cambridge University Press since 2006; the journal *Comparativ—Zeitschrift für Globalgeschichte und vergleichende Gesellschaftsforschung*, published by Leipzig University Press since 1991; and the *Global History Review* (*Quanqiushi pinglun*), published by Capital Normal University in Beijing since 2004.
3. For a global history blog (which also contains information about graduate programs) and the Toynbee Prize in global history, see http://toynbeeprize.org.
4. Pomeranz's work triggered quite intense debates, and many further contributions to that field have been published. See, for example, Kenneth Pomeranz, "Ten Years After: Responses and Reconsiderations," *Historically Speaking* 12, no. 4 (September/October 2011):20–25; and Peer Vries,, *State, Economy and the Great Divergence: Great Britain and China, 1680s–1850s* (London: Bloomsbury, 2015).
5. An example from the 1990s is Gungwu Wang, ed., *Global History and Migrations* (London: Westview, 1996). This research trend was also shared by other academic fields. A more recent example is Dirk Hoerder and Donna Gabaccia, eds., *Connecting Seas and Connected Ocean Rims: Indian, Atlantic, and Pacific Oceans and China Seas Migrations from the 1830s to the 1930s* (Leiden, the Netherlands: Brill, 2011).
6. For organizations, see the Network of Global and World History Organizations website at http://research.uni-leipzig.de/~gwhisto/home.

References

Aydin, Cemil. 2007. *The Politics of Anti-Westernism in Asia: Visions of World Order in Pan-Islamic and Pan-Asian Thought*. New York: Columbia University Press.

Bayley, Christopher A. 2004. *The Birth of the Modern World: Global Connections and Comparisons, 1780–1914*. Oxford, UK: Blackwell.

Beckert, Sven. 2014. *Empire of Cotton: A Global History*. New York: Knopf.

Beckert, Sven, and Dominic Sachsenmaier. eds. 2018. *Global History, Globally*. London: Bloomsbury.

Bender, Thomas. 2002. *Rethinking American History in a Global Age*. Berkeley: University of California Press.

Bentley, Jerry H. 1996. *Shapes of World History in Twentieth-Century Scholarship: Vol. 14. Essays on Global and Comparative History*. Washington, DC: American Historical Association.

Bose, Sugata. 2009. *A Hundred Horizons: The Indian Ocean in the Age of Global Empire*. Cambridge, MA: Harvard University Press.

Chaliand, Gérard. 2014. *A Global History of War: From Assyria to the Twenty-First Century*. Philadelphia: University of Pennsylvania Press.

Cheek, Timothy. 2016. *The Intellectual in Modern Chinese History*. Cambridge, UK: Cambridge University Press.

Conrad, Sebastian. 2010. *Globalisation and the Nation in Imperial Germany*. Cambridge, UK: Cambridge University Press.

Conrad, Sebastian. 2016. *What Is Global History?* Princeton, NJ: Princeton University Press.

Cooper, Frederick. 2001. "What Is the Concept of Globalization Good For?" *African Affairs* 100 (339): 189–213.

Crossley, Pamela. 2008. *What Is Global History?* Cambridge, UK: Polity.

Dalby, Andrew. 2001. *Dangerous Tastes: The Story of Spices*. Berkeley: University of California Press.

Duara, Prasenjit. 2009. *The Global and Regional in China's Nation-Formation*. New York: Routledge.

Dubois, Laurent M. 2004. *Avengers of the New World: The Story of the Haitian Revolution*. Cambridge, MA: Belknap.

Engel, Jonathan. 2006. *The Epidemic: A Global History of AIDS*. New York: HarperCollins.

Fuchs, Eckhardt, and Benedikt Stuchtey, eds. 2002. *Across Cultural Borders: Historiography in Global Perspective*. Lanham, MD: Rowman & Littlefield.

Gabaccia, Donna, & Katharine M. Donato. 2015. *Gender and International Migration: From the Slavery Era to the Global Age*. New York: Russell Sage.

Goldblatt, David. 2016. *The Games: A Global History of the Olympics*. New York: Norton.

Grafton, Anthony. 2006. "The History of Ideas: Precepts and Practice, 1950–2000 and Beyond." *Journal of the History of Ideas* 67 (1): 1–32.

Huber, Valeska. 2011. *Channelling Mobilities: Migration and Globalisation in the Suez Canal Region and Beyond*. Cambridge, UK: Cambridge University Press.

Iggers, Georg, Q. Edward Wang, and Supriya Mukherjee. 2008. *A Global History of Modern Historiography*. Harlow, UK: Pearson.

Iriye, Akira. 2002. *Global Community: The Role of International Organizations in the Making of the Contemporary World*. Berkeley: University of California Press.

Iriye, Akira. 2013. *Global and Transnational History: The Past, Present, and Future*. New York: Palgrave.

Kaufmann, Thomas DaCosta, Catherine Dossin, and Béatrice Joyeux-Prunel, eds. 2015. *Circulations in the Global History of Art*. New York: Routledge.

Lieberman, Victor. 2003. *Strange Parallels: Vol. 1. Southeast Asia in Global Context, c. 800–1830*. Cambridge, UK: Cambridge University Press.

Lieberman, Victor. 2009. *Strange Parallels: Vol. 2. Mainland Mirrors. Europe, Japan, China, South Asia, and the Islands: Southeast Asia in Global Context, c. 800–1830*. Cambridge, UK: Cambridge University Press.

Lim, Jie-Hyun, Barbara Walker, and Peter Lambert, eds. 2013. *Mass Dictatorship and Memory as Ever Present Past*. New York: Palgrave.

Liu, Lydia H. 1999. *Tokens of Exchange: The Problem of Translation in Global Circulations*. Durham, NC: Duke University Press.

Lucassen, Jan, ed. 2006. *Global Labor History: A State of the Art*. New York: Peter Lang.

Lucassen, Jan, and Leo Lucassen. 2009. "The Mobility Transition Revisited: What the Case of Europe Can Offer to Global History." *Journal of Global History* 4 (3): 347–377.

Majumdar, Rochona. 2010. *Writing Postcolonial History*. London: Bloomsbury.

Manela, Erez. 2015. "The Politics of Smallpox Eradication." In *The Cambridge World History: Vol. VII. 1750–Present*, edited by John R. McNeill and Kenneth Pomeranz, 237–257. Cambridge, UK: Cambridge University Press.

Manning, Patrick. 2003. *Navigating World History: Historians Create a Global Past*. New York: Palgrave Macmillan.

Manning, Patrick. ed. 2008. *Global Practice in World History: Advances Worldwide*. Princeton, NJ: Markus Wiener.

Mazlish, Bruce. 1998 "Comparing Global History to World History." *Journal of Interdisciplinary History* 28 (3): 385–395.

Mazlish, Bruce, and Alfred D. Chandler. eds. 2005. *Leviathans: Multinational Corporations and the New Global History*. Cambridge, UK: Cambridge University Press.

Mazlish, Bruce, and Akira Iriye. eds. 2004. *The Global History Reader*. New York: Routledge.

McKeown, Adam. 2004. "Global Migration, 1846–1940." *Journal of World History* 15 (2): 155–189.

McNeill, John R. 2012. *Global Environmental History: An Introductory Reader*. New York: Routledge.

McNeill, William H., and John R. McNeill. 2003. *The Human Web: A Bird's Eye View of World History*. New York: Norton.

Megill, Alan. 2004. "Intellectual History and History." *Rethinking History* 8 (4): 549–557.

Mignolo, Walter D. 2000. *Local Histories/Global Designs: Coloniality, Subaltern Knowledges, and Border Thinking*. Princeton, NJ: Princeton University Press.

Moyn, Samuel, and Andrew Sartori, eds. 2013. *Global Intellectual History*. New York: Columbia University Press.

Mühlhahn, Klaus. 2009. *Criminal Justice in China—A History*. Cambridge, MA: Harvard University Press.

Ogle, Vanessa. 2015. *The Global Transformation of Time 1870–1950*. Cambridge, MA: Harvard University Press.

Olstein, Diego. 2015. *Thinking History Globally*. New York: Palgrave.

Osterhammel, Jürgen. 2006. *Europe, the "West" and the Civilizing Mission*. London: German Historical Institute.

Osterhammel, Jürgen. 2014. *The Transformation of the World: A Global History of the Nineteenth Century*. Princeton, NJ: Princeton University Press.

Pernau, Margrit, and Dominic Sachsenmaier, eds. 2016. *Global Conceptual History: A Reader*. London: Bloomsbury.

Pomeranz, Kenneth. 2001. *The Great Divergence: China, Europe, and the Making of the Modern World Economy*. Princeton, NJ: Princeton University Press.

Riello, Giorgio. 2013. *Cotton: The Fabric That Made the Modern World*. Cambridge, UK: Cambridge University Press.

Reilly, Thomas, Stephen Kaufman, and Angela Bodino, eds. 2003. *Racism: A Global Reader*. New York: Sharpe.

Robertson, Roland. 1995. "Glocalization: Time–Space and Homogeneity–Heterogeneity. In *Global Modernities*, edited by Mike Featherstone, Scott Lash, and Roland Robertson, 25–44. London: Sage.

Rockefeller, Stuart A. 2011. "Flow." *Current Anthropology* 52: 557–578.

Sachsenmaier, Dominic. 2011. *Global Perspectives on Global History: Theories and Approaches in a Connected World*. Cambridge, UK: Cambridge University Press.

Sachsenmaier, Dominic. 2014. "Cultural and Religious Exchanges." In *Architects of World History*, edited by Jerry Bentley and Kenneth Curtis, 109–129. Hoboken, NJ: Wiley-Blackwell.

Sachsenmaier, Dominic. 2016. "The Evolution of World History." In *Introducing World History* (*Cambridge History of the World*, vol. 1), edited by David Christian and Marnie Hughes-Warrington, 56–83. Cambridge, UK: Cambridge University Press.

Sachsenmaier, Dominic, and Andrew Sartori. 2018. "Global Intellectual History." In *Global History, Globally*, edited by Sven Beckert and Dominic Sachsenmaier. London: Bloomsbury.

Sartori, Andrew. 2008. *Bengal in Global Concept History: Culturalism in the Age of Capital*. Chicago: University of Chicago Press.

Service, Robert. 2010. *Comrades! A History of World Communism*. Cambridge, MA: Harvard University Press.

Sluga, Glenda. 2013. *Internationalism in the Age of Nationalism*. Philadelphia: University of Pennsylvania Press.

Smith, Bonnie G., ed. , 2004–2005. *Women's History in Global Perspective*, vols. 1–3. Urbana: University of Illinois Press.

Steinmetz, George. 2014. "Comparative History and Its Critics: A Genealogy and a Possible Solution." In *A Companion to Global Historical Thought*, edited by Prasenjit Duara, Viren Murthy, and Andrew Sartori, 412–436. Oxford, UK: Wiley.

Tilly, Charles. 1984. *Big Structures, Large Processes, Huge Comparisons*. New York: Russell Sage Foundation.

Tyrell, Ian. 2007. *Transnational Nation: United States History in Global Perspective Since 1989*. New York: Houndmills.

van der Linden, Marcel. 2008. *Workers of the World: Essays Towards a Global Labor History*. Leiden, the Netherlands: Brill.

van der Linden, Marcel, and Magaly Rodríguez García, eds. 2016. *On Coerced Labor: Work and Compulsion After Chattel Slavery*. Leiden, the Netherlands: Brill.

Wang, Q. Edward. 2010. "Globalization, Global History, and Local Identity in 'Greater China.'" *History Compass* 8 (4): 320–329.

Wasserstrom, Jeffrey. 2009. *Global Shanghai, 1850–2010*. New York: Routledge.

Weinbaum, Alys E., ed. 2008. *The Modern Girl Around the World: Consumption, Modernity, and Globalization*. Durham, NC: Duke University Press.

Woolf, Daniel. 2011. *A Global History of History*. Cambridge, UK: Cambridge University Press.

Xu, Luo. 2007. "Reconstructing World History in the People's Republic of China Since the 1980s." *Journal of World History* 18 (3): 235–250.

CHAPTER 8

TRANSDISCIPLINARITY

DANIEL E. ESSER AND JAMES H. MITTELMAN

THIS chapter assesses transdisciplinarity as an approach to both research and teaching in the emerging field of global studies, as well as its relevance to relatively more established interdisciplinary fields such as international studies and regional studies. It takes into account historical precursors and explores how transdisciplinarity impinges on the division of labor among scholars engaged in disciplinary knowledge production and dissemination. Arguing that structural reconfiguration can involve cutting against conventions and establishing new ones, we consider the impetus for amplifying cross-fertilization in global studies. This also provides an opportunity to rethink disciplinarity not only theoretically but also as a practical constraint on complex problem-solving. Inasmuch as disciplines are the prevalent frame of reference for traversing modes of knowledge generation and learning in the academy, we focus on stretching disciplinary boundaries as a by-product of acute problem-solving. At the same time, we reaffirm the importance of disciplinary methodological innovations as building blocks for multimodal study designs and stress the centrality of methodologically rigorous approaches, whether transdisciplinary or not.

In the social sciences, disciplines originated in the West during the nineteenth century, coincident with the rise and power of the market economy (Wallerstein 1996; Abbott 2001). By the 1890s, universities had gradually formed departments and institutionalized disciplinarity, but at somewhat different times: Germany preceded the United States and the United Kingdom. From a global vantage point, however, this move had a Eurocentric element to it. Although no one individual became the touchstone of non-Western thinking, writers whose ideas transcended disciplines, such as Frantz Fanon, are compelling. This Martinique-born psychiatrist arguably contributed more original insights to the social sciences on the themes of domination, subordination, race, liberation, and revolutionary violence than did any of his contemporaries working within scholarly disciplines. Meanwhile, some Western scholars, including Albert Einstein, lamented an education that gives priority to specialization over "an understanding of and a lively feeling for values." Einstein maintained that the former could turn out "a well-trained dog [rather] than a harmoniously developed person" (Einstein 1952). In contrast, a rounded education develops what he deemed "precious" abilities: an appreciation of beauty and ethics. Foreshadowing Wallerstein's (1996) and Abbott's (2001) arguments, Einstein thus evoked American philosopher John Dewey's (1916: 304) early concerns about the wave of vocationalism sweeping campuses and the compartmentalization of higher education in the service of capitalism.

In view of sensibilities about the pernicious effects of disciplinary specialization, we explore the potential of transdisciplinarity as a means to complement disciplinary research, though not to dispense with it, and to grasp complexes of power and wealth in the twenty-first century. Transdisciplinarity does not seek to replace scholarly disciplines but, rather, address vexing global problems that defy analyses from narrow perspectives. Challenges and opportunities brought by transnational migration, global diasporas, and cross-border agglomerations such as Shenzhen–Hong Kong, Tijuana–San Diego, and Ciudad Juárez–El Paso benefit from thinking that focuses on problem-solving instead of epistemological compliance imposed or, as Foucault (1985) claimed, enforced by institutional silos.

A springboard for reflecting on this task is Robert Cox's (1981) important distinction between problem-solving theory and critical theory. The former takes the world as it is and attempts to make it "work smoothly" (p. 129ff). The prevailing order thereby sets the parameters for thinking about how to address concrete problems. The strength of this type of analysis is that it limits the number of variables and allows for precision in formulation. By comparison, critical theory challenges the dominant framework assumed by problem-solving and probes historical origins. It calls for reflexivity on theorists' own positions and social standpoints (Cox 1981: 129; see also Brincat 2016). Critical theory hence requires historical depth, normative assessment, and reasoning about alternative futures. Clearly, problem-solving and critical theory are not a binary. Both perspectives seek to build understanding and inform or enable action. They can be complementary ways to advance a global perspective. For instance, analysts in these two traditions may similarly advocate for a tax on international financial transactions as a way to reduce world inequality. The institutionalization of such a tax would indicate systemic reflection while also producing funds for development needs in the Global South.

THREE PATHS

One route for comprehending such vast issues is to push beyond globalization studies and encompass competing configurations of analytical power. Globalization is a core concept in global studies. The former is one construct among others in the matrix of the latter (see Steger and Wahlrab 2017; this issue is further discussed later). This distinction requires constructive interrogation of the predominance of national-level inquiries in the social sciences as well as in cognate disciplines. Although scholars from various disciplines have advocated "postnational" heuristics (Appadurai 2003; cf. Sassen 2000) to capture cross-scalar flows of people, capital, and ideas, the contemporary—and indeed inter-regional—pivot toward nationalistic populism risks reactionary political momentum against the rise of global studies as a mode of transdisciplinary scientific inquiry. Yet it is precisely the uneven dynamics of globalization that lie at the heart of the revival of the national project, and global studies is therefore ideally suited for investigating it.

Another option is to innovate within the field of international studies, while retaining its emphasis on the nation state as the primary actor and drawing on valuable research on rival nationalisms and how they undergird practices of contemporary governance. Undoubtedly, nation states continue to serve as primary drivers of international regulation and cooperation. Galvanizing research carried out in the tradition of disciplinary inquiry holds particular promise when it foregrounds the tensions resulting from scientific discoveries produced through different methodological approaches. A necessary criterion for this option to render valuable new insights on chronic global challenges is an epistemological openness to variation in validity standards that characterizes adjoining social science disciplines. As scholars, we witness and engage in conversations and procedures that often pit truth claims and protocols rooted in one discipline against epistemological consensus in another. A focus on global studies as a field that transcends the ontological fixation on "the national," along with methodological nationalism, provides an opportunity to retool processes of transdisciplinary knowledge generation. At the same time, it risks opening up an already broad front of multidisciplinary disagreement.

The third course is taken by specialists in world regions, who see global phenomena through the lenses of myriad localities and with more texture than do devotees of the macro orientations. There is ample evidence that amid persistent criticism from disciplinary positions, area studies has lost none of its relevance. Its legacy is alive when it comes to grappling with some of the world's most pressing problems; examples include migration studies, urban studies, and global health.

What might be read as a largely semantic debate is, in fact, constitutive. Eponymic framing is consequential because it orients the next generations of intellectuals, some of whom will become thought leaders of the future. In addition, although disciplinary knowledge sets overlap and can be combined, sharpening the distinctions among them also highlights transitions in the conduct of knowledge production and transmission. And debates about them concern shifts in lived experience in the twenty-first century, as well as in values and the exercise of power. In the following sections, we gauge what can be learned from these tensions and discuss prospects for embracing transdisciplinary inquiry.

GLOBAL STUDIES

According to Jan Nederveen Pieterse (2013), global studies has much in common with some other types of studies. It joins together globalization studies and international studies. In his formulation, global studies is marked by its aspirations for universality; emphasis on interdisciplinarity; efforts to recenter the social sciences toward systemic dynamics; and incorporations of micro, macro, and meso levels of analysis. Moreover, its epistemology permits critical reflexivity while its methodology foregrounds mixed strategies, such as ethnography and varied modes of mining data sets, with the aim of grounding measures and findings in local conditions (Esser and VanderKamp 2013). Similarly, Manfred Steger (2015: 5) delimits global studies in terms of four prisms that constitute a framework: the prisms of globalization, transdisciplinary framing, the dynamics of space, and a critical cast of mind.

But it is worth asking, What, if anything, makes global studies distinctive? After all, globalization research is also an interdisciplinary, multilevel, and, in keeping with Steger's (2015) explication, often critical endeavor (Mittelman 2004). It, too, uses multiple methods and seeks to be worldwide in scope. Indeed, Nederveen Pieterse's (2013) conclusion qualifies his main arguments: "The difference between studies of globalization/global studies should not be overdrawn. There are analytical differences, but they exist more as a potential than reality" (p. 511). For him, the keywords "global" and "globalization" basically matter insofar as they facilitate understanding.

The point to underscore is that both global and globalization studies concern the dynamics of capitalism in all its varieties and in sundry domains. Conceptually, however, the risk lies in any attempt to encapsulate all phenomena in a single, totalizing framework, irrespective of whether it is named "global" or "globalization" studies (Mittelman 2013: 516). While avoiding this trap, one can adopt the rubrics "global" and "globalization" for encouraging rich debates about empire, imperialism and sub-imperialism, and the governance of capitalism. The key criterion is not simply to investigate political, economic, and social dynamics at different scales and polities but to focus on how these dynamics interact across scales and systems. Analyses of global governance must therefore not be constrained to "the global" but, rather, seek to uncover how agendas and resulting actions unfold concurrently at multiple scales. Research on global phenomena, such as climate change, can view national formations and the interstate system in more fruitful ways than do orthodox state-centric studies. For instance, Leo Panitch and Sam Gindin's *The Making of Global Capitalism* (2012) skillfully explains the intricate connections between capitalism and the US state, which, they maintain, has served as an informal empire and superintended the restructuring of other states. In comparison to the mainstream tradition of positivism, which seeks to separate variables and facts and values, global and globalization studies have the greater potential for developing engaged theory and methods.

INTERNATIONAL STUDIES

Global and globalization studies alike seek to move beyond territorial notions of the nation state and take into account the time and space dimensions of social relations. As Eve Darian-Smith and Philip McCarty (2016) remind us, "international studies implicitly reaffirm the national" (p. 3). Yet this move should not entail a premature farewell to old paradigms. In "saying good-bye to international relations," Susan Strange (1996: xvi), a maverick intellectual who was often ahead of her times, seems to have underestimated the mainstream's resistance to innovations that break with its conventions of separate specializations in social research. State-centered thinking in its many iterations is alive, although it is not well from the standpoint of critical theorists. Semblances of realism appear, for example, in analyses of transnationalism, soft power, and rising powers. These conceptualizations have traveled from the West to the East and the Global South, where they are embraced—often coupled with nationalism—and frequently take the form of southern realism that is decentered but nonetheless replicates hegemonic knowledge generation rooted in conceptualizations of an international order that reflect colonial legacies and structures of inequality.

Critical theorists want to rethink the national project as it relates to the social project— that is, to understand the state as a constellation of social forces—and strengthen efforts to link, or relink, economic reform and social policy. These researchers are committed to using their work to benefit those at the margins, which, it should be added, is the focus of subaltern studies. This mode of inquiry interrogates history and shows that peasants frequently play key roles in effecting social transformations in postcolonial areas. A historiographic method is employed to excavate specific formations, as in the work of Russian and Finnish scholars (Hentilä 2010; Koposov 2009) who elicit memories to explore evolving patterns of politics. Recast in such critical form, international studies sheds light on the socially constructed interests (as well as the silences that result from them) of national actors in the global political economy.

REGIONAL STUDIES

Studies of a particular world region typically offer more contextual grounding—greater cultural and historical specificity—than do the other two approaches. Moreover, they may materialize as stepping stones for both interregional and intraregional comparisons. Regionalists mobilize local knowledge and affirm that even with globalization's deterritorializing tendencies, "place matters" (Dreier et al. 2001). In this vein, Clifford Geertz (1968), who certainly also had an interest in global phenomena, observed that Muslims in Indonesia and Morocco bow toward the same place when they pray, but they do so from different directions. He also pointed out that his understanding of Weber, Durkheim, and other great authors changed when he viewed their work through the lens of his ethnographic knowledge (as indicated in Dirks 2012: B4). Geertz's ontological discovery underscores the potential inherent in multiscalar scholarship not just for knowledge production as such but also more broadly to challenge the appropriation (and in some cases expropriation) of leading scholars' work by specific disciplines. To reduce Weber and Durkheim to sociology, or characterize Geertz merely as "an anthropologist," risks downplaying their enormous, continuous influence on the social sciences writ large. Reading Gramsci while traveling in rural Mozambique during that country's revolutionary period of the mid-1970s, one of us (JM) had much the same experience: Gramsci's insights on passive revolution, civil society, and wars of movement and maneuver took on new meanings that JM had not previously discovered. At approximately the same time, Edward Said's (1979) landmark study of Orientalism also chronicles the author's own discovery of distinctiveness that led him to discern global ways of framing friends and enemies, "we" and "they," in-groups and outliers. These intellectual journeys down the path and across the lands of "the Other" can serve to broaden cognitive horizons in ways that approximate knowledge generation prior to the institutionalization of scholarly disciplines (Sherwood et al. 2007).

Inasmuch as Western paradigms have undervalued autonomous discourses in the Global South, some regional, or area, specialists have consistently highlighted the importance of local knowledge production and a critical perspective of global knowledge governance (Mamdani 2011: 12). The global is thus viewed from the standpoint of the local, with an attempt to grasp the interactions between them. The objective is to come to grips with internally, rather than externally, driven research questions. Paralleling such indigenous attempts to reorganize knowledge, postcolonial scholars in North America and Europe welcome locally produced approaches in different areas of the world. What colonialism had devalued or sought to erase from the mind (Kumar 2011) is increasingly appreciated in some quarters of regional studies, including in the context of understanding the pressures of globalization.

Clearly, the initial waves of area-studies thinking in the West were colored by colonial and Cold War interests. National security concerns provided impetus for the US National Defense Education Act Title VI, which developed expertise on world regions and in foreign languages. After 1989, however, US government funding for area studies declined until the 2001 attacks on the Pentagon and the World Trade Center, icons of American military power and a globalizing economy. The events of September 11, 2001, and the US-led, multitrillion-dollar "global war on terror" prompted government, foundations, and universities to support studies of the Middle East, Islam, and transnational challenges such as global organized crime.

In the second decade of this century and after, peril lies in militarizing funding for regional studies so that it serves the purposes of the state's conception of homeland security rather than the core aims of a university in non-authoritarian societies—namely fostering democratic citizenship, promoting critical thinking, and defending academic freedom. These intellectual missions are increasingly put to the test in the wake of the Arab Spring's peaceful protests, followed by violent conflicts in areas of the Middle East and North Africa. The southern flank of the Mediterranean stretches across the Sahara's vast Sahel, a complex desert landscape where state power is weak; borders are porous; and multiple networks of ethnic groups, clans, militias, and criminal organizations intermingle and vie with one another. This complexity presents enormous challenges to policy intellectuals and theoretically minded researchers. Regional studies as a field is ideally suited to providing granular analyses that speak to cross-scalar dynamics by anchoring global research in local contexts and comparative insights.

TRANSDISCIPLINARY PERSPECTIVES

The transcendence of disciplinary knowledge production is not merely an epistemological agenda; it constitutes a formidable material challenge. As claimed at the outset of this chapter, the division of labor among different disciplinary specializations is an artifact of global capitalism, and scholarly work conducted outside of disciplinary confines remains a social as well as material venture. Disciplines continue to provide ontological security and rewards to those who follow established paths of knowledge generation. Innovation is encouraged insofar as it does not challenge institutionalized rationales of validity. Unsurprisingly, then, "disciplinary antagonisms that have remained unresolved for decades . . . imply that interdisciplinary scholars are dilatants or argue that interdisciplinary research is superficial in its efforts to draw connections across theoretical approaches and bodies of literature" (Darian-Smith McCarty 2016: 3). Indeed, such pushback can be traced to the moment of ideational inception. Basarab Nicolescu (2010) recalls French scholar Pierre Duguet (1972), who proposed a workshop organized by the Organisation for Economic Co-operation and Development (OECD) to be held under the title of "transdisciplinarité," a term for which Duguet is usually credited. The OECD, however, was "afraid to confuse some representatives of [its] member countries" (Nicolescu 2010: 20) and opted for "interdisciplinarity" instead. The material motivation for this choice is readily apparent.

Similarly, the interdisciplinary field of development studies, or international development as it is often known in North America, has been slow to adopt transdisciplinary perspectives. A review of two of the field's most widely read scholarly journals illustrates this limited salience to date. Only eight of literally thousands of articles published in *World Development* between 1991 and 2016 mention "transdisciplinary" or "transdisciplinarity." The earliest in this sample to do so, an introductory article by Neva Goodwin (1991) on "global issues," contended that in order "to understand the contemporary issues which have a global dimension, we will need to employ multi-, inter-, and transdisciplinary approaches" (p. 13). More recently, Lauren Crawshaw et al. (2014) lamented in their article in *World Development* that "most studies to date have focused on the *why* rather than *how* transdisciplinarity can be used" (p. 489). The pattern is comparable with regard to contributions to *Third World Quarterly*. To date, the journal has published seven papers containing explicit references to "transdisciplinary" or "transdisciplinarity," the earliest among them focusing on transborder labor migration amid global capitalist restructuring (Wise and Márquez Covarrubias 2008).

Despite its birth pains, however, a transdisciplinary approach to research on knotty global problems holds practical promise through forefronting problem-solving instead of requiring disciplinary norm cohesion. It challenges silos of knowledge production *in the process* of generating nuanced explanations that draw from across the social (and increasingly also the natural) sciences. The issues of intentionality and application are central to this foray.

Extending Crawshaw et al.'s (2014) aforementioned critique to the realm of global studies, we must ask, Does the field global studies provide an opportunity to substantiate the methodological strengths of transdisciplinarity? And do transdisciplinary perspectives help address nagging global challenges? Darian-Smith and McCarty (2016) posit that "the goal of transdisciplinarity is to move beyond the limits of the disciplines and provide new ways of organizing knowledge and modes of thinking" (p. 5). They echo Nicolescu's (1996/2002) earlier definition of transdisciplinarity as "that which is at once between the disciplines, across the different disciplines, and beyond all discipline" (Nicolescu 2010: 22). This depiction of transdisciplinarity is theoretically bold and intellectually exciting, but it is also prone to reinforce skepticism amid still scant examples of its robust impact on scholarship. In contrast, we propose that global studies is best served by demonstrating, rather than advocating, the virtues of transdisciplinarity through concrete applications.

The rise of intersectional scholarship on global issues provides several examples. Extending Kimberlé Crenshaw's (1989) groundbreaking argument regarding overlapping social identities amid systems of domination and oppression, scholars in international studies, regional studies, and indeed global studies have highlighted the fluidity and interdependence of social categories across scales. Kalpana Wilson (2011), for instance, shows how foreign-aid donors' representations of women in the Global South often remain essentialist. Women are portrayed as worthy recipients of foreign aid in order to help them unlock their economic potential. This treatment, Wilson argues, mirrors colonial depictions of female workers' value in an exploitative global economic system, creating a parallel between historical and contemporary exploitative practices of local labor by global interests. Malini Ranganathan (2014) engages Gramscian constructs of subaltern political agency by tracing how payment for water provides marginalized urban dwellers in India with a means to bargain for greater symbolic recognition. Her work showcases how global discourses of capitalism co-determine outcomes at subnational levels. And she goes one step further by suggesting that such instances of insurgent citizenship (Holston 2008) are harbingers of institutional reconfiguration "from below," not just in a structurally hierarchical sense but also geographically in global hegemonies.

Toward Rigor in Transdisciplinarity

The question of rigor looms large in this genre of studies and indeed all research that ventures beyond the confines of intradisciplinary methodological agreement. There is a risk that in the quest to escape disciplinary boundaries and their resulting epistemological and ontological constraints, transdisciplinary scholarship will devalue methodology writ large. This reframing may well be "potentially emancipatory in that it explicitly seeks to free up our ways of thinking and our organization of knowledge in the academy" (Darian-Smith and McCarty 2016: 5). Meanwhile, one must be cautious about inadvertently transforming global studies into the study of everything, where anything goes. Much reaffirmation of the viability of scholarly disciplines stems from an appreciation of the methodological innovation carried out within them. Although disciplinary boundaries can seem opportunistic and confining, disciplines' most limiting effect on problem-solving is not their fragmentation of knowledge and methods but, rather, their tendency to make absolute truth claims. As much as epistemological emancipation is necessary, methodological detachment from established disciplines is likely to result in protracted turf wars over scholarly terrain for mitigating formidable world challenges.

We therefore envision transdisciplinarity in global studies as a distinct perspective on knowledge generation that draws strategically from methodological advances in disciplinary social science scholarship. *The itinerary would both relax disciplinary borders and deeply integrate knowledge sets.* Such a conceptualization of transdisciplinarity also has important implications for how to teach global studies. On the one hand, the "liberating and empowering" (Darian-Smith and McCarty 2016: 18) effect of a "global transdisciplinary framework" as an approach to higher education amid "a dizzying array of apparently disconnected and chaotic events" (p. 19) is not to be dismissed. Unlike disciplinary frameworks, transdisciplinarity does not constrain inquiries through internal consensus on particular questions that are deemed more important than others. As a result, transdisciplinarity as pedagogy can leverage its relatively brief ideational history and its inherent skepticism of hegemonic knowledge canons by encouraging rather than disciplining innovative scientific inquiry.

On the other hand, transdisciplinarity in global studies must not be framed and practiced as a transcendence of established methodological arguments. In fact, teaching transdisciplinarity requires even more careful and extensive methodological education. Under transdisciplinary knowledge structures, the appropriateness of methods derives from the questions addressed and does not flow uncritically or mechanically from any disciplinary methodological canon. This impels global studies instructors as well as their colleagues in cognate interdisciplinary fields to teach wider ranges of methods than is common in any one social science discipline.

In the transdisciplinary turn to global studies, scholars need to secure methodological rigor. This requires methods curricula that offer a variety of study designs and critical reflection on their genesis, suitability for, and limitations in respect to specific research questions. Global studies curricula should therefore ensure that transdisciplinary courses are linked to methods training reflecting multiple disciplinary toolboxes and exposing students to myriad epistemological traditions.

CONCLUSION

Ongoing vulnerabilities manifest hauntingly with global climate change, economic inequality, and transborder migration. The application of a neoliberal policy framework to these problems is accompanied by disinvestment in public education in many countries, increased pressure to produce more applied research at the expense of basic inquiry, spiraling debt incurred by university students, and a proliferation of overseas educational initiatives prized as market opportunities. In this context, higher education institutions are rapidly restructuring their global(ization), international, and regional studies profiles. Military-strategic and corporate actors' analytical approaches can be embodied under all these banners, irrespective of the adjectival form, and put mounting pressure on university curricula to transform education into a narrowly functional and instrumental enterprise (Denskus and Esser 2015).

Under current political and economic conditions, a key challenge is to continue to experiment with how to realize the promise of transdisciplinarity in global studies. It encompasses pluralism in research and curriculum and counters knowledge hegemonies. Ongoing debates among scholars who embrace this emerging approach, along with their colleagues whose persuasions lie in the production of research and teaching within social science disciplines, are emblematic of intellectual health. We are generalizers and particularizers, knowers and doers, and advocates of different knowledge sets. The ontology is ever changing in a world in which humanity has not yet reached a post-historical future. Beyond naming global, international, and regional clusters of knowledge, transdisciplinarity faces the daunting task of explaining the complex layering of them. This is a top priority in the work ahead.

REFERENCES

Abbott, Andrew. 2001. *Chaos of Disciplines*. Chicago: University of Chicago Press.

Appadurai, Arjun. 2003. "Sovereignty Without Territoriality: Notes for a Postnational Geography." In *The Anthropology of Space and Place*, edited by Setha M. Low and Denise Lawrence-Zúñiga, 337–349. Oxford, UK: Blackwell.

Brincat, Shannon. 2016. "Traditional, Problem-Solving and Critical Theory: An Analysis of Horkheimer and Cox's Setting of the 'Critical' Divide." *Globalizations* 13 (5): 563–577.

Cox, Robert W. 1981. "Social Forces, States, and World Orders: Beyond International Relations Theory." *Millennium* 10 (3): 126–155.

Crawshaw, Lauren, Sonia Fèvre, Lampheuy Kaesombath, Bounlerth Sivilai, and Fongsamouth Southammavong. 2014. "Lessons from an Integrated Community Health Education Initiative in Rural Laos." *World Development* 64: 487–502.

Crenshaw, Kimberlé Williams. 1989. "Demarginalizing the Intersection of Race and Sex: A Black Feminist Critique of Antidiscrimination Doctrine, Feminist Theory and Antiracist Politics." *University of Chicago Legal Forum*, special issue on Feminism in the Law: Theory, Practice and Criticism: 139–167.

Darian-Smith, Eve, and Philip McCarty. 2016. "Beyond Interdisciplinarity: Developing a Global Transdisciplinary Framework." *Transcience* 7 (2): 1–26.

Denskus, Tobias, and Daniel E. Esser. 2015. "Countering the Risks of Vocationalisation in Master's Programmes in International Development." *Learning and Teaching* 8 (2): 72–85.

Dewey, John. 1916. *Democracy and Education: An Introduction to the Philosophy of Education.* New York: Macmillan.

Dirks, Nicholas. 2012, August 17. "Scholars, Spies, and Global Studies." *Chronicle Review* Section B: B4–B5.

Dreier, Peter, John Mollenkopf, and Todd Swanstrom. 2001. *Place Matters.* Lawrence: University Press of Kansas.

Duguet, Pierre. 1972. "Approach to the Problems." In *Interdisciplinarity: Problems of Teaching and Research in Universities*, edited by Léo Apostel, Guy Berger, Asa Briggs, and Guy Michaud, 11–22. Paris: Organisation for Economic Co-operation and Development.

Einstein, Albert. 1952, October 5. "Education for Independent Thought." *New York Times.* http://mczcm.wordpress.com/2006/12/19/albert-einstein-education-for-independent-thought. Accessed October 4, 2013.

Esser, Daniel E., and Emily E. VanderKamp. 2013. "Comparable and Yet Context-Sensitive? Improving Evaluation in Violently Divided Societies Through Methodology." *Journal of Peacebuilding & Development* 8 (2): 42–56.

Foucault, Michel. 1985. *Discipline and Punish: The Birth of the Prison.* Harmondsworth, UK: Penguin.

Geertz, Clifford. 1968. *Islam Observed: Religious Development in Morocco and Indonesia.* New Haven, CT: Yale University Press.

Goodwin, Neva R. 1991. "Introduction." *World Development* 19 (1): 1–15.

Hentilä, Seppo. 2010. "The Finnish–German Brotherhood of Arms as Politics of Memory." Paper presented at the seminar on "History, Memory, Politics," Helsinki Collegium for Advanced Studies, Helsinki, Finland, April 20.

Holston, James. 2008. *Insurgent Citizenship: Disjunctions of Democracy and Modernity in Brazil.* Princeton, NJ: Princeton University Press.

Koposov, Nikolay. 2009. *De l'imagination historique.* Paris: Éditions de l'École de hautes etudes en sciences sociales.

Kumar, Malreddy Pavan. 2011. "Postcolonialism: Interdisciplinary or Interdiscursive?" *Third World Quarterly* 32 (4): 653–672.

Mamdani, Mahmood. 2011. "The Importance of Research in a University. *CODESRIA Bulletin*, nos. 3–4: 10–13.

Mittelman, James H. 2004. "What Is Critical Globalization Studies?" *International Studies Perspectives* 5 (3): 219–230.

Mittelman, James H. 2013. "What's in a Name? Global, International, and Regional Studies." *Globalizations* 10 (4): 515–519.

Nederveen Pieterse, Jan. 2013. "What Is Global Studies?" *Globalizations* 10 (4): 499–514.

Nicolescu, Basarab. 2002. *La transdisciplinarité, manifeste* [1996]. English translation: *Manifesto of Transdisciplinarity*. New York: State University of New York Press, 2002.

Nicolescu, Basarab. 2010. "Methodology of Transdisciplinarity: Levels of Reality, Logic of the Included Middle and Complexity." *Transdisciplinary Journal of Engineering & Science* 1 (1): 19–38.

Panitch, Leo, and Sam Gindin. 2012. *The Making of Global Capitalism: The Political Economy of American Empire*. London: Verso.

Ranganathan, Malini. 2014. "Paying for Pipes, Claiming Citizenship: Political Agency and Water Reforms at the Urban Periphery." *International Journal of Urban and Regional Research* 38 (2): 590–608.

Said, Edward. 1979. *Orientalism*. New York. Vintage.

Sassen, Saskia. 2000. "The Global City: Strategic Site/New Frontier." In *Democracy, Citizenship and the Global City*, edited by Engin F. Isin, 48–61. London: Routledge.

Sherwood, Stephen, Donald Cole, and Charles Crissman. 2007. "Cultural Encounters: Learning from Cross-Disciplinary Science and Development Practice in Ecosystem Health." *Development in Practice* 17 (2): 179–195.

Steger, Manfred B., ed. 2015. *The Global Studies Reader*. 2nd ed. Oxford, UK: Oxford University Press.

Steger, Manfred B., and Amentahru Wahlrab. 2017. *What Is Global Studies? Theory and Practice*. London: Routledge.

Strange, Susan. 1996. *The Retreat of the State: The Diffusion of Power in the World Economy*. Cambridge, UK: Cambridge University Press.

Wallerstein, Immanuel, ed. 1996. *Open the Social Sciences: Report of the Gulbenkian Commission on the Restructuring of the Social Sciences*. Stanford, CA: Stanford University Press.

Wilson, Kalpana. 2011. "'Race,' Gender and Neoliberalism: Changing Visual Representations in Development." *Third World Quarterly* 32, no. 2: 315–331.

Wise, Raúl Delgado, and Humberto Márquez Covarrubias. 2008. "Capitalist Restructuring, Development and Labour Migration: The Mexico–US Case." *Third World Quarterly* 29 (7): 1359–1374.

FURTHER READING

Anievas, Alexander, Nivi Manchanda, and Robbie Shilliam, eds. 2014. *Race and Racism in International Relations: Confronting the Global Colour Line*. London: Routledge.

Darian-Smith, Eve, and Philip McCarty. 2017. *The Global Turn: Theories, Research Designs, and Methods for Global Studies*. Oakland: University of California Press.

International Consortium of Critical Theory Programs. 2016. http://directory. criticaltheoryconsortium.org/about.

Mittelman, James H. 2010. *Hyperconflict: Globalization and Insecurity*. Stanford, CA: Stanford University Press.

Sil, Rudra, and Peter J. Katzenstein. 2010. *Beyond Paradigms: Analytic Eclecticism in the Study of World Politics*. New York: Palgrave.

Tickner, J. Ann. 2014. *A Feminist Voyage Through International Relations*. New York: Oxford University Press.

CHAPTER 9

···

PROBLEM ORIENTATION

···

PAUL BATTERSBY

How are social problems identified? Where and how do problems begin and when, if ever, are they resolved? Definitions of the word "problem" are manifold, and the range of potential subjects for study is vast. The word implies deficiency, obstacle, and absence, but it also carries an implicit assumption that there is some identifiable thing or phenomenon that needs to be solved, and which can be solved if the right principles and right measures or prescriptions are applied. Problems can be highly complex, with multiple possible explanations and multiple possible responses to an identified question, proposition, or challenge. Can there then ever be a true or accurate statement of a problem? From a positivistic standpoint, natural and social phenomena should and can be studied objectively; relationships identified through rigorous data collection, testing, and analysis; and conclusions validated by their apparent consistency. However, *the* problem is arguably always in some way a social construct reflecting the current state of knowledge by which *it* is identified and defined, and the priorities of those who claim authority to seek and present solutions. The search for answers is then influenced in some way by the partiality of the observer, and the process of inquiry is, despite any appearance of methodological orderliness, inescapably anarchic, ad hoc, and incomplete (Bacchi 2009; Feyerabend 1991; Koppman, Cain, and Leahey 2015; Strange 1994; Fischer, Greiff, and Funke 2012). If knowledge is contestable, and desirably so if contestation is what drives discovery, then any problem, however proposed, should be subject to ongoing critical interrogation and reflexive reformulation.

This chapter introduces a global studies approach to the analysis of *problématiques*—a category of problem in which threads of causality are intricate, extensive, laterally related, and often hidden from direct view. Rapid population growth, urban pollution, and many other problématiques of modernity are attributable to scientific and technological innovations that enabled the formation of an interconnected global world but which have catalyzed new vulnerabilities—that is, "manufactured" new uncertainties or risks (Beck 1999; Giddens 1990: 59). Global analysis is thus concerned with the identification of patterns of cause and effect within complex and evolving social systems in which human subjectivity has a major role in determining social outcomes. Trajectories of change can be orderly or unanticipated and disruptive, and interpretations of change are colored by a sense of individual or collective vulnerability, prejudice, fear, or pessimism (Dean 1998)—hence the urgency in seeking a commensurably dynamic mode of thought.

Reasoning thus, effective problem recognition and response is less a matter of theoretical elegance, or even coherence, than of "muddling through," ideally toward a common or "shared" conception of what is at stake and why (Denzau and North 1994; Denzau, Roy, and Minassians 2016; Lindblom 1959: 79). The global method elaborated in this chapter identifies patterns of irregular migration to present a worked example of how such exploratory and creative inquiry might proceed. In so doing, it advances the claim that transdisciplinary thinking in global studies is a form of *"global* thinking" that mobilizes multiple perspectives in pursuit of a more nuanced, "multilevel" understanding of social phenomena (Bernstein 2015; Darian-Smith and McCarty 2016; Ghemawat 2014; Lawrence 2010; Steger and Wahlrab 2016). A global problem orientation accepts that new knowledge can form at the interstices of different systems or schools of thought. This creative–imaginative technique encourages the use of divergent models or paradigms in tandem to enable thick description and deep analysis of complex problem spaces. It is a hazardous enterprise to eschew disciplinary confinements in favor of an open form of chaotic inquiry commensurate with this age of aberrant globalization (Feyerabend 1991; Luhmann 2013; Osborn 1957; Sil and Katzenstein 2010; Treffinger, Schoonover, and Selby 2013;).

GLOBAL ORIENTATIONS

Are social problems then entirely imagined or manufactured? There is a tangible risk of being injured or killed in a traffic accident, and it would be nonsensical to argue that road fatalities are an invention of the human imagination. Speed is a major cause of vehicle accidents on the open road, but there are many other road safety risk factors to consider, including driver skills, vehicle roadworthiness, road conditions, driver age, and alcohol or drug consumption (New South Wales Government 2013; Solomon 2015). We can rank all known causal factors by their relative contributing effects to a series of accident events and then calculate by frequency how and where intervention should be weighted. However, there is still wide scope for interpretation of the evidence. Practical recommendations for addressing dangerous driving diverge with the priorities of the observer: lowering vehicle speed limits, as preferred by traffic authorities, or, acknowledging that speed is a relative phenomenon, better driver training, as preferred by many motoring organizations (Solomon 2015). The order of dispute increases with the scale and complexity of the issue area selected. Consider the so-called "Middle East problem" of the early twenty-first century and its historical antecedent, the "Eastern Question" of the nineteenth and early twentieth centuries. Both the question and the answers given reflect largely Western strategic interests and agendas and a West-centric geographic imagination. Prescriptions have ranged from military intervention and colonial rule to diplomacy and economic assistance. Yet, whether we look to the post-World War I formation of Arab states or to the twenty-first-century "War on Terror," efforts to rearrange political relations in this geopolitical space have not resulted in a durable pattern of regional co-existence or in settled systems of internal state governance (Bacevich 2016: 36; Blair 2016; Fromkin 1989; Schumacher, 2014).

Although the previous analogies are unrelated, they emphasize the contingent nature of problem knowledge and therefore problem "solutions." Circumstances alter and new factors emerge to disrupt existing problem spaces. New forms of psychotropic drugs, for example, add to the risks of driver impairment and erratic road behavior. The rapid uptake of mobile communication technologies also impacts the rate of distracted driving-related accidents and deaths in countries such as the United States and Australia (McEvoy et al. 2005; National Highway Traffic Safety Administration, 2016). Empirical research can quantify damage done and identify patterns of causal relations to guide future decision-making. Scientific findings are always subject to interpretation and to question, as indeed are all forms of data. This is how knowledge is advanced, but data are also open to invention and manipulation for political or commercial gain.

The purpose of this excursion into the nature of empirical knowledge is to foreground the role of perspective or standpoint in defining problem orientations. Despite extensive research into the causes and nature of climate change, and despite ever-increasing strictures imposed upon processes of data collection and interpretation by scientific communities, politically the "science" of global warming is kept in doubt. In perverse contrast, national economic fates are daily exposed to speculative and abstract estimation of risk in opaque and often volatile international financial markets. Finance risk is calculated by the weighted probability that economic gains will be won or forgone over a period of commodified time—a probability that is gauged by factoring in a range of circumstances that might be expected to prevail for the duration of a financial transaction. But here, as elsewhere, *the problem of potential financial loss is fashioned as much by what has yet to happen as what has happened* and also by educated or instinctive guessing of the latter. Risk formulae at best offer only a conditional surety that the future will unfold as anticipated. Risk management is a world of the imagination, influenced by feelings and calculations of fear, vulnerability and certainty, trust and mistrust. Although the trend toward automation, from financial trading to driverless vehicles, is driven by the aspiration to reduce and, where possible, eliminate human error and the human element from complex decision-making, human subjectivity at some stage necessarily, or ideally, still comes into play.

Whereas many kinds of problems can be identified and relatively straightforward answers sought through processes of linear-particular reasoning, problématiques are of a different order of complexity. Causal relationships within such *polymorphic* problem spaces are often indistinct, dispersed, and heterogeneous, rendering the identification of *global* patterns impossible without a commensurably dynamic mode of inquiry. Here, problem framing is guided by theoretical models chosen, not quite at random, from the fields of cultural anthropology and international political economy, specifically from the contemporaneous work of Arjun Appadurai and Susan Strange. Appadurai's conceptualization of "scapes" captures the complex irregularities of contemporary globalization, while Strange reminds us of the deep structures of institutionalized power that shape global relations. Although both framed their definitive ideas in the late twentieth century, both provide divergent but mutually intelligible representations of a global world that is entirely commensurate with the world of today. Appadurai (1996: 32) proposes five "imaginative landscapes" to map out complex "fluid" and "irregular" movements or "flows" of globalization: "ethnoscapes" (multidirectional and globalizing flows of people), "financescapes" (flows of capital), "ideoscapes" (the topography of ideas), "mediascapes" (flows and cultural imprints of globalized images), and "technoscapes" (multidirectional and multimodal patterns of technological evolution and technology-mediated exchange). Susan Strange (1994: 6) identifies four "structures of power" that govern the global political economy: security (the protection of interests, be they state, corporate, or individual), production (the capacity to produce wealth), finance (the power to create and allocate credit), and knowledge. Culture, if conceived differently, is pivotal to each model. Ideas and knowledge, despite their amorphous nature, are a source of immense power and, Strange asserts, "the knowledge structure determines what knowledge is discovered, how it is stored, and who communicates it by what means to whom and on what terms" (p. 121). In other words, knowledge is a form of cultural power that, as much as finance or military might, influences who gets what and how.

Within Strange's realism is the realization that "hard" power structures emerge out of fluid dynamics of social interaction shaped by ideas and identities (Strange, 1994: 121–138). The world of states is de-centered but not dismissed in Appadurai's "modeling" of the global; indeed, states are acknowledged as major topographical impressions of dominant global ideas about sovereignty, national community, and order. The possibility of a world without states was perhaps a more seductive notion in the aftermath of the Cold War, but the rise of the security state in the early twenty-first century, coupled with a strident popular rejection of globalization in the globalized West, points to fresh "disjunctures" in the relationship between deterritorialized capital, states, and what Manfred Steger (2008) terms the "global imaginary." Substantial hard power remains corralled within the nation-state, and state-makers are reluctant to cede authority to international institutions even though states acting in isolation are demonstrably ill-suited to addressing problems of a transnational and global nature. Global power relations are undergoing a reordering; however, neither the deterritorialization of capital nor the resurgence of great power competition is so complete as to disqualify either the state or the capital as pivots for the analysis of global social change.

One outcome of this blurring of realist and constructivist modes of thought is the confirmation that there are many degrees of commensurability between very broad images of the world (Appadurai, 1996; Barkin 2010; Denzau and North 1994; Ghemawat 2014). The challenge for problem analysis in this chaotic age is to find ways to conceive, explain, and then tentatively propose how "global problématiques" might be addressed. Selecting Appadurai's flows of people, finance, and ideas and synthesizing these with Strange's structures of security, production, and knowledge, three axes of inquiry—law–security, finance–production, and people–knowledge (Figure 9.1)—are construed to illuminate complex connections between multiple and multilayered social, economic, political, and cultural patterns that, in the context of this chapter, render persons vulnerable to criminal and legal exploitation of their person and their labor.

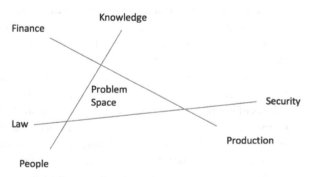

FIGURE 9.1 Axes of inquiry.

There could easily be further additions to this framework—for example, a gender–power axis to underscore the consequences of globalization for women and for transgender and intersex people. Yet, the operating codes of the global system, as it is currently configured, remain highly gendered, to the extent that gender–power relations affect social outcomes across all three axes. Although the notion of an axis might at first suggest linear framing, these intersecting lines of inquiry merely serve as a reference grid for the conception of a dynamic problem space, in which explanations of *the* problem can be assembled from a range of vantage points. Trafficked persons, for example, are caught between sovereign state institutions that prioritize state security, on the one hand, and international humanitarian and human rights laws that prioritize individual welfare, on the other hand. A person's life opportunities are shaped by her or his access to knowledge and finance, which in turn are shaped by the person's place within global–local production structures, with entrenched attitudes toward gender a defining factor. Illegal entry into a foreign country is therefore conceivably merely one step in a pattern of decisions and movements related, thickly or thinly, to unjust global distributions of opportunity and to the aggressive pursuit of power. The challenge here is not to focus on criminality or poverty, or power politics in isolation, but to examine their dynamic interrelationships; to test that is the explanatory strength of transdisciplinary global studies.

STATING THE PROBLEM: HUMAN TRAFFICKING AS HUMAN EXPLOITATION

The enslavement, in whatever form, of another human being is criminalized in international and national law through ratifications and accessions to the Convention Against Transnational Organized Crime, to which the "Protocol to Prevent, Suppress and Punish Trafficking in Persons" (hereafter "Trafficking Protocol" 2000) and the "Protocol Against the Smuggling of Migrants by Land, Sea and Air" (hereafter "Smuggling Protocol" 2000) are appended. At an operational level, trafficking and smuggling are treated as common elements of the crime of "modern-day slavery" (INTERPOL, 2016). In legal terms, trafficking is distinguished by the element of coercion for "the purpose of exploitation" to perform physical labor (Trafficking Protocol, 2000, Article 3a, p. 42). Trafficked persons are so, in objective legal terms, because they have been displaced and put to work against their will by dint of threats to their person or families, deception, or blackmail—or all three. The Trafficking Protocol is concerned with trafficking across international borders, but as discussed later, the definition given has much wider application. The Smuggling Protocol makes no reference to coercion in its objective definition, implying a degree of volition of the part of smuggled persons, but as with the Trafficking Protocol, it explicitly apportions criminal responsibility to those who facilitate illegal entry into a state (Smuggling Protocol 2000, Articles 5–6, pp. 55–56). This definitional distinction, however, raises questions of human agency and the degree of involuntariness that must be established in law for a person to be treated principally as a "victim" of trafficking or smuggling once he or she has passed border controls to become an illegal migrant worker.

The overwhelming purpose of both protocols is to focus international attention on the issue of human exploitation by transnational organized crime groups, but exploitative practices are perpetrated by more than just transnational criminals. Forced and unlawful movements of people can occur across but also within state borders. Temporary enslavement of laborers in the service of the state and the conscription of children into government or rebel armies are forms of trafficking that do not necessarily involve cross-border mobility (INTERPOL, 2016; Trafficking Protocol 2000, Article 3a, p. 42). The *scope* of human exploitation widens as new categories are added. The International Labor Organization (ILO) adopts a broad definition of trafficking, recast as forced labor, to include conditions in which workers are denied their legal entitlements to a fair wage, a safe working environment, and reasonable working hours (ILO 2015). Viewed critically, this broadening of terms extends the register of ILO responsibilities under its "decent work" agenda. Importantly, however, it also foregrounds the material connections between exploitation and social disadvantage, and it de-centers transnational crime in the analysis of causality. Refocusing thus, a conceptual shift in emphasis is permitted toward issues of global social justice, governance failure, and the coercive practices of legal commercial entities (ILO 2014a).

Research efforts have intensified, and research techniques have become more refined, with the consequence that estimates of the *scale* of human exploitation have been significantly revised up, from 2.4 million trafficked persons cited in the mid-2000s to 20.9 million persons working under conditions of forced labor in 2015 (ILO 2008, 2015). Illicit activity can never be comprehensively quantified. "The numbers" derive from extensive fieldwork but also from much deduction, and there are thus many opportunities for misinterpretation, sensationalist headlines, and misdirected moral crusades (Kessler 2015). Research specialists engaged by the ILO and the United Nations Office on Drugs and Crime (UNODC) acknowledge limitations but defend the integrity of their data on grounds of methodological rigor and collective expertise (ILO 2014b, 2015; UNODC 2010).

With these caveats in mind, the available data on human exploitation (as forced labor) reveal patterns that correspond at an intuitive and theoretical level with established models of global injustice. ILO statistics indicate that the largest concentrations of forced labor are in Asia and the Pacific[1] (11.7 million) and Africa (3.7 million) (ILO 2016).[2] UNODC data, as might be expected, are orientated more toward the transnational crime dimension of trafficking and smuggling, and because of this emphasis, they reflect the gendered nature of commercial sex work and domestic servitude, with 49% and 21% of trafficking victims globally being women and girls, respectively (UNODC 2014: 5). Unintentionally perhaps, the Trafficking Protocol, in listing sexual exploitation ahead of other forms of forced labor, strengthens the association between commercial sex work and human trafficking. The ILO's sampling captures the extent of forced labor in a broader range of industries, including agriculture, fisheries, and construction, in which men and boys are in the majority (ILO 2014a: 45–46, 2016). At issue here is not the savoriness or morality of occupation but, rather, the perpetuation of imbalances of power.

The factors that place people at *risk* of exploitation are both individual and systemic. Despite high rates of economic and population growth in Asia and Africa, significant pockets of extreme poverty persist, and extreme income inequalities within countries and across regions encourage licit and illicit flows of people in search of higher wages (ILO 2014a). In India, an emerging BRICS (Brazil, Russia, India, China, and South Africa) economy of 1.3 million people, depending on which estimates one trusts, between 20% and

30% of the population were living in absolute poverty in the first decade of the twenty-first century (World Bank, 2016). This in a country that is home to globally significant multinational conglomerates such as the Tata and Aditiya Birla groups. Disparities along the people–knowledge axis are stark, and they are startling compared to the developmental gains made by India's East Asian neighbors. Poverty is most prevalent in rural areas, where illiteracy rates are higher and social mobility is heavily constrained by distance (or remoteness) and caste. Economic hardships are compounded by the pressure of culturally defined social obligations that encourage the accumulation of unserviceable family debts. Deep structural irregularities persist due to governmental failure to properly regulate exploitative financial and employment practices, for which reasons debt bondage endures, however unlawfully, as an economic option for the poor (Kannan 2014; "Forced Labour in India" 2012; Knight 2012; Mehta 2016; Roy, Blomqvist, and Clark 2012: 158–159; World Bank 2016).

Returning to the law–security axis at a macro level of analysis, with major emphasis on security, global trafficking risk has increased in the early twenty-first century because of the seemingly "endless wars" that have engulfed Afghanistan, Iraq, Libya, and Syria in the Middle East and Colombia in Latin America (Bacevich 2016). National and subnational power struggles interleaved with regional and global interstate power politics have caused the displacement of millions. There were an estimated 64.5 million "forcibly displaced persons" worldwide in 2015: 21.3 million international refugees, 40.8 million conflict-affected internally displaced persons, 3.2 million asylum seekers, and a further 19.3 million persons displaced by natural disasters (United Nations High Commissioner for Refugees [UNHCR], 2016). Loci of forced displacement strongly correlate with loci of protracted conflict: Syria (11.6 million), Iraq (4.9 million), Afghanistan (4.4 million), the Democratic Republic of Congo (2.9 million), and Colombia (7.2 million) (UNHCR 2016). Insecurity has forced people to abandon homes and homelands and risk everything to seek social and economic opportunity in another country, leaving them prey to criminal exploitation. Traffickers charge asylum seekers between $4,000 and $6,000 for the opportunity to risk their lives and find refuge in Europe (Europol-INTERPOL 2016). The sheer scale of this disruption is unprecedented, and it was unanticipated by security planners who played a key role in spectacularly failed attempts to conclusively "resolve" conflict in the Middle East.

The risks of illicit migration are substantially borne by those who cross international borders illegally, not those who facilitate and profit from the people trade. For employers in licit industries, legal risk is evidently outweighed by potential economic gains, which suggests that irregularities within labor markets are as much a contributing factor to labor exploitation as criminal opportunism. Poverty is not necessarily the primary driver but, rather, relative economic opportunity. Millions of illegal economic migrants find their way across state borders by their own volition and by relatively simple means: on foot, by road, or by air. Relatively affluent women, meaning those who are not poor within their country of origin, often willingly submit to smuggling rings in the expectation of earning higher incomes abroad (Rao and Presenti 2012: 254–257; Grant 2014). Undocumented workers are exceptionally vulnerable to exploitation, primarily underpayment or non-payment of wages—a common form of financial crime—and because of their illegal status, they are beyond the protection of law unless they take the financially disastrous step of surrendering to authorities. The reality is that for people trafficked internationally and those forced to work in illegal conditions at home, in the initial stages of the procurement/recruitment process at least, an element of agency or market choice may be involved. All of this suggests that strategies to ameliorate trafficking risk must deal with the structural reasons for why people become inured to the circumstances of their exploitation.

PROBLEM RESPONSE

Modern mass population displacements highlight significant structural weaknesses in the evolving global system that governments in the developed and developing worlds are best placed, if reluctant, to tackle. The available statistical data on forced labor, displacement, inequality, and poverty serve as indices, if qualified, of systemic tolerance for abuse and suffering. It is common practice to apportion responsibility for the worst aspects of globalization, depending on one's political leanings, to a standard combination of factors: the failings of authoritarian leaders and corrupt institutions, the malicious operations of organized criminals and of course terrorists, the aggressive pursuit of commercial self-interest by transnational corporations, or the under- or over-regulation of financial markets and trade. Yet, the distorted framing of *the* problem at a global policy level is as much to blame.

Despite agreement on the socioeconomic dimensions of trafficking (and smuggling), the scope of governmental response is stunted by the prioritization of state security and the protection of state interests over human development. Heightened international attention to the subterranean machinations of terrorist organizations since the September 11, 2001, terrorist attacks has resulted in a skewing of official representation of the problem. Human trafficking is bracketed with a range of state security threats, inter alia, "piracy . . . illicit cross-border trafficking in arms . . . trafficking by non-State actors in nuclear, chemical and biological weapons, their means of delivery and related materials, trafficking in conflict minerals and the movement of terrorists and their funds" (Rice 2012: 1). Consequently, in official political discourse, response is framed primarily a law enforcement issue, with all forms of irregular human mobility inevitably, and explicitly, equated with transnational organized crime and terrorism (Zeldin 2016). This has obvious implications regarding the kinds of mitigation strategies in which states are prepared to invest (contrast with the approach set forth in Protocol P029, Protocol of 2014 to the Forced Labor Convention, 1930). Stricter national legal measures against trafficking and smuggling are necessary steps in curbing the global people trade, but an integrated global systemic approach is surely needed if the full spectrum of structural "disorders" that encourage human exploitation are to be treated to lasting effect.

The challenges or risks presented by irregular human mobility are multidimensional and multilayered. As stated previously, trafficking is construed and constructed as a crime against the state, an infringement of state sovereignty, and a violation of criminal law. Yet, *the* problem of human trafficking is as much a consequence of irregularities in the governance systems created to criminalize and penalize those caught in the complex webs of the global people trade as it is the illicit behaviors of transnational criminals (Lee 2011: 149). International protocols single out "victims" of crime for special legal protection against punishment, and yet in state-level immigration law and policy domains, in countries with immigration detention programs such as Australia, asylum seekers endure incarceration. People fleeing conflict undoubtedly avail themselves of transport services offered by trafficking and smuggling networks, but it could be argued that they are thus doubly entitled to humane treatment as victims of circumstance. Neither category of stranger is welcomed but instead condemned and conflated, through association, with trafficking criminals and with terrorists.

Without strong motives or incentives to disregard the rule of law, there would be no supply of trafficked or smuggled persons to foster and to feed illicit trade networks. In 2015, irregular migration into the European Union, principally from the Middle East, reached 1 million persons (Europol-INTERPOL 2016). This creates the short-term challenges of accommodating those fleeing conflict or persecution in accordance with international norms, preventing the deaths of refugees in transit, and generally re-establishing regulatory controls over the movement of people across state borders. The irony is that tighter, more effective border policing increases the premiums. Thinking divergently, stricter border controls might well enhance, not constrain, the people trafficker "business model," where no incentives are offered to people who would prefer to enter foreign countries by the front door. Transnational trafficking (and smuggling) networks are a last resort for persons fleeing conflicts not of their own making in the Middle East, Africa primarily, and Asia (Europol-INTERPOL 2016: 10). In other words, if there were alternative legal avenues sufficient to accommodate all persons seeking asylum in the world today, trafficking in persons across international borders might be a vastly more governable challenge. Logically, if there were more attractive legal employment options available to those disadvantaged by illiteracy (knowledge structure) and by their location within global supply chains (production structure), fewer people would be drawn into exploitative and criminal networks.

The fetishizing of border security and border protection exemplifies a paradox of globalization. States have reacted to increased global population flows by striving to consolidate territory and tighten regulation of cross-border movements. For a variety of practical and political reasons to do with geographical sensitivity, incongruent laws regarding irregular migration, and widely uneven levels of professional competence and resources between national police forces, many countries struggle to cooperate effectively to address irregular cross-border movements of people. Weak enforcement and limited regional cooperation open opportunities for traffickers to mobilize small-scale urban and rural assistance networks that enable the large-scale smuggling of persons. This systemic flaw was aptly and horribly illustrated by the discovery in southern Thailand of mass graves containing the remains of Rohingya asylum seekers who were murdered or allowed to perish from disease and neglect while inhumanely corralled in forest transit camps.[3] Allegations abound that Thai government officials, including police and military personnel, and nearby villagers colluded with traffickers to conceal the existence of the camps, and the graves, in return for financial rewards (Davis and Cronau 2015; Stoakes 2015). The Rohingya were there, illegally, arguably because there were no legal avenues for them to seek refuge in Thailand and no international obligation on the part of the Thai state to offer asylum.[4]

Thailand has the labor demand to temporarily absorb irregular migrants, for whom there are ample employment opportunities, as there are for millions of migrant workers from neighboring countries who reside in the country legally and illegally. The market for labor in lightly regulated economic sectors reveals the ugly side to human competitiveness and acquisitiveness. Thailand also has a poor record of protecting the rights of unskilled migrant workers who are routinely underpaid and forced to labor in poor conditions, with migrant women workers exploited substantially more than migrant men. Rohingya asylum seekers have also been coerced into working as virtual slave labor in Thailand's fishing industry (Errighi, Mamic, and Krogh-Poulsen 2016; Press 2016). Their plight exemplifies how a person's position on all three axes of inquiry pursued here influences her or his life options. As a people, the Rohingya are regarded as a security threat in Myanmar, where they are deliberately marginalized by the state. Stateless and powerless, they are at the mercy of those with the power to exploit them for private gain.

State securities are, as Barry Buzan (1983) notes, "complex" and deeply interrelated with issues of economic opportunity, law, and justice. Governance failures, or "gaps" in systems of governance, have major implications for the security of people and long-term implications for the security of states. Such gaps are bridgeable, and bridges—tentative, shaky, and fragile as they might be—can be built out of the social infrastructure of globalization that, for example, connects affluent consumers to exploited labor through the products they consume. People in democratic societies especially bear some responsibility for the actions of their governments that pursue military operations overseas and hence bear some responsibility for the human consequences of these operations. One of the most effective ways to limit mass irregular migrations, and hence the trafficking and smuggling of persons, is to curtail military adventurism by state and non-state actors alike (law–security axis); fast track sustainable economic development in regions of greatest economic need (production–finance axis); concentrate efforts to facilitate gender equity in social and economic outcomes (people–knowledge axis); and not abandon these critical issues to uncertain global market forces, particularly the global market for military power. The remedy to the "bads" of globalization is not the outright rejection of globalism but, rather, the reconfiguration of public and private responses to the opportunities and risks presented by global change. Unfortunately, political leadership is lacking here, and the list of indictments is long: appeasing reactionary public sentiment, encouraging public indifference to acts of unconscionable cruelty at home and abroad, fuelling or at best tolerating public hatred of irregular migrants, and failing to accept that increased human mobility as much as capital mobility is a part of the globalization that state policymakers have long embraced (Bauman 2016).

Whether viewed at a macro or a micro level, it is evident that the underlying causes of human exploitation are systemic. Opinion is divided between those who advocate a primary role for deregulated markets in promoting development and those who regard market dynamics as inherently regressive because they are weighted against those least equipped to compete. The Smuggling Protocol acknowledges that people are pushed to move by adverse "socio-economic circumstances" and enjoins signatory states to "combat" these drivers by addressing "poverty and underdevelopment" (Smuggling Protocol 2000, Article 15, 3, p. 62). Economic data on wealth distribution present compelling evidence that globally, inequality has been steadily rising for more than a quarter of a century in developed and developing countries (Anand and Segal 2015: 967–970; Piketty 2014). Looking to the finance–production axis of this analysis, from a macro perspective it can be argued that the neoliberal valorization of open, liberal markets as the most efficient way to allocate wealth has rendered the lives of people who are dependent on wage incomes more precarious (Ostry, Loungani, and Furceri 2016). Neoliberal models favor footloose investment and labor market flexibility, restrained only by the theoretical premise of natural equilibrium. Global tolerances for destruction and human exploitation, such as those touched upon here, suggest that the price of this equilibrium is unconscionably high.

Substantial declines in global poverty during the twentieth century are attributable to capitalist economic growth in East Asia, especially China, where state institutions have played a
decisive role. The logical conclusion to be drawn is that development strategies that are likely
to be most effective are those most appropriate to local conditions, including those where
the state plays the role of initiator and regulator and where liberal democracy might not be
prerequisite to the realization of basic needs (Rodrik 2011; Roy et al. 2012: 226–227). The absence of liberal democratic institutions, however, does not mean the absence of negotiation
and compromise; otherwise, how could a global system of national states produce extensive
international cooperation arrangements on matters of trade, security, finance, and sustainable development? Democratic ideas are clearly not universally adopted, and there are many
models of democracy, but this does not close off avenues for what John Dryzek (2010) terms
"deliberative governance" at the global level, even if public voice is often constrained at the
nation-state level, even in democracies, by varying degrees of censorship. Indeed, the theory
and practice of problem identification through deliberation suggest significant efficiency
dividends are realized through extensive consultation between technocrats and "lay persons"
(Lidskog 2000; Stevenson and Dryzek 2014). It is important to know who is being exploited,
where, how, and why, and this requires skilled investigation through open communication,
to the extent that people are at liberty to speak. Global coordination of localized responses
to the challenges outlined previously—through the cultivation of public awareness of labor
rights, promotion of social enterprises, and other forms of localized collective development
actions—can bring about positive social and economic results. Global governance is as much
about the exercise of leadership in the advancement of ideas, and especially in the cultivation
of "shared mental models" of global problématiques. The closure of gaps between divergent
images of globalization is inescapably part of the answer.

Conclusion

Global studies is a new transdisciplinary field of inquiry that accommodates the creative
exploration of ideas as an essential complement to rigorous analysis and critical interpretation. The problématique explored in this chapter is illustrated with structured data
interpreted through an adaptable, and adaptive, framework of inquiry. Statements of the
complexities of the chosen problem space are balanced with consideration of possible, and
plausible, responses. Two mental models of globalization are employed as framing devices
to capture the fluidity of global relations and the contingent reality of structures of power
and governance. This is one form of "*global* thinking," in which macro- and micro-level
concerns are discussed within a single problem space. The actions proposed might at first
appear straightforward because they give the impression of reducibility to simple matters of
economic justice and the pursuit of international cooperation. If answers or prescriptions
appear simple, their implementation is anything but. Global "orienteering" is justified by the
reality of multiple and complex interrelationships between contributing or causal factors
that spill across conventional policy and disciplinary domains. Patterns of power need to
be broken open to illuminate pathways toward the eventual elimination of human exploitation. Interventions to address all forms of forced migration require integrated strategies that
provide legal protection for trafficked persons and those seeking asylum. Instead, however,

the policy space for governing human exploitation is fragmented between agencies that deal with displaced persons, law enforcement, labor rights, and national security. The consequences of actions in an aberrant world are never certain, for which reason attempts to construct certainty or control outcomes will always generate unanticipated and unintended results. Actual and potential failures of governance, however, need to be considered against likely human costs of inaction and the reality that effective power to effect change in the lives of vulnerable people still resides in the hands of state institutions, imperfect as they are. There are imperatives to act to achieve generally accepted global priorities to end hunger, protect life, and preserve the planet. Yet, in all of this, there is a nagging concern that a critical piece of the jigsaw is missing.

Global integrity, so often read purely as legal compliance, can be usefully defined not as strict adherence to a set of rules but, rather, as openness to the possibility that we might be misguided. Mental models of the world can be rendered progressively more accurate through reflexive analysis, refined methodologies, and negotiated agreement on terms. Much valuable empirical research has been done on the factors that perpetuate disadvantage and injustice. New techniques of representation, be these indices of governance or peace, or matrices of environmental risk, offer finer-grained insights into the structures that impede or assist the cause of global justice. Agreement, then, through the development of "shared mental models" of global problématiques is prerequisite and possible. Perhaps too much faith is placed in the capacity of organizations to self-regulate, and to learn, and too little emphasis given to the deliberate exploitation of human weakness and human suffering by those who occupy positions of authority and trust. The abuse of power is widespread, and agreed rules regarding fundamental human rights, at least, need to be respected, internalized, and incorporated into practice. Otherwise, what value is there in calling for a more just global order and advocating the rule of law everywhere?

One watchword is "adaptability," and this chapter advances a tentative, creative–reflexive mode of problem orientation that is highly adaptable, sufficient to grapple with the unpredictability of globalization and to accommodate the role of power in human affairs. It is inspired by models of creative problem-solving that embrace divergent thinking as a necessary corollary to convergent problem definition. It questions linear "flow charts" of global change and rigid bureaucratic models of control without avoiding responsibility for offering prescriptive guidelines. It is possible to engineer what Luhmann (2008; 233) terms "preadaptive advances" in the means of governance by constructing appropriate legal and institutional infrastructures in an imaginative transnational space mapped out using the kind of divergent axial analysis proposed here. Policymakers can choose to become tuned in to such transdisciplinary methodologies or otherwise remain "tone deaf" to unfamiliar, alternative sources of insight and knowledge (Rodrik 2011: 83).

NOTES

1. Regional estimate includes forced labor in Central Asia.
2. Estimates are for 2012 and based on data collected during a ten-year period from 2001 to 2011. See International Labour Organization (2012, c. 2016).
3. The Rohingya are a Muslim minority people who inhabit Rakhine State, northwestern Myanmar, where separatist insurgencies with Islamist overtones have flared periodically since Myanmar's independence from Britain in 1948. A resurgence in violence beginning

in late 2012 drove Rohingya from their homes, with many hundreds of thousands seeking asylum in neighboring countries (Gangully 2016; International Crisis Group 2016; Parnini, Othman, and Ghazali 2013).

4. Thailand, like most Association of Southeast Asian Nations (ASEAN) countries, is not a signatory to the 1951 Refugee Convention.

REFERENCES

Anand, S., and P. Segal. 2015. "The Global Distribution of Income." In *Handbook of Income Distribution*, edited by A. B. Atkinson and F. Bourguignon, Vol. 2A, 937–979. Amsterdam: Elsevier. http://www.economics.ox.ac.uk/materials/papers/13376/anand-segal-handbook-pdf-mar15.pdf.

Appadurai, A. 1996. *Modernity at Large: Cultural Dimensions of Globalization*. Minneapolis: University of Minnesota Press.

Bacchi, C. 2009. *Analysing Policy: What's the Problem Represented to Be?* Frenchs Forest, New South Wales, Australia: Pearson.

Bacevich, A. J. 2016. "Ending Endless War: A Pragmatic Military Strategy." *Foreign Affairs* 95 (5): 36–44.

Barkin, J. S. 2010. *Realist Constructivism: Rethinking International Relations Theory*. Cambridge: Cambridge University Press.

Bauman, Z. 2016. *Strangers at Our Door*. Cambridge, UK: Polity.

Beck, U. 1999. *World Risk Society*. Cambridge, UK: Polity.

Bernstein, J. H. 2015. "Transdisciplinarity: A Review of Its Origins, Development, and Current Issues." *Journal of Research Practice* 11 (1): Article R1. http://jrp.icaap.org/index.php/jrp/article/view/510/412. Accessed June 26, 2016.

Blair, D. 2016. "Why the Middle East Might Just Be a Problem That Can't Be Solved—Least of All by Arab Dictators." *Telegraph*, February 16. http://www.telegraph.co.uk/news/worldnews/middleeast/12160391/The-Middle-East-might-just-be-a-problem-that-cant-be-solved-least-of-all-by-Arab-dictators.html. Accessed August 8, 2016.

Buzan, B. 1983. *People, States and Fear: The National Security Question in International Relations*. London: Wheatsheaf.

Darian-Smith, E., and P. McCarty. 2016. "Beyond Disciplinarity: Developing and Global Transdisciplinary Framework." *Transcience* 7 (2): 1–26.

Davis, M., and P. Cronau. 2015. "Migrant Crisis: Rohingya Refugees Buried in Mass Graves Near Thailand Authorities, Survivor Says." http://www.abc.net.au/news/2015-06-22/rohingyas-secret-graves-of-asias-forgotten-refugees/6561896 Accessed October 21, 2016.

Dean, M. 1998. "Risk, Calculable and Incalculable." *Soziale Welt* 49 (1): 25–42.

Denzau, A. T., and D. C. North. 1994. "Shared Mental Models: Ideologies and Institutions." *Kyklos* 47: 3–31.

Denzau, A. T., R. K. Roy, and H. P. Minassians. 2016. "Learning to Cooperate: Applying Deming's 'New Economics' and Denzau and North's 'New Institutional Economics' to Improve Inter-organizational Systems Thinking and Performance." *Kyklos* 69 (3): 471–491.

Dryzek, J. 2010. *Foundations and Frontiers of Deliberative Governance*. Oxford, UK: Oxford University Press.

Errighi, L., I. Mamic, and B. Krogh-Poulsen. 2016. *Global supply chains: Insights into the Thai seafood sector*. Bangkok: ILO. http://www.ilo.org/public/libdoc/ilo/2016/490688.pdf Accessed December 26, 2016.

Europol-INTERPOL. 2016. "Migrant Smuggling Networks: Joint Europol-INTERPOL Report" (Executive Summary). http://www.interpol.int/News-and-media/News/2016/ N2016-062. Accessed May 26, 2016.

Feyerabend, P. 1991. *Against Method*. 2nd ed. London: New Left Books.

Fischer, A., S. Greiff, and J. Funke. 2012. "The Process of Solving Complex Problems." *Journal of Problem Solving* 4, no. 1 (Winter): 19–42. doi:10.7771/1932-6246.1118

"Forced Labour in India: Toil and Trouble." 2012. *Economist*, November 3. http://www.economist.com/news/asia/21565685-where-slavery-persists-all-name-toil-and-trouble. Accessed November 30, 2016.

Fromkin, D. 1989. *A Peace to End All Peace: The Fall of the Ottoman Empire and the Creation of the Modern Middle East*. New York: Holt.

Gangully, M. 2016. "Bangladesh Should Accept, Protect Rohingya Refugees." *Dispatches*. Human Rights Watch, November 23. https://www.hrw.org/news/2016/11/23/bangladesh-should-accept-protect-rohingya-refugees. Accessed January 4, 2017.

Ghemawat, P. 2014. "Global Problem Solving Without the Globaloney." *Stanford Social Innovation Review*, Fall.

Giddens, A. 1990. *The Consequences of Modernity*. Stanford. CA: Stanford University Press.

Grant, M. G. 2014. "The Price of a Sex-Slave Rescue Fantasy." *New York Times*, May 29. https://www.nytimes.com/2014/05/30/opinion/the-price-of-a-sex-slave-rescue-fantasy.html?_r=0. Accessed December 28, 2016

International Crisis Group. 2016. "Myanmar: A New Muslim Insurgency in Rakhine State." Asia Report no. 283, December 15. https://d2071andvipowj.cloudfront.net/283-myanmar-a-new-muslim-insurgency-in-rakhine-state.pdf. Accessed December 16, 2016.

International Labour Organization. 2008. "ILO Action Against Trafficking in Human Beings." http://www.ilo.org/wcmsp5/groups/public/@ed_norm/@declaration/documents/publication/wcms_090356.pdf. Accessed October 4, 2016.

International Labour Organization. 2012. "ILO Global Estimate of Forced Labor: Results and Methodology." http://www.ilo.org/wcmsp5/groups/public/---ed_norm/---declaration/ documents/publication/wcms_182004.pdf. Accessed December 29, 2016.

International Labour Organization. 2014a. *Profits and Poverty: The Economics of Forced Labour*. Geneva: International Labour Office.

International Labour Organization. 2014b. "Protocol of 2014 to the Forced Labour Convention of 1930." http://www.ilo.org/wcmsp5/groups/public/---ed_norm/---declaration/documents/ publication/wcms_321414.pdf. Accessed December 29, 2016.

International Labour Organization. 2015. "ILO Expert Workshop on Measuring Modern Slavery: Geneva, 27–28 April 2015." http://www.ilo.org/wcmsp5/groups/public/---ed_norm/ ---declaration/documents/meetingdocument/wcms_390001.pdf. Accessed October 4, 2016.

International Labour Organization. c. 2016. "Statistics on Forced Labour, Modern Slavery and Human Trafficking." http://www.ilo.org/global/topics/forced-labour/policy-areas/statistics/lang--en/index.htm. Accessed December 31, 2016.

INTERPOL. 2016. "Trafficking in Human Beings." https://www.interpol.int/Crime-areas/ Trafficking-in-human-beings/Trafficking-in-human-beings. Accessed November 29, 2016.

Kannan, K. P. 2014. *Interrogating Inclusive Growth: Poverty and Inequality in India*. New Delhi: Routledge.

Kessler, G. 2015. "The False Claim That Human Trafficking Is a '$9.5 billion business' in the United States." *Washington Post*, June 2. https://www.washingtonpost.com/news/

fact-checker/wp/2015/06/02/the-false-claim-that-child-sex-trafficking-is-a-9-5-billion-business-in-the-united-states. Accessed October 27, 2016.

Knight, S. 2012. "Debt-Bondage Slavery in India." *Global Dialogue* (Online) 14 (2): 62–72.

Koppman, S., C. L. Cain, and E. Leahey. 2015. "The Joy of Science: Disciplinary Diversity in Emotional Accounts." *Science, Technology, & Human Values* 40 (11): 30–70. doi:10.1177/0162243914537527

Lawrence, R. J. 2010. "Beyond Disciplinary Confinement to Imaginative Transdisciplinarity." In *Tackling Wicked Problems Through the Transdisciplinary Imagination*, edited by V. Brown, J. A. Harris, and J. Y. Russell, J Y, 16–30. London: Earthscan.

Lee, M. 2011. *Trafficking and Global Crime Control*. London: Sage.

Lindblom, C. E. 1959. "The Science of Muddling Through." *Public Administration Review* 19 (2): 79–88.

Luhmann, N. 2008. *Law as a Social System*, translated by K. A. Zeigert. Oxford, UK: Oxford University Press.

Luhmann, N. 2013. *Introduction to Systems Theory*, translated by P. Gilgen. Cambridge, UK: Polity.

McEvoy, S. P., M. R. Stevenson, A. T. McCartt, M. Woodward, C. Haworth, P. Palamara, and R. Cercarell. 2005. "Role of Mobile Phones in Motor Vehicle Crashes Resulting in Hospital Attendance: A Case-Crossover Study," *British Medical Journal*, July 12. doi:10.1136/bmj.38537.397512.55

Mehta, M. N. 2016. "Weddings Condemn India's Poorest to Penury." *Hindustan Times*, August. http://www.hindustantimes.com/analysis/weddings-condemn-india-s-poorest-to-penury/story-NiEPbMONCdI8K5vy2eyshM.html. Accessed December 14, 2016.

Press, B. 2016. "The Social Inclusion and Exclusion of Migrants in Thailand." In *Permanently Temporary: Examining the Impact of Social Exclusion on Mekong Migrants*, edited by Mekong Migration Network. http://www.mekongmigration.org/wp-content/uploads/2016/10/Permanently-Temporary-Eng-mmn-printed-version.pdf. Accessed December 29, 2016.

National Highway Traffic Safety Administration. 2016. "Traffic Safety Facts: Distracted Driving 2014." US Department of Transportation report no. DOT HS 812 260. https://crashstats.nhtsa.dot.gov/Api/Public/ViewPublication/812260. Accessed November 16, 2016.

New South Wales Government. 2013. "Behavioural Risk Factors in NSW Crashes and Casualties, 2000–2012." http://roadsafety.transport.nsw.gov.au/downloads/behavioural-risk-factors.112013.pdf. Accessed August 8, 2016.

Osborn, A. F. 1957. *Applied Imagination: Principles and Procedures of Creative Writing*. New York: Scribner's.

Ostry, J. D., L. Loungani, and D. Furceri. 2016. "Neoliberalism Oversold?" *Finance and Development*, June: 38–39. http://www.imf.org/external/pubs/ft/fandd/2016/06/ostry.htm. Accessed July 29, 2016.

Parnini, S. N., M. R. Othman, and A. S. Ghazali. 2013. "The Rohingya Refugee Crisis and Bangladesh–Myanmar Relations." *Asian Pacific Migration Journal* 72 (1): 133–146.

Piketty, T. 2014. *Capital in the Twenty-First Century*. Cambridge, MA: Harvard University Press.

"Protocol Against the Smuggling of Migrants by Land, Sea and Air, Supplementing the United Nations Convention Against Transnational Organized Crime." 2000. United Nations, *Treaty Series*, vol. 2241, p. 507; Doc. A/55/383. Entered into force: January 2004. https://treaties.un.org/Pages/ViewDetails.aspx?src=TREATY&mtdsg_no=XVIII-12-b&chapter=18&clang=_en. Accessed December 2, 2016.

"Protocol P029—Protocol of 2014 to the Forced Labour Convention, 1930." Entered into force: November 9, 2016. International Labour Organization, Geneva, 103rd ILC session (June 11, 2014. http://www.ilo.org/dyn/normlex/en/f?p=NORMLEXPUB:12100:0::NO ::P12100_ILO_CODE:P029 Accessed December 15, 2016.

"Protocol to Prevent, Suppress and Punish Trafficking in Persons, Especially Women and Children, Supplementing the United Nations Convention Against Transnational Organized Crime." 2000. United Nations, *Treaty Series*, vol. 2237, p. 319; Doc. A/55/383. Entered into force December 25, 2003. https://treaties.un.org/Pages/ViewDetails.aspx?src=TREATY&mtdsg_no=XVIII-12-a&chapter=18&clang=_en. Accessed December 2, 2016.

Rao, S., and C. Presenti. 2012. "Understanding Human Trafficking Origin: A Cross-Country Empirical Analysis." *Feminist Economics* 18 (2): 231–263.

Rice, S. 2012. "Statement by the President of the Security Council." United Nations Security Council, S/PRST/2012/16, April 25. http://www.securitycouncilreport.org/atf/cf/ %7B65BFCF9B-6D27-4E9C-8CD3-CF6E4FF96FF9%7D/IPS%20S%202012%2016.pdf. Accessed May 16, 2016.

Rodrik, D. 2011. *The Globalization Paradox: Democracy and the Future of the World Economy.* New York: Norton.

Roy, K.C., H. C. Blomqvist, and C. Clark. 2012. *Economic Development in China, India and East Asia: Managing Change in the Twenty First Century.* Cheltenham, UK: Elgar.

Schumacher, L. R. 2014. "The Eastern Question as a Europe Question: Viewing the Ascent of 'Europe' Through the Lens of Ottoman Decline." *Journal of European Studies* 44 (1): 64–80.

Sil, R., and P. J. Katzenstein. 2010. *Beyond Paradigms: Analytic Eclecticism in the Study of World Politics.* Houndmills, UK: Palgrave Macmillan.

Solomon, R. 2015. "Why Australia's Speed Fixation Won't Lower the Road Toll." ABC Radio National, "Ockham's Razor." October. http://www.abc.net.au/radionational/programs/ ockhamsrazor/why-speed-isn't-the-only-factor-in-the-road-toll/6831300 Accessed August 6, 2016.

Steger, M. B. 2008. *The Rise of the Global Imaginary: Political Ideologies from the French Revolution to the Global War on Terror.* Oxford, UK: Oxford University Press.

Steger, M. B., and A. Wahlrab. 2016. *What Is Global Studies? Theory and Practice.* London: Routledge.

Stevenson, H., and J. Dryzek. 2014. *Democratizing Global Climate Governance.* Cambridge, UK: Cambridge University Press.

Stoakes, E. 2015. "Thailand Human Trafficking Death Toll Far Greater Than Feared, Claims Rights Group." *Guardian*, May 6. https://www.theguardian.com/global-development/ 2015/may/06/thailand-human-trafficking-mass-grave-burma-rohingya-people. Accessed September 29, 2016.

Strange, S. 1994. *States and Markets.* 2nd ed. London: Continuum.

Treffinger, D. J., Schoonover, P. F., and Selby, E. C. 2013. *Educating for Creativity and Innovation: A Comprehensive Guide for Research-Based Practice.* Waco, TX: Prufrock Press.

United Nations High Commissioner for Refugees. 2016. "UNHCR Global Trends: Forced Displacement in 2015." http://www.unhcr.org/en-us/statistics/unhcrstats/576408cd7/ unhcr-global-trends-2015.html. Accessed December 2, 2016.

United Nations Office of Drugs and Crime. 2014. "Global Report on Trafficking in Persons 2014." http://www.unodc.org/documents/data-and-analysis/glotip/GLOTIP_2014_full_report.pdf. Accessed June 18, 2015.

(UNODC) United Nations Office of Drugs and Crime. 2010. *Global Report on Trafficking in Persons 2014*. Vienna: UNODC. http://www.unodc.org/documents/data-and-analysis/glotip/GLOTIP_2014_full_report.pdf Accessed June 18, 2015.

World Bank. 2016. "India's Poverty Profile." http://www.worldbank.org/en/news/infographic/2016/05/27/india-s-poverty-profile. Accessed October 28, 2016.

Zeldin, W. 2016. "Turkey: People Smuggling to Be Declared a Terrorist Act." *Global Legal Monitor*, March 9. http://www.loc.gov/law/foreign-news/article/turkey-people-smuggling-to-be-classified-as-terrorist act. Accessed December 17, 2016.

CHAPTER 10

··

WORLDVIEW ANALYSIS

··

MONA KANWAL SHEIKH

THIS chapter discusses the concept of worldview and how it is relevant for the field of global studies. Although the study of worldviews is relevant to a wide range of phenomena related to global studies, it is particularly relevant to understanding communities of activists who hold transnational worldviews, such as those who commit violent acts justified with reference to religious traditions. Adding to this, the study of worldviews requires the transdiciplinary approach that a global studies framework can offer.

Since 2001, when New York and Washington, DC, were struck by horrifying acts of terrorism, it has become a mainstream political reaction in the West to dehumanize the perpetrators and describe them as being devoid of any sort of legitimation because they defy authorities within a nation-state paradigm. Although all acts of terrorism are condemnable, the moral denouncement should not stand in the way of enhancing better analysis of why people embrace such acts of violence and how they see their actions legitimized by transnational worldviews. A global studies framework can stimulate thinking in a direction that gets us closer to an understanding of the significance of *the transnational*. From an authoritative nation-state viewpoint, political opponents and terrorists may be seen as pure evil, devoid of any perspective worth trying to understand. The problem with this position is that by ignoring the alternate transnational worldview of these actors, important insights may be overlooked that can point toward ways of de-escalating conflicts and reducing violence—insights about the lenses through which perpetrators of violence view the world. In the field of conflict analysis, there is an increasing focus on the role of narratives as more than mere strategic assets of the conflicting parties. A main contention in the literature that deals with the escalation and de-escalation of conflicts is that one of the tools to avoid escalation is precisely to avoid playing into the conflict imagery by which the opposing party is driven. If, for instance, Islamists perceive secularism as a threat and connect secular ideologies to images of oppression, imperialism, and dictatorship, then it seems counterproductive to suggest secularism as the solution to violent manifestations of Islamism—as was the proposal in American think tank reports immediately after the September 9, 2001, terrorist attacks. Another illustrative example is the way events unfolded during the 1993 Waco, Texas, siege, in which the FBI established contact with the leader of the Branch Davidian sect, David Koresh. Although negotiations took place over many days, the outcome was tragic because the FBI did not have the proper tools to de-escalate a situation in which Koresh was seemingly playing out an interpretation of biblical imagery.

Surveys of militant actors affiliated with different religious traditions show that whether we are talking about the ongoing suicide bombings of the Pakistani Taliban, the attacks by extremist Jews or Christians in the 1990s in Israel and the United States, or the series of more recent attacks on Muslims carried out by militant monks in South and Southeast Asia or the Islamic State movement, they all justify their acts through particular religious understandings of social reality. These religious understandings are by their nature trans-national, and they provide alternative views of the world and bases for the legitimation of actions that are not permitted in the standard nation-state paradigms.

The literature analyzing the utterances and communication materials of violent activists from different religious traditions shows that they interpret events not according to secular national points of view but, rather, according to religious imagery; likewise, they defend their political activities with reference not to secular law but to religious principles and precepts (Jerryson 2011; Juergensmeyer 2003; Mahmood 1997; Marty and Appleby 2004, 1995; Sheikh 2016). This adds a transnational dimension to their actions and ascribes a spiritual significance to their struggle. At the same time, however, violent activists also in-terpret their religious purposes and self-understandings according to their particular social and political settings. To scrutinize how these different purposes and principles become entangled, ending up reinforcing and feeding into each other, is, as I will show, one of the principal aims of worldview analysis.

Particularly within global studies (Juergensmeyer 2003; Wilson 2012) and the interdisci-plinary field of terrorism studies, there have been attempts to understand how the prolifera-tion of violence is linked to the dispersion of ideas, including myths and religious doctrines (McCoy and Knight 2015; Rowland and Theye 2008). These analyses have often been ac-cused of being too simplistic, upholding a one-way relationship between the reservoir of ideas, myths, and doctrines on one side and action on the other. This chapter addresses some of the methodological fallacies linked to causality claims because worldview analysis views those ideas and doctrines in a wider cultural context, as part of a worldview that does not "cause" actions but provides a framework of legitimation for them. Still, the discussion on how worldviews matter is relevant for larger debates that are not only about violent be-havior but also about the dynamics between mind, values, ideas, and ideology, on the one hand, and human behavior, on the other hand.

Although the examples in this chapter focus on religious violence, as was mentioned at the outset of the chapter, the applicability of worldview analysis is much broader and is relevant to a broad range of phenomena in global studies and in the social sciences more generally. Furthermore, worldview analysis is relevant to a wide range of national and trans-national worldviews, not just those related to religious traditions. Hence, it is an entry point for understanding diverse views of the world.

This chapter first reviews the most dominant definitions and applications of the world-view concept as it has been used in the study of global phenomena in the social sciences, and it discusses how they differ from the way the concept of ideology is applied. Second, it critically discusses the link between worldview and behavior. Finally, it focuses on the methods to study worldviews and the epistemological assumptions that enable the study of worldviews through the analysis of speech and narratives.

WHAT IS A WORLDVIEW?

The term *worldview* is derived from the German word *Weltanschauung*—a concept originally coined by the German philosopher Immanuel Kant (1790/1952) in his work *Critique of Judgment*. The term was introduced in a classical Kantian passage emphasizing the human mind's ability to make sense of the infinite character of the world:

> If the human mind is nonetheless to be able to think the given infinite without contradiction, it must have within itself a power that is supersensible, whose idea of the noumenon cannot be intuited but can yet be regarded as the substrate underlying what is mere appearance, namely, our intuition of the world [Weltanschaaung]. (p. 111)

The word, used first by Kant and later popularized by Georg Wilhelm Friedrich Hegel, is used to broadly to refer to philosophies of life, holistic ideologies, and cultural or religious perspectives.

Kant introduced the concept of *Weltanschauung*, composed of *Welt* (world) and *Anschauung* (view or outlook), to describe the human ability to create order in a complex world that is full of infinite possibilities for perception. For Kant, a worldview was hence a comprehensive vision that enables human beings to see and experience and come to term with the world (Kant 1952: 111).

Kant's philosophical understanding of worldview has been applied in an empirical sense by contemporary psychologists who translate worldviews to cognitive schemata—tools that enable us to come to terms with the multifaceted character of the world by reducing the complexity of experience (Beck 1979: 12–13; DiMaggio 2003: 265; Fiske and Linville 1980: 544; Hastie 1981; Janoff-Bulman 1989: 115; Koltko-Rivera 2004: 25). However, the concept of schemata is designed for its empirical application to the cognitive processing of events, objects, and situations, whereas worldview remains a more abstract concept with hypothetical objects (Koltko-Rivera 2004: 26).

In sociology, Max Weber, one of the founding fathers of the field, was the most influential "practitioner" of the concept of worldview. For Weber, worldviews were central elements of empirical investigation and explanation, and in his studies he demonstrated the value of applying worldview analysis in social sciences. Weber's claim about the pre-eminence of Calvinism and a Protestant ethic in the development of capitalism stands out as the most famous example (Weber 1905/2000). His preoccupation with religious worldviews in general and particularly the religious societies of India and China reflected the connection he saw between social action and the outlook of religious traditions.

Although the concept of worldview has traveled across different academic disciplines and been subjected to numerous definitions, there are two major approaches in the literature that deals with worldviews. The first adapts worldviews within a cognitive framework and is primarily interested in how people develop shared worldviews as cognitive structure, which they apply to make sense of and come to terms with the world (Cobern 1996; Janoff-Bulman 1989; Johnson, Hill, and Cohen 2011; Kearney 1984). The second approach is more interested in the sociopolitical consequences of developing and sharing assumptions about social reality and is often taken on by social constructivists (Johnson et al. 2011; Koltko-Rivera 2004; Overton 1991; Redfield 1952; Rowland and Theye 2008; Wolman 1973).

More than representing entirely distinct understandings of worldviews, these trends delineate a difference in how worldviews are applied with respect to varying scientific aims. In the cognitive approach, worldview analysis is aimed at studying differences in behavior, anticipated behavior, and attitudes. It stems from a natural science perspective or model seeking to predict, control, and alter behavior. The cognitive approaches are a direct adaption of Kant's definition of worldviews as a meaning-making device that shapes perception and cognition and that enables people to come to terms with the world (Hiebert 2008; Janoff-Bulman 1989; Johnson et al. 2011). In this approach, worldviews are relevant as a *human ability* to create order, meaning, and value in a chaotic world.

The social constructivist way of adapting the worldview concept represents another angle on why worldviews matter: Here, worldviews are relevant as *narratives* that explain a person's place in the world, identify adversaries, and link the person to a purpose—worldly or transcendent (J. A. Edwards 2014; Røislien 2007; Rowland and Theye 2008). This approach is more interested in the way worldviews influence, shape, and explain behavior, processes, and outcomes and the way they become contested or remain uncontested—that is, whether they are the subject of conflict or the subject of consensus.

Within the social constructivist approach, a worldview is often divided into two parts— one that defines what *is* and one that defines what *ought* to be (Johnson et al. 2011: 37; Koltko-Rivera 2004: 4). This makes worldviews both ontological and normative. Goldstein and Keohane note that propositions about the world consist of so-called *principled beliefs* that refer to the ideas people hold of what is good and bad, right and wrong, and just and unjust; as well as *causal beliefs* that represent road maps people use to attain goals and realize objectives (Goldstein and Keohane 1993: 9–10; see also Bottici and Challand 2010: 321; Rowland and Theye 2008: 58). At the same time, they point out that beliefs have to be accepted as authoritative by the leaders of movements, groups, or nations in order to be powerful.

Rowland and Theye (2008: 56), who particularly examine religious or mythic worldviews, define these as part of the epistemic genre that explains a person's place in the world, identifies a villain to be fought, and links the individual to a transcendent purpose that can be achieved through violence. For social scientists, this conceptualization is useful because it outlines the structure of a worldview consisting of particular perceptions and action-directions. This understanding is congruent with what Mark Juergensmeyer and I described in 2013 as an *epistemic worldview*—a concept that draws on Michel Foucault's concept of episteme, the structure of knowledge that is the basis of an understanding of how reality works, and Pierre Bourdieu's notion of habitus, the social location of shared understandings about the world and how it should work. Whereas the concept of episteme is related to broader trends in culture, a worldview is often applied narrowly to the outlook of individuals or social groups—and it is exactly the dynamics between these levels that are interesting. The concept of habitus is relevant in this context because it represents the same sort of fusion between inside and outside factors that is important for worldview analysis: It refers to a framework in which individual actors experience, think, and act, and it creates linkages between social setting and ideas (Bourdieu 2004).

In many ways, the term worldview resembles the concept of ideology, and the two words are often used interchangeably. Although there are clearly overlaps in the way many scholars understand these two concepts, ideology is often defined in a more narrow way as a group's shared *social–political orientation* (Bell 1960; Mannheim and Wirth 1936) and, hence, applied primarily as a political concept. For instance, Mannheim and Wirth argue that ideology is the whole outlook of a social group—"its total Weltanschauung," which is conditioned by its position in history (p. 193). Ideology typically refers to well-established political ideas, reflected in different governments and political movements, but also draws on the influence that Karl Marx has had on the very idea of ideology. The concept of ideology is still heavily influenced by the way it was introduced in Marxist literature—as an expression of material interests and power (Althusser 2001; Mannheim and Wirth 1936; Marx 1872). It is often applied as a theoretical concept that is identical to Marx's conception of ideology—that is, as a "distorted vision of reality" or superstructure that conceals the true nature of things and makes people perceive things that are not in accordance with objective reality. In this usage, ideology is an illusion or fiction, a false consciousness that renders people incapable of coming to terms with capitalist organization and thus leads to alienation (Marx 1872). This usage actually makes ideology irrelevant in itself or relevant only as a rhetorical tool to enhance matters that are viewed as being "more real." Thus, the concept of ideology is often applied in literature that is in search of underlying truths behind what people say—that is, their real intentions, which are often condensed to being a matter of maintaining and gaining power or privilege. The Marxist interpretation of religion as a drug that prevents people from acknowledging their social conditions still haunts current approaches to religion and ideology; this interpretation strips religion of any importance in itself. This has especially been true of political science and international relations, in which ideology and religion have often been viewed in instrumental terms (Thomas 2005).

The discursive trends that characterize the study of ideology in the social sciences reflect an inclination toward the mere reading of canonical texts (of movements, political parties, ideologues, etc.) for the purpose of cataloguing their ideas. Methodologically speaking, there is hence a tendency of privileging text over practice and definitional claims over empirical evidence. As such, studies of ideology reflect an anthropological and sociological deficit by excluding analyses of practices from textual reading and a hermeneutical deficit by excluding various existing interpretations (Crone, Gad, and Sheikh 2008).

By contrast, worldview analysis should represent a much broader outlook that bears the potential to incorporate an insider-oriented attempt to understand the reality of a particular worldview: its social, ethical, political, and spiritual aspects and how they come together into a coherent whole (Juergensmeyer and Sheikh 2013). Such analysis is concerned with the worldviews of those who articulate them and is hence close to the methodologies dominant within the fields of ethnography and anthropology. In this usage, "world view refers to the way the world looks [to] people looking out" (Redfield 1952: 30).

In summary, a promising set of discursive practices have developed around the application of worldviews that are observant of the reasoning and narrative of the study object, as well as the social setting that conditions it. In contrast to how ideology is often studied, the guiding idea in worldview analysis is not to verify or falsify the ideas people hold but, rather, to bring them to the fore. The goal is to understand the subjects' own propositions about reality. What matters are the concepts they use, the categories they invoke, the imagery they paint, and the systems of representation that are part of their overall narratives.

LINKING WORLDVIEWS TO BEHAVIOR

Different academic disciplines have developed their own reasons for engaging with worldviews. In sociology, as already explained, this kind of analysis gained a central position due to the way Max Weber integrated both theological ideas and social theory in his studies of religion and society in India and China and also in developing his understanding of the link between Protestant ethics and capitalism. Also, thinkers such as Robert Bellah and Peter Berger have integrated theological points of view into their sociological analyses, and social thinkers such as Pierre Bourdieu and Anthony Giddens have acknowledged the social relevance of viewpoints from within religious traditions.

Social psychologists focus on worldviews in order to study how human beings encounter the world. They apply worldview analysis to study the formation of collective attitudes and the way different communities relate to one another (Goplen and Plant 2015; Greenberg, Solomon, and Pyszczynski 1997; Johnson et al. 2011; Koltko-Rivera 2004; Major et al. 2007; McGregor et al. 2001). The goal of the inquiry is often to understand the mechanisms through which people develop prejudice, engage in processes of othering, and deploy strategies to uphold their subjective beliefs when facing threats from competing worldviews.

Anthropologists focus on worldviews to describe and compare certain ways of life (Hiebert 2008; Redfield 1952; Sapir 1949). They use worldview analysis to examine how groups acquire their most fundamental values and ideas of the good life and how they develop different customs and institutions. Compared to social psychologists, anthropologists focus less on the cognitive and perceptive dimensions of worldviews and more on the affective and moral dimensions (Hiebert 2008: 15). Anthropologists have by disciplinary habit been more disposed to take other people's perspectives seriously, and thus they have accommodated religious points of view more easily. This has been true of well-known anthropologists such as Clifford Geertz, Louis Dumont, Mary Douglas, Stanley Tambiah, and Talal Asad.

In political science, the interest in worldviews primarily reflects an interest in how ideas and beliefs condition particular political outcomes and action (Blyth 1997; Bottici and Challand 2010; Goldstein and Keohane 1993; Røislien 2007; Rowland and Theye 2008). These include the use of overt physical force, violence, or annihilation. Political science has been much influenced by the Marxist way of approaching ideology and religion, and combined with the influence of the modernization narrative that created the dichotomy between religion and real science, it has only recently begun to take seriously the question of how religion matters for the field (Fox 2006; Fox and Sandler 2004; Hurd 2007a; Lynch 2000; Petito and Hatzopoulos 2003; Philpott 2002; Sheikh 2012; Thomas 2005).

For social sciences and global studies in general, the relevance of studying worldviews also lies in their connection to action (Johnson et al. 2011; Koltko-Rivera 2004: 23). Worldviews matter inasmuch as they have an impact on human action or because they can justify certain acts. In order for worldview analysis to be a useful tool in social sciences that can open up insights relevant to questions of escalation and de-escalation of conflicts (as mentioned at the beginning of this chapter), it needs to abstain from the simple causality questions that create straight lines from A (worldviews) to B (violence). Instead, the focus on the "how" question is far more interesting, such as how the perpetrators viewed the world in a way that would allow violent actions to be carried out. The goal is to understand the subject's framework for thinking about reality and acting appropriately within a perceived understanding of the world (Juergensmeyer and Sheikh 2013).

There are three important traps to avoid when conducting worldview analysis. The first is the assumption that behavior is *only* determined by worldviews. The second is the proposition that worldviews actually determine action and hence come before an action. The third is an essentialist and static concept of worldviews that is detached both from those who hold the views and from the interaction with a social world.

Samuel P. Huntington's (1993, 1996) well-known clash of civilizations thesis represents many of these fallacies. For Huntington, global politics is about the politics of civilizations, and worldviews are the cultural traits that represent civilizations. His proposition about world conflict rests on the implicit assumption that religion and civilizations are coherent—that is, that all Muslims share the same beliefs, all Christians share the same beliefs, and so on. Although numerous people claim adherence to the same traditions, their interpretation results in different worldviews—that is, their principled beliefs on what is right or wrong and their causal beliefs on how to achieve their objectives can be contradictory. For instance, a main tenant of violent Islamism is that orthodox behavior in times of crisis—that is intensifying prayers, paying alms, performing the pilgrimage, and so on—is not considered to be sufficient when religion is under attack. Armed jihad gains primacy over prayers or orthodox ways of worship.

In contrast to the static portrayal of worldviews, a more flexible definitional boundary drawing acknowledges that worldviews are shared in a pattern of association that is usually contiguous with other social boundaries, such as a particular ethnic or religious community. This means that there are concentric circles of social realities that coalesce with particular worldviews. For example, among right-wing Christian Protestants in the American rural West and South, some share an even more extremist Christian identity variety. Although the inner levels of these concentric circles are not always socially distinct, there are often social markers. For example, the right-wing movements are dominated by economically distressed heterosexual White men; this is a social category in which one would find few Blacks, Asians, or Hispanics, virtually no women in leadership roles, and no openly homosexual men or women (Juergensmeyer and Sheikh 2013).

The social boundaries of a movement's followers—those who agree with the central tenets and narrative story that dominate a particular epistemic worldview—may be more difficult to demarcate. If we think, for instance, of the al Qaeda organization as the people who worked directly under the leadership of Osama bin Laden before his death in 2011, the number was likely to be only in the hundreds. But if one includes all those who were influenced by, and to some extent sympathetic with, the general jihadi worldview that identified the United States as an opponent of Islam and insisted on militant resistance on the part of concerned Muslims, the number was much greater—in the thousands and perhaps even the millions.

Huntington's thesis constructs a simple cause-and-effect relationship between worldview and action, in which differences in worldviews inevitably lead to a clash. It is crucial, however, for anyone working on the dynamics between worldviews and political outcomes to recognize that we cannot assume a straightforward causal relationship between belief and action (Goldstein and Keohane 1993: 11). The questions how *much* worldviews matter and when *exactly* they matter will always be difficult to answer with scientific accuracy because methodologically it is difficult to enter the minds of people with a ruler that can measure this precisely.

A more accessible question is the following: Under what conditions can we assert a stronger relationship between worldviews and actions? Worldviews in which principled and causal beliefs are characterized by a very low level of ambiguity and a high level of simplicity are for instance more prone to enable or justify extreme action. When actors have a combination of well-defined principled beliefs, in which notions of identity, justice, and truth are very clear, and simple causal beliefs, in which the pathway to achieve their objectives is powerfully defined, they are in possession of a strong narrative. For example, narratives in which the world is seen through cosmic war images, and adversaries are identified as absolute enemies while the subject is identified as part of a heroic vanguard, are more likely to have a stronger mobilizing capacity toward violent or confrontational action directions. Imagined singularities can be remarkably powerful and turn into self-fulfilling prophecies by imprinting images of a sharply divided world in which identities cannot be reconciled. The Copenhagen School of security study has conceptualized this process as one of securitization: the intersubjective establishment of an existential threat with a saliency considerable enough to have significant political effects (Buzan, Wæver, and Wilde 1997; Wæver 1995). To make securitizing moves can involve, for instance, the claim that religion is existentially threatened and that action according to normal procedures will not be able to address the threat in time or efficiently enough, and that therefore extraordinary measures are both needed and justified.

In this light, the narrative of a civilizational clash in itself stages a dichotomous vision of the world—the cosmic war—with oppositions on an absolute scale (Juergensmeyer 1992). Not only has this image imprinted itself in academic fields but also it has successfully been adapted by both religious and secular zealots. Although Huntington's original idea of a civilizational clash has been strongly criticized for being too simplistic and scientifically inadequate (Bottici and Challand 2010; Sen and Gates 2006: 10), it can still be helpful if we apply it as a cognitive lens that can display how some people perceive and organize the world and use it as a basis for action.

Hence, there are two ways of conceptualizing a link between worldview and action. The first is a simple and linear cause–effect relationship in which X leads to Y, and the second is a looser relationship in which X is related to Y, either by way of enabling certain kinds of behavior or by justifying behavior. In the second case, worldviews are seen as playing a role in guiding human behavior, leading it onto certain action tracks while obscuring other tracks without asserting direct causality (Goldstein and Keohane 1993: 12).

The literature that treats worldviews as a precondition for political outcomes considers worldviews as road maps for action. From this perspective, it is interesting to study how principled and causal beliefs come to structure certain action preferences. In order to understand this approach, it is helpful to turn to Pierre Bourdieu's (2004: 479) concept of classification struggles. With this concept, he focuses on the classification processes that characterize the struggles to classify the social world. According to Bourdieu, classification struggles are struggles over the dominant "principles of vision and di-vision," and it is through these processes of classification that social collectivities are formed and the world is divided (Bourdieu 1984: 483, 2004; Gorski 2013).

An analysis of classification struggles would examine how one's study objects engage in a definitional struggle to assert their truth about the social world itself and their opponents, how identities are evoked, and how they gain a mobilizing capacity. An example of a clas-sification struggle is the doctrinal confrontations between religion and secularism. In conflict situations, there is a security dilemma between two meta-narratives, where one side is securitizing freedom and secularism against what is represented as aggressive reli-giosity, and the other side is securitizing freedom and religion against what is represented as aggressive secularism. In both meta-narratives, extraordinary security–political action is justified with reference to ideas about sovereignty, governance, and order, and both sides frame their war as defensive, as just, and as principal. Doctrines such as freedom, secu-larism, and religion appear to be especially inclined to securitization because their content is heavily disputable and, thus, they amount to what discourse theorists would categorize as empty signifiers (Sheikh 2014).

Bourdieu moves his analytic lens away from predicting war between cultures toward examining how cultural conflict is played out in a social–political battlefield. His framework analyzes the game of position takings—that is, the ways in which vital players, representing opposed factions, project their own schemas, truths, or dominance over others (Bourdieu 1984: 174–175; Gorski 2013: 243). These vital players, or specialists as Bourdieu calls them, have the authority to speak for a social collectivity—to articulate its history, political opinions, needs, and demands—and they therefore play a vital role in the maintenance of a group's boundaries and the mobilization of its members (Bourdieu and Thompson 1991: 173).

Such a position wears strategic lenses but still represents an interesting aspect of world-view analysis. Like Bourdieu's approach, a worldview analysis can shed light on how worldviews become espoused, defended, and disseminated in a relational context and also how they attain strong mobilizing effects—which has real political implications. Such an analysis does not reduce worldviews to being only an instrument, although it is interested in the effects they produce. The dynamic study of worldview entails that we study how vital players and members of the communities or groups we want to study enter into con-flict or competition with one another and simultaneously make both themselves and their opponents the object of classificatory practices.

Methods and Principles to Analyze Worldviews

Being aware of the interaction between worldviews and their social setting is one of the most important tasks of worldview analysis. The interdisciplinary trend that Mark Juergensmeyer and I labeled *sociotheology* in 2013 emerged out of the observation that in parts of socio-logical and political science literature, theology and religious idea were ignored or deemed irrelevant. The secularization thesis has had profound effects on the social sciences (Asad 2003; Hurd 2007b), and particularly in the United States, the gap increased between the-ology and the study of religious ideas, on the one hand, and approaches that did not consider religion to be of any *sui generis* importance, on the other hand. The approaches that tended to be reductionist and unappreciative of the significance of religious ideas and imagery were criticized, however, particularly after 2001, when religion was actively reintroduced to the social science agenda.

Sociotheology was a call to incorporate into social analysis the insider-oriented attempt to understand the reality of a particular worldview and to recover an appreciation for a field increasingly banished from the halls of secular academe: theology. The insider perspective on a religious worldview is, after all, what the field of theology has classically been about, long before the advent of the modern academic disciplines: attempts to structure the social, ethical, political, and spiritual aspects of a culture's ideas and meanings into a coherent whole (Juergensmeyer and Sheikh 2013).

In recent decades, there have been huge divisions, again particularly in the US context, between theology and religious studies—the latter having branded itself as more scientific due to its "neutral" perspective on religion. Theology fell into disrespect among social sciences due to three limitations in the way that it was predominantly practiced: It had only one religious tradition as its frame of reference, it asserted normative truth claims about its analyses, and its analysts often ignored the social context in which the ideas they studied emerged and were cultivated.

Sociotheological worldview analysis is different in that it can be applied to any tradition and even a secular outlook. Epistemologically, it brackets truth claims asserted by the subjects in the study or by the analysts themselves, and it takes seriously the social location in which a view of the world emerges and the social consequences of a particular way of thinking about reality. The point is to try to understand the reasoning behind the truth claims, not to verify them (Juergensmeyer and Sheikh 2013).

The sociotheological approach to worldviews is based on the acknowledgment that many of the phenomena that modern people since the time of the European Enlightenment have called religion are related to other aspects of society, from economic and political factors to matters of social identity. For this reason, sociotheological analysis seldom is limited to a study of religion in the narrow sense, as if there were a separate cluster of actions and ideas relating to a notion of transcendence and of spiritual transformation that is unaffected by other aspects of public and private life.

This framework for studying worldviews is part of a Weberian heritage in which the study of ideas in relation to action is a natural way of approaching social phenomena. But it is also built on epistemological revolutions across disciplinary borders that embraced a dynamic view on inside and outside factors driving the individual. One example is the Strong Program associated with the Edinburgh School of the sociology of science, which holds that all human knowledge and ideas, including religious ones, contain some social components in their formation process. Another relevant methodological revolution has come from within discursive psychology and social psychology that dissolved the mind–body dichotomy by developing a new concept of the mind (D. Edwards and Potter 1992; Gee 1992; Harré and Gillett 1994). The dynamic view of the mind–body relationship is part of what has been called the *second cognitive revolution* that challenged the idea that mental and psychological entities exist in a self-contained way.

The same sort of bridge building between inside and outside perspectives has taken place within the field of theology. Here, one of the pioneers was George Lindbeck, who developed a cultural–linguistic concept of religious doctrines by bridging anthropology and a Wittgensteinian philosophy of language that probed the relationship between language and culture, on the one hand, and experience and belief, on the other hand. Together, the approximations of the fields of psychology and theology (the mind and belief) and sociology (the context) as two poles in the same discursive dynamics have contributed to eroding a rigid dichotomy between theology, psychology, and the social sciences.

One of the implications of studying worldviews from this perspective is that it is more prone to take seriously the words of violent activists than instrumentalist or essentialist approaches to religion and ideology. Words are exactly the means by which an analyst can enter the mind. To understand a perception of reality—an epistemic worldview—requires the sociotheological tasks of recovering the internal logic of a certain perception of reality and placing it within its social milieu. It also requires understanding the relationship between people who share a certain worldview and the social and power structures of the world around them. The task is similar to the hermeneutical approach to the interpretation of texts—an approach that has been employed in cultural sociology as well—in attempting to understand the range of ways that statements and social events have been perceived from various perspectives.

NARRATIVES AS A PATHWAY TO WORLDVIEWS

In worldview analysis, narratives are taken seriously not only as superficial rhetoric but also as claims that can shape the social reality of human beings as well as their justifications for acting in certain ways. Narratives are accounts that create themes, plots, and drama (Bamberg and McCabe 2000). When people tell stories, they construct sequences and consequences, which is why narratives at their most basic level make sense of social action and history (Czarniawska-Joerges 2004: 11). The function of these narratives is to provide order and explanations and to distribute responsibility (J. A. Edwards 2014: 1; Riessman 2005: 85). Contained in these narratives are people's justifications, defenses, and rationalizations for action.

Religious or epistemic worldviews are often characterized by mythic narratives. These narratives provide people with stories of greatness, heroism, suffering, and victimhood (J. A. Edwards 2014: 85; Rowland and Theye 2008). Often, these stories of past legacies are activated in a direct relationship with the present undertaking of a political or religious project (Sheikh 2016).

Using narratives as a way to enter people's minds and understand their worldviews reflects an interest in the "how" questions related to worldviews rather than the causal questions. Narrations are always linked to *framing*: They showcase not only the elements of which the actor speaks but also *how* the actor speaks of these elements. The puzzling aspect of narratives is not just what they tell but also how they tell it. Values, sentiments, and ideas of ethics are demonstrated through the way people portray heroes, enemies, and landmarks and the way they distinguish right or wrong, just or unjust, and good or bad.

An argument resembling the Marxist position on ideology that is sometimes used to dismiss the relevance of narratives and listening to one's study objects is that interviewees do not realize their own motivations and hence would be unable to explain them. The implicit assumption is that the observer, for instance, would be in a better position to understand the minds of terrorists than would the terrorists themselves. The idea that people are not fully capable of analyzing their own motives and reasons for acting is also more broadly shared due to the complexities and multiple identities that characterize human beings.

In any attempt to conduct worldview analysis, it is therefore paramount to have a method and methodology to study the link between mind, motivations, and worldviews, on the one hand, and the narratives enabling or justifying violence, on the other hand. Although ethnographic work is priceless with regard to understanding the context and culture of the people one is studying, another dimension is also to make explicit the assumptions that enable an analysis of narratives to simultaneously say something about the mind or the worldviews of these people.

The sociotheological approach is based on a dynamic view of the mind–body dichotomy and is congruent with those strands of discursive and social psychology that dissolve this dichotomy. Scholars within these traditions do not view discourse as the product or expression of thoughts or the mind lying behind it; rather, these are immanent in discursive practice. Hence, beliefs or emotions cannot be isolated or identified outside of the context in which they are expressed, and as argued by psychologists Harré and Gillet (1994), the mind (e.g., beliefs, emotions, attitudes, and intentions) only comes into existence in the performance of actions. The mind with all that it contains, instead of being a separate entity, is actualized through "the telling," and this facilitates a more dynamic view of the relationship between psychological entities and the social world.

In the field of global studies, as in all other academic ventures, what then distinguishes a good analysis from a bad one is the ability of the researcher to go behind superficial appearances. When confronted with ideas and perceptions that are strikingly different from one's own, the challenge is to understand the way that words are used as well as the concepts inherent in these words, and it is this aspect, requiring cultural empathy, that can be helped by ethnographic methods. At the beginning of the nineteenth century, the Prussian philologist Wilhelm von Humboldt put forward the idea that there is a link between linguistic communities and their mode of apprehending reality. Humboldt is often credited with establishing the idea that language and worldview are inextricably linked, maintaining that language gives us the concepts of history, destiny, nation, and morality. This view fundamentally challenges the Cartesian dualism between *res cogitans* and *res extensa*, but it also pushes us toward a culturally sensitive approach to concepts and ideas. In the global era, the challenge to worldview analysis is to embrace this scientific agenda and find efficient ways of managing contemporary conflicts and manifestations of violence—manifestations that require solid methods to analyze and comprehend the vertical dynamics between worldviews and action and also the horizontal dynamics between the precepts, imageries, and grievances that stem from transnational views of religion, politics, and society. Global studies represents one such attempt to advance this transdisciplinary research.

ACKNOWLEDGMENTS

I thank Samyia Beg for excellent research assistance and senior researcher Manni Crone for her critical review of this chapter.

REFERENCES

Althusser, L. 2001. *Lenin and Philosophy and Other Essays*. New York, NY: Monthly Review Press. Translated from the French by Ben Brewster. .

Asad, Talal. 2003. *Formations of the Secular: Christianity, Islam, and Modernity*. Palo Alto, CA: Stanford University Press.

Bamberg, M., and A. McCabe. 2000. *Narrative Identity: Special issue of Narrative Inquiry*. Amsterdam: Benjamins.

Beck, A. T., ed. 1979. *Cognitive Therapy of Depression*. The Guilford Clinical Psychology and Psychotherapy Series. New York: Guilford.

Bell, D. 1960. *The End of Ideology: On the Exhaustion of Political Ideas in the Fifties*. Glencoe, IL: Free Press.

Blyth, M. M. 1997. "'Any More Bright Ideas?'" The Ideational Turn of Comparative Political Economy." *Comparative Politics* 29: 229–250. doi:10.2307/422082

Bottici, C., and B. Challand. 2010. *The Myth of the Clash of Civilizations*. New York: Routledge.

Bourdieu, P. 1984. *Distinction: A Social Critique of the Judgement of Taste*. Cambridge, MA: Harvard University Press.

Bourdieu, P. 2004. *In Other Words: Essays Towards a Reflexive Sociology*, Repr. ed. Cambridge, UK: Polity.

Bourdieu, P., and J. B. Thompson. 1991. *Language and Symbolic Power*. Cambridge, MA: Harvard University Press.

Buzan, B., O. Wæver, and J. D. Wilde. 1997. *Security: A New Framework for Analysis*. Boulder, CO: Rienner.

Cobern, W. W. 1996. "Worldview Theory and Conceptual Change in Science Education." *Science Education* 80 (5): 579–610.

Crone, M., U. P. Gad, and M. K. Sheikh. 2008. "Review Essay: Dusting for Fingerprints: The Aarhus Approach to Islamism." *Distinktion: Journal of Social Theory* 9: 189–203. doi:10.1080/1600910X.2008.9672970

Czarniawska-Joerges, B. 2004. *Narratives in Social Science Research*. Thousand Oaks, CA: Sage.

DiMaggio, P. 2003. "Culture and Cognition." http://www.annualreviews.org/doi/full/10.1146/annurev.soc.23.1.263 Accessed August 5, 2016.

Edwards, D., and J. Potter. 1992. *Discursive Psychology*. London: Sage.

Edwards, J. A. 2014. "The Mythology of Suffering and Redemption in the Discourse of al Qaeda." In *Myth in the Modern World: Essays on Intersections with Ideology and Culture*, edited by D. Whitt and J. R. Perlich, 83–101. Jefferson, NC: McFarland.

Fiske, S.T., and P. W. Linville. 1980. "What Does the Schema Concept Buy Us?" *Personality and Social Psychology Bulletin* 6: 543–557. doi:10.1177/014616728064006

Fox, J. 2006. "The Multiple Impacts of Religion on International Relations: Perceptions and Reality." http://www.ifri.org/files/politique_etrangere/4_2006_Fox.pdf

Fox, J., and S. Sandler. 2004. *Bringing Religion into International Relations*. New York: Palgrave Macmillan.

Gee, J. P. 1992. *The Social Mind: Language, Ideology, and Social Practice*. New York: Bergin & Garvey.

Goldstein, J., and R. O. Keohane. 1993. "Ideas and Foreign Policy: An Analytical Framework." In *Ideas and Foreign Policy: Beliefs, Institutions, and Political Change*, edited by J. Goldstein and R. O. Keohane, 3–30. Ithaca, NY: Cornell University Press.

Goplen, J., and E. A. Plant. 2015. "A Religious Worldview Protecting One's Meaning System Through Religious Prejudice." *Personality & Social Psychology Bulletin* 41: 1474–1487.

Gorski, P. S. 2013. *Bourdieu and Historical Analysis*. Durham, NC: Duke University Press.

Greenberg, J., S. Solomon, and T. Pyszczynski. 1997. "Terror Management Theory of Self-Esteem and Cultural Worldviews: Empirical Assessments and Conceptual Refinements." *Advances in Experimental Social Psychology* 29: 61–139.

Harré, R., and G. Gillett. 1994. *The Discursive Mind*. Thousand Oaks, CA: Sage.

Hastie, R. 1981. "Schematic Principles in Human Memory." In *Social Cognition: The Ontario Symposium*, edited by E. T. Higgins, C. P. Herman, and M. P. Zanna, Vol. 1, pp. 39–88. Hillsdale, NJ: Erlbaum.

Hiebert, P. G. 2008. *Transforming Worldviews: An Anthropological Understanding of How People Change*. Grand Rapids, MI: Baker Academic.

Huntington, S. P. 1993. "The Clash of Civilizations?" *Foreign Affairs*: Summer. https://www.foreignaffairs.com/articles/united-states/1993-06-01/clash-civilizations

Huntington, S. P. 1996. *The Clash of Civilizations and the Remaking of World Order*. New York: Simon & Schuster.

Hurd, Elizabeth. 2007a. *The Politics of Secularism in International Relations*. Princeton, NJ: Princeton University Press.

Hurd, Elizabeth. 2007b. "Theorizing Religious Resurgence." *International Politics* 44: 647–665.

Janoff-Bulman, R. 1989. "Assumptive Worlds and the Stress of Traumatic Events: Applications of the Schema Construct." *Social Cognition* 7: 113–136. doi:10.1521/soco.1989.7.2.113

Jerryson, M. K. 2011. *Buddhist Fury: Religion and Violence in Southern Thailand*. New York: Oxford University Press.

Johnson, K. A., E. D. Hill, and A. B. Cohen. 2011. "Integrating the Study of Culture and Religion: Toward a Psychology of Worldview." *Social and Personality Psychology Compass* 5: 137–152. doi:10.1111/j.1751-9004.2010.00339.x

Juergensmeyer, M., ed. 1992. *Violence and the Sacred in the Modern World*. London: Cass.

Juergensmeyer, M. 2003. *Terror in the Mind of God: The Global Rise of Religious Violence*. 3rd ed. Berkeley: University of California Press.

Juergensmeyer, M. and M. K. Sheikh. 2013. "A Sociotheological Approach to Understanding Religious Violence." In *The Oxford Handbook of Religion and Violence*, edited by M. Juergensmeyer, M. Kitts, and M. K. Jerryson, 620–643. New York: Oxford University Press.

Kant, I. 1952. *The Critique of Judgment*. Oxford, UK: Clarendon. (Original work published 1790)

Kearney, M. 1984. *World View*. Novato, CA: Chandler & Sharp.

Koltko-Rivera, M. E. 2004. "The Psychology of Worldviews." *Review of General Psychology* 8: 3–58. doi:10.1037/1089-2680.8.1.3

Lynch, Cecelia. 2000. "Acting on Belief: Christian Perspectives on Suffering and Violence." *Ethics & International Affairs* 14: 83–97.

Mahmood, C. K. 1997. *Fighting for Faith and Nation: Dialogues with Sikh Militants*. Series in Contemporary Ethnography. Philadelphia: University of Pennsylvania Press.

Major, B., C. R. Kaiser, L. T. O'Brien, and S. K. McCoy. 2007. "Perceived Discrimination as Worldview Threat or Worldview Confirmation: Implications for Self-Esteem." *Journal of Personality and Social Psychology* 92: 1068.

Mannheim, K., and L. Wirth. 1936. *Ideology and Utopia: An Introduction to the Sociology of Knowledge*. London: K. Paul, Trench, Trubner.

Marty, M. E., and R. S. Appleby. 1995. *Fundamentalisms Comprehended*. Chicago: University of Chicago Press.

Marty, M. E., and R. S. Appleby, eds. 2004. *Fundamentalisms Observed*. Chicago: University of Chicago Press.

Marx, K. 1872. *Das Kapital Kritik der politischen Oekonomie*. Hamburg, Germany: Verlag von O. Meissner.

McCoy, J., and W. A. Knight. 2015. "Homegrown Terrorism in Canada: Local Patterns, Global Trends." *Studies in Conflict & Terrorism* 38: 253–274. doi:10.1080/1057610X.2014.994349

McGregor, I., M. P. Zanna, J. G. Holmes, and S. J. Spencer. 2001. "Compensatory Conviction in the Face of Personal Uncertainty: Going to Extremes and Being Oneself." *Journal of Personality and Social Psychology* 80: 472–488. doi:10.1037//0022-3514.80.3.472

Overton, W. F. 1991. "Historical and Contemporary Perspectives on Developmental Theory and Research Strategies." In *Visions of Aesthetics, the Environment & Development: The Legacy of Joachim F. Wohlwill*, edited by J. F. Wohlwill, R. M. Downs, L. S. Liben, and D. S. Palermo, 263–312. Hillsdale, NJ: Erlbaum.

Petito, Fabio, and Pavlos Hatzopoulos. 2003. *Religion in International Relations: The Return from Exile*. London: Palgrave Macmillan.

Philpott, Daniel. 2002. "The Challenge of September 11 to Secularism in International Relations." *World Politics* 55: 66–95.

Redfield, R. 1952. "The Primitive World View." *Proceedings of the American Philosophical Society* 96: 30–36.

Riessman, C. K. 2005. "Narrative Analysis." In *Narrative, Memory & Everyday Life*, 1–7. Huddersfield: University of Huddersfield.

Røislien, H. E. 2007. "Living with Contradiction: Examining the Worldview of the Jewish Settlers in Hebron." *International Journal of Conflict and Violence* 1: 169–184.

Rowland, R. C., and K. Theye. 2008. "The Symbolic DNA of Terrorism." *Communication Monographs* 75: 52–85. doi:10.1080/03637750701885423

Sapir, E. 1949. *Culture, Language, and Personality: Selected Essays*. Berkeley: University of California Press.

Sen, A., and H. L. Gates. 2006. *Identity and Violence: The Illusion of Destiny*. New York: Norton.

Sheikh, M. K. 2012. "How Does Religion Matter? Pathways to Religion in International Relations." *Review of International Studies* 38 (2): 365–392.

Sheikh, M. K. 2014. "Doctrinal War." *E-International Relations*. http://www.e-ir.info/2014/01/15/doctrinal-war

Sheikh, M. K. 2016. *Guardians of God—Inside the Religious Mind of the Pakistani Taliban*. Oxford, UK: Oxford University Press.

Thomas, Scott M. 2005. *The Global Resurgence of Religion and the Transformation of International Relations. The Struggle for the Soul of the Twenty-First Century*. New York: Palgrave Macmillan.

Weber, Max. 2000. *The Protestant Ethic and the "Spirit" of Capitalism and Other Writings*. New York: Penguin/Putnam. (Original work published 1905)

Wæver, O. 1995. "Securitization and Desecuritization." In *On Security*, edited by R. D. Lipschutz, 46–85. New York: Columbia University Press.

Wilson, E. K. 2012. *After Secularism: Rethinking Religion in Global Politics*. New York: Palgrave Macmillan.

Wolman, B. B. 1973. *Dictionary of Behavioral Science*. New York: Van Nostrand Reinhold.

CHAPTER 11

THE ANTHROPOCENE THESIS

SIMON DALBY

> The old picture of stable natural systems that humanity can choose to interfere with or not should be replaced by the picture of a restless planet on which humanity is a constant enduring force.
>
> —Dale Jamieson (2014: 234)

As philosopher Dale Jameson suggests in this epigraph, we are living in times in which old assumptions about humanity's place in the larger scheme of things seem to be in need of a dramatic update. New understandings in natural sciences emphasize both the interconnectedness of human and non-human systems and the scale of the transformations that the global economy is causing. The term "Anthropocene" is widely used to suggest that we are now in a new geological situation in which humanity is actively remaking its circumstances and doing so in ways that affect the Earth in numerous ways all over the globe (Davies 2016). Although global studies has focused on the interconnectedness of human activities, this "Anthropocene thesis," the argument that we now live in a new geological era, means that global studies also needs to incorporate non-human systems into how it understands the "global."

Crucially, the new understanding made possible by Earth system sciences, one that posits "the Anthropocene thesis," requires us to understand humanity simultaneously as a globally interconnected cultural and economic phenomenon and as a geological scale material actor. This requires substantial rethinking on the part of the social sciences and humanities, a task that has begun in the past few years and is quickening pace as the full scale of the climate challenge in particular becomes clear to scholars (Hamilton et al. 2015). Earth system scientists make it clear that we have left the very stable conditions of Earth history since the last age ended approximately 12,000 years ago, the period usually known as the Holocene, and entered a new period now often called the Anthropocene, the age of humanity.

The interconnectedness and the transformation of the non-human world are two ways of looking at the same phenomena. Globalization has accelerated the interconnections between parts of the world, incorporating most of us into a global economy while transforming landscapes, and substantial parts of ocean ecosystems to supply us with food, fiber, and other materials while absorbing our wastes. How we should now conduct our inquiries, who we understand ourselves to be, and how we should act in light of the new recognition of our role in shaping the planet raise important scholarly and political questions. The discussion of the Anthropocene in the past decade emphasizes the importance of thinking these things through precisely because how we do so matters in terms of how we are likely to act to shape the future, the next stage of planetary history—one now shaped increasingly by human decisions.

The sheer scale of human activities now makes the modern ideas of an external environment, or nature separate from humanity, inadequate and, indeed, downright misleading as a way of understanding the human condition (Bonneuil and Fressoz 2016). It turns out that humanity has had much more profound effects on the planet than we realized until recently. It also turns out that our assumptions that we were citizens or relatively isolated states wherein the important decisions that matter are taken is also missing crucial aspects of how collective human actions shape how we live. Much of the discussion of the Anthropocene by social scientists is about who should now act how in light of the new insights from Earth system scientists about how geophysical and biophysical cycles shape the planetary surface.

It matters that the Anthropocene is a geological term, not a biological, geographical, or historical one. The use of the term suggests a much bigger shift in human circumstances than traditional thinking about environment, even discussions of global environmental change, has encompassed. It also suggests to historians in particular that they need to bring nature back into the human story and that the history of modernity, with its assumptions that humanity can be studied without focusing on its larger natural context, is no longer appropriate (Chakrabarty 2009; Emmett and Lekan 2016). Bruno Latour (2013) suggests that perhaps what we need is nothing less than a combination of geology and history as "geostory." Enlightenment assumptions of nature as a backdrop and of humanity as relatively autonomous from the rest of the planet are no longer tenable premises for serious inquiry into the human condition.

But not all geologists have been happy with the use of the term. In the science of stratigraphy, the study of Earth's very long-term biological and geological history recorded in accumulated sedimentary rocks, it is not at all clear that the notion of the Anthropocene fits well with the traditional ways of designating distinct periods of life or other geophysical phenomena of the Earth (Finney and Edwards 2016). So while the term has become commonplace in popular discussions, and is growing in use in the social sciences, it is important to note that physical scientists have been engaging in an intense series of arguments about its appropriateness as a scientific concept and, if one accepts that present circumstances are novel enough to require a new geological designation, how the beginning of this era, or maybe epoch, will be marked in geological sediments. What the "golden spike" that marks the beginning of the Anthropocene should be turns out to be a discussion of what is the most significant consequence of human activities that will leave a permanent record in Earth's history. This once again involves historians and social scientists in the discussion. Welcome to the Anthropocene, where the traditional division of natural and human studies no longer makes much sense in a rapidly changing world!

GLOBAL UNDERSTANDINGS

The rise of global studies in the academy reflects the new understanding of the planet as one of increased human interconnection, a sense of globality as the human context that has deepened since the middle of the twentieth century (van Munster and Sylvest 2016). This "sense of the global" has emerged gradually in human thinking, in part as a result of European exploration at the beginning of its imperial expansion, and subsequently in the nineteenth century as scientific research gradually filled in some of the gaps in knowledge. The assumption of a single world as an arena of political competition is the key assumption in what we now call geopolitics (Agnew 2003). But until very recently, much of this worked with an implicit understanding of a fairly stable planet, with separate species mixes in various parts of it, and one in which the species that European explorers and naturalists found were usually understood to be indigenous to particular places. Climates, too, related to particular places and were understood as caused by physical phenomena in those places. Those climates, driven by phenomena not well understood by Europeans, frequently disrupted their assumptions of fairly stable and predictable annual cycles. When drought caused crop failure, frequently this allowed imperial administrators to blame the weather rather than colonial administration for the human misery that resulted (Davis 2001).

Only later in the nineteenth century, but mostly in the twentieth century, as scientific efforts in meteorology in particular tried to construct data sets throughout the world, using standardized measuring systems on land and shipboard weather observations, did the interconnectedness of weather patterns gradually become clear (Edwards 2010). With this came a growing understanding of the global climate as one interconnected system. Likewise, assumptions of a stable geological arrangement of the planet led to the dismissal of early suggestions of continental drift. Until a convincing theory of plate tectonics emerged in the twentieth century, it was not clear just how dynamic a place the planet actually is. Now we understand that apparently stable continents are in fact in motion, and natural systems are both interconnected and mobile. This does not mean the laws of physics change; it means that they play out in a much more dynamic way than most Victorian era academics, the people who invented the academic disciplines that subsequently dominated universities in the twentieth century, understood.

The rapid rise of European power in the nineteenth century, which was a combination of industrial innovation based on steam engines and the expansion of imperial power to provide direct access to raw materials and markets for goods, gradually extended trading links throughout the world and moved peoples and products around the globe. The ecological consequences of potatoes from South America to Europe, rabbits to Australia, horses to the Americas, and numerous other changes began the transformation of the species mixes in all areas of the world (Crosby 1986). Slowly, too, the combustion of fossil fuels began to change the amount of carbon dioxide in the atmosphere. Although the likely heating effects of this were understood in the nineteenth century, the scale of the transformation had to await the rapid expansion of the use of petroleum in the latter part of the twentieth century before its consequences became a matter of concern.

The twentieth century accelerated these interconnections and began to provide such things as increasingly accurate weather forecasts on the basis of the vast accumulation of promptly reported meteorological readings. Two wars that stretched around the world, the rapid spread of telegraph systems, and then radio, sped up the flow of information and the sense of an instantaneous presence in the world. The sense of a single globe was enhanced by concerns about radioactive fallout after the bombing of Hiroshima and Nagasaki and the subsequent detonation of numerous nuclear bombs in the atmosphere (Masco 2015). The fallout products traveled round the world in the atmosphere, endangering people everywhere. The sense of global insecurity tied the arcane science of nuclear physics to the political rivalries of rulers in Washington, Moscow, London, and subsequently Paris, Beijing, Jerusalem, Delhi, Islamabad, and elsewhere.

Connected to rising concerns about the damage being done by industrial pollution, such things as the ecological consequences of pesticide use and toxic effluent from factories, coal smoke in industrial regions, and the alarms about radioactive fallout led to a rising consciousness about environmental damage and also both political movements to tackle the worst problems and the genesis of environmental studies programs to bring social science and humanities to study these issues. Simultaneously, concerns about famine and food shortages related to the very rapidly growing human population raised fears of global resource shortages and, borrowing from population biology formulations and conservation practices, discussions of the Earth's carrying capacity.

Studies of such "limits to growth" (Meadows et al. 1972) produced a widespread discussion of the environmental issues in the early 1970s. Reacting to this, leaders of some of the postcolonial underdeveloped states objected that this focus on environment and the insistence that it was a global problem was little more than a ploy by the rich developed nations to limit the development options of the poor areas of the planet all in the name of a global concern. The compromise solution to this apparent standoff took until the mid-1980s to work out. The formulation of "sustainable development" codified by the World Commission on Environment and Development (1987) in its report, *Our Common Future*, suggested that development could be made compatible with environmental concerns, although quite how this was to be done was rarely clear.

In the meantime, extended discussions of the potential of a major nuclear war to drastically, albeit temporarily, disrupt climate had raised the possibility of humanity changing the atmosphere on a global scale. The prospect of a nuclear winter added impetus to the nuclear disarmament campaigns of the early 1980s, linking global concerns with geopolitics once again. The huge chemical disaster at Bhopal in 1984, the nuclear meltdown at Chernobyl in 1986, and the unusually warm summer in the United States in 1988 all raised awareness that environmental destruction needed to be addressed. The recognition that artificial climate change was occurring and could cause drastic changes to the Earth system emerged at approximately the same time, and it fed into larger concerns with the future of the planet just as the cold war confrontation was ending in the late 1980s. It stimulated further scientific research on the interconnected nature of the Earth system, a discussion that, by the year 2000, had progressed so far that Paul Crutzen (2002), the scientist credited with bringing the term into popular use, had come to understand that the transformation of the Earth system was so profound as to deserve the specification of present times in terms of a new geological epoch, the Anthropocene.

AN ANTHROPOCENE
GOLDEN SPIKE?

If we live in a new era, then logically we must have passed some historical moment at which we crossed from the previous geological epoch into the current one. But once one tries to distinguish our time from the previous times, and do so by selecting a point at which the new era begins, things quickly become complicated (Davies 2016). Thinking in terms of geological epochs requires using the geological criteria normally used to distinguish one period from another to specify the boundary point at the beginning of the new epoch. Because the geological history of our planet deals with the distant past, geological time periods are usually marked by the transition from one set of species preserved in the fossil record in rocks to another distinctly different grouping. The key points of transition in the rock records are usually marked with a "golden spike" literally hammered into rocks somewhere on the planet to mark the transition boundary. The Anthropocene idea focuses on the present, and there are not any obvious fossil combinations that can mark an obvious transition simply because they have not had time to accumulate in sedimentary deposits that will eventually turn into rocks.

The question of when the Anthropocene began is thus a technical matter in discussions of geology, and not all geologists are convinced that the terminology of the Anthropocene is useful in terms of defining a new geological epoch. This mostly is not a discussion about the scale of the current transformations but, rather, a technical one about the appropriate beginning of the epoch, whether the transformations will be long-lasting, and hence whether such a designation is useful in terms of stratigraphy. It is difficult to imagine oneself as a geologist millions of years in the future looking at sedimentary rocks and saying, "Ah, yes, here is that sedimentary rock layer where we see the products of that weird bipedal species that turned huge quantities of rock into air for some obscure purposes and in the process caused the sixth extinction event in the planet's history." But to establish that we do live in a new geological era with the necessary technical detail to satisfy stratigraphers requires something that is plausible in these terms.

This is not a technical quibble. Rather, it is a simple recognition that geology looks back to planetary history and does not usually deal with the present. Clearly, if humanity's influence is only a matter of thousands of years of biological disruption, it is not significant in comparison with the millions of years timescales geological science usually deals with in designating epochs. Although present circumstances are clearly novel, there is not necessarily much utility to the study of geology in this new designation if purely technical matters of stratigraphy are all that is under consideration. In the words of Autin and Holbrook (2012), two skeptical stratigraphers,

> Identification of a basal boundary for the Anthropocene and the suggestion that the concept can be validated with a global stratigraphic marker is at best a bit premature. A distinct stratigraphic marker should have been forming since anthropogenic change began. As practicing stratigraphers, we are taken aback by the claim that scientists currently have sufficient evidence to define a distinctive and lasting imprint of our existence in the geologic record. (p. 60)

Although the lasting imprint on the geological record may not be clear, the transformation of the human condition certainly is. But "scientists from disciplines other than stratigraphy embrace the concept of Anthropocene while not appreciating the nuances of its application to formal stratigraphic practice" (p. 61).

Nonetheless, whatever the finer definitional points in terms of current changes (Brown et al. 2013),

> There is enough geomorphological evidence to support the contention that human activities in the later part of the present interglacial have been the dominant (but not necessarily over-whelming) drivers in many, but not all, sediment-flux systems from the scale of individual hill slopes to large catchments, and as a consequence have recognizably altered the nature of terrestrial, and parts of the marine, sedimentary records. (433)

Hence, although there may be a serious scientific discussion on the theme in geology, for most of the rest of the scientific community, a new term that emphasizes that humanity is currently changing how the Earth system operates is a most useful terminological innovation.

Bringing geological knowledge into global studies is not going to be easy to do in ways that satisfy both geologists and social scientists, but it needs to be done if geologists are to understand the causes of the new forces shaping the Earth system and social scientists are to understand the new context within which global social and economic matters are unfolding. We live in an increasingly artificial world, one in which cities, roads, dams, and pipes are the context for the global consumer culture. Decisions about what to make for that culture, such as concrete, plastics, or new entities, now shape the future geology of the planet. Assumptions of a given stable environmental backdrop to human affairs, or of the persistence of benign conditions for human flourishing into the future, are simply not a valid starting point for global studies if the long-term trajectory of humanity or its future matters.

The Human Age

The questions of when humanity might have started having such a large-scale influence, who among humanity is most responsible, and how that has implications for who should do what now have profound implications for how global studies formulates its research questions and how the subject is researched and taught. The planet has had a relatively very stable climate for approximately the past 12,000 years since the last ice age retreated. The Holocene has been an unprecedented period compared to the previous half million years. It has been a time when the carbon dioxide levels in the atmosphere have been remarkably stable, hovering slightly under 300 parts per million (ppm). This unusually stable period gave rise to what we know as civilization, setting in motion changes to the planet and to humanity that have brought us to the present situation in which we now know at least the broad outlines of the interconnected stories of human and planetary history.

Crucial to all this has been the emergence of humanity, the only species to systematically use fire to change its condition and shape its surroundings (Pyne 2012)—not the only species to use tools, but clearly one that has developed the art much further than any other, and also one with the most developed use of language. Clearly, humanity was a contributing factor to the dramatic reduction of other large mammals after the last ice age, one that has gone with the expansion of our species to inhabit most areas of the terrestrial surface of the planet, even with small settlements in Antarctica. The discussion about the beginning of the Anthropocene needs to take these matters into consideration because when the human signature on planetary processes is first clearly discernable is a key part of the discussion.

Should the Holocene actually be termed the Anthropocene given that human actions including hunting and the early stages of agriculture may have had discernable effects on the climate system despite the relatively small numbers and low level of technology? If the early agricultural activities of humanity generated small but significant amounts of methane from deforestation, farm animals, and paddy fields, might this have been enough to prevent the Earth slipping back into another ice age as had happened in previous interglacial periods (Ruddiman 2005)? Although the answer may not be certain, the very fact that geologists are asking such questions suggests that humanity is a factor in the biosphere that is more significant than has been realized until recently.

This raises difficult questions for traditional notions of environment that have usually assumed a fairly stable given context for humanity (Davies 2016). The history of agriculture is about changing species and the gradual transformation of land use in the more fertile areas of the planet. Even the tropical rain forests have had their species mix changed quite substantially by human activities that frequently favor certain tree species that can regenerate more rapidly. If rain forests have been changed, then assumptions about a pristine nature into which humanity recently intruded are fundamentally misconstruing our environmental context. Romantic premises of an untouched nature are simply wrong—a European colonial era projection that obscures the more profound transformations we are living through.

Notions of "sustainable development" do not provide easy answers either; it is no longer clear what needs to be sustained where in a rapidly changing world. If humanity has been changing its habitat effectively since the end of the last ice age, then the question of precisely what "physical sustainability," to use the terminology from Our Common Future (World Commission 1987), means is much more complicated than has been assumed until recently. Clearly, there is no environment "out there" separate from human actions, and our thinking has to recognize that humanity, or at least the rich and powerful parts of it that are making crucial decisions about what gets made how and where, has taken its fate into its own hands, albeit without recognizing the full consequences of what has been done until very recently.

Another suggestion for what might be considered the beginning of the Anthropocene is the early years of the seventeenth century when the carbon dioxide levels in the atmosphere briefly dipped to their lowest level in centuries (Lewis and Maslin 2015). The cause of this may have been the reforestation of substantial portions of the Americas in the sixteenth century. This was the result of the massive reduction in the native population following the introduction of infectious diseases by Europeans to the Americas during the early explorations and conquests starting with Columbus' voyages at the end of the fifteenth century. If colonization caused populations to die off, agriculture to be abandoned, and hence the large-scale growth of trees in areas that had previously been cleared, leading to carbon dioxide being pulled out of the air in substantial quantities, then there is a clear connection here between human activity linking the global spread of European influence with the global climate. That this in turn triggered societal and economic disruptions related to failed harvests due to bad weather across much of the world in the seventeenth "cata-strophic century" (Parker 2013) suggests a link between climate and human history that is a credible starting point for the Anthropocene.

This discussion suggests that humanity has been inadvertently shaping the conditions of its own existence for a long time. Nonetheless, the Industrial Revolution marks the begin-ning of the large-scale use of fossil fuels that set in motion the gradual and, more recently, rapid change in the composition of the atmosphere that is causing climate change. Given this geological scale transformation, the Earth system science literature that discusses the Anthropocene frequently suggests that the first phase of the epoch began in the late eight-eenth century with the Industrial Revolution (Steffen et al. 2007). The key technology is the steam engine, first as a power source for mines and early factories and then as a source of locomotion both for railway engines and ships. While the combustion of coal causes local pollution problems, as Chinese citizens are frequently reminded these days, it also generates carbon dioxide and, in the short term, shades the Earth with soot, or "black carbon," and aerosol emissions.

The larger transformations set in motion by the Industrial Revolution, and the enhanced communications made possible by railways and steamships, also facilitated the rapid expan-sion of European power in the nineteenth century, incorporating many of the ecosystems of the planet much more directly into the global economy (Hornborg et al. 2007). These ecological transformations, and the spread of agriculture in the Americas in particular, are also part of the Industrial Revolution phase of the Anthropocene. Although carbon dioxide levels in the atmosphere rose slowly from pre-industrial levels close to 280 ppm to more than 300 ppm during this period, it was not until the mid-twentieth century that they really began to rise rapidly.

In the aftermath of World War II, industrial production expanded rapidly, and once the European economies had recovered from wartime disruptions, the spread of automobiles and suburban high-consumption lifestyles powered by petroleum in addition to coal be-came a global phenomenon. Trade expanded even more rapidly than economic growth, ushering in what is now understood as globalization, a phenomenon that is part and parcel of the extraordinary transformation of Earth, a period now often appropriately termed "the great acceleration" (McNeill and Engelke 2016). This period, which has seen the rise of carbon dioxide to 400 ppm and the rapid expansion of the human population to 7 billion, is also marked by the construction of huge cities and effectively the urbanization of hu-manity. To feed and supply these burgeoning cities, resources have been extracted from all over the planet, and rural transformations to feed and fuel the cities have proceeded apace. The unprecedented transformation of the human condition has meant dramatic changes to many ecological systems both directly in terms of land use change and indirectly as a result of fishing, hunting, deforestation, and infrastructure construction. The "great acceleration," as the Earth system thinkers term this period, has transformed global ecologies and led to widespread extinctions in the process of constructing what is effectively an increasingly artificial world (Steffen et al. 2011). It is worth emphasizing that when *Our Common Future* (World Commission 1987) was written in the mid-1980s, carbon dioxide levels in the at-mosphere were close to 350 ppm.

The extraordinary rise in human population, partly as a result of hygiene improvements and at least rudimentary public health systems in many places and partly as industrial ag-riculture transformed how people are fed, coincides with the nuclear age. Nuclear fallout, consisting in part of novel artificial radionuclides, was spread throughout the world and deposited in sediments worldwide. Hence, it presents a clear point in the sedimentary record of the planet, the proverbial golden spike marking the new era in the geological record. This will also have the advantage of being relatively long-lived given the slow rate of decay of some of the long-lasting isotopes. It coincides roughly too with the emergence of plastiglomerates, the new layers of sediment composed of plastics that are starting to accumulate in some areas where they are washed up on beaches and become incorporated in sandy deposits, some of which may eventually be turned into a new version of conglomerate. The weight of evidence in favor of a mid-twentieth century designation as the start of the Anthropocene is growing. Nuclear isotopes, novel substances, massive amounts of concrete, biological extinctions, and numerous other changes to the planet point to this as the sensible geological point at which a new epoch can be said to have started (Waters et al. 2016).

The rise of Asian economies, particularly that of China, in the past few decades has added hugely to the productive capabilities of humanity, but it has made the term acceleration especially apt as a descriptor of our current circumstances. Although the recent global economic disruptions following the financial problems of 2008 may have slowed the economies of Europe and America and temporarily slowed the emissions of carbon dioxide; in the aftermath of these events the upward trend continues. Acceleration has resumed, and with it the increasingly alarming concern that planetary boundaries are being rapidly transcended. Although such trends raise numerous suggestions that the Anthropocene is the prelude to a massive crash in ecological systems and that climate disruptions of catastrophic proportions are looming (Potsdam Institute 2012), some Earth scientists at least are examining the possibilities of a further better phase of the Anthropocene for humanity. It is hoped that this will be a period when humanity takes seriously the possibilities of a "sustainable Earth" and arranges its affairs so that it does not violate crucial planetary boundaries and hopelessly compromise the conditions of the Earth's "safe operating space."

PLANETARY BOUNDARIES

If such a prospect is to unfold, then thinking about the global ecosystem as a single entity that cannot be transformed endlessly without disruptive consequences is essential. Although there are obviously some "limits to growth," as the previous discussion regarding the 1970s suggested, given the abilities of technology to innovate and make new things and materials in new ways, resource constraints are much less of an issue than neo-Malthusian frameworks suggested. In the case of climate change, the problem is too much fossil fuel, not too little, and the most important goal for geological politics in the next few decades is to ensure that most of the remaining unburnt fossil fuels on Earth stay in the ground (Princen, Manno, and Martin 2015). Obviously, there are ecological limitations, but how these affect the increasingly artificial assemblage of entities that now make urban life possible is not so easy to specify. Humanity is effectively making the future, but it has no effective governance mechanisms in place to shape that future. There is a large gap between what the biosphere can safely cope with and the governance arrangements that humanity has so far dreamt up to deal with issues in the Anthropocene (Galaz 2014).

To tackle these issues obviously requires numerous social and political innovations, but also some clear indications of what the "safe operating space" for humanity is and what thresholds we need to avoid crossing if the nightmare scenarios of ecological catastrophe are to be avoided (Rockstrom et al. 2009). The safe operating space formulation is an attempt to quantify changes to the planet system and to alert human decision-makers to thresholds beyond which it is obviously unwise to go. Where these might be is not clear in many cases, but in a few it is fairly obvious. At the Copenhagen climate conference in 2009, world leaders agreed to limit the average global heating to less than 2°C, a figure then agreed as the upper limit of what was safe. During the Paris climate conference in December 2015, delegates came to a broad agreement that humanity should not push the planet beyond a 1.5°C warmer average global temperature, even though it was clear at that conference that humanity is currently on a trajectory likely to lead to an increase in temperature at least twice that, if not more. Nonetheless, the aspirational statement clearly points to recognition of that crucial Earth system boundary. To keep within this boundary requires limiting carbon dioxide concentrations to less than 350 ppm, approximately the level in the 1980s when *Our Common Future* was published (World Commission 1987).

In the 2015 updated version of the Earth system boundary formulation (Steffen et al. 2015), the climate change boundary is the first of nine systems of concern. Second is the matter of changes in biospheric integrity. This concerns the rapid reduction and extinction of many species and the possibility of maintaining genetic resources and biodiverse communities to allow for evolution to continue in the future, even if this is done in conditions of artificially constructed habitats and artificial ecosystems (Lorimer 2015). Humanity has already exterminated many species, and both direct action in changing habitat and hunting and indirect action in terms of pollution and climate change threaten many more. Biological diversity is so threatened that sometimes the current time period is discussed in terms of the sixth planetary extinction event (Kolbert 2014), an indication that this boundary is also in danger of transgression unless human action changes soon.

The third Earth system boundary is stratospheric ozone depletion. Chlorofluorocarbons and other ozone-depleting substances threaten to reduce the efficacy of the ozone layer in the high atmosphere and, in the process, allow more dangerous "ultraviolet B" radiation to reach the surface of the planet. This threatens terrestrial life forms, and not just humans. The relatively good news concerning this boundary is that international action to stop the production of the most dangerous ozone-depleting substances several decades ago has limited the depletion, and although the ozone layer still experiences substantial reductions over the poles each spring and the "holes" are not shrinking yet in the way that ozone protocol authors hoped in the 1980s and 1990s, they are no longer becoming more extensive each year.

Fourth is the issue of ocean acidification, which has been increasing recently due to the increase in carbon dioxide in the atmosphere. When some of this increased atmospheric concentration becomes dissolved in the surface waters of the oceans, it increases acidity and in the process becomes a problem for marine animals that have difficulty secreting aragonite, the form of calcium carbonate in their shells. Keeping atmospheric concentrations below the 350 ppm volume threshold, deemed appropriate for the climate change planetary boundary, should solve this problem because it will reduce acid concentrations to below levels that affect sea animals.

Fifth is the matter of biogeochemical flows, notably of nitrogen and phosphorous in the original 2009 formulation (Rockstrom et al. 2009) but with the addition of other minerals in the 2015 version. This boundary is concerned with preventing a major anoxic ocean event should too much fertilization occur because of terrestrial run-off due to artificial fertilizers applied in agriculture. This now also needs to be amended to prevent large-scale freshwater pollution. Regional variations also need careful consideration because, as with the other planetary boundary conditions, they vary widely throughout the planet.

The sixth boundary concerns changes in land use that impact biosystem integrity and are also associated with climate change. Currently, the boundary marker used is the amount of remaining forest cover on the planet. Tropical forests are most important given their eco-system functions and their carbon dioxide trapping potential. Boreal forests are also impor-tant because their removal changes the regional energy dynamic in the Arctic, where global warming is rapidly occurring. Recent research has emphasized the dramatic role human actions have played in changing the composition of assemblages of species; the arrival of ag-riculture has substantially altered terrestrial ecosystems in many areas of the world (Lyons et al. 2016).

Seventh is fresh water use. Throughout the world, humanity has dammed many rivers and diverts flows for agriculture, industry, and urban use. This changes natural flows and challenges water provision for ecosystems; hence, it is associated with both climate change issues and biodiversity. Human systems are dependent on fresh water not only for drinking and hygiene but also for industrial and agricultural production, and the possible disruption of these systems by water shortages has been an ongoing concern to environmentalists.

Eighth is the degree of atmosphere aerosol loading, which relates to the addition of soot, nitrates, and sulfates to the atmosphere as a result of the use of diesel fuel and other forms of combustion. Concerns about the possible role of these pollutants in reducing the intensity of the monsoon rains, essential to agriculture in much of South Asia in particular, make this another planetary boundary that needs to be monitored.

Ninth is the matter of the addition of numerous novel entities into the Earth system, the overall impact of which is obviously considerable even if it is very difficult to pro-duce any single measure of where the threshold might be. Numerous new substances and chemicals have been synthesized and are now widely produced by industry. Nanoparticles, microplastic particles, and polymers, in addition to a huge international trade in chemical wastes, make attention to the potential but mostly unknown hazards of these substances necessary in monitoring the operation of the Earth system, although as yet there is no ob-vious way to calculate the overall damage or where thresholds may lie.

All this requires thinking carefully about human activities on the largest scale and thinking about what we make and what kinds of economic activities are appropriate for running a small planet without transcending the boundaries. The latest iteration of the ideas of sustainable development, codified in the 2015 United Nations sustainable development goals, implies that humanity needs to remain within the conditions that have pertained to the planetary system for the historical period. The "safe operating system" authors (Steffen et al. 2015) note that

> this approach implies that the PB [planetary boundaries] framework, or something like it, will need to be implemented alongside the achievement of targets aimed at more immediate human needs, such as provision of clean, affordable and accessible energy and the adequate supply of food. (p. 7)

All these matters need attention in thinking about sustainable development goals and how the future can be shaped so that the next phase of the Anthropocene is more sustainable and, crucially, that it operates within the safe operating space. The alternative may be a very grim and violent future for large parts of humanity, one that should be avoidable if intelligent policies are undertaken in a timely manner. This discussion is going to be an important component of any academic endeavor in coming decades that takes the notion of global studies seriously. Human circumstances are increasingly artificial, and the political consequences require urgent attention by scholars, activists, and policymakers.

FROM GLOBAL STUDIES TO ANTHROPOCENOLOGY?

The significance of this "Anthropocene thesis" is profound for global studies and the future of world politics. Humanity is rapidly changing the planet and in the process placing us in a position in which there are few "natural" (i.e., untouched) ecosystems that we can preserve. Human actions have "domesticated" wild species with dramatic consequences for both animals and diseases, moving around ecological components and reassembled them in farms, gardens, parks, zoos, and, once they spread beyond their boundaries, increasingly artificial landscapes. Vast amounts of concrete have been created in the past few decades, a new geological form that adds to the argument that the Anthropocene really is different from the Holocene (Waters et al. 2016). These artificial landscapes are the world of the Anthropocene made by the processes of globalization. This is now the context in which global studies operates, one in which thinking in terms of a relatively untouched environment somewhere beyond humanity no longer makes sense any more than state boundaries do as the containers of culture.

Our artificial landscapes are criss-crossed with all the social, economic, and cultural innovations that global studies concerns itself with in attempting to grapple with the current human condition. As the original formulation of sustainable development made clear (World Commission 1987), the planet is very unevenly divided in human terms between wealthy and impoverished. Since *Our Common Future* was published, the rapid growth of the Asian economies and the huge expansion of the use of fossil fuels and numerous other resources have accentuated the divisions within and between states. This, too, is key to the climate change discussion; the poor and marginalized are frequently those most in danger of extreme events, more intense storms, food price spikes, droughts, and other disruptions. Victims of the "slow violence" of environmental change (Nixon 2011), these people are usually least responsible for setting climate change in particular in motion.

Global studies brings an engagement with the multiplicity of cultures and economic modes that are the current human story to the Anthropocene discussion. Looking to the diversity of human experience in an interconnected world emphasizes one of the key weaknesses in many of the Anthropocene formulations that rely heavily on the natural sciences—that is, the tendency to invoke a singular humanity and in the process to avoid questions of relative responsibility, and the dramatically different consequences that current transformations are going to have for people in different places and with different economic capabilities (Malm and Hornborg 2014). Crucial to the discussion of who should do what to shape the future are matters of who has the decision-making power over which energy systems will be built and used; which uses agricultural land is put to; which species are protected from habitat destruction, overfishing, and toxic pollution; and such things as how and where coastal mangrove forests are planted to protect coasts from storm surges and flooding (Moore 2015).

The Anthropocene thesis makes it clear that these are the most important political decisions of our times because they literally shape the future context for human existence. The future geology of the planet is now substantially a matter of how the rich and powerful decide on whether coal and petroleum remain key energy sources for future generations or whether, given accelerating climate change, they are rapidly phased out and energy systems that do not generate greenhouse gases replace them to power the cities where the majority of humans now live. The future of the Anthropocene is neither good nor bad; rather, it is a matter of political decisions (Dalby 2016). Geopolitics is now literally about the geological contexts that are being built by current generations of engineers and about whether these structures are made with carbon-intensive concrete or with more ecologically benign materials. How various human cultures tackle these questions is crucial to the next phase of economic globalization and its geological consequences.

Bringing these matters of global political economy and ecological transformation together into a single mode of thinking is a task for scholars of the present—one that challenges both conventional academic boundaries and modes of scholarship (Gopel 2016). Just as global studies explicitly challenges the frequent national boundaries of traditional academic work, so too the juxtaposition of globalization and geological politics requires much further conceptual innovation. Bonneuil and Fressoz (2016) suggest that we all need to rethink our professional identities and, in trying to link what academic study has so frequently set apart, re-imagine our professional identities as "Anthropocenologists." Although the term is not pretty, and it is not easy to pronounce, it does suggest rather forcefully the necessity of re-imagining ourselves, our research, and our teaching in a vocabulary appropriate for our times. The Anthropocene thesis requires nothing less.

REFERENCES

Agnew, J. 2003. *Geopolitics: Revisioning World Politics.* New York: Routledge.

Autin, Whitney J., and John M. Holbrook. 2012. "Is the Anthropocene an Issue of Stratigraphy or Pop Culture?" *GSA Today* 22 (7): 60–61.

Bonneuil, C., and J.-B. Fressoz. 2016. *The Shock of the Anthropocene.* London: Verso.

Brown, Anthony G., Stephen Tooth, Richard C. Chiverrell, et al. 2013. "The Anthropocene: Is There a Geomorphological Case?" *Earth Surface Processes and Landforms* 38: 431–434.

Chakrabarty, Dipesh. 2009. "The Climate of History: Four Theses." *Critical Inquiry* 35: 197–222.

Crosby, A. 1986. *Ecological Imperialism: The Biological Expansion of Europe 900–1900.* Cambridge, UK: Cambridge University Press.

Crutzen, Paul J. 2002. "Geology of Mankind—The Anthropocene." *Nature* 415: 23.

Dalby, S. 2016. "Framing the Anthropocene: The Good, the Bad, and the Ugly." *Anthropocene Review* 3 (1): 33–51.

Davies, J. 2016. *The Birth of the Anthropocene.* Berkeley: University of California Press.

Davis, Mike. 2001. *Late Victorian Holocausts: El Nino Famines and the Making of the Third World.* London: Verso.

Edwards, P. N. 2010. *A Vast Machine: Computer Models, Climate Data, and the Politics of Global Warming*. Cambridge, MA: MIT Press.

Emmett, Robert, and Thomas Lekan, eds. 2016. "Whose Anthropocene? Revisiting Dipesh Chakrabarty's 'Four Theses.'" *RCC Perspectives: Transformations in Environment and Society*, no. 2.

Finney, Stanley C., and Lucy E. Edwards. 2016. "The Anthropocene Epoch: Scientific Decision or Political Statement?" *GSA Today* 26 (3): 4–10.

Galaz, V. 2014. *Global Environmental Governance, Technology and Politics: The Anthropocene Gap*. Northampton, MA: Elgar.

Gopel, M. 2016. *The Great Mindshift: How a New Economic Paradigm and Sustainability Transformations Go Hand in Hand*. Berlin: Springer.

Hamilton, C., C. Bonneuil, and F. Gemmenne, eds. 2015. *The Anthropocene and the Global Environmental Crisis*. Abingdon, UK: Routledge.

Hornborg, Alf, John R. McNeill, and Joan Martinez-Alier, eds. 2007. *Rethinking Environmental History: World System History and Global Environmental Change*. Lanham, MD: Altamira.

Jamieson, Dale. 2014. *Reason in a Dark Time: Why the Struggle Against Climate Change Failed—And What It Means for the Future*. Oxford, UK: Oxford University Press.

Kolbert, Elizabeth. 2014. *The Sixth Extinction: An Unnatural History*. New York: Holt.

Latour, Bruno. 2013. "Facing Gaia: Six Lectures on the Political Theology of Nature." The Gifford Lectures, Edinburgh. http://www.bruno-latour.fr/node/486. Accessed July 2, 2015.

Lewis, S. L., and M. A. Maslin. 2015. "Defining the Anthropocene." *Nature* 519 (March 12): 171–180.

Lorimer, J. 2015. *Wildlife in the Anthropocene: Conservation After Nature*. Minneapolis: University of Minnesota Press.

Lyons, S. K., K. L. Amatangelo, A. K. Behrensmeyer, et al. 2016. "Holocene Shifts in the Assembly of Plant and Animal Communities Implicate Human Impacts." *Nature* 529: 80–83.

Malm, A., and A. Hornborg. 2014. "The Geology of Mankind? A Critique of the Anthropocene Narrative." *Anthropocene Review* 1 (1): 62–69.

Masco, J. 2015. "The Age of Fallout." *History of the Present: A Journal of Critical History* 5 (2): 137–168.

McNeill, J. R., and P. Engelke. 2016. *The Great Acceleration: An Environmental History of the Anthropocene Since 1945*. Cambridge, MA: Harvard University Press.

Meadows, D. H., D. L. Meadows, J. Randers, and W. W. Behrens III. 1972. *The Limits to Growth*. New York: Universe Books.

Moore, J. 2015. *Capitalism in the Web of Life*. London: Verso.

Nixon, R. 2011. *Slow Violence and the Environmentalism of the Poor*. Cambridge MA: Harvard University Press.

Parker, G. 2013. *Global Crisis: War, Climate Change and Catastrophe in the Seventeenth Century*. New Haven, CT: Yale University Press.

Potsdam Institute for Climate Impact Research and Climate Analytics. 2012. *Turn Down the Heat: Why a 4°C Warmer World Must Be Avoided*. Washington, DC: The World Bank.

Princen, T., J. P. Manno, and P. L. Martin, eds. 2015. *Ending the Fossil Fuel Era*. Cambridge, MA: MIT Press.

Pyne, Stephen J. 2012. *Fire: Nature and Culture*. New York: Reaktion Books.

Rockström, J., Will Steffen, Kevin Noone, et al. 2009. "A Safe Operating Space for Humanity." *Nature* 461: 472–475.

Ruddiman, William F. 2005. *Plows, Plagues, and Petroleum: How Humans Took Control of Climate*. Princeton, NJ: Princeton University Press.

Steffen, Will, Paul Crutzen, and John R. McNeill. 2007. "The Anthropocene: Are Humans Now Overwhelming the Great Forces of Nature?" *Ambio* 36 (8): 614–621.

Steffen, Will, Åsa Persson, Lisa Deutsch, et al. 2011. "The Anthropocene: From Global Change to Planetary Stewardship." *Ambio* 40: 739–761.

Steffen, Will, K. Richardson, J. Rockstrom, et al. 2015. "Planetary Boundaries: Guiding Human Development on a Changing Planet." *Science* 347 (6223): 1259855.

Waters, C. N., J. Zalasiewicz, C. Summerhayes, et al. 2016. "The Anthropocene Is Functionally and Stratigraphically Distinct from the Holocene." *Science* 351(6269). doi:10.1126/science. aad2622

World Commission on Environment and Development. 1987. *Our Common Future*. Oxford, UK: Oxford University Press.

Further Reading

Bonneuil, C., and J.-B. Fressoz. 2016. *The Shock of the Anthropocene*. London: Verso.

Hamilton, C., C. Bonneuil, and F. Gemenne, eds. 2015. *The Anthropocene and Global Environmental Crisis: Rethinking Modernity in a New Epoch*. Abingdon, UK: Routledge.

Kolbert, Elizabeth. 2014. *The Sixth Extinction: An Unnatural History*. New York: Holt.

Rockstrom, Johan, and Mathias Klum. 2015. *Big World Small Planet: Abundance Within Planetary Boundaries*. New Haven, CT: Yale University Press.

Van Munster, Rens, and Casper Sylvest, eds. 2016. *Assembling the Planet: The Politics of Globality Since 1945*. London: Routledge.

Wapner, P., and H. Elver, eds. 2016. *Reimagining Climate Change*. New York: Routledge.

CHAPTER 12

....

GLOBAL EPISTEMOLOGY

....

MOHAMMED A. BAMYEH

CAN there be a global epistemology—that is, a way of assessing different approaches to the study of global processes? How to analyze any social process depends on how we decide to see it in the first place. This does not mean that we will always see what we wish to see; only that the decision to see in a particular way—that is, to emphasize one dimension of a phenomenon over another—will produce in us the impression that what we are observing is either "true" or at least the most relevant angle for our interests, even though it may be a very small part of the larger, more meaningful, more complex whole. Those who focus on the political economy of globalization, for example, may believe that globalization consists only of political economy. Those who focus on power dynamics will likely be predisposed to assess it as just the latest iteration of imperial or high politics. Those who are highly sensitized to questions of "hegemony" will tend to believe that globalization as they see it presents a clear tale of their cherished concept.

The perspectives listed previously are not necessarily "wrong" inasmuch as they are deeply myopic. Myopia means that the analysis is not necessarily an error but that it is relevant only to one dimension of a problem that is more complex than the analysis has made it to appear. This perspectivist problem is especially weighty in the study of *global* phenomena because these are by definition extremely complex and wide-ranging in their implications, given their worldwide scope and that they affect all spheres of life, including economy, culture, and politics. It is curious, therefore, that no epistemology has developed specifically in relation to the study of global processes. This is likely because most globalization experts saw no practical or empirical ways to draw on a rich philosophical tradition, or perhaps because they assumed that they could, without any epistemology, identify what was most compelling about something as huge as global processes. In this chapter, I first outline the scope of global epistemology and then devote the rest of the chapter to highlighting some perspectivist issues that illustrate what it may consist of.

The scope of global epistemology is vast, but it can be captured in two general approaches. The first approach identifies local phenomena that could be explained in terms of global processes. Here, the global is made to explain the local. The second approach targets global phenomena directly so as to identify their general patterns. Usually, this is the opposite of the former approach: Local or situational phenomena are brought together to explain the global. Both approaches have underlying epistemological assumptions. The most radical of those is the assumption that all local phenomena could be "translated" into a global script—whether as ingredients of a large process, as similes and parallels of each other, or as variations on a single large theme.

In light of the previous discussion, one would expect global approaches to knowledge to be intensely communicative. One provides an analysis of an event in Haiti because it explains something that has happened in Taiwan, for example. In global analysis, the two countries would be brought together not through evocative metaphors, nor for the sake of theory building about culture or personality in a way that is familiar to anthropologists especially and other social scientists. Rather, in global analysis especially, these disparate locations are brought together in order to demonstrate how they are linked and how they affect each other in ways that may be invisible to most of their inhabitants. We see elements of that approach in Karl Marx's (1867) introduction to *Das Kapital*, in which he reminds his German readers not to confuse it as a book about England just because his examples are drawn from the English experience: "The story is about you."

One apparent advantage of this approach is that it makes distant places and even times appear more intimate and familiar because they are part of the same (or at least analogous to) posited global processes. The distant therefore comes to life, without us having to experience it directly, because it has been described in a way that links it up to what we experience—or at least in a way that makes us understand better what we already experience. That distant location or time about which we may know nothing otherwise has become sensible to our imagination; sometimes what is accepted as proper "explanation" may be nothing more than a manner through which the explanandum is made to fit into an image of the world to which we were already committed.

But to someone *not* already committed to global narratives in the fashion described previously, the approach just outlined would appear to be completely unfounded. Knowledge that is new, original, or worthwhile, one might say, is knowledge that challenges rather than confirms our already held beliefs, including deep ones. From an epistemological viewpoint, therefore, not only must the global character of any phenomenon be demonstrated rather than asserted but also one must show how an explanation in global terms reveals more interesting or worthwhile facets of it, along with justifying criteria for such judgments.

Neither approach, however, is the end of the road, given the assumption of complexity associated with anything global. If an approach we take to explain the fate of any local community or social fact in global terms becomes compelling enough, it will tend to invite more analytical work precisely because "compelling" is the adjective we tend to use to suggest that a certain portrayal is inviting more analytical work. For "compelling" is what we say when we believe that we are finally approaching a significant meaning but are not confident enough that we are there yet. And one meaning may be said to be more significant than another when it accounts for more facets of any phenomenon, such as when it brings together both objective and subjective factors.

For example, once we acquire a real interest in some community hitherto unknown to us, we cease to be satisfied with it being described simply as "victimized," "vulnerable," or "oppressed" by external forces. Such descriptors no longer appear to give us an adequate sense of the agency and humanity of the people we are talking about. Rather, the discourse of pure victimhood gives us the sense of people as passive characters in a world of objective, large structures. The language of pure vulnerability tells us nothing about how people organize themselves or what they do to address challenges they face—for example, in times of war, atrocities, and all other apparently uncontrolled processes.

From a global perspective, the work of external forces on the local would be expected to be constant, which means that we should expect unceasing yield of human creativity in response. Therefore, the compelling global narratives are those that tell us not simply tales of objective, large structures but of agents who create new meanings as they confront new problems. Local knowledge tends to appear global enough when it conveys a larger theoretical proposition, shows similarities across cases in different locations, or reveals structural linkages across widely dispersed spaces or times. This would be the analysis of the specialist. But do local individuals or communities also do the same thing? That is, under what conditions do they themselves discover the generalizability of their own conditions; learn that their own local story has the potential to be a global story—that is, the story of someone else far away; or comprehend the global systems in which they are presumably embedded?

If we are interested in the last set of questions, then by implication we would be interested in a global epistemology that is communicative in its nature—that is, not only the epistemology of the specialist but also that of the ordinary person who we assume to be party to a global process, whether consciously or not. If the underlying assumption is that global life, global structures, or global processes are inescapable, then any epistemology that is said to be "global" gains validity to the extent that it is sensible to the broadest spectrum of those presumably affected by it. That is precisely why especially when it comes to global phenomena, we must speak of epistemologies that possess globally communicative capacities. Epistemology, the theory of knowing, often appears necessary to develop after various ways of looking at the same thing have begun to reveal their myopia and omissions—that is, reveal that they cannot communicate to all those presumably affected by the domain of knowledge it covers. Next, I suggest a few elementary building blocks of global epistemologies so conceived.

ELEMENTS OF GLOBAL EPISTEMOLOGY

Meso-Level Analysis (Not Macro)

Global analysis is by definition an analysis of large categories. That is true of local-level analysis as well, to the extent that the intended result is to show the local to be an instance of or illustration of something very large. In itself, using large categories is not a problem, but it quickly becomes such when the analysis suggests that (1) it presents a "solution" to a problem it diagnoses and (2) it endows the large category it analyzes with collective agency so that the category itself, rather than specific authorities, institutions, or groups, appears to be acting on the world. Understood this way, large categories are rarely helpful if they are the centerpiece of the analysis, even though they may appear analytically sound. But they rarely help us identify the *specific* agent who is producing phenomena, nor do they help us identify practical ways to solve problems.

For example, the rise of right-wing populism in Europe in recent years is said to be tied to a broad social perception that migrants cannot be integrated into host societies because of their "culture." However, there is nothing more immobilizing than positing such a large category as "culture" as the root of a problem. A meso-level analysis, by contrast, allows for a more precise diagnosis, when for example it descends from the category of "culture" and explores more specific areas, such as the structure of opportunities, social capital, various "subcultures," patterns of mutual help, or any other meso-level aspect of the social life of large communities. Macro analysis in terms of "culture," by contrast, rarely gives us clear guidance as to what we could do.

This logic can be extended to various problems. For example, there is usually no *practical* point in blaming "modernity," or even "capitalism," for a whole series of problems, even though the charge may be sound factually and analytically. Although such an analysis may help us understand the root of one problem or another, it is increasingly obvious that such understanding has only limited pragmatic venues. Explanations in terms of large categories tend to be immobilizing and discouraging precisely because they are posited as both "true" and "inescapable," which means that there is no point in trying to do anything about them if we lack the means to act on large categories, which is usually the case. So we either become perpetually depressed and in need of therapy or helpful substances or something like an unusually helpful god. But if we think of "analysis" not simply as a venue for "truth" but more importantly as the type of inquiry that should give one energy to live on, and of science as something that is evaluated in terms of its usefulness to life, then the level of analysis we opt for needs to be appropriate for such missions.

Normal Flow of Trouble (Not "Crisis")

Those seasoned in global studies are familiar with the profuse use of the term "crisis" to describe all sorts of phenomena, ranging from short-lived episodes to periodic fluctuations and long-term processes. "Crisis" has been applied to describe such things as financial turbulence, refugee flows, and electoral uncertainties, and it has encompassed all sorts of economic, political, and cultural discussions attendant to global phenomena. As a term, "crisis" evokes the image of a cataclysm, to be followed (at some usually unspecified period) by a resolution in the form of total overhaul of the system that caused the crisis, by technical adjustment that takes the system just a few steps away from the brink, or by yet another "crisis." But what is the difference between "crisis" and "normal troubles"? A global epistemology would require a clarification of the difference between the two, but especially when the term "crisis" is used, because "crisis" suggests a greater seriousness of the problem and anticipates weighty outcomes, whereas ordinary troubles occasion the functioning of any system. In the analysis of global processes, is it possible that what is often called "crisis" is little more than natural oscillations and adjustments to pressures produced by the very interconnection of the world?

The normalcy of trouble should in fact be expected in any system that is established enough to behave as a system—that is, established enough to compel influential participants to save it every time it seems to be faltering, and to suggest to most other ordinary participants that it is worth saving (if for no reason other than that the alternative may not be obvious). We saw that tendency, for example, during one of the darkest moments of the global economy in the 2008 financial crisis. Everyone *agreed* that that was a crisis worthy of the name, but hardly any participant opted to exit from the system then, and the crisis was managed despite its enormous scale and unparalleled cost. It was managed by technical adjustments, the accumulation of (presumably temporary) debt, and a few extra regulations. Of course, something similar to it could happen again, and a recurrence may be a feature of the system that we have. But the notion of "crises" suggests that the system that produces them cannot manage them, when, as the aftermath of 2008 demonstrates, we cannot anticipate how the system will be made to adjust to the specter of doom, until it must.

The notion of "normal trouble," by contrast, gives us two perspectivist advantages over the notion of "crisis": (1) Trouble is constant, and (2) it is a regular feature of the system. This applies to financial markets just as it does to the movement of peoples throughout the world. The fact that millions of people risk their lives in waves of illegal migrations, and continue to join such adventures despite their awareness of the perils and other disincentives paraded by receiving countries, suggests that the force that is producing these waves is irrepressible. But are they crises? In other words, are population movements a challenge to a global system or a normal byproduct of it (and as such constant and ordinary)? The difference between the two terms is not a simple matter of sophistry but, rather, of how to imagine a response: When a phenomenon is recognized as an ordinary trouble—that is, as an ordinary feature of the system—then the system can be asked to make room for it. If it is a crisis—that is, a counter-systemic movement (that may be generated by the system itself)—then it cannot be resolved within the bounds of the existing system, and we have a warlike situation between a system and its determined enemies.

A look at the profile of sending countries of migrants may help us identify push factors that constantly produce troubles aimed at only one feature of the global system, a feature that contradicts its own globality: the existence of borders against the movement of people but not against the movement of other things, such as capital and goods. Within this perspective, we can further identify two more specific push factors: (1) the tendency of the movement of people to follow routes along which economic links have already been established, as demonstrated by Saskia Sassen (1990, 1999); and (2) as is more recently evident, the movement of people out of situations characterized by absence of hope. Neither is about simple inequality in a world system. Rather, both concern the *context* in which persons and communities contemplate various options that they recognize to be available to them at any given point.

We know that people can live with gross inequalities as long as there is some realistic hope of improving one's condition by known and available means, however slightly. One can endure civil war, as the Syrians have done for the first three years of theirs, as long as there is a realistic hope of a solution soon, even an unsatisfactory one. But to the extent that the world becomes hopeless, one has to expect those who experience it as such to try to create hope in ways that only yesterday had appeared unimaginable. In doing so, they prove their humanity to their own selves. They become active agents and are no longer simple victims. They may be driven by war, by economics, or by famine. The mistake we make is that we try to distinguish them on the basis of the type of force that drives them out—that is, whether they are "economic" or "political" refugees. But more important is the gravity of such a force, its capacity, whatever its type, to generate hopelessness in the world and make it unlivable.

If forces that generate hopelessness are part of the global system, we should expect the same system to compel people to invent new sources of hope on an ongoing basis. The fact that sometimes they do so in ways that are very dangerous suggests that in one way or another, they view the world at large as their theater. The trouble they seek to overcome is the existence of borders vis-à-vis their own movement. And that itself is a source of trouble only when it contradicts the absence of borders in the face of other forces that make the system into a global system: goods, capital, and cultural messages.

Seeing the Agent (Not the Circumstance)

Global epistemology requires types of explanation that are neither entirely "objective" nor one-sided—for example, the claim that climate change will cause or is already causing revolutions, wars, and so on. One here should remember Amartya Sen's (1983) analysis of the causes of famines: They are not caused by droughts, by evidence of the fact that many world regions have suffered long droughts but no famines. Rather, famines tend to be associated most with the absence of an accountable political system.

If we apply this perspective to the environment, the pertinent social question would not simply consist of describing what nature is doing but also whether we as a society are organized in such a way as to allow us to handle effectively whatever problems are handed to us by nature. The Low Countries, for example, came into being in spite of nature, not because of it. Nomadic life in the desert was a way of social organization that allowed society to make use of an otherwise inhospitable nature. Humans do not simply conquer nature but, rather, organize themselves first in such a way so that they can handle its challenges. The fact that we often confuse this ancient self-organization with a modern attitude that abuses and disregards and destroys nature does not help us gain analytical clarity. Because then we do not see how, for example, the challenge of even a typhoon may be met more successfully by a society that has known how to deal with it than by another that never acquired that knowledge (Adger et al. 2005; Peters-Guarin, McCall, and van Westen 2012; Samaddar et al. 2015). Neither do we see, as Richards (2016) shows, how evolving local knowledge helped stem the tide against the spread of the Ebola virus.

The question therefore is not what external, objective forces are doing to us but, rather, how communities are organized to address their challenge. And because the work of external forces is constant and varies in shape and intensity, we should look more into human organizational creativity as a constant and varied impulse. In the globalization narratives, more compelling than tales of victimhood are tales of agents who craft innovative responses as they confront new challenges.

Complex Connectivity (Not Hegemony)

Students of global order, and before them students of world-system analysis, are used to such terms as "core" and "periphery" and also to describing cultural and ideological global hierarchies in terms of "hegemony." Those terms have indeed provided valuable insights into global relations, especially in pointing out the role of historical processes, including colonialism, in shaping the modern world. However, like all successful terms, they reach a point when their explanatory power becomes exhausted. This is generally the case when terms begin to be used ritualistically or mechanically rather than as ways to explicate new knowledge. Once a "hegemony" has been exposed, we are already one step beyond it; relations in the world may continue to be characterized by hegemonies of one form or another, but once we have identified the condition, the next step would be to see what the person who is presumably caught up in its thralls is doing about it.

Critics of globalization frequently stop short of that level of critique. In my own position as editor of an international sociological journal, I have repeatedly offered readers from around the world an opportunity to provide me with counter-hegemonic narratives—that is, examples of local contributions to sociological knowledge that are little known outside of their local environments, written in any language, and produced in any format, scholarly or otherwise. I thought of this as an attempt to provide "positive knowledge"—that is, knowledge that goes beyond the simple and already well-known critique of the "hegemony" of Western knowledge. The dearth of response to my efforts suggested to me that hegemony is perhaps maintained in part by those who complain about it: they no longer know how to operate should they be given a chance to work *without* hegemony.

What we call "local knowledge" may be such because it is not yet available in formats that allow it to be communicated beyond the local level. But the communication and translation of that knowledge is part of the responsibility of those intellectuals concerned about global knowledge, and *especially* about hegemony. For "critique" alone does not create lasting communities of belief, only episodic oppositions that cannot last if not followed with alternative, affirmative knowledge. And by "alternative knowledge," I do not necessarily mean "true," objective, or positivist knowledge, only *ways of seeing* that should come into existence after an original critique.

In addition, sometimes terms that purport to describe inequalities in world systems, such as core, periphery, and hegemony, cover up more than they reveal. This is not because inequality is not important. Rather, it is because global phenomena are by nature complex. A relationship that may be said to be hegemonic in one respect may also bring into being unsuspected possibilities and creativities, which require being investigated on their own terms even as we may continue to be suspicious of the power imbalances and unequal access that gave rise to them. In his work on transnational film, for example, Randall Halle (2014) has explored what he calls "complex connectivity," precisely as an alternative term to hegemony. Here, complex connectivity is the manner through which cultural creators and funders operating in different countries and film traditions find new ways to foster global film that had not been imaginable in a previous era in which film everywhere (apart from Hollywood) was expected to be a national endowment. Although power imbalances remain part of systems characterized by "complex connectivity," simply focusing on such imbalances does not help us understand the full scope of what is being created, nor to understand or appreciate the creativity of participants who are less privileged within such connectivities.

Community Comes into Existence by Knowledge (Not Necessity)

Perhaps one of the least explored roles of epistemology concerns the ways by which knowledge, specifically social knowledge, participates in bringing communities into being. By mapping out the social science landscape in the Arab region, for example, a recent Arab social sciences report (Bamyeh 2015), along with the various activities surrounding it in different countries, helped bring into being the social science community that it described.

The individual social scientists who came to form that community had of course existed before, but not as a self-conscious, networked group across many countries. The same is true of other types of communities, including national ones: A social community comes into awareness of its distinct identity, or at least gains more such awareness, to the extent that it is described. Sometime, it is described defensively—that is, in relationship to or in the context of an increasing awareness of an encroaching outside world. But in either case, we often forget this community-making role of knowledge that is a fundamental part of the work of intellectuals (Bamyeh 2012).

The role of discourse, including learned discourse, in giving shape to social communities is perhaps one of the least appreciated facts of social knowledge, perhaps due to the learned assumption that science explores rather than creates reality. Obviously, not all such discourses are equally effective, but the salience of any knowledge depends on whether an audience finds it to speak to what it believes to be its authentic circumstances. For example, there were times when the "working class," as an object of knowledge, was a highly effective and relevant category of analysis both because working classes in many areas of the world existed as self-conscious communities with strong organizations, and because social sciences developed intercommunicative traditions of addressing this term. Sometimes, however, that old clarity becomes blurry, whether because an old social community begins to define itself in different terms, or because the social science discourse about it has become frozen in old debates and thus no longer seems to generate knowledge that appears relevant to its current life. It is precisely such situations that call anew for a socially communicative epistemology: an epistemology that gives effective voice to a cluster of scattered feelings for which the loudest expression could for a time be populist politics. But that would be the case only because an epistemology proper to articulate things more intelligibly has not yet taken shape.

The Human Actor (Not the Structures) at the Center of Analysis

A large part of the globalization critique may be described as anti-human, ironically precisely as it shows deep concern for downtrodden humanity. This anti-humanity comes in two forms: excessive economism, which reduces the full complexity of the human actor to just one facet (which then is said to be "determining"), and a focus on victimhood, which does the same thing, namely by presenting the human as a non-actor, a mere recipient of systemic troubles and in need to be saved (by someone else).

Practitioners of either approach seem to be unaware of their myopias, even though those who understand globalization as a purely economic process also sometimes add non-economic factors as footnotes, and largely insofar as these seem to help "explain" economic processes. From an epistemological viewpoint, such analyses are always myopic because they emphasize only one side of a complex operation, because they posit that one side as "determining" of all else, and because they highlight human passivity over activity.

Although these analytic preferences may be partially traced to a widespread version of traditional Marxist analysis, they are also traceable to another approach that could not be farther removed from Marxism, namely the contemporary neoliberal perspective. Ironically, both seem to say the same thing: The economy is the fundamental starting and end point of any discussion of human emancipation. The reason why this analytical proposition may be said to be anti-human is not because economics are not important but, rather, because it ignores the various ways by which humans create meaning and culture out of their situations, including all kinds of illegalities.

Second, victim stories are anti-human: Victims are objects of sympathy, but it is a great deduction of their humanity if we only see them as victims, rather than as agents capable of doing something creative within a miserable environment. Some of the most popular films to discuss such problems as underdevelopment or oppression, such as *Darwin's Nightmare* (2004) or *The Devil Came on a Horseback* (2007), sketch out a starkly troubling perspective in which local inhabitants appear as no more than passive victims waiting to be saved by White Western heroes. *The Devil Came*, in particular, has not been viewed as a racist film only because it seems to portray the victims in Darfur, even though it is nothing more than the story of the "heroism" of a White US marine who single-handedly tries to save poor Africans. The latter appear in the film only as corpses, spectators, or mute characters staring at the camera and waiting for the White man to explain their story.

Conclusion

Clearly, a global epistemology must be a humane epistemology, in which those who are presumably subject to large forces are allowed to speak and express how they themselves live, know, learn, and grow, and not simply how they suffer. Because suffering, in the final analysis, should itself serve as an invitation to knowledge. The more varied the sources of this suffering, and the longer it lasts, the more comprehensive is the scope of knowledge it calls forth. A global epistemology gains much by linking itself up to that heritage of profuse knowledge.

References

Adger, W. Neil, Terry P. Hughes, Carl Folke, Stephen R. Carpenter, and Johan Rockström. 2005. "Social–Ecological Resilience to Coastal Disasters." *Science* 309 (5737): 1036–1039.

Bamyeh, Mohammed A. 2012. "The Social Dynamism of the Organic Intellectual." In *Intellectuals and Civil Society in the Middle East*, edited by Mohammed A. Bamyeh, 1–28. London: Tauris.

Bamyeh, Mohammed A. 2015. *Social Sciences in the Arab World: Forms of Presence*. Beirut: Arab Council for the Social Sciences.

Darwin's Nightmare [Motion picture]. 2004. Directed by Hubert Sauper. Produced by Hubert Sauper et al. Distributed by International Film Circuit.

Halle, Randall. 2014. *The Europeanization of Cinema: Interzones and Imaginative Communities*. Urbana: University of Illinois Press.

Marx, Karl. 1867. *Das Kapital*. Hamburg, Germany: Verlag von Otto Meisner.

Peters-Guarin, Garciela, Michael K. McCall, and Cees van Westen. 2012. "Coping Strategies and Risk Manageability: Using Participatory Geographical Systems to Represent Local Knowledge." *Disasters* 36 (1): 1–27.

Richards, Paul. 2016. *Ebola: How a People's Science Helped End an Epidemic*. London: Zed.

Samaddar, Subhajyoti, Muneta Yokomatsu, Frederick Dayour, Martin Oteng-Ababio, Togbiga Dzivenu, Mujeeb Adams, and Hirohiko Ishikawa. 2015. "Evaluating Effective Public Participation in Disaster Management and Climate Change Adaptation: Insights from Northern Ghana Through a User-Based Approach." *Risk, Hazards & Crisis in Public Policy* 6 (1): 117–143.

Sassen, Saskia. 1990. *The Mobility of Labor and Capital: A Study in International Investment and Labor Flow.* Cambridge, UK: Cambridge University Press.

Sassen, Saskia. 1999. *Guests and Aliens.* New York: New Press.

Sen, Amartya. 1983. *Poverty and Famine: An Essay on Entitlement and Deprivation.* Oxford, UK: Oxford University Press.

The Devil Came on a Horseback [Motion picture]. 2007. Directed by Ricki Stern and Anne Sundberg. Produced by Jane Wells and Gretchen Wallace. Distributed by Break Thru Films.

CHAPTER 13

GLOBAL STUDIES VERSUS INTERNATIONAL STUDIES

SARA R. CURRAN

INTERNATIONAL studies scholarship as defined by the International Studies Association (ISA) is dedicated to understanding international, transnational, and global affairs.[1] It boasted more than 7,000 members in 2017, including academics, practitioners, policy experts, private sector workers, and independent researchers. Founded in 1959, it hosts seven publications that cover the gamut of topics related to security, conflict, peace and reconstruction, cross-border interactions, human rights, interactions of global actors and organizations, foreign policy, teaching, and policy applications. It is a diverse collective of scholars and practitioners primarily concerned with the "affairs" of international interactions. As Hey (2004: 397) notes, the predominating topics, theories, and evidence published in the leading journal of the ISA, *International Studies Quarterly*, along with the association's presidential addresses, are those of international relations and political science, particularly the work of scholars who study conflict.

Chernotsky and Hobbs (2015) define international studies as "a field of inquiry that examines the broad array of human relationships that involve cross-border interaction" (p. 3). In this sense, scholarship in the field is defined by national borders and anchored by the paradigmatic state-centric assumption of the primacy of nation-states (Blanton and Breuning 2016). In reaction to debates in the field and the recognition of the heavy emphasis on political science theory and methods, in recent years the ISA has introduced two new journals to accommodate a greater array of disciplinary scholarly publication venues. One is *International Political Sociology*, which includes critical social science approaches from scholars in sociology, anthropology, and geography. The other journal is *International Interactions*, which invites scholarship at the intersection of conflict and political economy. However, the association's approach to interdisciplinary as agglomeration rather than integration is reminiscent of development approaches that failed to understand the distinction between "women in development" and "gender and development" (Razavi and Miller 1995).

As this volume's collection of chapters attest, the premise of global studies begins with a transdisciplinary integration. At its core, global studies critiques social science and postmodern approaches, challenging the taken-for-granted categories and boundaries that inadvertently reify systems of power and marginalize inquiries into the "undoing" of those categories, boundaries, and systems of power through the intensification and dynamics of various forms of globalization (see Chapter 1, this volume). The field is united, not by theory, methodology, or a set of assumptions but, rather, by the very questioning of old assumptions, the generation of new conceptual domains, the application of mixed methodologies, and the building of knowledge through the multiperspectival lenses of space and time, necessitating analyses of processes, recursive reflection, mutability, and dialectics (Appadurai et al. 1997).

The purpose of this chapter is to focus on the distinctiveness of international studies and its contributions to global studies. In the first section, I place the field into historical context. My point is not to diminish the value of international studies as a field of scholarship but, rather, to understand the value of what knowledge it can offer, as well as the inevitable boundedness of the field. The second section describes the institutional presence of international studies programs across hundreds of campuses, including thousands of professors and tens of thousands of students in the United States, Europe, and throughout the world, that offers a richly endowed resource that will inevitably continue to enrich traditional disciplines and vitalize emergent fields such as global studies. This latter perspective is the focus of the third section of this chapter.

EMERGENCE AND ESTABLISHMENT OF INTERNATIONAL STUDIES SCHOLARSHIP AND CURRICULAR PROGRAMS

The emergence of international studies in the United States is closely tied with the disciplinary endeavors of area studies. In fact, histories of area studies are frequently identified as the antecedents of international studies. Often, historians will point to the interwar period of the twentieth century and the so-called awakening of America to its place in the world as the moment when the American Council of Learned Societies or the Social Science Research Council led the call for an international studies academic enterprise (Bigelow and Legters 1964; Lambert 1980). However, McCaughey's (1984) *International Studies and Academic Enterprise* traces the institutionalization of area studies and international studies within academia from the early nineteenth century. Although McCaughey argues that the academic enterprise was a relative latecomer among the disciplines represented within the humanities and social sciences, it comes into full force by the time of World War I. Nevertheless, with early roots closely associated with religious missions, and then to a lesser extent foreign affairs and those interested in language and travel, the field remained relatively untouched by academia. By this, McCaughey means that those claiming to be international studies scholars and associating professionally were not those hired within academia. Often, they pursued training through extracurricular, individual intent and hands-on experience, and they associated with each other in non-academic, learned societies such as the American Oriental Society. Throughout much of the nineteenth century, these gentlemen scholars intended to take their learning and put it into practice, including evangelizing throughout the "hinterlands." To the extent there was academic training, it was in philology, particularly the languages of the Middle East, and the study of the Orient.

During this time, European universities and learned societies, particularly English and German organizations, often provided a source of expertise and training for these American international studies scholars. McCaughey's (1984) point in tracing the roots of area and international studies is to indicate the deep and persistent strain of practicality and mission-driven, colonizing inclinations of the earliest contributors to the field. It was during the latter half of the nineteenth century that language and civilization studies were established, and many of the recruits to those programs were ministers in training (p. 17). Although few of these graduates entered the academy, the "second-generation" international studies scholars were the children of some of these missionaries. They arrived on the small number of campuses with sincere interest in knowledge for knowledge's sake and substantial and deep language and cultural studies experience. Although they may have put aside their parents' missionary tendencies, they remained rooted in that experience (McCaughey 1984). Their perspectives and experiences shaped the establishment of area studies programs at Chicago, Columbia, Cornell, Harvard, Johns Hopkins, and Yale. Throughout the last decades of the nineteenth century, programs were also established at public universities, including the University of California and the University of Washington. McCaughey estimates that by the end of the nineteenth century, 13% of PhDs granted in the humanities and social sciences were awarded to those in international studies (p. 35). As programs had grown, so had opportunities for teaching within the academy. By the end of that century, 35% of PhDs were entering the academy. Even so, an almost equal proportion (30%) still pursued missionary work (p. 38). McCaughey argues that by 1911, the 7,000 protestant missionaries evangelizing on most continents were the main sources of American academic knowledge about the "non-Western" world (p. 53).

It was the two world wars and the interwar period that truly galvanized both international studies and a growing number of area studies programs. During World War I, the student constituency for international studies shifted dramatically away from missionaries to include journalists, particularly those who were war correspondents or wanted to be war correspondents. Commercial and military interests resulting from American trade and military exploits also provided constituencies of students keen to pursue international studies training. After World War I, a sizeable number of American newspapers set out to become definitive sources of foreign news coverage, beyond just war correspondence. Although these correspondents may not have been steeped in area studies knowledge, their books and reporting whetted the appetite for deeper understanding. At the same time, their reporting sowed the seeds of doubt about their objectivity and capacities. Notably, several of the more intrepid and famous correspondents "went native" and stayed abroad more often than returning home. Their questionable allegiances and objectivity led to something of a decline in both the prestige and the number of foreign correspondent positions (McCaughey 1984: 60). At the same time, the US government's interest in investing in national capacities in language and area studies was growing. George Kennan's opportunity to return to graduate study of Russian with government funding and the promise of a job in the US Foreign Service is the emblematic case of both the enclosure of international and area studies within the academy and the explicit linkage to public service and American national interests (p. 66). It was during this time that a clearly established alignment of area studies and US government service occurred. Area studies training became a career trajectory within the Foreign Service, and becoming a diplomat was viewed as a form of public service that included an intellectual endeavor for highly trained elites. This was not without a great deal of ambivalence among those elites who filled the academy and the Foreign Service; that ambivalence remains a constant theme in both realms to this day (Barnes and Farish 2006; Bender 1997; Engerman 2007; Solovey 2001).

The greatest boost for international studies came from World War II and American entry into the war. A significant American military, commercial, and government international expansion, alongside a concomitant growth of, and investment in, American universities, and support from major philanthropic interests led to a significant growth in international studies programs and experts housed in the academy (Barnes and Farish 2006; Bender 1997; Cummings 2002; Engerman 2007; McCaughey 1984; Mitchell 2003, Solovey 2001). McCaughey argues that besides physics, no other American academic enterprise benefitted more from the national war mobilization than did international studies. Academics were brought into the halls of government to lend insights on far-flung areas of the world where the United States had strategic interests (McCaughey 1984). The role of the American government in supporting the academic enterprise of area and international studies materialized after the war's conclusion and with the rise of the Cold War.

Beginning in the 1950s, major philanthropic entities such as the Rockefeller Foundation and the Ford Foundation marshaled significant resources for area and international studies, beginning with the Ford Foundation's Foreign Area Fellowship Program in 1950. Their investments were soon matched by the Carnegie Corporation. Crucial to the catalyzing of these investments were the American Council of Learned Societies and the Social Science Research Council. Nevertheless, while the academy expanded throughout the country after the war, and international studies expanded along with it, the proportion of international or area studies PhDs dropped relative to the overall production of PhDs in the social science and humanities. The Ford Foundation's International Training and Research Program imbued the relatively small number of PhDs and their advisors within area and international studies with significant importance and power. The major goals of the Ford Foundation were to advance the national good and then international human welfare through significant investments in higher education, particularly area and international studies. Within three years, from 1960 to 1962, Cornell University, Harvard University, Columbia University, UCLA, the University of California at Berkeley, the University of Chicago, Indiana University, the University of Pennsylvania, Princeton University, the University of Washington, Stanford University, the University of Wisconsin, and Yale University had received institutional grants to establish non-Western studies on a permanent and comparable footing as other disciplines. Alongside these private investments, the Ford Foundation worked closely with the US Congress and Senator Fulbright to establish Title VI funding, with appropriations growing from $500,000 in 1960 to $13 million in 1965. Much of this was focused on national need and national mobilization to better understand the world and influence its trajectory economically and ideologically (McCaughey 1984).

The formal establishment of a professional association of scholars and practitioners dedicated to international studies emerged during this period. Ole Holsti (2014) and Henry Teune (1982) provide informal histories about the founding of the ISA in 1958, as both served as presidents of the professional association. In their description, they articulate the profound desire at the time of its founding to shape the world through moral suasion, both practically and empirically. This included two dimensions—one practical—the inclusion of foreign policymakers and practitioners, as well as economists, psychologists, political scientists, biologists, and geographers deeply engaged with resolutely seeking to eliminate war and creating a more civilized, progressive world. The personal histories of the early leaders of the field were forged as refugee intellectuals from World Wars I and II, as well as soldiers on the battlefields. They were some of the same individuals who founded, for example, the *Journal of Conflict Resolution*, the New School, the RAND Corporation, as well as populating the emerging curricular programs in area and international studies across higher education institutions in the United States (Bessner 2017; Holsti 2014). Although of a different substance, theirs was a mission-oriented agenda, just like that of their nineteenth-century, antecedent colleagues.

The second and related dimension defining the establishment of the ISA and the research agenda it professed to pursue was to create a space for scholars of international relations who found the American Political Science Association stifling for its empiricism and who sought to develop theories beyond realism. The realism theory prominent in political science thought at the time offered a value-neutral agenda that the founders of the ISA found perplexing. This normative agenda of the ISA founders meshed well with other members' practical mission, seeking to create a more peaceful world. As Guilhot (2008, 2011) cogently argues, international relations scholars have chafed over their place within political science. The ISA and investments in international studies became a fertile intellectual ground for colonization, and that has remained true throughout its history as a field, notwithstanding the notable theoretical diversification of social science scholarship in recent decades. Teune (1982) notes the continued preeminence of scholarship explaining international systems of states and the role of scholarship in international relations, law, organization, problems of conflict and cooperation, or war and peace. Secondarily, he notes, there are two sets of "younger" scholars keen to either understand global interdependencies and local contingencies or apply development theories (whether Marxist or non-Marxist) (p. 10). Teune's prescience about the emergence of younger scholars and the need for the ISA to accommodate their theoretical interests outside of international relations seems to have been largely ignored, according to reviews of the science published in the association's journals. The predominance of international relations or scholars of conflict and war is notable (Blanton 2009; Hey 2004; Szanton 2001; Vitalis 2002; White, Malik, and Chrastil 2006).

The ISA continued in the latter half of the twentieth century to enclose mostly scholars of international relations and foreign affairs. At the same time, the ranks of the professoriate identified with international studies became far more diverse. As US universities grew during the 1960s through the 1980s, their ranks were filled with both international and area studies scholars with training in anthropology, communication, geography, sociology, history, languages, and religions, and these scholars had received funding to support an increasing array of rich encounters of complexities and nuance. Their empirical insights from the field combined with a cultural turn in the social sciences that started with the ideas of Thomas Kuhn and continued with the insights of Clifford Geertz and moved onto the theories of Michel Foucault, Jacques Derrida, and Claude Levi-Strauss (Bender 1997).

This diversification of international studies scholars raised dilemmas not only within the ISA but also beyond it, including some crises of identity among area studies faculty. By the 1990s, it seemed that finding a place for area studies within international studies was particularly problematic (Cummings 2002; Lee 2015; Mitchell 2003). Edited volumes and intellectual histories noted a need for a new international studies or global studies (Chernotsky and Hobbs 2015; Cooper and Packard 1997; Cummings 2002; Darian-Smith and McCarty 2017; Lee 2015; Mirsepassi, Basu, and Weaver 2003; Szanton 2001, 2004; Waters 2000). For example, there is the striking study of the application of social science in Africa that turned on its head assumed categories and causal arguments about development (Cooper and Packard 1997) or Solovey's (2001) analysis of Project Camelot and the consequential episte-mological revolution. Although these scholars and their successors drew upon postmodern conceptualizations or approaches, their empirically grounded fieldwork and confrontations with both real and imagined hierarchies, relations, identities, and distresses meant that they assumed a certain sensibility about the relativity of knowledge and the practices of their crafts (Chernotsky and Hobbs 2015; Mirsepassi et al. 2003; Waters 2000). This ontological reflexivity of area studies scholarship points to the possibilities for contributing to a robust field of global studies scholarship—a field that was distinct from the scholarship defined by the ISA (Hey 2004; Lambert 2001).

Ongoing Disjuncture Between International Studies Scholarship and Pedagogy

The debates about enclosure did not go unnoticed within the ISA and the pages of its sanctioned journals. Recently, two noted crises received some attention. One notes the disjuncture between scholarship and pedagogy in the field (Blanton 2009; Blanton and Breuning 2016; Breuning and Ishiyami 2007; Breuning and Quinn 2011; Brown, Pegg, and Shively 2006; Dolan 2011; Hey 2004; Ishiyama and Breuning 2004). The second notes the possible competition between political science departments and international studies degrees, programs, and schools for limited institutional resources (Chin 2009; Knotts and Schiff 2015; White et al. 2006).

The latter warrants a brief description, as it provides an update on the earlier description of international studies' intellectual history and it frames the notable disjuncture between pedagogy and scholarship. White et al. (2006) argue that many international studies programs borrow heavily from international relations courses in political science and that most other offerings are less coherent. Knotts and Schiff (2015) confirm the overlap, but they find that most political science chairs are not particularly threatened by the establishment of international studies programs and note that it depends on the stature of the program and the prestige perceived with enrolling in one or the other major. Strikingly, chairs of political science programs perceive international studies as equivalent degrees to international relations in both theory and practice (Knotts and Schiff 2015), even if the former includes faculty and courses under a larger umbrella. Both White et al. and Knotts and Schiff argue forcefully for greater definitional clarity about the field, and both strongly suggest subsuming it within political science to lend greater methodological coherence (Knotts and Schiff 2015: 147; White et al. 2006: 102).

Claims by some about the need for intellectual and pedagogical coherence followed a series of articles published in journals hosted by the ISA during the early 2000s. These are similar to many arguments by disciplinary advocates in response to interdisciplinary initiatives (Calhoun 2017). In these, the focus is primarily on undergraduate training, where most of the enrollment growth has occurred in recent decade (Chernotsky and Hobbs 2015; Hobbs 2012). These studies include surveys of international studies programs via systematic reviews of institutional websites (Breuning and Ishiyama 2007; Brown et al. 2006; Ishiyama and Breuning 2004), surveys of directors of international studies programs (Blanton 2009; Blanton and Breuning 2016), and studies of the learning outcomes resulting from international studies training (De Soto, Tajalli, and Villarreal 2016). These research projects coincided with a significant debate about the extent to which international studies should or should not be more closely aligned with political science traditions (Breuning and Ishiyama 2004; Hey 2004; Ishayam and Breuning 2004). Much of the emphasis on the debate in this scholarship is about the structure, mostly identifying a predominant sense of institutional "homelessness" that is rarely anchored by a cumulative pedagogical core that starts with an introduction, builds skills and knowledge systematically, and concludes with a capstone. Although the authors of these studies of the field make note of long lists of courses from across disciplines and pedagogical missions that are inclusive of disciplines and of cross-cultural competencies (namely language study and area studies training), they dismiss the multiperspective, multidisciplinarity of the program structures as not rigorous enough because it is missing a sequential learning (Hey 2004). As Hey aptly notes, such critiques miss the larger point about how international studies programs are not disciplinary endeavors and applying a disciplinary logic to the pedagogical structure makes little sense. It would be difficult not to observe that these accounts, although published in the professional journals of the ISA and pursuing objective, quantitative analyses of programs, appear to be attempts to enclose the field within political science.

Consistently represented in these reviews of international studies curricular programs are the "large umbrella" or "big tent" approaches. Furthermore, international studies programs are recognized for emphasizing interdisciplinary skills and subject matter, gaining cosmopolitan outlooks, and problem-solving (De Soto et al. 2016; Dolan 2011; Hobbs 2012). Also, the premise of most international studies programs is the global challenges confronting contemporary generations, such as human rights, climate change, refugees, and poverty (Hobbs 2012). In addition, courses comprising the major, or available as part of a set of electives, reflect an entire array of offerings from across the arts and sciences (Brown et al. 2006; Kelleher 2005). Finally, area studies foci are predominant components of an undergraduate major (Brown et al. 2006; Kelleher 2005). Such diversity of course offerings and inclusively comprehensive articulations of missions and learning goals are similar to most global studies curriculum. As Calhoun (2017) notes, the possibilities and instantiation of such human capital breadth and depth of training could have only emerged from decades of investments in higher education capacity to contribute to area, international, and global knowledge by numerous sources (as described in the preceding section).

Nevertheless, strikingly absent from the political science-directed analyses of international studies programs are observations about the faculty comprising the collective enterprise. We know little from these analyses of international studies programs about faculty disciplinary backgrounds, their pedagogical goals, or their research. Their absence in the description about the formation and sustenance of the program shortchanges any possible insights about what is to be gained by the interdisciplinarity of the field. Furthermore, there seems to be little assessment of the area studies strengths of the faculty. This is a glaring blind spot in the assessments and leads to the failure of the authors to fairly understand the remarkable contribution of area studies to the appeal and richness of international studies for undergraduate learning. Chernotsky and Hobbs (2015), Hobbs (2012), and Hobbs, Chernotsy, and Van Tassell (2010) argue forcefully for a far more explicit interdisciplinarity that already describes international studies programs and that requires acknowledgment. The roots of that interdisciplinarity and the strength of that discplinarity are precisely anchored by the successes of area studies projects (Calhoun 2017). Consequently, such academic programs might help extend and clarify the contributions of international studies scholarship, beyond political science. As Calhoun (2017) writes,

> The area studies projects at their best were not so much about idiographic particulars as about the notion that there were and are different ways to be human, to be social, to be political, and even to have markets—and therefore that the pursuit of more general knowledge required attention to specific historical and cultural contexts and patterns. Such knowledge could be of broad application without being abstractly universal. And indeed, the area studies fields contributed to major analytic perspectives that far transcended their initial sites of development. (p. 121)

I argue that the disjuncture between scholarship and pedagogy within international studies as articulated in the pages of the profession's journals is unlikely to disappear, unless international studies programs are enclosed within political science or international studies programs are reconceived in a new field. Given the similar articulations and disciplinary diversities of global studies and international studies faculty, there is a space for articulating a global studies agenda that is very distinct from international studies and that harkens back to the earlier successes resulting from an area studies approach (Lee 2015). This new pedagogical landscape, while built on area studies and less on international studies, can also incorporate the theoretical and methodological challenges inherent in addressing globalization, global complexities, and global interdependencies.

DISTINCT SPACE FOR GLOBAL STUDIES APART FROM INTERNATIONAL STUDIES

One of the more unusual, critical analyses of international studies appeared in the 2009 issue of *International Studies Perspectives*. In it, Chin (2009) employs a critical social science and postmodern lens to critique the lack of explicit attention to race and application of implicit racialized codes within the fields of international relations and international studies. The critique is one that is likely to be understood and more easily picked up by global studies scholarship and pedagogy, given the reflexive ontology proposed by Chin. As opposed to political science critiques of international studies pedagogy, which fueled numerous references and commentary, this one appears to have fallen on deaf ears. The absence of remark is notable and relevant to my argument. Chin offers the following in the conclusion:

> When it comes to race, the stance of dismissiveness is a luxury that our profession can ill afford if it is to continue to make sense of an increasingly complex world at large and help impart it to a younger generation socialized by promises of the freedom to choose. At the end of the day, informed choices demand a higher standard and outcome than that of indifference or even tolerance: They require greater knowledge and discussions of the complex manner in which the "self" and the "other" are co-constructed, for better and for worse, in this social world. (p. 98)

Surprisingly, Chin is located at one of the more prestigious schools of international studies (American University), her work is in the field of political economy, and she recently served as a leading administrator of higher education at her institution. Chin's own work examines trends toward securitization of transnational migration and refugees—a contemporary global studies research field with foundations in the field of international studies and international relations. The silence in response to her provocative essay, especially in contrast to similarly timed discussions about international studies programs, speaks volumes about the extent to which international studies is enclosed by political science and distinct from global studies.

International studies scholarship and the efforts to enclose it within academia bound the research enterprise closely to a predominantly US-centric, international relations, and international systems perspective on world order. Because of the preceding emphasis and associated existential threats during the Cold War, important investments by the US government and leading foundations led to the strengthening of interdisciplinary area studies and international studies curricular programs, including significant hiring of humanities and social science scholars.

By the late 1970s, these investments had matured, and they coincided with a concomitant turn in the humanities and social sciences toward critical social science and postmodern inquiries. Thus, as faculty hiring continued apace and enrollments grew, international studies curricular programs became far more expansive and less closely tied to a narrow agenda that had previously and primarily been curated by political scientists. By the early 2000s, this disjuncture between international studies scholarship and pedagogy found a voice that continues to be heard in ongoing debates within professional associations and journals. The debates, both their vocal and silent responses, define a widely delineated space for global studies to define itself as distinct from international studies. Global studies research programs are distinct from international studies scholarship in important ways, but their respective curricular programs and pedagogy are more closely aligned in contemporary times. Global studies programs will be able to call upon the breadth and depth of area studies scholars, including their critical social science and postmodern approaches to explanation. Doing so will afford the possibility of closely aligning scholarship and pedagogy, providing a foundation for a vibrant field of transdisciplinarity. The opportunity for global studies stands in stark contrast to international studies, which may have been an antecedent to global studies, but remains stuck within an enclosure defined intellectually by political science.

In the last decades of the twentieth century and early years of this century, the demands for international studies training have grown rapidly. In response, institutions of higher education have made room for pedagogical innovations on behalf of international studies. In addition, substantial extramural funding leveraged internal resources that continued to refresh and grow higher education faculty, especially those trained in critical social science and postmodernity and with research agendas that encompassed international, global, and local themes. Far from being "homeless," these faculty are rapidly redefining international studies pedagogy into global studies pedagogy, and their research is far from the enclosed space of international studies.

NOTE

1. International Studies Association website, https://www.isanet.org/ISA/About-ISA, accessed September 1, 2017.

REFERENCES

Appadurai, A., J. Bhabba, S. Collins, and A. Guneratne. 1997. "Area Studies, Regional Worlds: A White Paper for the Ford Foundation." Chicago: The Globalization Project, The University of Chicago. http://regionalworlds.uchicago.edu/areastudiesregworlds.pdf.

Barnes, T. J., and M. Farish. 2006. "Between Regions: Science, Militarism, and American Geography from World War to Cold War." *Annals of the Association of American Geographers* 96 (4): 807–826.

Bender, T. 1997. "Politics, Intellect, and the American University, 1945–1995." *Daedalus* 126 (1): 1–38.

Bessner, D. 2017. *Democracy in Exile: Hans Speier and the Rise of the Defense Intellectual.* Ithaca, NY: Cornell University Press.

Bigelow, D. K., and L. H. Legters, eds. 1964. "The Non-Western World in Higher Education." *Annals of the American Academy of Political and Social Science* 356.

Blanton, R. G. 2009. "Surveying International Studies Programs: Where Do We Stand." *International Studies Perspectives* 10: 224–240.

Blanton, R. G., and M. Breuning. 2016. "What Makes International Studies Programs Successful? A Survey-Based Assessment." *International Studies Perspectives* 17: 136–153.

Breuning, M., and J. Ishiyama. 2004. "International Studies Programs: For What Purpose and for Whom? A Rejoinder to Hey." *International Studies Perspectives* 5: 400–402.

Breuning, M., and J. Ishiyama. 2007. "International Studies Major: Claims and Content of Programs at Primarily Undergraduate Institutions in the Midwest." *International Studies Perspectives* 8: 121–133.

Breuning, M., and J. Quinn. 2011. "International Studies Minor in Practice: Program Offerings and Student Choices." *Journal of Political Science Education* 7: 173–195.

Brown, J., S. Pegg, and J. W. Shively. 2006. "Consensus and Divergence in International Studies: Survey Evidence from 140 International Studies Curriculum Programs." *International Studies Perspectives* 7: 267–286.

Calhoun, C. 2017. "Integrating Social Sciences: Area Studies, Quantitative Methods, and Problem-Oriented Research." In *The Oxford Handbook of Interdisciplinarity*, edited by R. Frodeman, J. T. Klein, and R. C. D. S. Pacheco, 117–130. Oxford, UK: Oxford University Press.

Chernotsky, H. I., and H. H. Hobbs. 2015. *Crossing Borders: International Studies for the 21st Century.* Thousand Oaks, CA: Sage.

Chin, C. B. N. 2009. "Claiming Race and Racelessness in International Studies." *International Studies Perspectives* 10: 92–98.

Cooper, F., and R. M. Packard. 1997. *International Development and the Social Sciences: Essays on the History and Politics of Knowledge.* Berkeley: University of California Press.

Cummings, B. 2002. "Boundary Displacement: The State, the Foundations, and Area Studies During and After the Cold War." In *Learning Places: The Afterlives of Area Studies*, edited by M. Miyoshi, 261–302. Durham, NC: Duke University Press.

Darian-Smith, E., and P. C. McCarty. 2017. *The Global Turn: Theories, Research Designs, and Methods for Global Studies.* Berkeley: University of California Press.

De Soto, W., H. Tajalli, and A. Villarreal. 2016. "Do International Studies Students Have a Broader Global Awareness Than Other College Students?" *Journal of Political Science Education* 12 (2): 216–219.

Dolan, C. 2011. "From Scratch: Designing and Implementing International Studies Program at a Small College." *International Studies Perspectives* 12: 428–446.

Engerman, D. C. 2007. "Bernath Lecture: American Knowledge and Global Power." *Diplomatic History* 31 (4): 599–622.

Guilhot, N. (2008). "The Realist Gambit: Postwar American Political Science and the Birth of IR Theory." *International Political Sociology* 2 (4): 281–304.

Guilhot, N. 2011. "Cyborg Pantocrator: International Relations Theory from Decisionism to Rational Choice." *Journal of the History of the Behavioral Sciences* 47 (3): 279–301.

Hey, J. 2004. "Can International Studies Research Be the Basis for an Undergraduate Curriculum? A Response to Ishiyama and Breuning." *International Studies Perspectives* 5: 395–399.

Hobbs, H. 2012. "Administering International Studies Curriculum: A Fast Growing Major in Search of a Home." Paper presented at the International Studies Association Annual Convention, San Diego, CA, April 1–4.

Hobbs, H., H. Chernotsy, and D. Van Tassell. 2010. "International Studies and the Global Community: Transforming the Agenda." In *The International Studies Encyclopedia*, edited by R. A. Denmark, vol. 7, 4598–4609. Chichester, UK: Wiley-Blackwell.

Holsti, O. R. (2014). "Present at the Creation." International Studies Association. http://www.isanet.org/Portals/0/Documents/Institutional/Holsti_ISA_West.pdf. Accessed October 13, 2017.

Ishiyama, J., and M. Breuning. 2004. "International Studies Programs at Liberal Arts Colleges and Universities in the Midwest: Characteristics and Correlates." *International Studies Perspectives* 5: 134–146.

Kelleher, A. 2005. "Does International Studies Have a Common Core? An Analysis of Seventy-Three Curriculum Programs." Paper Presented at the Annual Meeting of the International Studies Association, Honolulu, HI.

Knotts, H. G., and J. Schiff. 2015. "Major Competition? Exploring Perceptions of International Studies Programs Among Political Science Chairs." *PS* 48 (1): 142–147.

Lambert, R. D. 1980. "International Studies: An Overview and Agenda", pp. 151–164. *Annals of the American Academy of Political and Social Science* 449 (May): R7–R7.

Lambert, R. D. 2001. "Domains and Issues in International Studies." In *Changing Perspectives on International Education*, edited by P. O'Meara, H. D. Mehlinger, & R. M. Newman, 30–48. Bloomington: Indiana University Press.

Lee, B. 2015. "Area and International Studies: Cultural Studies." In *International Encyclopedia of the Social and Behavioral Sciences*, edited by J. Wright, pp. 933–937. Oxford, UK: Elsevier.

McCaughey, R. A. 1984. *International Studies and Academic Enterprise: A Chapter in the Enclosure of American Learning.* New York: Columbia University Press.

Mirsepassi, A., A. Basu, and F. Weaver, eds. 2003. *Localizing Knowledge in a Globalizing World: Recasting the Area Studies Debate.* Syracuse, NY: Syracuse University Press.

Mitchell, T. 2003. "Deterritorialization and the Social Sciences." In *Localizing Knowledge in a Globalizing World: Recasting the Area Studies Debate*, edited by A. Mirsepassi, A. Basu, and F. Weaver, 148–170. Syracuse, NY: Syracuse University Press.

Razavi, S., and C. Miller. 1995. *From WID to GAD: Conceptual Shifts in the Women and Development Discourse*, vol. 1. Geneva: United Nations Research Institute for Social Development.

Solovey, M. 2001. "Project Camelot and the 1960s Epistemological Revolution: Rethinking the Politics–Patronage–Social Science Nexus." *Social Studies of Science* 31 (2): 171–206.

Szanton, D. 2001. "Area and International Studies in the United States: Intellectual Trends." In *International Encyclopedia of the Social and Behavioral Sciences*, edited by N. Smelser and P. Baltes, 692–699. Oxford, UK: Elsevier.

Szanton, D. 2004. "Introduction: The Origin, Nature and Challenges of Area Studies in the United States." In *The Politics of Knowledge: Area Studies and the Disciplines*, edited by D. Szanton, 1–33. Berkeley: University of California Press.

Teune, H. 1982. "The ISA." International Studies Association. http://www.isanet.org/Portals/0/Documents/Institutional/Henry_Teune_The_ISA_1982.pdf. Accessed October 13, 2017.

Vitalis, R. 2002. "International Studies in America." *Items & Issues* 3: 1–29.

Waters, N. L., ed. 2000. *Beyond the Area Studies Wars: Toward a New International Studies*. Hanover, NH: Middlebury College Press.

White, T. J., A. Malik, and R. Chrastil. 2006. "International Studies and Political Science." *Academic Exchange Quarterly* 10 (4): 101–106.

CHAPTER 14

···

INEQUALITY FROM THE PERSPECTIVE OF THE GLOBAL SOUTH

···

MANORANJAN MOHANTY

Two paradoxes of inequality stare at us glaringly in the twenty-first century. One is the discernible phenomenon of individuals, groups, regions and, even more important, nations, religions, and cultures asserting their claim to equal dignity in all areas of the world. All constitutions affirm the right to equality before law for all citizens. The United Nations Charter framed in 1945 declares all nations as equal, as do many subsequent international covenants. At the same time, the trend of increasing social and economic inequality within and between countries and regions has been prominently noticeable in recent decades. Inequality of incomes in countries such as the United States, India, and China has continued to rise, with occasional slight fluctuations. Discrimination on the basis of caste in India, race in the United States and South Africa, ethnicity in China and many other countries, and gender in all countries persists even though laws prohibit it (Human Rights Council 2016). Sexual violence continues to be a phenomenon in all areas of the world. Caste discrimination in general and atrocities on dalits—the former "untouchable" castes in India—remain a troubling trend. As the contradiction between formal political equality among citizens and actual inequality in society and economy has continued to create tensions throughout the world, the warning by B. R. Ambedkar, the social revolutionary and Chair of the Drafting Committee of the Indian constitution, while introducing the bill to adopt the constitution on November 25, 1949, acquires even greater significance not only for India and the Global South but also for the entire world. He observed that in politics, India recognized the value of "one man one vote," but in social and economic life it "continues to deny the principle of one man one value." He urged his colleagues to "remove this contradiction at the earliest possible moment, or else," he warned, "those who suffer from inequality will blow up the structure of political democracy which this Assembly has laboriously built up" (Ambedkar 1949).

The other paradox is the growing justification of prevailing inequalities by regimes in the name of achieving economic growth or stability of the system. The very basis of neoliberal reforms launched in the 1990s was to unleash forces of entrepreneurship and give them maximum incentives for profit without caring if that led to increasing inequalities. In 1991 and 1992, when there was a debate in China as to whether the expansion of a free market economy would cause greater polarization in Chinese society, Deng Xiaoping, the architect of China's reforms, said that the "reform and open door" must be pursued to achieve China's economic growth and the Communist Party of China (CPC) was there to prevent polarization (Deng Xiaoping 1992). After four decades of reforms, China—which was once one of the world's most egalitarian societies—had become one of the most unequal societies, its Gini coefficient being higher than that of the United States (Table 14.1). India has been on the same path, and reducing inequality has not been a top priority for any regime in recent decades. To avoid tensions among people resulting from the reforms, most countries introduced a set of populist measures to provide relief from destitution and hunger and to reduce the size of the population living below the "poverty line." Accomplishments such as reducing the size of the population living below the poverty line from 39% in 2001 to 29% in 2017 in India or from 30% in 1985 to 2% in 2015 in China and aiming to lift the remaining poor population above the poverty line by 2020 were indeed laudable. But these measures did not address the problem of stark inequalities of income, status, wealth, and power within these countries (Thorat and Newman 2012). The de-emphasis on equality as a goal was clearly discernible in the past two decades with the depoliticization of terms of discourse during the neoliberal era. Inequality was replaced by "exclusion," and oppressed groups were called "marginalized"; programs of "inclusion" were designed for them (Mohanty 2000).

The irony was that in many of these countries, debates stressing the value of equality had been raging for more than 2,000 years. In India in the fifth-century BCE, the Buddha challenged the caste system of Brahmanism and initiated a new cultural and spiritual movement for equality of all humans (Omvedt 2003). That has remained part of the many conflicting streams of culture and religion in India. Gandhi's concept of *swaraj* (self-rule), Ambedkar's focus on social equality, and the Indian freedom struggle's affirmation of the right to equality that was enshrined into the Indian constitution showed that equality was a cherished value. But the social and economic policies in Independent India did not uniformly reflect it, and in India's neoliberal phase there was a clear de-emphasis on equality (Dubey and Thorat 2012). Moreover, one could point to traditional societies as being distinctly unequal. Brahmanism in India stratified society into unequal groups. Confucianism presented a hierarchy of social relationships in China by defining five sets of relationships: father–son, husband–wife, elder brother–younger brother, teacher–disciple, and king–subject. With the revival of popularity of Confucianism in contemporary China, it is interesting to note how harmony and order have been highlighted more than equality (Gao 2017: 242). When Buddhism entered China and, later, when Christianity and Islam became a part of Chinese culture, they challenged that notion. But it was not just the ancient traditions of the East that were non-egalitarian. In ancient Greece, Plato, too, believed in the hierarchy of human abilities: wisdom, spirit, and appetite, respectively, possessed by philosophers, royals, and workers, with slaves outside this sphere having only physical abilities. Aristotle also believed in that stratification of humans, allowing, however, that equality among the citizens should be promoted as an ideal, for without it there would be a revolution. He advocated the exercise of power by aristocracy to manage a polity. This line of thought was challenged even then, and by the time of the Renaissance and the Enlightenment, many social movements in Europe had asserted the equality of humans (Lakoff 1964). "All men were created equal"

Table 14.1 Inequality in China, India, and the United States

Country	Survey Year	Share of Income in Percent of Total Income				Gini Index
		Poorest 10%	Poorest 20%	Richest 20%	Richest 10%	
China	2001	1.8	4.7	50	33.1	44.7
	2005	1.8	5.0	47.9	32.0	42.5
	2012[a]	2.05	–	–	31.43	42.16
	2014	–	–	–	37.2[c]	0.469[c,1]
India	1999–2000	3.9	8.9	43.3	28.5	32.5
	2005	3.8	8.6	42.4	28.3	33.4
	2011[a]	3.56	8.26	43.97	29.77	35.1
	2014	–	–	–	–	33.6
US	2000	1.9	5.4	45.8	29.9	40.46
	2010[a]	1.62	–	–	29.4	40.46
	2014[b]	1.6	5.2	45.1	29.2	0.394[d]

[a]Data from World Data Atlas, "World and Regional Statistics, National Data, Maps, Rankings," https://knoema.com/atlas; accessed March 3, 2017.

[b]Data from "Release of OECD Inequality Update 2016: Income Inequality Remains High in the Face of Weak Recovery" (November 24, 2016), http://www.oecd.org/social/income-distribution-database.htm; accessed March 3, 2017.

[c]Data from World Inequality Database, "Income Inequality, China, 1978–2015," http://wid.world/country/china; accessed March 5, 2017.

[d]Gini coefficient.

Sources: United Nations Development Programme, "Human Development Report," 2006, 2010, 2011, 2013, 2015; The World Bank, "World Development Indicators," 2012, 2013; Organisation for Economic Co-operation and Development, "StatExtracts: Income Distribution and Poverty," 2014.

became a creed that entered political declarations in the eighteenth century. In the three ancient traditions of India, China, and Greece, the justification of inequality rested on the proclaimed need for ensuring sociopolitical stability. Maintaining order in society was the primary value for the elites, which they prescribed as the goal of the whole society. It could be peace and order or economic growth or maintenance of the elite power in one form or another. It is remarkable that these ways of thinking recurred continuously throughout history in these countries and elsewhere up to contemporary times to justify prevailing levels of inequality. In the United States and Europe, the Plato version of the argument for inequality resounds in the twenty-first century. In China, Confucius is rehabilitated as the source of humanism and moral living for social and political order, but indirectly accepting discrimination and inequality as the country rises as a global superpower with a free market economy guided by the power of a communist party. In India, Ambedkar's reaffirmation of the Buddhist concept of equality and the liberal democratic values of the French Revolution—liberty, equality, and fraternity (fraternity to be replaced by human solidarity)—has been neglected and remains only in the thinking of social movements dedicated to this cause. The Brahmanic notion of varnashrama dharma characterizing the caste order propounded by modern-day Hindutva theorists as a "non-hierarchical functional division of labour" has had a new lease on life. Thus, in all three settings of the modern West, China, and India, the attempt to build a society of equality, freedom, and dignity for all has continued to face serious obstacles (McGill 2016).

These two paradoxes—unprecedented assertion of equality in the face of rising inequality and justifications for equality even though they have been presented and challenged from time to time for more than 2,000 years—clearly indicate that the coming decades will witness intense struggles by forces demanding faster realization of conditions of equality while other forces view them as causing disruptions in their strategies of growth and stability. Because both sets of forces possess various kinds of strength, these situations will continue to generate tensions, alienation, and dislocations including violent confrontations. Global developments in the first decades of the twenty-first century show that the struggle for equality may have emerged as the defining feature of the century.

Although this point is most conspicuous from the perspective of the Global South, it is no less evident in the Global North. In other words, the common perception that societies in the Global North are more equal than those in the Global South should also be critically examined.

It should be clarified here that the terms Global South and Global North are debated concepts, and they are used here primarily for heuristic purposes. In recent years, the term "Global South" has replaced the term "Third World," which was used during the Cold War from the 1960s through the 1980s to refer mostly to former European colonies and had a political potency with an anti-imperialist and anti-hegemony thrust (Prashad 2007). The First World and Second World then referred to the two superpowers, the United States and the Soviet Union, and their allies, respectively, whereas the Third World generally referred to developing countries. The term "developing country" is still used by many, indicating the relatively low ranking in the world in terms of gross domestic product (GDP). The United Nations Development Programme and the World Bank rank countries in terms of national income as high-income countries, middle-income, lower middle-income, and low-income countries. During the past three decades of neoliberal globalization, the terms "emerging economies" and "emerging markets" have acquired currency; these terms focus on the extent of expansion of the free market economy and economic growth. Incidentally, the reference to countries and nations as merely "markets," ignoring many other aspects of the lives and history of people and their civilizations, is questionable.

The term Global South mainly refers to the countries of Asia, Africa, and Latin America (ASAFLA), even though, strictly speaking, many of them are located north of the equator. Political economies of Western Europe and North America have defined the characteristics of Global North, which has a relatively higher per capita income, free market economy, and liberal democratic polity. But there are problems in the way that these categories are defined. Japan, located in Asia, is actually part of the Global North in terms of its national income per capita. China, the world's second largest economy in terms of GDP since 2010, very much belongs to the category of developing countries or Global South in terms of national income per capita, despite its accelerated growth. More important, there are islands of Global North in terms of high income, living standards, and infrastructure in the Global South, and there are islands of Global South—poor and vulnerable sections and regions—in the Global North. When we use any of these terms—Global South, Third World, developing country, or ASAFLA—three elements are stressed. First, located in the southern part of the world, these countries are mostly former colonies or semi-colonies that are engaged in consolidating their independence. Second, their economic conditions remains underdeveloped compared to those of the former colonial powers or developed countries of Europe and North America. Third, they are currently engaged in transforming the unequal global order, where the Global North enjoys more political, economic, technological, and cultural power than the Global South and accordingly has framed the rules of global govern ance during the past 200 years of colonial and postcolonial history. Undoubtedly, the term Global South has gained currency because some of the key elements in the other terms have lost centrality or have gained negative connotations (Williams, Meth, and Willis 2014).

With these clarifications, in this chapter, I first first discuss the concept of inequality and the various meanings associated with it. Then, I take up how the problems of economic and social inequalities have been addressed in the Global South. The debates over caste in India are used to illustrate some of the important questions with regard to addressing problems of structural inequalities. Next, I take up the discussion of how liberal democracy treats the issue of inequality and how it is handled in regimes governed by communist parties. I describe the experiences as deferred liberalism and acquiescent socialism. The latter is based on a discussion of China's reforms and their implications for promoting equality.

I contextualize this chapter keeping in view the century of anti-colonial struggles in ASAFLA and the postcolonial history, including the recent decades of globalization. Some key concepts define their character. One is the concept of *swaraj*, which was advocated by Mohandas Gandhi. He argued that swaraj, or self-rule, meant not only replacing colonial rule with rule by people of the country but also self-realization or self-determination of each individual, group, and region. It meant multidimensional freedom from various kinds of bondages or dominations. In the same vein, another concept is relevant—that of *jiefang*, described by Mao Zedong, which, like Gandhi's movement, focused on the struggle against political domination of all kinds, including feudalism and colonialism. In the postcolonial setting, another concept became relevant—that of *samata*, the notion of social equality propounded by Ambedkar and popularized in the 1990s even though Ambedkar had advocated it in the course of writings and acts in programs in his lifetime. It was in India in 1990 after the implementation of the Mandal Commission report, which required special provisions to improve the backward castes, that Ambedkar's philosophy of equality acquired great currency. Yet another critical concept is *ubuntu*, "I am because you are"—the Zulu notion of mutual interdependence of people irrespective of race and color or other social divisions. The *ubuntu* discourse of Nelson Mandela tried to establish a relationship of harmony among the Blacks and Whites and others in South Africa aimed at establishing social equality (Mohanty 2018).

In the post-Soviet era of globalization, there is a very different trend in the rising wave of capitalist free trade throughout the world. But even in the global era, capitalist economies have faced crises of one kind or another, and global political interventions of the United States and its allies have faced challenges. The debates raged around the crisis of capitalism that unfolded in 2008, and movements such as "Occupy Wall Street" and the "1% versus 99%" placed on center stage the question of growing inequality under the present phase of capitalism. The climate change crisis acquired alarming proportions, with countries of the Global South, especially China and India, contributing massively to global warming. This led thinkers who speculated on the global future to draw attention to the challenges of the era of Anthropocene (Falk 2017). Cultural and religious crises and terrorist actions that have become increasingly serious in recent years gave rise to fresh reflections on the causes of alienation of communities and regions leading to multiple cycles of violence and counterviolence (Juergensmeyer 2008). Many economists throughout the world noted the growing dangers of the rising trend of inequality (Stiglitz 2012). Piketty's (2014) historical analysis based on statistical data on income and wealth taxes from approximately the past 200 years showed how the concentration of wealth was a persisting trend in Europe and the United States except for the period of 1913–1948 and was likely to grow in the twenty-first century. It was a powerful warning that initiated a worldwide debate, with many not sharing his conclusions. Some pointed out that he neglected the fact that capitalism in its current phase produced growth of output without providing adequate employment (Patnaik 2014, 2016). Warnings have been given at different points in time by many others (Amin 1997, 2009; dos Santos 2010; Nayyar 2013). Since these developments and debates comprised the foundation of the United Nation's (UN) Sustainable Development Goals (SDG) formulated in 2015, they might collectively be called the SDG moment. They represented an acknowledgment of persisting problems on a global scale. Whereas equality and freedom in a multidimensional framework informed the swaraj, jiefang, samata, and ubuntu moments, the SDG moment recorded an acquiescence of prevailing inequality with dangerous consequences for the global future.

Inequality as a Power Relationship

Two issues have emerged as critical to the meaning of inequality at this point of the twenty-first century. One is that inequality is not just about the uneven possession or quantitative difference in which individuals, groups, regions, or other entities are placed. It is about the conditions that allow certain groups to dominate over others. Inequality is a power relationship. This is important to consider because unequal power relations propel the process of more inequality on increasingly more fronts. At the same time, unless sources of power in income, wealth, knowledge, culture, and other capacities are shared, the power relationship cannot become equitable. The second issue that has emerged in recent years is the recognition that inequality is a cumulative condition and cannot be reduced to any one aspect, even though some aspects may be more impor-tant than others in a specific context. For example, universal adult franchise, one of the most valued achievements of modern history, provided political equality to all citizens as voters irrespective of social origin, education, income, and wealth. But economic ine-quality, caste, gender, religion, and racial discrimination severely limit political equality in real life. Therefore, the centrality of power and the multidimensionality of inequality have stood out as the crucial elements in the definition of inequality in recent years (Mohanty 1983).

Those who dismiss the idea of equality as a utopian value that can never be attained mistake it for what Aristotle called "numerical equality" or what might be called arith-metic equality. Mechanically giving equal quantity to everyone is what is meant in this use of the concept. Proponents of this view often are heard saying "Five fingers are never equal," "No two humans are equal," or similar statements. Such views take equality as sameness. Justification of prevailing inequalities as "natural" results from such thinking. This view is widespread because the elites of society who wield power lend their support to such views. When such views were firmly challenged and equality became a cherished value as a result of a civilizational movement of humankind, then this view took another form. It was said that equality was the goal, but it would take time—a long time—to reach that goal. To achieve that end, the argument went, there must be economic growth and social stability, peace and order. This put equality as a lower order value preceded by peace and order.

Once we are clear that equality is not about mechanical "leveling" of living conditions, we have to identify the main elements of this concept. Equal respect for every human being and access to life conditions that a civilization at a historical moment considers necessary for the fulfillment of the creative potentiality of a human being are the two main elements of the concept of equality. Each of these elements is broad and can be subject to a variety of interpretations (Beteille 1977). Respect for a human being involves respecting his or her language, culture, and religion. This basic concept is affirmed by Buddha's affirmation of the divinity in each being, including human beings; the dec-laration of "Aham Brahmashmi" ("the divine is in me") in the ancient Indian texts, the Upanishads; and the description in the Bible and Koran that all humans are chil-dren of God. But power divisions in society have made them abstract, and inequality has persisted in multiple forms. In the twenty-first century, the demand is to set it in concrete. Even though in 1948 the *Universal Declaration of Human Rights* asserted the equality of all humans, the rights of nations to self-determination, the rights of indige-nous people, and many other movements for the equality of all humans have remained constrained by competition for power and the forces of economic and political he-gemony. The anti-colonial struggles and the Third World movement championed this trend until the 1980s; the socialist and communist movements affirmed equality as a value and a policy objective until the collapse of the Soviet Union in 1991. Since then, the worldwide spread of neoliberal reforms has subordinated equality as a value and a policy objective to achieving productivity, growth, and political stability—hence the paradox of declining equality even as the rhetoric of equality continues to resound.

INEQUALITY: MULTIPLE SOURCES

The multidimensional aspects of equality have had a complex history. The liberal democratic path focused on universal adult franchise and equality before law. In other words, political equality was put at the center. Modern liberal democracies such as the United States and India included it in their constitutions and have evolved elaborate structures of independent judiciary to ensure that no citizen can be denied rights on account of social origin, religion, race, caste, and gender. It was realized, however, that disadvantaged sections historically placed lower in social structures due to inherited conditions or for other reasons needed opportunities to make up for their disadvantages. Hence, the concept of equality of opportunity became popular. To provide equal opportunity to all sections of society with regard to education, the common school system emerged in the United Kingdom, which in the past had been famous for its elite schools and colleges for the aristocracy not only in the United Kingdom but also in its colonies throughout the world. In the United States, the neighborhood school system and public universities were open to all. In India and many postcolonial countries, government schools were set up to provide educational opportunities for all children irrespective of caste, class, and religion.

Similarly, the public health systems in the United Kingdom and India provided common access to health care. In addition, equal wages for equal work was a great advancement in this process. The welfare state emerged as the new agency of providing equal opportunities to all sections of society. The state was more active in the Global South because it had higher levels of poverty, malnutrition, and social inequality. It was realized, however, that in both the Global South and the Global North, "equality of opportunity" operating in an unequal social order still favored the privileged, better off, powerful sections, and unless special support was accorded to the more disadvantaged, inequality would persist. It was realized in the pre-liberalization era that in the context of economic reforms, inequalities were likely to be further widened. Hence, there was believed to be a need to set aside "reservation" of seats in the legislature and positions in government jobs and university placement in countries such as India and for "affirmative action" or "equal opportunity" initiatives in many countries of the Global North, especially the United States (Galanter 1984; Sheth 2004).

THE INDIAN MODEL OF FIGHTING
SOCIAL INEQUALITY

The Constitution of India, which came into force in 1950, provided for "reservation" of seats in the legislatures at the state assemblies and in Parliament for the Scheduled Castes (SCs; former so-called "untouchable castes" constitute approximately 16% of India's population) and Scheduled Tribes (STs; the numerous tribes living mostly in hilly areas, which comprise approximately 7% of the population); the number of seats set aside for them was to be proportionate to their percentage of the population. It also provided reservation in civil services for the SCs and the STs proportionately. Although the constitution had provided it initially for 10 years, reservation has continued to be the state policy, and all political parties have been committed to continuing it. In 1990, the Indian government, with V. P. Singh as Prime Minister, implemented the Mandal Commission report, which recommended reservation in civil services and elsewhere for the "socially and educationally backward classes." After some violent resistance from upper caste youth, this reservation for "OBCs" (other backward classes; mainly cultivating castes who were poorly represented in bureaucracy and the education sector) has also been implemented. Reservation of seats for OBCs was also gradually extended to educational institutions, schools as well as colleges. In addition to caste groups, there was reservation for women of at least one-third of the strength, also provided in rural local government and urban bodies under the 73rd and 74th Amendments of the Indian constitution in 1992. However, the campaign for a similar reservation for women in Parliament and state assemblies led to the introduction of a law in Parliament that failed to pass (Shirin Rai et al. 2006). In India, religious minorities such as Muslims have suffered much exclusion, as exposed by the Sachar Committee report in 2006. But measures to rectify this inequality have stalled in debates among political parties (Z. Hasan 2009).

The Indian experiment in reservation has exposed some important dimensions of the prevailing approaches to promoting equality. The liberal democratic approach values equality of opportunity and insists on the principle of fair competition for various positions. Therefore, the insistence on the principle of merit is common. This is where there emerge two lines of action. One is to take "affirmative action" by giving support to the weaker sections. For example, in the United States, educational facilities and some living amenities were provided to Blacks, and thereafter the policy was to employ merit-based selection. In Canada and some Scandinavian countries, government-funded public health systems and educational facilities for all residents provide an even better framework for "equality of opportunities." But in countries such as India, these measures are considered inadequate and hence the need for reservation of seats set aside for the marginalized groups. Occasionally, the reservation system in India has invited criticism from those who think that it is an unfair system denying "equal opportunity" to many who happen to be born to upper caste families. Countering that viewpoint is the powerful argument that for centuries some castes have suffered discrimination and humiliation, and it is necessary to continue giving them protection in legislatures, services, and education. The other argument is that quality of services was affected adversely because the candidates with lower marks had been admitted to professional institutions for higher education and were poorly trained. That argument appeared specious because every educational system had to cater to an uneven group of students and train them to acquire a certain level of skill and knowledge. In India, the reservation debate has periodically been highly charged. The merit argument had much backing among the elites, who were still dominated by the upper castes. Many reserved posts remained vacant because there were not enough candidates from the SCs and STs who qualified for the posts. Even the small number who did qualify generally adopted the cultural moorings of the upper caste. Many sectors, such as the defense forces, the police, and the judiciary, remained outside the sphere of reservation. Although there were powerful laws to prevent atrocities against the SCs and STs, prescribing tough punishment—the 1989 legislation was given more teeth in 2015—the number of atrocities remained high. This showed that the prevailing policies had many gaps.

RESERVATION AND AFFIRMATIVE ACTION

Although the elites claimed that affirmative action and reservation were enough to promote equality, in fact these measures were inadequate. In reality, these measures had become an alibi for not taking fundamental measures to address long-standing inequalities of caste, race, and gender. Because such inequalities had a strong basis in the economy and culture, comprehensive reforms were required. For example, in India most dalits were landless agricultural laborers. Therefore, access to productive resources such as land and credit was key to the development of the oppressed. In order to use it profitably, they must have education and proper health conditions. But in India, land reforms have failed to provide adequate land to the poor. The SC and ST finance corporations have too few funds to provide enough credit and intervene effectively in the bleak situation. The corporate sector has firmly declined to provide reservation for the SCs, STs, and OBCs on the ground that doing so would adversely affect their global competitiveness. Some dalit entrepreneurs have taken the initiative to establish the Dalit Indian Chamber of Commerce and Industry (DICCI). They take the view that they can take advantage of the opportunities provided by the globalization process and make a profit. However, the DICCI is a small initiative in the vast arena of dalit deprivation.

In India, inequality in the education and health sectors remains high, and this has been accentuated in the era of market economy globalization. State funding for education and health was cut substantially under policies of fiscal discipline, which affected the poor sections of society, especially the SCs, STs, and OBCs. Private schools, colleges, and universities sprang up, attracting students from the wealthy sections of society. The standards of education in government schools declined so badly that parents had to seek resources to send their children to expensive private schools. Due to pressure from people's movements, the government of India enacted the Right to Education Act in 2009, which was applauded as a substantial measure to promote equality because it provided free and compulsory elementary education for children aged 6–14 years. Alas, implementation of this measure failed, and although enrollment improved significantly, the dropout rate was high, especially among SC and ST children. Poverty and social conditions of the families were clearly a factor. A similar situation occurred with regard to health care. Public hospitals were starved of resources and the quality of their services declined considerably, resulting in the mushrooming of private clinics and corporate hospitals attracting those who could afford them. Thus, the neoliberal economy generated new inequalities as the state retreated from social welfare. The argument that economic growth with free enterprise would create enough opportunities for all to buy social services was not vindicated in practice, either in the Global South or in the Global North. This new inequality was particularly evident in the case of the people in the tribal regions in South Asia (Nathan and Xaxa 2012).

In the cultural realm, attitudes toward dalits and adivasis (tribal people) remained prejudiced; just as in other areas of the world, many Whites have continued to treat people of color differently as well. Gender disparity also persists because patriarchy has had a strong basis not only in the economy but also in Indian culture. The idea that all humans, irrespective of identity, deserve equal respect was still not imparted in early education or in early childhood socialization in family and society. Debates on continuing cultural degradation and humiliation of the oppressed groups, especially the dalits in India, show the serious magnitude of this phenomenon (Guru, 2011; Ilaiah 2009).

Thus, the measures of reservation and affirmative action have been grossly inadequate in reducing inequality even though they must be defended as a minimum step to recognize and tackle the problem of social inequality. Many critics argued that what was needed was a "structural affirmation" involving economic, cultural, and political measures that addressed the roots of long-standing inequalities. Currently, reservation has become an alibi for not taking adequate structural measures. Advertising that one entity was "an equal opportunity organization" or that "its diversity index" was better than average or that reserve seats were filled was not enough. This is why Ambedkar gave a call for the "annihilation of caste," which was also the title of his monumental essay in 1936 in which he asked dalits to "educate, organise and agitate'" (Ambedkar 1936). Finding that the Hindu religion was not amenable to social transformation from within, he converted to Buddhism in the final years of his life. He demonstrated that economic, political, and cultural measures were equally important in addressing the question of inequality. But important issues were raised by many other liberal democrats as well as Marxists, both in theory and in practice. Whereas the former insisted that any program in the name of reducing inequality must not deny freedom to citizens, the latter debated on the stages of social development to promote equality.

PRIORITY OF LIBERTY OVER EQUALITY: DEFERRED LIBERALISM

The discourse on justice in a democracy gave centrality to the idea of the freedom of the individual. The formulation of John Rawls that "justice was fairness" rested on this idea. Through education, employment facilities, and so on, the state had to create the minimum conditions to enable individuals to exercise freedom. But in no case should the state play this role to infringe on the rights of the individual so as to violate principles of political liberalism. The debate regarding the relationship between freedom and equality that was ongoing among the social contract theorists in seventeenth- and eighteenth-century Europe has persisted into contemporary times. It is generally believed that John Locke gave priority to liberty, whereas Jean-Jacques Rousseau gave priority to equality, even though there are many complex arguments over their positions. The establishment of the communist party regime in Russia and fascist states in Germany and Italy greatly influenced this debate in the second half of the twentieth century. The Soviet state had undertaken tasks in the name of promoting equality that restricted freedom of citizens. The fascist regime had a program of providing welfare to all as a part of its racist agenda. Therefore, it was understandable to give priority to liberty. But as scholars such as C. B. Macpherson have noted, recalling the argument of Rousseau, such a perspective became one of possessive individualism in which individuals were mainly viewed as propertied agents engaged in making personal profit. That more likely caused greater inequalities in society. Instead, individuals could be perceived as creative beings working together with others to promote the welfare of all. This argument recorded a high point of the radical stream within liberalism. Thereafter, capitalism took the neoliberal turn, experiencing a moment of triumph with the collapse of the Soviet Union in 1991. The promise of resolving the dichotomy between liberty and equality by making the two interdependent, which Rousseau and his successors advocated, was given up for a new wave of capitalism that promoted individual freedom and enterprise. This era can be called one of deferred liberalism because it opted for treating equality as a second-order value, giving priority to liberty. The emergence of the United States as the single superpower exercising hegemony throughout the world and Western capital and technology, especially communication and information technology, as the driving force of global development provided the political support to the new wave of thought that asserted superiority of Western values, culture, and religion. That ran counter to the trends that had risen since the anti-colonial struggles, affirming equality and dignity of nations, cultures, religions, and people's right to self-determination. As a result, confrontations emerged in different areas of the world regarding the question of equality. The rise of terrorism and fundamentalism, including violent terrorist attacks conducted by Islamic groups and counter-attacks by the United States and its allies, may have many causes, but the demand for equality is one of them (Mohanty 1983).

THE MARXIST APPROACH TO INEQUALITY: ACQUIESCENT SOCIALISM IN CHINA

China's experience during the past half century—the Cultural Revolution (CR) under the leadership of Mao Zedong (1966–1976) and the reforms initiated by Deng Xiaoping—reasonably illustrates the Marxist approach to reducing inequality. The CR reaffirmed the centrality of the equality principle in socialism and communism. Capitalism, it was argued, negated the equality principle by appropriating the surplus value of labor and accumulated profit, denying labor its due. Hence, socialism sought to alter the production system by introducing collective and state ownership and used state power to ensure that workers got their due. Before the CR, the CPC under Mao's leadership had already established people's communes, recalling the model of Paris Communes of 1871, to put into practice collective ownership of land. Under this system, from 1958 until 1978, land was collectively owned by the village community, and wages were distributed according to work points given to laborers. This and many other institutions of socialist construction of the Mao era were dismantled, and a new system of what was later called "socialist market economy" was introduced with the launching of "reforms and open door" policies in 1978 under the leadership of Deng Xiaoping. Mao's economic policies were criticized by Deng and colleagues for promoting equality prematurely even before material conditions of production had developed. Hence, the Deng era reforms focused on the single point of "economic construction." Reforms meant changing state and collective ownership to private, joint, and multiple forms of ownership that promoted growth of production. Making all production units oriented toward market and bearing gains and losses depending on their performance in the competitive market economy. Open door meant opening the opportunities to procure capital and technology from abroad as well as from within the country and producing for the market. Agricultural land, still owned by the village, was now contracted to households on a long-term basis, allowing household members the freedom to allocate labor and thus allowing many of them to join rural industries or migrate to cities for work. A principle that was enforced without exception was the "production responsibility system." Instead of workers getting fixed wages for work, now their wages depended on their contribution to the profit of the enterprise. Hard-working workers producing more output received more wages. If the unit suffered losses, the workers received less wages and less or no bonuses. Mao-era wage policy was denounced as "every one eating from the iron bowl," with the implication that both the lazy and the hard-working laborer received the same compensation. There were many other fundamental changes in the economy along this line (Mohanty 2014).

The reforms in China achieved spectacular success, raising Chinese people's living standards, introducing world-class infrastructure in the cities, allowing China to grow into the status of the world's second largest economy by 2010, and achieving a pride of place in the global community. But this path of development has given rise to many serious problems, including a growing inequality and the rise of disparities among social groups, regions, and ethnic communities, along with a persistent gender gap. Rural–urban disparities in income, educational and health facilities, and employment opportunities grew faster during the course of reforms, although they had shown encouraging signs in the first decade of reforms when rural industries and collective investment in welfare improved the conditions in the countryside. By 2000, CPC leaders were talking about the "three rural problems": environmental degradation, distress migration from the countryside, and the crisis of the floating population—urban residents who were not entitled to the same amenities as the city's registered citizens (with city *hukou*). The high degree of corruption and widespread phenomenon of consumerism, selfishness, and the breakdown of moral behavior were some of the trends recognized by China's leaders. The anti-corruption campaign of Xi Jinping exposed the magnitude of some of these problems.

The China experience showed that there were no easy ways to implement the principle of equality. Marx had made a distinction between two principles, one for the socialist stage and another for communism. The socialist principle of "from each according to his/her ability, to each according to his/her work" ("her" is added) meant that because workers will avail the results of their labor, they will work to the best of their ability. But still there would be a valuation of their work, and accordingly they would receive wages as per the value of their work. In other words, there would be inequality of wages because socialism was regarded as a transitional system to communism. In the communist stage of social development, however, the principle of distribution would be "from each according to his/her ability, to each according to his/her need." According to Marx, the productive forces would have developed well and workers' self-management system put in place, resulting in full satisfaction of every person's needs. In the socialist stage, there would be inequality, but much less than that under capitalism. This is where Mao Zedong had advocated a faster pace of reduction of inequality, and the rule was not to exceed the ratio of one to eight. Gradually, three major differences had to be addressed: manual and mental labor, rural and urban societies, and factory worker and farm peasant roles. Priority was to be given to reducing these inequalities even if it led to a slower rate of economic growth. On this issue, Deng Xiaoping radically departed from Mao. According to Deng, economic growth must be given priority. He theorized that socialism was a long historical period of transition and China was in the "primary stage of socialism," which was likely to also be a long period.

He wanted China to adopt a market economy, management system, and science and technology from the advanced capitalist countries and apply them to China's specific conditions, maintaining full control by the communist party. Indeed, that has led to the present stage of China's development, one marked by tremendous economic success but accompanied by serious sociopolitical and ecological problems (Mohanty 2017). Today, China boasts of some of the world's top billionaires, and the income disparities are stunningly high.

Thus, socialist experiments have settled for tolerating high degrees of inequality—social, economic, and political. Political inequality is manifest in two ways. One is the monopoly of power by the communist party and the other is the rise of the new class of bourgeoisie that is a major participant in the market economy and therefore wields power. This phenomenon of what can be called "acquiescent socialism" is regarded by many as a system of developing capitalism with Chinese specificities maintaining and reproducing inequalities old and new. China's reforms have coincided with the growth of neoliberal globalization, and China has taken full advantage of it and has championed the principles of globalization and free trade while some countries have experienced nationalist and protectionist waves. The socialist agenda of promoting equality has been relegated to the background by most communist parties in power.

The SDG Moment and the Global South

Deferred liberalism that promoted free enterprise and an acquiescent socialism that focused on economic growth both converged to shape the political economy of the Global South. Neoliberal economic reforms were adopted by India, China and the other BRICS countries—Brazil, South Africa, and Russia (which although not geographically located in the south, it is economically in close proximity). Reducing inequality had become a low priority. In India under the Congress-led regime, for example, there were a spate of poverty reduction and welfare support programs, such as the Rural Employment Guarantee Act, 2005, and the Food Security Act, 2013. Under the BJP-led regime, bank accounts for obtaining credit and support for startup programs were made available to help the poor. China had been more successful in reducing poverty by region-specific support programs. But the fact that poverty is rooted in unequal access to productive resources is not taken into account in either case. As a result, inequality persisted and even increased. Persistent inequality was a major cause of alienation, protest, and resistance.

In addition, the phenomenon of economic inequality was seen together with lack of respect for culture, religion, and knowledge systems of the communities of the Global South. Just as economic exploitation had occurred with cultural subjugation during the colonial times, the era of globalization had produced a peculiar semblance with that experience. In fact, anti-colonial struggles had largely succeeded in regaining cultural confidence of the southern countries and built up postcolonial cultural and educational systems to promote indigenous knowledge. That had been under threat in the face of a global capitalist drive that was welcomed enthusiastically by local elites. There were, no doubt, continuing challenges to the globalization policies that used the local elite to extract natural resources from the ASAFLA countries. Global corporations used the creed of free trade to establish themselves in the resource-rich countries—some characterize it as resource-cursed countries—and not only remove their minerals but also use those countries as markets for their products. Thus, according to critics, economic exploitation and cultural subjugation went together, making a mockery of national independence promised by the charter of the UN. Post-national global community was meant to enhance autonomy of the local, national, and regional entities to interact on terms of equality and dignity. On the other hand, inequality between the units at every level had increased.

In 2015, the UN General Assembly adopted the SDGs for 2015–2030. They replaced the MDGs (Millennium Development Goals of 2000–2015), which constituted a landmark declaration in contemporary history. Yet the 17 global goals with 169 targets only marginally focused on reducing inequality. Besides a commitment to the promotion of gender inequality in goal 5, it declared a commitment to work for "reducing income inequality within and among countries" (goal 10). All the goals were certainly laudable and were necessary for human development, and they would also impact on reducing inequality (Sachs 2015). But the thrust on the specific welfare programs did not have a coherent focus on the major issues of the age, namely the demand for equality and freedom for struggling people. The fact that income inequality was part of the problem of cumulative inequalities was hardly appreciated. Reduction of arithmetic inequality or quantitative trends in raising income of the lower strata was only one aspect, whereas many other dimensions of discrimination and oppression remained active. From this viewpoint, the SDGs seemed to be meant to service the globalization agenda of the dominant global elite, which also included the elite of the Global South. These goals were meant to manage the tensions generated by the expansion of the free market economy and aid the economic growth agenda. Hence, the SDG moment represented the historic acquiescence with prevailing inequalities in the contemporary world.

Whereas the anti-colonial era upheld the movement for swaraj and jiefang and the post-colonial global society stressed the vision of samata and ubuntu, the globalization era diffused and redirected historical processes toward a new version of the unequal world. The SDGs embodied that. But forces unleashed by the movements for swaraj, jiefang, samata, and Ubuntu in the Global South had resounded in the Global North as well. Therefore, struggles for equality were bound to continue on a global scale even when the power elites throughout the world sought to dilute the equality movements to promote their agenda of economic growth driven by the free market. The Buddha's challenge presented more than 2,000 years ago has continued to confront twenty-first century elites in the Global South as well as in the Global North, who are preoccupied with economic growth and political stability. If that challenge for the equal dignity of all goes unheeded, the likelihood is greater for continued alienation and violence in the global future.

Note

1. Hazrat Hassan, "The Gap Between China's Rich and Poor Is Growing," *Foreign Policy News* (May 17, 2016), http://foreignpolicynews.org/2016/05/17/gap-chinas-rich-poor-growing.

REFERENCES

Ambedkar, B. R. 1936. "Annihilation of Caste." Undelivered speech.

Ambedkar, B. R. 1949. "Speech Moving the Resolution for Adoption of the Constitution of India." https://indiankanoon.org/doc/792941. Accessed August 1, 2018.

Amin, Samir. 1997. *Capitalism in the Age of Globalization*. London: Zed.

Amin, Samir. 2009. *Seize the Crisis!* New York: Monthly Review Press.

Beteille, Andre. 1977. *Inequality Among Men*. London: Basil Blackwell.

Deng Xiaoping. 1992. "Excerpts from Talks Given in Wuchang, Shenzhen, Zhuhai and Shanghai, January 18–February 21, 1992." http://www.olemiss.edu/courses/pol324/dengxp92.htm. Accessed October 5, 2017.

dos Santos, Theotonio. 2010. "Development and Civilisation." *Social Change* 40 (2): 95–116.

Dubey, Amaresh, and Sukhdeo Thorat. 2012. "Has Growth Been Socially Inclusive During 1993–94–2009–10?" *Economic & Political Weekly* 47(10): 43–53.

Falk, Richard. 2017. "The World Ahead: Entering the Anthropocene?" In *Exploring Emergent Global Thresholds: Towards 2030*, edited by Richard Falk, Manoranjan Mohanty, and Victor Faessel, 19–47. New Delhi: Orient BlackSwan.

Galanter, Marc. 1984. *Competing Equalities: Law and the Backward Classes in India*. Berkeley: University of California Press.

Gao, Ruiquan. 2017. "The Unarticulated Conception of Equality in Early Confucianism, and Its Relation to Modern Conceptions." In *Reconceptualising Confucian Philosophy in the 21st Century*, edited by Yao Xinzhong, 241–256. Singapore: Springer.

Guru, Gopal, ed. 2011. *Humiliation: Claims and Context*. New Delhi: Oxford University Press.

Hassan, Hazrat. 2016. "The Gap Between China's Rich and Poor Is Growing." *Foreign Policy News*, May 17. http://foreignpolicynews.org/2016/05/17/gap-chinas-rich-poor-growing. Accessed March 3, 2017.

Hasan, Zoya. 2009. *Politics of Inclusion: Caste, Minorities and Affirmative Action*. New Delhi: Oxford University Press.

Human Rights Council. 2016. *Report of the Special Rapporteur on the situation of human rights defenders*. See http://ap.ohchr.org/documents/dpage_e.aspx?si=A/HRC/31/55. Accessed August 1, 2018.

Ilaiah, Kancha. 2009. *Post-Hindu India*. New Delhi: Sage.

Juergensmeyer, Mark. 2008. *Global Rebellion: Religious Challenges to the Secular State, from Christian Militias to al Qaeda*. Berkeley and Los Angeles: University of California Press.

Lakoff, Stanford. 1964. *Equality in Political Philosophy*. Boston: Beacon Press.

McGill, Kenneth. 2016. *Global Inequality: Anthropological Insights*. Toronto: University of Toronto Press.

Mohanty, Manoranjan. 1983. "Towards a Political Theory of Inequality." In *Equality and Inequality*, edited by André Béteille, pp. 243–291. New Delhi: Oxford University Press.

Mohanty, Manoranjan. 2000. *Contemporary Indian Political Theory*. New Delhi: Sanskriti

Mohanty, Manoranjan. 2014. *Ideology Matters: China from Mao Zedong to Xi Jinping*. New Delhi: Aakar Books.

Mohanty, Manoranjan. 2017. "Development as Civilizational Movement: Counter-hegemonic Prospects from Asia, Africa and Latin America." In *Exploring Emergent Global Thresholds: Towards 2030*, edited by Richard Falk, Manoranjan Mohanty, and Victor Faessel, 76–103. New Delhi: Orient BlackSwan.

Mohanty, Manoranjan. 2018. *China's Transformation: The Success Story and the Success Trap.* New Delhi: Sage.

Nathan, Dev, and Virginius Xaxa. 2012. *Social Exclusion and Adverse Inclusion: Development and Deprivation in India.* New Delhi: Oxford University Press.

Nayyar, Deepak. 2013. *Catch Up: Developing Countries in the World Economy.* Oxford, UK: Oxford University Press.

Omvedt, Gail. 2003. *Buddhism in India: Challenging Brahmanism and Caste.* New Delhi: Sage.

Patnaik, Prabhat. 2014. "Capitalism, Inequality and Globalisation: Thomas Piketty's Capital in the Twenty First Century." *International Journals of Political Economy* 43 (3): 55–69.

Patnaik, Prabhat. 2016. "Capitalism and Its Current Crisis." *Monthly Review* 67 (8): 1–13.

Piketty, Thomas. 2014. *Capital in the Twenty First Century.* London: Belknap Press.

Prashad, Vijay. 2007. *The Darker Nations: A People's History of the Third World.* New York: New Press.

Rai, Shirin, Farzana Bari, Nazmunnessa Mahtab, and Bidyut Mohanty (2006). "South Asia: Gender Quotas and the Politics of Empowerment–A Comparative Study." In *Women, Quotas and Politics*, edited by Dahlerup, Drude, pp. 222–246. London, New York: Routledge.

Sachs, Jeffrey D. 2015. *The Age of Sustainable Development.* New York: Columbia University Press.

Sheth, D. L. 2004. "Reservation Policy Revisited." In *Class, Caste, Gender*, edited by Manoranjan Mohanty, 207–226. New Delhi: Sage.

Stiglitz, Joseph. 2012. *The Price Inequality.* London: Lane.

Thorat, Sukhdeo, and Katherine S. Newman. 2012. *Blocked by Cast: Economic Discrimination in Modern India.* New Delhi: Oxford University Press.

Williams, Glyn, Paula Meth, and Katie Willis. 2014. *Geographies of Developing Areas: The Global South in a Changing World.* London: Routledge.

CHAPTER 15

FEMINIST PERSPECTIVES IN GLOBAL STUDIES

VALENTINE M. MOGHADAM

WHAT has feminist scholarship contributed to global studies? How do feminist approaches differ? To what extent do feminist contributions meet what Steger identified in Chapter 1 of this volume as the four central pillars or framings of global studies: globalization, transdisciplinarity, space and time, and critical thinking? This chapter addresses these questions through a focus on three areas of feminist research: (gendered) globalization, violence against women and armed conflict, and transnational social movements. As will be evident, the three areas of research are interconnected in that "globalization-from-above" generates or exacerbates inequalities, tensions, and conflicts, whereas social movements— including transnational feminist networks and locally based women's rights groups that ally with them—are manifestations of "globalization-from-below." Feminist economists (both macro- and micro-economists), sociologists (largely those associated with world society, world-systems, or gender stratification theories), and political scientists (comparativists, theorists, and those in the international relations field) have been the most prominent contributors to global studies. Their research has spanned micro, meso, and macro levels of analysis, tackling the gender dynamics of the global economy and the interstate system; social movements, feminist organizations, and international organizations; and the individual and household effects of larger socioeconomic and political processes. Methods of feminist research in global studies range from quantitative to ethnography, but in general feminist researchers are cognizant of the "intersectionality" of gender, class, and race/ethnicity. In examining processes associated with globalization, feminist scholars also have addressed the persistent conundrum of structure and agency: How does change occur, by whom, and under what conditions?

This chapter examines feminist perspectives, critiques, and contributions to global studies during the past three decades, including my own research, with a focus on the feminist political economy approach. To anticipate the analysis, I note here that the era of neoliberal globalization has given rise to a number of contradictory and paradoxical developments. These include ever-increasing female educational attainment and greater female labor force participation amid widening income inequality, periodic crises, rising unemployment, wage stagnation, and continued violence against women; democracy promotion alongside the "war on terror," imposed regime changes, and the relative decline of US hegemony; and the proliferation of women's movements supported by the United Nations' (UN) global women's rights agenda notwithstanding the persistence of hypermasculinity and patriarchy.

To begin, I explain the global women's rights agenda as it frames some of the discussion that follows. It consists of a large and growing number of initiatives, notably world conferences and international treaties, sponsored by the UN, signed by governments, and embraced by women's rights groups. An important treaty and norm is the Convention on the Elimination of All Forms of Discrimination against Women, known by its acronym CEDAW (which is also the acronym for the committee that reviews signatory-government periodic reports as well as non-governmental organization [NGO] shadow reports). Adopted in 1979, following the first World Conference on Women (Mexico City, 1975) and during the Decade for Women (1976–1985), CEDAW came into force in 1981 and to date has been ratified by nearly all states, although its provisions have not necessarily been implemented in full. Antecedents to CEDAW include the 1952 UN Convention on the Political Rights of Women; the 1957 Convention on the Nationality of Married Women; the 1960 UNESCO Convention against Discrimination in Education; and the 1962 UN Convention on Consent to Marriage, Minimum Age for Marriage, and Registration of Marriage. Since then, other international standards and norms concerning women's rights include Security Council Resolution 1325 on women, peace and security; ILO Convention 183 on maternity protection (2000; revised from the 1952 version); and Goal 3 of the Millennium Development Goals (2000–2015), which pertained to ending gender gaps in education and political participation. Since 2010, UN Women—the agency that incorporated the three preceding entities on women—has been tasked with monitoring, researching, and advocating for women's rights and gender equality. One task is to monitor the integration of gender issues across the 16 new Sustainable Development Goals.

The many standards, norms, and treaties that constitute the global women's rights agenda have been adopted in varying degrees across countries and are the subject of considerable feminist inquiry. However, they are vulnerable to the volatilities of the global economy and of the interstate system. The neoliberal era has in fact both undermined and exacerbated patriarchal forms of gender relations, in at least two ways. First, by drawing more women into the global economy, it has removed many women from local and household patriarchal controls, allowing for the formation of a professional class of employed women and a female working class. At the same time, much of the work available to women—especially working-class women and today's educated young people—is irregular, precarious, temporary, or exploitative. In addition, patriarchal backlashes have occurred in some areas, especially where men have been left behind or otherwise threatened by women's gains.

Second, both the UN's global women's rights agenda and democracy-promotion initiatives by the United States and European Union have encouraged women's political participation and representation. In August 2016, 46 countries had met or exceeded the UN's recommended 30% benchmark; among that group were Algeria and Tunisia (the United States ranked 96th; see Interparliamentary Union 2016). As these efforts have coincided with the emergence of large populations of educated and assertive women engaged in both civil society and political society, the result has been to weaken patriarchal gender relations and bring about pro-women legislative and policy reforms. At the same time, competition and rivalries among male-dominated states and militant movements have generated invasions and occupations, armed conflicts, and horrific forms of violence against women.

Paradoxically, these conflicts have been supported by some women, whether in government or in the society at large (discussed later).

As a result of the contradictions and paradoxes, progress and setbacks, and the push and pull of collective action and entrenched structures, feminist global studies have themselves revealed different emphases. Some studies have emphasized women's agency and empowerment, whereas others highlight the structures of constraint and oppression; some advocate for policy reforms in line with institutional imperatives, whereas others stress the need for systemic change; and some scholars engage in innovative theoretical work that may or may not be welcomed or acknowledged by colleagues in the mainstream of their disciplines. This chapter can make references only to a small number of those studies and scholars in the three sections that follow—on the gendered nature of globalization, violence, and social movements—while also underscoring the compelling nature of the more radical critiques and proposed alternatives to the prevailing global order.

GENDERING GLOBALIZATION

Globalization is a complex and multidimensional process whereby the mobility of capital, products, ideas, organizations, and movements takes on an increasingly global form (Moghadam 2005: 35). Although it has come under attack in recent years, it remains the current stage of the capitalist world-system, characterized by the global expansion of capitalist relations of production, the spread and promotion of democracy, the diffusion of the UN-promoted women's rights agenda, the worldwide growth of feminist movements and networks, the speed of communications, and the spread of Islamist movements and political parties. It is perhaps an irony of history that neoliberalism, feminist movements, Islamist movements, and anti-globalization movements spread at roughly the same time (Moghadam 2013a).

A key postulate of feminist global studies is that globalization in its varied dimensions is gendered. The economic dimension—privatization, the introduction of "flexible" labor markets, outsourcing, financialization, and the emphasis on entrepreneurship—affects women and men differently, while the political dimension can be imbued with culture-laden concepts of masculinity and femininity (Marchand and Runyan 2000). The study of globalization reveals possibilities for change in gender relations, with opportunities for cross-border collective action, domestic coalition-building, and progressive legal and policy reforms. But it also reveals the entrenchment of structural or systemic obstacles.

Since the 1970s, a prodigious literature has emerged on the effects of economic processes on working women's lives, and we may identify three "waves" of such feminist global studies. The first set of studies focused on modernization, development, and female labor; the second focused on structural adjustment policies and women; and the third focused on globalization and women's work and domestic lives. Early modernization marginalized women from the productive process, creating "housewifization" and marginalization (Mies 1986; Saffioti 1978), but subsequent development processes not only integrated female labor but also relied on it for industrial growth and exports, especially in Southeast Asia and along the US–Mexico border (Elson and Pearson 1981; Joekes 1987; Nash and Fernandez-Kelly 1984; Sen and Grown 1985). Structural adjustment policies intensified women's productive and reproductive burdens and were marked by male bias (Elson 1990). Neoliberal global-ization was accompanied by flexible and "feminized" labor markets (Standing 1989, 1999), along with an outflow of female migrant workers and the persistence of unacceptable levels of violence against women (True 2012). Financialization led to growing income inequalities and reckless market behavior that culminated in the 2008 Great Recession and new aus-terity measures, all of which had specific effects on women, work, and welfare (Moghadam 2011; Rubery 2015; Walby 2015).

When feminist research on globalization emerged in the 1990s, two approaches began to define the field. One was the materialist and political economy approach that brought attention to how states, multinational corporations, and institutions of global governance have created a *global economy* in which female labor plays a distinct role, albeit in dif-ferent ways across regions and within societies (Dunaway 2001; Peterson 2003). The other was the postcolonial and post-structuralist approach emphasizing the signs, symbols, and representations of globalization as a *masculine* project in which *scattered hegemonies* subsumed subordinate sectors, countries, and social groups, but where women were able to act toward self-empowerment (Bergeron 2001; Grewal and Kaplan 1994; Marchand 2000; Marchand and Parpart 1995). The field of gender and globalization has expanded, but many studies continue to be characterized by the two approaches; in both, scholars examine the interplay of structure and agency, although with different emphases and methodologies. For example, in the first approach, the economic zones of the capitalist world-system constitute the analytical point of departure, within which women's collective action toward resistance and self-empowerment takes shape in different ways, with the implicit or explicit assump-tion that a sort of global social democracy would be a solution to contemporary gender and social inequalities (Moghadam 2005; Walby 2009). The second approach evinces a tendency toward methodological individualism, without broad recommendations of epochal shifts but with examples of ways that women in particular settings have negotiated globalized structures to their own advantage (Desai 2009; Sylvanus 2016). A third approach, currently largely confined to feminist studies of the democratic welfare states of the European Union, is to focus on particular institutions—national or supranational—as sites of contestation, change, and empowerment (Krook and Mackay 2015; Rai and Waylen 2008). Across these approaches, therefore, we find feminist analyses of macro-level structural processes, meso-level institutions, and micro-level forms of action.

Precarity, Care, and Class

New research on the changing global class structure has included investigations into the so-called "precariat" (Standing 2011), where a large part of the world's female labor force is located. The era of globalization compelled a shift from manufacturing to services as the main source of employment; along with the spread of information-based systems and technologies, this shift generated a new economy emphasizing flexibility in the labor market and in employment relations. Flexibility entailed the erosion of the standard (in-dustrial) employment relationship and an increase in precarious work, which is poorly paid and insecure. Researchers may use "precarity" in a broad sense, but for Guy Standing (2011), the precariat is located in the services sector, in irregular/insecure forms of labor such as retail and hospitality, temp agencies, and call centers. The precariat includes part-time or fixed-term workers, those on "zero contracts" and subcontracted workers, along with interns. Educated young people with university education have few, if any, prospects of the kind of stable, full-time jobs or careers that their parents and grandparents were guaranteed during the "golden age" of Third World development or the "golden age of capitalism" in Western countries. Educated young women may have the necessary training and credentials as well as civic skills, but they face either very high unemployment rates or "flexible" jobs that do not enable them to embark on professional careers. In some countries, they face the burden of traditional gender bias and are either excluded from certain positions in the public sector or face quotas that limit their access (because men are favored). Standing rightly notes that precarious workers have *rights insecurity* in that they are not beneficiaries of pensions or other social benefits. This has been a characteristic of vast sections of the global labor force generally, and the female labor force specifically, but in recent years it has encompassed populations that in the past would be guaranteed stable work and good benefits.

If we accept world-system theory's postulate that the contemporary capitalist world-system consists of the three economic zones of core, periphery, and semi-periphery (Chase-Dunn 1998), we can acknowledge that forms of the female labor force—including the female precariat—will vary by world-system location, country, and social class. In the core, many working-class and lower middle-class women have lost the decent jobs and benefits they may have previously enjoyed, a condition exacerbated by the Great Recession. But even before that, Barbara Ehrenreich's (2001) celebrated ethnographic study *Nickel and Dimed* elucidated the precarious employment conditions of working-class and low-income American women. What might be called the Americanization of the global economy occurred with economic globalization, as non-standard and precarious jobs spread across Europe as well as in developing countries. Women in such jobs remain outside social security programs because the state does not extend benefits that private employers will not or cannot cover. In Bangladesh, a peripheral country, women account for almost 85% of workers in the garment industry (Oxfam 2014). These jobs, although often better for women than subsistence farming, offer minimal job security or physical safety: Most of those killed by the collapse of the Rana Plaza garment factory in April 2013 were women.

Bangladesh is also famous for the microcredit revolution. There remains some disagreement as to the extent of microcredit's contribution to poverty alleviation in Bangladesh or elsewhere. What seems clear, however, is that the goals of privatization and poverty reduction underpin the promotion of entrepreneurship and microfinancing, targeted in large measure to women. Many income-generating projects that focus on low-income women largely operate on the basis of a market approach notwithstanding the claim of women's empowerment as the goal. Such projects do not enable the establishment of productive women-owned businesses with growth potentials; rather, they keep women in what the International Labor Organization (ILO) calls the "vulnerable worker" category. Because women are often oriented toward traditional homemaking occupations that generate little income, they are trapped in survivalist activities (Beneria 2001).

The economic problems and burdens that working-class and lower-income women face are exacerbated by the growing inequality that numerous countries have been experiencing across the neoliberal era. Studies show that in more economically unequal societies, fewer women complete higher education, fewer women are represented in the legislature, and the pay gap between women and men is wider (Oxfam 2014; Wilkinson and Pickett 2009). The recent rapid rise in economic inequality in most countries, therefore, is a serious blow to efforts to achieve gender equality. At the same time, women's lower wages, precarity, and unemployment both reflect and contribute to overall social and income inequality.

As neoliberal globalization was unfolding across the past decades, women's labor force participation increased, whether for labor supply-side reasons (women's economic need, educational attainment, and fewer children) or for demand-side reasons (employers' preference for low-cost non-unionized labor in manufacturing, the need for professionals in certain public and private services, or equal-opportunity laws mandating the hiring of women). In the wake of the Great Recession, however, data show that young women's labor force participation decreased, globally, from 50.5% in 1992 to 40.5% in 2012 (ILO 2012: Table 5, p. 19). In countries of the Middle East and North Africa, where there had been a slow but steady increase in female involvement in manufacturing in countries such as Morocco, Tunisia, Egypt, Jordan, and Turkey, more recent data show declines, suggesting a contraction of the female working class. Women may be withdrawing because of precarious work conditions and the absence of supports for maternal employment in the expanding private sector (Ilkkaracan 2012; Moghadam 2016).

As Johanna Brenner (2001) has pointed out, Marx and Engels knew that capitalism would have the tendency to draw women into wage labor and that this would create the material basis for their independence from men. But they overlooked the limitation that women's role in biological reproduction placed on women's independence. Feminist political economy has detailed how women's care work underpins both production and social reproduction and in many instances compensates for the state's inadequate welfare provisions (Folbre 1997, 2012). Cooking and cleaning, childcare, and elder care are the responsibility of all but the wealthiest women, and neither value nor status is attached to caregivers within the household. As such, the sexual division of labor has remained remarkably resilient. Studies show that women's care work is a causal factor in the gender differences in leisure time, income, promotions, and pensions (UN Women 2015).

Another aspect of the changing global class structure that is also tied to the gender dynamics of globalization is paid care work by female migrants. Such labor may be beneficial to sending countries such as the Philippines, Sri Lanka, and Indonesia, in that remittances support families at home while also contributing to the national income. But migrating women workers often encounter oppressive working conditions as well as the perverse reality of caring for other people's children and elderly relatives while their own remain thousands of miles away.

Women's domestic and caring responsibilities shape women's labor force participation and influence employment arrangements; the availability of migrant female labor does the same. For example, studies by the Organisation for Economic Co-operation and Development (OECD) find that European women's labor force participation aligns with the presence or absence of child care facilities (Thévenon 2013). In the oil-rich countries of the Persian Gulf, rates of female labor force participation are now the highest in the region of the Middle East and North Africa—at approximately 40–50%—because in these very small countries all the (educated) women who want to work find jobs in the public sector and because they all have nannies, imported from Southeast Asia. What is more, the labor force statistics include migrant workers. Elsewhere in the region, women's labor force participation is low, certainly because of weak economic conditions, discriminatory legislation, the contraction of public sector employment and the absence of decent work in the private sector, but crucially because women from low-income and working-class households do not have access to either paid maternity leave of a culturally acceptable duration or affordable and quality childcare facilities (Moghadam 2016).

If working women throughout the world are concentrated at the lower rungs of the stratification ladder, those at the top may enjoy far better living standards and life options, although not compared to their male peers. As a number of studies have shown, men are over-represented at the top of the income ladder and hold more positions of power as ministers and business leaders. In 2014, just 23 chief executives of Fortune 500 companies and only 3 of the 30 richest people in the world were women (Oxfam 2014). Nonetheless, a kind of "1% feminism" may be identified, exemplified by Facebook's Sheryl Sandberg, whose book, *Lean In* (2013), was addressed to highly paid professional women who did not make as much as their male peers. The recommendation that women "lean in" to demand the kinds of promotions, bonuses, and pay raises their male colleagues more easily obtain is found in texts and speeches geared toward highly paid professional women (in legal and medical services, the entertainment industry, media, and the corporate world), but it is less relevant to women in low-paid service jobs. Equal pay for equal work is certainly a valid feminist demand, but so is the presence of precarious work, low or stagnating wages, and the lack of institutional supports for working mothers. Structural inequalities systematically prevent progress for large segments of the world's current or potential female labor force. Economic advantages and disadvantages spill over into the domain of "human capabilities" (Drèze and Sen 1999; Nussbaum 2000: 70–110). The presence of very wide income inequalities that characterize many areas of the world would call into question the validity of the notion of "equality of opportunities."

VIOLENCE, ARMED CONFLICT, PEACE, AND SECURITY

Feminist studies on violence against women (VAW) have been both prodigious and prominent. Starting with second-wave US feminist concerns with "wife battering," research and advocacy has spread across the world to encompass sexual harassment at the workplace and on the streets, harmful traditional practices, and sexual abuse during armed conflict. Feminist scholarship has sought to show how gender inequality is inextricably tied to both intra- and interstate violence (Caprioli 2005; Hudson et al. 2012; womanstats.org) and how women's involvement in peace movements should be recognized and rewarded (Cockburn 2010). This approach examines VAW within micro and macro processes to assert that gender inequality correlates with VAW as well as with violence generally and also to postulate that the presence or absence of women in political life matters for the propensity of a state to engage in war.

Violence against women is present across cultures, historical periods, and political systems; it occurs in contexts of the politicization of ethnicity, wars, and criminal activity. Wife battering and sexual harassment have been documented in countries throughout the world, but culture-specific forms of VAW include date rape/campus rape, compulsory veiling, forced marriage, honor killings, female feticide, dowry deaths, bride fattening, acid attacks, and virginity tests. Such violence takes place within the home, on the streets, and at workplaces, universities, clinics, and prisons; some, such as compulsory veiling or punishments for adultery or premarital sex, may be state-sanctioned. Intimate partner violence (IPV) accounts for the majority of women's experience of violence. Resources remain limited even though VAW has become a major focus of feminist advocacy and mobilization. Studies have shown that in most countries, less than half of the women who experienced violence sought help of any sort, and among those who did, most looked to family and friends as opposed to the police and health services (McCleary-Sills 2016; see also Klugman et al. 2014: Chap. 3).

Scholarly interest in domestic and sexual violence blossomed in the 1970s when feminist movements in the United States and Great Britain called attention to the high rates of men's violence against their wives. Feminist scholars suggested that patriarchy reinforced men's unequal access to power and material resources through both subtle and overt forms of violence. Wife abuse, within this tradition, is viewed as both a byproduct and a producer of unequal gender relations: Violence prevents women from challenging men's authority in the home and reinforces their subordinate position within the gender hierarchy. A feminist analysis of domestic violence focuses on the contexts within which men hurt women; the physical and non-physical forms of violence that maintain men's power over women; and the gendered implications of VAW for individual survivors, their families, and society (Moghadam and Fahlberg 2017). In other words, women's inequality is the central explanatory variable in feminist scholarship on domestic violence, although not the exclusive one.

The varied forms of VAW are regarded by many scholars as examples of *structural violence*—that is, rooted in unequal gender relations, patriarchal laws and norms, geopolitics, and economic inequalities rather than solely in individual pathology. Feminist social theory locates VAW in (gendered) power asymmetries that manifest themselves at micro, meso, and macro levels. Across time and space, men have been socialized into hegemonic masculinity or hypermasculinity and accorded privileges and entitlements, whereas women have been subject to men's supervision or control within the family, placed in subordinate roles in other societal domains, and often considered as sexual objects. One line of inquiry suggests that violence by men against women is not solely a resource for reinforcing men's dominance over women but also a strategy for men to claim and maintain power over other men. Connell and Messerschmidt (2005) contend that the patriarchal social structure produces a hierarchy among men that shapes conceptions of hegemonic masculinity and requires that individual men adopt particular, often aggressive and competitive, behaviors in order to assert their dominant status in relation to other men. Although idealized notions of masculinity and the legal or normative resources for enacting these vary across communities, masculinity scholars argue that in every society women's bodies have become a common vehicle through which men perform their dominance over other men as well as over women (Moghadam and Fahlberg 2017). One need only think of wars, gangs, and authoritarian state policies as sites for such hypermasculine competition and power struggles and the fallout for women. As a result, sexual assault, IPV, femicide, sexual harassment, and other forms of gender-based violence continue to remain high, even as feminist notions of equality between men and women seep into social norms and public policies. As Walby (2009) has argued, violence is entrenched in the economy, polity, and society, perpetrated by state and non-state actors alike.

The interstate system of the current era of neoliberal globalization is complicit in VAW in at least three ways. First, it produces conflicts and wars. Second, it produces economic pressures and crises, or "economic violence" (Fabián 2010: 18). Macroeconomic policies that induce unemployment may generate tensions in households or communities, exacerbate hegemonic masculinities, and increase IPV. Third, numerous states retain discriminatory laws or laws that expressly place women in a subordinate position in the family or society at large. Feminist scholarship further examines how geopolitical interests and interventions by regional or global powers in support of contested states or non-state rebels ignites hypermasculinity and thus controls over women in the family or the household (Winter 2017); this is quite apart from the pervasive sexual abuse that typically accompanies armed conflicts and refugee waves (Leatherman 2011). Examples since just the late twentieth century abound and include Afghanistan, Liberia, Somalia, the former Yugoslavia, Rwanda, Iraq, the Democratic Republic of Congo, northern Nigeria, and Syria. Scholarship in the field of feminist international relations has examined both sexual misconduct in peacekeeping operations and the "uniformly shallow approach to gender" on the part of the North Atlantic Treaty Organization (NATO) and even the UN, especially in connection with peacekeeping, and it emphasizes the long-standing privileging of militarized states in the international system (Hebert 2012). In these ways, macro-level processes intersect with pre-existing gender inequalities and forms of male privilege to perpetuate VAW, including domestic violence.

Palestinian feminist researchers have tied the persistence of "honor killings" and the spread of veiling to the Israeli occupation of the West Bank and the economic strangle hold of the impoverished Gaza Strip (Shalhoub-Kevorkian 2001). Zahia Smail Salhi (2010) has argued that the Algerian state's patriarchal laws as well as what she defines as "private violence" indirectly enabled the "Islamist femicide" of the 1990s when Islamist extremists took up arms against the state. The unprecedented violence experienced by Syrian women since 2012 is a direct consequence of a protracted internationalized civil conflict in which the Syrian state, supported by Iran and Russia, and the armed rebels, supported by Turkey, Saudi Arabia, Qatar, the United Arab Emirates, and a number of Western countries, battle for supremacy. The rise of ISIS in Iraq and Syria, and now also in Libya, only occurred in the wake of destabilization policies of Western countries and regional allies. (Similarly, the resurgence of the Taliban in Afghanistan, and now Pakistan as well, is a result of the US policy of destabilizing the modernizing Democratic Republic of Afghanistan in the 1980s.) "Femicide" in Guatemala, Honduras, El Salvador, and the Mexican city of Ciudad Juarez may be associated with US immigration and deportation policies, economic difficulties within communities, and weak or complicit state responses to criminal activity (Godoy-Paiz 2008; Olivera 2006; Staudt 2008).

As noted previously, the political economy of VAW (True 2012) locates much of the violence that women encounter and the male dominance that underpins it in state policies and economic crises, as well as in armed conflict, militarism, invasions, occupations, and wars. As a result, the sexual abuse of women during periods of armed conflict has been a long-standing practice of state and non-state combatants. Furthermore, sex trafficking—certainly rooted in patriarchy and male entitlement—has been enabled by globalization's porous borders, ease of communication and travel, and periodic economic crises.

Buvinic et al. (2012) argue that there are first-round and second-round differential impacts of violence on gender relations, inequality, and equality. First-round channels include an increase in mortality and morbidity, especially of men and children, along with a higher incidence of widowhood; forced displacement and migration; asset and income loss due to disruption of markets, infrastructure destruction and damage, and deaths of household members; and sexual and gender-based violence. Second-round impacts, which may be viewed as household coping strategies, are changes in marriage and fertility; political and civic participation; labor reallocation; and children's human capital. The conflicts in Cambodia, Rwanda, Sierra Leone, East Timor, and Guatemala generated massive male deaths; the same occurred earlier in Germany and Russia during World War II. The resulting unbalanced sex ratios could lead to later marriage and lower fertility; widowhood also contributes to lower fertility. The shocks of conflict produce specific coping strategies that may include women assuming primary responsibility for ensuring the survival of families. Women and girls may increase their labor, especially in areas with a low sex ratio, thus adding to their productive and reproductive burdens; or they may lose their livelihood and descend into destitution or prostitution. Buvinic and colleagues cite a study of 50 countries that found significant increases in gender-based violence following conflict (Buvinic et al., 2102: 120). To compound the tragedy, women in sub-Saharan Africa who were raped became HIV-positive. Such forms of VAW can lead to, or perpetuate, individual and household poverty. Poverty also results from the inevitable infrastructural destruction that occurs during periods of armed conflicts and wars (Moghadam 2013b).

In that connection, the violence that some women perpetrate on other women cannot be denied. Certain women in positions of political power have been complicit in invasions, occupations, civil wars, coups d'état, and the arming of rebels (sometimes in the name of "humanitarian intervention"), as well as nuclear arms development. Their counterparts in violent extremist movements include the misguided groupies of ISIS, the Chechen "Black Widows," and the suicide killers of Sri Lanka's Tamil Tigers. It is some consolation, however, that such women represent a very small proportion of the world's politically active and empowered women. And for every female warmonger or terrorist there are countless women activists, trade unionists, and political party members who eschew violence by both state and non-state actors. For such women, ensuring security at home should not come at the expense of the undermining of women's security elsewhere.

Ending Violence Against Women

Advocacy and activism have taken various forms: awareness-raising through various media; the passage of laws and training of law enforcement; Take Back the Night marches; the establishment of battered women's shelters and hotlines for women victims of domestic violence and workplace harassment; the strengthening of Title IX offices and protocols at US universities; measures to prosecute rapists and traffickers at national and international levels; women's peace movements; and transnational networks dedicated to ending sexual abuse during armed conflict, supporting women victims, and advocating for an end to militarism. In short, strategies to prevent or eliminate VAW involve complex responses for a complex problem, including social protection; access to justice, media, education, economic opportunities; and engaging men, communities, and families.

Recognizing the pervasive reality of VAW, and in response to both scholarship and advocacy, the UN has issued a number of recommendations throughout the decades. In 1985, the UN General Assembly adopted the Resolution on Domestic Violence; 1989 was the year of the Convention on the Rights of the Child, with a focus on sexual exploitation and trafficking. In 1993, galvanized by the violence against women occurring in Bosnia and Rwanda, the UN's General Assembly issued a Declaration on Eliminating Violence against Women (EVAW) and also established the International Criminal Tribunal for former Yugoslavia. Echoing feminist research, the UN defined violence against women as

> a manifestation of historically unequal power relations between men and women, which has led to domination over and discrimination against women by men and to the prevention of the full advancement of women, and that violence against women is one of the crucial social mechanisms by which women are forced into a subordinate position compared with men. (http://www.un.org/documents/ga/res/48/a48r104.htm)

The year 1994 saw many steps taken on EVAW: the establishment of the International Criminal Tribunal for Rwanda; the Special Rapporteur on Violence Against Women, its causes and consequences; the International Conference on Population and Development; the adoption of the Convention of Belém do Pará, which was legally binding at the regional level in Latin America; and the US Violence Against Women Act, which also created services for survivors. Later in the 1990s, the UN established the Trust Fund to End Violence Against Women; the International Criminal Court was founded; and in 1999 the UN International Day for EVAW was designated for November 25, which has become an important tool for advocacy and activism.

In October 2000, the Security Council passed Resolution 1325: Women, Peace, and Security. As Josephine Beoku-Betts (2016) notes in her analysis of its application to the case of Sierra Leone, SCR 1325 rests on the four pillars of women's participation, prevention of violence, protection of women, and promotion of a gender perspective. It designates rape by combatants a war crime, stipulates that UN peacekeepers must ensure the protection and integrity of women and girls as well as civilians in general, and encourages the participation of women's organizations in post-conflict and peacebuilding strategies. SCR 1325 was followed in later years by a number of other resolutions focusing on conflict and post-conflict, notably SCR 1820, adopted in June 2008, with the main goal of strengthening the commitments already made.

The role of the UN's Special Rapporteur on Violence Against Women has been an important part of the UN's global women's rights agenda; it is also a significant way of highlighting the global problem and its structural and ideational foundations. Radhika Coomaraswamy (1994–2003) criticized the academic discipline of anthropology for the concept of "cultural relativism," which had been used by community and national leaders as a way to reject notions of women's human rights, including freedom from domestic violence. Her successor, Yakin Erturk of Turkey (2003–2009), submitted a report in 2007 on the intersection of culture and violence against women that acknowledged a new anthropological conceptualization of culture but reiterated the critique of cultural relativism (Dauer 2014: 3, 5). Succeeding Erturk in 2009, Rashida Manjoo of South Africa highlighted the relevance of concepts of intersectionality and structural violence to analyze and interrogate VAW, and in September 2014 she issued a report examining the problem through the lens of citizenship.

As a result of the UN's global women's rights agenda, as well as feminist mobilizations across countries, at least 119 countries have passed laws on domestic violence, 125 have laws on sexual harassment, and 52 have laws on marital rape. Availability of data on VAW has increased significantly (Alarcon 2016; see also The World's Women statistical database at http://unstats.un.org/unsd/gender/worldswomen.html). Today, the problem of domestic violence and VAW is recognized throughout the world, and it continues to be the subject of scholarship, advocacy, and policy initiatives. In July 2017, for example, the Tunisian parliament passed its strongest law yet on violence against women, the result of years of Tunisian feminist advocacy. Women's rights groups throughout the world call for ending VAW through implementation of the UN's women's rights agenda to facilitate cultural and normative changes; legal and institutional measures, including more effective prosecution of perpetrators; socialization and education for gender equality and non-violence; reduced military spending; and the realization of human development and human security to end some of the material bases for VAW.

Women's Movements/Women in Movement

The women's rights movement has been the subject of considerable scholarly analysis (Basu 1995; Beckwith 2007; Chafetz and Dworkin 1986; Ferree and Hess 2000; Moghadam 2005; Molyneux 2001; Taylor 1989; Walby 2011; West and Blumberg 1990). Feminist theorizing has focused on national-level factors such as the growth of the population of educated women with grievances about their second-class citizenship; waves and varieties of feminism; the evolution of women's movements and campaigns; and cross-regional similarities and differences in mobilizing structures, cultural framings, and strategies. Research also distinguishes *feminist movement* as a social movement guided by feminist ideas from *women's movement* as defined by a demographic group or constituency, with the former being a subset of the latter.

West and Blumberg (1990) identified the following forms of women's mobilizations: in grassroots protests for economic survival; in racial/ethnic and nationalist struggles (see also Jayawardena 1986; Tétreault 1994; L. West 1997); in "social-nurturing/humanistic protests"; and in women's rights or feminist protests. In each of these types, and also in each individual case, cultural framings are crafted in ways that resonate not just with the activists themselves but also with the state, society, and potential recruits in mind. One common frame is that of maternalism (West and Blumberg's "social-nurturing/humanistic" category), which is found in women's peace, anti-war, and anti-militarist movements and organizations throughout the world. Also known as *social motherhood* (Di Marco 2009) and *activist motherhood* (Naples 1998), it is a surprisingly universal, resilient, and versatile way of framing problems, claims, and goals (Carreon and Moghadam 2015). As with the anti-authoritarian Mothers and Grandmothers of the Plaza de Mayo in Argentina (Arditti 1999), the audacious anti-war American group Code Pink: Women for Peace (Moghadam 2015), and Israel's anti-occupation Machsom Watch (Kutz-Flamenbaum 2012), women's organizations may strategically leverage traditional gender roles to frame their activism and participation in political and civic life in socially acceptable terms, but such activism can also extend far beyond traditional gender roles as mothers, wives, and daughters to challenge the political status quo. In other cases, women's rights groups eschew the maternalist discourse in part because of its entrenchment in state policies or the wider culture; they will instead deploy the discourse of "gender equality," "equal citizenship," or "women's human rights." Women's rights or feminist activists may strategically adopt the motherhood frame, just as they may strategically deploy religious frames, but scholars recognize these as fault lines that may divide women's movement activists. Complexity within women's activism and organizations remains an understudied aspect of women's movements, whether local or transnational. Indeed, research on women's movements and feminist activism must reconcile what may appear to be parallel phenomena: women's experiences and activism at the local or grassroots level (Basu 1995) and transnational responses to economic and political globalization (Moghadam 1996, 2005, 2015).

Throughout the world, self-defined feminist or women's rights mobilizations have tended to adopt the UN's women's rights agenda. As scholarship and the historical record show, feminist movements respond to women's oppression or subordination or second-class citizenship, and they aim for women's autonomy or legal equality or enhanced participation. In this connection, they engage with states, civil-society actors, fellow citizens, and supranational institutions. These engagements and encounters are not without tensions and ambivalences. As noted previously, the state may be complicit in VAW. Civil society organizations may follow the dominant cultural script and promote male leadership, or they may be hostile to the feminist agenda. Certain supranational organizations may be responsible for the promotion of economic policies that harm working-class and poor women. The UN may be less influential than in the past. Nonetheless, women's movements recognize these as institutional forces, in what I have previously called a kind of *critical realism* (Moghadam 2005: 29). Whereas social movements—in all their diversity otherwise—are generally thought to act in opposition to the state, women activists maintain a dual positioning, which enables them to pursue both confrontational and assimilative strategies of engaging with the state as well as with institutions of global governance. A similar set of approaches may be found among transnational feminist networks (TFNs), which bring together women from three or more countries around a common critique and goal. TFNs may focus their research and advocacy on economic policies and their adverse effects on women; on religious fundamentalisms and women's human rights; or on militarism, war, and peace. The Women's World March/Marche Mondiale des Femmes, which began as an initiative of feminists in Québec, Canada, has a more expansive mandate as it stands against patriarchy, violence, and capitalism. A number of TFNs engage with supranational institutions such as the World Bank, despite their criticism of its economic policies (Moghadam 2005, 2013a, 2015).

Research on forms of women's collective action shows that women's movements are not "identity movements" but, rather, democratic and democratizing movements. Women's organizing tends to be inclusive, and women's movement activism often involves the explicit practice of democracy (Barron 2002; Beckwith 2007; Eschle 2000; Ferree and Mueller 2004; Moghadam 2005). This is especially the case with women's rights or feminist movements, which often practice democracy internally as well as ally themselves with other democratic movements, organizations, networks, and parties. Women's movement activism and advocacy—whether in the form of social movements, transnational networks, or professional organizations—contribute to the making of vibrant civil societies and public spheres, which are themselves critical to sustaining and deepening democracy. In Morocco and Tunisia, the presence of numerous women in the 2011 Arab Spring protest movements, along with the demands of women's rights groups and their record of promoting pro-women legal and policy changes, shaped the non-violent nature of those protests and ensured egalitarian and democratic outcomes, certainly compared with other countries that experienced the Arab Spring (Moghadam 2017).

To reconnect this section to the chapter's first section, contemporary women's rights movements are linked to globalization in at least three ways. First, the diffusion of the UN's global women's rights agenda creates an environment conducive to women's movements, their legitimacy, and their access to resources. CEDAW, for example, is clear that its provisions obtain across cultures and religions, stating in Article 2 that "States Parties . . . undertake . . . to take all appropriate measures, including legislation, to modify or abolish existing laws, regulations, customs and practices which constitute discrimination against women."[1] Activists refer to CEDAW as an international norm because it is an important source for defining gender inequalities and relations in order to legitimize the claims of the movement in opposition to the state. Many Muslim-majority countries signed and ratified CEDAW with reservations that pertained to conflicts with Sharia or with national legislation. For that reason, a key objective of many women's rights groups has been to pressure governments to remove the reservations and to comply with all CEDAW provisions.

Second, the emergence of transnational feminist networks and collective action across borders were responses to the adverse effects of structural adjustment and neoliberal economic policies; the spread of various forms of religious fundamentalism; and the persistence of patriarchy, violence, and conflicts. In this example of globalization-from-below, activist groups take advantage of the opportunities afforded by the spread of the new information and computer technologies as well as the political space for feminist activism created by the UN's global women's rights agenda.

Third, many nationally based women's groups have formed to protest patriarchy and VAW, which activists view as reinforced or exacerbated by aspects of globalization. As noted previously, economic hardships have been accompanied by spikes in domestic violence, while the spread of religious fundamentalism has led many governments to compromise women's human rights (Di Marco and Tabbush 2011; Moghadam 2005). Globalization also has engendered reaction in the form of right-wing populist movements, secular and religious alike, which are inimical to the feminist agenda.

CRITIQUES AND ALTERNATIVE VISIONS

Whether as ideology, movement, or academic study, feminism has encountered some self-criticism. A number of scholars have argued that feminism has lost its way—especially in the United States, where it has colluded with neoliberalism and war as well as the dominant ideology of individualism. Johanna Brenner (2001) argues that second-wave American feminism has been co-opted by reliance on state policy or by such institutionalized forms as women's studies programs and feminist journals. Brenner focuses on the constraints that capitalism and patriarchal culture alike place on American working-class women, calling for a revitalization of a movement to challenge both patriarchy and capitalism. Similarly, Hester Eisenstein (2009) asserts that feminism has become de-radicalized and co-opted into the capitalist project. Through the promotion of strategies such as microcredits, she maintains, intergovernmental organizations and NGOs not only use gender expertise for their own purposes but also undermine the developmental state, public sectors, and social provisioning. Globalizing institutions seek to remake women after their own image—to make and proliferate neoliberal subjects amenable to markets. Asserting that the post-structuralist, post-Marxist turn in feminism was the pathway to this co-optation, Eisenstein calls on academic feminists to eschew analyses that focus on "individual and private acts of resistance" and turn toward a "structural analysis of global capitalism" (p. 212). Similarly, Angela McRobbie (2009) critiques a "faux feminism" and de-politicized feminism that applauds such spectacles as young women "acting out" and becoming aggressive and even violent as purported marks of feminism. Highlighting what she calls a *patriarchal ownership* of feminism, she argues that governance feminism, especially in the form of gender mainstreaming, as well as other forms of institutionalized feminism, renders feminist movement politics unnecessary, even passé. Marysia Zalewski and Anne Runyan (2013) discuss feminist "imbrication in the violences of neoliberalism and global governance" (p. 293). While using the term "feminist violences" in a broader perspective to include feminist disruptions of the status quo, they critically examine the way some prominent women leaders who self-define as feminists are "implicated in propping up and giving cover to international neoliberal policies, program and militarized 'humanitarian' interventions" (p. 299).

Nancy Fraser (2013) also has critiqued "lean in" feminism. She writes of her "fear that the movement for women's liberation has become entangled in a dangerous liaison with neoliberal efforts to build a free-market society." Her critique of "a one-sided focus on 'gender identity' at the expense of bread and butter issues" was entirely apt, as was the statement that "we absolutized the critique of cultural sexism at precisely the moment when circumstances required redoubled attention to the critique of political economy." American feminism in particular contributed three ideas to the development of neoliberalism, she writes: the critique of the family wage, the rejection of "economism" in favor of the politicization of the personal and individual expression, and the critique of welfare state paternalism. All of these were in line with neoliberalism's promotion of flexible labor markets, the sidelining of social justice and equality demands, and the end of the developmental state.[2]

It was therefore inevitable that American feminists would find themselves on opposing sides of the Democratic nomination race in the run-up to the November 2016 presidential election. The dividing line was between those who supported the socialist candidate Bernie Sanders and those who supported the mainstream Democratic candidate Hillary Clinton, regarded by many left-wing feminists as too closely aligned with neoliberalism and militarism.

A number of gender-and-development scholars have similarly cast a critical eye on strategies that call for integrating women in labor markets not for the sake of gender equality or women's empowerment but, rather, to make markets operate more effectively and efficiently and also to stimulate growth. Sylvia Chant (2012) criticizes the World Bank's heralded *World Development Report 2012: Gender Equality and Development* for its promotion of "smart economics" and obfuscation of how its own macroeconomic policy prescriptions have generated economic difficulties and crisis. Adrienne Roberts and Susanne Soederberg (2012) criticize the report for "the central role accorded to leading financial corporations like Goldman Sachs in the formulation of the key World Bank recommendations." They view the goal of the report as "to deepen and consolidate the fundamental values and tenets of capitalist interests" (p. 949). Sakiko Fukuda-Parr (2016) has noted that the MDGs put the focus on poverty eradication to the neglect of income inequality and ignored the role of the developmental state in implementing the goals. My own review of the celebrated book, *Half the Sky*, by Kristoff and WuDunn (2010) is critical of its neglect of macroeconomics and the international state system (Moghadam 2010). I argue that the book's emphasis on individual action, local efforts, and small-scale activities makes the authors overlook the larger structural and systemic dynamics that prevent poverty eradication, stall or set back development efforts, and perpetuate or create gross inequalities within and across countries. A better alternative is a return of the developmental state, this time feminist and egalitarian.

CONCLUSION

In Chapter 1 of this volume, Steger does not refer to any feminist studies of globalization. The present chapter, however, has elucidated the extent of feminist contributions to global studies, with a focus on studies of globalization, violence and armed conflict, and women's social movements. It is indeed difficult to imagine global studies *without* analysis of the way that gender is inscribed in power relations, social inequalities, economic development and growth, state policies, and war-making. This chapter also has drawn attention to the varied feminist approaches to global issues. Perhaps most cogent is the feminist political economy approach that elucidates both the pervasive nature of gender inequality and the capacity of feminist and women's movements to challenge the status quo toward a more egalitarian social order. Feminist scholars within the political economy approach may strategically deploy language akin to the "business case" for women's participation and rights, especially in their policy-oriented work, but they are cognizant that real change comes about through social movement activism and concerted coalition-building.

NOTES

1. CEDAW (http://www.un.org/womenwatch/daw/cedaw/text/econvention).
2. A rather harsh rejoinder, "White Feminist Fatigue Syndrome," by Brenna Bhandar and Denise Ferreira da Silva (2013), actually confirms Fraser's argument in that it is steeped in a postmodernist discourse, refers to "White feminists" versus "Black" and "Third World" feminisms, and erroneously charges "Marxist and socialist feminist thought that continues to fail, in many ways, to account for race, histories of colonization, and the structural inequities between the so-called developed and developing nation-states." Evidently, Bhandar and Ferreira da Silva have not encountered the world-systems scholar Wilma Dunaway or read the devastating anti-capitalist and anti-imperialist critiques by "White" feminists in transnational feminist networks such as Marche Mondiale, Madre, and Code Pink.

REFERENCES

Alarcon, Diana. 2016. "Women's Empowerment in the UN Development Agenda." Paper presented at the Conference on Women's Empowerment and International

Organizations: Achievements, Opportunities, and Constraints, Northeastern University, Gender and Development Initiative (April 22). Available at https://www. northeastern.edu/cssh/internationalaffairs/wp-content/uploads/sites/2/2016/05/ GAD-Conference-Report-short-17-May-2.pdf

Arditti, Rita. 1999. *Searching for Life: The Grandmothers of the Plaza de Mayo and the Disappeared Children of Argentina*. Berkeley: University of California Press.

Barron, Andrea. 2002. "The Palestinian Women's Movement: Agent of Democracy in a Future State?" *Critique: Critical Middle Eastern Studies* 11 (1): 71–90.

Basu, Amrita. 1995. *The Challenge of Local Feminisms: Women's Movements in Global Perspective*. Boulder, CO: Westview.

Beckwith, Karen. 2007. "Mapping Strategic Engagements: Women's Movements and the State." *International Feminist Journal of Politics* 9 (3): 312–338.

Beneria, Lourdes. 2001. "Shifting the Risk: New Employment Patterns, Informalization, and Women's Work." *International Journal of Politics, Culture, and Society* 15 (1): 27–53.

Beoku-Betts, Josephine. 2016. "Holding African States to Task on Gender and Violence: Domesticating UNSCR 1325 in the Sierra Leone National Action Plan." *Current Sociology* 64 (6): 654–670.

Bergeron, Suzanne. 2001. "Political Economy Discourses of Globalization and Feminist Politics." *Signs: Journal of Women in Culture and Society* 26 (4): 983–1006.

Bhandar Brenna, and Denise Ferreira da Silva. 2013. "White Feminist Fatigue Syndrome." *Critical Legal Thinking*, October 21. http://criticallegalthinking.com/2013/10/21/ white-feminist-fatigue-syndrome.

Brenner, Johanna. 2001. *Women and the Politics of Class*. New York: Monthly Review Foundation.

Buvinic, Mayra, Monica Das Gupta, Ursula Casabonne, and Philip Verwimp. 2012. "Violent Conflict and Gender Inequality: An Overview." *World Bank Research Observer* 28: 110–138.

Caprioli, Mary. 2005. "Primed for Violence: The Role of Gender Inequality in Predicting Internal Conflict." *International Studies Quarterly* 49 (2): 161–178.

Carreon, Michelle, and Valentine M. Moghadam. 2015. "'Resistance Is Fertile': Revisiting Maternalist Frames Across Cases of Women's Mobilization." *Women's Studies International Forum* 51: 19–30. doi:10.1016/j.wsif.2015.04.002

Chafetz, Janet Saltzman, and Gary Dworkin. 1986. *Female Revolt: Women's Movements in World and Historical Perspective*. Totowa, NJ: Rowman & Allanheld.

Chant, Sylvia. 2012. "The Disappearing of 'Smart Economics'? The *World Development Report 2012 on Gender Equality*: Some concerns about the preparatory process and the prospects for paradigm change." *Global Social Policy* 12(2): 198–218.

Chase-Dunn, Christopher. 1998. *Global Formation: Structures of the World-Economy*. Lanham, MD: Rowman & Littlefield.

Cockburn, Cynthia. 2010. "Getting to Peace: What Kind of Movement?" *OpenDemocracy*. April 19. www.opendemocracy.net.

Connell, Raewyn, and James Messerschmidt. 2005. "Hegemonic Masculinity: Rethinking the Concept." *Gender & Society* 19 (6): 829–859.

Dauer, Sheila. 2014. "Introduction: Anthropological Approaches to Gender-Based Violence." In *Anthropological Approaches to Gender-Based Violence and Human Rights*, edited by Sheila Dauer, Melissa A. Beske, Janet Chernela, Rebecka Lundgren, Melissa K. Adams, and Shannon Speed, eds., Working Paper no. 304: 1–15. Lansing: Michigan State University, Gender, Development, and Globalization Program.

Desai, Manisha. 2009. *Gender and the Politics of Possibilities: Rethinking Globalization.* Lanham, MD: Rowman & Littlefield.

Di Marco, Graciela. 2009. "Social Justice and Gender Rights." *International Social Science Journal* 191: 43–55.

Di Marco, Graciela, and Constanza Tabbush, eds. 2011. *Feminisms, Democratization and Radical Democracy.* Buenos Aires: UNSAM EDITA.

Drèze, Jean, and Amartya Sen. 1991. *Hunger and Public Action.* Oxford, UK: Clarendon.

Dunaway, Wilma A. 2001. "The Double Register of History: Situating the Forgotten Woman and Her Household in Capitalist Commodity Chains." *Journal of World-Systems Research* 7 (1): 2–29.

Ehrenreich, Barbara. 2001. *Nickel and Dimed: On (Not) Getting By in America.* New York: Holt.

Eisenstein, Hester. 2009. *Feminism Seduced: How Global Elites Use Women's Labor and Ideas to Exploit the World.* London: Zed.

Elson, Diane, ed. 1990. *Male Bias in the Development Process.* London: Macmillan.

Elson, Diane, and Ruth Pearson. 1981. "Nimble Fingers Make Cheap Workers: An Analysis of Women's Employment in Third World Export Manufacturing." *Feminist Review* (Spring): 87–107.

Eschle, Catherine. 2000. *Global Democracy, Social Movements, and Feminism.* Boulder, CO: Westview.

Fabián, Katalin, ed. 2010. *Domestic Violence in Postcommunist States: Local Activism, National Policies, and Global Forces.* Bloomington: Indiana University Press.

Ferree, Myra M., and Beth Hess. 2000. *Controversy and Coalition: The New Feminist Movement Across Four Decades of Change.* 3rd ed. London: Routledge.

Ferree, Myra M., and Carol Mueller. 2004. "Feminism and the Women's Movement: A Global Perspective." In *The Blackwell Companion to Social Movements*, edited by D. Snow, S. Soule, and H. Kriesi, 576–607. London: Blackwell.

Folbre, Nancy. 1994. *Who Pays for the Kids? Gender and the Structures of Constraint.* London: Taylor & Francis.

Folbre, Nancy, ed. 2012. *For Love and Money: Care Provision in the United States.* New York: Russell Sage Foundation.

Fraser, Nancy. 2013. "How Feminism Became Capitalism's Handmaiden—And How to Reclaim It." *The Guardian*, October 13.

Fukuda-Parr, Sakiko. 2016. "From the Millennium Development Goals to the Sustainable Development Goals: Shifts in Purpose, Concept, and Politics of Global Goal Setting for Development." *Gender & Development* 24 (1): 43–52.

Godoy-Paiz, Paula. 2008. "Women in Guatemala's Metropolitan Area: Violence, Law, and Social Justice." *Studies in Social Justice* 2 (1): 27–47.

Grewal, Inderwal, and Caren Kaplan, eds. 1994. *Scattered Hegemonies: Postmodernity and Transnational Feminist Practices.* Minneapolis: University of Minnesota Press.

Hebert, Laura. 2012. "Analyzing UN & NATO Responses to Sexual Misconduct in Peacekeeping Operations." In *Making Gender, Making War: Violence, Military and Peacekeeping Practices*, edited by Annica Kronsell and Erika Svedberg, 107–120. New York: Routledge.

Hudson, Valerie M., Mary Caprioli, Bonnie Ballif-Spanvill, and Chad F. Emmett. 2012. *Sex and World Peace.* New York: Columbia University Press.

İlkkaracan, İpek. 2012. "Why so Few Women in the Labor Market in Turkey?" *Feminist Economics* 18 (1): 1–37.

International Labour Organization. 2012. *Global Employment Trends for Women 2012.* Geneva: International Labour Organization.

Interparliamentary Union. 2016. *Women in National Parliaments.* Geneva: Interparliamentary Union.

Jayawardena, Kumari. 1986. *Feminism and Nationalism in the Third World.* London: Zed.

Joekes, Susan. 1987. *Women and the World Economy.* New York: Oxford University Press.

Klugman, Jeni, Jennifer McCleary-Sills, Julieth Santamaria, et al. 2014. *Voice and Agency: Empowering Women and Girls for Shared Prosperity.* Washington, DC: The World Bank.

Kristof, Nicholas D., and Sheryl WuDunn. (2010). *Half the Sky: Turning Oppression into Opportunity for Women Worldwide.* New York: Vintage.

Krook, Mona, and Fiona Mackay, eds. 2015 *Gender, Politics and Institutions: Towards a Feminist Institutionalism.* London: Palgrave Macmillan.

Kutz-Flamenbaum, Rachel V. 2012. "Mobilizing Gender to Promote Peace: The Case of Machsom Watch." *Qualitative Sociology* 35: 293–310.

Leatherman, Janie L. 2011. *Sexual Violence and Armed Conflict.* Medford, MA: Polity.

Marchand, Marianne. 2000. "Reconceptualizing 'Gender and Development' in an Era of 'Globalization.'" In *Poverty in World Politics: Whose Global Era?* edited by Sarah Owen Vandersluis and Paris Yeros, 119–147. Basingstoke, UK: Macmillan.

Marchand, Marianne, and Jane Parpart, eds. 1995. *Feminism, Postmodernism, Development.* London: Routledge.

Marchand, Marianne, and Anne Sisson Runyan, eds. 2000. *Gender and Global Restructuring: Sightings, Sites and Resistances.* London: Routledge.

McCleary-Sills, Jennifer. 2016. "Progress and Pitfalls in Expanding Voice and Agency: The Case of Violence Against Women." Paper presented at the Conference on Women's Empowerment and International Organizations: Achievements, Opportunities, and Constraints, Northeastern University, Gender and Development Initiative, April 22. https://www.northeastern.edu/cssh/internationalaffairs/wp-content/uploads/sites/2/2016/05/GAD-Conference-Report-short-17-May-2.pdf

McRobbie, Angela. 2009. *The Aftermath of Feminism: Gender, Culture and Social Change.* London: Sage.

Mies, Maria. 1986. *Patriarchy and Accumulation on a World Scale: Women in the International Division of Labour.* London: Zed.

Moghadam, Valentine M. 1996. "Feminist Networks North and South: A Case Study of DAWN, WIDE, and WLUML." *Journal of International Communication,* special issue on International Feminism(s) 3 (1): 111–126.

Moghadam, Valentine M. 2005. *Globalizing Women: Transnational Feminist Networks.* Baltimore, MD: Johns Hopkins University Press.

Moghadam, Valentine M. 2010. Review of *Half the Sky: Turning Oppression into Opportunity for Women Worldwide,* by Nicholas D. Kristof and Sheryl WuDunn. *Perspectives on Politics* 8 (1): 284–286.

Moghadam, Valentine M. 2011. "Women, Gender, and Economic Crisis Revisited." *Perspectives on Global Development and Technology* 10: 30–40.

Moghadam, Valentine M. 2013a. *Globalization and Social Movements: Islamism, Feminism, and the Global Justice Movement.* Lanham, MD: Rowman & Littlefield.

Moghadam, Valentine M. 2013b. "Toward Human Security and Gender Justice: Reflections on Afghanistan and Iraq." In *Globalization, Social Movements and Peacebuilding,* edited by Jackie Smith and Ernesto Verdeja, 97–133. Syracuse, NY: Syracuse University Press.

Moghadam, Valentine M. 2015. "Transnational Feminism and Movement Building." In *The Oxford Handbook of Transnational Feminist Movements*, edited by Rawwida Baksh and Wendy Harcourt, 53–81. New York: Oxford University Press.

Moghadam, Valentine M. 2016. "A Female Precariat in the Middle East?" Paper presented at the RC-02 session on "Changes in the Global Class Structure: The Precariat in the North and South," International Sociological Association Forum, Vienna, Austria, July 10–14.

Moghadam, Valentine M. 2017. "Explaining Divergent Outcomes of the Arab Spring: The Significance of Gender and Women's Mobilizations." *Politics, Groups, and Identities* (online), January 31. http://dx.doi.org/10.1080/21565503.2016.1256824.

Moghadam, Valentine M., and Anjuli Fahlberg. 2017. "Domestic Violence and Violence Against Women." In *Wiley–Blackwell Encyclopedia of Social Theory*, edited by Bryan Turner, C. Kyung-Sup, Cynthia Epstein, et al. New York: Wiley–Blackwell.

Molyneux, Maxine. 2001. *Women's Movements in International Perspective: Latin America and Beyond*. London: Palgrave Macmillan.

Naples, Nancy A. 1998. *Grassroots Warriors: Activist Mothering, Community Work, and the War on Poverty*. New York: Routledge.

Nash, June, and Maria Fernandez- Kelly, eds. 1984. *Women, Men, and the International Division of Labor*. Albany, New York: SUNY Press.

Nussbaum, Martha. 2000. *Women and Human Development: The Capabilities Approach*. Cambridge, UK: Cambridge University Press.

Olivera, Mercedes. 2006. "Violencia Feminicida: Violence Against Women and Mexico's Structural Crisis." *Latin American Perspectives* 33 (2): 104–114.

Oxfam. 2014. *Even It Up: Time to End Extreme Inequality*. London: Oxfam.

Peterson, V. Spike. 2003. *A Critical Rewriting of Global Political Economy: Integrating Productive, Reproductive, and Virtual Economies*. New York: Routledge.

Rai, Shirin, and Georgina Waylen, eds. 2008. *Global Governance: Feminist Perspectives*. London: Palgrave Macmillan.

Roberts, Adrienne, and Susanne Soederberg. 2012. "Gender Equality as Smart Economics? A critique of the 2012 World Development Report." *Third World Quarterly* 33 (5): 949–968.

Rubery, Jill. 2015. "Austerity and the Future of Gender Equality in Europe." *ILR Review* 68 (4): 715–741.

Saffioti, Heleith. 1978. *Women in Class Society*. New York: Monthly Review Press.

Salhi, Zahia Smail. 2010. "Gender and Violence in Algeria: Women's Resistance Against the Islamist Femicide." In *Gender and Diversity in the Middle East and North Africa*, edited by Zahia Smail Salhi, 161–184. London: Routledge.

Sandberg, Sheryl. 2013. *Lean In: Women, Work, and the Will to Lead*. New York: Knopf.

Sen, Gita, and Caren Grown. 1985. *Development, Crises, and Alternative Visions*. New York: Monthly Review Press.

Shalhoub-Kevorkian, Nadera. 2001. *Femicide in Palestinian Society*. New York: UNIFEM.

Standing, Guy. 1989. "Global Feminization Through Flexible Labor." *World Development* 17 (7): 1077–1095.

Standing, Guy. 1999. "Global Feminization Through Flexible Labor: A Theme Revisited." *World Development* 27 (3): 583–602.

Standing, Guy. 2011. *The Global Precariat: The New Dangerous Class*. London: Bloomsbury.

Staudt, Kathleen. 2008. *Violence and Activism at the Border: Gender, Fear, and Everyday Life in Ciudad Juarez*. Austin: University of Texas Press.

Sylvanus, Nina. 2016. *Patterns in Circulation: Cloth, Gender and Materiality in West Africa.* Chicago: University of Chicago Press.

Taylor, Verta. 1989. "Social Movement Continuity: The Women's Movement in Abeyance." *American Sociological Review* 54: 761–775.

Tétreault, Mary Ann, ed. 1994. *Women and Revolution in Africa, Asia, and the New World.* Columbia: University of South Carolina Press.

Thévenon, Olivier. 2013. "Drivers of Female Labour Force Participation in the OECD." OECD Social, Employment and Migration Working Papers, no. 145. Paris: Organisation for Economic Co-operation and Development.

True, Jacqui. 2012. *The Political Economy of Violence Against Women.* Oxford and New York: Oxford University Press.

UN Women. 2015. *Progress of the World's Women 2015–16: Transforming Economies: Realizing Rights.* New York: United Nations.

Walby, Sylvia. 2009. *Globalization and Inequalities: Complexity and Contested Modernities.* London: Sage.

Walby, Sylvia. 2011. *The Future of Feminism.* London: Polity.

Walby, Sylvia. 2015. *Crisis.* London: Sage.

West, Guida, and Rhoda Lois Blumberg, eds. 1990. *Women and Social Protest.* New York: Oxford University Press.

West, Lois, ed. 1997. *Feminist Nationalism.* New York: Routledge.

Wilkinson, Richard, and Kate Pickett. 2009. *The Spirit Level: Why Greater Equality Makes Societies Stronger.* New York: Bloomsbury Press.

Winter, Bronwyn. 2017. *Women, Insecurity, and Violence in a Post-9/11 World.* Syracuse, NY: Syracuse University Press.

World Bank. 2012. *World Development Report 2012: Gender Equality and Development.* Washington, DC: World Bank.

Zalewski, Marysia, and Anne Sisson Runyan. 2013. "Taking Feminist Violence Seriously in Feminist International Relations." *International Feminist Journal of Politics* 15 (3): 293–313.

CHAPTER 16

....

DECOLONIZING GLOBAL STUDIES

....

EVE DARIAN-SMITH

IN the wake of the 2016 US presidential election, there has been much hand-wringing and angst among the center-left trying to understand just what happened and why they were so taken by surprise with the results. Unfortunately, the genuine disbelief in the election results is reminiscent of the public reaction voiced after the September 11, 2001, terrorist attacks. Back then, many US citizens asked, "How could *they* hate us so much?" whereas now the question is "How could *we* hate ourselves so much?" Although there are many complicated issues at play, the general consensus seems to be that globalization and the forces of global capital have left many White middle-class Americans impoverished and feeling marginalized. This is an entirely new experience for these constituencies (although not so new for non-Whites whose legacies of immigration and former slavery have forced many to exist on the margins of society for centuries).[1] Despite the differences of voting across race and ethnic lines, according to the French economist Thomas Piketty (2016), "Trump's victory is primarily due to the explosion in economic and geographic inequality in the United States over several decades and the inability of successive governments to deal with this" (see also Rasmus 2016). As argued by Cosmin Cercel (2016), along with many others, "We should have seen this [Trump] coming" (p. 2).

This chapter explores why scholars associated with the field of global studies were surprised by the results of the US presidential election and why there may be a need to decolonize the field as it is emerging, particularly in the Global North. After all, global scholars are acutely aware of "globalization and its discontents," to borrow from the title of Joseph Stiglitz's (2002) groundbreaking book. In this chapter, I ask, What does this failure to anticipate support for Donald Trump suggest with respect to the field of global studies, particularly as it evolves in the United States? How is it possible to ensure that global studies remains relevant and "real" in the sense that it does not become an intellectual arena of primarily privileged White scholars cut off from unexpected political activism and social movements that they fail to see let alone comprehend? In other words, what steps can be taken so that in the future scholars in the Global North may not be so taken by surprise about what is happening as a result of unfolding global processes manifesting on their own domestic fronts?

This chapter responds to this question by arguing for the need to decolonize global studies—to decolonize the basic building blocks that have dominated the past three centuries of Western thought (Mutua and Swadener 2011; Santos 2007, 2014). Writes Oliver Stuenkel (2016), "Our Western-centric world view thus leads us to under-appreciate not only the role non-Western actors have played in the past and play in contemporary international politics, but also the constructive role they are likely to play in the future." For global studies scholars, this means decentering the dominance of a White privileged world view that naturally assumes that such a world view leads the rest at home and abroad. It also means actively seeking to understand social and political relations from the standpoint of non-Western communities, particularly the standpoints of postcolonial and Indigenous peoples who globally constitute a much larger population than Euro-Americans. I argue for the need to decolonize Western thinking precisely because histories of marginalization and being "cut out" of the positive impacts of global capitalism have long been the experience among many non-Western peoples of the world. Learning from these alternative subject positions and experiences offers a way to rethink the current phase of globalization as it impacts those living in the Global North and the Global South. At the very least, it highlights that "thinking globally" is not a singular practice but, rather, highly diverse and pluralistic, encompassing ways of thinking that scholars clinging to a Western-centric worldview perhaps cannot yet imagine (Darian-Smith 2015a).

The decolonizing of Western knowledge could and should be made on many fronts, but this chapter focuses on what I consider are three of major significance: (1) the need to pluralize histories, (2) the need to depoliticize human rights, and (3) and the need to repoliticize global capitalism. In most scholarship produced within mainstream academia, these three fronts would typically be analyzed separately, but I want to push their mutually constitutive interdependencies as they intertwine over decades and even centuries.

I divide the chapter into three parts and begin in the first part with a discussion about decentering modernist frameworks. In the second part, I look back in time to the work of the African American postcolonial scholar W. E. B. Du Bois, whose insights revealed the deep interconnections between crises of humanity wrought by global capitalism in an earlier nineteenth-century colonial era of open markets and laissez-faire capitalism. Then in the third part, I explore current Indigenous activism surrounding Standing Rock in North Dakota as an illustration of contemporary human rights abuses and conflict wrought by neoliberal capitalism. Both Du Bois and Standing Rock underscore the need to decolonize conventional ways of presenting the past as an unfolding narrative of Western nations' superiority and dominance. They point to the politicization of human rights rhetoric despite its aspirations of objectivity and neutrality in the post-World War II era. Moreover, they highlight the need to analyze and theorize a global political economy not as operating as an "invisible hand" bringing unintended social benefits to the general population but, rather, as a deeply political and, in many instances, violent force of subjugation, oppression, and expulsion (Sassen 2014). Finally, these two examples urge scholars to think beyond state geopolitical units—or at least not to begin analysis as if the nation-state formation is a given and "society" naturally correlates and coalesces to it. Rather, postcolonial and Indigenous perspectives remind us that modern nation-state formation emerged within competing historical contexts and a dynamic global political economy. These non-Western perspectives suggest that to better understand a shifting national political landscape—such as that dramatically unfolding within the United States—requires situating the national domestic sphere within culturally contingent, highly politicized, and often violent global economic processes.

DECENTERING MODERNIST FRAMEWORKS

Global studies is a critical and interdisciplinary field that embraces both the humanities and the social sciences.[2] As such, global scholarship is not bound by the "scientific" knowledge of economists (who did not anticipate the 2008 global economic recession) or the state-centered models used by most sociologists and political scientists (who did not anticipate Brexit or Trump). In contrast to mainstream social science disciplines, global scholars are aware of the power of ideology, religion, ethics, and emotion in shaping people's everyday social relations (Appiah 2006). Global scholars appreciate the significance of history, narrative, and memory in framing a person's sense of self and respective world view. They recognize the gross inequalities that have emerged throughout the world as a result of free-market neoliberal policies put into place since the late 1970s (Brown 2015; Collier 2008). They are versant in ideological frameworks such as the "clash of civilization" rhetoric and Islamophobia espoused by Samuel Huntington and others since the 1990s (Huntington 1993; see also Said 2001). Global scholars are knowledgeable about a range of global crises, such as mass migrations and regional conflicts that are in large part driven by a global political economy from which US capitalists have profited handsomely. Why, then, were global scholars so taken aback when reactionary political chaos experienced for decades throughout the world in postcolonial contexts finally exploded on the US domestic front?

I argue that global studies scholars did not anticipate Trump because they remain constrained in their understanding of the interconnections across time and space that informs global issues, processes, and crises. Despite the expanding intellectual horizons in recent years of many global scholars to include such things as climate change, dispossession, security, and ongoing terrorism, global scholarship remains largely entrenched in modernist presumptions, theories, and logics. This in turn has prevented scholars from entirely breaking free of mainstream conceptual and analytical frameworks such as individualism, rationalism, liberalism, secularism, democracy, sovereignty, and the conventional building blocks of society understood in terms of nation-states and their respective citizenry. One consequence of this enduring state-centered mode of thinking is that many global scholars—like their colleagues from across the US–Euro academy—were not able to fully appreciate the forces behind the widespread popular support that ensured Trump's presidential victory.

In an effort to understand the US presidential election, some commentators point to the rise of right-wing politics across a number of countries in an effort to understand the rise of conservative politics as a global phenomenon (Moffitt 2016). They see similarities in Trump's United States with Putin's Russia, Erodoğan's Turkey, Temer's Brazil, Orbán's Hungary, Kaczyński's Poland, or Brexit in Britain. Of course, right-wing politics are playing out differently in these countries, but there are commonalities of racism, xenophobia, and ultra-nationalism. Against this conventional mode of comparative analysis, I suggest that seeing parallels and commonalities across nation-states provides some insights but does not fully explain the rise and formation of reactionary politics throughout the world.

Conservative politics is a symptom of deep structural shifts across time and space. In other words, analyzing crises of democracy requires a deeper probing than that offered by a conventional modernist understanding of politics framed and analyzed in terms of electoral politics, swings in governments, changing laws, citizen's rights, and ideologies of state-nationalism (Maier 2013; Streeck 2014).

No one is suggesting that issues of state governance and citizenry are not important. However, what I am suggesting in this chapter is that it is essential to problematize nation-state formation as an unfolding and, in many cases, fraught process and to not assume that what constitutes the "state" is a fixed and given entity. Moreover, it is important to recognize that conventions of a right/left political spectrum do not operate in every state context, particularly in countries and on continents with deep histories of colonialism and neocolonialism.[3] Looking at parallels across nation-states presents a temporally shallow reading of events that discounts deep histories of capitalist exploitation, colonial oppression, and social marginalization that have gone into the making of modern nations and their foundational myths of cultural homogeneity (Anderson 1983). In short, as scholars, we need to analyze pluralist and interconnected global histories to better understand how the legacies of time play out in the national politics of the present.

Global studies scholars should also appreciate the limits of nation-states to deal with the havoc that a deregulated global political economy has created during the past three decades. Unpleasant as it is to admit, nation-states alone cannot fix today's global challenges such as climate change, depletion of natural resources, regional conflict, and mass migrations which are fueling domestic population's anger, insecurity, and disenfranchisement. What the world is experiencing is the meltdown of the modern nation-state in the face of overwhelming global crises.[4] This can be seen most obviously in poorer regions of the world, such as sub-Saharan Africa, which suffers from the destabilization wrought by decades of decolonization. Against such grim images of human suffering and injustice, most scholars in the Global North cannot imagine the United States or Europe experiencing the tragic circumstances experienced by many countries and regions in the Global South. Ingrained biases of Western privilege prevent many of us from grasping that modern industrialized nation-states may not be able to manage their citizenry in the face of global crises (Porter 2016). As a result, and quite understandably, many scholars cling to modern liberal concepts such as individualism, rationalism, liberalism, secularism, democracy, and sovereignty. But it is the argument of this chapter that rather than cling to possibly outmoded conceptual frameworks, these terms themselves need to be critically interrogated in the context of the twenty-first century (Güven 2015; Sanín-Restrepo 2016).

Global scholar David Held wrote in 2002 that we need to recognize "the necessary partiality, one-sidedness and limitedness" of state-based reason especially "when judged from the perspective of a world of 'overlapping communities of fate'—where the trajectories of each and every country are tightly entwined" (p. 57). Fortunately, more and more global scholars—many of them informed by the contributions of global history—are increasingly sensitive to the need to decenter the nation-state.[5] With the enormous power of multinational corporations and a wide range of non-state actors eclipsing conventional notions of state governance, these scholars are keen to not reify a modernist framework or assume the norms of democracy are secure. As argued by Steven Levitsky and Daniel Ziblatt (2016), professors of government at Harvard University, the rules of democracy are changing. Moreover, increasingly more global scholars are anxious to recognize that new modes of political, economic, and cultural formation—what Saskia Sassen (2008) calls "global assemblages"—criss-cross borders and localities and regions, reconfiguring geopolitical conventions of territory, centrality, and power (Lantham 2016).

Often unconsciously, much of the new global studies scholarship draws upon standpoint theory, which was first introduced by Dorothy Smith in 1977 in her groundbreaking book, *Feminism and Marxism*. Standpoint theory underscores that there are many different perspectives and subject positions and that these standpoints represent variations in people's ways of knowing and experiencing the world. Building on this feminist platform, standpoint theory in the context of global studies suggests that all subject positions and experiences—not just those of women—should be valorized and included in analyses of political, social, cultural, and economic processes. This means more than simply widening the liberal framework to recognize and include non-White/non-Western peoples as members of the nation-state.[6] More profoundly, it means that global studies scholars should be sensitive to the existence of alternative imaginings of one's place in the world and plural historical narratives and memories of how one arrives at that place. This awareness may include different epistemologies, logics, and sets of social and political relations that do not correlate with taken-for-granted concepts of state and citizenship. These alternative epistemologies may even counter or directly challenge taken-for-granted ideologies such as nationalism and capitalism (Santos 2007, 2014).

Elsewhere, I and my co-author Philip McCarty have written about the decentering of the nation-state as a characteristic of global studies scholarship (Darian-Smith and McCarty 2017). We suggest that this decentering is more than a questioning of the conventions of geopolitical analysis because it also involves decentering the predominance of "First World" knowledge and Western-centric concepts, logics, and world views. Decentering as an ethical commitment is related to decolonialism as an intellectual commitment. I argue that both are vital if global studies scholarship (as it is practiced in the Global North) is to imagine alternative futures beyond modernist frameworks and so retain its analytical relevance in a world of shifting postnational asymmetries of economic, political, religious, and cultural power (Darian-Smith 2015b).

W. E. B. Du Bois and Global Racism

One of the earliest postcolonial scholars to think like a contemporary global historian was W. E. B. Du Bois, the first African American to receive a doctoral degree from Harvard University in 1895. Du Bois was trained as a historian and sociologist, and he taught economics as well. He brought his considerable insights about colonialism and slavery to bear on a systemic and structural understanding of global capitalism that wrought inequality and racial oppression throughout the history of the United States.

An extensive body of literature exists on Du Bois and his role in US race relations, and I cannot do his writings and activism justice in this brief chapter. However, what is often eclipsed in this extant body of writing, and what I wish to focus on, is that Du Bois was central in configuring racism and marginalization as a global issue by drawing connections between Black oppression and the victimization of others throughout the world. Du Bois' international activism and writings on global oppression in the decades following World

War II solidified his interpretation of the history of the world as embedded within a global political economic system. Specifically, the Holocaust affirmed Du Bois' thinking that the same economic and political forces that created the oppression of African peoples in the colonial margins could also create oppression and genocide at the centers of Western imperial states, most notably Germany and the United States. This realization informed Du Bois' questioning of the taken-for-granted Western model of international relations that foregrounded the modern nation-state in binary relations of colonizer/colonized, center/periphery, and superiority/inferiority. The events of World War II were pivotal in challenging a center/periphery model of European domination and consolidating Du Bois' understanding of a full circle of oppression such that centers of European imperialism were subject to mass racial violence analogous to the violence perpetrated at their colonial edges (Figure 16.1).

Moreover, World War II helped Du Bois move beyond a schema of black, brown, yellow, and white races and solidified his thinking that racism based on pseudoscientific hereditary distinctions of skin-tone classification was empirically unsound. Du Bois, who was a long-standing friend of the German American anthropologist Franz Boas, shared with Boas a deep skepticism of social Darwinism and biological explanations of racial inferiority.

W.E.B. DuBois, founder of the NAACP and opponent of imperialism: "In college I replaced my hitherto egocentric world by a world centering and whirling about my race."
photo credit: Schomburg Center of the New York Public Library

FIGURE 16.1 W. E. B. DuBois, founder of the NAACP and opponent of imperialism: "In college, I replaced my hitherto egocentric world by a world centering and whirling about my race."

Source: Schomburg Center of the New York Public Library.

Nonetheless, when Du Bois visited Germany in 1936 and became aware of the atrocities that the Nazis perpetrated on Jews, homosexuals, and other minorities who biologically looked exactly like themselves, he was deeply troubled. This realization forced Du Bois to think more imaginatively about the production of race, such that religion, cultural heritage, and socioeconomic status were folded into his understanding of the global dimensions of racism to involve Blacks, Jews, Roma, and other cultural and religious minorities. In this process, Du Bois built upon his early pre-war writings that called for Blacks to be equally treated to develop a more nuanced interpretation of racism that enabled him to frame the oppression of African Americans as a violation of universal human rights more generally. This understanding of human rights as a universal entitlement was brought home to the American public through his increasingly radical commentaries and activism in the 1940s and 1950s.

Du Bois' thinking of race in the context of Jewish persecution took on new nuances and complexities. In 1952, three years after visiting Poland (and specifically the Warsaw ghetto), Du Bois (as cited in Darian-Smith 2012) wrote in the journal *Jewish Life* that the result of his visits

> was not so much clearer understanding of the Jewish problem in the world as it was a real and more complete understanding of the Negro problem. In the first place, the problem of slavery, emancipation, and caste in the United States was no longer in my mind a separate and unique thing as I had so long conceived it. It was not even solely a matter of color and physical and racial characteristics, which was particularly a hard thing for me to learn, since for a lifetime the color line had been a real and efficient cause of misery. It was not merely a matter of religion. I had seen religions of many kinds—I had sat in the Shinto temples of Japan, in the Baptist chapels of Georgia, in the Catholic cathedral of Cologne and in Westminster Abbey. No, the race problem in which I was interested cut across lines of color and physique and belief and status and was a matter of cultural patterns, perverted teaching and human hate and prejudice, which reached all sorts of people and caused endless evil to all men. So that the ghetto of Warsaw helped me to emerge from a certain social provincialism into a broader conception of what the fight against race segregation, religious discrimination and the oppression by wealth had to become if civilization was going to triumph and broaden in the world. (p. 489)

To counter this global system of racial oppression, Du Bois increasingly turned to the growing conversations around universal human rights that erupted in the fifth and last Pan-African Congress, held in Manchester, UK, in 1945. At this historic meeting, the pan-African movement dovetailed with self-determination movements that had emerged throughout the 1940s to create a much wider front against Western imperialism. The Congress was symbolically and politically important: It involved not only Black Africans but also Afro-Caribbeans and Afro-Americans in the common call for independence from imperial control and demands for recognition of human rights. It is in this context that Du Bois and the National Association for the Advancement of Colored People (NAACP) played significant roles in leading the charge against European colonial regimes and arguing for the need to recognize universal human rights in order to secure lasting world peace.

At the historic five-week-long United Nations Conference on International Organization held in San Francisco in 1945, Du Bois, along with many other postcolonial activists, forcefully argued that recognizing human rights throughout the world was essential for securing world peace (Lauren 2003: 177–198). He was concerned that the language of the proposed United Nations (UN) Charter should speak not only about nations and states but also to the rights of individuals and races of people (Borgwardt 2005: 193). He argued that the UN Charter must refer to the "essential equality of all races" and help the millions of oppressed colonial subjects to have a voice in governmental processes (Aptheker 1978: 11). Furthermore, Du Bois (as cited in Lauren 1983) declared that the UN Charter should

> make clear and unequivocal the straightforward stand of the civilized world for race equality, and the universal application of the democratic way of life, not simply as philanthropy and justice, but to save human civilization from suicide. What was true of the United States in the past is true of world civilization today—we cannot exist half slave and half free. (p. 21)

Du Bois' concept of world civilization was important for underscoring the inclusivity of all peoples, both colonizers and colonized. Moreover, by calling for universal citizenship, Du Bois highlighted the view that the enforcement of human rights should not be left to nation-states but, rather, protected through the mechanism of the international/transnational UN entity.

Du Bois, along with many other postcolonial activists, hoped that the establishment of the United Nations in 1945 and the Universal Declaration of Human Rights in 1948 would bring global recognition to the plight of formerly colonized peoples and provide a platform for their inclusive participation in establishing world peace. Unfortunately, this hope was quickly dashed for expedient political reasons. Du Bois' anti-colonial and anti-racist rhetoric put him and his camp in direct conflict with the White Southern Democrats, who were led to a large degree by Texas Senator Tom Connally. Connally was committed to the principle of states' rights and the limiting of federal (and international) oversight over the Southern states' institutionalized racism through Jim Crow laws. Significantly, Connally's domestic concerns and determination to resist wording about human rights being put into the UN Charter dovetailed with the federal government's foreign policy toward anti-colonialism. Emerging Cold War tensions with the Soviet Union made it an imperative that the United States maintained control over its Pacific island colonies as strategic military outposts. Hence, conversations about anti-colonialism and support for independence movements raised by many of the attending state representatives were quickly shelved by the US delegation, and authority over US Pacific colonies moved to the veto-protected Security Council. In short, Du Bois' insight that racism was a globally interconnected system of oppression (which in his view had been affirmed by the events in Nazi Germany) was silenced or ignored by a US government anxious not to displease Western colonial powers and US allies in the emerging Cold War (Dudziak 2000: 11; see also Darian-Smith 2012: 498).

Despite the United States agreeing to the establishment of a UN Commission on Human Rights, the San Francisco conference was regarded by many non-Western nations, as well as by all the attending activist associations, as a grave disappointment. Rayford Logan, a pan-African activist and advisor to the NAACP, "angrily denounced the UN Charter as a 'tragic joke'" (as cited in Anderson 2003: 55). Du Bois summed up his disappointment in a letter to the editor of the journal *Foreign Affairs*, stating, "While the San Francisco Conference took steps to prevent further wars in certain emergencies they did not go nearly far enough in facing realistically the greatest potential cause of war, the colonial system" (as cited in Aptheker 1978: 16). In a private telegraph, Du Bois further commented, "We have conquered Germany but not [its] ideas. We still believe in white supremacy, keeping negroes in their places and lying about democracy, when we mean imperial control of 750 million human beings in colonies" (as cited in Anderson 2003: 51). Publically, he railed against the failings of the UN Charter for perpetuating the paternal oppression of the European nations, writing in the *New York Post* (as cited in Aptheker 1982),

> What guarantees ought to be set up by international action to safeguard human rights? So far as the mass of civilized men are concerned, such guarantees have been repeatedly stated but only in part realized. So far as the majority of human beings are concerned, they have for the most part not even been initiated. The usual reason given is that colored folk, colonial peoples, lower classes, have no conception of "rights," could not use them if they had them, and naturally do not have them. We greater folk will guide and guard them when once we get our own rights. But is it not barely possible that one of the reasons human rights are not realized in Germany, England and the U.S. is just because they can be flouted at will in Nigeria, Java, Fiji and among the natives of South Africa? (pp. 2–3)

In 1950, Du Bois ran for the US Senate on the American Labor Party ticket in New York. The next year, at the height of the Cold War and McCarthyism, he was indicted under the Foreign Agents Registration Act for his involvement in the Peace Information Center and his association with Soviet-affiliated peace efforts. After being acquitted, Du Bois went on a speaking tour and gave public talks such as that before an audience of 15,000 in the Coliseum of Chicago. There, he declared—in language as applicable today as it was then— the need to disentangle corporate interests from governmental power and to socialize the economy (Du Bois 1968):

> Big business in the United States is forcing this nation into war, transforming our administration into a military dictatorship, paralyzing all democratic controls and depriving us of knowledge we need. . . . There is no way in the world for us to preserve the ideals of a democratic America, save by drastically curbing the present power of concentrated wealth; by assuming ownership of some natural resources, by administering many of our key industries, and by socializing our services for public welfare. This need not mean the adoption of the communism of the Soviet Union, nor the socialism of Britain, nor even the near-socialism of France, Italy or Scandinavia; but either in some way or to some degree we socialize our economy, restore the New Deal, and inaugurate the welfare state, or we descend into military fascism which will kill all dreams of democracy. (pp. 377–378).

Despite many supporters, Du Bois was increasingly marginalized by both Black and White activists and political organizations, and the "NAACP essentially abandoned him" (Darian-Smith 2012: 501). In the context of the Cold War, his views were seen as highly problematic and, for some, even traitorous. This distancing from Du Bois by Black and White activists correlated with the US government's targeting as "communist" anybody who linked domestic racial struggles with the international anti-colonial movement. As his marginalization and disillusionment mounted, Du Bois became increasingly more active in overseas political organizations and communities focused on self-determination, such as the small expatriate community that existed in Ghana (Gaines 2007).

In contrast to Du Bois' escalating political and social marginalization within the United States, he was often treated as a hero in international circles. He was well received in Britain, and when he was traveling for 10 weeks in China in 1959, the occasion of his 91st birthday was given national celebration and his plea for the unity of China and Africa widely broadcast (Du Bois 1968: 405). In his later writings, Du Bois mused on the injustices of American imperialism, writing sadly that the United States is still a land of magnificent possibilities. It is still the home of noble souls and generous people. But it is selling its birthright. It is betraying its mighty destiny. . . . Today we are lying, stealing, and killing. No nation threatens us. We threaten the world. (pp. 419, 415)

Du Bois and Trump

In the context of the new US administration under Donald Trump, Du Bois' words ring across the decades with poignancy and foreboding. Trump's racist and xenophobic slogans, embrace of capitalist elites, promotion of violence against his critics for being "un-American," and evoking of Cold War rhetoric together underscore circulatory logics of exclusion and authoritarianism across time and space, decades and continents. Du Bois' extraordinary insights shed light on the present. He appreciated that the violence and oppression experienced in the colonies were linked to the violence and oppression experienced within European imperial centers. The common element in the lives of both the colonized and the colonizer is the logics of an exploitative global political economy that disproportionately impacts marginalized communities at home and abroad, in turn justifying overt and covert racism.

In thinking about the decolonizing of Western knowledge in terms of (1) pluralizing histories, (2) depoliticizing human rights, and (3) repoliticizing a global political economy, Du Bois offers an astute postcolonial perspective of import to global studies scholars. First, Du Bois was intimately aware of the need for nation-states to maintain a singular cultural identity and suppress pluralized histories and subjectivities under colonial and postcolonial rule. Today's worldwide backlash of ultra-nationalism in the face of uncompromising global diversity and global migrations would not have surprised Du Bois in the least. Second, Du Bois—himself the target of McCarthyism—would not be surprised by Trump's dismissal of civil and political rights in the stamping out of "unpatriotic" criticism. Nor would Du Bois be taken aback with Trump's endorsement by the Ku Klux Klan and white supremacy groups, or his explicit appeals to Islamophobia. Du Bois spent his entire life fighting Jim Crow laws and the politicization of human rights at home and on a global stage (Darian-Smith 2012; Moyn 2012). Third, Du Bois would have clearly seen historical continuities between the "robber baron" era of the latter half of the nineteenth century and today, in which a supposed apolitical global political economy justifies and naturalizes mass inequality and a global color line. Trump's embrace of corporate power that unabashedly makes a sham of the checks and balances of government evokes an earlier period when a plantation economy helped create the modern United States and democracy was merely a radical aspiration. In short, if Du Bois were alive today, I am confident that he would have anticipated the appeal of Trump to disempowered Whites, who until recent decades had driven the country's political agenda and determined its nationalist identity.

THE GREAT SIOUX NATION AND GLOBAL CAPITALISM

While the United States—and the world—was consumed by the 2016 US presidential campaigns, Indigenous communities mobilized an international protest in North Dakota against the laying down of an oil pipeline. The Dakota Access Pipeline protest, also known by the hashtag #NoDAPL, was a grassroots demonstration by Native communities against the building of a pipeline under the Missouri and Mississippi Rivers. The Dakota Access Pipeline is part of a massive underground project that runs more than 1,000 miles carrying oil from the Bakken oil fields in North Dakota southward through Iowa to holding tanks in Patoka, Illinois. The original plan to run the underground pipeline under the Missouri River near Bismarck (the capital city of North Dakota) was rejected because of its potential threat to municipal water supplies and natural wetland and waterway crossings. As a result, the plan for construction was moved to cross under the Missouri River, approximately half a mile from the Standing Rock Indian Reservation. Members of the reservation view the pipeline as threatening their clean water supply as well as violating their ancestral burial grounds. These sites are considered essential to their sense of identity and historical narratives connecting them to place and territory (Bravebull 2016).

For many months, the #NoDAPL protest was entirely ignored by mainstream media, reflecting a general lack of interest in the United States for anything pertaining to Native peoples. However, as the number of supporters swelled to thousands and international media began spreading news of the protest throughout the world, it was no longer possible to disregard events on the domestic front. By September 2016, news stories started appearing detailing the use of attack dogs by security workers on protesters, which injured a number of them. Global attention was furthered when the Standing Rock Chairman Dave Archambault II spoke before the Human Rights Commission of the United Nations in Geneva on September 20, 2016. He argued that the United States had violated its nineteenth-century treaties with the tribe and that by supporting the pipeline, it had violated the tribe's human rights and sovereignty (Medina 2016; Figure 16.2).[7] In October, public attention

FIGURE 16.2 Standing Rock Chairman Dave Archambault II speaking before the Human Rights Commission of the United Nations in Geneva on September 20, 2016.

grew further as stories circulated widely on social media of armed soldiers in riot gear using tear gas, tanks, and other military equipment to clear protest camps. Calls for the arrest of high-profile journalists and celebrities who had joined the protest also helped bring attention to the movement, as did a new song released by Neil Young called "Indian Giver" ("Neil Young Honors Dakota Access Pipeline Resistance" 2016).

The Standing Rock Indian Reservation is the sixth largest reservation in the United States and a highly symbolic region overlaid with violence and memories of the US colonial government's treatment of Native peoples. In 1874, gold was discovered in the Black Hills, land considered sacred to the Sioux. The US government tried to force the purchase of the land, but the offer was rejected by the leader Sitting Bull. What ensued was war and devastation, with the Sioux initially victorious against the US army at the Battle of Little Bighorn but ultimately overcome and forced to surrender. In 1877, the US government took the Black Hills from the Sioux and split the tribal lands into two smaller reservations (Keeler 2016). Against this background of historical violence and deep memories of betrayal and failure by the US government to stand by its treaties and legal promises, the Dakota Access Pipeline protest takes on a particularly poignant symbolism. As noted by LaDonna Bravebull Allard (Bravebull 2016), Standing Rock's Historic Preservation Officer,

> We must remember we are part of a larger story. We are still here. We are still fighting for our lives, 153 years after my great-great-grandmother Mary watched as our people were senselessly murdered. We should not have to fight so hard to survive on our own lands.

Arguably, Standing Rock, as a site of postcolonial conflict, has more than historical symbolism. Many tribal members do not view themselves as "protestors" of global capitalism but, rather, "protectors" of water and Mother Earth. They present an alternative understanding of people's place in the world as part of a holistic system that incorporates water, sun, trees, and animals and that sponsors a sense of collaboration, cooperation, inclusivity, and a caretaker obligation to protect nature for past and future generations.[8] Many tribal communities argue that resisting the pipeline is essential because there is much more at stake than extractive industries seeking profit, an argument that expressly flies in the face of Milton Friedman's rationale of neoliberal economics. For many journalists and non-Native supporters who joined the Standing Rock camps, there was a sense of amazement at this alternative narrative of how to live in the world. According to Raul Garcia (2016),

> Even when we were talking about politics, the sacredness of it all was what tribe members conveyed as important. The respect of the people overcame any thought of animosity, and the solemnity of the place and the need to protect nature inspired peaceful unity. This indigenous vision of sacred air, sacred water and sacred land was striking to me. I live in Washington, D.C., where polarized rhetoric dominates the landscape, and where, since the presidential election season, distasteful attacks are rampant. Visiting the camps and understanding the spirituality driving this struggle against corporate profit was an eye-opening and humbling experience.

Importantly, the sense of water as sacred also presents alternative ways of organizing political power that counter the dominant international order that is organized through nation-states and which has long been dominant, particularly since post World War II. The prominent Native American cartoonist Ricardo Caté, from Kewa Pueblo, graphically

FIGURE 16.3 "United Nations," one of the most spectacular and strengthening images at Standing Rock are the hundreds of flags representing Native Nations, Indigenous peoples, and non-Native political allies, all standing in solidarity.

Source: https://indiancountrymedianetwork.com/culture/arts-entertainment/nodapl-trump-mother-earth-funny-cartoons-ricardo-cate/?mqsc=ED3863763.

demonstrates the need to reorganize global power in his cartoon titled "United Nations," which shows hundreds of flags at Standing Rock representing Native Nations, Indigenous peoples, and non-Native political allies all standing in solidarity (Figure 16.3). Winona LaDuke, Executive Director of Honor the Earth, a Native American environmental group, has also drawn attention to the need to reorganize political power by declaring, "This is a moment of opportunity, a moment for cities and nations and people all over the world to stand up and demand that no more rivers be poisoned, and no more people be sacrificed" (LaDuke 2016). But as noted in a UN statement issued by members of the Permanent Forum on Indigenous Issues, "Actions such as these [blocking the pipeline] tend to occur in different parts of the world and are often misunderstood and described as rebellious, backward thinking and unilateral opposition to development" (United Nations 2016). Members went on to state,

> Therefore, we call on the United States government to establish and implement, in conjunction with indigenous peoples concerned, a fair, independent, impartial, open and transparent process to resolve this serious issue and to avoid escalation into violence and further human rights abuses.

The details of the Dakota Access Pipeline are complicated and not entirely transparent to the general public. What is known is that because of the manipulation of permit laws that treat the pipeline as small construction projects, it was able to be exempt from review under the Clean Water Act and the Environmental Policy Act. This exemption was brought to the attention of the Environmental Protection Agency (EPA), the Department of the Interior, and the Advisory Council on Historic Preservation, which together asked the US Army Corp of Engineers for a formal environmental impact assessment. According to the Council (as cited in *Indian Country Today* Staff 2016), the

> EPA recommended that the Corps' draft Environmental Assessment "be revised to assess potential impacts to drinking water and the Standing Rock Sioux Tribe. . . . Based on our improved understanding of the project setting, we also recommend addressing additional concerns regarding environmental justice and emergency response actions to spills/leaks."

Notes Dallas Goldtooth, an organizer with the Indigenous Environmental Network (as cited in *Indian Country Today* Staff 2016),

> It is impressive to see these federal agencies stand up in support of the Standing Rock Lakota Nation and acknowledge the tribe's right to be consulted on any extractive development that impacts lands, water, and peoples within their territory. And although a full EIS [environmental impact statement] is a welcome step to hold Dakota Access accountable, the only way we can truly protect the land and water is by rejecting such dirty oil projects, enacting just transition policy towards renewable energy, and keeping fossil fuels in the ground.

During the later months of 2016, the protest camps swelled into the thousands with Native and non-Native supporters. The #NoDAPL movement was widely acclaimed to be unprecedented in terms of support of Indigenous rights in the United States (Street 2016). But as the winter cold set in, tensions mounted between protestors and security agents eager to have the camps disband. Reports of water cannons spraying activists in a deliberate attempt to inflict injury in the frozen landscapes of North Dakota brought international condemnation. Security forces declared they would physically break up the camps. On December 2, 2016, approximately 2,000 military veterans arrived to support the activists and pledged to form a human shield to protect them from police. Fortunately, on December 4, the US Army Corps of Engineers announced that it would not issue a permit for an easement through federally owned land and would halt construction until a full environmental impact review had been made. Although this was viewed throughout the world as a victory for Indigenous peoples, it was short-lived. In January 2017, the Trump administration signed a presidential memorandum that granted an easement to continue construction of the pipeline over reservation land. Despite legal protests by the Cheyenne River Sioux, construction continued and was complete by April 2017, and by June 2017 the pipeline was commercially in operation.

Native Americans and Trump

Violence against the world's Indigenous peoples has been occurring for centuries (Samson and Gigoux 2016). Historically, Indigenous communities have been disproportionately impacted by early European colonial ventures in search of natural resources and cheap labor. The United States, first under British colonialism and then under independent rule, participated in the subjugation of Indigenous peoples. Indians, subject to the practices of colonialism and imperialism, were often the targets of genocide, racism, and dispossession (Forbes 2008). One result of these deep historical antagonisms is that Native Americans remain the most socioeconomically marginalized of all ethnic communities in the country.

Conflict surrounding the Dakota Access Pipeline points to enduring colonial legacies that play out in attempts by multinational corporations, now in overt alliance with US federal agencies, to dispossess Native Americans of their sovereign rights to land and resources. There is a long history of violent land-grabbing by Whites of Indian lands (McNally 2016). For many tribal leaders, the recent conflict over the pipeline is understood as the continuation of war against them. Trump has openly criticized tribes and vowed to privatize reservation land to further exploit natural resources. Against great uncertainty about the future, John Echohawk (2016), Executive Director of the Native American Rights Fund, declared,

> As Native people we have been down this road before. For over 500 years we have endured the invasion of our homelands, endured the horrific and failed termination, assimilation and boarding school policies of the federal government, and in more recent times we have fought past administrations' attacks on Indian country and the environment and won. Since the Trump administration has not announced any Native policy positions, we look forward to the opportunity to work in partnership and educate them about Native rights. But make no mistake, we are firmly committed to continue our fight to protect Native rights and tribal sovereignty—and fight we will. We stand by our commitment as "Modern Day Warriors." . . . We encourage our brothers and sisters and our allies to be brave, take courage, remember our ancestors, and continue to stand firm with us for justice.

What does resistance to the Dakota Access Pipeline suggest about better understanding the shifting political landscape within the United States? How can the historically most marginalized communities in the country help us understand the groundswell of support for Trump in the 2016 presidential election? What do the alternative world views and standpoints of Native peoples offer in terms of rethinking scholarly conventions about how mainstream politics and governance operate within the parameters of the nation-state? In other words, how do Indigenous perspectives help us decolonize the building blocks of Western knowledge and think more creatively and inclusively about our collective futures?

One possible answer lies in the writings of Judith Butler and Athena Athanasiou, who in their book, *Dispossession: The Performative in the Political* (2013), call for disenfranchised communities to come together, often in desperation, to assert their collective stance against exploitation, discrimination, and erasure. Butler and Athanasiou are concerned with how groups of people perform their dispossession in positive ways, calling for new alliances and new ways of belonging and being that do not neatly correlate to nationalist frameworks or hinge on capitalist dogma of property ownership and self-interested individualism (Figure 16.4). In the context of the Dakota Access Pipeline demonstrations, Butler and Athanasiou's concluding words from their book seem most appropriate:

> If there is a crowd, there is also a media event that forms across space and time, calling for the demonstrations, so some set of global connections is being articulated, a different sense of the global from the "globalized market." And some set of values is being enacted in the form of collective resistance: a defense of our collective precarity and persistence in the making of equality and the many-voiced and unvoiced ways of refusing to be disposable. (p. 197)

FIGURE 16.4 Standing Rock solidarity march in San Francisco, November 2016.

Source: https://en.wikipedia.org/wiki/Dakota_Access_Pipeline_protests#/media/File:Stand_with_Standing_Rock_SF_Nov_2016_11.jpg.

In thinking about the decolonizing of Western knowledge in terms of (1) pluralizing histories, (2) depoliticizing human rights, and (3) repoliticizing a global political economy, protesters of the Dakota Access Pipeline offer an Indigenous perspective of import to global studies scholars. First, Indigenous peoples are intimately aware that their history was silenced in the making of the modern United States. Manipulated laws, broken treaties, absconded funds, lies, and cheating all featured in the ways Whites treated Indigenous peoples and to this day filter through their ongoing relations (Washburn 2016). Hence, Native Americans were not surprised—as most scholars were—by the explicit manipulation of "truth" by Trump and the Republican Party to further their political agendas (*New York Times* Editorial Board 2016).

Second, Native Americans have intimately experienced the politicizing and denouncing of Indigenous rights in defense of the national polity. It should be remembered that on the international level, in 2007, as 144 states adopted the United Nations Declaration on the Rights of Indigenous Peoples, four countries voted against it—the United States, Australia, New Zealand, and Canada. On national and local levels, Native Americans have been denied basic political and civil rights for centuries. Hence, they would not have been surprised by Trump threatening those opposing him with violence, calling for harsher voting procedures for minorities, denouncing free journalism, and explicitly violating norms of governance and accountability.

Moreover, Native Americans would not have been surprised by the interference of Russia in the United States' national political process by cyber-hacking and other underhanded disclosures of confidential information. After all, the capacity of tribes to run their own internal affairs has been taken out of their hands by federal agencies for centuries, and the concept of tribes as sovereign nations is constantly under legal attack by the Supreme Court and successive governmental administrations. Moreover, Indigenous peoples throughout the world, and particularly in Latin America, are deeply aware of how both the United States and Russia interfered in their countries domestic politics throughout the decolonization and Cold War eras. Russia now continuing its international strategies by interfering in the political and civil rights of US citizens would probably seem disturbingly familiar.

Finally, with respect to decolonizing the concept that a global political economy is politically neutral, Native American perspectives offer much insight. They have been at the forefront of the politics of capitalism and dispossession for centuries, first with respect to land-grabbing of their territories for agricultural purposes and, more recently, for mining and extractive industries (Svampa 2015). Native peoples—in the United States and throughout the world—have never been fooled by the apolitical myths of capitalism that have been so heavily embraced and endorsed in the neoliberal policies of the past 40 years.

Conclusion

In this chapter, I have called for the decolonizing of Western knowledge. There is much at stake in this call. If it can be achieved, decolonizing Western knowledge may help US and European scholars more fully understand what is going on "over there" in the Global South and appreciate that in fundamental ways, the binary between a Global South and a Global North no longer holds. It may also help scholars in wealthy industrialized nations better understand their own increasingly multiracial, multiethnic, and multireligious societies and the political ramifications and social contradictions of that reality. Perhaps most important, decolonizing contemporary knowledge and its future production may help scholars better see the mutually constitutive relations and systemic interconnections across time and space that inform and shape the current global political landscape and that come to ground and manifest in national domestic politics.

In our current postnational era, global scholars are uniquely poised to help in the problematizing and decolonizing of the concepts of "statehood" and "democracy" in an effort to better understand the reassertion of reactionary politics throughout the world and how best to counter that trend. As champions of critical interdisciplinary scholarship, global scholars can help decolonize knowledge production and promote a more inclusive global intellectual framework that embraces plural ontologies, epistemologies, and non-Western world views (Darian-Smith and McCarty 2017). This may in turn promote more nuanced understandings of what is going on in terms of ordinary peoples' responses to the forces of globalization, feelings of marginalization and insecurity, and crises of identity in a world of vast multiethnic and multireligious diversity. In my view, this represents the extraordinarily exciting promise and value of global studies as an emerging field of inquiry.

Who better to help white elite scholars better understand the United States' shifting domestic landscape than those who live among us but from whose standpoint we rarely think or imagine. African Americans and Native Americans carry within their collective memories silenced narratives of the past, as well as intimate knowledge of the politicizing of human rights and the legacies of exploitative global capitalism. It is from their experiences that privileged scholars may learn new insights. Learning to see from the standpoints of postcolonial and Indigenous subjectivities suggests that "democracy" and "nationalism" are not all they can and should be for those who live on the margins of the state. African Americans and Native Americans show us that global capitalism, in both its colonial and postcolonial iterations, is a highly politicized process that carves up society between "winners" and "losers" and in that process creates enormous conflict and disenfranchisement. In short, what some of Trump's supporters have been experiencing during the past three decades, others have been cumulatively experiencing, in some cases, for centuries.

Unfortunately, what is being experienced are new conflicts and tensions as the numbers of impoverished people grow in ways that have been difficult to imagine within the enclave of the US–Euro academy. In contrast, non-Western scholars have long anticipated the growing populations of the disempowered, with scholars such as Yash Ghai, a Kenyan academic in constitutional law, writing portentously in 2000,

> The globalization of economies has also brought cultures into greater contact, and made most states multi-ethnic, with contradictory consequences. On one hand, there is greater knowledge of other cultures that produces a sympathetic understanding of diversity and emphasis on human solidarity. On the other hand, globalization itself has produced a sense of alienation and powerlessness in the face of new global forces, in which one's identity depends even more fundamentally on one's culture, while that culture may be perceived to be under threat from external forces. (p. 1095)

What is becoming clear is that the United States and other industrialized countries in the Global North are now part of what is typically thought of as the Global South (Sanín-Restrepo 2016). As Du Bois argued so insightfully years ago, the binary between "us" and "them" is not obvious given that we are connected through the forces of global capitalism. According to Du Bois, it is inevitable that the logics of oppression exercised at the edges of imperialism will ultimately return to settle in, and perhaps implode, the centers of Western nationalism. In order to keep pace with this interconnected geopolitical global reality, scholars need to take seriously alternative epistemologies and ways of viewing the world that may not correlate with dominant Western sensibilities and the taken-for-granted principles of liberal democracy. Transcending modernist conceptual frameworks—as argued by the protestors at Standing Rock—may provide insights into how to better understand and envisage our own immediate postnational contexts and uprisings of "public disorder" (Body-Gendrot 2016). It may also help scholars counter and resist reactionary political, economic, and social trends that seek to silence intellectual capacities to imagine alternative futures that may not be bound by Western-centric concepts of individualism, rationalism, liberalism, secularism, democracy, and national sovereignty. Given the backlash against the status quo and rise of authoritarianism throughout the world, it is clear that the dominant assemblages of power are not creating global equality and justice for all. In this context, decolonizing the basic building blocks that have dominated the past three centuries of Western thought may well become an imperative for the emerging field of global studies.

Notes

1. As noted by George Yancy (2016), an African American philosopher, "For many Black people, making America 'great again' is especially threatening, as it signals a return to

a more explicit and unapologetic racial dystopia. For us, dreaming of yesterday is not a privilege, not a desire, but a nightmare." Yancy is one of 200 professors placed on the Professor Watchlist, a website created by a conservative youth group known as Turning Point USA.

2. See Juergensmeyer (2014), Nederveen Pieterse (2013), Duve (2013), Sparke (2013), Darian-Smith (2015b), McCarty (2014), Middell (2014), and Steger (2015).

3. This was demonstrated in an important conference, "'The Rise of the Global Right?" organized by the Society of Global Scholars in the Global Studies Department at the University of California at Santa Barbara, November 2016 (http://www.global.ucsb.edu/news/event/591).

4. While multinational corporations and global financers stand on the sidelines cheering the demise of nation-states as they eagerly amass enormous profit, their glory days are doomed to be short-lived. As Joseph Stiglitz (2012) and other leading economists are quick to acknowledge, corporations need state and global governance mechanisms in order to do business. In a totally deregulated and privatized finance sector, economic profits cannot be sustained over time and with any predictability.

5. Global historians have been particularly important in problematizing the nation-state and forging new modes of inquiry that contextualize nations within intercontinental flows of ideas, cultures, resources, and movements of people (Bentley 2013; Conrad 2016; Hughes-Warrington 2005; Pernau and Sachsenmaier 2016). Together, these scholars call for the removal of the "analytical shackles of 'methodological nationalism'" (Zürn 2013: 416). As a relatively new subfield of inquiry, global historians reflect upon historiographical conventions and point to the limitations of national histories that have dominated the past 200 years in the US–Euro academy. They are keen to explore how modes of cultural exchange and conceptual translation that flowed across state boundaries and diverse cultures shaped events, including the very construction of nations and nationalist identities. So instead of taking the nation-state as a given and then making comparisons between them, global historians explore how nations developed over time as a product of transnational events, complex social relations, and geopolitical forces (Frühstück 2014; Goebel 2015).

6. Some Indigenous peoples do not wish to be "recognized" in this way and reject attempts to incorporate/subsume their identities and subjectivities within what they regard as a colonial framework that has violently subjugated them over centuries (Coulthard 2014; Moreton-Robinson 2015; Simpson 2014).

7. Presenting an appeal to the UN has an important history in Native American politics. In 1977, the American Indian Movement sent delegates to the International NGO Conference on Discrimination Against Indigenous Populations in the Americas, held at the UN offices in Geneva. According to commentators, this was a "watershed event, the very first UN conference with Indigenous delegates, the first direct entry of Native peoples into international affairs, the first time that Native peoples were able to speak for themselves at the UN. Some governments felt so threatened that they prevented delegates from participating and persecuted them upon their return" (John Curl, http://ipdpowwow.org/Archives_1.html; see also Notes 1978).

8. According to a UN statement issued by the UN members of the Permanent Forum on Indigenous Issues: "For indigenous peoples, the environment is a living entity that contains our life sources as well as our sacred sites and heritage. The environment is an important part of our lives and any threats to it impacts our families, ancestors and future generations. It is therefore imperative that the United States respects and recognizes the

intrinsic, inter-related rights of Sioux and their spiritual traditions, history, philosophy, and especially their rights to their lands and territories" (United Nations 2016).

REFERENCES

Anderson, Benedict. 1983. *Imagined Communities: Reflections on the Origin and Spread of Nationalism*. London: Verso.

Anderson, Carol. 2003. *Eyes off the Prize: The United Nations and the African American Struggle for Human Rights, 1944–1955*. Cambridge, UK: Cambridge University Press.

Appiah, Kwame Anthony. 2006. *Cosmopolitanism: Ethics in a World of Strangers*. New York: Norton.

Aptheker, Herbert, ed. 1978. *The Correspondence of W. E. B. Du Bois: Volume III: Selections, 1944–1963*. Amherst: University of Massachusetts Press.

Aptheker, Herbert, ed. 1982. *Writings by Du Bois in Periodicals Edited by Others, Volume 4: 1945–1961*. Millwood, NY: Kraus-Thomson.

Bentley, Jerry H., ed. 2013. *The Oxford Handbook of World History*. Oxford: Oxford University Press.

Body-Gendrot, Sophie. 2016. *Public Disorder and Globalization*. New York: Routledge.

Borgwardt, Elizabeth. 2005. *A New Deal for the World: America's Vision for Human Rights*. Cambridge, MA: Belknap.

Bravebull Allard, LaDonna. 2016. "Why the Founder of Standing Rock Sioux Camp Can't Forget the Whitestone Massacre." *Yes! Magazine*, September 3. http://www.yesmagazine.org/people-power/why-the-founder-of-standing-rock-sioux-camp-cant-forget-the-whitestone-massacre-20160903. Accessed December 1, 2016.

Brown, Wendy. 2015. *Undoing the Demos: Neoliberalism's Stealth Revolution*. New York: Zone.

Butler, Judith, and Athena Athanasiou. 2013. *Dispossession: The Performative in the Political*. Cambridge, UK: Polity.

Cercel, Cosmin. 2016. Darker with the Day: Notes on Fascism, Exception and Primitive Accumulation. *Critical Legal Thinking*, November 18. http://criticallegalthinking.com/2016/11/18/darker-day-notes-fascism-exception-primitive-accumulation.

Collier, Paul. 2008. *The Bottom Billion: Why the Poorest Countries Are Failing and What Can Be Done About It*. Oxford, UK: Oxford University Press.

Conrad, Sebastian. 2016. *What Is Global History?* Princeton, NJ: Princeton University Press.

Coulthard, Glen Sean. 2014. *Red Skin, White Masks: Rejecting the Colonial Politics of Recognition*. Minneapolis: University of Minnesota Press.

Curl, John. nd. "The Geneva Conference, 1977. A Documentary History of the Origin and Development of Indigenous Peoples Day." http://www.ipdpowwow.org/the-geneva-conference-1977/. Accessed May 25, 2018.

Darian-Smith, Eve. 2012. "Re-Reading W.E.B. Du Bois: The Global Dimensions of the Us Civil Rights Struggle." *Journal of Global History* 7 (3): 485–505.

Darian-Smith, Eve. 2015a. "Global Studies—The Handmaiden of Neoliberalism?" *Globalizations* 12 (2): 164–168.

Darian-Smith, Eve. 2015b. "The Constitution of Identity: New Modalities of Nationality, Citizenship, Belonging and Being." In *The Handbook of Law and Society*, edited by Austin Sarat and Patricia Ewick, 351–366. Malden, MA: Wiley-Blackwell.

Darian-Smith, Eve, and Philip C. McCarty. 2017. *The Global Turn: Theories, Research Designs, and Methods for Global Studies.* Berkeley, CA: University of California Press.

Du Bois, W. E. B. 1968. *The Autobiography of W. E. B. Du Bois: A Soliloquy on Viewing Life from the Last Decade of Its First Century.* New York: International Publishers.

Dudziak, Mary L. 2000. *Cold War and Civil Rights: Race and the Image of American Democracy.* Princeton, NJ: Princeton University Press.

Duve, Thomas 2013. "European Legal History: Global Perspectives." Paper presented at Colloquium, Max-Planck Institute for European Legal History, Frankfurt, Germany, September 2–4.

Echohawk, John. 2016. "NARF Will Stand Firm for Justice and for Native Rights During the Trump Administration." Native American Rights Fund, November 17. https://www.narf.org/narf-will-stand-firm-justice-native-rights-trump-administration.

Forbes, Jack. 2008. *Columbus and Other Cannibals: The Wétiko Disease of Exploitation, Imperialism, and Terrorism.* rev. ed. New York: Seven Stories Press,

Frühstück, Sabine. 2014. "Sexuality and Nation States." In *Global History of Sexuality*, edited by Robert Marshall Buffington, Eithne Luibheid, and Donna Guy, 17–56. London: Wiley-Blackwell.

Gaines, Kevin K. 2007. *American Africans in Ghana: Black Expatriates and the Civil Rights Era.* Chapel Hill: University of North Carolina Press.

Garcia, Raul. 2016. "We Are Missing 90% of the Dakota Access Pipeline Story." *Earthjustice*, November 22. http://earthjustice.org/blog/2016-november/we-re-missing-90-percent-of-the-dakota-access-pipeline-story?gclid=CN3sidKu7NACFdm6wAodUA4EnQ#

Ghai, Yash. 2000 "Universalism and Relativism: Human Rights as a Framework for Negotiating Interethnic Claims." *Cardoza Law Review* 21: 1095–1140.

Goebel, Michael. 2015. *Anti-Imperial Metropolis: Interwar Paris and the Seeds of Third World Nationalism.* Cambridge: Cambridge University Press.

Güven, Ferit. 2015. *Decolonizing Democracy: Intersections of Philosophy and Postcolonial Theory.* Lanham, MD: Lexington Books.

Held, David. 2002. "Culture and Political Community: National, Global, and Cosmopolitan." In *Conceiving Cosmopolitanism: Theory, Context, Practice*, edited by Steven Vertovec and Robin Cohen, 48–58. Oxford, UK: Oxford University Press.

Hughes-Warrington, Marnie, ed. 2005. *Palgrave Advances in World Histories.* Basingstoke, UK: Palgrave Macmillan.

Huntington, Samuel P. 1993. "The Clash of Civilizations?" *Foreign Affairs* 72 (3): 22–49.

Indian Country Today Staff. 2016. "Dakota Access Pipeline: Three Federal Agencies Side with Standing Rock Sioux, Demand Review." *Indian Country Today*, April 28. https://indiancountrymedianetwork.com/news/environment/dakota-access-pipeline-three-federal-agencies-side-with-standing-rock-sioux-demand-review. Accessed December 1, 2016.

Juergensmeyer, Mark 2014. "The Origins of Global Studies." Interview with Manfred Steger and Paul James, *Globalizations* 11 (4): 539–547.

Keeler, Jacqueline. 2016. "The Vicious Dogs of Manifest Destiny Resurface in North Dakota." http://www.telesurtv.net/english/opinion/The-Vicious-Dogs-of-Manifest-Destiny-Resurface-in-North-Dakota-20160906-0028.html. Accessed December 1, 2016.

LaDuke, Winona. 2016. Excerpt from speech cited in press release. "Twin Cities Deliver No Dakota Access Resolutions." City of Minneapolis. September 5, 2016. https://

d3n8a8pro7vhmx.cloudfront.net/honorearth/pages/2276/attachments/original/ 1472921805/Twin_Cities_DAPL_resolutions_press_release_FINAL.pdf?1472921805. Accessed May 25, 2018.

Lantham, Robert. 2016. *The Politics of Evasion: A Post-Globalization Dialogue Along the Edge of the State*. New York: Routledge.

Lauren, Paul Gordon. 1983. "First Principles of Racial Equality: History and the Politics and Diplomacy of Human Rights Provisions in the United Nations Charter." *Human Rights Quarterly* 15 (2): 1–26.

Lauren, Paul Gordon. 2003. *The Evolution of International Human Rights*. 2nd ed. Philadelphia: University of Pennsylvania Press.

Levitsky, Steven, and Daniel Ziblatt. 2016. "Is Donald Trump a Threat to Democracy?" *New York Times*, December 16. http://act.moveon.org/go/7246?t=16&akid=175026.179164 34.1YJEM3. Accessed December 1, 2016.

Maier, Peter. 2013. *Ruling the Void: The Hollowing of Western Democracy*. London: Verso.

McCarty, Philip C. 2014. *Integrated Perspectives in Global Studies*. Rev. ed. San Diego: Cognella.

McNally, Robert Aquinas. 2016. "The Nod and a Wink Slaughter: What California's Native Genocide Looked Like." *Indian Country Today*, December 21. https:// indiancountrymedianetwork.com/history/events/nod-wink-slaughter-californias-native-genocide-looked-like/?mqsc=ED3863570.

Medina, Daniel A. 2016. "Standing Rock Sioux Takes Pipeline Fight to UN Human Rights Council in Geneva." NBC News. https://www.nbcnews.com/storyline/dakota-pipeline-protests/standing-rock-sioux-takes-pipeline-fight-un-human-rights-council-n651381. Accessed December 1, 2016.

Middell, Matthias. 2014. "What is Global Studies All About?." *Global Europe—Basel Papers on Europe in a Global Perspective* 105: 45–49.

Moffitt, Benjamin. 2016. *The Global Rise of Populism: Performance, Political Style, and Representation*. Palo Alto, CA: Stanford University Press.

Moreton-Robinson, Aileen. 2015. *The White Possessive: Property, Power, and Indigenous Sovereignty*. Minneapolis: University of Minnesota Press.

Moyn, Samuel. 2012. *The Last Utopia: Human Rights in History*. Cambridge, MA: Belknap.

Mutua, Kagendo, and Beth Blue Swadener, eds. 2011. *Decolonizing Research in Cross-Cultural Contexts: Critical Personal Narratives*. Albany: SUNY Press.

Nederveen Pieterse, Jan. 2013. "What is Global Studies?." Special issue, *Globalizations* 10 (4): 499–514.

"Neil Young Honors Dakota Access Pipeline Resistance in New Song." September 18, 2016. http://www.telesurtv.net/english/news/Neil-Young-Honors-Dakota-Access-Pipeline-Resistance-in-New-Song-20160918-0012.html. Accessed December 1, 2016.

New York Times Editorial Board. 2016. "Truth and Lies in the Age of Trump." *New York Times*, December 11: 10.

Notes, Awesasne. 1978. *Basic Call to Consciousness*. Rooseveltown, NY: Mohawk Nation. [rev. ed. 2005]

Pernau, Margrit, and Dominic Sachsenmaier. 2016. "History of Concepts and Global History." In *Global Conceptual History: A Reader*, edited by Margrit Pernau and Dominic Sachsenamier, 1–17. London: Bloombury.

Piketty, Thomas. 2016. "We Must Rethink Globalization, or Trumpism Will Prevail." *The Guardian*, November 16. https://www.theguardian.com/commentisfree/2016/nov/16/ globalization-trump-inequality-thomas-piketty.

Porter, Eduardo. 2016. "A Dilemma for Humanity: Stark Inequality or Total War." *New York Times*, December 6. http://www.nytimes.com/2016/12/06/business/economy/a-dilemma-for-humanity-stark-inequality-or-total-war.html?smid=pl-share.

Rasmus, Jack. 2016. "Why Trump Won—And What's Next." *Counterpunch*, November 10. http://www.counterpunch.org/2016/11/10/why-trump-won-and-whats-next.

Said, Edward. 2001. "The Clash of Ignorance." *The Nation*, October 3.

Samson, Colin, and Carlos Gigoux. 2016. *Indigenous Peoples and Colonialism: Global Perspectives*. Cambridge, UK: Polity.

Sanín-Restrepo, Ricardo. 2016. *Decolonizing Democracy: Power in a Solid State (Global Critical Caribbean Thought)*. Lanham, MD: Rowman & Littlefield.

Santos, Boaventura de Sousa, ed. 2007. *Another Knowledge is Possible: Beyond Northern Epistemologies*. London: Verso.

Sassen, Saski. 2008. *Territory, Authority, Rights: From Medieval to Global Assemblages*. Princeton, NJ: Princeton University Press.

Sassen, Saski. 2014. *Expulsions: Brutality and Complexity in the Global Economy*. Cambridge, MA: Belknap.

Simpson, Audra. 2014. *Mohawk Interruptus: Political Life Across the Borders of Settler States*. Durham, NC: Duke University Press.

Smith, Dorothy. 1977. *Feminism and Marxism*. Vancouver, British Columbia, Canada: New Star Books.

Sparke, Matthew. 2013. *Introducing Globalization: Ties, Tensions, and Uneven Integration*. Hoboken, NJ: Wiley-Blackwell.

Steger, Manfred B., ed. 2015. *The Global Studies Reader*. 2nd ed. Oxford: Oxford University Press.

Stiglitz, Joseph. 2002. *Globalization and Its Discontents*. New York: Norton.

Stiglitz, Joseph. 2012. *The Price of Inequality: How Today's Divided Society Endangers Our Future*. New York: Norton.

Streeck, Wolfgang. 2014. *Buying Time: The Delayed Crisis of Democratic Capitalism*. London: Verso.

Street, Paul. 2016. "Behind Standing Rock: Native N. America vs. Capitalist Ecocide." http://www.telesurtv.net/english/opinion/Behind-Standing-Rock-Native-N.-America-vs.-Capitalist-Ecocide-20160915-0002.html. Accessed December 1, 2016.

Stuenkel, Oliver. 2016. "Why the West Struggles to Understand the BRICS." *Global Policy*, December 19. https://www.globalpolicyjournal.com/blog/19/12/2016/why-west-struggles-understand-brics.

Svampa, Maristella. 2015. "Commodities Consensus: Neoextractivism and Enclosure of the Commons in Latin America." *South Atlantic Quarterly* 114 (1): 65–82.

United Nations. 2016. "UN Statement from Mr. Alvaro Pop Ac, Chair of the Permanent Forum on Indigenous Issues, and Ms. Dalee Dorough and Chief Edward John, Members of the Permanent Forum on Indigenous Issues on the Protests on the Dakota Access Pipeline (North Dakota, USA)." https://www.un.org/development/desa/indigenouspeoples/news/2016/08/statement-on-protests.

Washburn, Kevin. 2016. "Another Broken Promise Addressed with the Return of 25,000 Acres to the MHA Nation in North Dakota." Indian Country Today, December 21. https://www.linkedin.com/pulse/another-broken-promise-addressed-return-25000-acres-mha-washburn?trk=prof-post.

Yancy, George. 2016. "I Am a Dangerous Professor." *New York Times*, December 4.

Zürn, Michael. 2013. "Globalization and Global Governance." In *Handbook of International Relations*, edited by Walter Carlsnaes, Thomas Risse, and Beth A. Simmons, 401–425. Thousand Oaks, CA: SAGE.

PART III

GLOBAL CONCERNS

Issues and Themes at the Core of Global Research and Teaching

CHAPTER 17

....

FINANCIALIZATION

....

RAVI K. ROY AND THOMAS D. WILLETT

THE term "financialization" has increasingly become part of the lexicon of global studies in recent years. This is especially the case since the global financial crisis of 2008–2009 (GFC). Definitions and understandings, however, are often imprecise, confused, and mired in emotionally charged references to the expanding wealth and power of the financial sector. We prefer to use the term more neutrally to refer to the increased role that the financial sector has been playing in economies over time. Strong financial sectors are necessary to support well-functioning economies. During the past four decades, the financial sector has facilitated economic growth on an unprecedented scale. During the same period, economic distortions caused by malfunctioning financial sectors have imposed enormous costs.

In this chapter, we discuss how the scope of activities performed by the financial sector has been expanding in recent decades in ways that are linked to globalization more generally. Following on from this, we analyze how some of this expansion has contributed to growing economic instability and turbulence. Finally, we outline four specific areas that must be addressed if the financial sector is to carry out its functions properly. Normative approaches in political economy, for example, have been emphasizing the importance of ideas in influencing the performance of economies, economic sectors, and organizations. Denzau and North's (1994) work on shared mental models (SMMs) provides a useful conceptual framework for helping us analyze the underlying rationale for contemporary trends in financialization as well as how faulty ideas have contributed to financial instability.

WHAT IS FINANCIALIZATION?

....

The financial sector has traditionally been responsible for performing a range of essential functions generally associated with deposit-taking and lending by banks for productive uses. In addition, the financial sector plays a vital role in the management and transfer of liabilities and assets through the trading of stocks, bonds, securities, insurance, and credit intermediation. According to economist John Kay (2015), "We need a finance sector to manage our payments, finance our housing stock, restore our infrastructure, fund our retirement and support new business" (p. 283).

The growth in the financial sector is in part due to the development of more efficient banking systems, increased international capital flows, and greater investment activity. Indeed, these developments have helped contribute substantially to higher economic growth in many developing countries. At the same time, however, they have exposed countries with poorly structured financial regulation and supervision regimes to increased turbulence and instability.

In advanced economies, the exponential growth in financialization in recent decades has been due, in considerable part, to increases in securities trading throughout the world. Indeed, securities trading generates most of the revenue within the finance industry. The global securities market involves the trading of negotiable financial products that represent the value of debts and equities on other real and paper assets. The explosion in the derivatives market during the past 30 years is particularly noteworthy. Simply stated, a derivative is a security whose value is based on other underlying assets, such as home market values, stock indexes, commodities, and bonds. Most of these financial instruments, such as asset-backed securities, provide vital services that, when designed and used sensibly, allow corporations and investors to hedge risks more efficiently. In a number of cases, however, this expansion went too far; such derivative contracts expanded to a level roughly three times the value of the underlying assets (Kay 2015: 2).

Given the previous discussion, it is not surprising that the term "financialization" has often been used pejoratively to refer to a country's growing reliance (some say over-reliance) on the financial sector vis-à-vis other "traditional" sectors of the economy (i.e., manufacturing and agriculture) as the driver of economic growth in recent decades. In the United States, for example, manufacturing contributes less than one-fourth of the country's $18.5 trillion gross domestic product (GDP); agricultural goods (and related products) contribute less than 4%. In contrast, the country's service sector contributes more than three-fourths of the United States' total GDP; financial services alone contribute more than 8% of total GDP. Although there is an ongoing debate regarding which industries should be included under the broad tent of the financial services sector, generally speaking, the Organisation for Economic Co-operation and Development (OECD) suggests that financial services now comprise nearly 20% of the total GDP of many of the world's developed economies. This economic profile is very different from that of 40 years ago when most of an advanced country's productive wealth was generated from manufacturing and other tangible value-added activities. The growth in the financial sector has contributed to the wealth of many individual investors, pension schemes, and investment funds. Indeed, a new global social class has emerged as a result of new income-creating opportunities that have accompanied an expanding financial sector. At the same time, the decline in manufacturing-based employment that accompanied de-industrialization during the past four and half decades has directly resulted in the systematic decline of the middle class in many nations throughout the world. Consequently, the income gap between social classes has been widening within many industrial nations.

As discussed later, when the financial sector grows beyond its proper scope and function, many of the economic benefits associated with increased financialization are often privatized, whereas many of the substantial costs tend to be socialized. When viewed from this perspective, we may consider a number of the developed industrial countries to be "over-financialized." However, the size and scope of the financial sector tend to vary widely from one country to the next. In many developing countries, for example, the financial sector tends to be "underdeveloped" and, therefore, limited in its ability to provide many of the essential functions that contribute to productive growth. Robust financial sectors are instrumental in supporting a process traditionally known as "financial deepening," which has proven to be especially critical during a country's early stages of development. Indeed, developing countries with more robust financial systems have had greater success in closing the income gap vis-à-vis wealthier nations. Therefore, when attempting to conduct any serious and objective appraisal of the appropriate size and scope of the financial sector, one must proceed using well-defined criteria that take into account the overall economic profile of a given country.

The Essential Functions Performed by the Financial Sector

The strength of any capitalist economy depends on its level of productive investment. Money is a key element in this process—it functions as a medium of exchange, a unit of account, and a store of value. A well-developed and robust financial sector is required to facilitate the management and investment of this money. If individuals and corporations were only able to invest their own money, the amount of financial capital available to support productive investment would be extremely limited. The financial system supports economic productivity by facilitating borrowing and lending among institutions and individuals. In addition, the financial system provides trade credits that enable buyers (e.g., securities traders) to make purchases now and pay later.

An integral part of the financial sector involves the banking system. The banking system plays a vital role in ensuring that depositors have access to their liquid assets on short notice without incurring penalties while at the same time facilitating the practice of "lending long" through its commitment guarantees of funds. This form of maturity transformation is essential to the operation of any modern economy and, under most circumstances, tends to work very well. This is because under normal economic circumstances, only a fraction of depositors will demand their money at any given time. Accordingly, a substantial portion of a bank's deposits can be lent out to finance productive activity.

During periods of financial turbulence, however, depositor fears can lead to capricious bank runs. In such instances, a given bank's short-term liquidity stores—which it is supposed to make available to its depositors on demand—can quickly disappear. Consequently, in modern economies, governments and central banks generally play an important role in ensuring the soundness of the banking system through deposit guarantees and the operations that they perform as "lenders of last resort." However, at the same time, such guarantees can create incentives (known as moral hazards) that may encourage banks to engage in high-risk lending practices. This is because such guarantees tend to shield banks from potential losses associated with high-risk investment activities should they go bad while also allowing them to keep the profits when their investments are successful. Government regulation is generally required, therefore, to temper moral hazard resulting from such explicit or implicit guarantees.

With the end of World War II and the US-led effort to support the reconstruction of Europe and Japan, financial systems became increasingly globalized. International economic development activities were principally focused on the expansion of global trade and productive growth. An international financing system was required to support these efforts. The Bretton Woods international monetary system and development-oriented international financial institutions (known popularly as IFIs), such as the International Monetary Fund (IMF) and the World Bank, have contributed greatly to what we now know as modern global finance. Next, we explore the connection between globalization and financialization in depth.

FINANCIALIZATION AND GLOBALIZATION

In a sense, according to Kay (2015: 13), "finance has always been global" because it has been historically interconnected with the rise of global trade. Since the 1950s, in particular, there have been vast reductions in the costs of global transportation and communication. Innovations in shipping and, more recently, the ability to transmit vast amounts of data in the blink of an eye through revolutionary developments such as fiber-optic-based communication have contributed greatly to this process. Indeed, technological breakthroughs in high-speed trading computers during approximately the past 25 years have enabled global investors to conduct billion-dollar transactions across the world instantaneously at any time. Political economist Eric Helleiner (1994) concisely summarizes the connection between economic globalization and financialization:

> "Economic globalization" is one of the more popular catch-phrases used to describe momentous changes in our era. And yet, as usual with such phrases, its precise meaning and significance remain poorly understood and even hotly disputed among academic specialists. Nowhere is this more true than with respect to the sector of the world economy where "globalization" is most developed: *the financial sector* [emphasis added]. For most people, the emergence of a twenty-four hour, globally integrated financial marketplace in recent years has been a phenomenon difficult to comprehend. International financial issues are, after all, widely perceived as arcane and highly technical. This perception is only reinforced by the fact that the new enormous movements of money across borders are seemingly invisible, taking place largely in the form of rapid blips on computer screens distributed around the planet. (p. 295)

The exponential growth in financial transactions taking place daily, coupled with the major expansion of trade throughout the world during the past 40 years, make it appear as though national boundaries are disappearing. In fact, many have been claiming that global financialization has diminished the capacity of governments to exercise national control over economic policymaking. Although such claims overstate reality, there can be no doubt that the rise of global financial markets has resulted in increased economic interdependence among nations. Simultaneous movements in the value of the various stock indexes following any given international financial event suggest the extent to which national economies throughout the world are interconnected.

In principle, the economic and financial interdependencies that have developed between nations would be expected to create strong incentives for their governments to engage in some kind of international coordination of their policies. Some progress has been made on this front. For example, "beggar thy neighbor" policies of competitive devaluations that exacerbated the Great Depression of the 1930s are now much less common. Nonetheless, most national governments retain a high degree of formal autonomy in domestic economic policymaking. The recent "Brexit" referendum, along with the United Kingdom's long-standing (and likely wise) decision to remain outside the Euro, provide vivid examples.

Although the threat of investment flight has inspired governments to adopt monetary and fiscal discipline in some instances, in general, nation-states are not passive victims of the "ruthless" and "unstoppable" forces of global financialization as is often argued. In fact, nation-states are often active and willing participants. After all, nation-state actors and sovereign governments make national public policies. Consequently, domestic political pres sure from interest groups, rather than international financial movements, often influence when, and to what degree, national governments choose to engage in the global economy.

Indeed, global financialization has simultaneously made it easier for governments to borrow large sums of foreign capital from international credit markets. For example, increases in international flows, made possible through global financialization, initially enabled countries such as Greece to run large national fiscal deficits while allowing them to avoid painfully high interest rates. Thus, for a time, the Greek government borrowed extensively from these international financial markets to support expensive domestic social policies while not having to internalize many of the costs. In fact, it was only with the onset of the crisis in 2010 that international financial markets began to limit the options of the Greek government (Willett and Srisorn 2014).

As the costs of many arcane government regulations became more apparent, and beliefs in the efficiency of the free market began to spread throughout the economics profession, governments in numerous countries began to adopt a series of financial deregulation and liberalization measures. Next, we discuss how this process unfolded historically.

THE RISE OF GLOBAL FINANCIALIZATION IN THE 1980S AND 1990S

Although the process of global financialization began gaining momentum in the advanced economies in the early 1980s, an increasing number of emerging market countries would later follow. In the United States, leading figures such as Treasury Secretary (and former CEO of Merrill Lynch) Donald Regan helped bolster financialization in the early 1980s by spearheading an aggressive financial liberalization agenda. This initiative was directed, in part, at the deregulation of the savings and loans industry. Toward this end, Donald Regan and others in the Reagan administration worked with sympathizers in the US Congress to begin systematically removing legal barriers that kept firms from taking advantage of historic investment opportunities in the securities markets.

Similar developments were taking place in Britain. Keen to take full advantage of these new global financial trends, Prime Minister Margaret Thatcher undertook a series of reforms in the mid-1980s aimed at addressing systemic problems that underlay her country's underperforming financial sector. Popularly known as London's "Big Bang,"

Thatcher's reform effort involved a comprehensive upgrade of London's fledgling computerized trading system as well as the adoption of new competitive policies governing commissions and fees. Big Bang would usher in a new era of securities trading. The historic financial deregulation and liberalization initiatives undertaken by Thatcher and Reagan in the early 1980s (within their respective countries) helped fuel some of the most spectacular "bull markets" that the world had ever seen. By the late 1980s, a speculative bubble began developing in both countries. Motivated by fears that the securities markets were overvalued, droves of investors began dumping their assets, thereby contributing to a massive financial crash in the fall of 1987.

In the late 1990s, President Bill Clinton's administration greatly expanded the deregulation drive that Ronald Reagan had initiated a decade earlier. The most important among these was the enactment of the Gramm–Leach–Bliley Act (aka the Financial Services Modernization Act of 1999). President Clinton signed into law a bill that largely reversed the historic Glass–Steagall Act of 1933, which sharply separated the roles of commercial banks from investment banks. The 1999 act helped inspire one of the most spectacular securities booms in history. Ten years later, however, many blamed the act for having contributed to the most horrific economic catastrophe since the Great Depression.

FINANCIALIZATION AND GLOBAL TURBULENCE IN THE TWENTY-FIRST CENTURY

Claims that contemporary global financialization has increased economic instability and turbulence have been fueled by a number of regional financial crises that have occurred during the past two decades, including Mexico in 1994, East Asia in 1997, Russia in 1998, and Argentina in 1999. More recently, the Euro Crisis has severely affected a number of the European economies (Roy, Denzau, and Willett 2007; Roy and Willett 2014; Steger & Roy 2010). These claims gained particular salience in the aftermath of the GFC. Here, we examine the GFC in detail.

The spark that appeared to ignite the GFC was the USs' subprime mortgage crisis of 2008. From there, the crisis spread quickly to other financial markets in the US and then to markets abroad. European countries that had invested heavily in US mortgage-backed securities were especially vulnerable. Almost half of US mortgage-related securities were held by the largest European banks and hedge funds, which with the blessing of regulators were negligently undercapitalized.

Recessions in advanced economies quickly followed. As conditions worsened, financial markets began to freeze, liquidity began drying up, trade slowed, and stock market values plummeted. Even countries that appeared to escape initial direct financial losses later suffered from capital flight as droves of investors began redirecting their money to safe havens. The resulting economic fallout ended up costing taxpayers, investors, and governments trillions of dollars. All of this, however, paled in comparison to the heartbreaking pain experienced by millions of innocent people who lost their jobs, pensions, life savings, homes, and livelihoods.

As discussed previously, the seeds of the GFC had been germinating for some time. Mortgage-backed securities, and the distorted housing market on which they were based, were a large source of the problem. In the late 1990s and early 2000s, in particular, borrowing limits were raised and down payment requirements for securing mortgage loans were substantially reduced. In many cases, buyers were able to secure loans with little or even no money down and/or without producing any documentation of their income.

Operating on the false belief that real estate values could only go up (and never down or remain stagnant), some of the world's most respected credit rating agencies, such as Standard and Poor's, overestimated the degree to which mortgage-backed securities could reasonably balance higher risk investments. In a number of cases, credit rating agencies intentionally assigned strong ratings to high-risk investments under pressure from the banks that commissioned them. A number of ethical economists and financial analysts attempted to warn the public and government regulators. Often, however, these alarm bells went largely unheeded by exuberant governments, traders, investors, financial institutions, and the public alike, who were unwilling to interfere with the mystical hand of the free and unfettered market.

As long as housing prices (and consequently home equities) continued to rise at substantial rates, the mortgage-backed securities industry thrived. Once housing price increases began to slow, however, things began to turn in the other direction. Many already extended borrowers could not make their mortgage payments, ultimately forcing them to declare bankruptcy or surrender their homes in foreclosure. Soon thereafter, the entire real estate market collapsed. Mortgage lending titans Fannie May and Freddie Mac teetered on the brink of insolvency. Mortgage-backed derivatives became suspect. Predictably, investors began dumping their assets. Major brokerage houses such as Bear Stearns and insurance giants such as AIG struggled to avoid bankruptcy.[1] The turmoil on Wall Street ultimately found its way down "Main Street." Declining consumer demand for "big ticket" items such as cars and other durable goods led some of America's most prestigious and well-branded companies to lay off large numbers of their workforce.

In the immediate aftermath of the crisis, questions abounded: What happened? Who was to blame? What should be done to clean up the mess? and Who should pay for it? Competitive pressures emanating from both within the financial services sector and the wider economy to develop innovative securities products, coupled with poorly designed and executed industry practices and government regulatory processes, were all contributing factors to growing financial instability and turbulence.

Mortgage-backed securities can be useful tools in helping reduce risks associated with certain investments under conditions when the financial system as a whole is functioning well. However, risks tend to increase substantially when the system is stressed. Although many, most notably US Federal Reserve Chairman Alan Greenspan, assumed that a competitive market would automatically generate the requisite incentives for investors to avoid inordinately high-risk behavior, this proved not to be the case. In fact, many financial institutions, which were operating, in part, on inordinate faith in highly flawed risk models, began "levering up" (Blyth, 2013). These institutions took on excessive debt positions by employing the use of opaque and exotic financial instruments that were supposed to abate substantial risk.[2]

Taming Financialization: Focus Areas for Well-Functioning Financial Sectors

Much has been learned from the painful experiences described previously. Although it is politically expedient to blame avaricious investors for the entirety of the crisis, the vast analysis governing the origins of the crisis has revealed multiple complex causes. The field of political economy is now awash with studies that could assist our efforts to mitigate future market crises.

Any serious discussion on how to promote well-functioning financial sectors must focus on the following four areas:

Begin with sound leadership. Currently, the industry is in dire need of genuine leadership and direction.

The decisions and behavior of leaders and participants must be guided by sound theory. Ideas and institutions matter to the performance of economies. Therefore, one must consider the pervading ideas driving human decisions and the consequent behavior that occurs within a given industry. Specifically, actors must possess correct, or at least reasonably accurate, ideas about the environments in which they operate.

Cooperation and communication within an interdependent economic system are essential. One must consider how the functions and activities of the financial sector affect, and are at the same time affected by, other organizations and individuals within a larger interdependent economic system. Specifically, financial actors must develop an awareness of how the various parts of the economy are interconnected.

Sound regulation and enforcement are crucial. Therefore, one must consider the structural soundness of both national and international regulatory systems. Specifically, we must promote sensible regulation and effective oversight that do not stymy the essential functions performed by the financial sector in facilitating economic growth.

To some extent, these four areas may interrelate. Let us examine each of them in more detail.

Begin with Sound Leadership

The financial sector needs leaders who can answer the fundamental questions of the industry: What is the aim of the financial sector? What purpose does it serve? Whom does it serve? As the financial system began to expand its influence beyond its traditional scope of functions, it became less connected with providing services to the real economy. As Kay (2015) argues, the finance industry became less concerned with "the facilitation of payments, the provision of housing, the management of large construction projects, the needs of the elderly or the nurturing of small businesses" (p. 283). Instead, he suggests, many of the leaders of the financial sector became focused on "the process of financial intermediation," which, he claims, has now "become an end in itself" (p. 283). Much of the activity that occurs within the financial services industry today involves trading paper (representing assets and liabilities) back and forth between a relatively small group of financial firms and institutions throughout the world (pp. 5–6). Effective public oversight and private sector leadership are jointly required to redirect the industry's focus on the essential functions outlined previously. Although the most important causes of the crisis were structural, the disgraceful, and in some cases criminal, behavior of a large number of participants in the financial sector contributed to the magnitude of the disaster. Therefore, leaders must improve the aims and culture in their institutions.

The Decisions and Behavior of Leaders and Participants Must Be Guided by Sound Theory

Complexities associated with increased global financialization have led to growing uncertainty, making rational prediction extremely difficult. Accordingly, Denzau and North (1994) have suggested that issues of uncertainty, rather than risk, tend to increasingly "characterize choice making" in the modern age (p. 3). In his book, *The End of Alchemy*, Mervyn King (2016), the former governor of the Bank of England, corroborates the claim that we live in a world fraught with radical uncertainty, not just risk, and need to adjust our thinking accordingly. Many mathematically sophisticated risk models were designed in a manner that failed to distinguish factors of risk from factors of uncertainty. In a world characterized by ubiquitous uncertainty, data are not enough; we must know how to interpret them. As W. Edwards Deming (2000) notes, "Use of data requires knowledge about the different sources of uncertainty" (p. 100). Sound theories, he argues, are essential in helping us comprehend situations and problems as well as interpreting data so that we can make better predictions and devise useful solutions.

Denzau and North (1994) emphasize the use of SMMs for helping us comprehend the importance of ideas in guiding our attempts to navigate political, social, and economic environments characterized by high levels of uncertainty. What are SMMs? How do they shape our understanding of economic environments and, consequently, our best options within them? According to the *World Development Report 2015: Mind, Society, and Behavior* (World Bank Group 2015), "Mental models include categories, concepts, identities, prototypes, stereotypes, causal narratives, and worldviews" (p. 62). Moreover, "Without mental models of the world, it would be impossible for people to make most decisions in daily life" or to "develop institutions, solve collective action problems, feel a sense of belonging and solidarity, or even understand one another" (pp. 62–63). The *World Development Report* was largely inspired by the work of Denzau and North (1994), who likewise argue that "the performance of economies is a consequence of the incentive structures put into place" that comprise "the institutional framework of the polity and economy" (p. 27).

Mental models can be verbal and non-verbal. The latter involves what Michael Polanyi (2009) refers to as "tacit knowledge," which is based on his assertion that "we can know more than we can tell" (p. 4). Moreover, Denzau and North (1994) claim that "individuals with common cultural backgrounds and experiences will share reasonably convergent mental models, ideologies, and institutions" (pp. 3–4).[3]

In a world mired in uncertainty, we can never be sure that any theory or SMM is 100% accurate. The 2015 *World Development Report* (World Bank Group 2015) reveals that "there is immense variation in mental models across societies, including different perceptions of the way the world 'works'" (p. 62). As statisticians George Box and Norman Draper (1987) pithily note, "All models are wrong, but some are useful" (p. 424). In certain instances, SMMs can help us fill in gaps in our knowledge with information and claims that are consistent with our world views (World Bank Group 2015: 63, 69). At other times, however, they may cause us to ignore data and feedback that are inconsistent or conflict with our deeply held beliefs and assumptions about the world.

Contemporary forms of "financialization" are often associated with a set of SMMs underlying economic globalization known as "neoliberalism" (Cerny 2008; Steger and Roy 2010). The neoliberal SMM collectively embodies various subsets or strands that jointly emphasize the virtues of market capitalism as espoused by classical liberal economists. These strands tend to range from "no-holds-barred" free market fundamentalism (as promoted by Friedrich Von Hayek and Milton Friedman) to more moderate and mainstream economic approaches emphasizing the positive role that government can play in correcting market failures and helping smooth out market cycles. Although financialization, as a concept, is not necessarily interwoven with neoliberalism per se, the ideas fueling many of the decisions made by those within the financial services sector in recent decades tend to be highly sympathetic with an extreme strand of neoliberalism known as "free market fundamentalism."

Although the adoption of sensible liberalization policies governing international capital flows has greatly helped improve global economic efficiency and growth, perverse liberalizations (i.e., those that simultaneously eviscerate essential capital controls and regulatory safeguards while shielding the financial system from excessively risky behavior) have served to increase the propensity for global economic turbulence. Such liberalization policies have contributed significantly to large capital flow surges that have quickly turned in the other direction, resulting in large disruptive reversals. In some cases, such surges and reversals reflect efficient responses to changing economic circumstances and government policies. However, in many cases, they cannot. Such perverse liberalization policies were often the conscious design of those who blindly followed free market fundamentalist rationales and/or the result of political pressures exerted by shortsighted special interests.

If those operating in the financial sector are to develop and implement sound financial liberalization policies and processes more effectively in the future, they must begin with sound SMMs. The quality of knowledge or theory in any field or practice depends on rigorous research and scrutiny. The validity of this knowledge is further determined through independent testing and verification by outsiders. In some important areas of the financial services sector, however, these activities have been negligently absent. Many practitioners rarely question or challenge the core underlying assumptions, axioms, and beliefs that inspire the activities and practices within the industry. Securities traders, for example, often operate in narrow professional silos (Tett 2015) according to highly similar (and in some cases detrimentally wrong) beliefs about how the world works. Consequently, contesting views emanating from outside industries and professions often fail to permeate, resulting in a high degree of confirmation bias within the financial services sector.

Although sometimes difficult to achieve, major shifts in SMMs are possible. For example, the devastating economic crises that have followed in the wake of international financial surges and reversals have led many economists and officials to rethink their positions regarding the universal liberalization of capital controls. In an article that has attracted considerable attention, titled "Neoliberalism Oversold?" IMF economists Ostry, Loungani, and Furceri (2016) argue that part of the neoliberal agenda promoting the complete liberalization of capital controls may have been extreme.[4] This view is consistent with the positions of mainstream neoliberals, such as Nobel Prize winner James Tobin and John Williamson (and others belonging to the Washington Consensus), who have long advocated the use of capital controls in environments that have been prone to market failure.

Cooperation and Communication Within an Interdependent Economic System Are Essential

The failure of many actors, including officials and financial sector participants, to recognize the growing complexity and interdependence of many financial activities is a major problem. As Hayek (1945) emphasized, one of the benefits of the competitive price system is that it reduces information costs for many actors. Unlike central planners, most actors may only require a certain amount of local knowledge about a particular area in order to operate efficiently. However, at the same time, important public and private actors must take into account the broader interdependencies within a larger system if they are to optimize potential gains for themselves and the others with whom they interact. The GFC was due, in part, to the fact that both the leaders of financial institutions and state regulators focused too narrowly on the risks assumed by individual firms. In doing so, they failed to see the systemic risks deeply embedded in the structure of the financial sector.

If the financial sector is to perform its job effectively and promote consistency and stability within the economy as a whole, then the actors operating within it must start by "minding the gaps" that exist throughout the complex and interdependent system. This entails looking beyond the parts that they perform within it. Participants who operate in the broader economic system must develop greater awareness about those who depend on their products and services, as well as those on whose services and products they depend. Many traders, for example, tended to be highly conversant with the technical process involved with trading mortgage-backed securities, but they knew surprising little about housing markets or the mortgage industry (Kay 2015). As Deming (2000) notes, "One may learn a lot about ice, yet may know very little about water" (p. 101).

Although isolated parts of an industry may operate very well on their own, they often do so to the detriment of the system as a whole. Fixing these structural problems will require leaders to do more than simply adopt new reforms and regulations. In fact, attempts to implement new reforms in a bad system will likely make things worse (Kay 2015: 7). Indeed, as the esteemed quality management guru Russell L. Ackoff (Ackoff and Rovin 2003) noted, "The righter we do the wrong thing, the wronger we become" (p. 1). Unfortunately, the official responses to the global financial crisis focused on tinkering with the existing system rather than overhauling it. The United States' Dodd–Frank legislation, for example, outlines a host of new regulations that in part mandate higher capital requirements for many financial institutions. Although Dodd–Frank represents on balance a step in the right direction, many experts argue that these reforms do not go nearly far enough (Admati and Hellwig 2013; Kay 2015; King 2016; Turner 2016).

Sound Regulation and Enforcement Are Crucial

Government officials have not done enough to ensure that current regulations are effectively enforced. Many point to the reversal of Glass–Steagall regulations as the main culprit. Deregulation, in and of itself, however, played only a partial role. Although the repeal of the Glass–Steagall Act, for example, allowed commercial banks to engage in certain risky investment banking activities, it was the pure investment banks, such as Lehman Brothers, that were directly hit by the crisis. Glass–Steagall would have done little to curtail high-risk financial behavior taking place within investment banking. Indeed, the Securities and Exchange Commission watched approvingly as these investment banks increased their leverage by taking on higher levels of debt.

Participants in the financial system have demonstrated an enormous capacity to either circumvent the spirit of regulatory rules or manipulate them to their own advantage. Consequently, many experts (with whom we agree) have been pressing for a smaller number of rules that are easy to understand and enforce across the industry. First, regulators need to enforce limits on the size of financial institutions and the manner in which they interconnect so that they are not "too big to fail." In addition, regulators must set higher capital requirements that financial institutions must hold, impose stricter regulations governing the amount of leverage that they may assume, and require them to maintain higher levels of liquidity to ensure their solvency through periods of volatility.

CONCLUSION

The financial sector performs many functions that are crucial to supporting a well-functioning market economy. However, the growth in the financial sector is related, in part, to the increase in high-risk securities trading in recent decades. The financial sector's deepening involvement in this highly volatile industry has made financial markets increasingly susceptible to financial crises. This is especially true in instances in which perverse incentive structures have taken root and proper regulatory oversight is wanting. At the same time, it must be noted that it would be impossible to eliminate the factors that contribute to financial crises entirely without simultaneously stifling the crucial functions performed through financial intermediation. The conundrum before regulators is to determine how they can effectively implement regulation that discourages excessive risk-taking while at the same time enabling the financial services sector to perform these essential functions. Most mainstream economists agree that we can maximize many of the gains, and at the same time minimize many of the likely losses produced by financialization, through the intelligent design of procedures and practices that promote more stable and predictable financial systems. Moreover, we can, and must, do more to discourage financial activities and practices that waste society's resources. This is so regardless of whether or not these activities lead directly to crises.

Leaders in the industry, and the public sector regulators who are supposed to oversee their activities, must begin by adopting a new philosophy or set of mental models that guide the core aims of the financial sector. In a world characterized by great (and ever-growing) uncertainty, it is difficult to predict which mental models will prove useful and which ones may be detrimental. The financial sector operates as a relatively closed system that not only engenders detrimental blind spots but also tends to reinforce high degrees of confirmation bias. Industry leaders must make a concerted effort to solicit and systematically incorporate outside views and independent analysis into their processes and activities.

Sound mental models, however, are not enough. Even if most individuals operating within the financial services sector were to abandon fundamentally flawed mental models, some actors would continue to seek to benefit themselves at the expense of the broader society. The drive to maximize short-term profits often tends to outweigh concerns about the possible long-term consequences for the entire economy. Calomiris and Haber (2014) document that political interests interacting with special interests have been a major factor contributing to the creation of fragile financial systems.

There are grounds for hope. For example, after the financial crisis of 1997–1998, a number of Asian countries undertook reforms to improve the regulation and supervision of their financial systems as well as reduce political cronyism in the lending process. There are many lessons that we should have gleaned from the Asian experience. Unfortunately, however, many of these went largely ignored by financial actors and government regulators in Western industrial economies.

Will the painful experience of the global financial crisis be enough to inspire similar kinds of learning among policymakers within the advanced economies? To date, the evidence is mixed. Although there is some evidence that views are beginning to change in positive directions, there is still a long way to go. Many experts believe that the revisions in financial regulations since the crisis have been far from sufficient to ensure safety and soundness of our financial system. To what extent further developments will ultimately translate into genuine, and much needed, transformations of the financial sector will remain an open question for some time to come.

Notes

1. AIG lost nearly $100 billion in 2008 related to the crisis. More than $30 billion of this loss was is in credit default swaps. The Federal Reserve Bank of New York was compelled to extend an $85 billion loan to keep the fledgling insurance giant from collapsing. Credit default swaps are the most common form of credit derivative contracts designed to insure against risk associated with a variety of debt securities, including municipal, corporate, and market bonds, as well as mortgage-backed securities. Credit default swaps are insurance contacts that are issued to protect lower rated securities against potential future defaults.
2. For further discussion of the role of faulty mental models in contributing to the crisis, see Willett (2012).
3. This is also true of those who engage in shared teaching and learning environments (see Oestmann and Oestmann, 2011).
4. The IMF's position on neoliberalism introduced here is highly nuanced. It specifically relates to the reconsideration of the view that countries should universally embrace the liberalization of capital controls in all circumstances. The IMF's reconsidered position does not involve a wholesale rejection of neoliberalism, the basic tenets of free markets, or the doctrine of capitalism more generally.

REFERENCES

Ackoff, R., and S. Rovin. 2003. *Redesigning Society*. Stanford, CA: Stanford University Press.

Admati, A. R., and M. F. Hellwig. 2013. *The Bankers' New Clothes*. Princeton, NJ: Princeton University Press.

Blyth, M. 2013. *Austerity: The History of a Dangerous Idea*. New York: Oxford University Press.

Box, G., and N. Draper. 1987. *Empirical Model-Building and Response Surfaces*. New York: Wiley.

Calomiris, C., and S. Haber. 2014. *Fragile by Design*. Princeton, NJ: Princeton University Press.

Cerny, P. 2008. "Embedding Neoliberalism: The Evolution of a Hegemonic Paradigm." *Journal of International Trade and Diplomacy* 2(1): 1–46.

Deming, W. E. 2000. *The New Economics for Industry, Government, Education*. 2nd ed. Cambridge, MA: MIT Press. (Original work published 1994)

Denzau, A. T., and D. C. North. 1994. "Shared Mental Models: Ideologies and Institutions." *Kyklos* 47: 3–31.

Hayek, F. A. 1945. "The Use of Knowledge in Society." *American Economic Review* 35(4): 519–530.

Helleiner, E. 1994. "The World of Money: The Political Economy of International Capital Mobility." *Policy Sciences* 27: 295–298.

Kay, J. 2015. *Other People's Money: The Real Business of Finance*. New York: PublicAffairs.

King, M. 2016. *The End of Alchemy: Money, Banking, and the Future of the Global Economy*. New York: Norton.

Oestmann, E., and J. Oestmann. 2011. "Assessment of Learning and Evaluation Strategies." In *Innovative Teaching Strategies in Nursing and Related Health Professions*, edited by M. J. Bradshaw and A. Lowenstein, pp. 531–562. Burlington, MA: Jones & Bartlett.

Ostry, J., P. Loungani, and D. Furceri. 2016. "Neoliberalism: Oversold?" *Finance & Development* 53 (2). http://www.imf.org/external/pubs/ft/fandd/2016/06/ostry.htm#author. Accessed November 11, 2016.

Polanyi, M. 2009. *The Tacit Dimension*. Chicago: University of Chicago Press. 2009 (Original work published 1966)

Roy, R. K., A. T. Denzau, and T. D. Willett, eds. 2007. *Neoliberalism: National and Regional Experiments with Global Ideas*. London: Routledge.

Roy, R. K., and T. D. Willett. 2014. "Market Volatility and the Risks of Global Integration." In *The Sage Handbook of Globalization*, edited by M. B. Steger, P. Battersby, and J. M. Siracusa, 283–2981088. Thousand Oaks, CA: Sage.

Steger, M. B., and R. K. Roy. 2010. *Neoliberalism: A Very Short Introduction*. Oxford, UK: Oxford University Press.

Tett, G. 2015. *The Silo Effect: The Peril of Expertise and the Promise of Breaking Down Barriers*. New York: Simon & Schuster.

Turner, A. 2016. *Between debt and the devil*. Princeton, NJ: Princeton University Press.

Willett, T. D. 2012. "The Role of Defective Mental Models in Generating the Global Financial Crisis." *Journal of Financial Economic Policy* 4 (1): 41–57.

Willett, T. D., and N. Srisorn. 2014. "The Political Economy of the Euro Crisis: Cognitive Biases, Faulty Mental Models, and Time Inconsistency." *Journal of Economics and Business* 76: 39–54.

World Bank Group. 2015. *World Development Report 2015: Mind, Society, and Behavior*. Washington, DC: World Bank. https://openknowledge.worldbank.org/handle/10986/20597. Accessed January 24, 2016.

CHAPTER 18

....

LABOR

....

RICHARD P. APPELBAUM

BUILDING fires, explosions, and collapses—not to mention health, safety, and wage and hour violations—are endemic features of factory production throughout the world. They provide a window into much that is problematic of global supply chains, and they show why the study of labor conditions is such an important aspect of understanding how the global economy works.

In China, for example, labor protests have beset Foxconn (also known as Hon Hai Precision Industry Company), the world's largest contract electronics manufacturer. It is a giant Taiwanese firm that reportedly employs 1.3 million workers worldwide. Its factories are assemblers of choice for consumer electronics: iPhones and iPads, Dell computers, Kindles, Play Stations, and Xboxes are among the products whose component parts are assembled at Foxconn for shipping to retail outlets throughout the world.

Between 2010 and 2013, 22 young workers at "Foxconn City"—a giant complex that at the time housed nearly a half million workers in the southern Chinese city of Shenzhen—committed suicide; most jumped to their deaths from the upper floors of the factory. The Foxconn workers took their lives because they were despondent about harsh working conditions, long hours, mandatory overtime to meet production deadlines, and home sickness: Chinese factory workers are among the hundreds of millions of migrants from impoverished regions in western China who have made their way to China's eastern provinces, where they find work in the export-oriented industries that have spearheaded China's meteoric rise as a world economic powerhouse. Foxconn's response to the suicides was initially to install nets below the upper stories of the factory, in order to catch would-be suicides, and compel new workers to sign an anti-suicide pledge. When labor rights activists at a tiny Hong Kong nonprofit (Students and Scholars Against Corporate Misbehavior) exposed this response to Foxconn's working conditions, it went viral in news media throughout the world—a public relations disaster for Apple, a company whose success is closely tied to its positive public image (Heffernan 2013). Apple responded by joining the Fair Labor Association (FLA), a US-based nongovernmental organization (NGO) composed at the time of apparel companies seeking to address working conditions in their supply chains. The FLA launched an investigation into working conditions in the Foxconn factory. Foxconn raised wages in its Shenzhen Longhua factory and moved much of its production to China's interior, where wages were lower and labor rights organizations less active (Chan, Ngai, and Selden 2016a). More recently, Foxconn has addressed its problems with suicidal and increasingly militant workers by replacing workers with robots. As of 2016, Foxconn had introduced approximately 60,000 robots into one of its factories, cutting the factory work-force in half, with plans to replace nearly one-third of its workers by 2020 (TCP 2015; Hsu 2016; Wakefield 2016).

In Bangladesh on April 24, 2013, a multistory building collapsed in the Savar indus-trial district of Dhaka, the capital of the country. The collapse of the Rana Plaza industrial building, which housed factories producing apparel for many leading brands, claimed 1,138 lives when the seven stories illegally added to the original two stories pancaked; thousands more were injured. When cracks first appeared the previous day, the businesses on the first floor closed their doors. But the factory workers in the upper stories were ordered to go back to work by the factory owners, who threatened them with loss of pay; Mr. Rana him-self assured them the building would be standing for 100 years. One hour later, the building collapsed.

These two tragedies—one in a rapidly emerging economic power and the other in an impoverished Third World country—reveal a great deal about the challenges faced by labor in today's far-flung system of global production.

THE CHANGING WORLD ECONOMY: CHALLENGES FOR LABOR

Outsourcing—a term used interchangeably with *subcontracting*—involves a firm's use of an external vendor to provide a business function that would otherwise be done by the firm itself (Appelbaum 2012). Although outsourcing is not new, it has become increasingly global since the early 1970s. Firms from the Global North have outsourced many of their manufacturing and service operations to lower wage countries throughout the world. This has been facilitated by advances in information technology, which has made it possible for a central firm (a brand or a retailer) to coordinate suppliers of its goods and services globally, and by containerization coupled with intermodal transport systems, which enable goods to be quickly and efficiently transported by sea and land. Activities ranging from low-cost manufacturing to high-end research and development, from financial services to logistics, can be thought of as links in a chain. They are variously described as comprising supply chains, commodity chains, global value chains, or global production networks.

Labor historian Nelson Lichtenstein has contrasted firm structure in the twentieth cen-tury with that of the twenty-first century as the difference between General Motors and Walmart (Lichtenstein 2005; see also Appelbaum and Lichtenstein 2006). During the twen-tieth century, at least in the industrial North, the paradigmatic firm was General Motors—a giant corporation that designed, manufactured, and marketed trucks and automobiles. General Motors was vertically organized, relatively bureaucratic, and inflexible. Although not all work was done in house, much of the principal manufacturing was done by General Motors itself: Hundreds of thousands of workers, working in General Motors factories, produced vehicles that General Motors designed and sold through its franchised outlets. General Motors workers were unionized and protected by US labor law. They were legally allowed to engage in collective bargaining and engage in strikes if their efforts to get what they regarded as their fair share of GM revenues were unsuccessful. Workers might have believed that the laws were stacked against them, and businesses might have claimed that the laws were stifling and impeded their ability to innovate and grow, but from the end of World War II through the early 1970s, this system contributed to the growth of a blue-collar middle class in the United States. Similar systems existed in Europe and other advanced industrial economies, whose parliamentary systems—which often resulted in politically strong pro-labor parties—empowered workers to a greater degree than was the case in the United States.

Giant retailers such as Walmart, in contrast, characterize the twenty-first century. Unlike General Motors, retailers do not themselves manufacture anything. Rather, they carry thousands of brands, from cheap clothing to high-end electronics. These brands, in turn, also do not manufacture anything. Rather, they design products, create image identification, and market that image: The actual manufacturing is done through extensive global networks of independently owned contract factories. This system of independent contracting, achieved by means of global supply chains, has completely changed the dynamic of labor–capital relations in the world today. A company such as Apple, for example, will outsource the hundreds of components that go into its computers or smartphones from numerous factories in many countries. Those components are then assembled in giant factories (e.g., the Foxconn factory) and then shipped to retail outlets throughout the world. The workers who make the goods and provide the services are employed by the contract factories, not the brands and retailers. This system is celebrated by business as providing flexibility: Companies can pick and choose factories based on anticipated needs, taking into account differences in labor costs, regulations, the cost of shipping, and other logistics. Such global outsourcing historically has involved networks of many small suppliers, although there now appears to be some consolidation of suppliers into a smaller number of large, powerful East Asian firms that are better equipped to work with the larger orders placed by major brands and retailers (Appelbaum 2008, 2009a, 2011; Appelbaum and Lichtenstein 2006, 2016). Nike, Adidas, Asics, Reebok, and every major athletic shoe brand place their orders with a Pou Chen factory, which reportedly accounts for one out of every six branded athletic shoes sold in the world today; every major electronics brand sources from the Taiwanese giant Foxconn. The emergence of giant transnational contractors—many of them Taiwanese or Chinese— is a relatively recent phenomenon, and it may eventually prove to be a counterweight to the power of the brands and retailers that hire them. As such giant contractors engage in upgrading and knowledge acquisition, they may also develop their own brands, becoming competitors with the companies they currently supply. But whether this will result in better working conditions is far from certain.

This global production system has significant implications for labor–capital relations. Brands and retailers are no longer legally responsible for working conditions (although they are responsible for product quality). It encourages brands and retailers to seek out the lowest cost factories with the weakest environmental enforcement. Bangladesh's history of factory fires and building collapses has not discouraged apparel manufactures from relocating there, as wages in China have gone up. This system significantly weakens workers' power: If they try to form unions or strike for higher wages, the brands and retailers can simply move their production to another factory or another country. There is no global enforcement mechanism analogous to the national enforcement that protected twentieth-century industrial workers in Europe and the United States: That is, national labor governance has yet to be replaced by a system of global labor governance. If an impoverished, low-wage country decides to crack down on factory violations and significantly raise wages, businesses will just look elsewhere—there remain many low-cost options throughout the world. Production may be global, but any realistic enforcement remains local—an asymmetry that greatly disadvantages and disempowers labor.

Sociologist Jill Esbenshade (2004) has described this shift from production as the shift from the social contract to a social accountability contract. Under the twentieth-century social contract that governed labor–capital relations in the advanced industrial world, there were three components: capital, labor, and the state. Big capital confronted big labor—two countervailing powers (Galbraith 1952)—with the state as maker and enforcer of rules. This tripartite system is currently enshrined in the organizational mandate of the United Nations' International Labour Organization (ILO), which has proven to be a weak and ineffectual system of global governance (discussed later). In contrast, under the twenty-first-century social accountability contract, the three principal actors are the brand or retailer, the contract factory, and the firms that are hired by the brands or retailers to monitor their contract factories. It is significant that two of the three key actors in the social contract system are missing: labor and the state. Workers, through their unions, no longer negotiate directly with the firms that employ them. Labor has no voice in this arrangement; indeed, effective unions are all but non-existent, the result of anti-union policies and outright repression. As for the state, in the developing countries in which the supply chains touch down, governments seldom, if ever, enforce whatever rules may exist.

Anti-Sweatshop Activism, Private Enforcement, and Reputation Management

Beginning in the 1990s, well-publicized revelations of labor abuses in Asian contract factories tarnished the images of major US brands such as Nike, Gap, and Walmart's Kathie Lee line (Appelbaum 2016). Anti-sweatshop campaigns put additional pressure on these companies to address the problems that were proving to be the norm rather than the exception. The emergence of firms that publicly express a commitment to behave in socially responsible ways is the direct result of revelations about corporate abuses, worker strikes, and activist campaigns that began in the 1990s and continue to the present.

Nike was the first major firm to garner worldwide media attention for abuses throughout its supply chain when in August 1992, *Harper's Magazine* published an article featuring a young Indonesian woman who worked 10 hours a day, six days a week, making Nike athletic shoes for 14 cents an hour. At this rate of pay, she would have needed to work for a full month in order to purchase the shoes she made—or 44,000 years to earn as much as basketball superstar Michael Jordan's $20 million endorsement. Human Rights Watch and the International Labor Rights Research and Education Fund filed a complaint with the US Trade Representative. Well-publicized strikes generated additional bad public relations for Nike (Ballinger 2016), which responded by adopting its first code of conduct. Nike's code prohibited forced labor, set minimum age and maximum hour requirements, and required compliance with local health and safety standards (Heuer and Ronkainen n.d.). Anti-Nike protests nonetheless spread throughout the United States and Europe. In the United States, students demonstrated against Nike's university links at Penn State University, Florida State University, the University of Illinois, the University of North Carolina, the University of Colorado, and the University of Michigan (Ballinger 2016). Nike then established a department responsible for addressing workplace issues in its contract factories, and it played a key role in the creation of the FLA, an NGO charged with overseeing labor practices in its members' garment and footwear factories.

In August 1995, it was discovered that 72 mostly female workers from Thailand were working as virtual slaves, some for as long as seven years, in a Los Angeles area factory surrounded by barbed wire. The women were sewing clothing for Montgomery Ward, Mervyns, BUM International, and LF Sportswear. The highly publicized "El Monte slave shop"—named for the Los Angeles working-class suburb where the women were kept in captivity—revealed that sweatshops were not limited to impoverished developing countries (Appelbaum 2009b; Bonacich and Appelbaum 2000; Miller 1997).

During the past three decades, a growing number of businesses have emphasized the importance of ethical environmental and labor practices. In 1970, codes of conduct setting labor and environmental standards were nearly non-existent; today, nearly 9 out of 10 *Fortune* Global 200 corporations have codes. All business schools now offer curricula centered on ethical business practices, and most major corporations often have a division devoted to implementing their codes of conduct. These efforts are variously termed corporate social responsibility, sustainability, and achieving a "triple bottom line," which ideally assigns equal value to profits, planet, and people. Whatever the effectiveness of this approach, successful or not, it has proven to be good public relations because it reassures customers that their purchases are not harming workers or despoiling the planet. Codes are typically adopted for a variety of reasons, including compliance with legal requirements, creating a shared company culture around ethical practices, and burnishing the corporate reputation (KPMG 2008: 3–4).

Numerous NGOs and for-profit businesses have been created to implement codes of conduct. NGOs typically provide oversight through developing model codes, offering training sessions, and accrediting the factory inspection companies (often for-profit firms) that do the actual auditing and compliance certification. Brands and retailers hire factory inspection companies to monitor their contract factories and report back any violations. Significantly, these reports are seldom made public: They are internal documents only, intended as a self-correcting mechanism, and outside of public scrutiny. The workers in the factories that are being monitored are seldom made aware of the findings, even though they are the ones most directly affected by any significant abuses.

If the triple bottom line is thought of as a three-legged stool, it is clear that the profit leg is necessarily the sturdiest: Corporations are under a legal responsibility to return value to their shareholders, and failure to do so can be harshly rewarded, particularly in publicly traded firms. Sustainable environmental practices can sometimes provide a second, fairly strong leg for the stool: Although a genuine ethical concern about doing environmental damage in some cases may be a motivating factor, businesses recognize that ecologically sustainable practices can open up new market opportunities. Conversely, doing ecological damage can be bad public relations, particularly in industries in which customers are likely to be environmentally conscious. Environmental efficiency can also cut costs, contributing to the profit leg of the stool. Walmart, to take the most prominent example, in 2005 launched its Carbon Disclosure Project, a well-publicized environmental campaign that would be good for both planet and profits: Walmart used the non-profit CDP (2016) to track, reduce, and publicly report its carbon footprint, thereby cutting energy costs across its global supply chain (Walmart 2016a, 2016b). Although this campaign has been criticized by some as a cynical "greenwashing" effort to improve public relations while lacking any positive environmental impact (Mitchell 2013), at least in this area, it is possible that a firm's economic and social objectives can coincide: Ecologically sustainable products now command a large market, and cost-cutting based on any criteria is essential to efficient supply chain management.

The third leg of the stool, social responsibility, is by far the least developed, and it is the first to go when competitive pressures are strong. Fair and reasonable wages and hours, strong enforced health and safety regulations, and the right to freedom of association are all weak or absent in contract factories throughout the world. NGOs have become highly active in this area—some working with corporations to provide a variety of monitoring services for purposes of self-enforcement and others as independent monitors (or, more often, industry watchdogs) that are highly critical of the corporate ability to self-regulate. Examples of the former include Global Social Compliance, Veritas, and PwC, a separate legal entity of PricewaterhouseCoopers International. Examples of the latter are numerous and include the Worker Rights Consortium (WRC), the FLA, the Maquila Solidarity Network, and the International Labor Rights Forum.

THE FAILURE OF SELF-REGULATION

Corporate social responsibility and its associated monitoring systems set aspirational standards and sometimes may result in improved working and environmental conditions. Yet overall, the system under which firms regulate their own supply chains has not proven effective. Despite the ubiquity of this approach, significant abuses continue. The flaws in self-monitoring were revealed in the early days of this approach: The El Monte "slave shop," discussed previously, was sewing garments for firms that were part of the Compliance Alliance, an organization of leading Los Angeles brands committed to monitoring their factories in the regional supply chain. Although orders may have originally been placed in monitored factories, they were quickly passed through to El Monte, a fact that somehow escaped the monitoring organizations.

Two decades later, under far more elaborate systems of self-monitoring, Bangladesh has been plagued by fires and building collapses that have claimed thousands of lives. All the major disasters that have occurred in Bangladesh's garment factories in recent years have occurred at those that were used by major brands and that had been repeatedly subjected to labor rights audits conducted for these same buyers. One study found that between 1990 and 2012, more than 1,000 people had died in Bangladesh factory fires. The same study undertook a detailed examination of six high-mortality incidents that had occurred since 2000, including the Rana Plaza collapse. In all of these cases, the major European and North American brands that were using the factories had codes of conduct with specific labor, health, and safety standards. All of the factories had recently been audited for compliance; none were found to have violations that might result in loss of life or serious injury. None of the audits were made available to the workers or the wider public (Ross 2016). Significantly, factory audits almost always lack transparency: They are internal reports to the brand or retailer, not public documents. Workers have no knowledge of the results of audits, even when the findings have clear implications for their health and safety. Nor do consumers have access to potentially embarrassing information that might spur the firms to action.

How could factory disasters claiming thousands of lives, and injuring thousands of others, have occurred in recently audited factories producing apparel for some of the world's largest brands and retailers, all of which profess socially responsible practices and claim to routinely monitor their contract factories to ensure compliance? One reason is that the factories in a firm's supply chain are often numerous and globally dispersed, often involving multiple levels of subcontracting through which contracted factories outsource some of their production to other factories. Because supply chains often consist of thousands of factories, only a small percentage can ever be inspected; a particular factory that is part of an auditing program is likely to be inspected only once every few years. Although it is difficult to know exactly how many factories are audited each year, one estimate is approximately 50,000 factories employing millions of workers. Walmart alone accounts for approximately 11,500 inspections (Clifford and Greenhouse 2013).

When audits are conducted, they are often superficial; auditors may be poorly trained, visits may be brief, and serious health and safety violations may go undetected because auditors may lack adequate training to detect hazardous chemical or electrical problems (O'Rourke 2000, 2003). In the case of Bangladesh, auditors were not adequately trained in terms of fire safety requirements or structural defects that might result in building collapse. Audits are seldom unannounced; they are typically planned well in advance, giving factory owners time to unlock fire exits or remove piles of clothing or equipment that may be blocking them; prepare a set of books that hide wage and hour violations; and warn workers that reporting violations could result in a loss of orders and, as a result, their jobs. Workers are often interviewed in the factory, leading to possible reprisals by management if they are seen as complaining. The monitoring firms themselves may have an interest in downplaying violations because reporting too many to the brand or retailer that hired them may entail costly corrective measures—a result that might be avoided in the future by hiring a less stringent auditor.

INTERNATIONAL EFFORTS AT REGULATION

Although some international governmental organizations seek to raise labor standards, they are mainly aspirational and operationally ineffective. In this section, two examples are discussed: the ILO and the United Nations (UN) Global Compact.[1]

The ILO is a UN agency, although its origins date back to the Versailles Treaty that ended World War I. It was conceived of as a tripartite international agency that involved shared power between representatives of government, employers, and workers. This was a unique form of international organization, in which organized labor played a leadership role as one of the key founders. Samuel Gompers, head of the American Federation of Labor, chaired the 1919 Labor Commission—composed of representatives from nine countries—that was responsible for drafting the ILO's constitution (ILO 2015a).

After the UN was created in 1945, the ILO became its first specialized agency the following year; it remains the only UN agency with such a tripartite organizational structure. In 1977, the ILO adopted its so-called MNE Declaration (the Tripartite Declaration of Principles Concerning Multinational Enterprises and Social Policy), which, revised in 2006, recognizes that "the advances made by multinational enterprises in organizing their operations beyond the national framework may lead to abuse of concentrations of economic power and to conflicts with national policy objectives and with the interest of the workers" (ILO 2006). The MNE Declaration—which is entirely voluntary and non-enforceable—calls on all parties to obey local laws and regulations, promote secure and safe employment, eliminate discrimination, respect human rights, and in general follow ILO conventions on workers' rights.

During the course of the twentieth and twenty-first centuries, the ILO enacted approximately 190 conventions governing workers' rights. Many of these were unified in the ILO 1998 Declaration on Fundamental Principles and Rights at Work, which combined a number of these conventions into four overarching human rights principles, embodied in eight core conventions, that all member nations stated are required to respect: freedom of association and the right to collective bargaining, the elimination of all forms of forced labor, the abolition of child labor, and the elimination of discrimination with respect to employment (ILO 2015b). These four fundamental rights are contained in eight core ILO Conventions.[2] Like the MNE Declaration, ILO Conventions lack the force of law: Although they may provide aspirational standards, they lack enforcement mechanisms and so are seldom honored outside of Europe (the United States has signed only two of the ILO's eight core labor-standard conventions; China has adopted none). Moreover, the very structure of the ILO Conventions reflects the ILO's tripartite organization, in that they assume some degree of symmetrical labor–capital relation exists in the signatory countries, along with a state apparatus that is willing and capable of enforcement. Although this might have been the case during the heyday of nationally based industrial century capitalism in the twentieth century, at least in the Global North, its applicability in a twenty-first-century world of global supply chains is questionable. When production occurs in countries in which independent unions are at best weak (if they exist at all) and corrupt governments are unlikely to enforce labor standards, the tripartite structure provides a weak foundation on which to build workers' rights (Appelbaum 2016).

The UN officially affirmed the importance of labor rights in 2000 when it launched the UN Global Compact. It presents itself as "the world's largest corporate sustainability initiative. . . . A call to companies to align strategies and operations with universal principles on human rights, labour, environment and anti-corruption, and take actions that advance societal goals." As of 2016, it had been signed by more than 9,500 companies with nearly 60 million employees and also 3,000 "non-businesses" (e.g., universities, business associations, NGOs, labor unions, cities, foundations, and public sector organizations) in 168 countries, and it had issued nearly 42,000 public reports (UN Global Compact 2018a, 2018b). The Compact is composed largely of businesses that profess ethical standards, and although it provides a vehicle for sharing best practices, it relies entirely on self-reporting and explicitly lacks any enforcement mechanism. Its members pledge to "voluntarily align their operations and strategies with ten universally accepted principles in the areas of human rights, labor,[3] environment and anti-corruption" (UN Global Compact 2018a). It draws on the UN's 17 Sustainable Development Goals, adopted by the UN's 193 member states as "a path over the next 15 years to end extreme poverty, fight inequality and injustice, and protect our planet" (UN Global Compact, 2018c). Under its own charter, the Global Compact makes clear that it is "not a code of conduct" but instead offers "a policy framework for organizing and developing corporate sustainability strategies." It is not legally binding, nor is it "a substitute for existing regulatory approaches"; rather, it is "a purely voluntary initiative designed to promote innovation in relation to good corporate citizenship" (UN Global Compact 2018d). The Compact explicitly states that "it is not designed, nor does it have the mandate or resources, to monitor or measure participants' performance. . . . It is not now and does not aspire to become a compliance based initiative" (UN Global Compact 2018d). The UN Global Compact's (2013) *Global Corporate Sustainability Report 2013* reports that

> 77% of companies report having taken some action to define their workers' right to freely form and join trade unions, and 59% claim they have taken steps to actually implement collective bargaining, although these results are self-reported without being subject to independent verification.

It is difficult to avoid the conclusion that however well intentioned, the UN Global Compact's main effect is to provide its members with the public relations benefit of being a part of "the world's largest corporate sustainability initiative."

WORKERS' STRUGGLES FOR BASIC RIGHTS

China has experienced an upsurge in strikes in recent years as workers in manufacturing export industries have demanded higher pay, retirement contributions, severance when factories close, and better working conditions. China's growing worker militancy has taken the form of wildcat strikes, unsanctioned by the government-controlled All China Federation of Trade Unions (ACFTU). Recent examples (from 2014) include strikes at the giant Yue Yuen shoe factory in Dongguan, where more than 30,000 workers making athletic shoes for Nike and other leading brands went on strike for two weeks, demanding not only that Yue Yuen make good on its contributions to their retirement fund but also that their union be reorganized and empowered to engage in collective bargaining. Workers also went on strike at an IBM factory and a Walmart store (Mitchell and Jopson 2014; Quan 2016; Reuters 2014). Strikes in one locale often inspire a wave of strikes elsewhere, especially when met with police violence, resulting in hundreds (by some estimates thousands) of strikes in China in recent years (Quan 2016).[4] China's recent labor history suggests that even China's repressive environment, in which independent unions and worker control of local branches of the ACFTU are not tolerated, worker militancy has begun to make some inroads into the country's state-controlled labor unions (Chan, Ngai, and Selden 2016b; Quan 2016). Workers have become increasingly aware of the importance of collective representation, and they have gained important organizational experience (Chan,

Ngai, and Selden 2016b). The Chinese government enacted a contract labor law in 2008 that guarantees workers some basic rights (Wang et al. 2009), and it has raised worker wages in the coastal provinces where most factory production occurs.

China's actions were in response both to concern with stemming worker unrest and because China is in the process of transitioning from economic expansion driven by state-led infrastructure investment and the manufacture of low-cost exports to expansion resulting from a growing Chinese middle class that consumes Chinese-made products. This rebalancing of the Chinese economy requires middle-class spending power and hence calls for higher wages. To the extent that other countries transition from export-oriented industrialization to middle-class status, improved working conditions—and perhaps some degree of independent labor empowerment—may also result.

China may not yet be the new "epicenter of world labor unrest" as was once claimed (Silver and Zhang 2009). The Xi government has tightened its controls over the internet and social media, and it has significantly cracked down on pro-labor NGOs, filing criminal charges against prominent labor and other human rights activists (Palmer 2017; Wong 2016). Still, the growth of labor militancy suggests that successful direct action on the part of workers is not impossible, even in a global economy in which restive workers can result in capital flight: Advances in workers' rights have historically resulted from "labor upsurges" rather than from continuous, if slow, progress (Clawson 2003). In 1944, the economic historian Karl Polanyi (1944/2001) argued that free-market capitalism entails a "double movement": Capitalists move to disembed the economy from social control, which results in a movement on the part of those who are adversely affected to bring the economy back under control by fighting for such things as social welfare protections and trade unionism (i.e., re-embedding). Sociologist Beverly Silver (Silver 2003, 2005, 2013; Silver and Karatasli 2015) has analyzed capital flows and resulting labor actions since the end of the nineteenth century, and she concludes that "where capital goes, labour–capital conflict shortly follows" (Silver 2003: 50). Businesses may relocate their production throughout the world in search of lower labor and other costs (Polanyi's first movement), but this "spatial fix" to ensure profitability inevitably mobilizes workers (the second movement). This strategy, Silver acknowledges, is most effective during the innovative phase of an industry, when competition is low and profits are high. In industries in which the work has become highly standardized and therefore competitive—which is to say most of the manufacturing being done in the world today—firms will be more resistant to granting concessions to militant workers (and may instead find it more profitable to replace workers with robots).

In industries in which there has been a consolidation of production—where major brands and retailers are sourcing their production from a small number of large manufacturers—workers' actions may prove successful, even when production is fairly standardized. In the case of both Nike (which sources much of its products from giant Pou Chen factories) and Apple (whose products are assembled in giant Foxconn factories), such consolidation has provided an opportunity for workers to engage in militant actions that have significantly disrupted supply chains. To the extent that giant contract factories account for a significant portion of their clients' products, worker action directed against the factories and their logistics operations can have a highly disruptive impact, particularly where just-in-time delivery is key to success (Appelbaum 2008, 2009a, 2011; Appelbaum and Lichtenstein 2006; Silver 2003, 2013).

Steps Forward: Achieving Workers' Rights in the Global Economy

Despite the many problems with the current system of corporate self-regulation and largely aspirational international standards, codes of conduct nonetheless set a public standard to which firms can be held accountable—a pathway to the "naming and shaming" that has resulted in some victories for anti-sweatshop activists. For example, in 2011, the Korean owner of PT Kizone, an Indonesian sportswear factory, stopped paying wages to the factory's 2,800 workers and fled Indonesia. The factory eventually went bankrupt and closed its doors. Under Indonesian law, the workers—many of whom had been earning only 60 cents an hour—were entitled to severance pay totaling $3.4 million, amounting to roughly a year's base income for each worker. Because the owner had absconded with the factory's revenues and could not be located, the brands that were using the factory were the only possible source of compensation: They had received product from the factory and had the funds to do so. Because the factory was an independent contractor, however, the brands were under no legal obligation to pay the severance. Nonetheless, Green Textile—the buying agent for Nike, adidas, and the Dallas Cowboys (the three brands using the factory)—eventually agreed to pay $1 million, and Nike contributed another $521,000. Adidas initially refused to contribute, but under pressure from colleges and universities that threatened to sever their adidas contracts, the company also contributed a reportedly significant (but undisclosed) amount (Hermanson 2016).

This example highlights two factors that, working together, provide one way forward for achieving worker's rights: strong national laws and activist "naming and shaming" pressures (especially when combined with economic sanctions). Indonesia had strong laws on the books, providing a legal basis for compensating the workers for their lost jobs. Even in a global production system, labor-friendly national laws can still provide a basis for enforcement. The Indonesian government worked closely with unions and activist NGOs to estimate the total severance that was legally owed Kizone workers. In addition, enormous public relations pressure was put on the brands that were using the factory at the time it closed. Nike and adidas goods were being sold under licensing arrangements with approximately 200 colleges and universities throughout the United States—educational institutions that belonged to the WRC, a Washington, DC-based NGO charged with enforcing its members' codes of conduct. University codes of conduct require that all products that include the university name, likeness, or logo, such as T-shirts, hoodies, or caps, are made under safe and decent workings condition. They also typically require that the brands operating under university licensing arrangements fully disclose the names and addresses of all factories throughout the manufacturing supply chain, ensure that their contract factories pay a living wage and permit their workers to form unions and engage in collective bargaining, and in general comply with ILO labor standards.

Although the motives for Green Textile and Nike agreeing to pay a combined total of $1.5 million are not clear, it seems likely that Nike put pressure on Green Textile to do so: Nike itself had recently been under criticism from universities for its initial failure to pay severance to workers at its Honduran contract factories Hugger and Vision Tex, but under university, labor union, and NGO pressure, it eventually agreed to provide $1.5 million in relief to the workers (for a full discussion, see WRC 2007; see also CSR 2010). Adidas eventually agreed to contribute to the workers' severance after a nationwide "badidas" campaign by United Students Against Sweatshops led 17 colleges and universities to cancel their contracts with the company (Anner, Bair, and Blasi 2013).[5] The Kizone example suggests that under some circumstances, firms are willing to assume some liability for workers' rights violations that occur in their independently owned contract factories.

The notion of joint or shared liability—the idea that firms could be held legally responsible for working conditions in the factories they hire—has been strongly resisted by brands and retailers. Nonetheless, in the aftermath of the Rana Plaza collapse, a major step forward was taken in this direction. A coalition of unions and workers' rights NGOs from different countries joined together and crafted the Accord on Fire and Building Safety in Bangladesh, a legally enforceable contract between corporations and unions that requires Bangladesh factories to be made safe. The brands and retailers are responsible for securing the funds that will be required to cover the cost of upgrading their factories; it is estimated that the total cost of meeting existing safety standards may exceed $1 billion. The Accord identifies various sources available to brands and retailers, including joint investments, providing loans, or offering business incentives to their factories. Contributions from governments and donors have also been obtained. As a last resort, however, the brands and retailers must cover the costs of renovations themselves. The signatories to the Accord also agree not to "cut and run"—leave Bangladesh to avoid the potential logistical and economic costs—until the process is successfully completed (Nova and Wegemer 2016).

Although the Accord covers only fire and building safety concerns (it does not touch on wage and hour issues), it is nonetheless an important step forward. It covers more than 1,600 factories and more than 2 million workers, accounting for half of all apparel production in Bangladesh, and it is administered by a committee that includes equal representation by workers and brands and also an ILO representative (Nova and Wegemer 2016). As of April 2018, it had been signed by more than 200 apparel brands, retailers, and importers from more than 20 countries in Europe, North America, Asia, and Australia; two global trade unions; and eight Bangladesh trade unions and four NGO witnesses. A total of 1,620 factories had been inspected for fire, electrical, and structural safety, identifying more than 134,000 violations, of which nearly three-fourths had been corrected; however, the most serious (and costly) violations remained to be addressed (Accord, 2018a, 2018b).[6]

The accord sets a precedent in that its commitments, including potential financial obligations, are binding and legally enforceable. Disputes are to be settled through international arbitration, and decisions are legally enforceable in each brand's or retailer's home country. This approach to joint liability is, in fact, a century old because it was used in the so-called "jobbers agreements" between the retailer buyer ("jobber") and the International Ladies Garment Workers Union, which had gained power in New York City's garment factories in the early twentieth century (Anner, Bair, and Blasi 2013, 2016). What is unique is its global scope: If it proves to be a viable approach to securing the right of workers to a safe environment, it could become a model for more far-reaching agreements.

Another approach would be to mandate labor standards in trade agreements—so-called "social clauses" that require acceptable working conditions be certified before goods can be shipped across borders. The creation of the World Trade Organization (WTO) in 1994 spurred a debate over whether such clauses, which would have included labor and environmental standards, should be included in trade agreements (ILO 2015c). Although free trade proponents prevailed in terms of the rules governing the WTO, were its charter to be modified to permit such agreements, the leading apparel importing countries could level the playing field because their brands would be required to comply regardless of where they produced their products. Such agreements could incorporate ILO conventions, but they would be enforceable under the dispute resolution mechanism of the WTO, which enables countries that are found to have been the target of WTO rule violations to engage in retaliatory trade sanctions against the violator. Such a change in the WTO charter is currently not possible, given the free trade assumptions under which the WTO was created. But given the recent global rise of nationalism and related calls for economic deglobalization (Nixon 2016), the WTO's neoliberal policies may well come under challenge in the future.

GLOBAL LABOR STUDIES

A growing number of university programs and institutes focus on global labor studies. Although numerous US undergraduate and graduate programs address domestic labor concerns, some also address labor within the context of globalized production networks. A partial list of programs that go beyond individual global labor course offerings includes the Joseph S. Murphy Institute for Worker Education and Labor Studies at the CUNY School of Professional Studies, the School of Labor and Employment Relations at the University of Illinois, San Francisco State University, the Global Social Change and Development Program at Johns Hopkins University, and labor centers at four University of California campuses (Berkeley, UCLA, Santa Barbara, and Santa Cruz). There is a 10-year old Global Labour University (GLU) that draws on a global network of trade unions, and universities, as well as the ILO ("International Masters Programmes for Trade Unionists" 2017). It offers a master's degree for trade unionists through university courses at the University of Campinas in Brazil, the University of Kassel/Berlin School of Economics and Law in Germany, Jawaharlal Nehru University in India, the University of the Witwatersrand in South Africa, and Penn State University in the United States.

The *Global Labour Journal*, launched in 2010 as the official journal of the International Sociological Association's Research Committee on Labour Movements, is co-hosted by the GLU, in partnership with the International Center for Development and Decent Work in Kassel, Germany, and the Center for Global Workers' Rights at Penn State University (*Global Labour Journal* 2017). All business schools offer courses that touch on global labor issues as well, primarily in terms of supply chain management but also framed in terms of corporate social responsibility. As labor has become increasingly globalized, so too has the study of its challenges and prospects—both through the lens of standard business school CSR programs and through the lens of the workers themselves.

CONCLUSION

As Karl Marx recognized more than a century and a half ago, workers in factories can be a potent source for change. Even in China, where independent labor organizations are not allowed, worker unrest has led to strikes and sometimes violent demonstrations (Chan 2016; Quan 2016). Although achieving workers' rights in a globalized production system can be difficult, gains have been made.

Globalization is currently under fire. The rise of nationalist movements throughout the world—reflected in the emergence of strong nationalist leaders in such countries as Russia, India, Turkey, China, and, with the 2016 election, the United States—may result in a growth of protectionism and an effort to bring manufacturing jobs back to the high-wage countries of the Global North. If and when such manufacturing jobs return, however, they will likely not employ large numbers of high-wage workers. If giant manufacturers such as Foxconn are prepared to automate their Chinese factories in the face of rising labor costs and worker militancy, it seems unlikely that returning production to the United States or Europe will result in a revival of the twentieth-century General Motors model. The past three decades have seen high-wage US workers unsuccessfully compete for jobs with low-wage Chinese workers, and the coming decades will see workers in both countries compete with no-wage robots.

NOTES

1. For a more extensive discussion, see Appelbaum (2016), from which this section is adapted.
2. The eight core Conventions are freedom of association and protection of the right to organize (No. 87), right to organize and collective bargaining (No. 98), forced labor (No. 29), abolition of forced labor (No. 105), minimum age (No. 138), worst forms of child labor (No. 182), equal remuneration (No. 100), and discrimination (No. 111). As of September 2015, 138 countries had ratified all eight core Conventions. The United States has ratified only two: the Conventions on the abolition of forced labor (No. 105) and the worst forms of child labor (No. 182). Nineteen countries have ratified seven, 9 countries have ratified six, 8 countries have ratified five, 5 countries have ratified four, 1 country has ratified three, and 2 countries have ratified two. For a complete interactive list of ratifications, see ILO (2015c).
3. The four labor-related principles are the ILO's four Fundamental Principles and Rights at Work (freedom of association and the right to collective bargaining, and the elimination forced labor, child labor, and workplace discrimination).
4. The Chinese government stopped reporting "incidents" (not all of which were strikes) in approximately 2003, at which time there were approximately 60,000 incidents involving several million workers. In the same year, more than 800,000 cases were brought by workers for official labor arbitration (White 2007).
5. These included Cornell University; Oberlin College; the University of Washington; Brown University; Rutgers University; Georgetown University; the College of William & Mary; Santa Clara University; Penn State University; Northeastern University; the University of Montana; the University of Minnesota Twin Cities, Crookston, and Morris; Oregon State University; Temple University; and Washington State University (United Students Against Sweatshops 2013).
6. A second agreement, also negotiated in the aftermath of the Rana Plaza collapse, operates in parallel with the Accord: the Alliance for Bangladesh Worker Safety (http://www.bangladeshworkersafety.org). The Alliance, initiated by Gap and Walmart and

comprising 29 largely US-based brands and retailers, also calls for safety inspections and remedial actions. Unlike the Accord, however, there is no suggestion of possible financial obligation on the part of the signatories, and it is not legally binding; it therefore avoids the precedent of joint liability.

REFERENCES

Accord on Fire and Building Safety in Bangladesh. 2018a. "Progress." http://bangladeshaccord. org/progress.

Accord on Fire and Building Safety in Bangladesh. 2018b. "Quarterly Aggregate Report," May 8. http://bangladeshaccord.org/wp-content/uploads/Accord_Quarterly_Aggregate_ Report_April_2018.pdf.

Anner, Mark, Jennifer Bair, and Jeremy Blasi. 2013. "Towards Joint Liability in Global Supply Chains: Addressing the Root Causes of Labor Violations in International Subcontracting Networks." *Comparative Labor Law and Policy Journal* 35 (1): 1–43.

Anner, Mark, Jennifer Bair, and Jeremy Blasi. 2016. "Learning from the Past: The Relevance of Twentieth-Century New York Jobbers' Agreements for Twenty-First-Century Global Supply Chains." In *Achieving Workers' Rights in the Global Economy*, edited by Richard P. Appelbaum and Nelson Lichtenstein, 239–258. Ithaca, NY: Cornell University Press.

Appelbaum, Richard P. 2008. "Giant Transnational Contractors in East Asia: Emergent Trends in Global Supply Chains." *Competition and Change* 12 (1): 69–87.

Appelbaum, Richard P. 2009a. "Big Suppliers in Greater China: A Growing Counterweight to the Power of Giant Retailers." In *China and the Transformation of Global Capitalism*, edited by Ho-fung Hung, 65–85. Baltimore, MD: Johns Hopkins University Press.

Appelbaum, Richard P. 2009b. *Report of the Los Angeles Jewish Commission on Sweatshops*. Los Angeles, CA: American Jewish Congress and LAJCS (January).

Appelbaum, Richard P. 2011. "Transnational Contractors in East Asia." In *The Market Makers: How Retailers Are Reshaping the Global Economy*, edited by Gary Hamilton, Benjamin Senauer, and Misha Petrovic, 255–269. New York: Oxford University Press.

Appelbaum, Richard P. 2012. In *Encyclopedia of Global Studies*, edited by Helmut K. Anheier and Mark Juergensmeyer. Newbury Park, CA: Sage

Appelbaum, Richard P. 2016. "From Public Regulation to Private Enforcement: How CSR Became Managerial Orthodoxy." In *Achieving Workers' Rights in the Global Economy*, edited by Richard P. Appelbaum and Nelson Lichtenstein, 32–50. Ithaca, NY: Cornell University Press.

Appelbaum, Richard P., and Nelson Lichtenstein. 2006. "A New World of Retail Supremacy: Supply Chains and Workers' Chains in the Age of Wal-Mart." *International Labor and Working-Class History* 70 (Fall): 106–125.

Appelbaum, Richard P., and Nelson Lichtenstein. 2016. "Introduction." In *Achieving Workers' Rights in the Global Economy*, edited by Richard P. Appelbaum and Nelson Lichtenstein, 1–15. Ithaca, NY: Cornell University Press.

Ballinger, Jeffrey. 2016. "Nike Chronology." University of Washington Center for Communication and Civic Engagement. https://depts.washington.edu/ccce/polcommcampaigns/NikeChronology. htm.

Bonacich, Edna, and Richard P. Appelbaum. 2000. *Behind the Label: Inequality in the Los Angeles Apparel Industry*. Berkeley: University of California Press.

CDP. 2016. "Driving Sustainable Economies: About Us." https://www.cdp.net/en.

Chan, Jenny, Pun Ngai, and Mark Selden. 2016a. "Apple, Foxconn, and China's New Working Class." In *Achieving Workers' Rights in the Global Economy*, edited by Richard P. Appelbaum and Nelson Lichtenstein, 173–189. Ithaca, NY: Cornell University Press.

Chan, Jenny, Pun Ngai, and Mark Selden. 2016b. "Dying for an iPhone: The Lives of Chinese Workers." *China Dialogue*, April 14. https://www.chinadialogue.net/article/show/single/en/8826-Dying-for-an-iPhone-the-lives-of-Chinese-workers.

Clawson, Dan. 2003. *The Next Upsurge: Labor and the New Social Movements*. Ithaca, NY: Cornell University Press.

Clifford, S., and S. Greenhouse. 2013. "Fast and Flawed Inspections of Factories Abroad." *New York Times*, September 1. http://www.nytimes.com/2013/09/02/business/global/superficial-visits-and-trickery-undermine-foreign-factory-inspections.html.

CSR. 2010. "NIKE, Inc. and Central General de Trabajadores de Honduras (CGT) Statement." *CSR Wire*. http://www.csrwire.com/press_releases/30124-NIKE-Inc-and-Central-General-de-Trabajadores-de-Honduras-CGT-Statement.

Esbenshade, Jill. 2004. *Monitoring Sweatshops: Workers, Consumers, and the Global Apparel Industry*. Philadelphia, PA: Temple University Press.

Galbraith, John Kenneth. 1952. *American Capitalism*. New York: Houghton Mifflin.

Global Labour Journal. 2017. https://escarpmentpress.org/globallabour.

Heffernan, Margaret. 2013. "What Happened After the Foxconn Suicides." *CBS Money Watch*, August 7. https://www.cbsnews.com/news/what-happened-after-the-foxconn-suicides.

Hermanson, Jeff. 2016. "Workers of the World Unite: The Strategy of the International Union League for Brand Responsibility." In *Achieving Workers' Rights in the Global Economy*, edited by Richard P. Appelbaum and Nelson Lichtenstein, 259–274. Ithaca, NY: Cornell University Press.

Heuer, William H., and Ilkka A. Ronkainen. n.d. "Nike in Southeast Asia: Case Study." http://www.swlearning.com/marketing/czinkota/int_mkt_7e/cases/NikeInSEAsia.doc.

Hsu, Sara. 2016. "Foxconn: From Worker Suicides to Plastic Workers." *The Diplomat*, May 29. http://thediplomat.com/2016/05/foxconn-from-worker-suicides-to-plastic-workers.

International Labour Organization. 2006. "Tripartite Declaration of Principles Concerning Multinational Enterprises and Social Policy." http://www.ilo.org/dyn/normlex/en/f?p=1000:62:0::NO:62:P62_LIST_ENTRIE_ID:2453910:NO.

International Labour Organization. 2015a. "Origins and History." http://www.ilo.org/global/about-the-ilo/history/lang--en/index.htm.

International Labour Organization. 2015b. "The Text of the Declaration and Its Follow-Up." http://www.ilo.org/declaration/thedeclaration/textdeclaration/lang--en/index.htm.

International Labour Organization. 2015c. "Ratifications of Fundamental Protocols and Conventions by Country." http://www.ilo.org/dyn/normlex/en/f?p=1000:10011:0::NO:100 11:P10011_DISPLAY_BY,P10011_CONVENTION_TYPE_CODE:2,F.

"International Masters Programmes for Trade Unionists." 2017. The Global Labour University. http://www.global-labour-university.org.

KPMG. 2008. "Business Codes of the Global 200: Their Prevalence, Content, and Embedding." https://www.kpmg.com/CN/en/IssuesAndInsights/ArticlesPublications/Documents/business-codes-global-200-O-0804.pdf.

Lichtenstein, Nelson. 2005. *Wal-Mart: The Face of Twenty-First-Century Capitalism*. New York: New Press.

Miller, Michael. 1997. "Sweatshop Workers to Get $2 million." *Reuters*, October 23. http://www.hartford-hwp.com/archives/45b/132.html.

Mitchell, Stacy. 2013. *Walmart's Assault on the Climate*. Institute for Local Self-Reliance (November). http://www.ilsr.org/wp-content/uploads/2013/10/ILSR-_Report_WalmartClimateChange.pdf.

Mitchell, T., and B. Jopson. 2014. "Official China Union Raises Stakes in Walmart Closure Programme." *Financial Times*. https://www.ft.com/content/2038fd78-b262-11e3-b891-00144feabdco.

Nixon, Simon. 2016. "Risk of Deglobalization Hangs Over World Economy." *The Wall Street Journal*, October 5. http://www.wsj.com/articles/risk-of-deglobalization-hangs-over-world-economy-1475685469.

Nova, Scott, and Chris Wegemer. 2016. "Outsourcing Horror: Why Apparel Workers Are Still Dying, One Hundred Years After Triangle Shirtwaist." In *Achieving Workers' Rights in the Global Economy*, edited by Richard P. Appelbaum and Nelson Lichtenstein, 17–31. Ithaca, NY: Cornell University Press.

O'Rourke, Dara. 2000. "Monitoring the Monitors: A Critique of PriceWaterhouseCoopers (PWC) Labor Monitoring." Unpublished manuscript, Department of Geography, University of California, Berkeley. http://nature.berkeley.edu/orourke/PDF/pwc.pdf.

O'Rourke, Dara. 2003. "Outsourcing Regulation: Analyzing Nongovernmental Systems of Labor Standards and Monitoring." *Policy Studies Journal* 31 (1): 1–29. http://nature.berkeley.edu/orourke/PDF/OutSourcingReg-PSJ.pdf.

Palmer, Alex W. 2017. "'Flee at Once:' China's Besieged Human Rights Lawyers." *New York Times*, July 25. https://www.nytimes.com/2017/07/25/magazine/the-lonely-crusade-of-chinas-human-rights-lawyers.html.

Polanyi, Karl. 2001. *The Great Transformation*. Boston: Beacon Press. http://inctpped.ie.ufrj.br/spiderweb/pdf_4/Great_Transformation.pdf. (Original work published 1944)

Quan, Katie. 2016. "Labor Transformation in China: Voices from the Frontlines." In *Achieving Workers' Rights in the Global Economy*, edited by Richard P. Appelbaum and Nelson Lichtenstein, 190–208. Ithaca, NY: Cornell University Press.

Reuters. 2014. "IBM China Workers Strike over Terms in $2.3 Billion Lenovo Deal." *Reuters.com*, March 6. http://www.reuters.com/article/2014/03/06/us-china-ibm-strike-idUSBREA250ZB20140306.

Ross, Robert J. S. 2016. "The Twilight of CSR: Life and Death Illuminated by Fire." In *Achieving Workers' Rights in the Global Economy*, edited by Richard P. Appelbaum and Nelson Lichtenstein, 70–93. Ithaca, NY: Cornell University Press.

Silver, Beverly J. 2003. *Forces of Labor: Workers Movements and Globalization Since 1870*. New York: Cambridge University Press.

Silver, Beverly J. 2005. "Labor Upsurges: From Detroit to Ulsan and Beyond." *Critical Sociology* 31 (3): 439–451.

Silver, Beverly J. 2013. "Theorizing the Working Class in Twenty-First Century Global Capitalism." In *Workers and Labour in a Globalised Capitalism: Contemporary Themes and Theoretical Issues*, edited by Maurizio Atzeni, 46–69. London: Palgrave Macmillan.

Silver, Beverly J., and Sahan Savas Karatasli. 2015. "Historical Dynamics of Capitalism and Labor Movements." In *The Oxford Handbook of Social Movements*, edited by Donatella Della Porta and Mario Dani, 133–145. Oxford, UK: Oxford University Press.

Silver, Beverly J., and Lu Zhang. 2009. "China: Emerging Epicenter of World Labor Unrest." In *China and Global Capitalism*, edited by Ho-fung Hung, 174–187. Baltimore, MD: Johns Hopkins University Press.

TCP. 2015. "Hon Hai Aims to Replace 30% of Its Workforce with Robots." *China Post*, June 26. http://www.chinapost.com.tw/taiwan/national/national-news/2015/06/26/439236/Hon-Hai.htm.

United Nations Global Compact. 2013. *Global Corporate Sustainability Report 2013*. https://www.unglobalcompact.org/library/371.

United Nations Global Compact. 2018a. "Who We Are." https://www.unglobalcompact.org/what-is-gc.

United Nations Global Compact. 2018b. *Guide to Corporate Sustainability: Shaping a Sustainable Future*. https://www.unglobalcompact.org/library/1151.

United Nations Global Compact. 2018c. "The SDG's Explained for Business." https://www.unglobalcompact.org/sdgs/about.

United Nations Global Compact. 2018d. "About the UN Global Compact: Frequently Asked Questions." https://www.unglobalcompact.org/about/faq.

United Students Against Sweatshops. 2013. "VICTORY! 'Badidas' Campaign Forces Adidas to Respect Indonesian Garment Worker Rights." http://usas.org/tag/pt-kizone.

Wakefield, Jane. 2016. "Foxconn Replaces '60,000 Factory Workers with Robots.'" *BBC News*, May 25. http://www.bbc.com/news/technology-36376966.

Walmart. 2016a. "Reducing Energy Intensity and Emissions." *Walmart 2016 Global Responsibility Report*. http://corporate.walmart.com/2016grr/enhancing-sustainability/reducing-energy-intensity-and-emissions.

Walmart. 2016b. *Walmart 2016 Global Responsibility Report*. http://corporate.walmart.com/2016grr.

Wang, Haiyan, Richard Appelbaum, Francesca de Giuli, and Nelson Lichtenstein. 2009. "China's New Contract Labor Law: Is China Moving Towards Increased Power for Workers?" *Third World Quarterly* 30 (3): 485–501.

White, Chris. 2007. "China's New Labour Law: The Challenge of Regulating Employment Contracts." Evatt Foundation Papers. http://evatt.org.au/papers/chinas-new-labour-law.html.

Wong, Chun Han. 2016. "Chinese Labor Activists Handed Suspended Sentences." *The Wall Street Journal*, September 26. http://www.wsj.com/articles/chinese-labor-activists-handed-suspended-sentences-1474913153.

Worker Rights Consortium. 2007. "Hugger de Honduras and Vision Tex." http://www.workersrights.org/Freports/Hugger%20de%20Honduras%20and%20Vision%20Tex.asp.

CHAPTER 19

THE TRANSNATIONAL CAPITALIST CLASS

WILLIAM I. ROBINSON AND
JEB SPRAGUE

THE study of the capitalist class has always, in a sense, been linked to that of globalization, insofar as Karl Marx and Frederick Engels (1848), in *The Communist Manifesto*, originally formulated the rise of a capitalist class as part and parcel of the creation of a world market and the outward expansion of the capitalist system. But for most of the nineteenth and twentieth centuries, those who studied the capitalist class assumed it to be a national phenomenon, and their studies focused on its emergence and development within particular nation-states. It was not until the late 1960s that social scientists began to discuss the rise of an *international* capitalist class as the rise and spread of multinational corporations (MNCs) in that decade seemed to be supplanting the earlier understanding of national corporations that merely operated abroad.[1] Such a notion took off in the following decade, in particular, with the publication in 1974 of Barnet and Muller's landmark study, *Global Reach: The Power of the Multinational Corporation*. In it, they observed that internationally footloose MNCs had come to touch every aspect of daily life, establishing through their activities a new international corporate economy. The spread of MNCs had spawned what they called a new "international corporate elite."

Barnet and Muller's (1974) study unleashed an explosion of interest in and research on the new global economy, and it paved the way for what would later come to be referred to as globalization. They discussed the growth of MNCs and such phenomena associated with it as international outsourcing and the spread of export-processing plants, or *maquiladoras*, utilizing young and super-exploited female labor, that drew the attention of scholars, journalists, activists, and other observers in the 1970s and 1980s.[2] Globalization studies have since spanned cultural, social, and political processes and have drawn in scholars from across the social sciences, humanities, area and regional studies, and from emerging inter/multidisciplinary fields such as environmental studies, migration studies, communications, and gender studies. Books and articles on the topic are now countless. However, much of the early focus on globalization centered on the notion of an emerging globalized economy based on new transnational systems of production, finance, and consumption, as well as worldwide economic integration. Scholars who study capitalism and class, especially from the disciplines of sociology and international relations, began to discuss transnational class formation, predicated on the idea that the study of the capitalist class should be located within research on the rise of these new transnational systems and the process of capitalist globalization.

Between the 1974 release of *Global Reach* and Leslie Sklair's publication in 1995 of *Sociology of the Global System* (discussed later), a number of notable studies pushed the idea of a rising inter- or transnational bourgeoisie. Economist Stephen Hymer noted in 1979 that an

> international capitalist class is emerging whose interests lie in the world economy as a whole and a system of international private property which allows free movement of capital between countries. . . .There is a strong tendency for the most powerful segments of the capitalist class increasingly to see their future in the further growth of the world market rather than its curtailment. (p. 262)

Dutch political economist Kees Van der Pijl (1984, 1989, 1998) analyzed the fractionation of capital along functional lines in the post-World War II period in advanced capitalist countries. Van der Pijl pointed to transnational class formation and the internationalization of different capitalist groups and their political projects as a consequence of the transnational expansion of capital. He developed the idea of an internationally class-conscious bourgeoisie and a "comprehensive concept of [capitalist class] control" at the international level. For their part, scholars from the "Italian school" in international relations—so-called because it has applied the theories of the early twentieth-century Italian Marxist, Antonio Gramsci, to the study of international relations—have theorized a global social formation beyond the logic of the nation-state (Cox 1987; Gill 1990). Robert Cox, one of the lead figures in this school, pointed to "an emergent global class structure" and an "international managerial elite" at its apex (Cox 1987: 271), whereas Stephen Gill identified a "developing transnational capitalist class fraction" (Gill, 1990).

It was Sklair, however, who pioneered the idea of a transnational capitalist class (TCC) in his 1995 book, *Theory of the Global System*, followed by his full-blown study in 2000 on the topic, appropriately titled *The Transnational Capitalist Class*. In that same year, sociologist William I. Robinson together with Jerry Harris published their seminal paper, "Towards a Global Ruling Class? Globalization and the Transnational Capitalist Class" (see also Robinson 1996, 2001), followed in 2004 by Robinson's *A Theory of Global Capitalism*. In subsequent years, Sklair and Robinson, both sociologists and scholars of globalization, have been seen as the leading proponents of the theory of a TCC who set the stage for this emerging subfield in globalization studies, and they have also been at the center of heated debates on the concept. Although Sklair and Robinson have distinct interpretations of the TCC, as we discuss later, what sets their theoretical work on the topic apart from the earlier research on an international capitalist class, and from critics of the concept, is their insistence on the *trans*national, rather than *inter*national, nature of the TCC, as a class group grounded in a global system as something beyond the international system of nation-states. In this regard, Sklair's "global system theory" and Robinson's "theory of global capitalism" broke with conventional Marxist analyses of classes and of national capitalism as well as with the world-system approach pioneered by sociologist Immanuel Wallerstein (2012), both of which take as their starting point a conception of capitalism organized through national economies and national capitalist classes interacting in an international system of states.

In what follows, we first summarize the early (or original) theoretical constructs of the TCC put forth by both Sklair and Robinson. This is followed by a review of more recent research on the TCC. Finally, we discuss some of the major debates regarding the concept and the objections put forth by critics. Given the natural limits to this chapter, we can only touch on some of the wide-ranging research that has appeared in recent years. As a caveat, we can do no more than tangentially reference the broader processes of economic globalization and transnational class formation that encase our more specific focus on the TCC.

SKLAIR AND ROBINSON:
FOUNDATIONAL PROPOSITIONS

Operating from an eclectic political economy approach, Sklair's theory of the TCC rests on four basic propositions. First, a TCC based on the transnational corporations (TNCs) is emerging that is more or less in control of the processes of globalization. For Sklair, as well as for Robinson and others researching the global economy (e.g., Dicken 2007), there is a critical distinction between an MNC and a TNC: The former is seen as a corporation from a particular nation-state that operates in a number of countries, whereas the latter is seen as a global corporation without a national identity, that may have executive offices in several countries, and that generally operates in numerous countries throughout the world. Second, the TCC is beginning to act as a transnational dominant class in some spheres. Third, the globalization of the capitalist system reproduces itself through the profit-driven culture–ideology of consumerism. Finally, the TCC is working consciously to resolve the crisis of global social polarization between wealth and poverty and the ecological unsustainability of the system. In turn, the TCC, according to Sklair (2000), can be analytically divided into four main fractions: (1) TNC executives and their local affiliates ("the corporate fraction"), (2) globalizing bureaucrats and politicians ("the state fraction"), (3) globalizing professionals ("the technical fraction"), and (4) merchants and the media ("the consumerist fraction") (p. 17). Above all, states Sklair, the TCC seeks "the establishment of a borderless global economy, the complete denationalization of corporate procedures and activities, and the eradication of economic nationalism" (p. 3).

Sklair (2000: 18–22) goes on to identify five respects in which the TCC is "transnational and globalizing": The economic interests of its members are increasingly globally linked rather than exclusively local and nation in origin, including the globalization of property, shareholding, and markets; the TCC "seeks to exert economic control in the workplace, political control in domestic and international politics, and culture–ideology control in everyday life through specific forms of global competitive and consumerist rhetoric and practices" (p. 19); members of the TCC "have outward-oriented global rather than inward-oriented local perspectives on most economic, political, and culture–ideology issues" (p. 20); members of the TCC tend to share similar lifestyles, particularly patterns of higher education (increasingly in business schools) and consumption of luxury goods and services: "Integral to this process including exclusive clubs and restaurants, ultra-expensive resorts in all continents, private as opposed to mass forms of travel and entertainment and, ominously, increasingly residential segregation of the very rich secured by armed guards and electronic surveillance" (pp. 20–21); and members of the TCC "seek to project images of themselves as citizens of the world as well as of their places of birth" (p. 21).

Finally, following Useem (1984), Sklair (2000) suggests that at the apex of the TCC there is an "inner circle" that acts as a collective political agent seeking to integrate global capitalism and to develop transnational political and economic policies that advance the interests that its members share in global capital accumulation:

> The concept of the transnational capitalist class implies that there is one central inner circle that makes system-wide decisions, and that it connects in a variety of ways with subsidiary members in communities, cities, countries, and supranational regions. Despite real geographic and sectoral conflicts, the whole of the transnational capitalist class shares a fundamental interest in the continued accumulation of private profit. What the inner circle of the TCC does is to give a unity to the diverse economic interests, political organizations, and cultural and ideological formations of those who make up the class as a whole. . . . The achievement of [the TCC's] goals is facilitated by the activities of agents and organizations that are connected in a complex network of local and global interlocks. A crucial component of the integration of the TCC is that most of the senior members of its inner circle will occupy a variety of interlocking positions [on corporate boards of directors, think tanks, charities, scientific and cultural bodies, universities, and other such institutions of civil society]." (pp. 21–22)

For both Sklair and Robinson, the study of the TCC must be located within a larger study of the qualitative transformation of world capitalism, critical to which is reconceptualization of the relationship of space and territory to classes and capitalism and the rise of transnational socioeconomic, political, and cultural spaces that cannot be conceived through a nation-state/interstate framework (this is of course a more general preoccupation of globalization studies). Sklair (1995) insists that

> state-centrists, transnational relations advocates and Marxists of several persuasions, while acknowledging the growing important of the global system in one form or another, all continue to prioritize the system of nation-states. . . . They all fall back on it to describe what happens in the world, and to explain how and why it happens. (p. 6)

In contrast, "the thesis on which this conceptual apparatus [the TCC] rests and on which any viable theory of the global system depends is that capitalism is changing qualitatively from an inter-national to a global system" (pp. 60–61). He goes on to develop his notion of transnational practices (TNPs) as the central analytical category for the global (as distinct from international) system and conceptualization of the TCC:

> TNPs are analytically distinguished on three levels, economic, political and cultural–ideological, what I take to constitute the sociological totality. In the concrete conditions of the world as it is, a world largely structured by global capitalism, each of these TNPs is typically, but not exclusively, characterized by a major institution. My contention is that the transnational corporation (TNC) is the major locus of transnational economic practices; what I shall term the transnational capitalist class is the major locus of transnational political practices; and the major locus of transnational cultural–ideological practices is to be found in the culture–ideology of consumerism. . . . The TNPs make sense only in the context of the global system. The theory of the global system based on transnational practices is an attempt to escape from the limitations of state centrism. (pp. 6–7)

For Robinson, global capitalism represents a qualitatively new stage in the ongoing and open-ended evolution of world capitalism, the fourth since the inception of the system with the conquest of the Americas in 1492. The mercantile period was followed by a stage of competitive industrial capitalism from the late eighteenth century into the early twentieth century and a stage of corporate, or monopoly, capitalism in much of the twentieth century—what he calls "nation-state capitalism." What is qualitatively new in this fourth stage of world capitalism, according to Robinson, are a globally integrated production and financial system, the TCC, and the rise of what he terms transnational state (TNS) apparatuses. Central to the development of Robinson's explicitly Marxist approach to the TCC is the work conducted in the 1970s by French political economist Christian Palloix, who suggested a clear historic sequence in the "internationalization of capital". The circuit of commodity capital was the first to become internationalized in the form of world trade; the circuit of money capital was the second, in the form of the flow of portfolio investment capital into overseas ventures; the circuit of productive capital is the most recent, in the form of the massive growth of TNCs in the post–World War II period (Palloix 1975, 1977). For Robinson, key to the rise of a TCC is this transnationalization of the circuit of productive capital, involving not merely the spread of TNC activities but also the restructuring, fragmentation, and worldwide decentralization of the production process.

According to Robinson (2004),

> Inherent in the notion of *inter*national is a system of nation-states that mediates relations between classes and groups, including the notion of national capitals and national bourgeoisies. *Trans*national denotes economic and related social, political, and cultural processes—including class formation—that supersede nation-states. The global economy is bringing shifts in the process of social production worldwide and therefore reorganizing world class structure. The leading elements among national capitals are in a process of fusing into a new configuration of transnational capital. The rise of transnational capital out of former national capitals is having a transformative effect on what were national capitalist classes. These are drawn by globalization into transnational chains that reorient the determinants of class formation. The leading capitalist strata worldwide are crystallizing into a TCC. (pp. 46–47)

In distinction to Sklair's eclectic political economy approach, Robinson advances his "theory of global capitalism" and the TCC through established Marxist categories. Contra Sklair, he views politicians, state managers, institutional bureaucrats, and leading journalists and intellectuals not as part of the TCC but, rather, as elites that form part of a larger global capitalist historic bloc—made up of the TNCs and transnational financial institutions, the elites that manage the supranational economic planning agencies, major forces in the dominant political parties, media conglomerates, and technocratic elites and state managers in both North and South. Robinson (2004) writes,

> My differences with his [Sklair's] "theory of the global system" revolve around his definition of the capitalist class as inclusive of professional and middle class groups (such as journalists), state bureaucrats, politicians, and technicians, and other strata that are not necessarily propertied. . . . I believe the capitalist class is a propertied class—the owners of capital—and that the TCC is that capitalist group which owns or controls the transnational capital. The task is to problematize the mechanisms of capitalist influence over non-propertied strata and over the state, and to analyze how coalitions are constructed and capitalist hegemony achieved. (p. 36)

Robinson (2004) provides the following definition of the TCC:

> This new transnational bourgeoisie or capitalist class is comprised of the owners of trans-national capital, that is, the group that owns the leading worldwide means of production as embodied principally in the transnational corporations and private financial institutions. This class is *trans*national because it is tied to globalized circuits of production, marketing, and finances unbound from particular national territories and identities, and because its interests lie in global over local or national accumulation. The TCC therefore can be located in the global class structure by its ownership and/or control of transnational capital. What distinguishes the TCC from national or local capitalists is that it is involved in globalized pro-duction and manages globalized circuits of accumulation that give it an objective class exist-ence and identity spatially and politically in the global system above any local territories and polities. As the agent of the global economy, *transnational capital has become the hegemonic fraction of capital on a world scale* . . . that fraction which imposes the general direction and character on production worldwide and conditions the social, political, and cultural char-acter of capitalist society worldwide. (pp. 7–48, emphasis in original)

Robinson characterizes the TCC as a global ruling class because it controls the levers of what he terms an emergent transnational state (TNS):

> This TCC is the new ruling class worldwide. . . . At the level of agency, the TCC, as represented by its inner circles, leading representatives, and politicized elements, is class conscious. It has become conscious of its transnationality. It has been pursuing a class project of capitalist globalization, as reflected in its global decision-making and the rise of a transnational state apparatus under the auspices of this fraction. The TCC is represented by a class-conscious transnational elite, made up of an inner circle of transnational capitalists, along with trans-national managers, bureaucrats, technicians, and leading ideologues and intellectuals in the service of the TCC. The transnational managerial elite, based in the centers of world capi-talism, is at the apex of the global economy, exercises authority over global institutions, and controls the levers of global policy-making. The TCC is increasingly a class-in-itself and for-itself. It is a *manifest agent of change*. (pp. 47–49, emphasis in original)

Robinson's idea of a TNS, more than any other aspect of his theory of global capitalism and more generally of TCC theory, has generated intense debate.[3] According to Robinson (2014),

> The members of the TCC and transnational managerial elites operate through the dense net-work of institutions that comprise a TNS apparatus as they manage their investments and pursue their political concerns around the world. And it is out of such networking that a politicized strata has been able to engage transnationally. The TNS is a web of decentered institutions, a fragmentary apparatus with a lack of supranational enforcement mechanisms or of institutional cohesion. There is certainly no systemic unity in an organizational sense. The U.S. national state is the closest thing to a center within the TNS. There is no central coordinating mechanism. But the degree of centralized cohesion of the network is *not* what determines that this network constitutes a TNS; rather, *it is the ability of the TCC and trans-national elites to operate institutionally through this network to coordinate policies and practices across borders in the effort to achieve its class interests, exercise class power at a transnational level, and develop a field of transnational power*. (p. 83, emphasis in original)

Here, a brief digression is necessary to draw a distinction between class analysis and elite analysis, as Robinson seems to be combining the two in the idea of this TNS. There is an ineluctable overlap between the notion of transnational elites and transnational capitalists and of those associated with the tradition of elite analysis with those from class analysis. Much debate in political sociology, political economy, and political science has centered on the relationship between classes and elites and whether or not these are commensurate analytical categories. In political sociology, elites generally refer to dominant political, socioeconomic, and cultural strata and, in particular, to capitalists and landlords, along with top-level managers and administrators of the state and other major social institutions and leadership positions in the political system. In Marxist-oriented approaches, capitalists are viewed as elites who own or manage means of production as capital, whereas other elites who are not necessarily capitalists occupy key decision-making positions in institutions, whether in private corporations, the state, political parties, or culture industries. In contrast, the "power elite" approach in the tradition of C. Wright Mills, author of the classic *The Power Elite* (1956), does not generally identify or analyze the capitalist class per se or elites of a capitalist state. The focus, influenced by Weberian analysis of status and power, tends to be on control over the major social institutions so that there are corporate elites, political elites, military elites, cultural elites, and so on (although there is also a long and theoretically rich scholarship of power elites in national capitalist societies that cannot be examined here [see Domhoff 2006]).

There is a broad and rapidly growing literature from a "power elite" perspective that examines the rise of *transnational elites* that we cannot take up here. One of the more notable studies in this regard is David Rothkopf's (2008) *Superclass*. Rothkopf, a former high-level US government official and Kissinger associate, interviewed several hundred of the top global elite and found considerable evidence for increasing social and cultural integration of global elites. What he calls "superclass" is the top echelons of the transnational elite. He observes,

> A global elite has emerged over the past several decades that has vastly more power than any other group on the planet. Each of the members of this superclass has the ability to regularly influence the lives of millions of people in multiple countries worldwide. Each actively exercises this power, and they often amplify it through the development of relationships with others in this class. (p. 9)

Describing his participation in the annual World Economic Forum retreats in Davos, Switzerland, Rothkopf notes that

> even the casual observer in Davos would have to conclude that had [C. Wright] Mills been writing today, he would have turned his attention from the national elite in America to a new and more important phenomenon: the rise of a global power elite, a superclass that plays a similar role in the hierarchy of the global era to the role that the U.S. power elite played in that country's first decade as a superpower. (p. 11)

Sklair and Robinson have continued to research and publish on the TCC. Sklair has written on the globalization of human rights, icon urban architecture as a hegemonic project of the TCC, and the transition from capitalist to socialist globalization (Sklair 2009, 2011, 2017). Robinson has written on the TCC in Latin America, the BRICS (Brazil, Russia, India, China, and South Africa) and the rise of a TCC in the Global South, militarization and the TCC, and global crisis and the TCC (Robinson 2003, 2008, 2014, 2015). Since their seminal works, there has been an explosion of research by a growing corpus of scholars from throughout the world as the TCC concept has become popularized and has demonstrated—at least in the view of its proponents—significant explanatory power in the age of globalization.

THE PROLIFERATION OF RESEARCH, CRITIQUE, AND DEBATE ON THE TRANSNATIONAL CAPITALIST CLASS

Much recent scholarship on the TCC has attempted to test TCC theory by studying the extent of transnational interlocking of corporate boards of directors (David, Westerhuis, and Schifeling 2014; Kentor 2005; Kentor and Jang 2006; Kentor, Sobek, and Timberlake 2011; Nolbert 2005; Staples 2006, 2008, 2012). An interlocking directorate occurs when a person affiliated with one organization sits on the board of directors of another organization. Such interlocking directorates among large corporates characterize the structure of modern capitalism and have been broadly studied in recent decades, dating back to Mill's (1956) classic work, *The Power Elite* (see also Fennema 1982; Fennema and Van der Pijl 1987; Mintz and Schwartz 1985; Mizruchi 1992; Stockman, Ziegler, and Scott 1985; Useem 1984). The evidence broadly shows that capitalist globalization has involved a sharp increase in *transnational* interlocking. What remain contested are the extent of this interlocking relative to nationally interlocked networks and the meaning of transnational interlocking for TCC theory.

Summarizing several years of his research on transnational interlocking of corporate boards, sociologist William K. Carroll published in 2010 *The Making of a Transnational Capitalist Class*, the most significant book-length work on the TCC since Sklair's and Robinson's foundational studies. Carroll argues,

> The increasingly integrated character of global capitalism does not in itself dictate a specific form of capitalist class organization. This is so because capital is not a unified macro subject but is divided microeconomically into competing units which themselves are positioned within and across national boundaries in an international political system, rendering tendencies towards global capitalist unity always tenuous. (p 41)

Thus, the question of the transnational capitalist class "cannot be reduced to the globalization of capitalism per se" (p. 2). He criticizes both Sklair and Robinson for failing to "map the transnational capitalist class's social organization" and for "relying primarily on aggregated statistical evidence . . . rather than sociological analysis of class organization" (p. 2).

For Carroll (2010), the principal empirical indicator of a would-be TCC is the interlocking of TNC boards of directors. Interlocking directorates, Carroll states,

> link individual members of the corporate elite—capitalists and organic intellectuals alike—in ways that help cement general class cohesion. Interlocks serve as channels of communication among directors, facilitating a common worldview and allowing for the integration of potentially contradictory interests based on property ownership alone. (p. 9)

Drawing on several data sets from the 1970s into the early 2000s on the boards of directors of the *Fortune* 500 corporations, he finds through network analysis a significant increase in transnational corporate interlocks and an emerging "transnational corporate policy network" involving a "network of overlapping memberships between corporate boards and such global policy planning boards as the Trilateral Commission and the World Economic Forum" (p. 36). He goes on to observe that in the decade 1996–2006, *"transnational interlocking becomes less the preserve of a few internationally well-connected companies, and more a general practice in which nearly half of the world's largest firms participate"* (p. 98, emphasis in original). These findings "support the claim that by the closing years of the twentieth century a well-integrated transnational corporate community had formed, and that neoliberal policy groups, themselves vehicles of globalization, were instrumental in its formation" (p. 54). Carroll reaches an ambiguous conclusion: "Whether this confirmed the arrival of a transnational capitalist class is partly a matter of semantics and partly a matter of substance (p. 54).

Other recent research confirms that unlike earlier epochs in the history of world capitalism, the concentration and centralization of capital involve the amassing and growing power not of national but, rather, of *transnational* capitalist groups. A 2011 analysis of the share ownerships of 43,000 TNCs undertaken by three systems theorists at the Swiss Federal Institute of Technology identified a core of 1,318 TNCs with interlocking ownerships (Vitali, Glattfelder, and Battiston 2011). Each of these core TNCs had ties to 2 or more other companies, and on average they were connected to 20. Although they represented only 20% of global operating revenues, these 1,318 TNCs appeared to collectively own through their shares the majority of the world's largest blue chip and manufacturing firms, representing a further 60% of global revenues—for a total of 80% of the world's revenue.

A major question for TCC theory remains the extent to which this structural integration of capitals transnationally—whether through transnational corporate interlocks, share ownership, or a variety of other mechanisms that integrate capitalists across borders (Robinson 2004)—also involves the development of a TCC consciousness and political protagonism in pursuit of TCC interests, as both Sklair and Robinson maintain. Drawing on the works of Useem (1984) and Mizruchi (1992), among others, that identify the political behavior of interlocking corporate networks at the national level, J. Murray (2013) notes that class consciousness and political action on behalf of global interests are integral to the formulation of the TCC, but systematic evidence linking the indicators of TCC formation with political behavior is largely missing. "If the claims of TCC theory are correct," he argues, "we should expect firms with a greater number of interlocks in the transnational network to be more likely to engage in political behavior on behalf of transnational class interests" (p. 6).

Using Carroll's (2010) data set and the LexisNexis Corporate Affiliations database, J. Murray (2013) sets out to test this hypothesis by measuring through regression analysis the relationship of participation in transnational corporate networks to political donations in the United States to political action committees (PACs), which serve as the principal vehicles for influencing US political parties and elections. PAC activity, he shows, is one key avenue through which the TCC acts to serve its transnational class interests. He finds that the more transnationally interlocked a firm is and the more centrally located it is within the transnational network, the more money it will contribute to PACs. He concludes, "Transnational centrality is a significant predictor of globally oriented political activity"

(p. 18). This finding suggests "a segment of the transnational business community has emerged as a class-for-itself" (p. 18).

Alongside the study of transnational corporate networks, another growing body of research has come from scholars throughout the world who have focused on the dynamics of TCC formation in specific countries and regions and on the rise of TCC groups in the former Third World. The spectacular rise of India and China and their integration into global capitalism have generated major interest among these researchers. An Indian contingent of the TCC emerged in the 1990s in conjunction with the transnationalization of the Indian state, particularly among Indian companies tied to the global information technology (IT) industry. By the twenty-first century, a number of powerful Indian conglomerates began to go global, setting up subsidiaries and operations on every continent. The transnationally oriented capitalist elites in India "differ sharply in their ideological orientation from the established business class, many of whom (represented by the Bombay Club) opposed unbridled globalization," observes Upadhya (2004), "In contrast to the old bourgeoisie, the IT business class emerged within the global economy and a liberalized environment" (p. 1, online edition). The IT industry, she states, "has produced a new kind of transnational capitalist class in India" (p. 1, online edition). The members of this class are

> distinguished by their global integration and relative autonomy from the "old" Indian economy dominated by the public sector and a nationalist capitalist class. The entry of multinationals into the IT industry has produced synergies that have helped it to grow and for these reasons the IT business class is also one of the most outspoken votaries of globalization. (p. 1, online edition)

A second pattern of TCC formation in India has involved the transformation and transnationalization of companies previously inserted into protected national circuits, such as Wipro, Arcelor Mittal, and, most illustrative, India's leading global corporation, the Tata Group. By 2011, the Tata Group ran more than 100 companies in 80 countries. It had become the single largest manufacturer in the United Kingdom—the old colonial power in India—having bought Jaguar, Land Rover, Corus (formerly British Steel), Tetley Tea, Brunner Mond (chemicals), and other holdings ("Tata for Now" 2011: 61).

In their study of business process outsourcing in India, Russell, Noronha, and D'Cruz (2016) note that from its inception in the wake of India's neoliberal opening to the global economy in the 1990s, the business has been global in outlook. They note that the type of capitalist class development currently underway in India

> has different implications to those spelt out in both the classical theories of imperialism and in world systems analysis. With regard to the theory of imperialism, here we see Indian capital developing, not so much in competition with other *national* capitals but in conjunction with their evolution. (p. 115)

The rising Indian TCC is promoting India's participation in an expanding globalized economy: "It is in this sense that the outward-reaching bourgeoisie is part of a transnational capitalist class, one that is materially grounded in supranational production processes and one that is fully conscious of where its interests lie" (pp. 115–116).

A number of studies have investigated the role of a TCC in Asia and Oceania (e.g., see the collection of essays in Sprague 2016). In discussing the global orientation and activities of Toyota as emblematic of Japanese TNC activity, Takase (2016) shows how Japanese TCC groups hold sway over policymaking and push for stronger global economic integration. Zhao (2008) identifies a powerful emerging TCC in China that collaborates with the Chinese bureaucratic state and that has also developed in consort with the massive entrance of foreign transnational capital into that country. Shen (2011) examines how transnational capitalists in Taiwan have exploited "nationalist" state policies as favorable opportunities for their cross-strait strategies of capital accumulation and integration. The outward orientation of Taiwanese transnational capital accelerated since family and business travel from Taiwan to China was opened in 1987 as Taiwanese investors have come to prefer the regimented labor system in China, profiting by subcontracting on the mainland.

There has been an explosion of studies on the TCC in Latin America.[4] Madrid (2009) has examined the TCC in El Salvador and its role in facilitating the Central American Free Trade Agreement. The trade agreement, she shows, sought to facilitate new patterns of transnational accumulation in Central America, and its passage was a "decisive victory for the Salvadoran contingent of the TCC in its struggle to wrestle the state from descendent nationally-based fractions of capital" (p. 98). Avilés (2008) discusses the formation of TCC groups in Colombia that, together with their counterparts in the United States, pursued "a transnational order of neoliberal economics and 'market democracies'" (p. 426). Watson (2015) analyzes how the United States and other major powers have pursued policies conducive to transnational capital and to the emergence of local TCC groups in the Caribbean. Sprague (2017; see also Sprague 2015a, 2015b) examines the role of TCC agents in the Caribbean in facilitating the integration of that subregion into new globalized circuits of accumulation, especially with regard to mining, migration and remittance flows, export processing, and tourism. Morton (2007) discusses how a TCC came about in Mexico as a result of economic restructuring from the 1970s into the twenty-first century, moving beyond the in-bond, or *maquiladora*, industry and into transnational agribusiness, among other activities, and coming to control the country's major business associations and eventually the state.

With regard to the greater Middle East region, Baker (2014) finds that the US invasion and occupation of Iraq opened up new opportunities for a section of the Iraqi elite to expand into transnational corporate circuits and to integrate into the ranks of the TCC. The country became a hothouse for broader TCC formation throughout the region as business groups from Jordan, Egypt, Kuwait, Turkey, Saudi Arabia, Lebanon, and elsewhere poured into post-invasion Iraq. Hanieh (2011) finds that the transnationalization of "Gulf capital" has been a "striking feature throughout the economies of the Middle East" in the 1990s and the 2000s. In particular, Palestinian capitalists, absent their own state, have globalized through association with Persian Gulf capitalist conglomerates. He observes that "Palestinian displacement throughout the Arab world meant that Palestinian diasporic capital generally evolved as an interlocked component of other regional Arab capitalist classes," especially in the Gulf (p. 83). In turn, Mirtaheri (2016) shows how the Gulf Cooperation Council has been the critical institutional setting for the rise of TCC groups in the region as well as a major forum through which power struggles among various transnational elites have been played out. Sener (2008) finds that as Turkey has integrated into global capitalist circuits since it first launched neoliberal reform in 1980, a new TCC has arisen through association with TNCs that have invested in the country and through the integration into theses circuits of previously nationally oriented, often family owned companies. The new TCC groups and transnationally oriented elites and middle strata, he shows, increasingly have more in common in terms of their consumption patterns, cultural practices, worldview, and identity with their counterparts throughout the world than with their fellow nationals. Most of the elites, managers, and technocrats he interviewed regarded themselves as "world citizens" first and foremost over national and other identities.

In Africa, observe Taylor and Nel (2002),

> dominant elite fractions have increasingly affected this transnationalization process through locking into the global. They have indulged in mergers or co-operative pacts with transnational corporations, moved their portfolios offshore, engaged in financial speculation, diversified their holdings outside the national space, and invested abroad. (p. 170)

They continue:

> Fractions of African elites are in themselves emerging as vital sections of the transnational capitalist class. Such sections have increasingly attempted to make use of the global capitalist system in a strategy aimed at bolstering their own position within the global historic bloc. . . . The close fit between interests of externally orientated elites and the type of project advanced by New Africa is increasingly evident [what they mean by New Africa is Africa's renewed integration into the global capitalist economy]. (p. 170)

In Europe, research has centered on the creation of the European Union as a project of a European-wide TCC, on the European Round Table of Industrialists (Van Apeldoorn 2001, 2014), and on the rise of new TCC groups in Eastern Europe on the heels of the fall of communism (Shields 2014). Shields shows how state managers and small business classes as "aspirant members of a transnational capitalist class" (p. 238) led the integration of Eastern European countries into post-Cold War global capitalism. Harris (2005, 2009, 2016) has discussed what he terms a "statist fraction" of the TCC in Russia, China, and the Persian Gulf states, in reference to state elites who together with private capitalists control sovereign wealth funds (SWFs) and state or joint state–private corporations. He argues that these TCC fractions are not so closely aligned with or restrained by the ideology and practices of Western liberalism. As such, they are able to take part more thoroughly in the operation of national state assets such as SWFs.

Some have argued that the rise of powerful state corporations and SWFs in the international arena signals a "decoupling" from the US and Western economy. Yet Harris (2009) observes that these state corporations have not turned inward to build up protected national or regional economies but, rather, have integrated into transnational corporate circuits. The SWFs have invested billions buying stocks in banks, securities houses, and asset management firms, including Barclays, Blackstone, Carlyle, Citigroup, Deutsche Bank, HSBC, Merrill Lynch, Morgan Stanley, UBS, the London Stock Exchange, and NASDAQ. Harris terms this phenomenon "transnational state capitalism": The activities of the SWFs and other state corporations underscore "the statist nature of the Third World TCC." There comes about, he argues,

> a merger of interests between transnational capitalists from both statist and private sectors that takes place over an array of joint ventures. It is not simply competition between state and private transnational capitalists (although that is one aspect), but rather the integration

of economic interests creating competitive blocs of transnational corporations seeking to achieve advantage in a variety of fields and territorial regions. (p. 13)

CONCLUSION: CRITICS, DEBATES, AND OPEN-ENDED RESEARCH AGENDAS

The contradiction of a globalizing economy within a nation-state-based system of political authority and the division of the world into approximately 200 territorial units remains an unresolved tension in globalization studies. Bound up with the debate on the TCC is the role of the nation-state in relationship to the global class structure or, more theoretically, the extent to which national states mediate transnational class relations. Is it possible for a TCC to exist within a world political structure based on sovereign nation-states and the interstate system? Hanieh (2011) writes, "The work of Robinson, Sklair and other transnational theorists is empirically rich and often contains powerful analysis of the activities of international corporations and the institutions that support them" (p. 85). He continues, in what is an emblematic objection to the global capitalism thesis,

> The weakness of the transnational approach, however, is its argument that the role of the nation state has declined and that it no longer forms the key institutional mediator of capitalist accumulation, having been replaced by an amorphous "transnational" state. While capital tends to expand and move at an ever-increasing pace across nation-state borders, and certainly conceives its field of activity at the inter-national scale . . . the accumulation and production of value must necessarily take place in territorially bounded and place-specific locations. This requires institutions that manage economic policy and ensure the continued maintenance of conditions favorable to capitalist accumulation. (p. 85)

For Marx, and for many Marxists after him, the capitalist class, although a global agent, is *organically national* in the sense that its development takes place within the bounds of specific nation-states and is by fiat a nation-state-based class. Early twentieth-century theories of imperialism, such as those advanced by Vladimir Lenin and Rudolph Hilferding, established the Marxist analytical framework of rival national capitals, a framework carried by subsequent political economists into the latter twentieth century via theories of dependency and the world-system and radical international relations theory, and for whom debate over the TCC often boils down to "imperialism versus globalization." It is no surprise, then, that among the strongest critics of the TCC thesis are traditional Marxists who adhere to the classical theory of imperialism, for whom the national organization of capitalist classes is immanent to the system, as is national rivalry and conflict among them. The modern-day adherents to this theory substitute analysis of the capitalist class for that of state competition, geopolitics, the struggle among nations for hegemony, and the domination of an "American empire."

Noted Marxist theoretician Ellen Meiksin Wood (2007) argues,

> As it stands, the conception of a transnational capitalist class and a transnational state apparatus owes more to that a priori assumption about the parallel development of capital and state than to any persuasive demonstration of how it operates in practice or how capital

transcends the contradictions in its relations with the state, in the relation among capitals or in the reproduction of capital by means of uneven development. p. 157)

For Van der Pijl (2001–2002), "the logic of capital drives societies forward to reconstitute themselves at the wider-than-national level" (p. 497). Nonetheless, "the reality of society as constituted around an axis of exploitation involving complex comprises along that axis, within and between classes, has so far proven to be a powerful brake on the tendency of the capitalist class to become really transnational" (p. 497). In dismissing the notion of a TCC, Canadian Marxists Leo Panitch and Sam Gindin (2013) claim that the processes associated with globalization are better understood in the context of inter-capitalist competition and US Empire. These processes "did not spawn a 'transnational capitalist class', loosened from any state moorings or about to spawn a supranational global state. 'National capital' did not disappear. Nor did economic competition between various centers of accumulation" (p. 11). John B. Foster (2015), editor of the Marxist journal *Monthly Review*, charges that "analysts within the transnational-capitalist-class model exaggerate the extent of transnational intercorporate linkages" and insists instead that the world political and class structure should be understood in terms of US domination over the ruling bloc of rich countries formed by the traditional "triad" of North America, Europe, and Japan.

Similarly, Samir Amin (2011) sees the world divided into national capitalisms. Critiquing the TCC thesis, he states that "capitalist societies are national societies and of this I am very insistent. They always have been and they always will be, in spite of transnationalization." He goes on:

> Globalization is an inappropriate term. Its popularity is commensurate with the violence of ideological aggression that has prohibited henceforth the utterance of "imperialism." For me, the deployment of true historical capitalism has always been globalized and has always been polarized and to this end, imperialist. Thus, collective imperialism is simply an old and enduring phenomenon in a new guise. This new form of imperialism is clearly built upon objective foundations and its character is determined by the strong transnationalization of the leading corporations. It implies a rallying towards a common political project: working together to manage the downtrodden world (global South), and to this end, placing it safely under the military control of the US armed forces and their subaltern allies within the triad (NATO, Japan). Yet this new demand does not wipe out the national character of the capitalist components within the triad.

Amin is both a Marxist political economist and a veteran scholar of dependency, world-systems, and related radical theories of underdevelopment that emerged in the second half of the twentieth century. World-systems scholars have argued that the North–South, or center–periphery, division of the world belies the analytical purchase of TCC theory. According to Arrighi (2001–2002), the increasing transnational character of capitalism cannot be taken "as evidence of an accelerated division of the world into a global bourgeoisie and a global proletariat as classes-in-themselves" because "the significance of North–South divisions in the global social structure has certainly not decreased and has probably increased in the age of globalization" (p. 472). The implications of the continued wealth gap between the former First and Third Worlds

> for processes of class formation on a world-scale are straightforward. The emergence of new forms of global integration and production processes via direct investment, combined with

the reemergence of older forms via financial flows, has consolidated rather than undermined the fundamental difference in the material conditions of class formation that separates the North form the South. (p. 473)

There have been lively debates among TCC and TNS scholars with regard to these criticisms, and Robinson, Sklair, and other scholars who research the TCC have replied to much of it (see Robinson 2014). No one writing on the TCC and the TNS has actually claimed that the nation-state is disappearing. They have insisted, rather, than the nation-state and its relationship to the larger global system are being transformed and that scholars need to think in new ways about the relationship of a now-transnational capitalist class to the nation-state and the interstate system. Similarly—and although they debate the issue among themselves—none have actually denied the significance of the North–South divide. They have argued, rather, that despite this divide, powerful TCC groups have emerged throughout the Global South whose interests lie in the global over national and regional economies and that core and periphery may be more fruitfully seen as denoting social groups in a transnational setting than core and peripheral nation-states. Also, no TCC scholar has negated the exploitative and repressive nature of the economic, political, and military policies of the powerful countries that are associated with imperialism, but rather that these practices seek to promote and defend global capitalism rather than the particular national interests of dominant groups in particular countries.

In 2011, approximately 100 scholars from several dozen countries throughout the world who research the TCC met in Prague for the International Conference on the Transnational Capitalist Class and Global Class Formation. The participants formed the Network for Critical Studies of Global Capitalism as a forum for shared research and debate. The association's inaugural conference, according to its website, was

> the first international conference devoted to transnational capitalist class (TCC) theory and global class formation. The conference set out to provide a place to share research, debate and explore this newly emerging network of scholars and activists focused around global capitalism and transnational class analysis.

The Network has since institutionalized biennial conferences, and its website provides a forum for scholarly research and debate on the TCC and on global capitalism. Panel sessions at its conferences have covered a wide range of topics, notably TCC and working-class formations, global elite networks, immigration and migration, the global economy, production networks and commodity chains, global finance, transformation of the nation-state, the transnational state, transnational governance, information technology and globalization, the military/industrial complex, and the state. The Network has published several books of conference proceedings (Haase 2013; G. Murray and Scott 2012; Sprague 2015a; Struna 2014). We direct those interested in following TCC research and debates to the Network's website at https://netglobalcapitalism.wordpress.com.

Acknowledgment

We thank Jason Struna for his comments and suggestions on an earlier draft of this chapter.

Notes

1. Notable among this research was Raymond Vernon's *Sovereignty at Bay*, published in 1971, which argued that multinational corporations had outgrown the nation-state and—with their ability to shift their activities from one location to another throughout the world—were undermining the traditional authority of the nation-state and its economic policymaking capacities.

2. Sklair (1995) provides a very useful summary of the first generation of research into what we now call economic globalization, including summaries of the literature on MNCs, what was termed in the 1980s the "new international division of labor," global commodity chains, and export assembly in free trade zones. He also provides a very useful overview of how the sociology of development converged with the emerging literature on economic globalization and world-systems theory in research on the diverse trends in economic globalization.

3. Robinson's theory of global capitalism, including the TNS and the TCC, has been the subject of a number of journal symposia dedicated to critiquing and debating his work. See, inter alia, symposia in the following journals: *Theory and Society* 30 (2), 2001; *Science and Society* 65 (4), 2001–2002; *Critical Sociology* 38 (3), 2012; *Historical Materialism* 15, 2007; and *Cambridge Review of International Affairs* 19 (3), 2006.

4. See, for example, Robinson's 2008 book-length study on the rise of a TCC and a TNS in Latin America, which we do not discuss here.

References

Amin, Samir. 2011. "Transnational Capitalism or Collective Imperialism." *Pambazuka News*, March 23. http://www.pambazuka.org/global-south/transnational-capitalism-or-collective-imperialism.

Arrighi, Giovanni. 2001–2002. "Global Capitalism and the Persistence of the North–South Divide." *Science and Society* 65 (4):469–475.

Baker, Yousef. 2014. "Global Capitalism and Iraq: The Making of a Neoliberal State." *International Review of Modern Sociology* 40 (2): 121–148.

Barnet, Richard J., and Ronald Muller. 1974. *Global Reach: The Power of the Multinational Corporation*. New York: Simon & Shuster.

Cox, Robert W. 1987. *Production, Power, and World Order*. New York: Colombia University Press.

David, Thomas, Gerarda Westerhuis, and Todd Schifeling, eds. 2014. *The Power of Corporate Networks*. New York: Routledge.

Dicken, Peter. 2007. *Global Shift: Mapping the Changing Contours of the World Economy*. New York: Guilford.

Domhoff, William G. 2006. *Who Rules America? Power, Politics, and Social Change*. 5th ed. New York: McGraw-Hill.

Fennema, Meindert. 1982. *International Networks and Banks and Industries*. The Hague, the Netherlands: Nijhoff.

Fennema, Meindert, and Kees Van der Pijl. 1987. "International Bank Capital and the New Liberalism." In *Corporate Relations*, edited by Mark S. Mizruchi and Michael Schwartz, pp. 298–319. New York: Cambridge University Press.

Foster, John Bellamy. 2015. "The New Imperialism of Globalized Monopoly-Finance Capital." *Monthly Review* 67 (3). http://monthlyreview.org/2015/07/01/the-new-imperialism-of-globalized-monopoly-finance-capital.

Gill, Stephen. 1990. *American Hegemony and the Trilateral Commission*. Cambridge, UK: Cambridge University Press.

Haase, Dwight. 2013. *Perspectives on Global Development and Technology* 12 (1–2) [special issue].

Hanieh, Adam. 2011. "The Internationalization of Gulf Capital and Palestinian Class Formation." *Capital and Class* 35 (1): 81–106.

Harris, Jerry. 2005. "Emerging Third World Powers: China, India, and Brazil." *Race and Class* 46 (3): 7–27.

Harris, Jerry. 2009. "Statist Globalization in China, Russia and the Gulf States." *Science and Society* 73 (1): 6–33.

Harris, Jerry. 2016. "Statism and the Transnational Capitalism Class in China." In *Globalization and Transnational Capitalism in Asia and Oceania*, edited by Jeb Sprague, 21–39. London: Routledge.

Hymer, Stephen. 1979. *The Multinational Corporation: A Radical Approach*. Cambridge, UK: Cambridge University Press.

Kentor, Jeffrey. 2005. "The Growth of Transnational Corporate Networks 1962–1998." *Journal of World Systems Research* 11 (2): 263–286.

Kentor, Jeffrey, and Yong Suk Jang. 2006. "Studying Global Interlocking Directorates: Different Questions, Different Answers." *International Sociology* 21 (4): 602–606.

Kentor, Jeffrey, Adam Sobek, and Michael Timberlake. 2011. "Interlocking Corporate Directorates and the Global City Hierarchy." *Journal of World Systems Research* 17 (2).

Madrid, Cori. 2009. "El Salvador and the Central American Free Trade Agreement: Consolidation of a Transnational Capitalist Class." *Perspectives on Global Development and Technology* 8 (2–3): 189–210.

Marx Karl, and Frederick Engels. 1848. *The Communist Manifesto*. Moscow: Progress Publishers.

Mills, C. Wright. 1956. *The Power Elite*. New York: Oxford University Press.

Mintz, Beth A., and Michael Schwartz. 1985. *The Power Structure of American Business*. Chicago: University of Chicago Press.

Mirtaheri, Seyed Ahmad. 2016. "The Political Economy of a Transnational Elite in the [Persian] Gulf Cooperation Council (GCC)." *Class, Race, and Corporate Power* 4 (1).

Mizruchi, Michael. 1992. *The Structure of Corporate Political Action*. Cambridge, MA: Harvard University Press.

Morton, Adam David. 2007. *Unravelling Gramsci: Hegemony and Passive Revolution in the Global Economy*. London: Pluto.

Murray, Georgina, and John Scott, eds. 2012. *Financial Elites and Transnational Business: Who Rules the World?* Northampton, MA: Elgar.

Murray, Joshua. 2013. "Evidence of Transnational Capitalist Class-for-Itself: The Determinants of PAC Activity Among Foreign Firms in the Global Fortune 500, 2000–2006." *Global Networks* 14 (2): 230–250.

Nolbert, Michael. 2005. "Transnational Corporate Ties: A Synopsis of Theories and Empirical Finding." *Journal of World-Systems Research* 11 (2): 289–314.

Palloix, Christian. 1975. "The Internationalization of Capital and the Circuits of Social Capital." In *International Firms and Modern Imperialism*, edited by Hugo Radice, 67–92. Harmondsworth: Penguin.

Palloix, Christian. 1977. "The Self-Expansion of Capital on a World Scale." *Review of Radical Political Economics* 9 (2): 17–28.

Panitch, Leo, and Sam Gindin. 2013. *The Making of Global Capitalism: The Political Economy of American Empire.* London: Verso.

Robinson, William I. 1996. *Promoting Polarchy: Globalization, U.S. Intervention, and Hegemony.* Cambridge, UK: Cambridge University Press.

Robinson, William I. 2001. "Social Theory and Globalization: The Rise of a Transnational State." *Theory and Society* 30 (2): 157–200.

Robinson, William I. 2003. *Transnational Conflicts: Central America, Social Change, and Globalization.* London: Verso.

Robinson, William I. 2004. *A Theory of Global Capitalism: Production, Class, and State in a Transnational World.* Baltimore, MD: Johns Hopkins University Press.

Robinson, William I. 2008. *Latin America and Global Capitalism.* Baltimore, MD: Johns Hopkins University Press.

Robinson, William I. 2014. *Global Capitalism and the Crisis of Humanity.* New York: Cambridge University Press.

Robinson, William I. 2015. "The Transnational State and the BRICS: A Global Capitalism Perspective." *Third World Quarterly* 36 (1): 1–21.

Rothkopf, David. 2008. *Superclass: The Global Power Elite and the World They Are Making.* New York: Farrar, Straus & Giroux.

Russell, Bob, Ernesto Noronha, and Premilla D'Cruz. 2016. "Transnational Class Formation: A View from Below." In *Globalization and Transnational Capitalism in Asia and Oceana*, edited by Jeb Sprague, 108–124. London: Routledge.

Sener, Tilmaz Meltem. 2008. "Turkish Managers as Part of the Transnational Capitalist Class." *Journal of World-Systems Research* 13 (2): 119–141.

Shen, Hsiu-hua. 2011. "Transnational or Compatriotic Bourgeoisie? Contesting Democracy Across the Taiwan Strait." In *Contested Citizenwhip in East Asia: Developmental Politics, National Unity, and Globalization*, edited by K. S. Chang and B. Turner, 115–132. New York: Routledge.

Shields, Stuart. 2014. *The International Political Economy of Transition: Neoliberal Hegemony and Eastern Central Europe's Transformation.* London: Routledge.

Sklair, Leslie. 1995. *Sociology of the Global System.* Baltimore, MD: Johns Hopkins University Press.

Sklair, Leslie. 2000. *The Transnational Capitalist Class.* Oxford, UK: Blackwell.

Sklair, Leslie. 2009. "The Globalization of Human Rights." *Journal of Global Ethics* 5 (2): 81–96.

Sklair, Leslie. 2011. "The Transition from Capitalist Globalization to Socialist Globalization." *Journal of Democratic Socialism* 1 (1): 1–14.

Sklair, Leslie. 2017. *The Icon Project: Architecture, Cities, and Capitalist Globalization.* New York: Oxford University Press.

Sprague, Jeb. 2015a. "The Caribbean and Global Capitalism." PhD dissertation, University of California, Santa Barbara.

Sprague, Jeb. 2015b. "From International to Transnational Mining: The Industry's Shifting Political Economy and the Caribbean." *Caribbean Studies* 43 (1): 71–110.

Sprague, Jeb. 2016. *Globalization and Transnational Capitalism in Asia and Oceania.* London: Routledge.

Sprague Jeb. 2017. "The Caribbean Cruise Ship Business and the Emergence of a Transnational Capitalist Class." *Journal of World-Systems Research* 23 (1): 93–125.

Staples, Clifford L. 2006. "Board Interlocks and the Study of the Transnational Capitalist Class." *Journal of World-Systems Research* 12 (2): 309–319.

Staples, Clifford L. 2008. "Cross-Border Acquisitions and Board Globalization in the World's Largest TNCs, 1995–2005. *Sociological Quarterly* 49: 31–51.

Staples, Clifford L. 2012. "The Business Roundtable and the Transnational Capitalist Class." In *Financial Elites and Transnational Business: Who Rules the World?* edited by Georgina Murray and John Scott, 100–123. Northampton, MA: Elgar.

Stockman, Frans N., Rolf Ziegler, and John Scott, eds. 1985. *Networks of Corporate Power.* Cambridge, UK: Polity.

Struna, Jason. 2014. *Global Capitalism and Transnational Class Formation.* New York: Routledge.

Takase, Hisanao. 2016. "Japanese Transnational Capitalists and Asia-Pacific Free Trade." In *Globalization and Transnational Capitalism in Asia and Oceania,* edited by Jeb Sprague, 40–55. London: Routledge.

"Tata for Now." 2011. *The Economist,* September 10.

Taylor, Ian, and Philip Nel. 2002. "'New Africa,' Globalization and the Confines of Elite Reformism: 'Getting the Rhetoric Right,' Getting the Strategy Wrong." *Third World Quarterly* 23 (1): 163–180.

Upadhya, Carol. 2004. "A New Transnational Capitalist Class? Capital Flows, Business Networks and Entrepreneurs in the Indian Software Industry." *Economic and Political Weekly* 39 (48): 5141–5151.

Useem, Michael. 1984. *The Inner Circle: Large Corporations and the Rise of Political Business Activity in the U.S. and U.K.* Oxford, UK: Oxford University Press.

Van Apeldoorn, Bastiaan. 2001. "The Struggle over European Order: Transnational Class Agency in the Making of 'Embedded Neo-Liberalism.'" In *Social Forces in the Making of the New Europe,* edited by Andres Bieler and Adam Morton, 70–89. London: Palgrave Macmillan.

Van Apeldoorn, Bastiaan. 2014. "The European Capitalist Class and the Crisis of Its Hegemonic Project." *Socialist Register* 50: 189–206.

Van der Pijl, Kees. 1984. *The Making of an Atlantic Ruling Class.* London: Verso.

Van der Pijl, Kees. 1989. "Introduction." *International Journal of Political Economy* 19 (3): 3–6.

Van der Pijl, Kees. 1998. *Transnational Classes and International Relations.* New York: Routledge.

Van der Pijl, Kees. 2001–2002. "Globalization or Class Society in Transition." *Science and Society* 65 (4): 492–499.

Vernon, Raymond. 1971. *Sovereignty at Bay: The Multinational Spread of U.S. Enterprises.* New York: Basic Books.

Vitali, Stefania, James B. Glattfelder, and Stefano Battiston. 2011. "The Network of Global Corporate Control." *PLoS One:* 1–36. http://www.scribd.com/doc/70706980/The-Network-of-Global-Corporate-Control-by-Stefania-Vitali-James-B-Glattfelder-and-Stefano-Battiston-2011.

Wallerstein, Immanuel. 2012. "Robinson's Critical Appraisal Appraised." *International Sociology* 27 (4): 524–528.

Watson, Hilbourne. 2015. *Globalization, Sovereignty and Citizenship in the Caribbean.* Mona, Jamaica: University of the West Indies Press.

Wood, Ellen Meiksins. 2007. "A Reply to My Critics." *Historical Materialism* 15: 143–170.

Zhao, Yuezhi. 2008. *Communication in China: Political Economy, Power, and Conflict.* Lanham, MD: Rowman & Littlefield.

CHAPTER 20

....

THE IMPACT OF GLOBAL FINANCIAL CRISES

....

WALDEN BELLO

THE interdependent nature of the global economy means that financial crises—and their responses—experienced in one country will immediately have implications throughout the world. Many global studies scholars have correctly highlighted the 2008 global financial crisis (GFC) as one of these cases, in which it created a turning point in both the objective development and public perception of neoliberal globalization. This chapter focuses on this case, showing the long-term impacts of the GFC on US politics and global economic policy.[1] In particular, I analyze what I consider to be the surprisingly inadequate response of the Obama administration, which accelerated the failure of Keynesianism and opened the door to Hillary Clinton's stunning 2016 electoral loss to the national populist Donald Trump.

The unfolding of the GFC brought Keynesian economics to the forefront, with neoliberalism beating a hasty retreat in the immediate aftermath of the crisis. Keynesian economists, particularly those in the Hyman Minsky school, had correctly anticipated the crisis, but even they were probably surprised by its severity.[2] But it was not only for the correctness of their financial analysis but for the policy tools they offered for dealing with the unfolding crisis that their expertise was sought. As the neoliberal par excellence Robert Lucas stated, "Everyone is a Keynesian in a foxhole."[3]

Even before Obama won the 2008 presidential election, the George W. Bush administration in Washington discarded the hands-off approach to the financial sector and brought the free-market recalcitrant in Congress to endorse the massive rescue of the banks via the Troubled Assets Rescue Program (TARP) of $700 billion to purchase the toxic securities of the top commercial and investment banks under the doctrine that the banks were "too big to fail." This was in addition to the Federal Reserve's infusion of credit via so-called "special purpose vehicles" to two troubled financial players—Bear Stearns and the American International Group (AIG). Government action also forced two investment banks, Goldman Sachs and Morgan Stanley, to convert themselves into holding companies of the big banks.

But Keynesianism's rise to prominence really took place during the Obama presidency. Government fiscal intervention and regulation of the banks were seen by the incoming administration and its advisers as the central instruments in stabilizing an unraveling system.

FAILURE ON THE FISCAL FRONT

In 2009, the Stimulus was enacted, with governments in the North running deficits of up to 10% of their gross domestic product (GDP) to counteract the economic downturn. The Group of 20 (G20), meeting in Pittsburgh, Pennsylvania, in September 2009, appeared to give the imprimatur to a new era of fiscal activism by urging the adoption and maintenance of stimulus programs as the key solution to the crisis.

Another key resolution that the G20 adopted was the creation of a new regulatory framework for the financial sector at both the national and the international level. Although everyone agreed on financial reform, the devil was in the detail, with some governments favoring the banning of derivatives and the imposition of some kind of financial transactions tax, and some governments, such as the United States, not willing to go that far.

The move on the fiscal front was disappointing, however. Christina Romer, the head of Barack Obama's Council of Economic Advisors, estimated that it would take $1.8 trillion to reverse the recession. Obama approved only less than half, or $787 billion, supported by the more conservative members of his economic team, leaving Romer isolated. In relation to the size of the economy, this was a stimulus that was smaller than the Chinese government's $585 billion package. To many Keynesians, such as Richard Koo, the United States already had the lesson of Japan to appreciate the importance of a massive fiscal stimulus. Despite much skepticism in policy and academic circles, noted Koo, the 140 trillion yen that the Japanese government spent to counter Japan's Great Recession in the 1990s prevented economic collapse:

> In reality, it was only because the government increased fiscal expenditures to the extent it did that the nation's standard of living did not plummet. Indeed, it is nothing less than a miracle that Japan's GDP remained at above peak bubble-era levels despite the loss of 1500 trillion yen in national wealth and corporate demand equal to 20 per cent of GDP, and it was government spending that made this miracle possible.[4]

What makes the Obama administration's restraint even less understandable is that the neoliberals were still in disarray, with a number of their leading lights supporting Obama's stimulus spending. One of them was Nobel Prize laureate Robert Lucas, the unofficial dean of the US neoliberalism. Another was John Cochrane, another University of Chicago neoliberal luminary, who stated his position in a way that Paul Krugman would have approved:

> Let's be clear what this issue is not about. Governments *should* run deficits in recessions, and pay off the resulting debt in good times. Tax revenues fall temporarily in recessions. Governments should borrow (or dip into savings), to keep spending relatively steady. Moreover, many of the things government spends money on, like helping the unfortunate, naturally rise in recessions, justifying even larger deficits. Recessions are also a good time to build needed infrastructure or engage in other good investments, properly funded by borrowing. For all these reasons, it is good economics to see deficits in recessions—and surpluses in booms. . . . We can argue whether the overall level of spending is too high;

whether particular kinds of recession-related spending are useful or not; whether particular infrastructure really is needed; and we certainly face a structural deficit problem. But those are not the issue either.[5]

Obama's apparent motive in cutting Romer's proposed stimulus by half was not economic but political: to signal the right in Congress that he was someone they could talk business with. According to Krugman and other Keynesians, this Solomonian decision may have prevented the economy from tanking, but it prolonged the stagnation, with GDP growth not rising above 2.25% and unemployment not declining below 7% from 2009 to 2013.[6]

THE LIMITS OF MONETARY POLICY

With the Obama administration unwilling to put into effect an aggressive stimulus program for fear of triggering a backlash from neoliberals, the one Keynesian mechanism that was left to stop the downward spiral was an expansive monetary policy. Here, the Fed, under Ben Bernanke, did act aggressively, radically bringing down the rate at which banks could borrow from the Fed from 2.5% to effectively zero. A wide range of channels opened to pump liquidity into the economy and radically raise effective demand:

> The Fed also expanded the definition of who could borrow and what classified as acceptable collateral. An entire alphabet soup of new programs was initiated. There was the $150 billion Term Auction Facility (TAF); $50 billion in swap lines for foreign central banks; the $200 billion Term Securities Lending Facility (TSLF); the $20 billion Primary Dealer Credit Facility (PDCF); the $700 billion Commercial Paper Funding Facility (CPFF); and the $1 trillion Term Asset-Backed Securities Loan Facility (TALF).[7]

The largest and longest-lasting Fed program was known as "quantitative easing," the formal name of the program being the Large-Scale Asset Purchase (LSAP) program. This involved the Fed buying long-term assets from banks, including agency debt, mortgage-backed securities, and long-term treasuries. This program was massive, with the Fed's balance sheet leaping from $800 billion in 2007 to $3.3 trillion by 2013.[8] The idea was that these purchases would enable banks to make loans to companies and households that would then spend, add to aggregate demand, and jumpstart the economy.

The slow pace of the recovery and continuing high unemployment showed that this second-best Keynesian method for overcoming a recession was disappointing in its results, although it did not trigger the inflation that the hardline neoliberals and neoliberal press such as The Wall Street Journal predicted. Again, there was a Keynesian explanation for this; this time, it was not the size of the program. Drawing from his experience in Japan during the 1990s, Richard Koo explained that the response of indebted corporations and households is to pay off their debts or "deleverage" instead of contracting new debt:

> The private sector began paying down debt after the debt-financed asset bubble collapsed, leaving only debt in its wake. This was both responsible and correct behavior for individual businesses and households, but as a result of their actions the economy as a whole experienced what are known as fallacy-of-composition problems. A fallacy of composition refers

to a situation in which behavior that is correct for individuals or companies has undesirable consequences when everyone engages in it.[9]

Thus, when corporations stop borrowing money even at zero interest rate because they are deleveraging, funds supplied to financial institutions by the central bank remain stuck within the financial system. The same disappointing results that met expansive monetary policy in Japan in the 1990s also greeted the post-Lehman dramatic expansion of the monetary base in the United States. The key implication here, writes Koo, is that "the effectiveness of monetary policy diminishes dramatically as the private sector switches from maximizing profit to minimizing debt."[10]

In the United States, the infusion of money by the Fed into the banks or "bank reserves" rose from less than $1 trillion in 2009 to $3 trillion in 2013, but currency in circulation, reflecting money released by the banks through loans to corporations and households, rose only from approximately $500 billion to approximately $1 trillion.

Far more effective in the Keynesian view is monetary stimulus that puts as much money as direct as possible in the hands of households that have a significant propensity to spend, meaning poor households. Mian and Sufi state, perhaps in an exaggerated manner to make a point, that

> a better approach would be to allow central banks to directly inject cash into the economy, bypassing the banking system altogether. The most extreme image that comes to mind is the chairman of the Federal Reserve authorizing helicopter drops of cash. The idea of directly injecting cash into the economy may at first seem crazy, but reputable economists and commentators have suggested exactly such a policy during severe economic downturns. Ben Bernanke, only a few years before he was chairman of the Fed, suggested helicopter drops for Japanese central bankers in the 1990's, earning the nickname "Helicopter Ben." *Financial Times* columnist Martin Wolf wrote in February 2013 that "the view that it is never right to respond to a financial crisis with monetary financing of a consciously expanded fiscal deficit—helicopter money, in brief—is wrong. It simply has to be in the tool kit. Willem Buiter used rigorous modeling to show that such helicopter drops would in fact help an economy trapped at the zero lower bound nominal interest rates. It would be best if the helicopters targeted indebted areas of the country to drop cash.[11]

THE BANKING REFORM THAT WASN'T

The most dismal failure of the Keynesian effort, however, occurred in the area of financial reform. When the financial crisis broke, there was one thing on which there was a virtual national consensus: Urgent reform of the financial system was needed so the crisis would not happen again. There were widespread expectations that with Barack Obama taking over as president during the depths of the crisis and the Democrats winning control of the House and Senate, banking reform was just around the corner. The new president captured the mood of the country when he warned Wall Street, "My administration is the only thing that stands between you and the pitchforks."[12]

Reform of the US financial system was not just the concern of Keynesian and progressive economists. Many economists and policymakers of a strong free market bent were, in fact, also supporters of tough penalties and robust rules on the big banks. What is amazing is that despite a common front uniting the vast majority of the public, economic policymakers, and economists, practically no real reforms have been implemented in the decade following the outbreak of the financial crisis.

To take the most obvious first, if one excludes outright fraudsters such as Bernie Madoff whose criminal wrongdoing began way before the crisis, no Wall Street senior executives have been jailed for the myriad white-collar crimes involved in the mortgage-backed securities and derivatives business, including "well documented illegal acts, such as authorizing document forging, misleading investors, and obstructing justice."[13] Lack of prosecution of people at the top has contributed to continuing lack of accountability among top executives, resulting in scandals such as the recent Wells Fargo scandal involving bank personnel creating false accounts under customers' names without the latter's knowledge.

Next, there is the question of executive pay. Despite opprobrium visited on AIG officials for pocketing bailout money from the government in 2009, executive pay has remained relatively unrestrained. Caps on the pay of top executives of the banks that were bailed out while they were indebted to government was one of the reasons that they rushed to pay back the government. This way, they were able to take advantage of tax loopholes such as the CEO bonus based on "performance." This loophole, as many have noted, had been one of the reasons for irresponsible executive behavior leading to the crisis. With the loophole ban lifted, between 2010 and 2015, the top executives at the 20 leading US banks pocketed nearly $800 million in stock-based "performance" pay—before the value of their company's stock had returned to pre-crisis levels. In other words, with shareholders who had held on to their stock still in the red, executives were reaping massive rewards that their banks could then deduct off their taxes.[14]

Interestingly, the biggest beneficiary of the bonus was John Stumpf, CEO of Wells Fargo, who received tax-deductible bonus pay between 2012 and 2015 totaling $155 million.[15] As noted previously, Wells Fargo is the focus of the most recent Wall Street scandal, this time involving setting up false accounts of customers without their knowledge.

Nationalization of the troubled banks such as Citi and Bank of America (BofA), which were propped up with more than $800 billion by the government at the start of the financial crisis, was one of the measures in the playbook of Keynesians such as Paul Krugman and Joseph Stiglitz. As Krugman stated,

> To end their zombiehood the banks need more capital. But they can't raise more capital from private investors. So the government has to supply the necessary funds. . . . But here's the thing: The funds needed to bring these banks fully back to life would greatly exceed what they're currently worth. Citi and BofA have a combined market value of less than $30 billion, and even that value is mainly if not entirely based on the hope that stockholders will get a piece of a government handout. And if it's basically putting up all the money, the government should get ownership in return.[16]

Again it was not economic rationality that was the reason the Obama administration did not take a route that other governments in Europe had taken. It was ideology. The Obama administration, said Robert Gibbs, the White House spokesman, believes "that a privately held banking system is the correct way to go."[17] Bank nationalization, even temporary nationalization, was said to be "anathema to large segments of the American public, not to mention to the banking lobby."[18] In any event, what eventually resulted was what amounted to a government charade of giving the banks "stress tests" in order to declare them healthy, even if some of them were insolvent or bordered on insolvency, so that they could raise the capital that would bring them back to good health. As Eichengreen writes,

> A less happy interpretation is that the Good Housekeeping Seal of Approval conferred by the tests was tantamount to a colossal government guarantee. The nineteen biggest banks received special attention. Treasury asserted that they were solvent. Nine of them, starting with Goldman Sachs and JP Morgan Chase, required no additional capital. Citigroup, Bank of America, and eight of their less pristine competitors would be adequately capitalized if the raised only an additional $75 billion of capital, or so the government averred. If they then got into trouble, it stood to reason that this would be due to events not of their own making, and that the authorities, having attested to their soundness, would bail them out.[19]

The total cost to taxpayers of bailing out the banks in 2008 and 2009 was $2.2 trillion—$900 billion through the US Treasury and $1.3 trillion through the Federal Reserve. The paradoxical result is that the big banks have become even bigger and more profitable and have continued to engage in many of the practices that led to the financial crisis. Derivatives trading that violated federal law led to JP Morgan paying $920 million in fines in 2013, and the bank continues to be the object of a wide-ranging criminal probe of charges that it misrepresented the quality of the mortgages it was packaging into bonds and selling to investors. Wells Fargo, for its part, has admitted to creating millions of accounts in clients' names that they did not know about. All the while, the CEOs of the two corporations, Jamie Dimon of JP Morgan and John Stumpf of Wells Fargo, were receiving high pay packages and multiple bonus payments in the banking business in 2015, with Dimon making $27 million and Stumpf $19 million.[20] Given these developments, it is difficult to argue that nationalization was not the better option.

Keynesian economists and policymakers also favored having the financial institutions pay a portion of the costs of the subprime crisis, instead of sticking all of these on bankrupt homemakers. This would have involved the government forcing banks to write down mortgages of indebted homeowners—that is, debt forgiveness or debt relief. This would have meant that the banks would take a large hit. The rationale for sharing the financial consequences of the housing crisis was that because both homeowners and creditors were responsible for driving the housing boom, it was only fair to have a "more even distribution of losses between debtors and creditors."[21]

Such an arrangement would also make macroeconomic sense because the lack of effective demand could be partly addressed by reducing the indebtedness of households in trouble. Indeed, top economists who met with President Obama and Vice President Joe Biden said that Obama "could have significantly accelerated the slow economic recovery if he had better addressed the overhang of debt mortgage debt left when housing prices collapsed."[22]

The problem was again ideological: That the banks had to be saved at all costs and having them bear part of the cost of the mess they created by forcing them to write down mortgages would have harmed their recovery. In the measured judgment of Mian and Sufi,

> When a financial crisis erupts, lawmakers and regulators must address problems in the banking system. They must work to prevent runs and preserve liquidity. But policy makers have gone further, behaving as if the preservation of the bank creditor and shareholder value is the only goal. The bank-lending view has become so powerful that efforts to help homeowners are immediately seen in an unfavorable light. This is unacceptable. The dramatic loss in wealth of

indebted home owners is the key driver of severe recessions. Saving the banks won't save the economy. Instead, bolstering the economy by attacking the levered-losses problem directly would save the banks.[23]

Ideological predisposition was very pronounced among economists, who ignored the fact that the banks were no longer in severe stress after the bailout of 2008 and 2009. According to Mian and Sufi,

> The bank lending view enjoys tremendous support among some in the economics profession, and they help lodge it in the public discourse of policies in severe recessions. The entire discourse becomes focused on the banking crisis, and potential solutions to the household-debt crisis are ignored.[24]

In fact, not only was the plight of households ignored but also the administration deliberately sabotaged the passage of measures to assist them:

> [A] policy that implied large losses for the lenders would have undermined Treasury's strategy for rehabilitating the financial system, which was based on the banks' earning their way back to health. Secretary Geithner opposed any form of intervention that meant losses for the banks. The Senate was quietly told that bankruptcy reform was not a priority of the Treasury, and legislation aimed at revising the [law] died a quick death.[25]

Of course, ideological predilection was greased by money. Mian and Sufi found that "campaign contributions by financial firms led congressional representatives to be more likely to vote for bank bailout legislation. . . . Some members of Congress desperate to get campaign funds have clearly been bought off by the financial industry."[26]

Another reform that was badly needed was to have banks increase their equity relative to the debt, thus decreasing the leverage and their willingness to take risks that had contributed to the financial crisis. And when banks do get distressed, the more equity they have makes them less susceptible to become insolvent. Moreover, as Admati and Hellwig note,

> If solvency risk is reduced, the likelihood of liquidity problems and runs is also reduced because depositors and other creditors are less nervous about their money. Moreover, beyond the bank's own ability to absorb losses without becoming distressed, the fraction of assets that a bank may have to sell after losses in order to recover its equity is smaller if it has more equity. Therefore, the contagion caused through asset sales and interconnectedness is weaker when banks have more equity. Increasing banks' ability to absorb losses through equity thus attacks fragility most effectively and in multiple ways.[27]

When the financial crisis began in 2007, the equity of some major financial institutions was 2% or 3% of their assets, and these thin margins of safety played a critical role in bringing about the crisis. The Basel I and II Accords that government bank regulators put together to regulate capital did little to prevent the crisis. Basel III, which regulators agreed to after the outbreak of the crisis, failed to address the basic problem that banks can easily "game" the regulation, with the agreement permitting banks' equity to still be as low 3% of their total assets.[28] "The weakness of Basel III," note Admati and Hellwig, "was the result of an intense lobbying campaign mounted by the bankers against any major change in regulation. This campaign has continued since. By now even the full implementation of Basel III is in doubt."[29]

The most ambitious effort at financial reform was the so-called Dodd–Frank Wall Street Reform and Consumer Protection Act of 2010. Authored by Senator Christopher Dodd and Rep. Barney Frank, this piece of legislation totaled 848 pages, which, as one authority has noted, "easily surpasses the 32 pages of the Federal Reserve Act of 1913 and the 37 pages of the Glass–Steagall Act of 1933, the earlier major pieces of banking legislation."[30]

Upon its being signed into law, President Obama said, "The American people will never be asked again to foot the bill for Wall Street's mistakes. There will be no more taxpayer-funded bailouts. Period."[31] It is fair to say, however, that this monumental and exceedingly complex and detailed law gave birth to a mouse. On this, both the right and the left agreed.

One of the main objectives of the law was supposed to be to eliminate moral hazard, especially that which came under the rubric of too-big-to-fail institutions. Yet assuring the big banks that they were too big to fail was what the legislation did by declaring that every banking organization larger than $50 billion was "systemically important." As Peter Wallison and Cornelius Hurley assert,

> Prior to the financial crisis, the policy option of government intervening was called "constructive ambiguity." It provided creditors with just enough uncertainty to keep the biggest banks from being subsidized. But the financial crisis and the Dodd–Frank response have turned government intervention into a perceived entitlement.[32]

Given their central role in triggering the financial crisis, there was a strong call for the banning or very strict control of derivatives. Dodd–Frank did nothing of the sort. Instead, it permitted investment banks to

> create innovative (toxic) derivative products (such as CDO-cube or synthetic CDs) that defy analysis by ratings agencies as well as by investors, with no required approval by the Securities and Exchange Commission or the new Consumer Financial Protection Bureau within the Federal Reserve as long as the products are sold only to professional investors.[33]

It left out regulation of cross-border derivatives trading, a process that had contributed to the crisis. Even the minimum demand of the reformers that derivatives trading must take place on electronic exchanges where they could be better monitored and put in the public record did not make it.

Following the financial crisis, there were calls to bring back the Glass–Steagall separation between retail banking and investment banking; its abolition during the Clinton administration had led the banks to engage in risky trades in search of high profits. This was not taken up by Dodd–Frank. Instead, the final version of the legislation adopted what came to be known as the Volcker rule, which, in its original formulation, would have banned banks from engaging in proprietary trading or using depositors' money to trade on the banks' own accounts and from owning or investing in a hedge fund or private equity fund. In addition, it would have set limits on the the liabilities that the largest banks could hold. The Volcker Rule already was a retreat from a Glass–Steagall Chinese Wall between commercial and investment banking. Still it was further watered down so that rather than banning proprietary trading, banks could still invest up to 3% of their equity in speculative trading. How the banks could twist the weak Volcker rule version that became law was illustrated by the $6.2 billion JP Morgan lost in speculative trading by an agent known as "London Whale" in 2012, which the bank initially claimed was within the parameters of the Volcker rule but eventually admitted violating securities laws and agreed to pay fines of more than $1 billion.[34]

WHY KEYNESIANISM FAILED

Banking reform in the United States was a case of the regulated capturing the regulators. Despite their severe crisis of legitimacy, the financial elite were able to resist reform. Despite a national consensus for radical reform of the banking industry, Keynesian reforms were stopped dead in their tracks.

Finance capital and its allies were able to wage skilled defensive warfare from their entrenched positions in the US economic and political power structure. This structural power had developed over the nearly 30 years of neoliberal hegemony, wherein the balance of power in government–business relations had shifted decisively in the direction of business.

Capital's Structural Power I: The Power of Inaction

The first line of defense in the deployment of this "structural power" was to get the government to rescue the banks from the financial mess they themselves had created. The banks flatly refused Washington's pressure on them to mount a collective defense with their own resources. The banks simply told government that they were responsible for their own balance sheets and not for dealing with any systemic threat. This is what Cornelia Woll so aptly called the "power of inaction" or the power to influence developments by not acting.[35] Even when Lehman Brothers was about to go bankrupt in the fall of 2008, the banks did not budge. Revealing the banks' sense of their strong bargaining position vis-à-vis government, Merrill Lynch CEO John Thain remarked that in hindsight the only thing he regretted in the tense days of negotiations leading up to the collapse of Lehman Brothers was that the bankers did not "grab [the government representatives] and shake them that they can't let this happen."[36] It was up to government to come up with the resources to save the banks and save the system, not the banks themselves.

The banks calculated correctly. The Bush administration pressured Congress to approve the $787 billion TARP and used this to recapitalize the banks, with the dividend for the government shares so low that Vikram Pandit, CEO of Citigroup, the most troubled Wall Street giant, exclaimed, "This is really cheap capital."[37] Accepting the banks' implicit position that "they were too big to fail," Treasury and Federal Reserve funds that went to the banks through various conduits either as capital for recapitalization or as guarantees eventually totaled $3 trillion.

Government action—and taxpayers' money—saved the day, but the banks also calculated correctly that despite pressures from Keynesian economists such as Paul Krugman and Joseph Stiglitz, nationalization was out of the question because it was "not the American way." So generous—or intimidated—was Washington that what should have been standard operating procedure—the firing of top management and the shake-up of the board of what were essentially insolvent institutions—was not even considered seriously.

Capital's Structural Power II: The Power of Action

To the power of inaction must be added the power of action. As demonstrated in the various cases cited previously—the debates over burden sharing between the banks and indebted homeowners, bank equity levels, and Dodd–Frank—Wall Street deployed massive lobbying and cash to accompany it. Indicative of the bank's lobbying firepower was the $344 million the industry spent lobbying the US Congress in the first nine months of 2009, when legislators were taking up financial reform. Senator Chris Dodd, the chairman of the Senate Banking Committee, alone received $2.8 million in contributions from Wall Street in 2007 and 2008. The result of the lobbying offensive was summed up by Cornell University's Jonathan Kirshner:

> [The] Dodd–Frank regulatory reforms, and provisions such as the Volcker rule, designed to restrict the types of risky investments that banks would be allowed to engage in, have . . . been watered down (or at least waterboarded into submission) by a cascade of exceptions, exemptions, qualifications, and vague language. . . . And what few teeth remain are utterly dependent for application on the (very suspect) will of regulators.[38]

Capital's Structural Power III: "Productive Power"

The third dimension of the structural power of the banks was ideological—that is, the sharing of its perspectives with key government personnel about the centrality of finance, about how the good health of the financial system was the key to the good health of the whole economy, including the government. Some analysts called this the bank-lending point of view. Others called it the Wall Street–Washington connection. Woll characterizes this as "productive power"—the joint production of world views, meanings, and interpretations that emerge from shared perspectives.[39] The perspective in question developed from the thorough discrediting of government interventionist approaches by the stagflation of the 1970s and 1980s and their yielding primacy to the supposed superior efficacy of private sector initiatives. It was a central part of the neoliberal revolution. Through education and close interaction, regulators and bankers had come to internalize the common dictum that finance, to do its work successfully, must be governed with a "light touch." By the late 1990s, according to Simon Johnson and James Kwak, this process had created a Washington elite world view "that what was good for Wall Street was good for America."[40]

Neoliberalism may have gone on the defensive with the financial crisis, but it was not without influence within the Obama administration, especially from 2009 to 2012, when the administration was forging its strategy to deal with the fallout from the financial crisis. The new regime's core economic technocrats had a healthy respect for Wall Street—notably Treasury Secretary Tim Geithner and Council of Economic Advisors' head Larry Summers, both of whom had served as close associates of Robert Rubin, who had successive incarnations as co-chairman of Goldman Sachs, Bill Clinton's Treasury chief, and chairman and senior counselor of Citigroup. More than anyone else, Rubin has, during the past two decades, symbolized the Wall Street–Washington connection that dismantled the New Deal controls on finance capital and paved the way for the 2008 implosion. During a period of nearly 20 years, Wall Street had consolidated its control over the US Treasury Department, and the appointment of individuals who had served in Goldman Sachs, the most aggressive investment bank on Wall Street, to high positions became the most visible display of the structural power of finance capital. Rubin and Hank Paulson, George W. Bush's Secretary of the Treasury, were merely the tip of the Goldman Sachs iceberg at the center of Washington politics.

Wall Street was afforded an opportunity to make an ideological counteroffensive when the financial crisis entered its second phase, which was dominated by Greece's sovereign debt crisis. During the debate on the fiscal stimulus, which involved governmental deficit spending and increased the national debt, and even as they enjoyed tremendous monetary support from the Federal Reserve and the Treasury, the banks and their Republican allies in Congress were able to change the narrative from the irresponsible banks to the "profligate state." Greece was painted as the future of the United States. One Wall Street economist stated,

> As federal and state debt mounts up, the US credit rating will continue to be downgraded, and investors will become reluctant to hold US bonds without receiving much higher interest rates. As in Greece, high interest rates on government debt will drive federal and state governments into insolvency, or the Federal Reserve will have to print money to buy government bonds and hyperinflation will result. Calamity would result, either way.[41]

Wall Street's hijacking of the crisis discourse and shifting the blame for the continuing slowdown on government convinced some sectors of the population that it was the Obama administration's pallid Keynesian policies that were responsible for the continuing stagnation, and this contributed to putting the administration on the defensive and moving slowly on bank reform. Cornelia Woll concludes that

> for the administration and Congress, the main lesson from the financial crisis in 2008 and 2009 was that they had only very limited means to pressure the financial industry into behavior that appeared urgently necessary for the survival of the entire sector and the economy as a whole.[42]

Technocracy and Political Demobilization

The structural power of Wall Street certainly contributed to making Obama less aggressive in pushing banking reform and taking state action that would decisively end the recession. But Woll's analysis is too deterministic an explanation for failure. The presidency is a very powerful position, and from 2009 to 2011, the Democrats also controlled the House and the Senate, which put them in a position of pushing decisive measures for recovery. Moreover, no other office can compare in terms of mobilizing the citizenry in support of reform. In other words, if power could be productive on the side of Wall Street, it could also be productive on the side of the administration. Here, the contrast between Obama and Franklin Delano Roosevelt is stark. Whereas Roosevelt used the presidency as a bully pulpit to rally the population, setting in motion the massive organizing drive of labor that became a key pillar of the New Deal, Obama wed a technocratic approach that demobilized the base that had carried him to the Wall Street-biased prescriptions of the conservative wing of his economic team. This pallid, pragmatic Keynesianism was precisely what people were not looking for in a period of deep uncertainty and crisis.

Building a mass base for reform would, of course, have necessitated an inspiring comprehensive alternative vision to the discredited neoliberal one. Perhaps it was precisely articulating such an agenda that Obama, with his pragmatic instincts, feared, for it could run out of his control. But such are the risks that must be taken by serious reformists. The opportunity that presented itself and the way it was wasted are well described by Eichengreen:

> An administration and a president convinced of the merits of a larger stimulus would have campaigned for it. Obama could have invested the political capital he possessed as a result of his recent electoral victory. He could have appealed to GOP senators from swing states like Maine and Pennsylvania. Going over the heads of Congress, he could have appealed to the public. But Obama's instinct was to weight the options, not to campaign for his program. It was to compromise, not confront.[43]

The derailment of progressive Keynesianism by Obama's conservative, technocratic Keynesianism resulted in a protracted recovery, continuing high unemployment, millions of foreclosed or bankrupt households fending for themselves, and more scandals on a Wall Street where nothing had changed. Obama did not pay for this tragic outcome in 2012, but Hillary Clinton did in 2016.

THE POLITICAL CONSEQUENCES
OF ECONOMIC FAILURE

If there is one certainty that emerged in the 2016 elections, it was that Clinton's unexpected defeat stemmed from her loss of four so-called "Rust Belt" states: Wisconsin, Michigan, and Pennsylvania, which had previously been Democratic strongholds, and Ohio, a swing state that had twice supported Barack Obama.

The 64 Electoral College votes of those states, most of which had not even been considered battlegrounds, put Donald Trump over the top. Trump's numbers, it is now clear, were produced by a combination of an enthusiastic turnout of the Republican base, his picking up significant numbers of traditionally Democratic voters, and large numbers of Democrats staying home.

But this was not a defeat by default. On the economic issues that motivate many of these voters, Trump had a message: The economic recovery was a mirage, people were hurt by the Democrats' policies, and they had more pain to look forward to should the Democrats retain control of the White House.

The problem for Clinton was that the opportunistic message of this demagogue rang true to the middle-class and working-class voters in these states, even if the messenger himself was quite flawed. These four states reflected, on the ground, the worst consequences of the interlocking problems of high unemployment and deindustrialization that had stalked the whole country for more than two decades due to the flight of industrial corporations to Asia and elsewhere. Combined with the financial collapse of 2007 and 2008 and the widespread foreclosure of the homes of millions of middle-class and poor people who had been enticed by the banks to go into massive indebtedness, the region was becoming a powder keg of resentment.

It is true that the working-class voters who voted for Trump or boycotted the polls were mainly White. But these were the same people who placed their faith in Obama in 2008, when they favored him by a large margin over John McCain. And they stuck with him in 2012, although the margins of his victory were for the most part narrower. By 2016, however, they had had enough, and they would no longer buy the Democrats' blaming George W. Bush for the continuing stagnation of the economy. Clinton bore the brunt of their backlash because she made the strategic mistake of running on Obama's legacy—which, to the voters, was one of failing to deliver the economic relief and return to prosperity that he had promised eight years earlier, when he took over a country falling into a deep recession from the Bush administration.

Thus, the basic lesson that can be drawn from the analysis offered in this chapter is that failed or even half-hearted policies have massive political consequences. Clearly, the response to the 2008 GFC had an impact on US politics, but considering the wider tentacles of American political and economic influence throughout the world, it had a global impact as well.[44]

Notes

1. This contribution is part of a larger study on the global financial crisis being done under the auspices of the Amsterdam-based Transnational Institute and the Center for Southeast Asian Studies of Kyoto University. It is published here with the permission of the Transnational Institute.

2. Hyman Minsky, *Stabilizing an Unstable Economy* (New Haven, CT: Yale University Press, 1982).

3. Quoted in Satyajit Das, *Extreme Money* (London: Penguin, 2011).

4. Richard Koo, *The Escape from Balance Sheet Recession and the QE Trap Koo* (Singapore: Wiley, 2015), 26.

5. John Cochrane, "Fiscal Stimulus, RIP," November 9, 2009, https://faculty.chicagobooth.edu/john.cochrane/research/papers/stimulus_rip.html.

6. Paul Krugman, *End This Depression Now* (New York: Norton, 2012), 117.

7. Atif Mian and Amir Sufi, *House of Debt* (Chicago: University of Chicago Press, 2015), 128.

8. Ibid. 125.

9. Koo, n 4, 26.

10. Ibid. 15–16. Or as Keynes himself states, "Although the amount of [an individual's] own saving is unlikely to have any significant influence on his own income, the reactions of the amount of his consumption on the incomes of others makes it impossible for all individuals simultaneously to save any given sums. Every such attempt to save more by reducing consumption will so affect incomes that the attempt necessarily defeats itself" (John Maynard Keynes, "The General Theory of Employment," *Quarterly Journal of Economics* 51: 84).

11. Mian and Sufi, n 7, 156–157.

12. Quoted in Cornelia Woll, *The Power of Inaction* (Ithaca, NY: Cornell University Press, 2014), 101.

13. Simon Johnson, quoted in Johan Lybeck, *The Future of Financial Regulation* (Cambridge, UK: Cambridge University Press, 2016), 408.

14. Institute for Policy Studies, "Executive Excess 2016: The Wall Street Bonus Loophole," August 31, http://www.ips-dc.org/executive-excess-2016-wall-street-ceo-bonus-loophole.

15. Ibid.

16. Paul Krugman, "Banking on the Brink," *New York Times*, February 22, 2009, http://www.nytimes.com/2009/02/23/opinion/23krugman.html.

17. Ibid.

18. Barry Eichengreen, *Hall of Mirrors* (Oxford, UK: Oxford University Press, 2016), 293.

19. Ibid. 296.

20. Emily Jane Fox, "Here's the Stunning Amount of Money Top Wall Street C.E.O.s Made in 2015," *Vanity Fair*, March 21, 2016, http://www.vanityfair.com/news/2016/03/wall-street-ceo-pay-2015.

21. Mian and Sufi, n 7, 150.

22. Ibid. 142.

23. Ibid. 133.

24. Ibid. 131.

25. Eichengreen, n 18, 317.

26. Mian and Sufi, n 7, 131.

27. Anat Admati and Martin Hellwig, *The Bankers' New Clothes* (Princeton, NJ: Princeton University Press, 2013), 95.

28. Ibid. 96.

29. Ibid. 96.

30. Johan Lybeck, *The Future of Financial Regulation* (Cambridge, UK: Cambridge University Press, 2016), 397.

31. Admati and Hellwig, n 27, 110.

32. Lybeck, n 30, 406–407.

33. Lybeck, n 30, 411.

34. Patricia Hurtado, "The London Whale," *Bloomberg*, February 23, 2016, https://www.bloomberg.com/quicktake/the-london-whale.

35. Woll, n 12, 56–60.

36. Ibid. 7.

37. Quoted in ibid. 40.

38. Jonathan Kirshner, *American Power after the Financial Crisis* (Ithaca, NY: Cornell University Press, 2014).

39. Woll, n 12, 50–56.

40. Simon Johnson and James Kwak, quoted in Woll, n 12, 52.

41. Peter Morici, "The United States Is Becoming Too Much Like Greece," *Fox News*, June 15, 2012, http://www.foxnews.com/opinion/2012/06/15/united-states-is-becoming-too-much-like-greece.html.

42. Woll, n 12, 102.

43. Eichengreen, n 18, 298–299.

44. The points I make here are more fully developed in Walden Bello, "How Obama's Economic Legacy Lost the Elections for Hillary Clinton," *Foreign Policy in Focus*, November 16, 2016, http://fpif.org/obamas-legacy-lost-elections-hillary.

References

Admati, Anat, and Martin Hellwig. 2013. *The Bankers' New Clothes*. Princeton, NJ: Princeton University Press.

Bello, Walden. 2016. "How Obama's Economic Legacy Lost the Elections for Hillary Clinton." *Foreign Policy in Focus*, November 16. http://fpif.org/obamas-legacy-lost-elections-hillary.

Cochrane, John. 2009. "Fiscal Stimulus, RIP." November 9. https://faculty.chicagobooth.edu/john.cochrane/research/papers/stimulus_rip.html.

Das, Satyajit. 2001. *Extreme Money*. London: Penguin.

Eichengreen, Barry. 2016. *Hall of Mirrors*. Oxford, UK: Oxford University Press.

Fox, Emily Jane. 2016. "Here's the Stunning Amount of Money Top Wall Street C.E.O.s Made in 2015." *Vanity Fair*, March 21. http://www.vanityfair.com/news/2016/03/wall-street-ceo-pay-2015.

Hurtado, Patricia. 2016. "The London Whale." *Bloomberg*, February 23. https://www.bloomberg.com/quicktake/the-london-whale.

Institute for Policy Studies. 2016. "Executive Excess 2016: The Wall Street Bonus Loophole." August 31. http://www.ips-dc.org/executive-excess-2016-wall-street-ceo-bonus-loophole.

Keynes, John Maynard. "The General Theory of Employment." *Quarterly Journal of Economics* 51: 84.

Kirshner, Jonathan. 2014. *American Power After the Financial Crisis*. Ithaca, NY: Cornell University Press.

Koo, Richard. 2015. *The Escape from Balance Sheet Recession and the QE Trap Koo*. Singapore: Wiley.

Krugman, Paul. 2009. "Banking on the Brink." *New York Times*, February 22. http://www.nytimes.com/2009/02/23/opinion/23krugman.html.

Krugman, Paul. 2012. *End This Depression Now*. New York: Norton.

Lybeck, Johan. 2016. *The Future of Financial Regulation*. Cambridge, UK: Cambridge University Press.

Mian, Atif, and Amir Sufi. 2015. *House of Debt*. Chicago: University of Chicago Press.

Minsky, Hyman. 1982. *Stabilizing an Unstable Economy*. New Haven, CT: Yale University Press.

Morici, Peter. 2012. "The United States Is Becoming Too Much Like Greece." *Fox News*, June 15. http://www.foxnews.com/opinion/2012/06/15/united-states-is-becoming-too-much-like-greece.html.

Woll, Cornelia. 2014. *The Power of Inaction*. Ithaca, NY: Cornell University Press.

CHAPTER 21

TRAFFICKING

PAUL AMAR

THE study of "trafficking" is essential to the scholarly agenda of global studies. The term relates to a set of illicit and criminalized forms of commerce and movement that constitute the transnational *other* of the normative, legalized "global" sphere. Conventional ways of thinking about trafficking and transnational crime can mystify or, worse, create moral panic or racialized misconceptions. Interdisciplinary, critical global studies scholarship can offer more useful approaches to the study of "trafficking" by exploring colonial history and political–economic relations and specifying the modes of global governance and state violence that have crystallized around formations of trafficking and anti-trafficking. Many of the dominant liberal legal and ideological formulations of globalization are defined through the repudiation of trafficking—trafficking in drugs, goods, sex, and labor, and even trafficking in information. So studying the illicit worlds of trafficking is key to understanding processes of globalization, as much as the study of trade, migration, development, and conflict.

Twenty-first-century regimes of global governance, and the commercial, legal, and cultural formations that undergird them, emerged historically through processes of criminalization and regulation. These rules defined the sphere of legality as standing in strict opposition to piracy, then to smuggling, and then in opposition to trafficking.

Piracy on the high seas was tolerated as long as it benefitted individual European monarchs or helped one empire challenge a rival (Little 2007). For example, in the sixteenth century, "privateers" (pirates contracted by one monarch to rob from another) seized shiploads of gold along the Caribbean route of the Spanish Main, the mainland coastal departure points and prime trade routes between the Americas and Iberia (Struett, Carlson, and Nance 2013). This embrace of piracy through privateering allowed England to challenge the sixteenth-century Atlantic supremacy of Spain. Subsequently, on the other side of the world, a pirate "commonwealth" in Madagascar, on the southeast African coast in the Indian Ocean, developed its own quasi-democratic codes and wreaked havoc in sea routes around the Horn of Africa that connected Europeans to Asia (Thomson 1994). But pirates were rarely truly neutral or autonomous. In fact, the actions of Madagascar pirates allowed the British merchants in charge of the East India Company not just to eliminate European (Dutch and Portuguese) rivals but also to sink local South Asian, Arab, and African merchants of the Swahili coast. The British could bribe, bluster, and blast their way through the pirate gauntlet.

The field of global studies and those in affiliated disciplines have made important contributions that set the term "trafficking" into the context of contemporary transnational debates (Carmack 2013; Gootenberg 2009). Global studies-oriented scholarship traces from where this term emerged historically and through which processes "trafficking" practices and "anti-trafficking" politics have seized global public imaginations.

In this chapter, I examine four spheres in which "trafficking" is currently constituted. First, I briefly examine the history of this term as it gradually took shape in relation to struggles over the meaning of "free trade" as well as in tension with terms such as piracy and smuggling. History demonstrates that these terms and the practices they describe did not necessarily operate at opposite ends of the moral and legal spectrum. In fact, they often overlapped and stirred contention, through which the essential norms of global commercial governance gradually emerged. Second, I examine the evolution of "trafficking" in the context of "drug wars," from the imperial Opium Wars in China in the early nineteenth century to the twenty-first-century "narco" battlegrounds of Mexico. Third, I trace how global studies-related research has developed critical lenses for analyzing the politics of "sex trafficking" and "human trafficking." This branch of trafficking politics has focused primarily on criminalizing the movements of women sex workers while displacing questions of women's agency, sexual rights, and autonomy (Shah 2014). But human trafficking politics has also come, more constructively, to challenge new patterns of forced labor in the global economy and to reveal forms of "new slavery" and indentured servitude—for example, in the United Arab Emirates (Kakande 2015; Kotiswaran 2017). Finally, I examine the term "trafficker" as selectively deployed along racial and social lines. I demonstrate how the discourse produces an obscuring pseudo-analysis of the violence of global capitalism that preserves the impunity of certain powerful actors, creates a monstrous misrepresentation of globalizing forms of violence, and stirs forms of moral and racial panic that enforce punishment and marginalization of the least powerful in the global system.

The analysis that follows maps the study of global trafficking by drawing upon scholars, some of whom explicitly identify with the field of global studies. The list of references at the end of the chapter brings together some of this new generation of interdisciplinary studies of global trafficking and related issues. Other scholars cited here have offered contributions that have furthered work in related disciplines that constitute the infrastructure of the global field, such as global history, postcolonial studies, transnational cultural studies, and critical political economy.

TRAFFICKING AND PIRACY AND SMUGGLING

Terminologies around "free trade" emerged historically in the context of processes of colonization, as well as of insurgency against colonial rule. "Trafficking" as a term came to signify the subversion or hijacking of "free trade" circulatory dynamics by extralegal actors trading in illicit goods. In the 1500s, Spanish theologians began to argue for "freedom of sea commerce" to protect the routes that connected Castille and Aragon to its New World conquests—that is, primarily to protect the shipment of gold looted from indigenous peoples (Scott 2000). During the American Revolution against the British, New Englanders were condemned as smugglers and pirates. The British Navy sealed American ports in order to crush the insurgency. In response, the insurgent Americans demanded "Free Trade." For the American rebels, a call for "free trade" meant something very different than it does today; the cry for "free trade" signified an appeal for the French navy, Spanish supply vessels, and Caribbean and North African pirates to breach the British blockade and come to the aid of the revolutionaries (Davis and Engerman 2006).

Two generations later, it was the British Navy, rather than one of its rebel adversaries, that demanded "free trade." In China in the 1830 and 1840s, British gunboats forced Free Trade on the Qing Dynasty's coastal cities. By ensuring submission of ports to so-called "free trade," the British East India Company aimed to displace Asian merchant elites and divert profits to London (Celikkol 2011). When examined in its contentious historical context, meanings of the term "free trade" flipped back and forth during centuries of complex struggle, along with the label of who was the legitimate merchant and who was the pirate or trafficker. Depending on the context, the term's meaning was harnessed closely to the interests of empire or rebellion, to whose blockade one was transgressing or enforcing.

In the early nineteenth century, a philosophical school of political economy emerged, influenced by the work of Scottish Enlightenment moral philosopher Adam Smith (who first published *Wealth of Nations* in 1776 during the British blockade of rebel American ports) and of British philosopher David Ricardo, whose pioneering economic conceptualizations, such as "the labor theory of value" (1817; Wood 1991; see also Cain 1999), were closely tied to his political work supporting "free trade." But for Ricardo, the banner of "free trade" signified a principled, liberal mobilization against slavery and particularly against inhumane slave-holding sugar cartels in the West Indies. In the nineteenth century, debates at the heart of the British Empire elaborated the notion of "free trade." This new language aimed to sanitize the image of global commerce and cleanse trade of its association with projects of conquest, violent seizure, slavery, racial colonialism, port blockades, and mercenarism (Fakhri 2014).

Jurists at the heart of the British Empire, in particular, drafted the founding frameworks for international law—commercial law and security doctrines—as this "free trade" politics began to turn against the violent seizure and disruption of commerce (piracy), on the one hand, and against the secret conveyance of goods (smuggling), on the other hand (Oxford LibGuides n.d.; Wachspress 2015). Together, these shifts constituted a new liberal (but still firmly colonial–imperial) world order in which violence was supposedly disentangled from trade through law and also in which secret, unregulated, untaxed commerce was purged through establishment of norms of transparency and accounting. However, history has demonstrated that the colonial and imperial power struggles, and the racial and moral dynamics that shaped this originary era of free trade policy and anti-trafficking regulation, persist. They have been displaced and aggravated by the division of the imaginary of the global between an enlightened world of market forces and a violent realm of trafficking and illegality.

Many of today's prohibitions against smuggling date back to this period. In that era, empires and states began to define and police their borders and to protect their mercantile commercial regimes by prohibiting secret shipments. Whereas efforts to arrest piracy focused on the violence of forced seizures, the control of smuggling focuses on rooting out its secrecy and unaccountability, acts of secretly conveying an object that is not necessarily illicit but is used for illicit purposes or sold for illicit gains, including evasion of tax and tariff once it secretly crosses a border or transgresses a security perimeter. In other words, the transnational commerce in narcotics is, of course, trafficking. But the act of se-cretly conveying drugs across a border is also smuggling. Bringing a legal product subject to a tariff across a border without paying that tariff is smuggling (Karras 2010). Secretly conveying a banned object into a prison or through an airport checkpoint is also smuggling.

International and domestic realms of law and policing around piracy and smuggling do overlap to some extent with the definition of control regimes around trafficking. But "trafficking," throughout the modern history of globalization, has remained an incredibly powerful, flexible, and ideologically manipulated concept. This is because the notion of trafficking stirs the imagination in particular ways; revives and animates racial and moral logics of colonialism; justifies extraordinary and unlimited forms of state power; and channels large-scale anxieties about agency, insurgency, mobility, and networking in the global commercial system.

"Drug War" Empires and Global History

In the twenty-first century, many world regions face the social devastation wrought by an epidemic of opiate addictions. The US Appalachian region has been flooded with megadoses of prescription painkillers imposed by a racket of profiteering doctors and pharmaceutical companies. The Middle East and Europe have been saturated with illicit heroin (an opiate) and opium, itself generated largely within Afghanistan. Warlords in Southwest Asia, both those allied with the US occupation of Afghanistan and those opposed to it, harvest and process poppies in order to fund this generations-old conflict, the same poppies that supply the booming "legal" opiate production by the global pharmaceutical companies (Brauer 2017; Chossudovsky 2005; Chouvy 2010; Muhawesh 2016).

But this is not the first time that Western legal drug industries have been at the center of an intersection of global controversies around pain, addiction, and wars in Asia. The Opium Wars in the 1830s and 1840s brought the British Empire and China to their first major standoff (with once more the militarization of Afghanistan and the neighboring Indus valley serving as the site of militarized cultivation and dispossession). This con-flict created the first dynamics through which the discourse of "trafficking" emerged and through which the power of the global drug trade embedded itself in the core of the global legal, commercial, and moral orders.

What interests collided to trigger the Opium Wars? And why is this history so important for global studies scholars to explore? The Opium Wars that erupted in the 1830s are a gen-erative case study of global commerce and conflict, as well as of colonial and anti-colonial struggles, because they reveal the intimate relationship between globalizing capitalism and its most criminalized adversaries—in this case between peddlers of addiction and vice and champions of civilizing, liberal trade. The Opium Wars are still remembered vividly in China as a moment of national humiliation, but global studies scholarship in general needs to be attentive to this era and its resulting global governance, legal, and cultural regimes.

In the early and mid-nineteenth century, the British Empire, with the private trading corporation the British East India Company at its heart, faced a series of major insurgencies and fiscal crises, as well as saturation of the markets for the Empire's products. Enslaved workers led mass revolts in Britain's plantation colonies, and abolitionism was winning the moral argument in London. Popular uprisings were sweeping India and southern Africa and challenging the East India Company's violent legacies of repression and expropriation of land, institutions, and power. Resentment also simmered in China. At this time, China was still an independent empire, headed by the dynastic Qing emperor, but British, French, and Japanese armed assaults and merchant aggressions were chipping away at its sovereignty.

Given the proclivity for criminalizing narcotics in the twentieth and twenty-first centuries, one might assume that Chinese merchants and consumers, and perhaps its "opium den" culture, were the origin points of opium trafficking in this era and the cause of the Opium Wars. But the opposite is true. The trafficking in and increased consumption by Chinese consumers of opium were the explicit commercial and military aim of the British Empire. British war-mongering was tied to its promotion of opium consumption and addiction. The British aimed to eliminate Chinese merchants who wanted to reduce opiate addiction and instead market and export more productive commodities from China to the British and European consumer markets.

As analyzed by Julia Lovell in her book, *The Opium War: Drugs, Dreams and the Making of China* (2011), the world's first global drug war began as the British Empire faced a funding crisis and a massive trade deficit: The cost of maintaining direct rule over India was exploding, and the British public was consuming huge amounts of tea from China, without Chinese consumers expressing interest in buying British goods (pp. 1–4). The solution to both problems was to use naval force to push China's Qing Dynasty's government to lift its ban on opium sales and to maximize British revenue by ensuring the addiction of China's coastal cities to consuming opiates that the British government itself would ship into China, mediating between producers in India and private merchants. Opium sales were going to salvage the British Empire's economy and prop up the empire's military budget of Britain. With poppies raised in British-controlled Afghanistan and India, processed in the British India capital of Calcutta, and then sold in the areas around what would become British Hong Kong and the interior provinces of China, opium sales would balance the books. And its mesmerizing, addictive effects would also quiet resistance and build literal and commercial dependence on British merchants throughout the region.

So the first global drug war was one in which Western law and free trade discourse bolstered a pro-drug regime, insisting on "free ports" and decriminalized consumption, but with the aim of propping up colonial plantations, merchant profits, and military operations. The Opium Wars consisted of two sets of battles, mostly along the coast of what would be developed into the British colonial possession of Hong Kong, where Chinese forces attempted to free themselves from the British opium merchants' stranglehold on their ports and their economy.

The Mexican Drug Wars and Post-NAFTA Globalization

More than a century later, another set of militarized efforts to restructure transnational trade and reconfigure global hegemonies played out through another series of drug wars, this time in the Americas. With increasing intensity since the 1980s and 1990s, ideological struggles between political mobilizations on the left and the right were displaced onto debates regarding the close relationship between neoliberalism and narcotrafficking. Global studies methods—combining analyses of political economy, social history, transnational governance of trade and crime, and cultural politics—can reveal the contexts of these shifts in uniquely powerful ways (Barndt 2004; Caulfield 2010; Clarkson 2008; White 2014).

Coming into force on January 1, 1994, the North American Free Trade Agreement (NAFTA) created a zone of lower trade tariffs and intensified economic, investment, and commercial integration between Mexico, the United States, and Canada. Although this agreement lowered duties (fees or tariffs) on trade, it did not address the question of government subsidies to producers in the United States. In addition, agricultural tariff quotas were negotiated bilaterally, which strengthened the United States' hand in securing trade imbalances that favored its producers even as it argued for market opening. This mix of barrier dropping and selective protectionism led to particular negative impacts, experienced disproportionately in Mexico and the border regions of the United States. These effects included food insecurity, displacement of agricultural workforce, and a flood of guns and arms products from the United States into Mexico (Ayres and MacDonald 2012; Cukier and Sidel 2006).

As some scholars have argued, drugs became a very "useful" shared currency for this NAFTA economy: Drugs served as a kind of illicit currency, untaxed and untraced. As the production hub of this violent new post-NAFTA order, Mexico provided a space where US industries (gun sellers, factory investors, and agribusiness) benefitted hugely, whereas laborers, farmers, and the average citizens of Mexico and the US border region suffered from explosive police corruption or terrorizing drug cartel governance (Bailey and Godson 2001). Paradoxically and perversely, many of these social problems and forms of violence were then blamed on Mexican migrants to the United States, when in fact migration trends were secondary effects, certainly not causes, of these NAFTA-era changes (Carlson 2013; Darlington and Gillespie 2017; Semple 2017).

In *The Illicit Global Economy and State Power*, H. Richard Friman and Peter Andreas (1999) analyzed presciently the impact that NAFTA's version of "free trade" would have in terms of the "narcotization" of the Mexican economy. What do "free trade agreements" have to do with the emergence of narcotraffic economies and regimes of violence in Mexico?

First, the NAFTA agreement led to the flooding of the Mexican agricultural market with cheap corn and food products, subsidized by US government aid, which eliminated the viability of rural agricultural economies in Mexico and wiped out millions of small farms and millions of farm-related jobs in the corn heartland, rendering people desperate enough to turn to the cultivation or sale of illicit agricultural products (including marijuana) in order to survive. This occurred at the same time that opening of the commercial border with the United States promoted the flooding of Mexican gun markets with cheap US weapons (Cook, Cukier, and Krause 2009) and also with the reduction of controls over transshipment of goods and money. Although NAFTA was articulated as a free trade agreement during a time in which the US government and its allies in Mexico and Colombia and throughout the world were also drafting draconian legal and military agendas for repressing and combatting drug economies, the structural effects of NAFTA ended up being at least as pro-drug, pro-violence, and pro-dispossession as its Opium War predecessor. But the difference between today's narco-wars and the nineteenth-century conflict is that today's drug wars mask the role of economic elites and seem to shift all responsibility for the profits and violence of trafficking (and associated gun industries and money laundering practices) onto the victim countries and onto those rural or urban-peripheral populations most harmed by the free trade regimes.

As a model for global studies scholarship, Curtis Marez' book, *Drug Wars: The Political Economy of Narcotics* (2004), blends transnational cultural and media analysis, global political economy, and postcolonial legal studies research. He argues that

> drug enforcement is part of a larger set of ideologies and practices that might be better described as the management of drug traffic. . . . The demand for drugs is not, strictly speaking, the enemy of state power, rather drugs demand is a sustaining object of power. (p. 2)

Sayek Valencia's *Capitalismo Gore* (2010; this title translates to English as either "Gore Capitalism" or "Slasher Capitalism") serves as a useful model for reimagining global capitalism and global studies through the lens of critical narcotraffic studies. In Valencia's vision, narco cultures and economies are not marginal or outside of conventional or formal productive economies and commercial circuits but, rather, represent the core logic emerging from and transcending neoliberalism. In this groundbreaking book, trafficking, or the figure of the narco (as cartel leader or even as agent of state or police that participates in economies of violence), is analyzed as shaping a global market of images of consumer desires and forms of capital, in collaboration with states and companies that superficially firmly oppose narcotrafficking. This focus on the violent and social formations of global capitalism, as it appropriates "narco" cultures, provides a critical alternative that complements new research on "narco-states" in the world system (Battersby and Siracusa 2011).

TRAFFICKING IN PERSONS AND GLOBAL AGENCY

In 2000, the United Nations (UN) passed the "Palermo Protocol" to "prevent, suppress and punish trafficking in persons, especially women and children." This served as an amendment to the landmark UN Convention against Transnational Organized Crime, also signed in 2000. The passage of this resolution marked the ratification on the global stage of a politics of "anti-trafficking" that diverged in important ways from the terms of the war on narcotrafficking that had come to saturate global imaginaries of crime since the 1980s. In some ways, the increasing visibility of "human trafficking" as a globally visible issue represented a victory for feminist organizers and labor rights movements that had long decried the trans-border nature of labor exploitation, the vulnerability of migrant workers, and the gendered and racialized character of migrant labor dilemmas. But, significantly, this moment also reflected the appropriation of the issue of human trafficking by evangelical neoconservative militants and missionaries, whose politics were diametrically opposed to those of the feminist and labor movements.

The pioneering work of Elizabeth Bernstein traces the historical connections between the twenty-first-century anti-sex trafficking movement, particularly among internationally minded evangelical Christian activists, and "carceral feminists" who are anti-trafficking and pro-criminalization (Bernstein 2007, 2010). She also describes how these contemporary links resonate with the mobilization against "White slavery" in the late nineteenth and early twentieth centuries. Campaigns against "White slavery" in this period appropriated the discourse of abolition and married it to conservative and moralistic attempts to stop single women from migrating on their own, or circulating outside of the sphere of domestic labor (de Vries 2005).

Feminist studies scholar Heather Berg (2015) has analyzed how global anti-trafficking policy makes "victims" out of sex workers through curtailments on mobility and work eligibility that "make workers more dependent on third party managers and less able to secure assistance when these parties abuse the power that the state has effectively granted them."

The work of globally oriented scholarship that sets Brazil into transnational and geopolitical context has generated a body of critical scholarship on how "human trafficking" or "sex trafficking" politics have confronted resistance from traditions of global and local organizing around HIV/AIDS, access to public health, workers' rights, and women and trans and Black struggles against police brutality and racketeering. Publications by Adriana Piscitelli, Laura Agustín, Ana Paula da Silva, Gregory Mitchell, Thaddeus Blanchette, and Paul Amar have exposed the economic, legal, and state-institutional stakes of struggle around the globalization of anti-trafficking politics as it focuses on sex work or prostitution in the Global South (Agustin 2007; Amar 2009, 2013; da Silva, Blanchette, and Bento 2013; Mitchell 2016; Piscitelli 2007). This set of publications based on distinct empirical research endeavors, as well as ethnography and media and legal studies, has converged around a set of distinct lines of analysis and trajectories of argument. First, it does not assume "victim" status for all those participating in sex work, and it critically examines the "rescuer" status of social movements that use "trafficking" discourse to speak for and criminalize workers "for their own good." Instead, this group of global studies-oriented scholars assesses working conditions and forms of structural and interpersonal violence through in-depth case studies rather than voyeuristic or scandal-focused portrayals. Second, these studies situate sex work in a broad spectrum of gendered and sexualized spheres of work and transnationally articulate labor struggles, engaging questions of domestic labor, care work, tourism, and textile factory labor. This research inserts sex worker issues into the context of other struggles with health care and bodily dignity (particularly for women, trans, racialized, and indigenous groups). Third, this group spotlights and sets into historical context the international and global circulation of norms that shape "trafficking"-related activities as a particular site for neocolonial or unaccountable state violence and police racketeering.

Racial Imaginaries of Trafficking and Imagining Realms of "Shadow" Globalization

How is trafficking represented today in global media and policy discourse? Has "migration" panic built on this? Why is it important to engage the field of "critical trafficking studies" today? And why is the field of global studies uniquely positioned to generate rigorous scholarship, illuminating analyses, and policy relevance in this area?

The study by Hall et al. (2013) and other cultural studies have examined racialized crime in the global public sphere and the wave of police corruption, social violence, and mass incarceration that followed the launch of the drug wars in the Americas, from the Crack Wars (Lusane and Desmond 1991; Murch 2015) in the United States to the cocaine-centered conflicts in Miami and Colombia in the 1980s and the narco-economies of the twenty-first century. Globally oriented scholarship in the fields of cultural studies, law and society, anthropology, and transnational criminology has traced how representations of race and morality have framed these conflicts in ways that mask where social violence originates and how economic dispossession is enacted. Media discourses and anti-crime policies worldwide during this period have represented the origin of violence and inequality in and around drug trafficking as a moral failing and sexual or bodily excess of the racialized poor rather than as the responsibility of those who benefit most by leveraging the historic contradictions of global "free trade" as it intersects with arms industries, money laundering, and systematic state and police corruption.

A number of global studies-oriented works in the field of cultural studies, media studies, and ethnic studies have confronted these systematic misrepresentations of trafficking as a product of monstrous race/gender cultures rather than as an effect of structures of capitalism and governance. These works, which focus more on "sex trafficking" or "human trafficking," include that by Elina Pettinen (2008), who describes how forms of global capitalism create a "shadow globalization" that reconfigures the bodies and representation of Baltic and Russian women sex workers. But this work tends to re-emphasize the passive role of women in these so-called "sex-scapes." Other more critical work, which draws upon the voices and agency of sex workers themselves, includes that by Laura Augustín (2007), who focuses on the assertions of migrants, racialized women, and sex workers and how their struggles for better working conditions, against police brutality, and for rights as workers, women, and/or migrants are hampered by the voyeurism and the horrific metaphors of globalization produced by "anti-trafficking" advocates.

Global studies-oriented scholarship that analyzes the racial representation of the struggles around narcotrafficking include many in-depth reports about the racially unequal rates of targeting, arrest, incarceration, and media (mis)representation of racialized peoples in the "drug war" (We Are the Drug Policy Alliance n.d.) Cinar and Bender (2007) explore how the militarization of the state around trafficking has created a new kind of "global city" where race and class divisions are exacerbated, and social resources and democratic institutions are "walled off" for populations identified with trafficking. In addition, media studies examinations have explored how "narco" stereotypes have come to animate television and cinema narratives in Latin America and other world regions in ways that exacerbate myths and generate new monsters around figures of race, gender, and sexuality (Benevides 2009).

What we call trafficking economies are still sometimes referred to as "black markets." As Hatsuda and Sakasai (2016) have analyzed, historically, it is no mere coincidence that terms such as "dark mirror," "shadow state," and "black markets"—used to describe the universe of trafficking crimes—resonate closely with the darkness-obsessed language of race, even in Japan, where ethnic orderings and the "racialization of class" function in wholly unique ways. Cedric Robinson, a founder of critical studies of race and globalization, would call these metaphors, and he would call the informal economies they misrepresent and subjective categories part of the founding structures of racial capitalism (Robinson 2005; see also Melamed 2011). But paradoxically, the discourse of trafficking produces a virulently racist, rather than race conscious, theory of racial capitalism that blames and hypercriminalizes its exploited victims and that targets rather than reveal the systematic legal, economic, and policing practices at its core.

In the 1980s and 1990s, on a global scale, the words "drug" and "trafficking" in English came to operate almost as the new "n-word," married to the ideological imaginary of racial capitalism. "Drug dealer," "drug-related crime," "trafficker": If any of these terms became attached to an individual or a community, then they were deemed outside the bounds of citizenship, more likely to face more police violence, unfair treatment by justice systems, or disproportionately high incarceration rates.

"Trafficking" as a framing of criminality and as a historic set of controls has consistently produced an obscuring pseudo-analysis of the violence of global capitalism that preserves the impunity of certain powerful actors while stirring forms of moral and racial panic that enforce punishment and marginalization of the least powerful in the global system (Fojas 2017). With a turn toward legalization and partial decriminalization of marijuana in Uruguay and some US states, and under discussion in many other countries, has the trafficking discourse turned a corner? Or have the key questions of violence, racialization, and economic dispossession been sidelined? These are urgent questions that global studies scholars are uniquely positioned to engage.

"Global trafficking" is not a set of phenomena that can be studied uncritically or without careful exploration of the ways that colonial violence, economic dispossession, missionary moralism, and legal/regulatory biases have instrumentalized this volatile term. Global studies, as an inherently critical and interdisciplinary enterprise—as represented by some of the groundbreaking work cited in this chapter—can fruitfully reshape the agenda of "trafficking studies" and center this nascent field as an important site with valuable lessons to offer scholars across the disciplines, as well as policymakers, community organizers, public advocates, journalists, and media makers.

REFERENCES

Amar, P. 2009. "Operation Princess in Rio de Janeiro: Policing 'Sex Trafficking,' Strengthening Worker Citizenship, and the Urban Geopolitics of Security in Brazil." *Security Dialogue* 40 (4–5): 513–541.

Amar, P. 2013. *The Security Archipelago: Human-Security States, Sexuality Politics, and the End of Neoliberalism.* Durham, NC: Duke University Press.

Andreas, P., and H. R. Friman. 1999. *The Illicit Global Economy and State Power.* Lanham, MD: Rowman & Littlefield.

Augustín, L. M. 2007. *Sex at the Margins: Migration, Labour Markets and the Rescue Industry.* London: Zed.

Ayres, J., and L. MacDonald, eds. 2012. *North America in Question: Regional Integration in an Era of Economic Turbulence.* Toronto: University of Toronto Press.

Bailey, J. J., and R. Godson. 2001. *Organized Crime and Democratic Governability: Mexico and the U.S.–Mexican Borderlands.* Pittsburgh, PA: University of Pittsburgh Press.

Barndt, D., ed. 2004. *Woman Working the NAFTA Food Chain: Women, Food and Globalization.* Toronto: Sumach Press.

Battersby, P., and J. M. Siracusa. 2011. *Crime Wars: The Global Intersection of Crime, Political Violence, and International Law.* Santa Barbara, CA: ABC-CLIO.

Berg, H. 2015. "Trafficking Policy, Meaning Making and State Violence." *Social Policy and Society Journal* 14 (1): 145–155.

Bernstein, E. 2007. "The Sexual Politics of the 'New Abolitionism.'" *Differences* 18 (3): 128–151.

Bernstein, E. 2010. "Militarized Humanitarianism Meets Carceral Feminism: The Politics of Sex, Rights, and Freedom in Contemporary Antitrafficking Campaigns." *Signs* 36 (1): 45–71.

Brauer, M. S. 2017. "Inside a Killer Drug Epidemic: A Look at America's Opioid Crisis." *New York Times*, January 6. https://www.nytimes.com/2017/01/06/us/opioid-crisis-epidemic.html.

Cain, P. 1999. "British Free Trade, 1850–1914: Economics and Policy." *Refresh* 29 (Autumn). http://www.ehs.org.uk/dotAsset/11cabff5-3f6a-4d69-bba0-1086d69be6c7.pdf.

Carlson, L. 2013. "Under NAFTA, Mexico Suffered, and the United States Felt Its Pain." *New York Times*, November 14. https://www.nytimes.com/roomfordebate/2013/11/24/what-weve-learned-from-nafta/under-nafta-mexico-suffered-and-the-united-states-felt-its-pain.

Carmack, R. M. 2013. *Anthropology and Global History: From Tribes to the Modern World-System*. Lanham, MD: Alta Mira Press.

Caulfield, N. 2010. *NAFTA and Labor in North America*. Champaign: University of Illinois Press.

Celikkol, A. 2011. *Romances of Free Trade: British Literature, Laissez-Faire, and the Global Nineteenth Century*. New York: Oxford University Press.

Chossudovsky, M. 2005. "The Spoils of War: Afghanistan's Multibillion Dollar Heroin Trade." *Global Research*, June 14. http://www.globalresearch.ca/the-spoils-of-war-afghanistan-s-multibillion-dollar-heroin-trade/91.

Chouvy, P.-A. 2010. *Opium: Uncovering the Politics of the Poppy*. Cambridge, MA: Harvard University Press.

Cinar, A., and T. Bender, eds. 2007. *Urban Imaginaries: Locating the Modern City*. Minneapolis: University of Minnesota Press.

Clarkson, S. 2008. *Does North America Exist: Governing the Continent After NAFTA and 9/11*. Toronto: University of Toronto Press.

Cook, P. J., W. Cukier, and K. Krause. 2009. "Illicit Firearms Trade in the Americas." *Criminology & Criminal Justice*, July 29. http://journals.sagepub.com/doi/abs/10.1177/1748895809336377.

Cukier, W., and V. W. Sidel. 2006. *The Global Gun Epidemic: From Saturday Night Specials to AK-47s*. Westport, CT: Praeger Security.

da Silva, A. P., T. G. Blanchette, and A. R. Bento. 2013. "Cinderella Deceived: Analyzing a Brazilian Myth Regarding Trafficking in Persons." *Vibrant: Virtual Brazilian Anthropology* 10 (2). http://www.scielo.br/scielo.php?script=sci_arttext&pid=S1809-43412013000200012.

Darlington, S., and P. Gillespie. 2017. "Mexican Farmer's Daughter: NAFTA Destroyed Us." *CNN Money*, February 9. http://money.cnn.com/2017/02/09/news/economy/nafta-farming-mexico-us-corn-jobs/index.html.

Davis, L. E., and S. L. Engerman. 2006. *Naval Blockades in Peace and War: An Economic History Since 1750*. New York: Cambridge University Press.

de Vries, P. 2005. "'White Slaves' in a Colonial Nation: The Dutch Campaign Against the Traffic in Women in the Early Twentieth Century." *Social and Legal Studies* 14 (1): 39–60.

Fakhri, M. 2014. "The Institutionalisation of Free Trade and Empire: A Study of the 1902 Brussels Convention." *London Review of International Law* 2 (1): 49–76.

Fojas, C. 2017. *Zombies, Migrants, and Queers: Race and Crisis Capitalism in Pop Culture*. Champaign: University of Illinois Press.

Gootenberg, P. 2009. *Andian Cocaine: The Making of a Global Drug*. Chapel Hill: University of North Carolina Press.

Hall, S., C. Critcher, T. Jefferson, J. Clarke, and B. Roberts. 2013. *Policing the Crisis: Mugging, the State and Law and Order*. London: Palgrave Macmillan.

Hatsuda, K., and A. Sakasai. 2016. "The Black Market as City: New Research on Alternative Urban Space in Occupied Japan (1945–52)." East Asia Studies Program, Princeton University event, March 7. http://arc-hum.princeton.edu/black-market.

Kakande, Y. 2015. *Slave States: The Practice of Kafala in the Gulf Arab Region*. New Alresford, UK: Zero Books.

Karras, A. 2010. *Smuggling: Contraband and Corruption in World History*. Lanham, MD: Rowman & Littlefield.

Kotiswaran, P. 2017. *Revisiting the Law and Governance of Trafficking, Forced Labor and Modern Slavery*. New York: Cambridge University Press.

Little, B. 2007. *The Buccaneer's Realm: Pirate Life on the Spanish Main, 1674–1688*. Washington, DC: Potomac Books.

Lovell, J. 2011. *The Opium War: Drugs, Dreams and the Making of China*. London: Picador.

Lusane, C., and D. Desmond. 1991. *Pipe Dream Blues: Racism and the War on Drugs*. Boston: South End Press.

Marez, C. 2004. *Drug Wars: The Political Economy of Narcotics*. Minneapolis: University of Minnesota Press.

Melamed, J. 2011. *Represent and Destroy: Rationalizing Violence in the New Racial Capitalism*. Minneapolis: University of Minnesota Press.

Mitchell, G. 2016. "Evangelical Ecstasy Meets Feminist Fury: Sex Trafficking, Moral Panics, and Homonationalism During Global Sporting Events." *GLO* 22 (3): 325–357.

Muhawesh, M. 2016. "US War in Afghanistan Is Fueling Global Heroin Epidemic and Enabling the Drug Trade." *MintPress News*, July 21. https://www.mintpressnews.com/global-war-terror-created-heroin-epidemic-us-afghanistan/218662.

Murch, D. 2015. "Crack in Los Angeles: Crisis, Militarization, and Black Response to the Late Twentieth-Century War on Drugs." *Journal of American History* 102 (1): 162–173.

Oxford LibGuides. n.d. "International Law: Origins & History: Privateering & Piracy." http://libguides.bodleian.ox.ac.uk/c.php?g=464195&p=3301381.

Penttinen, E. 2008. *Globalization, Prostitution and Sex-Trafficking: Corporeal Politics*. Abingdon, UK: Routledge.

Piscitelli, A. 2007. "Corporalidate em Confronto: Brasileiras na Industra do Sexo na Espanha." *Revista Brasileira de Ciências Sociais* 22 (64): 17–33.

Robinson, C. J. 2005. *Black Marxism: The Making of the Black Radical Tradition*. Chapel Hill: University of North Carolina Press.

Scott, J. B. 2000. *The Spanish Origin of International Law: Francisco de Vitoria and His Law of Nations*. Union, NJ: The Lawbook Exchange.

Semple, K. 2017. "Mexico Ready to Play the Corn Card in Trade Talks." *New York Times*, April 2. https://www.nytimes.com/2017/04/02/world/americas/mexico-corn-nafta-trade.html.

Shah, S. P. 2014). *Street Corner Secrets: Sex, Work, and Migration in the City of Mumbai*. Durham, NC: Duke University Press.

Smith, A. 1776. *Wealth of Nations*. London: Methuen.

Struett, M. J., J. D. Carlson, and M. T. Nance, eds. 2013. *Maritime Piracy and the Construction of Global Governance*. New York: Routledge.

Thomson, J. 1994. *Mercenaries, Pirates, and Sovereigns: State-Building and Extraterritorial Violence in Early Modern Europe.* Princeton, NJ: Princeton University Press.

Valencia, S. 2010. *Capitalismo Gore.* Santa Cruz de Tenerif, Spain: Melusina.

Wachspress, M. 2015. "Pirates, Highwayman, and the Origins of the Criminal in Seventeenth-Century English Thought." *Yale Journal of Law & the Humanities* 26 (2): Article 4. http://digitalcommons.law.yale.edu/yjlh/vol26/iss2/4

We Are the Drug Policy Alliance. n.d. "Race and the Drug War." http://www.drugpolicy.org/race-and-drug-war.

White, C. M. 2014. *A Global History of the Developing World.* New York: Routledge.

Wood, J. C., ed. 1991. *David Ricardo: Critical Assessments.* vol. 2. London: Routledge.

CHAPTER 22

....

MIGRATION

....

SUCHENG CHAN

EVER since the ancestors of anatomically modern humans walked out of Africa to populate the Earth, human migration has been a powerful generative force integral to the unfolding of global prehistory and history. In the existing literature, most authors define migration as large-scale, intentional, and permanent relocation across time and space. In this chapter, I expand how migration is conceptualized in three ways. First, considered as a topic in global studies, I treat migration not just as movements across *inter*national boundaries (a framework in which nation-states are the units of analysis) but, rather, as a global, *trans*national process that increases the interconnectedness of human societies within what John L. Brooke calls a "earth-system" composed of the atmosphere, the geosphere, and the biosphere (Brooke 2014: 28). It is within this multilayered system that human life has evolved, and migration has played a critical role in that evolution. For that reason, this chapter has a section on the interrelationship between migration, on the one hand, and changes in the climate and the environment, on the other hand. Second, in the debate regarding whether globalization is a "new" phenomenon that began only in the 1970s with the restructuring of the global economy, I take the side of scholars who argue that globalization is not something that is only a few decades old; rather, the current form of globalization is simply the latest stage in a process that began centuries and, indeed, millennia ago. If migration has been a key strand in the evolution of globalizing forces, as I propose in this chapter, then it is appropriate to begin the analysis of migration with a discussion of the prehistoric movements of humans as they spread out into all the habitable continents of the world. Hence, my analysis begins with prehistoric migration, seen from the perspective of the longue durée. Third, I pay particular attention (and allot the most space) to involuntary migration. Although different forms of coerced migration have been more common than voluntary ones, forced migration has received relatively less attention from scholars who write about migration. Voluntary and involuntary migrations are usually treated as separate fields of academic inquiry, each generating its own body of writings. Involuntary migration includes the forcible removal of indigenous peoples from their habitats; the coerced migration of indentured servants, "transported" convicts, and enslaved peoples; the mass deportation of entire communities and ethnic cleansing; the post-conflict repatriation of former belligerents; the flight of refugees; and contemporary human trafficking. People who have migrated under coercion cannot be dismissed or forgotten because their experiences constitute the dark underside of human migration. Therefore, instead of focusing only on voluntary migrations, this chapter addresses multiple forms of migration. Each type of migration is discussed only very briefly, but the cited sources serve as introductions to the pertinent existing literature.

PREHISTORIC MIGRATION

As late as the 1980s, archaeologists, paleoanthropologists, and comparative linguists debated whether the *Homo* genus evolved in a single site of origin or multiple ones. Geneticists have now offered definitive answers by using deoxyribonucleic acid (DNA) genome sequencing techniques, expedited by supercomputers and statistical models, to analyze the DNA that can still be recovered from the fossils of bones and teeth that archaeological excavations have unearthed, as well as DNA from living populations in various locations throughout the world today. Whereas archaeologists date these fossils to estimate when hominins (bipedal proto-humans who made and used tools) first reached certain locations, geneticists trace the evolution and mobility of hominins by analyzing the DNA in the mitochondria (mtDNA) of females and the Y chromosome (Y-DNA) of males. Mitochondria are tiny energy generators located outside the nuclei of cells in the space between the cell nuclei and the cell walls. The mtDNA is passed down from mothers only to their daughters. The Y chromosome is passed down from fathers only to their sons. Humans have 23 pairs of chromosomes; one member of each pair comes from the father and the other from the mother. There is one pair that determines the sex of an embryo: Females have an XX combination, whereas males have an XY coupling. The Y chromosome does not recombine during conception, so it has been called "non-recombining Y" (NRY). However, in recent years, scientists have discovered that *intra*-Y chromosomal recombination does occur, so the nomenclature is being changed to the "male-specific region" (MSR) of the Y chromosome (Zegura, Karafet, and Hammer 2009). By taking DNA samples from people living in different areas of the world today, geneticists are able to track the geographic dispersal of our ancestors by examining the mutations (random "copying mistakes" made in the DNA sequence as cells divide over and over again to form organisms) in the genomes of divergent populations. These mutations are passed down from generation to generation, creating specific genetic lineages. People who share the same genetic markers belong to the same haplogroup, which indicates they share common ancestors. Such genetic sleuthing based on the DNA mutations found in different populations in various localities has enabled geneticists to decipher the most likely routes our ancestors took as they spread out from Africa to the rest of the world (Bellwood 2013; Cavalli-Sforza and Cavalli-Sforza 1995; Stringer 2012; Wells 2002, 2007).

Combining the findings of archaeologists, paleoanthropologists, comparative linguists, geneticists, and climatologists, it is now widely accepted that all hominins evolved in Africa approximately 2.5 million years ago from an earlier genus of great apes. Anthropologists named the earliest hominin *Homo habilis*. A later hominin, *Homo erectus*, existed in Africa between 2 million and 300,000 years ago. Some of its members began to disperse out of Africa more than 1 million years ago, and their fossils have been found as far away as northern China and on the island of Java in Indonesia. Another species, *Homo neanderthalensis*, populated areas of West Asia (a region commonly called the Middle East but not including Egypt) and southern Europe between 125,000 and 35,000 years ago (Fagan 1990: 74–89; Groves 2013). Several other species of hominins also existed, but all except the descendants of *H. erectus* became extinct (Hertler, Bruch, and Märker 2013: 13).

Homo sapiens, our own species, arrived on the scene approximately 195,000 years ago. Their oldest remains have been found in a site named Omo Kibish in southern Ethiopia that dated to 195,000 years ago (Aubert et al. 2012). Until recently, it had been postulated that *Homo sapiens* migrated out of Africa approximately 70,000 years ago. In 2018, however, researchers announced that they had found a fossilized jaw bone in a collapsed cave in Israel that is between 177,000 and 194,000 years old, which pushes back the date of exit from Africa by 100,000 years (St. Fleur 2018). It is not yet certain whether all scholars have reached a consensus regarding this dating. Regardless of when *H. sapiens* migrated out of Africa, they went northward from East Africa and crossed the Sinai Peninsula to reach the northern Arabian Peninsula and the Levant region of West Asia. Some geneticists argue that they then moved along the Indian Ocean littoral to Southeast Asia and Australia (Stringer 2012; Wells 2007). Others disagree that such a "southern route" was ever used (Stoneking and Harvati 2013: 28). What had not been disputed until recently is that by approximately 45,000 years ago, *H. sapiens* had reached Australia. However, a multidisciplinary analysis of material objects found in the excavations of an Aboriginal rock shelter at the Madjedbebe site in northern Australia indicates that humans lived there as early as 65,000 years ago (Clarkson et al. 2017).

During the Last Glacial Maximum (24,000 to 18,000 years ago), when huge, thick ice sheets covered most of North America and northern Eurasia (Europe and Asia combined), so much water was locked up in the ice that the sea level was more than 300 feet lower than the current level. At that time, the Sunda continental shelf joined mainland Southeast Asia to the present-day islands of Sumatra, Kalimantan (Borneo), Java, and Bali. Only 19 miles of water separated Sunda from Wallacea—a large island encompassing today's smaller islands named Sulawesi, Timor, the Malukus, and the thousands of islands that make up the Philippines. The distance from Wallacea to the Sahul continental shelf (composed of the island of New Guinea, the continent of Australia, and the island of Tasmania) was approximately 60 miles. Crossing such distances required the know-how to build seaworthy boats and to navigate open waters (Fagan 1990: 126–127; Sémah and Sémah 2013).

How *H. sapiens* spread into East Asia is still being debated. Two routes have been proposed: a northeasterly land route across the huge landmass of Eurasia, traversing Central Asia to reach East Asia, and an alternate route from tropical Southeast Asia that turned northward toward East Asia. *H. sapiens* had reached China by 60,000 years ago, where they eventually replaced the *H. erectus* who had found their way there much earlier (Zhang and Hung 2013: 209). *Homo sapiens* also migrated from West Asia to Europe sometime between 45,000 and 35,000 years ago (Manco 2016), where they coexisted with *H. neanderthalensis* until the latter went extinct. To survive in the very cold regions of Eurasia, they had to master the use of fire both for warmth and for cooking, as well as the ability to sew warm clothing using eyed needles made of bone to join together animal hides and pelts (Hisock 2013: 41). That tiny but utterly crucial tool, the needle, was invented approximately 20,000 years ago (Ponting 2007: 28).

Approximately 15,000 years ago, *H. sapiens* living in Siberia and what is presently called the Russian Far East crossed the Beringia land bridge, which had existed before sea levels rose as ice sheets melted and submerged it to form the Bering Strait, and landed in North America (Fagan 2003; Meltzer 2013). They then spread out until some of them reached the southernmost part of South America by approximately 10,000 years ago. What southward routes they took is still being debated among scholars (Bellwood 2013: 83–93; Dillehay 2000; Ruhlen 2009; Southerton 2013; Zegura et al. 2009). It is now known, however, that Native Americans descended from two ancestral groups: a northern branch that includes the Athabascans in Canada and the Navajo and Apache in the United States, and a southern branch that includes all the other indigenous peoples of North, Central, and South America (Zimmer 2018).

This first cycle of globalization undertaken by anatomically modern human migrants occurred over a period of approximately 70,000 years. As a mini-glacial period known as the Younger Dryas (12,800 to 11,700 years ago) ended and ice sheets melted, causing the sea level to rise, formerly connected lands became separated by immense expanses of water, thereby breaking the link between Afro-Eurasia, on the one hand, and the Americas and Australia, on the other hand. More than 11,000 years would pass before all the habitable continents were once again connected by humans—this time traveling in wind-propelled sailing ships. Before that happened, the peoples known collectively as Melanesians, Micronesians, and Polynesians had managed to navigate across thousands of miles of open ocean to colonize islands in the Pacific Ocean between 3,000 and 1,000 years ago (Anderson 2013; Bellwood 1979; Carson 2013; Lewis 1972; Thorne and Raymond 1989).

CLIMATE, ENVIRONMENT, AND MIGRATION

As the climate and the environment have changed over long geological epochs, migration has been a key asset that has enabled humans to survive. The Earth's climate goes through very long cycles, oscillating between extremely cold, dry glacial periods and warmer, more humid interglacial ones. Long-term climate change is affected by the elliptical shape of the Earth's orbit around the sun, the tilt of the Earth's rotational axis, and how that axis wobbles. The critical factor is how much sunlight falls on the northern hemisphere, where the largest land masses, North America and Eurasia, are located. The astronomically induced temperature swings are amplified by conditions on Earth itself, such as the amount of greenhouse gases in the atmosphere and changes in the patterns of air and ocean currents. The size of the ice sheets also plays a role: The larger they are, the more they can reflect the sun's radiant energy back into space, thereby making the temperature on Earth colder. These factors taken together have caused ice sheets and glaciers to form and melt, sea levels to fall and rise, the ecological niches of different kinds of vegetation to retreat and advance, deserts to turn into green belts and then back to deserts depending on the amount of rain available (a phenomenon most visible in the history of the Sahara Desert), and animals and humans to migrate for the sake of survival and the reproduction of their species (Mithen 2003: 11–13).

Until humans learned to farm 9,000 years ago, they depended on their ability to forage and gather edible plants—their leaves, fruit, nuts, seeds, and roots—and to hunt terrestrial animals and catch marine mammals, shellfish, and fish to feed themselves. Such methods of food acquisition required mobility. Whenever and wherever sources of subsistence diminished or when climate change made certain habitats inhospitable for human survival, humans migrated to locations where more abundant sources of food could be found or to regions with a more salubrious climate where they neither froze to death nor died of dehydration from excessive heat. Three accomplishments facilitated their movement. First, after domesticating certain plants, migrants discovered that they could carry the seeds of those plants with them to be sown in new locations for future harvests. Second, after horses, donkeys, cattle, goats, sheep, pigs, camels, yaks, reindeer, and llamas were domesticated, these self-propelling animals could be herded from one location to another wherever pastures and water could be found. These animals provided and continue to provide meat, milk, hides, hair, and wool; some of them also served and continue to serve as essential beasts of burden. Both the seeds and the animals were and continue to be *portable* sources of food. Third, domesticated horses enabled their riders to travel for much longer distances and at a much faster speed than humans could do on foot (Anthony 2007). Domesticated camels allowed humans to move across deserts. Even after wheeled carts had been invented, horses and camels remained the vehicles of choice in many areas of the world (Bulliet 1990).

Geography has fundamentally shaped humans' migratory paths. The world's ecosystem is divided into belts running in an east–west direction. In the northern hemisphere, moving from the far north to the equator are the tundra, boreal forests (also known as the *taiga*) of evergreen coniferous trees, deciduous forests of trees with broadleaves that fall in autumn, the *steppe* (grasslands), deserts, high plateaus and massive mountain ranges, as well as fertile riverine plains and equatorial rainforests. In the southern hemisphere, the ecological zones exist in the reverse order. In both hemispheres, the location of different kinds of vegetation depends not just on latitude but also on elevation, as well as distance from the ocean, with its moderating effect on temperature and humidity. Of these ecological belts, the Eurasian steppe, a cold grassland, has served as a superhighway of human migration. Long before the invention of the railroad, migrants on horseback could travel thousands of miles across the steppe, where they encountered few topographical barriers (the main barrier was the Altai mountain range). The 5,000-mile-long Eurasian steppe stretches from Hungary in the west to northeast China in the east. Over millennia, horse-riding nomadic groups, tribal confederations, and empire-builders who spoke Turkic and Mongolic languages have traveled across its vast expanse, herding their animals, conquering territory, and raiding, as well as trading with, sedentary agrarian communities (Christian 1998; Cunliffe 2015; Khazanov 1994). The Eurasian steppe's counterparts in the other continents are the prairies in Canada and the United States, the pampas in South America east of the Andes mountain range, and the savanna in sub-Saharan Africa.

In other ecological zones, rivers and their valleys have served as crucial migratory routes. The world's oldest and most enduring civilizations developed in the valleys of major rivers, such as Egypt along the Nile River; Mesopotamia (today's Iraq) between the Euphrates and Tigris rivers; China along the Yellow and Yangzi rivers; and India along the Indus, Ganga (Ganges), and Brahmaputra rivers. Some migrants relied on both river valleys and grasslands to take them to distant places. In sub-Saharan Africa, for example, approximately 500 groups of people who speak Bantu languages have been the continent's most active long-distance migrants. They spread out from their original habitat in West Africa located in the borderland between present-day Nigeria and Cameroon and migrated eastward and southward until they became the most widely dispersed peoples south of the Sahara. Some of them followed rivers as they migrated, whereas others traversed the savanna—Africa's tropical grassland (Davidson 1995: 20–21; Newman 1995: 140–149).

During the past two centuries, a human-made factor has exacerbated nature's impact. As the Industrial Revolution advanced and as fossil fuels have become the main sources of energy, the amount of greenhouse gases—carbon dioxide, methane, nitrous oxide, and chlorofluorocarbon compounds—has increased at an accelerating rate. Unlike oxygen and nitrogen, the two most abundant gases in the atmosphere that have little impact on temperature, greenhouse gases trap part of the sun's radiant energy and prevent it from re-radiating back into space, thereby warming the lower atmosphere and the surface of Earth. Life on Earth has depended on this greenhouse effect: Without it, the Earth would be too cold for human habitation. However, as increasingly more carbon dioxide is produced with the burning of fossil fuels, and as increasingly more trees, which are major absorbers of carbon dioxide, are cut down to produce lumber and fuel and to make space for more farmland and built-up centers of population, the Earth is warming up much faster than it would if left to the forces of nature. As the Greenland and Antarctica ice sheets melt, people living in low-lying islands or coastal areas where the highest ground is only a few feet above sea level worry about where they can move as their habitats disappear into the ocean. Global warming also makes droughts more widespread and long-lasting, with significant negative impacts on agriculture. As chemical fertilizers, pesticides, and industrial wastes pollute increasingly more sources of water, clean water will be more difficult to find. All these developments are certain to generate an increasing number of climate or environmental "refugees" in the foreseeable future who will be impelled to migrate for the sake of survival.

INVOLUNTARY MIGRATION

The most important contexts for large-scale involuntary migration have been empire-building and wars. The two have almost always coexisted. Empires, by definition, are multi-ethnic societies in which a dominant ethnic group controls one or more subordinate ethnic groups. Empires can be classified according to their location (overseas or in contiguous areas), the motive for creating them (for settlement, for trade, for natural resource exploitation, or for religious proselytizing), the method of rule (direct or indirect), and the trajectory of their historical development (whether they remained as empires, evolved into nation-states, or disintegrated).

Involuntary Migration in Western European Maritime Empires

The common conception of empires is based on the Western European model. Beginning at the dawn of the sixteenth century, the Portuguese, Spaniards, Dutch, British, and French began to venture overseas to establish colonies of settlement in sparsely populated areas with temperate climates, as well as colonies of trade and natural resource exploitation in more densely populated regions in tropical climes. In the nineteenth century, Germans and Belgians joined these colonial powers. Most European emigrants, commonly called settlers or colonists, went to what they thought of as "empty" continents—the Americas,

Australia, and the southern portion of East Africa—that were, in fact, not so empty. The land that Europeans claimed became theirs only because they succeeded in removing a vast majority of the indigenous inhabitants—now called Native Americans in the United States, First Peoples in Canada, and Aborigines and Torres Strait Islanders in Australia—from the more desirable arable land (Banner 2005). The indigenous peoples perished in large numbers as a result of having no immunity to "Old World" diseases (Cook 1998; Thornton 1987; Verano and Ubelaker 1992), being killed in the "Indian Wars," and being forcibly removed to "reservations" usually located on unproductive land (Bowes 2016; Dunbar-Ortiz 2015; Jahoda 1995). Those living on islands in the Pacific Ocean and the Caribbean Sea suffered proportionately the largest losses: Most were literally decimated and some groups went extinct. The indigenous peoples who managed to survive the onslaught of European settlers—an onslaught that some scholars have called genocide (Levene 2008)—thus became involuntary migrants in the Americas and Australia. The indigenous peoples in Siberia met a similar fate. Even though the Russian Empire was a land empire, its conquest of Siberia bore strong similarities to how the European overseas empires gained control over the Americas and Australia (Lincoln 1994). A relatively new term, *settler colonialism*, is increasingly used to describe this form of empire-building or colonialism.

European immigrants did not just want land to establish farms for their own subsistence; some also wanted to use the land to generate profits by planting commercial crops, particularly sugar, tobacco, and cotton to be sold in national and international markets, or by mining precious metals and minerals. Both cash-crop agriculture and mining required workers able to perform long hours of strenuous labor. In the early years of British immigration to North America, the English penal system played a role in the peopling of North America and later of Australia. Convicts, debtors, poor street urchins, Irish dissenters, and participants in various protest movements were "transported" to North America as indentured servants. After the 13 British colonies declared their independence and became the United States, the new nation declined to continue serving as the dumping ground for England's unwanted people. So the British used Australia for the same purpose (Brooke and Brandon 2005; Hughes 1988; Jordan and Walsh 2007). Because indentured servants could gain their freedom once their term of service was over, plantation and mine owners increasingly turned to unfree labor—Africans who were enslaved for life, with that status passing down to their offspring—as their preferred source of labor.

The trans-Atlantic slave trade carried more than 12.5 million enslaved Africans from sub-Saharan Africa to the western hemisphere from the beginning of the sixteenth century until the 1860s. Almost half of them departed from West Central Africa; most of the rest left from ports along the West African coast stretching from the Upper Guinea region to the Gold Coast, the Bight of Benin, and the Bight of Biafra. Less than 5% came from southeastern Africa and the island of Madagascar. The mortality rate was high during the infamous Middle Passage. Consequently, only approximately 11 million arrived alive. Brazil received more than 5 million of them. The Caribbean islands, highly prized as "sugar islands," and Mexico took in another 5.4 million. The United States became home to the rest of the Middle Passage's survivors. Between 1501 and 1641, approximately three-fourths of the enslaved Africans sailed in Portuguese and Spanish ships. From 1642 to 1807, British and Portuguese ships were the main carriers. France, the Netherlands, the United States, and several other countries also participated in the slave trade. Even after Britain made the slave trade illegal in 1807 and used the British Navy to patrol shipping lanes in the Atlantic

Ocean, Portuguese and Spanish ships continued to carry on the trade (Davis 2006; Eltis and Richardson 2010; Klein 2010; Klein and Vinson 2007). Only decades after the trade ended was chattel slavery itself abolished—the laggards being the United States in 1863, Cuba in 1886, and Brazil in 1888. Although the Atlantic slave trade is the best known, there also existed a trans-Saharan and an Indian Ocean trade in enslaved Africans. In the non-Western areas of the world, enslaved persons were used in a wider range of work than in the Americas (Campbell 2004; Chatterjee and Eaton 2006; Christopher, Pybus and Rediker 2007; Segal 2001).

After slavery ended, part of the labor shortage was met by keeping the freed men and women economically dependent on their former masters and partly by the migration of Indian and Chinese contract laborers to work in the Caribbean sugar islands and in plantations growing other cash crops that the European powers had established in Southeast Asia, East Africa, and Latin America. Derisively called "coolies" and treated with brutality, they nevertheless differed from enslaved Africans in one fundamental respect: Legally, they were not chattel (Meagher 2008; Northrup 1995; Tinker 1993; Young 2014). Pacific Islanders were also involuntarily shipped to tropical Queensland in northeastern Australia to work on sugar plantations (Banivanua-Mar 2007; Saunders 1982).

Involuntary Migration and Land Empires

Although paradigmatic, overseas empires were by no means the only kind of empire. Land empires that grew by incorporating contiguous territories emerged centuries before the overseas ones did so. The largest land empires were located in Eurasia. The Mongol and Russian empires both stretched across almost the entire span of northern Eurasia. During the thirteenth and fourteenth centuries, the Mongols swept westward across the steppe from their homeland in Mongolia all the way to eastern Europe, as well as southward into China, where they ruled as the Yuan Dynasty (1271–1368). Because they were not a populous people, they tended to assimilate into the cultures of the peoples and lands they conquered rather than forcing the subjugated populations to adopt Mongol ways (Morgan 2007; Rossabi 2011). The Russian Empire grew in the opposite direction. In the late fifteenth century, the principality of Muscovy began to expand eastward toward the Ural Mountains and then across Siberia all the way to the shores of the Pacific Ocean. Russian and Ukrainian Cossacks, fur trappers, and peasants (especially after the serfs were emancipated in 1861) used Siberia's rivers and tributaries to help make their way through the thickly wooded taiga. (Siberia's major rivers flow northward into the Arctic Ocean, but many of their tributaries flow in a more or less east–west direction so that when portages on land between the rivers and streams were found, travelers could persevere in their journeys toward the Pacific Ocean.) As the number of Russians increased, the indigenous peoples in Siberia and in the Russian Far East became minuscule minorities in their native habitats (Forsyth 1992; Slezkine 1994; Wood 2011). The Russians also claimed lands lying between Moscow and the Baltic Sea. The final phase of their empire-building took them southward to the Caucasus Mountains and Central Asia, which they conquered in the 1860s (Kappeler 2013; Khodarkovsky 2004; Sunderland 2004).

South of the steppe, the Chinese empire that was alternately unified and fragmented under successive dynasties spread southward from the valley of the Yellow River, where the

Han Chinese civilization first emerged, until it reached the shores of the South China Sea. Those dynasties that were expansive sent millions of migrants to colonize and secure the new frontier regions, pushing aside the indigenous peoples and forcing them to move into adjoining hilly areas or to migrate southward into mainland Southeast Asia. Over many centuries, Chinese imperial armies subdued the regions that now make up northeastern, southwestern, and northwestern China. The empire reached its largest extent during the Qing Dynasty (1644–1911). In distant frontier regions, soldiers who had fought in these campaigns were allotted some land so that they could grow their own food, in the process becoming soldier–migrants. A combination of Chinese officials and co-opted local elites governed the newly acquired territories (Fitzgerald 1972; Lary 2012; Perdue 2010; Wiens 1954). The Indian subcontinent and West Asia were also home to many large land empires, the most notable being the Mughal Empire in India (1528–1857), a succession of Persian (Iranian) empires, and the Ottoman Empire (1299–1922). Each of the Eurasian land empires grew by a combination of military conquest; using soldiers-cum-settlers to hold the newly acquired regions; sociocultural absorption of the indigenous peoples in some, but not all, instances; establishing bureaucracies to administer extensive territories with multiethnic populations; building roads; and designating official languages with which to transmit orders and laws. Soldiers played a leading role as involuntary migrants—involuntary because they were conscripts who had no say over their fate. Some of them were prisoners of war captured during earlier conflicts who were then enslaved to serve the victors.

The European overseas empires, as well as the short-lived Japanese overseas empire (1895–1945), all disintegrated either as a result of defeat in war or because the colonized people's independence struggles succeeded in driving the colonial powers out during the four decades following the end of World War II. Some of the major land empires, in contrast, have evolved into modern nation-states without losing much, if any, of their territories. China, Russia, and the United States all reached their current size via the process of incorporating contiguous territory—the classic manner in which land empires were built.

Involuntary Migration as Punishment

Involuntary migration has often been used as a form of punishment. Exiling dissidents has long been used for this purpose, but during the twentieth century, the scale of punitive deportations increased exponentially. Although the term *ethnic cleansing* did not come into popular usage until the early 1990s when inter-ethnic conflicts resulted in Yugoslavia splitting into several countries, the phenomenon had existed long before that. The Russian Empire and its successor state, the Soviet Union, sent political dissidents and criminals into exile in Siberia (Viola 2007). After the Qing rulers in China conquered Xinjiang in northwestern China in the eighteenth century, that far-off territory was used as a location to which people were banished (Perdue 2010). In 1915, when a group of reformist politicians in the disintegrating Ottoman Empire, until then a multiethnic polity, developed a robust sense of Turkish nationalism and tried to make Turkey into an ethnically homogeneous nation-state, they gave orders to massacre an estimated 1.5 million Christian Armenians and pushed those who had not yet been killed into the Syrian Desert, where they died of hunger, thirst, and heat exhaustion—a genocide that the present Turkish government refuses to acknowledge (Akçam 2006; Suny 2015). After World War I, a compulsory "population exchange" in 1923 forced more than 1 million Greeks living in Turkey to move to Greece and approximately 355,000 Turks in Greece to move to Turkey (Hirschon 2003; Naimark 2001: 17–56). The Assyrians, a smaller ethnic group, were likewise massacred by Turkish troops in 1924 (Donef 2014). Like the Armenians, both the Greeks and the Assyrians were Christians.

During World War II, Joseph Stalin (1878–1953) and Adolf Hitler (1889–1945) both forced multitudes to become involuntary migrants. Stalin sent millions of people into "internal exile" not only in Siberia but also in Kazakhstan and other areas of Central Asia. These mass deportations, which involved uprooting entire ethnic groups, should not be conflated with the exile of political dissidents sent to harsh labor camps, the *gulag*, in Siberia. The first ethnic community to be forcibly "transferred" comprised 170,000 Koreans from the Russian Far East, where they had settled during the mid-nineteenth century. Piled into railway cattle cars that took them across thousands of miles to not-yet-settled lands in Russian-colonized Kazakhstan and Uzbekistan in Central Asia in 1937, they found no food, shelter, or medicines upon arrival, which led to the death of approximately one-fourth of that group (Pohl 1999: 9–20).

The Koreans' internal exile became the blueprint for how to remove other ethnic groups expeditiously just before and during World War II. Stalin singled out ethnic groups that dwelled along the northwestern, western, southwestern, and eastern borders of the Soviet Union for "total deportation." He feared that some of these peoples might act as fifth columns should war break out with Nazi Germany and later Japan. In addition to the Koreans, the "punished peoples" included Finns and Germans who had settled in Russia over several centuries; Kalmyks living in a region northwest of the Caspian Sea; Karachais, Ingushetians, Chechens, and Balkars from the North Caucasus; Meskhetian Turks from the South Caucasus; and Crimean Tatars, Greeks, Jews, Kurds, Bulgarians, and Armenians, who lived either on the Crimean Peninsula that juts southward into the Black Sea or on the steppe lands north of that body of water, were all forcibly removed from their areas of settlements (Polian 2004: 92–171). After Nazi Germany invaded the Soviet Union in 1941, the Nazis used members of some of these ethnic groups as forced laborers. When the Soviet Red Army recaptured the German-occupied areas in 1944, these people and their fellow co-ethnics were branded as traitors and subject to wholesale expulsion despite the fact that tens of thousands of Chechens, Ingushetians, Meskhetian Turks, and Crimean Tatars had served and were still serving in the Red Army.

In terms of numbers, almost 200,000 Crimean Tatars, who are Muslims, were expelled to Central Asia. Loaded onto railway box cars with all the windows and doors bolted shut and given no food or water, many captives died en route. The trains had to stop to toss out corpses. No food, shelter, or means of earning a living awaited them upon arrival in their places of exile. Approximately 100,000 of them died. The Muslim peoples in the Caucasus mountain region, who had long resisted Russian colonial rule, were deported to Kazakhstan and Siberia. One-fourth of the more than half a million Chechen deportees, the largest group among the Muslim residents of the Caucasus, died. Ninety-eight thousand Kalmyks, the only practicing Buddhists in the Soviet Union, were sent to Siberia, where approximately half of them perished. People in Estonia, Latvia, Lithuania, part of Finland, eastern Poland, and part of Romania were likewise exiled to Siberia and Kazakhstan. Between 1.2 and 1.5 million ethnic Germans, who were scattered widely on Soviet soil with the largest concentration in the valley of the Volga River, were similarly deported, mainly to Kazakhstan (Ahonen et al. 2008: 23–26; Naimark 2001: 85–107; Nekrich 1981; Pohl 1999; Polian 2004: 124–139).

During the same period, Hitler launched a campaign to bring ethnic Germans living outside of Germany back to the fatherland. There were 3.2 million ethnic Germans in Czechoslovakia, 1.7 million in France, 1 million in Poland, more than 1 million in the Soviet Union, 786,000 in Romania, 623,000 in Hungary, and more than half a million in Yugoslavia before the war in Europe began (Ahonen et al. 2008: 15). Proclaiming that more space was needed to house these returnees, Nazi Germany set out to conquer Europe. Hitler's scheme involved what might be called a demographic transfusion: As many "racially superior" ethnic Germans as possible would be gathered within an enlarged German heartland while "racially inferior" non-Germans would be banished to the fringes or killed outright. (Unlike the Soviet Union, Germany did not have a Siberia or Central Asia to which unwanted people could be sent.) In 1939, Stalin and Hitler agreed secretly in the Molotov–Ribbentrop Pact to divide up Central and Eastern Europe. The most drastic measure they took was to split Poland into three sections: Eastern Poland would go to the Soviet Union, western Poland to Germany, and central Poland (named the General Government or Governorate) would be administered jointly by the Germans and Soviets. Soon thereafter, however, Germany gained the right to be the sole administrator in exchange for turning Lithuania (initially allotted to Germany) over to the Soviet Union. Both countries invaded Poland in September 1939, during which more than 75,000 Poles were killed and more than 2 million were slated for forcible removal. The Nazis took several million Poles to Germany and rounded up those who remained in the General Government area in order to use them as forced laborers. They were treated so harshly that a significant portion died (Lukas 2012). The land and houses from which Poles had been uprooted were given to the incoming ethnic Germans. Hitler's ultimate goal was to wipe out all traces of Poland as an independent nation-state. When he decided to exterminate the Jews, not only those in Germany but also the ones in all the countries that the Nazis had invaded and occupied, six of the major extermination camps were set up in Poland, which had the largest number of Jews before it was partitioned in 1939. Jews were rounded up and taken to these extermination camps for the sole purpose of being killed, unlike those confined in other concentration camps, who were forced to engage in hard labor while they still had the strength to do so (Ahonen et al. 2008: 11–42). Six million perished during the Holocaust.

Lest it be thought that only totalitarian regimes would engage in coercive population removals, during World War II the United States "evacuated" and incarcerated 120,000 people of Japanese ancestry, two-thirds of them American citizens, in what were euphemistically called "relocation camps" on the pretext of "military necessity." Canada did the same thing to Japanese Canadians (Daniels 1981). To be sure, these Japanese Americans and Japanese Canadians did not perish in large numbers; still, they were involuntarily removed and confined.

Involuntary Migration and the Dissolution of Empires

Although involuntary migrations have almost always resulted from empire-building and wars, the end of wars and the dissolution of empires have also engendered involuntary migrations. Massive movements of people occurred as World War II came to an end in both the European and Pacific theaters of war. As many as 3.5 million ethnic Germans were expelled from Poland, 3.2 million from Czechoslovakia, almost 2 million from the Soviet Union, 400,000 from Hungary, 300,000 from Romania, and an additional 1 million from other areas of Central and Eastern Europe. Along the way, angry people who had suffered so much while under German occupation beat up and killed some of the fleeing ethnic German men and raped the women. Soldiers of the Red Army also participated in these acts of vengeance. Not just the Nazi regime but also the German people as a whole were held collectively responsible for Nazi war crimes. Those who fled landed in the American, British, French, and Soviet occupation zones in post-war Germany. Many of them, as well as German prisoners of war, were used as forced labor to clear the debris and rebuild bombed out cities and infrastructure. The terms of Germany's unconditional surrender made it clear that the use of German forced labor after the war would be a part of the reparations that Germany had to pay. Italians and Hungarians, who had fought on the side of the Germans, were also expelled from the regions they had occupied (Ahonen et al. 2008: 61–109; Cohen 2012; Connor 2007; de Zayas 2006; Polian 2004: 239–303; Reinisch and White 2011).

When war in the Pacific theater ended in August 1945, there were approximately 6.5 million Japanese outside of Japan, 3.5 million of whom were military personnel deployed in all the areas of Asia that Japan had conquered and colonized between 1895 and 1945, including Taiwan, Korea, northern and eastern China, Malaya, Singapore, Indonesia, the Philippine, Burma, and numerous islands in the Pacific Ocean. Japan and the French Nazi-collaborationist Vichy government agreed that in exchange for Japan not attacking the French colonies in Southeast Asia, Japanese troops could be stationed in and transit through French Indochina. Thailand also used diplomacy to fend off a Japanese invasion. Upon Japan's unconditional surrender, US Navy ships took most of the Japanese— both prisoners of war and civilians—back to Japan. The repatriation process took longer than might have been expected because the victors—the Russians, Chinese, British, and Americans—wanted to use Japanese prisoners of war to clean up the wartime destruction. By the end of 1946, 5.1 million Japanese had been repatriated (Dower 1999: 48–58).

The most notable example of how decolonization and massive population exchanges go hand in hand occurred in 1947 when the Indian subcontinent, the "crown jewel" of the British Empire, was partitioned into an independent, Hindu-majority but determinedly secular India and an independent Islamic republic, Pakistan. An estimated 10–15 million people moved on foot, in carts drawn by donkeys and oxen, in motor vehicles, and in trains across the new international borders—Muslims going to East and West Pakistan, and Hindus moving from both wings of Pakistan to India. At least 1 million people died and thousands of women were raped while in transit (Khan 2007; Zamindar 2007). In West Asia, as the British left Palestine, which they had held as a League of Nations "Mandate," 700,000 Palestinians fled from their homes when the state of Israel was established in 1948 to accommodate Jews who wished to migrate there from all over the world where they had settled. Palestinian refugees are still living in squalid, overcrowded camps in neighboring countries. One of the key sticking points in round after round of failed peace talks between the Israelis and the Palestinians is the latter's insistence on their "right of return" to the homes they had been forced to leave seven decades ago—a right that Israel seems determined to never grant them.

Involuntary Migrants as Refuge-Seekers

Europe's experience in dealing with 30 million displaced persons in the aftermath of World War II (Cohen 2012; Marrus 1985; Reinisch and White 2011) led to a realization that policies must be formulated with regard to who can be considered as refugees. The United Nations established the office of the United Nations High Commissioner for Refugees in 1950 and produced two documents, the 1951 Convention Relating to the Status of Refugees and the 1967 Protocol Relating to the Status of Refugees, in which the word "refugee" acquired a specific meaning in international law. Refugees are defined as persons outside of their countries of origin to which they cannot return because they have a "well-founded fear of persecution for reasons of race, religion, nationality, r membership in a particular social group or political opinion" (Loescher and Loescher 1994: 2–17, 98–139, quote on p. 100). They are entitled to certain kinds of protection, including being housed and fed while awaiting one of three options: to be repatriated to their countries of origin when conditions there permit their safe return; to be locally integrated in the countries of first asylum where they initially land; or to be resettled in "third countries," also known as countries of second asylum. Most important, they have a guarantee of non-refoulement: They cannot be forced to return to their countries of origin where they may be persecuted by their own governments. Refugees and asylum-seekers are thus *politically defined* persons because it is the nation-states from which they fled that are persecuting them. Asylees differ from refugees in that they can apply for asylum after they have already entered the countries from which they seek asylum, whereas refugees must be "processed" before they are allowed to travel to the countries of resettlement. Given the precise manner in which *refugees* has been defined, in a previous publication (Chan 2004: xxiv) I coined the term *refuge-seekers* to include not only "real" refugees but also those who are escaping poverty, other social ills, or natural disasters—people usually considered as "economic migrants" who cannot claim the same protection given to refugees.

Since the 1950s, there has been an almost constant stream of refuge-seekers throughout the world. The Cold War and several hot "proxy wars" fought between countries that sided with the "Free World," led by the United States, and those that were allied with the Soviet Union, leader of the Communist bloc, generated large outpourings of refuge-seekers. In addition, civil wars and military coups d'état in Asia, Africa, and Latin America have added to the number of people seeking refuge. Chinese and Koreans escaped from their countries as the Chinese Civil War (1945–1949) and the Korean War (1950–1953) came to an end. The communists emerged victorious in mainland China, whereas the Korean Peninsula was divided into two, with North Korea joining the communist bloc and South Korea the US-led bloc. From Europe came Hungarian and Czechoslovakian refuge-seekers in 1956 and 1968, respectively, who were also escaping from communist regimes. In Africa in the 1960s, refuge-seekers flowed out of conflict zones in Algeria, Sudan, Rwanda, and Mozambique. Approximately 10 million refuge-seekers left East Pakistan for India during a civil war that resulted in the establishment of an independent Bangladesh in 1971. In Latin America, Fidel Castro's victory in Cuba in 1959 generated an unending stream of anti-communist refuge-seekers bound for the United States—an exodus that is still ongoing to this day. (With the re-establishment of diplomatic relations between the United States and Cuba in 2015, the refuge-seekers will, in time, become regular immigrants if the administration of President

Donald J. Trump so allows). During a military coup against Chilean president Salvador Allende in 1973, 200,000 Chilean refuge-seekers left the country, while a military takeover of Uruguay during the same year led to the exodus of 200,000 Uruguayans.

The outflow of refuge-seekers increased so greatly from the 1970s onward that international conferences had to be convened to deal with them. The wars that the United States fought in Vietnam, Laos, and Cambodia in the late 1960s and early 1970s produced approximately 2 million refuge-seekers as communist regimes came to power in all three countries in 1975. During the course of two decades, the United States and approximately 60 other countries took them in under agreements forged during two international conferences in 1979 and 1989. The Soviet invasion and occupation of Afghanistan (1979–1989) caused 5 million Afghans to become refuge-seekers in neighboring Iran and Pakistan. An off-and-on civil war in Somalia in the late 1980s and early 1990s sent 1 million or more Somali refuge-seekers to neighboring Ethiopia and Kenya, a significant number of whom have been resettled in the United States. In Rwanda in the early 1990s, during a civil war between Tutsis and Hutus, more than 1 million people fled the inter-ethnic bloodletting. As Yugoslavia disintegrated in the early 1990s, 4 million people became either internally displaced persons or refugees (Bon Tempo 2008; Loescher and Loescher 1994; Marfleet 2006).

In the Middle East, an exodus of refuge-seekers, many of them quite well-to-do, began as an Islamic republic was established in Iran in 1979. During the first Persian Gulf War in 1990 fought by the United States and its allies against Iraq's Saddam Hussein, who had invaded Kuwait, 4 million persons, including 1 million migrant workers from many foreign countries, were displaced. In the aftermath of the September 11, 2001, attacks against New York City and Washington, DC, the United States invaded first Afghanistan, where Al Qaeda's leader, Osama bin Laden, was hiding out, and later Iraq under the false pretext that Saddam Hussein had weapons of mass destruction. The United States, which has absorbed the largest proportion of most post-World War II refugee outflows, has been uncharacteristically stringent with regard to admitting refuge-seekers from those two war-torn countries. Many of the refugee applicants had worked as interpreters and translators for the US armed forces and the US State Department and had been promised sanctuary should their lives become endangered. But only a tiny fraction of them has been admitted into the United States. During approximately the past five years, as an estimated 5 million Syrians became refuge-seekers during Syria's civil war, they, along with refuge-seekers from other conflict zones, are finding that the doors into the European Union, the United States, and Australia are closing fast. With President Donald J. Trump in the White House, the doors of the United States have closed even tighter. Canada and Germany have been the only two Western countries willing to accept sizable numbers, but the souring public mood in Germany is forcing the government to reduce the size of that influx. In several countries in both Western and Eastern Europe, xenophobic populist political parties are now fanning the flames of public phobia about the danger of admitting "terrorists." There are now at least 20 million refuge-seekers in the world and a far larger number of internally displaced persons.

Refuge-seekers are not the only involuntary migrants in the contemporary world. Human trafficking is a multi-billion dollar business with a global reach. There are no accurate statistics on the dimensions of this trade due to its clandestine and illegal nature. Most tragically, young women, including pre-teen girls, are trafficked into countries throughout the world, where they are forced to become prostitutes and virtual domestic slaves. There is a difference between human trafficking and human smuggling. In the former case, victims are kidnapped or sold into servitude against their will—that is, they are involuntary migrants. In the latter case, people who are smuggled into countries in which they hope to find jobs or personal safety pay large sums of money to underworld entrepreneurs who make huge profits dealing in human cargo. The smuggled people and their families back home are held in debt bondage until they pay off what they owe. Some unfortunate ones end up in the same circumstances as those who are victims of trafficking. However, even though they are badly exploited by both the smugglers and the employers who hire them, they began their journeys as voluntary migrants. As countries that had welcomed immigrants and refugees in the past begin to limit the number of people they are now willing to admit, human smuggling has become one of the few options available to determined individuals who wish to find their way into more prosperous nations where they hope to have a better life (Hepburn and Simon 2013; Kyle and Koslowski 2011).

VOLUNTARY MIGRATION

The literature on voluntary migration has been dominated by studies of immigration into the United States, with the main focus on European immigration—both the "old" immigrants from the British Isles, France, Germany, and the Scandinavian countries who arrived from the early seventeenth century onward and the "new" immigrants from Central, Eastern, and Southern Europe who came in large numbers from the 1880s to 1924. Generally, the "old" immigrants were lured by the possibility of acquiring cheap farmland, whereas the "new" immigrants came for jobs in a rapidly industrializing and urbanizing United States. The number of immigrants burgeoned after railroads and steamships were invented, offering safer and cheaper transportation from various points in Europe across the Atlantic Ocean to multiple destinations in the Americas. However, sailing ships continued to be used for voyages to Australia because the steamships could not carry enough coal in their holds to last the much longer voyage until coaling stations were established along the way. Most studies in the existing literature are about immigrants from a single European country, but some scholars have synthesized a large body of writings on multiple immigrant groups (Daniels 1990; Hatton and Williamson 1998; Nugent 1992; Zahra 2016). Since the 1960s, there has been a growing literature on immigrants from Mexico and, to a lesser degree, other countries in Latin America, and studies of immigrants from Asia have also become an important subfield in US immigration history (Chan 1991; Foley 2014; Lee 2015; Romo and Mogollon-Lopez 2016; Takaki 1989).

Approximately 55 million Europeans had migrated to the Americas by the early 1920s. Between three-fifths and two-thirds of them settled in the United States, and Canada, Brazil, Argentina, and Uruguay took in a large portion of the rest (Baily and Miguez 2003; Nugent 1992). There are no precise statistics on the *net* intake because records were not kept on how many of the immigrants returned to their countries of origin. Given the fact that some migrants went back and forth, it is also not known how many of those counted as immigrants were repeat entrants who had already been counted previously upon their first arrival. Brazil needed immigrants to develop its rubber and coffee plantations, while the descendants of enslaved Africans continued to work in its vast sugar cane plantations in the tropical region of northeastern Brazil. Argentina needed immigrants to develop its cattle industry in the pampas and to work in its industrial labor force. So many Italian immigrants flocked to Argentina that approximately 40% of Argentinians today are descendants of Italians. But economic factors were not the only determinants of the immigrants' settlement patterns or what occupations they chose. Social factors also played significant roles. Emigrants from a particular European country often came from the same region(s) within that country. They also congregated in the same rural or urban areas upon arrival in the receiving countries. Family members and friends who had migrated to certain localities and found employment in certain occupations encouraged their relatives and friends to follow them to the same locations to take up similar occupations, in the process creating chain migrations. Instead of being "uprooted" (Handlin 1951/2002), they "transplanted" their socioeconomic networks in the new countries (Bodnar 1987).

Unregulated immigration ceased when the US Congress passed restrictive legislation in 1921 and 1924 to greatly reduce the influx, introducing a quota system that diminished the numbers from Central, Eastern, and Southern Europe, as well as from Japan. Aspiring Japanese immigrants were kept out by the phrase "aliens ineligible to [sic] citizenship"—a concept delineated in previous legislation and US Supreme Court decisions. A series of Chinese exclusion laws had already restricted Chinese immigration beginning in 1882. Canada and Australia also limited the number of Asian and other non-White immigrants (Freeman and Jupp 1992; Knowles 2007). During the Great Depression and World War II, there was a lull in the volume of migrants worldwide. In the immediate post-World War II years, war-torn European countries trying to recover economically admitted "guest workers" from overseas to fill new job vacancies, but voluminous global migration did not pick up again until the 1960s when the United States amended its national-origins quota system and Canada and Australia ended their "White Canada" and "White Australia" policies, respectively. The post-1960s immigrants have come from many countries in all the habitable continents. Their presence has had significant demographic, cultural, social, economic, and even political impacts on the receiving countries (Portes and Rumbaut 2014; Reimers 1992). In the traditional immigrant nations and, more recently, in certain countries within the European Union (Boswell and Geddes 2011), the percentage of foreign-born, non-White immigrants is growing steadily while the proportion of people of European ancestry is decreasing. In response, status anxiety among White people is fueling increasingly strong anti-immigrant sentiments. When nativists proclaim they want to "take the country back," what they mean is that they want to return to the days when White people dominated all spheres of life.

Aside from immigrants who intend to become permanent settlers, there is a growing number of migrants who sign contracts that allow them to enter certain countries as low-paid, low-skilled service workers. Women outnumber men in this migrant stream. They find employment as nannies for children, caregivers for elderly people, house cleaners, waitresses, kitchen helpers, "escorts" or "hostesses" in bars and gentlemen's clubs, seamstresses, manicurists, and salespeople (Chang 2000; Ehrenreich and Hochschild 2004). Women from Southeast Asia, South Asia, and North Africa have flocked to oil-rich countries in the Middle East to work as caregivers and house cleaners (Gunatilleke 1987). The major source countries for women workers headed to the Middle East are almost all Islamic societies because their Muslim Arab employers feel more comfortable with fellow Muslims living in their homes. The recent slump in the price of oil has created massive unemployment among the workers who are trapped in Persian Gulf countries—trapped because their employers have withheld their passports, a common tactic to prevent workers from moving to other employers or fleeing home. Male migrants find employment as farm workers, construction workers, and in the various trades, where they are employed by contractors who pay them wages far below those received by White workers doing similar work. They cannot protest because many of them enter the country without the required documents and will be deported if caught. These migrants go not only to the traditional countries of immigration but also to economically better off societies within the same geographic regions where their own countries are situated (Caballero-Anthony and Menju 2015). For example, men and women from Indonesia seek work in Malaysia, whereas Malaysians seek work in more prosperous Singapore. Young women in poverty-stricken Cambodia and Myanmar are lured to more economically developed Thailand, where they are told they will be offered "respectable" jobs but, instead, find themselves held as virtual slaves in brothels. Filipinas go to Hong Kong, Taiwan, Japan, and many other countries throughout the world to work as caregivers, house cleaners, and "hostesses," even though many of them have college degrees (Parreñas 2011, 2015). They do so because the Philippine economy is unable to provide employment for all those who seek work. Millions of Filipino men are employed as waiters, cooks, room attendants, and musicians on cruise ships and ships of the US Navy and US Merchant Marines. Filipino crew also serve in ships registered in dozens of other nations (Fajardo 2011). All these migrant workers who hail from so many countries send a huge amount of remittances back home to support family members left behind.

Today's most fortunate migrants are those with higher education and technical skills. There is, in fact, a global competition for such workers in the so-called STEM (science, technology, engineering, and management) sectors of the economy. Both Canada and Australia use a point system to choose which aspiring immigrants to admit. The largest number of points is given to those who have at least a Bachelor of Arts or Bachelor of Science degree, are fluent in English (and/or French in Canada), and are younger than age 45 years. In contrast, the two major selection criteria the United States uses are family reunification and the admission of persons with skills needed in the economy at particular moments. Because family reunification slots take up the largest portion of each year's quota, in addition to the annual immigration quotas, the United States now issues special visas, usually good for six years with the possibility of renewal, to persons who can show evidence of extraordinary accomplishments, such as awards received and leadership in their professions. These individuals include not just STEM experts but also nurses, artists, musicians, star athletes, and (for a time) even sushi chefs, regardless of their level of education. Applicants must usually be sponsored by employers who have already promised them jobs, but some exceptional individuals are allowed to sponsor themselves. The British and Germans have been the most numerous among the knowledge experts migrating to fill such job slots throughout the world, but the Irish, New Zealanders, Chinese, Indians, and Filipinos are fast catching up (Basri and Box 2008; Bhagwati and Hanson 2009; Chiswick 2011). In the 1960s, there was much concern about how the less developed countries that were losing their well-educated people were suffering from a "brain drain." However, because some countries, such as the Philippines, are producing more well-educated people than their economies can absorb, and because there are certain benefits from sending their citizens abroad who can later return with new knowledge and expertise that can benefit their countries of origin, the anxiety over brain drain has lessened. The concept of "brain circulation" has become the new accepted norm. Migration for permanent settlement, the global circulation of talent, and the peripatetic circuits of service-sector workers constitute the newest chapter in the history of human migration that began a long, long time ago.

REFERENCES

Ahonen, P., Gustavo Corni, Jerzy Kochanowski, et al. eds. 2008. *People on the Move: Forced Population Movements in Europe and the Second World War and Its Aftermath*. Oxford, UK: Berg.

Akçam, T. 2006. *A Shameful Act: The Armenian Genocide and the Question of Turkish Responsibility*, translated by P Bessemer. New York: Metropolitan Books.

Anderson, A. 2013. "Polynesia, East and South, Including Transpacific Migration." In *The Global Prehistory of Human Migration*, edited by P. Bellwood, 320–326. Sussex, UK: Wiley Blackwell.

Anthony, D. W. 2007. *The Horse, the Wheel, and Language: How Bronze-age Riders from the Eurasian Steppes Shaped the Modern World*. Princeton: Princeton University Press.

Aubert, M., A. W. G. Pike, C. Stringer, A. Bartsiokas, L. Kinsley, S. Eggins, M. Day, and R. Grün. 2012. "Confirmation of a Late Middle Pleistocene Age for the Omo Kibish 1 Cranium by Direct Uranium-series Dating." *Journal of Human Evolution* 63(5): 704–710.

Baily, S. L., and E. J. Miguez, eds. 2003. *Mass Migration to Modern Latin America*. Wilmington, DE: Scholarly Resources.

Banivanua-Mar, T. 2007. *Violence and Colonial Dialogue: The Australian–Pacific Indentured Labor Trade*. Honolulu: University of Hawaii Press.

Banner, S. 2005. *How the Indians Lost Their Land: Law and Power on the Frontier*. Cambridge, MA: Belknap.

Basri, S., and S. Box. 2008. *The Global Competition for Talent: Mobility of the Highly Skilled*. Paris: Organisation for Economic Co-operation and Development.

Bellwood, P. 1979. *Man's Conquest of the Pacific: The Prehistory of Southeast Asia and Oceania*. New York: Oxford University Press.

Bellwood, P. ed. 2013. *First Migrants: Ancient Migration in Global Perspective*. West Sussex, UK: Wiley Blackwell.

Bhagwati, J., and G. Hanson, eds. 2009. *Skilled Immigration Today: Prospects, Problems, and Policies*. New York: Oxford University Press.

Bodnar, J. 1987. *The Transplanted: A History of Immigrants in Urban America*. Updated ed. Bloomington: Indiana University Press.

Boswell, C., and A. Geddes. 2011. *Migration and Mobility in the European Union*. New York: Palgrave Macmillan.

Bowes, J. P. 2016. *Land Too Precious for Indians: Northern Indian Removal*. Norman: University of Oklahoma Press.

Brooke, A., and D. Brandon. 2005. *Bound for Botany Bay: British Convict Voyages to Australia*. Kew, UK: The National Archives.

Brooke, J. L. 2014. *Climate Change and the Course of Global History*. Cambridge, UK: Cambridge University Press.

Bulliet, R. C. 1990. *The Camel and the Wheel*. New York: Columbia University Press.

Caballero-Anthony, M., and T. Menju, eds. 2015. *Asia on the Move: Regional Migration and the Role of Civil Society*. Tokyo: Japan Center for International Exchange.

Campbell, G., ed. 2004. *Structure of Slavery in Indian Ocean Africa and Asia*. London: Cass.

Carson, M. T. 2013. "Micronesian Archaeology." In *The Global Prehistory of Human Migrations*, edited by P. Bellwood, 314–319. West Sussex, UK: Wiley Blackwell.

Cavalli-Sforza, L. L., and F. Cavalli-Sforza. 1995. *The Great Human Diasporas: The History of Diversity and Evolution*. New York: Basic Books.

Chan, S. 1991. *Asian Americans: An Interpretive History*. Boston: Twayne.

Chan, S. 2004. *Survivors: Cambodian Refugees in the United States*. Urbana: University of Illinois Press.

Chang, G. 2000. *Disposable Domestics: Immigrant Women Workers in the Global Economy*. Cambridge, MA: South End Press.

Chatterjee, I., and R. M. Eaton, eds. 2006. *Slavery in South Asian History*. Bloomington: Indiana University Press.

Chiswick, B. R. ed. 2011. *Highly-Skilled Immigration in a Global Labor Market*. Washington, DC: American Enterprise Institute Press.

Christian, D. 1998. *A History of Russia, Central Asia and Mongolia. Vol. 1: Inner Eurasia from Prehistory to the Mongol Empire*. Malden, MA: Blackwell.

Christopher, E., C. Pybus, and M. Rediker. 2007. *Many Middle Passages: Forced Migration and the Making of the Modern World*. Berkeley: University of California Press.

Clarkson, C., Z. Jacobs, B. Marwick, et al. 2017. "Human Occupation of Northern Australia by 65,000 Years Ago." *Nature* 547: 306–310.

Cohen, G. D. 2012. *In War's Wake: Europe's Displaced Persons in the Postwar Order*. New York: Oxford University Press.

Connor, I. 2007. *Refugees and Expellees in Post-War Germany*. Manchester, UK: Manchester University Press.

Cook, N. D. 1998. *Born to Die: Disease and the New World Conquest, 1492–1650*. Cambridge, UK: Cambridge University Press.

Cunliffe, B. 2015. *By Steppe, Desert and Ocean: The Birth of Eurasia*. New York: Oxford University Press.

Daniels, R. 1981. *Concentration Camps, North America: Japanese in the United States and Canada During World War II*. Malabar, FL: Krieger.

Daniels, R. 1990. *Coming to America: A History of Immigration and Ethnicity in American Life*. New York: HarperCollins.

Davidson, B. 1995. *Africa in History: Themes and Outlines*. Revised and expanded ed. New York: Touchstone.

Davis, D. B. 2006. *Inhuman Bondage: The Rise and Fall of Slavery in the New World*. New York: Oxford University Press.

de Zayas, A. M. 2006. *A Terrible Revenge: The Cleansing of the East European Germans*. 2nd revised and updated ed. New York: St. Martin's Griffin.

Dillehay, T. D. 2000. *The Settlement of the Americas: A New Prehistory*. New York: Basic Books.

Donef, R. 2014. *The Hakkâri Massacres: Ethnic Cleansing by Turkey, 1924–25*. Sydney, Australia: Tatavla.

Dower, J. W. 1999. *Embracing Defeat: Japan in the Wake of World War II*. New York: Norton.

Dunbar-Ortiz, R. 2015. *An Indigenous Peoples' History of the United States*. Boston: Beacon.

Ehrenreich, B., and A. R. Hochschild, eds. 2004. *Global Woman: Nannies, Maids, and Sex Workers in the New Economy*. New York: Holt.

Eltis, D., and D. Richardson. 2010. *Atlas of the Transatlantic Slave Trade*. New Haven, CT: Yale University Press.

Fagan, B. M. 1990. *The Journey from Eden: The Peopling of Our World*. London: Thames & Hudson.

Fagan, B. M. 2003. *The Great Journey: The Peopling of Ancient America*. Updated ed. Gainesville: University Press of Florida.

Fajardo, K. B. 2011. *Filipino Crosscurrents: Oceanographies of Seafaring, Masculinities, and Globalization*. Minneapolis: University of Minnesota Press.

Fitzgerald, C. P. 1972. *The Southern Expansion of the Chinese People*. New York: Praeger.

Foley, N. 2014. *Mexicans in the Making of America*. Cambridge, MA: Belknap.

Forsyth, J. 1992. *A History of the Peoples of Siberia: Russia's North Asian Colony, 1581–1990*. Cambridge, UK: Cambridge University Press.

Freeman, G. P., and J. Jupp, eds. 1992. *Nations of Immigrants: Australia, the United States, and International Migration*. Oxford, UK: Oxford University Press.

Groves, C. 2013. "Hominin Migration Before *Homo sapiens*: Out of Africa—How Many Times?" In *The Global Prehistory of Human Migration*, edited by P. Bellwood, 18–25. West Sussex, UK: Wiley Blackwell.

Gunatilleke, G., ed. 1987. *Migration of Asian Workers to the Arab World*. Tokyo: United Nations University Press.

Handlin, O. 2002. *The Uprooted: The Epic Story of the Great Migration That Made the American People*. 2nd ed. Philadelphia: University of Pennsylvania Press. (Original work published 1951)

Hatton, T. J., and J. G. Williamson. 1998. *The Age of Mass Migration: Causes and Economic Impact*. New York: Oxford University Press.

Hepburn, H., and R. J. Simon. 2013. *Human Trafficking Around the World: Hidden in Plain Sight*. New York: Columbia University Press.

Hertler, C., A. Bruch, and M. Märker. 2013. "The Earliest Stages of Hominin Dispersal in Africa and Eurasia." In *The Global Prehistory of Human Migration*, edited by P. Bellwood, 9–17. West Sussex, UK: Wiley Blackwell.

Hirschon, R., ed. 2003. *Crossing the Aegean: An Appraisal of the 1923 Compulsory Population Exchange Between Greece and Turkey*. New York: Berghahn Books.

Hisock, P. 2013. "The Human Colonization of Australia." In *The Global Prehistory of Human Migration*, edited by P. Bellwood, 55–60. West Sussex, UK: Wiley Blackwell.

Hughes, R. 1988. *The Fatal Shore: The Epic of Australia's Founding*. New York: Vintage.

Jahoda, G. 1995. *Trail of Tears*. San Antonio, TX: Wingspress.

Jordan, D., and M. Walsh. 2007. *White Cargo: The Forgotten History of Britain's White Slaves in America*. New York: New York University Press.

Kappeler, A. 2013. *The Russian Empire: A Multiethnic History*. New York: Routledge.

Khan, Y. 2007. *The Great Partition: The Making of India and Pakistan*. New Haven, CT: Yale University Press.

Khazanov, A. M. 1994. *Nomads and the Outside World*. 2nd ed., translated by J. Crookenden. Madison: University of Wisconsin Press.

Khodarkovsky, M. 2004. *Russia's Steppe Frontier: The Making of a Colonial Empire, 1500–1800*. Bloomington: Indiana University Press.

Klein, H. S. 2010. *The Atlantic Slave Trade*. 2nd ed. Cambridge, UK: Cambridge University Press.

Klein, H. S., and B. Vinson, eds. 2007. *African Slavery in Latin America and the Caribbean*. 2nd ed. New York: Oxford University Press.

Knowles, V. 2007. *Strangers at Our Gates: Canadian Immigration and Immigration Policy, 1540–2006*. Rev. ed. Toronto: Dundurn Press.

Kyle, D., and R. Koslowski, eds. 2011. *Global Human Trafficking: Comparative Perspectives*. 2nd ed. Baltimore, MD: Johns Hopkins University Press.

Lary, D. 2012. *Chinese Migrations: The Movement of People, Goods, and Ideas over Four Millennia*. Lanham, MD: Rowman & Littlefield.

Lee, E. G. 2015. *The Making of Asian America: A History*. New York: Simon & Schuster.

Levene, M. 2008. "Empire, Native Peoples, and Genocide." In *Empire, Colony, Genocide: Conquests, Occupation, and Subaltern Resistance in World History*, edited by A. D. Moses, 183–204. New York: Berghahn Books.

Lewis, D. 1972. *We, the Navigators: The Ancient Art of Landfinding in the Pacific*. Honolulu: University of Hawaii Press.

Lincoln, W. B. 1994. *The Conquest of a Continent: Siberia and the Russians*. Ithaca, NY: Cornell University Press.

Loescher, G., and A. D. Loescher. 1994. *The Global Refugee Crisis: A Reference Handbook*. Santa Barbara, CA: ABC-CLIO.

Lukas, R. C. 2012. *The Forgotten Holocaust: The Poles under German Occupation, 1939–1944*. New York: Hippocrene Books.

Manco, J. 2016. *Ancestral Journeys: The Peopling of Europe from the First Adventurers to the Vikings*. Rev. and updated ed. London: Thames & Hudson.

Marfleet, P. 2006. *Refugees in a Global Era*. New York: Palgrave Macmillan.

Marrus, M. R. 1985. *The Unwanted: European Refugees in the Twentieth Century*. New York: Oxford University Press.

Meagher, A. J. 2008. *The Coolie Trade: The Traffic in Chinese Laborers to Latin America, 1848–1874*. Bloomington, IN: Xlibris.

Meltzer, D. J. 2013. "The Human Colonization of the Americas: Archaeology." In *The Global Prehistory of Human Migration*, edited by P. Bellwood, 61–69. West Sussex, UK: Wiley Blackwell.

Mithen, S. 2003. *After the Ice: A Global Human History, 20,000–5,000 B.C.* Cambridge, MA: Harvard University Press.

Morgan, D. 2007. *The Mongols*. 2nd ed. Malden, MA: Blackwell.

Naimark, N. M. 2001. *Fires of Hatred: Ethnic Cleansing in Twentieth-Century Europe*. Cambridge, MA: Harvard University Press.

Nekrich, A. M. 1981. *The Punished Peoples: The Deportation and Fate of Soviet Minorities at the End of the Second World War*. New York: Norton.

Newman, J. L. 1995. *The Peopling of Africa: A Geographic Interpretation*. New Haven, CT: Yale University Press.

Northrup, D. 1995. *Indentured Labor in the Age of Imperialism, 1834–1922*. New York: Cambridge University Press.

Nugent, W. 1992. *Crossings: The Great Transatlantic Migrations, 1870–1914*. Bloomington: Indiana University Press.

Parreñas, R. S. 2011. *Illicit Flirtations: Labor, Migration, and Sex Trafficking in Tokyo*. Stanford, CA: Stanford University Press.

Parreñas, R. S. 2015. *Servants of Globalization: Women, Migration, and Domestic Work*. 2nd ed. Stanford, CA: Stanford University Press.

Perdue, P. C. 2010. *China Marches West: The Qing Conquest of Central Eurasia*. Cambridge, MA: Belknap.

Pohl, J. O. 1999. *Ethnic Cleansing in the U.S.S.R., 1937–1949*. Westport, CT: Greenwood.

Polian, P. 2004. *Against Their Will: The History and Geography of Forced Migrations in the U.S.S.R.* Budapest, Hungary: Central European University Press.

Ponting, C. 2007. *A New Green History of the World: The Environment and the Collapse of Great Civilizations*. rev. ed. London: Penguin.

Portes, A., and R. G. Rumbaut. 2014. *Immigrant America: A Portrait.* 4th ed. Berkeley: University of California Press.

Reimers, D. M. 1992. *Still the Golden Door: The Third World Comes to America.* 2nd ed. New York: Columbia University Press.

Reinisch, J., and E. White, eds. 2011. *The Disentanglement of Populations: Migration, Expulsion, and Displacement in Post-War Europe, 1944–1949.* New York: Palgrave Macmillan.

Romo, H. D., and O. Mogollon-Lopez. 2016. *Mexican Migration to the United States: Perspectives from Both Sides of the Border.* Austin: University of Texas Press.

Rossabi, M. 2011. *The Mongols and Global History.* New York: Norton.

Ruhlen, M. 2009. "Migrations to the Americas." In *Ancient Human Migrations: A Multidisciplinary Approach*, edited by P. N. Peregrine, I. Peiros, and M. Feldman, 112–126. Salt Lake City: University of Utah Press.

Saunders, K. 1982. *Workers in Bondage: The Origins and Bases of Unfree Labour in Queensland, 1824–1916.* London: University of Queensland Press.

Segal, R. 2001. *Islam's Black Slaves: The Other Black Diaspora.* New York: Farrar, Straus & Giroux.

Sémah, F., and A-M. Sémah. 2013. "Pleistocene Migrations in the Southeast Asian Archipelago." In *The Global History of Human Migration*, edited by Peter Bellwood, 49–54. West Sussex, UK: Wiley Blackwell.

Slezkine, Y. 1994. *Arctic Mirrors: Russia and the Small Peoples of the North.* Ithaca, NY: Cornell University Press.

Southerton, S. G. 2013. "The Human Colonization of the Americas: Population Genetics. In *The Global Prehistory of Human Migration*, edited by P. Bellwood, 70–76. West Sussex, UK: Wiley Blackwell.

St. Fleur, N. 2018. "In Cave in Israel, Scientists Find Jawbone Fossil from Oldest Modern Human Out of Africa." *New York Times*, January 25, 2018.

Stoneking, M., and K. Harvati. 2013. "Early Old World Migrations of *Homo sapiens*: Human Biology." In *The Global Prehistory of Human Migration*, edited by P. Bellwood, 26–37. West Sussex, UK: Wiley Blackwell.

Stringer, C. 2012. *Lone Survivors: How We Came to Be the Only Humans on Earth.* New York: St. Martin's Griffin.

Sunderland, W. 2004. *Taming the Wild Field: Colonization and Empire on the Russian Steppe.* Ithaca, NY: Cornell University Press.

Suny, R. G. 2015. *"They Can Live in the Desert but Nowhere Else": A History of the Armenian Genocide.* Princeton, NJ: Princeton University Press.

Takaki, R. 1989. *Strangers from a Different Shore: A History of Asian Americans.* Boston: Little, Brown.

Tempo, C. L. B. 2008. *Americans at the Gate: The United States and Refugees During the Cold War.* Princeton, NJ: Princeton University Press.

Thorne, A., and R. Raymond. 1989. *Man on the Rim: The Peopling of the Pacific.* North Ryde, New South Wales, Australia: Angus & Robertson.

Thornton, R. 1987. *American Indian Holocaust and Survival: A Population History Since 1492.* Norman: University of Oklahoma Press.

Tinker, H. 1993. *A New System of Slavery: The Export of Indian Labour Overseas, 1830–1920.* 2nd ed. London: Hansib.

Verano, J. W., and D. H. Ubelaker, eds. 1992. *Disease and Demography in the Americas.* Washington, DC: Smithsonian Institution Press.

Viola, L. 2007. *The Unknown Gulag: The Lost World of Stalin's Special Settlements*. New York: Oxford University Press.

Wells, S. 2002. *The Journey of Man: A Genetic Odyssey*. New York: Random House.

Wells, S. 2007. *Deep Ancestry: Inside the Genographic Project, the Landmark DNA Quest to Decipher Our Distant Past*. Washington, DC: National Geographic.

Wiens, H. J. 1954. *China's March toward the Tropics*. Hamden: Shoe String Press.

Wood, A. 2011. *Russia's Frozen Frontier: A History of Siberia and the Russian Far East, 1581–1991*. London: Bloomsbury Academic.

Young, E. 2014. *Alien Nation: Chinese Migration in the Americas from the Coolie Era Through World War II*. Chapel Hill: University of North Carolina Press.

Zahra, T. 2016. *The Great Departure: Mass Migration from Eastern Europe and the Making of the Free World*. New York: Norton.

Zamindar, V. F. Y. 2007. *The Long Partition and the Making of Modern South Asia: Refugees, Boundaries, Histories*. New York: Columbia University Press.

Zegura, S. L., T. Karafet, and M. Hammer. 2009. "The Peopling of the Americas as Viewed from the Y Chromosome." In *Ancient Human Migrations: A Multidisciplinary Approach*, edited by P. N. Peregrine, I. Peiros, and M. Feldman, 127–136. Salt Lake City: University of Utah Press.

Zhang, C., and H. Hung. 2013. "Eastern Asia: Archaeology." In *The Global Prehistory of Human Migration*, edited by P. Bellwood, 209–216. West Sussex, UK: Wiley Blackwell.

Zimmer, C. 2018. "In the Bones of a Buried Child, Signs of a Massive Human Migration to the Americas." *New York Times*, January 3, 2018.

CHAPTER 23

....

WAR AND MILITARIZATION

....

JAIRUS VICTOR GROVE

A vital part of global studies is understanding the role that warfare has played in global political life and how it is changing in intensity and form. The complexity of these issues in the scope and character of combat significantly complicate how we understand the global generally and specifically how we investigate other frames of analysis, from economics to politics and culture.

In 1919, British Major General J. F. C. Fuller wrote (as cited in Fuller 1984),

> In war, more especially modern wars, in which weapons change rapidly, one thing is certain, and this is—that no army of fifty years before any date selected would stand "a dog's chance" against the army existing at the date, not even were it composed entirely of Winkelrieds and Marshal Neys. (p. 62)

This was an accurate assessment of the strategic thinking about modern warfare in the first half of the twentieth century. Like modernism, modern warfare followed a progressivist telos in which each successive stage of development was to be an irreversible improvement on the stage that proceeds it. Technological change was a line moving forever upwards, never turning around or declining. Under that paradigm of military thought, weaponry and fighting style were thought to follow a simple linear diffusion model in which "competition produces a tendency towards sameness in competitors" (Kenneth Waltz as cited in Goldman and Eliason 2003: 8). Technic and technique were thought to be innovated by the great powers, generally with the support of heavy industrial and capital-intensive "Science." Advances then defused from center to periphery or were actively transferred from center to periphery as dictated by the security or financial interests of European and American metropoles (Goldman and Eliason 2003: 8). This description of the linear diffusion pattern and the advantage of modernity was roughly accurate in describing military development and patterns of war, with a few notable exceptions, throughout the early modern and modern period, reaching its peak during World War II.

I do not argue that there was a period or break after which a modernist approach to war ceased to be operative. But I do suggest that the acceleration and intensification of globalization, particularly in the spread of technical knowledge and the means of destruction, culminated in a period in which there was and continues to be a precipitous decline in the strategic value of force and a parallel fragmentation and proliferation of collective violence.

This transition did not happen all at once, neither is there one sufficient explanation of a "break." However, there were several necessary conditions that entered into a relay of positive feedbacks resulting in a severe mutation of global warfare.

In this chapter, I sketch out how I have come to understand this historical transformation as a process, and its trajectory, given the trajectory of the contemporary state in which we find ourselves. Along the way, I hope to provide some insight on how to think about the problem of war as well as the shortcomings of existing concepts and definitions of war used in the fields of international relations, security studies, and war studies. I do not try to develop a replacement definition. Instead, I argue throughout the chapter that the changing nature of war should itself be treated as a problematic for research and investigation rather than trying to settle on another definition of war that fails to keep up with the dynamic character of empirical reality.

I first introduce the problem of what Mary Kaldor (2012) describes as "new wars" or a form of conflict endemic to globalization. I then lay out the attributes I think best distinguish contemporary war from earlier forms of war. Next, I develop what I call *late globalization* as a period in which key characteristics of globalization and warfare become increasingly indistinguishable. Finally, I extend the analysis of late globalization, particularly its algorithmic character, to describe the possible near future of warfare.

OLD WARS, COLD WARS, NEW WARS?

The question of whether the post-Cold War period, or what I more loosely periodize as late globalization, has created "new wars" of a categorical or conceptually different type has been hotly debated in international relations, security studies, and war studies (Kaldor 2012). The crux of this fight has been about the nature of conflicts and what is driving the nature of conflicts that emerge after the loss of bipolar hegemonic ordering. Although a rigorous academic debate, unlike many other academic fights, the opposing sides of this argument bleed directly into policymaking and military planning throughout the world. What Gerard Toal described as a sense of "geopolitical vertigo" after the Cold War has been further amplified by the September 11, 2001 (9/11), terrorist attacks in the United States; the 7/7 attacks in London; the attacks in Mumbai, India; the favela wars in Brazil; the cartel wars in northern Mexico; as well as the bloody so-called "ethnic conflicts" that dominated the 1990s, such as the Rwandan genocide and the Balkan conflict (Tuathail and Dalby 1998). The vertigo endures in the form of a continuing impasse in ideological and strategic thinking about the structure of global order (Milevski 2016).

Contemporary conflicts are transdimensional in character. By *transdimensional*, I mean that although the conflicts are local in character, they are connected by interest, solidarity, blood, or curiosity to other distant spaces that in turn reinforce and resupply those local conflicts in ways that defy settled definitions of civil wars, proxy wars, or internationalized conflicts. In particular, security practices and practitioners and military hardware move from place to place with little regard to national or allied allegiance in tandem with increasingly feverish commitments to national security. I concur with Kaldor (2012), who writes that in "new wars," the "distinction between internal and external, between aggression (attacks from abroad) and repression (attacks from inside the country), or even between local and global, are difficult to sustain" (loc. 230–231).

In addition to the complex spatial character of contemporary conflicts, there is also a vexing temporal element in which old fights take on a contemporary significance made possible by real-time constituencies created in vast media-saturated "imagined communities" that are significantly influenced by constant Twitter updates, even if some of those constituencies have little or no actual historical connection. Making use of Walter Benjamin's thinking on literature, Benedict Anderson (1991) theorizes that the virtual simultaneity of print media creates imagined communities essential to the making of national culture. However, the social media age no longer requires "imagination" to create the verisimilitude of simultaneity. Mediated experience is for all practical purposes now simultaneous, and the result has not always been amplified versions of the same nationalism Anderson theorized. Instead, the complex territoriality of affiliation, attention, and identification created by social networks fractializes constituencies that more and less overlap with existing nation-states. The possibility of real-time diaspora and even the production of new publics, sometimes temporary, complicates questions of nationalism, patriotism, and partisanship (Glezos 2016). In some cases, the consumption model of old media is transformed by new media platforms to allow forms of direct, nonterritorial participation, as in the case of GoFundMe accounts for military equipment or real-time technical or medical assistance in conflict areas via digital networks (Grove 2015).

In contradistinction to the more technology-driven narrative for transformation, Kaldor (2012) insists that identity politics in postcolonial states are the heart of so-called new wars. I find Kaldor's emphasis on identity and cosmopolitanism unpersuasive as a historically unique attribute of what makes "new wars" new. Furthermore, I do not accept the cartography of her diagnosis, which sees new wars as *native* to postcolonial or post-Soviet states. I argue that the shift by states and other forms of organization from war to security and the subsequent breakdown in the distinctions between combat and policing drive the proliferation of what Kaldor calls "new wars." I concur with Kaldor that these wars are characterized by heavy civilian casualties, crime networks, blurry lines of enmity, complex humanitarian crises, and indiscernibly civil and internationalized participants. But the claim that identity and fundamentalism are key attributes of "new" conflict is, I think, unsustainable. After all, historically, all wars have had identity at their core. One need only look at the vile racial depictions of enemies by all sides in World War II and its material double of flagrant civilian bombing, or the Japanese use of Korean prisoners for rape and medical experimentation, to see the virulence of identity politics in twentieth-century great power conflicts (Harris 2002; Lindqvist 2011). Further back in the history of Europe, the common use of rape and disfigurement in the Thirty Years War, and the indiscriminate warfare against Native American civilians and non-combatants in the United States until the early twentieth century are just a few examples of the intensity of identity politics in other periods of global history. I am not sure how one distinguishes these racially motivated atrocities as somehow distinct from the identity politics of Bosnia or the Congo. As McNeill (2009) and others have noted about the critical role of French nationalism in the rise of Napoleon, it is difficult, if not impossible, to mobilize soldiers to fight without the mobilization of identity politics.

Rather than blame a new "tribalism" as Kaldor (2012) does, what I see unifying contemporary conflicts is an archipelago or assemblage of security and insecurity. By an *assemblage*, I mean a loose and diverse ecological web of policing practices that are shared at conventions and state-sponsored international training exchanges; global arms dealers; criminal organizations; private interests and attention to threats now seen as interdependent; the structural transformations of travel, communication, and destructive capability; and at the same time the increasing marketization/monetization via arms sales and other security resources that support the conflicts that global intervention and attention create.

In focusing on the transformation of the technology and political economy of war, I do not want to ignore identity. As discussed previously, identity is amplified and reinvented in ways that mirror the novelty of the new media of contemporary life. However, unlike Kaldor (2012), I resist the idea that "identity" is a problem confined to the "failed states" of the lingering colonial cartographic imagination that always finds "tribal hatred" in Africa or the Middle East. Ethnonationalist violence is a global problem that thrives in the violent streets and ballot booths of the United States and Europe. Thus, rather than pathologize the conflict in the Congo as a difference in kind, it is, I think, more valuable to see how identity is mutating and finding new points of connection through religious and civilizational identification rather than just the nineteenth-century categories of nationalism. Christian nationalism in the United States and Flemish nationalism in Belgium are useful examples of how nineteenth-century forms of national consciousness can mutate to accommodate contemporary revivals of religious or local imaginaries.[1]

LATE GLOBALIZATION AND THE PERSISTENCE OF WAR

Any list of major drivers would have to include the unprecedented industrialization and commercialization of light arms during each of the world wars, the truly globalized network of arms dealers that developed throughout competitive security assistance programs during the Cold War, and the global arms bazaar that metastasized after the Cold War into a multibillion-dollar market with almost no regulations (Feinstein 2011). Of course, these state-led markets did not just drive globalization. They were in turn transformed by globalization as the flow of licit and illicit currency, the expansion of commercial markets, and the denationalization of commercial interests intensified (Nordstrom 2007). The nascent global market in low-cost, automatic, light weapons also amplified anti-colonial struggles, which further drove the creation of new clients, markets, and conflicts. As an example of this exchange back and forth between globalization and war, the AK-47 reverberated through nearly every major rebellion and independence movement. After its invention in 1946, the AK-47 helped create a new global network for the trafficking of licit and illicit small arms and images, proliferating as a symbol of national independence (Bolton, Sakamoto, and Griffiths 2012). The rifle even made its way onto the flag of Mozambique, further reinforcing the "brand" of the already nearly ubiquitous weapon (Forrer 2013).

The emergence of the postcolonial political order also changed the security infrastructure of dispossession, and the transnationalism of financial interests itself created new demands for warlike capabilities outside of the state (Abrahamsen and Williams 2007; Sassen 2010). European and North American states that could once take whatever they wanted from colonies now had to rely on corporations and trade agreements, which were variously themselves reliant on state military intervention and private military forces or what James Ferguson (2006) calls the "governing of extraction." What takes place between the end of World War II and September 11, 2001, is a flattening of the access to modes of warlike violence and a saturation of capability such that better and worse weapons platforms and fighting capability lose their footing (Krause 1995). It is worth noting that the declining efficacy of great powers was apparent much earlier. Signs of the "leveling effect" of martial globalization were already evident in the Chinese Communist Revolution (1946), Korean War (1950), and the French defeat at Dien Bien Phu (1954), and it was undeniable by the time of the Algerian and Vietnamese wars of independence (1962 and 1975, respectively).

Without overstating the point, it can confidently be stated that after World War II the value of force, as a currency for compelling opponents to accept one's own will, declines continuously (Clausewitz 1989). Unfortunately, the resulting era of cheap violence, although being somewhat antagonistic to colonial control and extreme international hierarchy, does not lead to a decline in the use of violence. Despite the claims of Goldstein, Mueller, and Pinker that war is on the decline, I argue instead that the declining value of force merely shifts what kinds of wars we fight (Goldstein 2012; Mueller 2007; Pinker 2012). To point to the absence of great power wars after World War II or the decline of traditional battle deaths after the Cold War is a bit like celebrating the decline of catapults after the discovery of gunpowder. War is not disappearing; it is changing.

It would be naive and presentist to assert that the transformation of warfare is *simply* the result of globalization, as neither process has that kind of unilinear causal explanation. War has always been a process of globalization, and it is difficult to name a period of globalization not intimately intertwined with warfare in the sense that both concepts give name to simultaneous processes of territorialization and deterritorialization, the erasing and drawing of new lines, the breaking and making of new relations, and creation and destruction across space–time (Deleuze and Guattari 1987). However, there is a difference that makes a difference in the contemporary relationship between war—what I call *late globalization*.[2]

By late globalization, I mean the period of renewed ethnonationalism, wall building, border militarization, authoritarian electoral success, right and left agendas against market liberalization, declining demand for global supply chains and commercial shipping, the crumbling of the European Union and other regional fora, and a multinational backlash against international institutions such as the United Nations and the International Criminal Court—all taking place simultaneously with unprecedented numbers of people on the move, drone programs premised on a universal jurisdiction, an unregulated global market in arms, a global slave trade eclipsing the height of the Middle Passage, and the first truly non-sovereign currencies with the rise of blockchain platforms such as Bitcoin (Bob 2012; Nickel 2014). In the wake of Brexit and the intensification of hostility against cosmopolitan ideals, the popular press is awash in headlines that read "Is Globalization Over?" Like the premature declarations of the end of the state and the end of history, globalization can continue, indeed even accelerate, with the intensification of processes of territorialization and provincialization. Reality shows that these logical contradictions are not material contradictions.

Late globalization is a way of describing a global system expanding, deepening, and thickening but with relations better characterized by inter-vulnerability rather than interdependence and heterogeneous fracturing, and diversification rather than flattening and homogenization. More succinctly, in the past two decades, the dark side of globalization has been vastly outpacing or at least showing itself to be semi-autonomous of ideologically progressive components of globalism. The cosmopolitanism of the Kantian variety is being eclipsed by a martial cosmopolitanism that thrives on particularistic and ethnonationalist identities and actors, while also globalizing the networks and supply lines of destructive capability, and the interests that globalize seemingly local conflicts. Therefore, it should not surprise us that the character of warfare is also taking on a depth of complexity, mutation, and unpredictability correspondent to late globalization. Warfare, like globalization more broadly, cannot be measured by agreed upon attributes derived from historical patterns. Some patterns still persist, but they are not sufficiently isomorphic to describe the current condition.

There are, of course, other stories to tell about globalization. Globalization also includes historical changes to our conceptions of human rights; globalization has played a significant role in making powerful social movements against the inevitability of war and violence; and globalization equally includes global labor movements, as it does the conditions those movements militate against. This chapter is not meant to be to the exclusion of those countervailing and more positive forces of globalization. However, there has been significantly more interest and scholarship on both the social and the political character of globalization, with much less scholarly work put into understanding the intimate role that war plays in the process of globalization (Barkawi 2006).

WHY WAR STILL MATTERS

There is a growing consensus among academics that available data point to war declining globally. The basis for this claim is well-founded if the question can be answered quantitatively, where the measurement is restricted to the number of battlefield deaths generated in a traditionally defined battle. Kaldor (2012) concludes in her study of war and globalization that all three of the major war databases from which Goldstein and Pinker draw their conclusion "are based on 'old war' assumptions.[3] For violence to be counted as a war, there has to be a state involved at least on one side and there has to be a certain number of battle deaths" (Loc. 4602–4604). I concur, and I view the problem of counting as twofold, at least. First, there are qualitative or intensive changes in warfare that are not themselves quantifiable within the existing framework of battlefield deaths but still suggest that war is expanding in a deleterious way. Land use, percentage of gross domestic product (GDP),[4] drain on human and intellectual capital, militarization and weaponization into every area of science and research, basing and deployment-related sexual violence, environmental damage, energy consumption, territorialization, and the rigidification of borders all suggest that the size and scope of war are beyond the narrow indicator of battlefield deaths (Dalby 2002; Enloe 2014; Goldstein 2005; Jones 2017; Klare, 2012; Moreno 2012).

Second, even if we are concerned first and foremost with human casualties from direct acts of lethal violence, our numbers are unhelpfully obscured by the definition of battlefield deaths. Consider, for instance, the 80,000 civilian deaths from Mexican cartel wars since 2006 (Hernández 2013). These deaths are the result of military conflicts between non-state groups and the Mexican state. The fights are over territory and legitimacy, and the intensity of violence is far beyond what any useful category of criminal activity could contain. Like the Favela wars of Brazil, the Mexican cartel wars represent a pattern of conflict not captured by existing and accepted definitions of war (Wacquant 2008). Furthermore, the problem of counting casualties is also now a weapon of warfare. The significance of *lawfare*, the clever neologism for the strategic and tactical opportunities and constraints of international norms and human rights, means that undercounting is often a highly politicized and even militarized practice (Kittrie 2016). Controversies regarding the casualties in both Persian Gulf Wars and the ongoing US drone program are two examples in which war is fought by other means via methodological fights over sampling eras, demography projections, accusations of politically motivated reporting, and even the ideological commitments of coroners (International Physicians for the Prevention of Nuclear War 2015). Reports concerning the numbers killed swing between multiple orders of magnitude. Therefore, even if battlefield deaths were a critical indicator of war's ebb and flow, there are very good reasons ethically and methodologically to broaden the scope of our inquiry.

The conceptual myopia in the study of warfare is compounded by a systemic bias of the field of international relations that sees little history and a lot of state-centric structure in the arrangement of global order. I do not want to argue that we should leave the state behind as outmoded, as many globalization theorists declared it in the wake of the Cold War. The state has to be brought back into a changing context. If international relations theory once thought of the globe as a kind desert landscape populated by a single homogeneous species of war, one wielding states competing for advantage, balance, or cooperation (depending on one's theoretical leanings), the picture developed here involves a richer ecosystem (Grove 2014). The state is one among a veritable rainforest of species. Some are relatively similar to states, such as terrorist organizations with institutionalized goals and human leadership. Others involve more alien and less analogous features, such as mobs, uprisings, insurgencies, global warming, industrial catastrophes, emergent pandemic diseases, computer viruses, solar flares, glitches, and other assemblages whose organization or control is less directed but sustainable and competitively superior to the state form.

It is also the case that states the world over are in productive and ambivalent relationships with a number of private militias that carry out the illegitimate violence that is often part and parcel of the state's official strategies, despite the seeming contradiction with the Weberian drive to maintain a monopoly over violence (Brown 2014). Achille Mbembe (2001) refers to the "privatization of public violence" as "private indirect government." In what Mbembe calls the postcolony, the "emasculation" of African state sovereignty results in a competitive market for security in which states dependent on exporting natural resources rely on militia groups to focus their profitable collaboration with multinational corporations (Mitchell 2013). Private security takes over when the state withdraws, often with sensationally excessive violence. The Janjaweed militias of Southern Sudan are emblematic of what Mbembe (2003) calls necropower, or the inversion of biopolitics in which sovereignty and governmentality deploy the management of death and killing, rather than liberal governance.

These indirect and increasingly nebulous relationships between states and non-state "security providers" are an attempt to hack the system rather than directly order it. Hacking is a vital concept for thinking about this difference between "ordering" a system that often fails, such as nation-building through force or the introduction of alien institutions versus capitalizing on an order, nudging it, and amplifying those characteristics that benefit the persistence of the state or organization, as in the case of privatized public violence.

There is, of course, no equilibrium nor Archimedean point on which a state gains total authority or an order breaks entirely from the state. However, dynamic equilibria shifting between creative state intervention and withdrawal in the making of warlike ordering and disordering practices are a defining characteristic of war in late globalization. The almost two decades-long slow wars in Iraq and Afghanistan led by the United States, Russian incursions into the Ukraine, and Israel's periodic destabilization of Lebanon are emblematic of a possessive investment in disorder. The adaptability or, more appropriately, elasticity (and perhaps plasticity) of a given organization or state relates to its success in taking advantage of a given order or disorder. To develop a theory of plasticity for institutional behavior, Karl Deutsch (1963) argues against the conventional wisdom on political power in international politics. Deutsch theorizes that power is in fact pathological, leading to sclerotic and brittle states and organizations. The logic behind his claim is that material power reduces the necessity of states and institutions to learn and adapt because the ability to martial force allows those institutions to cheat or forestall otherwise necessary changes in norms and practices. According to Deutsch, successful institutions are those that have "integrity," which he defines as the ability to modulate their plasticity or adaptability. Too much plasticity and one has no identity; too little plasticity and the global environment leaves one behind, and decline sets in as the efficacy of force inevitably diminishes.

In the case of disorder, often "terrorist" or insurgent groups more successfully surf the more turbulent subsystems via loose, plastic connections and organizational structures. However, if the logic of the previous argument follows, the "terrorist" groups' affinity or attraction to disorder carries little chance of nudging or steering the self-organized, emergent order toward calmer waters (enmity or agonism that is less violent or destructive) in that their "adaptive advantage" is mutually dependent on the disorder relative to hegemonic global order (Kilcullen 2010).

A similar relationship may exist between states in which a state is invested in the persistent disorder of other states, as in the case of Africa, in which a persistent disorder benefited the expropriation of resources as well as proxy conflicts between the United States and the Soviet Union during the Cold War. It is important that tumult, combat, violence, and even genocide not be seen as chaos in the sense that there is no consistency or patterning to them. In all these cases, the possibility of persistence and regularity arises, but they are often undesirable because of the suffering they engender. However, these orders are regularly in intimate connection with even the most "stable" liberal order. States that become dependent on disordering practices are unlikely to be capable of institutionalizing those practices sustainably. The enormous cost of these long-term conflicts in the case of the United States is exemplary. The geopolitics of sabotage and managed disorder have run up an enormous strategic and financial debt, as well as having long-term corrosive effects on the democratic institutions engaged in them. If we consider that the ecology of Saddam Hussein, the Mujahedin, the Taliban, al-Qaeda, ISIS/Daesh, and Boko Haram is also the same ecological order of Cold War covert operations, regime-change and nation-building policies, as well as state-based security assistance in the form of arms and training and then the privatized arms market, then we begin to see how unsustainable disordering practices are.[5] Following Deutsch (1963), power can delay the necessity of change and adaptation, but in doing so power becomes pathological and self-destructive, or what Deutsch calls a "self-destroying system" (pp. 249–250). Late globalization is riddled with the consequences of these practices throughout the Middle East and increasingly in Europe and the Asia–Pacific region.

THE FUTURE PRESENT:
ALGORITHMIC GEOPOLITICS

The age of the internet was, like globalization, prophesied to be the end of history. The internet was to be a place where information wanted to be free and therefore the barriers of entry to the market and government would be horizontalized, thus creating unforeseen opportunities for democratization and entrepreneurship.[6] It is difficult to imagine late globalization without speed-of-light financial trading, global telecommunication networks, real-time news coverage, and just-in-time production. The internet and the vast infrastructure of wires, fiber-optic cables, and satellites that enable it are the fabric of late globalization. The hope for a global democratic public sphere and equitable market place has been significantly curtailed by Twitter demagoguery, legions of misogynistic and racist trolls, infrastructure sabotage, DDoS attacks, and increasingly geopolitically motivated hacking and cyberwarfare.

The ubiquity of the internet and digital communications such as email and SMS texting have also ushered nearly ubiquitous surveillance in democratic and authoritarian states alike (Deibert 2013). Again, surveillance and codebreaking are not new to states or even democratic states. Many of the agencies and technologies, even the computers themselves, that enable monitoring of all cell phone and internet traffic were developed by the Allied forces during the fight against fascism. Alan Turning's Enigma machine was created to break Nazi codes, and John Von Neumann used the first computer, which he built from scratch, to model nuclear explosions and strategy alike (Dyson 2012). Again, what is characteristic of war in the age of late globalization is the scale and intensity of what is now a full-blown algorithmic geopolitics. The inter-vulnerability of digital networks has created both new capabilities for the mobilization of violence and a target-rich environment for new kinds of attack. There is no stable high ground when the means of destruction (i.e., networks) is also the access point and vulnerable to attack. The result is an escalating war of all against all that includes states, corporations, organizations, and individuals, with varying degrees of equivalent capability.

Even the lines of enmity are quite blurry, as is demonstrated in the fights over figures such as Edward Snowden and groups such as Wikileaks and Anonymous. Are these groups "fronts" for geopolitical interests such as Russia? Are traditional geopolitical powers simply taking advantage of a naive faith in leak-based transparency? Are these organizations themselves shifting alliances and allegiances? Or do these organizations lack the consistency of interest and leadership to make those determinations in the first place? Gabriella Coleman (2015) has made the strongest case for a post-leadership model of Anonymous. According to Coleman's analysis, there is consistency in the organization established through shared codes of conduct rather than centralized leadership or agenda setting. The blurriness of capability and enmity is not due to conceptual error or insufficient data. Rather, the blurriness is in the empirical. Warfare in late globalization, particularly digital warfare and digitally augmented warfare such as drones and other automated weapons platforms, is messy and getting messier. Kaldor (2012) makes a similar point that "new concepts are always fuzzy" (Loc. 4529–4529). However, I emphasize that the lack of conceptual clarity is because of the real empirical complexity rather than the newness of the concept (Kaldor, 2012).

Ian Shaw (2016) has identified the US war in Vietnam as a critical juncture for the development of electronic and drone warfare. Weaponized versions of the Firebee drone were deployed, but according to Shaw, more important was the development by the CIA's Phoenix program of techniques of targeted assassinations. Furthermore, the inclusion of the electromagnetic spectrum as a critical component of the theory of "full-spectrum dominance" was critical to the development of contemporary drone warfare, as well as cyberwar. The NATO engagement in Bosnia and later Kosovo also made use of the now emblematic Predator drone. However, the rapid proliferation in the development and deployment of unmanned vehicles did not take place until after the 9/11 improvised bombings of the Pentagon and the World Trade Center. Similarly, although surveillance capability improved consistently throughout the twentieth century, the use and capability took an exponential leap after 9/11, led in no small part by the US government, and then rapidly globalized through US-based firms (Deibert 2013).

The Global War on Terrorism laid out by George W. Bush in the 2002 National Security Strategy Directive represented a paradigm shift in the attentiveness and responsiveness to danger by states on a global scale (Ansorge 2016). Contrary to its name, the global scope of the War on Terrorism belied the extraordinarily local focus of the monitoring and targeting of infrastructure and human beings determined to be threatening. Individuals and small groups with assumed loose networks and therefore global mobility became the focus of the new war.

Despite President Barack Obama's insistence during both of his administrations that the Global War on Terrorism was over, in practical terms, US policy has pursued an unprecedented integration of travel, financial, criminal justice, and military surveillance via bilateral relationships, as well as alliance structures such as NATO, the Five Eyes, and international organizations such as the United Nations, which account in part for the rapid mirroring of capabilities and practices throughout the world (Bamford 2012; Shirkman 2013). The microlevel at which danger is now being pursued, combined with the very real mobility of money, weapons, and combatants and the newly available funding doled out by the US Department of Homeland Security, has transformed law enforcement agencies at federal, state, and local levels into combatants in the new war. Although the civil–military distinction is maintained legally, the armaments and broad-sweeping emergency powers of the police closely resemble military force (Balko 2013). In addition, although the intensity of force and surveillance is somewhat elastic in relationship to crises, the general trend is moving toward a securitization of state functions at all levels of government. As the methods, means, and targets of different agencies and departments overlap, the pressure and support for the expansion of capabilities running the gambit from state-sponsored hacking to the deployment of drones no longer distinguish between home and abroad, citizen and stranger, in the way that states classically have done so. The US Department of Defense has for some time transferred technology directly to police departments, but the level of sophistication and destructive capability has significantly increased since the transfer program was established in 1997 (US Department of Defense, 2007). Although the United States has certainly been a forerunner in the transition from war to security, countries such as Israel, China, and Russia have certainly provided a global model kept apace with the United States in the blurring of military actions and policing, along with the blurring of changes in policy and practices that reflect increasingly little distinction between security operations at home and abroad. In fact, in many ways, Russia and China have outpaced the United States in their ability to adapt and take advantage of the multidimensional strategy space made possible by algorithmic geopolitics (McLeary 2015).

Beyond great powers, countries such as France are also heading toward a state of indiscernibility between domestic policing, immigration, and foreign military operations in the development and deployment of digital warfare techniques. Anthropologist Didier Fassin (2013) has described at length the militarization of French policing techniques, particularly in the highly racialized spaces of the banlieues around Paris. However, I doubt even Fassin knew how prescient his critique would be. The French response to the November 2015 Paris attacks by individuals claiming allegiance to the Islamic State escalated to open combat in many of the same neighborhoods Fassin studied. Under the auspices of martial law, warlike combat was soon directed toward refugees, culminating in the burning and dismantling of one of the largest makeshift refugee camps in Calais, euphemistically known as "the Jungle." Since the Paris and Nice attacks, martial law has become a chronic feature of French life (Zaretsky 2016). The United States is leading the world in the development of domestic digital surveillance and drone deployment, but UK and French surveillance systems and the use of digital warfare techniques by Russia and China against their own citizens as well as foreign adversaries reflect Kenneth Waltz's claim that competitors mirror one another (Goldman 2005). The problem, of course, for the neorealist focus on state mirroring is that the nation-states are being joined by insurgent groups, corporations, and individuals in the use of drones, digital surveillance, and warlike operations (Bamford 2016; Opray 2016). David Kilcullen (2015) describes at length how the 2008 Mumbai attackers made use of open source surveillance techniques such as news media, civilian GPS, and public digital communication networks such as Skype and Instant Messenger to organize an invasion that took the full capacity of the Indian state to bring to an end. The globalization of threats in the form of increasingly small and diverse enemies, as well as the mobility of those enemies, resonates with the hyper-attention of states and non-states alike (Peters et al. 2011). The result is a continuing demand for the development and deployment of digital warfare capability in the network of the internet and the physical world. The size and scope of the massive $2 billion National Security Agency (NSA) data center in Utah give some scale to the intensity of the demand, but so does the now trillion-dollar industry of cybersecurity (Bamford 2012). Industry projections estimate that cybersecurity will be a $6 trillion a year market by 2021 (Morgan, 2016). Similar projections in growth are forecasted for private security in the physical world, as the global markets for private military and private policing continue to expand (Stevens 2004).

In part, the expansion of agencies such as the NSA is as important as the robots and networks themselves in that the goals and capabilities of digital warfare are shaped by the availability and interpretability of useable data information. The trail of email, consumer purchases, wire transfers, websites visited, books read, blogs commented on, and places visited with one's cell phone or other trackable devices come to define all individuals more than their citizenship or the content of their political positions. Individuals take the form of meta-data, IP addresses, account numbers, and GPS coordinates. We live, as one commentator described it, as data shadows in our globalized world (Schneirer 2008). There is a dense ecosystem created by data generation, data collection, the autonomous algorithms that sort and make sense of the data and the demand to further narrow those interpretations within the confines of state security interests, creating what Ansorge (2016) calls "hyper-legibility." Unlike mere visibility, legibility requires that those doing the surveilling know what they are seeing. To make sense or make legible the sheer volume of what can be seen requires increasing reliance on forms of inhuman and unaccountable sorting practices, the consequences of which vary from being denied a credit card to being targeted by a drone (Chamayou 2015).

CONCLUSION: LATE GLOBALIZATION AND TRANSDIMENSIONAL WARFARE

Although war and globalization have always been dynamic partners in expansion and innovation, the beginning of the twenty-first century has witnessed a kind of phase shift in which the diversity of actors, capabilities, locations, durations, and lethalities of war are multiplying and speciating rather than converging or diffusing. Therefore, the argument over whether there is "more" or "less" war after the Cold War is, I believe, the wrong question, not because the frequency or lethality of war is not morally or strategically significant but, rather, because the question itself lacks the conceptual rigor to describe the complexity of the empirical world. Any consensus on the definition of war at this moment is an unhelpful reductionism (Bousquet 2016). Rather than being theoretically useful, a consensus on war merely so that it can be counted rather than described will lead us to intellectually wander back to "old war thinking" (Kaldor 2012, Loc. 127). The period of late globalization we have now entered is characteristically nonsystemic. The level of turbulence exceeds the capacity to settle conceptually. I do not suggest that we do away either with the debates over what constitutes war or with the concept itself. The conceptual debate is generative, if it is empirically engaged, of the attentiveness that is necessary to keep war's mutating expansion from becoming normal or acceptable. Instead, there is more value than ever in describing and mapping the ways in which older, blunter definitions of war infiltrate other, more mundane activities such as waste siting, tourism, or energy policy (Lisle 2016). Rather than being a measurable, discrete phenomenon, war in the age of late globalization should be a problematic—that is, a site for investigation and research about the shifting terrain of politics, violence, mobility, technology, and commerce.

NOTES

1. William Connolly (2008) describes the strange ambivalence between evangelical nationalism in the United States, free market ideology, and older forms of patriotism forming what he calls the "evangelical–capitalist resonance machine."
2. The concept of *lateness* is inspired by Elizabeth Povinelli (2011) to draw attention to the long, slow aftermath of settler-led violent globalization, and its character is not fully captured by Foucault's notion of biopower.
3. Goldstein concludes that the declining number of battlefield deaths, particularly since the end of the Cold War, suggests that international institutions such as the U.N. are having a systemic effect on the prevalence of war in the international system. Pinker goes a step further to suggest a kind of moral evolution on the part of the human race as, he argues, a general decline in violence such as violent crime in addition to the decline in inter-state warfare

4. The percentage of GDP spent on the military has decreased since the end of the Cold War but has been steadily increasing since 2001. However, the decline after the Cold War, like the decline in battle deaths, does not accurately reflect the shift from military expenditures to "security" expenditures. It is worth considering that the measured decline in spending may instead reflect changes in spending because the security infrastructure of most developed countries vastly overshadows their militaries in size and cost. (See http://data.worldbank.org/indicator/MS.MIL.XPND.GD.ZS?end=2015&start=1988&view=chart&year=2015.)

5. This narrative is reconstructed much more elegantly in Bacevich's (2016) *America's War*. Rashid Khalidi (2009) extends this analysis back to the beginning of the Cold War and adds the additional role of the Soviet Union in making the expanding disorder of the present.

6. In a debate with Apple co-founder Steve Wozniak, Stewart Brand argued that the dialectic of the information age was one between the increasing value of knowledge and the decreasing cost of access to that knowledge (Brand 1985: 49).

REFERENCES

Abrahamsen, R., and M. C. Williams. 2007. "Securing the City: Private Security Companies and Non-State Authority in Global Governance." *International Relations* 21: 237–253.

Anderson, B. 1991. *Imagined Communities: Reflections on the Origin and Spread of Nationalism*. London: Verso.

Ansorge, J. 2016. *Identify and Sort: How Digital Power Changed World Politics*. New York: Oxford University Press.

Bacevich, A. 2016. *America's War for the Greater Middle East: A Military History*. New York: Random House.

Balko, R. 2013. *Rise of the Warrior Cop: The Militarization of America's Police Forces*. New York: Public Affairs.

Bamford, J. 2012. "The NSA Is Building the Country's Biggest Spy Center (Watch What You Say). *Wired*, March 15. http://www.wired.com/threatlevel/2012/03/ff_nsadatacenter. Accessed October 8, 2013.

Bamford, J. 2016. "Terrorists Have Drones Now. Thanks, Obama." *Foreign Policy*. https://foreignpolicy.com/2016/04/28/terrorists-have-drones-now-thanks-obama-warfare-isis-syria-terrorism. Accessed January 22, 2017.

Barkawi, T. 2006. *Globalization and War*. Lanham, MD: Rowman & Littlefield.

Bob, C. 2012. *The Global Right Wing and the Clash of World Politics*. Cambridge, UK: Cambridge University Press.

Bolton, M., E. E. Sakamoto, and H. Griffiths. 2012. "Globalization and the Kalashnikov: Public–Private Networks in the Trafficking and Control of Small Arms." *Global Policy* 3: 303–313.

Bousquet, A. 2016. "War." In *Concepts in World Politics*, edited by F. Berenskoetter, pp. 91–106. Thousand Oaks, CA: Sage.

Brand, S. 1985. *Whole Earth Review*. May 1985.

Brown, W. 2014. *Walled States, Waning Sovereignty*. Brooklyn, NY: Zone Books.

Chamayou, G. 2015. *A Theory of the Drone*. New York: New Press.

Clausewitz, C. 1989. *On War*. Princeton, NJ: Princeton University Press.

Coleman, G. 2015. *Hacker, Hoaxer, Whistleblower, Spy: The Many Faces of Anonymous*. London: Verso.

Connolly, W. 2008. *Capitalism and Christianity, American Style*. Durham, NC: Duke University Press.

Dalby, S. 2002. *Environmental Security*. Minneapolis: University of Minnesota Press.

Deibert, R. 2013. *Black Code: Surveillance, Privacy, and the Dark Side of the Internet*. Toronto: Signal.

Deleuze, G., and F. Guattari, F. 1987. *A Thousand Plateaus: Capitalism and Schizophrenia*. Minneapolis: University of Minnesota Press.

Deutsch, K. 1963. *The Nerves of Government: Models of Political Communication and Control*. New York: Free Press.

Dyson, G. 2012. *Darwin Among the Machines: The Evolution of Global Intelligence*. Philadelphia, PA: Basic Books.

Enloe, C. 2014. *Bananas, Beaches and Bases: Making Feminist Sense of International Politics*. Berkeley: University of California Press.

Fassin, D. 2013. *Enforcing Order: An Ethnography of Urban Policing*. Cambridge, UK: Polity.

Feinstein, A. 2011. *The Shadow World: Inside the Global Arms Trade*. New York: Farrar, Straus & Giroux.

Ferguson, J. 2006. *Global Shadows: Africa in the Neoliberal World Order*. Durham, NC: Duke University Press.

Forrer, J. 2013. "10 Photos That Show How the AK-47 Has Become a Global Political Symbol." https://mic.com/articles/77515/10-photos-that-show-how-the-ak-47-has-become-a-global-political-symbol. Accessed September 12, 2017.

Fuller, J. 1984. *Machine Warfare*. Carlisle, PA: US Army War College.

Glezos, S. 2016. "Virtuous Networks: Machiavelli, Speed and Global Social Movements." *International Politics* 53 (4): 534–554.

Goldman, E. 2005. *Information and Revolutions in Military Affairs*. New York: Routledge.

Goldman, Emily O., and Leslie C. Eliason, eds. 2003. *The Diffusion of Military Technology and Ideas*. Stanford, CA: Stanford University Press.

Goldstein, J. 2005. *The Real Price of War: How You Pay for the War on Terror*. New York: New York University Press.

Goldstein, J. 2012. *Winning the War on War: The Decline of Armed Conflict Worldwide*. New York: Plume.

Grove, J. 2014. "Ecology as Critical Security Method." *Critical Studies on Security* 2 (3): 366–369.

Grove, N. 2015. "The Cartographic Ambiguities of HarassMap: Crowdmapping Security and Sexual Violence in Egypt." *Security Dialogue* 46 (4): 345–364.

Harris, S. 2002. *Factories of Death: Japanese Biological Warfare, 1932–1945, and the American Cover-Up*. New York: Routledge.

Hernández, A. 2013. *Narcoland: The Mexican Drug Lords and Their Godfathers*. London: Verso.

International Physicians for the Prevention of Nuclear War. 2015. "Body Count: Casualty Figures After 10 Years of the "War on Terror: Iraq, Afghanistan, Pakistan." https://purl.stanford.edu/rs154fr6978. Accessed December 15, 2016.

Jones, R. 2017. *Violent Borders: Refugees and the Right to Move*. London: Verso.

Kaldor, M. 2012. *New and Old Wars: Organised Violence in a Global Era*. 3rd ed. Cambridge, UK: Polity.

Khalidi, R. 2009. *Sowing Crisis: The Cold War and American Dominance in the Middle East*. Boston: Beacon.

Kilcullen, D. 2010. *Counterinsurgency*. New York: Oxford University Press.

Kilcullen, D. 2015. *Out of the Mountains: The Coming Age of the Urban Guerrilla*. London: Hurst.

Kittrie, F. 2016. *Lawfare: Law as a Weapon of War*. New York: Oxford University Press.

Klare, M. 2012. *The Race for What's Left: The Global Scramble for the World's Last Resources*. New York: Picador.

Krause, K. 1995. *Arms and the State: Patterns of Military Production and Trade*. Cambridge, UK: Cambridge University Press.

Lindqvist, S. 2011. *A History of Bombing*. New York: New Press.

Lisle, D. 2016. *Holidays in the Danger Zone: Entanglements of War and Tourism*. Minneapolis: University of Minnesota Press.

Mbembe, A. 2001. *On the Postcolony*. Berkeley: University of California Press.

Mbembe, A. 2003. "Necropolitics." *Public Culture* 15 (1): 11–40.

McLeary, P. 2015. "Russia's Winning the Electronic War." *Foreign Policy*, October 21. https://foreignpolicy.com/2015/10/21/russia winning-the-electronic-war. Accessed January 22, 2017.

McNeill, W. 2009. *Keeping Together in Time: Dance and Drill in Human History*. Cambridge, MA: Harvard University Press.

Milevski, L. 2016. *The Evolution of Modern Grand Strategic Thought*. New York: Oxford University Press.

Mitchell, T. 2013. *Carbon Democracy: Political Power in the Age of Oil*. London: Verso.

Moreno, J. 2012. *Mind Wars: Brain Science and the Military in the Twenty-First Century*. New York: Bellevue Literary Press.

Mueller, John E. 2007. *The Remnants of War*. Ithaca: Cornell University Press.

Nickel, J. 2014. "What Future for Human Rights?" *Ethics & International Affairs* 28 (2): 213–223.

Nordstrom, C. 2007. *Global Outlaws: Crime, Money, and Power in the Contemporary World*. Berkeley: University of California Press.

Opray, M. 2016. "Revealed: Rio Tinto's Plan to Use Drones to Monitor Workers' Private Lives." *The Guardian*, December 8. https://www.theguardian.com/world/2016/dec/08/revealedrio-tinto-surveillance-station-plans-to-use-drones-to-monitors-staffs-private-lives. Accessed September 12, 2017

Peters, J. E., S. Seong, A. Bower, et al. 2011. *Unmanned Aircraft Systems for Logistics Applications*. Santa Monica, CA: RAND Corporation.

Pinker, S. 2012. *The Better Angels of Our Nature: Why Violence Has Declined*. New York Toronto London: Penguin Books.

Povinelli, E. 2011. *Economies of Abandonment: Social Belonging and Endurance in Late Liberalism*. Durham, NC: Duke University Press.

Sassen, S. 2010. "A Savage Sorting of Winners and Losers: Contemporary Versions of Primitive Accumulation." *Globalizations* 7(1–2): 23–50.

Schneirer, B. 2008. "Our Data, Ourselves." *Wired*, May 15. http://www.wired.com/politics/security/commentary/securitymatters/2008/05/securitymatters_0515. Accessed September 24, 2013.

Shaw, I. 2016. *Predator Empire: Drone Warfare and Full Spectrum Dominance*. Minneapolis: University of Minnesota Press.

Shirkman, P. 2013. "Obama: 'Global War on Terror' Is Over." *US News and World Report*, May 23. http://www.usnews.com/news/articles/2013/05/23/obama-global-war-on-terror-is-over. Accessed September 24, 2013.

Stevens, B. 2004. "Factors Shaping Future Demand for Security Goods and Services." In *The Security Economy*, 17–34. Geneva, Switzerland: Organisation for Economic Co-operation and Development.

Tuathail, G., and S. Dalby, S. 1998. *The Geopolitics Reader*. New York: Routledge.

US Department of Defense. 2007. "Title10Sec2576a.pdf." https://www.gpo.gov/fdsys/pkg/USCODE-2010-title10/pdf/USCODE-2010-title10-subtitleA-partIV-chap153-sec2576a.pdf. Accessed August 6, 2018.

Wacquant, L. 2008. "The Militarization of Urban Marginality: Lessons from the Brazilian Metropolis." *International Political Sociology* 2 (1): 56–74.

Zaretsky, R. 2016. "France's Perpetual State of Emergency." *Foreign Policy*, July 16. https://foreignpolicy.com/2016/07/16/frances-perpetual-state-of-emergency. [Accessed January 22, 2017.

CHAPTER 24

GLOBALIZATION AND SECURITY

MONICA DUFFY TOFT AND ALLARD DUURSMA

A year after the al-Qaeda attacks on the World Trade Center and the Pentagon on September 11, 2001, President George W. Bush stated in the "US National Security Strategy 2002" that the United States is threatened less by conquering states than by failing ones (US National Security Council, 2002). This statement illustrates how globalization has fundamentally changed the security landscape. Globalization has made it possible for terrorist groups to recruit, transport arms, and communicate transnationally. In addition, terrorist groups often operate within failed states, which blurs the lines between security concerns at the domestic, international, and transnational levels. The emergence of failed states as a matter of high politics is just one example of how globalization affects security. This chapter provides an overview of the ways in which globalization has changed what security is and how security can be achieved most effectively.

This chapter proceeds in four sections. The first section provides a brief overview of the literature on globalization and security, highlighting a disconnect between the state-centric security literature and the focus on transnational linkages within the literature on globalization. The second section shows the importance of accounting for the effects of globalization when studying security. Globalization has made the threat environment more diverse and complicated for understanding the dynamics of the states system, as reflected in the emergence of failed states as high politics, the advent of the human security concept, and the development of the Responsibility to Protect (R2P) doctrine that holds states responsible for keeping their citizens free from injury or harm within their borders. These three trends exemplify how contemporary security issues have come to overlap at the domestic, international, and transnational levels while simultaneously reveal an inadequate accounting of the interrelations between these different levels. The third section addresses core issues at the domestic, international, and transnational levels and how they are challenging or reinforcing the more traditional basis of legitimacy and authority of states and the state system. The final section discusses several implications of the impact of globalization on security.

THE LITERATURE

Globalization

Globalization essentially refers to increasing political, economic, and social linkages between states. It is therefore unsurprising that when defining globalization, political scientists have tended to emphasize the political links (Mandelbaum 2002: 35–36; Shaw 2000: 10), economists, the economic links (Frieden and Rogowski 1996: 26–27; Prakash and Hart 1999: 2), and sociologists, the social links (Mittelman, 2000: 6; Spybey 1996: xi). Emphasizing the political dimension of globalization, Held (1995) defines globalization as the

> stretching and deepening of social relations and institutions across space and time such that, on the one hand, day-to-day activities are increasingly influenced by events happening on the other side of the globe and, on the other, the practices and decisions of local groups or communities can have significant global reverberations. (p. 20)

Focusing on economic aspects of globalization, Bhagwati (2004) asserts that globalization is reflected in the "integration of national economies into the international economy through trade, direct foreign investment (by corporations and multinationals), short-term capital flows, international flows of workers and humanity in general, and flows of technology" (p. 4). Finally, a telling example of a cultural definition of globalization is put forward by Alex Inkeles (1998), who describes globalization as the "movement of national populations away from diverse indigenous cultural patterns towards the adoption of attitudes, values and modes of daily behavior that constitute the elements of a more or less common world culture" (p. xiv).

In short, globalization refers to the expanding interaction beyond the borders of states to reach a global scale, but depending on their academic discipline, scholars have given different weight to whether this expanding interaction is political, economic, or social in nature. For this reason, some have simply defined globalization as the "intensification of economic, political, social, and cultural relations across borders" (Holm and Sorensen 1995: 4).

It also follows from the previous definitions that globalization is characterized by activities increasingly taking place outside the formal domain of the nation-state. The growing economic, cultural, and even political transnational linkages reduce the power of governments at the state level because governments cannot effectively use their internal policy instruments to regulate these links (Falk 1997: 124–125; Held 1995; Ohmae 1995; Rosenau 1996: 251). Indeed, globalization processes are not hindered or prevented by territorial or jurisdictional boundaries. Examining the impact of globalization from a political–economic perspective, Susan Strange (1996: 46) argues in this regard that the progressive integration of the world economy has shifted the balance of power away from states and toward world markets. Globalization thus broadens and weakens boundaries at the same time.

Security

Williams (2012) defines security as "the alleviation of threats to cherished values" (p. 1). This definition is purposely kept broad by Williams because what constitutes a security threat to what type of referent object is contested in the literature. Security has traditionally been understood as the protection of the state against internal and external threats (Carr 1946; Mandelbaum 1988; Mearsheimer 2001; Walt 1987; Waltz 1979). In addition, the state is not only seen as the referent object in need of protection, but also understood to be the most significant threat to other states. In order to be secure, states compete with other security-seeking states. This results in an international system of self-help, which leads states to pursue unilateral competitive policies to increase their security (Bull 1977; Buzan 1991; Waltz 1959, 1979). Indeed, Walt claimed in 1991 that the main focus of security studies is easy to identify: "It is the phenomenon of war" between states (p. 212). Hence, the security studies literature tends to be state-centric.

Furthermore, the security literature tends to focus on the material power of states as opposed to nonmaterial sources of power. From this perspective, a state with a large military capacity can protect its borders, population, and physical assets (Deudney 1995; Waltz 1979). Following this logic, Mearsheimer (2001) defines power simply as "nothing more than specific assets or material resources that are available to a state" (p. 57).[1] This definition is not unique in terms of its narrow understanding of power. The security literature has predominantly focused on military resources that a state can use to protect itself against attacks from other states. Yet, because economic resources can be converted into military resources, the economic capacity of a state is generally also considered to be a major source of power (Ripsman 2005).

In summary, scholars studying security have predominantly been concerned with the state as both a referent object in need of protection and the most significant security threat to the state and states system. In addition, great material sources of power—economic and/or militarily—have traditionally been viewed as the means to ensure security, whereas nonmaterial sources of power have been downplayed or ignored altogether.

The Disconnect: States Versus Ideas

A strong disconnect thus exists between an increasing political, economic, and social interaction beyond state boundaries and the state-centric nature of the security studies literature (Aydinli 2012; Cha 2000). As a result of globalization, the security agenda has broadened beyond the conception that the state is the only referent object in need of protection. Buzan (1997) notes in this regard,

> What can be clearly observed is that the state is less important in the new security agenda than in the old one. It still remains central, but no longer dominates either as the exclusive referent object or as the principal embodiment of threat. (p. 11)

Indeed, advances in human mobility, communication, and technology are forcing policymakers to elevate the importance of transnational security (Matthew and Shambaugh

1998: 167). A telling example in this regard is that the globalized world economy and advances made in communication technology from the early 1990s onward make it easier for terrorist groups to organize and carry out transnational attacks (Cha 2000: 393; Enders and Sandler 2006; Mandel 1999; Ripsman and Paul 2010: 31–32). Other transnational actors that have made the threat environment more diverse as a result of globalization include insurgent movements and criminal networks.

The state has also lost some of its relevance as the guarantor of security as a result of globalization. Due to its historical focus on external threats from other states, the state as an institution struggles to cope with transnational threats that have emerged as a result of globalization (Matthew and Shambaugh 1998; Ripsman and Paul 2010: 4). Activities increasingly take place outside of the formal domain of the state, resulting in the state being less in control (Reinicke 1998; Rosenau 1996). Other agents of security now include bureaucracies, corporations, international organizations, nongovernmental organizations, social movements, religious organizations such as the Catholic Church, and private security companies (Cha 2000; Rosenau 1996; Spybey 1996). For example, private security companies can contribute to security by intervening in conflicts in which states are unwilling to intervene, often making these types of conflicts less intractable (Shearer 1998).

Although it is clear that globalization has had a profound impact on what security is, who it is for, what constitutes a threat, and how security can be achieved, the globalization–security relationship has received relatively little scholarly attention. As explained by Aydinli (2012),

> While traditional security issues have been largely occupied with external threats, with the advance of globalization, security issues and challenges have become increasingly transnational and multilevel. Security studies must speed up its efforts to find ways of further conceptualization of multilevel and nonlinear understandings. (p. 232)

Globalization has resulted in a shift from fellow states as allies and opponents to a host of substate and transnational actors as allies and opponents. In order to mitigate existing security threats, a wide range of different actors need to cooperate domestically, internationally, and transnationally (Cha 2000: 397; Davis 2003: 7). The next section identifies some key trends to illustrate why it is crucial to take into account the impact of globalization when studying international security.

Key Trends

Globalization is an ongoing process. This means that the effect of globalization on security can change over time. Nevertheless, three major themes of the globalization–security relationship stand out: (1) the emergence of failed states as a matter of high politics, (2) the development of the human security concept, and (3) the rise of the R2P doctrine. Together, these three trends show how the threat environment has become more diverse in recent times, particularly from the early 1990s onward.

Emergence of Failed States as High Politics

According to political scientist Robert Rotberg (2003), weak states suffer from three types of deficiencies. First, as a result of a weak and poorly maintained military apparatus, weak states are unable to protect their citizens. Rotberg describes this as a security deficiency. Second, weak states suffer from a participation deficiency. Political participation is often absent or highly restricted in weak states. In addition, civil society tends to be absent, or at the very least dysfunctional, in weak states. Third, weak states suffer from an infrastructure deficiency. Weak states are often unable, for example, to collect taxes effectively. This often results in a poorly maintained physical infrastructure and large donor debt (Rotberg 2003: 3). A weak state is usually labeled a failed state when all of its governing structures have collapsed (Bates 2008b; Howard 2008; Zartman 1995).

Although scholars have debated whether weak and failed states have become increasingly common (Bates 2008a; Jackson and Rosberg 1982; Rotberg 2003), it is clear that following the end of the Cold War, the issue of weak and failed states rose to the domain of high politics. The reason why failed states have become a vital security concern is that in a globalized world, weak and failed states can be used as bases and for sanctuary by transnational terrorist and insurgent groups from which to carry out operations against targets throughout the world (Mohsen 2003). Governments of failed states lack the ability or the willingness to crack down on these groups operating in their countries. Yet, at the same time, failed states often maintain what Jackson and Rosberg describe as external sovereignty: the recognition of sovereignty by other states rather than an actual ability to fulfill the functions of a state. This limits foreign states in terms of what they can do to target violent groups operating in failed states (Piazza 2008; Takeyh and Gvosdev 2002).

Moreover, in a globalized world, states cannot easily prevent hostile non-state actors from recruiting from and organizing in failed states throughout the world (Hegghammer 2010; Ripsman and Paul 2010: 33). The globalized world economy and the compromised borders of weak and failed states make it possible to move weapons across the borders (Enders and Sandler 2006; Piazza 2008). In addition, advances in communication technology from the early 1990s onward have allowed people and groups to organize on a global scale (Cha 2000: 393; Mandel 1999; Ripsman and Paul 2010: 31–32). Indeed, although the majority of terrorist attacks are still conducted domestically (LaFree and Dugan 2007; LaFree, Dugan, and Miller 2014: 146–172), terrorist groups have shown an increasing ability to attack targets globally, of which the attack on the World Trade Center in New York on September 11, 2001, is the most prominent example (Aydinli 2012: 232; Ripsman and Paul 2010: 53), as are the more recent attacks in France (2015) and Belgium (2016).[2]

That failed states have moved to the domain of high politics is clearly reflected in policies developed by states to strengthen weak and failed states. States have responded to global terrorism originating from failed states by making failed status a security priority, particularly in the wake of the attack on the World Trade Center on September 11, 2001 (Traub 2011). As mentioned previously, President George W. Bush stated in the "US National Security Strategy 2002" that the United States is threatened less by conquering states than by failing ones (US National Security Council 2002). Similarly, in the "National Strategy for Combating Terrorism" published in February 2003, the US State Department noted, "Our economic strength will help failing states and assist weak countries in ridding themselves of terrorism" (p. 2). Nevertheless, the response to transnational terrorism has also been heavily military oriented, with a war in Afghanistan as a primary example (Ripsman and Paul 2010). Similarly, Russia has responded to the terrorist threat of Chechen separatists by bolstering the national security state (Fish 2005). In summary, while globalization has increased the threat from global terrorism, states tend to respond to this threat with relatively traditional military means.

Human Security

Global terrorism poses a military threat to the state in the sense that it challenges the state's monopoly on violence. Yet, as a result of globalization, the security agenda has widened beyond solely military threats to the state. The rapid changes in the global environment have led to the emergence of nontraditional security threats, including migration, global crime, trafficking in humans, instability in financial markets, threats to job security, the spread of disease, and internal conflicts (Davis 2003; Fukuda-Parr 2003; Matthew and Shambaugh 1998; Rudolph 2003). Echoing these new security challenges that emerged as a result of globalization, *Human Development Report 1994* (United Nations Development Programme 1994) noted that

> the concept of security has for too long been interpreted narrowly: as security of territory from external aggression, or as protection of national interests in foreign policy or as global security from the threat of a nuclear holocaust. It has been related more to nation-states than to people. (p. 22)

Accordingly, the report redefined the concept of security as safety from chronic threats and protection from sudden hurtful disruptions in the pattern of daily life (p. 22). Human security thus essentially means safety for people from both violent and non-violent threats. It refers to both freedom from fear and freedom from want (MacFarlane and Khong 2006; Paris 2001: 90).

The human security concept not only shifts the emphasis from the state to the individual as the referent object in security studies, but also shifts the focus from narrow national security concerns to a much broader set of security concerns. Indeed, *Human Development Report 1994* identifies seven types of security: economic, food, health, environmental, personal, community, and political security (United Nations Development Programme 1994: 24–25). That the security agenda is increasingly being set by nontraditional security concerns in the post-Cold War period is also reflected in a burgeoning literature that expands the type of security threats (Booth 2007; Buzan, Wæver, and Wilde 1998; Krause 1998).

The broadening of the security agenda has been criticized as not being useful for policymakers. If human security means almost anything, policymakers cannot use the concept to prioritize among competing policy goals. In other words, the human security concept provides policymakers with little guidance because it encompasses everything from physical security to psychological well-being (King and Murray 2001; Paris 2001). For this reason, Buzan et al. (1998) argue that rather than solely employing the human security concept, a more fruitful approach is to study a diverse set of possible referent objects for security separately.[3]

In summary, the human security concept moves away from the state as the sole referent object that needs to be secured, as well as broadens the security agenda with nontraditional security concerns. Globalization processes are at the heart of this wider security agenda. Yet, how globalization exactly will affect human security still remains unclear (Davis 2003). As noted in *Human Development Report 1997* (United Nations Development Programme, 1997), "The great unanswered question is whether the winds of globalization will be viewed as a great opportunity or a great threat, as a fresh breeze or a violent hurricane" (pp. 9–10). What is clear, however, is that globalization has forced policymakers to adopt wider security agenda. Reflective of this change, a wide variety of theorists have argued that the definition of security must be (or has been) expanded to include new dimensions of security relating to economics, development, health, migration, and security of the person. Nevertheless, broadening the security agenda leads to a relatively vague concept of security.

Responsibility to Protect as a Doctrine That Holds States Accountable

Although the human security concept has been criticized for having relatively little value for policy, it has been at the heart of the emergence of the R2P doctrine that holds states accountable for insuring that their citizens are free from injury or harm for mass atrocities (Bellamy 2005; Bellamy and Williams 2011; MacFarlane and Khong 2006). Reflecting a shift from the state as the referent object to the individual, an ad hoc commission consisting of members of the UN General Assembly was set up in 2001 to examine how the international community should respond to gross and systematic violations of human rights in light of the sovereignty of states. In its final report, this commission—known as the International Commission on Intervention and State Sovereignty—reframed sovereignty as a responsibility, not a license to kill (Evans 2009; International Commission on Intervention and State Sovereignty 2001).

The commission thus essentially asserted that the security of humans as individuals overrides the sovereignty of a state. In its final report, the commission highlighted two ways in which globalization has contributed to this reframing of sovereignty. First, the report noted that globalization and growing interdependency prompt other states to become "engaged positively both in promoting prevention, and also in calling for intervention in situations that seem to be spiraling out of control" (International Commission on Intervention and State Sovereignty 2001: 7). Second, the report noted that the revolution in information technology has resulted in an unprecedented awareness of conflicts wherever they may be occurring, with compelling images of the resultant suffering on television and in other mass media, which has "created a domestic political cost for inaction and indifference" (pp. 6–7).[4]

The report published by the International Commission on Intervention and State Sovereignty (2001) was the basis for a document adopted at the 2005 World Summit held September 14–16, 2005, which stipulated that (1) states have R2P their people; (2) states have the responsibility to assist other states to protect their people; and (3) states should be prepared to take collective action, in a timely and decisive manner, through the UN Security Council, in accordance with the Charter, including Chapter VII, on a case-by-case basis to help protect populations from genocide, war crimes, ethnic cleansing, and crimes against humanity (UN General Assembly, 2005).

The R2P doctrine was subsequently confirmed in UN Security Council Resolution 1674 (2006) and even evoked in Libya when the UN Security Council issued Resolution 1973, which reiterated the responsibility of the Libyan authorities to protect the Libyan population and authorized UN member states to take all necessary means through the use of air attacks to "protect civilians and civilian populated areas under threat of attack in the Libyan Arab Jamahiriya, including Benghazi, while excluding a foreign occupation force of any form on any part of Libyan territory."[5] Although one might assume that the humanitarian intervention in Libya by NATO reflects a global consensus on the application of the R2P doctrine to this case, states have welcomed the doctrine unevenly. Russian President Vladimir Putin, for example, described Resolution 1973 as a "medieval call for a crusade" (Bryanski 2011). African leaders issued similar objections against the NATO intervention. Mauritanian President Mohamed Ould Abdel Aziz, the chair of the African Union panel concerned with the situation in Libya, immediately rejected any form of military intervention in the Libyan crisis. Aziz specifically stated a solution to the crisis must "adhere to the value we place in respecting territorial unity and integrity, as well as the rejection of all foreign military intervention, whatever form it takes" ("African Union Urges Restraint" 2011).[6] Particularly among smaller states in the international system, concern emerged that R2P would give permission to larger states to intervene in their domestic affairs freely.

THE GROWING POWER OF IDEAS: CHALLENGES TO THE LEGITIMACY OF THE STATE AND THE STATE SYSTEM

It follows from the trends that as a result of globalization, security issues increasingly overlap at the domestic, international, and transnational levels. Yet, what is missing from the current literature on security is a proper sense of the interrelations of these different levels. The domestic, international, and transnational levels arguably interact mostly on issues of identity and ideas that either reinforce or challenge the traditional basis of legitimacy and authority of states and the state system. On one hand, globalization arguably reinforces the Western liberal democracy as the global political model. On the other hand, the rise of this political model has generated significant pushback. Finally, in addition to driving cultural homogenization, globalization has in some cases increased nationalist and populist sentiment from feelings of displacement and dislocation.

Democracy

In a highly influential book—*End of History*—published in 1992, political scientist Francis Fukuyama heralded the triumph of Western liberal democracy over other types of political models. Fukuyama's thesis was welcomed in Western policy circles because it explained how the world would be more secure as a result of the spread of liberal democracy. Indeed, many observers have noted that the spread of liberal democracy not only reduces the risk of interstate war but also makes states more secure from within (Inkeles 1998; Keohane and Nye 1977; Mandelbaum 2002). The assertion that security can be attained through the promotion of democracy, development, and free markets is reflected in the "democratic enlargement" strategy (Cha 2000: 393). For example, it is noted in the 2002 "US National Security Strategy" that "a strong world economy enhances our national security by advancing prosperity and freedom in the rest of the world" (US National Security Council 2002: 17). In his letter introducing this strategy, President George W. Bush's stated, "The United States will use this moment of opportunity to extend the benefits of freedom across the globe. We will actively work to bring the hope of, and free trade to every corner of the world." Globalization thus plays a central role in the democratic enlargement strategy because it can facilitate the spread of liberal democracy. In a RAND issue paper, analyst Lynn Davis (2003) notes in this regard, "Global technological and economic developments offer opportunities to promote economic prosperity and advance political freedom, which in turn hold out the possibility of ameliorating the transnational threats and, indirectly, some of their underlying causes" (pp. 4–5).

Religion

Although the democratization of states has turned into a global phenomenon, this trend has not gone unchallenged. Democratization generates significant support and resistance, particularly from religious forces. The political influence of religion has significantly increased during the past 40 years, at least in part as a result of globalization (Toft, Philpott, and Shah 2011). While Toft, Philpott, and Shah (2011) show how religious actors both advance and retard moves toward democracy in the current era of globalization that began in the 1970s, Falk (1997) explains how extremist, religious actors often reject globalizing tendencies: "Only by retreating to premodern, traditionalist orientations does it now seem possible to seal of sovereign territory, partially at least, from encroachments associated with globalized lifestyles and business operations" (pp. 131–132). Islamic fundamentalist groups, for example, have challenged state authority and the international system through the Middle East and Asia. From 1940 onward, Islam has been involved in a disproportionately high number of civil wars compared with other religions (Toft 2007). Similarly, Islam terrorist groups are responsible for most international terrorist attacks from the 1990s onward (Hoffman 1999; Rapoport 2001).

Whereas the spread of religion and the increasing salience of religion can be understood as a response to globalization, other globalizing processes have made religion, itself a transnational phenomenon, a more potent force. Globalization has enhanced the ability of substrate fundamentalist groups to organize transnationally and to meet virtually. As a result of the rise of the internet, states now face "networked" asymmetric adversaries and allies. While Catholics were empowered to challenge autocrats throughout Latin America and Eastern Europe in the 1970s and 1980s, in the 1990s, the internet became a virtual sanctuary where supporters of an Islamic global jihad could relatively safely communicate and recruit (Cha 2000: 393; Moghadam 2008). In addition, the internet created what Ranstorp (2007) describes as a "virtual university of Jihad" that can provide militants with advice and instruction that reaches a huge audience (p. 31). Accordingly, the internet has made it possible for al-Qaeda and other Islamist networks to set up networks that are self-generating. Ironically, the increasing salience of religion as a political model is thus both a response to globalization and made possible through globalizing processes (Toft et al. 2011).

Moreover, although religion can be viewed as a response to globalization, it can also be understood as a globalizing process in itself. By its very nature, religion is transnational and thus a force of globalization. Religious ties often override state authority and legitimacy. Adherents are first and foremost loyal to their religious community. In other words, religion compels people across states to engage in similar forms of behavior and share similar beliefs and values. From this perspective, the spread of religion is a boundary-broadening process. A telling example in this regard is the term *global* jihad.

The increasing importance of religion in the political domain thus poses a challenge to the state. This shows that globalization has not resulted in a homogeneous set of ideas. On the contrary, rather than being clearly victorious as Fukuyama (1992) predicted, the Western-style liberal democracy is competing with alternative political models, some based in religion.

Nationalism

Globalization processes have made borders less sacrosanct. Trade, investment, and the internet move easily across national borders. Yet, national borders still matter. Globalization drives cultural homogenization, but it simultaneously reinforces nationalist and ethnic sentiment as it compels people to promote and defend their ethnic, religious, and/or linguistic identities in response to the homogenizing effect of globalization (Cha 2000: 394–395; Mittelman 1994: 432). For instance, the increasing anxieties in Western Europe over an influx of migrants and refugees from Africa, Eastern Europe, the Middle East, and South Asia reflect how, despite globalization, societies are still very much concerned with the preservation of their historically grounded national identity (Weiner 1992; Toft 2003; Adamson 2006; Côté, Mitchell and Toft 2019).[7] Ethnically homogeneous societies particularly value preserving their ethnic identity. One need only think of Japan, which only recently revealed that it had negative population growth. Why? Because of its reluctance to accept foreigners into the country. For similar reasons, states are more willing to accept migrants when these migrants share the host country's dominant language, religion, or race (Fekete 2004; Weiner 1992). Nevertheless, a growing commitment to universal human rights has somewhat delegitimized ethnicity as a criterion to accept or reject immigrants (Adamson 2006: 181), although it nevertheless remains strong, as the recent flows into Europe as a result of the Syrian civil war demonstrate.

Migration is not a new phenomenon, but the interaction between migration and other globalization processes produces new security threats (Côté, Mitchell, and Toft 2019). For instance, global criminal networks are increasingly involved in facilitating people to migrate. Similarly, refugee flows are increasingly viewed as a channel for international terrorism (Adamson 2006; Fekete 2004; Ibrahim 2005). That the 19 members of al-Qaeda were able to live and train in the United States in preparation for their attack on the World Trade Center and the Pentagon on September 11, 2001, raised concerns regarding the cross-border mobility of people and international terrorists. Examples in Europe include the terrorist attacks in Madrid on March 11, 2004; in London on July 7, 2005; in Paris on November 13, 2015; and in Brussels on March 22, 2016. Incidents such as these result in refugee issues increasingly being perceived as a matter of high politics, which requires the involvement of ministries of defense and internal security (Adamson 2006; Weiner 1992: 91). That migration is increasingly perceived as the domain of high politics is a telling example of how globalization has complicated the alleviation of security threats. States are struggling to change those structures that are pushing migrants to leave their home countries, because these structures exist beyond the boundaries of states facing high levels of immigration (Mabee 2009).

CONCLUSION

Globalization processes have challenged traditional notions of security. There has been a rethinking about what needs to be secured, what constitutes a threat, and how security can be best achieved. First and foremost, there has been recognition of the need to go beyond the conception that security solely entails military competition between states. The growing global interconnectedness has transformed the types of security threats. With subnational actors such as al-Qaeda being able to recruit, transport weapons, and communicate transnationally, security threats are no longer solely international but also transnational.

Furthermore, as a result of globalization, security no longer solely entails the protection of the state. Other referent objects now include the environment, the economy, and people as individuals. The idea that the human is a referent object in need of protection has particularly gained prominence as reflected in the R2P doctrine.

Accounting for the effect of globalization on security has also had major implications regarding the allocation of resources to enhance security and policy priorities. A telling example in this regard is President George W. Bush's statement in September 2002 that the United States is threatened less by conquering states than by failing ones (US National Security Council 2002). This means that if the United States seeks to alleviate security threats, it needs to prevent states from failing rather than solely increasing its traditional military capabilities to protect it against military threats from rival states.

In addition, when policymakers seek alternative ways to enhance their country's security, they will need to take into account nontraditional sources of power. Some studies have highlighted how globalization has made economic power more important (Ripsman and Paul 2010), but the scholarly understanding of the effect of globalization on ideational sources of power is limited. This is a major gap in research because the growing importance of transnational ideas—such as democracy, religion, and nationalism—makes it difficult to calculate the power of a state. Nye has introduced the concept of soft power to account for power based on attraction rather than power based on coercion and inducement (Nye 2004: 5; Nye 2007: 389). The concept of soft power has mainly been used to explain how values such as cosmopolitanism and democracy are universally attractive, increasing the soft power of states committed to these values (Nye 2004: 11). Yet, the concept could equally well be used to explain the attractiveness of potential recruits to join such entities as al-Qaeda and the Islamic State. In summary, transnational sources of power offer both opportunities and challenges to states.

Globalization already has had a profound impact on security. This effect is likely to grow even further in the future. An expanding network of transnational interconnections will continue to challenge the autonomy of the state. Moreover, tensions between states and non-state actors are likely to grow. Although these changes will by no means make the state redundant as a security provider, as a result of globalization, solely focusing on the behavior of states and military power is no longer a viable approach to study security.

Notes

1. See also Waltz (1979).
2. Nevertheless, statistical evidence about whether failed states are likely to host terrorist groups that commit transnational attacks is mixed. Whereas some studies find that states plagued by chronic state failure are indeed more likely to host terrorist groups that conduct transnational attacks (Coggins 2014; Piazza 2008), other studies show that weak—but not failing—states are more likely to host transnational terrorist groups (Stewart 2011). There has to be some order and infrastructure in place from which to engage in their activities. Finally, despite these contradicting studies, it is clear that not every failed state necessarily poses a global security threat. For example, the implosion of the Democratic Republic of Congo had few repercussions beyond the region and primarily affected the Congolese population (Traub 2011).
3. Buzan et al. (1998) focus on the following referent objects of security: the military sector, the environmental sector, the economic sector, the societal sector, and the political sector.
4. See also Jakobsen (2002).
5. Note, however, that R2P has been applied selectively. Whereas humanitarian intervention has taken place in the Ivory Coast and Libya based on the concept of R2P, the international community has not intervened in Darfur or Syria. See Badescu and Bergholm (2009), Bellamy and Williams (2011), and De Waal (2007).
6. See also De Waal (2013).
7. Refugee flows from the Global South are increasingly perceived as a security threat in Western countries, but note that the vast majority of refugees travel from development countries to other development countries (Weiner 1992). Rather than a threat to the national identity of the state, refugees from one development country to another are often perceived as a military threat because refugee-sending states may violate borders in pursuit of dissidents. From the perspective of the country that produces the refugees, the refugee flows are a security threat because the regional countries might intervene to prevent the negative spillover effects of the refugee flows (Salehyan 2008, 2010).

References

Adamson, F. B. 2006. "Crossing Borders: International Migration and National Security." *International Security* 31: 165–199.

"African Union Urges Restraint on Both Sides." 2011. *The Star*, March 21.

Aydinli, E. 2012. "Conclusion: Seeking Conceptual Links for Changing Paradigms." In *Globalization, Security, and the Nation State: Paradigms in Transition*, edited by E. Aydinli and J. N. Rosenau, 231–240. New York: State University of New York Press.

Badescu, C., and L. Bergholm. 2009. "The Responsibility to Protect and the Conflict in Darfur: The Big Let-Down." *Security Dialogue* 40: 287–309.

Bates, R. H. 2008a. *When Things Fell Apart: State Failure in Late-Century Africa.* Cambridge, UK: Cambridge University Press.

Bates, R. H. 2008b. "State Failure: Aid, Taxation, and Development in sub-Saharan Africa." *Annual Review of Political Science* 11: 1–12.

Bellamy, A. J. 2005. "Responsibility to Protect or Trojan Horse? The Crisis in Darfur and Humanitarian Intervention After Iraq." *Ethics & International Affairs* 19: 31–54.

Bellamy, A. J., and P. D. Williams. 2011. "The New Politics of Protection? Côte d'Ivoire, Libya and the Responsibility to Protect." *International Affairs* 87: 825–850.

Bhagwati, J. 2004. *In Defense of Globalization.* Oxford, UK: Oxford University Press.

Booth, K. 2007. *Theory of World Security.* Cambridge, UK: Cambridge University Press.

Bryanski, G. 2011. "Putin Likens U.N. Libya Resolution to Crusades." Reuters, March 21. https://www.reuters.com/article/us-libya-russia-idUSTRE72K3JR20110321.

Bull, H. 1977. *The Anarchical Society: A Study of Order in World Politics.* London: Macmillan.

Buzan, B. 1991. *People, States and Fear: An Agenda for International Security Studies in the Post-Cold War Era.* London: Harvester Wheatsheaf.

Buzan, B. 1997. "Rethinking Security After the Cold War." *Cooperation and Conflict* 32: 5–28.

Buzan, B., O. Wæver, and J. D. Wilde. 1998. *Security: A New Framework for Analysis.* London: Rienner.

Carr, E. H. 1946. *The Twenty Years' Crisis, 1919–1939: An Introduction to the Study of International Relations.* London: Macmillan.

Cha, V. D. 2000. "Globalization and the Study of International Security." *Journal of Peace Research* 37: 391–403.

Coggins, B. L. 2014. "Does State Failure Cause Terrorism? An Empirical Analysis (1999–2008)." *Journal of Conflict Resolution* 59 (3): 455–483.

Côté, I., M. Mitchell, and M.D. Toft, eds. 2019. *People Changing Places: New Perspectives on Demography, Migration, Conflict, and the State.* New York: Routledge.

Davis, L. E. 2003. "Globalization's Security Implications." RAND Issue Paper. Santa Monica, CA: RAND Corporation.

De Waal, A. 2007. "Darfur and the Failure of the Responsibility to Protect." *International Affairs* 83: 1039–1054.

De Waal, A. 2013. "African Roles in the Libyan Conflict of 2011." *International Affairs* 89: 365–379.

Deudney, D. 1995. "Nuclear Weapons and the Waning of the Real-State." *Daedalus* 124: 209–231.

Enders, W., and T. Sandler. 2006. *The Political Economy of Terrorism.* Cambridge, UK: Cambridge University Press.

Evans, G. 2009. *The Responsibility to Protect: Ending Mass Atrocity Crimes Once and for All.* Washington, DC: Brookings Institution Press.

Falk, R. 1997. "State of Siege: Will Globalization Win Out?" *International Affairs* 73: 123–136.

Fekete, L. 2004. "Anti-Muslim Racism and the European Security State." *Race & Class* 46: 3–29.

Fish, S. M. 2005. *Democracy Derailed in Russia: The Failure of Open Politics.* Cambridge, UK: Cambridge University Press.

Frieden, J. A., and R. Rogowski. 1996. "The Impact of the International Economy on National Policies: An Analytic Overview." In *Internationalization and Domestic Politics*, edited by R. O. Keohane and H. V. Milner, pp. 25–47. Cambridge, UK: Cambridge University Press.

Fukuda-Parr, S. 2003. "New Threats to Human Security in the Era of Globalization." *Journal of Human Development* 4: 167–179.

Fukuyama, F. 1992. *The End of History and the Last Man.* London: Penguin.

Hegghammer, T. 2010. "The Rise of Muslim Foreign Fighters: Islam and the Globalization of Jihad." *International Security* 35: 53–94.

Held, D. 1995. *Democracy and the Global Order: From the Modern State to Cosmopolitan Governance.* Palo Alto, CA: Stanford University Press.

Hoffman, B. 1999. "Terrorism Trends and Prospects." In *Countering the New Terrorism,* edited by I. Lesser, J. Arquilla, B. Hoffman, et al., pp. 7–38. Washington, DC: RAND Corporation.

Holm, H.-H., and G. Sorensen. 1995. "Introduction: What Has Changed?" In *Whose World Order? Uneven Globalization and the End of the Cold War.* Boulder, CO: Westview.

Howard, T. O. 2008. "Revisiting State Failure: Developing a Causal Model of State Failure Based Upon Theoretical Insight." *Civil Wars* 10: 125–146.

Ibrahim, M. 2005. "The Securitization of Migration: A Racial Discourse." *International Migration* 43: 163–187.

Inkeles, A. 1998. *One World Emerging.* Boulder, CO: Westview.

International Commission on Intervention and State Sovereignty. 2001. *The Responsibility to Protect: Report of the International Commission on Intervention and State Sovereignty.* Ottawa, Ontario, Canada: International Development Research Centre.

Jackson, R. H., and C. G. Rotberg. 1982. "Why Africa's Weak States Persist: The Empirical and the Juridical in Statehood." *World Politics* 35: 1–24.

Jakobsen, P. V. 2002. "The Transformation of United Nations Peace Operations in the 1990s: Adding Globalization to the Conventional 'End of the Cold War Explanation.'" *Cooperation and Conflict* 37: 267–282.

Keohane, R. O., and J. S. Nye. 1977. *Power and Interdependence: World Politics in Transition.* Ann Arbor: University of Michigan Press.

King, G., and C. J. L. Murray. 2001. "Rethinking Human Security." *Political Science Quarterly* 116: 585–610.

Krause, K. 1998. "Critical Theory and Security Studies: The Research Programme of 'Critical Security Studies.'" *Cooperation and Conflict* 33: 298–333.

LaFree, G., and L. Dugan. 2007. "Introducing the Global Terrorism Database." *Political Violence and Terrorism* 19: 181–204.

LaFree, G., L. Dugan, and E. Miller. 2014. *Putting Terrorism in Context: Lessons from the Global Terrorism Database.* London: Taylor & Francis.

Mabee, B. 2009. *The Globalization of Security: State Power, Security Provision and Legitimacy.* New York: Palgrave Macmillan.

MacFarlane, S. N., and Y. F. Khong. 2006. *Human Security and the UN: A Critical History.* Bloomington: Indiana University Press.

Mandel, R. 1999. *Deadly Transfers and the Global Playground.* New York: Praeger.

Mandelbaum, M. 1988. *The Fate of Nations: The Search for National Security in the Nineteenth and Twentieth Centuries.* Cambridge, UK: Cambridge University Press.

Mandelbaum, M. 2002. *The Ideas That Conquered the World: Peace, Democracy, and Free Markets in the Twenty-First Century.* New York: PublicAffairs.

Matthew, R. A., and G. E. Shambaugh. 1998. "Sex, Drugs, and Heavy Metal: Transnational Threats and National Vulnerabilities." *Security Dialogue* 29: 163–175.

Mearsheimer, J. J. 2001. *The Tragedy of Great Power Politics.* London: Norton.

Mittelman, J. H. 1994. "The Globalisation Challenge: Surviving at the Margins." *Third World Quarterly* 15: 427–443.

Mittelman, J. H. 2000. *The Globalization Syndrome: Transformation and Resistance*. Princeton, NJ: Princeton University Press.

Moghadam, A. 2008. *The Globalization of Martyrdom: Al Qaeda, Salafi Jihad, and the Diffusion of Suicide Attacks*. Baltimore, MD: Johns Hopkins University Press.

Mohsen, A. 2003. "Challenges of the Terrorist Phenomenon in the Twenty-First Century." In *Meeting the Challenges of Global Terrorism: Prevention, Control, and Recovery*, edited by D. K. Das and P. C. Kratcoski, pp. 117–130. Lanham, MD: Lexington.

Nye, J. S. 2004. *Soft Power: The Means to Success in World Politics*. New York: PublicAffairs.

Nye, J. S. 2007. "The Place of Soft Power in State Based Conflict Management." In *Leashing the Dogs of War: Conflict Management in a Divided World*, edited by C. A. Crocker, 389–400. New York: US Institute of Peace Press.

Ohmae, K. 1995. *The End of the Nation State: The Rise of Regional Economies*. New York: Free Press.

Paris, R. 2001. "Human Security: Paradigm Shift or Hot Air?" *International Security* 26: 87–102.

Piazza, J. A. 2008. "Incubators of Terror: Do Failed and Failing States Promote Transnational Terrorism?" *International Studies Quarterly* 52: 469–488.

Prakash, A., and J. A. Hart. 1999. "Globalization and Governance: An Introduction." In *Globalization and Governance*, edited by A. Prakash and J. A. Hart, 1–24. London: Routledge.

Ranstorp, M. 2007. "The Virtual Sanctuary of al-Qaeda and Terrorism in an Age of Globalization." In *International Relations and Security in the Digital Age*, edited by J. Eriksson and G. Giacomello, pp. 31–56. New York: Taylor & Francis.

Rapoport, D. C. 2001. "The Fourth Wave: September 11 in the History of Terrorism." *Current History* 100 (650): 419–424.

Reinicke, W. H. 1998. *Global Public Policy: Governing Without Government?* Washington, DC: Brookings Institution Press.

Ripsman, N. M. 2005. "False Dichotomy: Why Economics Has Always Been High Politics." In *Guns and Butter: The Political Economy of the International Security*, edited by P. Dombrowski, 15–31. Boulder, CO: Reinner.

Ripsman, N. M., and T. V. Paul. 2010. *Globalization and the National Security State*. Oxford, UK: Oxford University Press.

Rosenau, J. N. 1996. "The Dynamics of Globalization: Toward an Operational Formulation." *Security Dialogue* 27: 247–262.

Rotberg, R. I. 2003. "Failed States, Collapsed Sates, Weak States: Causes and Indicators." In *State Failure and State Weakness in a Time of Terror*, edited by R. I. Rotberg, pp. 1–28. Washington, DC: Brookings Institution Press.

Rudolph, C. 2003. "Globalization and Security." *Security Studies* 13: 1–32.

Salehyan, I. 2008. "The Externalities of Civil Strife: Refugees as a Source of International Conflict." *American Journal of Political Science* 52: 787–801.

Salehyan, I. 2010. "Weapons of Mass Migration." *International Studies Review* 12: 640–642.

Shaw, M. 2000. *Theory of the Global State: Globality as an Unfinished Revolution*. Cambridge, UK: Cambridge University Press.

Shearer, D. 1998. *Private Armies and Military Intervention*. Oxford, UK: Oxford University Press.

Spybey, T. 1996. *Globalization and World Society*. Cambridge, UK: Polity.

Stewart, P. 2011. *Weak Links: Fragile States, Global Threats, and International Security*. Oxford, UK: Oxford University Press.

Strange, S. 1996. *The Retreat of the State: The Diffusion of Power in the World Economy.* Cambridge, UK: Cambridge University Press.

Takeyh, R., and N. Gvosdev. 2002. "Do Terrorist Networks Need a Home?" *Washington Quarterly* 25: 97–108.

Toft, M. D. 2003. *The Geography of Ethnic Violence: Identity, Interests and the Indivisibility of Territory.* Princeton, NJ: Princeton University Press.

Toft, M. D. 2007. "Getting Religion? The Puzzling Case of Islam and Civil War." *International Security* 31: 97–131.

Toft, M. D., D. Philpott, and T. S. Shah. 2011. *God's Century: Resurgent Religion and Global Politics.* New York: Norton.

Traub, J. 2011. "Think Again: Failed States." *Foreign Policy*, June 20.

UN General Assembly. 2005. "2005 World Summit Outcome." New York: UN General Assembly.

United Nations Development Programme. 1994. *Human Development Report 1994.* Oxford, UK: Oxford University Press.

United Nations Development Programme. 1997. *Human Development Report 1997.* Oxford, UK: Oxford University Press.

US National Security Council. 2002. "The National Security Strategy of the United States of America." Washington, DC: US National Security Council, September.

US State Department. 2003. "National Strategy for Combating Terrorism." Washington, DC: US State Department, February.

Walt, S. M. 1987. *The Origins of Alliance.* Ithaca, NY: Cornell University Press.

Walt, S. M. 1991. "The Renaissance of Security Studies." *International Studies Quarterly* 35: 211–239.

Waltz, K. N. 1959. *Man, the State, and War: A Theoretical Analysis.* New York: Columbia University Press.

Waltz, K. N. 1979. *Theory of International Politics.* London: Addison-Wesley.

Weiner, M. 1992. "Security, Stability, and International Migration." *International Security* 17: 91–126.

Williams, P. 2012. "Security Studies: An Introduction." In *Security Studies: An Introduction*, edited by P. Williams, 1–12. Abingdon, UK: Routledge.

Zartman, W. 1995. *Collapsed States: The Disintegration and Restoration of Legitimate Authority.* Boulder, CO: Rienner.

CHAPTER 25

....

HUMAN RIGHTS

....

MICHAEL FORMAN

HUMAN rights is a hope and a way of articulating demands for justice. At least twice, at the end of World War II and again following the Cold War, the world was promised that human rights would reign supreme. The pledge remains unfulfilled. Indeed, it is once again under attack. Freedom of conscience, thought, and speech are regularly curtailed as technological advances hailed to foster these rights also become tools of technological domination. Torture and disappearances continue to be practiced. Hundreds of thousands of refugees cross borders only to serve as pawns in domestic and international politics, to be rejected and thrown into camps. Millions more are internally displaced by wars, environmental degradation, and development projects. Women, children, and members of sexual minorities are common victims of violence. Social rights are everywhere the object of relentless and effective attack by a triumphant neoliberalism. Well over 2 billion people worldwide, many of them in the Global North, cannot attain an adequate standard of living. Indigenous groups and ethnic and national minorities still find themselves unable to sustain, let alone develop, their cultures or participate in the lives of the larger national communities of which they are part. In summary, despite important successes, there is much evidence of the failure of human rights.

To examine the validity of this conclusion, which I believe premature, I propose to reconstruct the modern notion of human rights, its foundations in history and in the ideas of the political theorists who framed it. Because the institutions which make up the contemporary human rights regime are the product of this history and embody these theories, this procedure highlights not only the limitations of human rights but also its potential as an emancipatory idea.

The study of human rights casts important light upon the normative transformations which are an important aspect of the emergent order global studies aims to elucidate. In effect, human rights is about the transnationalization of justice claims, understood as both values and a system of laws which might govern the ability of global citizens to articulate their demands and of national and transnational institutions to make good on these. From this perspective, a reconstruction of human rights should also be of assistance to those who might raise evaluative claims about globalization because it tells how we got here and what paths might have been taken. To this effect, this chapter proceeds by examining the historical issues to which early rights claims responded, the central articulations of these responses in political theory, the imperfect institutionalization of these claims, and the potential routes for the expansion of human rights, always keeping in mind the political, and thus contingent, quality of these developments.

THE CRISIS OF EARLY EUROPEAN MODERNITY

The crisis of early European modernity first manifested toward the late fifteenth century. It was marked by three distinct, although interrelated, trends: the emergence of new socioeconomic structures, the development of new political orders, and the deep normative transformations which sometimes followed and sometimes led these changes. I discuss each of these trends in turn, with the caveat that the connections between them do not admit of a strict pattern of linear causality; rather, events and trends were in constant interaction, mutually transforming each other, often in contradictory manners.

The first of these trends might be summarized as the emergence of capitalism, that is of a form of social organization, production, and distribution marked by the prevalence of the commodity form, especially the commodification of land, labor, and money. Although both local and long-distance trade were present in Medieval Europe, their impact was marginal to the lives of most people. This would change as markets and manufacturing grew in various centers, especially the Italian states, after the fourteenth century. The fall of Constantinople weakened these Mediterranean centers and made way for new mercantile powers first in Portugal and Spain and then in the Netherlands, France, and England. Soon, the so-called Columbian exchange brought new products, new liquidity, and new territories which would fuel a nascent mercantile capitalism and provide the resources for state-building projects. Yet, there was much in European institutions, laws, customs, ideas, and social arrangements to slow down these trends: Land was not yet a commodity, free labor was largely unavailable, and usury was a sin.

Effectively, the development of capitalism amounted to a veritable social revolution. For example, by the mid-sixteenth century in rural England, feudal practices stood in the way of the commercialization of agriculture. Peasants had rights to the use of the land and to residence upon it—rights the landed aristocracy could not readily abrogate. The Catholic Church, itself a part of these arrangements, had a stake in their preservation. Yet, by the time of Henry VIII, the sheep had begun to "devour human beings themselves and devastate and depopulate fields, houses, and towns" (More, 1964: 24). Over the next three centuries, English lands would be commodified and subsistence agriculture would give way to commercial production and the massive displacement of the peasantry. With variations, these processes were reproduced in much of northwestern Europe over the following four centuries.

Just as important were the concurrent consolidation and centralization of power which would produce new forms of sovereignty and organize the new sovereigns into an international system of states usually dominated by a handful of powers. In effect, beginning in the late fifteenth century, monarchs sought to consolidate their rule, monopolize the means of violence, and eliminate feudal prerogative. This process resulted in the formation of a system of sovereign territorial states centered on the new absolutisms of England, France, Spain, and Portugal, as well as the Dutch commercial empire. Always in conflict with each other, monarchs such as Ferdinand II of Spain, Elizabeth I of England, and Louis XIV of France sought to replace the scalar sovereignty arrangements of the Middle Ages with centralized monarchies.

Early European modernity also saw significant normative changes, from the first inklings of modern science to the Protestant Reformation. The ideas of Luther, Calvin, and other reformers made way for new conceptions of individuality and introduced normative plurality. The conquest of the Americas stimulated the transformation of the European world view because it presented important conceptual challenges. Indeed, for the Europeans, the conquered populations of the Americas did not fit the traditional categorical scheme which until then only knew three types of people: Christians, Muslims, and Jews. In response, Europeans constructed the naturalized classificatory schemes which would result in modern concepts of race. At the same time, some thinkers and theologians expressed shock at the treatment of these populations. Thus, justifications for colonialism and rejections of it saw the light.

In summary, normative plurality would deeply affect European views of the self and sensibilities around the treatment of human beings; new ways of organizing political authority would enhance royal power and interact with the emergence of the financial systems and capitalist forms which in turn would support state building, give states new purposes, and make way for multiple ideas about the good life. These processes, which continue today, involved extraordinary violence, social dislocation, and genocide—precisely the conditions human rights aims to address. Liberalism was one theoretical and institutional solution to this crisis. Human rights and the democratic republic would eventually provide a frame for understanding, containing, and managing these developments.

LIBERALISM: THE BIRTH OF HUMAN RIGHTS

Liberalism, in the broadest sense, is a comprehensive doctrine (Rawls) and a tradition in political theory which advances three fundamental principles. First, it holds that the individual is prior to society in the sense that his or her goals are the highest goods. Respectively, society and the state are the stage and the instrument for the realization of the individual's purposes. In turn, society and the state are justifiable only if they can be said to be founded upon the self-interested consent of rational individuals. To this end, the state and its laws must recognize that political power is fundamentally dangerous to its own legitimate purposes and thus in need of containment. These doctrines emerged in the context of the consolidation of modern sovereignties which, as Jean Bodin (1993) observed not long after the 1572 Massacre of Saint Bartholomew, were to be thought of as absolute, permanent, and indivisible.

Against the background of the confessional conflicts which fueled the English civil wars of the mid-seventeenth century, Thomas Hobbes (1981) took up Bodin's notion of sovereignty and grounded it in a conception of individuality. In part, his aim was to construct a narrative of legitimation which would not rely on tradition or religious authority. His innovation consisted in conceiving of both individuals and sovereigns as autonomous, equal in their capacity to harm each other, indivisible, rational, and always hostile to each other. Given these assumptions, the only legitimate route out of a state of nature, which was also a state of war, would be the rational, self-interested consent of these sovereign individuals. This was a desperate response to a desperate situation. It was fundamentally illiberal because, other than minimal residual rights, subjects retained no effective claims against the sovereign. A powerful account of the modern state formation, it did not protect the property rights necessary for capitalist accumulation or provide for the freedom of conscience through which confessional conflicts might be alleviated and individual self-realization fostered.

It was John Locke who built a narrative to address these issues. His point of departure was the quintessential individual subject, equal in dignity and claims to every other individual. This was also a propertied subject, the owner of a body. From this flowed a series of legitimate claims to personal autonomy, to the respect and benevolence of others, and to the material goods necessary for survival and flourishing. Unlike the Hobbesian individual, the Lockean's rights were grounded in an effective, albeit inefficient, natural law: "Reason, which is that law, teaches all mankind who will but consult it, that, being equal and independent, no one ought to harm another in his life, health, liberty, or possessions" (Locke 2003a: 263–264). This procedure permitted the elaboration of a pre-political condition which encompassed all the elements of civil society: property rights, complex households, and commercial relations facilitated by money—all of this absent a state. Political power, "a right of making laws with penalties of death and consequently all less penalties, for the regulating and preserving of property" (p. 262), had to accommodate these assumptions, especially because it was both fundamentally dangerous and necessary for the preservation of natural rights. Given the possibilities for abuse and the relatively benevolent circumstances which gave birth to civil government, Locke proposed that political power would be narrowly defined by its purposes as well as by institutional arrangements such as the separation of powers. The notion of a rights-bearing individual thus provided legitimate political power with both its foundation and its limits. This was important for later understandings of property and for creating the space for individuals to pursue their own life-plans. This account offered a solution to the crisis of early European modernity because it addressed the structural, institutional, and normative changes underway.

Embodied in law, Locke's notion of property articulates the claims necessary to the conduct of business. Ownership of things flows from the conscious extension of the subject's body upon nature, labor, and so from self-ownership. Most significant in this respect is the claim to landed estate. While recognizing the proposition that "the Lord hath giveth the earth to all men in common," and so of usufruct rights and of the provisos that spoilage and sufficiency might limit the extent of property, Locke also held that individuals might appropriate the land by mixing their labor and possessions with those portions of creation which none had enclosed before: "The grass my horse has bit, the turfs my servant has cut, and the ore I have digged in any place where I have a right in common with others become my property, without the assignation or consent of anybody" (Locke, 2003a: 275). Significantly from the viewpoint of capitalist social structures, self-ownership also implied the right to sell one's labor. Consequently, enclosing English gentry and English colonial settlers had, in Locke's view, an original claim to appropriate land and treat it as a commodity, as well as to buy and sell labor. Locke's arguments, then, justified the Parliamentary Enclosure Acts, beginning in 1700, and the common law understandings of property which would ease the way for capitalist development in England and its settler colonies.

These arguments also prepared the way for modern conceptions of human rights. Most significantly, reliance on natural law, by definition universal, sets standards higher than those any sovereign might impose. Thus, Locke defended the circumscription of royal authority soon associated with the 1689 English Bill of Rights. Significantly, he elaborated criteria for discerning usurpation and tyranny to argue that these put government at war with society which could legitimately defend itself (Locke 2003a).

But Locke's theory of rights did not end with landed property or the assertion of constitutional rule of law. It was important that individuals be free to pursue their life-plans. Locke's main concern was freedom of conscience. This argument also flows from the assumption of a quintessential rights-bearing subject to limit the sovereign prerogative. Locke argued for religious toleration as moral standard, as a requirement for private institutions, and as a rule for limiting the reach of the state. In moral terms, he held that toleration was "the chief characteristical mark of the true Church" whose real function was to order "men's lives according to the rules of virtue and piety" (Locke 2003b: 390). If toleration characterized the true faith and the true church, the state itself had to exhibit this value. To this end, Locke came to conceive of churches as private clubs whose powers were limited by both individual consent and civil law. Civil law was itself limited by the goals of the original social contract: the protection of life, health, liberty, and estate. How someone used these rights was not up to the sovereign who had no original authority to guide individuals toward salvation and no power to secure it. Church and state had different realms of competence. If they shared anything, this was a duty of toleration. In effect, Locke resolved confessional conflict by removing religion from the realm of politics, thus opening the door for later arguments around freedom of expression and other forms of personal autonomy.

Locke's account of rights is productive. For example, the assumption of a natural equality of powers and dignity makes it necessary to seek justification for any existing inequalities. While Locke went on to absolve socioeconomic inequalities and inequalities among genders, his argument demands the justification of inequalities, thus opening a door for those who would challenge them.

In time, Locke's account of the rights-bearing individual as a foundation for society and the state would lead to much broader conceptions of rights. Eighteenth-century thinkers radically elaborated upon his ideas. Beccaria, for example, extended individual rights into new standards for retributive justice, going so far as to argue against capital punishment. Condorcet (1988) addressed social inequalities. Believing that poverty was partly the result of illegitimate laws, he proposed to alleviate it by "applying the calculation of probabilities to human life and the uses of money" in order to establish social insurance (pp. 273–274, my translation). Similarly, he proposed a universal right to free public instruction because "well directed instruction corrects the natural inequality of faculties ... much as good laws remedy the natural inequality in the means of subsistence" (p. 276). Twentieth-century social movements advocating for labor, women, and excluded minorities, and theorists such as Marshall, Pogge, Okin, and Rawls reprised these themes to challenge social inequities. Before this, however, Rousseau had to add an important element to the idea of rights.

Rousseau was the *enfant terrible* of the Enlightenment: He pointed out many embarrassing truths about modernity—truths that later critics such as Marx, Weber, and Marcuse would term alienation, rationalization, and technological domination. His solution was a scheme for popular sovereignty which "taking men as they are and laws as they might be ... [would] bring together what right permits with what interest prescribes, so that justice and utility do not find themselves at odds" (Rousseau 2011: 156). The political solution Rousseau proposed placed the act of legislation in the hands of the governed so sovereignty would rest with the people. They would be ruled by laws which gave them a common purpose and fashioned them into a community. In effect, Rousseau evoked the ancient tradition of republicanism to enhance individual rights while also constructing a society characterized by rights to freedom, equality, and solidarity—all of these later recognized as human rights.

Rousseau's solution is as problematic as it is necessary because "political philosophy has never really been able to strike a balance between popular sovereignty and human rights, or between the 'freedom of the ancients' and the 'freedom of the moderns'" (Habermas 2001: 116). Already in the eighteenth century, if not before, many observers saw in emergent mass politics an inherent threat to the claims of privileged minorities. By the twentieth century, it was also clear that underprivileged and excluded groups might avail themselves of the protection of rights regimes. In fact, in the wake of the Holocaust, this was one of the inspirations behind the Universal Declaration of Human Rights. Yet, at the same time, it is also clear that popular sovereignty is the ultimate defense for rights. Thus, today, we observe popular majorities in the Global North using their political rights to oppress women, immigrants, religious and ethnic minorities, and others in broad challenges to the notions of human rights. We also see these minorities and their allies defend these rights with varying degrees of effectiveness not only through the courts, which as the example of Nazi Germany suggests can be ineffective, but also through the processes of popular sovereignty. This tension between popular sovereignty and human rights cannot be resolved in theory. The solution, if there is one, is political and so necessarily temporary.

In any event, the solutions Locke and Rousseau offered concerned the national level. They gave little guidance with respect to the relations among states. For a Europe long plagued by wars, this was of the utmost importance: There is no more severe threat to human rights than war. It is here that the contribution of cosmopolitan theorists was key.

Liberal ideas got a first false start at the beginning of the sixteenth century with the Salamanca school. Its most important thinker was Francisco de Vitoria, whose concerns were fueled by the treatment of colonized peoples. Vitoria, for example, elaborated a notion of individuality which conceived of an autonomous and self-motivated subject capable of formulating his own plans and bound only by natural law and his own consent. Among other things, this implied that "true faith" had to be promulgated but could not be compelled (Vitoria 2015).

More important was Vitoria's 1530 intervention in the debates over the right of Spain to conquer and convert the indigenous peoples of the Americas. In practice, his account of hospitality came too late: Already in 1493, Pope Alexander VI had promulgated the infamous Doctrine of Discovery. Against this, Vitoria argued that the Pope could not transfer this *dominium* because he was not the master of the entire *seculum*. Furthermore, he held that "the barbarians [already] possessed true public and private dominion" by right of first occupancy, a well-established claim in international law which applied in this case (Vitoria 1991: 264). Finally, Vitoria explored the question of *commercium*; by this he meant not so much trade as a claim to hospitality. This entitled Europeans to be received as guests and even as inhabitants and to respond in kind should they be received with aggression: "the *Spaniards have the right to travel and dwell in those countries so long as they do no harm to the barbarians*" (Vitoria 1991: 278, emphasis in original). But it did not give them authority to impose their own rule or faith. This response was consistent with European practices, which at the time did not include immigration laws. What is important here is that Vitoria argued that indigenous peoples were entitled to the same kinds of claims as Europeans, including a law-governed international order.

Kant did not cite Vitoria, but his sources on international law, Puffendorf and Grotius, likely were familiar with Vitoria. By considering emergent international law, Kant added a crucial element to the story of human rights: secular cosmopolitanism. He argued for a universal morality embodied in institutions and laws furthering individual rights, peace, and toleration. In his scheme for "Perpetual Peace," he extended the social contract model to the international level (Kant 1991a). If Hobbes proposed that individuals who sought peace had to agree to relinquish their ineffective right to everything, Kant called upon states to give up their right to everything, their absolute sovereignty and warlike posture, in exchange for peace, and in the name of moral progress and happiness. To accomplish this, three conditions had to be met. First, following Rousseau, Kant held that states which would participate in the project had to sport republican constitutions. Second, international law could not be left to unenforceable principles; rather, it had to rely on a *Foedus pacificum*. This "pacific federation" amounted to a transformation of the very idea of sovereignty: States would retain their identities while coming together to will laws, thus extending the principle of public autonomy to a new level. Third, this agreement would accord with conditions for universal hospitality similar to those of which Vitoria spoke. States would agree to respect each other's citizens and each other's domestic laws in order to form a larger community eventually encompassing the whole of humanity.

Kant was surely aware of the difficulty of establishing a cosmopolitan order. He rested his hopes on self-interest, itself a function of a "hidden plan of nature" embodied in the "unsocial sociability of men" (Kant 1991b: 44–46, 50–52). This amounted to an innate tendency toward competition and cooperation best realized in markets. Thus, Kant associated peace with commerce, itself more profitable and in line with the moral law than colonialism and slavery.

In summary, in addressing the triple crisis of European modernity, theorists ranging from Vitoria and Locke to Rousseau, Condorcet, and Kant argued for principles of respect and reciprocity which, supplemented by self-interest, would bind citizens and perhaps the whole of the human community. This is the origin of the idea of universal human rights. Its key elements aim to address the capitalist social relations, the system of sovereign states, and the normative plurality which have been generalized to include much of the planet. If the principles of human rights, as individual rights and as popular sovereignty, first received official articulation in the French Declaration of the Rights of Man and the Citizen (1789), this document served to frame many struggles throughout the world, beginning with the Haitian Revolution, continuing through the revolutions of the Spanish colonies in the Americas and the labor movements of nineteenth-century Europe and the Americas, and on to the Universal Declaration of Human Rights. In effect, the idea of human rights contains a normative core which bears critical expansion and proposes the institutional frameworks which, in various guises, have inspired modern developments ranging from the United Nations and the African Union to the European Union, the Inter-American Court of Human Rights, and, most important, the International Bill of Human Rights, to which we now turn.

THE INTERNATIONAL HUMAN RIGHTS
REGIME: SOLUTIONS AND ONGOING PROBLEMS

The idea of human rights is now part of international and regional law, and many national constitutions, from South Africa and Colombia to South Korea, make specific reference to this term. Although in the popular discourse, especially in the United States, accounts of human rights mostly address issues such as torture, the suppression of freedom of expression, and genocide, the scope of human rights is much broader. For example, the African (Banjul) Charter on Human and People's Rights makes colonialism a crime against humanity and stresses the collective rights to autonomy of families and peoples. In fact, the most widely recognized human rights document, the 1948 Universal Declaration of Human Rights (UDHR), also includes extensive claims to economic and social justice.

The UDHR was not the first international document to announce the legitimate claims of individuals and peoples. The League of Nations, for example, took on a variety of human rights functions, including the abolition of slavery and the incorporation of bodies such as the International Labour Organization. Earlier, most of the rights enunciated in the UDHR were fought for at the domestic and international levels in the period between the French Revolution and the beginning of World War II. Feminists struggled for the personal, civil, and political rights of women. Similarly, the labor movement in the West and elsewhere, such as Latin America, was able to attain rights such as social security after fighting for political rights. Although, in this case, the efforts of radicals associated with Bakunin or Marx should not be underestimated, it was liberal socialist programs associated with figures such as Bernstein and Jaurès that juridified working-class claims. Later, movements in various places upheld the rights of religious and racial/ethnic minorities. Finally, many struggled against colonialism and for the right of peoples to rule themselves. The Declaration incorporates these demands into goals that United Nations (UN) members, in principle, proclaim as their own.

The UDHR embodies a long list of civil, political, social, economic, and cultural claims. Efforts to include a rights document linked to the UN Charter originated with the interventions of Latin American jurists, activists, and states in the months preceding its establishment. The formulation of the UDHR itself included consultation with scholars, activists, and political actors from throughout the world. It yielded an edifice of rights. René Cassin, one of the framers, used the metaphor of the Greek portico to describe it. The steps, which recognize the importance of human dignity and the relevance of human rights to peace and justice, stand for the Preamble. The first two articles, proclaiming principles such as freedom and equality, are the foundation of the edifice. The first of four columns represents personal liberties such as the rights to life and freedom as well as the right not to be subjected to torture; the second stands for civil rights such as freedom of movement and asylum; the third symbolizes rights associated with popular sovereignty, such as freedom of expression and the right to participate in government; the fourth corresponds to economic, social, and cultural rights, such as the claims to social security, holidays, and remuneration ensuring "an existence worthy of human dignity." Finally, the three concluding articles make up the pediment—that is, the conditions which would enable people to secure their rights, including the rule of international law.

The Declaration aims to prevent the repetition of the crisis of the first half of the twentieth century. By the early 1940s, there was broad agreement among political actors and scholars that the appeal of communism and fascism in the interwar period followed from dire economic conditions, themselves the product of the fluctuations of self-regulating markets. Polanyi (1944), for example, showed that because land, labor, and money were part of life itself, their subjection to markets introduced deep insecurities which led people to seek the protection of authoritarian regimes. Consequently, preserving democracy and human rights required social protection. Ideas such as these, along with the arguments of Keynesian economics, would motivate political actors ranging from American Democrats to European Social Democrats to promote what amounted to a social contract between capital, labor, and the state. The UDHR articulates these intentions. The initial goal was to give the Declaration the force of law through one instrument which would embody civil, political, social, economic, and cultural rights. This is not what happened.

The codification of the Declaration stalled in the context of the Cold War and the domestic politics of both the United States and the Soviet Union. It was not until 1966 that the two other key elements of the International Bill of Rights took shape. They did so in the form of the International Covenant on Civil and Political Rights (ICCPR) and the International Covenant on Economic, Social, and Cultural Rights (ICESC). The former covers roughly the first 21 articles of the UDHR, making little mention of the rest. The latter, after short reference to the earlier articles, focuses on the next 7 articles. Nominally, the United States and its allies promoted the ICCPR, whereas the Soviet Union pushed for the ICESC. In practice, neither camp gave its full support to either convention. In any event, the conventions would only achieve enough ratifications to enter into force in 1976. Each binds only the states which ratified it, and in both cases, states parties added significant exceptions and reservations, important players have yet to ratify both documents.

These delays notwithstanding, an elaborate system for the governance of international human rights now exists. The UN and other intergovernmental organizations have built an extensive apparatus to monitor and make human rights effective. The scope of international human rights instruments has also grown significantly. In the past half century, approximately a dozen new international human rights instruments have been enacted to address, for example, the rights of children and of victims of enforced disappearances. Work with a focus on the rights of persons with disabilities is proceeding. These developments mostly address the first two pillars of the Declaration, although elements of the Convention on the Elimination of All Forms of Discrimination Against Women, the Convention on the Rights of All Migrant Workers, and the Indigenous and Tribal Peoples Convention also bear upon social, economic, and cultural rights. Unfortunately, ratification of these conventions has been very limited.

Regional systems have also grown alongside the global human rights regime. In fact, the Inter-American system came into being before its UN equivalent. The settling of internal conflicts and the elimination of political repression have come to be its main concerns. More recently, a human rights system has also grown out of the Organization of African Unity and its successor, the African Union. Unfortunately, despite some effective efforts on a smaller scale, there is no Asian equivalent to these regional regimes.

The best developed regional human rights system is in Europe. Soon after its establishment, the Council of Europe adopted the European Convention on Human Rights (1950); ten years later, it adopted the European Social Charter. These instruments embody much of the UDHR and create the European Court of Human Rights and the European Committee of Social Rights to oversee compliance. The Court focuses largely on civil and political rights and has come to accept the applications of individuals against states parties, in itself an important departure from prevalent ideas of sovereignty. Along these lines, its watershed accomplishment is its 1978 decision in *Ireland v. United Kingdom*. In this case, the Republic of Ireland initiated action against the United Kingdom in connection with the treatment of prisoners accused of terrorist acts. The Court ruled in favor of the plaintiff; the United Kingdom complied with the ruling. This has set an authoritative precedent for human rights in Europe.

Important advances relevant to the idea of human rights have also been made in international humanitarian law, the aspect of the law of nations which regulates the conduct of war with respect to both combatants and the treatment of civilians. Two sets of developments have been important for human rights: international tribunals and the extension of international humanitarian laws, including the Convention on the Prevention and Punishment of the Crime of Genocide, which entered into force in 1951.

In the aftermath of World War II, tribunals were established in Nuremberg and Tokyo to prosecute officials for violations of the law of war, thus denying them sovereign immunity. These tribunals expanded on the legal concepts of "crimes against humanity" and "war crimes" to include not only the treatment of prisoners of war but also the treatment of civilian populations under the control of belligerents. They also prepared the way for a succession of special tribunals which have addressed crimes against humanity in a variety of settings, from Bosnia to Rwanda and Liberia, among others. It is of course true that these tribunals embody victor's justice. Thus, for example, the bombing of Nagasaki was not treated the same way as Rape of Nanjing or the Bombing of Wuhan. Nonetheless, the crimes are real, even if the pace at which these tribunals have proceeded has been far from satisfactory. Also, the principles formulated by the special tribunals have made their way into the precept of universal jurisdiction. It holds that any court has subsidiary jurisdiction in matters of crimes against humanity if the closest courts cannot or will not act. This very controversial notion has been adopted by some European and South American courts. It has also been embodied in the 1998 Rome Statute of the International Criminal Court, although in this case jurisdiction is largely limited to states parties.

There have been other developments in international humanitarian law. Inspired by crimes against humanity in Rwanda and the former Yugoslavia, the UN adopted the principle of the Responsibility to Protect (R2P), which holds that in the case of a serious threat to human rights, a variety of measures (from mediation to peacekeeping force) will be enacted. This principle is controversial not only because it challenges established notions of sovereignty but also because it might open the door to neocolonial enterprises under cover of human rights. Other important developments in international humanitarian law highlight gender-based violence and the persecution of ethnic minorities in the prosecution of war crimes. Furthermore, the original Geneva Convention has been extended, and three additional protocols relating to the treatment of victims of war have been added since 1949. Most states have ratified the main conventions. Unfortunately, the United States, which has been involved in conflicts for most of this time, has not ratified the protocols; furthermore, since the early years of the twenty-first century, the United States has constructed a rationale for excluding informal combatants from the jurisdiction of the Geneva Conventions and other instruments of humanitarian law.

As this brief overview suggests, the international human rights regime is very much a work in progress. And a halting progress it has been. This is not surprising because both the interests involved and the political processes which have shaped the implementation of human rights embody the contradictions in the very idea of human rights as a way of articulating the demands for justice of the lowly and oppressed.

LIMITATIONS AND PROSPECTS

Human rights is a productive idea whose scope has expanded significantly since it first took shape during the Enlightenment. It is "predicated on an existential willingness to feel empathy and compassion for the victim, the oppressed, and the disenfranchised" and so on a cosmopolitan sensibility (Bronner 2004: 145). Its power, in the final analysis, depends on its ability to grasp the minds of people who wield it in a quest for justice. This power ebbs and flows. The reasons are many. They include conceptual weaknesses embodied in the extant human rights regime, its norms, its paradoxical connections to the modern system of states, and the uncertainties of politics.

One important line of criticism has been conceptual. Human rights depends on a model of individuality that introduces assumptions which make the apparently universal subject much less so. Also, despite its cosmopolitan spirit, the liberal notion of rights is founded upon absolutist conceptions of sovereignty which effectively make states only morally accountable and complicate the global realization of an international human rights regime.

The liberal notion of the subject, based on the assumption that the normative condition of individuals is absolute autonomy, is problematic. From different perspectives, MacIntyre (1981) and Santos (2014), for example, conclude that the foundational liberal account of the subject fails to consider the importance of communities, of interstate relations and colonialism, perhaps even of nature, in the construction of values or a meaningful life. Instead, the liberal notion obscures power relations. Indeed, as, for example, Marx (1994) and Dewey (1988: 185ff) note, liberal individuality is an abstraction leading to a conception of freedom which ignores social, cultural, and ideological power. Actual individuals are not to be found in isolation; they only exist in relation with each other. Their identities—be they social, cultural, or political—are constructed in institutions and through conflicts rooted in the structure of society, both domestic and global. If so, understandings of just claims can only attain validity when they shed light on the power inherent in conflicts which might pit different interests, such as transnational corporations and particular societies, or sections of capital (e.g., manufacturing and finance), or social classes, against each other. This powerful line of criticism suggests that human rights may be deficient as an approach to the study of society. However, the notion of rights is productive enough to integrate these critiques while proposing institutional arrangements capable of preserving these claims.

Along these lines, Nussbaum (2006) shows that the core liberal assumption of a fair original contract presumes a rough original equality of power and capacities among parties which only propertied adult male heads of household might exhibit. The rights of children, the elderly, the disabled, and even adult women, if they figure at all, seem particular claims (pp. 27–45). Locke's (2003a: 286–299) account of the household bears out this critique. His presentation of non-political forms of power—those of parents, husbands, and employers—suggests that male heads of household are the ones who retain the power to sign the contract. In response, Nussbaum repositions liberal rights in the notion of capabilities as fundamental entitlements first articulated by Sen (2009). The "capabilities approach" aims at human flourishing and extends substantive claims to include such items as bodily health, emotional development, play, and being able to live with other species (Nussbaum 2006: 76–78). In practice, however, capabilities require the juridification of claims and, so, a notion of rights. Because only states and intergovernmental organizations are potential guarantors of claims, only a rights approach would seem viable.

A further charge against human rights holds that its Western origins and the nature of the claims it deems basic are not universally compelling (Rorty 1999). Recognizing the significance of these challenges, human rights scholars have attempted to address the problem of cultural translation. Best known is Rawls' effort to extend his arguments about justice and political liberalism to the global scene. Agreeing with Kant that a world state is neither possible nor desirable, Rawls (1999) offers a "realistic utopia" grounded in the assumptions that "the great evils of human history . . . follow from political injustice" and that social policies "establishing just (or at least decent) basic institutions" will eventually overcome these injustices (pp. 6–7). His solution is to reformulate liberal principles in accordance with norms of public reason which ought to be acceptable to non-liberal peoples. Similarly, Forst (2012) proposes a "substantive individual moral right to justification," a claim to expect good reasons when power is deployed or substantive rights are denied to anyone. This conception of a just order requires that two criteria be met: reciprocity and generality. In other words, any demands or claims must be at least potentially mutual and the reasons offered must be commonly acceptable to those involved. This would apply at both the domestic level and the transnational level (pp. 2, 38).

From cosmopolitan premises, Rawls and Forst then propose that rights arguments should be both open to contestation and persuasive because they are always necessarily incomplete and amenable to extension. Human rights is then a specific way of formulating demands for justice in the modern context characterized by capitalism, a system of centralized sovereign states, and normative plurality. Thus, the concerns that inspired human rights and popular sovereignty claims have themselves been generalized beyond the region that gave them birth. At any rate, from a normative viewpoint, the liberal solution builds on a long history with a variety of origins beyond Europe. If only because they are solutions to problems that affect all of humanity, liberalism's most significant moral precepts were already part of many ethical codes (Appiah 2007: 45–68). Indeed, liberalism shares its normative core, the duty to reciprocity and generality, with many world views: Kant's categorical imperative articulates the same core idea as, for example, the Christian golden rule and the Confucian principle of humanness. In summary, the philosophy which underpins the idea of human rights is not "an exclusively European product but instead a *production* of humanity that has been situated in Europe as a center" (Dussel 2013: 45).

A further contention against the universality of human rights returns to the claim that some rights, namely civil and political rights, are more "basic" than others. Certainly, as the history of the implementation of the UDHR illustrates, the Global North, especially the United States, has prioritized civil and political rights. Observing this, Santos (2014), for example, has argued that human rights is historically and epistemologically limited to these terms which, in his view, are at best insufficient. Instead, he offers the notion of "good living," a translation of the Spanish "*buen vivir*," itself a rendering of the Aymara *sumak kawsay.* This term, which articulates demands raised by indigenous activists in South America, suggests that claims for human flourishing must include a good life marked by reciprocity, material sufficiency, a positive relationship with nature, and respect for different ways of life. In practice, however, in the current institutional context these demands can only become effective when embodied in law as just claims, so indigenous movements from Nunavut to Patagonia have demanded human rights. It is thus that Ecuador and Bolivia, for example, have incorporated the notion of *el buen vivir* into their constitutions, making it part of a regime of rights.

In fact, the most significant strengths and weaknesses of human rights and the efforts to actualize this ideal are political and so contingent. For example, alongside the personal, civil, and political rights associated with Locke and Rousseau, the UDHR includes rights concomitant with the demands of the labor movement and of women, ethnic minorities, and former colonial peoples. Even more, as Glendon (1998) convincingly argues on the basis of both internal and external evidence, the UDHR must be read as an integral document, in the civil law tradition. Where the common law tradition treats legislation as a menu from which particular elements may be served, civil law jurisprudence reads the law as an integral document: Each element depends on all others and supports all others—very much what Cassin had in mind when he drew the image of the Declaration as a Greek portico. The Declaration presents rights as mutually supportive and extends to circumstances which, likely, never occurred to its framers. The disaggregation and limitation of rights Santos and other critics highlight results from political choices and conflicts, rather than conceptual difficulties as such.

If the promise of human rights remains unfulfilled and is perhaps in crisis in the early decades of the twenty-first century, we must also look to political and economic factors associated with the intensification of neoliberal capitalist globalization. Emerging from the economic crises of the late 1970s, neoliberalism is ideology and program. As ideology, it proposes that self-regulating markets are the standard for justice. As a program, neoliberalism has engaged in the opening of product and financial markets, the elimination of the social net and the reduction of social consumption, as well as the privatization of state functions ranging from public utilities to, in the most extreme cases, prisons, policing, and military. From the standpoint of human rights, on the one hand, neoliberal policies have contributed the transnationalization of the commercial aspect of law and the institutions which enforce it (e.g., the World Trade Organization). This has the potential for the transnationalization of other areas of law and rights. On the other hand, neoliberalism directly undercuts the practices of social and economic rights and potentially weakens the scope of political rights and alternate ways of being by placing key decisions beyond the reach of popular sovereignty and raising the stakes for social conflicts.

There are significant parallels between neoliberal processes and the crisis of early European modernity. Expanding capitalist relations generate deep social change by undermining long-established ways of life, including gender structures and forms of production, while they also weaken regimes of social protection where they exist at all. Modern practices of sovereignty, always associated with violence, generate counterviolence just as new technologies of destruction and social control enhance the capacity to do harm. Thus, as global networks of terrorism have spread, liberal states have curtailed traditional rights, claiming that "a constitution is not a suicide pact" (Ignatieff 2004: 9). The intensification of interactions resulting from mass migrations and new technologies of communication highlights normative plurality while simultaneously increasing social isolation. Finally, increased economic activity aggravates climate change and other environmental catastrophes. Not surprisingly, increased insecurity has called forth demands for protection premised on parochialism, authoritarianism, and the rejection of human rights. It is thus that political movements embracing religious fundamentalism, racial supremacy, and integral nationalism have enjoyed a revival in the early decades of the twenty-first century, often availing themselves of the mechanisms of popular sovereignty to curtail human rights.

At the same time, a cosmopolitan imaginary has also gained strength (Steger 2008). Consistent with this development, the ideal of human rights also has a hold of the minds of the disadvantaged, the excluded, and the oppressed. With various degrees of success, Latin American activists seek to include social, economic, and cultural claims and the right to a livable environment in constitutions and argue in favor of international tribunals expressing themselves on this matter (Rodríguez and Rodríguez 2015). Again with mixed results, in the face of precisely the same tensions which have fueled the reaction against human rights, grass-roots campaigns from Tahrir Square to Barcelona and New York have framed their demands for justice in human rights terms, often extending the very meaning of the concept to cover new claims or redress old wrongs (Forman 2016).

Conclusion

Human rights is a project whose realization remains uncertain. At its core, it addresses an edifice of just claims to permissions, protections, and goods which persons may raise against each other and before the state. Rights may have a variety of sources, but conceptually and pragmatically they are tied to the law. Their effectiveness depends on moral compulsion and coercive force (Habermas 1998). To claim something as a matter of right, as opposed to, for example, charity or love, is to hold someone to an enforceable obligation. The broad notion of human rights, expressed in the International Bill of Human Rights and elsewhere, articulates its provisions in international law but, in the final analysis, leaves it up to sovereign states to recognize and enforce their own responsibilities under this law. Thus, even if we hold that the underlying moral bases for human rights are the standards against which we judge positive law, actual institutional orders, and social practices, these demands are ultimately tied up with political authority and circumscribed by the claims of sovereignty. Consequently, human rights often falls short precisely when and where it is most needed. Also, those people who most need rights are often juridically or customarily precluded from claiming them. But it is also the case that human rights provides an extraordinarily productive language that activists widely use to articulate justice claims in the modern world.

References

Appiah, K. A. 2007. *Cosmopolitanism: Ethics in a World of Strangers.* New York: Norton.
Bodin, J. 1993. *Les six livres de la République*, edited by G. Mairet and M. Bergeron. Chicotumi, Quebec, Canada.

Bronner, S. E. 2004. *Reclaiming the Enlightenment: Towards a Politics of Radical Engagement.* New York: Columbia University Press.

Condorcet, N. 1988. *Esquisse d'un tableau historique des progrès de l'esprit humain*, edited by Alain Pons. Paris: Flammarion.

Dewey, J. 1988. *The Public and Its Problems.* Athens: Ohio University Press.

Dussel, E. 2013. *Ethics of Liberation in the Age of Globalization and Exclusion*, translated by E. Mendietta, et al. Durham, NC: Duke University Press.

Forman, M. 2016. "Marcuse in the Crisis of Neoliberal Capitalism: Revisiting the Occupation." In *The Great Refusal: A New Cycle of Struggle out of the Ashes of the Economic Collapse*, edited by P. Funke, A. Lamas, and T. Wolfson, 29–55. Philadelphia, PA: Temple University Press.

Forst, R. 2012. *The Right to Justification: Elements of a Constructivist Theory of Justice*, translated by J. Flynn. New York: Columbia University Press.

Glendon, M. A. 1998. "*Propter honoris respectum*: Knowing the Universal Declaration of Human Rights." *Notre Dame Law Review* 73: 1153–1176.

Habermas, J. 1998. *Between Facts and Norms: Contributions to a Discourse Theory of Law and Democracy*, translated by W. Rehg. Cambridge, MA: MIT Press.

Habermas, J. 2001. "Remarks on Legitimation Through Human Rights." In *The Postnational Constellation: Political Essays*, edited and translated by M. Pensky, 113–112. Cambridge, MA: MIT Press.

Hobbes, T. 1981. *Leviathan or the Matter, Forme, & Power of a Commonwealth Ecclesiasticall and Civill*, edited by C. B. Macpherson. New York: Penguin.

Ignatieff, M. 2004. *The Lesser Evil: Politics in an Age of Terror.* Princeton, NJ: Princeton University Press.

Kant, I. 1991a. "Perpetual Peace: A Philosophical Sketch." In *Political Writings*, edited by H. Reiss, translated by H. B Nisbet, 93–130. Cambridge, UK: Cambridge University Press.

Kant, I. 1991b. "The Idea of a Universal History with a Cosmopolitan Intent." In *Political Writings*, edited by H. Reiss, translated by H. B. Nisbet, 41–53. Cambridge, UK: Cambridge University Press.

Locke, J. 2003a. "The Second Treatise of Government: An Essay Concerning the True, Original, Extent, and End of Civil Government." In *Political Writings*, edited by D. Wooton, 261–386. Indianapolis, IN: Hackett.

Locke, J. 2003b. "A Letter Concerning Toleration." In *Political Writings*, edited by D. Wooton, 390–436. Indianapolis, IN: Hackett.

MacIntyre, A. 1981. *After Virtue: A Study in Moral Theory.* London: Duckworth.

Marx, K. 1994. "On the Jewish Question." In *Political Writings*, edited by J. O'Malley, 28–56. Cambridge, UK: Cambridge University Press.

More, T. 1964. *Utopia*, edited by E. Surtz. New Haven, CT: Yale University Press.

Nussbaum, M. 2006. *Frontiers of Justice: Disability, Nationality, Species Membership.* Cambridge, MA: Harvard University Press.

Polanyi, K. 1944. *The Great Transformation.* New York: Farrar & Rinehart.

Rawls, J. 1999. *The Law of Peoples with the Idea of Public Reason Revisited.* Cambridge, MA: Harvard University Press.

Rodríguez Garavito, C., and D. Rodríguez Franco. 2015. *Juicio a la exclusión: El impacto de los tribunales sobre los derechos sociales en el Sur Global.* Mexico, D.F.: Siglo Veintuno.

Rorty, R. 1999. "Human Rights, Rationality, and Sentimentality." In *The Politics of Human Rights*, edited by O. Savić, 67–84. London: Verso.

Rousseau, J.-J. 2011. "On the Social Contract or Principles of Political Right." In *Political Writings*, edited and translated by D. A. Cress, 155–252. Indianapolis, IN: Hackett.

Santos, B. de S. 2014. *Epistemologies of the South: Justice Against Epistemicide*. Boulder, CO: Paradigm.

Sen, A. 2009. *The Idea of Justice*. Cambridge, MA: Harvard University Press.

Steger, M. 2008. *The Rise of the Global Imaginary: Political Ideologies from the French Revolution to the Global War on Terror*. Oxford, UK: Oxford University Press.

Vitoria, F. 1991. "On the American Indians." In *Political Writings*, edited and translated by A. Pagden and J. Lawrence, 231–292. Cambridge, UK: Cambridge University Press.

Vitoria, F. 2015. *De actibus humanis: Sobre los actos humanos* (Bilingual edition), edited and translated by A. Sarmiento. Stuttgart, Germany: Frommann-Holzboog.

FURTHER READING

Falk, R. 2009. *Achieving Human Rights*. New York: Routledge.

Goodhart, M. 2005. *Democracy as Human Rights: Freedom and Equality in the Age of Globalization*. New York: Routledge.

Lutz-Bachmann, M., and A. Nascimento, editors. 2014. *Human Rights, Human Dignity, and Cosmopolitan Ideals: Essays on Critical Theory and Human Rights*. Burlington, VT: Ashgate.

Pogge, T. 2002. *World Poverty and Human Rights: Cosmopolitan Responsibilities and Reforms*. Cambridge, UK: Polity.

Tagore, R. 1931. *The Religion of Man*. New York: Macmillan.

Talbott, W. J. 2010. *Human Rights and Human Well-Being*. New York: Oxford University Press.

CHAPTER 26

....

DEMOCRACY

....

JAN AART SCHOLTE

GLOBAL studies (in my understanding) investigates social relations as practiced and experienced in transworld, planetary, terra-earth spaces. This emergent field of research and learning explores how people live collectively in global domains as a distinctive kind of social place. The motivating premise is that, particularly with accelerated globalization in contemporary history, society has specific transplanetary qualities that bear thorough examination in their own right. This is by no means to discount the importance of other arenas (e.g., local, national, and regional) of culture, ecology, economy, geography, history, politics, and psychology. But it is to affirm that global relations have their own major significance, whereby globality shapes society across other scales, at the same time as the global is also shaped by these other spheres.

As many chapters in this handbook highlight, global studies requires theory, both explanatory and normative. Theorization of the global can substantially draw upon concepts and analytical frameworks that have been developed previously in other fields of social enquiry. However, substantial revision or even wholesale transdisciplinary reconstruction of inherited theory may also be required in order to make fuller sense of globality. In this vein, this chapter reconsiders one of the lynchpins of normative theory, namely democracy. What does (or could) democracy entail in global social spaces? How can global studies help to rethink ideas and practices of democracy to make them more fitting for contemporary society?

Democracy (*demos-kratos*, "people's power") is a core value of a good society in many life-worlds. Particularly in modern political theory and practice, it is generally maintained that all affected people (often dubbed "the public") should have due participation in and control over the decisions that shape their collective lives. Democratic mindsets moreover generally believe that "people's power" can promote other key qualities of living well, such as justice, liberty, morality, peace, prosperity and solidarity.

Democracy lies at the heart of modern notions of legitimacy. Prevailing norms have it that to obtain a right to govern, an authority must adequately involve and answer to the subjects of its rule. Failure to meet this standard has provided major fuel for modern revolutions: in France and the Thirteen colonies in the late eighteenth century; across Europe and Latin America in the nineteenth century; in decolonization struggles across Africa, Asia, and the Middle East in the twentieth century; and in a further wave of revolts against one-party rule and military government in recent history.

All of the movements just mentioned involve *national* democracy. In this context, "the people" take the form of a nation, and the ruling apparatus for that population takes the form of a territorial state. Thus, on the established modern principle, democracy entails collective self-determination of a nation through "its" territorial state. To be sure, in practice it has proved well-nigh impossible to achieve seamless democratic fits between country, nation, and state that all affected parties endorse. Indeed, modern history has seen territorial borders perpetually contested, national identities continually questioned, and state constitutions repeatedly revised. Nevertheless, the underlying vision of democracy constructed around the country–nation–state has remained robust for several centuries.

Yet now, as elaborated later in this chapter, contemporary globalization poses challenges to these core premises of modern democracy. In terms of geography, for example, increased global connectivity means that the spaces of social relations frequently do not correspond (fully) to country realms. In terms of the public, "all affected people" in global affairs generally do not fall (only) into distinct national groupings. In terms of governance, rules for global spaces usually do not emanate (wholly) from states.

If inherited cornerstones of modern democracy are substantially contradicted, then what form(s) can and should people's power take in today's more global society? This question has preoccupied substantial research and practice since the mid-1990s (Archibugi, Koenig-Archibugi, and Marchetti 2012; Bray and Slaughter 2015; Held 1995). Later sections of this chapter critically review a variety of suggestions made in that work for advancing democracy in global affairs. Some of these proposals relate to institutional design, whereas others relate to the deeper structures of politics. Each of the institutional and the deeper structural formulas holds some promise, but each also has conceptual and/or practical limitations. Hence, the democratization of global spaces may better happen through some combination of these propositions, although the precise character of such a mixture will no doubt remain contested.

Before proceeding to elaborate these points, a brief methodological note is in order. My analysis of democracy in global politics derives largely from 20 years of field-based studies. This research has included participant observation of multiple global governance settings as well as interviews with approximately 1,000 official and activist practitioners in 50 countries (O'Brien et al. 2000; Scholte 2004, 2011, 2012, 2017). From 2008 through 2014, I also co-convened dialogues in a Building Global Democracy program, which involved several hundred participants from diverse geographical regions, societal sectors, academic disciplines, and ideological perspectives (Scholte 2014, 2015; Scholte, Fioramonti, and Nhema 2016). Certainly, as indicated by the references in this chapter, my thinking on democracy in a global world also builds on pertinent academic literature. However, the assessment comes more particularly from my direct engagement with individuals and groups across the planet who have sought concretely to promote people's power in global politics. To understand democracy in a global world, it seems vital to learn from practitioners as well as philosophers and to listen to a plethora of voices around the world rather than to refer only to professional theorists in the North Atlantic region. To the extent that this chapter presents alternative (and possibly more relevant) ideas about democracy in the contemporary global world, it is a consequence of the research methods employed. Indeed, these methodological principles of transculturalism and research–practice engagement are arguably also pertinent for the full span of global studies.

A More Global World: Challenges
to Modern Democracy

Global social relations encompass transactions and interdependencies that connect people on a planetary scale (Scholte 2005). Through global linkages, people's lives are interwoven no matter where on the Earth they might be located. Prominent instances of global connectivity include climate change, many public health challenges, long-range air travel, the Internet, transborder value chains, cross-world finance, intercontinental migration, satellite communications, transplanetary leisure (e.g., in much contemporary cuisine, film, music, and sport), and global knowledge (e.g., professional sciences, certain memories, and various ideologies).

Global social connectivity is by no means entirely new to contemporary history. Indeed, the initial exodus of humans from Africa to other continents some 400 generations ago might be considered the first instance of globalization. Other early manifestations of globality include the world religions, transoceanic trade, the Seven Years' War (across Africa, Asia, Europe, and North America in 1756–1763), and nineteenth-century colonialism. However, recent globalization has comprehensively increased the amount, range, frequency, speed, intensity, and impact of transplanetary relations. Hence, the vocabulary of globality and the field of global studies have understandably appeared in recent times and not before.

Among the many challenges raised by contemporary accelerated globalization are acute concerns about democracy. Perceptions that affected people lack sufficient voice and influence in global politics have already spurred half a century of popular resistance. Instances include mobilizations against the Bretton Woods institutions from the 1970s, against multilateral trade agreements from the 1990s, against climate (non)policies and global financial markets from the 2000s, and against global migration in the 2010s. Movements such as the World Social Forum and Occupy have particularly highlighted global democracy issues. In 2016, calls to "get our country back" also energized Brexit in the United Kingdom and the election of Donald Trump in the United States of America.

What—at a deeper level—underlies this widespread unease about globalization and democracy? Three structural mismatches between global connectivity and established democratic practice can be highlighted, namely regarding geography, contours of the public, and governance apparatuses. To this extent, democracy constructed in a country–nation–state framework jars with a more global world, and alternative formulations are also wanted. Global studies as a new transdisciplinary enquiry invites such reflection and reinvention.

Geography Beyond Countries

In respect of geography, contemporary accelerated globalization has disrupted the modern equation of "society" and "country," with the associated assumption that the space of democracy corresponds with a country unit. This is not to argue that countries—and territory more generally—are not important spatial spheres in a global world. But it is to suggest that constructions which limit the location of democracy to countries are unsustainable.

For example, global relations such as offshore finance, intercontinental missiles, and human rights movements are not confined by country borders. Global ecological changes, global diseases, and global corporations likewise confound social organization in terms of bounded territories. Moreover, some global relations have a "supraterritorial" quality, with a geography that transcends territorial place, territorial distance, and territorial borders. For instance, a foreign exchange rate cannot be plotted with longitude and latitude; it prevails across the global economy at the same time. An email transmits instantaneously anywhere across the planet, irrespective of the territorial distance between sender and recipient. Global warming transpires with no heed of socially constructed territorial frontiers.

If many key social relations in a more global world do not map neatly onto country units—or indeed territorial space more generally—then democratic arrangements built in relation to individual countries cannot deliver adequate people's power. If democracy is contained within country spaces, but the forces that democracy is meant to control are not, then people's power correspondingly falls short. It is not that country-based democracy is irrelevant for global democracy but that it is not enough. If social geography involves more than countries, then democracy must also.

Publics Beyond Nations

Global relations furthermore challenge modern democracy's presumption that "the people" takes form wholly and solely as a nation. To be sure, communities constructed around a shared "homeland" and associated bonds of language, ritual, history, and so on provide an important source of identity and solidarity in today's global world. Indeed, sometimes global forces affect people specifically along national lines—for example, in cases of national diasporas, global market effects on national currencies, and global cultural threats to marginalized languages. Moreover, many people appeal to national collective self-protection in attempts to fend off perceived global dangers. Thus, by no means is the national demos dead in globalized conditions.

However, in global relations, "all affected people" do not always and only fall into a national grouping (Fraser 2007; Habermas 2001). For instance, contemporary politics witness frequent references to a "global community" of humankind as a whole. In such situations, the demos encompasses all human beings across the world. Such universalist claims maintain that transplanetary ecology, disease, infrastructure, knowledge, and so on significantly impact *Homo sapiens* everywhere. Likewise, assumptions of a species identity underpin policies of "human rights," "humanitarian assistance," and "global public goods." Indeed, many persons today characterize themselves as "global citizens" alongside, or even instead of, their national citizenship. In other cases, the operative demos in contemporary global politics can be regional, as is deliberately pursued in projects of African *Union* and European *Union*.[1]

On still other occasions, appeals to collective fate in today's global world have a social-sectoral character. Such nonterritorial solidarities can relate to age, caste, class, disability, faith, language, gender, race, sexual orientation, and more. With regard to religion, for example, many Buddhists form "world fellowships," many Christians see their "home" in a universal Church, many Muslims identify their "people" in terms of a supraterritorial *Ummah*, and so on. Global class solidarities have taken form in intercontinental associations such as Slum Dwellers International, La Vía Campesina (of peasants), and the World Economic Forum (of global corporate managers). In contemporary politics, oppressed groups often globalize their community to advance struggles for Dalit power, disabled rights, gender justice, indigenous peoples, LGBT pride, and racial equality. Some global networks combine several subordinations, for instance, as women of African descent or as gay migrants.

In summary, constructs of the demos in democracy—"the people" in "people's power"—are highly plural in today's global world. "Publics" take shape as nations, the human species, regions, and a host of nonterritorial groupings. Moreover, the same person may embrace multiple collective identities in global politics —for example, being variously Sámi, Swedish, European, human, indigenous, lesbian, woman, and/or young. Hence, one may better speak of global "demoicracy" with multiple peoples often coming in overlapping and shifting combinations (Bohman 2007).

Governance Beyond States

Compounding the complexities of geography and publics are complexities of governance in contemporary global politics (Scholte 2010). Democracy brings people's power to the regulatory arrangements of a society. In the case of modern society, those governance processes have focused almost entirely on the state—that is, a public, unified, centralized, hierarchically organized, bureaucratic, territorial, sovereign authority apparatus. Thus, modern democracy has been understood as bringing the participation and control of a nation to bear on "its" state. The various institutions to achieve this people's power vis-à-vis the state include universal franchise, referenda, popularly elected representative assemblies, bills of rights, ombudspersons, and so on.

Just as countries and nations remain important in globalized politics, so states also continue to play a prominent role in regulating global spaces. Governments often figure substantially in efforts to order ecology, economy, knowledge, and polity in today's global world. Indeed, on the whole, no other type of regulatory organization currently has as many resources to hand as the state. So the democratization of global affairs is in part a matter of democratizing states. National governments, legislatures, and courts need better to promote public voice and influence in global politics.

However, it is also vital to recognize that state engagement with global arenas operates differently than state regulation of territorial realms. For instance, today's state usually governs transplanetary circumstances not by itself but collectively through global and regional intergovernmental organizations (IGOs). These formal institutions of public international law have their own offices, staff, and budgets. Examples of the official multilateralism of IGOs include the World Trade Organization (WTO) and the Gulf Cooperation Council (GCC). In many other cases, states collaborate in global regulation through transgovernmental networks (TGNs). These informal associations of ministers and/or officials have no basis in treaty and no own resources, but they can be highly influential in constructing regulatory norms and transferring them between countries. Examples of the unofficial multilateralism of TGNs include the Group of Seven (G7), the Group of Twenty (G20), and the Nuclear Suppliers Group (NSG).

It is far from evident that established practices of democracy through the state are adequate to bring people's power sufficiently to bear on IGOs and TGNs. After all, through these venues, states (especially more powerful states) take actions that can significantly impact publics beyond their own territorial jurisdictions; however, those "outside" populations have few democratic channels to the "foreign" state that affects them. Even citizens of a given state often have little means of influence over "their" government's global governing, which is generally little debated in state elections and little controlled through state courts and legislatures. Moreover, IGO bureaucracies such as the European Union (EU) Commission and the United Nations (UN) Secretariat can have their own governing impacts beyond the reach of the democratic processes of their member states. For example, how far can citizens of Malawi use their national government to be heard at the International Monetary Fund (IMF)?

In addition to issues around states and their multilateral arrangements, further democratic problems arise with respect to regulation of global relations through non-state arrangements (Dingwerth 2007). Recent decades have seen a large expansion of private global governance, where societal rules are made and implemented through non-governmental actors, as well as public–private combinations. State-based democracy has little role in regulatory organizations like the Forest Stewardship Council (FSC), the Internet Engineering Task Force (IETF), the International Accounting Standards Board (IASB), and the World Fair Trade Organization (WFTO). In such situations, too, more than state channels of public participation and control are needed.

To reiterate, none of the above discussion is to suggest that countries, nations, and states—and associated modern constructions of democracy—are disappearing in today's more global society. However, it is equally plain that the dynamics of a global world involve geography beyond countries, publics beyond nations, and governance beyond states. Democracy in global politics therefore requires innovations beyond modern theories and practices with their unsustainable premise that society is reducible to country–nation–state units.

Global Democracy: Institutional Designs

As noted earlier, considerable research and practice of recent decades has responded to the shortcomings of democracy in respect of global affairs. The many proposed institutional constructions for greater "people's power" in today's more global world can be broadly catalogued under six headings: communitarianism, multilateralism, world federalism, multistakeholderism, deliberative forums, and resistance struggles. The following discussion reviews the main features, promises, and limitations of each approach. Like any summary, this account cannot do justice to the full variety and nuance of the arguments. Nevertheless, a compact overview can conveniently identify broad debates and trends, which can in turn feed into, and be developed further by, emergent global studies.

Communitarianism

A first strand in contemporary global democracy theory and practice downplays the need for suprastate institutions and instead maintains that even in the face of heavily globalized circumstances, people's power is best realized through smaller populations rooted in bounded territorial spaces. Communitarianism argues that a veritable demos—in the sense of a deep and lasting bond of collective identity and solidarity—is only available on national and local scales (Dahl 1999; De Wilde 2011; Miller 1995). All larger entities—global human-kind, regional communities, and nonterritorial publics—are from a communitarian per-spective shallow, artificial, and unsustainable. Similarly, communitarian democracy views with skepticism all regional and global governance institutions, both public and private, in preference for handling global issues through local and national arrangements.

Much communitarian politics focuses on the national scale. These perspectives hold that the territorially defined nation is always the primary and overriding demos, also in today's global world. In this view, national self-determination through a sovereign state remains the optimal institutional formula for democracy. Moreover, in order to promote and protect the nation amid global flows, the state should, in the communitarian eyes, carefully monitor and, where necessary, restrict links with "the outside world." Communitarian democracy may thus sometimes call for "de-linkage" and "de-globalization," including state controls on transborder communications, investment, trade, and travel (Bello 2004).

Other variations of communitarianism devolve still further and promote self-sustaining local communities as the optimal site of democracy in the contemporary global world (Hines 2000). Such "localist" constructions of people's power are found in some ecological initiatives (e.g., for "food sovereignty"), aboriginal movements (e.g., in Aotearoa, Buganda, and Navajo), and secessionist strivings (e.g., in Abkhazia, Catalonia, Somaliland, and Tibet). In these cases, even the larger nation-state is regarded as too "distant" from "the people," understood as a smaller population grounded in a scaled-down territory.

Communitarian approaches have attracted broad and diverse audiences across the global world. These territorialist visions of democracy amid globalization are embraced in widely varying forms, including old-style nationalism in Russia, new-style populism with Trump, old-style statism of the Bolivarian Alliance in Latin America, and new-age "small-is-beautiful" environmentalism. Communitarianism is thus not inherently "left" or "right" in political orientation and has sometimes produced unexpected alliances—for example, across party–political lines in the Brexit referendum.

Communitarian democracy certainly offers some significant possibilities for people's power vis-à-vis global relations. Many people feel empowered "at home" in "their" countries and localities, speaking a "native" language, performing "traditional" political rituals, and so on. Moreover, state and substate governments—especially those with large resources—can be substantially harnessed to the will of their resident populations and make substantial impacts on global flows in the name of those territorial constituencies. Hence, communi-tarian democracy is anything but obsolete in contemporary globalized circumstances.

However, communitarianism also has notable limitations as a formula for democracy in a global world. For one thing, many local and national regimes in practice provide little participation and control to "their" people. Local mafias and autocratic states abound across the planet. Moreover, even territories with apparent "free and fair" politics witness substantial popular disillusion with modern liberal democracy, as reflected in low party membership and poor voter turnout. Meanwhile, critical theories suggest that the modern state is an inherently oppressive apparatus—for example, of class domination (according to Marxism), patriarchy (according to feminism), knowledge/power (according to post-structuralism), neo-imperialism (according to postcolonialism), or anthropocentrism (ac-cording to post-humanism).

Yet, even putting aside these deeper critiques of territorial democracy, communitarianism also falls short in its own terms. Suppose that every dictator worldwide were removed: People would still not always and only find their chief political bond with the territorial community around them. Contrary to communitarian expectations, many persons deeply embrace regional citizenship, humanitarian action, transnational religious solidarity, and so on. Indeed, many national and local governments have quite dubious democratic records toward nonterritorial publics under their jurisdiction. Consider how often states have oppressed subordinate castes, underclasses, people with disability, persons of color, sexual minorities, and women. Not surprisingly, then, such groups have often looked to regional and global spaces to pursue voice and influence—for example, in the International Dalit Solidarity Network, StreetNet International, the International Disability Alliance, Pan-Africanism, global LGBT mobilizations, and the World March of Women.

In material terms, too, communitarian constructions of democracy often fall short in global circumstances. Even the strongest national or local government cannot exercise "sovereign" (in the sense of absolute, supreme, unilateral, and comprehensive) control over global flows that affect its territory. For example, the Federal Reserve Bank has quite limited command of the globally circulating US dollar and the globally held US government debt. If even the USA is so constrained, then what of nation-states in Bhutan, Bolivia, and Burkina Faso? Meanwhile, for all its localist aspirations for bottom-up autonomy, the Freifunk movement of wireless networks cannot operate outside the regional and global regime of internet registries.

Finally, even local authorities and nation-states with the most democratic internal arrangements have dubious democratic credentials when they impact publics outside their jurisdiction. For instance, how are governments in China and Norway democratically accountable for their climate change impacts on people in Bangladesh? How do governments in Brazil and Canada democratically answer for their food security impacts on people in Ghana? Underlining this point, "global vote" initiatives have invited "foreigners" to cast informal "ballots" in the elections of other countries.

Multilateralism

One possible (partial) corrective to the shortcomings of communitarianism lies in multilateralist designs of global democracy (Keohane, Macedo, and Moravcsik 2009; Moravcsik 2004). Whereas communitarianism prescribes people's power in a global world through unilateral actions of local and national governments, multilateralism builds on the principle of "joint" and "pooled" sovereignty of democratic territorial regimes. The notion is that such governments (especially nation-states) can through cross-border collaboration "add up" to global democracy. On this premise, there need be no democratic deficits in global politics as long as the constituent territorial units are democratic. In this view, the principal challenge is to democratize all states, which can then democratize their collective arrangements.

Thus, from a multilateralist perspective, global democracy is available through IGOs and TGNs composed of democratic states. For example, the UN and the G20 would provide sufficient people's power in their governance of global spaces provided that their member states offered due participation and control to their respective populations. The democratic member governments would also ensure that IGO secretariats such as the EU bureaucracy and the IMF staff were duly accountable to the people whom they affect.

Certainly, multilateralist democracy has points in its favor. Effective governance of global relations demands substantial elements of global cooperation, and it is clearly better for people's power if such collaboration occurs among democratic rather than autocratic states. The Southern Common Market (MERCOSUR) is arguably in better democratic shape than the Shanghai Cooperation Organization (SCO). In principle, democratic governments from all continents could work together through the World Health Organization (WHO) for global policies of disease control that duly consider all affected people across the planet.

That said, multilateralist democracy also has notable shortfalls, beginning with the problem, already mentioned in relation to communitarianism, that states often fail tests of democracy. Many member states of IGOs and TGNs do not meet even modest criteria of people's power, such as open elections and impartial courts, let alone more ambitious practices of popular involvement. Meanwhile, every modern state the world over has, to one degree or another, denied sufficient access and influence to structurally subordinated groups such as ethnic minorities and women. Thus, it seems unlikely that any multilateral arrangement will ever consist of only and wholly democratic states.

Even if these deep-rooted problems of state-based democracy were somehow overcome, IGOs and TGNs would still face severe capacity deficits. Most multilateral institutions fall far short of the budget, staff, and other resources required to fulfill their tasks. Thus, even if IGOs and TGNs were composed entirely of securely democratic states, the resulting people's power would be limited so long as the interstate organizations lacked the tools to make effective responses to global problems. For the moment it appears highly unlikely that member states will provide multilateral institutions with anything close to the necessary levels of competences and means.

These circumstances of weak state-based multilateralism have encouraged the expansion of private global governance. When governments do not provide the functionally required levels of regulation for global connections such as financial markets and the internet, then space is created for nongovernmental actors to govern instead. The resulting private global regulation—for example, through the Internet Corporation for Assigned Names and Numbers (ICANN) and the Wolfsberg Group of International Financial Institutions—operates with little state oversight, either unilateral or multilateral. Global democracy through IGOs and TGNs is clearly not enough in situations where non-state organizations do the actual governing.

Other democratic shortcomings of multilateral governance relate again to the global institutions themselves. For example, certain important IGOs and TGNs significantly impact people whose states are not members of the regime. The G20 has important worldwide consequences, but its members comprise only around 10% of the nation-states. Likewise, the Organisation for Economic Co-operation and Development (OECD) has transplanetary reach, but it has only 35 member states. Restricting permanent membership of the UN Security Council to 5 states also contradicts multilateralist democracy.

Moreover, even when states are nominally equal members of a multilateral institution, they rarely have equivalent opportunities of voice and influence. For instance, all member governments are represented on the executive boards of the IMF and the World Bank, but their votes are weighted as a function of their highly unequal shares in the capital base of those agencies. At the WTO, the principle of state equality is compromised by the so-called "green room" practice of private consultations among smaller groups of (often more powerful) governments.

Finally, multilateralist designs of global democracy are fragile given the large political distance that generally separates national democratic practices from IGOs and TGNs. States are usually represented in these multilateral forums by professional civil servants who are far removed from domestic elections, legislatures, and courts. Individual citizens are rarely able to engage in IGOs and TGNs via "their" parliaments. Indeed, advocacy groups often bypass national democratic processes and instead directly engage with multilateral institutions themselves.

World Federalism

A third general approach to global democracy seeks to avoid institutional shortcomings of communitarianism and multilateralism by providing for formal direct citizen participation in suprastate governance (Archibugi 2008; Cabrera 2010; Tännsjö 2008). World federalism envisions a multi-tiered planetary government in which the regional and global levels are subject to the same sorts of liberal–democratic mechanisms of participation and control as apply to modern local and national governments. This perspective thereby prescribes global democracy through regional and global plebiscites, with regional and global political parties, for regional and global parliaments. Likewise, in world federalist designs, regional and global human rights instruments supplement state-based bills of rights, regional and global citizenship complement national citizenship, and regional and global civil society mobilize people alongside local and national activism.

Recent history has seen some concrete steps in conformity with world federalist democracy. For example, several regional institutions (e.g., in Central America and Europe) have acquired directly elected parliaments. In addition, national lawmakers have come together in several worldwide initiatives, such as Global Legislators for a Balanced Environment (GLOBE) and the Parliamentary Conference on the WTO. States have established a host of regional and global human rights regimes, several of which include suprastate tribunals such as the International Criminal Court (ICC). Considerable transborder civil society collaboration has developed to pursue a plethora of public-interest concerns.

However, the scale of such world federalist developments falls well behind the pace of globalization and the accompanying expansion of regional and global governance, both public and private. Regional and global political parties are severely underdeveloped. Most regional regulatory institutions lack directly elected legislatures, and popularly elected global parliaments remain a very distant prospect. Suprastate human rights apparatuses struggle to obtain recognition and compliance. Regional and global civil society initiatives, although sometimes notable (in cases such as Amnesty International and Médecins sans Frontières), are on the whole small and difficult to sustain.

In addition to these practical shortcomings, world federalism is also open to the previously mentioned deeper critiques of modern liberal democracy. Critical theories argue that world federalism merely regionalizes and globalizes the inherent flaws of modern national democracy. As a result, one would obtain regional and global capitalist hegemony (on Marxist readings), regional and global governmentality (on post-structuralist readings), regional and global patriarchy (on feminist readings), or regional and global anthropocentrism (on post-humanist readings). Indeed, critical theories could regard world federalism as a recipe for less, rather than more, democracy.

From a postcolonialist perspective, world federalism could also be faulted with Western imperialism (Rao 2010). Such a critique notes that however well-intentioned, world federalists presume the universal applicability of constructions of people's power that were developed in the specific historical context of modern White male middle-class Europe and the Americas. Today's proponents of world federalism, too, tend to be predominantly Western modern elite White men, with limited popular followings in wider global society. To this extent, critics may wonder how broadly and deeply the democratic roots of world federalist democracy can run.

Multistakeholderism

A fourth stream of global democracy thought and practice departs from the previous three approaches by looking beyond conventional liberal institutions of nation-states, political parties, and parliaments. Multistakeholder democracy reconfigures "representation" in governance, with a focus on functional rather than territorial constituencies. Such regulatory arrangements construct participation in decision-taking processes in terms of sectoral positions. Typically, multistakeholder bodies allocate seats for business, civil society, and government. Some also reserve roles for academe, consumers, marginalized groups, and technical circles. The underlying multistakeholder argument is that representation which relates to functional roles offers affected people suitable participation and control in (global) governance processes (Hallström and Boström 2010; Macdonald 2008).

One early instance of multistakeholder global governance is the International Labour Organization (ILO), founded in 1920, with delegates from employers, governments, and workers. Another pioneer is the International Organization for Standardization (ISO), founded in 1947, with participation from academe, consumer associations, government, industry groups, and nongovernmental organizations (NGOs). However, the multistakeholder principle has seen its main rise since the 1990s, with a proliferation of new arrangements for issue areas such as agriculture, corporate social responsibility, education, environment, and health. Concurrently, multistakeholder ideas have motivated IGOs and TGNs increasingly to pursue policy initiatives together with functional associations such as business federations, trade unions, and women's groups.

In some important respects, multistakeholder governance can bolster democratic prospects in a more global world. For one thing, reserving decision-taking positions for different affected sectors has brought a framework of systematic representation to private regulatory bodies such as the FSC and ICANN. In addition, stakeholder consultation by IGOs and TGNs opens channels of direct citizen access to multilateral institutions. More broadly, multistakeholder arrangements widen democratic horizons by inviting affected people to organize themselves not only on national lines but also in relation to whatever categories they deem relevant for their political participation in a given policy area. In particular, stakeholder communities need not be defined by territorial boundaries, which offers greater political space for the various nonterritorial publics that populate global politics.

However, many multistakeholder practices have also fallen short of their democratic promises. For example, many civil society associations complain that IGOs and TGNs do not seriously listen to and act upon stakeholder consultations. Meanwhile, multistakeholder decision-making apparatuses can be captured by insiders—that is, small circles of veteran participants who monopolize the key decision-making positions. Moreover, co-opted insiders can sometimes lose sight of their intended role as critical scrutinizers of the multistakeholder regime. In addition, stakeholder "representatives" can practice limited accountability toward their supposed "constituencies," with shortfalls in transparency, consultation, evaluation, and redress vis-à-vis their "people." Then the profile of multistakeholder bodies can show considerable geopolitical, social, and cultural hierarchies—for example, such that the "representatives" are disproportionately from the Global North, professional classes, and Westernized groups. In these ways and more, multistakeholderism can lose much of its democratic shine.

Deliberation

Along with multistakeholder governance, deliberation is another more recently developed theory and practice for the democratization of global politics (Dryzek 2010; Smith and Brassett 2008). In this approach, people's power is sought not through direct involvement in decision-taking processes but through engagement with a surrounding "global public sphere" of discussion and debate. The motivating principle of deliberative democracy is that affected people can enhance their participation in and control over the governance of global relations through dialogue: exchanging information, expressing views, elaborating principles, and developing proposals. Deliberation is thereby said to give the demos/demoi voice and—through pressures of "public opinion"—influence. The challenge for practice is then to design effective frameworks for deliberation.

Global deliberative democracy can be observed in a number of contemporary initiatives. For instance, the World Economic Forum (WEF), founded in 1971, has assembled global elites for public policy discussions at its annual meeting in Davos, as well as at various other gatherings throughout the year. The World Social Forum (WSF) was launched in 2001 to assemble social movements for deliberations concerning alternative global orders. The Internet Governance Forum (IGF) has since 2006 convened global, regional, and national deliberations about the regulation of this global communications apparatus. Further civil society forums have become a regular fixture alongside meetings of the UN, the G7, and other IGOs/TGNs. More ad hoc deliberative democracy regarding global affairs occurs through the press, new social media, civil society workshops, academic conferences, café encounters, and other settings where affected people come together to discuss and debate.

Deliberative forums certainly offer citizens important opportunities for involvement in global affairs. If designed well, these dialogues can include wide-ranging people in broad explorations of actual and prospective orderings of global spaces. Democratic deliberation can encompass diverse positions, embrace dissent, prize argumentation above interest lobbying, and make space for marginalized people. In such ways, deliberation can open larger democratic engagement—in terms of participants as well as views—than is generally found in decision-taking institutions.

That said, deliberative democracy has the major limitation of lacking decision-taking competence. Forums, mass media, workshops, and the like can shape the landscape of decision, but they do not actually decide. However much such dialogues might advance public participation and public control, it is bureaucracies which generally institutionalize the rules in contemporary society. Hence, for fuller effect, deliberative democracy has to be coupled with a complementary democratization of formal decision mechanisms.

Deliberation also has limited democratic consequence if it is merely talk, without accompanying mobilization to advance public will. Open and inclusive dialogue on global affairs can be significantly empowering for affected people, but the resulting visions and proposals want implementation as well. For that greater impact, one needs—in addition to ideas and vision—personal and group energy, effective organization, sufficient resources, and clever tactics, along with enough self-critique to maintain the movement's own democratic credentials.

Finally, global deliberative democracy is compromised to the extent that affected people have unequal access to the deliberative arenas. For example, the WEF is mainly the preserve of large corporations and major states. Meanwhile, only persons with sufficient funds can attend a faraway global WSF meeting. Likewise, the IGF and other civil society forums around the UN are disproportionately populated by individuals with structural advantages of age, class, gender, language, nationality, race, and region. Exclusion from deliberation also applies to people for whom open public debate is culturally alien as a mode of political expression. Thus, if full democracy entails that all affected people have *equivalent* possibilities of participation and control, then current global deliberative processes fall well short of that standard.

Resistance

Sixth in this classification of global democracy strategies is counter-hegemonic action (Amoore 2005). This category overlaps with previous schemes in instances such as radical localism (e.g., in food sovereignty movements) and more deeply critical deliberation (e.g., in certain quarters of the WSF). However, otherwise the preceding five approaches generally work within the prevailing social order. That is, they pursue democracy through *reform of existing institutions* rather than through *transformation of underlying societal structures*. In contrast, a resistance approach prescribes that veritable democracy requires dissidence toward and transcendence of embedded power hierarchies. Invoking notions of agonistic politics (Mouffe 2005)—where conflict can be positively productive—resistance perspectives hold that any reigning governance arrangement is liable to capture by repressive forces. Hence, (global) democracy is advanced when people refuse whatever arbitrary domination rules the day.

Counter-hegemonic resistance to established patterns of global politics is witnessed in various activities. Street demonstrations are one readily recognizable way to confront prevailing global power structures. Examples include "IMF riots" in the Global South as early as the 1970s, the so-called Anti-Globalization Movement around the turn of the millennium, and Occupy sit-ins during 2011–2012. Other resistance can involve noncompliance with existing rules (e.g., by anarchist hackers) and refusal of prevailing governance regimes (e.g., the Government of India's withdrawal from the Non-Proliferation Treaty). Meanwhile, everyday grass-roots dissent might involve actions such as boycotting products, parodying rulers, politicizing art (e.g., through graffiti, music, and theater), or turning off mainstream television news. In some cases, resistance movements pursue global democratic transformation through armed struggle, as seen in various anti-colonial scenarios.

In addition to employing diverse tactics, pursuit of global democracy through resistance encompasses widely varying strategic visions. For example, anti-capitalist movements seek democratic transformation of global order through a transcendence of surplus accumulation and associated class inequalities. Feminist resistances aim at overcoming global-scale patriarchal structures. Religious revivalisms target the prevailing secularism of global modernity. Postcolonialist struggles oppose arbitrary hierarchical binaries (e.g., north/south, man/woman, white/color, and straight/queer) in search of alternative and more empowering modes of identity politics. Poststructuralist theory and practice refuses the oppressive "governmentality" of disciplining discourses (e.g., global neoliberalism in the present day). Ecocentrists resist an anthropocentric global order in favor of an "earth democracy" that cares for the full web of life. As these examples indicate, global resistance has many streams that can as readily deviate from as ally with one another.

Agonistic democracy certainly opens important avenues for greater people's power in a global world. For example, resistance can provide involvement and influence for persons who generally obtain little hearing through reformist designs of global democracy. Thus, groups which are substantially locked out of the state, multilateral institutions, and multistakeholder bodies (e.g., Dalits, indigenous peoples, peasants, sexual diversities, urban poor, women, and youth) may turn to resistance as a way of political participation. In addition, resistance looks beyond institutional obstacles to popular voice and impact by also emphasizing deeper structural hindrances to democracy. Fuller people's power in global affairs will likely remain elusive unless embedded geopolitical, social, cultural, and ecological hierarchies are overcome. Indeed, the historical record suggests that governance regimes only make larger institutional advances on democracy in response to sustained counter-hegemonic resistance—for example, when feminist struggles exacted women's suffrage or when labor activism prompted social democracy. Without the pressures of resistance, the potentials of other approaches to global democracy are arguably limited.

That said, resistance offers no inherent panacea for global democracy either. A major practical difficulty is that these contestations of undemocratic world orders have generally been small-scale, fragmented, and short-lived. Contemporary global politics has not witnessed large sustained impactful opposition coalitions of the kind that spearheaded anti-colonialism in the twentieth century. Another challenge for many resistance movements has been to move beyond protest to proposal. Although counter-hegemonic visions of alternative globalizations are often rich in intuitive appeal, they can also be rather vague and/or impracticable. For example, what is entailed more precisely by a feminist global care economy or a post-human political ecology? Moreover, nothing guarantees that counter-hegemonic resistance leads to attractive outcomes, as experiences such as Stalinism and "Islamic State" attest. Indeed, some resistance movements can themselves have weak democratic credentials (low transparency, authoritarian leadership, male dominance, and so on).

Summary

Hence a wide range of institutional designs are available for the democratization of global politics. Some of these schemes reaffirm the democratic potentials of local and national government. Others seek people's power through expanded and reformed regional and global regulatory apparatuses, both public and private. Still others look to promote democracy outside governance bodies with deliberative and resistance programs.

All six strategy types distinguished here involve potential opportunities as well as possible limitations. How the promises and perils pan out in practice depends on the contextual conditions that surround particular scenarios. In current circumstances, for example, a multistakeholder approach might offer most for a democratic global governance of HIV/AIDS, whereas a resistance approach might most advance overall people's power in global finance. Given such variation, it could better serve global democracy to choose strategies pragmatically rather than ideologically. In other words, one should not embrace or reject any approach dogmatically, and instead carefully evaluate what each avenue could contribute in a given situation.

Indeed, the resulting judgment might be to combine several streams of action as the optimal way to advance people's power in the specific global context at hand. For instance, the food sovereignty movement has blended communitarianism in its local democracy strivings, multistakeholder democracy through the Committee on World Food Security, and resistance struggles against global corporate power. In another issue area, popular voice and influence vis-à-vis global digital spaces might be maximized through a mix of democratically based state legislation, multilateralism in the International Telecommunication Union (ITU), multistakeholder arrangements such as ICANN, deliberation at the IGF, and resistance through the Internet Social Forum (ISF). Hence, the menu of global democracy strategies set out here does not always require either–or choices and may on the contrary invite combining several courses.

GLOBAL DEMOCRACY: DEEPER STRUCTURES

The preceding section described and evaluated a variety of institutional designs to bring people's power into global affairs; however, the question of global democracy also extends further to the deeper ordering of society. As the discussion of resistance has already indicated, constraints on participation and control by affected people may lie not only in the ways that regulatory agencies operate but also in the overall organization of society. Indeed, no amount of institutional reform will yield adequate people's power if democratic failings in the "metagovernance" of social structure are not also addressed.

Indeed, as discussed earlier in this chapter, it is shifts in several deeper social structures which have prompted the contemporary need to reinvent democracy. Primary ordering principles of modern society assumed that geography would be organized in terms of countries, that community would be organized in terms of nations, and that governance would be organized in terms of states. As these patterns give way to others, precepts and practices of democracy need to adjust as well.

The remainder of this chapter discusses three further questions of deeper structure that need attention when pursuing democracy in globalized politics. The first concerns political economy and shortfalls of people's power which result from current highly unequal distributions of resources globally. A second metagovernance problem relates to politics of meaning and democratic deficits in prevailing ways of handling cultural diversity and difference in global affairs. A third deeper structural challenge for global democracy lies with existing anthropocentric patterns of political ecology. Across these three issues, the argument is that certain systemic changes are needed in order for all affected people to obtain due say in global politics. Note that a *transdisciplinary* global studies which encompasses economics, politics, culture, and ecology—as well as their interconnections—is especially suited to this structural analysis of planetary democracy.

Political Economy: Redistributing Resources

Like any democracy, people's power in global affairs has a crucial economic aspect. The public as a whole cannot have adequate voice and control in global politics so long as some or all affected persons lack sufficient material resources to pursue active political involvement. The presence of universal suffrage, impartial courts, stakeholder bodies, deliberative forums, and resistance movements is of limited practical use for people who must spend every ounce of energy securing basic subsistence. According to World Bank (2017) estimates, 10.7% of humanity lived on less than US$1.90 in 2013, and further large numbers have little more. Many others (disproportionately women) are overburdened with household cares that leave little scope for democratic engagement in wider society.

Alongside these obstacles of absolute poverty are additional hindrances to democracy that arise from economic inequalities. Even if all humanity were to have secure material welfare, unbalanced distributions of resources would still enable some people to have undue voice and influence relative to others. This is evident, for example, when concentrated financial and media power sways elections.

Today's global world, sees enormous economic gaps. For example, the global-scale Gini coefficient (measuring the distribution of household incomes) may lie as high as 70 (Milanovic 2012), compared with the EU average of around 30. As of 2008, the top 5% of households worldwide earned 245 times more than the bottom 25% (Milanovic 2013). As of 2014, the wealthiest 1% of humanity owned 48.2% of all assets, whereas the bottom 50% held less than 1% (Credit Suisse 2014: 11). Such staggering inequalities—where a global public includes multibillionaires alongside landless peasants—put paid to any genuine democracy. Due opportunities for participation go hand in hand with equitable distributions of resources.

On this political economy diagnosis, any program of democratic global politics would require major elements of poverty eradication and resource redistribution. The two are intertwined inasmuch as elimination of absolute poverty depends on redistribution in order to provide basic education, health, and shelter for those who currently lack them. Likewise, proposals for universal basic income, which would guarantee a living wage for everyone across the planet, depend on transfers of resources from the higher endowed.

However, redistribution for democracy does not stop with raising all human lives above a subsistence level. It extends also to providing all people with the material bases to engage meaningfully in public life. These additional resources could include time outside work to broaden political awareness, learning English as the de facto lingua franca of global governance, internet access for effective political communication, and travel funds to attend face-to-face global gatherings. Increased economic productivity from technological advances and the like can generate some of these extra resources for democratic participation. However, fuller democratization of global politics also requires significant transfers from the greater to the lesser endowed.

Global redistribution involves resource transfers between as well as within countries. Even if national redistribution could bring every country's Gini coefficient to the Scandinavian level of around 25, large economic inequalities between countries would continue to impede global democracy. Proactive redistribution among countries has already occurred on a modest scale, for example, through the regional policy of the EU and so-called "development assistance" from the Global North to the Global South. However, much larger transfers could be achieved by means of global taxes—for example, on financial transactions, profits of transnational corporations, patent registrations, and international airline and cruise tickets. Revenue from global taxes that mainly impact the well-off could be reallocated to provide greater life chances for those with fewer means.

Finally, a more level material playing field for contemporary democracy could be reached through reconstructions of global regimes. Today's large global economic inequalities result in good part from rules that give arbitrary advantages to the rich and powerful. For example, the use of certain national currencies as global monies—particularly the US dollar since 1945—has accrued enormous material gains to the countries concerned. A regime based on suprastate currency units (e.g., the existing but only modestly used Special Drawing Right) could reduce these unwarranted privileges. More even global economic distribution could also be advanced through rule changes with respect of global communications, intellectual property, migration, and trade (Scholte et al. 2016).

In summary, institutional designs of whatever kind offer only a limited recipe for global democracy if they are not coupled with global distributive justice. Unfortunately, most writing and advocacy on communitarianism, multilateralism, world federalism, multistakeholderism, and global deliberative democracy have not addressed problems of economic inequality. Global capitalism as currently organized—leaving several billion people in destitution and a few million with enormous wealth—forms a major structural barrier to meaningful democracy.

Political Culture: Renegotiating Differences

Alongside problems associated with economic structure, other metagovernance challenges for global democracy have a cultural character. "Culture" refers here to processes of constructing, communicating, and consuming meaning—through language, symbols, rituals, and other practices. Democracy is realized not only through institutional set-ups and political–economic arrangements but also through life-worlds and life-ways. Meaningful democracy requires that the people involved *feel* that they have due voice, participation, and control. Veritable democracy is not a top-down dictionary definition but a bottom-up lived experience.

Chief among the cultural challenges for democracy in contemporary global affairs is the question of difference. People live the contemporary global world very differently. These divergences are manifested in highly variable vocabularies, beliefs, values, rituals, narratives, and aesthetics. Pronounced cultural conflicts arise in global politics with regard to matters such as death penalties, divine will, ecological care, and sexual practices. How can people's power be constructed so that it is experienced to be democratic across multiple and, in some respects, incommensurable life-worlds?

For instance, an elderly Black rural straight Muslim woman career of the mentally ill in Africa experiences a very different global world than a young White metropolitan agnostic able-bodied queer man banker in Europe. Yet both can be deeply affected—and sometimes quite directly interconnected—by global lending, climate change, global disease, global trade, global migration, and so on. What kind of global-scale democracy can encompass and honor such cultural differences?

Western modernity has generally responded to cultural difference by prescribing universal assimilation to its own lifeworld. Thus, "the West" is held to have attained the most enlightened knowledge, which the rest of humanity should emulate. The "advanced countries" are in this view leading the way on a single path of progress that the "less developed" should follow. From this perspective, deviations from Western rationalities are "backward," and the response to cultural difference is to erase it, as everyone everywhere boards the same historical train with its Western locomotive. Indeed, many advocates and critics alike have assumed that "globalization" entails cultural homogenization through the universalization of Western–modern lifeways.

The presumption of assimilation to Western models has also underpinned many theorizations of democracy in today's global world. For example, widely cited Freedom House reports have rather indiscriminately applied one set of (Western–modern) definitions and indicators of democracy across the planet. As noted previously, world federalist thinking similarly advocates that all humanity should adopt the formula of competitive multiparty elections, civil society activism, bills of rights, impartial courts, and so on. Also in an assimilationist vein, multilateralist formulas for global democracy assume that all parties across the planet will organize themselves in terms of a modern country–nation–state and follow the rules of Western diplomacy.

To be sure, Western life-worlds and their particular forms of democracy have provided countless people with meaningful experiences of political voice and influence. However, it does not follow that Western–modern designs provide the only or necessarily always the most suitable framework for democracy across all cultural contexts. For example, so-called "failed states" may result from a cultural misfit between modern institutions and local contexts rather than from "backwardness." Indeed, Western modernity has historically accumulated much undemocratic violence toward difference. Consider, for example, the suppression of indigenous peoples, the colonization of the Global South, and the neoliberalization of former communist-ruled areas.

Critiques of the undemocratic cultural imperialism of Western modernity have often been articulated from a multiculturalist position. Rejecting the monoculturalist aspirations of assimilationism, multiculturalism holds that humanity is divided into mutually exclusive "identities" with deeply incommensurate life-worlds. One common multiculturalist formulation identifies a global-scale "clash of civilizations" with different religious heritages (Huntington 1997). Multiculturalism can also highlight other purportedly irreconcilable oppositions—for example, between aboriginal and modern life-worlds, between queer and straight lifeways, or between older and younger generations. Communitarian emphases on cultural incompatibilities between nations also reflect a multiculturalist outlook.

For multiculturalism, deep divergences over fundamental values make it advisable to limit interactions and interdependencies between different life-worlds in global politics.

It is assumed that beyond superficial exchanges, encounters of difference invariably breed insecurity and violence. Hence, cross-cultural contacts are best minimized, and ambitions for global cooperation are best tempered. For multiculturalists, the default position for democracy in a global world is cultural separation and respectful mutual tolerance.

Although multiculturalism has advantages over assimilationism in terms of recognizing the existence and importance of difference, other cornerstones of this approach are untenable. For one thing, humanity does not divide neatly into discrete cultural groupings. Difference is far more complex than a "clash of civilizations" or other binary oppositions of "the self" and "the other." In practice, culture involves multiple and intersecting lifeways, as variously connected with age, ethnicity, faith, gender, nationality, profession, sexual orientation, and more. The notion of carving up the global population into a single set of neatly separated and self-contained "cultures" is unworkable. There is no "American," "Islamic," "youth," or other "identity" unto itself. Within each supposed cultural unit, there are dense cross-cultural linkages that dissolve its supposed coherence. Democracy in a global world needs a much more sophisticated and nuanced understanding of difference than multiculturalism provides.

In any case, far-ranging and profound global interconnectedness in today's society puts paid to any multiculturalist scheme for separatism. Contemporary global travel, communications, migrations, value chains, financial flows, ecological changes, and so on mean that encounters among cultural differences are inescapably frequent and intense. Different religions cannot sidestep each other in a global city. Different sexual practices cannot bypass each other in global media. Different academic disciplines cannot—and should not—evade each other in the face of global research and policy challenges. The multiculturalist prescription of handling difference by avoiding it is simply not practicable in a deeply global world.

So how does one neither deny difference (with assimilationism) nor skirt difference (with multiculturalism), but instead engage and negotiate difference? An alternative of "transculturalism" would construct global democracy with and through (rather than against) difference (Mignolo and Schiwy 2003; Welsch 1999). In such a vision, cultural difference is not a problem to be overcome but, rather, an opportunity to be seized. Following a transculturalist path, diversity and incommensurability of life-worlds do not obstruct democracy but, rather, widen possibilities for dynamic, creative, adaptive expressions of people's power.

Space limitations prevent full elaboration here of seven core tenets that could underpin a transculturalist global democracy (Scholte 2015). In brief, however, a first pillar would entail deep reflexivity on the part of everyone involved in a given global negotiation. Reflexivity (which is so lacking in assimilationist strategies) means that each participant in a global dialogue seeks to be (a) maximally aware of their specific contextualized position in relation to the policy problem and (b) acutely conscious that other parties come at the issue from different cultural locations. Second, transculturalist ethics involve high sensitivity to knowledge/power relations, whereby social structures assign some life-worlds greater force than others. Open acknowledgment of, and honest discussion about, such cultural hierarchies can help reduce their impact and counter arbitrary silencing of subordinated voices. Third, transculturalism depends on recognizing the kind of complexity and nuance of diversities that multiculturalism generally fails to appreciate. In this way, democracy can honor the intricacies of actually lived political experiences rather than slip into artificially simplified and essentialized identity politics that are readily exploited by demagogues. Fourth, transculturalism has a default position of celebrating cultural diversity. Thus, difference is welcomed as a positive resource unless and until a specific concrete situation presents an unpalatable challenge (e.g., female genital cutting or neo-Nazism). Yet, even when confronted by differences that seem morally offensive, transculturalism prescribes a fifth tenet of humility. This recognition of the severe limits of one's experience—how little one understands of unfamiliar circumstances—can encourage a course of dialogue and persuasion rather than immediate polarization and violence. Humility in turn fosters a sixth principle of transculturalism, namely deep listening to otherness. This practice involves concentrated, meticulous, patient attention in order maximally to hear the cultural other. One does not have to agree with or like the bearer of difference, but deep listening can generate understanding of how others have come to believe what they do, thereby enhancing possibilities for trust and cooperation. Finally, transculturalist politics urge learning for mutual change. Whereas conventional approaches often presume that life-worlds are fixed, transculturalism posits that ways of knowing are forever in flux and that encounters with difference can, when constructively pursued, enrich the experiences of all parties.

These seven tenets of transculturalism can in principle be applied to most of the previously discussed institutional designs for democracy in a global world. True the paradigm runs counter to communitarianism, which has little time for cultural complexity, celebrations of diversity, humility in the face of unpalatable differences, deep listening, and learning toward mutual change. However, tenets of transculturalism can be enacted in—and advance democracy through—multilateral institutions, world federalist schemes, multistakeholder arrangements, deliberative forums, and resistance movements.

That said, implementing transculturalism presents major challenges. The current global world is steeped in deeply entrenched habits of both West-centric assimilationism and segregational multiculturalism. Reorientation to a largely untried alternative knowledge politics requires substantial doses of imagination and courage.

Political Ecology: Democracy Within a Web of Life

As much, if not more, creativity and struggle are wanted to address—and reconstruct—the underlying ecological structure of democracy. Indeed, modern democratic theory and practice have generally remained silent regarding ecology, on the assumption that people's power is a question of "society" as divorced from "nature." Yet, ecological changes of the contemporary more global world arguably call into question the tenability of this anthropocentric construction of democracy.

Modern democracy has treated the human species in isolation from the wider web of life. As such, democracy of the country–nation–state has embodied the anthropocentrism born of early modernity: It concerns rule by, for, from, of, to, and within humanity. Modern people's power involves no rights and responsibilities beyond *Homo sapiens*.

Anthropocentrism is an ecological structure—that is, a socially constructed ordering of relations between human beings and the overall biosphere. Its core premises include (1) separating humanity and its society from "the environment"; (2) assuming the superiority and greater importance of the human species over other life; (3) affirming the prerogative of *Homo sapiens* to exploit the rest of nature for humanity's sole benefit; and

(4) regarding the ability to master and alter nature—with "science" and "technology"—as the foremost human achievement. Like other social structures—perhaps even more so—anthropocentrism is so deeply embedded in modern democracy that it is rarely made explicit, let alone challenged.

Yet, contemporary globalization has involved ecological developments that demand greater awareness and closer scrutiny of anthropocentrism. Population growth, climate change, resource depletions, and various pollutions are bringing large and increasing global-scale human interventions into the web of life on Earth. In this light, new vocabulary of an "Anthropocene" has attracted increasing attention to designate an emergent era in which the human species figures as a significant autonomous force in eco-systemic processes.

If the proposition of an Anthropocene is accepted, then it calls into question the ecological silence in prevailing constructions of democracy. What may be wanted is a shift from "citizenship" (with its focus on rights and responsibilities among human beings) to "eco-ship" (with an alternative emphasis on care for the broader web of life). The precise form of such "post-humanism" is far from clear (Cudworth and Hobden 2017), but explorations of "earth democracy" and "Gaian democracy" are suitably underway (Madron and Jopling 2003; Shiva 2005).

Conclusion

This chapter has enquired into the conditions and prospects of democracy in contemporary globalized social relations. The discussion first established that today's intensified globality substantially contradicts modern constructions of democracy based on country-nation–state containers. The chapter then described and evaluated six general institutional designs for advancing people's power in a more global society. It was suggested not to apply any model singly or rigidly but, rather, to promote democratic global politics through combinations of the approaches, with variation depending on the concrete situation at hand. The remainder of the chapter argued that in addition to institutional steps, democratization of today's global world also requires shifts in the "metagovernance" of deeper structures. In this regard, particular attention was given to economic redistribution, alternative cultural politics, and reconsidered political ecology.

Certainly, the institutional and structural aspects of democracy are mutually constitutive and co-dependent. Thus, undemocratic deeper structures are reflected in, and also perpetuated by, undemocratic institutional arrangements. Likewise, democratization of structures (through resource redistribution, transculturalism, and post-humanism) would generate, and also depend on, democratization of institutions (through some combination of communitarian, multilateral, world federalist, multistakeholder, deliberative, and resistance measures). Institutional governance and structural metagovernance are two sides of the democratic coin. Strategies for global democracy need to encompass both.

prospects for such democratization of global affairs are rather discouraging at the time of this writing in 2017. Adversarial communitarian multiculturalism marks many national governments and public spaces. In this environment, world federalism is scarcely discussed, multilateralism is generally stalled, multistakeholderism is mostly limited to technical standard-setting, and resistance is sporadic. Global economic redistribution and new political ecologies struggle to get attention, let alone application. Skeptical readers may regard this chapter as wistful intellectual speculation.

Yet, such dismissals could be premature. After all, ideas of modern democracy related to the country–nation–state took several centuries to move from initial articulation to substantial implementation. Indeed, as late as the 1930s, prevailing views still assumed that national self-government was a distant prospect for the Global South. Then it took but three decades for apparent pipedreams to become common sense. The years ahead may well also take quick and unexpected turns, and it will be vital to have good ideas ready when future moments are ripe for advances in democratic global politics. It is a key normative task for global studies to foster such ideas and encourage the accompanying practices.

NOTE

1. In this chapter, "regional" refers to macro-regions covering multiple countries rather than micro-regions within a country.

REFERENCES

Amoore, Louise, ed. 2005. *The Global Resistance Reader*. Abingdon, UK: Routledge.

Archibugi, Daniele. 2008. *The Global Commonwealth of Citizens: Toward Cosmopolitan Democracy*. Princeton, NJ: Princeton University Press.

Archibugi, Daniele, Mathias Koenig-Archibugi, and Raffaele Marchetti, eds. 2012. *Global Democracy: Normative and Empirical Perspectives*. Cambridge, UK: Cambridge University Press.

Bello, Walden. 2004. *Deglobalization: Ideas for a New World Economy*. London: Zed.

Bohman, James. 2007. *Democracy Across Borders: From Dêmos to Dêmoi*. Cambridge, MA: MIT Press.

Bray, Daniel, and Steven Slaughter. 2015. *Global Democratic Theory: A Critical Introduction*. Cambridge, UK: Polity.

Cabrera, Luis. 2010. "World Government: Renewed Debate, Persistent Challenges." *European Journal of International Relations* 16 (3): 511–531.

Credit Suisse. 2014. *Global Wealth Report 2014*. Zurich: Credit Suisse Research Institute.

Cudworth, Erika, and Stephen Hobden. 2017. *The Emancipatory Project of Posthumanism*. Abingdon, UK: Routledge.

Dahl, Robert A. 1999. Can international organizations be democratic? A skeptic's view. In *Democracy's Edges*, edited by I. Shapiro and C. Hacker-Cordón, 19–36. Cambridge, UK: Cambridge University Press.

De Wilde, Jaap. 2011. "The Mirage of Global Democracy." *European Review* 19 (1): 5–18.

Dingwerth, Klaus. 2007. *The New Transnationalism: Transnational Governance and Democratic Legitimacy*. Basingstoke, UK: Palgrave Macmillan.

Dryzek, John S. 2010. *Foundations and Frontiers of Deliberative Governance*. Oxford, UK: Oxford University Press.

Fraser, Nancy. 2007. "Transnationalizing the Public Sphere: On the Legitimacy and Efficacy of Public Opinion in a Post-Westphalian World." *Theory, Culture & Society* 24 (4): 7–30.

Habermas, Jürgen. 2001. *The Postnational Constellation*. Cambridge, UK: Polity.

Hallström, Kristina T., and Magnus Boström. 2010. *Transnational Multi-Stakeholder Standardization*. Cheltenham, UK: Elgar.

Held, David. 1995. *Democracy and the Global Order*. Cambridge, UK: Polity.

Hines, Colin. 2000. *Localization: A Global Manifesto*. London: Earthscan.

Huntington, Samuel P. 1997. *The Clash of Civilizations and the Remaking of World Order*. New York: Simon & Schuster.

Keohane, Robert O., Stephen Macedo, and Andrew Moravcsik. 2009. "Democracy-Enhancing Multilateralism." *International Organization* 63 (1): 1–31.

Macdonald, Terry. 2008. *Global Stakeholder Democracy: Power and Representation Beyond Liberal States*. Oxford, UK: Oxford University Press.

Madron, Roy, and John Jopling. 2003. *Gaian Democracies*. Totnes, UK: Green Books.

Mignolo, Walter D., and Freya Schiwy. 2003. "Transculturation and the Colonial Difference: Double Translation." In *Translation and Ethnography: The Anthropological Challenge of Intercultural Understanding*, edited by Tullio Maranhão and Bernhard Streck, 12–34. Tucson: University of Arizona Press.

Milanovic, Branko. 2012. "Global Income Inequality by the Numbers: In History and Now." Policy Research Working Paper No. 6259. World Bank Development Research Group, Poverty and Inequality Team, Washington, DC.

Milanovic, Branko. 2013. Author's personal communication with Professor Thomas Pogge, Yale University, January 4, citing unpublished data provided by Branko Milanovic, Lead Economist at the World Bank.

Miller, David. 1995. *On Nationality*. Oxford, UK: Oxford University Press.

Moravcsik, Andrew. 2004. "Is There a 'Democratic Deficit' in World Politics? A Framework for Analysis." *Government and Opposition*, 39 (2): 336–363.

Mouffe, Chantal. 2005. *On the Political*. London: Routledge.

O'Brien, Robert, Anne-Marie Goetz, Jan Aart Scholte, and Marc Williams. 2000. *Contesting Global Governance: Multilateral Economic Institutions and Global Social Movements*. Cambridge, UK: Cambridge University Press.

Rao, Rahul. 2010. *Third World Protest: Between Home and the World*. Oxford, UK: Oxford University Press.

Scholte, Jan Aart. 2004. *Democratizing the Global Economy: The Role of Civil Society*. Coventry, UK: Centre for the Study of Globalisation and Regionalisation.

Scholte, Jan Aart. 2005. *Globalization: A Critical Introduction*. 2nd ed. Basingstoke, UK: Palgrave Macmillan.

Scholte, Jan Aart. 2010. "Governing a More Global World." *Corporate Governance* 10 (4): 459–474.

Scholte, Jan Aart, ed. 2011. *Building Global Democracy? Civil Society and Accountable Global Governance*. Cambridge, UK: Cambridge University Press.

Scholte, Jan Aart. 2012. "A More Inclusive Global Governance? The IMF and Civil Society in Africa." *Global Governance* 18 (2): 185–206.

Scholte, Jan Aart. 2014. "Reinventing Global Democracy." *European Journal of International Relations* 20 (1): 3–28.

Scholte, Jan Aart, ed. 2015. *Global Cooperation Through Cultural Diversity: Remaking Democracy?* Global Dialogues 8. Duisburg, Germany: Centre for Global Cooperation Research.

Scholte, Jan Aart. 2017. "Polycentrism and Democracy in Internet Governance." In *The Net and the Nation State: Multidisciplinary Perspectives on Internet Governance*, edited by Uta Kohl, 165–184. Cambridge, UK: Cambridge University Press.

Scholte, Jan Aart, Lorenzo Fioramonti, and Alfred Nhema, eds. 2016. *New Rules for Global Justice: Structural Redistribution in the Global Economy*. London: Rowman & Littlefield International.

Shiva, Vandana. 2005. *Earth Democracy*. Boston, MA: South End.

Smith, Will, and James Brassett. 2008. "Deliberation and Global Governance: Liberal, Cosmopolitan, and Critical Perspectives." *Ethics & International Affairs* 22 (1): 69–92.

Tännsjö, Torbjörn. 2008. *Global Democracy: The Case for a World Government*. Edinburgh, UK: Edinburgh University Press.

Welsch, Wolfgang. 1999. "Tranculturality—The Puzzling Form of Cultures Today." In *Spaces of Culture: City, Nation, World*, edited by Mike Featherstone and Scott Lash, 194–213. London: Sage.

World Bank. 2017. "Poverty Overview." http://www.worldbank.org/en/topic/poverty/overview.

CHAPTER 27

....

IMPOVERISHMENT IN
THE ANTHROPOCENE

....

UPENDRA BAXI

"POVERTY" is a term usually used in global social policy literature, but for the most part, one really means impoverishment—a term that I have recommended for nearly three decades. Since the late 1980s,[1] I have urged, to no avail, that scholars as well as political and significant social movement actors everywhere should endeavor to distinguish between "poverty" and "impoverishment"—the latter being a dynamic process of social, economic, and political decisions whereby certain people are made and kept impoverished.

When social and political choices are made between acceptable levels of impoverishment and models of development, these place economic development and growth at a higher footing than social welfare, social protection, and human rights. These choices are guided, first, by the meta-decision that counsels that "poverty" cannot be altogether eliminated; it can only be alleviated by some addressal of its worst aspects, such as hunger, thirst, shelter, and health, generally known as "absolute poverty" or "extreme poverty." This kind of extreme impoverishment has been a target of eradication from the world scene. Other forms of impoverishment—conditions of "relative poverty"—are associated with ills of social vulnerability and exclusion generally, causing human disempowerment and human rightlessness. These conditions, circumstances, and contexts are left to be managed over time by policies and programs of "poverty" alleviation. Furthermore, as discussed in detail later, these policies of alleviation entail the twin notions of a "social minimum" and "core rights."

World "poverty" has been at the center of global concern since the advent of the Third World. The United Nations, since the 1974 international population conference, has accentuated monitoring the implementation of their goals and recommendations. The Cairo International Conference on Population and Development,1994, recommended actions be taken to "measure, assess, monitor and evaluate progress towards meeting the goals of its Programme of Action." This is so primarily because of the effects of deindustrialization, which was a planned policy of colonial administration,[2] although other causes may also be located—such as the nature of pre-colonial rule, internecine regional and ethnic conflicts, systemic governance corruption, slow emergence of an active civil society, and patterns of geopolitics. I do not burden this essay with further listing of "causes" and itineraries' of these processes and a vast literature but certainly impoverishment is not a causeless effect, even when many causes contribute to the effect of relative or absolute "poverty." Ever since violent and nonviolent (as in the case of India) struggles for self-determination from colonial sovereignty and governance prevailed, and (in Frantz Fanon's (2008) words) "black skins and white masks" appeared on national scenes, the Euromerican tendency has been to blame the "darker nations"[3] for failing to display leadership, thus perpetuating the nature of precolonial rule, internecine regional and ethnic conflicts, systemic governance corruption, slow emergence of an active civil society, and patterns of geopolitics. I do not burden this chapter by further listing the "causes" and "itineraries" of these processes (and a vast literature), but certainly impoverishment is not a causeless effect, even when many causes contribute to the effect of relative or absolute "poverty." Poverty alleviation and the allied notion of "failed states" have been used as an international law category for humanitarian intervention (Falk 2014a, 2014b; Orford 2005). The "population bomb" argument has also been countered by the idea that development is the "best contraceptive" (Ehrlich 1968/1995). Since the 1974 international population conference, the United Nations (UN) has accentuated monitoring the implementation of their goals and recommendations. The Cairo International Conference on Population and Development (1994) recommended actions be taken to "measure, assess, monitor and evaluate progress towards meeting the goals of its Programme of Action." Certainly, high population growth (especially in India and China) has enabled barbaric exploitation of human suffering and the production of human rightlessness, and this is not limited to the Global South.[4]

Many international normative developments have all but effaced the claim for compensation, rehabilitation, and resettlement of the Third World peoples. The most notable was the effort by the Third World to have the General Assembly of the UN enact a minimal obligation on the developed nations to aid the Third World countries and the effort to enunciate the New International Order and the World Information Order. The failures are as notable as they are instructive. So are some recent efforts at resolute demands for international reparations. The 2001 United Nations World Conference against Racism, Racial Discrimination, Xenophobia and Related Intolerance (Durban, South Africa) reinforced demands for reparations against the Euro-American world both for the "crimes against humanity" of African colonialism and for the Atlantic slave trade. In its place, "aid" and "trade" have been urged as accelerating economic development, indeed to a point of supplementation by the international financial institution-prescribed "bitter medicine" of polices directed to "structural adjustment."[5]

William Easterly (2003) finds that

> IMF [International Monetary Fund] and World Bank adjustment lending lowers the growth elasticity of poverty, that is, the amount of change in poverty rates for a given amount of growth. This means that economic expansions benefit the poor less under structural adjustment, but at the same time economic contractions hurt the poor less.

But he is sensitive to a "political economy" perspective that suggests "growth under structural programs is less pro-poor than in economies not under structural adjustment programs" even when "contractions under structural adjustment hurt the poor less than contractions not under structural adjustment programs" (Easterly 2003). Serious questions have been raised about this; for example, Edwin M. Truman (2001), in his comments on Easterly's paper, finds that adoption of "a broad and misleading definition of structural adjustment lending by the IFIs [international financial institutions]" tends to "lump essentially all types of IMF lending together with various types of World Bank structural adjustment lending." He also maintains that

> it is one thing to think that adjustment in an economy, no matter how defined or supported, has a minimal direct and immediate impact on the informal sector and, therefore, on poverty, but that is not the same as being irrelevant. In the longer run, the overall efficiency of the economy does matter because we expect that as a consequence of growth the poorest will move from the informal sector to the formal sector.

The articulation, near the end of the Cold War, of the "right to development" eventually led to the eight Millennium Development Goals (MDGs) that were established following the Millennium Summit of the United Nations in 2000, following the adoption of the United Nations Millennium Declaration. All 189 UN member states (there are currently 193) and at least 22 international organizations committed to help achieve the MDGs by 2015. The goals and the accompanying targets were geared specifically to eradicate extreme poverty and hunger; achieve universal primary education; promote gender equality and empower women; reduce child mortality; improve maternal health; combat HIV/AIDS, malaria, and other diseases; ensure environmental sustainability; and develop a global partnership for development. Annual reports were published by the UN concerning the various states of achievement of the goals and targets.

The goals were welcomed as setting an international development paradigm, especially privileging vulnerable humans and entities in nature. Expectations were high (and the goals frequently met with an extended timeline) and attainments incommensurate. Many found the enunciation of goals unclear and ambivalent; many simply found the goals to be unrealistic, setting a "legitimacy" trap. Others questioned methods of measurement and reportage. Still others raised the question of the efficacy of international action and collaboration (Kabeer 2005; Rosenfield, Maine, and Freedman 2006). The UN Millennium Development Program (since 1995) is now substituted by the Sustainable Development Programme,[6] which also defines the talk about post-development. In this "postist" world, we need to distinguish four related but differing notions: post-Fordism, post-development, post-neoliberalism, and post-human.[7] These trends continue to reinforce the same normative tendency of making governance and development human-rights friendly without laying down any precise obligation to remove global "poverty."

This chapter does not explore Third Worldism as a state of disorganized global social consciousness, the rights of reparation due to colonialism, and related areas such as the conditions and circumstances of high indebtedness of the "developing" countries and the austerity regimes as an antidote. Instead, it focuses on impoverishment and justice as these begin to appear from the vantage point of the Anthropocene.

SOCIAL MINIMUM AND CORE RIGHTS

The twin notions of social acceptance of "minimum" and "core" rights have guided the itineraries of the normative endeavor to relate "poverty" alleviation with images and standards of human rights, particularly "freedom from want" and a progressively more just (egalitarian) world order. These notions were long in gestation but found a clear enunciation in the labors of the UN treaty body on Economic, Social and Cultural Rights (ESCR) only in 2001. The ESCR does not mention "poverty" as such, although it provides the "rights to work, an adequate standard of living, housing, food, health and education, which lie at the heart" of the Covenant and which have "a direct and immediate bearing upon the eradication of poverty." It was only in 2001 that, in a major instrument adopted by the UN ESCR Committee, an effort was made to "integrate" human rights with anti-"poverty" strategies (Committee on Economic, Social and Cultural Rights (CESCR) 2001). Although Article 28 of the Universal Declaration of Human Rights entitled "everybody" to "a social and international order in which the rights and freedoms set forth in this Declaration can be fully realized," it is generally doubted that the Declaration recognized global impoverishment. A mere comparison with the Charter of Philadelphia, the cornerstone of the International Labour Organization, proves this point (Supiot 2012). The way the Committee proceeded with this task is crucial, and its key features are summarized next.

First, the Committee makes an important prefatory statement that although "human rights are not a panacea," they "can help to equalize the distribution and exercise of power within and between societies" (CESCR 2001, para. 6). Certainly, reiterating the world of human rights as a panacea does not help us grasp the contemporary predicament. Richard Falk poignantly highlights living on the edge when speaking about the "community of despair" within which one has to perform human rights.[8] If the normative limits of human rights (rules and standards) stand clearly acknowledged, so are stressed the normative and institutional opportunities of concerted action by global social policy and protest actors. The CESCR's statement that impoverishment affects all nations is noteworthy because it helps dispel the standard myth that it is a structural property only of the darker nations (para. 5).

Second, in finding that in "all States, women and girls bear a disproportionate burden of poverty, and children growing up in poverty are often permanently disadvantaged," the Committee adopts the view that "greater empowerment of women in particular is an essential precondition for the eradication of global poverty" (CESCR 2001, para. 5). Third, it recognizes "poverty's broader features, such as hunger, poor education, discrimination, vulnerability and social exclusion"; this reference to broader features notes that this "understanding of poverty corresponds with numerous provisions" of the ESRC Covenant (para. 7). Particularly, vulnerability and social exclusion define the salient features of later efforts at defining human rights.[9]

From these follow, fourth, the notion of "core rights." In 1990, the Committee adopted the view that "core obligation" lay in ensuring "the satisfaction of, at the very least, minimum essential levels of each of the rights" enunciated in the Covenant. It even stated that in the absence of such rights and obligations, the Covenant "would be largely deprived of its *raison de etre*" (CESCR 2001, para 15). It states explicitly that the "core obligations give rise to national responsibilities for all States and international responsibilities for developed States, as well as others that are 'in a position to assist'" (para. 16). The core obligations exist at all times, including "conflict, emergency and natural disaster"; the obligations have "great relevance to some individuals and communities living in the richest States" and cast corresponding duties on the ratifying states, "an obligation to move as expeditiously and effectively as possible towards the full realization of all the rights in the Covenant" (para. 16).

The Committee accordingly recommended "strongly . . . the integration of international human rights norms into participatory, multi-sectoral national poverty eradication or re-duction plans," adding that such "anti-poverty plans have an indispensable role to play in all States, no matter what their stage of economic development" (CESCR 2001, para. 19). However, it also reiterated that "the structural obstacles confronting developing States" anti-poverty strategies lie beyond their control in the contemporary international order (para. 21). It identified some of these as "unsustainable foreign debt, the widening gap be-tween rich and poor, and the absence of an equitable multilateral trade, investment and financial system" (para. 21).

Welcome as this paradigm is, there are a few issues that still should be considered. The Committee makes a mighty shift in considering human rights as integral to development policies and programs but is quite reluctant in extending even core human right obligations to multinational corporations and direct foreign investors. Not recognized is the global so-cial fact that these latter are among the chief "structural obstacles" to "poverty" alleviation policies.

The Committee also begins to include such general metanorms as "non-discrimina-tion" and "social inclusion." But the types of economic inequality vary, as all development economists learn early on: Interstate and global inequalities of income, consumption, as-sets, wealth, and enjoyment are difficult to measure in simple, single, and stark indicators. Whereas gender economics specify many forms of inequality between men and women, the many struggles of the ancient indigenous communities depict civilizational inequalities. Not all peoples exposed to human rights violations and human- and global structure-imposed social suffering seek Paretean maximization or the social wealth-maximizing satisfaction of their preferences. People living with disabilities, LGBT folks, refugees and asylum-seekers, survivors of mass disasters and catastrophes caused by multinational enterprises, and victims of human trafficking display a different kind of social vulnerability. The general point is that not all discrimination results in the same or similar inequalities and vulnerabilities, and "core" human rights norms do not extend to all human rights norms and standards.

A further question is raised by movements such as the Occupy and the 99/1% movements. They are different from movements such as the Czech uprising and the Arab Spring, which seek long-deferred core human rights. Margot Salomon (2011: 3) has captured this mood rather well when she asks,

> While human rights law is concerned with poverty, should it also be concerned with the fact that the poor are poorer *than others*? For a code premised on meeting universal minimum standards and levels of rights, why should it matter that others have more? (emphasis in the original)

In any event, normativity has lately flourished (founded on the Committee statement thus far examined), having yielded MDGs that in turn have been replaced by Sustainable Development Goals (SDGs) and the Agenda 2030 framework at the UN. We do not here ex-amine these developments save to observe that, aspirationally, the linkages between global social policy and impoverishment are understood at least as posing normative priority (Pogge 2010; Prada 2011).

THE ALIBI TENDENCIES

Much has been written positing a human right to poverty alleviation, and some very practical steps have been suggested to achieve "real-world justice" (to borrow the phrase from Thomas Pogge).[10] We mention here only in passing the UNESCO contribution to the need to promote international cooperation in combating poverty from a human rights perspective. It has valuably explored human rights dimensions of impoverishment in four volumes addressing some philosophical, legal, political science, and economic perspectives. Normatively, alleviation from impoverishment is considered an aspect of intergenerational justice, and both national and global theories of justice approach alleviation this way. It is considered difficult universally to prescribe a timeline even for a minimal management of impoverishment. That is the Cold War rationale for the "manifesto rights" in the UN ESRC. To grasp this rationale is a difficult task, but some salient trends can be readily identified.

First is the politics of denial in the sense that ESCRs are not legally human rights because they are said not to be enforceable at law courts, can never be "violated" as enforceable human rights can be, and are aspirational rather than having any duty-creating aspects. This view is mistaken, but it persists. Very few actors—political leaders and parties, civil servants and intergovernmental bureaucrats, and international organizations—ever fully publicly state that their decisions may cause and aggravate impoverishment. Few acknowledge causal links between systemic governance corruption and impoverishment; few acknowledge that public action against it is a measure of impoverishment alleviation, despite the United Nations Convention against Corruption (which entered into force on December 14, 2005); it recognizes that corruption is no longer a local matter but, rather, a transnational phenomenon that adversely affects all societies and economies, making international cooperation to prevent and control it essential. The political production of social indifference is often ingrained in bureaucratic cultures of the state (Herzfeld 1993).

Second, the notions of intergenerational justice are themselves very complex. How many generations may one encompass in this notion? Do we owe any duties to past generations? And may the existing generation decide on the composition (through population planning methods and recombinant DNA life science techniques) of the membership of future generations? Or, may future generations be pre-empted from the definition of problems and their solutions? These and many related issues have been addressed by emerging climate change justice theories but also stand aggravated now by the law, governance, and politics of systemic anthropogenic climate change and harm.

Third, the theoretical inclination to focus on income impoverishment has led everyone concerned to think about and practice multidimensionality and intersectionality. The United Nations Development Programme now rightly insists that like "development, poverty is multidimensional" but "this is traditionally ignored by headline money metric measures of poverty." It published the inaugural Multidimensional Poverty Index in the "2010 Human Development Report" and, as summarized in a later report (UNDP 2016), it refines monetary measures of poverty by

> considering overlapping deprivations suffered at the same time. The index identifies deprivations across the same three dimensions as the HDI (Human Development Index) and shows the number of people who are multi-dimensionally poor (suffering deprivations

in 33% or more of weighted indicators) and the number of deprivations with which poor households typically contend with. It can be deconstructed by region, ethnicity and other groupings as well as by dimension, making it an apt tool for policymakers.

But the difficulty of attending to complex causes of impoverishment and the structural forces and linkages to the global economy that exacerbate it often provide good alibis for passing on to infinite future generations the tasks, and burdens, of justice.

Fourth, states unite on the theme that even core human rights only obligate governments, not non-state actors—especially the communities of multinationals and direct foreign investors, or the "corporate legal humanity" (Grear 2006, 2011). The result is corporate Neanderthalism (despite all the talk about corporate social responsibility),[11] which creates toxic and epidemiological torts and mass disasters—catastrophes with immunity in the face of law. Normatively, "free" market fundamentalisms create conditions of emergence of (what I have called) the trade-related and market-friendly human rights paradigm in conflict with the paradigm of the Universal Declaration of Human Rights (Baxi 2012a); existentially, the suffering humanity of mass disasters and catastrophes witness this in their re-victimization and struggles for the "right to have rights."[12]

The fifth complex of reasons is furnished in the name of theories of international and global justice. Empirically, the Global South peoples and governments have insisted variously on the rank injustice of long periods of colonization and the evils of subjugation, slavery, plunder, deindustrialization, racism and apartheid, high indebtedness, and mass impoverishment; the demands have been addressed not so much in terms of reparation and rehabilitation for the acts of colonization but, rather, in terms of trade and aid. The latter has not even reached the promised target of 3% of gross domestic product of the developed countries, although policymakers sometimes assert such concepts as "the common heritage of mankind." Although there is no universal and binding definition of what constitutes the common heritage of mankind principle, which wavers between the notions of *res nullius* and *res communis*, a general definition would at least include five elements, as identified by Frakes (2003: 9):

> First, there can be no private or public appropriation; no one legally owns common heritage spaces. . . . Second, representatives from all nations must manage resources since a commons area is considered to belong to everyone. Therefore, governments are relegated to the role of representing their people. As popular management is practically unfeasible, a special agency to coordinate shared management must administer commons spaces in the name of all mankind. . . . Third, all nations must actively share with each other the benefits acquired from exploitation of the resources from the commons heritage region. Private entities seeking profits would have to perform a service that benefited all of mankind. Equitable distribution is intrinsic to the principle, but the application is ambiguous, necessitating a balance between economic benefit-sharing and environmental protection. Fourth, there can be no weaponry or military installations established in commons areas. Armed conflict is unlawful in the commons since every nation has a stake in maintaining the peace. Fifth, the commons should be preserved for the benefit of future generations, and to avoid a "tragedy of the commons" scenario.

Further normative accretions are "sustainable development,"[13] "the right to development,"[14] and ethical practices in trade and investment.[15] Yet projects such as the New International Economic Order and the World Information Order have been totally laid aside, and the complexity (as well as contradictions) between the World Trade Organization and human rights persist (Aaronson 2001; Aaronson and Jamie Zimmerman 2007).

All this is different from being and staying poor as a social and individual virtue, whether by ethical or spiritual practices or monastic vows of abstinence from wealth. Spiritual poverty is not impoverishment but, rather, a chosen way of life, into which as a matter of human rights the state and the law may not intervene. A certain sense of urgency of devotion mandated the following statement: "The poor you will always have with you, but you will not always have me" (Matthew 26:11). Certainly, charity may only be practiced as a virtue when there exist alms-receiving "poor." The complication is a naturalization of impoverishment. The New Testament also states, "Blessed are the meek, for they shall inherit the earth" (Mathew 5:5). Although a few millennia do not matter in cosmic time, the impoverished now claim a social, economic, and cultural human right to have miracles happen unto them.

Allied but different remain the images of the "culture of poverty."[16] This culture is said to arise when the "poor" perpetuate by an intergenerational "cultural" trait an aversion to work or to overpopulate beyond the means of livelihood support. The dependency on welfare rather than work is said to be characteristic of many citizens and migrant communities in Europe and the United States, and the removal of this trait passes on as welfare system reform. P. Bourgois (2001a: 11906) rightly critiques this perspective:

> From a theoretical perspective, the legacy of the culture of poverty debate has impoverished research in the social sciences on the phenomenon of social suffering, everyday violence, and the intimate experience of structural oppression in industrialized nations. Most importantly, by remaining mired in debates driven by identity politics, researchers have minimized the painful experience of day-to-day survival among the persistently poor.

The cultural trait and transmission approach raises wider questions about the distinction between an (Weberian) "ideal type" and a stereotype, and to the extent it does so in state policy and law, all that may be said is the following: If spiritual poverty is to be considered a matter of moral and ethical non-market choice, the culture of poverty suggests a stereotype of the impoverished as the basis of policy and law, which have been rightly questioned.

The Late Holocene and the Early Anthropocene

Recently, there has been some public discussion about the "end times" of the human rights era. Although much of this discourse is still seized by the now discredited idea that human rights are the gifts of the West to the East, we also hear about a neo-Westphalia era rather than the post-Westphalia era (Hopgood 2013). But concerns about global impoverishment arose only with the ushering in of the post-Westphalian international legal order, with the advent of biophilic decolonization and the traumatic phases of the Cold War.

In terms of geological time theory, this glacial global change in attitudes and dispositions occurred in the late Holocene era (lasting nearly 10,000–12,000 years), which has just recently been said to have been replaced by an Anthropocene era. In the late Holocene, we witnessed the great efflorescence of international human rights law and jurisprudence as well as environmental law and jurisprudence, which reflected a "new vision of international law, relations, and organization."[17] Although the validity of these concerns is accepted even today, Anthropocene law and jurisprudence cast (and craft) these differently, deeply, and urgently. We consider here only one question: whether impoverishment makes much sense in an era in which human species extinction is said to loom large in the current discourse. We return to this question after describing the larger challenges to human thought and action posed by the Anthropocene.

A multitude of difficulties surround the very act of naming the current era as "Anthropocene." This term must be officially certified by the verdict of an Anthropocene Working Group of the Subcommission on Quaternary Stratigraphy, but very few doubt that a profound change popularly known as "global warming" and "climate change" is "occurring and that is anthropogenic." As is well known, the Holocene is a geological epoch that began after the Pleistocene at approximately 9,700–12,000 BCE and continues to the present. Recently reported is the recommendation of a special subcommittee of the International Geography Commission (at Cape Town International Geographical Congress on August 29, 2016) that the new era should be named Anthropocene, beginning from 1950.[18] It is also certain that the decades of climate skepticism are nearly over, giving way to political and popular conviction that the "weight of evidence," on which science forever relies for its progress, overwhelmingly demonstrates today that climate change has already happened and will occur at a rapid pace in the near future.

Even as this chapter is being written, many of the Solomon Islands are actually disappearing as sea levels rise. Glaciers are melting, and the phenomenon of climate refugees is fast becoming a reality. Global temperatures are soaring, forest cover is disappearing, desertification advances, a large amount of biodiversity is extinct, and some unpredictable changes in Earth behavior are happening. To be sure, the Anthropocene is more than climate change, which is "only the tip of the iceberg" (how cruel this saying now sounds); it also relates to the fact that

> humans are (i) significantly altering several other biogeochemical, or element cycles, such as nitrogen, phosphorus and sulphur, that are fundamental to life on the Earth; (ii) strongly modifying the terrestrial water cycle by intercepting river flow from uplands to the sea and, through land-cover change, altering the water vapour flow from the land to the atmosphere; and (iii) likely driving the sixth major extinction event in Earth history. . . . Taken together, these trends are strong evidence that humankind, our own species, has become so large and active that it now rivals some of the great forces of Nature in its impact on the functioning of the Earth system.[19]

In this sense, we are entering in the Anthropocene a "geological age of our own making" (Chapman, Stainforth, and Watkins 2015; von Storch 1999). Not merely are humans themselves becoming a "force of nature" in "the sixth major extinction event in Earth history." It may also be the time of our own unmaking if the urgency of human action is not sufficiently realized. Audra Mitchell (2016) pluralizes "extinction" by providing categories "for several subjects of extinction" and "ample grounds for revisiting the doctrines of species encoded in the images of 'biodiversity'; 'humanity'; 'unloved' subjects; and 'absent or non-relational subjects.'" She expounds and explores ingrained hierarchies and the violence of exclusions and inequalities embedded in dominant discourses, identifying possibilities for "plural ethico-political responses to mass extinction." She urges that we differentiate between "the disappearance of the species *Homo sapiens* and the 'figural' extinction . . . of the normative figure of 'humanity' produced by Western European humanism, modernity and capitalism."[20] At the same time, anthropogenic climate change is not merely the cause of many catastrophes and crises: It is said at the same time to mark a new opportunity to restructure our governance, social traditions, and the global management of "nature." What is indicated is thus not "thinking out of the box" but, rather, smashing the box itself!

Doing this implies many things. One needs to listen carefully to those who alert us all to climate change catastrophes without succumbing to climate change conspiracy narratives. Also needed is the ability to differentiate "dangerous" or "catastrophic" scenarios of "abrupt" climate change and global warming from the medium- and long-term harms to the planet. The decision to name certain forms of climate change as "catastrophic" or "abrupt" is made by earth and climate scientists in terms mainly of their nonlinearity, and as entailing certain "thresholds," risks, and "vulnerabilities," the latter of which are more apt for a justice-based global policy analysis. The chief concerns here are the large ice sheets in Greenland and Antarctica and the ocean's thermohaline circulation, although many others are also discussed.[21]

Doing this does not at all detract from the understating that all types of climate change are truly hurtful for the survival of the human species, non-human species, objects in Nature, and the planet. The fact that such distinctions are difficult to make or maintain does not make them un-worthwhile. The *degree* of policy and action urgency varies, although the same *kind* of urgent attention and care must attach to all threats of human and non-human extinction. In this sense, for example, adaptation and mitigation of climate refugees are now more urgent than the goal of achieving an eventual post-carbon economy.

It is true that although theories about environment/ecological justice and global justice that evolved in the last decades of the Holocene era provide valuable beginnings, these may not uncritically and entirely extend to climate change justice approaches. The circumstances and tasks of justice in the Anthropocene era make different sorts of claims than cosmopolitan theories of environmental and global justice. Now is demanded a sort of planetary loyalty and multispecies solidarity, tasks that we never before posed so insistently. One has also to find a new dynamic of anthropomorphism that embraces all living begins and even unloved beings in Nature. Claire Colebrook (2014) rightly identifies the three senses of extinction: the now widely discussed sixth great extinction event (which we have begun to imagine and witness, even if in anticipation); extinction by humans of other species (with the endangered species of the "red list" evidencing our destructive power); and self-extinction, or the capacity for us to destroy what makes us human. All three senses of extinction require a nuanced conception of climate. Climate is at once an enclosing notion, imagined as the bounded milieu that is unavoidably ours, and a disturbing figure, for it is with the recognition that there is climate, or that the human species is now recognizable as a being that for all its seeming diversity is nevertheless bound into a unity of destructive power. She is correct in stating that

> we are at once thrown into a situation of urgent interconnectedness, aware that the smallest events contribute to global mutations, at the same time as we come up against a complex multiplicity of diverging forces and timelines that exceed any manageable point of view. (p. 9)

The prospect of extinction—the end of humanity—is a theme strongly associated with the growing understanding of the advancement of the Anthropocene. The probable extinction of the human species makes a strong "call for the consolidation of 'humanity' in the face of its possible demise" (A. Mitchell 2016: 28). What role, if any, does the idea of human rights possess in the face of the ultimate extinction of the human species? Human rights theory discourse has failed to pose this problematique, but global social movements have deployed, at times successfully, the idea of human rights in many a climate negotiation.[22] However, the instrumental uses of the "currency" of human rights enunciations do not frontally address the problem of mass extinction, or what it may mean to say "human," thus raising the question of whether human rights law and jurisprudence or even the moral/ethical idea of human rights have any contribution to make in averting this prospect.

Climate change and global warming raise again, and urgently, the question of territoriality. The doctrine of sovereign equality of all states is the cornerstone of post-Westphalian international law, orderings, and organizations. Indirect global governance is an exception to the norm of consent-based application of international law. It has been the grundnorm of all UN and many specialized agencies and activities. Despite manifest discontent with this, the late Holocene human rights and environmental law movements and norms have also been based on state consent. The Anthropocene, however, brings back the problematique of direct global governance—at least in the sense that the extinction of the human species, and other forms of dangerous climate change, lies beyond the capabilities of individual states. How then is one to blueprint a post-post-Westphalian order of international law, relations, and organization in the early Anthropocene?

Closely related to the foregoing is the question of the communities of multinational corporations and direct foreign investors who claim immunity and impunity from domestic and global law with regard to causation of mass disasters and social catastrophes. In effect, this continues to contribute to the privatization of governance, at all levels, from local to the global.[23] This privatization is made manifest by the three D's that mark the current form of globalization—denationalization, disinvestment, and deregulation—in ways that make human rights more market-friendly and trade-related. How may dangerous climate change be fought and governance refashioned to meet the tasks ahead?

Equally closely allied to privatization are processes of the securitization of information, simultaneous with its global diffusion through the internet, and the questions of transformations in science and technology in light of the crisis generated by the Anthropocene. The elementary insight that scientists and technologists are human beings, embedded in social practices and beliefs, is submerged from the view that considers them as abstracted beings, specializing in abstract categories and practical material uses. Not merely are we victims of "two cultures" of science and humanities (as C. P. Snow long ago stated) and thinking of science as "cultures of no cultures" rather than a culture of many cultures; we also stumble on the notion of public participation and responsibility (the more apt term is *response-ability*, a favorite of Jacques Derrida), but we tend to think of lay public opinion as less worthy than rule by experts.[24] However, such participation is increasingly thought of as belatedly but firmly bringing in the local to national, supranational, and international levels yet also as efficient in the economic sense.[25] And to what extent may concerns about impoverishment be resolved by participatory decision-making in this epoch?

Toward a Conclusion

How do we address the new forms of impoverishment effected by the Anthropocene? Most cruelly, to the already vexed situation of human refugees now stands added an altogether novel category, the phenomenon of climate refuges caused mainly by the submerging of whole territories due to the rise in sea levels. They suffer not just the loss of a dwelling place (as Heidegger would have it) but also the loss of their very nativity and community (as Hannah Arendt expresses this) (Peters 2002).

All of this therefore demands a new theorizing toward climate change justice. In addition to confronting the problematique of justice to infinite generations, we need to ask uncomfortable questions regarding the nature of old Holocene human rights. Clearly, we need to posit, as early environmentalists were wont to do, a collective human right of all peoples, species, and planet to survive endlessly into the future and to develop planetary loyalty into the future. Such an all-encompassing collective human right will be the starting point of any exploration of rights and justice in the early Anthropocene. Human rights and justice would clearly be "less anthropocentric than the present"; benefit society as a whole, not just individual victims; enable litigants and non-governmental organizations to challenge environmentally destructive or unsustainable development on public interest grounds; and "give environmental concerns greater weight" in the shaping and making of a global social change framework (Boyle 2010: 507).

All this is valuable, but we also need to cultivate new ways of being, belonging, and reflecting on the intransigence of the Anthropocene. We certainly need to develop rapidly "a thorough notion of global environmental justice" that is "locally grounded, theoretically broad, and plural—encompassing issues of recognition, distribution, and participation."[26] Equally, there is a "vital need" to face "critically-informed, reflexive, epistemically humble and renewing engagements with the question of who 'we' are in the Anthropocene age." How may such a cluster of rights—which is "transformed" by a non-universal, non-essentialist notion of the "human"—also carry the capacity for a "diverse entanglement with nature–culture" that might "co-inform a liberatory, restorative ontology, epistemology and ethics adequate to Anthropocene futures" and, above all, develop "an *in*justice-sensitive set of practices faithful to delivery of inclusion, compassion and resilience in a climate-threatened world"? (Grear 2015: 246).

The tendency to consider radical evil as natural has always been problematized by the idea of justice and the ideals of human rights. This idea and these ideals orient us toward moral outrage, social action, and even ethical and epistemological insurgency; theirs is the province and function of speaking truth to power and protesting the barbarisms of power. The capacity for future-building these ideas becomes ever more crucial when humanity probably verges on extinction. The question no longer is whether human rights and justice ideals have a future but, rather, how, when fully renovated, these may impact the future now unfolding before us all. Perhaps, a willing suspension of the questions concerning the relationship between discursive and nondiscursive reality should accompany the assumption that theories about justice and human rights do matter, even in an advancing Anthropocene era.

REFERENCES

Aaronson, Susan Ariel. 2001. "Seeping in Slowly, How Human Rights Concerns Are Penetrating the WTO." *World Trade Review* 6 (3): 413–449.

Aaronson, Susan Ariel, and Jamie Zimmerman. 2007. *Trade Imbalance: The Struggle to Weigh Human Rights in Trade Policymaking*. Cambridge, UK: Cambridge University Press.

Adelman, Sam. 2010. "Human Rights and Climate Change." In *Human Rights and Climate Change*, edited by Stephen Humphreys, pp. 1–34. Cambridge, UK: Cambridge University Press.

Adelman, Sam. 2016. "Climate Justice, Loss and Damage and Compensation for Small Island Developing States." *Journal of Environment and Human Rights* 7 (1): 32–53.

Alley, Richard B. 2007. "Wally Was Right: Predictive Ability of the North Atlantic 'Conveyor Belt' Hypothesis for Abrupt Climate Change." *Annual Review of Earth and Planetary Sciences* 35: 241–272.

Alston, Phillip. 1985. "The Shortcomings of a 'Garfield the Cat' Approach to the Right to Development." *California Western International Law Journal* 15: 510–523.

Alston, Phillip, ed. 2001. *People's Rights*. New York: Oxford University Press.

Anghie, Anthony. 2015. "Legal Aspects of the New International Economic Order." *Humanity* 25 (6): 145–158.

Arendt, Hannah. 1994. *The Origins of Totalitarianism*. New York: Harcourt.

Bair, Jennifer. 2015. "Corporations at the United Nations: Echoes of the New International Economic Order?" *Humanity* 6 (1): 159–171.

Baxi, Upendra. 1983. "The New International Economic Order, Basic Needs, and Rights: Notes Towards the Development of the Right to Development." *Journal of Indian Society of International Law* 23: 225–243.

Baxi, Upendra. 1988. "Introduction." In *Law and Poverty: Critical Essays*, edited by Upendra Baxi, pp. v–xxxvi. Bombay: Tripathi/Lexis/Nexis.

Baxi, Upendra. 2005. "Global Development and Impoverishment." In *The Oxford Handbook of Legal Studies*, edited by Mark Tushnet and Peter Cane, 455–483. Oxford, UK: Oxford University Press.

Baxi, Upendra. 2007. *Human Rights in a Posthuman World: Critical Essays*. Delhi: Oxford University Press.

Baxi, Upendra. 2012. "Epilogue: The Changing Paradigms of Human Rights." In *Law Against the State: Ethnographic Forays into Law's Transformations*, edited by Julia Eckert, Brian Donahoe, Christian Striirrpel, and Zerrin Ozlem Biner, 266–285. Cambridge, UK: Cambridge University Press.

Baxi, Upendra. 2013a. "International Development, Global Impoverishment, and Human Rights." In *Routledge Handbook of Human Rights Law*, edited by Scott Sheeran and Sir Nigel Rodley, 597–613. London: Routledge.

Baxi, Upendra. 2013b. *The Future of Human Rights*. 3rd ed. Delhi: Oxford University Press.

Beitz, Charles. 1999. *Political Theory and International Relations*. Princeton, NJ: Princeton University Press.

Beitz, Charles. 2011. *The Idea of Human Rights*. New York: Oxford University Press.

Benhabib, Seyla. 2011. *Dignity in Adversity: Human Rights in Troubled Times*. Cambridge, MA: Polity.

Berger, Peter. 1976. *Pyramids of Sacrifice*. New York: Anchor Press.

Birdsall, Nancy, and Francis Fukuyama. 2011. "The Post-Washington Consensus: Development After the Crisis." *Foreign Affairs* 90 (2): 45–53.

Birmingham, Peg. 2006. *Hannah Arendt and Human Rights: The Predicament of Common Responsibility*. Bloomington: Indiana University Press.

Bourgois, P. 2001a. "Culture of Poverty." In *International Encyclopedia of the Social & Behavioral Sciences*, edited by N. J. Smelser and Paul B. Baltes, pp. 11904–11907. Oxford, UK: Pergamon.

Bourgois, P. 2001b. "Poverty, Culture Of." http://www.philippebourgois.net/Encyclopedia%20Culture%20of%20Poverty%202001.pdf.

Boyle, Alan. 2010. "Human Rights or Environment Rights? A Reassessment." *Fordham Environmental Law Review* 18: 471–511.

Breton, Albert, Giorgio Brosio, Silvana Dalmazzone, et al., eds. 2009. *Governing the Environment: Salient Institutional Issues*. London: Elgar.

Brigg, Morgan. 2002. "Post-Development, Foucault and the Colonisation Metaphor." *Third World Quarterly* 23: 3421–3436.

Cai Dapeng, and Li Jie. 2014. "Efficiency, Privatization, and Political Participation: A Theoretical Investigation of Political Optimization in Mixed Duopoly." https://www.researchgate.net/publication/237242659.

Chapman, Sandra C., David A. Stainforth, and Nicholas W. Watkins. 2015. "Limits to the Quantification of Local Climate Change." *Environmental Research Letters* 10 (9): 094018.

Chaudhry, Moshmi, et al. 2012. "Participatory Gender-Sensitive Approaches for Addressing Key Climate Change-Related Research Issues: Evidence from Bangladesh, Ghana and Uganda." Working Paper no. 19, CGIAR Research Program on Climate Change, Agriculture and Food Security.

Clark, Timothy. 2015. *Ecocriticism on the Edge: The Anthropocene as a Threshold Concept*. London: Bloomsbury.

Colebrook, Clare. 2014. *Death of the Posthuman: Essays on Extinction, Vol. I*. Ann Arbor, MI: Open Humanities Press.

Committee on Economic, Social and Cultural Rights. 2001. "Substantive Issues Arising in the Implementation of the International Covenant on Economic, Social and Cultural Rights: Poverty and the International Covenant on Economic, Social and Cultural Rights." Twenty-fifth session, Geneva, April 23–May 11.

Crowder, Michael. 1968. *West Africa Under Colonial Rule*. Evanston, IL: Northwestern University Press.

Crutzen, P. J., and J. Lelieveld. 2001. "Human Impacts on Atmospheric Chemistry." *Annual Review of Earth and Planetary Sciences* 29: 17–45.

Davis, Jeremy. 2016. *The Birth of the Anthropocene*. Berkeley: University of California Press.

Derrida, Jacques. 1995. *Gift of Death*. Chicago: University of Chicago Press.

Duignan, Peter, and H. Lewis Gann, eds. 1975. *Colonialism in Africa, 1870–1960*. Cambridge, UK: Cambridge University Press.

Easterly, William. 2003. "IMF and World Bank Structural Adjustment Programs and Poverty." http://www.nber.org/chapters/c9656.

Ehrlich, Paul Ralph. 1995. *The Population Bomb*. Cutchogue, NY: Buccaneer Books. (Original work published 1968)

Escobar, Arturo. 1992. "Imagining a Post-Development Era? Critical Thought, Development and Social Movements." *Social Text* 31/32: 20–56.

Falk, Richard. 2009. *Achieving Human Rights*. New York: Taylor & Francis.

Falk, Richard. 2014a. *(Re)Imagining Humane Global Governance*. New York: Routledge.

Falk, Richard. 2014b. *Humanitarian Intervention and Legitimacy Wars: Seeking Peace and Justice in the 21st Century*. London: Routledge.

Fanon, Frantz. 2008. *Black Skin, White Masks*, translated by Richard Philcox. New York: Grove Press. (Original work published 1952)

Frakes, Jennifer. 2003. "The Common Heritage of Mankind Principle and the Deep Seabed, Outer Space, and Antarctica: Will Developed and Developing Nations Reach a Compromise?" *Wisconsin International Law Journal* 21: 409–434.

Galeano, Eduardo. 2008. *Open Veins of Latin America: Five Centuries of the Pillage of a Continent*. New York: Monthly Review Press. (Original work published 1971)

George, Susan. 1988. *A Fate Worse than Debt*. New York: Grove Press.

George, Susan. 1989. *How the Other Half Dies*. New York: Rowman & Littlefield 1989);

Gibson-Graham, J. K. 2005. "Surplus Possibilities: Postdevelopment and Community Economies." *Singapore Journal of Tropical Geography Lecture Series* 26 (1): 4–26.

Gilman, Nils. 2015. "The New International Economic Order. A Reintroduction." *Humanity* 6 (1): 1–16.

Glover, Jonathan. 1999. *Humanity: A Moral History of the Twentieth Century*. London: Cape.

Grear, Anna. 2006. "Human Rights–Human Bodies? Some Reflections on Corporate Human Rights Distortion, the Legal Subject, Embodiment and Human Rights Theory." *Law and Critique* 17 (2): 171–199.

Grear, Anna. 2011. "The Vulnerable Living Order: Human Rights and the Environment in a Critical and Philosophical Perspective." *Journal of Human Rights and the Environment* 2 (1): 23–44.

Grear, Anna. 2015. "Deconstructing the Anthropos: A Critical Legal Reflection on 'Anthropocentric' Law and Anthropocene Humanity." *Law Critique* 26: 225–249.

Guéneau S., and P. Tozzi. 2008. "Towards the Privatization of Global Forest Governance?" *International Forestry Review* 10 (3): 550–562.

Hall, Rodney Bruce, and Thomas J. Biersteker. 2004. *The Emergence of Private Authority in Global Governance*. Cambridge, UK: Cambridge University Press.

Hassan, Ghada Farouk, Ayman El Hefnawi, and Mohab El Refaie. 2011. "Efficiency of Participation in Planning." *Alexandria Engineering Journal* 203: 212.

Herzfeld, Michael. 1993: *The Social Production of Indifference: Exploring the Symbolic Roots of Western Bureaucracy*. Chicago: University of Chicago Press.

Hopgood, Stephen. 2013. *The Endtimes of Human Rights*. Ithaca, NY: Cornell University Press.

Houghton, R. J. 2007. "Balancing the Global Carbon Budget." *Annual Review of Earth and Planetary Sciences* 35: 313–347.

Jenks, Bruce. 2015. "From an MDG World to an SDG/GPG World: Why the United Nations Should Embrace the Concept of Global Public Goods." Development Dialogue Paper no. 15, September.

Kabeer, Naila. 2005. "Gender Equality and Women's Empowerment: A Critical Analysis of the Third Millennium Development Goal." *Gender and Development* 13: 13–24.

Kesby, Alison. 2012. *The Right to Have Rights: Citizenship, Humanity, and International Law*. Oxford, UK: Oxford University Press.

Khan, Adil Hasan. 2016. "International Lawyers in the Aftermath of Disasters: Inheriting from Radhabinod Pal and Upendra Baxi." *Third World Quarterly* 37 (11): 2061–2079.

Lee, Maria, Chiara Armeni, Javier de Cendra, et al. 2013. "Public Participation and Climate Change Infrastructure." *Journal of Environmental Law* 25 (1): 33–62.

Lewis, Oscar. 1961. *The Children of Sanchez: Autobiography of a Mexican Family*. New York: Random House.

Lewis, Oscar. 1966a. *La Vida: A Puerto Rican Family in the Culture of Poverty in San Juan and New York*. New York: Random House.

Lewis, Oscar. 1966b. "The Culture of Poverty." *Scientific American* 215: 19–25.

Loewe, Markus. 2015. "Post 2015: How to Reconcile the Millennium Development Goals (MDGs) and the Sustainable Development Goals (SDGs)?" The German Development Institute (DIE) Briefing Paper no. 18/2012.

Maddison, Angus. 1990. "The Colonial Burden: A Comparative Perspective." In *Public Policy and Economic Development*, edited by Maurice Scott and Deepak Lal, pp. 361–375. Oxford, UK: Clarendon.

Mamdani, Mahmood. 2001. *When Victims Become Killers: Colonialism, Nativism, and the Genocide in Rwanda*. London: Currey.

Marks, Stephen P., ed. 2008. *Implementing the Right to Development: The Role of International Law*. Geneva/Boston: Friedrich Ebert Stiftung/Program on Human Rights in Development, Harvard School of Public Health.

McNeill, H. R., and Peter Engelike. 2016. *The Great Acceleration: An Environmental History of the Anthropocene Since 1945*. Cambridge, MA: Harvard University Press.

Menke, Christoph. 2007. "The 'Aporias of Human Rights' and the 'One Human Right': Regarding the Coherence of Hannah Arendt's Argument." *Social Research* 74 (3): 739–762.

Mgbeoji, Ikechi. 2003. *Collective Insecurity: The Liberian Crisis, Unilateralism & Global Order*. Vancouver: University of British Columbia Press.

Michelman, Frank. 1996. "Parsing 'A Right to Have Rights.'" *Constellations* 3 (2): 200.

Mitchell, Audra. 2016. "Beyond Biodiversity and Species: Problematizing Extinction." *Theory, Culture & Society* 33 (5): 23–42.

Mitchell, Bruce. 2005. "Participatory Partnerships: Engaging and Empowering to Enhance Environmental Management and Quality of Life?" *Social Indicators Research* 71: 123–144.

Moore, Jason W., ed. 2015. *Anthropocene or Capitalocene? Nature, History, and Crisis of Capitalism*. Oakland, CA: PM Press.

Mosley, Layna. n.d. "Privatizing Global Governance? Dilemmas in International Financial Regulation." www.unc.edu/~lmosley.

Nederveen Pieterse, Jan. 1996. "The Development of Development Theory: Towards Critical Globalism." *Review of International Political Economy* 3 (4): 541–564.

Nino, Carlos Santiago. 1966. *Radical Evil on Trial*. New Haven, CT: Yale University Press.

Orford, Anne. 2005. *Reading Humanitarian Intervention: Human Rights and the Use of Force in International Law*. Cambridge, UK: Cambridge University Press.

Osborn, Derek, Amy Cutter, and Farooq Ullah. 2015. "Universal Sustainable Development Goals: Understanding the Transformational Challenge for Developed Countries: Report of a Study by Stakeholder Forum." https://sustainabledevelopment.un.org/content/documents/1684SF_-_SDG_Universality_Report_-_May_2015.pdf.

Osiel, Marc. 1997. *Mass Atrocity, Collective Memory and the Law*. London: Transaction Publishers.

Peters, Michael Aam. 2002. "Earthsongs: Ecopoetics, Heidegger and Dwelling." *The Trumpeter* 18 (1).

Philippopoulos-Mihalopoulos, Andreas. 2007. *Absent Environments: Theorising Environmental Law and the City*. London: Routledge/Cavendish.

Pogge, Thomas. 1999. *World Poverty and Human Rights: Cosmopolitan Responsibilities and Reforms*. Princeton, NJ: Princeton University Press.

Pogge, Thomas. 2001. "Eradicating Systemic Poverty: Brief for a Global Resources Dividend." *Journal of Human Development* 2 (1): 59–77.

Pogge, Thomas. 2007. *Real World Justice: Grounds, Principles, Human Rights, and Social Institutions*. Cambridge, UK: Polity.

Pogge, Thomas, ed. 2010. *Poverty and Human Rights: Who Owes What to the Very Poor?* Paris: UNESCO.

Prada, Maritza Formisano. 2011. *Empowering the Poor Through Human Rights Litigation.* Paris: UNESCO.

Prashad, Vijay. 2007. *The Darker Nations: A People's History of the Third World.* New York: New Press.

Purdy, Jedediah. 2015. *After Nature: A Politics for the Anthropocene.* Cambridge, MA: Harvard University Press.

Rajmani, Lavnya. 2010. "The Increasing Currency and Relevance of Rights-Based Perspectives in the International Negotiations on Climate Change." *Journal of Environmental Law* 22 (3): 391–429.

Rammel, R. J. 1997. *Death by Government.* New York. Transaction Publishers.

Ravallion, Martin. 2016. "Toward Better Global Poverty Measures." *Journal of Economic Inequality* 14: 2227–2248.

Ravallion, Martin. 2016. *The Economics of Poverty.* Oxford, UK: Oxford University Press.

Rosenfield, Allan, Deborah Maine, and Lynn Freedman. 2006. "Meeting MDG-5: An Impossible Dream?" *Lancet* 368 (9542): 1133–1135.

Salomon, Margot E. 2011. "Why should it matter that others have more? Poverty, inequality, and the potential of international human rights law." *Review of International Studies* 37 (05): 2137–2155. Available at LSE Research Online, November 2011 (p.3) at: http://eprints. lse.ac.uk/39547. Accessed July 28, 2018

Sands, Philippe. 2003. *Principles of International Environmental Law.* 2nd ed. Cambridge, UK: Cambridge University Press.

Schellnhuber, Hans Joachim, Wolfgang Cramer, Nebojsa Nakicenovic, et al., eds. 2006. *Avoiding Dangerous Climate Change*, pp. 7–24. Cambridge, UK: Cambridge University Press.

Schlosberg, David. 2004. "Reconceiving Environmental Justice: Global Movements and Political Theories." *Environmental Politics* 13 (3): 517–540.

Schlosberg, David. 2007. *Defining Environmental Justice: Theories, Movements, and Nature.* Oxford, UK: Oxford University Press.

Schellnhuber, H. J., Cramer, W., Nakicenovic, N., Wigley, T. M. L., and Yohe, G. W. 2006. *Avoiding Dangerous Climate Change*, pp. 7–24. Cambridge: Cambridge University Press.

Semenza, Jan C., D. E. Hall, D. J. Wilson, et al. 2004. "Public Perception of Climate Change: Voluntary Mitigation and Barriers to Behaviour Change." *American Journal of Preventive Medicine* 5 (5): 479–487.

Sengupta, Arjun. 2002. "On the Theory and Practice of the Right to Development." *Human Rights Quarterly* 24: 837–889.

Sepúlveda, Magdalena, and Carly Nyst. 2012. "The Human Rights Approach to Social Protection." Helsinki: Ministry for Foreign Affairs of Finland.

Snow, C. P. 1961. *The Two Cultures and the Scientific Revolution.* Cambridge, UK: Cambridge University Press.

Steffen, Will, Paul J. Crutzen, and John R. McNeill. 2007. "The Anthropocene: Are Humans Now Overwhelming the Great Forces of Nature?" *Ambio* 36 (8): 614–621.

Steffen, Will, Jacques Grinevald, Paul Crutzen, and John McNeill. 2011. "The Anthropocene: Conceptual and Historical Perspectives." *Philosophical Transactions of the Royal Society A* 369: 842–867.

Supiot, Alain. 2012. *The Spirit of Philadelphia: Social Justice vs. the Total Market.* London: Verso.

Traweak, Sharon. 1992. *Beamtimes and Lifetimes: The World of High Energy Physicists.* Cambridge, MA: Harvard University Press.

Truman, Edwin M. 2001. "Comment on IMF and World Bank Structural Adjustment Programs and Poverty by William Easterly." Paper presented at the NBER Conference on Management of Currency Crises, Peterson Institute for International Economics, Washington, DC, March 28.

United Nations. 1987. *Report of the World Commission on Environment and Development: Our Common Future*, Anexure 1, 'Summary of Proposed Legal Principles for Environmental Protection and Sustainable Development Adopted by the WCED Experts Group on Environmental Law.' New York: United Nations.

United Nations. 2015. *Transforming Our World: The 2030 Agenda for Sustainable Development.* New York: United Nations.

United Nations Development Program, 2016. "Human Development Reports, 2016. Multidimensional Poverty Index (MPI)." Available at: http://hdr.undp.org/en/content/multidimensional-poverty-index-mpi. Accessed July 28, 2018.

Valiante, Marcia. 2009. "Privatization and Environmental Governance." In *Governing the Environment: Salient Institutional Issues*, edited by Albert Breton, Giorgio Brosio, Silvana Dalmazzone, et al., pp. 43–86. London: Elgar.

Vishwanathan, Shiv. 2016. *Science, Population and Development* (Book review). *Manushi* 74/75: 68–69. www.manushi.in/docs/5868. Book Review.pdf. Accessed September 1, 2016.

von Storch, Hans, ed. 1999. *Anthropogenic Climate Change.* New York: Springer.

White, John. 1978. "The New International Economic Order: What Is It?" *International Affairs* 54 (4): 630.

Zaborowski, Holger. 2000. "On Freedom and Responsibility: Remarks on Sartre, Levinas and Derrida." *Heythrop Journal* 41: 47–65.

NOTES

1. See Upendra Baxi, ed. "Introduction," in *Law and Poverty* (Bombay/Lexis/Nexis, 1989). See also Upendra Baxi, "Global Development and Impoverishment," in *The Oxford Handbook of Legal Studies*, eds. Mark Tushnet and Peter Cane (Oxford, UK: Oxford University Press, 2005), 455–483; Upendra Baxi, "International Development, Global Impoverishment, and Human Rights," in *Routledge Handbook of Human Rights Law*, eds. Scott Sheeran and Sir Nigel Rodley (London: Routledge, 2013a), 597–613.

2. See Peter Duignan and H. Lewis Gann, eds. *Colonialism in Africa, 1870–1960* (Cambridge, UK: Cambridge University Press, 1975); Angus Maddison, "The Colonial Burden: A Comparative Perspective," in *Public Policy and Economic Development*, eds. Maurice Scott and Deepak Lal (Oxford, UK: Clarendon, 1990); Michael Crowder, *West Africa Under Colonial Rule* (Evanston, IL.: Northwestern University Press, 1968).

3. Vijay Prashad, *The Darker Nations: A People's History of the Third World* (New York: New Press, 2007). See also the works of Eduardo Galeano, especially *Open Veins of Latin America: Five Centuries of the Pillage of a Continent* (New York: Monthly Review Press, 2008).

4. Jonathan Glover, *Humanity: A Moral History of the Twentieth Century* (London, Cape, 1999). See also Shiv Vishwanathan, "*Science, Population and Development*" (Book review), *Manushi* 74/75 (2016), 68–69, www.manushi.in/docs/5868. Book Review.pdf,

accessed September 1, 2016; Paul Ralph Ehrlich, *The Population Bomb* (Cutchogue NY, Buccaneer Books, 1968; Reprint edition, 1995).

5. Susan George, *How the Other Half Dies* (New York: Rowman & Littlefield, 1989); Susan George, *A Fate Worse Than Debt* (New York: Grove Press, 1988); Peter Berger, *Pyramids of Sacrifice* (New York: Anchor Press, 1976). See also the Special Issue of *Journal of Social Philosophy* 37 (2006), 3; R. J. Rammel, *Death by Government* (New York: Transaction Publishers, 1997); Mahmood Mamdani, *When Victims Become Killers: Colonialism, Nativism, and the Genocide in Rwanda* (London: Currey, 2001); Ikechi Mgbeoji, *Collective Insecurity: The Liberian Crisis, Unilateralism & Global Order* (Vancouver: University of British Columbia Press, 2003); Carlos Santiago Nino, *Radical Evil on Trial* (New Haven, CT: Yale University Press, 1966); Marc Osiel, *Mass Atrocity, Collective Memory and the Law* (London: Transaction Publishers, 1997).

6. United Nations, *Transforming Our World: The 2030 Agenda for Sustainable Development* (New York: United Nations, 2015); Bruce Jenks, "From an MDG World to an SDG/GPG World: Why the United Nations Should Embrace the Concept of Global Public Goods," Development Dialogue Paper no. 15 (September 2015); Markus Loewe, "Post 2015: How to Reconcile the Millennium Development Goals (MDGs) and the Sustainable Development Goals (SDGs)?" German Development Institute Briefing Paper no. 18/2012; Derek Osborn, Amy Cutter, and Farooq Ullah, "Universal Sustainable Development Goals: Understanding the Transformational Challenge for Developed Countries: Report of a Study by Stakeholder Forum" https:// sustainabledevelopment.un.org/content/documents/1684SF_-_SDG_Universality_Report_-_May_2015.pdf (2015). See also the Global Network for the Right to Food and Nutrition, www.rtfn-watch.org/fileadmin/media/rtfn-watch.org.

7. Morgan Brigg, "Post-Development, Foucault and the Colonisation Metaphor," *Third World Quarterly* 23 (2002), 3421–3436; Arturo Escobar, "Imagining a Post-Development Era? Critical Thought, Development and Social Movements," *Social Text* 31/32 (1992), 20–56; Nancy Birdsall and Francis Fukuyama, "The Post-Washington Consensus: Development After the Crisis," *Foreign Affairs* 90, no. 2 (2011), 45–53; Jan Nederveen Pieterse, "The Development of Development Theory: Towards Critical Globalism," *Review of International Political Economy* 3, no. 4 (1996), 541–564; J. K. Gibson-Graham, "Surplus Possibilities: Postdevelopment and Community Economies," *Singapore Journal of Tropical Geography Lecture Series* 26, no. 1 (2005), 4–26.

8. Richard Falk, *Achieving Human Rights* (New York: Taylor & Francis, 2009), at1. See also Richard Falk, *(Re)Imagining Humane Global Governance* (New York: Routledge, 2014a), especially 183–192.

9. ECA, ILO, UNCTAD, UNDESA, UNICEF, "Social Protection: A Development Priority in the Post-2015 UN Development Agenda: Thematic Think Piece," www.un.org/millenniumgoals/pdf/Think Pieces/16_social_protection.pdf; Magdalena Sepúlveda and Carly Nyst, "The Human Rights Approach to Social Protection" (Helsinki: Ministry for Foreign Affairs of Finland, 2012).

10. Thomas Pogge, *Real World Justice: Grounds, Principles, Human Rights, and Social Institutions* (Cambridge, UK: Polity, 2007). See also Charles Beitz, *Political Theory and International Relations* (Princeton, NJ: Princeton University Press, 1999); Thomas Pogge, *The Idea of Human Rights* (New York: Oxford University Press, 2011); Thomas Pogge, *World Poverty and Human Rights: Cosmopolitan Responsibilities and Reforms* (Princeton, NJ: Princeton University Press, 1999); Thomas Pogge, "Eradicating Systemic

Poverty: Brief for a Global Resources Dividend," *Journal of Human Development* 2, no. 1 (2001), 59–77.

11. Upendra Baxi, *The Future of Human Rights*, 3rd ed. (Delhi: Oxford University Press, 2013b), Chaps. 8 and 9.

12. Hannah Arendt, *The Origins of Totalitarianism* (New York: Harcourt, 1994), 292; Alison Kesby, *The Right to Have Rights: Citizenship, Humanity, and International Law* (Oxford, UK: Oxford University Press, 2012); Frank Michelman, "Parsing 'A Right to Have Rights,'" *Constellations* 3, no. 2 (1996), 200; Christoph Menke, "The 'Aporias of Human Rights' and the 'One Human Right': Regarding the Coherence of Hannah Arendt's Argument," *Social Research* 74, no. 3 (2007), 739–762; Peg Birmingham, *Hannah Arendt and Human Rights: The Predicament of Common Responsibility* (Boomington: Indiana University Press, 2006); Seyla Benhabib, *Dignity in Adversity: Human Rights in Troubled Times* (Cambridge, MA: Polity, 2011).

13. United Nations, *Report of the World Commission on Environment and Development: Our Common Future* (popularly known, after the Chairperson, as Bruntland Report), and see particularly Anexure 1 providing the "Summary of Proposed Legal Principles for Environmental Protection and Sustainable Development Adopted by the WCED Experts Group on Environmental Law" (New York: United Nations, 1987). See also Philippe Sands, *Principles of International Environmental Law*, 2nd ed. (Cambridge, UK: Cambridge University Press, second edition, 2003); David Schlosberg, *Defining Environmental Justice: Theories, Movements, and Nature* (Oxford, UK: Oxford University Press, 2007), exploring, in particular, the difference between "environmental" and the "ecological" justice; Andreas Philippopoulos-Mihalopoulos, *Absent Environments: Theorising Environmental Law and the City* (London: Routledge/Cavendish. 2007).

14. See Upendra Baxi, *Human Rights in a Posthuman World* (Delhi: Oxford University Press, 2007), Chapters 3 and 4; Arjun Sengupta, "On the Theory and Practice of the Right to Development," *Human Rights Quarterly* 24 (2002), 837–889; Stephen P. Marks, ed. *Implementing the Right to Development: The Role of International Law* (Geneva: Friedrich Ebert Stiftung/Program on Human Rights in Development, Harvard School of Public Health, 2008); Philip Alston, ed. *People's Rights* (New York: Oxford University Press, 2001); Philip Alston, "The Shortcomings of a 'Garfield the Cat' Approach to the Right to Development," *California Western International Law Journal* 15 (1985), 510–523.

15. Anthony Anghie, "Legal Aspects of the New International Economic Order," *Humanity* 25, no. 6 (2015), 145–158; Nils Gilman, "The New International Economic Order: A Reintroduction," *Humanities* 6, no. 1 (2005), 1–16; Jennifer Bair, "Corporations at the United Nations: Echoes of the New International Economic Order?" *Humanity* 6, no. 1 (2015), 159–171; John White, "The New International Economic Order: What Is It?" *International Affairs* 54, no. 4 (1978), 630; Upendra Baxi, "The New International Economic Order, Basic Needs, and Rights: Notes towards the Development of the Right to Development," *Journal of Indian Society of International Law* 23 (1983), 225–243.

16. Oscar Lewis, *The Children of Sanchez: Autobiography of a Mexican Family* (New York: Random House, 1961); Oscar Lewis, *La Vida: A Puerto Rican Family in the Culture of Poverty in San Juan and New York* (New York: Random House, 1966a); Oscar Lewis, "The Culture of Poverty," *Scientific American* 215 (1966b), 19–25; P. Bourgois, "Poverty, Culture Of," http://www.philippebourgois.net/Encyclopedia%20Culture%20of%20Poverty%202001.pdf (2001b); Upendra Baxi quoted in Adil Hasan Khan, "International Lawyers in the Aftermath of Disasters: Inheriting from Radhabinod

Pal and Upendra Baxi," *Third World Quarterly* 37, no. 11 (2016), 2061–2079, quoted on p. 2067.

17. Sands, *Principles of International Environmental Law*; see also the introduction to the volume by Sir Robert Jennings urging a new "vision."

18. *The Holocene, A Major Interdisciplinary Journal Focusing on Recent Environmental Change* (London: Sage).

19. Will Steffen et al., "The Anthropocene: Conceptual and Historical Perspectives," *Philosophical Transactions of the Royal Society A* 369 (2011), 842–867 at 843; P. J. Crutzen and J. Lelieveld, "Human Impacts on Atmospheric Chemistry," *Annual Review of Earth and Planetary Sciences* 29 (2001), 17–45; R. J. Houghton, "Balancing the Global Carbon Budget," *Annual Review of Earth and Planetary Sciences* 35 (2007), 313–347.

20. See Claire Colebrook, *Death of the Posthuman: Essays on Extinction, Vol. I.* (Ann Arbor, MI: Open Humanities Press, 2014); Audra Mitchell, "Beyond Biodiversity and Species: Problematizing Extinction," *Theory, Culture & Society* 33, no. 5 (2016), 23–42 at 29. See also Timothy Clark, *Ecocriticism on the Edge: The Anthropocene as a Threshold Concept* (London: Bloomsbury, 2015); Jeremy Davis, *The Birth of the Anthropocene* (Berkeley: University of California Press, 2016); H. R. McNeill and Peter Engelike, *The Great Acceleration: An Environmental History of the Anthropocene Since 1945* (Cambridge, MA: Harvard University Press, 2016); Jason W. Moore, ed. *Anthropocene or Capitalocene? Nature, History, and Crisis of Capitalism* (Oakland, CA: PM Press, 2015); Jedediah Purdy, *After Nature: A Politics for the Anthropocene* (Cambridge, MA: Harvard University Press, 2015).

21. See Stephen H. Schneider and Janica Laneg, n.d. "An Overview of 'Dangerous' Climate Change," https://pdfs.semanticscholar.org/8ceb/db78e277e744e1734c4c4a9c00f95d44 2bf7.pdf, accessed September 11, 2016). See also Hans Joachim Schellnhuber, et al., eds. *Avoiding Dangerous Climate Change* (Cambridge, UK: Cambridge University Press, 2006); Richard B. Alley, "Wally Was Right: Predictive Ability of the North Atlantic 'Conveyor Belt' Hypothesis for Abrupt Climate Change," *Annual Review of Earth and Planetary Sciences* 35 (2007), 241–272.

22. See Lavnya Rajmani, "The Increasing Currency and Relevance of Rights-Based Perspectives in the International Negotiations on Climate Change," *Journal of Environmental Law* 22, no. 3 (2010), 391–429; Sam Adelman, "Human Rights and Climate Change," in *Human Rights and Climate Change*, ed. Stephen Humphreys (Cambridge, UK: Cambridge University Press, 2010), 159–180; Sam Adelman, "Climate Justice, Loss and Damage and Compensation for Small Island Developing States," *Journal of Environment and Human Rights* 7, no. 1 (2016), 32–53.

23. See Marcia Valiante, "Privatization and Environmental Governance," in *Governing the Environment: Salient Institutional Issues*, eds. Albert Breton ct al. (London: Elgar, 2009); S. Guéneau and P. Tozzi, "Towards the Privatization of Global Forest Governance?" *International Forestry Review* 10, no. 3 (2008), 550–562; Rodney Bruce Hall and Thomas J. Biersteker, *The Emergence of Private Authority in Global Governance* (Cambridge, UK: Cambridge University Press, 2004); Layna Mosley, "Privatizing Global Governance? Dilemmas in International Financial Regulation," n.d., www.unc.edu/~lmosley.

24. C. P. Snow, *The Two Cultures and the Scientific Revolution* (Cambridge, UK: Cambridge University Press, 1961); Sharon Traweak, *Beamtimes and Lifetimes: The World of High Energy Physicists* (Cambridge, MA: Harvard University Press, 1992). Jacques Derrida, *Gift of Death* (Chicago: University of Chicago Press, 1995); Holger Zaborowski, "On Freedom

and Responsibility: Remarks on Sartre, Levinas and Derrida," *Heythrop Journal* 41 (2000), 47–65; Baxi, "International Development, Global Impoverishment, and Human Rights."

25. See Bruce Mitchell, "Participatory Partnerships: Engaging and Empowering to Enhance Environmental Management and Quality of Life," *Social Indicators Research*, 71 (2005), 123–144; Ghada Farouk Hassan, Ayman El Hefnawi, and Mohab El Refaie, "Efficiency of Participation in Planning," *Alexandria Engineering Journal* 203 (2011), 212; Cai Dapeng and Li Jie, 2014, "Efficiency, Privatization, and Political Participation: A Theoretical Investigation of Political Optimization in Mixed Duopoly," https://www.researchgate.net/publication/237242659, 2014; Maria Lee, Chiara Armeni, Javier de Cendra, et al., "Public Participation and Climate Change Infrastructure," *Journal of Environmental Law* 25, no. 1 (2013), 33–62; Jan C. Semenza D. E. Hall, D. J. Wilson, et al., "Public Perception of Climate Change: Voluntary Mitigation and Barriers to Behaviour Change," *American Journal of Preventive Medicine* 5, no. 5 (2004), 479–487; Moshmi Chaudhry et al., "Participatory Gender-Sensitive Approaches for Addressing Key Climate Change-Related Research Issues: Evidence from Bangladesh, Ghana and Uganda," Working Paper no. 19, CGIAR Research Program on Climate Change, Agriculture and Food Security (2012).

26. David Schlosberg, "Reconceiving Environmental Justice: Global Movements and Political Theories," *Environmental Politics* 13, no. 3 (2004), 517–540 at 518; particularly important here is his discussion (pp. 532–537) of critical pluralism and the idea of "unity without uniformity."

CHAPTER 28

....

RELIGIOUS GLOBALISMS

....

JEFFREY HAYNES

LIKE other social agents, religion participates in and is affected by globalization, which is a continuous, historically based, multifaceted process. In some periods, it is especially speedy and influential. Globalization's pace increased from approximately 1870 until the start of World War I in 1914. This was partly because during those four decades, "all parts of the world began to feel the impact of the international economy, and for the first time in history it was possible to have instant long-distance communication (telegraph, radio) between people" (Warburg, 2001: 2). After World War II ended in 1945, globalization's speed, density, and impact expanded again—as it did once more after the Cold War came to an end in 1989 (Haynes 2007: 65–95).

The overall impact of processes of globalization led to a situation of "globalism." Globalism is "a state of the world involving networks of interdependence at multicontinental distances, linked through flows of capital and goods, information and ideas, people and force, as well as environmentally and biologically relevant substances" (Keohane 2002: 31). Thus, whereas *globalization* denotes the speed at which these connections grow—or diminish, *globalism* refers to the reality of being interconnected. The concept of globalism "seeks to . . . understand all the inter-connections of the modern world—and to highlight patterns that underlie (and explain) them" (Nye 2002: 2). Speck (2016) avers that "globalism" should be contrasted with "territorialism." The former refers to a beneficial-for-all "interconnectedness [which] is a good thing because it is what drives progress towards more prosperity and freedom everywhere" (p. 29). "Territorialists," on the other hand, regard interconnectedness as "mainly a threat. What is good and healthy is attributed to the natives and what is dangerous comes from the outside" (p. 29).

This chapter first examines the nature of post-Cold War globalization and its impact on religious approaches to international relations. The second section examines religious resurgence and the emergence of a post-secular international environment. The third section discusses the issue of religious globalisms, and the fourth section examines competing religious globalisms in a global forum, the United Nations, and outside of it.

What Do Globalization and Globalism Imply for Religious Understandings of the World?

How do globalization and globalism change our understanding of the involvement of religion in international relations—beyond the general idea that globalization implies increasing interdependence between states and peoples, including religious persons? In other words, what would a religion-centered or -focused globalism look like, and how would it affect our understanding of international relations? One approach is to view the issue in relation to a Western-directed "globalization," which some view as a thoroughly comprehensive and malign Westernizing process. This form of globalization is often judged to be *inherently* undesirable, a process whereby Western—especially American—capitalism and culture seek to dominate the globe, sweeping aside non-Western cultures, including those heavily influenced by religious belief and traditions. A second aspect of this view is that, in general, the Western world is made rich at the expense of the poverty of many non-Western areas of the world, areas compelled to bear the brunt of an unjust and unequal globalizing process. This is possible, it is asserted, because Western capitalist interests determine trading terms, interest rates, and dominance of highly mechanized production via control of important international institutions, such as the World Trade Organization.

An alternative view emphasizes that globalization offers enhanced opportunities for international cooperation in relation to various issues, including social development and improved human rights, as well as conflict resolution and peace-building. In this view, globalization is believed to enhance the chances of international cooperation to resolve a range of economic, developmental, social, political, environmental, gender, and human rights concerns and injustices. The quarter century since the end of the Cold War is seen to offer unprecedented opportunity for collective efforts involving both states and non-state actors, including religious entities, to tackle a range of pressing global concerns. In the early 1990s, the optimistic promise of progress was given a name: "new world order," briefly a focus of then US President George H. W. Bush. Soon, however, new wars—for example, between Iraq and the West and the contemporaneous implosion of Yugoslavia—encouraged Bush to switch US focus back to traditional international relations concerns: war, peace, and how to get more of the former and less of the latter.

Both "pessimistic" and "optimistic" views of globalization are in agreement that it is a multifaceted process of change, inter alia, affecting states, governments, industrial companies, local communities, and individuals. Religious entities, leaders, and actors are not exempted. Scholarly discussions of the relationship between religion and globalization typically concentrate on increased cultural pluralism and how religions organizations respond (Beyer 2013). Some religious actors react positively to globalization, developing a benign religious globalism that tolerates, accepts, or endorses pluralism. This includes "some Christian ecumenical movements or the Baháʾís. Other groups emphasise the differences and confront the non-believers in an attempt to preserve their particular values from being eroded by globalisation. So-called fundamentalist Christian, Muslim, and Jewish movements are well-known examples" (Warburg 2001: 3).

In other words, relationships between religion and globalization are characterized by tension between forces that lead, on the one hand, to *integration* in the context of globalization and, on the other hand, to *resistance* to it. Here, "integration" refers to religious processes that both promote and follow from processes of globalization. "Resistance" implies the opposite: criticism of and often mobilization against the perceived malign effects of globalization. According to Reychler (1997), the growing impact of religious discourses on international relations is a response to a

> world where many governments and international organizations are suffering from a legitimacy deficit. . . . Religion is a major source of soft power. It will, to a greater extent, be used or misused by religions and governmental organizations to pursue their interests. It is therefore important to develop a more profound understanding of the basic assumption underlying the different religions and the ways in which people adhering to them see their interests. It would also be very useful to identify elements of communality between the major religions.

Juergensmeyer (2005) argues that some religious organizations and movements enjoy more legitimacy than some governments and international organizations. He contends that in particular "radical religious ideologies have become the vehicles for a variety of rebellions against authority that are linked with myriad social, cultural, and political grievances." How did religion assume such social, political, and cultural importance given that only a few decades ago it was seen to be a waning force?

A clue to the newly significant position of religion in international relations is to be found in the changing nature of international interactions after the Cold War, exemplified by a growing presence of religious entities at important global fora, such as the United Nations (UN; Haynes 2014). First, the UN is today a focal point for alternative, sometimes competing or clashing, religious globalisms. Second, their presence at the UN is reflective more widely of the increasing international importance of "values," "norms." and "behavior" following the end of the Cold War. In particular, many religious actors at the UN are concerned with various aspects of human rights, including an interest in international development, such as how poverty-stricken people can improve their positions. However, achieving improved and more equitable international development is not simply a moral or theological concern. As Lynch (2012) notes, when faith-based organizations (FBOs) ponder international development, they typically move from initially moral dimensions to consider a highly material factor: "neoliberal competition of the 'market' [in] international development." From there, it is but a short jump to begin to ponder on how more generally the conditions what Wilson and Steger (2013) refer to as "neoliberal globalization" appear to encourage or exacerbate an unjust and polarized world, in which the rich and powerful benefit disproportionately.

The UN-sponsored Millennium Development Goals (MDGs) were an important focal point from the late 1990s in relation to questions about international development (Boehle 2010). (MDGs are listed at http://www.un.org/millenniumgoals.) It is not surprising, however, that many religious actors are interested in international development, as it is an issue intimately tied to many theological interpretations of the world. In this context, we can note the important involvement of various Christian entities—including the World Council of Churches, United Methodist Church, Religions for Peace, and Caritas Internationalis—in formulation of the MDGs. Muslim FBOs, including Islamic Relief and Qatar Charity Organization, also worked with UN development agencies, including the United Nations Development Programme and the World Bank, in relation to the MDGs. In summary, announcement of the MDGs in the late 1990s led to a focus of FBO activities in seeking to help redress international development shortfalls, especially in the poorest developing countries. FBOs were interested in the general thrust of improvements to international development, with specific interest in the following MDG goals: arresting the spread of HIV/AIDS and, in relation to gender issues in particular, reducing infant deaths, providing universal primary education, and reducing adult illiteracy (Haynes 2007).

The MDGs were stimulated by egregious failures of economically liberal structural adjustment programs (SAPs) in the 1980s and 1990s. Despite significant ideological and financial commitment from several UN agencies, including the World Bank and the International Monetary Fund (IMF), the general failure of SAPs to overcome development shortfalls in developing countries where they were applied led to strong critiques from many quarters, including secular non-governmental organizations (NGOs), grass-roots movements, and some religious actors. The common accusation was that both the World Bank and the IMF promoted and supported a narrowly economistic conception of development via SAPs, which crucially lacked a holistic focus on human development (Joshi and O'Dell 2013). Critics of SAPs, including from religious sources, wanted to see a shift away from state and market-led approaches to broader, more holistic, conceptions of development, focusing on interactions of civil society, human development, and grass-roots participation. To pursue this different vision of development, many religious actors, including those noted previously, developed "human development" outlooks in the 1990s, which focused, inter alia, on opening development spaces to non-state actors in order to augment development work undertaken by both international agencies and states. The result was that from this time, development-orientated religious entities became "legitimate actors in the field of development and humanitarian aid" (Petersen 2010: 2). A World Bank study, Voices of the Poor (2000), helped cement the importance of "religion" in the context of development, not least by the assertion that many poor people in the developing world had more confidence in their religious leaders than in their governments.

In summary, the advent of the MDGs in the late 1990s coincided with a new global governance focus on civil society involvement in development—including activities of both secular and religious NGOs—that collectively sought to move on from the egregious failures of SAPs to arrive at improved methods to achieve qualitative international development improvements. From the perspective of religious globalism, interfaith agreement about the MDGs in particular and approaches to improve international development more generally reflect the emergence of an ecumenical religious globalism on the issue. Emerging in the 1990s, it brought together like-minded actors from different religious faiths in pursuit of reversing development shortfalls following post-Cold War globalization. "The ecumenical movement is fueled by the thrust for religious globalism" (Standish 1998: 230). Before turning to the issue of religious globalisms in more detail, it is useful to explain how religion has moved from marginality to centrality in international relations, thus making an examination of religious globalisms both necessary and topical.

RELIGIOUS RESURGENCE AND POST-SECULARISM

During most of the twentieth century, religion had a very minor role in international relations. It was only after the Cold War ended and the Soviet Union imploded that we began to see increasing numbers of examples of religious involvement in international relations. From the early 1990s, as seen in the aforementioned conflicts involving Iraq and the West and the disintegration of Yugoslavia, conflicts involving self-identified religious actors came to the fore. Such was the overall impact that these conflicts, coupled with the effect of the September 11, 2001, terrorist attacks, led many to view the post-Cold War world as an unexpected "post-secular" environment.

First, a few terms need defining. *Secularism* is the state or quality of being *secular*, the end result of a process of secularization, whereby religion becomes significant less publicly important. For decades, secularism was a term strongly associated with "rational" Western social science. In this context, "secular" implied a profound lack of reference to or concern with a transcendent order, involving a divine being or beings, such as God or gods. Over time, the notion of secularism became normatively associated in Western social science both with universalist pretensions and with a claim to superiority over each and every set of religious ideas, irrespective of origin, content, philosophy, or approach. During the twentieth century, secularism developed into an ideology, characterized by domination, marginalization, and, often, belittling of religious ideas. After World War II, leaders of "modernizing" governments, especially in the developing world, widely expressed the view that reducing the public importance of religion was essential in order to secure generalized social, political, and economic "progress," marked by measurable steps toward "modernization" and "development." Inexorably, the idea of the secular characterized normatively desirable attributes, such as tolerance, common sense, justice, rational argument, public interest, and public authority. "Religion" was pejoratively regarded as the antithesis of secularism.

Today, however, it is often claimed that things have changed and that we now inhabit a "post-secular" international environment. According to Geoghegan (2000),

> Secularism is a complex and multifaceted process which emerged out of the European wars of religion in the sixteenth century, postsecularism is a heuristic and political device to address aspects of that process. *Postsecularism is a contested concept that lends itself to ambiguity. It could suggest a deeply antagonistic stance toward secularism, involving the call for a resurgent religiosity, where "post" really implies "pre"—a dismantling of the secular culture of the past few centuries.* (pp. 205–206, emphasis added)

A focus on "post-secularism" follows growing numbers of monographs, book chapters, journal articles, and conference papers that collectively testify to renewed interest in the role of religion in international relations. Many scholars also point to a "resurgent," "returning," or "rejuvenated" religion, a fundamental component of a no-longer-secular or "post-secular" global environment (Haynes 2013; Micklethwait and Wooldridge 2009; Toft, Philpott, and Shah 2011). The analytical and conceptual problem, however, is that the expression "post-secular"—rather like the earlier term, postmodern—is both vague and hotly debated. Or, as Geoghegan (2000) states, the post-secular is a "contested concept that lends itself to ambiguity" (p. 205).

What might characterize post-secular international relations, where religious globalisms might play an important ideological, social, and political role? It is difficult to argue persuasively that we live in an age characterized by a "dismantling of the secular culture of the past few centuries." One starting point to assess whether international relations is becoming "less secular" (or even "more religious") is to gauge whether state foreign policies are becoming more attuned to religious issues. This is because despite all the important changes of the past few decades—such as the end of the Cold War, the demise of the Soviet Union, the collapse of the communist counter-challenge to liberal democracy/capitalism, the sustained impact of globalization, and the rise of China—very few countries officially have a leading role for religion in their foreign policies. Among them, we could take account of two very different theocracies—Iran and Saudi Arabia—and also include the United States during the presidency of George W. Bush (2001–2009); Israel, especially concerning the contested issue of control of Jerusalem; and India during the rule of the Hindu-nationalist Bharatiya Janata party (1996–2004 and 2014 to the present). Each of these countries has had governments that in recent years, albeit intermittently, appear to take religion "seriously" in their foreign policies (Haynes 2008; Warner and Walker 2007). Yet this does not imply that there is a discernible trend in this regard that might suggest that governments in general are ditching traditional and embedded secular national interest concerns—such as national security, protection of trade and territory, or seeking to dissuade potential enemies from embarking on conflict with them—for religious concerns.

If it is not states that are engaging in international relations with more religion-focused policies, then evidence of post-secularism, and by extension the growing importance of religious globalisms, might be seen in the growing array of transnational non-state actors. The past few decades have seen increased importance of various moral and ethical concerns in international relations, often captured under the catch-all rubric of "human rights" or "justice." During the course of the twentieth century, the rise and fall of two extremist secular ideologies—fascism and communism, which led in both cases to extreme tyranny and to the deaths of millions of people at the hands of the state—fatally shook the perceived moral superiority of secular thinking and ideas over religious ones. Clearly, religion did not have a monopoly on conflict and repression, and by the end of the Cold War the certainty of a superior secular world order was severely shaken. The demise of optimism about the perceived "superiority" of rational secular values gave way to growing willingness to accept that maybe, after all, "religion" *might* have something to tell us about how to run international relations better—that is, ideas and values stemming from religious beliefs might conceivably assist in states' developing cooperation and undermining chances of conflict while helping provide an ethical framework for improved international collaboration. In this way, "religion" began its public international rehabilitation, and although the September 11, 2001, attacks rather set things back in this regard, they did not prove fatal. In summary, after the Cold War, religious norms and values began to reassert themselves, seeking to regain moral and ethical salience, in a significantly changed context for international relations.

Religious resurgence and its corollary, post-secularism, characterize international relations in various, often imprecise, ways. Two of the world faiths in particular—Christianity and Islam—now have regular involvement in international affairs in various ways (Haynes 2013). For example, in nominally Christian, although actually increasingly secular, Western Europe, Muslim immigrant communities seek to assert themselves publicly, gaining in confidence that they are pushing with the tide, in a changing environment in which religion, following years of marginalization, is making something of a public comeback in the context of the flowering of civil society. Christianity, on the other hand, provided the framework for the recent controversial debate about the abortive European constitution while also apparently providing a role model, in the specifically politicized guise of Christian democracy, for the electoral ascendant Justice and Development Party in Muslim-majority

Turkey (Haynes 2012). At the same time, it is not correct to talk of a single Christian globalism or an Islamic globalism for the simple reason that within each of these faiths there are various approaches to understanding how the world works and why it works as it does and, finally, what the faiths can do about it.

In summary, the recent renewed significance of religion in international relations is mainly due to the increased impact of non-state religious actors at the level of civil society both within and between countries. It is "religious" ideas and values, sometimes expressed in the terminology of "religious globalisms," and their impact on social and political questions and controversies that have taken center stage.

RELIGIOUS GLOBALISMS: HOW MANY AND WHAT TYPE?

How might one try to understand the concept of "religious globalism(s)" in international relations? Although it is relatively easy to identify key actors, such as the Roman Catholic Church and the Organisation of Islamic Cooperation, in this regard (for a survey of such actors, see Wilson and Steger 2013), how might we try to evaluate their influence on international outcomes? One approach, which I adopt in the remainder of this chapter, is to examine two distinct kinds of actors with very different approaches to religious globalism. First, there are religious actors projecting religious globalism at the leading global forum, the UN, such as the Roman Catholic Church and the Organisation of Islamic Cooperation. To be active at the UN necessarily implies that an organization will conduct itself in accordance with the UN's norms and values, expressed both in the UN Charter and in the Universal Declaration of Human Rights (1948). Second, there are influential actors not represented at the UN, such as Islamic State, that present a religious globalism reflecting quite different norms and values, which do not conform to those of the UN.

In the literature, there tends to be a dichotomy developed between "religious" and "secular" actors that, it is suggested, seek to present different visions of globalism. For Bellah (2012), religious globalism is expressed via global civil society:

> But for the creation of a viable and coherent world order, a world civil society is surely an essential precondition, and dare I say it, any actual civil society will have a religious dimension, *will need not only a legal and an ethical framework, but some notion that it conforms to the nature of ultimate reality.* The biggest immediate problem is the strengthening of global civil society, and . . . *perhaps the religious communities of the world may have something to contribute to that global civil society, and indeed, that their participation may be essential for its success.* (emphasis added)

In the quotation, Bellah presents the idea of an ethical framework central to a religious globalism that forms a component of global civil society. Steger (2013) avers that

> religious globalisms struggle against both market globalism and justice globalism as they seek to mobilize a religious values and beliefs [sic] that are thought to be under severe attack by the forces of secularism and consumerism. . . . Religious globalisms strive for a global religious community with superiority over secular structures. (p. 104)

For Carette and Miall (2012), the focus, values, and content of global governance debates are significantly influenced "by the moral resources that 'religions' offer and agencies of global governance need an awareness of what religious actors are doing and sensitivity to religious difference" (p. 3).

Steger (2013) asserts that there is a dichotomous relationship between, on the one hand, "religious globalism" and, on the other hand, "market globalism" and "justice globalism." This perceived dichotomy, I suggest, misrepresents and oversimplifies a more complex, fragmented, and shifting relationship between religious and secular globalisms, which I examine later. Wilson and Steger (2013) seek to present a dichotomy between the religious and the secular with roots in the "mounting global crises and the emergence of the post-secular" (p. 481). They contend that the "post-secular is both a description of and a response to shifting global realities in the twenty-first century. It describes the crisis of secular rationalism, brought about in many ways by an overemphasis on economic rationalism and neoliberalism" (p. 481). They aver that "the post-secular offers a way of resisting, reforming, and potentially revolutionizing these dominant secular, rationalist, neoliberal frameworks that presently shape global politics and society" (p. 481). In particular, this implies, they claim, "that the intersection between the post-secular and emerging global political ideologies of market and justice globalisms is having a profound impact on religious movements, generating 'religious globalisms' that offer alternative responses to global crises around finance, poverty, and climate" (p. 481).

This approach is superficially attractive—that is, religious versus secular globalisms, reflecting alternative visions of the good life and the way forward for humanity. I argue, however, that religious globalisms can take various forms, and not all express overt opposition to neoliberal globalization as reflected, for example, in failed SAPs endorsed by the World Bank and the IMF. It is clear, however, that the post-Cold War era is a time of deep globalization, coinciding with both an international religious resurgence and increased prominence of ethical and moral (often overlapping with religious) concerns in debates about values, norms, and behaviors, including at the UN (Haynes 2014). As a result, religious views and opinions are now often heard in relation to ethical and moral controversies, concerning not "only" neoliberal economic policies but also in relation to international development, "climate change, global finance, disarmament, inequality, pan-epidemics and human rights" (Carrette and Miall 2012: 3).

We have also seen that post-Cold War globalization paved the way for the new, highly unexpected, opening for religious and spiritual energies in international relations, albeit a development with variable impacts. Today's religious resurgence is not one-sided or easily interpreted. It can perhaps best be understood as part of a double-edged post-Cold War increase in impact of religion in international relations, including debates about global governance. On the one hand, widespread inter- and intrareligion conflicts are a significant, possibly increasing, source of domestic and international strife. On the other hand, it is widely accepted that if "benign" and "cooperative" religious principles and practices could be applied meaningfully in relation to such conflicts, then such "emancipatory religious and spiritual perspectives in world order thinking and practice" might improve matters (Falk 2004: 137). Falk conceptualizes this as a shift to what he calls "humane global governance," which he understands as a moral and ethical regime that may well involve religious world views. For Falk, a "humane global governance" that involves only secular (state and non-state) actors explicitly excludes an important component from the study and practice of global public policy: religious and spiritual dimensions of human experience. In this context, the UN, the world's only universal international organization concerned with issues of global governance, offers the most potentially useful environment. The World Conference on Religion and Peace (also referred to as the "United Nations of Religions") asserted in 2001 (as quoted in Berger 2003) that

> religious communities are, without question, the largest and best-organized civil institutions in the world today, claiming the allegiance of billions of believers and bridging the divides of race, class and nationality. They are uniquely equipped to meet the challenges of our time: resolving conflicts, caring for the sick and needy, promoting peaceful co-existence among all peoples. (p. 2)

From this, we might infer that religious globalism necessarily is concerned with improving things, including in relation to resolving conflict and more generally promoting peaceful coexistence. Discussions of international religious resurgence and its impact on global public policy overlap with another current debate in international relations: the extent to which today's international environment is no longer overwhelmingly secular but is instead increasingly affected by religious norms, beliefs, and values, leading to post-secular international relations. Reflecting these concerns, the UN has changed over time from a position in which religion was largely absent from its deliberations to one in which religion is more prominent. Reflecting this change, debates about global governance at the UN underwent a shift in emphasis from exclusively secular and material to include moral and ethical issues, which frequently overlap with faith-based concerns. But this is not to suggest that there was a religious versus secular approach to the issues. As discussed next, religious globalisms are by no means uniform and reflect ideological divisions within faith traditions.

In recent years, the UN has become a focal point for conflict and competition, with polarization notable between "conservative" and "liberal" religious globalisms. In other words, religious globalisms may be either "conservative" or "liberal," and their stance is linked to an ideological view of the world rather than necessarily as a result of their religious characteristics. For example, the issue of women's rights is articulated by reference to "family values" or by a "woman's right to choose," and international development debates highlight the moral and ethical necessity of advancing the position of the poorest people.

COMPETITIVE RELIGIOUS GLOBALISMS

Islam

An example of the difficulty of trying to pitch "a" religious against a secular globalism is that no religious world view is set in stone, reflective of just one unchanging set of understandings and values. This can be seen in relation to Islam. David Littman (1999) asserts that the UN has seen an increase in Islam's international influence and involvement, with "Islamism grow[ing] stronger at the United Nations." The Organisation of Islamic Cooperation (OIC) is the key focal point for Islam at the UN. The OIC is the only significant international organization organized by religious faith; there is, for example, no comparable Christianity-focused entity.

The OIC is a 57-member intergovernmental organization, established in 1969. Its raison d'être is to be "the collective voice of the Muslim world" that works to seek "international peace and harmony among various people of the world" (https://www.oic-oci.org/page/?p_id=52&p_ref=26&lan=en)—in effect, to be a proponent of an Islamic globalism highlighting a specific set of values toward building global peace and cooperation, assuredly in the mind of the OIC, a key tenet of Islam. During its lifetime, the OIC has primarily functioned as a forum for senior Muslim figures to discuss religious political issues while asserting the desirability of a path of moderation in international relations. Although the OIC professes to be the primary voice of the *ummah*, working to extend the global growth and influence of Islam, it has instead been dogged for decades by competition between its leading member states: Egypt, Iran, Pakistan, and Saudi Arabia. Dogan (2005) avers that *if* the OIC could overcome interstate rivalry, it would be more than capable of helping Muslims and Muslim states pull together to deliver "a unified ethical approach to such issues as international terrorism, international development, and democracy. This role of the organization is critical for both ending 'clashes' between 'civilizations' and bringing peace to the 'Greater Middle East'" (p. 1).

Kayaoğlu (2011) notes that

> while differences exist among the non-secular Muslim-majority states as well as between them and the secular Muslim-majority states, these states sometimes overcome their differences and present a formidable bloc within the UN. As in the Danish Cartoon Crisis, these states have increasingly brought Muslim agendas, grievances, and demands to the UN. (p. 7)

The "formidable bloc" of Muslim countries to which Kayaoğlu refers has an organizational focus: the OIC. This is notable in relation to "Muslim solidarity" in the context of the collective endeavor to get UN agreement on a binding international resolution condemning "defamation of religions." The issue was first raised in 1999, and during the next dozen years the OIC led the campaign. Over time, the measure, which was initially widely, albeit rather vaguely, supported by many UN members, including non-Muslim-majority countries, became highly controversial, and no agreement was achievable. The issue developed into an increasingly polarized confrontation involving, on one side, the OIC, Muslim states, and some Muslim NGOs, such as the Muslim World League. Opposing the pro-defamations of religion coalition was an alliance of Western states and non-state actors, including secular and religious NGOs. Under the leadership of the OIC, the Muslim campaign crystallized in a series of resolutions at the UN. The starting point was to claim that the justification for the "defamation of religions" measure was to be found in various UN human rights documents that made combating defamation of religions necessary and, as a result, governments were duty-bound to take steps to this end. The argument was that following September 11, 2001, and attendant talk about conflict between civilizations, there were strong reasons to increase religious dialogue and tolerance, and it was agreed that a defamation of religions measure was a necessary step forward. That is, if there was a strong measure to make religious hate speech unacceptable, then there was said to be a greater chance to develop civilizational coexistence. Although the plea was that governments should make all necessary efforts to combat "defamation of religions," it was by no means clear what this measure would practically imply. On the other hand, the issue of "defamation of religions" was a reflection of a shared Islamic approach to what

Muslims the world over viewed as an increasingly serious issue of their right to be treated with respect and dignity (Kayaoğlu 2011).

Although the issue of "defamation of religions" united Muslims at the UN, this is not to suggest that more generally the Muslim *ummah* is unproblematically united, projecting a unified religious globalism. Throughout the Middle East and North Africa (MENA), religious minorities are being squeezed, and their security is being compromised (Fox 2015). The situation was encouraged by the Arab Spring of 2011 and its aftermath, whereby state weakness or breakdown combined with the impact of politically assertive religious actors to add increasing pressure on religious minorities to convert to the dominant religious tradition or, failing that, to flee for their lives.

The post-Arab Spring context of state weakness/breakdown facilitated the rise of Islamic State, which, like al-Qaeda before it, purports to speak for "all Muslims," reflective of a religious world view that sees the world in structural terms with ordinary Muslims subjugated by their ungodly rulers in tandem with supportive Western governments. Islamic State thrives on, and perpetuates, egregious sectarian division both within the Muslim *ummah* and outside of it. Given the widespread diminution of state capacity in the MENA following the Arab Spring and the linked expansion of aggressive Sunni entities, notably Islamic State, it seems highly likely that the short and medium term will feature many sectarian conflicts in the MENA, which will cause significant friction and, in some cases, result in out and out conflict between warring sectarian groups. Tensions between (Shiite) Iran and the Saudi Arabian-led (Sunni) Gulf Cooperation Council (GCC) are likely to remain high in the next few years—not least because each is seen to support one sect of Islam only. However, not all Shia movements will necessarily be pro-Iranian, and not every Salafi or Wahhabist Sunni movement kowtows to Saudi Arabia. Indeed, there are significant Shiite minorities in GCC countries, as well as a growing (Sunni) Salafi movement in Iran. Sectarian tensions also reflect socioeconomic disparities and are likely to escalate if governments do not address these fundamental issues. For example, Bahrain and Saudi Arabia, where economic inequality between Sunni and Shia is greatest, are more likely to see tensions rise compared to other countries in the region. Globalization, represented by influential satellite television channels and social media, will play a growing, perhaps pivotal, role in spreading antigovernment rhetoric and sectarian mistrust. In addition, during the next 20 years, there are likely to be growing tensions within Sunni and Shiite communities. Sunni Islam is particularly likely to become increasingly factionalized. As Salafist groups grow in prominence throughout the world, a backlash may emerge from moderate Sunnis. Correspondingly, Shiite Islam contains a number of internal divisions. In terms of religious globalisms, these divisions within the Muslim *ummah*, which are likely to get worse as the tentacles of Islamic State spread across the MENA, highlight how difficult it is to understand religious globalisms in the singular.

Christianity

> Conservative religious groups have for years engaged in clashes over family policy. Much of their activism aims to preserve traditional families against what they decry as an *onslaught of feminism, abortion and gender politics*.
>
> —Bob (2012: 14–15, emphasis added)

> While health policy is usually framed as a part of the secular political domain, it touches upon combustible religious values and engages powerful alliances across religious divides. *Catholics and Mormons; Christians and Muslims; Russian Orthodox and American fundamentalists find common ground on traditional values and against SRHR issues at the UN.*
>
> —Norwegian Agency for Development Cooperation (NORAD, 2013: 1, emphasis added)

As the quotations make clear, religious globalisms are not uniform with regard to the issue of women's sexual and reproductive health rights (SRHR). This highly controversial issue pits conservative religious globalisms against liberal religious globalisms, mainly from within the broad Christian tradition. Contemporary campaigns at the UN seeking to uphold "family values" bring together Christian actors from a variety of Christian faiths—Catholics, Mormons, Protestants, and the Russian Orthodox Church—as well as conservative Muslims; in effect, they are working from the same understanding of religious globalism that, for both Christians and Muslims alike, reflects key, overlapping tenets of their different faiths. The interfaith bloc, led by the Roman Catholic Church, constitutes an influential grouping at the UN, projecting a distinctly conservative social agenda with overlapping religious globalisms. Liberals regard the conservatives as motivated by "premodern" ideas about gender issues, family politics, and women's health, working in effect to resist the advance of women's sexual and reproductive health rights. According to NORAD (2013), to the liberals, the conservatives work

> ceaselessly to contest, obstruct and delay the development of relevant UN agendas. Their influence does not reflect their number but is largely due to a striking ability to build alliances across religious boundaries as well as elicit the support of religious communities around the world. (p. 1)

Why would a diverse array of mainly Christian actors at the UN work together on pursuing a particular set of women's sexual and reproductive health rights? As previously noted, as a secular forum, debates at the UN necessarily "take place in the context of a secular global public policy sphere." This produces norms, values, and expressions that strongly influence potential "non-liberal" ideas by "causing" them to "align [their] frame to match the dominant [liberal] discourse" (Kayaoğlu 2011: 17). Thus, conservative religious actors at the UN seeking to oppose what they regard as liberal SRHR policies do not believe it appropriate or feasible if they want to make progress to express their arguments in terms of their religious values (based on community, personal responsibility, and traditional patriarchal understandings of the family and women's place within it). Instead, they couch their concerns in religiously neutral concerns with an ambiguous notion—that is, "family values"—enabling them to overcome what openly expressed conservative religious values would produce: "limited access to discursive and institutional opportunities at the UN" (Samuel 2007, cited in Kayaoğlu 2011: 17). Consequently, if anti-SRHR groups wish to be successful, they find it necessary to "concentrate on countering the pro-abortion"—that is, liberal—groups' agendas and declarations through blocking or weakening the pro-choice language in UN documents. They also adjust the frame of their discussions by arguing for concepts such as the "natural family" and referring to God as the "creator" in order to bypass theological differences and find non-Christian language (Samuel 2007, cited in Kayaoğlu 2011: 17).

Conservative religious globalisms' strategy in relation to SRHR developed from the early 1990s. This was a time when religion generally became much more important at the UN than it was during the preceding decades (Lehmann 2016). The starting point for the Christian conservative campaign was two UN conferences in 1994 and 1995: Cairo ("population growth") and Beijing ("women and gender"). At the 1995 Beijing conference, Christian "conservatives claimed that lesbians had launched a 'direct attack on the values, cultures, traditions and religious beliefs of the vast majority of the world's peoples'" (Bob, 2012: 2, quoting Human Rights Watch, 2005: 84–85). These conferences marked the beginning of a concerted anti-liberal campaign in relation to SRHR, initially led by the pope, the Vatican, and, more generally, the Roman Catholic Church. As Chao (1997) notes, at this time, "the Catholic Church became a leading actor on the conservative wing" (p. 48). This propelled the then pope, John Paul II, to overall leadership of the global conservative faith-based struggle. This was directed against "what the secular world would call progressive: the notion, for example that humans share with God the right to decide who will and who will not be born" (p. 48). This is not to imply, however, that to be Catholic is *necessarily* to be conservative. Instead, we can note a polarization between "conservative" and "liberal" Catholics—a competition played out at the UN: "Catholic NGOs with ECOSOC accreditation range from the liberal 'pro-choice' activist group Catholics for choice [sic] to the most fervent 'pro-life' campaigners in American Life League" (NORAD 2013: 11).

Conservative Catholic campaign leadership was added to by supportive involvement of mainly US-based Protestant evangelicals and conservative Muslims from various countries. Bob (2012: 36) argues that this "Baptist–burqa" alliance seeks mutual benefit in working together via a shared concern with "pro-family values." The "Baptist–burqa" alliance was resilient and managed to endure a key setback due to the terrorist attacks of September 11, 2001, whose impact otherwise was to divide (further) the Christian and Muslim worlds. The augmentation of the conservative Catholic campaign by additional conservative religious sources highlights the entities' shared conservative ideological orientation and their dispersed geographical locations: Conservative Catholics from Italy were joined by traditionalist Muslims from, inter alia, Egypt and Pakistan, while right-wing evangelical Protestants joined the campaign mainly from the United States.

This is not to suggest that conservative Christian "pro-family" religious actors have it all their own way at the UN. They are challenged by a smaller group of liberal, "pro-choice," Christian NGOs at the UN, which works with like-minded secular NGOs and supportive governments from, inter alia, Norway, Switzerland, and Canada. This "pro-choice" liberal network is coordinated by an NGO umbrella group, Women Action 2000, and comprises 30 mainly regional networks from sub-Saharan Africa, Europe, the Middle East, Asia Pacific, Latin America, the Caribbean, and North America. Christian NGOs active in the "pro-choice" network include Catholics for a Free Choice and Ecumenical Women 2000+ (Petersen, 2010, as quoted in NORAD 2013: 5):

> The liberal Catholics for Choice [sic], which has been accredited to ECOSOC since 1998 . . . strives for gender equality and reproductive rights as argued by Norway and the EU. However, this is the exception to the rule which illustrates the fact that Catholic NGOs are not ruled or run by the Vatican. (p. 13)

In summary, there are various Christian groups, including Catholic NGOs, that express different perceptions of a desirable religious globalism that represent different understandings of what it means to be Christian in relation to "family values."

Conclusion

The aim of the chapter was to survey how globalization and globalism change our understanding of the involvement of religion in international relations. I sought to go beyond the general idea that globalization implies increasing interdependence between states and peoples, including religious persons, with what happens in one area of the world affecting what happens elsewhere. I aimed to examine what differing religious globalisms look like and how their interaction affects our understanding of international relations.

The chapter demonstrated that competing expressions of "conservative" and "liberal" religious globalisms vie for influence and authority at the UN in relation to various issues, including "family values." Following foundational UN conferences in the 1990s, the networks developed into antagonistic, broad-based, highly competitive coalitions that focus on the UN as the key forum to advance their conflicting campaigns. The chapter also examined an alternative religious globalism, expressed by Islamic State, that is not represented or pursued at the UN.

This chapter showed that religious globalisms are ways of understanding the global environment as expressed through specific religious world views. Although the literature tends to see a dichotomous relationship between religious and secular globalisms, with the former being in opposition to the latter, the chapter showed that the situation is more complicated. This chapter contends that there are various religious globalisms and that it is not a straightforward dichotomous relationship between religious and secular globalisms. The situation was put in focus by the impact of post-Cold War globalization and the contemporaneous return of religion to international relations, which had much to say about the "soulless" nature of market-based globalization and the advance of capitalism to the detriment of religious values and norms.

References

Bellah, R. 2012. "Is Global Civil Society Possible?" February 2. University of California, Santa Barbara, Orfalea Center and Walter H. Capps Center. http://www.global.ucsb.edu/luceproject/papers/pdf/RobertBellah.pdf. Accessed July 27, 2017.

Berger, J. 2003. "Religious Nongovernmental Organizations: An Exploratory Analysis." *Voluntas* 14 (1): 15–39.

Beyer, P. 2013. *Religion in the Context of Globalization*. London: Routledge.

Bob, C. 2012. *The Global Right Wing and the Clash of World Politics*. Cambridge, UK: Cambridge University Press.

Boehle, J. 2010. "The UN System and Religious Actors in the Context of Global Change." *Crosscurrents* 60 (3): 383–401.

Carette, J., and H. Miall. 2012. "Big Society or Global Village? Religious NGOs, Civil Society and the UN." Briefing Paper.

Chao, J. K. T. 1997. "The Evolution of Vatican Diplomacy." *Tamkang Journal of International Affairs* 1 (2): 35–63.

Dogan, N. 2005. "The Organization of the Islamic Conference: An Assessment of the Role of the OIC in International Relations." Paper prepared for the Third ECPR General Conference, Budapest, Hungary, September 2005.

Falk, R. 2004. *Declining World Politics. America's Imperial Geopolitics.* London: Routledge.

Fox, J. 2015. *Political Secularism, Religion, and the State.* Cambridge, UK: Cambridge University Press.

Geoghegan, V. 2000. "Religious Narrative, Post-Secularism and Utopia." *Critical Review of International Social and Political Philosophy* 3 (2–3): 205–224.

Haynes, J. 2007. *Religion and Development: Conflict or Cooperation?* New York: Palgrave Macmillan

Haynes, J. 2008. "Religion and Foreign Policy Making in the USA, India and Iran: Towards a Research Agenda. *Third World Quarterly* 29 (1): 143–165.

Haynes, J. 2012. "Religion and Democracy: The Case of the AKP in Turkey." In *Religion, Politics, Society & the State*, edited by J. Fox, 73–88. Boulder, CO: Paradigm.

Haynes, J. 2013. *An Introduction to International Relations and Religion.* 2nd ed. London: Pearson.

Haynes, J. 2014. *Faith-Based Organizations at the United Nations.* New York: Palgrave Macmillan.

Human Rights Watch. 2005. *World Report.* New York: Human Rights Watch.

Joshi, D., and R. O'Dell. 2013. "Global Governance and Development Ideology: The United Nations and the World Bank on the Left–Right Spectrum." *Global Governance* 19: 249–275.

Juergensmeyer, M. "The Role of Religion in the New Global Order." In Europe. *A Beautiful Idea?*, edited by Rob Rieman, pp. 17–25. Tilburg: Nexus Institute.

Kayaoğlu, T. 2011. "Islam in the United Nations: The Liberal Limits of Postsecularism." Paper presented at the conference, "The Postsecular in International Politics," University of Sussex, Brighton, UK, October 27–28.

Keohane, R. 2002. "The Globalization of Informal Violence, Theories of World Politics, and the 'Liberalism of Fear.'" *Dialog-IO* Spring: 29–43.

Lehmann, K. 2016. *Religious NGOs in International Relations.* London: Routledge.

Littman, D. 1999. "Islamism Grows Stronger at the United Nations." *Middle East Quarterly* 6 (3): 59–64.

Lynch, C. 2012. "Religious Humanitarianism in a Neoliberal Age." The Religion Factor Blog, September 12. http://religionfactor.net/2012/09/12/religious-humanitarianism-in-a-neoliberal-age. Accessed May 29, 2013.

Micklethwait, J., and A. Wooldridge. 2009. *God Is Back: How the Global Rise of Faith Is Changing the World.* Harmondsworth, UK: Penguin.

Norwegian Agency for Development Cooperation (NORAD). 2013. "Lobbying for Faith and Family: A Study of Religious NGOs at the United Nations." Oslo: NORAD.

Nye, J. 2002. "Globalism Versus globalization." *The Globalist*, April 15. https://www.theglobalist.com/globalism-versus-globalization/. Accessed March 9, 2016.

Petersen, M.-J. 2010. "International Religious NGOs at the United Nations: A Study of a Group of Religious Organizations." *Journal of Humanitarian Assistance*, November. http://sites.tufts.edu/jha/archives/847. Accessed May 29, 2013.

Reychler, L. 1997. "Religion and Conflict." *International Journal of Peace Studies* 2 (1). http://www.gmu.edu/programs/icar/ijps/vol2_1/Reyschler.htm. Accessed March 9, 2016.

Speck, U. 2016. "From Trump to Merkel: How the World Is Divided Between Fear and Openness." *The Observer* (London), March 3, p. 29.

Samuel, June. 2007. *Adapting to Norms at the United Nations: The Abortion and Anti-Abortion Networks*, Ph.D. Dissertation, University of Maryland, College Park.

Standish, R. 1998. *Liberty in the Balance*. Rapidan, VA: Hartland.

Steger, M. 2013. *Globalization: A Very Short Introduction*. 3rd ed. Oxford, UK: Oxford University Press.

Toft, M. Duffy, D. Philpott, and T. S. Shah. 2011. *God's Century. Resurgent Religion and Global Politics*. New York: Norton.

Warburg, M. 2001. "Religious Organisations in a Global World: A Comparative Perspective." Paper presented at the 2001 international conference, "The Spiritual Supermarket: Religious Pluralism in the 21st Century," London School of Economics, London, April, 19–22, 2001.

Warner, C., and S. Walker. 2007. "Thinking About the Role of Religion in Foreign Policy: A Framework for Analysis." *Foreign Policy Analysis* 7: 113–135.

Wilson, E., and M. Steger. 2013. "Religious Globalisms in the Post-Secular Age." *Globalizations* 10 (3): 481–495.

World Bank. 2000. *Voices of the Poor*. Washington, DC: World Bank.

World Conference on Religion and Peace. 2001. "'Rejecting Terrorism, Promoting Peace with Justice: Religions Respond.' A Statement by the Executive Committee of the World Conference on Religion and Peace, October 24, 2001, New York." http://iccnow.org/documents/9-11-2001ReligionsforPeace.pdf. Accessed March 9, 2016.

....

CHAPTER 29

ART AND THE CULTURAL TRANSMISSION OF GLOBALIZATION

....

LINDA WILLIAMS

THERE is no precise historical juncture that can be identified as the point when globalization began to influence the visual arts. The term *globalization* itself only came into common usage by the late twentieth century, although its history as a process of socio-political transformation is, of course, centuries old (James and Steger 2014). Cultural responses to this process also have a long history with complex geopolitical origins that no doubt could be traced back along ancient migratory trade routes such as the Silk Road. In Europe, the cultural engagement in unfolding globalization was greatly extended by maritime circumnavigations of the world from the sixteenth century, when notions of a vast *New World* began to shape how people in young nation-states recalibrated the contours of their "imagined" communities (Anderson 1991). Hence, the imagery of the globe—of distant lands, exotic islands, or brave "new" worlds—combined with various imperialist tropes were commonplace in late sixteenth- and seventeenth-century art, literature, and letters. Not least in Anglophone culture, in which they often appeared in the works of major poets such as Shakespeare, Donne, Marvell, or Milton (M. Frank, Goldberg, and Newman 2016; Lim 1998; Mentz 2015). Shakespeare wrote from England of the shimmering new global horizons of the seventeenth century:

> O, wonder!
> How many goodly creatures are there here!
> How beauteous mankind is! O brave new world,
> That has such people in 't!
>
> —*The Tempest* (1611)

From the outset, however, early modern concepts of the global were tempered by the context of emergent nationalism and a robust colonial discourse imbued with world-destroying implications for subaltern peoples and unforeseen ecological consequences (Crosby 2003; Grove 1997). And by the twentieth century in England, Aldous Huxley's futuristic vision of the price of global modernity was much less sanguine than those of earlier writers:

> "What you need," the Savage went on, "is something *with* tears for a change. Nothing costs enough here."

—*Brave New World* (1932)

Cultural concepts of the global were also shaped by the deep shift in Western economies beginning in early modernity and now remaining *within* what Peter Sloterdijk (2014) refers to as the "world *interior* of capital." It is important to acknowledge this function of art as a "soft" agent of the extensive channels of international capital, a role it continues to occupy today. Yet this has never been its sole function because, paradoxically, art also has the capacity, as Franz Kafka (1904/1977) noted, to act "like an axe, to break up the frozen sea inside us." And it this transformative capacity of art that offers counternarratives to what has now been conceived as an advanced form of global socioeconomic *Empire* (Hardt and Negri 2000). As material culture, art is generally less capable of avoiding everyday contingencies than are poetry and philosophy, for example, yet since the reception of art is not based primarily on either language or literacy, this same materiality and the persuasive power of images can be powerful conduits for shaping transnational social imaginaries.

The concept of the social imaginary has gained considerable critical traction in the humanities (Appadurai 1996; Castoriadis 1987/1998; Connery 1996; James 2015; Taylor 2004), and the concept of a *global* imaginary is also gaining momentum (C. Frank 2010; Steger 2008). And while a unilateral social image of the global is clearly inconceivable in a highly contested geopolitical field of intensifying inequalities, the struggle to visualize a global imaginary has become a consistent theme of contemporary visual art. This aesthetic objective to visualize globalizing processes draws largely on a late twentieth-century cultural turn toward what George Modelski (2008: 11) called connectivism, in which globalization is viewed primarily as a condition of interdependence. This is particularly the case with themes of social justice and global ecological change in contemporary art, as discussed in greater detail later, but it also applies to the openness and connectivity of the global art markets that artists must negotiate. The connectivist approach to globalization, moreover, should be distinguished from an institutional approach that in the case of art applies to the persuasive power of cultural institutions, now commonly referred to as the culture industry, that effectively facilitate global art markets. Modelski observed,

> Both connectivity and openness are the product of a set of organizational and institutional arrangements. They derive from the organizations that originate and manage these flows; the regimes that facilitate and govern them; the matrices of mutual trust that sustain them; and the systems of knowledge that guide them. (p. 12)

If relations between the interior and exterior worlds of global capital are deeply contested, the same applies to the field referred to in developed countries as "contemporary art," produced by the "creative class" as an essential attribute of financially successful cities (Florida 2005). It is a field of cultural production disseminated by galleries and national biennales[1] and then endorsed by museum collections, art dealers, and private collectors. Yet it is also a field of critical discourse and social critique. Hence, the term "contemporary art" represents a frequently conflicted domain of social consensus confirming the way the world recognizes its most recent cultural self-images and that has, moreover, included many attempts to incorporate art from the "outside" into the interior of late modern culture.

Sloterdijk (2014; 265) identifies the Great Exhibition of 1851 in London as a turning point when the world was "transfigured by luxury and cosmopolitanism" from the far reaches of empire. Yet European maritime expansion had ensured that London's Crystal Palace was anything but "an agora or a trade fair beneath an open sky, but rather a hothouse that has drawn inwards everything that was once on the outside" (p. 12). In the field of contemporary art, there are comparable problems in how the global mainstream appropriates what it perceives as marginal. This is not just a recent problem; there are many well-known examples of cultural appropriation in late nineteenth- and early twentieth-century art, such as the use of Japanese or Polynesian art by the post-impressionists or the use of African tribal art by the cubists. Such examples were facilitated, on the one hand, by the rise in the market for Japanese prints and, on the other, by the establishment of the major European ethnographic museums from the 1870s (followed by the first Venice Biennale of 1895). Such examples are often regarded as colonizing gestures toward "primitivism" despite the fact that the artists themselves viewed the works they adapted as sophisticated and saw plagiarizing them as a form of admiration.

In the current discussion, however, rather than engaging in an ethnographic account of the diversity of "outsider" art, my focus is on art that can be described as late modern, which is to say, as art originating in a system of largely Western aesthetic values that, by default, are clearly located *within* the field of global capital. The fact that such art is no longer exclusively Western has become clearer during the past two decades by the global focus on contemporary Asian art and, more recently, on art from the global war zone of the Middle East. As, for example, the huge growth in the Western market for Chinese art attests, recent Asian art is as enmeshed in the world interior of capital as the European or American art that is more closely aligned with Western traditions. Notwithstanding claims for a new cultural internationalism, however, as Lotte Philipsen (2010; 80–83) has noted, the formal media of non-Western contemporary art has a conceptual framework that is essentially a product of Western processes of modernity. This is not to say that this global art of the contemporary condition does not have its own pluralities, dissensions, or forms of immanent critique but, rather, that it is delimited by its place *inside* a Western paradigm and exclusive cultural regime where the pressures of the art market mitigate against the agency of art as a form of social critique.

This global art market originated in seventeenth-century Holland, as distinct from other coeval colonial states such as Catholic Spain, Portugal, or France, where art patronage came mainly from the church and court, and England, where acquiring artworks was still largely a privilege of the court and aristocracy. Whereas in the Netherlands by the age of colonial expansion, there was a thriving middle-class art market for which Dutch artists produced large numbers of paintings (Montiaz 1989).[2] These works often referenced the effects of early globalization, to which I turn briefly before discussing art in the transdisciplinary field, where it has become a significant agent in the transmission of cultural globalization.

NEW WORLDS

An early form of global capitalism first emerged in the sixteenth and seventeenth centuries when European nation-states competed for imperial supremacy of the oceans. Although long before the era of mass consumption, Dutch art of this period effectively redefined the "cultural biography" of objects as luxury commodities (Kopytoff 1986), yet it also had the capacity to reveal their less stable meanings as objects of desire.

There is, for example, a detectable, if inchoate sense of tension in the imagery of maps and geographers' globes featured in many seventeenth-century still life or genre pictures. These works were produced at a time when the Western imagination was still shaped by theocentric ontologies and was turning only gradually toward the new economic logic of modernity. In Dutch paintings of this time, the cartographic aim to record with precision the outlines of new lands was at first moderated by attempts to anchor new territories in more familiar traditions by framing them with personifications of the natural elements, biblical narratives, or mythological figures. As the art historian Svetlana Alpers (1983: 122) has observed, however, Dutch map makers were known as "world describers," a term that she also aptly ascribes to Dutch painters with their heightened skill in carefully depicting the material details of everyday life. Although this "mapping impulse" of Dutch art, as Alpers calls it, certainly shaped new forms of secular landscape painting, it also inclined artists toward achieving greater ethnographic accuracy, where in maps of Africa or South America, for example, continental coastlines were flanked by careful representations of indigenous peoples (although this certainly did not extend to African slaves shipped to sugar plantations in Dutch Brazil).

The art of the new Dutch Republic also referred to geographers' globes, often rendered as objects as easily grasped as any of the other luxury items on a desk or table. Yet such worlds were also defined by the vast new horizons offered by early telescopes and by the new microscopes that revealed previously unknown dimensions of the physical world. This new lens technology complemented traditional juxtapositions of scale between near and far, small and large, that, as Alpers (1983) acknowledges, had long occupied the artists of Northern Europe. Lenses were also adapted by Dutch and Flemish artists to achieve greater refinement in painted details such as reflections in glass or metal. Hence, as this golden age of Dutch art brought greater visual acuity and focus to a European imaginary reshaped by global colonialism, it also drew on technological advances that offered new lines of enquiry into other kinds of worlds.

Of course, the maps and globes featured in Dutch art were also tools of global mercantile expansion. Companies such as the Dutch VOC (United East India Company, 1602), West India Company (1621), or the British East India Company (1600) were the first of many later multinational companies, including HSBC and BP in London and the Dutch-based ING and Shell. In the seventeenth century, early multinational corporations were new gateways for the trade of luxury goods shipped from afar to Europe. This was a naval trade greatly enabled by technological advances such as the magnetic compass, paper, and gunpowder, which were all invented by the Chinese (Brook 2008: 19). The Low Countries in particular were important channels for the trade in material culture (Rittersma 2010), not least in cosmopolitan cities such as Antwerp or in the bustling city of Amsterdam, where in Braudel's (1984) account,

> Everything was crammed together, concentrated: the ships in the harbor, wedged as tight as herrings in a case, the lighters plying up and down the canals, the merchants who thronged to the Bourse, and the goods that piled up in warehouses only to pour out of them. (p. 236)

Antwerp, Amsterdam, and other Dutch cities such as Delft were also centers for the production and trade of paintings with mainly secular subjects, such as still life, landscapes, genre pictures, and portraits. Dutch bourgeois preferences for paintings typically showed "little of colonial working life, concentrating rather on colonial benefits to trade, art and science" (Westermann, 1996: 114) while conveying a palpable sense of confidence in national prosperity. The popular genre of still life especially provided a quiet retreat of sorts from the busy pace and noise of the city while also conveying allusions to global horizons: where imported consumer goods such as exotic fruits and foreign flowers were placed beside Pacific Ocean nautilus shells fashioned as wine goblets, or next to pipes for American tobacco and Chinese export porcelain.

In Dutch art of the secular baroque, such imperial luxury goods are typically depicted with skillful verisimilitude, responding to the sumptuous effects of color and light arrayed across domestic objects in ways that suggest a celebration of new forms of consumption. Yet these pictures also suggest an inchoate sense of tension in the way flowers, fruit, or glassware were so often combined with the canonical imagery of still life as *memento mori*, where skulls, hourglasses, or flickering candle flames signified the vanity of human endeavors. Such references imbued these pictures with a certain ambiguity about the accumulation of worldly wealth that, if not derived from an ambivalence about globalization as such, suggests an unease with the emergence of capital as its driving force that, as discussed later, remains a persistent theme in contemporary art. The historian Simon Schama wrote of dual value systems underpinning seventeenth-century Dutch culture, in which the one "embraced money; power; authority; the gratification of appetite" while the other "invoked austerity; piety; frugality; parsimony; sobriety; the vanity of worldly success; the exclusive community of sacred congregation; the abhorrent" (Schama 1979: 113)—a tension he later went on to describe as an "embarrassment of riches" (Schama 1987).

Schama's account is certainly plausible, especially in light of Weber's (1905/1965) famous essay on the role of Calvinist salvation anxiety in the spirit of capitalism. Yet, on the other hand, an iconography that juxtaposes new forms of wealth and excess with mortality and decay may also plausibly indicate the nascent signs of a more secular and immanent form of critique. In the context of a new republic recently released from the heavy yoke of Spanish occupation, the experience of a colonization was not foreign to the Dutch people. This obviously did little to prevent the Dutch from profiting from the slave trade as much as other European states. But along with the kind of Calvinist restraint that recoiled from the Spanish baroque, the experience of colonialism may have contributed to an emergent aesthetic that allowed for abundance but drew a line against triumphalism.

The abundant imagery of flowers, fruit, and wine in Dutch still life pictures evoked reflections on mortality through images of dead animals such as birds, rabbits, or fish that were to be prepared as food. Dead animals are also a recurring feature of contemporary art, where they are reconstructed through taxidermy and often appear in a strange new poetic alluding to questions of the industrialized production of animals or global species extinctions. The contemporary Dutch taxidermist company Darwin, Sinke & Tongeren, on the other hand, sells stuffed animals in exhibitions with titles such as *New Masters* in homage to the seventeenth-century Dutch still life. In 2015, the company exhibited examples of its taxidermy in London, where the British artist Damien Hirst bought every item for his private collection. Hirst's artworks from the early 1990s of animals preserved in glass tanks of formaldehyde are well known as modern *memento mori*, although his more recent meditations on death have focused in greater detail on objects saturated by global capital, the subject of the following section.

GLOBAL LIQUIDITY

Hirst refers to the currency of diamonds rather than money as such, although their monetary status is clear enough in his paintings and display cabinets with synthetic diamonds.[3] In his major work *For the Love of God* (2007), references to big money are more explicit because Hirst had a London jeweler construct a platinum replica of an eighteenth-century human skull, embellishing it with the original teeth and 8,600 flawless diamonds at 1,106.18 carats valued somewhere around £10–14 million. On his website,[4] Hirst gave some clues to his thinking about this work:

> It becomes necessary to question whether they are "just a bit of glass," with accumulated metaphorical significance? Or [whether they] are genuine objects of supreme beauty connected with life.[5]
>
> The cutthroat nature of the diamond industry, and the capitalist society which supports it, is central to the work's concept. . . . The stones "bring out the best and the worst in people . . . people kill for diamonds, they kill each other."[6]

These questions seem reasonable enough, but the work was also designed to maximize publicity and, in effect, comments more eloquently on the global art market than on extractive mining or blood diamonds. Hirst marketed the skull for £50 million, and it remains controversial whether or not the artist later sold it for this sum to an anonymous consortium. What it did achieve, however, was a tryst with the media in partnership with an image of a wealthy celebrity artist, vigilant in the protection and promotion of his own brand while also managing a fashionably sardonic refutation of the romantic myth of the heroically impoverished artist.

By contrast, the artists of the Danish art collective Superflex have for some years made elaborate artworks aimed as direct hits on the global system of corporate capitalism. For example, their 2009 video, *The Financial Crisis*, took advantage of the stock market crash of 2008 and subsequent volatility in global markets to call attention to how global liquidity is manipulated in ways that leave most people with little sense of control. Superflex had an actor perform as a traditional hypnotist seeking to control viewers into believing they were the "invisible hand" of the market. Viewers were then addressed as if—in a hypnotized state—they had assumed the personality of one of the global financial elite and hence would suddenly be able to wake from the nightmare of their financial insecurity to become fully alert to how capital actually works. Like their work *Flooded McDonald's* (2009), in which global sea level rise appears to swamp the global fast-food franchise, *The Financial Crisis* puts satirical humor to good effect so that political critique is close enough to the rhetorical surface of the work to become part of the joke. Later, in an exhibition held in Mexico City, *The Corrupt Show and Speculative Machine* (2014), Superflex offered the idea of copying corruption as a useful tool for political sedition. Held on the grounds of a Jumex Mexican fruit juice plant to which the factory workers were invited, the exhibition featured banners of "bankrupt banks" displaying the corporate logos of the failed companies the workers once trusted. Viewers were also invited to participate in a work called *Copy Light/Factory*, encouraging them to appropriate intellectual property, trademarks, global brand ownership, and patents by scanning or photocopying. In ridiculing the corporatization of everyday life, Superflex also provided all the components of popular domestic lamp products so that people could make their own lamps from contemporary design copyrights. In a similar spirit, the group has also opened free shops as artworks. Indistinguishable from ordinary shops, there are no references to art, Superflex, the sponsors, or the word "free" so that buyers only realize there is no cost involved when they receive a printed bill for zero. Superflex's elaborate strategies include publications on political critique and seminars during which the public is invited to question how global corporations impact on people's everyday lives. Superflex's work is clearly a dedicated attempt to provoke counter-narratives to those sanctioned by multinational companies, and it often succeeds because it combines these questions with shrewd satire and innovative ways of engaging its audiences through artworks.

In her work *RMB City* from 2009, digital artist Cao Fei invited the public to visit her virtual city in the online world of *Second Life*. Named after the abbreviation for the Renminbi, the currency of the People's Republic of China, the City Planning for *RMB City* can be viewed at https://www.youtube.com/watch?v=9MhfATPZAog. This playful reflection on life in a Chinese global megacity is followed in other sequences based on the activities of a number of digital avatars living in the city. At first glance, the world of RMB City appears to be an attractive site of hybrid Eastern and Western mythologies—complete with a big floating panda bear and giant sinking statues of Chairman Mao. But RMB City also acknowledges history, as one of the avatars, Uncle Mars, explains to the baby "Little China Sun" (*Live in RMB City*, https://www.youtube.com/watch?v=61k679iP2xU):

> The buildings of this city are merely incarnations of your parents. In another time and space, they reverberate with the hollow shells of despair.

This is a real-world memory inside RMB City, where heroic Chinese modernity meets hard labor and the deepening gulf between wealth and poverty. Moreover, even in the futuristic, super-flat contours of *Second Life*, where dirt or pain are rarely seen, Cao Fei includes tanks, container ships, belching smokestacks, and the unmistakable signs of pollution gushing from giant drains. Yet her gentle satire on global capital is ambivalent: RMB City is polluted and there are metaphoric shadows that can be glimpsed in the flatness of this digital world, yet it also offers a buoyantly optimistic vision of the potential of technology and the future of China in the world.

Other approaches to money in contemporary art also appear to have a satirical edge, yet this too is frequently ambiguous, as in the case of the German artist Hans-Peter Feldmann, who works in art-multiples based on the playful reconfiguration of traditional taxonomies of apparently arbitrary images drawn from everyday life. In 2010, Feldmann was awarded the prestigious $100,000 Hugo Boss art prize that includes an exhibition at the Guggenheim in New York City. Following this, in 2011, Feldman devised *The Art and Money Project*, an installation at the Guggenheim where 100,000 real $1 bills were fixed to the walls. Feldmann's gesture could be read as a statement that the collapsing of distinctions between art and money simply represents a basic category error, yet it could also be understood as a recognition that institutions such as the Guggenheim play a powerful role in determining which artworks become global investments. And it is perhaps for this reason that Cao Fei has carefully constructed a "Guggenheim of the Virtual World" in her RMB City. Understandably, Feldmann took his money home after the exhibition, unlike the British artist Jimmy Cauty and his friend Bill Drummond, who, after becoming wealthy in the 1980s following their years in the successfully edgy band KLF, decided to send a message to the culture industry with an utterly insouciant project: *K Foundation Burn a Million Quid*. This project was undertaken with real money in August 1994, when it was also filmed.

Artists who do not share such celebrity status are often dissatisfied with the money galleries apportion to them on the sale of their works, and they occasionally make these concerns explicit, as for example in the 2009 work *Distribution of Wealth* by the Seattle-based arts collective SuttonBeresculler. These artists took a pile of 100 $1 bills and cut them neatly into proportioned pieces to expose the small remuneration received by artists from dealers and galleries. Blake Fall-Conroy's *Minimum Wage Machine* (2008–2010), on the other hand, was concerned with more general inequality in the social distribution of wealth. For this project, the artist made a hand-operated vending machine that released one penny for approximately 5 seconds of turning, or $7.67 an hour—a sum representing the minimum wage received by 1.8 million Americans in 2010, while at the same time a further 2.5 million people were paid less than the minimum wage.[7]

The theme of money persists in more recent art, as in Vienna in 2015, where an entire series of exhibitions was based on art about money. Photographs of vaults filled with gold bars were joined by virtual art platforms on which the group Cointemporary sold art online for Bitcoin currency, and a work by Tom Molloy, *Swarm* (2006), comprised a swarm-like mass of dollar bills folded as paper planes that appeared to have pierced the gallery walls. The walls of the world's galleries, this work seems to suggest, are as malleable to the flow of capital as the international market that rapidly adapts to most art-based social critiques through the processes of exclusivity and commodification. Hence, one of the most contemptuous anti-establishment gestures in modern art, the common urinal Marcel Duchamp transformed as a dada *Fountain* in 1917, by 2002 sorely disappointed auctioneers at Phillips de Pury & Luxembourg when it fetched a mere £1,185,000.

DISPLACED WORLDS

As much of the world's history of art patronage indicates, however, there is no cultural law demonstrating how big money compromises aesthetic value, yet on the other hand, when art is valued for the density of its saturation by market value alone, its affective meanings become warped. Apart from their effect on art, inflated art market values also obviously reveal massive differences between the cultural agency of a privileged few and that in the world of the poor, where even the prospect of *functioning* urinals or clean water is unlikely. Nonetheless, new cultural geographies of inequality have become another major theme of contemporary art, where such artworks are negotiated in the constantly shifting spaces between their means of production and the exclusive sites of their reception in contemporary galleries or the even more rarified domains of corporate philanthropy. These are the main outlets for artists adapting to the aesthetics challenges of representing shifting geopolitical boundaries (Belting, Birken, and Buddensieg 2011; Harris 2011; Philipsen 2010) or migratory cultures (Bal and Hernandez-Navarro 2011; Barriendos Rodriguez 2011) as they attempt to offer viable alternatives to the stream of mass media images in which the anguished face of one refugee seems to meld seamlessly with so many others. Although art in public spaces appears to offer alternative avenues to the usual outlets for artists, access and funding for art to urban sites also require negotiation with civic bodies and developers. And because urban artworks are often publicly contentious, a common solution is often the kind of aesthetic compromises that litter cities with dreary large-scale objects, directing the business of the cutting edge either to ephemeral public artworks or right back into the domain of the gallery.

In 2009, the French Algerian artist Kader Attia brought the shantytowns and markets of North Africa into the public event of the Biennale of Sydney with a work called *Kasbah*. Attia recycled materials similar to those recycled as roofs by people in urban slums throughout the world: corrugated iron, old doors, scrap metal, along with the ubiquitous satellite dish. This was not a work inviting an easy stroll through an exotic kasbah because the makeshift roofs completely covered the floor so that visitors were required to walk on top of them. It is difficult to gauge what visitors made of the overworked symbolism implied by trampling over the roofs of the poor, but at least the point appeared to be to make the physical negotiation of the work noisy and difficult and to alert people to watch their step.

In an earlier work, *Ghost* (2007), Attia filled a room with the hollow shapes of enrobed Muslim women made entirely out of tinfoil, kneeling uniformly in prayer. This work was purchased by the influential British collector George Saatchi, who included it the Saatchi Gallery exhibition *Unveiled: New Art from the Middle East*, and it is described on the Saatchi website as follows:

> Attia's figures become alien and futuristic, synthesising the abject and divine. Bowing in shimmering meditation, their ritual is equally seductive and hollow, questioning modern ideologies—from religion to nationalism and consumerism—in relation to individual identity, social perception, devotion and exclusion.[8]

Whatever Attia's own perception may be of women at prayer, the romanticization of the other in such art-speak obfuscation seems to filter out the lived experience of a largely hidden world rather than bringing us closer to understanding it. It also exposes the risk that the incorporation of cultural difference into the established art system might ultimately lead to a homogeneity that is "equally seductive and hollow."

Other works are less at risk of mystification, such as those by the Indian artists of RAQS Media Collective, who created a series of hollow and partial figures in white fiberglass, *Coronation Park*, for the 2015 Venice Biennale. This work was a direct reference to a neglected park of that name in Delhi, where there are still a range of grandiose marble statues of monarchs, viceroys, and colonial officials from the days of the British Raj. For some years, RAQS has been engaged in a robust investigation of concepts of time and how history can be read in the present, and *Coronation Park* brings that intellectual focus to bear on the ultimate hollowness at the center of imperial power. The transitory nature of colonial authority is made clear enough in these figural sculptures to be generally accessible, not only because they are grounded in history but also because there were circular discs on the plinths with imaginary epitaphs that brought the History of Great Men into the realm of common personal emotions. Hence, beneath one rather pompous-looking figure, RAQS wrote, "The crowd would laugh at him. And his whole life was one long struggle not to be laughed at." On the plinth of another was written, "It was at this moment, as he stood there with the weapon in his hands, that he first grasped the hollowness, the futility," and by a figure that seemed to embody the gradual entropy in the pursuit of power, RAQS wrote, "In the end he could not stand it any longer and went away."

The focus on how emotional life intersects with history also influences the work of the expatriate Iranian artist Sherin Neshat. Neshat's work questions normative codes of behavior for women, particularly (although not exclusively) in Islamic regimes. Her photographs, videos, and films have a compelling poetic quality drawing on her experience of how gender boundaries are prescribed in both Islamic and Western countries and also how these boundaries shape profoundly the limits of what is possible for people to feel for one another or for their place in the world. The Guggenheim online account of Neshat's approach provides basic information about her background in a way that allows viewers to draw their own conclusions about the artworks.

Brief biographical outlines are usually all that remain of lives lived in prosperous countries, whereas the lives of countless others in poorer places remain unrecorded, and women especially become part of the anonymous mass conceived as global "population." Sometimes this is because in some cultures the lives of ordinary women are not viewed as eventful, but it is probably more often because vast numbers of people are regarded as living somewhere "outside" social and historical narratives, especially those who for one cause or another find themselves in exile.

Like Neshat, the Palestinian Mona Hatoum has also lived in both Western and Islamic countries. In an early video work from 1988, *Measures of Difference*, Hatoum recited letters she received from her home in Beirut and translated from Arabic to English. These intimate letters were from her mother, written to a daughter exiled by war. The soundtrack of the letters is accompanied by a series of discrete photos of Hatoum's mother in the privacy of the shower and then superimposed with the Arabic script of the letters. And, as if in a private reverie while washing, the mother also confides her reflections on patriarchy. Hence, *Measures of Difference* responds directly to the wars of the Middle East while confronting some of the rigid gender hierarchies that add to the suffering of women in the region. The key feature of this work, however, is that it binds these major social issues into a much smaller and personally reflective story, so it is as if the artwork itself is Hatoum's reply to her mother across almost insurmountable boundaries. The old feminist dictum that the personal is political takes on new meaning in this work, which has the counterintuitive effect of making it both public and extending to many in others in the world with comparable cause to reflect on both misogyny and the personal consequences of war. Hatoum does not present such things as global abstractions but, rather, as artworks derived from specific circumstances and an approach to agency analogous to what Bruno Latour (2005) described as "what actors achieve by scaling, spacing, and contextualizing each other" (p. 174).

Hatoum's ability to visualize the affective qualities of personal life transformed by conflicting global interests in the Middle East was put to good effect in 2005 when her artwork *Mobile Home* was exhibited in London. This was an installation in which the ordinary stuff of domestic life—used furniture, household objects, children's toys, and worn suitcases—was shunted along very gradually on wires between two defining metal bollards of the type used in urban crowd control. Arrayed as they were between the bollards, the objects were oddly familiar—perhaps of glimpses of life in refugee camps seen on television screens, yet also easily recognized as items of daily routines of people anywhere in the world. There were also odd laundry items pegged to lines hanging above the objects that were also on the move, highlighting the sheer frustration that involuntary migrants face in maintaining even the most basic requirements of family life. Hatoum's tactic of using familiar objects to reach across cultural boundaries was also evident in her work of 2011, *Suspended*, in which a room was filled with children's swings, each inscribed with a street map of one of the world's capital cities. In this case, however, it was the viewers who were mobile and whose passage through the room created enough movement for the cities on the swings to shift in relation to each other—in anticipation, perhaps, of ever-increasing numbers of involuntary migrations throughout the world.

The use of everyday objects as common ground between artist and viewer was also an important element in an artwork by the Indian artist Subodh Gupta. Gupta's monumental sculpture *Line of Control* (2008) was a response to the potentially explosive border dispute between India and Pakistan over territory in Kashmir. The five states recognized under the international Treaty on the Non-Proliferation of Nuclear Weapons do not include countries such as India, Pakistan, Israel, and North Korea, although it is widely known that they also have the capacity to use nuclear weapons. Gupta's acknowledgment of the lethal potential of regional disputes between such nuclear powers is instantly recognizable in his reconfiguration of the shape of the mushroom clouds known to people everywhere following the nuclear destruction of Hiroshima and Nagasaki, Japan, in 1945. Gupta's cloud is also recognizably regional because it is made of hundreds of the kind of steel pots, pans, and bowls that are used daily by millions of people throughout the subcontinent, regardless of geopolitical boundaries, religion, or cultural differences. In India, these mass-produced objects are instantly familiar as signs of the kind of shared experiences to which national boundaries are entirely irrelevant—just as local differences would become insignificant in comparison to the scale of nondiscriminatory destruction that would result from a nuclear war. Gupta's work was first exhibited in the Tate Triennial in London and later sold by Euro-American art dealers and publishers Hauser and Wirth to the Indian collector Kiran Nadar. It is currently on public display in the foyer of Nadar's museum of art in New Delhi.

Art materials used by the Kurdish artist Hiwa K also refer to conflict in the Middle East as the result of global incursions into the region. His powerful work *Bell*, presented at the 2015 Venice Biennale, included videos of foundry workers casting a large metal bell in the Kurdish city of Sulaymaniyah in northern Iraq using metal from military hardware abandoned in Kurdistan. The bell is modeled on the famous Liberty Bell in Philadelphia, a national icon of American independence, which the artist placed in a wooden frame in front of the videos. Although Hiwa K's allusion to the American gift of independence to Iraq was clearly ironic, he also acknowledged a range of other vested interests because the metal of the bell was taken from weaponry sold by companies from more than 40 countries to supply different armed forces in the region. Hiwa K's work is a well-crafted example of cultural resilience in a region devastated by years of war. It also evinces a sense of determined cultural resistance in the artist's reference to the history of art in Iraq, with sculpted reliefs on the bell's surface depicting the ancient Mesopotamian artifacts in the Baghdad Mosul Museum that were stolen or destroyed by ISIS.

Other artwork aimed at ISIS comes from the recently formed Edge of Arabia art and art education collective, founded by Abdulnasser Gharem, an artist from Riyadh (and until 2014, also a lieutenant colonel in the Saudi army). Gharem's works often feature stealth bombers or tanks embellished with the intricate decorative imagery of Islamic architecture, along with scaled-down sculptural models of global icons such as the Capitol Dome in Washington, DC, and the Dome of the Rock in Jerusalem. Gharem has openly advocated the arts as a viable alternative for disaffected youth drawn to ISIS, public remarks to which the conservative Saudi regime has not objected. Gharem is also known as the highest selling living Gulf artist who has donated proceeds of sales to Edge of Arabia. The practice of art in Saudi Arabia, however, is clearly not without risk, as was demonstrated recently by the case of the Palestinian poet Ashraf Fayadh. Fayadh, the son of refugees and a member of Edge of Arabia, was condemned to be beheaded in 2015 for the religious crime of apostasy, with his poems used as evidence. After an international outcry from arts organizations and human rights groups, and following legal appeal, his sentence was commuted to eight years in prison and 800 lashes. Fayadh is currently in prison, although as a mark of the global status of artists' rights, the director of advocacy for the International Humanist and Ethical Union (IHEU), Elisabeth O'Casey, recently read one of his poems to the UN Human Right's Council,[9] a committee that includes Saudi delegates:

> Prophets have retired
> so do not wait, for a prophet to be resurrected for you.
> And for you,
> for you the observers bring their daily reports
> and earn their high wages.
> How much money is necessary
> for a life of dignity.

Issues of human justice in a global context of shifting geopolitical boundaries and involuntary migration are important themes in contemporary art, as Mona Hatoum's 2013 work, *Hot Spot*, also suggests. Constructed in stainless steel, this is a cage-like construction of the globe in which land masses and continents are outlined in red neon that projects an artificial glow of light across the gallery. This large globe is accompanied by a Peters Projection map of the world on an adjacent wall. As with the maps and globes of early modern Dutch art, there is a sense of tension in Hatoum's work between the realist's aim to accurately describe the world and the aim to represent the affective qualities of a world of conflicting human interests. Hatoum's glowing red globe also suggests a world now endangered by climate change, another key theme of contemporary art and the focus of the concluding section.

Global Ecologies

Although artists have always responded to the non-human world, it is really only during the past two or three decades that environmental critique has become a theme of contemporary art. This is a wide international field, emerging with the proliferation of environmental activism from the 1970s and since becoming a global network in which green activists, non-governmental organizations, and artists often work together across international boundaries. One of the earliest icons of this globalizing green movement was the iconic photograph of the earth taken from space in 1972 by the astronauts of Apollo 17, known as the *Blue Marble*. It was associated not only with the idea of global ecology but also with the notion of a "blue planet" in which the oceans comprise 71% of the world's surface. Yet most environmental art of the late twentieth century focused on more terrestrial ecologies, and the "oceanic turn" in the arts and humanities came after the turn of the century.[10] The global circulatory system of the world's oceans provides a powerful image of ecological interdependence analogous to Lynn Margulis' (1998) model of complex Earth systems understood as a "symbiotic planet." Yet the oceans are also conduits of military expansion and provide a fluid medium for the perpetual international trade in raw materials and consumer goods, most of which continue to be shipped across the world.

In 1608, Hugo Grotius (1608/1916) published his defense of the rights of the VOC or Dutch East India Company based on the concept of the freedom of the seas as the natural conduit of free trade:

> The OCEAN, that expanse of water which antiquity describes as the immense, the infinite, bounded only by the heavens, parents of all things . . . the ocean which . . . can neither be seized, nor enclosed; nay, which rather possesses the earth than is possessed. (p. 37)

Yet as Braudel (1981: 402) observed, the "asymmetry" in global power relations and "the triumph of the West" began when European nations gained world supremacy of the oceans that Grotius represented as immense bodies "beyond" possession. Braudel asked why it was the Europeans rather than capable Chinese or Arab navigators who claimed the globe, and he concluded that along with certain global wind patterns and the sturdy construction of Western vessels, the Western hegemony of the seas was enabled by the driving momentum of merchant capitalism combined with new practical discoveries (p. 415). Whatever the definitive causes, however, by the seventeenth century, the intercontinental routes defined by the "trade winds" were dominated by Europe. And as Sloterdijk (2014) suggests, this required a significant readjustment of the European imaginary away from old Ptolemaic beliefs to the recognition that "what they called the earth was revealed as a waterworld" (p. 40). Steve Mentz (2015) has taken this imaginative shift into the realm of global ecologies in his account of the unforeseen environmental consequences of the early modern "age of shipwrecks." Drawing on Sloterdijk's focus on the "waterworld" of modernity, Mentz disputes the notion that the Anthropocene as an era of global environmental decay was initiated by the rise of industrialization in the late eighteenth century (p. xv). As I have also argued elsewhere (Williams 2016), Mentz proposes that it was the processes of "wet globalization" in the sixteenth and seventeenth centuries rather than the Industrial Revolution as such that destabilized traditional ways of understanding the natural world and precipitated an age of ecological crisis.

This crisis has become a major theme of contemporary environmental art, in which the world's oceans are increasingly being viewed as a metaphor for what Modelski (2008) calls connectivist concepts of global. As Hester Blum (201) has aptly observed, however, the ocean is not simply a metaphor. Like other ecological systems, it has an extra-discursive ontological status that also happens to be largely incompatible with everyday human "ter-restrial" requirements. As such, global oceans consistently resist human efforts to define and control them, yet as Philip Steinberg (2001) notes, the ocean is also clearly a socially constructed space:

> As various ocean uses and the contradictions among them intensify, and as each of these constructions conflicts with the spaces of representation being constructed by everyday ac-tors outside the imperatives of capitalism's dominant (and contradictory) spatial practices, it seems likely that the ocean will become a site for imagining and creating social institutions and relations, for land as well for sea. (p. 209)

In relation to our current concerns about art and the processes of globalization, this raises the question of how contemporary artists have responded to our social relations with the oceans, especially as a way of understanding the processes of globalization.

One outstanding exception to how environmental artists in the twentieth century tended to elide the blueness of the planet was Allan Sekula's major long-term art project on the oceans (1989–1995), which, if not primarily ecocritical, did investigate the crucial agency of the world's oceans in processes of globalization. Sekula's *Fish Story* culminated in a 1995 book of the same title that combined photographs he had exhibited and a text in which he described his work as an interpretation of "the imaginary and material geographies of the advanced capitalist world" (Sekula 1995: 202).

Sekula's (1995) text effectively traced the history of seafaring in the modern age as a pro-cess of globalization from the period of Dutch maritime expansion (p. 45), while the critical realist edge of his photography depicted images of industrial ports all over the world and the ordinary workers who maintained them. Sekula's photos dramatized how, during the late twentieth century, the world's seaports and the lives of those who lived in them were transformed by the impact of late capitalism:

> If the stock-market is the site in which the abstract character of money rules, the harbor is the site in which material goods appear in bulk, in the very flux of exchange. . . . But the more regularized, literally containerized, the movement of goods in harbors, that is, the more rationalized and automated, the more the harbor comes to resemble the stockmarket. (p. 12)

As containerization became seamlessly standardized by the late 1960s, loading and unloading times were regulated just as tasks that were once performed be merchant seamen and dock workers became mechanized. Sekula suggested that because the ocean was such a primary force in globalization, such workers were in a privileged position to witness the politics of global trade. And he argued that this also enabled them to catch occasional glimpses of the contradictions and secrets of global relations in such instances of his account of the Danish sailors who discovered a broken crate, revealing how Israel was secretly shipping American weapons to Iran in the 1980s (p. 32).

As Elizabeth Deloughrey (2010) has remarked of the Atlantic Ocean, as an agent of mo-dernity, the ocean has often been understood in terms of its capacity to absorb waste: the wasted lives of slaves, militarization and radioactive waste, and the industrialized waste of heavy metals. Although there are visible forms of pollution, such as the great islands of plastic in the five main oceanic gyres,[11] much of the sea often still looks like a shining, pristine expanse of water. Effectively, the most insidious forms of oceanic pollution remain invisible to the human eye so that ocean acidification, mercury poisoning, and pollution by microplastics (Andrady 2011), along with the almost imperceptible effects of ocean warming, are slowly but surely afflicting every ocean on Earth. These invisible processes of oceanic pollution are analogous to what Rob Nixon (2013) aptly described as the "slow violence" of widespread environmental erosion. This slow assault on the world's oceans, furthermore, represents a risk not only to human food supplies but also to a diverse range of ocean creatures threatened with extinction (Herr and Gallard 2009; Kolbert 2014).

The slow violence of ocean pollution is entirely at odds with a powerful Western cultural tradition in which the sea has long appealed to the romantic imagination as an emblem of the power and mystery of nature (Isham 2004). This wild, unsullied image of the ocean that has arguably had a significant impact on the Western imagination of global space is now effectively fouled and endangered by human excess. It is a powerful material contradiction that is entirely incompatible with the imagery of global oceans at the level of affects that has formed the basis of recent environmental art responding to escalating threats to global ecologies, some of which is situated in the ocean itself.

The British artist Jason deCaires Taylor has installed an artwork called *Inertia* off the coast of Cancún in the Gulf of Mexico at a depth of five meters in the Caribbean Sea. Lodged firmly on the seafloor, the cast-concrete sculpture depicts a man in a pair of shorts slouching on a sofa with a plate of fast food, watching television. The figure appears to be lethargic and so absorbed in the screen that he appears entirely indifferent to the life in the tropical waters around him. Located on the seabed in 2011, the work itself has since accrued different types of marine algae beneficial to the marine environment as they produce carbon carbonates and form the basis of coral formations. Most of de Caires Taylor's artworks are located underwater in similar marine environments as silent commentaries on anthropogenic changes to the oceans in sea-level rise and pollution. And just to the south of this site, on the shores of the largest biosphere resort in Mexico, at Sian Ka'an, the artist Alejandro Duran collects plastic objects washed up on the shore. Duran has identified plastic waste from more than 50 countries on six continents that he collects and sorts into various colors and shapes before photographing it. The artificiality of the plastic colors forms a sharp contrast to the reserve, and the artist arranges the objects as it they have been washed up by the tide as waves of human waste.

Most of the world's oxygen is produced by the oceans and is vital to both human and oceanic life. Oxygen is something we readily identify as a human necessity, and as such, it is something the Australian artist Janet Laurence refers to regularly in her artworks through the tubes and apparatuses of hospital resuscitation units. Laurence combines these with fragile specimens such as coral, shells, or fish skeletons presented in a range of glass jars and cases. By exhibiting her work *Deep Breathing/Resuscitation of the Reef* in 2015 in Paris during the United Nations Climate Change Conference, or COP21, she sought a way of bringing global attention to the vulnerability of Australia's Great Barrier Reef. In her work *Coral Collapse* (2015–2016), Laurence aimed to imaginatively resuscitate the Great Barrier Reef itself with the same thin plastic pipes taken from hospital resuscitation equipment and glass jars—translucent materials that she later photographed underwater. In these works, equipment from hospital units is brought to bear metaphorically on reefs made vulnerable by ocean warming and coral bleaching, and if the connections between the art materials and the reef are at first oblique, the general fragility of the imagery is an effective means of encouraging the viewer to make the imaginative leap in joining human illness with the visually seductive images of an underwater world that is slowly dying.

One of the least visible results of how the world's oceans absorb CO_2 is the drop in calcium carbonates that plankton such as the microscopic creatures known as foraminifera need to build their exoskeletons. This is a serious problem with the potential to erode entire food chains, but there is a massive gulf between the human world and the habitats of invisible marine creatures that is difficult to breach imaginatively. The Scottish artist Anne Bevan, however, has attempted to render this process visible through her fragile sculptural reconstructions of microscopic foraminifera. Bevan is best known for her poetic installations that explore the metaphoric qualities of seawater, such as in *Moon Pool* (2002), for example, in which the poetry of the ocean was brought into a forest. In her work *Source* (2001), Bevan tested the quality of seawater transported from Venice in glass bottles that were compared with the northern waters of Scotland before combining them both in Orkney Harbor—a confluence drawing attention to the environmental vulnerability of water and its global circulation. In *Nova* (2007), Bevan explored a deeper dimension of global ecologies by contracting the spatial distinctions between microscopic and astronomical scale by escalating the scale of marine plankton and illuminating them in ways that suggested strange new worlds. In 2012, Bevan joined a scientist and writer in making *Particle (Things Unseen)*, which revealed the minute, complex forms of the foraminifera and exposed their vulnerability to climate change and ocean acidification. Artists are in an advantageous position to reveal the poetics of these unseen worlds in which biological conditions as fundamental as ocean chemistry are being changed by the global processes of modernity.

Contemporary artists may have a number of possible new worlds in mind as they take on the challenges of how the most effective forms of global agency often seem to reside in the electronic flow of capital and its connection with military satellite surveillance of the world. In this sense, the prospect of a dystopian global future seems as possible as a more utopian world in which international collaboration succeeds in addressing global problems such as climate change. Occasionally, the two prospects appear in the same artwork, as in *Brave New World* (1999) by Theo Eshetu, an artist of English and African descent. This work comprises a large globe constructed in a vast mirrored space onto which video images were projected. In order to see this work, viewers had to lean through an open window into the mirrored room. As viewers leaned into the space, their reflections were repeated across hundreds of mirrored surfaces so that they appeared to surround the globe, giving the impression that the world is imagined as something *inside* each viewer. On the globe itself, there are constantly changing videos with evocative images drawn from a diverse range of cultures, from the sacred scenes of a mass in an Ethiopian church to secular icons such as the Statue of Liberty in New York, sword dancers in Bali, and brash Western television advertisements. The viewer is located in a position of global surveillance where everything can be seen as a vibrant media spectacle. On the other hand, because the globe is contained by the mirrored reflections of viewers, it becomes difficult for them to avoid the inference that their own local perception of global diversity becomes part of the work itself. Hence, as in other themes in contemporary art articulating global processes, *Brave New World* points to an uncertain future in which the agency of the global citizen essentially becomes the implied core of the project. Effectively, such artists invite us as viewers to reconceive the world as it is presented through such new global imaginaries.

NOTES

1. From the first Venice Biennale of 1895, there are currently more than 50 such major art events, including the world's "hottest" in the Californian desert and the "coolest" in Antarctica, both scheduled to open in 2017. In addition, the Biennial Foundation was initially registered in 2009 with the Chamber of Commerce in the Netherlands.

2. The renowned English diarist John Evelyn went to Rotterdam in 1641, where he was "amazed" at the huge number of artworks for sale. Evelyn noted that even local farmers had houses "full of them." Evelyn bought some, along with maps and atlases he later purchased in Amsterdam (Evelyn 1930: 21–27).

3. Cubic zirconia or synthetic diamonds are worth approximately $20 per carat compared to natural diamonds, which are valued at approximately $1,500 per carat, but this increases with stones of greater weight.

4. http://www.damienhirst.com/for-the-love-of-god.

5. Damien Hirst and Gordon Burn, *On the Way to Work* (London: Faber & Faber, 2001), 162.

6. Damien Hirst, cited in "Epiphany: A Conversation with Damien Hirst," in Hans Ulrich Obrist, *End of an Era* (London/New York: Other Criteria/Gagosian Gallery, 2012), no pagination.

7. US Department of Labor, Bureau of Labor Statistics, "Labor Force Statistics from the Current Population Survey," http://www.bls.gov/cps/minwage2010.htm (accessed May 7, 2016).

8. https://www.saatchigallery.com/artists/kader_attia.htm?section_name=unveiled.

9. The "UN Human Rights Council, 32nd Session (13th June–1st July 2016): General Debate on Item 4—Human Rights Situations of Concern: Elizabeth O'Casey," is reported on the IHEU website at http://iheu.org/iheu-reads-poem-banned-in-saudi-for-apostasy-to-delegates-at-un (accessed July 3, 2016).

10. This despite influential publications such as Rachel Carson's *The Sea Around Us* (1951) or the increased focus on marine mammals in popular culture.

11. In 2015, NASA's Scientific Visualization Studio produced a video of global plastic pollution in the five major oceanic gyres: https://svs.gsfc.nasa.gov/4174 (accessed January 15, 2016).

REFERENCES

Alpers, Svetlana. 1983. *The Art of Describing: Dutch Art in the Seventeenth Century.* Chicago: University of Chicago Press.

Anderson, Benedict. 1991. *Imagined Communities.* rev. ed. London: Verso.

Andrady, Anthony L. 2011. "Microplastics in the Marine Environment." *Marine Pollution Bulletin* 62: 1596–1605.

Appadurai, Arjun. 1996. *Modernity at Large: Cultural Developments of Globalization.* Minneapolis: University of Minnesota Press.

Bal, Mieke, and Miguel A. Hernandez-Navarro, eds. 2011. *Art and Visibility in Migratory Culture, Conflict, Resistance and Agency.* Amsterdam: Rodopi.

Barriendos Rodriguez, Joacquin. 2011. "Global Art and the Politics of Mobility: (Trans)Cultural Shifts in the International Contemporary Art-System." In *Art and Visibility in Migratory Culture: Conflict, Resistance, and Agency*, edited by M. Bal and Miguel A. Hernandez-Navarro, 313–334. Amsterdam: Rodopi.

Belting, Hans, Jakob Birken, and Andrea Buddensieg, eds. 2011. *Global Studies: Mapping Contemporary Art and Culture*. Ostifildern, Germany: Hatje Cantze Verlag.

Blum, Hester. 2010. "The Prospect of Oceanic Studies." *Proceedings of the Modern Language Association* 125 (3): 670–677.

Braudel, Fernand. 1981. *The Structures of Everyday Life: Civilisation and Capitalism 15th–18th Century, Volume 1*, translated by S. Reynolds. London: Phoenix Press.

Braudel, Fernand. 1984. *The Perspective of the World: Civilisation and Capitalism 15th–18th Century, Volume 3*, translated by S. Reynolds. London: Phoenix Press.

Brook, Timothy. 2008. *Vermeer's Hat: The Seventeenth Century and the Dawn of the Global World*. New York: Bloomsbury.

Carson, Rachel. 1951. *The Sea Around Us*. London: Unicorn.

Castoriadis, Cornelius. 1998. *The Imaginary Institution of Society*, translated by Kathleen Blamey. Cambridge, MA: MIT Press. (Original work published 1987)

Connery, Chris. 1996. "The Oceanic Feeling and the Regional Imaginary." In *Global/Local: Cultural Production and the Transnational Imaginary*, edited by R. Wilson and W. Dissanayake, 284–311. Durham, NC: Duke University Press.

Crosby, Alfred. 2003. *The Columbian Exchange: Biological and Cultural Consequences of 1492*. Westport, CT: Praeger.

Deloughrey, Elizabeth. 2010. "Heavy Waters: Waste and Atlantic Modernity." *Proceedings of the Modern Language Association* (Special feature on oceanic studies) 125 (3): 703–712.

Evelyn, John. 1930. *The Diary of John Evelyn*, edited by William Bray, vol. 1. London: Dent.

Florida, Richard. 2005. *Cities and the Creative Class*. New York: Routledge.

Frank, Cheryl. 2010. "Global Warming and Cultural/Media Articulations of Emerging and Contending Social Imaginaries: A Critical Realist Perspective." In *Interdisciplinarity and Climate Change*, edited by R. Bhaskar et al., 100–115. Oxford, UK: Routledge.

Frank, M., J. Goldberg, and K. Newman, eds. 2016. *This Distracted Globe: Worldmaking in Early Modern Literature*. New York: Fordham University Press.

Grotius, Hugo. 1916. *The Freedom of the Seas, or the Right Which Belongs to the Dutch to Take Part in the East India Trade*, edited by James Brown Scott, translated by Ralph can Deman Magoffin. New York: Oxford University Press. (Original work published 1608)

Grove, Richard, H. 1997. *Green Imperialism: Colonial Expansion, Tropical Island Edens and the Origins of Environmentalism, 1600–1860*. Cambridge, UK: Cambridge University Press.

Hardt, Michael, and Antonio Negri. 2000. *Empire*. Cambridge, MA: Harvard University Press.

Harris, Jonathan, ed. 2011. *Globalization and Contemporary Art*. Oxford, UK: Wiley-Blackwell.

Herr, Dorothée, and Grantly R. Gallard. 2009. *The Ocean and Climate Change: Tools and Guidelines for Action*. Gland, Switzerland: IUCN.

Hirst, Damien. 2012. "Epiphany: A Conversation with Damien Hirst." In *End of an Era*, by Hans Ulrich Obrist. London/New York: Other Criteria/Gagosian Gallery.

Hirst, Damien, and Gordon Burn. 2001. *On the Way to Work*. London: Faber & Faber.

Isham, Howard. 2004. *Image of the Sea: Oceanic Consciousness in the Romantic Century*. New York: Lang.

James, Paul. 2015. *Urban Sustainability in Theory and Practice*. London: Routledge.

James, Paul, and Manfred Steger. 2014. "A Genealogy of 'Globalization': The Career of a Concept." *Globalizations* 11 (4): 417–434.

Kafka, Franz. 1977. "'Letter to Oskar Pollak' January 27, 1904." In *Letters to Family, Friends, and Editors*, edited by M. Brod, 15–16. New York: Schocken. (Original work published 1904)

Kolbert, Elizabeth. 2014. *The Sixth Extinction: An Unnatural History*. London: Bloomsbury.

Kopytoff, Igor. 1986. "The Cultural Biography of Things: Commoditization as Process." In *The Social Life of Things: Commodities in Cultural Perspective*, edited by A. Appaduri, 64–91. Cambridge, UK: Cambridge University Press.

Latour, Bruno. 2005. *Reassembling the Social: An Introduction to Actor-Network-Theory*. Oxford, UK: Oxford University Press.

Lim, Walter, S. H. 1998. *The Arts of Empire: The Poetics of Colonialism from Raleigh to Milton*. London: Associated University Press.

Margulis, Lynn. 1998. *Symbiotic Planet: A New Look at Evolution*. New York: Basic Books.

Mentz, Steve. 2015. *Shipwreck Modernity Ecologies of Globalization: 1550–1719*. Minneapolis: University of Minnesota Press.

Modelski, George. 2008. "Globalization as Evolutionary Process." In *Globalization as Evolutionary Process: Modelling Global Change*, edited by G. Modelski, T. Devzas, and W. Thompson, 11–29. London: Routledge.

Nixon, Rob. 2013. *Slow Violence and the Environmentalism of the Poor*. Cambridge, MA: Harvard University Press.

Philipsen, Lotte. 2010. *Globalizing Contemporary Art: The Art World's New Internationalism*. Aarhus, Denmark: Aarhus University Press.

Rittesma, Rengenier C., ed. 2010. *Luxury in the Low Countries: Miscellaneous Reflections on Netherlandish Material Culture from 1500 to the Present*. Brussels, Belgium: Faro.

Schama, Simon. 1979 "The Unruly Realm: Appetite and Restraint in Seventeenth Century Holland." *Daedalus* 108 (3): 103–123.

Schama, Simon. 1987. *The Embarrassment of Riches: An Interpretation of Dutch Culture in the Golden Age*. New York: Vintage.

Sekula, Allan. 1995. *Fish Story*. Rotterdam, the Netherlands: Richter Verlag.

Sloterdijk, Peter. 2014. *In the World Interior of Capital*. Cambridge, UK: Polity.

Steger, Manfred. 2008. *The Rise of the Global Imaginary: Political Ideologies from the French Revolution to the War on Terror*. Oxford, UK: Oxford University Press.

Steinberg, Philip E. 2001. *The Social Construction of the Ocean*. Cambridge, UK: Cambridge University Press.

Taylor, Charles. 2004. *Modern Social Imaginaries*. Durham, NC: Duke University Press.

US Department of Labor, Bureau of Labor Statistics. 2016. "Labor Force Statistics from the Current Population Survey." http://www.bls.gov/cps/minwage2010.htm. Accessed May 7, 2016.

Weber, Max. 1965. *The Protestant Ethic and the Spirit of Capitalism*, translated by T. Parsons. London: Unwin. (Original work published 1905)

Westermann, Marriët. 1996. *A Worldly Art: The Art of the Dutch Republic 1585–1717*. London: King.

Williams, Linda. 2016. "The Anthropocene and the Long 17th Century 1550–1750." In *The Cultural History of Climate Change*, edited by T. Bristow and T. Ford. London: Routledge.

CHAPTER 30

....

URBANIZATION

....

PETER J. TAYLOR

In the early twentieth-first century, it was first reported that a majority of human beings throughout the world were living in urban places. Furthermore, this urbanization trend showed no signs of abating: Sometime later in the twenty-first century, urban dwellers are expected to constitute more than 75% of humanity. Widely commented upon, this could be seen as merely an interesting new settlement geography—a spatial reorganization toward more concentration—or, more profoundly, as a critical change in the nature of the human condition. From the latter interpretation there came suggestions that historically we had entered the "first urban century" and biologically that we are now an "urban species" (Glaeser 2011). Given that this thinking coincided with two other epochal discourses relating to global-scale activities and planetary climate change, the twenty-first century, our times, has been framed as a special period of unprecedented change. But how exactly does the urbanization fit into this complex human predicament? The prime purpose of this chapter is to explore how this question might be answered within the remit of global studies. Is urbanization somewhat less profound in its role in contemporary change than globalization and climate change? I argue no, it should be viewed on a par with the other two epochal phenomena because all three are fundamentally interrelated.

This position is not widely appreciated, although there are some notable exceptions (e.g., Bulkeley 2013; Sassen 1991) the mainstream literatures in global studies and climate change studies will reveal. In textbooks and "Reader" collections of papers, cities feature hardly at all. In the case of globalization, for instance, a very popular way of framing debates has been a typology of positions—"hyperglobalists," "skeptics," and "transformationalists"—each of which is ultimately defined by how the contemporary state is changing: either being eroded, being enhanced, or being restructured, respectively (Held et al. 1999; Taylor 2000). There is little or no place for cities in such a state-centric way of thinking. It reflects a more general issue for understanding cities in social science research traditionally disciplined to search out social, economic, and political processes of change, again framed nationally. This has been transfigured in contemporary social science into urbanization being treated as very much secondary to globalization. There is a precedent: In an earlier form of modernity involving the rise of unparalleled numbers of large cities in the nineteenth century, urbanization has been treated as secondary to industrialization. Of course, the "Industrial Revolution" is today indicted for initiating anthropogenic climate change. And again, the study of the latter is led by research programs that are explicitly framed by states: the Intergovernmental Panel on Climate Change (personnel are chosen by states) whose research feeds into the UN Framework Convention on Climate Change (for states to negotiate policy). Therefore, in order to satisfy our prime purpose, there needs to be a corollary resolve to move discussion beyond an uncritical receipt of state-centrism in global and planetary studies.

This chapter is organized into four substantive sections. The first provides a historical context treating contemporary globalization as a third manifestation of such worldwide integration since the late nineteenth century in the following sequence: imperial → American → corporate globalizations. The decisive role of a shifting but consistently rampant urbanization across all three globalizations is described. The second section focuses on today's corporate globalization and illustrates how this is being produced and reproduced by a world city network. The focus is on the structure and dynamics of the latter underpinning contemporary globalization. The final two sections present more recent conceptualizations that locate urbanization in a planetary frame. This has been developed most fully as "planetary urbanization," a way of thinking that treats contemporary urban process as inclusive across all parts of the Earth—land, sea, and air. An extension of this idea historically links the urban with anthropocentric climate change on a much longer timescale than conventionally considered. These two sections are unambiguously bringing cities to center stage in global studies. However, in conclusion, the argument is made that cities should not be portrayed as opposed to, or as alternative to, states; rather, it is the interplay of city/state relations that matters. But before moving forward to the substantive sections, this chapter begins with a short note on concepts and approaches to urban studies. This is to make clear to urban scholars the approach adopted in this chapter and, more important, to clarify some key distinctions for the majority of readers who will not be city specialists.

A Note on Concepts in Urban Studies

Perhaps the reader might have noticed that in the first paragraph of this chapter I used the terms urban/urbanization, whereas the concepts of city/cities were employed in the second paragraph. Although with distinctively different etymologies, in common practice city and urban are used interchangeably: I expect no reader to have experienced a problem of understanding due to my introducing cities in the second paragraph. But it is also easy to understand how they are different, notably through their opposites: Urban contrasts with rural; city differs from town. Both these oppositions are about dissimilar places. In the case of urban, the key difference is demographic: An urban place denotes a population concentration that generates a high population density compared to a rural place. In the case of the city, the key difference is more functional: A city is a large, complex, busy place compared to a smaller, simpler, quieter town.

The images that form in our minds when using urban/rural and city/town support these binary pairings. However, in this chapter, I do not focus on urban or city as simply places; both are treated as processes. In other words, they are not viewed as fixed entities; rather, they depict incessant changing human relations whose outcomes at any one point in time are the places we think of as urban and city. Using a process approach in this context is sometimes difficult to envisage because of the social science penchant, previously noted, to conceive human processes as being just one of sociocultural, economic, or political relations. Both urban and city are complex processes, a cacophony of practices that incorporate and transcend the standard three types of human relations. I consider the urban and city concepts each in turn.

The title of this chapter is "urbanization," and this has been long employed as a measurement in urban studies (K. Davis 1965); indeed, just such a measure was used to begin this chapter. Taking a given space or territory, usually a country, the degree of urbanization is the proportion of people living in cities and towns. As always, measurement is employed to engage in comparisons, and this has taken two forms in this case. First, comparing measures at one point in time produces the familiar notion of differences between countries, essentially a focus on places, represented by variation in urbanization across bounded territories. Second, comparing measures over time in one country provides an indication of change, specifically an urban process usually increasing through time. It is this process form of urbanization that Harvey (1996, 2012) argues is to be preferred over the concept of cities, which he states, implies place rather than process. I contest the latter later, but before then, the limitations of urbanization measures need rehearsing. As most commonly used, they are actually measures about states, urban process within their territories. But such a bounded approach to urban process is anathema to the human relations and practices that generate urbanization (and cities). Whatever boundaries politicians or researchers impose, with respect to urban process the resulting containers are inherently porous. By curtailing the scope of the urban in urbanization measurement, the resulting state-centric measures are partial and therefore problematical. However, this is not the case with total measures of urbanization worldwide. Global measurement transcends political boundaries, thereby avoiding the problematic: This is discussed later as planetary globalization (Brenner 2014a).

Harvey's view of cities as just places is not the only way to view them. Furthermore, having identified their opposite as "town," which is also recognized as being urban, suggests urban process should be divided into two distinct processes: city-ness and town-ness. This separation has been made in terms of spatial relations of urban centers (Taylor 2013; Taylor, Hoyler, and Verbruggen 2010). The first set of relations is essentially local: the connections that each urban center has with its hinterland. This is town-ness, where the scale of the local may vary and is conventionally described as urban hierarchies. The second set of relations is non-local: the interconnections between urban centers. This is city-ness, where relations are more horizontal than vertical and are described as intercity networks. The key point is that all urban centers encompass both processes; urban centers differ in the balance between their town-ness and their city-ness. In global studies, focus has been on the latter process through discourses on global cities: This is discussed later as world city network (Taylor and Derudder 2015).

One final point needs to be made concerning the question of reification. In arguments presented in this chapter, there is reference to cities doing practical things such as coordinating or enabling. This is a shorthand way of referring to cities as complex entities with the inherent capacity to make such practices collectively possible. Change is generated by the myriad agency of people and institutions that constitute the city-ness. I am not referring to the political actions of city governments, although the latter may be a relevant part of the wider capacity.

CITIES IN THREE GLOBALIZATIONS

Some definitions of globalization view it as a set of human relations that are worldwide in scope and integrated to create a specific material world or global economy. Viewed this way, there have been three such processes creating distinctive global economies. In each case, important cities have operated as local–global nexuses enabling and shaping variegated global practices. Providing this global capacity has set in motion a spiraling development process based on historically unparalleled urbanization.

Imperial Globalization

In 1904, the political geographer Halford Mackinder declared the world had reached global closure—there were no lands left to colonize. This was the culmination of European expansion, which, by the end of the nineteenth century, had created an integrated global economy whose structure was defined by imperial relations—formal (colonies), informal (unequal treaties), and internal (frontiers)—whereby the rest of the world provided European countries (and latterly the United States and Japan) with agricultural commodities and raw materials. Different territories tended to specialize in one commodity, creating severe economic dependency relations with distant markets. In effect, this was a worldwide division of labor structured as one large functional region with global commodity flows from the periphery servicing a North Atlantic industrial core.

The resulting immense urban growth was famously recognized at the time by Adna Weber (1899); this has been more accurately corroborated by more recent historical demographers (Chandler 1987). Whereas historically cities with populations of more than 1 million have been very rare, there were 16 in 1900. There were three types of fast-growing cities: (1) the great imperial capitals in Europe—the largest being London, Paris, and Berlin; (2) industrial cities in Europe—the largest being Manchester, Glasgow, and Rhine-Ruhr; and (3) dependent cities beyond Europe dealing with the logistics of relaying products to Europe—the largest being Buenos Aires, Shanghai, and Calcutta. Within this economic structure, there was a US replication where New York functioned as the business and commercial capital complemented by industrial cities in the manufacturing belt (Chicago, Cleveland, Pittsburgh, and Detroit) and local supply cities in the West (Denver and San Francisco) and South (Atlanta and Dallas). Below these new large cities, there was a vast array of smaller cities creating a first modern urban world in an integrated global economy.

American Globalization

This second global economic integration grew in the first half of the twentieth century out of the US arrangements described previously and became fully developed in mid-century when the United States emerged from World War II with an expanded economy when all rivals had different degrees of severely war-damaged economies. This enabled American firms to dominate the world economy that included restoration of European and Japanese economies in the "post-war boom." There were two main elements: (1) Leading American firms became known as "multinational corporations" through having production units located in different countries, and (2) leading European firms emulated American management practices and technological advances. Despite the wave of decolonization and a challenge to this process by communist countries, the dissipation of the latter well before the end of the century created an intensified version of the old "core–periphery" international division of labor.

Massive urbanization continued unabated so that by 1950 there were 67 cities with populations of more than 1 million. But the new globalization featured more than increasing and reorientated urban growth; its key feature was a new landscape of consumption. While New York became the world's financial center, increased mass production was matched by the development of mass consumption. Increased productivity translated into higher wages so that levels of consumption soared in what J. K. Galbraith (1958) famously announced in the 1950s as the "affluent society." Across US cities, suburbia became the primary landscape of this new world of consumption, epitomized by the decentralized metropolis of Los Angeles. *Americanization* is the term used to describe the diffusion of this way of living beyond the United States. It encompassed Western Europe after 1950 in the "post-war boom" and then diffused to middle classes throughout the world, finally including the erstwhile communist countries late in the century. The shopping mall came to symbolize modern cities in the American mode worldwide.

Corporate Globalization

This third global economic integration is an extension of Americanization as numerous non-US firms became multinational corporations, with Japanese and German firms in particular initially challenging American economic dominance. But this is much more than a diffusion of American practices as leading firms became "transnational corporations" and later "global corporations" through realizing the new organizational potential of the technology merger between the communication and computer industries in the 1970s: An electronic infrastructure provided firms with an enhanced global capacity. It enabled them to create a "new international division of labour" (Frobel, Heinrich, and Kreye 1980) with industrial production moving to poorer regions of the world in a highly integrated global economy undergirding what Manuel Castells (1996) termed "global network society." This production shift firmly established corporations with their global strategies as the dominant players, not just economically but also politically (e.g., through lobbying) and culturally (e.g., through sponsorships). Corporate globalization is our contemporary globalization, an ongoing process of worldwide integration involving corporations from countries throughout the world, now importantly including China.

As a cumulative product of the previous two globalizations, corporate globalization has accelerated urbanization: There are currently more than 500 cities with populations of more than 1 million. What were exceptionally rare cities before the three globalizations have become commonplace today. The outcome is a much more complex and variegated global urbanization that has initially generated two quite distinct literatures. The mega-city literature focuses on the unique demographic sizes of contemporary cities and the many problems this entails. Initially defined by UN-Habitat as cities with more than 8 million people, the threshold currently used is 10 million. The vast majority of these cities are in poorer areas of the world, and the debates that ensue are concerned mainly with their travails generating both positive interpretations (e.g. Neuwirth's (2006) "shadow cities") and more despairing negative interpretations (e.g., M. Davis' (2006) "planet of slums"). The global/world city literature focuses on city functionalities and as such directly addresses corporate globalization. Because of this, I focus on research within this approach first.

World City Network as Edifice of Corporate Globalization

The rise of multinational corporations was first linked to cities as new worldwide centers of economic power by Hymer (1972). Linking his precocious thesis to global economic decentralization (i.e., Frobel et al.'s (1980) new international division of labor), a new role for cities was discovered as "command and control centers," the necessary organizational frame for the new global economy. There were two main theses offered. Friedmann (1986; Friedmann and Wolff 1982) postulated a "world city hierarchy," an up-scaling of prior "national urban hierarchies," now layered in three large world regions—Americas, Euro-Africa, and Asia. New York, London, and Tokyo were the leading world cities for each region, below which an array of other important cities were ranked. Sassen (1991, 1994) focused on a select group of cities with global capacity that she termed "global cities," which were deemed to be unique to corporate globalization; New York, London, and Tokyo were her working examples. Despite the understandable coincidence of both treating the same three cities as key cases, the two approaches were quite different. Friedmann provided the first popular representation of global urbanization as a hierarchy of important urban places; Sassen laid out a specific urban process, global city formation. It is her city-as-process that has been extended to constitute world city network as the critical urban frame of corporate globalization (Taylor 2001).

It has been noted that the emergence of corporate globalization derived from the new instantaneous global communication opportunities opening up in the 1970s. Initially, firms developed production strategies whereby they could take advantage of low-cost transport and cheap labor to forge global commodity chains for secondary sector production. This stimulated a globalization of tertiary activities by firms providing financial, professional, and creative services for their globalizing corporate clients. In the 1980s, they followed clients to new markets and thereby exported their services through new offices throughout the world. By the early 1990s, service firms' intranets criss-crossed the world as flows of expert knowledge to support corporate globalization. Very quickly, these service firms moved on from being corporate followers to becoming corporate players in their own right: Finding themselves in new markets, they soon produced their own global office strategies. By the turn of the century, these knowledge flows in and through cities reached new levels of density and diversity. According to Castells' (1996), an "informational world" had replaced the "industrial world" so that modernity now took the form of a global network society in which these "advanced producer services" had become part of a new "quaternary sector" of the corporate global economy.

The firms providing advanced producer services—numerous financial and banking services, advertising, accountancy, various consultancies, real estate, law, and so on—are to be found in the internal agglomeration of major cities throughout the world, specifically located in their hallmark clusters of skyscrapers connected by rooftop satellite dishes in a vast global infrastructure network. The result is a dynamic world city network of global service centers enabling contemporary globalization. In Sassen's (1991, 1994) global cities thesis, service production and consumption come together: These cities are both markets for advanced producer services (corporate headquarters) and where financial, professional, and creative services are produced. But because both users and providers of advanced producer services use the global capacities of cities to pursue their various global strategies, it is a vast network of cities—going far beyond Sassen's specific "global cities"—that constitute the spatial framework of the contemporary global economy. Thus, in what follows, the focus is on service corporations and how they use cities in their everyday work. Note that this choice of economic sector is based not on corporate size—except in financial services, most service corporates are relatively modest in size—but, rather, on their strategic position. One way of looking at them is to interpret advanced producer services as the "indicator sector" in the current global economy. By analogy with an "indicator species" in ecological habitats, the success of this indicator sector in today's city-ness is a pointer to how the "global habitat" is operating.

This global city-ness process is illustrated using empirical results from an ongoing research program carried out under the auspices of the Globalization and World Cities (GaWC) Research Network (http://www.lboro.ac.uk/gawc) since 1998. The subject of these studies is intercity relations that highlight the worldwide roles of cities in contemporary globalization. The research is premised on an interlocking network model whereby advanced producer service firms "interlock" cities through their workflows (of ideas involving information, knowledge, professional know-how, plans, strategies, direction, etc.) across worldwide office networks. Because data on this commercial work are impossible to access (for both confidentiality and sheer scale reasons), direct measurement of workflows is impossible; the model enables indirect measurement of workflows in the form of estimates of potential flows between individual offices within firms. These are simply based on the idea that more important offices generate more workflows; there are more flows within a firm between two cities with important offices than between two cities with less important offices. Importance is measured by size and function of a firm's office in a given city. The workflows through a single firm's office network are estimated; the aggregation of many firms' flows constitute the world city network as estimates of gross flows between cities servicing corporations throughout the world (Taylor 2001).

Data on leading firms in financial services, accountancy, advertising, law, and management consultancy have been collected since 2000 to monitor changes in the world city network. This reflects variations and fluctuations in the demand for advanced producer services and therefore indicates dynamics of an evolving corporate globalization. One hundred firms were researched in 314 cities in 2000, and 175 firms were researched in 526 cities in 2013. From these data, the aggregate of all potential workflows of a city can be computed, which defines its "global network connectivity." For ease of comparison, results for each city are presented as its percentage of the highest city score. Table 30.1 shows the top 20 cities in 2000 and 2013, and Table 30.2 shows the percentage changes across this time. These can be interpreted as showing cities in terms of their degrees of integration into the world

Table 30.1 Top 20 Cities in the World City Network, 2000 and 2013

	2000			2013	
Rank	City	GNC	Rank	City	GNC
1	London	100.00	1	London	100.00
2	New York	97.64	2	New York	92.66
3	Hong Kong	70.71	3	Hong Kong	78.31
4	Paris	69.92	4	Paris	71.62
5	Tokyo	69.08	5	Singapore	65.62
6	Singapore	64.54	6	Shanghai	63.66
7	Chicago	61.57	7	Tokyo	63.63
8	Milan	60.36	8	Beijing	62.09
9	Los Angeles	59.94	9	Sydney	62.06
10	Toronto	59.48	10	Dubai	61.33
11	Madrid	59.45	11	Chicago	59.63
12	Amsterdam	59.03	12	Mumbai	58.81
13	Sydney	57.86	13	Milan	58.58
14	Frankfurt	56.71	14	Moscow	57.20
15	Brussels	55.72	15	São Paulo	57.19
16	São Paulo	54.10	16	Frankfurt	56.88
17	San Francisco	50.75	17	Toronto	55.06
18	Mexico City	48.49	18	Los Angeles	54.90
19	Zurich	48.49	19	Madrid	54.44
20	Taipei	47.73	20	Mexico City	53.20
	Cities in the 2013 List			Cities in the 2000 List	
21	Mumbai	47.67	21	Amsterdam	52.68
31	Shanghai	42.78	23	Brussels	51.98
34	Moscow	42.17	28	San Francisco	47.87
36	Beijing	42.00	31	Zurich	47.42
54	Dubai	36.26	41	Taipei	43.14

GNC, global network connectivity.

city network (Table 30.1) and the changing worldwide geography of corporate globalization (Table 30.2).

Without concentrating on the details of these results, there are many interesting and important processes in the global economy that can be noted. First, the world city network appears to be very resilient. Despite major movements in the world economy during the period in question (dot.com bubble—rapid expansion—severe financial crisis—austerity), there are only five changes between the top 20 cities. This resilience is especially marked at the top of the ranking. London and New York remain by far the most connected cities, followed by Hong Kong and Paris in both lists. Note that it is Hong Kong as leading Asian city rather than Tokyo as originally identified by both Friedmann and Sassen. Cities from "emerging markets" are among these leading cities: São Paulo and Mexico City appear in both lists, and they are joined by Mumbai, Shanghai, Moscow, and Beijing in 2013. The latter represent important changes that are occurring in the world city network: a "West" to "East" shift. This is especially

Rank	City	% Change
	Table 30.2 Connectivity Changes of Top 20 Cities from 2000 to 2013	
1	Dubai	4.45
2	Shanghai	2.94
3	Beijing	2.65
4	Moscow	2.44
5	Mumbai	1.57
6	Hong Kong	0.86
7	Mexico City	0.70
8	Paris	0.65
9	Sydney	0.60
10	London	0.52
11	São Paulo	0.31
12	Singapore	0.20
13	New York	0.16
14	Frankfurt	−0.14
15	Toronto	−0.21
16	Zurich	−0.22
17	Chicago	−0.32
18	Milan	−0.37
19	Brussels	−0.70
20	San Francisco	−0.73
21	Madrid	−0.84
22	Amsterdam	−0.87
23	Los Angeles	−0.88
24	Tokyo	−0.97
25	Taipei	−1.33

shown in the changes (see Table 30.2), with western European and US cities showing relative decline compared to Asian cities. The swapping of positions between Toronto and Sydney is part of this broader pattern. A key outcome of this shift is the remarkable position of Chinese cities in the top echelons of the network, with 3 of the top 8 cities in 2013. In complete contrast, there are two Pacific Asian cities that have the largest relative decline: Tokyo and Taipei. The former represents a divergence from the pioneering research by Friedmann and Sassen and reflects the Japanese economy's opposite trajectory to that of China; the latter is a special case of a Chinese city politically separate from China and thereby suffering as a consequence. Finally, mention should be made of Dubai, which records by far the highest relative increase in global network connectivity. Partly due to a low starting point, this is nevertheless a remarkable trajectory that illustrates the additional need for more subtle interpretations of world city network analyses (Bassens 2013; Taylor et al. 2014).

Before leaving the world city network, there are two provisos that require airing. First, the evidence discussed previously is the tip of a very large iceberg, with myriad cities throughout the world contributing to corporate globalization. Focusing on the leading cities indicates an important dynamic, but this corporate globalization is present in every urban locale throughout the world. Second, the development of advanced producer services is just one process among a myriad of processes that constitute dynamic city-ness within corporate globalization. We move on now to an approach that provides a broader vista on the urbanization within corporate globalization.

Planetary Urbanization I: The Contemporary Thesis

Pioneered by Neil Brenner at the Urban Lab, Harvard University, and Christian Schmid at ETH Zurich, a fresh way of looking at contemporary urbanization is being developed that transcends the binary oppositions introduced in the opening text of this chapter. Taking particular exception to the concept of "the city" with its implication of isolation, they embrace the concept of urbanization as a process to counter such supposed separateness. In this, they compare with the analytics of the world city network with its emphasis on cities always in the plural (Jacobs 1969), but they take this position much further. This is an exciting development for three related reasons. First, it broadens the vision of being urban to encompass much that has traditionally been considered non-urban. Second, in this, it shows potential for transcending the society/nature dichotomy that so much research on globalization appears to avoid. Therefore, third, it is building a new urban language to engage with the twenty-first century as special historical moment starting with the adjective "planetary" rather than the more simple "worldwide" or "global": Welcome to planetary urbanization (Brenner 2014a).

The planetary urbanization approach builds upon familiar recent researches and observations on how urbanization processes are changing. This change is much more than the mega-city emphasis on demographic size; the actual configuration of cities is altering away from the classic conceptualization of the concentric ordering of cities around its center. Large amorphous urban regions with variegated functionality have been "discovered" throughout the world since Gottmann (1961) described "megalopolis," the string of US East Coast cities from Boston to Washington, DC. Today, such urban forms are deemed to exist, or are in the process of formation, across all settled continents (Harrison and Hoyler 2015). But this transcending of traditional borders is not a simple case of decentralization; rather, there is a complex mix of variations both centralizing (Glaeser 2011) and turning cities inside out, described by Lang (2003) as "edgeless cities." Brenner, Schmid, and colleagues draw these concepts and ideas together as planetary urbanization using an untypical (i.e., overtly urban) Marxist analysis that brings urbanization to center stage: Henri Lefebvre's (1970) treatise on urban revolution.

In this hugely influential work, Lefebvre (1970) places urbanization in the context of cycles of capitalist development that incessantly disrupts sociospatial structures. Through this process, urbanization massively expands and in turn changes the parameters of society. The limit of this process is the final elimination of the "non-urban," annihilating "rural" as something "outside" the urban. Lefebvre termed this "complete urbanization." What has subsequently been termed globalization Lefebvre interprets as the advent of this worldwide condition, which is planetary urbanization.

Lefebvre's dialectic of "implosions/explosions" is central to understanding planetary urbanization (Brenner 2014a). The myriad processes of mutating agglomerations that are conventionally considered as urbanization are coupled with the equally crucial transformation of "operational landscapes" worldwide. And this is more than the relatively commonplace idea of the rural being constructed by the urban (for the classic study, see Cronon 1991); the mutuality between these spaces is paramount. Thus, planetary urbanization is more than territorial as depicted on maps; it is oceanic, subaquatic, atmospheric, and includes the subterrain. This is explicit in all the various infrastructures that are integral to this urbanization process, as well as being equally evident in its effects on climate change and environmental pollution. Both communication satellites and concentrations of plastic in the Arctic Ocean are manifestations of planetary urbanization. This goes way beyond the elimination of the rural; planetary includes elimination of the "wild," conventionally "untouched" but now besmirched by urbanization everywhere. This is the uneven operationalization of an entire planet.

A particularly interesting empirical output from this approach focuses on visualization, attempting to transcend conventional cartographies that portray data territorially (i.e., neatly bounded). These studies employ a range of global depictions, including Friedmann's (1986) global urban hierarchy and results from world city network analysis, but also include historical visualizations covering all three globalizations described previously (Urban Theory Lab-GSD 2014). But this approach is not simply "global" in its one-scale meaning. Countries famous for their stretches of "un-urban-ness" are reinterpreted as essentially urban: Schmid (2014) convincingly illustrates "rural Switzerland" to be a myth. More broadly using a collection of contemporary images—including nightlights, land cover, transport routes, and human ecological footprints—Brenner (2014b) explores the notion of the Mediterranean being urban.

Planetary urbanization is an invitation to rethink so much—conceptually, theoretically, epistemologically, and methodologically. And given its radical provenance, it engages with the politics of change that is neglected in the world city network approach. The latter describes a global urban world to understand it better, with some pointers toward the need for a "network politics" and transborder policymaking to challenge bounded, territorial governance. In contrast, planetary urbanization incorporates bottom-up political action that is simultaneously local and global. Starting with Lefebvre's (1970) "right to the city," or better still Harvey's (2006, 2012) right to change ourselves by changing the city, this is to develop what the "right to make planetary urbanization" might mean.

PLANETARY URBANIZATION II: A HISTORICAL THESIS

Although differences between the two approaches to studying urbanization under conditions of contemporary globalization have been emphasized, they do share one important feature that is typical of much contemporary scholarship: treating the current condition of humanity as unprecedented. This chapter started with expressions of the twenty-first century as unique, and the urban dimension of this claim is central to both world city networks and planetary urbanization. In the case of the former, worldwide instantaneous communication has created a new sociospatial world—Castells' (1996) network society incorporating Sassen's (1991) global cities—that has no historical parallels. For planetary urbanization, the uniqueness claim is integral to the argument that today we are experiencing the limits of an urbanization process that is now "complete." This is why the former section was titled the "contemporary" thesis; here, it is complemented with an historical urban thesis that is similarly planetary.

Of course, using Lefebvre means incorporating a Marxist historiography into planetary urbanization—changing "cycles of capitalism since the Industrial Revolution"—which accords with conventional historical thinking on anthropogenic climate change. The consensus is that the latter is approximately 200 years old; it is an artifact of industrialization, sometimes referred to as "carboniferous capitalism." Such thinking again pushes urbanization to the margins, more a consequence than a cause of past planetary transformation. But cities are much older than this; urbanization is a process that is measured in millennia, not centuries. Therefore, what pre-modern cities lack in demographic quantities, they can counterbalance with vast amounts of time. This line of reasoning has produced a new urban thesis on anthropogenic climate change in a two-step argument that entails combining two quite distinct literatures (Taylor 2017: Taylor, O'Brien, and O'Keefe 2017).

The first step is William Ruddiman's (2003, 2010, 2013) identification of two periods of human impact on climate change: a short, rapid "industrial effect" and a long, slow "preindustrial effect." The first is familiar; the second is novel and, Ruddiman argues, of comparable importance because of its longevity of eight millennia. His method is to focus on the two key greenhouse gases, carbon dioxide and methane, which he traces in the atmosphere by comparing the Holocene (i.e., the current interglacial period) with past interglacial periods. Deviations show a rise in carbon dioxide starting approximately 8,000 years ago and a rise in methane starting approximately 5,000 years ago. He attributes both to "agricultural revolutions"—for the former, land clearances making way for dryland cereals, and for the latter, the development of wetland cereal farming. Of course, the use of this familiar, indeed conventional, historiography of production "revolutions"—agricultural coupled with industrial—for the two speeds of anthropogenic climate change omits urbanization.

The second step is to insert Jane Jacobs' (1969) "cities first thesis" into the argument. She posits that the invention of agriculture was an urban innovation, a solution to the escalating food demands of expanding cities. Therefore, cities precede agriculture, a position that completely overturns conventional archaeological understanding of at least a century's standing (Soja 2000; Taylor 2013). The ensuing debate revolves around definitions of cities and their deployment for identifying very early cities. The traditional archaeological focus on monumental architecture limits cities to the past 5,000 years, long after the development of agriculture, but more functional definitions of cities, as used by Jacobs (1969), push cities, small but multiple, back to times compatible with agriculture (Smith, Ur, and Feinman 2014; Taylor 2012, 2015). The basic difference between these two positions concerns the role of cities as either supply vehicle responding to agricultural surpluses as traditionally conceived (Childe 1950) or a demand mechanism generating agricultural necessities à la Jacobs. Taking the latter position, Ruddiman's two contrasting periods of human effect on climate change can both be reinterpreted as the effects of urbanization, early and modern. Furthermore, the different timings for rises of the two greenhouse gases in the long, slow effect on climate change can be related to two phases of urban development: the initial cities equate with dryland agriculture, and the development of large riverine cities equates with wetland agriculture. In fact, Ruddiman's overall historiography matches Soja's (2000) three "urban revolutions" (modern/industrial is the third) at 8,000, 5,000, and 200 years before the present (Taylor, O'Brien, and O'Keefe 2015). Beyond this, synchronization research is required to link early land cover clearance (Kaplan et al. 2010) to the growing evidence from new airborne laser scanning technology showing new networks of ancient cities throughout the world from Amazonia to Cambodia.

If anthropogenic climate change is indeed a function of urban demand over many millennia, it follows that there has been a planetary urbanization over this long period. The Holocene is like no other interglacial period; it has been altered by human beings through their urbanizations. Indeed, this has been a time of mutually recursive relations: Urbanization has been instrumental in generating a uniquely long, relatively stable climatic period that provided the environment for cities to prosper and expand. It is in this sense that a historical planetary urbanization can be postulated despite the lack of worldwide operational landscapes that are integral to contemporary planetary globalization. But the relatively stable climate as an urbanization effect appears to be coming to an abrupt end.

Being historical does not make historical planetary globalization only of historical interest. The designation of urban demand as the prime generator of anthropogenic climate change has critical resonance for contemporary climate science policymaking. As noted previously, currently the research base is very state-centric, feeding into interstate negotiations at UN climate change conferences: The result is a prevailing focus on energy supply, making policy to cut carbon emissions. The demand side—the huge consumption processes that have been so glaringly prominent since American globalization and have reached über proportions in the cities of corporate globalization—is sidelined in this global policymaking practice (Taylor 2016, Taylor, O'Brien, and O'Keefe 2016). Urbanization in contemporary globalization is not only crucial for understanding human effects on climate change but also critical for developing policies to mitigate and adapt to a changing planet.

Conclusion

This chapter has shown that viewing globalization through urbanization has the potential to generate a deeper rethink of globalization than provided by studies generated through social science disciplinary lenses. Instead of up-scaling conventional ideas and concepts by simply substituting "national" with "global"—as in "global civil society," "global governance," and "global economy"—and thereby reproducing old disciplinary separations, bringing cities into the argument promotes a more transdisciplinary thinking. In this chapter, a distinctive grounding of ideas is evidenced through linking the twenty-first century's three epochal changes identified in the introduction. Urbanization, globalization, and anthropogenic climate change are intimately entwined and should be understood as such.

Such a large topic and so little space, this chapter has perforce been treating complex subjects in a fleeting manner that is rather more assertive than nuanced. This conclusion briefly introduces and discusses two caveats that require airing to make the overall argument slightly more reputable.

First, a focus on cities prioritizes flows and routes over territories and places, which is entirely appropriate for studying globalization. But flows and places are complimentary, they exist together. Emphasis on the former should not be interpreted as dismissing the relevance of the latter. Thus, this chapter should not be interpreted as an addition to the literature implying an imminent ending of the state. There are examples in which global cities are viewed as replacements for states (Knight 1989), but this is not the position taken here. Rather, cities and states represent different complexes of human activities premised upon flows and places, respectively. Thus, a key area of study is their interrelations (Taylor 2013). City/state relations vary immensely over time and space; currently, both are instrumental in enabling and reproducing global relations and planetary changes. The obvious example of the continuing importance of the state is China, with its distinctive urbanization trajectory a consequence of changing state policy. In the 1960s, China was the only country to experience a decline in urbanization; since the 1980s, however, it has experienced the greatest rural–urban migration in human history.

Second, it has been noted that studies of cities in globalization elicit a huge bias toward larger cities, especially those in the richer areas of the world (Robinson 2006). This chapter might be viewed as an example of this tendency. However, the introduction of town-ness alongside city-ness, although not followed up in the subsequent arguments, does accept an urbanization that includes local and non-local and therefore urban places of all sizes. The key point is that a weakness of the "global city" concept is that there is no such thing as an "un-global city." Globalization is pervasive, and elements of its cacophony of processes can be found in every urban place, and much further afield in the planetary urbanization thesis. Jacobs (1969) famously argued that all cities need other cities; it might be added that the latter be of many sizes. Contemporary globalization has its particular worldwide network of cities in an urban landscape that is planetary.

REFERENCES

Bassens, D. 2013. "The Economic and Financial Dimensions." In *Global City Challenges: Debating a Concept, Improving the Practice*, edited by M. Acuto and W. Steele, 47–62. London: Palgrave.

Brenner, N., ed. 2014a. *Implosions/Explosions: Towards a Study of Planetary Globalization*. Berlin: Jovis Verlag.

Brenner, N. 2014b. "Is the Mediterranean Urban?" In *Implosions/Explosions: Towards a Study of Planetary Globalization*, edited by N. Brenner, pp. 428–459. Berlin: Jovis Verlag.

Bulkeley, H. 2013. *Cities and Climate Change*. London: Routledge.

Castells, M. 1996. *The Rise of Network Society*. Oxford, UK: Blackwell.

Chandler, T. 1987. *Four Thousand Years of Urban Growth: An Historical Census*. Lampeter, UK: Mellon Press.

Childe, V. G. 1950. "The Urban Revolution." *Town Planning Review* 21: 3–17.

Cronon, W. 1991. *Nature's Metropolis: Chicago and the Great West*. New York: Norton.

Davis, K. 1965. "The Urbanization of the Human Population." *Scientific American* 213 (3): 40–53.

Davis, M. 2006. *Planet of Slums*. London: Verso.

Friedmann, J. 1986. "The World City Hypothesis." *Development and Change* 17: 69–83.

Friedmann, J., and G. Wolff. 1982. "World City Formation: An Agenda for Research and Action." *International Journal of Urban and Regional Research* 6: 309–344.

Frobel, F., J. Heinrich, and O. Kreye. 1980. *The New International Division of Labour.* Cambridge, UK: Cambridge University Press.

Galbraith, J. K. 1958. *The Affluent Society.* London: Penguin.

Glaeser, E. L. 2011. *Triumph of the City.* London: Macmillan.

Gottmann, J. 1961. *Megalopolis: The Urbanized Northeastern Seaboard of the United States.* New York: Twentieth Century Fund.

Harrison, J., and M. Hoyler, eds. 2015. *Megaregions: Globalization's New Urban Form?* Cheltenham, UK: Elgar.

Harvey, D. 1996. "Cities or Urbanization?" *City* 1: 38–61.

Harvey, D. 2006. *Spaces of Global Capitalism: Towards a Theory of Uneven Geographical Development.* London: Verso.

Harvey, D. 2012. *Rebel Cities: From the Right to the City to the Urban Revolution.* London: Verso.

Held, D., A. McGrew, D. Goldblatt, and J. Perraton. 1999. *Global Transformations: Politics, Economics and Culture.* Cambridge, UK: Polity.

Hymer, S. 1972. "The Multinational Corporation and the Law of Uneven Development." In *Economic and World Order from the 1970s to the 1990s,* edited by J. Bhagwati. London: Collier-Macmillan.

Jacobs, J. 1969. *Cities and the Wealth of Nations.* New York: Vintage.

Kaplan, J. O., K. M. Krumhardt, E. C. Ellis, W. F. Ruddiman, C. Lemmen, and K. K. Goldewijk. 2010. "Holocene Carbon Emissions as a Result of Anthropogenic Land Cover Change." *Holocene* 21: 775–791.

Knight, R. V. 1989. "The Emergent Global Society." In *Cities in a Global Society,* edited by R. V. Knight and G. Gappert, pp. 24–43. Newbury Park, CA: Sage.

Lang, R. E. 2003. *Edgeless Cities: Exploring the Elusive Metropolis.* Washington, DC: Brookings Institution.

Lefebvre, H. 1970. *The Urban Revolution.* Minneapolis: University of Minnesota Press.

Mackinder, H. J. 1904. "The Geographical Pivot of History." *Geographical Journal* 23: 421–442.

Neuwirth, R. 2006. *Shadow Cities: A Billion Squatters, a New Urban World.* London: Routledge.

Robinson, J. 2006. *Ordinary Cities: Between Modernity and Development.* London: Routledge.

Ruddiman, W. F. 2003. "Humans Took Control of Greenhouse Gases Thousands of Years Ago." *Climate Change* 61: 262–293.

Ruddiman, W. F. 2010. *Plows, Plagues, and Petroleum: How Humans Took Control of Climate.* Princeton, NJ: Princeton University Press.

Ruddiman, W. F. 2013. "The Anthropocene." *Annual Review of Earth and Planetary Sciences* 41: 1–24.

Sassen, S. 1991. *The Global City: New York, London, Tokyo.* Princeton, NJ: Princeton University Press.

Sassen, S. 1994. *Cities in a World Economy.* Thousand Oaks, CA: Pine Forge Press.

Schmid, C. 2014. "A Typology of Urban Switzerland." In *Implosions/Explosions: Towards a Study of Planetary Globalization,* edited by N. Brenner, pp. 398–427. Berlin: Jovis Verlag.

Smith, M. E., J. Ur, and G. M. Feinman. 2014. "Jane Jacobs' 'City First' Model and Archaeological Reality." *International Journal of Urban and Regional Research* 38: 1525–1535.

Soja, E. W. 2000. *Postmetropolis: Critical Studies of Cities and Regions.* Oxford, UK: Blackwell.

Taylor, P. J. 2000. "Embedded Statism and the Social Sciences 2: Geographies (and Metageographies) in Globalization." *Environment and Planning A* 32: 1105–1114.

Taylor, P. J. 2001. "Specification of the World City Network." *Geographical Analysis* 33: 181–194.

Taylor, P. J. 2012. "Extraordinary Cities: Early 'City-Ness' and the Origins of Agriculture and States." *International Journal of Urban and Regional Research* 36: 415–437.

Taylor, P. J. 2013. *Extraordinary Cities: Millennia of Moral Syndromes, World-Systems and City/State Relations*. Cheltenham, UK: Elgar.

Taylor, P. J. 2015. "Post-Childe, Post-Wirth; Response to SMITH, Ur and Feinman." *International Journal of Urban and Regional Research* 39: 68–71.

Taylor, P. J. 2017. "Cities in Climate Change." *International Journal of Urban Sciences* 21 (1): 1–14.

Taylor, P. J., and B. Derudder. 2015. *World City Network: A Global Urban Analysis*. 2nd ed. London: Routledge.

Taylor, P. J., B. Derudder, J. Faulconbridge, M. Hoyler, and P. Ni. 2014. "Advanced Producer Service Firms as Strategic Networks, Global Cities as Strategic Places." *Economic Geography* 90: 267–292.

Taylor, P. J., M. Hoyler, and R. Verbruggen. 2010. "External Urban Relational Process: Introducing Central Flow Theory to Complement Central Place Theory." *Urban Studies* 47: 2803–2818.

Taylor, P. J., G. O'Brien, and P. O'Keefe. 2015. "Human Control of Climate: Introducing Cities." *Environment and Planning A* 47: 1023–1028.

Taylor, P. J., G. O'Brien, and P. O'Keefe. 2016. "Eleven Antitheses on Cities and States: Challenging the Mindscape of Chronology and Chorography in Anthropogenic Climate Change." *ACME: An International Journal for Critical Geographies* 15: 393–417.

Taylor, P. J., G. O'Brien, and P. O'Keefe. 2017. "Anthropogenic Climate Change Is Urban Not Modern: Towards an Alternate Critical Urban Geography." *ACME: An International Journal for Critical Geographies* 16 (4): 781–803.

Urban Theory Lab-GSD. 2014. "Visualizing an Urbanized Planet—Materials." In *Implosions/Explosions: Towards a Study of Planetary Globalization*, edited by N. Brenner, pp. 460–475. Berlin: Jovis Verlag.

Weber, A. 1899. *The Growth of Cities in the Nineteenth Century: A Study in Statistics*. New York: Macmillan.

CHAPTER 31

....

MULTICULTURALISM

....

NANDITA SHARMA

IN 2010, German Chancellor Angela Merkel declared that attempts to build a "multicultural" society had "failed, utterly failed." She prefaced her declaration by telling a meeting of her Christian Democratic Union party ("Merkel Says German Multicultural Society Has Failed," 2010) that at

> the beginning of the [19]60s our country called the foreign workers to come to Germany and now they live in our country. We kidded ourselves a while, we said: "They won't stay, sometime they will be gone," but this isn't reality.

She thus made it clear that the failure that she identified was to be laid at the feet of those socially represented as (im)migrants (regardless of their actual citizenship status), whom Merkel declared were not properly "integrating" and must begin to do so.

In 2011, British Prime Minister David Cameron similarly declared that the "doctrine of state multiculturalism" had failed. Like Merkel, the central issue for Cameron was that "multiculturalism" encouraged "separatism" rather than "integration." Making his comments in the context of a speech on radicalization and Islamic extremism, Cameron ("Full Transcript, David Cameron" 2011) added that

> under the doctrine of state multiculturalism, we have encouraged different cultures to live separate lives, apart from each other and the mainstream. We have failed to provide a vision of society to which they feel they want to belong. We have even tolerated these segregated communities behaving in ways that run counter to our values. . . . This hands-off tolerance has only served to reinforce the sense that not enough is shared.

Cameron declared that such "British tolerance" would end. "Instead of encouraging people to live apart," he stated, "we need a clear sense of shared national identity." He concluded that "frankly, we need a lot less of the passive tolerance of recent years and much more active, muscular liberalism."

For Merkel and Cameron, multiculturalism was juxtaposed to "integration," a key aspect of which was uniculturalism or "making sure immigrants speak the language of their new home" and "ensuring that people are educated in elements of a common culture and curriculum."[1] In his 2011 speech, Cameron stressed that this commonality was that of a "British national identity." He added, "It's that identity—that feeling of belonging in our countries—that is the key to achieving true cohesion" ("Full Transcript, David Cameron" 2011). For Cameron, like Merkel, it was those people constituted as (im)migrants in Britain—again, even if they were in fact co-citizens—who were to blame for the failure to learn how to be normatively "British."

The British government continued to problematize multiculturalism in its 2012 paper, "Creating the Conditions for Integration." In it, some of the "problems" created by multiculturalism were identified, including "public bodies bending over backwards to translate documents up to and including their annual report into a variety of foreign languages" and "men and women disciplined for wearing modest symbols of Christian faith at work, and . . . legal challenges to councils opening their proceedings with prayers, a tradition that goes back generations, brings comfort to many and hurts no one" (cited in Walford 2012). "This," British Communities Secretary Eric Pickles claimed, "is the politics of division" (cited in Walford 2012).

The Meanings of Multiculturalism

What does this proclaimed "end of multiculturalism" tell us about multiculturalism and about the politics that have given it meaning during the past several decades? It is worthwhile starting with the understanding that multiculturalism is both a *fact* of human societies and, since the 1970s, the *governmentality* of nation-states concerned with maintaining the imaginary character of "nation-ness" while contending with the demands for equality from those historically excluded from membership in the "nation" (Anderson 1991). If multicultural refers to the coexistence of numerous ways of life within a single political community, human societies are multicultural and have been for a very long time. The idea that human societies were in the past—or are now—"homogeneous" is a myth. For example, throughout the world patriarchal social relations have famously created separate "cultures" and even separate physical spaces and spheres of activity for men and women. People in the ruling class have always had a much different way of life compared to that of the people whose wealth they expropriate and whose labor they exploit. They eat different food, wear different clothes, listen to different music, find different things beautiful, have different ideas about how best to raise their children and form their families, and so on. Indeed, within each class, numerous fragments exist, each with its own distinct "lifestyle" (Bourdieu 1984).

Moreover, the global spread of racism that accompanied European imperialism has, since the seventeenth century, postulated the idea that there exist wholly different "types" of people, separate "races," each with its own discrete "culture." European empires, of course, depended on bringing these supposedly different "races" together in order to secure the labor and the territory necessary to make imperialism profitable and practical. From the nineteenth century onward, the negative duality of heterosexual/homosexual also proliferated the existence of multiple cultures. Thus, within the "relations of ruling," people categorized as men or women, conqueror or colonized, bourgeoisie or worker, White, Native, Black, or Asian, straight or queer have lived within the *same* political space and time, but because they have experienced these extremely differently, multiple cultures have developed (Smith 1990). In this historical understanding of society, multiculturalism is simply a long-standing fact of our world, nothing to be debated or disputed and certainly nothing that could just simply "end."

In its dominant or "common-sense" meaning, however, multiculturalism is understood both as a relatively new phenomena and as a consequence of the immigration of non-White people into nation-states imagined as belonging to members of "White nations." It was in 1971 when the Canadian nation-state described itself as "multicultural," the first to do so. This pronouncement came on the heels of Canada's 1965 revisions to its immigration policy, which had been based on the subordination and, at times, outright exclusion of all those racialized as non-White and, as such, portrayed as "inassimilable" into the White Canadian "nation." This is why, when we think of multiculturalism, we view it as a governmental policy granted—or taken away—by the state. Because those who govern nation-states view themselves as the standard bearers and protectors of "society," it is thought that these states can decide to either promulgate a policy of multiculturalism that calls for the tolerance of those who are said to have introduced heterogeneity into society—most especially those not just legally but also socially constituted as "immigrants"—or dictate that such tolerance has ended.

It is worthwhile noting, particularly as students of global studies, that the period in which multiculturalism was first proclaimed and later denounced as government policy is precisely the period when many new neoliberal reforms were rolled out. This mirrors a dominant, but I argue not a wholly accurate, strand within global studies, which conflates processes of globalization with those of neoliberalism. Nonetheless, it is true that the neoliberal restructuring of state policies has both expanded and intensified capitalist social relations throughout the world. All of the following have allowed states to strengthen the hand of capital against labor: the growing privatization of state-owned resources; weakening or eliminating regulations governing industry, the environment, and health and social welfare; and further liberalizing the global movement of capital and commodities while imposing further immigration restrictions on the movement of labor. As discussed later, the neoliberal period of capitalism has brought increasingly more people, places, and things into the capitalist market. This has led some political theorists to declare that there is no longer any "outside" to capitalism (Hardt and Negri 2000).

This is the global context in which we can best understand the rise—and the subsequent fall—not of multiculturalism per se but of the *governmentality* of multiculturalism. Notably, multiculturalism was practiced (if not always enacted into law) by nation-states formed out of the former British Empire, such as the United States, Canada, Australia, and New Zealand, all of which had long imagined themselves as "White nations." Multiculturalism was also proclaimed in the newly nationalized state of Great Britain, which lost its imperial status in the early 1960s, and, later, in other select European states. Multiculturalism represented the state's effort to manage the tension between the "national" and the "global" that neoliberalism brought to the fore. Through multiculturalism, nation-states called for the tolerance of "foreigners." Hence, the focus of multiculturalism was on "foreign" *people*—on "immigrants." Indeed, state multiculturalism cannot be understood outside of the context of the immigration reforms of the mid-1960s and 1970s.

It cannot be underestimated how much the entry, and eventual citizenship, of some non-White people acted as a shock to the legitimating rationale for the existence of these nation-states. After all, the new liberalized immigration policies allowed for the entry of some of the very people *against whom* these states had defined their "nationhood" and, hence, their national sovereignty. As a growing number of people in the Rich World comprised biopolitical groups defined historically as *not* fitting always-already racist ideas of national belonging, tensions grew. Multiculturalism, thus, was an "answer" of sorts to the question of the slowly growing presence—and power—of non-White people in national spaces long imagined as being *for* Whites or Europeans.

However, contrary to conventional wisdom, multiculturalism also provided a method to *maintain* the "White-ness" that defined and legitimated these nation-states. And it is in this sense that multiculturalism was part of the governmentality of neoliberalism. Far from weakening the racialization of national membership, the discourses and policies of multiculturalism further empowered Whites by encouraging them to "tolerate" others in what could only still be presumed to be "*their* nation." As Ghassan Hage (2000) has insightfully noted, the state's granting of power of Whites to tolerate their Others was fundamentally based on the recognition and maintenance of their power to *not* tolerate the Other when they chose not to do so. Thus, policies of multiculturalism represented the power of Whites to re-centralize themselves in ideas of nationhood.

State policies of multiculturalism, of course, also reflected the increased power of anti-racist movements and their struggle against not only the racialization of political membership within the Rich World but also what was now called "neo-imperialism" in its former colonies. Nevertheless, official multiculturalism policies did not represent a commitment by the state to end racism and move into a new anti-racist present and future, as is often claimed. Instead, in an effort to maintain—or, perhaps better, to regain—its legitimacy, the state shifted its official discourse from one of forced assimilation to the discourse of toleration. What elites, especially, but not only, in the state allowed was for some public representation of what "immigrants" (or "ethnics," as they were often called) wore, what they ate, and what they did in their leisure time. Elites readily displayed non-White people as living evidence of the state's claim to no longer being racist. Nonetheless, folkloric song and dance, and perhaps especially food, represented the *separate-ness* of "their culture," as well as the tolerance of both the White "nation" and the state for this separation. It is this opportunistic aspect of multiculturalism that gives life to the prevalent sense among anti-racist critics of multiculturalism that non-Whites have simply been set on a national and international stage to perform an elaborate phantasm of an anti-racist society that has never materialized. Himani Bannerji (2000: 90) states, "It is as though we asked for bread and were given stones."

However, from the start of state multiculturalism, some Whites, particularly those who had become part of the working precariat or feared becoming so, deeply resented multiculturalism and viewed even simple, symbolic acts of "inclusion" as a threat to their racialized proximity to White elites. Given the way that state multiculturalism was enacted, and despite their different takes on state multiculturalism, both dominant and working-class Whites imagined that "immigrant" or "ethnic" others had a wholly separate "culture." By the second decade of the 2000s, White elites joined working-class Whites in publically bemoaning the supposed lack of "integration" by "(im)migrants" (many of whom were co-citizens). Indeed, elites often called for the end of multiculturalism in the name of the "White working class," whose security they professed to care about even as they actively worked to breach it through neoliberal policy changes.

MULTICULTURALISM, THE NATION-STATE, AND IMMIGRATION

The way that nation-states enacted multiculturalism shored up the binary figures of the "immigrant" and its privileged opposite, the "national citizen." This is why societies described as "multicultural" are those widely understood to have had people of different "nations" immigrating to national territories and why "debates" on multiculturalism so easily segue into "debates" over immigration. How many of "them" should "we" let in? More of "them" or less? Indeed, should "we" let "them" in at all? The politics of multiculturalism, thus, cannot be fully understood without reference to both nationalism and, especially, to the immigration policies that are said to be the locus through which the "foreigner" enters a mythically homogeneous nationalized society.

Obsession with the "foreigner" is an elemental aspect of societies imagined as national. Indeed, it is impossible to imagine either nations or nation-states *without* their social boundaries and their legal borders against "foreigners." Indeed, as I have argued elsewhere, immigration restrictions and regulations on the entry of "foreigners" is what *defines* the national form of state power (Sharma, forthcoming). It is also what makes it unique in world historical terms. Whereas imperial-states were known for restricting mobility *out* of their territories so that people could be kept as the state's subjects, thus ensuring that there were people to tax and a workforce and/or force to fight in the state's military, nation-states have constructed themselves by regulating and restricting free mobility *into* their territories. Indeed, the nationalization of state sovereignty normally entails the enactment of immigration controls against those who, at a particular historical conjuncture, will not be included in the "nation."

Nation states, unlike the imperial-states that preceded them, are thus always-already defined as *limited* communities (Anderson 1991). "Nations" have been defined as made up of a discrete biopolitical "population" that, as Foucault (1997) insightfully understood, "must be defended" against their others. This is as true for the others within the state's territories as it is for those outside of them. Nation-states, especially the more powerful ones, do, of course, dominate people outside of their nationalized territories. However, unlike imperial-states, they do not *incorporate* these others into their political community by making them formal subjects of the state. Instead, nation-states maintain those outside of their current territorial boundaries as "non-nationals." Nation-states, thus, are particularly adept at making "foreigners." And, in this, immigration and citizenship policies are crucial.

Historically, far from being mere bureaucratic instruments, blandly but fairly applied across the board, setting limits to national belonging through immigration policies has largely relied on racism, the ideology that purports that there are different "types" of people, each of whom can be placed into biologically and/or culturally "distinct" groups that are differently valued in society. Sexism has been crucial in this regard. States claim that in order to protect "their" national populations, women's sexuality and their capacity to produce new life in the territory of the nation-state must be controlled. Thus, whereas women said to be *of* the "nation" are encouraged, sometimes through cash payments, to have more babies, women imagined as belonging to other "nations," particularly when these are negatively racialized, are discouraged from doing so and are often demonized when they do.

By determining who it will admit and who it will not, immigration policies thus work to define the "nation" on which the state stakes its legitimacy to rule. In the process, normative ideas of what it means to be a "national" man or woman are produced. Two historic examples make this process clear. The first immigration policy of the United States, the 1875 Page Act, expressly barred the entry of three categories of persons: "coolies" (ostensibly, a term used to describe people working as indentured laborers, but in this case, primarily a racialized term to describe *all* manual laborers from China), women deemed to be "prostitutes," and "criminals." Meanwhile, Canada, which in 1914 enacted its first controls over people's entry into what was then still British imperial territory, moved to restrict the entry of co-British subjects from India who were deemed to be unfit for membership in the emergent "Canadian nation." For both governments, the issue was not the *entry* of persons per se. Indeed, before and after these immigration restrictions were imposed, hundreds of thousands of people moved to the United States and Canada. What these restrictions did, therefore, was shape who was viewed as worthy of national membership. They also shaped the *pattern* of migration because people racialized as European remained free from such restrictions for some more years. All others were rejected because they fell outside of the limits identifying the "White nation."

The differences organized by regulations and restrictions on immigration, however, were never meant only as a way to prevent the movement of those who had been cast as "undesirable." Instead, many persons deemed to be "undesirable" lived and worked in these nation-states but did so in highly subordinated conditions. Gilles Deleuze and Félix Guattari (1987) have termed the process by which people are not physically excluded but are unevenly incorporated into nation-states "differential inclusion." This works against non-citizens, but it also works against those who are juridically co-citizens but who are negatively racialized.

Because the "nation" is often a stand-in for the "race," people associated with distant "nations" continue to be regarded as "immigrants." Even when they have obtained formal national citizenship, they are labeled as "second-generation immigrants" or "persons with an immigrant background." These terms are commonly employed in "multicultural societies" to describe those who are physically within the nation-state but represented as not being *of* the "nation." Second, the legal status one is given by the state, ranging from "citizen" to "immigrant" and "illegal," also dramatically alters how a person will experience life. Most aspects of life—from work to education, love, and the ability to feel secure in the knowledge that one is recognized as a member of society—are shaped by which status a person is accorded by the state.

Hence, immigration controls not only construct highly discriminatory criteria for "national belonging" but also shape how the territory of the nation-state is positioned within the highly competitive global system of capitalist investment, production, and profit. Differently including those who are excluded from the "nation" and, for a growing number and proportion of people, from the juridical status of "permanent resident" is highly lucrative for both the state and capital. Thus, restrictions on the freedoms and rights of persons deemed "undesirable" and/or "immoral" have worked not only to prevent certain people from entering nation-states but also to lessen the *claims* they can make on the state and its "nation" in terms of rights, entitlements, and belonging. Such politics of identity are highly material. Being socially and/or legally categorized as "not belonging" in a nation-state works to lessen the wages people can wrest from employers.

Neoliberalism and Multiculturalism

The chickens truly came home to roost with the advent of neoliberal reforms. Workers in the Rich World nation-states found that workers in the Poor World states—workers to whom they had not extended any significant solidarity in the past—had been made cheaper to employ and weaker with regard to bargaining power than even they had been. Workers in the Rich World experienced the process they termed "offshoring" when from the early 1960s onward, capital began to move its production sites to areas where there were few, if any, legal protections for workers and where trade union membership was made exceedingly difficult, if not impossible. Unfortunately, continuing the lack of global solidarity shown in the past, many of the workers in the Rich World who became un- or underemployed as a result of offshoring blamed the Poor World workers for taking "their jobs," thereby shoring up the nationalist entitlement that contributed to the neoliberal strategy of capital—and contributed to its success at maintaining divisions between workers. The neoliberal circle was squared as the products made in these newly competitive sites—products often owned by capital based in the Rich World—entered the vast consumer markets of the Rich World, making any strategy of re-shoring largely uncompetitive.

It was not only state policies governing social welfare, labor protections, and political rights that were affected by neoliberal restructuring. Immigration policies also underwent neoliberal reform. A significant shift in the (im)migration statuses of newly recruited workers took place. Increasingly, people were shifted into state categories of most rights and entitlements available to citizens and permanent residents. By the mid-1970s, throughout the world, as much as one-third of all people migrating did so under state-enforced conditions of unfree labor (Gardezi 1995). In Canada, for example, "non-immigrant workers" (or "temporary foreign workers") were legally bound to work for a state-specified employer and in a state-specified occupation while given no avenue to convert their status to "permanent resident."[2] Citizenship, therefore, was beyond reach for these workers. This made these "foreign workers" both cheaper to employ and much more structurally susceptible to the demands of employers compared to workers with the status of "permanent resident" or "citizen." They embodied the quintessential neoliberal workforce that employers were demanding and that states were increasingly providing: "flexible" and "disposable."

In other states—particularly the United States and, to a lesser extent, Europe—there were very few official routes of entry for workers. Consequently, increasingly more people were forced into the state category of "illegal alien." Indeed, in the United States, "illegal" is the largest immigration category of people (Pew Hispanic Center 2006). These workers are among the most "competitive" workforce because their wholesale lack of rights within nation-states ensures that they work for the lowest wages and in the "3D" (dangerous, dirty, and degrading) jobs. The production of a large "illegal" workforce is thus part of the neoliberal restructuring of state immigration policies. Thus, along with how one is racialized and gendered, one's immigration and citizenship status matters. As increasingly more states shift their immigration recruitment schemes to "managed" or "temporary migrant worker programs," most of which categorize people into subordinate immigration statuses and deny them access to national citizenship, these programs operate as a neoliberal technique of ensuring greater labor market competition.

Neoliberalism, of course, also shapes the *culture* of nationalized societies. For those workers with national citizenship status and a strong sense of "national" belonging, the 1970s were a period of a growing malaise. All that was imagined as a "Third World import"—be it commodities or human beings—was singled out by government leaders, the corporate-owned media, and even many labor union leaders as the main *cause* of workers' increasing insecurities. White workers were led to believe that their "rightful" place at the head of the "nation" was under attack, not by capital or states utilizing neoliberal strategies but, rather, by "foreign" workers. The dominant discourse of neoliberalism came to be one that saw the "national" space being illegitimately "taken over" by "foreigners." Within nation-states, White workers viewed themselves as under siege by (im)migrant others. Crucially, they also viewed themselves as having been "betrayed" by "their" nation-state.

It is this cultural context that needs to be taken into account to understand the popular and policy framework of multiculturalism. In such a climate, in which the state's legitimacy in acting for the (presumed White) "nation" was being called into question by a key constituency, multiculturalism can be read as an effort by nation-states to both manage and contain the foreign Other in such a way that the state could be seen as acting for the (again, presumed White) "nation." While regressive changes were made to (im)migrants' ability to hold and exercise their rights, White workers were also increasingly cajoled into making themselves more "competitive" with these "foreigners." People were encouraged to "tolerate" the Other and make themselves more like them. In both sets of prescriptions, it was all those who were "foreign" who were said to have caused such massive changes. Unsurprisingly, this situation could not last. And it did not.

The ever-proliferating declarations of "the end of multiculturalism" by various heads of state mark a significant shift in the governmentality of neoliberalism. In particular, it marks the return of demands for formal assimilationist policies (now reclassified as "integration") wherein a reified, glorified, and depoliticized "national culture," one shorn of its tolerance of all things "foreign," is upheld. Recently, British Prime Minister Cameron once again entered the fray with a January 2016 call to end what he termed the "passive tolerance" of "separate" communities. In continuing his earlier declaration of the "end of multiculturalism," he used terminology previously mobilized largely by the far right: the trope of "One Nation." He stated (as cited in Mason and Sherwood 2016), "We will never truly build One Nation unless we are more assertive about *our* liberal values, more clear about the expectations *we* place on those who come to live here and build *our* country together" (emphasis added).

Toward this aim, Cameron singled out Muslim women. He claimed that in Britain, there were 38,000 Muslim women unable to speak English and a further 190,000 who had only limited English language skills. Presenting this as a significant "problem" for the "nation," Cameron raised the possibility of deporting those who showed no progress in speaking relatively fluent English after two and a half years. He stated (as cited in Mason and Sherwood 2016), "You can't guarantee you can stay if you are not improving your language." Such changes were justified, in part, by linking the inability to speak English with terrorism. Cameron stated, "If you're not able to speak English, not able to integrate, you may find therefore you have challenges understanding what your identity is and therefore you could be more susceptible to the extremist message coming from *Daesh*" (i.e., the terrorist group Islamic State or ISIS). Cameron is far from alone in this position. Leading organizations, including the mainstream media, call for something increasingly termed "British Islam," or what Anya Hart Dyke (2009), writing in the liberal newspaper *The Guardian*, calls "an Islam that encourages Muslims to be more British."

The post-multiculturalism national paradigm is one in which the *no-longer-tolerated* Other must be eradicated (culturally or physically). The return to such assimilationist policies is representative of a rise in both the state's tolerance of racism and its own active practice of it, of which "racial profiling" is only the tip of the iceberg. The post-multiculturalism world also signals the further loss of power for anti-racist movements and their demands for the end of a racialized idea of political membership. Consequently, alongside the "hollowing out" of the rights and entitlements associated with citizenship, autochthonous ideas of "native-ness" have come to trump citizenship. There has been a hardening of nationalism in which even the ocant ability of people from the Poor World to be granted national citizenship in the Rich World is viewed as "too much." Today, a growing number of people with a sense of governmental belonging increasingly demand that one must be "native" to the "nation," not "just" its citizen. In this version of the racist discourse of "blood and soil," one must be "native" to the "national soil." Such a racialized criteria, of course, has a much higher threshold than the gaining of juridical citizenship status. Whereas one can "naturalize" into citizenship and thus accrue the rights associated with it, autochthonous rights require that one be able to prove ancestral ties with the biopolitical group said to be "native" to the territory of the state. The global rise in the discourse of autochthony thus represents a hardening of the distinction between "citizen" and "non-citizen" (or juridical "foreigner") into an even less negotiable hardening between "natives" and "immigrants."

This is a highly uncanny version of "native-ness," one with often multiple contenders. Originally a category of subjugation imposed by imperial-states upon their colonial subjects, in today's post-multiculturalism world it has become a signifier of "true" national "belonging." Indeed, with the expansion of juridical citizenship to some Others, an autochthonous identity has become a rampart from which to attack the "non-natives" in a manner that allows one to claim to *not* be racist because such attacks are presented as simply a re-assertion of "natural rights." Together, they signal a growing acceptance of the existence of a fundamental distinction between "natives" of the "nation" and their foreign-Others, "immigrants."

This can be seen in the strategic use of a rhetoric of the beleaguered and threatened status of the White "natives" of Europe or of Whites in the United States, Canada, Australia, and New Zealand.[3] Those imagining themselves as "Europeans" or as "Whites" increasingly claim the status of "native-ness" in an attempt to hold on to the historic privileges of "European-ness" (and, later, "Whiteness"), which they gained through imperialism. Throughout Europe, the nationalism of far-right parties increasingly relies on their racialized self-identification as the "indigenous people of Europe," the "natural" nationals of specific state territories. In their deployment of a discourse of autochthony, far-right parties, including the British National Party (BNP), France's National Front (Front National), the Swiss People's Party (Schweizerische Volkspartei), Germany's National Democratic Party (Nationaldemokratische Partei Deutschlands), Austria's Freedom Party (Freiheitliche Partei Österreichs), Belgium's Flemish Interest (Vlaams Belang), Holland's Party for Freedom (Partij voor de Vrijheid), the Swedish Democrats (Sverigedemokraterna), the Danish People's Party (Dansk Folkeparti), Norway's Progress Party (Bokmål: Fremskrittspartiet; Nynorsk: Framstegspartiet), Finland's Finns Party (Perussuomalaiset were called the True Finns until 2011), Latvia's National Alliance (officially titled "All for Latvia!—For Fatherland

and Freedom"; Nacionālā apvienība "Visu Latvijai!—Tēvzemei un Brīvībai/LNNK"), Italy's Northern League (Lega Nord), Greece's Golden Dawn (Λαϊκός Σύνδεσμος—Χρυσή Αυγή), Hungary's Movement for a Better Hungary (Jobbik Magyarországért Mozgalom), Romania's Greater Romania Party (Partidul România Mare), and the Slovak National Party (Slovenska Narodna Strana), center the need to "protect" Europeans from "immigrant invaders."[4]

All the previously mentioned parties target (im)migrants as the group that prevents "their nation" from succeeding (how that success is measured differs among these parties). All advocate the use of violence or other means to prevent the people they view as "out of place" in Europe from settling there and/or "returning" them to their proper "homes." For them, "native Europeans" and "migrants" cannot coexist. Such a sentiment was expressed by Laszlo Toroczkai, mayor of Asotthalom, Hungary (elected in 2013 with 71.5% of the vote), who in 2015, when speaking in regard to the movement of people fleeing war in Syria, Iraq, and Afghanistan through the town, stated (as cited in Yardley, 2015), "Migration is just going to lead to bloody conflict" (p. 45).

The success of these far-right parties can be better understood in their relationship to that which is positioned as the "mainstream" in Europe. In Belgium, where the Vlaams Belang is among the most successful of the far-right political parties in Europe, official federal state policy since 1989 has insisted that "migrants" "integrate" (Ceuppens and Geschiere 2005: 397). By this, it does not mean "integrate" into the markets for labor, housing, or commodities because those constituted as "migrants" are well-integrated. Rather, from the viewpoint of the state, the continuous demand that "migrants integrate" is a way to permanently isolate them politically because they are not able to "integrate" into a racialized understanding of "national" belonging which has been almost completely *depoliticized*. It is in this context that the political category of "native"—and the politics of autochthony—arises.

In Europe, Islamophobia is a central part of the public proclamations of far-right political parties and movements. Prefiguring Merkel's and Cameron's declarations of the end of multiculturalism—and the British Prime Minister's demand that Muslim women speak English as a condition of their continued residence in the United Kingdom—Vlaams Belang's leader, Filip Dewinter (cited in Moolenaar 2009), declared in 2009 that "Islamophobia [is] a duty" for "Europeans." Calling Islam an "insidious poison" inside Europe, he argued that "we really need to stop the 'multi-culture' and dare to communicate the superiority of our civilization. Europe is a continent of citadels and cathedrals, not of mosques and minarets." He added, "If we are not cured of our excessive tolerance and are not prepared to confirm the superiority of our European identity, then Europe is like a bird to a cat." Again, prefiguring the political mainstream by only a handful of years, the Vlaams Belang proposal for "keeping Europe European" is the repatriation of those "immigrants" who "reject, deny or combat" "Flemish culture" as well as certain "European values." Here, too, Muslim women are the main biopolitical group against whom the "nation" is defined. Dewinter also commented that women wearing the hijab have "effectively signed their contract for deportation."

None of this has prevented the growing popularity of the Vlaams Belang party. In 2006, it was only narrowly defeated for control of Belgium's second largest city, Antwerp. In 2007, the party won 17 seats in the national elections—just 1 less than Belgium's largest party, the Flemish Liberal Party. Although more recently its electoral support has diminished, this is largely due to the adoption of its politics by less controversial parties, such as the successful

New Flemish Alliance. Like the Vlaams Belang, this party not only demands Flemish independence but also insists that only Dutch should be spoken in Flanders and that "migrants" must be made to "integrate." It does so without openly espousing Islamophobia, but it does, however, reject multiculturalism.

The electoral success of parties with similar autocthonous messages is evident elsewhere in Europe. The slogan of the French Front National is the autochthonous "les Francais d'abord" (or the "First French"). In Switzerland, the Swiss People's Party ran under the slogan "Masseneinbürgerrung stoppen!" ("Stop mass naturalizations!") during the 2015 elections. Its main plank—anti-immigration—is informed by autochthonous discourses: The party became internationally infamous for its use of racist election posters, including one showing veiled Muslim women accompanied by the question, "Where are we living, Baden or Baghdad?"

In January 2016, a proposal by the Swiss People's Party in the region of Ticino (on the border with Italy) that gave priority for "native" Swiss over "foreigners" in the labor market was passed by the cantonal parliament ("Ticino Initiative" 2016). The slogan for such an initiative was "Ours First" ("Primi i nostri").

In Austria, the far-right Freedom Party's slogan is "Mehr mut für unser Wiener blut" ("More courage for our Viennese blood"). The next rhyming line, "too many foreigners does no one any good," is indicative of its proposal that Austria put a halt to all immigration. It, too, has made significant electoral gains, coming in second place in state elections in Upper Austria in September 2015. Later that year, it won 31% of the vote in Vienna. In Finland, the far-right Finns Party, which has anti-immigration at the top of its agenda, became the parliament's second largest party after the 2015 elections, receiving almost 18% of the vote. This allowed the party to join the current government coalition. In September of that year, Finland began border checks for "migrants." Demonstrators in support of such measures were filmed holding signs stating, "It is enough. Close the borders!" ("Protesters Form Human Wall Against Refugees" 2015).

In Denmark, the Danish People's Party argues that it is the state's "moral responsibility to the people of Denmark to keep Denmark Danish." The party's founder, Pia Kjærsgaard, has stated that immigration is neither "natural" nor "welcome" in Denmark. The party's current leader and member of the Danish parliament, Kristian Thulesen Dahl, has described his party as anti-Muslim and recently stated, "We will not accept a multi-ethnic transformation of the country." In 2015, the party received 21.1% of the vote in the Danish general election. In Sweden, the Swedish Democrats (Sverigedemokraterna), with early links to groups named Keep Sweden Swedish and White Aryan Resistance, maintain that "indigenous Swedish" people are being threatened by "immigrants." In a recent public advertisement campaign, the Swedish Democrats stated that if elected, "Native Swedes" would be "welcome back to a Better Sweden." Here, too, Muslim people are its main target. Niclas Nilsson, a Swedish Democratic city counselor in the city of Kristianstad, recently complained that "Swedish people don't feel at home anymore," adding that "the problem we have is basically with the Muslims. They have difficulty assimilating, so much of their culture is based on Islam." This, he says (as cited in Crouch 2014), dilutes "Swedishness." He was following in the footsteps of Jimmie Åkesson, the leader of the Swedish Democrats, who recently called for a total ban on the immigration of asylum seekers to Sweden, stating, "You will not enter our country because it is full" ("Åkesson: 'Stay Away, Refugees, Sweden Is Full'" 2015). The Swedish Democrats are currently the third largest party, with 49 seats in the parliament (Riksdag).

The Netherlands, which, like Belgium, classifies people as either autochthons or allochthones as part of its official policy, has seen the rise of the Partij voor de Vrijheid (the Party for Freedom (PVV)). Its leader, Geert Wilders, is openly Islamophobic, stating that Muslims are trying to "colonie" Holland (cited in Beaumont 2010). In the name of defending "Western civilisation as well as Dutch culture," Wilders campaigns to end all Muslim immigration to the Netherlands and "repatriate" Muslims currently living there. In 2007, he told the Dutch parliament that "Islam is the Trojan Horse in Europe. If we do not stop Islamification now, Eurabia and Netherabia will just be a matter of time." In the 2017 parliamentary elections, the PVV received the second highest number of votes and won 20 seats, an increase from the 12 seats it held in the outgoing parliament (Graham 2017). Like other far-right parties in Europe, its greater success has been measured by the adoption of its platform by mainstream political parties. In Holland, too, anti-immigration has been mainstreamed as part of the "defense" of the "nation."

The previously mentioned groups are only some of the most electorally popular parties in Europe that run on a nationalist platform of autochthony against "immigrants" (many of whom are co-citizens). There are, of course, many other such movements with less (but not totally absent) electoral success. Germany's neo-Nazi National Democratic Party (NPD) also campaigns on the relationship between ideas of "race" and "place." Running under the party's slogan, "Money for granny instead of Sinti and Roma," one of its lead candidates, Udo Voigt, told Reuters (as cited in Martin 2014), "We say Europe is the continent of White people and it should remain that way." For an avowed nationalist party, "Europe" figures very large: Voigt added that "we want to make sure that even in 50 years' time an Italian, a Frenchman, an Englishman, an Irishman and a German are still recognizable as European and cannot be mistaken for Ghanaians or Chinese." Toward this goal, the NDP platform includes the expulsion of the more than 12 million people whom it considers "racially impure" from Germany. Voigt won a seat in the European Parliament in its 2014 elections. That year, the NDP also held two state assemblies as well as hundreds of seats on local councils.

On its website, the BNP claims that

> the nationalisms of Europe champion the right of the traditional peoples of Europe to be recognized as the indigenous inhabitants of their lands, and to be accorded the moral right to the special status and right to self-preservation that all native peoples enjoy.

Donna Treanor (2013), London Regional Secretary of the BNP, stated that due to immigration, "in a few decades the British people will become a minority in their historical homeland. This is genocide, which is defined by international law." She defends such a statement by arguing that the UK government had contravened the UN Convention against genocide by allowing immigration to cause "psychological trauma of the indigenous British people becoming a minority in their own homeland."

We need to pay attention to such rejections of multiculturalism—however milquetoast such policies are—and the autochthonous discourses that have reframed resurgent nationalisms based on the demand that the "original" or "native" culture be preserved against immigrant encroachers. Such expressions of nationalism are one response to the increasingly global processes of capitalist expansion, which is often expressed culturally as *rootlessness*. In reactionary fashion, the retort is to claim to be *rooted* in the "nation" through ideas of native-ness (or indigeneity). Such responses can be read not only as a misrecognition of contemporary nation-state policies of neoliberalism but also as further evidence that the bogey of "multiculturalism" has insulated the global system of capitalism and the equally global system of nation-states by drawing attention to workers who are deemed to "not belong" to the "nation" and who are therefore portrayed as illegitimate makers of claims on the "nation" and "its" state. In such a way, the discourse of multiculturalism has enabled a re-imagining of the "nation" for neoliberal times.

CONCLUSION

As much as multiculturalism was a policy to manage social relations in a particular historical conjuncture—that period between the start of neoliberal policies in the mid- to late 1960s and their political maturation in the 1980s—the end of multiculturalism is best understood as a populist response to the political maturation of neoliberalism as well as the greater reach these policies have given to capital. Contrary to some theories of the relationship between neoliberalism (or capitalist globalization) and the state, the expansion of capitalist social relations has only *strengthened* the nation-state, particularly its ideological apparatuses that legitimate its coercive powers through the nationalist interpellation of "the People." The end of multiculturalism signals a more muscular nationalism. Such events further signal the importance of paying attention to nationalisms and the nation form of state power in the field of global studies.

Policies on multiculturalism and those on immigration are the Siamese twins of the post-World War II era of postcoloniality and the ascendency of the nation-state as the only legitimated form of political community formation. It is thus important to conclude this discussion of multiculturalism by recognizing that in the postcolonial new world order, free mobility throughout the world has become largely prohibited and illegalized. The state has the power to more or less unilaterally revoke people's freedom to move across nationalized territories (Motomura 2006: 15–37). People do not have the *right* to enter any nation-state other than the one that official recognizes them as its citizens. Without such rights, the right to leave the state whose nationality they hold is meaningless. Even more so, immigration restrictions are increasingly murderous, as attested to by the growing body count of people trying to circumvent border controls. Under international law, it is the nation-state that has the right to determine who gets in and what status those who enter are given. It is this right of national sovereigns that allows states to discriminate against (im)migrants, both those who are currently migrating and those placed in the racialized social category of "immigrant" regardless of their actual citizenship status.

This confers no small power on the citizenry. Indeed, holding citizenship, particularly the coveted citizenship of the Rich World nation-states, marks the racist politics of superiority and domination over others. In the "post-civil rights" era when explicit discrimination against "races" has been delegitimized (although this appears to be changing), the sovereign *national* right to exclude non-nationals is what has made it possible, in part, for states to continuously enact the racialization of the "nation." Polls and debates on immigration reinforce the power of those with a strong sense of national entitlement to act as the state themselves (Hage 2000). Of course, the power to exclude "immigrants" plays no small part in the neoliberal reorganization of nationalized labor markets. By recruiting workers through "managed migration" schemes that classify people as "temporary foreign workers" or by severely restricting legal avenues to migration so that increasingly more people are cast as "illegals," immigration policies need to be seen as part of the ideological apparatuses of nation-states—one with, of course, enormous material consequences.

As I have argued elsewhere, restrictive immigration policies are as much about *differentiating* among those within the nation-state as they are about restricting *access* to the territory of the nation-state (Sharma 2006). The border, therefore, is not just the physical boundary separating national state territories but also, perhaps more important, an ideological *line of difference* that authorizes the state to carry out practices against non-nationals that are often unconstitutional and that are deemed politically unacceptable, undemocratic, and even manifestly unjust if/when carried out against citizens or possibly even permanent residents. For this reason, it is important to go against ideas of "race," as Paul Gilroy (2002) has persuasively argued, but also to go against ideas of "nation" and against the power of national states to enact this "nation."

Notes

1. The political leaders of Germany or the United Kingdom are far from alone in making such demands. Numerous states throughout the world have implemented "integrationist" measures, including demanding that the "national language" be spoken by applicants for citizenship (e.g., Australia and Canada).
2. Some "temporary foreign workers" did gain the right to apply to convert their status to "permanent resident." In 1992, under Canada's Live-in Caregiver Program, migrant domestic workers became eligible to apply for landed status after two years of continuous employment as domestic servants in Canada (Sharma 2006).
3. Public opinion on race has changed over time as well. In the 1950s, surveys show, most White Americans believed that Black Americans faced substantial discrimination but that they themselves experienced little. Today, despite gaping disparities between Black and White Americans in income, education, health care, home ownership, employment, and college admissions, a majority of White Americans now believe they are just as likely, or more likely, to face discrimination as Black Americans (Hannah-Jones 2013).
4. See more at the Left Flank website (https://left-flank.org/2014/01/12/brown-international-european-far-right/#sthash.MiukBLEI.TOUpZcX0.dpuf).

References

"Åkesson: 'Stay Away, Refugees, Sweden Is Full.'" 2015. *The Local*, October 17. http://www.thelocal.se/20151017/kesson-stay-away-refugees-sweden-is-full. Accessed February 12, 2016.

Anderson, B. 1991. *Imagined Communities: Reflections on the Origin and Spread of Nationalism*. London: Verso.

Bannerji, H. 2000. *The Dark Side of the Nation: Essays on Multiculturalism, Nationalism and Gender*. Toronto: Canadian Scholars Press.

Beaumont, P. 2010. "Geert Wilders, the Ultra-Right Firebrand, Campaigns to be Holland's Prime Minister." *The Observer*, May 15. http://www.theguardian.com/world/2010/may/16/geert-wilders-pvv-holland-netherlands. Accessed February 10, 2016.

Bourdieu, P. 1984. *Distinction: A Social Critique of the Judgment of Taste*, translated by Richard Nice. Cambridge, MA: Harvard University Press.

Ceuppens, B., and P. Geschiere. 2005. "Autochthony: Local or Global? New Modes in the Struggle over Citizenship and Belonging in Africa and Europe." *Annual Review of Anthropology* 34: 385–407.

Crouch, D. 2014. "The Rise of the Anti-Immigrant Sweden Democrats: 'We Don't Feel at Home Any More, and It's Their Fault'" *The Guardian*. http://www.theguardian.com/world/2014/dec/14/sweden-democrats-flex-muscles-anti-immigrant-kristianstad. Accessed February 12, 2016.

Deleuze, G., and F. Guattari. 1987. *A Thousand Plateaus: Capitalism and Schizophrenia*, translated by B. Massumi. Minneapolis: University of Minnesota Press.

Dyke, A. H. 2009. "We Want a More British Islam." *The Guardian*, March 2. http://www.theguardian.com/commentisfree/belief/2009/mar/02/religion-islam-quilliam-imams. Accessed March 14, 2016.

Foucault, M. 1997. *"Society Must Be Defended": Lectures at the Collège de France, 1975–1976*. New York: Picador.

"Full Transcript, David Cameron, Speech on Radicalisation and Islamic Extremism, Munich, 5 February 2011." *New Statesman*, February 5. http://www.newstatesman.com/blogs/the-staggers/2011/02/terrorism-islam-ideology. Accessed March 9, 2013.

Gardezi, H. 1995. *The Political Economy of International Labour Migration*. Montreal: Black Rose Books.

Gilroy, P. 2002. *Against Race: Imagining Political Culture Beyond the Color Line*. Cambridge, MA: Harvard University Press.

Graham, P. 2017. "Who Won the Dutch Election and What Does It Mean for Geert Wilders and the Far-Right in the Netherlands and Europe?" *The Telegraph*, March 16. http://www.telegraph.co.uk/news/2017/03/16/won-dutch-election-does-mean-geert-wilders-far right-netherlands. Accessed August 3, 2017.

Hage, G. 2000. *White Nation: Fantasies of White Supremacy in a Multicultural Society*. New York/Annandale, NSW, Australia: Routledge/Pluto Press.

Hannah-Jones, N. 2013. "Race Didn't Cost Abigail Fisher Her Spot at the University of Texas." *The Wire*, March 18. http://www.theatlanticwire.com/national/2013/03/abigail-fisher-university-texas/63247. Accessed July 19, 2014.

Hardt, M., and A. Negri. 2000. *Empire*. Cambridge, MA: Harvard University Press.

Martin, M. 2014. "German Party Accused of Neo-Nazi Traits Set for EU Parliament." Reuters, May 21. http://uk.reuters.com/article/uk-eu-election-germany-neonazis-idUKKBN0E112M20140521. Accessed February 14, 2016.

Mason, R., and H. Sherwood. 2016. "Migrant Spouses Who Fail English Test May Have to Leave UK, Says Cameron." *The Guardian*, January 18. http://www.theguardian.com/uk-news/2016/jan/18/pm-migrant-spouses-who-fail-english-test-may-have-to-leave-uk. Accessed March 14, 2016.

"Merkel Says German Multicultural Society Has Failed." 2010. BBC News, October 17. http://www.bbc.com/news/world-europe-11559451. Accessed November 2, 2012.

Moolenaar, L. 2009. "Islamophobia Is a Duty for Everyone." *Gazet van Antwerpen*, March 2. http://www.filipdewinter.be/%E2%80%9Cislamophobia-is-a-duty-for-everyone%E2%80%9D-gazet-van-antwerpen. Accessed February 7, 2016.

Motomura, H. 2006. *Americans in Waiting: The Lost Story of Immigration and Citizenship in the United States*. Oxford, UK: Oxford University Press.

Pew Hispanic Center. 2006. "Estimates of the Unauthorized Migrant Population for States Based on the March 2005 CPS." Washington, DC: Pew Hispanic Center, April 26.

"Protesters Form Human Wall Against Refugees at Finnish–Swedish Border." 2015. Deutsche Welle, September 19. http://www.newsjs.com/url.php?p=http://www.dw.com/en/protesters-form-human-wall-against-refugees-at-finnish-swedish-border/a-18724593. Accessed February 10, 2016.

Sharma, N. 2006. *Home Economics: Nationalism and the Making of "Migrant Workers" in Canada.* Toronto: University of Toronto Press.

Sharma, N. Forthcoming. *Home Rule: Natives, Migrants and the Making of National Sovereignty.* Durham, NC: Duke University Press.

Smith, D. 1990. *The Conceptual Practices of Power: A Feminist Sociology of Knowledge.* Toronto: University of Toronto Press.

"Ticino Initiative Prioritising Locals for Jobs Declared Valid." 2016. Swissinfo.ch, January 26. https://www.swissinfo.ch/eng/cross-border-workers_ticino-initiative-prioritising-locals-for-jobs-declared-valid/41920212. Accessed February 9, 2016.

Treanor, D. 2013. "Question Time for Patriots—London." British National Party, January 3. https://bnp.org.uk. Accessed March 6, 2013.

Walford, C. 2012. "'We Need Community Cohesion': Ministers' Pledge to End Era of Multiculturalism by Appealing to 'Sense of British Identity.'" *Daily Mail Online*, February 21. http://www.dailymail.co.uk/news/article-2104049/Eric-Pickles-signals-end-multiculturalism-says-Tories-stand-majority.html. Accessed March 6, 2013.

Yardley, J. 2015. "Has Europe Reached the Breaking Point?" *New York Times Magazine*, December 15.

CHAPTER 32

······································

THE FEMALE BODY IN GLOBAL MEDIA

······································

TUIJA PARIKKA

GLOBALIZATION as an abstraction could easily result in a sense of indifference unless examined and made sense of in the context of the most mundane surfaces of ordinary life, the manifestations of the body. One can only watch in awe as disfigured or distressed faces, and mutilated body parts are excessively circulated, and at times celebrated, in the global media. For example, a 2010 UK campaign, "Safer Travel at Night" by Transport for London, informed passengers of the dangers of illegal cabs using a poster that mingled the playful nightlife of young women with the ultimate horror of a sexual attack in the confined, darkened space of a cab. The image highlighted a deeply terrified face of an urgently pleading woman trying to reach out. The title read, "Stop, no. Stop, please, no please. Please stop taking unbooked minicabs," and merged her plea for bodily integrity with advice for action. In 2014, the "Safer Travel at Night" campaign continued on social media with a #homesafeselfie hashtag that encouraged young women to let their friends know they made it home and thus survived the threat of unlicensed drivers which was connected with immigration outside of the European Union by, for example, Newsweek (Draper 2014). What is the relationship between the female face of horror sinking into the blackness of an illegal cab and fears of the global? Does her face signify distress at the emergence of non-EU migration as the embodiment of the Other?

This chapter discusses how the female body is subjected to being "played" in the global media and what that reveals of gender and minority-majority relationships and of global aims and fears. At a time of increased global conflicts and a heightened urgency to compete for scarce global resources, one cannot fail to notice the simultaneously increasing circulation of such gender imagery that fuses the sexual with the violent—"sexy violence." This chapter therefore focuses on such sexy violence imagery that cannot be thoroughly explained by theories of objectification, liberation, or commodification of women but, rather, calls for new explanations regarding the relationship between the body, globalization, and media. As the field of global media studies has become increasingly international and intercultural (Murphy and Kraidy 2003; Miller and Kraidy 2016), the limitations of universalizing interpretations of the workings of globalization have also become more apparent. A transdisciplinary space has opened for hybrid approaches aiming at transcending linguistic, geographic, cultural, and other boundaries in the construction of some of these alternative explanations.

Globalization has an unarguably long history of its own as a concept rooted in economic, social, and political interactions between nations over time. Some argue (Mattelart 2010) that we often fail to recognize, or even deny, the historicity of the phenomena that contribute to the construction of certain beliefs about globalization, and we consent to its meaning and significance. Similar to Mattelart, Fairclough (2006) emphasizes the interconnectedness of the material and symbolic processes. The material reality of globalization with its flows of money, goods, people, and technological infrastructures is supported and shaped by a discursive reality. Globalization as a consequence of modernity is mixed with ways of talking about it that contribute to its construction. Instead of reducing globalization to material processes, the social constructivist approach ties globalization processes with languages used to describe it.

In Mattelart's (2010) view, for example, language and ideology of corporate globalization have fused with world communication and resulted in a new totalizing ideology that is often advertised as a "happiness-for-all" ideology. Recently, diffusion of happiness-for-all ideologies has become complicated by other processes, such as flows of people, that come into conflict with global media discourses sustaining the happiness ideologies, especially in the West. In these conflicts, the gendered body is increasingly being used to imagine and work through such conflicts.

Speeding up of diffusion of various ideologies is enabled by the material reality of technological innovations, including the internet, mobile phones, and various social media platforms (Albarran 2010; Boyd-Barrett 2006; Flew 2007; McMillin 2007; Rantanen 2005) which is shifting attention to the digital in many areas of investigation. In addition to the ubiquitousness of digital media technologies (Flew 2007; McNair 2006; Miller and Kraidy 2016; Morley 2006), the material reality of media globalization is often understood in terms of the expansion of media markets, corollary to joining the interests of the media owners with content. Many view this as a fundamentally Euro-American phenomenon because of the role of the United States as the leader of global capitalism. On the other hand, some argue that the systemic evidence for this is missing (Hafez 2007), and the role of the United States will, in fact, be overshadowed by the rapid technological development of such Asian countries as China and India (Boyd-Barrett 2006).

In addition to globalization as processes and discourses, such as happiness-for-all discourses, many works focus on the relationship between globalization and especially gender through economic, political, or cultural (media) perspectives (Beneria, Berik, and Floro 2015; Desai 2009; Gill 2007a; Hedge 2011; Momsen 2010; Ponzanesi 2014) and approach globalization primarily as a context for various gender representations, discourses, and concerns. Gill (2007a) and Gill and Orgad (2015), for example, discuss localization of advertising that is made to fit local cultural, national, and ethnic settings while also being economically and culturally significant in the processes of globalization. Construction of gender and sexuality in advertising imagery often link such desired and pursued goals as independence and control over one's own body with commodities to be bought and thus make the bodies devoid of political significance.

From the perspective of liberation, such imagery can be interpreted as women's celebration of their own bodies and highly pursued freedoms. Yet, women can simultaneously be put on display to be gazed upon. Merging such contradictory ideas often results in the commodification of the female body, which can perhaps best be understood as visual styles or looks that fuel processes of global capitalism in the context of globalization (Gill 2007a). This is quite typical of post-feminist sensibilities that, in Gill's (2007b) and Gill and Orgad's (2015) views, fetishize young female bodies and construct them in contradictory discourses that are closely connected with post-feminism and neoliberalism with its emphasis on self-managed and self-regulated individualism. Also, in McRobbie's (2009) view, media in post-feminist consumer cultures takes up the tasks of the feminists of earlier eras in promoting women's many freedoms while negating what is political about the body. Furthermore, in the context of the "post-girlpower" era (Dobson and Harris 2015), girls are not only allowed to be active but also expected to be self-actualizing subjects.

Commodification, especially in the context of global capitalism, is one such subdiscourse of globalization that extensively shapes the reality of globalization in ways that threaten to negate what is political about the images and discourses of the body and further support global capitalism and neoliberal values and beliefs. Regardless of the dominance of the language of commodification embedded in globalization processes, however, globalization is not approached here for its power to result in commodification of objects but, rather, for its *socially constitutive* role in redrafting gendered and sexualized bodies in world communication. The female face is surely objectified in the "Safer Travel at Night" campaign, discussed previously, as the viewer gazes into the subject's watery and terrified eyes; yet the campaign is founded on the idea of women having a freedom to occupy a public space alone at night. Objectification and liberation discourses cannot, however, be reduced to commodification discourse here but, rather, connect the meanings of the image with the fear and danger of the outside Other beyond the European and Western borders. From this perspective, the question is no longer merely about women's rights to their bodies and bodily integrity, subjecting women to the primarily male gaze on markets in political or economic terms; rather, the power of definition of the fear of the global Other in the making of a woman is at stake.

In sexy violent imagery, in other words, globalization as discourse can contribute to the constitution of bodies as sexualized and gendered in ways that escape the traditional problematic of objectification, liberation, or commodification of women's bodies. In this sense, bodies are not only a medium of culture, as Bordo (2003) maintains, or the "oldest medium" (Kraidy 2013), but also a medium for globalization discourses and culture. Although bodies, nor femaleness or maleness, are not considered as a biological fact or a natural given here, the sexualized and gendered body is not reduced to purely discursive effect either. The raw materiality of the body remains beyond the discursive realm, although it cannot be accessed as a specific object. As such, it can only be conceived by studying meanings, manifestations, and relations (Heinämaa 1997; Irigaray 1985, 1993). Meanings, or imagery, fusing the sexual with the violent examined herewith functions as *imaginaries* that could be described as "something we believe to be something else" (Lacan 1968: 175) and that are, as such, fueled and shaped especially but not exclusively by globalization discourses and processes.

Therefore, in this context, this chapter is specifically interested in how the *images* of the female bodies enter into the function of globalization *imaginaries*. In imagery of this kind, the body as a signifier fuses with the signified and becomes an amalgam for fears and aims of the global. This approach emphasizes perhaps what is instrumental about the manifestations of female bodies in the workings of the global media. If play is a disguise for something else beyond the manifest content or meaning (Ruggil, McAlliter, and Menchaca

2004), how does "playing" with the female body function to describe "something we believe to be something else"? Furthermore, how does the female body as "played" function as a conduit for addressing gender, racial, and ethnic relationships, and overall, our ambivalent relationship with the global?

The global media has become the primary site for both politicizing meanings and conflicts rooted in globalization and resolved through the female body. The cases addressed in this chapter are all empirically conflicted by the contestation of the global economic or political order through the female body in the global media. The first case consists of a music video, "Bitch Better Have My Money," by Rihanna. Her music video is examined as an expression of resistance primarily to the racialized aspects of the global economic order. The second case is a Canadian advertising campaign, notorious for its associations with domestic violence, which is examined particularly as a gendered response to the workings of the global economic order. The third case, the *New York Times* article and an adjacent video footage documenting the killing of an Afghan woman, Farkhunda Malikzada, is read as an ethnic challenge to the primacy of a Western "self" in globalization.

RACIALIZATION OF THE WHITE FEMALE BODY IN THE WESTERN ECONOMIC ORDER

In 2015, popular Barbadian artist Rihanna released a single, "Bitch Better Have My Money." The song is an example of trap music, and various sources ranked it as the best song or in the top twenty-five of the year, ranging from the top ten to the top twenty in fourteen countries. The video won the best pop video and the best styling award at the UK Music Awards in 2015.[1]

In Rihanna's song, sexy violence is constituted through the eroticization of the White, female body and its mutilation in the name of extortion of money from her White husband who is overwhelmingly interested in economic matters and who fails to give the non-White woman what is hers. The video begins with a scene from an affluent home where a White woman puts on her makeup, jewelry, and clothes against the background of traditional signs of bourgeois habitus: soothing classical melodies, orchids, vases, and paintings. After kissing the cheek of a contemplating, oblivious husband, she steps into an elevator carrying a Pomeranian. She does not interact with a poorer woman who is standing in the back of the elevator. The non-White woman in the elevator is signified in stark opposition to the White woman. Dressed and made up in dark colors, wearing dark hair, under dark light barely illuminating her darker complexion and face, the next scene shows the non-White woman driving toward her house in the darkness of night and laboriously dragging a large trunk toward the building. In the next scene, the encounter between the non-White woman and the White woman in the elevator is not shown, but as the doors open, only the White woman's Pomeranian and the poorer woman dragging her trunk emerge. Together with her accomplices, the poor woman laboriously heaves the trunk into the car for a violent journey. Now naked in the back of the car, the White woman is subjected to torture and abuse, all the while the poorer women make calls to the White husband to extort money. As anger and aggression build, the women return to his home for the final scenes, in which knives, chainsaws, and plastic gloves are introduced, together with images of sprayed blood and the disgusted husband who is now tied to his chair and unable to avert his eyes from the scene. The final scene reveals to viewers the non-White woman relaxing in the trunk, which is filled with money, as she smokes a blunt (marijuana rolled in cigar paper) in the money bath.

Lena (2008) argues that rap music and videos take the listener and the viewer into the middle of class struggles between dominant and subordinate groups. In music, dominant ideologies can be resisted and objects and practices disarticulated and rearticulated in new contexts to negotiate social and cultural change, which potentially results in new alliances across audiences. Whereas many rap videos introduce the viewer to the "hood" and Black inner-city life associated with dangers from the perspective of the exotic other (Lena 2008), Rihanna's video begins with the opposite perspective. Rihanna begins by penetrating the upper class home as the safe haven and imagining that as the site of ultimate neglect in that the White husband consistently, and at times quite ignorantly, fails to respond to demands expressed by Rihanna's character to get his wife back. In this way, the imagined security and pleasures of the White bourgeois space become disarticulated and rearticulated in the context of the privacy of the non-White women, who are, rather, constructed through the bonds of loyalty and rambunctious play. In Rihanna's video, class struggle is racialized[2] as an opposition between Whites and non-Whites but does not parallel with power, and lack thereof, in a conventional way. The economic power of the White couple may produce emotional and social blindness but also resistance to power, in a Foucauldian vein, through sacrificing the White female body in an attempt to make the White male *see* what is expelled from his economic order: the non-White woman, beyond the definition of her as its Other.

Thus, in her invisibility, the non-White woman captures and "plays" the White woman while abusing her. The non-White women place her in and take her out of the trunk, which is like a treasure chest in children's stories and games, and it metaphorically becomes a conduit for the White male's wealth and possessions, including the wife, who now becomes the non-White women's toy. Such "play" functions as a private violent occurrence to them that makes visible not only her Whiteness but also the Whiteness of the economic and political order. Subcategories of Whiteness, such as ethnicity, do not take over to make Whiteness difficult to "see" (Dyer 1997: 228) but, rather, are amplified through reflecting Whiteness against the failures and ineffectiveness of authorities looking for her. The legal system is ridiculed for its ineffectiveness: If the body of the White female becomes located outside of Whiteness among non-White women, authorities cannot find it; they cannot see it. This underlying distinction of the private and the public becomes racialized in this case: In the privacy of the non-White women, the White female body is invisible to the non-White women other than as a "toy" of the moment, which paradoxically makes her Whiteness visible. In the privacy of her own home, the Whiteness of her female body becomes invisible again, and she is the signifier of the husband's possessions.

In Irigaray's (1985) view, Western societies are based on the exchange of women, which provides the foundation for our social, symbolic, and economic order; men "make commerce of them," not with them. Hence, the female body is often conceived as an abstraction reduced to its price, to "that of being a product of man's 'labor,'" and functions as a "mirror of value of and for man" (pp. 172–173, 177). In Rihanna's video, the non-White women are constructed as seeking to capitalize on such economic order in terms of pursuing a Subject position of trade in making commerce with a White male through the exchange of the

White female body. Her status as a woman on the market is corollary to the construction of her bourgeois sensibilities and the signs of his wealth on her appearance. And yet the White male refuses the "offers" of the non-White women, as if not acknowledging or "seeing" them as partners in trade until he witnesses his wife's bloody and violent death. Is it in her final mutilation by the non-White women that her Whiteness is imagined as revealed to him, if only to mark the edge of his economic power and culture, and to meet that of the non-White woman?

This suggests that his economic order becomes challenged, not in gendered terms, but in racial terms; the White female body is not visible to the husband until sacrificed by the non-White woman, as if suggesting her capacity to destroy not one but all of his possessions. Thus, the victory of the non-White woman is palpable in that she, in the end, bathes in his money and her blood. The White woman is not only located outside of the culture of Whiteness but also has vanished altogether, and threatens to take him with her. Yet even though he is extorted by her "death," he does not become dislocated or deterritorialized. Paradoxically, what is challenging about the economic power of the White male is also affirmative of that power as a result of sacrificing the potential object of exchange and its value to him.

What can be said of the relationship of women and its racialization? Although the non-White women cannot emerge as Subjects of economic order, they can be constructed as disturbing it through sacrificing the White female body in the process of undoing the hierarchization of "race," as established in the early dichotomous scenes of the video. The possibility for cultural exchanges between White and non-White women in this context is ultimately complicated by class that is imagined as aligned with a sense of one's place in the economic and social order; what the expelled can say to the Other of such order is frustrated by anger that is acted out on a "toy" until the "toy" becomes disfigured and banalized by having new eyelashes and a mouth repainted on her, just like children often do to their dolls, until the "toy's" final disembodiment. The White male stands outside of such cultural collapses and retains his definition power in the global economic order, global competition, and the status of White, affluent men.

Grossberg (2011) maintains that authentic rock music articulates private desires and feelings into shared language that becomes an expression of a community. Articulation of non-White women challenging the global economic power of White men through sacrificing a White woman transforms any private feelings to a social statement and commentary beyond entertainment. Political discourse is not always antagonistic of the logic of the marketplace, as Lena (2008) concludes, and yet in this case it takes the sacrifice of another woman to be racial–political, although that sacrifice compromises the gender–political. Gender and racial political discourse, in other words, is not difficult to articulate because it would be antagonistic to the logic of the marketplace but, rather, because it would be antagonistic to the racialization of that marketplace. Both the White and non-White women are here constructed outside of the logic of economic exchange in different ways and can only enter that exchange through the hostile puppetry of the other. Sacrificing the White, female body, after all, affirms the gendered logic of the marketplace with nothing for the non-White woman to exchange with a White male, leaving her with the mere pleasure of revenge.

Other attempts to address the question of female economic agency and economic order in popular music include Lady Gaga's "Bad Romance," in which she seeks to overthrow the phallogocentric logic of the age-old sexual and economic contract by subverting an old scenario, that of selling herself for sex. Although her action merges sex and money, she escapes construction of herself as a prostitute, and the traditional discourses of porn, and ultimately burns the male body in her video (Parikka 2015b). And yet, through sacrificing him, there is no one to trade with, and nothing to trade with, which speaks to the fears of economic marginality in a world that no longer functions merely as a context for gender discourses but, rather, is constitutive of gender, the sexual, and, at times, racial identities. The following discussion of a Canadian ad campaign, "Look Good in All you Do," focuses on how fears of economic marginality in the world can radically seep into constitution of gender and even be capitalized on in the process, expressing economic aims.

At the Edge of Culture: Love and Loss of the Female Body

Traditionally, in the context of Western imaginings regarding the beauty of the female body, aging marks the significant loss of beauty. Yet in the context of many recent contemporary mediated imaginings, it is not aging that yields bodies to the process of decline but, rather, another kind of harm, violence, whereby the beauty of the female body becomes painstakingly and meticulously both established and then disfigured. In such imagery, women can be claimed to be victims of their own beauty (Parikka 2015b), like, for example, in a Bulgarian fashion magazine image featuring a face of a young woman with a black eye while bearing the culturally accepted signs of the beautiful.

Such imagery often encourages readings that are closely connected with domestic violence. Yet playing with the idea of beauty and its simultaneous destruction can also escape the domestic violence discourse whereby the female body is conceived as attaining its status as beautiful in a usually heterosexual relationship with a male who takes possession of her and harms her; being a victim of beauty thus implies being a victim of someone's (a man's) beauty and, as such, a victim of his actions. This connotation can easily at first sight be attached to "Look Good in All You Do," a 2011 Canadian advertising campaign for a hair salon consisting of a series of ads featuring carefully coiffed battered women.

In one of the ads, a woman posing on a couch appears serious with her black eye, while the man standing behind the couch smiles slightly. At first sight, the man is constructed as holding a position of dominance over her because of his standing position and the necklace he holds in his hands as an instrument of affection and potential harm. As an example of sexy violence imagery, the image fuses her sex appeal, constructed through heels, short dress, looks, and pose, with signs of violence and the subsequent threat of it.

And yet she remains outside of the traditional victim-of-abuse discourse. The sign of her "Hair" marks her victory in managing to look good beyond the reduction of her to discourses of victimhood. The Hair, which repeats the colors of the couch on which she is sitting, remains as her uncompromised possession regardless of his actions or inactions. Here, the sexual and economic markets merge in terms of him perhaps possessing her but her possessing the final token of victory, her looks, in ways that confirm a victory of one over the other in an unconventional manner. The "Hair" crowns her as the winner in an imaginary competition.

However, in such sexy violence imagery, the meaning for competition seems to be missing; a woman can be perceived as drawing the last straw but for no apparent reason. Even in the context of a domestic violence awareness campaign, "Why Is It So Hard to See Black and Blue?" the position of the woman indicates not defeat but, rather, traditional feminine posture, even if beaten up. She is unarguably framed as a victim, but as one who, even if she chose to wear the dress that should never warrant violence, as the caption states, will again and again become sexualized by her pose and blond hair. The female body signified as beautiful, as an expression in itself, is not constructed as carrying meaning and purpose if located outside of male–female binarism, unless seen through the language of competition. Her currency (beauty) may be male defined, but it is through her victory in not only retaining beauty but also capitalizing on it that marks her not necessarily as a victim of domestic violence much longer but, rather, a subject on economic markets, within economic discourse, where she assumes a position in a relationship of exchange beyond the traditional definition of her as a passive beauty who cannot trade. In this way, the economic merges with the sexual unexpectedly.

Part of the spirit of this era is the waning of politicized public values and common good. Democratic public values are, rather, characteristic of past eras (Giroux 2011; Parikka 2015a) and become replaced by individualistic discourses on domestic violence, in this case, in support of economic globalization. As McRobbie (2009) notably has argued, such discourses with notions of empowerment and choice are also characteristic of post-feminist social and cultural landscape. In the sexy violent imagery, however, competition, achievement, and status beyond the discourse of victimhood not only align with the language of economic globalization in the context of post-feminist neoliberal economies but also in a sense exceed it. Symbolic disfigurement of "her" can render her as an economic subject by choice, as a sign of economic empowerment. An image of battered beauties in the globalization imaginaries may well serve not as an expression of fears of domestic violence but, rather, as fears of economic marginality, and aims of achieving a market status of one's own through self-punitive means to the extent that the "victim of violence" assumes agency and responsibility for her construction as an economic agent capable of capitalizing on her "victimhood." From this perspective, aging and violence are no longer threats to one's beauty; the threats, rather, are losses in the economic sphere. Ironically, positioning the female body with agency in economic discourse has always been the goal of many feminist agendas, but rarely, if ever, in such cultural terms.

It is no wonder that sexy violence imagery often yields to certain melancholic undertones. In Kristeva's (1989) view, melancholia results from the loss of an object that one both loves and hates. The lost object is embedded within oneself because of the love of it, and because of the hate of it, one begins to hate oneself as a bad self. In this context, the loved and hated object, the beauty of the female body, becomes infused with melancholia for its assumed role in economic discourse.

Such sexy violence imagery firmly grounds gender, sexual, and racial identities in the processes, realities, and discourses of globalization that speak to the neoliberal ideologies of global capitalism rooted in the ideas of competition for power, dominance, and economic resources. To draw on those resources, and to fight marginalization, mediated identities become perhaps most malleable, shifting, and playable, but not necessarily truly transformative unless uprooted from the discourses of globalization. The normative foundations of globalization discourses, and their assumed ethnic subject positions, ultimately become "played out" through the body of Farkhunda Malikzada, an Afghan woman represented by the *New York Times* and the local cell phone recordings of her killing, which is the subject of the following discussion.

UNDOING GLOBAL BINARIES: PLAYING THE BODY OF FARKHUNDA MALIKZADA

In *Strangers to Ourselves*, Kristeva (1991) conceives strangers as living within us as the other side of ourselves, the recognition of which saves us from detesting what is strange about the other. In her view, it is the recognition of the difference of ourselves that makes ourselves problematic, even impossible. In the contemporary context, however, it is the Other who is rather recognized as problematic. Many accounts of the representation of Muslims and Islam in the media before September 11, 2001, and after (Culcasi 2011; Falah 2005; Halim and Meyers 2010; Hedge 2011; Parikka 2015b; Pippert 2003; Said 1997) point out how the oppressed female victims "over there" need to be rescued by the West. Us-versus-them binaries within which Muslim women are defined as Others (Parikka 2015b) often serve geopolitical agendas and enable a Western transcendence from the local to the global. In such cases, the Muslim female Other often functions to overcome the threat of White marginality introduced by globalization and helps ensure the Western becoming and subjectivity as a form of imperialist force.

Such Othering discourse is at first sight again thematically reproduced in a December 26, 2015, *New York Times* article, "Flawed Justice After a Mob Killed an Afghan Woman." Rubin (2015) follows up on the story of an Afghan woman named Farkhunda Malikzada, who earlier that year had visited a Muslim shrine and was falsely accused of burning pages of the Quran. In fact, she was found to have been confronting the custodian of the shrine, as well as a fortune teller, for exercising practices that were fundamentally against Islam, such as exploiting women by charging them money for amulets in support of superstitious beliefs. This prompted the custodian to snap at her; he added burnt pages of an old Quran to a pile of old amulets that she apparently was burning in a trash can. The custodian then made an announcement to people on the street: "'A woman burned the Quran. I don't know if this one is sick or mentally disturbed, but what kind of Muslim are you? Go and defend your Quran'" (Rubin 2015). After a quick exchange of words, she was pulled down by the crowds shouting "Kill her," which marks the beginning of frenzied events leading to her violent death.

The story constructs Farkhunda Malikzada as the victim par excellence within the Western women's rights discourse. The largest part of the text narrates the flaws that exist in the Afghan justice system, regardless of the money poured in by the United States and European countries and efforts to educate Afghans on the issues and practices of law. According to Rubin (2015), "mob justice" was condemned and the public pressured the legal system to televise the trial and find the killers guilty. However, after an appeal that happened behind closed doors, those guilty verdicts were overturned. From this perspective, the Afghan government failed to signal the severity of compromising women's rights in public. As such, this incident could be read as once again affirming the superiority of the Western justice system in the area of defining women's rights, especially after the West had tried to protect Afghan women by financing the education of Afghan-born lawyers in the hopes of changing the justice system and thus saving Afghan women from the hands of local men.

What is perhaps more perplexing than the often-circulated Othering discourse by the West of the imagined East is the inclusion of a video footage accompanying the story. The video material was recorded by the killers and bystanders themselves using their cell phones, and it was posted on social media to document what a shopkeeper near the shrine described as a game: "They were like kids playing with the sack of flour on the floor."

Remediated video footage intersects with the women's rights discourse of the *New York Times*, and complicates the Othering discourse; video recording, in this case, provides access to the uncanny (Kristeva 1991) of what should have remained hidden but does not and is constructed as profoundly disturbing. The fear of the uncanny attaches it to the outside of "us," and yet it comes out in some circumstances and becomes part of our consciousness.

The imperialistically charged belief in the transformative power of Western education of the Other is resisted by the "playing" of Farkhunda Malikzada's body in the video of the cell phone clips whereby one man tenderly cradles the cheeks of an official, while pleading with him to give Farkhunda Malikzada to them. To the extent that her body is the official's to give to the pleading man as if it were a present marks an irreversible turn in the course of events. The officers help her once, then let her fall into the crowd where, to her horror, she loses her hijab. The violence is now not only gendered but sexualized as well. "It is very difficult to determine responsibility if you don't know what killed her," a court employee said (as cited in Rubin 2015). As an Afghan voice, the article begins to construct an argument "making sense" from the Afghan perspective: "*Who* is the guy who hit the first blow? *Who* is the one whose blow killed her? . . . *If it's violence*, who is responsible for this violence?" (Rubin 2015, emphasis added). The interpretation of whether the killing of Farkhunda Malikzada should even be considered a form of violence or not reveals the limits of the Western discourse of reason that, in this case, is supposed to function as the ultimate ivory tower against the uncanny (Kristeva 1991).

Death and the feminine are often archetypal topics for our experiences of the uncanny (Kristeva 1991) and connected with anxiety. Anxiety has an object. In this case, Western interpretation of violent "playing" the body reveals anxiety about the global Other, the Middle East. Uncanny, rather, constructed by the remediated Afghan video footage, can be associated with challenging the Western self as the omnipotent educator of others while becoming Othered itself.

If some other cases (Parikka 2015b) where Afghan maleness is rendered problematic, and potentially a violent global force, Western maleness is typically envisioned as heroic, which enables the Western conception of Otherness whereby the female body occupies a central place and function to "fix" meanings of various global forces and agendas. And yet in this case, such resolution is not available. Western constructions of itself and its Other are met with the constructions of collective sociality of men's play through Farkhunda Malikzada's body that functions beyond Western definition power. If, as Appadurai (2006) maintains, our anxieties about globalization have increased, as well as our fears of marginality that globalization evokes, cases such as these concretize fears through the uncanny. The female body may function to discursively dissolve, enforce, or alleviate conflicts embedded in the processes and discourses of globalization but also allow a culture to collapse.

The preoccupation with sexy violence in the global media does not necessarily offer a solution to global concerns but, rather, plays out the fears, aims, and anxieties about globalization through subjecting the female body to violence and aggression. Articulation of the agency of the Other through the mediation of the uncanny, however, suggests refusal to support Western understanding of itself, played through the imagery of the female body taking up its place in the imaginaries of globalization. Agamben (as cited in Butchart 2010) describes a relation of exception in terms of inclusion of something through its exclusion. Remediated video footage, in this case, thoroughly disturbs such inclusionary practices by the construction of the uncanny that serves to confuse the interior and exterior boundaries of a Western self. Globally mediated concerns, or unconcerns, contribute to fragmentation of any assumed unity of the interiority of a self. Whether there was a woman who was violated in the killing is subjected to fragmented meanings that call for a Western self to doubt itself.

CONCLUSION

In this context, I have attempted to explore how the contemporary media imagery of the female body functions in globalization imaginaries and, in particular, how we, through the female body, aim at addressing some of the most compelling issues of our time, including gender and minority–majority relationships. In such projects, the female body is subjected to being "played" in the global media, as if embodying aims, fears, and anxieties about globalization.

A Western self as inherently *White* became thoroughly frustrated by Rihanna's music. In her video, relationships of exchange were never purely economic, but complicated by racialization and gender, which speaks to the deep cultural repository of meanings regarding the logic of economic exchange of commodities, and the embedded elements of sacrifice, often overlooked by globalization ideologies. The frustration with the logic of the prevailing (global) economic order manifested itself through violence on the body of the White female. The question whether visually graphic violence was conceived as *violence* (similarly to Farkhunda Malikzada's case) in the video makes the body of the White female take on political meanings in racial terms. The abuse and torture of her body revealed the fundamental fragility of the White female body: When located outside of the economic order within which it functions and finds its value, in relation to a White male in this case, it becomes invisible and loses its value, much like the non-White woman in her own exclusion. This could perhaps mark the beginning of alliances across audiences, as Lena (2008) suggests, and a source for the political. A central question is whether the economic inequalities become reduced a concern that requires a non-White woman to sacrifice the White female body or whether the relationships of exchange can be imagined anew in terms of gender as well. In the absence of this, the White female body remains as a conduit for frustrations about the global economic order while keeping it fundamentally intact.

The meaning of violence was again contested in a Canadian ad campaign; to the extent that the female body functioned in the globalization imaginaries with its economic imperatives, the "woman" could be constructed as having agency on the global economic markets through her success at overlooking the cost of violence on her body, be it a result of domestic violence or some other kind of mutilation. This speaks to the excesses and self-punitive aspects of post-feminist cultures that come into contact with the "economic" of globalization.

Although global knowledge-based societies tend to depoliticize economic and other inequalities, and that Mattelart (2010), for example, is critical of, cases examined in this context also suggest that the "female body" functions in globalization imaginaries often in unexpected ways and can even contribute to returning the political into debates about globalization. For example, in Farkhunda Malikzada's case, contestation of the definition of a subject of violence was largely introduced by cell phone recordings of the mob that killed or watched her killing. Watching Farkhunda Malikzada being killed was framed by the women's rights discourse of the *New York Times* with its positions of subjectivity, agency, and responsibility, and yet the disarticulation of the Western discourse by the Afghan interpretations constructed the ultimate uncanny. The uncanny is no longer secluded from challenging the Western definition power of a "woman" but, rather, subjecting a Western self to fragmentation by destabilizing the interior and exterior boundaries set forth by media, region, culture, or religion. Is the "female body" in the process of acquiring a newly defined, politicized role in our attempts to express fears and anxieties not only of the global but also of its reshaping of a Western self in relation to its traditional Others?

Even if a "woman" or a "female body" functions politically in globalization imaginaries, "she" is not necessarily self-defined but subjected to outside forces of definition that help define or challenge the relationships and insecurities between and within the West and its Other, now speaking, and the Western (economic) self itself as gendered. In these case studies, this is exercised through primarily seeing "her" as bearer of violent acts on her body, the playing of which disguises not only our fears of the global but also ourselves in the global.

REFERENCES

Albarran, A. B. 2010. *The Media Economy.* London: Routledge.

Appadurai, A. 2006. *Fear of Small Numbers: An Essay on Geography of Anger.* Durham, NC: Duke University Press.

Beneria, L., G. Berik, and M. Floro. 2015. *Gender, Development, and Globalization: Economics as If All People Mattered.* New York: Routledge.

Bordo, S. 2003. *Unbearable Weight: Feminism, Western Culture, and the Body.* Berkeley: University of California Press.

Boyd-Barrett, O., ed. 2006. *Communications Media, Globalization, and Empire.* London: Libbey.

Butchart, G. 2010. "The Exceptional Community: On Strangers, Foreigners, and Communication." *Communication, Culture & Critique* 3 (1): 21–25.

Culcasi, K. 2011. "Mapping the Middle East from Within: (Counter)Cartographies of an Imperialist Construction." *Antipode* 44 (4): 1099–1118.

Desai, M. 2009. *Gender and the Politics of Possibilities: Rethinking Globalization.* Lanham, MD: Rowman & Littlefield.

Dobson, A. S., and A. Harris. 2015. "Post-Girlpower: Globalized Mediated Femininities." *Continuum: Journal of Media & Cultural Studies* 29 (2): 143–144.

Draper, L. 2014. "Exclusive: London Cabbies Say Uber is Dangerous Because of 'Immigrant Drivers.'" *Newsweek.*

Dyer, R. 1997. *White*. New York: Routledge.

Fairclough, N. 2006. *Language and Globalization*. London: Routledge.

Falah, G.-W. 2005. "The Visual Representation of Muslim/Arab Women in Daily Newspapers in the United States." In *Geographies of Muslim Women: Gender, Religion, Space*, edited by G.-W. Falah and C. Nagel, 300–320. New York: Guilford.

Flew, T. 2007. *Understanding Global Media*. New York: Palgrave Macmillan.

Gill, R. 2007a. *Gender and Media*. Cambridge, UK: Polity.

Gill, R. 2007b. "Postfeminist Media Culture: Elements of Sensibility." *European Journal of Cultural Studies* 10 (2): 147–166.

Gill, R., and S. Orgad. 2015. "The Confidence Cult(ure)." *Australian Feminist Studies* 30 (86): 324–344.

Giroux, H. A. 2011. "The Crisis of Public Values in the Age of the New Media." *Critical Studies in Media Communication* 28 (1): 8–29.

Goldberg, D. 2005. "Racial Americanization." In *Racialization: Studies in Theory and Practice*, edited by K. Murji and J. Solomos, 87–103. Oxford, UK: Oxford University Press.

Grossberg, L. 2011. "Is There a Fan in the House: The Affective Sensibility of Fandom." In *The Media Studies Reader*, edited by L. Oullette, 458–465. New York: Routledge.

Habermas, J. 1999. *The Structural Transformation of the Public Sphere: An Inquiry into a Category of Bourgeois Society*. Cambridge, MA: MIT Press.

Hafez, K. 2007. *The Myth of Media Globalization*. Boston: Polity.

Halim, S., and M. Meyers. 2010. "News Coverage of Violence Against Muslim Women: A View from the Arabian Gulf. Communication." *Culture & Critique* 3 (1): 85–104.

Halverson, J., S. W. Ruston, and A. Trethewey. 2013. "Mediated Martyrs of the Arab Spring: New Media, Civil Religion, and Narrative in Tunisia and Egypt." *Journal of Communication* 63 (2): 312–332.

Hedge, R. S., ed. 2011. *Circuits of Visibility: Gender and Transnational Media Cultures*. New York: New York University Press.

Heinämaa, S. 1997. "What Is a Woman? Butler and Beauvoir on the Foundations of Sexual Difference." *Hypatia: Journal of Feminist Philosophy* 12 (1): 20–39.

Irigaray, L. 1985. *This Sex Which Is Not One*. Ithaca, NY: Cornell University Press.

Irigaray, L. 1993. *Sexes and Genealogies*. New York: Columbia University Press.

Kraidy, M. M. 2013. "The Body as Medium in the Digital Age: Challenges and Opportunities." *Communication and Critical/Cultural Studies* 10 (2–3): 285–290.

Kristeva, J. 1989. *Black Sun: Depression and Melancholia*. New York: Columbia University Press.

Kristeva, J. 1991. *Strangers to Ourselves*. New York: Columbia University Press.

Lacan, J. 1968. *The Language of the Self*, translated with notes and commentary by A. Wilden. Baltimore, MD: Johns Hopkins University Press.

Lena, J. C. 2008. "Voyeurism and Resistance in Rap Music Videos." *Communication and Critical/Cultural Studies* 5 (3): 264–279.

Mattelart, A. 2010. "An Archaeology of the Global Era: Constructing a Belief." In *International Communication: A Reader*, edited by D. K. Thussu, 313–328. New York: Routledge.

McMillin, D. C. 2007. *International Media Studies*. Hoboken, NJ: Blackwell.

McNair, B. 2006. *Cultural Chaos: Journalism, News, and Power in a Globalized World*. New York: Routledge.

McRobbie, A. 2009. *The Aftermath of Feminism: Gender, Culture, and Social Change*. London: Sage.

Miller, T., and M. Kraidy. 2016. *Global Media Studies*. Cambridge, UK: Polity.

Momsen, J. 2010. *Gender and Development*. New York: Routledge.

Morley, D. 2006. *Media, Modernity, and Technology: The Geography of the New.* New York: Routledge.

Murji, K., and J. Solomos, eds. 2005. *Racialization: Studies in Theory and Practice.* Oxford, UK: Oxford University Press.

Murphy, P. D., and M. M. Kraidy, eds. 2003. *Global Media Studies: An Ethnographic Perspective.* New York: Routledge.

Parikka, T. 2015a. "Democracies at Odds: Ostracized Public Values and Viable Social Concerns." *Medijiske Studie Media Studies* 6 (12): 41–44.

Parikka, T. 2015b. *Globalization, Gender, and Media: Formations of the Sexual and Violence in Understanding Globalization.* London: Lexington Books.

Pippert, W. 2003. "Media Coverage of Arabs and Arab Americans." In *Journalism Across Cultures*, edited by F. Cropp, C. Frisby, and H. Mills, 65–78. Hoboken, NJ: Blackwell.

Ponzanesi, S., ed. 2014. *Gender, Globalization, and Violence: Postcolonial Conflict Zones.* New York: Routledge.

Rantanen, T. 2005. *The Media and Globalization.* London: Sage.

Rubin, A. J. 2015. "Flawed Justice After a Mob Killed an Afghan Woman." *New York Times*, December 26.

Ruggil, J. E., K. S. McAllister, and D. Menchaca. 2004. "The Gamework." *Communication and Critical/Cultural Studies* 1 (4): 297–312.

Said, E. W. 1997. *Covering Islam: How the Media and the Experts Determine How We See the Rest of the World.* New York: Pantheon.

Notes

1. "Bitch Better Have My Money" (https://en.wikipedia.org/wiki/Bitch_Better_Have_My_Money).
2. *Racialization* can be understood as "race-inflected social situations" (Goldberg 2005) or, in this context, discursive situations whereby group boundaries become defined in terms of race (Murji and Solomos 2005).

Further Reading

Appadurai, A. 2013. *The Future as Cultural Fact: Essays on the Global Condition.* London: Verso.

Boyle, K. 2015. *Media and Violence: Gendering the Debates.* London: Sage.

Butsch, R., ed. 2009. *Media and Public Spheres.* New York: Palgrave Macmillan.

Chopra, R., and R. Gajjala. 2011. *Global Media, Culture, and Identity.* New York: Routledge.

Darling-Wolf, F. 2015. *Imaging the Global: Transnational Media and Popular Culture Beyond East and West.* Ann Arbor: University of Michigan Press.

Dines, G., and J. M. Humez, eds. 2014. *Gender, Race, and Class in Media: A Critical Reader.* 5th ed. Thousand Oaks, CA: Sage.

Fraser, N. 2013. *Fortunes of Feminism: From State-Managed Capitalism to Neoliberal Crisis.* London: Verso.

Fraser, N.2014. *Transnationalization of the Public Sphere*, edited by K. Nash. Cambridge, UK: Polity.

Gill, R., and C. Scharff, eds. 2011. *New Femininities: Postfeminism, Neoliberalism, and Subjectivity.* New York: Palgrave Macmillan.

Kearney, M. C., ed. 2012. *The Gender and Media Reader*. New York: Routledge.

Kraidy, M. M. 2005. *Hybridity: The Cultural Logic of Globalization*. Philadelphia, PA: Temple University Press.

Kraidy, M. M., ed. 2013. *Communication and Power in the Global Era: Orders and Borders*. New York: Routledge.

Krijnen, T., and S. van Bauwel. 2015. *Gender and Media: Representing, Producing, Consuming*. New York: Routledge.

Lievrouw, L. A., and S. Livingstone. 2006. *Handbook of New Media*. Thousand Oaks, CA: Sage.

Machin, D., and T. van Leeuwen. 2007. *Global Media Discourse: A Critical Introduction*. London: Routledge.

McMillin, D. C. 2007. *International Media Studies*. Malden, MA: Blackwell.

Mirrlees, T. 2013. *Global Entertainment Media: Between Cultural Imperialism and Cultural Globalization*. New York: Routledge.

Ross, K. 2014. *The Handbook of Gender, Sex and Media*. Malden, MA: Wiley.

Sarikakis, K., and L. Regan Shade, eds. 2008. *Feminist Interventions in International Communication: Minding the Gap*. Lanham, MD: Rowman & Littlefield.

Shohat, E., and R. Stam. 2014. *Unthinking Eurocentrism: Multiculturalism and the Media*. 2nd ed. New York: Routledge.

Smith, C., F. Attwood, and B. McNair. 2017. *The Routledge Companion to Media, Sex and Sexuality*. New York: Routledge.

Tasker, Y., and D. Negre, eds. 2007. *Interrogating Postfeminism: Gender and the Politics of Popular Culture*. Durham, NC: Duke University Press.

Tomlinson, J. 1999. *Globalization and Culture*. Cambridge, UK: Polity.

CHAPTER 33

DIGITAL CONNECTIVITY

TANIA LEWIS

THE title of this chapter sums up what has been a remarkable shift in the nature of global information and communication systems as well as the everyday experiences of communicative culture and technology in the past few decades. Central to this is a transition from a relatively one-way, broadcast or transmission culture to a communicative ecology of networked devices, spaces, flows, and temporalities. Although *information* and *communication* are still terms that have some descriptive power in capturing how we use today's digital media and communication technologies, *connectivity* has in many ways become the key metaphor for how we adopt, adapt, and experience the digital in our daily lives. Indeed, one could argue that connectivity has become a kind of new social ontology that shapes all aspects of our daily lives.

The broadly encompassing nature of the phrase "digital connectivity" captures the fact that for many of us, digital technologies have become so enmeshed in our everyday lives as to become relatively invisible, a taken-for-granted element of daily social practices that usually only comes to our conscious attention when we experience moments of *dis*connection or indeed when we take time to reminisce about our practices in the past. Ironically, the very ubiquity of today's communicative technology—the embeddedness of the digital in our routines and habits and the way in which the technologization of every aspect of daily life has become both normative and naturalized in many areas of the world—paradoxically makes it increasingly difficult to research and write about these same technologies. In a world where social, political, economic, media, technological, and communicative systems have become supremely converged, it becomes increasingly difficult to extract oneself from the socio-technological networks one wants to interrogate.

As media anthropologist John Postill (2012) has noted, a related challenge is how to critically engage with the social and historical changes associated with the digital realm while we are in the very midst of these transformations. We often reflect on this ourselves in daily life when we note the speed of technological change and the difficulty of finding a contemplative space or time for reflecting on such change. This is often experienced as a sense of *over*connectedness—as an inability to disconnect or distance oneself from being continually *on* (to use an electronic analogy), linked up and linked in (Chayko 2017; Mackenzie 2007; Walsh, White, and Young 2008).

Another challenge in critically thinking and writing about the topic of digital connectivity in a global studies context is the sheer enormity of the task. The growing globalization of digital technologies and practices has seen the digital realm entering into complex articulations with some of the key issues shaping our world today, including public health; social justice; human rights; gender, race, and age inequality; poverty; environmental sustainability; migration; and international relations. For instance, in relation to public health and environmental sustainability, one of the hidden impacts of the growing place of digital devices in people's lives is the rise of "e-waste." Media scholars Maxwell and Miller (2008) list the major environmental and health problems associated with a growing reliance on digital technologies in everyday life, from the toxic pollution produced from today's electronic media (e.g., the cadmium contained in mobile phones) and the growing impact of e-waste, much of which is exported to the Global South, to the large amount of energy required both to produce digital technologies and associated infrastructure and to maintain and use said technologies. The example of global e-waste points to the way in which digital connectivity is in many ways an all-encompassing topic (an *ur* theme). Certainly, it is central to the majority of topics under discussion in this book, particularly financialization, labor, media industries, migration, religious globalisms, civil society, citizenship, and justice movements.

Finally, the term digital connectivity also needs to be qualified in terms of another key global studies concern, namely inequality. Many people in the world, even in so-called developed nations, are still not connected, have poor quality or limited access, and/or do not have the level of digital literacy or participation required to fully engage with the online community (International Telecommunication Union (ITU) 2017; Ofcom 2017; Poushter 2017; Thomas et al. 2016). For instance, as recent figures released by the ITU indicate, although young people throughout the world lead the way in internet adoption—in developed countries, 94% of young people aged fifteen to twenty-four years use the internet—this drops to 67% in developing countries and only 30% in least developed countries such as in areas of Africa. In addition, internet use continues to be marked by a global gender divide, with the proportion of women using the internet worldwide being 12% lower than that of men (ITU 2017).

So how then to tackle a topic that is globally differentiated, constantly evolving, and imbricated in diverse ways in many of our everyday practices? What I aim to do in this chapter is focus on a topic that one might not immediately associate with the realm of digital connectivity—food and digitization. When *Time* magazine named the top ten things that "broke the internet" in 2014 (Grossman 2014), in between a globally distributed image of Kim Kardashian's naked derriere on the cover of *Paper* magazine and web traffic about the new iPhone 6 release was a most unlikely candidate for viral popularity, was a kickstarter for potato salad. As the story goes, when all-around ordinary guy Zack "Danger" Brown got a craving for potato salad, he decided to raise the $10 needed to purchase the ingredients online but ended up making $55,000 and rather more potato salad than expected. In fact, he produced the largest vat of potato salad ever, and he used the cash raised to support local non-profit organizations that fight hunger.

This seemingly banal example speaks to the relevance of food, in its everyday ordinariness, as a marker of the growing digitization of daily life. During the past decade, the world of food, from home cookery to restaurant food "hubs" and food politics, has been quietly colonized by the digital. Meanwhile, the digital realm has been invaded by all things food related, from endless food snapshots on Facebook and Instagram to the rise of YouTube food channels. Paradoxically, despite the large amount of scholarship that has emerged in recent years on the impact of the digital on our everyday lives and social relations, as Deborah Lupton (2017) notes, there has been very little critical academic engagement with the topic of digital connectivity and food.

I suggest, then, that food is a particularly generative space through which to understand the complex evolution and impact of the digital realm and digital connectivity today. On the one hand, food purchasing, cooking, and eating, like digital media, are profoundly ordinary and in many ways invisible—tied to the repetitive habits, rituals, and rhythms of daily life. On the other hand, both the realm of food and the space of digital connectivity have become highly politicized and contested spaces. If, as US farmer–activist Wendell Berry (2009) has famously said, "eating is an agricultural act," then the seemingly banal habit of checking one's "smart" phone similarly triggers a complex network of political, economic, environmental, and governmental associations.

In this chapter, I provide a "cook's tour," so to speak, of the realm of digital food—from the banal and the everyday to the political potentials and limitations of culinary and agricultural connectivity—as a way of *grounding* and *materializing* our everyday engagements with the digital. The first section discusses the role of digital connectivity in relation to lifestyle and consumption. Discussing the rise of food photography on social media, I emphasize both its role as a marker of lifestyle and consumer identities as well as the way shared food snapshots enact and embody intimate and distant relationships and forms of sociality. In the next section on cultural economies of participation, I discuss the growing role of ordinary people as key participants in online food culture in terms of the rise of "prosumerism" via video sharing platforms such as YouTube. I then map the shift from web 2.0's dreams of connection, creativity, and sharing to the growing monetization of digital food communities. In the third section of the chapter, I turn to questions of food politics and the digital, as well as the antinomies of connectivity. Here, I discuss the constraints and affordances of digital connectivity in relation to food politics and food activism. The final section discusses the growing role of major food players in social media and the limits of data sharing and so-called informational transparency in an era of data monitoring and "big data."

FOOD PHOTOS: FROM CONSPICUOUS PROSUMPTION TO DIGITAL SOCIALITY

When we think of the digital realm and food, one of the key themes that comes to mind is the enormous number of images of food with which we engage every day, whether via smartphone apps or social media platforms, most of which are produced and shared by ordinary people. Digital photography and easily accessible platforms for sharing have resulted in an explosion in the social use of amateur photography, with the internet and particularly social media saturated with selfies and endless images of people's pets (Murray 2008). Similarly, in the past few years, a huge amount of food imagery has been uploaded on Facebook, with snapshots of restaurant meals increasingly competing with images of people's own culinary creations.

With the growing use of mobile photo-sharing services such as Instagram, the traffic of everyday amateur food photography has both intensified and also become more aestheticized and curated. If our followers on Instagram are more often than not people to whom we are "linked" via taste groups or communities of practice, one way in which we might understand the circulation of imagery, and especially food imagery, might be as a performance of lifestyle, identity, and good taste. Personally crafted and curated food images thus represent a kind of conspicuous culinary consumption or what we might term conspicuous "prosumption," as amateur digital media production is often badged.

Such imagery draws and extends upon a wider, lifestyle media ecology of cookery TV shows such as *MasterChef* and those of celebrity chefs. Associated with the global spread of middle-class forms of lifestyle culture and associated modes of consumerism, "foodie"-oriented social media can be seen as the ultimate customized and personalized extension of and engagement with lifestyle media and culture (de Solier 2005, 2013). The rise of aestheticized images of people's home cookery flowing through social media provides an intimate connection between people's domestic practices and wider lifestyle trends. At the same time, technologies of geolocation provide a powerful link to people's mobile engagements with food outside of the home—whether food shopping or dining out (as those who have visited a restaurant website with their smartphone only to be alerted by TripAdvisor as to what they should be ordering from the menu will attest).

Although crafted food photos on Instagram and Flickr can be read as performances of personal culinary capital, others see the imagery on social media as a marker not so much of narcissistic selfie-ism and consumer individualism but instead as an extension of practices of sociality. Anthropologist Daniel Miller, who has recently headed up a large global team of researchers investigating "why we post" (UCL 2016), argues that much of what we post image-wise is not so much about the self as it is about our relationship with others (e.g., see Miller 2011). If we frame digital image sharing as essentially social, the images of baked birthday cakes, lovingly prepared evening meals, and brunches at a local café with friends that form our daily news updates in social media feeds can be read as performing relations of care and love toward others as much as they reflect self-identity. For Miller's team of global anthropologists, rather than purely enacting a form of social distinction, the images that others post to your page and/or share with you by and large construct a shared sociality.

Cultural Economies of Sharing, Participation, and Ordinary Expertise

What does "the social" in social media mean here? How does, for instance, the use of social media platforms and apps to capture and share images of home cooking and dining out speak to broader digital disruptions in everyday interpersonal and social relations? José van Dijck (2013), in *The Culture of Connectivity*, argues that "within less than a decade, a new infrastructure for online sociality and creativity has emerged, penetrating every fiber of culture today" (p. 4). A key way in which this has been understood in much media and cultural studies work has been in terms of the rise of cultures of sharing and participation, and in this section I briefly discuss the digital foodscape through the lens of the sharing or collaborative cultural economy (Belk 2014; Schor 2014).

In their book *YouTube: Online Video, and Participatory Culture*, Jean Burgess and Josh Green (2009) suggest that digital media engagement is no longer about consumers and producers, professionals and amateurs, non-commercial versus commercial players but instead needs to be understood in terms of "a continuum of cultural participation" (p. 57). Enabled by the affordances of web 2.0 and by video conversion and sharing technology, websites such as YouTube have heralded a dramatic shift from the digital consumer as passive downloader to an upload and exchange culture of creativity and prosumerism.

In my own work during the past decade on the evolution of lifestyle and lifestyle media, I have been similarly interested in the rise of a participatory culture in digital space, particularly in relation to sharing advice about managing everyday life or what I term "ordinary expertise" via online platforms (Lewis 2008, 2010, 2012; Lewis, Martin, and Sun 2016). In the digital foodscape, in particular, we have seen the growing role of so-called ordinary people providing advice and demonstrating expertise in food and cooking, accompanied by an increasingly blurred line between professional and celebrity chefs and amateur cooks. These displays of ordinary expertise around food are perhaps most evident on YouTube, where food videos and food channels constitute a substantial proportion of the content.

A recent survey of internet users in the United Kingdom found that 31% had used YouTube when searching for information online, with internet users aged sixteen to twenty-four years even more likely to have used YouTube (39%) or social media (39%) to access information (Ofcom 2017). According to Google, which owns YouTube, cooking and food comprise the fastest growing genre on the video-sharing service. In ethnographic research I have been conducting with colleagues during the past three years on transformations in household use of digital media, we have similarly noted the growing presence of laptops and other devices in the kitchen, with householders accessing recipes online and watching YouTube clips to learn how to make a dish or master a particular cooking technique.

Although YouTube has enabled anyone to participate in the distribution and sharing of ordinary, amateur expertise, the practices of exchange associated with social media and collaborative platforms more broadly have of course become increasingly monetized, with YouTube known these days as much for personal branding, entrepreneurialism, and micro-celebrity (Marwick 2016) as a space for advice. A highly visible example of this shift is *Sorted Food*, a cookery channel that began when a group of dietarily challenged men started making food videos for their circle of friends and that developed into what the SORTEDfood website (2016) describes as a

> global movement of over a million people who share a passion for food, friends and laughter. From absolute cooking beginners to kitchen pros, SORTEDfood is the place to learn how to cook your way, share inspiration around recipes and have a laugh with friends all around the world.

YouTube's top global performer in its cooking channel offerings, *Sorted Food* is supported primarily through advertising revenue and sponsorship. Likewise, the rise of live video platforms such as Nom, a start-up created by one of the co-founders of YouTube, reflects the growing commercialization of sharing platforms as well as an increasingly blurred line between amateurs and professionals, foodies and fans. As it has been described, Nom.com is a "live, interactive video *community* and app for foodies . . . presents a mix of professional cooks alongside an open-ended platform that will let anyone direct, produce and host 'your own food show' " (Lunden 2016, emphasis added).

The ability for anyone to make and upload live video feeds of their domestic cookery takes YouTube's capacities to a new level, although Nom as it currently stands is very much a glossy, overtly commercialized concern without the somewhat dirty do-it-yourself aesthetic, feel, and presumably appeal of YouTube. Nevertheless, like *Sorted Food* and YouTube more broadly, these spaces draw on the rhetoric and practices of sharing, community, friendship, and participation but in ways that are increasingly tied to a normative, neoliberal logic of entrepreneurialism. Whereas in the early days of social media, the spread of digital connectivity seemed to represent an opening up and democratization of media and communication systems, today such connectivity increasingly comes with an often invisible price tag. As Nick Couldry (2015b) argues in his call to understand and interrogate social media platforms *as institutions*, the utopianism of connected sociality needs to be recognized as "a playground for deep economic battles about new forms of value, value generated from data, the data that we generate as we act online" (p. 641). Our everyday digital engagements then unwittingly become forms of free labor for corporations and marketers, a point I discuss further later in this chapter.

Apptivism and Connected Consumption

Although digital social relations are clearly intrinsically shaped and constrained by what we might term "compromised connectivities," Couldry's (2015b) metaphor of the battleground speaks to the ways in which digital socialities are underpinned by complex interplays of contestation and hegemony. For example, although social media may be increasingly commercialized, the participatory and connective affordances of digital culture have also enabled various forms of popular political engagement, from WikiLeaks to the Black Lives Matter movement. Likewise, in the arena of food politics, the digital turn has seen the rise of various forms of what Schneider et al. (2018) call "digital food activism," from apps oriented toward ethical consumption to digital food hubs that aim to undermine global agribusiness.

In this section, I unpack what the affordances of digital connectivity might suggest for food activism and particularly alternative food movements. In what ways might digital tools and platforms be politically enabling for linking up food activists? How might we understand forms of digital political engagement in the face of the fundamental monetization of the "social" in social media? As Deborah Lupton (2015) suggests in her book, *Digital Sociology*, "digital technologies have created new political relationships and power relations" (p. 189), and this is no more evident than in the increasing power struggles over information, data, visibility, and transparency that mark the contemporary digital foodscape and the rise of digital forms of "food citizenship" (Booth and Coveney 2015; Gómez-Benito and Lozano 2014; Wilkins 2005).

A key area here is the growing use of app-driven engagement or what has been termed "apptivism." In the food space, the rise of apptivism is linked to broader consumer movements concerned with the politics and ethics of commodity consumption and the rise of global agribusiness—movements that have a long history in terms of consumer advocacy and anti-globalism/anti-consumerism (Binkley and Littler 2011; Goodman, DuPluis, and Goodman 2012). In the context of the contemporary foodscape, there has been a particular and growing concern with the disconnection between consumers and the origins of and production processes behind their food—from questions about health and food safety to concerns about animal welfare and the exploitation of Third World producers.

A large number of food apps have emerged that attempt to create conditions of what we might term "connected consumption" but via virtual means, whether through enabling individual consumers to access information about the origins of a food product's ingredients via a barcode scanning app or through linking consumers to a broader community of ethical citizens. A free app called OLIO is a good example of the latter. OLIO aims to connect neighbors with each other and/or with local businesses to exchange any edible surplus food they might have, with app users being able to post and share images of their unused food with the OLIO community and then search for items in the near vicinity. On its website, OLIO also emphasizes the potential benefits of the app for business, noting that the act of advertising and sharing leftover food can bring in new customers, reduce food waste (and disposal costs), and also help business "connect with your community." Meanwhile, the website's pitch to consumers sums up both the potential and the limitations of apptivism or what has been termed more derogatively "clicktivism": "Here at OLIO we believe that small actions can lead to big change. Collectively, one rescued carrot or cupcake at a time, we can build a more sustainable food future" (OLIO, 2016). As per apptivism more broadly, OLIO emphasizes a kind of civic-minded digital consumerism in which the act of sharing leftover food is framed as a potentially collective and transformative act ("a food sharing revolution"). If value-driven acts of consumption have become a new stage for enactments of civil society and political agency, then what US sociologist Juliet Schor (1999) has termed "the new politics of consumption" has found its ultimate match in the just-in-time, connected affordances of personalized digital apps. At the same time, there are obvious limits to this kind of privatized, consumer-driven approach to "revolutionizing" food practices. Indeed, one could argue that such forms of apptivism in the case of food may deflect from rather than contribute to changing the reality of global agribusiness by offering a quick ethical fix or salve for guilty First World consumers.

Although the political impact of apptivism might be questionable, what potentially collective and structural challenges might the digital turn and web 2.0 in particular offer? One key argument made by social movement theorists is that despite the attempt by corporate players to appropriate web 2.0 for commercial ends, the digital realm can also be understood as a space of political action inhabited by a new generation of citizens who have been variously described as "cyberprotesters" and "e-activists" (Fuchs 2006; Meisner 2000; Pickerill 2003; Van de Donk et al. 2004). In the highly politicized and embattled area of food politics, the tools of the digital realm have enabled a range of social and political actors to come to the fore, from farmers and chefs to restaurateurs and consumers. These various players have been able to use digital platforms and social media to connect, organize, and increase the visibility of a range of food issues, from sustainability and food safety to animal rights. Online interactive food documentaries such as *A Five-Step Plan to Feed the World* (http://www.nationalgeographic.com/foodfeatures/feeding-9-billion), Peter Gilmore's app for iPad (http://www.pollen.com.au/pages/peter-gilmore.html), and "ethical shopping" websites such as *Follow the Things* (http://www.followthethings.com/grocery.shtml) make visible and materialize the politics of production behind the "commodity chains" or "networks" that bring us Israeli avocados grown on illegally seized Palestinian land or bananas grown by Nicaraguan banana workers who have sued Dole, one of the largest food corporations in the world, for exposing them to a banned pesticide linked to severe health problems.

FROM SOCIAL MEDIA ACTIVISM TO ALTERNATIVE FOOD NETWORKS

Beyond rendering otherwise hidden commodity networks visible and transparent and enabling consumers to start to reconnect their consumption to once distant producers and processes, the digital realm also offers powerful opportunities for more collectivized forms of virtual–civic engagement that aim to challenge political and business interests. As political communications theorist Zizi A. Papacharissi (2010) argues,

> These commercially public spaces may not render a public sphere, but they provide hybrid economies of space where individuals can engage in interaction that is civic, among other things. These spaces are essential in maintaining a politically active consciousness that may, when necessary, articulate a sizeable oppositional voice in response to concentrated ownership regulation. (p. 129)

Ginevra Adamoli's (2012) research on the role and impact of social media on the food movement in the United States is a generative case in point. Focusing in particular on the 2011 "Right to Know Rally," she demonstrates the ways in which a number of major offline protests in which activists demanded that the US government introduce genetically modified organism (GMO) food labeling throughout the country were the result of a long-running online grass-roots campaign.

Initially launched by the Organic Consumers Association, an online grass-roots, nonprofit organization concerned with "health, justice, and sustainability," a year prior to the street protests, the campaign was picked up by a range of social actors. These figures used a variety of online tools to communicate, organize, and plan the protests but also to continue anti-GMO activism via social media after the offline protests were complete. Adamoli's (2012) research indicates that although social media users were aware of the limitations of Facebook in terms of privacy and data monitoring, the platform had huge benefits in terms of enabling a wide range of diverse actors and networks to organize collectively online, resulting in significant impacts offline, including policy change.

Another key area in which digital connectivity has enabled significant alternative forms of political organization and community building is in the environmental space. For instance, although still a nascent area of research, critical scholarship has begun to emerge on the role of social media in shaping and enabling various alternatives to globalized food (Hearn et al. 2014). In an article on "the online spaces of alternative food networks in England," Elizabeth Bos and Luke Owen (2016) explore the way in which online space offers opportunities for reconnection with the "complex systems of food provisioning" that have worked "to distance and disconnect consumers from the people and places involved in contemporary food production" (p. 1). Studying eight alternative food networks and twenty-one online spaces, they examine the ways that producers and citizens alike are increasingly integrating the digital into their practices in order to enable reconnections with food and with local and rural production and to build alternatives to global agribusiness. As their research on online food networks suggests, digital networks are as much about intensifications of the local and connections to place as they are about global connectivity.

An example of this is the Open Food Network, which is based on open source technology developed by US food hubs Local Dirt and the Oklahoma Food Cooperative (Local Dirt 2016; Oklahoma Food Cooperative 2016; Open Food Network 2015), although Local Dirt also has a Facebook presence. Aimed at developing alternative foodscapes through linking multiple players from consumers, food hubs, and farmers to various local food enterprises, the network has been taken up by food communities throughout the world. Traditionally, the development of connected localized and regional food systems has been hampered by problems of scale and networking, particularly how to collectivize efforts and scale-up in a cheap and efficient manner while still adhering to key social and environmental drivers. Here, the connective affordances of web platforms have enabled distributed local systems to expand and collectivize. Crucially, the networked spaces built here are inhabited by a range of civic and social actors from community groups to farmers shifting digital food activism away from atomized individual or household consumption practices to the collective construction of alternative foodways.

COMPLICATING CONNECTIVITY: SOCIAL MEDIA WARS AND DATA DIVIDES

Whereas the Open Food Network is based on open source software enabling it to (in part) bypass proprietary software and platforms, our predominant engagement with the digital realm today is largely through what Papacharissi (2009) characterizes as "commercially public spaces" (p. 242). These are spaces not only owned by commercial interests but also increasingly dominated by corporate revenue flows and commercial content. In the domain of food, the top global agricultural and fast-food corporations are all major users of social media (Stevens et al. 2016), with many companies dedicating major staff and resources to managing their social media presence and strategies, while Twitter, Facebook, and, increasingly, Instagram draw a significant proportion of their revenue from online advertising.

Controversial agricultural players such as Monsanto, described by Bennett (2014) as America's "third-most-hated company," have invested heavily in a social media presence. Whereas Monsanto's internet outreach director once described the internet as "a weapon," Monsanto's more recent social media-based tactics have been rather softer, with the company attempting to reframe public debate around biotech along sustainability lines. Rebranding itself via Twitter using discourses of "sustainable development" and "biological conservation," Monsanto has sought to counter the attacks of anti-GMO activists through a "be part of the conversation" campaign in which members of the public are invited to ask questions about the company and its practices. On Monsanto's "The conversation" webpage are images of various members of the public along with thought bubbles containing questions and answers, positioning the company as an interlocutor in a larger public dialogue around nutrition, health and safety, population growth, and environmentalism (Monsanto 2015; Peekhaus 2010).

Although few GMO critics are likely to buy Monsanto's repositioning itself via social media as a sustainable corporate citizen, Monsanto's use of Twitter to suggest it is in open interactive dialogue with the community foregrounds what Couldry (2015a) describes as the seductive "myth of natural collectivity" (p. 620) associated with social media. Here, communicative power asymmetries appear magically erased by the apparently flat networks that circulate the tweets of teenagers and those of global corporate CEOs. In reality, the new media landscape, although in many ways representing a radical break with so-called "legacy" or old media companies, is still nevertheless dominated by corporations that seek to channel, control, and, above all, monetize the everyday connective practices of digital "audiences."

Any discussion of questions of power and inequity in the new digital era must necessarily account for two byproducts of connectivity that are key targets for corporate players: audience labor and the traces of data left behind by social interactions.

Although new media platforms have enabled audience members or users a tremendous degree of creativity and interactivity and, of course, the capacity to create content, digital engagement, through the act of demonstrating one's lifestyle and consumer preferences through likes on Facebook or through producing food videos for YouTube, can provide a kind of "free labor" (Terranova 2000). As van Dijck (2013) argues, although social media initially emerged out of a participatory, community-based ethos of creativity and exchange, "connectivity quickly evolved into a *resource* as engineers found ways to code information into algorithms that helped brand a particular form of online sociality and make it profitable in online markets" (p. 4, emphasis added).

In this space, people's everyday interactions and practices through digital media can be potentially converted into valuable commodities that are exchanged between digital media companies and advertisers (Fuchs 2010). This creeping commercial exploitation of everyday forms of digital interactivity is also evident, for instance, in the subtle exploitation of daily life practices and experience that is often referred to as the "experience economy." An example in the domestic food space is the rise of "free" life guides such as WhatsCook, a "service" sponsored by the mayonnaise manufacturer Hellmann's that connects people to real chefs via WhatsApp. Aiming to help householders cook meals based on what is in their refrigerators, the commercial subtext behind such services, aside from the positioning of Hellmann's as a benevolent provider of free advice, is the collection of personalized data on food and lifestyle preferences that advertisers then use to target their advertisements, marking a broader monetization of the so-called "social" exchanges in social media (Lupton 2017).

In an article on the "Googlization of everything," Brice Nixon (2016) draws attention to the similarity between Google's striving to "dominate" the internet and old media businesses that accumulate capital in order to extract value from their audience. As Nixon argues,

> Even in the digital era, processes of communication are also processes of capital accumulation specifically because communicative capitalists control audience activities of cultural consumption and exploit audience laborers (either directly or indirectly). In the digital era, communication is still capital. (p. 229)

Relatedly, another key area in which new media has converted audience engagement into a potential resource is through the generation of data. As Lupton (2018) contends, "In the context of the digital data economy, digitised information about food- and eating-related habits and practices are now accorded commercial, managerial, research, political and government as well as private value" (p. 74). Although the much discussed arena of big data and data mining is a space in which theoretically anyone can play, it is the large commercial food players who are often best placed to use data to their own ends. Thus, if the "digital divide" was once framed primarily in terms of access, the structural issues and inequities we increasingly face in a digital environment concern control and management of data (Rodino-Colocino 2006; see also Selwyn 2004), or what Mark Andrejevic (2014) calls the "big data divide." As Stevens et al. (2016) note in an article on social media and agro-food, "The food and beverage industry is at the forefront of interactive marketing and new types of digital targeting and tracking techniques. Food retailers have taken over social media marketing companies to gain more data and enhance their marketing strategies" (p. 103).

Linked to concerns regarding the capture and commercialization of personal data is the rise of what has been termed dataveillance—that is, the use of digital forms of connectivity to monitor either individuals or groups. Perhaps the most concerning use of data surveillance for political actors such as food or environmental activists lies in the potential for data abuse by internet service providers that are required by law in many countries to monitor internet traffic but also have the capacity to mine, monitor, and censor or block content.

Communications surveillance, of course, involves much more than monitoring internet use by corporations and governments. Although this chapter does not discuss the broader emerging ecology of data-linked devices and bodies, the rise of a range of technologies, such as RFID tagging and geolocation, enables constant connectivity and monitoring. As noted previously, in the food arena, this has played out in the consumer space in which GPS enables apps such as TripAdvisor to make restaurant and menu recommendations based on one's location and one's previous preferences (through profiling). At a broader level, such processes also tap into a concern regarding quantifying and managing the social and life itself (Lupton 2014, 2015). In the realm of agrobusiness, the rise of "smart" farming, for instance, has resulted in the use of geo-tagged animals, data-driven production techniques, and the use of drones to monitor crops and animals over large distances. Connectivity here is increasingly about the rationalization and efficiency of systems—with potential benefits in terms of food production and food "security"—but often at the cost of environmental and ethical scrutiny.

Conclusion: Decoding Digital Foodscapes

In this chapter, I have used the somewhat unlikely topic of food to discuss digital connectivity, focusing in particular on the substantive social and political dimensions of everyday digital engagements and the relations between the privatized food realm and global concerns from ethical consumption to GMO food. Such issues speak to the heart of global studies issues pertaining to civil society engagement, citizenship, and justice, as well as growing concerns regarding the need for processes of governance and regulation in an increasingly marketized global economy.

Although food traditionally conjures up images of groundedness, of materialism and naturalism, the digital realm would seem to represent the opposite. At once everywhere and nowhere, today's digital media appears immaterial and intangible, its encoded processes and infrastructure largely invisible to everyday users. Mapping key ways in which food consumers, producers, corporations, and activists engage with the digital realm, however, has enabled us to *materialize* some of the ways in which contemporary digital connectivity is articulated to and enabling of certain kinds of social relations, political engagement, as well as economic logics.

As discussed, what we might term "digital food" is a far from unified space and consists of a range of fields of practices and values that, like the digital environment itself, are constantly evolving and shifting. The varied ways in which food-related practices are articulated via new media platforms (from open source food hubs to Instagram-ed culinary creations) indicates the difficulty of offering easy generalizations about the capacities and constraints of the digital realm. Nevertheless, the world of digitally mediatized food is framed by certain key tensions or paradoxes, which speak to the broader experience of digital sociality today—that is, the price of communicability, community, and connection (or "compromised connectivity" as I have termed it) and the dialectic of visibility/invisibility that lies at the heart of encoded and data-ized social relations.

Speaking to the first issue, as discussed previously, in the arena of food politics and particularly the alternative food movement, digital connectivity has become central to contemporary food politics and activism. For instance, social media has enabled affordable and accessible ways of mobilizing, linking, and collectivizing diverse and distant players to protest against GMO food. For alternative food producers and food communities, new media platforms have provided the communicative and connective infrastructure for re-scaling "local" food hubs in order to offer real feasible alternatives to globalized food chains and retailers.

As Stevens et al. (2016) state,

> Flexible networks enable communities to join for a common cause in opposition against industrial food production, the horizontal links can bypass industrial–economic institutions and the interpersonal communication supports the social connections important to alternative food networks. This provides an opportunity for actors that do not fit industrial production standards, in which farmers play a greater role and the social and environmental origins of food products are emphasised. (p. 103)

At the same time, the growing recognition of the need for advanced digital literacy and programming skills in environmental and social movements and the increasing development and sharing of open source alternatives to social media platforms speak to a recognition of the limitations of the "everyday" forms of social connectivity provided through proprietorial devices and software. As van Dijck (2013) argues, although the rise of platformed spaces for sociality might have initially offered seemingly "neutral" spaces for the sharing of information and communication, the programming, formalization, and customization of these spaces along commercial lines means that everyday online social relations increasingly constitute practices and sites for capital to extract value as much as they offer tools for creating alternatives to normative commercialized foodscapes. Of course, another key limitation here is the fact that large swathes of the world—from the substantial proportion of people who are "disconnected" in the Global South to the large numbers of people still experiencing the ongoing "digital divide" in countries such as the United States—do not necessarily engage in or have access to the connective realm (Dimon 2013). For food activists, such a realization requires maintaining a constant, critical reflexivity toward the progressive participatory promise of the media tools and infrastructure that are increasingly dominating our daily lives.

Relatedly, a second fundamental dialectic at work across the digital food landscape is that of visibility/invisibility. Much of the digital activism oriented toward food consumers, for instance, is concerned with making visible the origins and conditions of global food production, often through the provision of information provided via apps or interactive online platforms. Political engagement and empowerment here are equated with informational transparency, with the notion that by revealing the elongated commodity chains or networks that underpin the workings of global agribusiness, we can challenge those processes and practices.

However, as Arthur Mol (2006) argues in relation to environmentalism in an era of digital technologies, although the possession of environmental information may enable reform, the rise of what he terms "a new informational mode of environmental governance" also raises critical concerns in relation to "new power constellations" (p. 511) around information access and use. As noted previously, the digitization of food through commercial apps such as WhatsCook can change our relationship to food in ways that are often hidden from view, embedded in an increasingly invisible algorithmic logic and culture. As Stevens et al. (2016) note, while "organizations in the agro-food system are challenged by the disruptive effects of erratic information flows, mass self-communication on social media also generates data for new forms of governance" (p. 103).

The somewhat utopian vocabulary of visibility, transparency, and connection then needs to be tempered by questions of governance and control, with a focus on understanding the social, cultural, and political economies of digital data processes and infrastructures. As critical technology gurus Arthur and Marilouise Kroker (2013) argue,

> Technological society is no longer understandable simply in terms of the globalizing spectacle of electronic images but in the more invisible, pervasive, and embodied language of computer codes. . . . When codework becomes the culture within which we thrive, then we must become fully aware of the invisible apparatus that supports the order of communications within which we live. (p. 7)

A critical media literacy today requires, as the Krokers suggest, the need for a deep appreciation of the coded infrastructures and often commercial logics and interdependencies that support the information and communication ecologies in which we increasingly live our lives. However, it also requires what we might call a material or infrastructural literacy or consciousness. Although digital connectivity is an increasingly taken-for-granted and ubiquitous part of daily life, we seldom stop to think about the vast arrays of material infrastructure required to support an increasingly globalized internet (Horst 2013). Such infrastructure triggers a larger set of political economy and governmental concerns in terms of maintenance, regulation, control, and security. But it also behooves us to ask key questions about—and to work to make visible—the potential environmental and social impact of digital infrastructure and energy-reliant "smart" communicative systems. Just as the food politics movement is seeking to build alternative sustainable ways of connecting all members of the food community, so too as increasingly digital citizens we need to build systems that take into account questions of e-waste and sustainable physical and digital infrastructure design (Maxwell and Miller 2011) and, as I have argued in this chapter, that foreground the social, political, ethical, and material elements that underpin and constitute our digital pathways.

REFERENCES

Adamoli, G. 2012. "Social Media and Social Movements: A Critical Analysis of Audience's Use of Facebook to Advocate Food Activism Offline." PhD thesis, College of Communication and Information, Florida State University, Tallahassee.

Andrejevic, M. 2014. "The Big Data Divide." *International Journal of Communications* 8: 1673–1689.

Belk, R. 2014. "You Are What You Can Access: Sharing and Collaborative Consumption Online." *Journal of Business Research* 67 (8): 1595–1600.

Bennet, D. 2014. "Inside Monsanto, America's Third-Most-Hated Company." Bloomberg, July 14. http://www.bloomberg.com/news/articles/2014-07-03/gmo-factory-monsantos-high-tech-plans-to-feed-the-world. Accessed September 22, 2016.

Berry, W. 2009. "Wendell Berry: The Pleasures of Eating." Center for Ecoliteracy, June 29. https://www.ecoliteracy.org/article/wendell-berry-pleasures-eating. Accessed September 22, 2016.

Binkley, S., and J. Littler, eds. 2011. *Cultural Studies and Anti-Consumerism: A Critical Encounter*. London: Routledge.

Booth, S., and J. Coveney. 2015. *Food Democracy: From Consumer to Food Citizen*. Dordrecht, the Netherlands: Springer.

Bos, E., and L. Owen. 2016. "Virtual Reconnection: The Online Spaces of Alternative Food Networks in England." *Journal of Rural Studies* 45: 1–14.

Burgess, J., and J. Green. 2009. *YouTube: Online Video, and Participatory Culture*. Cambridge, UK: Polity.

Chayko, M. 2017. *Superconnected: The Internet, Digital Media and Techno-Social Life*. Los Angeles: Sage.

Couldry, N. 2015a. "The Myth of 'Us': Digital Networks, Political Change and the Production of Collectivity." *Information, Communication & Society* 18 (6): 608–626.

Couldry, N. 2015b. "Illusions of Immediacy: Rediscovering Hall's Early Work on Media." *Media, Culture & Society* 37 (4): 637–644.

De Solier, I. 2005. "TV Dinners: Culinary Television, Education and Distinction." *Continuum: Journal of Media and Communication* 19 (4): 465–481.

De Solier, I. 2013. *Food and the Self: Consumption, Production and Material Culture* London: Bloomsbury.

Dimon, L. 2013. "This Is How Disconnected the World Is in the Internet Age." Mic, November 3. https://mic.com/articles/71111/this-is-how-disconnected-the-world-is-in-the-internet-age#.aXMnFyE3T. Accessed September 22, 2016.

Fuchs, C. 2006. "The Self-Organization of Social Movements." *Systemic Practice and Action Research* 19 (1): 101–137.

Fuchs, C. 2010. "Social Media and Capitalism." In *Producing the Internet: Critical Perspectives of Social Media*, edited by T. Olsson, 25–44. Göteborg, Sweden: Nordicom.

Gómez-Benito, C., and C. Lozano. 2014. "Constructing Food Citizenship: Theoretical Premise and Social Practices." *Italian Sociological Review* 4 (2): 135–156.

Goodman, D., E. M. DuPluis, and M. K. Goodman. 2012. *Alternative Food Networks: Knowledge, Practice, and Politics*. London: Routledge.

Grossman, S. 2014. "Top 10 Things That Broke the Internet." *Time*, December 1. http://time.com/3587943/things-that-broke-the-internet. Accessed September 22, 2016.

Hearn, G., N. Collie, P. Lyle, J. Hee-Jeong Choi, and M. Foth. 2014. "Using Communicative Ecology Theory to Scope the Emerging Role of Social Media in the Evolution of Urban Food Systems." *Futures* 62: 202–212.

Horst, H. A. 2013. "The Infrastructures of Mobile Media: Towards a Future Research Agenda." *Mobile Media & Communication* 1 (1): 147–152.

International Telecommunication Union. 2017. "ICT Facts and Figures 2017." June. http://www.itu.int/en/ITU-D/Statistics/Pages/facts/default.aspx. Accessed August 1, 2017.

Lewis, T. 2008. *Smart Living: Lifestyle Media and Popular Expertise*. New York: Lang.

Lewis, T. 2010. "Branding, Celebritization of the Lifestyle Expert." *Cultural Studies* 24 (4): 580–598.

Lewis, T. 2012. "'There Grows the Neighbourhood': Green Citizenship, Creativity and Life Politics on Eco-TV." *International Journal of Cultural Studies* 15 (3): 315–326.

Lewis, T., F. Martin, and W. Sun. 2016. *Telemodernities: Television, and Transforming Lives in Asia*. Durham, NC: Duke University Press.

Local Dirt. 2016. "Local Dirt: Buy, Sell and Find Local Food." http://localdirt.com. Accessed September 22, 2016.

Lunden, I. 2016. "Nom.com, a Foodie-Focused Live Video Network from YouTube's Steve Chen, Launches with $4.7M." *TechCrunch*, March 9. https://techcrunch.com/2016/03/09/nom-com-a-foodie-focused-live-video-network-from-youtubes-steve-chen-launches-with-4-7m. Accessed September 22, 2016.

Lupton, D. 2014. "Self-Tracking Modes: Reflexive Self-Monitoring and Data Practices." Paper presented at the Imminent Citizenships: Personhood and Identity Politics in the Informatic Age workshop, August 27, 2014, Australian National University, Canberra. http://papers.ssrn.com/sol3/papers.cfm?abstract_id=2483549.

Lupton, D. 2015. *Digital Sociology*. Abingdon, UK: Routledge.

Lupton, D. 2018. "Cooking, Eating, Uploading: Digital Food Cultures." In *The Bloomsbury Handbook of Food and Popular Culture*, edited by K. LeBesco and P. Naccarato, 66–79. London: Bloomsbury.

Mackenzie, A. 2007. "Wireless Networks and the Problems of Over-Connectedness." *Media International Australia* 125: 94–125.

Marwick, A. E. 2016. "You May Know Me from YouTube: (Micro-)Celebrity in Social Media." In *A Companion to Celebrity*, edited by P. D. Marshal and S. Redmond, 333–350. Malden, MA: Wiley.

Maxwell, R., and T. Miller. 2008. "E-Waste: Elephant in the Living Room." *Flow*, December 2. https://www.flowjournal.org/2008/12/e-waste-elephant-in-the-living-room-richard-maxwell-queens-college-cuny-toby-miller-uc-riverside. Accessed April 26, 2017.

Maxwell, R., and T. Miller. 2011. "Eco-Ethical Electronic Consumption in the Smart Design Economy." In *Ethical Consumption: A Critical Introduction*, edited by T. Lewis and E. Potter, 141–155. London: Routledge.

Meisner, M. 2000. "E-Activism: Environmental Activists Are Using the Internet to Organize, Spoof and Subvert." *Alternatives Journal* 26 (4): 34–38.

Miller, D. 2011. *Tales from Facebook*. London: Polity.

Mol, A. P. J. 2006. "Environmental Governance in the Information Age: The Emergence of Informational Governance." *Environment and Planning C: Government and Policy* 24 (4): 497–514.

Monsanto. 2015. "A Sustainable Agriculture Company." http://www.monsanto.com/pages/default.aspx. Accessed September 22, 2016.

Murray, S. 2008. "Digital Images, Photo-Sharing, and Our Shifting Notions of Everyday Aesthetics." *Journal of Visual Culture* 7 (2): 147–163.

Nixon, B. 2016. "The Old Media Business in the New: 'The Googlization of Everything' as the Capitalization of Digital Consumption." *Media Culture and Society* 38 (2): 212–231.

Ofcom. 2017. "Adults' Media Use and Attitudes: Report 2017." June. https://www.ofcom.org.uk/__data/assets/pdf_file/0020/102755/adults-media-use-attitudes-2017.pdf. Accessed August 1, 2017.

Oklahoma Food Cooperative. 2016. "The Oklahoma Food Cooperative." http://oklahomafood.coop. Accessed September 22, 2016.

OLIO. 2016. "About OLIO." http://olioex.com/about. Accessed September 22, 2016.

Open Food Network. 2015. "Open Food Network." https://openfoodnetwork.org. Accessed September 22, 2016.

Papacharissi, Z. A. 2009. "The Virtual Sphere 2.0: The Internet, the Public Sphere and Beyond." In *The Routledge Handbook of Internet Politics*, edited by A. Chadwick and P. N. Howard, 230–245. Abingdon, UK: Routledge.

Papacharissi, Z. A. 2010. *A Private Sphere: Democracy in a Digital Age.* Cambridge, UK: Polity.

Peekhaus, W. 2010. "Monsanto Discovers Social Media." *International Journal of Communication* 4: 955–976.

Pickerill, J. 2003. *Cyberprotest: Environmental Activism Online.* Manchester, UK: Manchester University Press.

Postill, J. 2012. "Media and Social Changing Since 1979: Towards a Diachronic Ethnography of Media and Actual Social Changes." Paper presented at the EASA 2012 Biennial Conference, Nanterre, Paris. https://johnpostill.com/2012/07/14/new-paper-media-and-social-changing-since-1979/. Accessed August 1, 2018.

Poushter, J. 2017. "Smartphones Are Common in Advanced Economies, But Digital Divides Remain." Pew Research Center, April 21. http://www.pewresearch.org/fact-tank/2017/04/21/smartphones-are-common-in-advanced-economies-but-digital-divides-remain/#. Accessed July 2, 2017.

Rodino-Colocino, M. 2006. "Laboring Under the Digital Divide." *New Media & Society* 8 (3): 487–511.

Schneider, T., K. Eli, C. Dolan, and S. Ulijaszek, eds. (2018). *Digital Food Activism.* London: Routledge.

Schor, J. 1999. "The New Politics of Consumption." *Boston Review.* http://new.bostonreview.net/BR24.3/schor.html. Accessed September 22, 2016.

Schor, J. 2014. "Debating the Sharing Economy." *Great Transition Initiative*, October. http://www.greattransition.org/publication/debating-the-sharing-economy. Accessed April 27, 2015.

Selwyn, N. 2004. "Reconsidering Political and Popular Understandings of the Digital Divide." *New Media & Society* 6 (3): 341–362.

SORTEDfood. 2016. "About SORTEDfood." https://sortedfood.com/about. Accessed September 22, 2016.

Stevens, T. M., N. Aarts, C. J. A. M. Termeer, and A. Dewulf. 2016. "Social Media as a New Playing Field for the Governance of Agro-Food Sustainability." *Current Opinion in Environmental Sustainability* 18: 99–106.

Thomas, J., J. Barraket, S. Ewing, T. MacDonald, M. Mundell, and J. Tucker. 2016. "Measuring Australia's Digital Divide: The Australian Digital Inclusion Index 2016." Swinburne University of Technology, Melbourne, for Telstra. doi:www.dx.doi.org/10.4225/50/57A7D17127384

Terranova, T. 2000. "Free Labor: Producing Culture for the Digital Economy." *Social Text* 18 (2): 33–58.

UCL. 2016. "Why We Post: Social Media Through the Eyes of the World." https://www.ucl.ac.uk/why-we-post. Accessed September 22, 2016.

Van de Donk, W., B. D. Loader, P. G. Nixon, and D. Rucht, eds. 2004. *Cyberprotest: New Media, Citizens and Social Movements.* London Routledge.

Van Dijck, J. 2013. *The Culture of Connectivity: A Critical History of Social Media.* Oxford, UK: Oxford University Press.

Walsh, S. P., K. M. White, and R. M. Young. 2008. "Over-Connected? A Qualitative Exploration of the Relationship Between Australian Youth and Their Mobile Phones." *Journal of Adolescence* 31 (1): 77–92.

Wilkins, J. L. 2005. "Eating Right Here: Moving from Consumer to Food Citizen." *Agriculture and Human Values* 22 (3): 269–273.

CHAPTER 34

···

MEDIA INDUSTRY

···

JACK LULE

THE media industry—local, national, and global media—might be surprised to find itself considered by many a global concern, sharing space with trafficking, poverty, and pandemics. However, the media industry has earned the concern. Three characteristics of the modern media industry in particular are cause for global apprehension:

First, the media industry has played a crucial role in fostering an uneven globalization, creating and maintaining the conditions for indiscriminate global capitalism and too often promoting an uncritical and unstudied narrative of the world's market economy, which has produced large, unequal distributions of wealth within nations and between nations. Economic globalization here is understood as a mythic tale, told to a world, that makes natural the buying and selling of products across borders and boundaries and celebrates profits, products, and consumption. The tale is told and celebrated even in the midst of vast inequalities that keep many mired in poverty.

Second, the media are themselves now huge transnational corporations (TNCs) that drive globalization even as they embody globalization. Not long ago, newspapers, magazines, television networks, and radio stations were primarily local media, owned and controlled by people of that place and serving those regional audiences. Media now are the epitome of economic globalization. Less than ten conglomerates, primarily Western, own or control much of the media industry. The oligopoly has led to the demise of public affairs reporting and independent, journalistic voices.

Finally, as global media grow in size and importance, they threaten local and regional cultural traditions. Food, fashion, music, film, and other expressions of local culture are compromised and endangered by ubiquitous Western media. Some states intercede to protect local industries and artists. Yet the national intercession can further imperil the independence of work and art.

The still-new millennium appears to be an era of media plenty. New media platforms, social media, and media technologies arise regularly and seem to offer the promise of multiple, varied, and independent voices. Yet, too often, new media are co-opted and eventually controlled by corporations and conglomerates or restricted and restrained by hostile governments. The media industry, indeed, is a global concern.

CREATING THE CONDITIONS FOR
GLOBAL CAPITALISM

Let me make a preliminary observation: Without the media industry, globalization and modern-day capitalism likely would not exist. The role of media in globalization can often be overlooked. But at every level and in every era, global capitalism has depended on the communication of recent, regular, and reliable information, much of that supplied by the media industry. Each iteration of media, from cave paintings to cell phones, manifests the importance of gathering, recording, and communicating economic information to humans. Cave paintings appear to be partially a record of fish and game found in particular areas. The Silk Road, the network of trade routes connecting Asia with the Mediterranean world, North Africa, and Europe, flourished when the Chinese invention of paper became more common along the route (Frankopan 2016). The new medium allowed permanent and portable records of debts and transactions.

In *Communication and Empire: Media, Markets, and Globalization, 1860–1930*, Dwayne Winseck and Robert Pike (2007) make the case that communication media were the foundation of globalization in that era:

> Globalization during the late nineteenth century and early twentieth was not shallow and fleeting, but deep and durable. The growth of a world-wide network of fast cables and telegraph systems, in tandem with developments in railways and steamships, eroded some of the obstacles of geography and made it easier to organize transcontinental business. These networks supported huge flows of capital, technology, people, news, and ideas which, in turn, led to a high degree of convergence among markets, merchants and bankers. (pp. 1–2)

In the twentieth century, newspapers, magazines, radio, television, film, and digital media all shaped economic globalization. Oliver Boyd-Barrett and Terhi Rantanen (1982) find that "the links between modernity, capitalism, news, news agencies and globalization are an outstanding but neglected feature of the past 150 years" (p. 2). Today, the media industry oversees instantaneous and voluminous flows of economic data and information throughout the world (Butterick 2015). Media outlets—such as London's *Financial Times*; Japan's *Nihon Keizai Shimbun*; China's *Jingji Cankao Bao*; and the United States' *Bloomberg News, Wall Street Journal*, and CNBC—provide markets with the data and information that fuel global capitalism.

But the media industry does more than supply information and infrastructure for globalization. The media also foster the conditions for global capitalism. Although media coverage of business is supposed to critically study and report on this significant aspect of economic, political, and social life, often the coverage is content to chart the rise and fall of markets and cheerlead for profit and expansion (Butterick 2015; Shaban 2014; Starkman 2013). Celebrations of global capitalism are a subtle but recurring motif in many media industry narratives, from breathless cover stories of CEOs to Hollywood blockbuster films. Manfred Steger (2008) states, "Globalization was never merely a matter of increasing flows of capital and goods across national boundaries" (p. 27). Rather, he says, "It constitutes a multidimensional set of processes in which images, sound bites, metaphors, myths, symbols and spatial arrangements of globality were just as important as economic and technological dynamics" (p. 27).

ADVERTISING AND MYTHIC EXHORTATIONS

The mythic exhortation and embrace of consumers, products, and markets is most readily seen in advertising and marketing, which drive consumption and expansion (Iqani 2015). With ceaseless commercials on radio and television, product placement in films, digital billboards, pop-up ads, broadsheets in bathroom stalls, and more, the media industry fills the day with appeals and enticements for consumption. Mike Featherstone (2008) has argued that

> commodities hence become free to take on a wide range of cultural associations and illusions. Advertising in particular is able to exploit this and attach images of romance, exotica, desire, beauty, fulfillment, communality, scientific progress and the good life to mundane consumer goods such as soap, washing, motor cars and alcoholic drinks. (p. 668)

Similarly, Arjun Appadurai (1996) states that "global advertising is the key technology for the worldwide dissemination of a plethora of creative and culturally well-chosen ideas of consumer agency" (p. 42). The following is just one example of the "well-chosen idea": The athletic apparel company Nike uses advertising to establish and maintain itself as a premium brand. The advertising associates Nike products with superior qualities, such as hard work, initiative, and success, as well as superior athletes, such as Michael Jordan, Tiger Woods, Maria Sharapova, and Serena Williams, to offer modern-day myths of exemplary figures—heroes—struggling and succeeding through adversity. Over more than 50 years, Nike has become the top apparel seller in the world, with sales in more than 150 countries, and its stock has become one of the market's top performers (Frisch 2009; Strasser and Becklund 1991). Other global brands, such as Apple, Coca-Cola, McDonald's, Mercedes-Benz, Budweiser, and countless others, also offer well-chosen ideas that equate fun, energy, relaxation, family harmony, and other emblems of a good life with the consumption of a product.

As Robert McChesney (2001) notes, "Economic and cultural globalization arguably would be impossible without a global commercial media system to promote global markets and to encourage consumer values." Elsewhere, McChesney and co-author Edward Herman call global media "the new missionaries of global capitalism" (Herman and McChesney 1997). They write,

> The global media are the missionaries of our age, promoting the virtues of commercialism and the market loudly and incessantly through their profit-driven and advertising-supported enterprises and programming. This missionary work is not the result of any sort of conspiracy; for the global media TNCs it developed organically from their institutional basis and commercial imperatives. Nor are the global media completely monolithic, of course, and dissident ideas make their occasional appearance in virtually all of them. But their overall trajectory of service to the global corporate system at many levels is undeniable. (pp. 37–38)

To be sure, the marriage of media and globalization can produce benefits. Private ownership of media can offer a sharp counterpoint to autocratic, state-controlled media under the heavy hand of government. In addition, popular global media events, from Hollywood blockbusters to international sporting events, bring relaxation and pleasure to millions throughout the world and provide glimpses of a global culture. And some media events, such as film, televisions shows, and music, can offer subtle portrayals of alternative cultural practices within repressive societies, from the education of young girls to the treatment of minorities. Often, however, the global media industry acts only to sustain and extend its competitive position and profit, using its vast resources to create and maintain a culture of consumption that enriches itself and its stockholders.

THE MEDIA OLIGOPOLY

To the casual observer, the global media industry might seem to be a bazaar of world-wide companies, firms, start-ups, and independents. Yet, in actuality, the media industry is controlled by a few transnational corporations. Different from a monopoly, in which a single company controls all of a product or service, an oligopoly shares control of the market with limited competition. For the media industry, the process has been relatively recent and rapid, underway only since the 1980s. But since that time, throughout the world, once small, local, and regional media companies—newspapers, magazines, radio stations, television and cable channels, book publishers, movie studios, internet sites, and more— have been bought and consolidated by a handful of huge global conglomerates, most of which were themselves once small and local (Straubhaar, LaRose, and Davenport 2016).

The result can go by other names, such as media consolidation, concentration, or convergence. By whatever name, in some estimates, six to ten companies own or control close to 75% of the world's media (Bagdikian 2004; Herman and McChesney 1997; McChesney 2014). Of those companies, three in particular stand out. Media scholar Ben Bagdikian (2004) calls them part of the "media monopoly." Robert McChesney (2000) calls them the "the holy trinity of the global media system" (p. 91). A brief review of their vast holdings is illustrative:

> *The Walt Disney Company*: Holdings include ABC television, which produces news shows such as *Good Morning America* and entertainment programs such as *Modern Family*; television production and distribution companies, such as Touchstone, Buena Vista, and the Muppets Studio; ABC radio networks, with more than seventy stations; ten other US TV stations and affiliated radio stations in major cities; top cable TV channels, including the Disney Channel, ESPN, ESPN2, ESPNews, ESPN International, Lifetime, A&E, E! Entertainment, and the History Channel; major film studios Pixar, Lucasfilm, Miramax, Touchstone, and Walt Disney Pictures; book publishers, including Hyperion Press and Disney Publishing; music recording companies, including the Hollywood, Mammoth, and Walt Disney labels; theme parks and resorts, including Disneyland, Disney World, and EuroDisney; Club Disney, a restaurant chain; the Disney Cruise Line; and Disney stores worldwide.
> *News Corp (formerly News Corp.) and its sister organization, 21st Century Fox*: Both founded by Rupert Murdoch, their holdings include the US Fox television network; more than twenty other US television stations; Fox News Channel; cable

channels such as FX, Fox Sports Net, the National Geographic Channel, and the Big 10 Network; interests in DirectTV; STAR television stations throughout Asia; interests in British Sky Broadcasting satellite TV service and other Sky TV channels throughout Europe, such as Sky Deutschland and Sky Italia; Twentieth Century Fox film studio, producer of films such as *Black Swan* and *Avatar*; Twentieth Television and other US and international TV producers and distributors; internet properties such as Hulu.com; more than 125 daily newspapers, including *The Times* (of London), the *New York Post*, and the *Wall Street Journal*, as well as 70% of Australia's newspaper circulation; and book publishers, including HarperCollins.

Time Warner Communications: Many entities bearing the Time Warner name have actually been spun off into independent entities, including Time Warner Cable, Warner Books, Warner Music, and Time Inc., with its magazines and websites. Holdings now include the following: Home Box Office, including HBO and Cinemax, with shows such as *Game of Thrones*, *Boardwalk Empire*, and *Entourage*; Turner Broadcasting System, including CNN, TNT, TBS, Cartoon Network, and Turner Classic Movies; Warner Bros. Picture Group, which produces movies such as the *Harry Potter* series and *Clash of the Titans*; New Line Cinema, which produces movies such as *A Nightmare on Elm Street* and *The Lord of the Rings*; Warner Bros. Television Group, with worldwide production, distribution, and broadcasting; and DC Comics, which includes characters such as Superman and Batman.

Other significant conglomerates in the media oligopoly include Comcast, which owns NBC Universal, CBS, Viacom, Bertelsmann, and Sony. For some observers, the growth of such conglomerates is a natural outcome of modern-day capitalism or the accepted result of successful business decisions. Yet this is not the case. The growth of these media conglomerates does not follow some presumptive law of economics, in which the strongest and best survive and get bigger. In fact, the media oligopoly is a political phenomenon. To become global conglomerates, companies must work ceaselessly to shape local, state, national, and international regulations, lobbying, marketing, and persuading officials and lawmakers, and toiling continually behind the scenes, until they receive necessary favors and concessions.

McChesney (2001) finds that a host of political decisions, including deregulation, support for market expansion, and government intervention, have paved the way for conglomerates to expand worldwide. He writes,

> The global media system is not the result of "free markets" or natural law; it is the consequence of a number of important state policies that have been made that created the system. The media giants have had a heavy hand in drafting these laws and regulations, and the public tends to have little or no input. In the United States, the corporate media lobbies are notorious for their ability to get their way with politicians, especially if their adversary is not another powerful corporate sector, but that amorphous entity called the "public interest."

Des Freedman (2008), in *The Politics of Media Policy*, agrees. "Media policy," Freedman says, "the systematic attempt to foster certain types of media structure and behavior and to suppress alternative modes of structure and behavior, is a deeply political phenomenon" (p. 1).

THE MASS PRODUCTION OF IGNORANCE

In many countries, the media industry is supported and protected by national governments so that it might fulfill important social and political roles, such as provide information and insights to citizens. Instead, the media industry uses that protection and support to further its profit-making, increase its holdings, and replace information and insights with trivial, sensational, and distracting drivel that crowds out insight and reflection.

The oligopoly's success thus has had ruinous results for the content of much media. The most profitable content for global media is that which can be mass-produced, published, and broadcast widely, sometimes simultaneously, in numerous countries. Such content thus rules the airwaves and often includes numerous reruns of US television shows and programming, such as *Game of Thrones* and *Scandal*; global sporting events, such as the Olympics or the World Cup; and celebrity entertainment programs, such as *Oprah* (Dionne 2015). Rather than producing local, homegrown programming on public problems and community issues, local media outlets often carry the mass-produced content of their conglomerate owners.

Relatedly, the oligopoly has thus overseen the demise of local, independent journalism and what was once called public affairs reporting. Media industry content often is escapist and apolitical. News and political coverage can upset and divide the populace, drive away viewers, and displease authorities. Despite the fact that nations such as the United States have laws like the First Amendment to protect and promote free inquiry by the press, the media industry cuts back on in-depth and investigative journalism. Herman and McChesney (1997) write, "Concentration of media power in organizations dependent on advertiser support and responsible primarily to shareholders is a clear and present danger to citizens' participation in public affairs, understanding of public issues, and thus to the effective working of democracy" (p. 1).

Throughout the world, news has become softer, lighter, and less challenging, with space and time given over to weather, celebrities, sensation, sports, recipes, and other less weighty fare. Reality shows, game shows, and cooking shows are non-labor-intensive and easy to produce. Local news broadcasting shows, investigative reporting, and documentaries are expensive. The escapist productions take up time, space, and resources that could be devoted to public affairs. British media scholar Greg Philo (2004) calls the result the "mass production of ignorance." Even when news covers events, Philo (2004) says, media "focus on dramatic, violent and tragic images while giving very little context or explanation to the events which are being portrayed" (p. 222). He blames the drive for ratings and profits:

> The development of television organised around crude notions of audience ratings is likely to make this situation worse. The irony is that in seeking to grab the attention of audiences, programme makers are actually fostering very negative attitudes towards the developing world and other international issues and in the long run will reduce audience interest. (p. 222)

Daya Kishan Thussu (2004), a former journalist in the Global South who now studies international media, decries what he calls the "poverty of news." Despite twenty-four-hour television news and online journalism outlets, he says, the "issues concerning the world's poor are being increasingly marginalised as a softer lifestyle variety of reporting appears to dominate global television news agendas" (Thussu 2004: 47). He critiques "real-time news as 24/7 infotainment" (Thussu 2009: 3). He finds that "media concentration has contributed to a tendency in journalism towards a socially dysfunctional focus on the 'bottom line'" (p. 3).

The results have been especially devastating for international news reporting. Foreign news bureaus are expensive to create and maintain. Throughout the world, media that once provided extensive foreign correspondence have disbanded staffs and shuttered bureaus. The *American Journalism Review* chronicled the damage in a cover story, "Retreating from the World: The Sharp Decline in Foreign Coverage" (Enda 2011). The magazine reported that eighteen US newspapers and two chains have shut down every one of their overseas bureaus in the dozen years since the magazine first surveyed foreign coverage. It cited a Harvard University study of US network news that found in the 1970s, 45% of the coverage was devoted to international news. In 1995, the total had dropped to 13.5% and decreases each year. "What's more," the review said, "an untold number of regional and local papers have dramatically decreased the amount of foreign news they publish. Television networks, meanwhile, slashed the time they devote to foreign news and narrowed their focus largely to war zones" (Enda 2011). A 2015 report by the Annenberg Media Center found the trend continues (Wadekar 2015). In late 2015, the McClatchy news service closed all its foreign bureaus, adding to the totals. Often, international coverage is now provided only for the most dramatic incidents, such as outbreaks of disease, airline disasters, or terrorist attacks.

The cutbacks are not just an American phenomenon. The BBC has seen hundreds of positions cut worldwide (Hennessy 2011; Martinson 2015). News media in China, India, and Japan have few correspondents outside their homeland. International news coverage is down throughout the world (Wadekar 2015). The irony is dismal. With twenty-four-hour news television, the creation of the World Wide Web, the expansion of mobile phones to villages in the most remote corners of the world, and the capacity for direct and immediate reporting from any place on the planet, the media industry provides less international news than ever.

Shahira Fahmy (2010) studied the amount of foreign affairs coverage in the aftermath of the September 11, 2001, terrorist attacks. Conventional logic would suggest, Fahmy says, that the dramatic and global events surrounding the terrorist strikes on the World Trade Center and the subsequent US wars in Afghanistan and Iraq, combined with the many advances of new media, would have produced a sharp rise in global news. The title of Fahmy's essay, however, is telling: "How Could So Much Produce So Little?" She concludes that news organizations must completely re-examine their commitment to foreign news:

> Editors have the ability and the responsibility to devote more space to high quality foreign news, including graphics and more photographs. Foreign news needs to move up the ladder of concern for the news industry. Foreign affairs coverage cannot remain far down the news scale. (p. 158)

Yet the world-wide media oligopoly has little economic or political incentive to increase its reporting of the world.

The Threat to Local Cultures

The consolidation and conglomeration of global media and the ubiquity of their products raise major concerns for local and regional cultural traditions. The dominance of Western companies is a central issue. The global media oligopoly is primarily owned and controlled by US and European firms. Decision-making about content, distribution, investment, and expansion is made far from the local cultures that will be affected by those decisions. Investments or programming that might be needed at the local level are unknown—literally foreign—to executives in far-off offices.

Because of this physical and cultural distance, the conglomerates sometimes distribute content unwanted by, or offensive to, those trying to observe or uphold local customs. Films involving sex, bloody violence, drug use, and other topics can go against cultural traditions. Such content sometimes leads to local protests and prohibitions. Violent film series, such as *Saw* and *Halloween*, are regularly banned in some countries. Sexually provocative fare of some shows on MTV International has caused consternation in numerous nations. Songs such as Katy Perry's hit single, "I Kissed a Girl," have been removed from airplay. The film *Brokeback Mountain* was prohibited in some nations for its depiction of homosexuality. The video game *Call of Duty: Modern Warfare II* caused dismay because of its dramatization of terrorism. A 2016 music video with Coldplay and Beyoncé, set in India, was criticized as "nothing more than an amalgamation of clichés about the country, from a peacock to temples to a fire eater, holy men and dancing girls" (Kapur 2016). Nations and cultures resent having media introduce such content into their lands by companies looking to sell products.

Local and regional industries, however, can offer few alternatives. Media productions, particularly in film and broadcast, can be prohibitively expensive. Most nations do not have the resources to support industries that can regularly produce programming to compete against the oligopoly. For example, Hollywood film studios bankroll multimillion-dollar movies with the world's most popular actors and actresses. One Hollywood film can cost more than entire nations spend on film production in a year. In addition, Western conglomerates then promote, market, and support their products on a global scale, using the many different platforms they control. Small local media industries must compete, often unsuccessfully, against transnational giants that control local publications, airwaves, advertising, theaters, television stations, and more.

The result is that entire cultural traditions of filmmaking and music are at stake in some locales. Nations must work diligently and redirect precious resources to preserve and protect their cultural heritage. The protection can take many forms, from quotas against Western fare to subsidies for local industries. For example, Ghana, Mali, and other African nations have passed legislation that seeks to support and protect distinctive music and dance traditions (Campbell 2015). European nations have also felt threatened by American cultural products. As early as 1989, the European Union (EU) instituted quotas to counter American television programming. The "Television without Frontiers" directive requires that EU states reserve a majority (more than 51%) of entertainment broadcast time for productions of European origin. The global film industry is a large concern. Italy provides subsidies to its struggling film companies, which work to keep alive the Italian tradition of filmmakers that includes Federico Fellini, Roberto Rossellini, and Bernardo Bertolucci. Then-French President Jacques Chirac strongly supported quotas on non-European productions. He argued he would not see "European culture sterilized or obliterated by American culture for economic reasons that have nothing to do with real culture" ("We Are Not an Average Nation," 1995).

Although Chinese leaders have sought the benefits of commercial interactions with Western media and conglomerates, they also strive to promote and maintain local and national culture and to resist possible convergence with Western culture (Su 2016). In some sense, China seeks the benefits of an economic globalization while resisting a cultural globalization. International communication scholars Paula Chakravartty and Yuezhi Zhao (2008) make a similar observation. They note that Chinese officials often avoid using the broad label of globalization. Instead, officials employ the more pointed phrase of economic globalization. The emphasis, Chakravartty and Zhao state, signifies "the Chinese state's attempt to integrate with the global market system on the one hand, and resist political and cultural assimilation into the American-dominated global capitalist order on the other" (p. 4).

Chakravartty and Zhao (2008: 4) suggest that the resistance to the West is often distilled simply to US–China interactions. China participates in economic globalization but with a wary eye on the United States. The wariness extends to Chinese media. For example, Liu Kang (2004), another scholar of communication in China, finds that Chinese journalists often balance their pursuit of press freedom with a nationalism shaped by long suspicion of US attempts to promote such freedom. Kang writes,

> Hence it becomes imperative that understanding China's freedom of press, political reform, and nationalism must take into account the U.S.–China relationship as a central component of China's "domestic" issues. Nothing remains purely "internal affairs" in China without the "interferences" of influences of the United States. (p. 130)

CULTURAL IMPERIALISM

Concern regarding the media oligopoly's influence on local cultures has found its way into communication theory. The thesis of "cultural imperialism" is that dominant cultures, often exemplified by Western states and corporations, impose their culture, either directly or indirectly, on others for economic and political gain. In the early years of debate over cultural imperialism, the 1970s and 1980s, the United Nations Educational, Scientific and Cultural Organisation (UNESCO) was often the site of impassioned controversy (Abel 1984). Developing nations wanted to limit the reach and access of large Western media to their people. They called for a New World Information and Communication Order (NWICO). Western nations resisted such limitations and claimed such restrictions violated free speech (Abel 1984). Ultimately, in 1984, the United States and the United Kingdom bitterly left UNESCO for almost twenty years, only rejoining when the issue was dropped (Fuchs 2015).

For many countries and cultures, however, cultural imperialism is still very much a concern. John Downing, Ali Mohammadi, and Annabelle Sreberny-Mohammadi (1995) point out its subtleties in a modern communication age. They note, "Imperialism is the conquest and control of one country by a more powerful one. Cultural imperialism signifies the dimensions of the process that go beyond economic exploitation or military force" (p. 482). Such imperialism, they say, often takes place in the very social fabric of some nations. The authors point out that colonial powers established educational structures and media systems in many countries that exist to this day and reflect Western culture. Current and prevalent media too, such as advertising, also reinforce Western culture. The authors state, "Subtly but powerfully, the message has often been insinuated that Western cultures are superior" (p. 482).

Scholars who study cultural imperialism or the less frequent term, electronic or digital colonialism, explore in particular the ways in which Western culture, especially American culture, might be imposed on other countries by the overwhelming presence and prevalence of modern Western cultural products. As media scholar Thomas McPhail (2006) argues, "All of the US multimedia empires, along with their extensive advertising networks, project and encourage US tastes, values, mores, history, culture, and language around the world" (p. 60). The large and aggressive reach of the oligopoly allows it to infiltrate, insinuate, market, and distribute Western music, food, fashion, appliances, cars, and nearly every other consumer item into the lives of others, sometimes swamping the ability of even the most resilient local cultures to sustain and offer alternatives. And the imposition has only intensified with what some have called "digital imperialism" (Wasik 2015).

For others, the issue of cultural imperialism is subtler. Some scholars argue that Western corporations are not often actively promoting Western political values. In his view of the implications of economic globalization and media, McChesney (2010) contends that the media oligopoly is not primarily interested in political ideology or Western cultural values. The oligopoly is interested in one thing: profit. McChesney states, "The global media system is better understood, then, as one that advances corporate and commercial interests and values, and denigrates or ignores that which cannot be incorporated into its mission" (p. 204). He continues,

> The logical consequence of a commercial media system is less to instill adherence to any ruling powers that be—though that can and does of course happen—than to promote a general belief that politics is unimportant and that there is little hope for organized social change. (p. 208)

Katharine Sarikakis (2008) studied media policies in the EU and reached a similar conclusion. She writes,

> The normative framework, necessary for the legitimization of policies that transformed the media across Europe, redefined the public in its relation to the media, as consumers of media services and accumulators of cultural goods, rather than as members of an informed and active citizenry. (p. 96)

The findings are in keeping with the work of critical theorists such as Theodor Adorno and Max Horkheimer, who argued in 2002 that a "culture industry," which produced simple and mindless entertainment, actually had great social, political, and economic importance. Such entertainment, they said, distracts audiences from critical thinking, sapping time and energy from social and political action and promoting passive political acquiescence.

Thus, in this view, the cultural imperialism of transnational conglomerates imposes consumer culture. The oligopoly has little interest or financial incentive to provide news and information necessary for active citizens or to promote local culture. People are encouraged to think of products, not politics and tradition. They are consumers, not citizens. The global oligopoly of media thus helps create a passive apolitical uninformed populace, uninterested in its own cultural traditions, which rises from the couch primarily for consumption.

The Resistance of Local Culture

Other scholars take yet another perspective. Although sensitive to the possibility of cultural imperialism or media imperialism, these writers suggest the thesis can have a simplistic, perhaps degrading view of developing countries. Cultural imperialism can imply that the cultures of developing countries are passive and weak when, in reality, these scholars state, the cultures are strong enough and resilient enough to reject or even adapt Western culture for their own purposes. Arjun Appadurai (1996), for example, finds that the intersection of global and local cultures brings about "a space of contestation in which individuals and groups seek to annex the global into their own practices of the modern" (p. 4). He argues, "There is growing evidence that the consumption of mass media throughout the world often provokes resistance, irony, selectivity, and in general, *agency*" (p. 7). And he concludes emphatically that "globalization is not the story of cultural homogenization" (p. 11).

In *Globalization and Culture: Global Mélange*, Jan Nederveen Pieterse (2004) argues that there are actually just three outcomes that result from the intersections of different cultures. Cultural differentialism implies that cultures are different, strong, and resilient. Differences will be retained and distinctive cultures will endure despite globalization and the global reach of American or Western cultural forms. Some scholars see danger in cultural differentialism, Pieterse acknowledges (p. 42). For them, it suggests that cultures are destined to conflict, portending a "clash of civilizations," as globalization continually brings cultures in contact with one another. A second outcome, cultural convergence, suggests that globalization will bring about a growing uniformity of cultures. A global culture, likely American culture, some fear, will engulf many local cultures, which will lose their distinctive characteristics (pp. 49–52). This outcome can lead to the "cultural imperialism thesis" and, more dramatically, a worldwide, homogenized, Westernized culture.

But Pieterse (2004) offers a third, more hopeful outcome. Cultural hybridity suggests that globalization will lead to an escalating mixture or blending of cultures, in which local cultures adopt and adapt aspects of other cultures to produce something new. This mélange, Pieterse suggests, can point the way to the creation of new and surprising cultural forms, from music to food and fashion. For Pieterse, this hybrid outcome is just as likely as differentialism and convergence. Indeed, he says, hybridity is common, occurs throughout history, and will occur more so in an era of globalization (pp. 59–72). He sums up the three paradigms as follows:

> Each paradigm involves a different take on *globalization*. According to cultural differentialism, globalization is a surface phenomenon only: the real dynamic is regionalization, or the formation of regional blocs, which tend to correspond with civilizational clusters. Therefore,

the future of globalization is interregional rivalry. According the convergence principle, contemporary globalization is westernization or Americanization writ large, a fulfillment in installments of the classical imperial and modernization theses. According to the mixing approach, the outcome of globalization processes is open-ended and current globalization is as much a process of easternization as of westernization, as well as of many interstitial influences. (p. 57)

The three outcomes provide an effective theoretical framework for considering the cultural implications of the media industry. By viewing the three outcomes on a kind of continuum, Pieterse's paradigms allow scholars to locate specific, historically situated meetings of global and local forms at any one point on the continuum. The violence surrounding the publication of Danish editorial cartoons of Mohammed can be understood as cultural differentialism. The overwhelming global popularity of US films such as *Avatar* can be viewed as cultural convergence. And the rise of musical forms such as Cuban hip-hop or French bluegrass can be viewed as cultural hybridity. The continuum also shows emphatically, however, how often the global media industry brings about the confluence of global and local culture.

THE PROMISE OF NEW MEDIA

For centuries, the media industry was the province of those with the money and power to own and operate hugely expensive enterprises, such as printing presses, broadcast stations, and film studios. However, the last half of the twentieth century saw explosive growth and development in what were called "new media." At first, new media referred to technologies such as fax machines, photocopiers, camcorders, audio cassettes, and VCRs. These technologies appeared to have democratizing potential; they placed the creation and production of media into the hands of many more people. And all of these media made their mark on social and political life. For example, audio cassettes were used to spread the sermons of the exiled Ayatollah Khomeini in Iran in the 1970s. Eventually, the Ayatollah built a base of support and led the Islamic Revolution. In the 1980s, photocopiers and fax machines helped produce "samizdat," the dissident, underground publications that evaded censorship in Eastern Europe and the Soviet Union (Kind-Kovacs and Labov 2013).

Eventually, however, those once-new media became old, and "new media" has come to refer to digital technologies, such as computers, tablets, and cell phones, and the social media that run on them, such as Facebook, Twitter, WhatsApp, and Snapchat. People increasingly use these media to communicate and collaborate as well as get information and news. In some sense, the media industry has indeed been opened up to many more people, as suggested by the title of a book by media scholar Clay Shirky (2008), *Here Comes Everybody*. Anyone with computer skills can become a publisher, broadcaster, or filmmaker. Some people thus have hopes that new media can erode the power of the media oligopoly and allow alternative voices within and across borders. They hope new media will enlarge the public sphere and offer the opportunity for more people to be involved with political action and civil society in ways that the traditional media industry does not.

And these new, digital media do have characteristics that can impact the media industry. New media are mobile, interactive, discursive, and participatory, very much in contrast to the old-guard media industry. Because of the low cost and ease of posting text, photos, video, music, and other material online, digital media allow for the possibility of multiple, varied voices and views that can reach more people, offer alternative products and approaches, and challenge and question those in power. For example, musicians and artists have been able to bypass the traditional media industry, place their work online, and find an audience. Citizens worldwide can post photos and dispatches from breaking news events via cell phones, computers, and webcams, disrupting traditional news channels. Activists from throughout the world can exchange information online and coordinate plans, demonstrations, and protests.

Some people and events from early in the millennium serve as exemplars for the possibilities and challenges facing new media. For example, in the early 2000s, one of the most read blogs in the world each day was beppegrillo.it, published by the Italian comedian turned political activist Beppe Grillo ("The World's Fifty Most Powerful Blogs" 2008). Offering biting satires of Italian and European politics, Grillo regularly protested against corruption and scandal in his country and the EU. He kept a running list of officials convicted of crimes. He had a "map of power" of the Italian stock exchange. He called the Italian leader, Silvio Berlusconi, "Psychodwarf." Such biting commentary likely would not appear in mainstream Italian media, which must be mindful of the power of politicians. In 2009, Grillo used his social media status and agitated Europe further by forming his own political party in Italy. He continues to question the EU through multiple media channels (Kirchgaessner 2015).

Iran offered another early example of the heightened role of new media. During 2009 presidential elections, protests, often led by young people, surprised and rocked the country. Some of the protests were met with force by the authorities. A twenty-six-year-old protester, Neda Agha-Soltan, was shot through the heart by a sniper. As she lay dying, graphic videos and photos of the young woman were taken by cell phones and posted on Twitter, linked to Facebook, and circulated throughout the world. "Neda" became a potent symbol for Iran's pro-democracy protesters, and her death increased international pressure on Iran. Although state forces held firm, the use of social media by protestors showed governments and people throughout the region the power of these media to organize and coordinate. The 2009 Iranian protests became known as the "Twitter revolution" (Keller 2010).

But perhaps the preeminent example of the disruptive power of new media was to take place soon after in Egypt, in what came to be called the "Facebook Revolution" (Taylor 2011). In late 2010 and early 2011, the people of Tunisia had overthrown their long-time dictator. Egypt, too, was stirring with protests against the thirty-year dictatorship of Hosni Mubarak. A social media campaign helped galvanize events. A Google official, Wael Ghonim, based in Cairo, took a leave of absence from his job. He created a Facebook page dedicated to photographs, videos, and other evidence that documented the horrific abuse endured by Egyptians under Mubarak. Others used the Facebook page and additional social media to organize large rallies in Tahrir Square.

Ghonim was detained by Egyptian authorities but, after worldwide protests, was released. He appeared on stage and rallied huge crowds in the square. One writer noted, "No turbaned ayatollah had stepped forth to summon the crowd. This was not Iran in 1979. A young Google executive, Wael Ghonim, had energized this protest when it might have lost heart" (Ajami

2011). On February 11, 2011, Mubarak stepped down as president of Egypt. Ghonim told an interviewer, "I want to meet Mark Zuckerberg [the founder of Facebook] one day and thank him. This revolution started online. This revolution started on Facebook" (as cited in Coll 2011).

As these events fade and find their place in history, scholars have used them to consider the still-evolving role of new media in social and political life. Malcolm Gladwell and Clay Shirky engaged in a memorable debate on the topic in an issue of *Foreign Affairs*. Gladwell (2010) had started the debate with an essay in *The New Yorker* that argued social media had been overhyped and overrated as a tool for social causes and political action. Gladwell said that the "strong-tie" connections of face-to-face, personal interactions were much more responsible for social action than the "weak-tie" connections of social media. Shirky was mentioned in the essay, and his book, *Here Comes Everybody* (2008), was called "the bible of the social-media movement" (Gladwell 2010). Not long after, Shirky responded with an essay in *Foreign Affairs* in which he argued that media had indeed been used effectively to effect social and political change in the Philippines, South Korea, Moldova, and elsewhere.

The following issue of *Foreign Affairs* then included an exchange of letters between the two (Gladwell and Shirky 2011). Gladwell wrote,

> The lesson here is that just because innovations in communications technology happen does not mean that they matter; or, to put it another way, in order for an innovation to make a real difference, it has to solve a problem that was actually a problem in the first place.

The social revolutions mentioned by Shirky, Gladwell said, would have happened with or without social media. Shirky's responded as follows:

> I would break Gladwell's question of whether social media solved a problem that actually needed solving into two parts: Do social media allow insurgents to adopt new strategies? And have those strategies ever been crucial? Here, the historical record of the last decade is unambiguous: yes, and yes.

Shirky went on: "Digital networks have acted as a massive positive supply shock to the cost and spread of information, to the ease and range of public speech by citizens, and to the speed and scale of group coordination."

Even as this exchange was being published, the uprisings of the Arab Spring occurred, and their "Facebook revolutions" seemed to contradict Gladwell's thesis. Yet, as the promise of the Arab Spring gives way to less optimistic political realities, there is still no consensus on whether new media can succeed in fostering social and political practices in ways that the traditional media industry cannot. Often, the promise of new media is overstated. New media voices can all too easily be silenced. In Egypt, for example, the government owns the internet service provider, Telecom Egypt. During the 2011 revolt, the government simply shut down the internet to prevent organizing through Facebook and other social media. New media can also be silenced in more primitive ways—by threatening people, by arresting them, and by killing them. Not only was Iran's Twitter revolution unsuccessful but also the government then used Twitter, Facebook, and other social media to track down, arrest, and imprison protest leaders.

The vulnerability of new media was shown dramatically in 2013 when Edward Snowden, a computer programmer who worked as a subcontractor for the US National Security Agency (NSA), accessed top-secret, classified documents that showed a large-scale NSA surveillance program. The NSA, Snowden demonstrated, was intercepting, collecting, and analyzing the media use of millions of Americans and others worldwide, including state leaders. The spying included mobile phone records, private online user data from sites such as Google, internet searches, emails, text messages, and more. Snowden leaked the information to reporters, and the resulting news articles awakened international outrage and condemnation that continue today. The revelations surely reveal the vulnerability of new media to political intervention.

New media do offer the possibility of alternative political voices and social realities. Websites, blogs, Twitter, Facebook, and other tools yet to come will continue to provide people with social and economic opportunities as well as challenges to government and authority worldwide. But the stakes are high, and many forces can be brought to bear against those in new media. Access can be blocked. Costs can become prohibitive. Lawsuits can be brought. Arrests can be made. And, more directly, those in new media can be brutally silenced. The Committee to Protect Journalists (2016) has found that online journalists make up an increasing number of the journalists murdered worldwide.

Finally, new media may have reached a point in their social and economic development in which the opposition between new media and the traditional media industry may no longer make sense. New media companies—Google, Facebook, and Apple—are among the largest and most valuable media properties in the world. Like traditional media corporations, they have begun to buy up and consolidate other media, such as Google's purchase of YouTube and Facebook's acquisition of WhatsApp. In 1988, Edward S. Herman and Noam Chomsky castigated the political economy of traditional media for "manufacturing consent." Today, the fundamental, commercial structure of new media, Chomsky says, has changed little. He states (as cited in Russon 2015),

> If you think about what the commercial media are, no matter what, they are businesses. And a business produces something for a market. The producers in this case, almost without exception, are major corporations. The market is other businesses—advertisers. The product that is presented to the market is readers (or viewers), so these are basically major corporations providing audiences to other businesses, and that significantly shapes the nature of the institution.

A GLOBAL CONCERN

The transformation of the media industry into a media oligopoly is more than just a significant economic development in the global marketplace. It has had numerous implications for global economics, politics, and culture. For this reason, understanding the media industry is crucial to the understanding of global studies. No aspect of the globalized world is untouched by the media industry.

The media oligopoly, to be sure, has benefits. Once consolidated, these transnational corporations are global employers, providing work for millions. In addition, these huge media companies excel at producing, marketing, and distributing commercial, escapist entertainment enjoyed throughout the world. In some countries, especially those under authoritarian control, some themes in that entertainment, such as the independence of women or importance of education, can resonate with political or cultural insights.

Yet the media industry deserves global concern and attention. It has helped bring about an era of uneven globalization and global capitalism, promoting uncritical narratives of a market economy with vast inequalities between and within nations. As an oligopoly, with less than a dozen corporations controlling content worldwide, the media industry embodies the excesses of global capitalism, emphasizing shareholder profits over the quality of its products and the responsibilities that have been entrusted to it. And as it blankets the world with its ubiquitous offerings, the global media industry imperils local cultures and traditions. Digital and social media seem to offer variety and the possibility of independent voices and agency, but, often, new media are too easily controlled or, conversely, become large, transnational corporations with the same failings as traditional media. The media industry merits concern and continued scrutiny. And global studies scholars play a pivotal role in this process.

References

Abel, E. 1984. *Many Voices, One World: The MacBride Report*. Paris: UNESCO.

Ajami, F. 2011. "Egypt's Heroes with No Names." *Wall Street Journal*, February 12.

Appadurai, A. 1996. *Modernity at Large: Cultural Dimensions of Globalization*. Minneapolis: University of Minnesota Press.

Bagdikian, B. 2004. *The New Media Monopoly*. Boston: Beacon.

Boyd-Barrett, O., and T. Rantanen. 1998. *The Globalization of News*. London: Sage.

Butterick, K. J. 2015. *Complacency and Collusion: A Critical Introduction to Business and Financial Journalism*. London: Pluto Press.

Campbell, H. 2015. "Imperialism and Anti-Imperialism in Africa." *Monthly Review* 67 (3, July–August).

Chakravartty, P., and Y. Zhao. 2008. "Introduction: Toward a Transcultural Political Economy of Global Communications." In *Global Communications: Toward a Transcultural Political Economy*, edited by P. Chakravartty and Y. Zhao, 1–20. Lanham, MD: Rowman & Littlefield.

Coll, S. 2011. "The Internet: For Better or Worse." *New York Review of Books*, April 7: 20.

Committee to Protect Journalists. 2016. "1186 Journalists Killed Since 1992."

Dionne, E. 2015. "15 Of the Most Popular American Shows Around the World." *Refinery29*, December 6.

Downing, J., A. Mohammadi, and A. Sreberny-Mohammadi. 1995. *Questioning the Media: A Critical Introduction*. 2nd ed. Thousand Oaks, CA: Sage.

Enda, J. 2011. "Retreating from the World." *American Journalism Review*, December/January.

Fahmy, S. 2010. "How Could So Much Produce So Little? Foreign Affairs Reporting in the Wake of 9/11." In *International Media Communication in a Global Age*, edited by G. J. Golan, T. J. Johnson, and W. Wanta, 147–159. New York: Routledge.

Featherstone, M. 2008. "Theories of Consumer Culture." In *Cultural Studies: An Anthology*, edited by M. Ryan, 667–682. Malden, MA: Blackwell.

Frankopan, P. 2016. *The Silk Roads: A New History of the World*. New York: Knopf.

Freedman, D. 2008. *The Politics of Media Policy*. Cambridge, UK: Polity.

Frisch, A. 2009. *Built for Success: The Story of Nike*. Toronto: Creative.

Fuchs, C. 2015. "The MacBride Report in Twenty-First-Century Capitalism, the Age of Social Media and the BRICS Countries." *Javnost—The Public: Journal of the European Institute for Communication and Culture* 22 (3).

Gladwell, M. 2010. "Small Change: Why the Revolution Will Not Be Tweeted." *The New Yorker*, October 4.

Gladwell, M., and C. Shirky. 2011. "From Innovation to Revolution: Do Social Media Make Protests Possible?" *Foreign Affairs*, March/April.

Hennessy, M. 2011. "Budget Cuts Force BBC to Scale Back Foreign Coverage." *Irish Times*, October 8.

Herman, E. S., and N. Chomsky. 1998. *Manufacturing Consent: The Political Economy of the Mass Media*. New York. Pantheon.

Herman, E. S., and R. McChesney. 1997. *The Global Media: The New Missionaries of Global Capitalism*. Washington, DC: Cassell.

Horkheimer, M., and T. W. Adorno. 2002. *Dialectic of Enlightenment: Philosophical Fragments*, translated by Edmund Jephcott. Stanford, CA: Stanford University Press.

Iqani, M. 2015. *Consumption, Media and the Global South: Aspiration Contested*. New York. Palgrave Macmillan.

Kang, L. 2004. *Globalization and Cultural Trends in China*. Honolulu: University of Hawaii Press.

Kapur, M. 2016. "Why India's Annoyed with Cold Play and Beyonce's New Video." CNN, February 5.

Keller, J. 2010. "Evaluating Iran's Twitter Revolution." *The Atlantic*, June 18.

Kind-Kovacs, F., and J. Labov, eds. 2013. *Samizdat, Tamizdat, and Beyond: Transnational Media During and After Socialism*. New York: Berghahn.

Kirchgaessner, S. 2015. "Beppe Grillo Calls for Nationalisation of Italian Banks and Exit from Euro." *The Guardian*, July 23.

Martinson, J. 2015. "BBC Cuts: What Will Have to Go?" *The Guardian*, September 7.

McChesney, R. 2000. *Rich Media, Poor Democracy: Communication Politics in Dubious Times*. New York: New Press.

McChesney, R. 2001. "Global Media, Neoliberalism, and Imperialism." *Monthly Review* 52 (10).

McChesney, R. 2010. "The Media System Goes Global." In *International Communication: A Reader*, edited by D. K. Thussu, 188–220. New York: Routledge.

McChesney, R. 2014. *Blowing the Roof off the Twenty-First Century: Media, Politics, and the Struggle for Post-Capitalist Democracy*. New York: Monthly Review Press.

McPhail, T. 2006. *Global Communication: Theories, Stakeholders, and Trends*. 2nd ed. Malden, MA: Blackwell.

Philo, G. 2004. "The Mass Production of Ignorance: News Content and Audience." In *International News in the Twenty-First Century*, edited by C. Paterson and A. Sreberny, 199–224. Luton, UK: University of Luton Press.

Pieterse, J. N. 2004. *Globalization and Culture: Global Mélange*. Lanham, MD: Rowman & Littlefield.

Russon, M. A. 2015. "Noam Chomsky: Buzzfeed and Vice Are 'Distorting Free Media' with Native Advertising." *International Business Times*, May 26.

Sarikakis, K. 2008. "Regulating the Consciousness Industry in the European Union: Legitimacy, Identity, and the Changing State." In *Global Communications: Toward a Transcultural Political Economy*, edited by P. Chakravartty and Y. Zhao, 95–112. Lanham, MD: Rowman & Littlefield.

Shaban, H. 2014. "What Has Become of Business Journalism?" *The New Yorker*, February 5.

Shirky, C. 2008. *Here Comes Everybody: The Power of Organizing Without Organizations*. New York: Penguin.

Starkman, D. 2013. *The Watchdog That Didn't Bark: The Financial Crisis and the Disappearance of Investigative Journalism*. New York: Columbia University Press.

Steger, M. 2008. *The Rise of the Global Imaginary: Political Ideologies from the French Revolution to the Global War on Terror*. New York: Oxford University Press.

Strasser, J. B., and L. Becklund. 1991. *Swoosh: The Unauthorized Story of Nike and the Men Who Played There*. New York: HarperCollins.

Straubhaar, J., R. LaRose, and L. Davenport. 2016. *Media Now: Understanding Media, Culture, and Technology*. 9th ed. Boston: Cengage.

Su, W. 2016. *China's Encounter with Global Hollywood: Cultural Policy and the Film Industry, 1994–2013*. Lexington: University Press of Kentucky.

Taylor, C. 2011. "Why Not Call It a Facebook Revolution?" CNN, February 24.

"The World's Fifty Most Powerful Blogs." 2008. *The Guardian*, March 9.

Thussu, D. K. 2004. "Media Plenty and the Poverty of News." In *International News in the Twenty-First Century*, edited by C. Paterson and A. Sreberny, 47–61. Luton, UK: University of Luton Press.

Thussu, D. K. 2009. *News as Entertainment: The Rise of Global Infotainment*. London: Sage.

Wadekar, N. 2015. "State of the Media: International Coverage in U.S. Journalism." Annenberg Media Center, September 24.

Wasik, B. 2015. "Welcome to the Age of Digital Imperialism." *New York Times Magazine*, June 4.

"We Are Not an Average Nation: An Exclusive Talk with Jacques Chirac." 1995. *Time*, December 11: 59.

Winseck, D., and R. Pike. 2007. *Communication and Empire: Media, Markets, and Globalization, 1860–1930*. Raleigh, NC: Duke University Press.

FURTHER READING

Castells, M. 2000–2004. *The Information Age: Economy, Society, Culture*. 2nd ed., 3 vols. Malden, MA: Blackwell.

Compaine, B., and D. Gomery. 2000. *Who Owns the Media? Competition and Concentration in the Mass Media*. 3d ed. Mahwah, NJ: Erlbaum.

Gurevitch, M., T. Bennett, J. Curran, and J. Woollacott, eds. 1982. *Culture, Society, and the Media*. London: Methuen.

Hanson, E. C. 2008. *The Information Revolution and World Politics*. Lanham, MD: Rowman & Littlefield.

Hardt, H. 1992. *Critical Communication Studies: Communication, History, and Theory in America*. New York: Routledge.

Hardy, J. 2014. *Critical Political Economy of the Media: An Introduction*. London: Routledge.

McLuhan, M. 1951. *The Mechanical Bride: Folklore of Industrial Man*. New York: Vanguard.

Picard, R. G. 2003. *The Economics and Financing of Media Companies*. New York: Fordham University Press.

Schiller, H. I. 1992. *Mass Communications and American Empire*. 2nd ed. Boulder, CO: Westview.

Taylor, P. M. 1997. *Global Communications, International Affairs and the Media Since 1945*. London: Routledge.

CHAPTER 35

....

GLOBAL SPORT

....

RICHARD GIULIANOTTI

WORLD sport often appears as one of the most powerful illustrations of globalization in action. Indicatively, global sport mega-events such as the Olympic Games or football's World Cup finals attract worldwide television audiences, involve at least the initial participation of athletes from more than 200 nations, feature sponsorship and advertising by the largest transnational corporations (TNCs), draw world leaders and celebrities into attendance, and produce epic moments of sporting action that live long in the global memory.

In this chapter, I examine the making of global sport from a critical social scientific perspective that is primarily rooted in the fields of sociology and global studies, while also being substantially influenced by allied disciplines such as anthropology, history, human geography, and political science. Following Robertson (1992), globalization is understood here as being defined by growing levels of global "compression" or connectivity and by greater degrees of global consciousness. A complex transnational process, globalization also harbors interrelated political, economic, social, and cultural dimensions.

Modern sports usually emerged through the adaptation, codification, and wider diffusion of earlier physical games or disciplines. A key period in the social development and spread of sports was from the 1870s through the 1920s when, according to Robertson (1992), wider globalization was experiencing its very rapid "take-off" phase. At this time, leading international sport federations such as the International Olympic Committee (IOC) and the Fédération Internationale de Football Association (FIFA; world football's governing body) were founded, while mega-events such as the Olympics and football's World Cup finals were either started or began to be planned (Guttmann 1994). Longer term, as discussed later, the political economies of sports have been marked by extensive processes of global integration, commercialization, and professionalization and, in turn, by the sharpening of transnational inequalities between nations and regions. Latterly, various "lifestyle" or "extreme" sports—such as surfing, snowboarding, and mountain biking—have emerged, often evading or rejecting the institutionalized, commercialized, and competitive ethos of established sports. Yet, even here, these postmodern pastimes have undergone "sportification"; for example, snowboarding was taken on by the mainstream international governing body, the Fédération Internationale de Ski (FIS), and incorporated within Olympic competition (Humphreys 2003).

In the following sections, I examine four critical areas of social scientific research and debate on global sport, relating to political economic issues, sport mega-events, the sport for development and peace (SDP) sector, and sociocultural issues of identity and belonging. The focus here is on elite-level professional global sport and how it is structured, interpreted, and experienced by diverse organizations and social groups, including athletes, officials, sponsors, and fans. While highlighting the major social processes within global sport, this discussion is also embedded in classic debates in social and global theory, notably in the tensions between political–economic structural forces and everyday forms of sociocultural agency.

POLITICAL ECONOMY OF GLOBAL SPORT

The political economy of global sport has grown very substantially in recent years and has received significant attention from social scientists. A particular focus has been on contemporary processes of commercialization or commodification and on the impacts of neoliberal social and economic policies on different sporting domains.[1] Evidence of these developments is provided by the financial scale of the world's largest sport clubs—such as Real Madrid and Manchester United in football, the Dallas Cowboys in American football, and the New York Yankees in baseball—which in 2014 were each valued at more than \$3 billion.[2]

To elaborate, commodification processes in global sport have been marked by the following interrelated developments:

- The growing economic value of top clubs, leagues, tournaments, and federations
- The huge growth in off-the-field earnings, notably from television contracts and sponsorship deals with global TNCs
- The greater transnational broadcasting of elite sport events and leagues such as the National Football League (NFL; American football), Major League Baseball (North American baseball league), the English Premier League (football), and the European Champions League (Europe's premier football club tournament)
- The greater international recruitment and movement of elite-level athletes in sports such as football, cricket, baseball, and basketball, as facilitated in part by the international liberalization of sport labor markets
- The deregulation of media markets, enabling TNCs to establish pay-television networks such as Sky/Fox television that broadcast throughout the world
- The cultivation of global supporters, audiences, and "consumers" by top athletes, sport clubs, and leagues

Taken together, these processes have engendered a "hypercommodification" of elite-level sport in the Global North from the late 1980s onward (Walsh and Giulianotti 2007). The crucial driving force here has been provided by the rise of transnational media corporations, which have themselves been developed largely on the back of sport-focused programming through subscription-based satellite and cable and then digital television platforms. For example, since the late 1980s, News Corporation, controlled by Rupert Murdoch and with subsidiaries based throughout the world, has acquired the rights for live broadcasting of elite-level UK football, American football and baseball, the Australian rugby league, and many other sports (Boyle and Haynes 2004; Rowe 2011). The television-based revenues of these leagues have undergone exponential growth: Most spectacularly, English Premier League football saw UK television contracts for live match coverage increase from an annual £11 million in 1988 to approximately £165 million in 1997 and subsequently to approximately £1.7 billion in 2016. In turn, this league has come to be globalized through television coverage in more than 210 nations (Millward 2011).

The world's highest-value sport clubs or "franchises" in football, baseball, American football, basketball, and other sports may also be understood as "TNCs." Alongside their multi-billion-dollar valuation, clubs such as Real Madrid and the New York Yankees have a global strategy for branding, engaging audiences (or consumers), media reach, and (particularly in football) labor recruitment (Giulianotti and Robertson 2009). Part of this global political economic expansion includes the staging of international games in "new market" territories. For example, to develop their global fan and consumer bases, the NFL plays games in London and Europe's leading football teams undertake preseason tours in North America, Asia, Australasia, and southern Africa. Major League Baseball is similarly expansionist due in part to the understanding that the sport is beyond its peak in popularity in North America (Klein 2006).

Arguably, elite-level global sports are moving toward instituting their own versions of Wallerstein's (1974, 2002) "world-system." This is evidenced, for example, in the structuring of complex and integrated transnational labor markets for the development, recruitment, or transfer of athletes. To apply Wallerstein world-system theory, these sport labor markets tend to be differentiated into three categories:

- First, in the largest "core" nations and regions, such as North America and Western Europe, we find major clubs and leagues, such as in the English, Spanish, Italian, and German football leagues, or North America's baseball and basketball leagues. These leagues and their teams recruit the best athletes from other core nations, as well as from peripheral and semi-peripheral regions.
- Second, there are "semi-peripheral" nations and regions that in recent times have included post-communist transition societies or the so-called BRICS (Brazil, Russia, India, China, and South Africa); these tend to recruit athletes from other semi-peripheral as well as peripheral labor markets—for example, Russian football clubs recruiting Brazilian players.
- Third, there are "peripheral" nations and regions, such as in sub-Saharan Africa, which have little development and weak governments. In sports such as football and athletics, the more developed peripheral nations—such as Nigeria and Ghana—have coaching and development systems that serve the recruitment interests of clubs and federations in core and semi-peripheral nations and regions.

Athlete development academies play an important role in institutionalizing these asymmetrical transnational labor markets. For example, in baseball, many North American clubs run academies in weaker societies such as the Dominican Republic and Puerto Rico, developing young athletes, the best of whom are incorporated cheaply into the major leagues, whereas inferior players are left to the local leagues or, with little alternative education or training, to find work somehow outside of sport. There are concerns that some vulnerable young athletes, such as African football players in Europe or exiled Cuban baseball players in North America, undergo forms of trafficking or other illegal detainment when being moved from peripheral to core sport labor markets (Esson 2015).

During approximately the past decade, in the sport context, Wallerstein's model has been complicated by the rise of new economic and political powers, such as Qatar, Russia, and China in football, India in cricket, and Russia in ice hockey. Pointing to the potential rise of "post-Westernization" global processes, these nations' sport development strategies have been varied and have included individual or mixed cases of creating their own lucrative competitive leagues, attracting the world's leading athletes, building strong influence in the governance of transnational sport, buying into the ownership and control of world-leading sport teams (notably in football), and staging the largest mega-events (Brannagan and Giulianotti 2015; Rumford 2007).

A further critical development in the political economy of global sport concerns the rise and influence of TNCs. In addition to media TNCs, sport has been the main field for the rapid growth of merchandise firms such as Nike, adidas, and Reebok since the 1970s, as registered by their transnational chains of production and consumption and as assisted through strong endorsement deals with leading athletes, sport teams, and tournaments. The endorsement deals between Michael Jordan and Nike in the 1990s set the mold (LaFeber 2002). Strategies of "corporate nationalism" have also been deployed by TNCs within sport—for example, world-leading national teams and organizations such as New Zealand rugby and Brazilian football teams are heavily wrapped in the marketing and branding of their main sponsors, including merchandise corporations such as adidas and Nike (Scherer and Jackson 2010).

As the interface between global sport, lifestyle, and consumer culture has become more complex, TNCs have driven the commodification of action or alternative sports such as skateboarding, surfing, and snowboarding. For example, the subscription television station ESPN created the "X Games," which showcases many of these new activities and is sponsored by diverse TNCs (Thorpe and Wheaton 2014: 344). Meanwhile, surfing and wider beach subcultures have been "recuperated" into global consumer culture through the product design and brand marketing strategies of apparel TNCs such as Billabong, Hollister, Nike, Quiksilver, and Rip Curl. Close association with these sports enables global corporations to attach the whiff of countercultural rebelliousness to their products (Laderman 2014).

One important theorization of global commodification processes that may be applied to sport is advanced by American sociologist George Ritzer (2004) through the concept of "grobalization." For Ritzer, grobalization is driven by three "grobal" forces: capitalism, via expansionist major corporations; Americanization, via US corporations and cultural products; and "McDonaldization," through transferring the highly efficient, predictable, and successful organizational principles of the McDonald's fast-food chain into other fields of social life. A powerful force of global homogenization, grobalization, in Ritzer's view, threatens to obliterate local cultural agency, creativity, and diversity, including in sport (Andrews and Ritzer 2007). We may identify grobal forces as being particularly evident at major elite sport events: These occasions are rationally organized to allow for suitable advertising breaks, television coverage is itself full of TNC marketing, and "American-style" entertainment of crowds within the stadium is also prevalent.

One limitation of Ritzer's (2004) thesis when applied to sport concerns his argument on the importance of American commercial influences. Instead, TNCs from throughout the world—adidas from Germany, Gazprom from Russia, Samsung from Korea, Sony from Japan, and so on—act as major sponsors for global sport events and federations, whereas North American sports are often eclipsed by other sporting disciplines, most obviously football, but also cricket and rugby, which appeal to many nations with large population bases.

The negative aspects of these global commercial processes have been perceived increases in the corruption of sport in two particular ways. First, the fixing of sport results or periods of play in sport competitions has been associated with criminal gambling syndicates that operate at a transnational level. For example, international cricket has faced several fixing scandals involving South Asian gangs and leading international teams and players. In football, match-fixing syndicates based in Southeast Asia have operated throughout Europe, Africa, and Latin America (Hill 2013). Second, international criminal investigations have been initiated and allegations of systematic corruption have been leveled at global sport federations (Jennings 2011). For example, following investigations led by US authorities, many leading FIFA officials have pleaded guilty to corrupt activities particularly in the distribution of television contracts; further investigations have centered on alleged corrupt activities involving top FIFA officials with regard to elections within football governance, and in the allocation of major tournaments to specific nations (Blake and Calvert 2015; Jennings 2011). At the International Association of Athletics Federations, a major corruption scandal has centered primarily on how leading officials and their associates conspired to suppress the positive doping results of athletes.[3]

In broad terms, the hypercommodification of elite-level global sport may be subject to a range of social, political, and normative criticisms, including the following: the fact that the emphasis on profit over play serves to intensify divisions between clubs and communities or between athletes and fans; sport clubs that are owned and controlled by wealthy individuals tend to have weaker relationships with their fan communities; some dedicated fans may have been "squeezed out" of attending elite sport events by the increasing cost of ticket prices (Dubal 2010); athletes from developing countries are apt to be exploited (Marcano and Fidler 2003); the "free market" in sport, as elsewhere, is inherently volatile, leading to a greater potential for sport teams and businesses to go bankrupt; and as financial gulfs have intensified between clubs and nations in many sports, competitive divisions have also increased.

Note that many sport clubs or leagues, particularly at the national level, are in positions to contain or control some of these negative impacts. For example, most German football clubs and English cricket clubs are majority or fully owned by their member supporters rather than privately controlled by individual owners and investors. In addition, North American sports leagues operate player draft systems and some revenue-sharing measures across teams, which are intended in part to facilitate a stronger competitive balance within these competitions. Moreover, there are regular outbreaks of protest, opposition, and criticism within the public sphere that are directed against the commercialization of sport: Fan groups stage protests against high ticket prices, journalists lambast the sale of television rights for sport events to pay-television networks, and local communities oppose decisions by local authorities to use scarce public funds for stadium-building projects rather than provision of key services such as schools and hospitals. Yet, in broad terms, these counterbalancing structures, measures, and movements are swimming against rapid neoliberal currents, which otherwise advance the commodification of elite-level sport.

Global Sport Mega-Events

For many cities and nations, the staging of sport mega-events, such as the Olympic Games or the "World Cup" finals in various sports, is viewed as an important opportunity for advancing their political–economic (including their commercial) transformation, as well as for pursuing their sociocultural interests on the global stage. Arguably, the study of these mega-events provides one important arena for the transdisciplinary field of global studies to contribute to our understanding of sport's centrality to wider transnational processes.

For social scientists, five key research themes are of particular relevance when examining global sport events. First, there is the issue of how the staging of these mega-events contributes to the making of "global cities." Sassen's (1991, 2002) path-breaking work on global cities represents an excellent example of global studies research. Sassen examined how London, New York, Tokyo, and other metropolises are at the worldwide epicenter of cross-border networked economies—for example, in finance, telecommunications, and new multimedia industries. In a broader context, global cities are also associated with different cultural attractions, multiethnic complexity, gentrification of old industrial areas, and excellent international travel hubs. Hosting sport mega-events may assist cities to maintain or to pursue "global" status, particularly through the long-term legacies of these events (Preuss 2004: 93–94). Although the real picture is far more complex and multifaceted, the Barcelona 1992 Olympics are widely presented as the best example of how such an event may catapult a significant city to global status. In more established global cities, staging such events may serve other purposes. For example, the London 2012 Olympics were used in part to develop post-event technology and media business centers and to intensify the gentrification of local housing estates (Cohen 2013; Giulianotti et al. 2015).

Second, strong forms of civic branding, nation branding, and place marketing are associated with the hosting of sport mega-events. Such branding is intrinsic to how cities and nations endeavor to market their new industries, images, and identities before global audiences of prospective investors, business partners, tourists, and other consumers (Herstein and Berger 2013; Knott, Fyall, and Jones 2013; Smith 2005). For the Olympics, the opening ceremonies and the specific event of the marathon race (which takes place through the city's main avenues and many landmarks) are particularly important for developing civic and national narratives. Event hosts have to be careful to ensure there is no mismatch between top-down branding by city authorities and the bottom-up experiences of visiting media, spectators, and other tourists. At the Beijing 2008 Olympics, for example, official city branding projected themes of cultural history and harmony, the international megalopolis, and a liveable (environmentally friendly) city; however, many visitors failed to understand these themes, with environmental associations having notably little impact (Zhang and Zhao 2009).

Third, global mega-events are utilized by host cities and nations to pursue different kinds of soft power on the transnational stage. The concept of "soft power" was forwarded by the American political scientist Joseph Nye (2004) to refer to "the ability to get what you want through attraction rather than coercion or payment." Soft power thus contrasts with hard power (e.g., military intervention or direct economic influence), and it reflects the more subtle, contemporary ways in which international influence is secured through the arts, education, sport, tourism, media, and other cultural spheres. In reality, hard and soft power are often interconnected, notably as North American or European nations exercise their military and economic powers globally alongside their seductive appeal through major sports events, festivals, galleries, theater, popular music, film, media, and wider tourism.

The staging of sport mega-events may be understood as playing a key role within the soft power strategies of different nations (Houlihan and Grix 2014). Qatar's successful bid to host the 2022 World Cup finals in football has been closely associated with its wider "sport diplomacy" strategy, which also features the staging of many other sports events, investment in international sport teams (e.g., Paris Saint-Germain and Barcelona), and development of international sport television platforms.[4] In the case of the Olympics, the London 2012 event helped the United Kingdom rank as the world's number one nation for soft power by *Monocle*, a leading high-end consumption magazine, in that year. The interconnections of hard and soft power are evidenced in the very heavy spending of nations that stage sport mega-events: Relatively extreme examples include the estimated $51billion spent on the 2014 Winter Olympics in Sochi and the anticipated $200 billion to be spent by World Cup 2022 host Qatar, including the development of a new city (Müller 2015; Smart 2015: 423).[5]

The soft power gained from hosting these events needs to be located within the nation's broader international context and standing. Certainly, the Beijing Games helped embed China more fully within international society. Yet, for Nye (2008), China still fails to match key Western indices of soft power, such as autonomous civil society organizations, solid liberal democracy, and institutionalization of human rights (see also Zhongying 2008).

Staging these events can be double-edged for host nations because the global spotlight may turn into a glare as the world's media investigate issues that are discrediting or damaging. In such cases, the gain in soft power is counterbalanced by forms of "soft disempowerment" within the global context (Giulianotti 2015). For example, after being chosen to host the World Cup finals, Qatar came under strong international political, public, and media pressure over allegations of systematic corruption in winning the vote, human rights abuses suffered by migrant workers, and the wider infringement of the liberties of women and LGBT people (Blake and Calvert 2015; Brannagan and Giulianotti 2015).

A fourth issue for sport mega-event research relates to security issues. Drawing together critical sociology, criminology, and human geography, this field of inquiry examines contemporary forms and systems of surveillance, security, and social control in and around sport mega-events in particular (Bennett and Haggerty 2012; Giulianotti and Klauser 2010; *Urban Studies* 2011). Indicatively, spending on security at sport mega-events has grown exponentially since the September 11, 2001 (9/11), terrorist attacks in the United States. For the summer Olympics pre-9/11, security budgets were estimated at $66.3 million (Barcelona, 1992), $108.2 million (Atlanta, 1996), and $180 million (Sydney, 2000). After 9/11, spending mushroomed to $1.5 billion (Athens, 2004), $6.5 billion (Beijing, 2008), and an estimated $2 billion (London, 2012) (Houlihan and Giulianotti 2012).

These events witness the extensive development of transnational professional networks and partnerships, notably as local security personnel are required to engage with the substantial security entourages that accompany the competing national sports teams and many global VIPs (e.g., heads of state and celebrities) in attendance (Armstrong, Giulianotti, and Hobbs 2016). Other partnerships arise between host cities and nations and the global security industry. For example, the Beijing Olympics saw large trade between China and overseas security corporations such as GE, Honeywell, IBM, LG, Panasonic, and Siemens.[6] In turn, these events possess a potent "security legacy," as new "security assemblages" and technologies are bequeathed for direction toward the surveillance and social control of local populations (Giulianotti and Klauser 2010; Haggerty and Ericson 2000). For example, approximately 2,000 closed-circuit television (CCTV) cameras were installed in Delhi in the run-up to the 2010 Commonwealth Games; in Germany, new public CCTV systems, including cameras with facial-recognition software, were introduced for the 2006 World Cup finals; and in China, CCTV systems, two-wheeled electric scooters, and event tickets containing RFID (radio-frequency identification) chips were among the new technologies employed for the 2008 Olympics.

Fifth, social research examines the politics of resistance and opposition that surround sport mega-events (Lenskyj 2008). A growing number of cities and nations in liberal democracies have had to drop their bids to host sport mega-events due to public concerns and opposition regarding a variety of issues, including very high staging costs, environmental impacts, security risks, and potential legal or policing restrictions on freedom of speech or movement. For the Olympic Games, recent examples of withdrawn planned bids include those by Boston, Hamburg, Munich, and Oslo. One consequence is that in the long term, the hosting of sport mega-events may become increasingly associated with the pursuit of international legitimation and soft power by non-democratic and authoritarian regimes.

Sport for Development and Peace

One of the fastest growing fields of activity within global sport has centered on the "sport for development and peace" (SDP) movement, which has in turn attracted substantial interest from academic researchers (Coalter 2013; Darnell 2012; Kidd 2008; Levermore and Beacom 2009; Schulenkorf and Adair 2014; Spaaij, Magee, and Jeanes 2014). SDP refers to many diverse organizations, social programs, and campaigns that utilize sport as a site or tool of intervention in order to promote different kinds of social development and peace-making throughout the world. Giulianotti (2011) has argued that the SDP sector encompasses

- private corporations and individual donors who support SDP work (e.g., Barclay's Bank, Coca-Cola, and Nike);
- national governments and their various ministries (e.g., education, international development, and sport), development agencies, and international embassies or missions;
- intergovernmental organizations, such as the United Nations (which, until 2017, had its own SDP office, the UNOSDP) and Commonwealth Secretariat;
- non-governmental organizations (NGOs) that coordinate or implement SDP programs at international, national, and local levels (e.g., Right to Play, Laureus, Peace and Sport, and International Platform on Sport and Development);
- sport governing bodies, such as the IOC, FIFA, and the Fédération Internationale de Volleyball (FIVB), which support development work; and

- campaigning NGOs and social movements which focus on SDP-related issues e.g. Amnesty International, Play the Game, War on Want.

To this, we might add celebrities in sport and other fields, who fund, endorse, and work on SDP projects (Wilson, van Luijk, and Boit 2015). Most SDP work is undertaken in developing countries by NGOs through projects targeted at young people, with the aim of improving health education, building peace in divided societies, upskilling participants for employment or training, and empowering girls and young women. Private corporations and donors, intergovernmental organizations, and sport governing bodies typically provide different resource and logistical support for these initiatives.

Social scientific research on international SDP encompasses in particular the disciplines of sociology, anthropology, management studies, social policy, social psychology, health sciences, and international relations.[7] Arguably, it is also a major research arena in which global studies has great potential to make a powerful contribution in the future. For social scientists in the SDP domain, a significant research driver has been the greater expectation that they should work closely with non-academic partners such as international governmental organizations and NGOs in order to investigate and help alleviate major social problems.

Two different, ideal–typical approaches tend to underpin actual SDP research; most actual studies of SDP usually combine both aspects to varying degrees.[8] The first, more positivist or pragmatic approach—particularly useful in health-focused studies—measures or otherwise assesses the specific impacts of SDP projects on diverse user groups. For example, Maro, Roberts, and Sorensen (2009) investigated the effectiveness of peer sport coaches in Tanzania for delivering HIV/AIDS education to young people.

The second, more interpretive or critical approach underpins a range of social scientific studies and examines how SDP activities are constructed with reference to cultural context and power relations. Anthropological studies, particularly in African communities, have highlighted the need for international SDP agencies to understand the complexities of local culture and politics when implementing projects (Armstrong 2007; Collison 2016; Hognestad and Tolleson 2004). In Liberia, for example, SDP activities among young people may inadvertently serve to reaffirm the generational divisions between powerful older generations watching these projects and the weaker younger people who are required to participate (Collison 2016).

Some critical sociological perspectives locate the SDP sector within the wider context of neoliberal economic and social policies through which Global North governments, institutions, and corporations exercise influence across much of the Global South (Coakley 2011; Darnell 2012; Hartmann and Kwauk 2011). These approaches critique some SDP projects for their individualistic focus (e.g., in promoting self-reliant "life skills") rather than challenging the power relations and structures that serve to reproduce deep social divisions and inequalities within these societies. Other perspectives have located the SDP sector within a wider, neoliberal "global civil society," wherein "tamed" NGOs compete among themselves to gain funding for projects that fit the interests and ideologies of neoliberal funding sources, such as intergovernmental organizations, Western governments, and large corporations (Giulianotti 2011; Kaldor 2003).

Arguably the strongest critical approach involves broadening the definitional range of SDP to encompass institutional and social actors that are normally excluded from discussions of the sector but that are nevertheless committed to using sport to advance particular social benefits (Giulianotti and Armstrong 2014). These actors include campaign groups and new social movements, which are focused on diverse social justice issues and arguments for the structural transformation of relations between the Global North and Global South. These progressive political positions chime with the critical stances of many social scientists, while leading campaign groups adopt critical and often oppositional relationships toward other types of SDP stakeholder. Activities here include campaigns against corruption in sport governing bodies, against sport merchandise companies for sweatshop factory conditions in developing countries, and against civil and human rights abuses by nations or corporations that are staging or sponsoring sport mega-events (Brownell 2012; Lenskyj 2008; Timms 2012).

SOCIOCULTURAL IDENTITY, CREATIVITY, AND BELONGING

As noted previously, the SDP sector, sport mega-events, and commercialization processes have all been marked at times by critical responses from different social groups and movements at everyday, grassroots level. Such expressions reflect the broader ways in which individuals and social groups engage creatively and critically, rather than passively, with global sport on a day-to-day basis. Social scientific approaches that recognize these forms of human agency are associated with micro-sociological or anthropological "bottom-up" research and draw particularly on qualitative and interpretive methods in order to investigate these social processes. Sport thus appears as a dynamic sociocultural field in which we may examine how globalization processes are constantly made and remade at the everyday level, and how it contributes to the shaping of new forms of belonging and identity at local, national, and transnational levels.

We may examine these processes within sport through the use of various concepts, such as creolization and hybridization, that are drawn from globalization theories (Appadurai 1995; Burke 2009; Hannerz 1992; Pieterse 2007). Creolization theory helps explain how global sports have been creatively adapted by different societies, including weak or peripheral ones, and often with highly effective results in international competition. For example, in cricket, Afro-Caribbean players from the West Indies developed exceptional skills in aggressive batting and ultra-fast bowling to dominate the game in the 1970s and 1980s. More radical cases of creolization have occurred when particular social groups transform existing games or sports in order to create their own sports. For example, the American sport of baseball might be viewed as a creolized version of the game of "rounders"; more recently, snowboarding may be viewed as a subculturally inspired, creolized variation on established snow sports. Hybridization theory is particularly useful in explaining how different societies with significant migrant communities create and re-create their identities through sport and other forms of physical culture. Archetti (1998) explored how hybridized forms of national, masculine identity were constructed in Argentina through football, polo, and tango dancing, particularly at times when the nation was being shaped by substantial migrant influences from Italy and Spain.

To return to our opening definition, we may see the crucial roles played by forms of global connectivity and consciousness in the making of transnational sport identities and cultures at the everyday level. The media (ranging from mass media to social media such as Facebook and Twitter) and travel and migration are two critical drivers of these processes. One consequence is the "disembedding" or "deterritorializing" of people; in other words, their cultural identities, practices, and forms of belonging are less tied to specific geographical locations and more fluid across physical spaces.

Sport fans provide some powerful illustrations of these processes. Two examples, often interrelated, are suggested. First, migration-based fans may continue to identify with their "home" club or nation despite having moved long distances away. For example, Scottish, Turkish, North African, and other migrant groups may continue to support their football teams from afar in North America or Europe (Giulianotti and Robertson 2007; McManus 2015). Similar practices occur with the large Irish diaspora in North America that follows Gaelic games such as Gaelic football and hurling. Satellite transnational television systems provide the most obvious ways in which these links with the "home" sport cultures are maintained. Looking beyond sport fans, we may consider also the case of migrant athletes: For example, Besnier (2012) has examined the complex experiences and identity dilemmas faced by rugby players from the Pacific Islands who seek escape, fun, and fortune by moving to Japan.

Second, media-based fans rely on the national or transnational mass media in order to inspire and sustain their identifications with specific sport teams. For example, many thousands of Norwegian football fans identify strongly with different English football clubs; this identification has been largely inspired by live Norwegian television coverage of English fixtures since the 1960s (Hognestad 2009). Social media contributes increasingly in this way as well, for example, through Facebook pages or Twitter feeds that enable virtual transnational communities of fans to exchange news and comments on their favored sport teams and players.

"Networked media sport" provides a specific field of inquiry for sport-focused researchers (David and Millward 2015; Hutchins and Rowe 2012). A key argument here centers on a perceived shift in the type and nature of communication that underpins media sport: That is, we have moved from a "first media age," defined by radio and television, to a "second media age," marked by broadband and wireless internet usage, mobile communications, and social media. Sociological theorizations of these processes tend to draw substantially on Castells's (2001) notion of the transnational "network society" and how power is closely associated with information and knowledge. In this context, we might highlight the scope for the transnational empowerment of sport media audiences. On the one hand, sport fans use these new media to access diverse sports media content, to express opinions, and to form new virtual communities that are largely beyond the immediate control of conventional mass media such as newspapers or television stations. On the other hand, further empowerment is highlighted by instances of transnational "sharing" or "piracy," for example, as internet broadband users utilize "live-streaming" techniques to view sport events for free, thereby avoiding making the intended subscription-based payments.

A final point to make here concerns the different forms of sociocultural identity and belonging that follow from these connectivity-focused processes of migration and mediatization. The concept of cosmopolitanism is particularly useful when it is deployed sociologically to refer to relatively high levels of interaction with other societies and cultures.

The term might be used here in two main senses. First, at the everyday level, sport may facilitate high levels of "banal cosmopolitanism," wherein these other societies and cultures are encountered in increasingly routine ways (Beck 2006). For example, increasingly more foreign athletes will travel abroad to join new sport leagues; more coaches encounter new ideas and methods from different nations, which are then brought into coaching at the everyday level; more international sport events and competitions take place; and television offers increasing coverage of international sport leagues. The net effect is that sport athletes and their audiences become banal cosmopolitans through such routine encounters.

Second, there are important issues relating to cosmopolitanism and different layers of identification and belonging. In summary, sport fans may sustain strong forms of local and national attachments and identifications alongside concerns for other social groups and cultures. One illustration is provided by "cosmopolitan patriots" who, to adjust Appiah's (2006) initial phrase, harbor appreciations of other sport teams along with support for their national sides. Other expressions of such cosmopolitanism involve more direct forms of identification with and support for different international athletes and teams. Overall, these expressions of cosmopolitanism point to the complex ways in which transnational identities and forms of belonging are constructed within and through sport, notably with hybridized or creolized outcomes, in the shape of local, national, and transnational identifications.

CONCLUSION

I have sought to demonstrate that sport provides one of the most vibrant, complex, and significant cultural fields for global studies scholars and other social scientists who are seeking to understand and explain contemporary transnational processes. Underpinned by intensified levels of global connectivity and consciousness, contemporary elite-level sport is marked by the increasing political–economic influences of commercialization and neoliberalization but also by the critical creativity, improvisation, and identity projects of social actors, groups, and movements at the everyday level. The interplay of these structure–agency tensions is highlighted in part within the important substantive research areas of sport mega-events and the "sport for development and peace" sector.

Academic research into global sport will continue to build strongly on these theoretical and substantive areas. Looking ahead, this work may develop in three interrelated ways that reflect the potential for closer collaboration between sociologists and other disciplines. First, through a deeper connection with philosophy and political science, a fuller interdisciplinary study of global governance in sport may follow, which pays adequate critical heed to founding principles of democracy, transparency, and social justice, as marked by the clear participation of relatively marginalized sporting communities.

Second, closer ties to political economy and human geography may help facilitate a stronger critical investigation and public debate on the commercialization of sport, such as on the distribution and valuation of scarce resources (e.g., sport event tickets) or the direction of public funds into pursuing the hosting of sport mega-events or the provision of sport-related facilities.

Third, deeper engagement with the disciplines of social anthropology and education may help strengthen our appreciation of the ways in which global sport is experienced, rejected, adapted, and transformed by individuals and social groups. The SDP sector is an ideal location for pursuing these rich, in-depth, cross-cultural studies, given that, as a rapidly growing field of activity in the Global South, there is a particular need to understand how social groups engage critically with different sporting experiences and their potential social benefits.

These three strands of future research are interrelated and should direct us toward specific lines of critical inquiry. By definition, the strongest organizations—be they corporations, sport governing bodies, governmental agencies, or other entities—are well able to pursue the realization of their own particular visions of global sport and other social fields. Yet, the most compelling and, indeed, defining qualities of global sport are made at the everyday level by social actors in how they play and interplay, create and re-create, or identify and differentiate themselves within sporting contexts. Global studies research would be best aimed at nurturing these qualities within global sport, to protect and advance the scope for improvisation, for the creative play of "grass-roots globalization."

NOTES

1. See, for example, Andrews and Silk (2012), Dubal (2010), Giulianotti and Robertson (2009), and LaFeber (2002).
2. See https://www.forbes.com/pictures/mli45fdlkd/1-real-madrid.
3. *The Guardian*, January 7, 2016.
4. *The Guardian*, November 14, 2015.
5. See also *Financial Times*, May 28, 2015.
6. *Bloomberg Business Week*, August 6, 2008.
7. For such interdisciplinary mixtures, see Gilbert and Bennett (2012), Levermore and Beacom (2009), and Schulenkorf and Adair (2014).
8. See, for example, Coalter (2007, 2013).

REFERENCES

Andrews, D., and G. Ritzer. 2007. "The Grobal in the Sporting Global." *Global Networks* 7 (2): 135–153.

Andrews, D., and M. Silk, eds. 2012. *Sport and Neoliberalism*. Philadelphia, PA: Temple University Press.

Appadurai, A. 1995. "Playing with Modernity: The Decolonization of Indian Cricket." In *Consuming Modernity*, edited by C. A. Breckenridge, 23–48. Minneapolis: University of Minnesota Press.

Appiah, K. A. 2006. *Cosmopolitanism: Ethics in a World of Strangers*. London: Lane.

Archetti, E. 1998. *Masculinities*. Oxford, UK: Berg.

Armstrong, G. 2007. "The Global Footballer and the Local War-Zone: George Weah and Transnational Networks in Liberia, West Africa." *Global Networks* 7 (2): 230–247.

Armstrong, G., R. Giulianotti, and D. Hobbs. 2016. *Policing the London 2012 Olympics*. London: Routledge.

Beck, U. 2006. *Cosmopolitan Vision*. Cambridge, UK: Polity.

Bennett, C. J., and K. D. Haggerty, eds. 2012. *Security Games*. London: Routledge.

Besnier, N. 2012. "The Athlete's Body and the Global Condition: Tongan Rugby Players in Japan." *American Ethnologist* 39: 491–510.

Blake, H., and J. Calvert. 2015. *The Ugly Game: The Qatari Plot to Buy the World Cup*. London: Simon & Schuster.

Boyle, R., and R. Haynes. 2004. *Football in the New Media Age*. London: Routledge.

Brannagan, P., and R. Giulianotti. 2015. "Soft Power and Soft Disempowerment: Qatar, Global Sport and Football's 2022 World Cup Finals." *Leisure Studies* 34 (6): 703–719.

Brownell, S. 2012. "Human Rights and the Beijing Olympics." *British Journal of Sociology* 63 (2): 306–327.

Burke, P. 2009. *Cultural Hybridity*. Cambridge, UK: Polity.

Castells, M. 2001. *The Internet Galaxy*. Oxford, UK: Oxford University Press.

Coakley, J. 2011. "Youth Sports: What Counts as Positive Development?" *Journal of Sport and Social Issues* 35 (3): 306–324.

Coalter, F. 2007. *A Wider Social Role for Sport*. London: Routledge.

Coalter, F. 2013. *Sport for Development*. London: Routledge.

Cohen, P. 2013. *On the Wrong Side of the Track? East London and the Post Olympics*. London: Lawrence & Wishart.

Collison, H. 2016. *Youth and Sport for Development: The Seduction of Football in Liberia*. Basingstoke, UK: Palgrave.

Darnell, S. 2012. *Sport for Development and Peace*. London: Bloomsbury.

David, M., and P. Millward. 2015. "Sport and New Media." In *Routledge Handbook of the Sociology of Sport*, edited by R. Giulianotti, 388–397. Abingdon, UK: Routledge.

Dubal, S. 2010. "The Neoliberalization of Football." *International Review for the Sociology of Sport* 45 (2): 123–146.

Esson, J. 2015. "Better off at Home? Rethinking Responses to Trafficked West African Footballers in Europe." *Journal of Ethnic and Migration Studies* 41 (3): 512–530.

Gilbert, K., and W. Bennett, eds. 2012. *Sport for Peace and Development*. Champaign, IL: Common Ground.

Giulianotti, R. 2011. "The Sport, Development and Peace Sector: A Model of Four Social Policy Domains." *Journal of Social Policy* 40 (4): 757–776.

Giulianotti, R. 2015. "The Beijing 2008 Olympics: Examining the Interrelations of China, Globalization and Soft Power." *European Review* 23 (2): 286–296.

Giulianotti, R., and G. Armstrong. 2014. "The Sport for Development and Peace Sector: A Critical Sociological Analysis." In *Global Sport-for-Development*, edited by N. Schulenkorf and D. Adair, 15–32. Basingstoke, UK: Palgrave.

Giulianotti, R., G. Armstrong, G. Hales, and D. Hobbs. 2015. "Sport Mega-Events and Public Opposition." *Journal of Sport and Social Issues* 39 (2): 99–119.

Giulianotti, R., and F. Klauser. 2010. "Security Governance and Sport Mega-Events: Toward an Interdisciplinary Research Agenda." *Journal of Sport and Social Issues* 34 (1): 49–61.

Giulianotti, R., and R. Robertson. 2007. "Forms of Glocalization: Globalization and the Migration Strategies of Scottish Football Fans in North America." *Sociology* 41 (1): 133–152.

Giulianotti, R., and R. Robertson. 2009. *Globalization and Football*. London: Sage.

Guttmann, A. 1994. *Games and Empires: Modern Sports and Cultural Imperialism*. New York: Columbia University Press.

Haggerty, K., and R. Ericson. 2000. "The Surveillant Assemblage." *British Journal of Sociology* 51 (4): 605–622.

Hannerz, U. 1992. *Cultural Complexity*. New York: Columbia University Press.

Hartmann, D., and C. Kwauk. 2011. "Sport and Development: An Overview, Critique, and Reconstruction." *Journal of Sport and Social Issues* 35 (3): 284–305.

Herstein, R., and R. Berger. 2013. "Much More Than Sports: Sports Events as Stimuli for City Re-Branding." *Journal of Business Strategy* 34 (2): 38–44.

Hill, D. 2013. *An Insider's Guide to Match-Fixing in Football.* London: McDermid.

Hognestad, H. 2009. "Transglobal Scandinavian? Globalization and the Contestation of Identities in Football." *Soccer & Society* 10 (3–4): 358–373.

Hognestad, H., and A. Tollisen. 2004. "Playing Against Deprivation: Football and Development in Nairobi, Kenya." In *Football in Africa,* edited by G. Armstrong and R. Giulianotti, 227–254. Basingstoke, UK: Palgrave.

Houlihan, B., and R. Giulianotti. 2012. "Politics and the London 2012 Olympics: The (In) Security Games." *International Affairs* 88 (4): 701–717.

Houlihan, B., and J. Grix. 2014. "Sports Mega-Events as Part of a Nation's Soft Power Strategy: The Cases of Germany (2006) and the UK (2012)." *British Journal of Politics and International Relations* 16 (4): 572–596.

Humphreys, D. 2003. "Selling out Snowboarding: The Alternative Response to Commercial Co-optation." In *To the Extreme: Alternative Sports, Inside and Out,* edited by R. E. Rinehart and S. Sydnor, 407–428. New York: State University of New York Press.

Hutchins, B., and D. Rowe. 2012. *Sport Beyond Television.* London: Routledge.

Jennings, A. 2011. "Investigating Corruption in Corporate Sport: The IOC and FIFA." *International Review for the Sociology of Sport* 46 (4): 387–398.

Kaldor, M. 2003. *Global Civil Society.* Cambridge, UK: Polity.

Kidd, B. 2008. "A New Social Movement: Sport for Development and Peace." *Sport in Society* 11(4): 370–380.

Klein, A. 2006. *Growing the Game: The Globalization of Major League Baseball.* New Haven, CT: Yale University Press.

Knott, B., A. Fyall, and I. Jones. 2013. "The Nation-Branding Legacy of the 2010 FIFA World Cup for South Africa." *Journal of Hospitality Marketing and Management* 22 (6): 569–595.

Laderman, S. 2014. *Empire in Waves: A Political History of Surfing.* Los Angeles: University of California Press.

LaFeber, W. 2002. *Michael Jordan and the New Global Capitalism.* New York: Norton.

Lenskyj, H. 2008. *Olympic Industry Resistance.* Albany: State University of New York Press.

Levermore, R., and A. Beacom, eds. 2009. *Sport and International Development.* New York: Palgrave Macmillan.

Marcano, A. J., and D. P. Fidler. 2003. *Stealing Lives.* Bloomington: Indiana University Press.

Maro, C. N., G. C. Roberts, and M. Sorensen. 2009. "Using Sport to Promote HIV/AIDS Education for At-Risk Youths: An Intervention Using Peer Coaches in Football." *Scandinavian Journal of Medicine & Science in Sports* 19: 129–141.

McManus, J. 2015. "Driven to Distraction: Turkish Diaspora Football Supporters, New Media and the Politics of Place-Making." *Sociological Research Online* 20 (2): 12.

Millward, P. 2011. *The Global Football League.* Basingstoke, UK: Palgrave.

Müller, M. 2015. "What Makes an Event a Mega-Event? Definitions and Sizes." *Leisure Studies* 34 (6): 627–642.

Nye, J. 2004. *Soft Power: The Means to Success in World Politics.* London: Public Affairs.

Nye, J. 2008. "Soft Power and the Beijing Olympics." *Real Clear World,* August 24. http://www.realclearworld.com/articles/2008/08/soft_power_and_beijing_olympic.html.

Pieterse, J. N. 2007. *Ethnicities and Global Multiculture.* Lanham, MD: Rowman & Littlefield.

Preuss, H. 2004. *The Economics of Staging the Olympics*. London: Elgar.

Ritzer, G. 2004. *The Globalization of Nothing*. Thousand Oaks, CA: Pine Forge Press.

Robertson, R. 1992. *Globalization*. London: Sage.

Rowe, D. 2011. *Global Media Sport*. London: Bloomsbury.

Rumford, C. 2007. "More Than a Game: Globalization and the Post-Westernization of World Cricket." *Global Networks* 7 (2): 202–214.

Sassen, S. 1991. *The Global City*. Princeton, NJ: Princeton University Press.

Sassen, S., ed. 2002. *Global Networks, Linked Cities*. London: Routledge.

Scherer, J., and S. Jackson. 2010. *Globalization, Sport and Corporate Nationalism*. New York: Lang.

Schulenkorf, N., and D. Adair, eds. 2014. *Global Sport-for-Development*. Basingstoke, UK: Palgrave.

Smart, B. 2015. "Sport and the Corporate World." In *Routledge Handbook of the Sociology of Sport*, edited by R. Giulianotti, 417–428. London: Routledge.

Smith, A. 2005. "Reimaging the City: The Value of Sport Initiatives." *Annals of Tourism Research* 32 (1): 217–236.

Spaaij, R., J. Magee, and R. Jeanes. 2014. *Sport and Social Exclusion in Global Society*. London: Routledge.

"Special Issue: Security and Surveillance at Sport Mega-Events." 2011. *Urban Studies* 48 (15).

Thorpe, H., and B. Wheaton. 2014. "Dissecting Action Sports Studies." In *A Companion to Sport*, edited by D. L. Andrews and B. Carrington, 341–358. Oxford, UK: Wiley-Blackwell.

Timms, J. 2012. "The Olympics as a Platform for Protest: A Case Study of the London 2012 'Ethical' Games and the Play Fair Campaign for Workers' Rights." *Leisure Studies* 31 (3): 355–372.

Wallerstein, I. 1974. *The Modern World System*. vol. 1. London: Academic Press.

Wallerstein, I. 2002. *The Decline of American Power*. New York: New Press.

Walsh, A. J., and R. Giulianotti. 2007. *Ethics, Money and Sport*. London: Routledge.

Wilson, B., N. van Luijk, and M. K. Boit. 2015. "When Celebrity Athletes Are 'Social Movement Entrepreneurs': A Study of the Role of Elite Runners in Run-for-Peace Events in Post-Conflict Kenya in 2008." *International Review for the Sociology of Sport* 50 (8): 929–957.

Zhang, L., and S. Zhao. 2009. "City Branding and the Olympic Effect: A Case Study of Beijing." *Cities* 26: 245–254.

Zhongying, P. 2008. "The Beijing Olympics and China's Soft Power." Brookings, September 4. http://www.brookings.edu/research/opinions/2008/09/04-olympics-pang. Accessed February 12, 2016.

....

CHAPTER 36

GLOBAL FOOD POLICIES

....

HILAL ELVER

Two of the major global challenges of our time are eliminating hunger and providing food security for all in times of climate change, natural resources scarcity, and increasing population in an economically highly unequal and culturally diverse world. These challenges are interconnected and variously embedded in global studies programs. They are best addressed by way of interdisciplinary approaches, enabling a better understanding of a group of distinct issue areas that had formerly been studied separately in traditional academic disciplines. Agricultural studies were long treated under the rubric of rural development policies, tending to focus only on the supply side of agricultural production at the national level. International trade was not viewed as a component of national policy, and the interdisciplinary approach was virtually unknown. Twenty-first-century global food policy is committed to such goals as the elimination of hunger and improvement of food security while at the same time protecting environmental resources and ecosystem services facing multiple threats from population growth, consumerism, industrial agriculture, climate change, and economic globalization.

The global studies approach, especially the stress on interdisciplinary understanding, is based on the study of the interplay of political, economic, ecological, social, and cultural factors. It evaluates policy from the perspective of critical thinking, seeking an integrated understanding of complex and multipolar food policy. The inclusion of a new generation of food policy studies within global studies programs will enhance the curriculum of global studies as well as bring to bear wider perspectives for the consideration of policymakers seeking to manage global food governance.

WHAT IS FOOD SECURITY?

....

Concepts of food security have evolved in the past thirty years to reflect changes in official policy thinking (Food and Agriculture Organization (FAO) 2006). A widely accepted definition of food security was adopted at the World Food Summit (WFS) in 1996, placing an emphasis on the multidimensional nature of the concept of food security. According to this definition, "Food security exists when all people, at all times, have physical and economic access to sufficient, safe and nutritious food that meets their dietary needs and food preferences for an active and healthy life" (FAO 2006). The WFS also formally affirmed "the right to adequate food," recognizing the ethical and human rights dimension of food security. Against this background, the analysis of food security as a social and political construct has gained increasing acceptance and influence.

A Short History of the Global Food Systems

Modern-day agricultural regimes date back to the late nineteenth century. According to Harriet Friedmann and Philip McMichael (1989), three distinct periods shaped food regimes: (1) from 1870 to 1914, during the period of British hegemony in the world economy; (2) from 1945 to 1973, under US hegemony in the post-World War II world economy; and (3) the corporate food regime in the 1980s, during the period of neoliberal globalization.

Today's food system is the continuation of the second and third regimes, which started in the early twentieth century. The period after World War II gave rise to production-oriented agricultural policy in developed countries. During this period, with the establishment of the United Nations (UN) and the FAO (in 1945), nationally focused food policies shifted into an international platform with the goal of eliminating hunger and ensuring food security for all. This undertaking was a reaction by the liberal West to the massive suffering that arose from hunger and famine during World War II and an accompanying determination to avoid its recurrence in the future.

During this period, population and economic growth, as well as the transformation of technical and productive capacities from a war economy to peaceful development, had enormous impacts on the agricultural sector. Starting in the 1950s, global agricultural yield steadily increased, which resulted in the production of more food than was consumed. As a result, there was overproduction on the supply side. Economic prosperity, rapid urbanization, and a growing middle class triggered intensive consumption and demand. This was especially present in the United States and, to a lesser extent, in post-war Europe as a result of American economic assistance. In this manner, the world experienced an early stage of the growing power of the productionist food system to overcome aggregate food shortages.

As a result, global food production has increased by one-third since the early 1960s and has outpaced human population growth. However, the increasing mechanization of agriculture had a negative impact on the portion of the labor force dependent on agriculture. It also had dramatic detrimental effects on subsistence farming (Grada 2009). This was the beginning of the gradual change of rural America and its farming system. The US government supported large-scale farmers with large subsidies to keep them content, which also had the effect of encouraging mono-cropping for export. Global agricultural trade mainly benefitted the United States. Later, the European Union made inroads on the global market with the help of Common Agricultural Policy. At the same time, high tariffs and subsidies protected their own industrial agriculture from competition.

During this period, international food aid was viewed as the major remedy to solving the problems of hunger and malnutrition in developing countries. But this aid was given sporadically and in response to emergency situations, and it served somewhat geopolitical interests. As such, it treated symptoms rather than addressing root causes or seeking structural changes in global agricultural policy. It was during this period that overproduction in developed countries resulting in the saturation of developing markets with cheap available food that undermined the viability of smallholder farmers in many developing countries.

In the 1970s, with the leadership of the United States and the World Bank, the production-oriented agricultural system was bestowed upon developing countries under the banner of the "Green Revolution" through high-yielding crop varieties and abundant use of water, fertilizers, and pesticides. These chemicals were already widely available due to high rates of wartime production leading to post-war surpluses. In this period, the geopolitical impact of hunger, food security, and population increase in developing countries became a major preoccupation for the developed world. Modernization and productivity were believed to be the only way to eliminate world poverty and attendant hunger and famine.

In the 1980s, the impact of the Green Revolution—ecosystem degradation, excessive resource consumption, water scarcity, and dependence on fossil fuels—was experienced by many developing countries. In reality, increased production, which caused serious environmental degradation, brought neither prosperity that was equitably distributed to the whole society nor helped eliminate hunger. The first "world food crisis" emerged in several developing countries with the culmination of the El Nino weather impact, the oil crises, and early tensions surrounding globalization. Famine spread throughout the southern hemisphere, from West Africa to Bangladesh (Otter 2010).

In the 1990s, the "structural adjustments" required by the World Bank, the International Monetary Fund, and other agencies brought sweeping economic liberalization, privatization, and major cutback from social policies. Although these fiscal and monetary policies were not directed specifically at the agricultural sector, many negative impacts on smallholder farmers and rural communities occurred. Instead of land reform, these policies brought deregulation of land markets; drastic cuts in farm subsidies; expanded use of biotechnologies and commodification of seeds; growing dependence on fossil fuel inputs; expansion of cash crops for export, such as animal food, biofuel, and niche luxury fruit, vegetables, and flowers for the global centers of overconsumption (Araghi 2008: 133).

CURRENT STATE OF GLOBAL HUNGER AND MALNUTRITION

Despite overflow of food production at the global level and significant progress in recent decades, hunger and malnutrition are still major problems. In 1990, approximately one in four people in the world suffered from hunger. In 2017, approximately 800 million people in the world did not have enough food to lead a healthy, active life, and more than 3 billion people suffered from the triple burden of malnutrition—undernutrition, micronutrient deficiencies, as well as overweight and obesity. Although food insecurity and hunger are problems mostly for developing countries, malnutrition, especially overweight and obesity, is a universal problem.

The previously cited data on food insecurity do not capture the full story. The way in which calculations are made and how acute, chronic, and hidden hunger (malnutrition) is framed must be critically examined. For instance, in sub-Saharan Africa, chronic food insecurity has been increasing rather than decreasing, as one in every four people is currently undernourished (World Food Program 2016). Although catastrophic famine is no longer a twenty-first-century problem, when severe drought occurs, which is more frequent and persists longer due to climate change, it can quickly lead to a serious famine, especially in fragile societal settings such as national and international armed conflict. As recently as January 2017, a "Global Food Security Alert" report stated that 70 million people in forty-five countries needed immediate emergency food assistance due to stresses associated with drought. Especially countries that are also experiencing protracted crises, such as Nigeria, Somalia, South Sudan, and Yemen, currently suffer from famine or are facing a credible risk of famine.

Geographical variations are also a cause of concern. Nearly two-thirds of the world's hungry people are in the Asia–Pacific region, where half of the world's population lives. Overall, 65% of the world's hungry people live in only seven countries: India, Pakistan, the Democratic Republic of Congo, Bangladesh, Indonesia, China, and Ethiopia. China is the only country in this group that has successfully reduced hunger in the past two decades.

The Most Vulnerable: Smallholders, Specifically Women Farmers

Hunger is predominantly a problem in developing countries, where the vast majority of the world's hungry (95–98%) reside. Yet, hunger and food insecurity do not threaten everyone equally within these societies. It is ironic that the majority of those who are food-insecure are peasants and smallholder farmers, who live in rural areas where agriculture is the main source of income. Farmers are actually the backbone of global food production, constituting more than one-third of the world's population and contributing two-thirds of the world's food production (Bello 2009: 15).

The rural poor suffer from hunger because they lack access to resources such as water, land, seeds, and markets; do not hold secure land tenure; and are bound by unjust sharecropping contracts or have properties that are so small that they cannot grow enough food both to feed themselves and to sell it (Ziegler et al. 2011: 3).

Yearly statistics do not take short-term undernourishment into account, and they neglect the household distribution of food, which negatively affects women and girls. Yet, until very recently, the role of women was not treated as a policy issue in the food and agriculture sector. This is a startling oversight considering that although women make up just over half of the world's population, they account for 60–70% of the world's' hungry. Moreover, in approximately the past decade, the ratio of women farmers has been steadily increasing in many developing countries. "Feminization of agriculture" is a new phenomenon because of male migration from rural areas to cities, and even abroad, to search for jobs. As a result, women are left behind to serve as primary caretakers, responsible for raising children, dealing with the elderly and sick, as well as being farmers and farmworkers. Numerous studies show that women spend a larger percentage of income on food for the family than do men. Moreover, women tend to prefer to cultivate food and vegetables to achieve better nutrition for family members, foregoing the appeal of cash crops that are more often the priority of men. Given these results, it is clear that empowering women with the resources they need to increase agricultural production and reshaping gender roles to give women more decision-making power are direct and effective ways to enhance global food security.

However, female farmers and farmworkers face discrimination due to culturally and socially constructed stereotypes of gender roles, impeding their ability to farm as effectively and productively as their male counterparts. One of the greatest disparities between male and female farmers is land ownership. Data from the FAO (2011) indicate that women own, on average, only 15% of land in developing countries and only 5% in Oceania, North Africa, and West Asia. This significant inequality in property rights creates barriers for women not only in terms of agricultural production but also when attempting to obtain credit, training, and other instruments of empowerment. The FAO estimates that if women are given the same access to agricultural production resources as men, their yields would increase by 20–30%, in turn increasing agricultural output in developing countries by 2.4–4% and reducing the amount of hungry people in the world by 12–17%. (FAO 2011; see also United Nations 2015b).

Minorities are also often disproportionately impacted by hunger and malnutrition compared to the majority population. Indigenous peoples are especially vulnerable to discrimination because they generally live in remote and climatically challenging regions and lack political representation. According to the most accepted indicators, indigenous peoples make up 5% of the world's population yet comprise approximately 15% of the world's poor (see the International Fund for Agricultural Development website at https://www.ifad.org). There is disagreement regarding who qualifies as "indigenous," making statistical assertions controversial. Many governments try to understate the size and obscure the visibility of their indigenous populations. This reality further complicates the task of assessing the extent of hunger and malnutrition being experienced by indigenous peoples in various national settings.

Indigenous peoples are frequently victims of official policies of displacement, being pushed out to remote areas with the least fertile and most ecologically fragile lands. Furthermore, their land and their livelihoods are generally precarious, being subject to development projects and predatory policies, including land grabbing, mining, and opportunistic claims in the event valuable minerals or other land uses emerge. Their typical vocation is based on subsistence farming. This puts their lifestyle at great risk under current world conditions due to environmental degradation and climate change.

GLOBALIZATION OF FOOD SYSTEMS AND ITS IMPACT ON FOOD SECURITY

Current food systems illustrate the way in which our diet and food choices are subject to the influence of neoliberal globalization, financialization, corporatization, and industrialization (Leguizamon 2016). Consumers are increasingly dependent on decisions made by geographically remote agro-industrial business executives, as well as the politics of international trade, climate change, and energy systems.

The rise of neoliberal market forces brought a new dimension to global food policy. Transnational companies have become major players through globalization of food markets tied to supermarket chains that now often control the entire value chain of food production "from farm to fork." Transnational agro-food global capitals disconnect production from consumption and then relink through the dynamics of buying and selling. (Friedmann 1994: 260).

The globalization of the food and agricultural sector became very strong and lucrative. This development has had an enormous influence on global diet, pushing consumers to eat increasingly more ready, frozen food as disseminated by fast-food companies. Changing diets are also the result of changing lifestyles—migrations from rural areas to urban centers that result in disconnecting the majority of the population from traditional forms of food production. Gradually, consumers have become addicted to the habits and tastes of the fast-food culture. Most developing countries are also becoming dependent on cheap food imports, abandoning self-sufficiency and nationally oriented agriculture and food policies.

As a result, smallholder farmers have been put under increasing pressure, and these small holdings have almost disappeared in some major markets, where local food systems frequently collapse, even though most of the world's more than 570 million farms continue to remain small and family run. Smallholder farms (less than two hectares) operate approximately 12% of the world's agricultural land but provide more than 70% of the food consumed in much of the developing world, contributing significantly to poverty reduction and food security. However, their contributions are under threat due to reduced investment support and marginalization of small farms in most national economic development plans. Instead of a direct connection with consumers, farmers have become contractors of the supermarket giants, with production that is driven by the market interests decided by supermarkets rather than the traditional tie between producers and consumers.

This is a global phenomenon, not just in developing countries. Even in Europe and the United States, smallholder and family farmers do not have power to compete with large-scale companies with respect to access to markets or independence to decide what they want to produce. Despite small farms currently being squeezed, now occupying less than one-fourth of the world's farmland, they continue to be major food producers globally (GRAIN 2014).

The percentage of Americans who live on farms declined from nearly 25% in the 1940s to approximately 2% today, and only 0.1% of the US population works full-time on a farm. At the same time, farm subsidies have remained high, but they mostly benefit large farms and agro-businesses rather than medium and smallholder farmers. In the United States, the agro-business lobby currently spends approximately $60 million each year to influence policymakers. It is thus not surprising that transnational agro-business interests are influential in decision-making mechanisms in domestic and international policy arenas.

Oligopoly of the transnational food corporations also has important consequences. A small number of giant corporations are dominating the current global food system by their control over the production, distribution, and market—that is, entire production chains—as reinforced by their influence on regulatory systems and trade regimes.

Resource Scarcities and Depletion of Biodiversity

Intensive industrial agriculture, practiced mostly by transnational corporations, is using already exhausted farmlands and depleted water resources to produce large amounts of export-oriented cash crops, animal food, and biofuel throughout the world. Agricultural land is almost exhausted at the global level because 75–90% of the land suitable for agriculture is already in use (Global Land Outlook 2017). Moreover, water scarcity is a major challenge because 40% of the land mass is arid. According to the World Bank, in the near future, 6% of the global gross domestic product (GDP) will be required to meet the demand for water. At the same time, the world population is in the process of shifting its diet to consume more meat-based food, which is more water-intensive than plant-based food. For example, whereas 1,500 liters of water is required to produce 1 kg of wheat, 16,000 liters of water is needed to produce 1 kg of meat.

As a result of a large and growing human population, the persistence of widespread malnutrition has a direct impact on the expanding agriculture that poses a threat to biodiversity. The goals of providing universal food security and protecting biodiversity are incompatible. The current agricultural system provides sufficient food on a worldwide basis, but in doing so it methodically undermines the capacity of agroecosystems to preserve biodiversity (Chappell and LaValle 2011).

The two problems of biodiversity loss and food insecurity are global in scope and cannot be viewed independently: In a world with limited resources, the methods used to address one necessarily involve choices affecting the other. Approximately 40% of the Earth's land surface is being used for agriculture; an estimated 16–40% of this land is already lightly to severely degraded. Moreover, 40% of species have experienced severe population declines.

Current human use of surface water, groundwater, and soil is almost unsustainable, and these are essentially non-renewable resources.

Large-Scale Land Acquisitions

As farmlands have become scarce, the competition over land has increased. Remaining farmland and water resources are subject to competition between animal food, biofuel, commodities, and human consumption. Smallholders and subsistence farmers are in particular danger in developing countries because large-scale land acquisitions are a major threat, especially in countries in which property rights are not secure and farmlands are still not entirely cultivated, such as in Africa, Latin America, and South Asia. Africa is the continent most affected by large land acquisitions. According to the World Bank, of 42 million hectares sold in less than a year, 75% of these sales took place in sub-Saharan Africa, mainly involving the production and export of food, animal feed, biofuel, timber, and minerals in Cameroon, Ethiopia, the Democratic Republic of Congo, Madagascar, Mali, Somalia, Sudan, Tanzania, and Zambia (Deininger et al. 2011).Of the investment-promotion agencies in Africa, 87% are actively promoting foreign agricultural investments, more than in any other region of the world. Transfer from customary to state land is also widespread as a precondition or means for transferring land to investors.

Industries such as mining and logging, agri-businesses, and infrastructure projects have major impacts on land acquisitions. Local communities are rarely consulted or compensated (De Schutter 2016). Although many of the deals remain secret, the Land Matrix documented more than 1,000 transnational land deals in recent years covering 38 million hectares of land that has been acquired in developing countries by large investors ("Act on It" 2015).

Unfortunately, governments of developing countries are willing to offer available lands to foreign investors in the hope of securing an economic miracle or, in some cases, simply because the governments are corrupt. These deals are generally concluded without considering long-term adverse impacts on ecosystems, sociopolitical consequences, and human rights violations. The majority of victims of land dispossession are peasants, pastoralists, indigenous and nomadic peoples, and transboundary communities, whose land management system is based on customary land tenure.

Although large-scale land acquisitions are defended as being helpful for economic development, they also increase poverty and food insecurity and displace people from rural areas to the peripheries of cities or barren lands. In many countries, peasants resist large land appropriations, sometimes with weapons; with outbreaks of violent conflict and political unrest, abused peasants are transformed into "criminals."

From the perspective of the right to food and their impact on small-scale farmers and local peoples' livelihoods, large-scale land investments should be carefully scrutinized. Often, locals either abandon or are forced to leave their lands, or they are forced to work for the foreign investors. Suddenly, their villages and their lands are turned into large-scale plantations with a high risk of human rights violations. If they do not directly lose their lands, subsistence farmers are often excluded from accessing vital resources such as water and are thus pushed further into poverty (Stephens 2011).

Excessive Use of Chemicals

Industrial agriculture heavily relies on the use of chemicals to increase production. Despite the harms associated with excessive and unsafe pesticide practices, it is commonly argued that intensive industrial agriculture, which is heavily reliant on pesticide inputs, is necessary to increase yields to feed a growing world population. This argument is reinforced by the effects of climate change and by the growing global scarcity of farmlands.

Pesticides are responsible for an estimated 200,000 acute poisoning deaths each year, 99% of which occur in developing countries, where health, safety, and environmental regulations are weaker and less strictly applied. Although records on global pesticide use are incomplete, it is generally agreed that use rates have increased dramatically during the past few decades (United Nations 2016a).

Pesticides cause an array of harms. Hazardous pesticides impose substantial costs on governments and have catastrophic impacts on the environment, human health, and society as a whole, encroaching upon a number of human rights, with groups such as farmworkers, communities living near agricultural lands, pregnant women, and children at elevated risk from pesticides.

Run-off from treated crops frequently pollutes the surrounding ecosystem and beyond, with unpredictable ecological consequences. Furthermore, reductions in pest populations upset the complex and delicate balance between predator and prey species in the food chain, thereby destabilizing the ecosystem. Pesticides can also decrease biodiversity of soils and contribute to nitrogen fixation, which can cause large declines in crop yields.

Scientists contend that it is possible to produce healthier, nutrient-rich food, with higher yields in the longer term, without current reliance on pesticides that pollute and exhaust environmental resources (International Assessment of Agricultural Knowledge, Science and Technology for Development 2009: 3).

Relying on Technology (Biotechnology)

In current food systems, technological tools and scientific advancements are being relied on as the best way to deliver more food, improve health, and prevent negative consequences. It is believed that ever more sophisticated science and technology will result in increased productive capacity to feed ever more mouths better and with fewer costly and damaging consequences (Lang and Heasman 2015). These tools are also under the control of powerful countries and large-scale oligopoly agri-businesses.

One of the major controversies in relation to biotechnology concerns genetically engineered (GE) seeds, which are featured as the way to overcome food insecurity for our overcrowded and overheated world. Although there is no consensus regarding the harmful effects of GE foods on human health and the environment, the majority of scientists are in agreement that GE foods should be dealt with cautiously, and labeling is necessary to protect consumers' right to know what they eat.

Despite the fact that the harmful effects of uncontrolled biotechnology and chemical- and fossil fuel-intensive agriculture to the environment, human health, and livelihoods of people are well documented, most research and development funding continues to be channeled to technologically driven large-scale projects. In contrast, alternative food systems, especially those in the domain of agroecology, are denied adequate funding. Due to the large profit margins of monoculture soy, corn, biofuel plants, and other commodity crops that heavily rely on GE, it is almost impossible to make the case for agroecology.

Nutrition, a New Universal Problem

Although hunger is a problem in developing countries, nutrition is a universal problem. Whereas more than 2 billion people suffer from malnutrition and vitamin deficiencies, more than 1.6 billion people are overweight or obese. This means that one in three people worldwide suffers from malnutrition. It is widely recognized that different manifestations of malnutrition often coexist, and many countries are confronted not only with malnutrition and micronutrient deficiencies but also with rising rates of overweight and obesity (Elver 2016a, 2016b).

The underlying causes of malnutrition are complex and multidimensional. Women and children are particularly susceptible to malnutrition, whereas poverty, gender inequality, and lack of access to adequate sanitation, health, and education services are aggravating factors. Poor nutrition among women and children threatens a "vicious cycle of malnutrition." One out of six children, roughly 161 million, is suffering from malnutrition. Each year, nearly 3.1 million children younger than age five years die because of malnutrition-related diseases. Malnourished children, even if they survive, are unable to grow properly and develop their full potential, which means they are usually not able to contribute much to the social well-being of their country.

Unfortunately, 66 million primary school-age children in developing countries are hungry when attending classes, including 23 million in Africa alone (World Food Program 2016). This statistic underlies the belief that hunger and malnutrition will have a strong generational impact on the future of the world. It is scientifically documented that even a short period of food insecurity during the first 1,000 days of life does irreparable damage to children's mental and physical capacity. The World Food Program calculates that $3.2 billion is needed per year to ensure that these 66 million hungry school-age children are provided with adequate food.

Women who are lactating and pregnant require more than the normal nutrient-rich diet. Malnourished mothers are more likely to give birth to underweight infants, which in turn are 20% more likely to die before the age of five years (World Food Program 2016). Diets that consist of less than 6% protein in utero have been linked with many deficits, including decreased brain weight, obesity, and impaired brain communication.

Nevertheless, half of women of reproductive age in West Africa are anemic. Not only does anemia contribute to almost one-fifth of global maternal deaths but also infants born to anemic mothers are more likely to be underweight ("Global Nutrition Report" 2015). Rural women are among those most victimized by malnutrition. Patriarchal norms and systemic discrimination in accessing land and other natural resources impede the ability of these women to provide appropriate nutritious food for themselves and their families, a pattern that produces intergenerational cycles of malnutrition.

Unhealthy Eating Habits and Noncommunicable Diseases

Today's food systems, which are dominated by industrial production and processing, as well as affected by trade liberalization and aggressive marketing strategies, are fostering unhealthy eating habits and creating a dependence on highly processed, nutrient-poor foods. Urban living conditions and changing lifestyles are also creating a dependence on highly processed, energy-dense yet nutrient-poor foods that are widely available to consumers. As a result, unhealthy eating habits are on the rise globally, especially in middle-income and developing countries.

The impact of industrial food systems on nutrition and public health is alarming. Ultra-processed foods contain high levels of sodium, sugar, trans fats, and saturated fats so that they are energy-dense yet lack nutritional value. Highly processed "junk food" is widely available in supermarkets throughout the world, and it is much cheaper than local fruit and vegetables of local farmers' markets. In addition to unhealthy ingredients, the food processing industry uses preservatives, artificial colorants, additives, and other chemicals in order to enhance the appearance, flavor, and shelf life of food products, and animals grown on factory farms are given growth hormones and antibiotics (Nestle 2013)

Consumption of unhealthy foods has been determined to be an important cause of several noncommunicable diseases (NCDs), which shorten life expectancy. According to the World Health Organization (WHO; 2015), four NCDs—heart failure, diabetes, cancers, and chronic respiratory diseases—are collectively responsible for almost 70% of all deaths worldwide, which is an alarming figure that is expected to increase to 75% by 2020. The WHO report indicates that an unhealthy diet is one of the major causes of NCDs and early mortality. Considering that 2 billion people are overweight or obese and 2 billion additional people are suffering from hidden hunger (micronutrient deficiencies), combatting malnutrition in all its forms and ensuring healthy diets for growing populations are major universal health challenges. These three forms of malnutrition can be found in the same country, the same family, and sometimes even the same person.

Worldwide data suggest that average sodium and sugar consumption is well above minimal physiological needs. Processed food consumers unknowingly consume three to five times more sodium than required, which is particularly troubling because such foods are mainly developed for consumption by children. For example, a global study conducted in 2015 reviewed 387 popular children's meals and found sodium levels to be dangerously high (World Action on Salt and Health 2015). Similarly, during the past 50 years, global sugar consumption has more than tripled, particularly in the form of sweetened beverages (Dylan 2012).

The overall picture is not beneficial for human health and also not ecologically sustainable from the perspective of planetary viability. In order to produce massive amounts of cheap, ultra-processed food, the current food system focuses on monoculture agriculture, excessive use of chemicals from farm to supermarket to ensure long shelf life, and the distribution of food through reliance on global supermarket chains.

The economic costs of malnutrition and its adverse impact on development are huge. During the next 20 years, NCDs will cost more than $30 trillion, representing 48% of the global GDP and pushing millions of people below the poverty line. By contrast, mounting evidence highlights how millions of deaths can be averted and economic losses reduced by billions of dollars if added focus is put on prevention ("The Global Economic Burden of NDC" 2011).

Global Food Governance: Efforts of the United Nations Organizations

Recognizing the growing threat of malnutrition in all its forms and its negative impacts on economic development, universal health, and efforts to reduce food insecurity, the international community has taken major initiatives to ensure global policy action.

Fighting against malnutrition requires multiple sectors to support each other, including agriculture, trade, investment, health, education, social policies, as well as human rights. The 2014 Second International Conference on Nutrition (United Nations, 2014), organized by the UN's WHO and FAO, acknowledged that

> current food systems are being increasingly challenged to provide adequate, safe and diversified and nutrient rich food for all that contribute to healthy diets due to, inter alia, constraints posed by resource scarcity and environmental degradation, as well as by unsustainable production and consumption patterns, food losses and waste, and unbalanced distribution.

It is also recognized that nutrition plays a crucial role in fulfilling the UN 2030 Agenda for Sustainable Development. In April 2016, the UN proclaimed the "Decade of Action on Nutrition," which presents a unique opportunity for the next ten years to ensure a coherent, inclusive, and transparent response to malnutrition, embedded within human rights (United Nations 2016b).

The right of everyone to safe, sufficient, and nutritious food is an encouraging policy initiative. Yet the world is not on track to reach this global target. It is essential to translate commitments into action. Unless global food systems move away from agro-industrial production methods, which are responsible for dietary unity and an abundance of ultra-processed food and beverages, it is highly improbable that the malnutrition challenge can be met. The current system is neither sustainable nor healthy. We need to transform today's dominant food system to a system that implements the principles and practices of agroecology, protects biological diversity, and respects human rights and food sovereignty. Only such a regime will be able to protect small-scale producers, traditional practices, and local food production and markets; eliminate discriminatory practices; and prioritize vulnerable groups to eliminate hunger and enhance food security while upholding sustainable food systems for future generations. Sustainable and healthy food solutions already exist at the micro level, and it must be remembered that the majority of the world's food is still produced by smallholder farmers. Yet what is lacking is the political will and scale of investment required to ensure that small-scale farmers receive the support they need to flourish economically and serve consumers instead of serving global food companies.

What Is the Future of Global Food Policy?

According to FAO projections, in order to feed the projected 9.7 billion global population by 2050, food production must increase by 60%. This is a formidable challenge. The majority of global food players and the agro-industrial lobby start any policy debate with this alarming sentence so as to divert the future of the global food problem in ways that make industrial agriculture the only solution.

Many believe that future food policy must be based on the capacity to produce more food using advances in technology. It is true that the world produces 17% more food per person today than it did thirty years ago. For the past two decades, due to mechanization and excessive use of chemicals, pesticides, and fossil fuels, the rate of global food production has increased faster than the rate of global population growth. Global GDPs continue to increase, with food production at a historic high. Currently, the world produces more than one and a half times the amount of food required to feed everyone on the planet, and yet chronic hunger remains widespread and 40% of available food is wasted or lost during various stages of the production chain.

A fundamental question is how the global community will solve hunger and food security challenges despite overproduction. Despite the earlier success of increased production, the FAO's future scenarios are not very optimistic about following that same path. Productivity cannot be sustained as was the case during the 1960s. The current conditions of the Earth's ecosystem will not tolerate production-based scenarios to increase food supply. While population has increased on every continent, most rapidly in Africa (from 1 billion to 2 billions), growing wealth and excessive consumption due to lifestyle changes and increased incomes of middle-class families are pushing food demand higher against planetary limits in times of climate change (United Nations 2015a).

At the same time, most of the root causes of hunger and malnutrition continue to exist. Poverty and inequality are the most crucial and persistent problems facing humanity, and they are not addresses effectively by mere increases in agricultural production. People making less than $2 a day—many of whom are resource-poor farmers cultivating very small plots of land—still cannot afford to buy food.

One of the major issues in the twenty-first century is the increasing concentration of global wealth and the gap between rich and poor. According to Oxfam (2015), in 2015, the richest 1% of people in the world owned 48% of global wealth, leaving 52% to be shared among the other 99% on the planet. In December 2016, Oxfam's report to the World Economic Forum dramatically announced that the eight richest individuals on Earth owned as much wealth as that owned by half the human race. This reality is very unnerving considering such social and political consequences to world peace, and it has definite relevance to the humane framing of food policy.

Political Unrest

The 2007–2008 worldwide food crisis caused by shortages and price spikes gave the world community a wake-up call with respect to the urgency of addressing food policy on a global scale. Subsequently, prices remained volatile, and they spiked again in 2011. These crises resulted partly from the manipulation of commodity prices for rice, wheat, corn, and soy and were partly due to the excessive subsidized production of biofuel at the expense of crops for food supply. As a result, the number of undernourished people in the developing world skyrocketed. Several countries experienced serious food riots and political unrests (FAO 2009). Yet, no comprehensive policy changes occurred at the global level despite significant international attention.

Although the world has been spared historical catastrophic famines and the numbers of violent conflicts and conflict-related deaths are less than in the past, it would be a grave mistake to suppose that war and hunger are no longer matters for concern. There are continuing expectations that many people will die in this century from starvation. Famines continue to occur, although with less regularity than in the past and only in places that have become economically severely stressed and in war-torn regions.

Armed conflict is one of the key reasons for lack of food and starvation. At the same time, food insecurity is one of the major underlying causes of armed conflict and displacement. It is important for countries not to become trapped in such vicious cycles. Increasing numbers of people are being caught in a "conflict trap" that keeps them in poverty and hunger. For instance, in 2014, more than 13 million people were uprooted by violence, mostly by conflicts in Syria, Afghanistan, and Somalia. An average of 42,500 people per day were forced to flee their homes. Approximately 60 million people are being displaced by conflict and persecution worldwide, the highest level ever recorded (von Grebmer et al. 2015: 3).

During situations of armed conflict, more people die directly from starvation and malnutrition than from weapons. Victims are disproportionately women and young children, who are extremely susceptible to malnutrition. Often in conflict zones, starvation is used as a political weapon, crops are destroyed or poisoned, and relief supplies are blocked (Ziegler et al. 2011).

Protracted conflicts disrupt livelihoods, limit trade, and restrict humanitarian access. Today's wars involve not only government military forces and insurgents but also paramilitaries and ethnic militia, criminal gangs, mercenaries, and international forces. Most "new wars" are civil wars, which increasingly spill over borders and disrupt livelihoods and food systems, forcing people to flee (de Waal 2015: 23). According to a January 2017 "Global Food Security Alert" report, 70 million people living in forty-five countries needed immediate emergency food assistance. In these countries, protracted political/armed conflict combined with drought conditions due to a variety of aggravating weather events.

Climate Change: A Threat Multiplier

Climate change, sustainable resource management, and food security are now widely considered to mount complex, interdependent, and urgent global policy challenges. The scientific community estimates that the average Earth temperature will rise 2–4°C by the end of the century, posing multiple threats to availability, accessibility, adequacy, and sustainability of food. It is expected that these developments will increase hunger between 10% and 20% by 2050 and that 65% of those affected will be in sub-Saharan Africa (Intergovernmental Panel on Climate Change (IPCC) 2014). In many areas of the world, such as sub-Saharan Africa and the Middle East, the adverse impacts of climate change, especially water scarcity, drought, and flood-related disasters, are already happening.

Although climate change has enormous negative impacts on agriculture and food production, agriculture occupies roughly half of the planet's habitable surface, uses globally 70% of fresh water, and together with the food system is responsible for 50% of the greenhouse gas emissions. In addition, growing demand for agriculture and pastureland is the primary driver of tropical deforestation and soil degradation. The direct and indirect impacts of intensive food production have contributed to the depletion of biodiversity. Marine resources are in increasing danger of becoming exhausted due to the activities of industrial fishing fleets. The search for foods with higher nutritious value and increasing demand have led to the exploitation of more than 90% of the world's marine fisheries ("The Global Food System" 2016: 2).

Understanding the specific impacts of climate change on food security is challenging because vulnerabilities are unevenly spread throughout the world and mitigation of and adaptation to climate change depend ultimately on the ability of diverse communities to manage risks and develop resilience. Moreover, climate change is perversely exerting its most severe negative impacts on those societies that have contributed least to global warming.

Manifestations of climate change, such as an increase in the frequency and intensity of extreme weather, drought, flooding, heatwaves, a rise in sea levels, and a decrease in the availability of water, diminish food security. Crop failure and a variety of harms to livestock, fisheries, and aquaculture will have negative effects on people's livelihoods, causing climate-induced food price volatility, nutritional deficiencies, and diminishing quality of land and soil suitable for agricultural production. The failure to enact appropriate policies will pose threats to global peace and security.

Furthermore, agricultural production continues to employ half of the global workforce. If the agricultural sector is adversely affected by climate change, so too will be the livelihoods of significant numbers of farmworkers and rural communities (High Level Panel of Experts on Food Security and Nutrition 2012). Farm and food workers already lack comprehensive social protection, suitable labor conditions, and often receive impoverishing compensation. Climate change will exacerbate problems of the agricultural sector even further. Climate change is already significantly impacting approximately 2 billion of the world's poor. If the "business as usual" continues without implementation of a series measures to combat climate change, this figure could rise 20% by 2050 (IPCC 2014).

Is There an Alternative Path?

A strong "agro pessimism" has emerged, partly as a result of the significant adverse effects of agricultural activities responsible for triggering climate change and degrading natural resources and partly as a result of the difficulty of the task of feeding a growing global population in the face of substantial challenges. As a result, the view has emerged that humankind will not be able to feed itself unless current industrial modes of agriculture are expanded and intensified, which is not only misleading if put forward as a solution but also ecologically extremely dangerous.

In the face of these facts, we need a paradigm shift as a prelude to a comprehensive policy reform that must include ethical, social, economic, and technological efforts to protect vulnerable sectors of society as a first priority. It will also be necessary to use every available tool to conserve natural resources and reduce adverse impacts of climate change while providing food security for all.

We need a new set of policies that will better deliver us to the future. First, we have to invest in alternative food production systems that use ecosystems in a balanced manner rather than exhausting natural resources and relying on the excessive use of chemicals and fossil fuels. There is a need to encourage a major shift from the current emphasis on industrial agriculture to transformative activities such as conservation agriculture (agroecology) that support local food movements, protect smallholder farmers, empower women, respect food democracy and related cultural traditions, maintain environmental sustainability, and facilitate a healthy diet. To achieve such a goal, there must be a new willingness to promote agroecology and to abandon the idea that all we need to do about food policy is continue expanding the output of industrial agriculture.

Second, the food system must be restructured so that quantity should not be the only goal. Although malnutrition is a formidable universal challenge, a commitment to "adequate and healthy food" should be highlighted. The quality of the food we consume must become as important as the quantity. This is the only way to reduce current levels of malnutrition in all its forms.

Third, the food system should make greater efforts to support the livelihoods and well-being of smallholder farmers, women, fisherfolk, and farmworkers. They are the backbone of the whole system, and globally the world continues to lose and demoralize its farmers instead of empowering them. Supporting smallholder farmers actually addresses the other two challenges. A resilient system cannot be built without smallholder farmer's and local peoples' increasing and meaningful participation. Sustainability requires mutually reinforcing economic, ecological, and social balance.

WHAT ROLE FOR GLOBAL STUDIES?

In the current world order, ecologic, economic, demographic, and social problems, as well as the inequality gap between rich and poor, make the human future highly uncertain. The impact of globalization further exacerbates such problems in the wider setting of interconnected geographic relations. Problems such as food security, once treated as a local issue, are now strongly affected by economic globalization. Balancing the local against the regional and global is very helpful when seeking to grasp the complexity of food systems. Also, balancing the rules of global economic order with ethical principles and human rights standards contributes to the development of a normative understanding of food policy. Such efforts strengthen the legal entitlement of people, which is more necessary than ever, considering the enormous economic power exercised by corporations. Protecting the human interest while diminishing food insecurity should operate as a high priority in any democratic and humane world order. If we adopt this outlook, we need principles of human rights that embody universally endorsed ethical values. Global studies can contribute to attaining this kind of enlightened understanding by prioritizing human rights in the context of global food policy.

During this time of globalization, greater attention than in the past needs to be given to the role and contribution of women and their special vulnerabilities, including the distorting effects of cultural and legal discrimination; demographic pressures and the lack of employment opportunities in rural areas; growing inequality and the absence of an adequate social safety net; marginalization and discrimination of minorities and indigenous peoples that threatens social peace; and the increasing numbers of internally displaced peoples and refugees generated by severe armed conflicts and climate-related disasters. To tackle these issues properly, we need to think and act with far greater imagination and higher quality comprehension than in the past. Global studies not only provides the intellectual tools but also offers such vulnerable groups an ethical orientation.

We need effective global governance for food security to encourage governments as duty bearers to respect, protect, and fulfill human rights of their citizens by making available and accessible adequate and healthy food for all at all times. Prioritizing a human rights approach during this time of predatory economic globalization seeks a protective edge and helps governments solve many problems that currently challenge states and that, if left unsolved, are likely to initiate political unrest. A human rights approach can provide citizens with various tools, such as accountability, justiciability, monitoring, transparency, participation in decision-making processes, and promotion of non-discrimination. Such initiatives will strengthen governments and increase the effectiveness of international organizations, thereby weakening reliance on market-based policies. It should be apparent that it is not possible to overcome the various dimensions of global food insecurity by investing false hopes in production-oriented, market-based policies. On the basis of extensive experience, it is naive to believe that an economistic approach will by itself produce humane and sustainable policies that ensure all people throughout the world, as a matter of right, will have access to sufficient and healthy food to meet their needs. Even if a human rights approach were adopted worldwide, which is almost impossible to imagine given current political realities, it would still be difficult to achieve the lofty goal of universal food security.

References

"Act on It: 4 Key Steps to Stop Land Grabs." 2015. *ActionAid*, May.

Araghi, Farshad. 2008. "The Invisible Hand and the Visible Foot." In *Peasants and Globalization*, edited by A. H. Akrem-Lodhi and C. Kay, 111–147. London: Routledge.

Bello, Walden. 2009. *The Food Wars*. Verso: London.

Chappell, M. J., and L. A. LaValle. 2011. "Food Security and Biodiversity: Can We Have Both?" *Agriculture and Human Values* 28: 3–26.

De Schutter, Olivier. 2016. "Tainted Lands: Corruption in Large-Scale Land Deals." Global Witness, November 15.

de Waal, Alex. 2015. "Armed Conflict and the Challenge of Hunger: Is an End in Sight?" In *Global Hunger Index*, 23. Washington, DC: International Food Policy Research Institute.

Deininger K., et al. 2011. *Rising Global Interest in Farmland*. Washington, DC: World Bank.

Dylan, Neel. 2012. "The Sugar Dilemma." *Harvard College Global Health Review*, October 24.

Elver, Hilal. 2016a. "The Challenges and Developments of the Right to Food in the 21st Century: Reflections of the United Nations Special Rapporteur on the Right to Food." *20 UCLA J. Int'l L. Foreign Aff. 1.*

Elver, Hilal. 2016b. "Interim Report of the Special Rapporteur on the Right to Food." Nutrition, A/71/282.

Food and Agriculture Organization (FAO). 2006. "Food Security Policy Brief." Issue 2. Rome, Italy: FAO.

Food and Agriculture Organization (FAO). 2009. "Hunger on Rise." FAO briefing paper. Rome, Italy: FAO.

Food and Agriculture Organization (FAO). 2011. "World Hunger Report 2011: High Volatile Prices Set to Continue." Rome, Italy: FAO.

Friedmann, Harriet. 1994. "Distance and Durability: Shaky Foundations of the World Food Economy." In *The Global Restructuring of Agro Food Systems*, edited by Philip McMichael, 258–276. Ithaca, NY: Cornell University Press.

Friedmann, Harriet, and Philip McMichael. 1989. "Agriculture and the State System: The Rise and Decline of National Agricultures, 1870 to the Present." *Sociological Ruralis* 29: 93–117.

Global Food Security Alert. January 25, 2017. Famine Early Warning System Network, US Aid, Washington DC.

Global Land Outlook. 2017. First Edition, UN Convention to Combat Desertification.

Global Nutrition Report: Actions and Accountability." 2015. Washington, DC: International Food Policy Research Institute.

Grada, Cormac O. 2009. *Famine: A Short History*. Princeton, NJ: Princeton University Press.

GRAIN. 2014. "Hungry for Land." May 28.

High Level Panel of Experts on Food Security and Nutrition. 2012. "Food Security and Climate Change." Rome, Italy: High Level Panel of Experts on Food Security and Nutrition and the Committee of Food Security, June. www.fao.org/3/a-me421e.pdf.

Intergovernmental Panel on Climate Change. 2014. *Climate Change 2014: Impacts, Adaptation, and Vulnerability: Summary for Policymakers: Working Group II Contribution to the Fifth Assessment Report of the Intergovernmental Panel on Climate Change*. Cambridge, UK: Cambridge University Press.

International Assessment of Agricultural Knowledge, Science and Technology for Development (IAASTD). 2009. "Agriculture at a Crossroads: Synthesis Report." Washington, DC: IAASTD.

Lang, T., and M. Heasman. 2015. *Food Wars*. 2nd ed. New York: Earthscan.

Leguizamon, A. 2016. "Disappearing Nature? Agribusiness, Biotechnology and Distance in Argentina Soybean Production." *Journal Peasant Studies* 43 (2): 313–339.

Nestle, Marion. 2013. *Food Politics: How the Food Industry Influences Nutrition and Health*. Los Angeles: University of California Press.

Oxfam. 2016. An Economy for the 1%: How Privilege and Power in the Economy Drive Extreme Inequality and How This Can Be Stopped.

Oxfam, 2016. "An economy for the 99%." Available at: https://www.oxfam.org/en/research/economy-99. Accessed August 1, 2018.

Oxfam. 2015. "Wealth: Having It All and Wanting More."

Stephens, Phoebe. 2011. "The Global Land Grab: An Analysis of Extant Governance Institutions." *International Affairs Review* 20 (1).

"The Global Economic Burden of NDC." 2011. Harvard School of Public Health, September.

"The Global Food System: An Analysis." 2016. BigPicnic, January.

United Nations. 2014. "The UN Rome Declaration 2014."

United Nations. 2015a. "UN Interim Report of the Special Rapporteur on the Right to Food (Climate Change): A/70/287." August 5.

United Nations. 2015b. "UN Report of the Special Rapporteur on the Right to Food: Integrating a Gender Perspective in the Right to Food: A/HRC/31/51." December 29.

United Nations. 2016a. "UN Report of the Special Rapporteur of the Right to Food (Pesticides): A/HRC/34/48." January.

United Nations. 2016b. "UN SR Right to Food, Elver Report on Nutrition: A/71/282." August 3.

Vitousek, Peter M., et al. 1997. "Human Domination of Earth's Ecosystem." *Science* 277: 494.

von Grebmer, K., et al. 2015. *Global Hunger Index: Armed Conflict and the Challenge of Hunger*. Bonn, Germany: Concern World Wide.

World Action on Salt and Health. 2015. "New International Study Reveals Dangerously High Levels of Salt in Children's Meals and Calls for Global Action NOW." August 18.

World Bank. 2016. A Water Secure world for All.

World Food Program. 2016. "Women and Hunger: 10 Facts."

World Health Organization. 2015. "Factsheets: Noncommunicable Diseases." January.

Ziegler, J., C. Golay, C. Mahon, and S. Way. 2011. *The Fight for the Right to Food: Lessons Learned*. Basingstoke, UK: Palgrave Macmillan.

CHAPTER 37

....

CLIMATE CHANGE

....

CLIVE HAMILTON

We all experience weather parochially, but local and regional weather is embedded in interlocking weather systems spanning the entire globe. So when human activity changes the climate, it becomes the global issue par excellence—one that will only gain in stature in the growing academic field of global studies. Climate change concerns not only every nation's future climatic regime but also the functioning of the planet as a whole. In addition to a warming world, extreme weather events are increasing in frequency, the oceans are becoming more acidic as they absorb more carbon dioxide from the atmosphere, ice masses from glaciers to the Arctic to Greenland are melting, sea levels are rising, and many plant and animal species are facing extinction. Some of these changes are now irreversible and will affect the Earth for thousands or tens of thousands of years (Archer 2009). Climate change is therefore about the conditions in which all humans will live, however much we may think we have isolated ourselves from the weather, as complacent New Yorkers learned when Hurricane Sandy, intensified by human-induced climate change, devastated the city in 2012.

We know all this as a result of a remarkable process of global scientific cooperation that has prompted—if all too slowly—a unique process of global political cooperation. Today, a vast network of measuring instruments covers the Earth's land masses, oceans, and ice sheets (Edwards 2010). Along with orbiting satellites bristling with sensors, the network comprises a truly global data collection and monitoring system. Meteorological agencies in all countries feed information into the system and rely on data supplied by other nations to forecast the national weather and assess the effects of global warming.

We know that the Earth's atmospheric layer is shared by all of us, not merely because we all breathe it but because we now understand that what we do in our daily lives may affect the climate in the remotest areas of the globe. The carbon dioxide emitted from a power station in Seattle affects the climate in Beijing, and the emissions from vehicle exhaust pipes in Beijing influence the climate in Nairobi. The more scientists have discovered about the global climate system, the more we appreciate that our local weather connects us all. At least, it does for those who are open to the lessons of climate science. For a number of reasons, others remain doggedly closed to them (Hamilton 2010: 95–133).

That the Earth's climate system rings the entire planet now seems obvious, yet it was not until the end of the nineteenth century that scientists first began to formulate a conception of a worldwide climate system operating in the planet's thin layer of atmosphere. Scattered early ideas suggesting a global system of climate were brought together in an 1896 book by Julius von Hamm, *The Earth as a Whole: Its Atmosphere and Hydrosphere*, and yet a popular handbook published in 1922, and still being published in 1961, argued that "the notion of a global climate made little sense" because the weather is too changeable between the poles and the tropics (Edwards 2010: 67–69).

Until that point, the climate had been thought of as a local or regional phenomenon, as the average patterns of daily weather. But especially since the end of World War II, climatologists began to understand that the weather is influenced not only by local factors— latitude, vegetation, proximity to mountains and seas, urban air pollution, and so on—but also by planetary phenomena such as variations in solar insolation, the great air circulation processes that drive the monsoons, and, crucially, the greenhouse effect (Edwards 2010: 80).

Solar radiation warms the Earth, but the heat would be mostly radiated back into space if it were not for the atmosphere trapping some of it, in the same way that the glass of a greenhouse traps heat and warms it more than the air outside. The idea of global warming is best dated from the pioneering work of Swedish chemist Svante Arrhenius, who, in a now-famous 1896 paper, made some remarkably accurate calculations concerning the influence of carbon dioxide and water vapor on the average temperature of the globe. "Arrhenius," writes Edwards, "may have been the first scientist to image that human activities might cause global climate change," although he was concerned with global cooling rather than global warming (Edwards 2010: 74).

The greenhouse gases that help block some of the infrared heat escaping the Earth include water vapor, carbon dioxide, methane, and several others of lesser impact. The main sources of human-induced global warming are carbon dioxide emissions from the burning of fossil fuels (coal, oil, and natural gas). In 1958, Charles David Keeling set up instruments to measure carbon dioxide on top of an extinct volcano in Hawai'i. It soon became evident that the concentration of carbon dioxide in the atmosphere was steadily increasing year on year. Keeling's first measurement in 1958 showed it at 315 parts per million (ppm), compared to the long-term pre-industrial level of the late eighteenth century of 280 ppm. In 1970, it had reached 325 ppm; it was 353 ppm in 1990, and accelerating through the 1990s and 2000s, in 2016 it broke through the 400 ppm mark, a level that had not been exceeded for 23 million years. Although scientists knew it was coming, it caused widespread alarm and rising anxiety among them and all who understand what is at stake.

The Keeling curve prompted some climate scientists to turn their minds to how industrial activity may be changing the climate, and by the late 1970s many began to worry that warming may cause serious harm. Scientists organized conferences to discuss their research, including an important one in Villach, Austria, in 1985, where it became clear that a broad consensus had emerged on the basic propositions of global warming. The issue began to filter into the political domain and the media in the United States and Europe. Developing countries began to take notice, too, because they would be the worst affected by a changing climate.

In 1988, the issue was debated in the United Nations General Assembly, leading to a declaration that climate change is a "common concern of mankind" (Bodansky 2001: 25). In a crucial development in the same year, the World Meteorological Organization and the United Nations Environment Programme (UNEP) founded the Intergovernmental Panel on Climate Change (IPCC). Although established by governments, the IPCC draws together the most qualified climate scientists from throughout the world to sift through and synthesizes all the latest scientific research, subjecting each of the major claims to the most rigorous scrutiny. In an unprecedented program of global scientific cooperation, approximately every five years it publishes the results of its work in three compendious reports—one on the science of climate change itself, one on the current and expected impacts of climate change, and one on the range of policies that might be adopted to counter global warming or adapt to it. Its fifth report was published in 2015. The evidence for human-induced global warming is drawn from a wide range of sources and is now mountainous.

GLOBAL POLITICS

The IPCC's reports provide the foundations for international negotiations and represent the most extensive, thorough, and influential global scientific collaboration ever attempted. Its first report in 1990 laid the groundwork for the vital global agreement reached in Rio de Janeiro in 1992, the United Nations Framework Convention on Climate Change. Soon ratified by virtually all nations of the world, the Convention's objective (under Article 2) was to stabilize greenhouse gas emissions at a level that would prevent "dangerous anthropogenic interference with the climate system." In recognition of the very unequal contributions of nations to global warming and the very unequal distribution of its harmful impacts—in summary, rich countries have caused the problem and poor countries will suffer most—Article 3.1 of the Convention required parties to make efforts in accord with their "common but differentiated responsibilities and respective capabilities"; that is, those most responsible for causing the problem, and those that can more easily afford to reduce their emissions, should take the lead.

The Convention and the two previously mentioned principles still underpin all international climate change negotiations. Although bilateral agreements and plurilateral agreements have played a significant role—none more so than the 2015 agreement between China and the United States—the global response to climate change has been governed by negotiations between the parties to the Convention. They meet formally each year at Conferences of the Parties (COPs), such as the landmark COP21 in Paris in late 2015. These global negations and the agreements they reach (or fail to reach) have a substantial, although variable, influence on each nation's greenhouse gas reduction efforts. Among rich nations, some take their international obligations more seriously than others, with the main influences being the seriousness with which they treat the scientific warnings, the political influence of the fossil fuel lobby, and the "ecological consciousness" of their citizens.

The 1992 Framework Convention was the product of hard-fought negotiations in which the divergent positions of various parties, which had been forming over the previous few years, clashed (Bodansky 2001; Oberthür and Ott 1999). Sharp divisions have bedeviled negotiations ever since, with each nation or party striving to play its role while protecting the "national interest." Climate change negotiations have brought into sharp focus the concept of *the national interest*, which in recent decades has come to be defined increasingly narrowly by economic impacts and the commercial interests of domestic businesses. The extent to which political leaders include protecting their citizens—not to mention the citizens of other nations and all future citizens—from the effects of dangerous climate change has been highly variable, and indeed the positioning of parties has changed as their governments have changed.

Climate change highlights, perhaps more clearly than any other issue, the difficulties and tensions created by the global order structured on the Westphalian state system—that is, the system, first agreed in Europe with the Peace of Westphalia in 1648, that divides the world into nations each with its own sovereignty over its territory. How does a nation defend its sovereignty when it cannot prevent other nations from transforming, perhaps dramatically, the conditions of life in one's own territory? Only a collective approach by humanity, acting in concert to respond to a common threat, holds any hope, because climate change operates above all territories as a planetary phenomenon. It is changing, if slowly, how nations and people think about themselves and their place in the world.

While negotiations are conducted between states, non-state actors have had an important influence. International non-governmental organizations (NGOs) acting outside of the state system attempt to influence the actions of states and indeed of each other. For our purposes, there are two main kinds.[1]

Business organizations such as those representing the world's coal industry and the nuclear power industry are the first kind.[2] Corporations that are otherwise in competition with each other have a common interest in stopping or shaping responses to climate change. At their most influential, they form alliances with state negotiators, as at times they have, for example, with the Australian government (Hamilton 2001). In recent years, the monopoly exercised by the fossil fuel industries has been challenged by the alternative energy industries, mainly wind and solar, which have grown rapidly in size and therefore in political sway. Finance industries have also begun exerting influence, generally in a positive direction, as they seek to reduce the risk of carbon-based assets.

The world view of business organizations is better described as "international" rather than "global" because they link the business interests of their members across national borders rather than taking a global approach to the problems of climate change.

Global environmental NGOs such as Greenpeace and the World Wildlife Fund are the second kind of non-state actors. Although best known for their public campaigning, they also engage in lobbying and produce policy papers to shape opinion. Although there have been important differences in strategy between the environmental NGOs, they often cooperate and, at times, coordinate their activities. The larger groups have made concerted efforts to establish offshoots in developing countries and forge ties of solidarity with kindred organizations in the South. They also exchange ideas and coordinate their activities with local, national, and international NGOs through a number of continent-wide Climate Action Networks, which help internationalize the perspectives of national NGOs. These networks amplify the voices of the poor and vulnerable of the Global South. Because they are more focused on protecting the global commons from dangerous climate change and promoting global solidarity with poor and vulnerable people throughout the world, the perspective of environmental NGOs is better described as "global" rather than "international."

At the COPs, environmental NGOs have had a substantial influence on various players. In the face of government and corporate resistance, their policy work and activism have helped frame proposals and outcomes more in keeping with what climate science states must be done to avoid dangerous climate change. They have influenced the negotiating stances of major parties, especially governments that aim to appeal to "green voters," and have helped shape the media messages that go out to the world from the conferences. They have also provided expert support for nations too small to have the scientific and other expertise needed to participate effectively in negotiations.

GLOBAL JUSTICE

Since the world met in Rio de Janeiro in 1992, international negotiations have been dogged by a critical question: Who is responsible?

Calculating each nation's annual and historical greenhouse gas emissions is relatively straightforward, and it is done using a system of greenhouse accounting agreed at the Kyoto COP in 1997. But allocating blame and responsibility for fixing the problem is much more difficult. Blame matters because, as an ethical principle, it would seem that those most to blame for causing the damage to the global climate have an obligation to do most to fix it. Although the answers have often been acrimonious, the question of blame invites us to view climate change as one for the citizens of the world as a whole.

So who is to blame? Is it those nations that now have the highest annual emissions? Those that have contributed most during the past 200 years? Those with high emissions per person, even if as small rich countries their overall emissions are less than those of a large poor country? And just as a fair tax system asks the rich to pay proportionally more, should we not take into account the principle of capacity to pay for emission reductions as well as the principle of polluter pays? What about poor people in rich countries whose personal emissions are low compared to those of rich people in poor countries who drive around in limousines and live in mansions? Are we global citizens with a responsibility to all, and especially the world's poor, or are we national citizens committed only to the "national interest"? And should those nations that have caused most disruption to the climate pay compensation to those nations that will be most damaged?

Posing these awkward questions suggests that at its heart the debate over how to respond to a warming world is an *ethical* one involving questions of global justice, despite the frequent framing of climate change as an economic question (Gardiner 2011). From the first day the global community began debating what to do, the negotiations have been mired, and at times wrecked, by differences over how to answer them. Nevertheless, the 1992 Framework Convention enshrined a number of principles that have guided negotiations. The principle of intergenerational equity declares that "the Parties should protect the climate system for the benefit of present and future generations of humankind." The principle of "common but differentiated responsibilities and respective capabilities" captures the greater historical contribution of rich countries to the accumulation of greenhouse gas emissions in the atmosphere and imposes a greater obligation on those that can afford it to reduce their carbon emissions. Of course, agreeing to a broad set of principles is easier than implementing them. When there is no international enforcement mechanism, it is even more difficult.

In the 1990s, a concept emerged that is globally cosmopolitan in form and intention. "Contraction and convergence" is an ethical principle and a practical solution based on the idea that every person in the world ought to have the same entitlement to pollute the atmosphere—that is, "converge" on an equal per person right to emit (Meyer 2004). But avoiding dangerous climate change demands that emissions per person fall to a very low level—that is, "contract" to that level—usually by 2050. Calculations indicate that to avoid the worst effects of climate change, average per person carbon dioxide emissions would need to decline to approximately 1 tonne of carbon dioxide equivalent, compared to emissions in 2014 of 16.5 tonnes in the United States, 7.6 tonnes in China, 1.8 tonnes in India and 0.5 tonnes in Nigeria.[3]

The principle of equal per capita rights can be operationalized only by joining it with the notion of a global carbon budget—that is, the upper limit of global carbon emissions from now until 2050 that is consistent with keeping warming below the internationally agreed limit of 2°C. Fair shares of the global carbon budget for each state are then calculated by combining the two, leaving it to each country and its monopoly on law-making to decide how best to fulfill its commitment. So under a contraction and convergence approach, fair shares of the global carbon budget would be allocated to each nation, but how that share is divided among individual citizens is left to those nations to decide. They may not allocate their national carbon budget in an equitable way.

Although the principle of contraction and convergence has not been formally adopted, and is unlikely to be, the language of climate change treaties has increasingly reflected the idea behind it. Some states, such as the United Kingdom, have calculated their emission reduction trajectories accepting that their "fair share" of global emissions in 2050 should be no more than the global per capita average (multiplied by their population) needed to limit warming to less than 2°C.

THE LOST YEARS, FROM KYOTO TO PARIS

When the COP was held in Kyoto in 1997, competing notions of fairness were exploited in pursuit of economic benefit. After exhaustive negotiations, the parties agreed to a protocol aimed at turning the principles enshrined in the Framework Convention into concrete, legally binding actions. The developed countries committed themselves to reduce their greenhouse gas emissions by certain percentages by 2012. The United States agreed to cut them by 7% compared to 1990 levels, the European Union by 8%, and Japan by 6%. (Australia demanded it be allowed to increase its emissions by 8% above 1990 levels and inserted a special loophole permitting a much higher increase (Hamilton 2001).) Recognizing their need to industrialize, and rich nations' responsibility for most emissions, developing countries were not obliged to limit the growth in their emissions, although it was implied that at some future point they would make such commitments.

Before an international treaty can enter into force and become legally binding on participating parties, it must be ratified by a specified number of nations. (Ratification usually means formal endorsement by a nation's legislature but may be done by presidential fiat.) While President Clinton was negotiating the protocol in Kyoto, the US Senate passed a resolution rejecting the treaty and any other treaty that imposed emission limits on some nations but not others. When George W. Bush became president in 2000, he announced that the United States would not be ratifying, which was almost a deathblow to the Kyoto Protocol. By 2005, enough parties had ratified the treaty for it to enter into force. Although the European Union was taking its commitment seriously, it was clear that the Protocol was wholly inadequate to tackle skyrocketing global carbon emissions and the increasingly apparent damage being caused by a warming world.

The search began for a new way to respond to the worsening problem. Global conditions were changing rapidly from those that gave rise to the Kyoto Protocol in 1997. Two stood out. First, the "top-down" approach of imposing, through negotiation, legally binding emission limits was no longer acceptable and had proven largely ineffective. Second, the profile of global emissions was changing radically, with China's extraordinarily rapid industrial growth causing it to surpass the United States and become the world's largest emitter of greenhouse gases in 2007. Today, China's emissions are double those of the United States. China's rapid economic expansion made it a far more powerful player in global politics. The reshaping of the global economy saw climate policy alliances shifting. Europe's influence has declined sharply; new blocs such as BRICS (Brazil, Russia, India, China, and South Africa) have emerged; and the most vulnerable nations, especially the low-lying small island states and Africa's poorest countries, have been increasingly isolated, although their isolation, combined with more confronting scientific forecasts, has made them more determined to demand strong actions.

When the nations of the world met at the climate change conference in Copenhagen in 2009, this global reordering was very apparent. Attempts to broker a new agreement were resisted by China, and the conference broke up in disarray. A period of deep gloom settled over activists, policymakers, and clean energy businesses, with no apparent way forward. But the process of rebuilding began. A new architecture emerged with two core components. The Kyoto-style top-down approach would be replaced by a "pledge-and-review" system in which every nation would, on the basis of its own assessment of its circumstances and obligations, pledge to reduce its emissions or the growth of its emissions and agree to review its contribution periodically (Zia 2013). There was an understanding that pledges would be expected from both developed and developing nations.

After a series of conferences and a great deal of work behind the scenes, including a historic bilateral agreement between China and the United States announced in September 2015, this new approach was agreed to by all parties at the Paris climate conference in December 2015. Since 2009, the Chinese Government, increasingly concerned about the impacts of climate change and severe urban air pollution, had shifted to a much more constructive approach. It also anticipates that its huge program of investment in renewable energy will see it become the global economic powerhouse for clean-energy technology.

China and the Reshaping of the Globe

From this very brief history, a number of conclusions can be drawn. First, the era of the United States' global hegemony is over. The post-Soviet era of a single superpower, following the Berlin Wall's collapse in 1989, lasted less than two decades. China is asserting itself as a countervailing force. An agreement between the United States and China was essential for a new global climate change agreement to emerge, and we should expect the same precondition in other matters of global affairs for the foreseeable future, perhaps until India attains a level of economic influence that creates a tripartite structure.

Second, China realized that it could exempt itself from emission reduction commitments but it could not exempt itself from the effects of a changing climate, including the domestic political unrest that environmental disputes cause throughout the "Middle Kingdom." In addition, a powerful nation that exempts itself from global agreements limits its own influence, particularly on questions that profoundly affect every nation.

The changing role of China in international efforts to respond to the threat of climate change undermines one of the central planks of global studies, namely the binary view of the world taken by many global studies scholars based on the legacy of colonialism (the "postcolonial perspective") and the understanding of globalization as the imposition on an unwilling South of the economic model and way of living of the North.

A glance at historical statistics for national greenhouse gas emissions shows the North to be responsible for bringing on climate change. And any familiarity with the history of negotiations and national actions from the early 1990s confirms the unwillingness of most rich nations to respond to the scientific warnings by cutting their emissions. The sharp division between North and South in the climate negotiations was predictable on purely moral grounds: "You caused the problem, you fix it."

However, with the rise of China to the position of a global economic power, with the carbon emissions to match, it must be accepted that the old world of North and South has been upended. Many scholars have argued that China's emissions do not count morally because a large portion of them is emitted making consumer goods exported to the North (Bonneuil and Fressoz 2016). The intention of this argument is to keep China firmly in the exploited South by continuing to attribute sole blame for climate change to the North and the capitalist world-system it established and still enforces. This perspective is an articulation of so-called dependency theory developed in Latin America in the 1960s and 1970s to explain continued subservience of developing countries after decolonization in the 1950s.

Yet any fair assessment of the example of China shows it is time to abandon simple notions of dependency. The facts speak against it. First, the share of China's total emissions arising from export manufacture has been approximately 30%, a figure that is declining as China reorients its economy toward domestic consumption, which every year erodes the basis of the postcolonial argument. Although there is a long history of American and European corporations relocating factories to poor countries with lax environmental laws to avoid stricter ones at home, it is simply not true that corporations in the North *imposed* their dirty factories on China as a means of exploiting cheap labor and weak environmental laws. Aware of its lack of capital, expertise, and certain intangible resources, China invited corporations in the North to bring their factories to China but under strict conditions (Economist Intelligence Unit 2004). Foreign corporations, even the most powerful ones, often found themselves at the mercy of hard-nosed domestic companies with which they were forced to enter joint ventures. Those that refused to play by Chinese rules were forced to leave.

So China *chose* the path of export-oriented industrialization as an act of national sovereignty, and it did so as the quickest way of enriching itself. This was part of a deliberate shift in official ideology and practice first announced by Deng Xiaoping and then pursued vigorously by subsequent leaders (Shirk 1993).[4] One sign of its astonishing success came in 2008 when the United States found that its ability to respond to the financial crisis was severely constrained because it had funded much of its public debt by borrowing from China's central bank. Far from being a product of unequal relations of power, exchange, and material flows throughout the world, China's massive greenhouse gas emissions are an expression of its sovereign power. If anything, compared to the United States, and certainly to Europe, global power and economic strength have tilted in China's favor, as will be attested to by many in Africa, where Chinese corporations have bought up huge swathes of land and resources. Arguably, China's coal-fueled growth has given it *too much* power over others.

China's rise as a global economic and political power has given rise to a widening split within the South at international climate change negotiations. For many years, developing countries had negotiated as a bloc under the banner of "G77 plus China." However, at the 2009 Copenhagen climate change conference, China adopted an intransigent stance leading to the effective collapse of negotiations, pursuing its own economic and geopolitical interests at the expense of the small island states and the most vulnerable countries.

In summary, the rise of China has fractured the old view of the world divided between the exploited South and the dominant North. To characterize China's astonishing economic growth rates in the 1990s and 2000s, and so its enormous greenhouse gas emissions, as the result of neocolonial manipulation puts entrenched belief before history. A new, more complex, subtle and dynamic framework is required.

Climate Change as the Product of Capitalism

If the North did not impose its polluting factories on China, it did export something much more transformational—capitalism. The imperative of capitalism is the need for capital to continually expand through constant questing for new markets or a greater share of old ones (Barry 2012). A stationary capitalism is a contradiction in terms. It is driven by the restless search for higher profits and the growth of "shareholder value." This is structured into and inseparable from the system itself. If anyone occupying its commanding heights became convinced that protection of the environment must come before profits and growth, then they would have no alternative but to resign. The improvement of living standards is incidental to the process of expansion of capital; it is not true that the rich get richer and the poor get poorer. Yet governments of right and left are united in their conviction that their first responsibility is to facilitate economic growth through providing conditions supportive of business. They insist that we can have both uninterrupted growth and a healthy environment. If only one were possible, then growth would undoubtedly come first, and the natural environment would go into terminal decline (as it arguably has).

This is why analysts such as Wright and Nyberg (2015) argue that "the threat of climate change is fundamentally connected with the expansion of global capitalism" (p. 6) and that businesses operate in an incentive system that encourages them to "devour the very life-support systems of a habitable environment" (p. 25). Angus (2016), too, writes of capitalism's "fundamental drive to grow and speed up, and its consequent tendency to override and rupture nature's essential processes and cycles" (p. 126). The expansion of capitalism in the nineteenth century became increasingly dependent on fossil fuels for energy, a trend that only intensified in the twentieth century. This gave enormous financial and political power to oil and coal corporations, a system that has been dubbed "fossil capitalism" (Angus 2016: 108; Malm 2016).

Harking back to the discussion of the role of non-state actors, when corporations organize to influence international treaty negotiations, they are doing more than protecting their commercial interests. They are defending a *system*, the global system of capitalism organized on neoliberal principles. In this goal, they mobilize an army of supporters—in the media, universities, think tanks, public institutions, and politics—whose function is to persuade the citizenry that climate change is not so serious as to require radical action and that the best way to respond is through the system itself.

China and World-Systems Analysis

Drawing on dependency theory, world-systems analysis emerged in the 1970s to counter modernization theory, the idea that all societies could be placed somewhere on a well-defined trajectory of economic and technological development. In modernization theory, each nation operates independently as it moves through the stages of development driven by the historical force of "progress." Underdeveloped countries were lectured by the rich to speed up the process by emulating the practices of modern states. In general, this meant opening up their economies to foreign corporations and withdrawing government from the economy. Adopting liberal democratic forms was preferable, although in practice the United States was not averse to sponsoring coups and insurgencies to topple democratically elected governments if they did not act in ways sympathetic to US corporations.

World-systems analysis rejected the idea of autonomous nations moving more or less quickly along the path of "development." The world is not made up of a collection of sovereign states but, rather, is composed of national components of a world system, with a few powerful ones occupying the "core" and the others consigned to the "periphery" (Wallerstein 1999: 192–197). The relationship between core and periphery has been one of unequal exchange, with the periphery providing raw materials at cheap prices, at times compelled by military force. In the nineteenth century, for example, Britain launched two wars against China in order to keep the supply of tea flowing.

The world system is driven by capitalist accumulation—that is, the endless imperative of capital to expand, mainly by finding new areas (geographically and socially) to draw into the commodity world. The world system began to take shape some five centuries ago. Its reach and power grew so that it now encompasses the entire world in a tightly knit system. The "globalization" of the 1990s and 2000s has only been a more intense phase. World-systems understanding has recently been mobilized by Bonneuil and Fressoz (2016), among others, to explain the climate crisis in terms of "unequal ecological exchange" whereby unequal flows of matter, energy, commodities, and capital between rich and poor countries have enabled the rich to become richer while imposing environmental degradation and exploitation on poor countries (pp. 224–225, 250–252).

The rise of China provides a fundamental challenge to world-systems understanding. It is true that China's growth is due to the opening up of the nation to capitalist accumulation, but it contradicts the other main elements of the approach. First, as discussed previously, capitalism took hold in China as a result of decisions by the Chinese Communist

Party and not because corporations or political powers in core countries imposed it. If there has been an "unequal ecological exchange" manifested in China's enormous emissions of greenhouse gases, it is because China invested heavily in manufacturing and infrastructure as a deliberate strategy. Second, if as a poor country China was firmly on the periphery, its rapid growth into a global economic powerhouse—its total gross domestic product is expected to exceed that of the United States within a decade or two—has moved it from the periphery to the core, which undermines the core–periphery analytical structure, which is one of subjugation. Third, the Chinese model of capitalism is very different from the neoliberal model characteristic of the West, with widespread state ownership or state control of all major businesses.[5] Although encouraged to grow aggressively, in the final analysis Chinese corporations serve the interests of the state rather than the other way around.

Thus, the rise of China (to take only the most striking example) both further unifies the world under the global system of capitalism and also divides it by demonstrating that capitalism can take sharply different forms and can itself, contrary to world-systems analysis, upset the core–periphery structure. It is a complex world in which the claim that "the prosperity of the rich countries is constructed by way of a monopolization of the benefits of the Earth and an externalization of environmental damages by the phenomena of dispossession and 'unequal exchange'" (Bonneuil and Fressoz, 2016: 225) is unhelpful when taken as a general rule.

A New Cosmopolitanism?

If climate change threatens the future prosperity and stability of all nations, indeed of life itself, perhaps it will give rise to a growing *cosmopolitan sentiment*, the sense among the world's citizens that "we are all in this together" and therefore must act collectively to respond to the danger. This is certainly the sentiment that is de rigueur in the rhetoric of leaders when they gather at climate change conferences.

In this form of cosmopolitanism, the world is viewed as "a community of people and not a set of countries" so that "ethical obligations and responsibilities are not defined or delineated by national borders" (Harris 2011b: 6–7). These sentiments are globalist rather than international in their recognition that "human beings, rather than states, ought to be at the centre of moral calculations" (Harris 2011a: x).

Although phenomena such as Brexit, Trumpism, and the rise of European xenophobia argue against it, there is evidence that this kind of sentiment is widespread in the world. It underpins the approach of influential NGOs. And some progressive nations negotiate with a view to balancing national interests with the interests of the poor and vulnerable wherever they may live. Chancellor Merkel's decision in 2015 to admit an unlimited number of Syrian refugees to Germany was an expression of this standpoint, despite the backlash.

There was also evidence at the 2015 Paris conference that a cosmopolitan sentiment is gaining ground. The meeting itself and the agreement that came out of it can be seen as taking a small but important step toward a more global view. Undoubtedly, rising anxiety prompted by the warnings of climate scientists led to more willingness to join a common cause rather than retreat to the realpolitik of nations jockeying to protect a narrow version of the national interest.

A concrete and promising expression of cosmopolitan thinking could be seen in the activities of those engaged in the so-called Lima–Paris Action Agenda (LPAA).[6] The LPAA brings together a multitude of non-state actors that are increasingly taking the initiative in combatting climate change. Thousands of representatives of provincial governments, city councils, businesses, financial institutions, and on-the-ground NGOs converged on the Paris conference eager to tell the world what they were doing, whether it be initiatives promoting cooperation in urban transport and electric vehicles, an international solar energy promotion alliance (initiated by India), or a group of major businesses committed to zero deforestation in their supply chains. Approximately 6,000 cities and local authorities signed on to the LPAA, committing themselves to the 2°C or less objective and, more to the point, adopting action plans to match. The ethos of the LPAA is a globalist one of sharing experience and supporting others.

In a strong sense, what these non-state actors do is crucial to what the state actors can credibly promise. Although one must be wary of hype and green-wash, the LPAA expresses, much more than national governments, the cosmopolitan commitments to the equal worth and dignity of each individual, active agency, personal responsibility, solidarity, and sustainability (Harris 2011b: 2).

The global approach of contraction and convergence (discussed previously) is built on the cosmopolitan belief that "the world is one domain in which there are some universal values and global responsibilities" (Harris 2011b: 5) and as such reflects a sense of global citizenship, particularly a sense of solidarity with those most vulnerable to the impacts of a changing climate. This is very much the starting point of the "climate justice" movement, a broad coalition linking climate change with human rights, equitable burden-sharing, and the well-being of the most vulnerable. By framing the issue in a way that directly links the activities of the rich to the lives of the poor, it meets the definition of cosmopolitanism as a "political philosophy of living in a global age" (Harris 2011b: 16).

However, cosmopolitanism is an elastic concept. Some environmental activists view themselves as global citizens acting on behalf of all peoples of the world. Many also view themselves as acting on behalf of non-human creatures and "the planet." On the other hand, some executives and high-level personnel of multinational corporations also view themselves as "citizens of the world," without attachment or loyalty to any particular nation, but active participants in the global marketplace. This kind of "free-market cosmopolitanism" reaches a grotesque apogee on *The World*, an ocean liner billed as "the only private residential community-at-sea."[7] The residents of the ship's 165 luxury apartments enjoy "one of the most exclusive lifestyles imaginable," living a stateless existence grounded only by visits to exotic ports.

Despite superficial appearances, the rootlessness of the super-rich and global technological workers militates against the emergence of the "thick ties" of common humanity needed to overcome our Westphalian norms and motivate us to consider the impacts of our actions on those far off. In other words, we need to *feel* our "cosmopolitan nearness" (Harris 2011b: 8), rather than regard the world as an abstraction while absolving ourselves of our moral responsibilities. Into the latter category we might also place those who dream excitedly of escaping a ruined Earth in a spaceship (Hamilton 2017).

Securitization of Climate Change

If there are signs of a growing global cosmopolitanism stimulated by the threat of global warming, there are powerful forces working against it, and none more so than the securitization of climate change, which serves to reinforce the "nation-centric" framing of the threat.

Climate change is already placing stresses on some societies and giving rise to instability. For example, human-induced climate change is believed to have contributed to the long-running war and humanitarian crisis in Darfur (UNEP, 2007). A severe drought in Syria, exacerbated by anthropogenic climate change, is believed to have helped precipitate the war in Syria that began in 2011 (Kelley et al. 2015). The ensuing flood of migrants to Europe created its own security problems. The Chinese Communist Party fears that its grip on power may be weakened if it does not respond to social unrest arising from severe urban air pollution, and it is conscious of the destabilizing effects of droughts in the country's north and flooding in the south, expected to be more intense in a warming globe.

Climate change stresses are also expected to cause tensions among nations as they compete for scarce resources. A landmark German report warned that "climate change will draw ever-deeper lines of division and conflict in international relations, triggering numerous conflicts between and within countries over the distribution of resources, especially water and land, over the management of migration, or over compensation payments" (Schubert et al. 2007: 1). It identifies a number of "conflict constellations" where social and environmental linkages bring destabilization and possible violence. The constellations include growing competition over scarce water resources; decline in food production leading to collapsing social systems; increasing migration and economic difficulties due to climate-induced storm and flood disasters; and rising migration pressures due to drought, soil degradation, and water scarcity exacerbated by a weak capacity of institutions to respond.

Military strategists now describe climate change as a "threat multiplier" and have begun to factor the effects of global warming into their planning scenarios (Brown, Hammill, and McLeman 2007). A 2014 Pentagon report noted, "We are considering the impacts of climate change in our war games and defense planning scenarios, and are working with our Combatant Commands to address impacts in their areas of responsibility" (Banusiewicz 2014). One early manifestation has been the increasing militarization of the Arctic, where melting sea ice has opened up opportunities for sea-floor exploration and exploitation of fossil fuel resources (Singh 2013). In the summer of 2007, Russia took the opportunity of an ice-free Arctic to symbolically stake its claim to deep-sea oil and gas reserves by sending a submarine to plant its national flag on the sea-floor beneath the North Pole.[8]

Thus, a number of complex forces are at work. In response to the most global phenomenon imaginable, one arising above all from the relentless logic of capitalism, we are witnessing the opening up of new opportunities for capital accumulation but also the likelihood of growing political destabilization from climate-induced migration, the multiplication of security threats, and greater preparedness for conflict between nations. Analytically, we are seeing a tug-of-war between global studies and international relations as ways of comprehending the world.

GLOBAL STUDIES IN THE EARTH SYSTEM

Global studies emerged in response to dissatisfaction with the way orthodox international relations framed issues as contests between sovereign states and the way this framing mischaracterizes global issues that transcend borders. The new approach emphasizes the "globality" of people and their concerns. Yet it may be that global studies is better founded not on the globality of shared human concerns but, rather, on the emergent understanding of the globality of the natural world. To explain why requires a little more science.

The emergence in the 1980s and 1990s of a new kind of ecological thinking known as Earth system science changed the way Earth scientists thought about climate change and its implications (Hamilton and Grinevald 2015). So far, we have considered only the climate. Yet the *atmosphere* is only one of five "spheres" that make up the Earth system. The others are the *hydrosphere*, comprising rivers, lakes, oceans, and water vapor in the atmosphere; the *cryosphere* or ice masses, including those at the poles, over Greenland, and the world's glaciers; the *biosphere*, consisting of all living things and their environments; and the *lithosphere*, the outer crust of the Earth. Beginning in the 1980s, scientists began to understand that each of these spheres is linked to the others. Together, they constitute a dynamic, integrated, complex Earth system that evolves through deep time but also may switch states quickly. In thinking about climate change and its effects, all of the spheres come into play— sea-level rise threatens low-lying Pacific islands, melting glaciers jeopardize water supplies in Peru, die-off in the Amazon forests could affect rainfall in Africa, and acidifying oceans (due to rising carbon dioxide concentrations) changes depositions on the ocean floor.

The essential problem of global warming arises because human beings during the past 200 years—and especially during the past 70 years—have been redistributing carbon around the Earth system. When we dig up and burn fossil fuels, we convert their stored carbon into carbon dioxide and dump it as waste into the atmosphere. Some is soaked up by vegetation, and some is absorbed by the oceans (making them more acidic). Over very long time scales, the carbon can be immobilized in fossils and rocks. But over years to millennia, some of it stays in the atmosphere, warming the globe, linking all future generations wherever they may live.

We now know that the impact of humans on the Earth system has become so powerful that we have changed the functioning of the Earth system as a whole, so much so that we have entered a new geological epoch, the Anthropocene, or the Age of Humans (Zalasiewicz et al. 2011). As the implications of this "earth-shattering" development sink in over the next two or three decades, perhaps humans will begin to think of themselves in a different way, as creatures with enormous but dangerous powers that somehow must be governed and controlled (Hamilton 2017). It is perhaps utopian to imagine that the arrival of the Anthropocene will give rise to a new spirit of global citizenship in the way envisaged by, for instance, the founders of the United Nations and the League of Nations before them. But it may compel nations, in the face of widespread breakdown of the natural systems that support life, to work much harder at cooperation, as no nation can solve the problem alone. If they do not, the future is bleak.

In a way, the advent of the Anthropocene brought humans together as a common entity for the very first time. Before its arrival, groups of humans—in towns, in regions, and in nations—were transforming the environments around them. At times, there were cross-border problems (emissions from smoke stacks in one country caused acid rain in neighboring countries). The arrival of the new epoch means that humans collectively are changing the way the Earth functions in its totality, even though it remains true that some humans are much more to blame than others. This is new in the history of humankind, and it has far-reaching implications for global studies. If we search for the foundations of global studies in intra-human relations alone, we are locked into a (Kantian) world of autonomous agents; but if those agents belong to the Earth system, they become "global" in a radically new way.

NOTES

1. A third group covers humanitarian organizations, such as the Red Cross, that campaign in the interests of the poorest and most vulnerable.
2. There has also been an internationally coordinated effort by climate science deniers (often with public or secret backing of fossil fuel corporations such as Exxon Mobil) to disrupt and undermine negotiations (Oreskes and Conway 2010).
3. https://en.wikipedia.org/wiki/List_of_countries_by_carbon_dioxide_emissions.
4. These facts have not prevented senior Chinese officials from themselves turning to world-systems arguments to defend their own position at climate talks (Bonneuil and Fressoz 2015: 227).
5. For an overview, see http://factsanddetails.com/china/cat9/sub58/item1884.html (accessed October 14, 2016).
6. For objectives, participation, and figures, see http://newsroom.unfccc.int/lpaa (accessed October 13, 2016).
7. See http://aboardtheworld.com (accessed October 13, 2016).
8. https://www.theguardian.com/world/2007/aug/02/russia.arctic (accessed October 13, 2016).

REFERENCES

Angus, I. 2016. *Facing the Anthropocene: Fossil Capitalism and the Crisis of the Earth System*. New York: Monthly Review Press.

Archer, D. 2009. *The Long Thaw: How Humans Are Changing the Next 100,000 Years of Earth's Climate*. Princeton, NJ: Princeton University Press.

Banusiewicz, J. 2014. "Hagel to Address 'Threat Multiplier' of Climate Change." US Department of Defense, October 13. http://www.defense.gov/News/Article/Article/603440. Accessed October 4, 2016.

Barry, John. 2012. "Climate Change, 'The Cancer Stage of Capitalism' and the Return of Limits to Growth." In *Climate Change and the Crisis of Capitalism*, edited by M. Pelling, D. Manuel-Navarrete, and M. Redclift, 129–142. London: Routledge.

Bodansky, D. 2001. "The History of the Global Climate Change Regime." In *International Relations and Global Climate Change*, edited by U. Luterbacher and D. F. Sprinz, 23–40. Cambridge, MA: MIT Press.

Bonneuil, C., and J-B. Fressoz 2016. *The Shock of the Anthropocene*. London: Verso.

Brown, O., A. Hammill, and R. McLeman. 2007. "Climate Change as the 'New' Security Threat: Implications for Africa." *International Affairs* 83 (6): 1141–1154.

Economist Intelligence Unit. 2004. "Coming of Age: Multinational Companies in China." White paper. *The Economist*. http://graphics.eiu.com/files/ad_pdfs/MNC_report.pdf

Edwards, P. N. 2010. *A Vast Machine: Computer Models, Climate Data, and the Politics of Global Warming*. Cambridge, MA: MIT Press.

Gardiner, S. 2011. *A Perfect Moral Storm: The Ethical Tragedy of Climate Change*. New York: Oxford University Press.

Hamilton, C. 2001. *Running from the Storm: The Development of Climate Change Policy in Australia*. Sydney: University of New South Wales Press.

Hamilton, C. 2010. *Requiem for a Species: Why We Resist the Truth About Climate Change*. London: Earthscan.

Hamilton, C. 2017. *Defiant Earth: The Fate of Humans in the Anthropocene*. Cambridge, UK: Polity.

Hamilton, C., and J. Grinevald 2015. "Was the Anthropocene Anticipated?" *The Anthropocene Review* 2 (1): 59–72.

Harris, Paul. 2011a. "Preface." In *Ethics and Global Environmental Policy: Cosmopolitan Conceptions of Climate Change*, edited by Paul Harris, ix–x. Cheltenham, UK: Elgar.

Harris, Paul. 2011b. "Introduction: Cosmopolitanism and Climate Change Policy." In *Ethics and Global Environmental Policy: Cosmopolitan Conceptions of Climate Change*, edited by Paul Harris, 1–19. Cheltenham, UK: Elgar.

Kelley, C., S. Mohtadi, M. A. Cane, R. Seager, and Y. Kushnir. 2015. "Climate Change in the Fertile Crescent and Implications of the Recent Syrian Drought." *Proceedings of the National Academy of Science of the USA* 112 (11): 3241–3246.

Malm, A. 2016. *Fossil Capital: The Rise of Steam Power and the Roots of Global Warming*. London: Verso.

Meyer, A. 2004. "Briefing: Contraction and Convergence." *Proceedings of the Institution of Civil Engineers—Engineering Sustainability* 157 (4): 189–192.

Oberthür, S., and H. E. Ott. 1999. *The Kyoto Protocol: International Climate Policy for the 21st Century*. Berlin: Springer.

Oreskes, N., and E. Conway. 2010. *Merchants of Doubt: How a Handful of Scientists Obscured the Truth on Issues from Tobacco Smoke to Global Warming*. London: Bloomsbury.

Schubert, R., et al.; German Advisory Council on Global Change. 2007. *Climate Change as a Security Risk*. London: Earthscan.

Shirk, S. 1993. *The Political Logic of Economic Reform in China*. Berkeley: University of California Press.

Singh, A. 2013. "The Creeping Militarization of the Arctic." *The Diplomat*, October 16. http://thediplomat.com/2013/10/the-creeping-militarization-of-the-arctic. Accessed October 10, 2016.

United Nations Environment Programme. 2007. "Sudan: Post-Conflict Environmental Assessment." Nairobi: United Nations Environment Programme.

Wallerstein, I. 1999. *The End of the World as We Know It: Social Science for the Twenty-First Century*. Minneapolis: University of Minnesota Press.

Wright, C., and D. Nyberg. 2015. *Climate Change, Capitalism, and Corporations: Processes of Creative Self-destruction*. Cambridge, UK: Cambridge University Press.

Zalasiewicz, J., M. Williams, A. Haywood, and M. Ellis. 2011. "The Anthropocene: A New Epoch of Geological Time?" *Philosophical Transactions of the Royal Society A* 369: 835–841.

Zia, Asim. 2013. *Post-Kyoto Climate Governance: Confronting the Politics of Scale, Ideology, and Knowledge*. London: Routledge.

CHAPTER 38

....

PANDEMICS

....

KATHRYN H. JACOBSEN

A pandemic is a global epidemic, and the determination that a pandemic is occurring is based on frequency, geography, and severity. To be considered a pandemic, a disease must be occurring frequently enough to meet the definition of an epidemic, which is an event in which new cases of disease are occurring at higher than expected rates (Barreto, Teixeira, and Carmo 2006). The typical statistic used to measure disease occurrence is the incidence rate, which is the number of new cases of a disease divided by the population at risk of the disease during a set time period, such as a week or a month. There is no predetermined incidence rate that constitutes an epidemic. If zero cases of a particular disease are typically present in a population, then an outbreak might be declared after just a few people become ill. If an infectious disease is regularly present at a particular incidence level (i.e., if the disease is endemic in a particular population), a substantial increase in that rate might constitute an epidemic. The words "outbreak" and "epidemic" are often used interchangeably, but some people consider an outbreak to be an event limited to one community or a limited number of people or places, whereas an epidemic is a more widespread occurrence.

Once the frequency criterion is met, a potentially pandemic disease must spread across a large geographic range. To epidemiologists—the public health scientists who seek to understand why diseases occur in particular populations and to apply that knowledge toward the prevention and containment of outbreaks—the defining feature of a pandemic is the disease epidemic adversely affecting multiple world regions at one time (Card 2012). A deadly emerging infectious disease that remains contained in one world region is a serious threat to global public health because of the potential for more widespread transmission, but it is not a pandemic event if local transmission of the pathogen is not occurring on several continents.

The third criterion for a pandemic, along with the incidence rate and the number of regions affected, is a consideration of severity. The word "pandemic" conveys a sense of risk and urgency (Doshi 2011). A global outbreak of a mild illness such as the common cold would generally not be considered a pandemic because the pathogen does not cause serious illness (morbidity), long-term disability, or death (mortality). By contrast, a virulent strain of influenza that is determined to be a serious risk to human health would likely be declared a pandemic flu once several countries in different areas of the world report locally acquired (rather than travel-associated) cases (Dupras and Williams-Jones 2012). A challenge with including severity as a criterion for a pandemic is that severity is not well defined. For example, it is not readily apparent whether a disease that is not highly contagious but kills a high percentage of the people it does affect (i.e., one that has a low infectivity but a high case fatality rate) would be considered severe. Similarly, a disease with a high infectivity rate but a very low case fatality rate might not meet the criterion for severity because the typical person who becomes ill has almost zero risk of death from the disease, but even with a low fatality rate, the cumulative number of deaths could be substantial if several billion people contracted the infection. The perception of risk by members of the general public might play more of a role in the determination of severity than the actual risk as determined by scientific calculations.

Other factors used to determine whether a pandemic is occurring include the widespread vulnerability of large populations to the disease; the speed of spread of the epidemic throughout the world; the novelty of the disease-causing agent, with an emerging infectious disease considered to be a greater threat than a well-known pathogen; and the contagiousness of the agent—the ability of the disease to be easily transferred from one person or place to another—although there is no firm requirement that a pandemic be caused by a highly infectious pathogen (Morens, Folkers, and Fauci 2009). In addition, political and financial considerations may factor into this determination (Kelly 2011). The World Health Organization (WHO) describes a series of stages in the development of a pandemic influenza event, but there is no formal global agreement about how the word "pandemic" is defined for influenza or for other diseases (Doshi 2011). The lack of one clear set of criteria for defining pandemics means that experts may reach different conclusions about whether a pandemic is occurring. The nebulous nature of pandemics makes case studies the best option for clarifying what pandemics are, why they occur, how various players respond to them, and how globalization and pandemics are connected.

HISTORIC RESPONSES TO PANDEMICS

Case Study: Cholera

Cholera is a bacterial infection that causes severe watery diarrhoea and can lead to a rapid death in victims who are unable to adequately replenish lost fluids and electrolytes. Cases of cholera have been reported in South Asia for centuries, with occasional spread along trading routes to neighboring countries. Approximately 200 years ago, as the British Empire was instigating rapid changes in global economic and political systems, an expanded network of international migration and shipping allowed cholera to be exported repeatedly from Asia. A series of devastating pandemics occurred in quick succession: A first wave in 1817–1823 was followed by a second in 1826–1838, a third in 1839–1855, a fourth in 1863–1874, a fifth in 1881–1896, and a sixth in 1899–1923 (Lee 2001).

Cholera moved across Asia and the Middle East, into Europe and North Africa, and across the Atlantic Ocean to the Americas, killing tens of millions of people (Lee and Dodgson 2000). Quarantines and blockades (the *cordon sanitaire*) that had been somewhat effective in controlling plague, a bacterial infection spread by rats, proved to be ineffective against a disease associated with poor sanitation. Perhaps more important, public health measures restricting travel had come to be viewed as impractical given the clear economic benefits of international trade (Huber 2006).

In response to the global cholera crises of the nineteenth century, a series of a dozen International Sanitary Conferences was held between 1851 and 1911 (Lee and Dodgson 2000). Although most of the representatives were from European nations, delegates from other countries participated in the scientific and political dialogues (Huber 2006). The resulting agreements about information sharing and travel rules during epidemics of cholera, plague, and yellow fever set the stage for modern global health communication and policy (Fidler 2005). A key aim of these International Sanitary Regulations (ISR) was to limit slowdowns of international trade and commerce during outbreaks by replacing piecemeal international agreements with global ones and by stipulating that decisions about public health policy should be based on scientific evidence rather than reactionary politics (Fidler 2005). In 1951, soon after WHO was established, the ISR was updated by a new set of rules that were subsequently renamed the International Health Regulations (IHR). These updates placed an even greater emphasis on "maximum security" with "minimal interference" on world travel and trade (Fidler 2005).

Cholera remains an infectious disease of special global concern, with all United Nations member states obligated under the IHR to immediately report cases to WHO. The global reporting and response system overseen by WHO is a valuable mechanism for continuous tracking of outbreaks of cholera and other emerging infections with pandemic potential. A seventh cholera pandemic, one sparked by a new strain of *Vibrio cholerae* called El Tor, began in 1961 and spread through much of Asia, Africa, and the Americas during the following decades (Mutreja et al. 2011). An emergent strain called *V. cholerae* O139 could spark an eighth pandemic at any time (Lee 2001).

Pandemics: Anxiety, Action, and Advocacy

The cholera case study highlights a typical pattern of response to pandemic events. The first reaction is often a desire for isolation. This collective anxiety about outside threats is accompanied by active attempts to keep the pathogen from crossing into new countries. During the early cholera pandemics, some ports were closed to ships from affected countries even though this proved to be a futile attempt to stop the spread of the waterborne pathogen. Similar types of isolationism continue to be the initial reaction to modern epidemics. For example, during the 2003 severe acute respiratory syndrome (SARS) pandemic and the 2014 Ebola outbreak in West Africa (which did not become a global pandemic), flight bans and border closures were quickly implemented by dozens of countries (Poletto et al. 2014).

When travel bans and other attempts to wall off an outbreak at its point of origin prove to be unsuccessful, the typical second phase of responding to a pandemic is to call for collective global action. The disease control conventions held during the early cholera pandemics led to the creation of the international laws that continue to guide pandemic responses today. The records from those gatherings of international delegates acknowledge the same tension between science and politics that has been apparent in more recent pandemics. They also highlight the difficulties of allowing countries to restrict migration for disease control purposes while at the same time attempting to mandate that borders remain open to trade.

Finally, a pandemic or the lessons learned from it may be used to promote other strategic goals, whether those are social, economic, political, or in some other domain. A cholera outbreak that started in Peru in 1991 and spread regionally was used to advocate for economic development, improved access to medical services, strengthening of the public health system, new food safety regulations, and the promotion of traditional medicine and indigenous rights; the epidemic also sparked several international spats and exacerbated tensions between some neighboring nations (Labonte 1992). Because of cholera's history, the presence of the disease is viewed as an effective rallying cry for changes that extend far beyond the immediate threat to health. Tensions arise when pandemic preparedness and response plans are suspected to be driven by commercial and political interests rather than by scientific evidence (McCloskey et al. 2014).

PANDEMICS AND GLOBAL SECURITY

Case Study: Influenza

Influenza is a respiratory pathogen that spreads through the air, and the viral disease can cause its victims to develop severe pneumonia and die. Because influenza viruses mutate quickly and have the capacity to cause severe illness and death in humans, pandemic influenza—or "pan flu," for short—is a major concern of epidemiologists. Large-scale influenza outbreaks are thought to have occurred every few decades throughout much of human history. The first true influenza pandemic likely occurred in 1510, soon after global shipping opened up the whole world to travelers (Kamradt-Scott 2012). Historical records record other pandemics occurring in the 1730s, 1760s, 1780s, 1830s, 1840s, 1890s, and several times thereafter (Morens and Fauci 2007).

The 1918–1920 pandemic has been carefully examined as a model of an epidemiological disaster. The pandemic caused an immense loss of human life, especially when factoring in that the world population 100 years ago was approximately one-fourth of its size today. The global number of deaths in 1918–1920 from influenza would be the proportional equivalent of approximately 50–80 million deaths today (Murray et al. 2006). This burden was magnified because so many of the victims were otherwise healthy young adults. Seasonal influenza outbreaks typically cause the most deaths among the very young, the very old, and the immunocompromised, but the highest fatality rates from the 1918 strain were among people in their twenties and thirties (Murray et al. 2006). The 1918–1920 pandemic has gained notoriety in part because of how it affected the course of World War I, which was fought mainly in Europe. However, death records from those years show that the excess mortality rate caused by influenza was substantially higher in places such as India and the Philippines than in most places in Europe and North America (Murray et al. 2006). An equivalent pandemic today might cause 20 million deaths in South Asia, 18 million deaths in sub-Saharan Africa, 13 million deaths in East Asia, 6 million in the Middle East, 2.5 million deaths in Latin America and the Caribbean, and several million deaths in Europe and other high-income countries (Murray et al. 2006).

Various strains of influenza viruses affect birds, pigs, humans, and a diversity of other animals. Influenza viruses frequently undergo small mutations called antigenic drift. Those minor but important changes are the reason why a new influenza vaccine must be developed every year. There are also larger changes called antigenic shift in which two very different types of influenza viruses (typically from two different animals) merge and form a novel strain of influenza. Two types of influenza affect humans, influenza A and influenza B. Influenza A strains are named for the configuration of hemagglutinin (H) and neuraminidase (N) proteins on the surface of the virus. The H1N1 strain was dominant after its emergence in 1918 until a new H2N2 strain emerged in Asia and caused a pandemic in 1957–1960 (Glezen 1996). The H2H2 strain was dominant until a new H3N2 strain identified in Hong Kong caused a costly pandemic in 1968–1972 (Glezen 1996). The level of disease severity caused by new influenza strains varies considerably, but an emergent event can lead to a dangerous new strain quickly circling the globe.

Approximately a century after the H1N1 pandemic of 1918–1920 wreaked havoc globally, a new strain of H1N1 emerged. The first cases were diagnosed in April 2009 in Mexico and the US state of California. Although the 2009–2010 strain did not cause severe disease in most people who contracted it, the virulence of the 1918–1920 H1N1 strain caused great anxiety about the new H1N1 strain (Girard et al. 2010). WHO considers a global epidemic of pandemic influenza to be occurring when a new strain emerges for which most humans have no immunity, the virus has the capacity to cause serious illness, and the virus begins spreading easily between humans (Doshi 2011). By June 2009, less than two months after the new strain was first identified, H1N1 had matured from "Phase 3" on WHO's pandemic influenza scale to the highest level, "Phase 6," which indicates widespread human infection in multiple world regions. Although WHO officials tried to emphasize that these phases represented where cases were occurring and were not an indication that the infection was becoming more virulent and causing an alarming number of deaths, these types of important qualifiers are not consistently understood by the public and may exacerbate collective anxiety (Chew and Eysenbach 2010). By the end of December 2009, cases had been reported by more than 200 countries (Girard et al. 2010).

Under the 2005 revision of the IHR, WHO declared H1N1 to be a "public health emergency of international concern" (PHEIC) in April 2009, soon after H1N1 was shown to be spreading between humans. This was the first time the PHEIC declaration had been used since the IHR revisions went into force in 2007 (Wilson, Brownstein, and Fidler 2010). The PHEIC declaration triggered mandated H1N1 surveillance, reporting, and communication by all United Nations member nations, and it allowed WHO to issue temporary recommendations about containment strategies and policies (Wilson et al. 2010). The state of emergency allowed funds for some types of research and coordination activities to be released, but the IHR does not ensure that low-income countries with limited epidemiological and laboratory capacity are offered the financial and technical support they require to be able to comply with the IHR (Wilson et al. 2010). For example, during the H1N1 pandemic, South Africa was the only sub-Saharan African country with the necessary laboratory infrastructure to fulfill national responsibilities under the IHR (Katz and Fischer 2010).

Currently, there are few good options available for slowing or stopping the spread of novel influenza viruses. After the onset of H1N1, several countries banned or quarantined travelers from North America, especially Asian countries that had been seriously affected by SARS (Katz and Fischer 2010). However, travel bans typically delay the onset of an epidemic in a country that closes its borders by only a few weeks (Ferguson et al. 2006). Widespread use of antiviral medication can substantially reduce the attack rate during an outbreak if the particular viral strain is susceptible to the medication rather than being resistant to it (Ferguson et al. 2006), but novel pan flu strains may not be tamed by existing medications. Vaccines are often highly effective in stopping the spread of influenza, but it usually takes months to develop, test, manufacture, and distribute a vaccine against a novel pathogen. If a pathogen spreads quickly through populations, nearly everyone will have contracted the infection and developed natural immunity from it (if they survive) before a vaccine is widely available (Ferguson et al. 2006). Strains of influenza that do not yet cause severe human disease and do not yet spread quickly between humans could at any time mutate into a more dangerous pathogen, and an H5N1, H7N9, or other emerging strain could become the next pandemic agent. Influenza is a zoonotic infection (i.e., one that primarily causes disease in animals), and it takes only one human encountering one infected bird, pig, or other animal to initiate a chain of events that can lead to another pandemic.

Anxiety: Pandemics as Security Threats

Influenza is perhaps the best example of a pandemic infection being reframed as a threat to security. The developing field of global health security merges the desire to protect human populations worldwide from a diversity of physical and social threats to health with the notion that pandemics create economic and political vulnerabilities that further jeopardize health and stability (Aldis 2008). By combining human security with national security, global health security blends humanitarianism with military and political responses (Aldis 2008). Global health security therefore emphasizes shared risks and responsibilities at the same time that it mandates viewing some countries as threats to global well-being even before any particular infectious disease event is occurring.

At the individual level, framing pandemics as security threats raises alarm without providing clear pathways toward solutions. Disaster movies suggest that pandemics lead to mass panic in which store shelves are stripped of their goods, roads are blockaded, mass violence ensues, the police and military must be called in to restore order, and eventually cities look like ghost towns with a few armed guards patrolling empty streets. The threat from disease outbreaks is portrayed as not merely the risk of a gruesome death from infection but also a threat to safety and security. Everyone could be out of work, out of food, and frightened of their neighbors. The reality is that during outbreaks, most people comply with public health regulations and are able to maintain relatively normal daily activities, and therefore even most serious epidemics do not result in mass chaos. This was observed in West Africa during the 2014 Ebola outbreak. Although schools were closed for nearly a year and health care services were severely disrupted, most households continued with farming or other small business activities. There were some skirmishes at health care facilities, but the outbreak did not lead to armed conflict or famine (Wilkinson and Leach 2014). However, the rhetoric around health security considers outbreaks to be threats even to those who avoid infection. By extension, epidemics that do not reach pandemic status can still endanger well-being globally by creating security vulnerabilities.

At the national and international levels, framing pandemics as security threats may shift discussions from science toward politics. This is not new. The naming of various influenza strains reveals the political nature of past pandemics. The so-called "Spanish flu" of 1918–1920 likely emerged either in China or on pig farms in the US state of Kansas (Palmer 2010). The pandemic did not start in Spain, and Spain was not heavily affected by it compared to the burden in neighboring countries. However, Spain was a neutral country during World War I and did not censor reports of cases, unlike neighboring countries that did not want reports of mass casualties from infections to be in the news, and those reports unfairly led to the flu being considered a Spanish phenomenon (Palmer 2010). Spain referred to the virus as "French flu" (Palmer 2010). When the H1N1 pandemic began in 2009, it was referred to as "swine flu" because the virus was a strain of porcine influenza that had mutated, crossed species, and begun to cause severe disease in humans and to spread easily from human to human in the absence of contact with pigs. The "swine flu" name caused confusion about how influenza is transmitted. The virus is an airborne one, but the name "swine flu" implied that it was caused by eating pork. As the pandemic intensified, some countries banned pork imports or culled herds of pigs even though these actions would have no effect on preventing the spread of H1N1 (Schein et al. 2012). When the term "Mexican flu" was introduced as an alternative way to describe the disease based on its first known location, it stigmatized Mexico and some countries imposed unfair travel bans on Mexicans (Schein et al. 2012).

As global health has become part of the global security agenda, the political response to pandemics has shifted from diplomatic efforts emphasizing state sovereignty toward legal agreements emphasizing state responsibility (Hoffman 2010). This approach may privilege more powerful states over weaker ones. During the 2009–2010 H1N1 pandemic, world maps of case reports showed almost no countries in Africa reporting any cases. Without strong national surveillance and laboratory systems, those countries were unable to test for H1N1. And without test results, they were simply left off the map. The continent looked like a place with no risk for influenza, even though those countries were almost certainly experiencing rates similar to the rates in other world regions. That visualization enabled African leaders to be sidelined in the global conversations about influenza response, and it did not help those countries petition for the technical assistance they needed to fulfill their responsibilities under IHR and to protect the health of their populations.

Pandemics presented as humanitarian crises might demand a coordinated global response that is uncomfortable for politicians and members of the public who are skeptical about globalization and who view isolationism as a way to keep out germs as well as other undesirable outside influences. By reframing pandemics as security threats, those politicians are empowered to implement travel bans and other restrictions and controls even when they might not be supported by science and have not been recommended by medical and public health experts. Global health security enables a supportive international response to a pandemic simultaneously to enable isolationism.

MODERN PANDEMICS AND GLOBAL HEALTH

Case Study: HIV/AIDS

Although the human immunodeficiency virus (HIV) likely emerged in Central Africa early in the twentieth century and then slowly spread throughout the world (Sharp and Hahn 2011), the acquired immunodeficiency syndrome (AIDS) that the virus causes was not recognized until the early 1980s, when a series of cases were diagnosed in the United States. The first responses to HIV were characterized by fear, judgment, and denial that further ostracized already marginalized populations (Prins 2004). The acronym "4H" was used in the United States to classify four populations as high-risk groups: homosexuals, heroin addicts, Haitians, and hemophiliacs (Gallo 2006). The *British Medical Journal* observed in 1989 that the stigma of HIV and AIDS was so great that listing AIDS as an underlying cause of mortality on death certificates could dishonor the memory of the deceased and have negative repercussions for surviving family members (King 1989). Many countries responded to the emergence of HIV by implementing restrictions on travel visas and migration by people with HIV infection (Duckett and Orkin 1989).

More than 5 million people worldwide were estimated to have contracted HIV by 1988, with the heaviest burdens in sub-Saharan Africa (2.5 million people, most of whom had acquired HIV heterosexually) and the Americas (2 million people, most of whom had acquired HIV through homosexual contact) (Chin, Sato, and Mann 1990). With cases occurring in every world region less than a decade after AIDS was first recognized, HIV could already be considered a pandemic. The term "pandemic," however, has not been consistently used to describe HIV. The Joint United Nations Programme on HIV/AIDS (UNAIDS) prefers to use the term "global epidemic" to emphasize that there is considerable variation by region in which populations are most at risk in different countries and regions (UNAIDS 2011). Avoiding the use of the term "pandemic" is also a way to destigmatize HIV and remove the fear associated with that term.

In 1990, WHO projected that up to 18 million people worldwide might be living with HIV by 2000, including approximately 6.5 million people in the Americas and 10.5 million people in sub-Saharan Africa (Chin et al. 1990). That projection turned out to be a serious underestimate. By 2000, more than 30 million people worldwide were estimated to be living with HIV, in addition to the nearly 20 million who were thought to have already died from the infection (Piot et al. 2001). The projected distribution of cases was also incorrect. By 2000, the number of people with HIV infection in sub-Saharan Africa was nearly ten times greater than the total number in the Americas, and the nearly 6.5 million cases in Asia were more than twice the number in the Americas (Piot et al. 2001). Although Africa bore the heaviest burden from HIV/AIDS, there was widespread recognition that this was truly a global epidemic.

A special session of the United Nations General Assembly in 2001 brought together political leaders from throughout the world to identify strategies for improving prevention, increasing access to antiretroviral medications, and reducing stigma and discrimination (Piot and Coll Seck 2001). Some of the rhetoric emphasized the destabilizing effect of AIDS in heavily burdened communities and countries, but HIV/AIDS was also reframed as a failure of public health and a symptom of socioeconomic disenfranchisement (Prins 2004). The HIV pandemic exacerbated existing economic inequalities and health disparities between and within countries (Benatar 2002). The resulting global strategy framework emphasized the need to bridge local needs and expertise with international funding and support. Several large global health initiatives were launched in the early 2000s, including the Global Fund to Fight AIDS, Tuberculosis and Malaria, which is a public–private partnership that began in 2002, and PEPFAR (the U.S. President's Emergency Plan for AIDS Relief), which was initiated in 2003 and provides antiretroviral drugs to millions of people in sub-Saharan Africa (Spicer et al. 2010). These efforts are complemented by networks of HIV advocates and advocacy organizations that have pushed since the beginning of the global epidemic to improve access to prevention, treatment, and social support (Colvin 2014).

Although HIV/AIDS remains a global health issue of critical importance, the outlook is quite different now than it was just 15 years ago. As access to antiretroviral therapy increases, HIV is transforming from a rapidly fatal infection to a chronic disease that often can be successfully managed for many years or even decades (Dutta, Barker, and Kallarakal 2015). The global HIV incidence rate remains far too high at nearly 2 million new cases per year, despite intensive efforts to promote prevention (UNAIDS 2016). However, the growing number of people living with HIV—nearly 37 million in 2014—is driven primarily by a great success in preventing deaths and extending survival for people with HIV infection (UNAIDS 2016). Local, international, and global networks of activists, scientists, political leaders, people living with HIV, and others have helped reduce the stigma of HIV/AIDS and support individuals, families, and communities affected by HIV/AIDS. By 2010, many countries had removed or were in the process of removing travel restrictions on people with HIV infection (Chang et al. 2013), reversing the isolationist trend observed 30 years ago at the beginning of the AIDS pandemic.

Action: Pandemics and International Cooperation

The global response to the HIV pandemic has almost single-handedly created the field of global health. Before HIV/AIDS, international health efforts primarily involved high-income countries contributing to improving child health in low-income countries through programs to combat tropical diseases and malnutrition (Koplan et al. 2009). In the new era of global health, there is a continued focus on health equity but a greater emphasis on multilateral, multidisciplinary initiatives built on global cooperation (Koplan et al. 2009).

A multitude of new intergovernmental agencies and government-funded entities were formed to address HIV/AIDS globally. UNAIDS was launched in 1996 to coordinate the United Nations' response to the pandemic (Smith and Whiteside 2010). The World Bank launched the Multi-country AIDS Program (MAP) in 2000 to provide multilateral support for national AIDS response plans (Spicer et al. 2010). The Global Fund was created by several wealthy countries in 2002 as a public–private partnership to facilitate multilateral rather than bilateral funding of HIV programs (Spicer et al. 2010). Major philanthropists such as the Bill & Melinda Gates Foundation joined the efforts to control HIV/AIDS (McCoy et al. 2009). Scientific collaborations with foundation funding, such as the International AIDS Vaccine Initiative, which was initiated with the support of the Rockefeller Foundation, sought to develop new tools to prevent and treat HIV

(Hanlin, Chataway, and Smith 2007). Also, despite continued stigma and discrimination, the LGBT community and other marginalized populations worked across national boundaries to advocate for action on issues related to HIV/AIDS (Parker and Aggleton 2003). Together, these initiatives represent an incredible diversity of forms of international cooperation as well as a very large amount of money being poured into HIV/AIDS prevention and control activities each year.

HIV has moved from being thought of as a pandemic to being framed as a chronic disease that demands a sustained response. This is partly because HIV has reached a state of endemicity—a term used to describe diseases that are present at a relatively constant rate in a population, rather than occurring at the higher than usual rates that define an epidemic—but also because of the recognized need for a sustainable, coordinated response to disease events.

Case Study: Noncommunicable Diseases as "Pandemics"

In the new era of global health—one in which shared global concerns garner worldwide attention, funding, and other support—the word "pandemic" has been adopted for use by a diversity of noncommunicable disease (NCD) advocacy groups (Allen 2017). The rise of global obesity was one of the first non-infectious conditions to which the term pandemic was applied (Egger and Swinburn 1997). The prevalence of obesity is increasing in every country worldwide (Swinburn et al. 2011), and a variety of factors related to the globalization of the food supply and dietary consumption patterns are credited with much of this growth (Popkin, Adair, and Ng 2012). Proponents of the expanded use of the term pandemic could make a case that obesity meets the traditional definition because it has increased in frequency, spread throughout the world, and is associated with serious risks to health. However, obesity is spreading slowly compared to a traditional infectious disease pandemic, so the public perception is that the risk associated with obesity is considerably less alarming than the risk associated with outbreaks of cholera, influenza, HIV, and other communicable conditions. Diabetes (van Dieren et al. 2010), cancer (Mellstedt 2006), violence against women (Bitzer 2015), and other noncommunicable conditions have also been presented as emerging pandemics, as have behavioral risk factors for NCDs, such as physical inactivity (Kohl et al. 2012) and tobacco use (Taylor and Bettcher 2000).

Advocacy: Pandemics as Agenda Setting

The obesity pandemic—if that term is considered acceptable to use for an NCD—is a slow-motion event that seems to be moving directly from epidemiological observation to advocacy about the health risks associated with excess weight, while skipping the intermediate response of collective anxiety that would typically be associated with an infectious disease pandemic. This is by design: The pandemic-related rhetoric that helped garner major resources for HIV/AIDS is being strategically deployed by advocates for expanded public health responses to NCDs (Jönnson 2014). By using language such as "pandemic" to connote life-threatening danger, various emerging non-infectious conditions can be advanced as priorities for global health funding and programming.

PANDEMICS AND GLOBAL STUDIES

The Constitution of the World Health Organization defines health as "a state of complete physical, mental, and social well-being and not merely the absence of disease or infirmity," adding that "the health of all peoples is fundamental to the attainment of peace and security and is dependent upon the fullest cooperation of individuals and states" (WHO 1948). Health is a function not only of biology but also of psychology, sociology, politics, and a variety of other socioeconomic and environmental factors. Similarly, pandemics do not occur solely as a result of biological events. Pandemics arise from a complex set of biological mechanisms, human behaviors, and human–environment interactions, and the speed with which global outbreaks are propagated or contained is dependent not only on medical and public health interventions but also on the accompanying social, policy, and economic responses.

Pandemics are global events that demand global preparedness strategies and global responses. The process of negotiating these shared plans, communicating about emergent events, navigating cooperative interventions, and implementing other critical responses to pandemics requires all involved parties to understand the science of pandemics and to understand the sociocultural perspectives of their collaborators from other countries. The complex pathways leading to the occurrence of pandemics and the complicated responses to them cannot be understood when only one disciplinary or cultural lens is applied (Nederveen Pieterse 2013). The success of global health interventions is dependent on experts in the biological, medical, and environmental sciences working alongside experts in the social sciences and policy, with all of the partners demonstrating global competence (Organisation for Economic Co-operation and Development 2016). Global problem-solving requires knowledge of the liberal arts, including the sciences, social sciences, and humanities; a critical understanding of recent and historic events that might provide insights about effective and ineffective actions; and excellent cross-cultural and interdisciplinary communication skills (Juergensmeyer 2014).

At their core, pandemics are the result of global interrelationships and other globalization processes. Global epidemics raise anxiety about global integration while at the same time serving as reminders of the benefits of global trade and travel and of the inconveniences associated with disruption to those exchanges of goods and people. Pandemics are threats to human security that simultaneously open opportunities for building camaraderie across borders, demonstrating shared humanitarian values, and improving global communication. Studies of pandemics are, by definition, global studies. The global literacy and global leadership skills that are central to academic global studies programs (Juergensmeyer 2014) are integral components of the toolkit required for pandemic preparedness and response.

REFERENCES

Aldis, W. 2008. "Health Security as a Public Health Concept: A Critical Analysis." *Health Policy and Planning* 23 (6): 369–375. doi:10.1093/heapol/czn030

Allen, L. 2017. "Are We Facing a Noncommunicable Disease Pandemic?" *Journal of Epidemiology and Global Health* 7 (1): 5–9. doi:10.1016/j.jegh.2016.11.001

Barreto, M. L., M. G. Teixeira, and E. H. Carmo. 2006. "Infectious Disease Epidemiology." *Journal of Epidemiology and Community Health* 60 (3): 192–195. doi:10.1136/jech.2003.011593

Benatar, S. R. 2002. "The HIV/AIDS Pandemic: A Sign of Instability in a Complex Global System." *Journal of Medicine & Philosophy* 27 (2): 163–177. doi:10.1076/jmep.27.2.163.2992

Bitzer, J. 2015. "The Pandemic of Violence Against Women: The Latest Chapter in the History of Misogyny." *European Journal of Contraception & Reproductive Health Care* 20 (1): 1–3. doi:10.3109/13625187.2015.1005445

Card, A. J. 2012. "Pandemicity and Severity Are Separate Constructs." *American Journal of Public Health* 102 (7): e12. doi:10.2105/AJPH.2012.300756

Chang, F., H. Prytherch, R. C. Nesbitt, and A. Wilder-Smith. 2013. "HIV-Related Travel Restrictions: Trends and Country Characteristics." *Global Health Action* 6: 20472. doi:10.3402/gha.v6i0.20472

Chew, C., and G. Eysenbach. 2010. "Pandemics in the Age of Twitter: Content Analysis of Tweets During the 2009 H1N1 Outbreak." *PLoS One* 5 (11): e14118. doi:10.1371/journal.pone.0014118

Chin, J., P. A. Sato, and J. M. Mann. 1990. "Projections of HIV Infections and AIDS Cases to the Year 2000." *Bulletin of the World Health Organization* 68 (1): 1–11.

Colvin, C. J. 2014. "Evidence and AIDS Activism: HIV Scale-Up and the Contemporary Politics of Knowledge in Global Health." *Global Public Health* 9: 57–72. doi:10.1080/17441692.2014.881519

Doshi, P. 2011. "The Elusive Definition of Pandemic Influenza." *Bulletin of the World Health Organization* 89 (7): 532–538. doi:10.2471/BLT.11.086173

Duckett, M., and A. J. Orkin. 1989. "AIDS-Related Migration and Travel Policies and Restrictions: A Global Survey." *AIDS* 3 (Suppl 1): S231–S252.

Dupras, C., and B. Williams-Jones. 2012. "The Expert and the Lay Public: Reflections on Influenza A (H1N1) and the Risk Society." *American Journal of Public Health* 102 (4): 591–595. doi:10.2105/AJPH.2011.300417

Dutta, A., C. Barker, and A. Kallarakal. 2015. "The HIV Treatment Gap: Estimates of the Financial Resources Needed Versus Available for Scale-Up of Antiretroviral Therapy in 97 Countries from 2015 to 2020." *PLoS Medicine* 12 (11): e1001907. doi:10.1371/journal.pmed.1001907

Egger, G., and B. Swinburn. 1997. "An 'Ecological' Approach to the Obesity Pandemic." *British Medical Journal* 315 (7106): 477–480.

Ferguson, N. M., D. A. Cummings, C. Fraser, J. C. Cajka, P. C. Cooley, and D. S. Burke. 2006. "Strategies for Mitigating an Influenza Pandemic." *Nature* 442 (7101): 448–452. doi:10.1038/nature04795

Fidler, D. P. 2005. "From International Sanitary Conventions to Global Health Security: The New International Health Regulations." *Chinese Journal of International Law* 4 (2): 325–392. doi:10.1093/chinesejil/jmi029

Gallo, R. C. 2006. "A Reflection on HIV/AIDS Research After 25 Years." *Retrovirology* 3: 72. doi:10.1186/1742-4690-3-72

Girard, M. P., J. S. Tam, O. M. Assossou, and M. P. Kieny. 2010. "The 2009 A (H1N1) Influenza Virus Pandemic: A Review." *Vaccine* 28 (31): 4895–4902. doi:10.1016/j.vaccine.2010.05.031

Glezen, W. P. 1996. "Emerging Infections: Pandemic Influenza." *Epidemiologic Reviews* 18 (1): 64–76.

Hanlin, R., J. Chataway, and J. Smith. 2007. "Global Health Public–Private Partnerships: IAVI, Partnerships and Capacity Building. *African Journal of Medicine and Medical Sciences* 36 (Suppl): 69–75.

Hoffman, S. J. 2010. "The Evolution, Etiology and Eventualities of the Global Health Security Regime." *Health Policy and Planning* 25 (6): 510–522. doi:10.1093/heapol/czq037

Huber, V. 2006. "The Unification of the Globe by Disease? The International Sanitary Conferences on Cholera, 1851–1894." *Historical Journal* 49 (2): 453–476. doi:10.1017/S0018246X06005280

Jönnson, K. 2014. "Legitimation Challenges in Global Health Governance: The Case of Non-Communicable Diseases." *Globalization* 11 (3): 301–314. doi:10.1080/14747731.2013.876174

Juergensmeyer, M. 2014. *Thinking Globally: A Global Studies Reader.* Los Angeles: University of California Press.

Kamradt-Scott, A. 2012. "Changing Perceptions of Pandemic Influenza and Public Health Responses." *American Journal of Public Health* 102 (1): 90–98. doi:10.2105/AJPH.2011.300330

Katz, R., and J. Fischer. 2010. "The Revised International Health Regulations: A Framework for Global Pandemic Response." *Global Health Governance* 3 (2): 1–18.

Kelly, H. 2011. "The Classical Definition of a Pandemic Is Not Elusive." *Bulletin of the World Health Organization* 89 (7): 540–541. doi:10.2471/BLT.11.088815

King, M. B. 1989. "AIDS on the Death Certificate: The Final Stigma." *British Medical Journal* 298 (6675): 734–736.

Kohl, H. W., 3rd, C. L. Craig, E. V. Lambert, S. Inoue, J. R. Alkandari, G. Leetongin, and S. Kahlmeier. 2012. "The Pandemic of Physical Inactivity: Global Action for Global Health." *Lancet* 380 (9838):294–305. doi:10.1016/S0140-6736(12)60898-8

Koplan J. P., T. C. Bond, M. H. Merson, K. S. Reddy, M. H. Rodriguez, N. K. Sewankambo, and J. N. Wasserheit. 2009. "Towards a Common Definition of Global Health." *Lancet* 373 (9679): 1993–95. doi:10.1016/S0140-6736(09)60332-9

Labonte, R. 1992. "South America's Cholera Pandemic Provides Lesson in Public Health, Politics." *Canadian Medical Association Journal* 147 (7): 1052–1056.

Lee, K. 2001. "The Global Dimensions of Cholera." *Global Change and Human Health* 2 (1): 6–17. doi:10.1023/A:1011925107536

Lee, K., and R. Dodgson. 2000. "Globalization and Cholera: Implications for Global Governance." *Global Governance* 6 (2): 213–236.

McCloskey, B., O. Dar, A. Zumla, and D. L. Heymann. 2014. "Emerging Infectious Diseases and Pandemic Potential: Status Quo and Reducing Risk of Global Spread." *Lancet Infectious Diseases* 14 (10): 1001–1010. doi:10.1016/S1473-3099(14)70846-1

McCoy, D., G. Kembhavi, J. Patel, and A. Luintel. 2009. "The Bill & Melinda Gates Foundation's Grant-Making Programme for Global Health." *Lancet* 373 (9675): 1645–1653. doi:10.1016/S0140-6736(09)60571-7

Mellstedt, H. 2006. "Cancer Initiatives in Developing Countries." *Annals of Oncology* 17 (Suppl 8): viii24–31. doi:10.1093/annonc/mdl984

Morens, D. M., and A. S. Fauci. 2007. "The 1918 Influenza Pandemic: Insights for the 21st Century." *Journal of Infectious Diseases* 195 (7): 1018–1028. doi:10.1086/511989

Morens, D. M., G. K. Folkers, and A. S. Fauci. 2009. "What Is a Pandemic?" *Journal of Infectious Diseases* 200 (7): 1018–1021. doi:10.1086/644537

Murray, C. J. L., A. D. Lopez, B. Chin, D. Feehan, and K. H. Hill. 2006. "Estimation of Potential Global Pandemic Influenza Mortality on the Basis of Vital Registry Data from the 1918–20 Pandemic: A Quantitative Analysis." *Lancet* 368 (9554): 2211–2218. doi:10.1016/S0140-6736(06)69896-4

Mutreja, A., D. W. Kim, N. R. Thomson, T. R. Connor, J. H. Lee, S. Kariuki, et al. 2011. "Evidence for Several Waves of Global Transmission in the Seventh Cholera Pandemic." *Nature* 477 (7365): 462–465. doi:10.1038/nature10392

Nederveen Pieterse, J. 2013. "What Is Global Studies?" *Globalizations* 10 (4): 499–514. doi:10.1080/14747731.2013.806746

Organisation for Economic Co-operation and Development (OECD) Programme for International Student Assessment. 2016. *Global Competency for an Inclusive World.* Paris: OECD.

Palmer, R. 2010. "A Disease—Or Gene—By Any Other Name Would Cause a Stink." *Nature Medicine* 16 (10): 1059. doi:10.1038/nm1010-1059

Parker, R., and P. Aggleton. 2003. "HIV and AIDS-Related Stigma and Discrimination: A Conceptual Framework and Implications for Action." *Social Science & Medicine* 57 (1): 13–24. doi:10.1016/S0277-9536(02)00304-0

Piot, P., M. Bartos, P. D. Ghys, N. Walker, and B. Schwartländer. 2001. "The Global Impact of HIV/AIDS." *Nature* 410 (6831): 968–973.

Piot, P., and A. M. Coll Seck. 2001. "International Response to the HIV/AIDS Epidemic: Planning for Success." *Bulletin of the World Health Organization* 79 (12): 1106–1112. doi:10.1590/X0042-96862001001200006

Poletto, C., M. F. C. Gomes, A. Pastore y Piontti, L. Rossi, L. Bioglio, D. L. Chao, et al. 2014. "Assessing the Impact of Travel Restrictions on International Spread of the 2014 West African Ebola Epidemic." *Eurosurveillance* 19 (42): 20936. doi:10.2807/1560-7917.ES2014.19.42.20936

Popkin, B. M., L. S. Adair, and S. W. Ng. 2012. "The Global Nutrition Transition: The Pandemic of Obesity in Developing Countries." *Nutrition Reviews* 70 (1): 3–21. doi:10.1111/j.1753-4887.2011.00456.x

Prins, G. 2004. "AIDS and Global Security." *International Affairs* 80 (5): 931–952. doi:10.1111/j.1468-2346.2004.00426.x

Schein, R., S. Bruls, V. Busch, K. Wilson, L. Hershfield, and J. Keelan. 2012. "A Flu by Any Other Name: Why the World Health Organization Should Adopt the World Meteorological Association's Storm Naming System as a Model for Naming Emerging Infectious Diseases." *Journal of Health Communication* 17 (5): 532–545. doi:10.1080/10810730.2011.626503

Sharp, P. M., and B. H. Hahn. 2011. "Origins of HIV and the AIDS Pandemic." *Cold Springs Harbor Perspectives in Medicine* 1 (1): a006841. doi:10.1101/cshperspect.a006841

Smith, J. H., and A. Whiteside. 2010. "The History of AIDS Exceptionalism." *Journal of the International AIDS Society* 13: 47. doi:10.1186/1758-2652-13-47

Spicer, N., J. Aleshkina, R. Biesma, R. Brugha, C. Caceres, B. Chilundo, et al. 2010. "National and Subnational HIV/AIDS Coordination: Are Global Health Initiatives Closing the Gap Between Intent and Practice." *Globalization and Health* 6: 3. doi:10.1186/1744-8603-6-3

Swinburn, B. A., G. Sacks, K. D. Hall, K. McPherson, D. T. Finegood, M. L. Moodie, and S. L. Gortmaker. 2011. "The Global Obesity Pandemic: Shaped by Global Drivers and Local Environments." *Lancet* 378 (9793): 804–814. doi:10.1016/S0140-6736(11)60813-1

Taylor, A. L., and D. W. Bettcher. 2000. "WHO Framework Convention of Tobacco Control: A Global 'Good' for Public Health." *Bulletin of the World Health Organization* 78 (7): 920–929. doi:10.1590/S0042-96862000000700010

UNAIDS. 2011. *UNAIDS Terminology Guidelines—Revised Version: October 2011.* Geneva: UNAIDS.

UNAIDS. 2016. *AIDS by the Numbers 2016.* Geneva: UNAIDS.

van Dieren, S., J. W. Beulens, Y. T. van der Schouw, D. E. Grobbee, and B. Neal. 2010. "The Global Burden of Diabetes and Its Complications: An Emerging Pandemic." *European Journal of Cardiovascular Prevention and Rehabilitation* 17 (Suppl 1): S3–S8. doi:10.1097/01.hjr.0000368191.86614.5a

Wilkinson, A., and M. Leach. 2014. "Briefing: Ebola—Myths, Realities, and Structural Violence." *African Affairs* 114 (454): 136–148. doi:10.1093/afraf/adu080

Wilson, K., J. S. Brownstein, and D. P. Fidler. 2010. "Strengthening the International Health Regulations: Lessons from the H1N1 Pandemic." *Health Policy and Planning* 25 (6): 505–509. doi:10.1093/heapol/czq026

World Health Organization. 1948. *Constitution of the World Health Organization.* New York: World Health Organization.

CHAPTER 39

ENVIRONMENTAL CRITIQUE

PATRICK BOND

In addition to global economic volatility, the threat of disease pandemics, and the potential for nuclear annihilation, there has been an overarching concern generating critical internationalist discourses and persistent (albeit ineffectual) multilateral governance efforts in recent decades: environment. The Anthropocene is now named for our current epoch, in which humans have fundamentally altered the Earth's geological and macro-environmental processes. Driven by the imperative of accumulating capital, powerful economic actors have structured society in a manner that now exceeds humankind's ability to exist within at least four "planetary boundaries": climate change, biosphere integrity, biogeochemical flows, and land-system change. But divergent interpretations of how to address environmental crises, especially the catastrophic threat of climate change, have generated different strategies and different scalar politics. These range from reliance on technical fixes and markets to advocacy of a strong regulatory regime enforced by not only states (from local to national to global) but also—in view of ongoing multilateral environmental governance failure—civil society campaigners.

The attention that the global studies field gives to environmentalism has so far been inadequate, given the scope of the challenge to multiple species' survival and the extent to which the field's core characteristics provide foundations of global environmental solutions: It is transnational, interdisciplinary, both contemporary and historical, postcolonial and critical, and aiming at global citizenship (Jurgensmeyer 2013). The most obvious links between these features and environmentalism are in addressing anthropogenic (human-induced) threats of exceeding "planetary boundaries"—for example, in climate change, species destruction and biodiversity loss, oceanic degradation, and ozone depletion. As the latter problem has already demonstrated, none of these macro-phenomena respect state boundaries, and all will require global governance strategies (in the case of ozone, the 1987 Montreal Protocol). Most other pollution and degradation events are of a localistic character, but it is at the global scale that we find universalizing ideologies within environmentalism that global studies' critical capacities can interrogate.

After all, there have been powerful statements of human and capitalist destruction of the natural environment for centuries, with a nineteenth century focus on soil degradation. Climate change was also identified as early as 1856 by Eunice Newton Foote and again in 1896 by Svante Arrhenius as a future threat in the event that atmospheric carbon dioxide

(CO_2) levels doubled, thus causing a 5° or 6°C increase in average temperatures. In 1972, the first Earth Summit was held in Stockholm and a popular book, *The Limits to Growth* (Club of Rome 1972), was released, which in turn jumpstarted multilateral concerns about sustainable development. The 1987 United Nations (UN) Brundtland Commission and the 1992 Rio Earth Summit followed, but soon, co-opted by corporations during the 1990s, the idea of "sustainability" was downgraded in favor of neoliberal ideologues' advocacy of export-led growth and the commodification of nature. Sustainable development concerns rose again at a 2002 UN Earth summit in Johannesburg, South Africa, which fused the UN's strategy with water privatizers, carbon traders, and mega-corporations supporting its "Global Compact"—a fundraising gambit (also reflecting adverse power relations, such as the demise of the Center on Transnational Corporations and Washington's refusal to pay its dues). Then, finding "Green Economy" rhetoric, biodiversity offsetting, and market-centric climate change policy as fertile soil at the 2012 Rio Summit, multilateral environmental strategies again flowered, leading to fears of a renewed corporate agenda termed "neoliberalized nature" (Büscher, Dressler, and Fletcher 2014).

For the period 2015–2030, Sustainable Development Goals are now the mantra of the UN and many other multilateral agencies (despite extensive critique of the realities they elide, such as by the scholar–activist network The Rules (2015)). The December 2015 Paris climate agreement was meant to be a landmark multilateral strategy to avoid climate catastrophe, but as the 2017 withdrawal of the United States indicated, the Paris deal was fatally flawed due to non-existent penalties for failing to cut greenhouse gas (GHG) emissions. The mid-2017 G20 gathering subsequently failed to impose even marginal carbon taxes that advocates as diverse as Naomi Klein, Joseph Stiglitz, and Nicolas Sarkozy had recommended against the United States. Instead, the European Union–California–China Plan B strategy was to commodify climate policy through carbon trading, which California Governor Jerry Brown relaunched in mid-2017 despite growing controversy over the efficacy and distributional impacts (Dorsey and Williams 2017) of what is sometimes termed "the privatization of the air" (Bond 2012).

CONTENDING PRINCIPLES OF ENVIRONMENTALISM

Underlying the surface rhetoric of the international environmental debate are narratives with divergent philosophical roots. The dominant approach is often termed "ecological modernization" due to its reliance on technological innovations, efficiencies, and the management of externalities aimed at improving environmental outcomes in a rational manner (for a critical discussion, see Harvey 1996). After initial development of the argumentation by researchers based in Berlin and Amsterdam (especially Joseph Huber, Martin Jänicke, and Udo Simonis), the approach was advanced by the World Business Council on Sustainable Development, established by Swiss construction billionaire Stephan Schmidheiny. Today, the commodification of nature occurs increasingly under the rubric of "payment for ecosystem services," aiming to "put a price" on the environment for the sake of valuing nature. Indeed, full-fledged environmental financialization is underway with carbon markets and other forms of emissions trading—as discussed in detail later—and virtual water sales, increasingly packaged in exotic investment instruments (most of which do not hold up under scrutiny) (Bracking 2016; Bond 2012). In ecological modernization's most advanced form, Deutsche Bank's Pavan Sukhdev initiated The Economics of Ecosystems and Biodiversity (TEEB 2018) within the UN Environment Program to "make nature's values visible" and thus "help decision-makers recognize the wide range of benefits provided by ecosystems and biodiversity, demonstrate their values in economic terms and, where appropriate, capture those values in decision-making."

TEEB's search for optimal resource use emphasizes "low-hanging fruit" that can achieve the least costly form of market-facilitated environmental management. Likewise, the World Bank's (2012: 174) *Inclusive Green Growth* mandated,

> Care must be taken to ensure that cities and roads, factories and farms are designed, managed, and regulated as efficiently as possible to wisely use natural resources while supporting the robust growth developing countries still need . . . [to move the economy] away from sub-optimalities and increase efficiency—and hence contribute to short-term growth—while protecting the environment.

Not mentioned by World Bank staff were capitalism's recent distortions, such as in the food system, carbon markets, and real estate, most proximately caused by financial speculation in commodities, nature, and housing. Nor would the Bank admit that overproduction tendencies in the world economy (most notably from China) are amplified by the "increased efficiency" required for successful export-led growth, nor that irrationality characterizes a large share of international trade. Silences in neoliberal versions of sustainability discourse tell us just as much about the real agenda behind co-optation of this sort.

This is the weak, corporate-dominated version of the sustainability narrative, but there was once a stronger one. Gro Harlem Brundtland's World Commission on Environment and Development (1987) defined "sustainable development" as meeting "the needs of the present without compromising the ability of future generations to meet their own needs." Moving beyond simple intergenerational equity, Brundtland also allowed mention of two central concepts that reflected the more favorable balance of forces for the environmental left (in 1987). First was "the concept of 'needs,' in particular the essential needs of the world's poor, to which overriding priority should be given." Second was "the idea of limitations imposed by the state of technology and social organization on the environment's ability to meet present and future needs." These relatively radical red and green agendas were briefly married in 1987. But John Drexhage and Deborah Murphy (2010) explain the demise of the term "sustainable development" as follows: "Over the past 20 years it has often been compartmentalized as an environmental issue. Added to this, and potentially more limiting for the sustainable development agenda, is the reigning orientation of development as purely economic growth."

It is worth dwelling on this artificial bifurcation because within the discipline of economics, two lines of argument had emerged by the early 1990s. First was the visionary work of Herman Daly, who edited the seminal *Toward a Steady State Economy* (1973) but then labored fruitlessly at the World Bank to inject environmental values into financial considerations. Daly (1996) had offered a tougher definition than Brundtland: "Development without growth beyond environmental carrying capacity, where development means qualitative improvement and growth means quantitative increase." (p. 220). At the World Bank, he found, this framing "just confirmed the orthodox economists' worst fears about the subversive nature of the idea, and reinforced their resolve to keep it vague" (p. 9). In his resignation speech, Daly (1996) proposed four environmental policy recommendations for both the World Bank and governments, centered on preserving an ecological inheritance that came to be known as "natural capital":

> Stop counting natural capital as income [by which he meant it should be a *debit* from a country's genuine savings each year, not just a *credit* for non-renewable resources sold that year];
>   Tax labor and income less, and tax resource throughput more [more recent iterations focus on the political economy of resource inputs and "decoupling" of growth from resources (e.g., Fischer-Kowalski and Swilling 2011)];
>   Maximize the productivity of natural capital in the short run, and invest in increasing its supply in the long run; and
>   Move away from the ideology of global economic integration by free trade, free capital mobility, and export-led growth—and toward a more nationalist orientation that seeks to develop domestic production for internal markets as the first option, having recourse to international trade only when clearly much more efficient. (pp. 88–93)

Daly (1996) grew frustrated by 1995 because

> although the World Bank was on record as officially favoring sustainable development, the near vacuity of the phrase made this a meaningless affirmation. . . . The party line was that sustainable development was like pornography: We'll know it when we see it, but it's too difficult to define. (p. 220)

On the other side of the bifurcation was World Bank chief economist Lawrence Summers (1991). He signed off on an internal memo (leaked to *The Economist*, which endorsed the idea) a few months prior to the Rio Earth Summit. The memo contained the following argument: "I think the economic logic behind dumping a load of toxic waste in the lowest-wage country is impeccable and we should face up to that." For Summers, in effect, sustainability at the global scale allowed evasion or evisceration of state regulations that should otherwise "internalize the externalities" associated with pollution or ecological damage. Summers' version meant simply displacing these externalities to wherever political power and economic wealth were negligible and the immediate environmental implications less visible. After all, Summers continued, inhabitants of low-income countries typically died before the age at which they would begin suffering prostate cancer associated with toxic dumping. And using the "marginal productivity of labor" as his guiding measure, Summers implied that low-income Africans were not worth very much anyhow, compared to those living in wealthier sites, nor were Africans' aesthetic concerns with air pollution as substantive as for wealthy Northerners. So sustainability would permit dumping toxic waste on poor people instead of halting the production of toxins.

"Your reasoning is perfectly logical but totally insane," rebutted Brazilian environment secretary José Lutzenburger (1992). He continued, "Your thoughts [provide] a concrete example of the unbelievable alienation, reductionist thinking, social ruthlessness and the arrogant ignorance of many conventional economists concerning the nature of the world we live in." Lutzenburger was fired by a conservative Brazilian president (who was later impeached for corruption), whereas Summers rose to the positions of US Treasury Secretary under President Bill Clinton, Wall Street investment advisor, Harvard University president, and President Barack Obama's economic czar, in which position he arranged trillions of dollars' worth of banking bailouts following the hazardous deregulation of banking for which he was the main champion. Due to the displacement of the "dirty industries," pollution largely generated in the North (or caused by Northern overconsumption) began to shift to new production sites in the South, such as Mexican maquiladora border manufacturing zones and the newly industrializing countries (Hong Kong, Singapore, Taiwan, South Korea, and then Indonesia, Malaysia, and Thailand), and eventually to the east coast of China and to South Asia.

In part because of rampant socioenvironmental unsustainability in these sites, the world started to hit what the Club of Rome (1972) had long warned would become planetary boundaries. The most serious threat is running out of the carrying capacity for GHGs that cause climate change. There are others: rapid biodiversity loss (a "sixth mass extinction" now underway), stratospheric ozone depletion (abated by the 1987 Montreal Protocol that phased out chlorofluorocarbons (CFCs) by 1996 but leaving atmospheric aerosols as a danger), oceanic degradation and acidification, crises in the biogeochemical nitrogen and phosphorus cycles, other resource input constraints, chemical pollution, freshwater adulteration and evaporation, and shortages of arable land (Magdoff and Foster 2011).

The scholarship on planetary boundaries emphasizes "maintenance of the Earth system in a resilient and accommodating state" and identifies current system threats through overshooting of climate change, biosphere integrity, biogeochemical flows, and land-system change (Steffen et al. 2015: 730; for a fusion of analysis with socioeconomic "undershoot," see Raworth 2017). Addressing these systemic threats, powerful institutions and companies are increasingly proposing technological silver-bullet fixes—which critics term "false solutions"—as environmental policy. These include

- dirty "clean energy": nuclear, "clean coal," fracking shale gas, hydropower, and hydrogen;
- biofuels, biomass, and biochar;
- carbon capture and storage (in which CO_2 is pumped underground); and
- other geoengineering gimmicks, such as genetically modified trees; sulfates in the air to shut out the sun; iron filings in the sea to create algae blooms (to sequester CO_2); artificial microbes to convert plant biomass into fuels, chemicals, and products; and large-scale solar reflection (e.g., desert plastic wrap).

However, many tech-fix strategies violate the precautionary principle; create land-grab pressure; have excessive capital costs; require increased energy; are unproven in technological terms; and are many years, if not decades, from implementation. For example, a strategy undergoing pilot testing in Iceland is the conversion of CO_2 into limestone-type rocks, but the cost (\$24 trillion to absorb the world's 40 billion tons/year of CO_2 emissions) is far beyond current capitalist budgeting parameters (Parenti 2017). One of the most controversial of the false solutions is carbon trading (discussed later), which continues to be advanced as a way to use market solutions to solve the world's greatest market failure—the externality of climate change (Bond 2012).

Climate Politics Commodified

The recent rounds of world climate negotiations culminating in Paris have revealed severe flaws in the character of the global economy, the role of the state in its transformation, and state–capitalist relations. The hope for the planet's survival has been vested in a combination of multilateral emissions rearrangements and national regulation, which since 1997 have hinged on the premise that market-centric strategies such as emissions trading schemes and offsets can allocate costs and benefits appropriately. In constructing market arrangements and, later, an accompanying UN Green Climate Fund to support emissions mitigation and climate change adaptation, there has necessarily arisen a high degree of uneven geographical development. The sources and impacts of GHG emissions are diverse, with "common but differentiated responsibilities" acknowledged since 2002, and compensation for "loss and damage" recognized as a vital component since 2012. But these global strategies are unfolding not within the parameters of state control of market dynamics. Instead, they remain subordinated to the ongoing neoliberal accumulation strategy of financialization.

This process is fraught with contradictions, resulting in amplified crises, and increasing resorts to both temporal and spatial fixes, as well as accumulation by dispossession—the three modes of capitalist crisis displacement (not resolution) identified by David Harvey (1982, 2003). For the purposes of exploring how the fixes affect society–nature relations, these concepts refer, respectively, to

- *globalization*'s ability to *shift* problems around spatially, without actually solving them;
- *financialization*'s capacity to *stall* problems temporally, by generating credit-based techniques—including securitization of toxic loans and commodified nature—that permit the purchase of products today at the expense of future arrears and defaults when the upside-down pyramid topples; and
- *imperialism*'s compulsion to *steal* from weaker territories via extra-economic extractive systems, variously termed "articulations of modes of production," "primitive accumulation," "uneven and combined development," the "shock doctrine," and accumulation by dispossession.

The shifting, stalling, stealing strategy is at the heart of the management and mismanagement of both capitalist crises and climate catastrophe, most obviously in 2008–20099 when vast taxpayer bank bailouts were required as financial bubbles burst, followed by three bouts of central bank "quantitative easing," as well as driving real interest rates negative so as to push currency into the economy as an artificial stimulant. These techniques, in turn, set the stage for another future round of subprime disasters, including further bubbles bursting, more sovereign and corporate debt defaults, inflation and devaluation of the dollar—as well as a faster push by capital into nature under the auspices of the "green economy." Harvey (2014) notes that moving these financial assets around is itself a generator of instability:

> Capital's ecosystem is riddled with inequalities and uneven geographical developments precisely because of the uneven pattern of these transfers. Benefits pile up in one part of the world at the expense of another. Transfers of ecological benefits from one part of the world to another underpin geopolitical tensions. (p. 168)

It should be the case, if crisis management is to be effective, that global governance resolves uneven environmental costs and benefits. Since 1997 in Kyoto, the United Nations Framework Convention on Climate Change Conference of the Parties (COP) summits have confirmed that instead of a strong regulatory approach, the chosen regime of emissions controls would emphasize market incentives. The Kyoto Protocol's binding commitments on wealthy countries to make emissions cuts were considered too onerous for the historic number one polluter, the United States. In 2015, China emitted 30% of the world's total, the United States 14%, the European Union 10%, India 7%, Russia 5%, and Japan 4%; Iran, Saudi Arabia, South Korea, Canada, Indonesia, Brazil, Mexico, and South Africa emitted between 1.5% and 2% (Fondation BNP Paribas 2017).

In addition to neutering Kyoto's binding commitments at the 2009 Copenhagen COP15, the US State Department promoted several other strategies to weaken meaningful multilateral climate policy. For example, after the COP17 in Durban in December 2011, US State Department adviser Trevor Houser bragged to the *New York Times* (as cited in Broder 2012),

> The Durban Platform was promising because of what it did not say. There is no mention of historic responsibility or per capita emissions. There is no mention of economic development as the priority for developing countries. There is no mention of a difference between developed and developing country action.

Considered historically since 1850, the US share is 29%, that of the European Union is 27%, and those of Russia and China are each 8% (Fondation BNP Paribas 2017). Fossil fuel companies are especially important climate debtors, with 90 firms responsible for nearly 60% of historic emissions, led by 7 private (Chevron, ExxonMobil, BP, Royal Dutch Shell, ConocoPhillips, Peabody Energy, and Total) and 7 parastatal (Saudi Aramco, Gazprom, National Iranian Oil Company, Pemex, Petroleos de Venezuela, Coal India, and Kuwait Petroleum) companies (Ekwurzel et al. 2017).

As neoliberalism gripped many aspects of local, national, and global public policy, especially in the run-up to the COP21 in Paris, the environmental managerial elites' strategy aimed at turning a medium-/long-term humanity-threatening prospect into a short-term source of speculative profit. Kyoto had permitted carbon trading initiatives (e.g., the European Union Emissions Trading Scheme, the Clean Development Mechanism, Joint Implementation offsets, the Reducing Emissions from Forest Degradation and Deforestation program, and other for-profit climate financing programs) so as to harness and direct liquid financial capital toward lower emissions productive investments, public transport, renewable energy, and various kinds of sinks. Market tactics were based on commodification of nearly everything that could be viewed as a carbon sink, especially forests but also agricultural land, and even the ocean's capacity to sequester CO_2 for photosynthesis via algae.

However, all the evidence suggests that the worst-ever case of market failure, as former World Bank chief economist Nicholas Stern (2007) described GHG emissions, cannot be solved by recourse to even more chaotic, crisis-ridden financial markets (Bond 2012; Lohmann 2006, 2012). Moreover, due to internecine competition between blocs influenced by national fossil fuel industries, the COPs appear unable to either cap or regulate GHG pollution at its source or jump-start the emissions trade in which so much hope is placed. The financial markets have been especially ineffectual, and in the first major round of carbon trading, centered in the European Union (along with a few outlying North American regional markets), the ceiling on annual market trades was $175 billion in 2011 (of which the European Union's contribution was $150 billion). With the post-2008 crash of markets and the 2010 closure of the Chicago carbon market, the value of annual existing emissions trading measured by the World Bank (2017) receded to just $32 billion in 2016. (In 2012,

Bank of America Merrill Lynch's main carbon trader, Abyd Karmali, was still projecting a $3 trillion world market by 2020.) The main reason was the decline in price from $33/ton to less than $4.4/ton from 2008 to 2013 and the inability to raise that price as Europe's polluters continued to successfully lobby for free emissions credits. Prices will remain low until at least 2019, European Union ETS expert Frank Watson (2017) reports, due to "a huge surplus of allowances, including hefty supply from auctions in 2017 and 2018." Europe is typical: Of the 15% of world CO_2 equivalent emissions that are covered by either carbon trading or a tax, only one-fourth of those carry a price above $10/ton. The countries with a price above $25/ton have achieved this with taxation, not carbon trading: Sweden, $126; Switzerland and Liechtenstein, $84; Finland, $66; Norway, $52; France, $33; and Denmark, $25.

Nevertheless, despite the sickly emissions trading environment and the inauguration of US President Donald J. Trump in January 2017, the Davos World Economic Forum hosted a discussion the day before he took power, titled "The Return of Carbon Markets." The markets were promoted especially by Stern. He and Stiglitz had been commissioned by Carbon Pricing Leadership Coalition chairs Ségolène Royal and Feike Sijbesma to report on pricing options in May 2017. Their High-Level Commission on Carbon Pricing (2017: 50) was enthusiastic about carbon trading ("cap-and-trade") and carbon taxation as means to raise the carbon price to "at least US$40–80/tCO2 by 2020 and US$50–100/tCO2 by 2030" so as to lower the rate of emissions to the two-degree temperature increase targeted at Paris.

The "return" of emissions trading is a misleading hope, based as it is on the vaguely market-promotional language in the Paris climate agreement and some tentative emerging market forays into emissions trading and taxation, notably several of the BRICS bloc (Brazil, Russia, India, China, and South Africa). A major new China–California–Canada (specifically Quebec and Ontario) nexus of carbon markets is anticipated given California Governor Jerry Brown's 2017 recommitment to the "cap and trade" system for his state (strongly supported by the oil lobby). His proposed 2018 climate summit will advance this strategy further. Yet, in expressing support for linkages to the eight Chinese local and pro-vincial schemes (Beijing, Shanghai, Tianjin, Guangdong, Hubei, Shenzhen, Fujian, and Chongqing), Brown himself warned, "We want to make sure it has full integrity and know exactly what's going on. And we can't say that today" (Henderson 2017).

But integrity is in short supply in the carbon markets, for various reasons. One is the price differential in China, which at the time ranged from $8.9/ton in Beijing to just €0.55/ton in Chongqing, with Shenzhen falling from a Chinese high of $10.5/ton in early 2013 to just $3.9/ton by mid-2016. But more generally, the following critiques of carbon markets were developed by the Durban Group for Climate Justice starting in 2004, and they remained relevant in 2018:

- The idea of inventing a property right to pollute is effectively the "privatisation of the air," a moral problem given the vast and growing differentials in wealth inequalities.
- The rising production of GHGs creates a nonlinear impact that cannot be reduced to a commodity exchange relationship (1 ton of CO_2 produced in one place accommodated by reducing 1 ton in another, the premise of the emissions trade).
- Corporations most guilty of pollution and the World Bank—which has historically been most responsible for fossil fuel financing—are the driving forces behind the market and can be expected to engage in systemic corruption to attract money into the market even if this prevents genuine emissions reductions.

- Many offsetting projects—such as monocultural timber plantations, forest "protection," and landfill methane-electricity projects—have devastating impacts on local communities and ecologies, and they have been heavily contested in part because the carbon sequestered is far more temporary (because trees die) than the carbon emitted.
- The price of carbon determined in these markets is unstable, having crashed by half in a short period in April 2006, by two-thirds in 2008, and by a further 80% from 2011 to 2013.
- There is a serious potential for carbon markets to become an out-of-control, multi-trillion dollar speculative bubble, similar to exotic financial instruments associated with Enron's 2002 collapse (indeed, many Enron employees populate the carbon markets).
- Carbon trading encourages small, incremental shifts and thus distracts from a wide range of radical changes needed in materials extraction, production, distribution, consumption, and disposal.
- The idea of market solutions to market failure ("externalities") is an ideology that rarely makes sense, especially not in derivatives markets in the wake of the world's worst-ever financial market failure (Bond 2012, pp. 32–33).

The Stiglitz–Stern High-Level Commission on Carbon Pricing (2017) did acknowledge some "incomplete and imperfect capital market" weaknesses that mitigate against carbon trading's effectiveness:

> The capital required to transition to low-carbon futures often faces large uncertainties, political risks, illiquid assets, and solid returns in the long term only. Aside from the standard credit constraints, investors lack the knowledge and information necessary to assess the quality of innovative, low-carbon projects. (p. 15)

The alternative strategy of putting a cap (without trading) on emissions similar to the 1987 Montreal Protocol's ban of CFCs to halt ozone hole expansion or the climate debt owed by the historic polluters to those suffering "loss and damage" from climate change was not considered worthy of mention in the Commission report. This refusal to either countenance an effective system of emissions capping or inject an element of historic justice reflects the success of the imperialist project, especially as managed by Todd Stern (2016) of the US State Department. WikiLeaks exposures of State Department cables and his emails to Hillary Clinton reveal the extreme measures that imperialists believed were necessary to take so as to avoid an emissions cap and reparations payments. These concerns—especially potential liabilities in the Paris agreement—were echoed by Trump in his June 1, 2017, abrogation of the Paris agreement, although the President was sorely misinformed (Stern 2016). But of crucial importance is that the other major emitters—including Brazil, Russia, India, China, and South Africa—were not particularly worried because pressure on them to reduce emissions (already negligible) would wane. Steffen Böhm, Maria Ceci Misoczky, and Sandra Moog (2012: 1629) have noted the "subimperialist drive" of carbon-intensive, extractive-oriented economies in many such non-Western countries, and the broader reticence about punishing Trump can be explained, as does Harvey (2003: 185), by recalling how the emerging markets fit into the world system:

> The opening up of global markets in both commodities and capital created openings for other states to insert themselves into the global economy, first as absorbers but then as producers of surplus capitals. They then became competitors on the world stage. What might be called

"subimperialisms" arose.... Each developing center of capital accumulation sought out systematic spatio-temporal fixes for its own surplus capital by defining territorial spheres of influence.

CLIMATE CRISIS CAPITALISM DISPLACEMENT STRATEGIES AND THEIR LIMITS

The attraction of carbon trading in the new markets, no matter its failure in the old, is logical viewed within context: a longer term capitalist crisis that has raised financial sector power within an ever-more frenetic and geographically ambitious system; the financial markets' sophistication in establishing new routes for capital across space, through time, and into non-market spheres; and the mainstream ideological orientation to solving every market-related problem with a market solution, which even advocates of a post-Washington Consensus and Keynesian economic policies share, with Stiglitz and Paul Krugman (2009) being the most famous. Interestingly, even Krugman (2013) had second thoughts, for after reading formerly pro-trading environmental economist William Nordhaus' (2013) *Climate Casino*, Krugman remarked, "The message I took from this book was that direct action to regulate emissions from electricity generation would be a surprisingly good substitute for carbon pricing." Krugman observed that Environmental Protection Agency regulation "will probably prevent the construction of any new coal-fired plants."

Krugman's reversal is the sort of hard-nosed realism that will be needed to disprove Klein's (2014) thesis that capitalist crisis and climate crisis are conjoined. Instead, however, capitalist financial markets have so distorted the playing field that the "green economy" and similar ecological-modernization narratives are bound to continue generating new, futile attempts at an ecological fix (Bracking 2016). According to Ariel Salleh (2010), "The current financial and climate crises are consciousness-raising opportunities all round, but green new deals designed to revive the faltering international system will delay fundamental change" (p. 215). In the same spirit, Samir Amin (2010), Africa's leading political economist, offered the following argument about economic theory applied to ecology:

> Capture of ecology by vulgar ideology operates on two levels: on the one hand by reducing measurement of use value to an "improved" measurement of exchange value, and on the other by integrating the ecological challenge with the ideology of "consensus." Both these maneuvers undermine the clear realization that ecology and capitalism are, by their nature, in opposition.

This capture of ecological measurement by vulgar economics is making huge strides. Thousands of young researchers, in the United States and, imitating them, in Europe, have been mobilized in this cause. The "ecological costs" are, in this way of thinking, assimilated to external economies. The vulgar method of measuring cost–benefit in terms of exchange value (itself conflated with market price) is then used to define a "fair price" integrating external economies and diseconomies. For Amin, there are obvious limitations to these sorts of reforms based on actually existing power relations within capitalism:

> It goes without saying that the work—reduced to mathematical formulas—done in this traditional area of vulgar economics does not say how the "fair price" calculated could become

that of the actual current market. It is presumed therefore that fiscal and other "incentives" could be sufficiently effective to bring about this convergence. Any proof that this could really be the case is entirely absent. In fact, as can already be seen, oligopolies have seized hold of ecology to justify the opening up of new fields to their destructive expansion. Francois Houtart provides a conclusive illustration of this in his work on biofuels. Since then, "green capitalism" has been part of the obligatory discourse of men/women in positions of power, on both the Right and the Left, in the Triad (of Europe, North America and Japan), and of the executives of oligopolies.

Amin (2010) faults Stiglitz for having "openly embraced this position," proposing "an auction of the world's resources (fishing rights, licenses to pollute, etc.). A proposal which quite simply comes down to sustaining the oligopolies in their ambition to mortgage further the future of the people of the South." If we set aside for the moment the moral challenges Amin raises about the maintenance of unfair North–South power relations, another part of the problem is that the market does not readily map on to natural phenomena that are only now being understood by the world's leading climate scientists, such as the sequestration of carbon in forests, oceans, and grasslands. As Harvey (2006) warns,

> The spatio-temporality required to represent energy flows through ecological systems accurately, for example, may not be compatible with that of financial flows through global markets. Understanding the spatio-temporal rhythms of capital accumulation requires a quite different framework to that required to understand global climate change. (p. 96)

The increased commodification of nature runs under such constraints of uncertainty into various limits, Harvey is quick to point out, in part because spatiotemporal rhythms of unstable financial markets now drive global-scale public policy, even when with regard to addressing the crucial problem of global climate change. Hence, there arose the notion in vulgar economic ideology that financial solutions really do exist for the purpose of mitigating GHG pollution. Exemplifying vulgarity in the expression of financial market power, there is no one better than Larry Summers, who as a leading US Treasury Department official arranged Wall Street bailouts in 1995 (Mexico), 1997–1998 (East Asia), and 2009–2010 (throughout the world but mainly helping Wall Street and the City of London) through extreme devaluations visited upon vulnerable countries and people. This tendency to devalue other people's wealth and lives harkens back to December 1991 when World Bank chief economist Summers (1991) wrote (or at least signed a memo written by Lant Pritchett) that "the economic logic behind dumping a load of toxic waste on the lowest-wage country is impeccable and we should face up to that. . . . African countries are vastly underpolluted."

The implications of Summers' (1991) analysis and strategy—which extreme as these words sound, in modified form still represent the ecological modernization philosophy to which the World Bank and its allies adhere—are that the United States and other Northern polluters should (1) *shift* problems associated with environmental market externalities to the South; (2) *stall* a genuine solution to the problems by instead opening up the field of pollution trading for a future market solution, using financialization techniques, derivatives, and imaginary "offsets" ostensibly aimed at building tomorrow's sinks so as to mop up today's dangerous forms of Northern pollution; and (3) *steal* more of the world's environmental carrying capacity—especially for GHG emissions—and perhaps pay a bit back through commodification of the air (resorting to mythical carbon markets and offsets) while denying climate debt responsibilities. Yet while emissions markets as tools for management of economic and ecological crises are attractive (to capital) in principle, they appear impossible to implement in practice, largely because of ongoing disputes about how the deeper capitalist crisis is displaced. Capitalist "crisis," Harvey (2010) states, is

> a condition in which surplus production and reinvestment are blocked. Growth then stops and there appears to be an excess over-accumulation of capital relative to the opportunities to use capital profitably. If growth does not resume, then the over-accumulated capital is devalued or destroyed. The historical geography of capitalism is littered with examples of such over-accumulation crises. (p. 45)

How does the capitalist system ultimately address this underlying tendency to overaccumulate? Harvey argues that

> in a general crisis, a lot of capital gets devalued. Devalued capital can exist in many forms: deserted and abandoned factories; empty office and retail spaces; surplus commodities that cannot be sold; money that sits idle earning no rate of return; declining asset values in stocks and shares, land, properties, art objects, etc. (p. 46)

(Climate change may well visit such destruction on vulnerable sites; after all, Hurricane Sandy causes $60 billion worth of devalorization in a few hours in October 2012, requiring New York mayor Michael Bloomberg to develop a $20 billion climate-proofing strategy for the city.) But in lieu of sufficient devaluation of overaccumulated capital, those responsible for crisis management attempt various other crisis displacement tactics.

One of these, the rise of carbon trading, can be compellingly understood using a theory of capitalist crisis developed in the tradition of Marxian political economy. Here, accumulation by dispossession allows capital to interact with society and nature on non-capitalist terrain, in search of scarce profits, in the way Rosa Luxemburg (1968) argued was central to capitalist crisis management a century ago. Throughout the world, there are a great many examples that Harvey (2003) traced back to Marx's idea of primitive accumulation, including

> conversion of various forms of property rights (common, collective, state, etc.) into exclusive private property rights; suppression of rights to the commons; . . . colonial, neocolonial and imperial processes of appropriation of assets (including natural resources) . . . and ultimately the credit system as radical means of primitive accumulation. (p. 145)

From such origins of understanding capitalist/non-capitalist power relations, a theory of imperialism emerged based on accumulation by dispossession, perhaps best articulated by Luxemburg (1968) in 1913:

> Accumulation of capital periodically bursts out in crises and spurs capital on to a continual extension of the market. Capital cannot accumulate without the aid of non-capitalist relations, nor . . . can it tolerate their continued existence side by side with itself. Only the continuous and progressive disintegration of non-capitalist relations makes accumulation of capital possible. (p. 347)

These concepts help us to better locate the carbon markets and other emissions trading and offset strategies as vehicles for displacing overaccumulated capital during a period of extended crisis. The Kyoto Protocol's opportunities for profit from the trade in rights to engage in environmental degradation are considered in *The Ecological Rift*, by John Bellamy Foster, Brett Clark, and Richard York (2010):

> By the perverse logic of the system, whole new industries and markets aimed at profiting on planetary destruction, such as the waste management industry and carbon trading, are being opened up. These new markets are justified as offering partial, ad hoc "solutions" to the problems generated non-stop by capital's laws of motion. . . . Such schemes continue to be advanced despite the fact that experiments in this respect have thus far failed to reduce emissions. Here, the expansion of capital trumps actual public interest in protecting the vital conditions of life. At all times, ruling-class circles actively work to prevent radical structural change in this as in other areas, since any substantial transformation in social–environmental relations would mean challenging the treadmill of production, and launching an ecological–cultural revolution. Indeed, from the standpoint of capital accumulation, global warming and desertification are blessings in disguise, increasing the prospects of expanding private riches. (pp. 70–71)

It is with political–ecological reasoning—seeing through the lens of capitalist crisis and, consequently, the more desperate search for profit (with an ever more intense capital–nature metabolism)—that we can substantially understand how overaccumulated capital found spatial, temporal, and imperialist routes to flow through during the past three decades, eventually landing in the emissions markets in the past decade. Financial markets are central to the story because they exploded in size and reach once the temporal fix began in earnest with liberalization and a shift to a higher interest rate regime in the late 1970s. As productive sector profit rates in the North declined and financial returns boomed, financial expansion into various exotic derivative investments permitted virtually any notional value to be marketed as a credit for packaging and onward sale, including emissions of sulfur dioxide in the United States in the early 1990s, carbon in Europe by the late 1990s, and a new round of sales of nature and its derivatives within both the North and the emerging markets in the coming decade. With this sort of lubrication, the commodification of the environmental commons proceeded apace, with water privatization, biopiracy, genetic modification, and other processes controlled by multinational corporations generating expectations for what became the world's largest artificial market—that is, carbon emissions.

The contradictions are extreme, as financial markets overextended geographically during the 1990s–2000s with investment portfolios diversifying into distant, risky areas and sectors. Global and national financial governance proved inadequate, leading to bloated and then busted asset values ranging from subprime housing mortgages to illegitimate emissions credits. Likewise, geopolitical tensions emerged over which sites would be most vulnerable to suffer devalorization of overaccumulated capital after 2008—that is, which regions or countries would bear the brunt of the deep financial sector and real economic downturns. The geopolitical context during the 2000s featured a sole military superpower oriented to neoconservative imperialism (especially in relation to US energy needs and hence inbuilt climate change denialism) but mitigated somewhat by a global class politics of neoliberalism. This arrangement has evolved somewhat since 2010, with BRICS becoming the most coherent emerging market network. But as BASIC countries' (Brazil, South Africa, India, and China) leaders Lula da Silva, Jacob Zuma, Manmohan Singh, and Wen Jiabao showed in 2009, they were perfectly willing to agree to a Copenhagen Accord that served

Northern—and elite Southern—interests of GHG emissions without constraint (Bond 2012). Competition in emissions laxity is the only way to describe the COPs under current circumstances, in which delegates have attended summits in carbon-intensive countries at which the UN Framework Convention on Climate Change secretariat was led by a carbon trader (Christiana Figueras) and each of the summit presidencies bore the market of local fossil industry power.

No better examples can be found of the irrationality of capitalism's spatial–ecological fix to climate crisis—and the limits of shifting–stalling–stealing strategies—than two remarks from London. First, in 2010, said Tory climate minister Greg Barker (as cited in Penman 2012), "We want the City of London, with its unique expertise in innovative financial products, to lead the world and become the global hub for green growth finance. We need to put the sub-prime disaster behind us." In that spirit, *World Finance* magazine's "Western European Commodities Broker of the Year" award in March 2012 went to Simon Greenspan, who bragged of his City of London firm (as cited in Penman 2012),

> At Tullett Brown we've only ever invested in areas of the market that have truly stood the test of time, such as gold and silver and property. When our analysts were looking for the next great area of growth it was fairly obvious to them. It was the planet, it was the environment.

Just days later, British financial authorities forced Tullett Brown into provisional liquidation, and at the executives' fraud trial a few months later, the suspects in this financial–ecological crime could not even afford a lawyer (Penman 2012).

Conclusion

Can the logic of capitalism generate repairs for the intrinsic damage being done during the Anthropocene or, specifically—because obviously not all humans are equally responsible— the "Capitalocene" (Moore 2013)? Some believe in a "green capitalism" strategy, including Al Gore (2009), often based on arguments by Paul Hawken, Amory Lovins, and L. Hunter Lovins (1999) (for a critique, see Tanuro 2014). But as Salleh (2012) argues, a serious consideration of externalized costs should include at least three kinds of surplus extractions, both economic and thermodynamic, never comprehensively incorporated by reformers: (1) the social debt to inadequately paid workers, (2) an embodied debt to women family caregivers, and (3) an ecological debt drawn on nature at large.

In contrast to the weak form of sustainability are concepts of the left, stressing distributional equity, non-materialist values, and a critique (and transcendence) of the mode of production. They include the environmental justice vision that African American activists in North Carolina began to articulate in the 1980s (Bullard 2000); "anti-extractivism" and the "rights of nature" articulated by Ecuadorean and Bolivian activists and constitutions (even if not in public policy, as noted by Accion Ecologica (2014)), along with the Andean indigenous peoples' versions of *buen vivir* (living well) and allied ideas (Council of Canadians and Global Exchange and Fundacion Pachamama 2011); "degrowth" (*décroissance*; Latouche 2004); post-gross domestic product "well-being" national accounting (Fioramonti 2014) such as Bhutan's Gross National Happiness, which emphasizes sufficiency; "the commons" (Linebaugh 2008); and eco-socialism (Kovel 2007). Strategies for transitioning to genuinely sustainable societies and economies are also hotly debated (Scoones, Leach, and Newell 2015; Swilling and Anneke 2012).

With such creative options flowering—albeit in sometimes reformist mode harking back to indigenous conservation, mere accounting reforms, and the slowing (not ending) of capitalism—determining genuine sustainability does ultimately depend on the nature of the critique of unsustainability. Perhaps the most popular systemic analysis comes from Annie Leonard's (2007) *Story of Stuff* film and book, which link the spectrum of extraction, production, distribution, consumption, and disposal. Klein's (2014) *This Changes Everything* puts the onus on capitalism for climate change. The opening for global studies analysts is obvious, insofar as these divergent ideologies are partly understood only when the world as a whole becomes the unit of analysis, as historical processes are made explicit, as critical postcolonial and indeed post-capitalist thinking is increasingly vital, and as narrow disciplinary boundaries inherited from the late nineteenth century (in most social sciences) are discarded. The logic of environmental catastrophe as a series of local symptoms within a global crisis can no longer be denied. As a result, this is where studies of global processes are not just an innovation but now a necessity.

References

Accion Ecologica Colectivo Miradas críticas del Territorio desde el Feminismo. 2014. "La vida en el centro y el crudo bajo tierra: El Yasuní en clave feminist." June 2. http://www.accionecologica.org/component/content/article/1754.

Amin, S. 2010. "The Battlefields Chosen by Contemporary Imperialism." *MRZine* 2, February. http://mrzine.monthlyreview.org/2010/amin070210.html.

Böhm, S., M. C. Misoczky, and S. Moog. 2012. "Greening Capitalism? A Marxist Critique of Carbon Markets." *Organization Studies* 33 (11): 1617–1638.

Bond, P. 2012. *Politics of Climate Justice: Paralysis Above, Movement Below*. Pietermaritzburg, South Africa: University of KwaZulu-Natal Press.

Bracking, S. 2016. *The Financialization of Power*. London: Routledge.

Broder, J. 2012. "Signs of New Life as UN Searches for a Climate Accord." *New York Times*, January, 24. http://www.nytimes.com/2012/01/25/business/global/signs-of-new-life-as-un-searches-for-a-climate-accord.html?pagewanted=all&_r=0.

Bullard, R. 2000. *Dumping in Dixie: Race, Class and Environmental Quality*. 3rd ed. New York: Routledge.

Büscher, B., W. Dressler, and R. Fletcher, eds. 2014. *Nature™ Inc.: Environmental Conservation in the Neoliberal Age*. Tucson: University of Arizona Press.

Carbon Pricing Leadership Coalition. 2017. *Report of the High-Level Commission on Carbon Prices*. Washington: World Bank Group.

Club of Rome. 1972. *The Limits to Growth*. New York: Universe.

Council of Canadians and Global Exchange and Fundacion Pachamama. 2011. *The Rights of Nature: The Case for a Universal Declaration on the Rights of Mother Earth*. Ottawa: Council of Canadians.

Daly, H., ed. 1973. *Toward a Steady State Economy*. San Francisco: Freeman.

Daly, H. 1996. *Beyond Growth: The Economics of Sustainable Development*. Boston: Beacon.

Dorsey, M., and J. Williams. 2017. "Why Pollution Trading Will Never Be the Climate Solution for California—Or Anywhere Else." *Alternet*, August 11. http://www.alternet.org/environment/why-pollution-trading-will-never-be-climate-solution-california-or-anywhere-else.

Drexhage, J., and D. Murphy. 201. "Sustainable Development: From Brundtland to Rio 2012." Background paper prepared for consideration by the High Level Panel on Global Sustainability, United Nations, New York. https://www.popline.org/node/216968.

Ekwurzel, B., J. Boneham, M. W. Dalton, R. Heede, R. J. Mera, M. R. Allen, and P. C. Frumhoff. 2017. "The Rise in Global Atmospheric CO_2, Surface Temperature, and Sea Level from Emissions Traced to Major Carbon Producers." *Climatic Change*, September 7. https://link.springer.com/article/10.1007/s10584-017-1978-0.

Fioramonti, L. 2014. *How Numbers Rule the World*. London: Zed.

Fischer-Kowalski, M., and M. Swilling. 2011. *Decoupling: Natural Resource Use and Environmental Impacts from Economic Growth*. New York: United Nations Environment Programme. http://wedocs.unep.org/handle/20.500.11822/9816.

Foster, J. B., B. Clark, and R. York. 2010. *The Ecological Rift*. New York: Monthly Review Press.

Fondation BNP Paribas. 2017. *Global Carbon Atlas 2017*. Paris: Fondation BNP Parisb. http://www.globalcarbonatlas.org/en/content/welcome-carbon-atlas.

Gore, A. 2009. *Our Choice*. New York: Rodale.

Harvey, D. 1982. *The Limits to Capital*. Oxford, UK: Basil Blackwell.

Harvey, D. 1996. *Justice, Nature and the Geography of Difference*. Oxford, UK: Basil Blackwell.

Harvey, D. 2003. *The New Imperialism*. Oxford, UK: Oxford University Press.

Harvey, D. 2006. *Spaces of Global Capitalism*. London: Verso.

Harvey, D. 2010. *The Enigma of Capital*. New York: Profile Books.

Harvey, D. 2014. *Seventeen Contradictions and the End of Capitalism*. New York: Oxford University Press.

Hawken, P., A. Lovins, and L. Hunter Lovins. 1999. *Natural Capitalism*. Boston: Little, Brown.

Henderson, P. 2017. "California to Discuss Linking Carbon Market with China." *Reuters*, June 2. https://af.reuters.com/article/commoditiesNews/idAFL1N1IY2H3.

High-Level Commission on Carbon Pricing. 2017. "Report of the High-Level Commission on Carbon Pricing." Washington, DC: World Bank, May 29. https://static1.squarespace.com/static/54ff9c5ce4b0a53decccfb4c/t/59244eed17bffc0ac256cf16/1495551740633/CarbonPricing_Final_May29.pdf

Jurgensmeyer, M. 2013. "What Is Global Studies?" *Globalizations* 10 (6): 765–769. doi:10.1080/14747731.2013.845956.

Klein, N. 2014. *This Changes Everything*. New York: Simon & Schuster.

Kovel, J. 2007. *The Enemy of Nature*. London: Zed.

Krugman, P. 2009. "Unhelpful Hansen." *New York Times*, December 7. http://krugman.blogs.nytimes.com/2009/12/07/unhelpful-hansen.

Krugman, P. 2013. "Gambling with Civilization." *New York Review of Books*, November 7. http://www.nybooks.com/articles/archives/2013/nov/07/climate-change-gambling-civilization.

Latouche, S. 2004. "Degrowth economics." *Le Monde Diplomatique*, November. https://mondediplo.com/2004/11/14latouche.

Leonard, A. 2007. *Story of Stuff Project*. http://storyofstuff.org.

Linebaugh, P. 2008. *The Magna Carta Manifesto: Liberties and Commons for All*. Berkeley: University of California Press.

Lohmann, L. 2006. *Carbon Trading: A Critical Conversation on Climate Change, Privatization and Power*. Uppsala, Sweden: Dag Hammarskjöld Foundation.

Lohmann, L. 2012. "Financialization, Commodification and Carbon: The Contradictions of Neoliberal Climate Policy." *Socialist Register*, 48.

Lutzenburger, J. 1992. "Letter to Laurence Summers." http://www.whirledbank.org/ourwords/summers.html.

Luxemburg, R. 1968. *The Accumulation of Capital*. New York: Monthly Review Press.

Magdoff, F., and J. B. Foster. 2011. *What Every Environmentalist Needs to Know About Capitalism*. New York: Monthly Review Press.

Moore, J. 2013. "Anthropocene or Capitalocene?" https://jasonwmoore.wordpress.com.

Nordhaus, W. 2013. *The Climate Casino*. New Haven, CT: Yale University Press.

Parenti, C. 2017. "If We Fail." *Jacobin*, August 29. https://jacobinmag.com/2017/08/if-we-fail.

Penman, A. 2012. "Tullett Brown Scammers Net £3.2 Million But Are "too Poor" to Defend Themselves in Court." *Mirror*, July 4. http://blogs.mirror.co.uk/investigations/2012/07/tullett-brown-scammers-net-32m.html.

Raworth, K. 2017. *Doughnut Economics*. New York: Random House.

Salleh, A. 2010. "From Metabolic Rift to Metabolic Value." *Organization and Environment* 23 (2): 205–219.

Salleh, A. 2012. "Women, Food Sovereignty and Green Jobs in China." Friends of the Earth Australia. http://www.foe.org.au/women-food-sovereignty-and-green-jobs-china.

Scoones, I., M. Leach, and P. Newell. 2015. *The Politics of Green Transformation*. London: Routledge.

Steffen, W., K. Richardson, J. Rockström, et al. 2015. "Planetary Boundaries: Guiding Human Development on a Changing Planet." *Science* 347 (6223):1259855. doi:10.1126/science.1259855

Stern, N. 2007. *The Economics of Climate Change: The Stern Review*. Cambridge: Cambridge University Press.

Stern, T. 2017. "Trump is Wrong on the Paris Climate Agreement. I Know Because I Negotiated It." *Washington Post*, May 31. https://www.washingtonpost.com/opinions/trump-is-wrong-on-the-paris-climate-agreement i know-because-i-negotiated-it/2016/05/31/ce3a680a-2667-11e6-ae4a-3cdd5fe74204_story.html.

Summers, L. 1991. "The Memo." Reprinted in *The Economist*, February 8, 1992. http://www.whirledbank.org.

Swilling, M., and E. Annecke. 2012. *Just Transitions: Explorations of Sustainability in an Unfair World*. Cape Town, South Africa: University of Cape Town Press.

Tanuro, D. 2014. *Green Capitalism: Why It Can't Work*. Toronto: Fernwood.

TEEB. 2018. The Economics of Ecosystems Services. http://www.teebweb.org/about/

The Rules. 2015. "SDGs." http://therules.org/tag/sdgs.

Watson, F. 2017. "EU Carbon Prices Rally to Four-Month High." New York: S&P Global Platts. https://www.platts.com/videos/2017/july/snapshot-eu-carbon-prices-rally-072717

World Bank. 2012. *Inclusive Green Growth*. Washington, DC: The World Bank.

World Bank. 2017. "Carbon Pricing Dashboard." http://carbonpricingdashboard.worldbank.org/map_data.

World Commission on Environment and Development. 1987. *Our Common Future*. Oxford, UK: Oxford University Press. http://www.un-documents.net/ocf-02.htm.

PART IV

GLOBAL CITIZENSHIP

Ideas and Institutions for an Emerging Global World

CHAPTER 40

....

CIVIL SOCIETY

....

KAREN BUCKLEY

CIVIL society is a concept—an idea—and a lived reality. It draws on long traditions of philosophical and political thought and individual actions that have settled it within a strong associational format of individuals and groups that perform a range of beneficial functions for society, such as reviving communities, training citizens, building habits of cooperation, providing an alternative to bureaucracy, and reinvigorating public life (Ehrenberg 2012). The changing meanings of civil society over time are thought to contain a common core as "the process through which individuals negotiate, argue, struggle against or agree with each other and with the centres of political and economic authority. Through voluntary associations, movements, parties, unions, the individual is able to act publicly" (Kaldor 2003b: 585). Accumulating empirical accounts of civil society activities of an international and global character build on these ideas and invest hope in civil society to foster good governance, ensure respect for human rights, promote peaceful conflict resolution, rebuild global democracy, and contest global governance (Anheier, Glasius, and Kaldor 2001; Kaldor 2003a, 2003b; O'Brien et al. 2000; Scholte 2002, 2011). Global civil society, in this context, signifies a "new understanding of civil society . . . [which represents] both a withdrawal from the state and a move towards global rules and institutions" (Kaldor 2003b: 588).

There is nevertheless much "restraint, hesitancy, ambiguity and skepticism amongst those who write about it" (Chandhoke 2005). For some, civil society has outlived its fortunes and is viewed as "a playground of upper-middle classes and their NGOs [non-governmental organizations], bankrolled by foreign donors to promote special hobbies or free-market agendas" (Sogge 2013: 787). Civil society, according to another view, is just not up to the challenge of presenting alternatives in the face of historically rooted concentrations of wealth and power. Ehrenberg (2012) notes,

> As important as they are, local activity, voluntary organizations, and good manners cannot protect equality or advance democracy in conditions of historic inequality and gigantic centers of private power. They cannot take on the historic concentrations of wealth and privilege that dominate contemporary life and distort democracy.

Others who are skeptical of civil society view it as a category that has been promoted by hegemonic powers or depoliticized in an effort "to discipline dissent and promote a false legitimacy for an oppressive capitalist order," whereas the postcolonialist view finds civil society "so steeped in Western theory and practice that, in an imperialist project, it invariably marginalises and silences other political cultures" (Scholte 2011: 35).

Conceptual Overview

A wide range of hopeful and critical voices is indicative of debate over the extent and nature of civil society. For its myriad debates, interpretations, and discussions, research on detailing and imagining civil society, global civil society, and associated social relations is constrained in how it conceives global social relations. Often, the novelty, scope, and intensity of "the global" appear to hasten either the fastening of the global as simply a new hierarchy in existing levels of analysis or a leap to the global so that the object of analysis becomes only those constituents of civil society that fit a new global frame of reference. These peculiarities of civil society research are examined later through drawing on existing studies on the nature and extent of civil society.

There is confusion in the research literature on civil society as to whether discussions on civil society refer to an "analytical concept" or an "actually existing social form" (Lewis 2002: 572). Sometimes, discussions on civil society refer to it simultaneously as both a vision, as shown in debates regarding future global constitutional visions, and a "messy reality," as shown in global-level negotiations (Kaldor 2005a: 23). This chapter adds a missing dimension to these discussions through engaging a critical dialogue between concept and reality in civil society research (Buckley 2013a, 2013b; Cox 1999, 2002; Gramsci 1971; Thompson 1963, 1978). This involves understanding "the historical variations that have altered the meanings of the concept in an ongoing dialectic of concept and reality" (Cox 1999: 5). This chapter explores variations in conceptualizations of civil society and global civil society particularly as they relate to global governance and contestation. This aims to set up an immediate dialogue within civil society research. Openness toward the boundaries of "theoretical and practical activity" is also considered to have longer term significance through providing "a basis for the subsequent development of an historical, dialectical conception of the world, which understands movement and change" (Gramsci 1971: 34–35).

The main body of this chapter explores some of the cumulative historical conceptualizations and experiences associated with civil society research on global governance and contestation. It notes the enduring influence of methodological and wider disciplinary constraints in explaining and understanding civil society and extrapolating to the global sphere of theory and practice. Creating a critical dialogue between concepts and realities of civil society involves recognizing that policymakers, development workers, political activists, and academic researchers are part of and engaged in the making of civil society. Recognizing that there are not exclusive boundaries between those invested in civil society, this chapter focuses on the reproduction of ideas on civil society by academic researchers. This aims to open a critical dialogue through which emerging research avenues could potentially present greater understanding of civil society, global civil society, and associated social relations.

Conceptual Constraints

The historical permutations of the concept of civil society have been well documented to show its changing meanings according to differing philosophies, contexts, and struggles. In the present context, civil society is likened to "a battlefield upon which different values, ideas and political visions are debated, contended and struggled over" (Howell and Lind 2009: 5). The perception that civil society draws on rich traditions of thought and is enlivened by current intellectual debate places it as an important social science (re)discovery that transcends conventional social science categories and cuts across disciplinary boundaries (Anheier 2005, 2014; Anheier et al. 2001). At the very least, it is thought, civil society has brought "a more concrete meaning of society back into sociology . . . community back in political science . . . and social capital [in economics]" (Anheier 2005: 2). It is entrusted to do more than that too, for, as Anheier (2005) states,

> it could involve an intellectual shift away from disciplinary specialization . . . moreover, in its transnational dimension, the term goes beyond the notion of the national state and the national economy, and allows us to examine critical aspects of globalization and the emergence of a new social, cultural and political sphere. (p. 1)

Although there appears to be much promise within civil society research to break down conventional disciplinary boundaries, the reality is that methodological and wider disciplinary constraints continue to shape its contemporary meanings in often quite problematic ways (Richmond 2011). Divergent approaches among civil society researchers are divided between, for example, systemic views focusing on civil society and the state, individualistic views emphasizing agency and social capital, and other views locating civil society institutions and organizations within the public sphere (Anheier 2005: 1; Anheier 2014: 335). The presence of divergent approaches does not ensure the coterminous presence of a contentious battlefield of ideas. Nor does it ensure that a wider spatial application of civil society to global spheres of authority and decision-making between movements, institutions, and organizations automatically effects more meaning to global social relations.

In terms of civil society research on global social relations, a broad methodological bifurcation can be seen to exist between functional and aspirational perspectives on civil society (Buckley 2013a, 2013b). According to functional views on civil society and its internationally corollary, civil society effortlessly assimilates into rational, individualistic, and often nationalistic methodologies, discourses, and fields of action. More aspirational perspectives on civil society, and in apparent contradiction, cohere easily with solidarity and global, often normative, frames of reference and action. The difficulty in achieving dialogue between perspectives, and indeed their tendency to speak past each other using alternate language and reference points (Chandler 2007; Kaldor 2007; Patomäki 2007), results in further constraints in negotiating the boundaries set around conventional social science categories such as the state, market, or society and makes more difficult the production of research that effectively cuts across disciplinary boundaries. These issues are further examined next alongside some key features of civil society research and debate, particularly extending to global conceptions of civil society.

Civil society research is notable for a host of enquiries into the emergence and growth of non-state actors, often referred to as civil society, the third sector, the non-profit sector, global social movements, or transnational activism. The Center for Civil Society Studies at Johns Hopkins University, the London School of Economics' *Global Civil Society Yearbook*, and the Centre for Civil Society in Durban, South Africa, are each significantly involved in mapping and measuring civil society (Munck 2006: 327). At a time when civil society was receiving increased interest more widely, the objective of a Johns Hopkins Center study (Salamon et al. 1999) on the non-profit sector was to fill the gaps in basic knowledge on the non-profit sector in the context of wider questioning of the capacity of the neoliberal Washington consensus to guide global economic policy and related suggestions that

> because of their unique position outside the market and the state, their generally smaller scale, their connections to citizens, their flexibility, their capacity to tap private initiatives in support of public purposes, and their newly rediscovered contributions to building "social capital," civil society organizations have surfaced as strategically important participants in this search for a "middle way" between sole reliance on the market and sole reliance on the state. (p. 5)

The following are viewed as vital elements of this comparative research agenda: supporting a vibrant non-profit sector; promoting better awareness of the sector among policymakers, business leaders, and the media; and increasing recognition of the non-profit sector as a major economic force and contributor to economic and social life.

The need for greater empirical data on global civil society was also one of the main driving forces of the *Global Civil Society Yearbook*, which adopted an empirical definition of global civil society as "the sphere of ideas, values, institutions, organizations, networks, and individuals located *between* the family, the state, and the market and operating *beyond* the confines of national societies, polities and economies" (Anheier et al. 2001: 17; emphasis in original). Later, finding themselves "increasingly critical of the dominant associational notion of global civil society often equated with international NGOs," the editors adopted a more normative definition (Anheier, Kaldor, and Glasius 2012: 3). Broadly conceived as "the medium through which individuals negotiate and struggle for a social contract with the centres of political and economic authority," this definition is unambiguously transferred to the global context by virtue of the transborder existence of social movements and groups (Kaldor 2007: 299). This definition of civil society includes its many versions: The activist version, to which Kaldor finds herself closest, is composed of peace, women, human rights, and global social justice movements; the neoliberal version is promoted by global institutions and Western governments to facilitate market reforms and parliamentary democracy; and the postmodern version is critical of the individualism of Western civil society and more expansive toward recognizing realms of "uncivility" and non-Western forms of checks on state power (Kaldor 2003b: 588–590).

A study on "building global democracy," focusing on how civil society can add to democratic accountability in global governance, similarly conceives the existence of global civil society as a reflection of increased global interaction and a necessary response to global policy challenges such as climate change, crime, infectious disease, financial stability, (dis) armament, identity politics, social inequality, and human rights (Scholte 2011: 1). The emergence of "global-scale" social relations and governance is therefore linked to a need for greater democratic accountability, and civil society is deemed one such avenue through which this may be achieved (p. 1). There is recognition that "ideas of 'civil society' must be employed carefully and critically so that the activities in question are not captured for hegemonic and imperialist ends—and thereby detract from democratic accountability" (p. 36). The simple existence of global social relations, however, is not enough to counteract the co-option of civil society for other ends.

Research on civil society, from that concerned with the non-profit sector (Salamon et al. 1999) to that focused on global civil society in global activism (Anheier et al. 2001) and global governance (Scholte 2011), aims to increase data on an emerging actor in a more global political economy. These conceptualizations of civil society reflect concern with supporting a vibrant non-profit sector, enhancing the role of civil society in global activism, or considering how civil society can contribute to more accountable global governance. In global activism and governance, in particular, civil society is carefully defined and employed. Debating the boundaries and realities of global civil society is "one of the ways we construct the public space we call civil society" (Kaldor 2005a: 24). It is carefully construed (Kaldor 2005b):

> If we include either markets or constitutional order in the definition of civil society, I believe we lose the political utility of the term, and that is the role of new political groups, associations, movements and individuals in contributing to and being enabled by an emerging global regulatory framework. (p. 44)

Global civil society is recognized as undemocratic, uneven, and Northern-dominated, but nevertheless within it is found "a potential for individuals—a potential for emancipation" (Kaldor 2003b: 591). This potential is linked to the wider positioning of global civil society as supplementary to traditional democracy and tendering support for an international law enforcement position to minimize violence at a global level (Kaldor 2003a: 148, 155–156).

Amid the richness, depth, and extent of civil society research, however, is continued reliance on bounded conceptions of civil society as a social sphere outside the state and market: In the *Global Civil Society Yearbook*, civil society is positioned between the family, market, and state and is elsewhere seen to refer to "social institutions that operate outside the confines of the market and the state" (Salamon et al. 1999: 3). At times, the positioning and inherent values of civil society appear to be too easily carried from the national to the global context through emphasizing the descriptively clear existence of individuals and groups that have global aspirations or engage on a global level. Global civil society is positioned within the emerging configurations of global politics as part of "an ongoing project . . . to reconstruct, re-imagine, or re-map world politics" (Lipschutz 1992: 391–392). Its spatial boundaries are perceived to be different due to its location "above and beyond national, regional, or local societies" (Anheier et al. 2001: 3). States and international organizations have been particularly influential in using similarly bounded understandings to depoliticize civil society and locate it primarily as a sphere of rational action and non-governmental organization. In this way, civil society is considered a legitimizing force that lends representation, participation, accountability, and transparency to global affairs—themes that are often mirrored in academic research. The harnessing by academic researchers of civil society's apparently unique position outside the state and market is described as a form of "civil society purism" that understands civil society as "a liberated base from which the despotic powers of markets and governments can be challenged and politically defeated" (Keane 2005: 26). Civil society purism influences some Gramscian understandings of civil society, locating it as a bounded sphere of contestation, despite the much more nuanced meaning that Gramsci brought to the concept (Buckley 2013a: 47–48). Civil society purism is also often accompanied by a leap to the global whereby global civil society is viewed as a central arena or public space for shaping new agendas and remaking world order.

The problem with this is that much as with many theories of civil society, their firm setting in the Western liberal tradition (Munck 2006: 326) does not convince that they can easily evade the harmful effects of liberal and neoliberal theory and policy and amount to meaningful forms of global resistance and emancipation. In this sense, "theories of global civil society perform similar functions in the world polity as did theories of domestic civil society within distinct national polities," with each providing answers to the question of how to govern effectively "with or without the consent of the governed"; global civil society is simply deemed necessary to protect liberal democratic values from power politics, war, and wealth (Bartelson 2006: 372–373, 390). The language of civil society and global civil society alone should challenge a deeper rethinking of democratic possibilities, structures, and ideas (Pasha and Blaney 1998: 419–420), whereas the persisting rhetoric and ideology of global liberal values (Chandler 2009) also demand that empirical manifestations of individual resistance are not axiomatically placed within wider emancipatory strategies.

Civil society cannot, therefore, be ensured as a category of resistance, but there is much more to it than that. The concept is not a static one, but the enduring influence of its associational format, likening to "social capital," and relationship to positivism are enduring features that do not easily escape the empirical and aspirational methodologies engaged in its formation. Empirical methods of mapping and measuring civil society can, for example, fall too easily into a "mathematical paradigm" (Obadare 2011: 427) that focuses the social sciences and humanities on systems of measurability and quantification rather than engaging further conceptual and political clarifications and meanings. Measuring civil society is considered, for example, *the methodological cornerstone of civil society research* (Obadare 2011: 427; emphasis in original).[1] Although there is value in mapping and measuring civil society, political and theoretical clarification is more urgent (Munck 2006: 330). Such clarification is equally lacking in aspirational methodologies that "fail to problematize global social relations at all . . . assuming that, indeed, some kind of global civil society is somehow rising that will, at some point, stand between the World Bank and markets" (Drainville 2004: 9).

In searching for greater political and theoretical clarification on the nature of global social relations, research on civil society remains important because the limitations of civil society research prevail in analysis of global social relations. These limitations are discussed under the categories of "Civil Society I" and "Civil Society II" approaches (Edwards and Foley 1997; Foley and Edwards 1996). The Civil Society I approach emphasizes the capacity of associational life, drawing on Alexis de Tocqueville's *Democracy in America* (1835) and Putnam's "social capital" (Putnam 1995, 2000), to foster a strong civil society and promote effective democratic governance. One of the aims of the Johns Hopkins project referred to previously, for example, was to establish the contributions of civil society in building social capital. The lineage of current interest on social capital traces through studies on the decline of social capital and emerging citizen disenfranchisement in the United States, drawing on Putnam, and related interest in citizen renewal and the strengthening of the voluntary sector. A strong civil society is often in this context considered to bridge social and political divides and generate "social capital" (Smith 1998: 93). At the same time, liberal, neo-Tocquevillian interpretations of civil society emphasize "the harmonious, plural and diverse nature of citizen action around shared public interests" such as democratization and poverty reduction (Howell 2011: 268). The Civil Society II approach, closer to Kaldor's (2003a, 2003b) version of activist civil society, derives from studies on Eastern European resistance to Soviet domination and highlights a strong civil society as protection against an undemocratic or unjust regime. The conceptual paradoxes that these understandings of civil society are considered to contain (Foley and Edwards 1996) can be similarly seen in understandings of global civil society. Often missing in civil society formulations is attention to "the political economy of discontent" linked to national and international economic restructuring and the dismantling of the welfare state, specifically "the impact of workplace, corporate, and governmental restructuring on individuals, families, and communities" (Edwards and Foley 1997: 674). Further missing is attention to "political factors that shape and explain the intersection of civil society and the political order" (Smith 1998: 94; see also Foley and Edwards 1996). There is one main difference, however: Transnational social movements are increasingly considered part of civil society even though they may not bridge social and political cleavages as earlier concepts of civil society were deemed to do (Smith 1998: 103). The inclusion of (global) social movements within (global) civil society has nevertheless turned toward neo-Tocquevillian solutions borne through unity and harmony and an "outside-in" ability to hold governance to account. This continues to overlook "the essential nature of civil society, namely as an arena of power relations, involving cooperation and contestation not only with governments and capital, but also within its own folds" (Howell 2011: 268). Similarly, social capital formulations of civil society lack emphasis on power, conflict, and social class (Schuurman 2003: 1002). Social capital persists as "a prime example of the way in which neoliberalism as the dominant politico-economic model of recent decades has managed to shape the narrative, language and conceptualization of civil society" toward producing a "consensus based understanding of social change . . . [which masks] relations of power between the economic, political and social spheres" (Bunyan 2014: 543–544).

The nature of a "consensus based understanding of social change" is worthwhile exploring further in the context of how civil society is researched in relation to global governance. The co-authored *Contesting Global Governance* gives an empirical snapshot of civil society interactions with key global governing institutions aiming to focus on "collision between powerful economic institutions and social movements in many countries [that] has led to a contest over global governance" (O'Brien et al. 2000: 2; see also Buckley 2013a). Similarly to related studies on movements that have gained access to global institutions (Scholte 2011) is a predominant focus on the functional capacity of civil society to address accountability gaps and legitimize, often in a top-down restricted manner, global governance. The conclusions of the study by Scholte make this clear, in which it is found that both civil society campaigners and the International Monetary Fund appear to confirm rather than transform the nature of transparency to "make 'markets' (read globalising capitalism) function more smoothly and to make 'knowledge' (read neoclassical economic analysis) more available and influential" (Scholte 2011: 87). The outcome is a clear empirical study that highlights many of the severe shortcomings of civil society engagements with global governance but that, as it concludes, mostly leaves out those "silenced actors" who proffer "alternative grounds of understanding" and advocate structural transformation beyond capitalism (Scholte 2011: 339–340). Instead, capitalism perseveres as "perhaps the deepest structure of global politics in terms of material circumstances," and "rationalism is arguably the deepest organising principle of ideational conditions in the contemporary more global world" (Scholte 2011: 339). Civil society research—particularly in relation to global governance and global activism, which is the focus of this chapter—silences some civil society voices (Buckley 2013a; Scholte 2011). This happens not just where NGOs are considered the main bearers of civil society—for example, in some global governance, peacebuilding, and development research—but also where global activism is confined to bounded interpretations of civil society.

The first World Social Forum (WSF) in 2001 marked a significant development in global activism. It is considered by many to mark a culmination of increasingly cross-border social activism directed against global governing gatherings and institutions such as the G8, the International Monetary Fund, and the World Trade Organization. The hope was that the time of protest had evolved into an opportunity for broad groupings of civil society to meet, exchange ideas, and build toward a global convergence of civil society opposed to neoliberalism, capital domination, and imperialism. According to one assessment of the forum, "deliberative democracy has flown off the pages of the theorists' scholarly works and become a real-life aspiration for civil society activists" (Albrow and Glasius 2008: 12). Habermas' public sphere is not the direct focus of the research mentioned previously, but the World Social Forum might be considered one among other possible "fora for deliberation on the complex issues of the contemporary world, in which the various parties to the discussion do not only represent state interest" (Kaldor 2003a: 148).

The broad principles governing the forum reflect many of the bounded ideas on global civil society explored so far in this chapter. The WSF Charter of Principles, for example, defines the forum as "an open meeting place for reflective thinking, democratic debate of ideas, formulation of proposals, free exchange of experiences and interlinking for effective action" (World Social Forum 2002). The forum does not intend

> to be a body representing world civil society. . . . It does not constitute a locus of power to be disputed by the participants [and it] is a plural, diversified, non-confessional, non-governmental and non-party context. . . . Neither party representations nor military organizations shall participate in the Forum . . . the World Social Forum is a movement of ideas that prompts reflection.

Whitaker, one of the founders of the WSF, describes the forum as an incubator for ideas and initiatives to create other possible worlds (Whitaker, Santos, and Cassen 2005: 68). He explains that it is organized around the conception of the forum as an "open space," not a movement, "based on the assumption that it is not the Forum that can change the world but the social movements and organisations engaged in that struggle" (p. 68). The contention that the forum is an open space, rather than a movement, has been the subject of much debate but, based on author observations at the Tunisia WSF International Council meeting in March 2015, largely appears to have been resolved toward a more predominant open space position.

Further assessment of the forum reflects many of these founding principles and extends the conception of the global public sphere as a necessary component of global democracy. The forum "serves as a foundation for a more democratic global polity," and we are reminded that "without a global public sphere, there can be no plural discussion of global issues" (Smith et al. 2008: 4). The forum, therefore, "allows people to actively debate proposals for organizing global policy while nurturing values of tolerance, equality, and participation" and "the activities of the WSF are crucial to cultivating a foundation for a more democratic global economic and political order" (pp. 3–4). It "constitutes a new body politic, a common public space where previously excluded voices can speak and act in plurality" (p. 13). The significance of the forum is here found in its description as a normative, inclusive, public sphere that serves a large plurality of ideas and enables participants to work together and help achieve global democracy. However, as "a new major space created by and for global civil society" (Patomäki and Teivainen 2004: 212), the conceptual paradoxes of civil society are clear here, too. The forum space aims to facilitate a global convergence of civil society, but the nature of this strategy, based on the previously mentioned precepts, means that "the political economy of discontent" (Edwards and Foley 1997), which is arguably the principal concern of forum participants, is susceptible to civic-consensual understandings of movement and change that disregard social relations of power and wealth both at the site of the forum and in relation to the global political economy more broadly (Buckley 2013a: 82–110). From an organizational perspective, it is also important to consider to what extent the forum reproduces economism and reinforces capitalist power relations at the site of the forum through focusing on technical fixes and "nonpolitical" modes of organization at the expense of more contentious issues surrounding funding and the political economy of the forum itself (Buckley 2013a; Teivainen 2007).

How then to recapture "the emancipatory thread of civil society that has been won away through the strategic instrumentalisation, depoliticisation and . . . securitization of civil society" (Howell 2011: 270)? There is increasing evidence that civil society research is becoming more responsive to concerns about civil society instrumentalization as a service provider, depoliticization, Western-centric NGOization, romanticization, and bounded conceptualization. Some developing research, discussed later, disrupts images of global civil society as the societal accompaniment to global governance and offers a more nuanced and considered approach toward rethinking global civil society. Meanwhile, research that focuses on civil society in Western liberal democracies (Bunyan 2014) and in relation to authoritarian states (Lewis 2013) offers insight into global social relations in a way that challenges the paucity of dialogue between research on civil society and that on global civil society. When the historical traditions of civil society thought are integrated into global civil society research, they more often form part of the onward, progressive, march of history of which global civil society is considered a part. In other research, bounded views of civil society are highlighted for hiding, on the one hand, "state-led redistribution of wealth through regressive fiscal and monetary policies, deregulation, and privatization" and, on the other hand, "broad state action to address the inequalities of civil society" such as the New Deal (Ehrenberg 2012). Further research, from a less state-centric view, has delved into the extent to which civil society is influenced and changed by its interaction with international organizations such as the World Trade Organization (Hopewell 2015; Wilkinson 2005). These studies call attention to civil society as an agent within global political structures without starting from the normative prescription that civil society involvement is inherently or axiomatically beneficial. Shepherd (2015) focuses on its limited discursive conditions of possibility through showing how the meaningful participation of civil society is taken for granted in United Nations peacebuilding discourse. There is increasing recognition that the analytical privileging of civil society in abstraction from the state and market is detrimental to activist versions of the concept (Buckley 2013a). It can result in the celebration of contestation and incomplete recognition of the intersecting and crisscrossing nature of global social relations between governing bodies, the market, and civil society.

Nevertheless, many policy and academic visions of the concept continue to attach to civil society a functional and uniform character and, as Lewis (2002) suggests, perceive civil society to stand outside of normal politicized social relations:

> Among some development policy-makers and policy-focused academics, an idea of civil society has become influential which tends to be deployed in ways which limit not only the diversity of local civil society understandings and struggles, but also the essentially political nature of the concept itself. (p. 570)

When understood as a static concept, often one that can be mapped and measured with relatively few problems, global civil society tends to take on the predominant character and function of a rational and instrumental civil society. This is analogous to the distribution of figures marching up and down pages and across centuries carrying out a series of regular maneuvers (Thompson 1965: 357; Thompson 1978: 271). The tendency to depoliticize civil society and neglect a focus on specific local experiences can also be found in normative accounts in which civil society's social contractual obligations, normally outlined in relation to state–civil society relations, are transferred to global spheres of authority. There is concern in some civil society research, however, that this leaves the micro everyday struggles of civil society relatively unaccounted for, creating a disjuncture between civil society and global civil society and further reinforcing already established methodological and disciplinary constraints. It is suggested, for example, that it is time to "explore the stories of the people who make up civil society" such that "it is through their everyday lives that civil society can be understood" (Peck 2015: 550). Meanwhile, it is argued that "deeper structures of state/civil society entanglements can be understood through an analysis of contextualized individual life trajectories" (Räthzel, Uzzel, and Lundström 2015: 154–155). A research emphasis on the individuals within civil society, as an alternative to further quantification and measurements of civil society, is elsewhere put forward (Obadare 2011).

It may be the case that sustained focus on the concrete lived realities and experiences of the people that make up civil society more cogently captures the spatial and contextual nuances of global civil society, but this is not possible without additional ontological attention to the nature of the global logics of power, distribution, and contestation. Rather than being bound by the constraints set by some methodological and disciplinary lens, global civil society could be understood as a flexible category comprised through historical accumulations of meanings and actions. In a study of Indian NGO activists as "strategic cosmopolitans," the discourses of civil society and international development are opened up to give an improved understanding of how Indian development organizations that are oriented toward presenting development alternatives engage with the global (Baillie Smith and Jenkins 2012):

> Considering the personal, and often relatively hidden, narratives of activists in local NGOs . . . provides the opportunity to develop a less institutionalised understanding of civil society, as not only being composed of different types of organisations but also of individuals and their everyday struggles, and their identification and pursuit of alternatives. (p. 641)

The promise of such approaches is not their specific focus on the "local," "individual," or "everyday" but, rather, the possibility that the local, multiple, and marginal might be additionally thought of as part of, rather than independent to, global logics of power and contestation (Agathangelou and Ling 2004: 29).

CONCLUSION

A note of caution is necessary in relation to the objective of this chapter to focus on global social relations in civil society research. The objective is neither to achieve a definitive picture of global social relations nor to create a transformative global civil society. It is, rather, to draw attention to how civil society is constituted and conceived and how global social relations are understood with respect to governance and contestation. The perspective put forward emphasizes the developing, approximate, and provisional nature of conceptualizing civil society and draws attention to dialectical complexity between related concepts and realities (Buckley 2013a, 2013b). Within this dialectic, civil society is constitutive of, but not reducible to, historical variations and accumulations of meanings, contexts, and struggles. Its full understanding is not restricted to the existing variation of theories. Indeed, these theories meet with significant methodological, disciplinary, and experiential constraints even while the presence of a contentious battleground between theories is suggested. Nevertheless, the normative aims of civil society researchers—whether to promote awareness of the non-profit sector as a major economic force, to enhance the emancipative potential of global civil society to reduce violence at a global level, to confront global policy challenges, or to achieve greater democratic accountability in the context of global-scale social relations—have an effect on how civil society is transcribed into the world. Civil society is, at the same time, constitutive of prevailing ideologies and paradigms. Although aiming to evade the constraints embedded in, for example, methodological nationalism, social scientific rationalism, positivism, mathematical paradigms, or neoliberal economism, current extrapolations toward global civil society still tend toward "global inaccessibility," making more difficult dialogue between expressions of lived experiences or realities and their conceptualization (Jameson 1990). The enduring influence of associational civil society, the reduction of civil society to "social capital," and the formative influence of liberalism and neoliberalism in the constitution and study of global civil society each lengthen civil society from its lived realities of power, conflict, and inequality. Attention to these lived realities can be redrawn through an understanding of civil society as a sphere of transversal hegemony (Buckley 2013a). This moves from the concrete opposition of hegemony and counter-hegemony or power and resistance within which the dual face of civil society is overemphasized to produce an exaggerated form of impenetrable neoliberal hegemony or over-voluntarist form of emancipatory counter-hegemony. A transversal understanding of hegemony draws attention to the theoretical and practical positioning of movements of civil society in relation to the global political economy and to their inherent negotiations and contestations over global social relations.

REFERENCES

Agathangelou, A. M., and L. H. M. Ling. 2004. "The House of IR: From Family Power Politics to the Poisies of Worldism." *International Studies Review* 6 (4): 21–49.

Albrow, M., and M. Glasius. 2008. "Democracy and the Possibility of a Global Public Sphere." In *Global Civil Society 2007/8: Communicative Power and Democracy*, edited by M. Albrow, H. Anheier, M. Glasius, M. Price, and M. Kaldor, 1–18. London: Sage.

Anheier, H. 2005. "Introducing the Journal of Civil Society: An Editorial Statement." *Journal of Civil Society* 1 (1): 1–3.

Anheier, H. 2014. "Civil Society Research: Ten Years On." *Journal of Civil Society* 10 (4): 335–339.

Anheier, H., M. Glasius, and M. Kaldor. 2001. "Introducing Global Civil Society." In *Global Civil Society 2001*, edited by H. Anheier, A. Glasius, and M. Kaldor, 3–22. Oxford, UK: Oxford University Press.

Anheier, H., M. Kaldor, and M. Glasius. 2012. "The Global Civil Society Yearbook: Lessons and Insights 2001–2011." In *Global Civil Society 2012: Ten Years of Critical Reflection*, edited by M. Kaldor, H. L. Moore, and S. Selchow, 2–26. Basingstoke, UK: Palgrave Macmillan.

Baillie Smith, M., and K. Jenkins. 2012. "Existing at the Interface: Indian NGO Activists as Strategic Cosmopolitans." *Antipode* 44 (3): 640–662.

Bartelson, J. 2006. "Making Sense of Global Civil Society." *European Journal of International Relations* 12 (3): 371–395.

Biekart, K. 2008. "Measuring Civil Society Strength: How and for Whom?" *Development and Change* 39 (6): 1171–1180.

Buckley, K. 2013a. *Global Civil Society and Transversal Hegemony: The Globalization-Contestation Nexus.* London: Routledge.

Buckley, K. 2013b. "Global Civil Society: The Dialectics of Concept and Reality." *Globalizations* 10 (2): 231–244.

Bunyan, P. 2014. "Re-conceptualizing Civil Society: Towards a Radical Understanding." *Voluntas* 25 (2): 538–552.

Chandhoke, N. 2005. "What the Hell Is Civil Society?" *OpenDemocracy*, March 17. https://www.opendemocracy.net/democracy-open_politics/article_2375.jsp. Accessed July 19, 2016.

Chandler, D. 2007. "Deriving Norms from 'Global Space': The Limits of Communicative Approaches to Global Civil Society Theorising." *Globalizations* 4 (2): 283–298.

Chandler, D. 2009. *Hollow Hegemony: Rethinking Global Politics, Power and Resistance.* New York: Pluto Press.

Cox, R. W. 1999. "Civil Society at the Turn of the Millennium: Prospects for an Alternative World Order." *Review of International Studies* 25 (1): 3–28.

Cox, R. W. (with M. G. Schechter). 2002. *The Political Economy of a Plural World: Critical Reflections on Power, Morals and Civilization.* London: Routledge.

de Tocqueville, Alexis. 1835 *Democracy in America.* London: Saunders and Otley.

Drainville, A. 2004. *Contesting Globalization. Space and Place in the World Economy.* Oxford, UK: Routledge.

Edwards, B., and M. W. Foley. 1997. "Social Capital and the Political Economy of Our Times." *American Behavioral Scientist* 40 (5): 669–678.

Ehrenberg, J. 2012. "The History of Civil Society Ideas." *Oxford Handbooks Online*, May. http://www.oxfordhandbooks.com/view/10.1093/oxfordhb/9780195398571.001.0001/oxfordhb-9780195398571-e-2. Accessed July 19, 2016.

Foley, M. W., and B. Edwards. 1996. "The Paradox of Civil Society." *Journal of Democracy* 7 (3): 38–52.

Gramsci, A. 1971. *Selections from the Prison Notebooks of Antonio Gramsci*, translated by Q. Hoare and G. N. Smith. New York/London: International Publishers/Lawrence & Wishart.

Hopewell, K. 2015. "Multilateral Trade Governance as Social Field: Global Civil Society and the WTO." *Review of International Political Economy* 22 (6): 1128–1158.

Howell, J. 2011. "Commentary: Crises, Opportunities and the Elephant in the Room." *Journal of Civil Society* 7 (3): 265–271.

Howell, J., and J. Lind. 2009. *Counter-Terrorism, Aid and Civil Society.* Basingstoke, UK: Palgrave Macmillan.

Jameson, F. 1990. "Cognitive Mapping." In *Marxism and the Interpretation of Culture*, edited by C. Nelson and L. Grossberg, 347–357. Champaign: University of Illinois Press.

Kaldor, M. 2003a. *Global Civil Society: An Answer to War.* Cambridge, UK: Polity.

Kaldor, M. 2003b. "The Idea of Global Civil Society." *International Affairs* 79 (3): 583–593.

Kaldor, M. 2005a. "Commentary on Mazlish: 'The Hijacking of Global Civil Society.'" *Journal of Civil Society* 1 (1): 23–24.

Kaldor, M. 2005b. "Commentary on Keane." *Journal of Civil Society* 1 (1): 43–44.

Kaldor, M. 2007. "Reply to David Chandler." *Globalizations* 4 (2): 299–300.

Keane, J. 2005. "Eleven Theses on Markets and Civil Society." *Journal of Civil Society* 1 (1): 25–34.

Lewis, D. 2002. "Civil Society in African Contexts: Reflections on the Usefulness of a Concept." *Development and Change* 33 (4): 569–586.

Lewis, D. 2013. "Civil Society and the Authoritarian State: Cooperation, Contestation and Discourse." *Journal of Civil Society* 9 (3): 325–340.

Lipschutz, R. D. 1992. "Reconstructing World Politics: The Emergence of Global Civil Society." *Millennium* 21 (3): 389–420.

Munck, R. 2006. "Global Civil Society: Royal Road or Slippery Path?" *Voluntas* 17: 325–332.

Obadare, E. 2011. "Revalorizing the Political: Towards a New Intellectual Agenda for African Civil Society Discourse." *Journal of Civil Society* 7 (4): 427–442.

O'Brien, R., A. M. Goetz, J. A. Scholte, and M. Williams. 2000. *Contesting Global Governance: Multilateral Economic Institutions and Global Social Movements.* Cambridge, UK: Cambridge University Press.

Pasha, M. K., and D. L. Blaney. 1998. "Elusive Paradise: The Promise and Peril of Global Civil Society." *Alternatives: Global, Local, Political* 23 (4): 417–450.

Patomäki, H. 2007. "The Role of 'Critical' in the Theory and Practice of Global Civil Society." *Globalizations* 4 (2): 312–317.

Patomäki, H., and T. Teivainen. 2004. *A Possible World: Democratic Transformation of Global Institutions.* London: Zed.

Peck, S. 2015. "Civil Society, Everyday Life and the Possibilities for Development Studies." *Geography Compass* 9/10: 550–564.

Putnam, R. D. 1995. "Tuning in, Tuning out: The Strange Disappearance of Social Capital in America." *PS: Political Science and Politics* 28 (4): 664–683.

Putnam, R. D. 2000. *Bowling Alone: The Collapse and Revival of American Community.* New York: Simon & Schuster.

Räthzel, N., D. Uzzell, R. Lundström, and B. Leandro. 2015. "The Space of Civil Society and the Practices of Resistance and Subordination." *Journal of Civil Society* 11 (2): 154–169.

Richmond, O. P. 2011. "Critical Agency, Resistance and a Post-Colonial Civil Society." *Cooperation and Conflict* 46 (4): 419–440.

Salamon, L. M., H. Anheier, R. List, et al. 1999. *Global Civil Society: Dimensions of the Nonprofit Sector.* Baltimore, MD: Johns Hopkins Center for Civil Society Studies.

Scholte, J.-A. 2002. "Civil Society and Democracy in Global Governance." *Global Governance* 8 (3): 281–304.

Scholte, J.-A. 2011. *Building Global Democracy? Civil Society and Accountable Global Governance*. Cambridge, UK: Cambridge University Press.

Schuurman, F. J. 2003. "Social Capital: The Politico-Emancipatory Potential of a Disputed Concept." *Third World Quarterly* 24 (6): 991–1010.

Shepherd, L. 2015. "Constructing Civil Society: Gender, Power and Legitimacy in United Nations Peacebuilding Discourse." *European Journal of International Relations* 21 (4): 887–910.

Smith, J. 1998. "Global Civil Society? Transnational Social Movement Organizations and Social Capital." *American Behavioral Scientist* 42 (1): 93–107.

Smith, J., M. Karides, M. Becker, D. Brunelle, C. Chase-Dunn, and D. Della Porta. 2008. *Global Democracy and the World Social Forums*. Boulder, CO: Paradigm.

Sogge, D. 2013. "Civil Society Studies: Two Compendia Compared." *Development and Change* 44 (3): 787–796.

Teivainen, T. 2007. "The Political and Its Absence at the World Social Forum: Implications for Democracy." *Development Dialogue* 49: 69–79.

Thompson, E. P. 1963. *The Making of the English Working Class*. London: Penguin.

Thompson, E. P. 1965. "The Peculiarities of the English." *Socialist Register* 2: 311–362.

Thompson, E. P. 1978. *The Poverty of Theory and Other Essays*. London: Merlin Press.

Whitaker, F., B. de Sousa Santos, and B. Cassen. 2005. "The World Social Forum: Where Do We Stand and Where Are We Going?" In *Global Civil Society 2005/6*, edited by M. Glasius, M. Kaldor, and H. Anheier, 64–86. London: Sage.

Wilkinson, R. 2005. "Managing Global Civil Society: The WTO's Engagement with NGOs." In *The Idea of Global Civil Society: Politics and Ethics in a Globalising Era*, edited by R. Germain and M. Kenny, 156–174. London: Routledge.

World Social Forum. 2002. "World Social Forum Charter of Principles." https://fsm2016.org/en/sinformer/a-propos-du-forum-social-mondial. Accessed July 28, 2016.

NOTE

1. For discussions on measuring civil society and a summary of critiques of the *Civicus Global Survey of the State of Civil Society*, see Biekart (2008).

FURTHER READING

Baker, G., and D. Chandler, eds. 2005. *Global Civil Society: Contested Futures*. New York: Routledge.

Löfgren, M. and H. Thörn, eds. 2007. "Global Civil Society: More or Less Democracy?" *Development Dialogue* 49: 1–173. http://www.daghammarskjold.se/publication/global-civil-society-less-democracy. Accessed July 19, 2016.

Germain, R. D., and M. Kenny, eds. 2005. *The Idea of Global Civil Society: Politics and Ethics in a Globalizing Era*. London: Routledge.

Hall, J., and F. Trentmann, eds. 2005. *Civil Society: A Reader in History, Theory, and Global Politics*. Basingstoke, UK: Palgrave Macmillan.

Kaviraj, S., and S. Khilnani, eds. 2001. *Civil Society: History and Possibilities*. Cambridge, UK: Cambridge University Press.

CHAPTER 41

....

CITIZENSHIP

....

HANS SCHATTLE

CITIZENSHIP is one of *the* big ideas in politics and society: Questions of "who belongs" and what sorts of responsibilities accompany belonging cut to the heart of social and political life in any community, and these matters spark much disagreement in our contemporary public debates. In most of the world's countries today, following decades of democratic transitions and consolidations, the basis of legitimate government rests on principles of human rights and consent of the people, as well as the public accountability and responsiveness of political leaders. This holds at all levels of domestic politics, from national governments to local authorities, and many scholars concerned about our collective capacity to solve the world's most pressing problems have advocated for these democratic principles to be deployed wholeheartedly into the international arena, as well, through the voices of civil society activists and by means of more responsive and accountable global governing institutions. Meaningful democratic citizenship everywhere depends on watchful and engaged publics to ensure that governments are effective and transparent and, when they are not, to end abuses of power or shortcomings in leadership and insist on change. This essential part of active citizenship—public participation in self-government and the monitoring of representatives in government—is not to be take for granted; it requires constant upkeep and nourishment.

For centuries, first city-states and, eventually, nation-states have functioned as the principal venues for upholding basic rights and carrying out corresponding obligations of citizenship. These range from compulsory duties such as taxation, military conscription, and serving on juries to voluntary duties such as voting (compulsory in some countries, such as Australia, Brazil, and Singapore), taking up a career in government service, getting involved in community organizations or interest groups, and speaking out on public issues. For most people, national citizenship remains the primary vehicle for political belonging, even amid the current era of globalization, and in fact, the legal mechanisms of national citizenship and border controls are becoming more significant in the present day, at least within the "developed" world. In many important respects, global integration has pushed nation-states to tighten up on citizenship as a way of reasserting sovereignty and authority—trying to restore the sense that countries are still at least partially able to control their destinies, after all. Global economic integration and a growing perception among discontented mass publics that international institutions are far from democratic or even legitimate in their decision-making have also prompted many people to think about citizenship and the question of "who belongs" in exclusionary terms. Amid high anxiety about the economic consequences of globalization and concern that the middle classes and working classes are negatively affected the most by the global market, public support has been rising for politicians, some of them textbook demagogues, promising crackdowns on immigration and withdrawal from economic collaboratives and trade agreements; witness Donald Trump's election as president of the United States; the decision by voters in Great Britain to exit the European Union; the ability of "far right" politicians throughout continental Europe to work their way into top leadership positions; and rising anti-immigration sentiments in East Asian polities, notably Japan and South Korea, that are still adjusting into their relatively new positioning as destination countries for migrants and refugees.

At the same time, rapid advances in global communication platforms and growing recognition of global economic interdependence as well as global cultural interconnectedness have brought the fates of vast populations closer together now than ever before, and this speaks to the ways in which citizenship now takes on global dimensions. Most people throughout the world still identify primarily as citizens of their respective countries—and the world's least advantaged people hardly have the luxury of thinking about citizenship at all—but growing numbers of individuals have also come to think of themselves as global citizens: as members and participants in communities that stretch beyond the boundaries of their home countries. Similar to the concept of citizenship more generally, the idea of global citizenship has plenty of its own internal divisions and variants. Although some individuals go as far to consider themselves literally as citizens of the world rather than citizens of any particular country, more commonly today's global citizens view the idea as complementary to national citizenship—as a metaphor that evokes elements of awareness, responsibility, participation, cross-cultural empathy, mobility, and competence in multiple, cross-cutting communities, from their immediate neighborhoods to the world at large. Some are highly privileged and see the world as their oyster for prosperity, whereas others are driven mainly by moral and ethical commitments and find resonance in the following immortal words attributed to Margaret Mead: "Never doubt that a small group of thoughtful, committed citizens can change the world."

Citizenship, then, is simultaneously a focal point for public debate, a platform for lived experiences to link up with political ideals, and a key integrating concept in global studies. Like global studies, the study of citizenship works across numerous academic disciplines: philosophy, law, political science, international relations, sociology, cultural anthropology, social psychology, business ethics, and educational studies—a field that recently has shown tremendous interest in global citizenship given how many schools and universities have elevated this specific concept as a key strategic objective in vision and mission statements. Keeping with the interdisciplinary nature of citizenship, this chapter first discusses some important "real-world" developments and lines of inquiry related to citizenship that are of particular interest in the field of global studies, and it examines how many important points of contestation now revolve around "who belongs" and what is required of the people who belong. Then the chapter outlines various approaches to studying global citizenship as well as critiques leveled against this concept from skeptics in the academy and in contemporary public debate. This section of the chapter also examines how the field of civic education has embraced the idea of global citizenship—and the related idea of global competency—before concluding with some comments about how citizenship and global citizenship fit within the larger endeavor of global studies.

THE CONTESTED NATURE AND RISING CONTINGENCIES OF CITIZENSHIP

Defining Citizenship

What is citizenship? This basic question prompts different kinds of answers depending on the chosen point of emphasis. One useful way to understand, consolidate, and mediate the range of competing interpretations on citizenship is to think of three definitional streams: (1) rights and corresponding duties; (2) democratic empowerment and participation; and (3) allegiance, belonging, loyalty, and identity. Across all three of these areas, membership and participation are two fundamental elements of citizenship in any political community (Schattle 2012).

Rights and duties reflect the most legally binding aspects of citizenship, tied to specific territorial and legal jurisdictions. British social theorist and historian T. H. Marshall (1963) provided the classic formulation of modern citizenship status as a trilogy of civil rights, political rights, and social rights. Also, the founding documents of the United Nations have upheld the basic principle of universal human rights and distinguished between civil and political rights (freedoms of speech, religion, assembly, and the rights to petition the government, vote, and receive proper treatment through "due process" within the legal system) and social and economic rights (rights to education, health care, basic living wages, fair and safe working conditions, unemployment insurance, and retirement pensions). Despite the advancement of human rights as an international norm after World War II, for the most part, political philosophers and social scientists have continued to distinguish between universal human rights regarded as applicable worldwide for all people and rights conferred by national citizenship within specific legal and territorial jurisdictions. Social theorist Charles Tilly (1996) offered one classic, state-based definition, casting citizenship as

> a continuing series of transactions between persons and agents of a given state in which each has enforceable rights and obligations uniquely by virtue of (1) the person's membership in an exclusive category, the native-born plus the naturalized and (2) the agent's relation to the state rather than any other authority the agent may enjoy. Citizenship thus forms a special sort of contract. (p. 8)

In contrast, democratic empowerment and participation relate with the extent citizens choose to raise their voices in the political arena and get involved in matters that affect their communities; these are the practices of citizenship, or what Alexis de Tocqueville famously labeled "habits of the heart." This leads into the psychological aspects of citizenship—the senses of allegiance, belonging, and loyalty that individuals feel toward their communities, regardless of their legal status. These elements of citizenship place emphasis not on citizenship as a formal legal institution but, rather, on the ways in which individuals and groups voluntarily take on civic engagement as a way of life. All three of these definitional streams of citizenship are major lines of inquiry in themselves, and the interdisciplinary journal *Citizenship Studies*, founded in 1996, has become a major venue for scholarship that explores not only how these varied aspects of citizenship are progressing within nation-states but also how new kinds of membership and participation transcend states and often rely more heavily on common affinities among diverse and dispersed groups of people: cultural citizenship, digital citizenship, environmental citizenship, feminist citizenship, sexual citizenship, transnational citizenship, and so forth. The founders of the journal marked the tenth anniversary of the publication with the following observation about the vitality of citizenship as part of an essential social contract (Isin and Turner 2007):

> Citizenship is vital partly because, when people put investments into their states, they can assume that they have a legitimate claim on that state when they fall ill, or become unemployed, or become too old to support themselves. The past contributions to the community become the basis of legitimate claims on the "commonwealth." In this respect, they can see or experience a clear connection between effort, reward and virtue. Citizenship in this way involves, often covertly, an education in civic culture in which, because citizens are patriotically proud of the society to which they belong, and they are therefore committed to defending its democratic institutions.

Globalization and Contention Regarding "Who Belongs"

Globalization, however, and "neoliberal" economic policies that have widened inequality within many societies have placed significant pressure on the social rights and social welfare provisions that for much of the twentieth century provided the basis for what Engin Isin and Bryan Turner (2007: 16), in the previous passage, call the "connection between effort, reward and virtue." Growing public doubt about whether globalization is worthwhile has increased support for exclusionary measures tightening access to national citizenship and undermining freedom of movement. Even as global economic interdependence, cultural hybridization and intertwinement, and advances in communications technology have rendered our world seemingly "smaller" and more connected than ever, the legal institution of national citizenship has sought to re-assert itself. Many destination countries are now stepping up efforts to keep migrants out or make their stays fraught with fear of getting caught and deported. The United States has already built walls and fences along 600 miles of the border with Mexico (which totals nearly 2,000 miles), and many Americans eagerly supported Donald Trump and his promises to expand this wall: "Build the wall!" was one of the most forceful rallying cries that dominated the Republican National Convention in the summer of 2016. Even under former President Barack Obama's seemingly more open and embracing administration, with its unsuccessful attempt to reform immigration policy and create a pathway to citizenship for the estimated 11 million unauthorized immigrants in the United States, deportations increased to a record level of 2.5 million people during the eight years of his presidency.

In Europe, immigration has become an exceptionally divisive issue that plays simultaneously into fears in the wealthier countries that their native citizens are losing out on jobs to newcomers and that immigration is bringing about all too rapid cultural transformation and, even worse, outright insecurity. Terrorist attacks in London, Paris and Brussels, in addition to a series of violent incidents across the continent often involving dual nationals, have only amplified these concerns. In the current decade, the continent's political leaders have struggled and, in many respects, failed to respond in a coordinated manner to the massive inflow of refugees into Europe in the aftermath of the Arab Spring revolutions in the Middle East, the civil wars in Libya and Syria, and the continued unrest elsewhere in Africa and also in Iraq and Afghanistan. Those who did manage to respond positively, such as German chancellor Angela Merkel, found themselves heavily criticized by considerable segments of their electorates. Greece has built a fence along its land border with Turkey in an attempt to deter migrants, and public antipathy toward the freedom of movement that accompanies citizenship in the enlarged European Union, with its twenty-eight member states including most of post-communist Eastern Europe, was one of the driving issues that prompted voters in the United Kingdom in June 2016 to opt in a national referendum for leaving the European Union. In all these cases, globalization has spurred calls for the closing of political borders and pushed a politics of protest driven by citizens who feel threatened by economic restructuring and cultural change and want to use the institution of national citizenship, narrowly and restrictively defined, as a bulwark against the relentless tide of globalization and immigration. In several European countries, voters have elected politicians from far-right, anti-immigrant political parties to represent them in national governments and have even, in the European Parliament, given these parties the mandate to turn against the very institution in which they serve.

All this underscores the contentious nature of "who belongs" and the readiness of anxious "native-born" (using Tilly's parlance) citizens throughout the "West" who have lost ground amid globalization to scapegoat immigrants. After all, immigrants are an easier target for retribution than global corporations that have abandoned hollowed-out factory towns, which now illustrate all too painfully how globalization has sharply widened inequality within nation-states by causing millions of workers in richer countries to lose their jobs to cheaper workers overseas. It is far more expedient, at least in the short term, for frustrated citizens—and politicians—to kick out immigrants than to formulate strategies to reclaim jobs that have already gone elsewhere or to retool their workforces for the "new" economy—with its jobs that in any case will not likely be located in what is left of these "blue-collar" communities. However, the anti-immigrant crowd has yet to move into majority status in these countries; counterprotests in support of immigrants and the contributions they make to their communities often take place alongside the rallies of far-right politicians, and many voters in the United Kingdom have voiced outrage at the prospect of being taken out of the European Union by a simple majority vote of 52%, with the "leavers" disproportionately composed of older voters criticized as depriving the next generation of its European future.

Some groups of migrants, in the era of Skype and relatively affordable air travel, manage to maintain important social and political ties in both their home countries and the communities in which they currently reside. Sociologist Peggy Levitt (2001), for example, showed how it has become feasible for "transnational villagers" to carve out niches of belonging simultaneously in two or more countries. In her study of immigrants from the Dominican Republic living in Boston, the relative proximity of the two communities (one time zone apart) helped facilitate the sustained transnational connections. Globalization has also increased migration among the most prosperous segments of the population—the "Superclass" (Rothkopf 2008) of investment bankers, management consultants, and technology mavens—living in so-called "super zips" that have become pockets of concentrated wealth far more "cosmopolitan" in atmosphere than the surrounding neighborhoods just a few miles away. In some developing countries, notably India, Malaysia, and Pakistan, as comparative politics scholar Kamal Sadiq (2009) has shown in detail, many unauthorized immigrants who make their way across porous national borders gain a foothold into their adopted countries by gradually obtaining (through either fraud or lenient government agencies) documents that ultimately have the effect of providing them with the same kinds of basic identification papers that typically go along with legal citizenship status, thus allowing them to enjoy the full benefits of citizenship without ever having to naturalize as citizens.

"Citizenship Gaps" and New Sources of Vulnerability, Dislocation, and Devaluation

For the most part, the "citizenship gap" encapsulated more than a decade ago by Alison Brysk and Gershon Shafir (2004), in which "the globalization of migration, production, regulation and conflict construct rights without sufficient institutions to enforce them, identities without membership, and participation for some at the expense of others" (p. 209), has only become more glaring. Most of the world's estimated 244 million migrants (as of June 2018) live in uncertain conditions, deprived of proper shelter, food, and clothing and forced into an endless stream of temporary jobs that fail to pay a living wage; this is especially the case for unauthorized migrants and asylum seekers, the latter lacking work permits in their countries of residence while they wait for decisions from national immigration bureaus regarding whether they will receive refugee status. Especially vulnerable are rejected asylum seekers who choose to go underground in their countries of residence, often working in notorious 3D jobs (dirty, dangerous, and demeaning) rather than returning to the countries they had fled. At the same time, many migrants have succeeded in raising their voices as political actors as they fight to close the "citizenship gap." Many have gained allies in domestic and transnational civil society organizations in articulating their interests; calling for reforms; and—above all—making the case that they, too, belong and bear rights in their new countries of residence, regardless of whether their immigration status is legally authorized. In this regard, the stories of transnational migrants are by no means consigned to exploitation but carry into voice and efficacy; the same social movement actors that have challenged economic globalization also have taken up the causes of migrants and refugees and worked with them as they organize to assert their interests.

Even full citizens within the world's constitutional democracies are now in a far more precarious state than before as a result of the economic and social dislocations traced to neoliberalism and its policies of deregulation, privatization, and "free" trade. Bryan Turner (2016) has concluded that "we are all denizens now" because of the "attenuated social and economic status of citizen under regimes of austerity and diminished rights and opportunities" (p. 679)—and the resulting diminishing life chances for all but the most wealthy and advantaged of citizens. The post-war social contract that set the stage for living wages, free education, and numerous social insurance provisions has eroded dramatically in the past generation. This virtual unraveling of social rights, along with declining "real" wages (adjusted for inflation) that have made it necessary for most households to have two full incomes for families to hold onto their status within the dwindling middle class, have also left growing numbers of citizens less inclined to participate in politics or even believe that they have a meaningful stake in political decisions. As Turner states,

> The emphasis on individualism and privatization means that the active citizen has become increasingly a passive consumer exercising individual choices in a society dominated by the market and commercial values. These social, economic, and political changes have ushered in the consumer denizen and the disappearance of the active citizen. (p. 685)

Therefore, Turner sees the protective aspects of citizenship as eclipsed by market forces and citizens downgraded into denizens who remain trapped in temporary jobs, earn lower incomes, pay lower taxes, expect less of the state in terms of public services, and, in turn, are not expected to be active in politics or to carry out military service.

Dislocated and devalued citizens are by no means the only segments of national populations whose interests as citizens are compromised in the era of globalization. The unfortunate rise in global terrorist networks, which gained even further momentum in 2015 and 2016 with a rash of bombings and mass killings throughout Europe and the United States, has changed the calculus of liberal democracies with regard to balancing competing sets of rights and obligations: The threat of suicide terrorism has prompted states to make numerous stark compromises on civil liberties and rights to privacy. The vast expansion of the National Security Agency (NSA) in the United States since the September 11, 2001, terrorist attacks and the revelations, due substantially to former NSA contract employee Edward Snowden, about the extent of government monitoring of the public and accumulation of online data (Greenwald 2014)—with numerous national intelligence agencies now collaborating and sharing information worldwide to spy on their publics—reveal how governments now assign greater importance to maintaining at least an illusion of security over a thoroughgoing preservation of civil liberties and an inclusive vision of "who belongs." This has prompted some governments to take more extreme measures of "securitization" that go as far as revoking citizenship status. This, too, is highly problematic, both in moral terms and in the ways in which it further weakens international security. As Canadian political theorist Patti Lenard (2016) has noted, "States that choose to revoke citizenship are effectively offloading responsibility for individuals they have deemed dangerous onto states that are often less able and willing to ensure that they are prevented from committing harm globally" (p. 88).

The mixed imperatives of open borders for capital yet tighter bureaucratic restrictions on the movement of people across borders have yielded a new climate of "securitization" that inhibits civil rights and political freedom. The story of citizenship in the twenty-first century, so far, has been marked by the rift between those embracing diversity and calling for greater inclusion and acceptance of immigrants (i.e., "No one is illegal!") and those demanding immigration quotas, border controls, harsher deportation regimes, and more widespread detention procedures for unauthorized immigrants and asylum seekers. Individual states, as their leaders mediate these disputed claims, have generally chosen to err on the side of caution, especially given unyielding concerns about terrorism and also the realization that in fact the economies throughout the "developed" world have been largely stagnant, at best, for what remains of the middle and working classes. Scholars and activists now lament how citizenship as a newly "globalizing regime for governing mobility" translates into a greater priority for securitization above all else (Rygiel 2010), and the next generation of theorizing on citizenship faces the challenge of pointing the way for basic rights and social inclusion to gain a stronger foothold in a difficult political climate.

GLOBAL CITIZENSHIP AND ITS CRITICS

The Idea of Global Citizenship Through History

Despite all the concern about the weakening of citizenship amid globalization, a more hopeful strain of thinking in citizenship studies has put forward the idea of global citizenship as a dynamic, action-driven concept that helps provide the language for political communities to catch up with the global economy and correct some of the inequities posed by global capitalism. Indeed, the communicative, cultural, entrepreneurial and technological aspects of globalization have opened up new opportunities for citizenship as democratic empowerment and participation, particularly through online platforms, that make it easier than ever for citizens to raise their voices and mobilize campaigns not only within their respective countries but also more widely into the international arena (Bennett and Segerberg 2013; Earl and Kimport 2013; Margetts et al. 2016). Current discourses of global citizenship emerged in the 1990s and 2000s, a period in which increasing public awareness of our interconnected world sparked an interest in finding a new political vocabulary to express the changing circumstances and inspire collective action, across international borders, to address global problems that states are simply not equipped to solve on their own and also push international institutions toward greater democratic legitimacy. Earlier iterations of what we now think of as variants of global citizenship long predate national citizenship. The idea of a cosmopolitan—a citizen of the universe—dates back at least as far as Socrates and also Diogenes, who wished to distance himself from his fellow Athenians, as well as Stoic thinkers from ancient Greece and Rome who linked the idea of civic virtue in one's local community with aspirations to live "in accordance with a universal code of good conduct" and to "feel a deep loyalty" to one's state, the polis, as well as the universal natural law of the (envisioned) cosmopolis (Heater 2004: 37–38).

As chronicled in detail by historian Derek Heater (2002, 2004), the normative appeal of a more expansive vision of citizenship transcending one's immediate political and social attachments attracted the interest of many philosophers and visionaries through the centuries, from Renaissance thinkers who sought to revive the ideas of the Stoics to figures such as Voltaire, Thomas Paine, and Immanuel Kant during the upsurge in intellectual activity in the late eighteenth century that accompanied the American and French Revolutions and the activists who hoped that the founding of the United Nations after World War II would lead to a world federation. Most illustrious among this cohort was Albert Einstein, who feared that the advent of nuclear weapons would condemn humanity to catastrophe without a world government to rein in this new threat (Heater 2002, 2004). However, the hardening of the Cold War instead relegated the United Nations to a forum for individual states to resolve their differences and try to work together on humanitarian, developmental, and environmental issues. In many respects, political theorist Hannah Arendt (1968), otherwise a champion of republican citizenship, delivered the sharpest rebuttal to

Albert Einstein when she wrote that a sovereign world government, "far from being the prerequisite for world citizenship, would be the end of all citizenship" (p. 81) given its inevitable distance, in her view, from democratic self-government and the potential for tyranny. Although some contemporary perspectives on global citizenship hearken to world government by advocating for more advanced global governing institutions (Archibugi 2008), more commonly the idea of global citizenship today refers to dispositions and mindsets of everyday people who engage not only within their immediate political communities but also beyond them (Lilley, Barker, and Harris 2015, 2017; Morais and Ogden 2010; Rhoads and Szelényi 2011; Schattle, 2008).

Contemporary Approaches to the Study of Global Citizenship

Contemporary scholarship has offered divergent ways of thinking about global citizenship as well as numerous approaches to studying this idea across academic disciplines. Two separate early contributions, from international relations theorist Richard Falk (1994) and sociologist John Urry (2000), identified what each of them considered as key segments of the population that were becoming prototypical global citizens: Taken together, Falk and Urry regarded global citizens as a mixture of global cosmopolitans embracing other cultures; global activists campaigning on behalf of causes such as human rights, environmental sustainability, and the elimination of world poverty; global reformers seeking more just and democratically responsive governing institutions; global managers working across the breadth of government, business, and civil society to address common problems facing the world; and global capitalists who pursue their economic interests without any strong bonds of political affiliation or engagement. It is more than worthwhile to add to these categories global educators—those who strive to prepare their students to navigate the fiercely competitive global marketplace and instill in the next generation not only academic knowledge and capabilities but also important personal qualities related to good citizenship, such as understanding, efficacy, and empathy.

One landmark early contribution to the contemporary study of global citizenship came in the form of moral philosopher Martha Nussbaum's call for schools (specifically American schools) to educate young people to think of themselves as global citizens as well as citizens of their country and their local communities. Following the Stoics, Nussbaum (1996) argued that political attachments and loyalties should be regarded as a series of concentric circles. She argued specifically that the outermost circle, encompassing all humanity, should take priority over one's more proximate political communities, for the sake of helping individuals better "recognize their moral obligations to the rest of the world" (p. 12); work across persistent barriers of ethnicity, gender, and social class; and thereby deliberate more effectively in solving problems that require international cooperation. Her position sparked a lively debate among numerous political thinkers who argued that Nussbaum was awarding too much privilege on allegedly abstract and remote global ties at the expense of more tangible and, in the eyes of her critics, morally credible local ties. Nussbaum later modified her call for a primary emphasis on a global identity to a preference for "globally sensitive patriotism" (Nussbaum 2008).

As a small yet lively cohort of political philosophers and international relations theorists elevated the conceptual profile of global citizenship at the dawn of the twenty-first century (e.g., Carter 2001; Held 1995, 1999, 2000; Linklater 1998), they were bolstered by momentous events in the history of global political activism. One watershed moment was the awarding of the 1997 Nobel Peace Prize to the International Campaign to Ban Landmines, the first major example of a campaign in which networks of activists used internet communication to convince 162 countries to sign a treaty banning landmines as a weapon of war. Another series of milestones came in the massive protests in 1999 outside the meeting of the World Trade Organization in Seattle, as well as meetings of the International Monetary Fund and the World Bank in 2000, that indicated how a new movement of global citizens—today's global justice movement—was rising to challenge the dominance of global corporations and American-led "neoliberalism" in economic power (Kaldor 2000; Mertes 2004; for a pre-Seattle view, see Broad and Heckscher 2003). These campaigns provided compelling new examples of transnational activism at almost exactly the moment when international relations scholars Margaret Keck and Kathryn Sikkink (1998) published their now-classic book detailing the longer history of political and social activism beyond borders, with a particular focus on women's campaigns in the nineteenth century to abolish slavery, establish voting rights, and end the practice of foot-binding in East Asia.

The more recent scholarship on global citizenship—one could classify it as a second wave of contemporary scholarship in global citizenship—has picked up where this first wave of literature left off: unpacking how the idea of global citizenship actually lives and breathes in practice—how at least limited numbers of people are trying to walk the walk as global citizens, not just talk the talk. Luis Cabrera, for example, has combined normative political theorizing with empirical, shoe-leather field research to bring the obvious but easily overlooked problem of international borders to center stage in scholarship on global citizenship, arguing that unauthorized immigrants and those who aid them carry out important aspects of global citizenship. This fits into his position that a valid practice of global citizenship contains "a very concrete 'legal dimension' of rights and responsibilities enacted within the global human community" in which individuals seek "to protect the core rights of individuals who do not share their state citizenship" (Cabrera, 2010: 258). Meanwhile, I have turned to the tools of critical discourse analysis and grounded theory construction to cast light upon the multiple practices of global citizenship, examining how a host of individuals have come to view themselves, in strikingly different ways, as global citizens and how institutions and organizations have chosen to work this concept into their specific missions and programs (Schattle 2008).

Civic Education: Global Citizenship and Global Competency

One reason why the idea of global citizenship has gained a high profile in the educational arena is the related imperative, accompanying the rise of neoliberalism, for schools and universities to turn out "globally competent" citizens. Fortunately, educators have by no means limited their understanding of global competency to mercenary economic considerations; instead, they have taken a far more comprehensive and even holistic view, placing emphasis not only on core academic skills but also on international understanding, cultural sensitivity, and language fluency (Hunter, White, and Godbey 2006; Olson and Kroeger 2001). A helpful and widely encompassing definition of "global competency" comes from educational studies scholar Fernando Reimers (2012), who views the concept as having three interdependent dimensions:

> (1) A positive disposition toward cultural difference and a framework of global values to engage in difference. This requires a sense of identity and self-esteem but also empathy toward others with different identities. An interest and understanding of different civilizational streams and the ability to see those differences as opportunities for constructive, respectful and peaceful transactions among people. This ethical dimension of global competency includes also a commitment to basic equality and rights of all persons and a disposition to act to uphold those rights.
>
> (2) An ability to speak, understand and think in languages in addition to the dominant language in the country in which people are born.
>
> (3) Deep knowledge and understanding of world history, geography, the global dimensions of topics such as health, climate and economics and of the process of globalization itself (the disciplinary and interdisciplinary dimension) and a capacity to think critically and creatively about the complexity of current global challenges.

Reimers summarizes these three dimensions as "the three A's of globalization: the affective dimension, the action dimension and the academic dimension." He notes that building global competency is important for two reasons: (1) People who pick up the relevant attributes and aptitudes have much better prospects in today's competitive global economy; and (2) without fostering a shift toward cosmopolitan values in today's world, societies run a higher risk of falling into cultural conflicts, both within countries and across "civilizations," along the lines of what Samuel Huntington (1996) feared in the aftermath of the Cold War. Global civic education, then, serves as both a means toward the desired ends of peace and prosperity and an end in itself for enriching the lives of individual students as well as the collective well-being of the next generation.

Other recent work in the field of educational studies has sought to clarify further the kinds of personal qualities and "learning capacities" that are associated with the idea of global citizenship. Australian researchers Kathleen Lilley, Michelle Barker, and Neil Harris (2017) have identified four "thinking tools" that correlate with global citizenship, which they label as *social imaginary* (responding to "intercultural challenges" and considering issues from multiple viewpoints), *criticality* (examining more critically one's own assumptions and positions, as well as the circumstances of change), *reflexivity* (being ready to "embrace and learn from engagement with different others"), and *relationality* (being able to "walk in the shoes" of others). As the authors conclude,

> It is important for students to understand that being and becoming a global citizen occurs in response to challenge, intercultural encounters, and dialogue with diverse others, including diverse co-nationals. . . . Being and becoming a global citizen is more than a technical efficiency; it involves a process of thinking differently. (p. 18)

Likewise, working across a range of issues, Veronica Boix Mansilla and Howard Gardner (2007) have framed "global consciousness" as a series of capacities, namely

> *global sensitivity*, or our awareness of local experience as a manifestation of broader developments in the planet; *global understanding*, or our capacity to think in flexible and

informed ways about contemporary worldwide developments; and *global self*, or a perception of ourselves as global actors, a sense of planetary belonging and membership in humanity that guides our actions and prompts our civic commitments. (p. 59)

Such multidimensional ways of thinking about global citizenship respond in part to prescriptions long articulated that educators take care that "multiple 'global citizen selves' are conceptualised not solely through the Western norm, but also through diverse perspectives that challenge Western humanism and that employ non-Western ontologies to define global citizenship" (Pashby 2011: 439).

Critiques of Global Citizenship from the Academy and Beyond

All the previously discussed developments underscore how the idea of global citizenship is no longer consigned to idle speculation, moral aspiration, or categorization exercises but, rather, has become a topic for empirical analysis that provides detailed examples of today's "actually existing cosmopolitanism" (Robbins 1998). However, the idea of global citizenship has sparked numerous critiques through the years, and the attacks come from several directions. One line of critique is that global citizenship as a concept ends up being too value neutral—that anyone can use the term to advance their chosen cause. This critique has been applied especially by those holding the view that corporations declaring themselves as global citizens have deployed the concept in a cynical sense merely to gain the upper hand in debates about the moral legitimacy of global capitalism, without making substantive progress on issues such as environmental sustainability or the treatment of workers (especially low-income workers for subcontractors); that "global citizenship" ends up being invoked for the cultivation of image above all else, used mainly for vacuous, even bogus claims that amount to nothing more than the rebranding of pre-existing corporate philanthropy programs.

A related critique has surfaced in the educational arena: that here, too, scores of schools and universities have used "global citizenship" simply as a way to rebrand existing international programs (i.e., study abroad) without clarifying sufficiently what exactly this idea really means. Worse, the critics of global citizenship allege, the concept can sow arrogance and hubris by causing students to believe that one can be a global citizen merely by living overseas for a semester. Study abroad programs poorly conceived and executed run the risk of lapsing into voyeuristic opportunities that indulge well-heeled students and fall short of providing meaningful engagement with the outside world.

Extending from this is the concern that global citizenship ends up being nothing more than a luxury for the affluent to contemplate: that even for many working-class people in the world's wealthier countries, and especially for people living in the more impoverished corners of the world, any concept of global citizenship is far away. Despite the good intentions of educators to transcend Western prisms, skeptics also worry about the potential for global citizenship to lapse into cultural imperialism. Political and cultural theorist Charles Lee (2014) has argued that the usage of global citizenship carries the danger of replicating oppressive aspects of colonialism, neoliberalism, and "Western" hegemony rather than overcoming or transcending them. South Africa-based educational studies scholars Nico Jooste and Savo Heleta (2017) have raised a similar objection:

> It is hard not to see global citizenship, as currently promoted in the North, as a push by the well-off parts of the world for solidarity with the "backward" South. Although this may sound extreme, we do not think it is too far off. This patronizing approach, which portrays the South as the problem, a helpless mass, which cannot survive without the assistance from the "enlightened" North, will not make the world a better, more equal place; it will only sow more divisions and animosity. (p. 47)

Still other critiques of global citizenship come from those who enforce precision over latitude in definitions of citizenship and dismiss global citizenship as an oxymoron, as a contradiction in terms, or as a vague and woolly metaphor. Recalling Aristotle, who argued that a meaningful difference exists between good citizens and good people, they argue that it is not realistic to expect citizens in a democracy to go any further than awarding top priority to the interests of their immediate political communities. In this critical view, expressed clearly and consistently through the years by political theorist David Miller (1999, 2011), citizenship rightly understood *must* revolve around duties shared by highly motivated and responsible people who know and trust each other well. In Miller's view, genuine republican citizenship has a chance at working only in clearly bounded political communities, although he has suggested that the idea of a "globally concerned citizen" might be practicable (Miller 2011):

> We can't have a relationship to all our fellow human beings that is genuinely a relation of citizen to citizen; what we can do is identify with them, show ethical concern for them, arrange our institutions to avoid global harms. In other words we can have citizenship that incorporates global concern; besides factoring in the beliefs and interests of our compatriots when collective decisions have to be made, we can take account of the concerns of people outside of the political community. How best to do this is of course a big practical problem. It may involve forms of dialogue such as inviting outside representatives into our assemblies to make their case. (p. 21)

In contrast with the skeptics, supporters of global citizenship and transnational democracy often take the position that the nation-state does not warrant elevation as a principal venue either for citizenship or for addressing problems at any level, domestic or international. As philosopher Daniel Weinstock (2001) has written,

> Nationalists who claim that broadening the scope of democratic institutions would erode the values of democracy and citizenship overestimate the naturalness of the fit between citizenship and democracy and the nation-state, and ignore the degree to which the modern nation-state itself had to overcome the same kinds of obstacles that transnational institutions face today in attempting to realize these values. . . . Nation-states have had to find ways of carrying on debates about distributive justice despite the absence of any widely shared understandings concerning the goods that institutions of distributive justice must allocate. And the institutional designers of the modern nation-state faced obstacles of language and size. (p. 66)

Scholarly critiques of global citizenship have been compounded by the resurgence in nationalist sentiments, often narrowly defined, that have marked the second decade of this century in response to high public anxiety about the social and economic inequalities that have widened in so many countries and are at least partly induced by globalization. Current debates in national political arenas tend to frame "globalism" in monolithic terms—as tantamount to economic globalization—and overlook the fact that several different kinds of "globalisms" have emerged in the present day—market globalism, imperial globalism, justice globalism, and jihadist globalism, as Manfred Steger (2005, 2008) has classified them. The critics of global citizenship also overlook the opportunities for citizens to counter market globalism with justice globalism—and that the movements challenging global capitalism are not necessarily seeking an outright rollback of globalization but, rather, a different, more ethically, socially, and politically responsive model of global collaboration and community building.

Likewise, we also see an unfortunate lack of understanding in public debates of the ways in which growing numbers of people throughout the world think about global citizenship in deliberate and meaningful ways that complement, not override, their allegiances as citizens of their respective countries and provide an important basis to think about their roles and responsibilities in multiple, overlapping communities both within their home countries and beyond them. Many people wrongly assume that there is only one kind of monolithic globalism—neoliberal economic globalization—that must be fended off with nationalism; the idea that there are multiple globalisms and that the voluntarily adopted practices of global citizenship can be harnessed to bring about a different kind of global community seems not to register. Lacking these sorts of nuances, many critics of the current regrettable circumstances in global politics and economics argue in rather simplistic terms that we are now shifting into an era of "deglobalization," meaning economic and political closure and retrenchment (Sharma 2016), or that nationalism has decisively triumphed over "globalism." One major challenge for scholars in global studies is to debunk arguments containing these kinds of mistaken assumptions with the facts on the ground.

CONCLUSION: CITIZENSHIP AND GLOBAL STUDIES—A MUTUALLY REINFORCING RELATIONSHIP

Global studies facilitates the exploration of citizenship from specific and broad perspectives. As a transdisciplinary field, global studies offers a far more liberating approach to the study of citizenship compared to political science because global studies does not privilege, let alone insist on the primacy of, domestic citizenship and its links to legal status and national governing institutions. A global studies perspective on citizenship takes on board the importance of democratic empowerment and participation in small-scale political settings, as well as the moral and civic character of good citizens, but it does not restrict the horizons of citizenship to domestic political and social interaction. Citizenship, meanwhile, offers the field of global studies a key integrating concept—encompassing and also convergent with the very essence of education as critical inquiry and reflection. Not only does citizenship provide an integrating function for university degree programs in global studies, as a concept that surfaces in courses across a wide range of academic disciplines, but also it fills an important role beyond the classroom, linking in critical ways many issues that arise in classroom discussions with extracurricular programs such as service learning, study abroad, and internship experiences. A strong citizenship component helps global studies programs strengthen in coherence and gain standing as a vital, even indispensable, academic offering for universities.

The transdisciplinary field of global studies also has a meaningful role in addressing the challenges that local communities face in strengthening social capital, which Robert D. Putnam (2007) defines as the presence of strong social networks and norms of reciprocity and trust. As Putnam has documented in detail, through research focused specifically on the United States and also applicable elsewhere, changing immigration patterns and growing cultural diversity have the promise to strengthen "social capital" in the long term but have had the effect of weakening social solidarity and social trust in the short term. As Putnam has noted, "The central challenge for modern, diversifying societies is to create a new, broader sense of 'we'" (p. 139). The open and pluralistic intellectual spirit offered by global studies can also encourage more open, inclusive, and respectful plural societies. Those working to advance a global studies perspective on citizenship should aim to offer today's fractious societies a toolkit for thinking more judiciously about how to mediate senses of loyalty and fulfill competing responsibilities across the multiple communities, at home and abroad, in which we are all morally implicated. As scholars and policymakers have argued for decades, we need feasible political solutions for numerous problems that remain beyond the capacities of states to resolve on their own, including environmental degradation; poverty; public health threats; abuses of human rights; nuclear proliferation; suicide terrorism; and growing displacements of migrants and refugees as well as the masses of unemployed, underemployed, and underpaid workers unable to flourish in the current global economic context. A return to nationalism or a push toward "deglobalization" will not solve these problems, whereas thinking about citizenship from a global viewpoint can help create the conditions for positive steps to emerge.

References

Archibugi, D. 2008. *The Global Commonwealth of Citizens: Toward Cosmopolitan Democracy.* Princeton, NJ: Princeton University Press.

Arendt, H. 1968. *Men in Dark Times.* New York: Harcourt, Brace & World.

Bennett, W. L., and A. Segerberg. 2013. *The Logic of Connective Action: Digital Media and the Personalization of Contentious Politics.* Cambridge, UK: Cambridge University Press.

Broad, R., and Z. Heckscher. 2003. "Before Seattle: The Historical Roots of the Current Movement Against Corporate-Led Globalisation." *Third World Quarterly* 24 (4): 713–728.

Brysk, A., and G. Shafir, eds. 2004. *People out of Place: Globalization, Human Rights, and the Citizenship Gap.* London: Routledge.

Cabrera, L. 2010. *The Practice of Global Citizenship.* Cambridge, UK: Cambridge University Press.

Carter, A. 2001. *The Political Theory of Global Citizenship.* London: Routledge.

Earl, J., and K. Kimport. 2013. *Digitally Enabled Social Change: Activism in the Internet Age.* Cambridge, MA: MIT Press.

Falk, R. A. 1994. "The Making of Global Citizenship." In *The Condition of Citizenship*, edited by B. van Steenbergen, 127–140. London: Sage.

Greenwald, G. 2014. *No Place to Hide: Edward Snowden, the NSA, and the U.S. Surveillance State*. Oxford, UK: Signal.

Heater, D. 2002. *World Citizenship: Cosmopolitan Thinking and Its Opponents*. London: Continuum.

Heater, D. 2004. *A Brief History of Citizenship*. New York: New York University Press.

Held, D. 1995. *Democracy and the Global Order*. Cambridge, UK: Polity.

Held, D. 1999. "The Transformation of Political Community: Rethinking Democracy in the Context of Globalization." In *Democracy's Edges*, edited by I. Shapiro and C. Hacker-Cordón, 84–111. Cambridge, UK: Cambridge University Press.

Held, D. 2000. "Regulating Globalization? In *The Global Transformations Reader*, edited by D. Held and A. McGrew, 420–430. Cambridge, UK: Polity.

Hunter, B., G. P. White, and G. Godbey. 2006. "What Does It Mean to Be Globally Competent? *Journal of Studies in International Education* 10 (3): 267–285.

Huntington, S. P. 1996. *The Clash of Civilizations and the Remaking of World Order*. New York: Simon & Schuster.

Isin, E. F., and B. S. Turner. 2007. "Investigating Citizenship: An Agenda for Citizenship Studies." *Citizenship Studies* 11 (1): 5–17.

Jooste, N., and S. Heleta. 2017. "Global Citizenship Versus Globally Competent Graduates: A Critical View from the South." *Journal of Studies in International Education* 21 (1): 39–51.

Kaldor, M. 2000. "'Civilising' Globalisation? The Implications of the 'Battle in Seattle.'" *Millennium* 29 (1): 105–114.

Keck, M. E., and K. Sikkink. 1998. *Activists Beyond Borders: Advocacy Networks in International Politics*. Ithaca, NY: Cornell University Press.

Lee, C. T. 2014. "Decolonizing Global Citizenship." In *The Routledge Handbook of Global Citizenship Studies*, edited by E. F. Isin and P. Nyers, 75–85. London: Routledge.

Lenard, P. T. 2016. "Democracies and the Power to Revoke Citizenship." *Ethics & International Affairs* 30 (1): 73–91.

Levitt, P. 2001. *The Transnational Villagers*. Berkeley: University of California Press.

Lilley, K., M. Barker, and N. Harris. 2015. "Exploring the Process of Global Citizen-Learning and the Student Mind-Set." *Journal of Studies in International Education* 19(3): 225–245.

Lilley, K., M. Barker, and N. Harris. 2017. "The Global Citizen Conceptualized: Accommodating Ambiguity." *Journal of Studies in International Education* 21 (1): 6–21.

Linklater, A. 1998. *The Transformation of Political Community: Ethical Foundations of the Post-Westphalian Era*. Columbia: University of South Carolina Press.

Mansilla, V. B., and H. Gardner. 2007. "From Teaching Globalization to Nurturing Global Consciousness." In *Learning in the Global Era: International Perspectives on Globalization and Education*, edited by M. M. Suárez-Orozco, 47–66. Berkeley: University of California Press.

Margetts, H., P. John, S. Hale, and T. Yasseri. 2016. *Political Turbulence: How Social Media Shape Collective Action*. Princeton, NJ: Princeton University Press.

Marshall, T. H. 1963. *Class, Citizenship and Social Class*. Cambridge, UK: Cambridge University Press.

Mertes, T., ed. 2004. *A Movement of Movements: Is Another World Really Possible?* London: Verso.

Miller, D. 1999. "Bounded Citizenship." In *Cosmopolitan Citizenship*, edited by K. Hutchings and R. Dannreuther, 60–80. London: Macmillan.

Miller, D. 2011. "The Idea of Global Citizenship." Nuffield's Working Papers Series in Politics, Nuffield College, Oxford, UK. https://www.nuffield.ox.ac.uk/politics/papers/2011/David%20 Miller_working%20paper%202011_02.pdf.

Morais, D. B., and A. C. Ogden. 2010. "Initial Development and Validation of the Global Citizenship Scale." *Journal of Studies in International Education* 15 (5): 455–466.

Nussbaum, M. C. 1996. "Patriotism and Cosmopolitanism." In *For Love of Country? Debating the Limits of Patriotism*, edited by J. Cohen, 3–20. Boston: Beacon.

Nussbaum, M. C. 2008. "Toward a Globally Sensitive Patriotism." *Daedalus* 137 (3): 78–93.

Olson, C. L., and K. R. Kroeger. 2001. "Global Competency and Intercultural Sensitivity." *Journal of Studies in International Education* 5 (2): 116–137.

Pashby, K. 2011. "Cultivating Global Citizens: Planting New Seeds or Pruning the Perennials? Looking for the Citizen–Subject in Global Citizenship Education Theory." *Globalisation, Societies and Education* 9 (3–4): 427–442.

Putnam, R. D. 2007. "*E Pluribus Unum*: Diversity and Community in the Twenty-First Century." *Scandinavian Political Studies* 30 (2): 137–174.

Reimers, F. 2012. "Educating for Global Competency." https://www.neafoundation.org/content/assets/2012/11/Educating%20for%20Global%20Competence%20by%20Fernando%20 Reimers.pdf.

Rhoads, R. A., and K. Szelényi. 2011. *Global Citizenship and the University: Advancing Social Life and Relations in an Interdependent World*. Stanford, CA: Stanford University Press.

Robbins, B. 1998. "Actually Existing Cosmopolitanism." In *Cosmopolitics: Thinking and Feeling Beyond the Nation*, edited by P. Cheah and B. Robbins, 1–19. Minneapolis: University of Minnesota Press.

Rothkopf, D. 2008. *Superclass: The Global Power Elite and the World They Are Making*. New York: Farrar, Straus and Giroux.

Rygiel, K. 2010. *Globalizing Citizenship*. Vancouver: UBC Press.

Sadiq, K. 2009. *Paper Citizens. How Illegal Immigrants Acquire Citizenship in Developing Countries*. Oxford, UK: Oxford University Press.

Schattle, H. 2008. *The Practices of Global Citizenship*. Lanham, MD: Rowman & Littlefield.

Schattle, H. 2012. *Globalization and Citizenship*. Lanham, MD: Rowman & Littlefield.

Sharma, R. 2016. "Globalisation as We Know It Is Over—and Brexit Is the Biggest Sign Yet." *The Guardian*, July 28. https://www.theguardian.com/commentisfree/2016/jul/28/ era-globalisation-brexit-eu-britain-economic-frustration.

Steger, M. B. 2005. "From Market Globalism to Imperial Globalism: Ideology and American Power After 9/11." *Globalizations* 2 (1): 31–46.

Steger, M. B. 2008. *Globalisms: The Great Ideological Struggle of the Twenty-First Century*. 3rd ed. Lanham, MD: Rowman & Littlefield.

Tilly, C., ed. 1996. *Citizenship, Identity and Social History*. Cambridge, UK: Cambridge University Press.

Turner, B. S. 2016. "We Are All Denizens Now: On the Erosion of Citizenship." *Citizenship Studies* 20: 679–692.

Urry, J. 2008. *Sociology Beyond Societies*. London: Routledge.

Weinstock, D. M. 2001. "Prospects for Transnational Citizenship and Democracy." *Ethics & International Affairs* 15 (2): 53–66.

CHAPTER 42

....

GLOBAL MOVEMENTS

....

DONATELLA DELLA PORTA

SOCIAL movement studies have long focused on the national level because the nation-state was considered as playing a major role in setting the political opportunities for protest. Although there had been some attention to mobilization in civil society at the international level, research on the topic had remained mainly confined to international relations. In international relations, important steps have been taken toward recognizing the political nature of the international politics of the states as well as the international organizations. First, constructivist approaches challenged the idea that states act on their inherent interests, focusing on the many ways in which interests (as identities) are indeed constructed. Those who have brought the transnational dimension back into international relations have also pointed to the complexity of international decisions that do not involve just states but also interest organizations and principled actors (Risse, Ropp, and Sikkink 1999). At the turn of the millennium, a wave of protests targeting globalization increased attention on transnational phenomena in social movement studies, spreading expectations about a fast trend toward globalization of protests, as effects of economic globalization and as a sign of cultural and political globalization (della Porta and Tarrow 2005). The next wave of protests, prompted especially by the financial crisis that started in 2008 and continued well into the 2010s, challenged this expectation, showing, in some respects at least, a return of attention to national politics.

In this chapter, I refer to both waves of protest to illustrate concepts and theories that have developed in global studies and other fields to address the transnational dimension of protest. I first provide the definition of social movements at the global level, moving then to an analysis of the characteristics of global movements in terms of organizational model, repertoire of action, and framing. I conclude by addressing the political, social, and cultural contexts in which these movements develop.

DEFINING THE GLOBAL MOVEMENT

....

We can consider *social movements* as interactions of mainly informal networks based on common beliefs and solidarity, which mobilize on conflictual issues by frequent recourse to various forms of protest (della Porta and Diani 2006: Chap. 1). In Sidney Tarrow's (2001) definition, *transnational* social movements are "socially mobilised groups with constituents in at least two states, engaged in sustained contentious interactions with power-holders in at least one state other than their own, or against an international institution, or a multi-national economic actor" (p. 11). *Global* social movements can be defined as transnational networks of actors that define their causes as global and organize protest campaigns and other forms of action that target more than one state and/or international governmental organization (IGO).

The *global justice movement* has been defined as the loose network of organizations (with varying degrees of formality, and even including political parties) and other actors engaged in collective action of various kinds on the basis of the shared goal of advancing the cause of justice (economic, social, political, and environmental) among and between peoples throughout the world. This wave of transnational protest has contributed empirical evidence and theoretical thinking on transnational forms of mobilizations. In particular, it helped with regard to rethinking the main toolkit for social movement studies. Although the ideal type of global movement includes globalization in the action, organization, and framing, the reality is that social movements with some global perspective have variations on the three levels. This has in fact pushed social movement scholars to reflect on the varying degrees of transnationalization of movements in their repertoire, networks, and identification processes.

TRANSNATIONAL REPERTOIRE OF ACTION

Social movements are characterized by the use of *protest* as a means of placing pressure on institutions. Although the creation of the nation-state focused protest at the national level, globalization is expected to generate protest at the transnational level against international actors. After some preliminary experiences in the 1980s, counter-summits multiplied during the succeeding decade, simultaneously with large-scale United Nations (UN) conferences (Pianta 2002). In the 1990s, transnational campaigns mobilized against the North American Free Trade Agreement (NAFTA) and the Multilateral Agreement on Investment (MAI); for the cancellation of poor countries' foreign debt (in the Jubilee 2000 campaign); and for a more social Europe (e.g., in the European Marches against Unemployment and Exclusion) (Cohen and Rai 2000; Edwards and Gaventa 2001; Khagram, Riker, and Sikkink 2002). Several protest campaigns continue to be organized at the transnational level, focusing on global problems such as poverty, taxation of capital, debt relief, fair trade, global rights, and reform of IGOs.

In November 1999, the widely covered protest against the third World Trade Organization (WTO) conference in Seattle brought attention to the intertwining of transnational and domestic forms of contentious politics. In the following years, intense international mobilizations in counter-summits, global days of action, and World Social Forums multiplied within a transnational cycle of protest. Large numbers of citizens from various countries marched against the International Monetary Fund (IMF) and World Bank meetings in Washington, DC, and Prague in 2000 and 2001, respectively; the European

Union (EU) summits in Amsterdam in 1997, Nice in 2000, and Gothenburg in 2001; the World Economic Forum in yearly demonstrations in Davos, Switzerland; the G8 summit in Genoa in 2001; and the Iraq War in hundreds of cities on February 15, 2003.

Transnational protest are certainly rare events because protests still tend to target the state or substate levels of government (Imig and Tarrow 2002; Rucht 2002). Organizations active at the transnational level have long used lobbying rather than street protest. Even if not numerous, transnational events are highly transformative, involving long-lasting cooperation between organizations rooted in various countries and thus furthering the development of new networks and frames (della Porta 2015). Transnational events are often embedded at various geographical levels with protest campaigns that contemporarily address several territorial levels of governance (Diani 2005; Rootes 2005). Transnational events have increased in frequency, in the forms of both the transnational convergence of protestors in a symbolic place and global days of action, with protests organized on the same day in hundreds of localities worldwide.

Many of these protests converged in the global justice movement that, at least in the beginning, built on the dissatisfaction by activists who had attempted to influence international organizations through lobbying and consultation tactics and moved instead to performing non-violent direct action and civil disobedience aiming at simultaneously influencing public opinion and demonstrating the activists' commitment (della Porta et al. 2006). One of the most used repertoires of action has been counter-summits—that is, arenas of "international-level initiatives during official summits and on the same issues but from a critical standpoint, heightening awareness through protest and information with or without contacts with the official version" (Pianta 2002: 35). During counter-summits, the symbolic penetration of no-go areas for demonstrators (red zones) represented a widespread tactic that resulted in frequent harsh confrontations with the police with increasing use of this disruptive tactic (della Porta, Petersen, and Reiter 2006).

Social forums are another commonly used repertoire of action. Different from a counter-summit, which is mainly oriented toward protest, the social forum is organized as a space of debate among activists. The first large scale-social forum to be organized, the World Social Forum (WSF), was indirectly oriented to "counter" another summit—because it was organized on the same date as an alternative to the World Economic Forum (WEF) held in Davos. It presented however an independent space for civil society organizations and critical citizens to gather. From the beginning, the WSF has mobilized large numbers of citizens from dozens of countries, and the same is true for other macro-regional forums, such as the European Social Forums, but also national and local forums. They in fact have involved thousands of organizations and tens of thousands of activists from different countries, social backgrounds, and with different ideological beliefs. In the search for "another possible globalization," the various forums became a "huge showcase for a large number of issues, groups, and claims" and so contributed to "the creation of an overarching identity and community as expressed in the vision of a meeting place for the global civil society" (Rucht 2005: 291).

Social forums aim in particular at the construction and exchange of alternative knowledge. The importance of communication is demonstrated by the relevance assumed not only by the internet but also by issues connected with it, from copyright to censorship of telecommunications. The production of counter-expertise and alternative knowledge is important for many organizations; for example, Attac presents itself as a movement for people's self-education oriented to action. Transnational campaigns against multi-national corporations have targeted Microsoft, Monsanto, and Nike through "naming and shaming" (Micheletti 2003: 3). Presenting consumption as a potential political act, ethical consumerism stresses the role of individuals in taking responsibility for the common goods in their everyday life through the boycott of bad products but also *buy*cotts of fair ones (environmental-friendly and solidaristic) as well as socially re-sponsible investment.

ORGANIZING BEYOND THE STATE

Social movements are *informal networks* linking a plurality of individuals and groups, more or less structured from an organizational standpoint. Whereas parties or pressure groups have defined organizational boundaries, with participation normally certified by a membership card, social movements are instead made of loose, weakly linked networks of individuals who believe they are part of a collective effort.

A global movement involves organizational networks active in different countries. Already in the 1990s, an increasing number of transnational social movement organizations have developed, with a particularly sharp increase in the Global South (Smith and Johnston 2002). More or less durable in time, networks have been created around various campaigns, sometimes with a special focus on an international organization (Fox and Brown 1998). Campaigns have mobilized against international treaties, such as those on arms or trade (e.g., NAFTA and MAI), and transnational events emerged around UN-sponsored world conferences on issues such as the environment and women's rights or for the abolition of debt for poor countries (e.g., Jubilee 2000). These produced further organizational net-working between development and human rights non-governmental organizations (NGOs), religious and non-religious not-for-profit associations, unions and environmental associations, as well as smaller and more informal groups. The European Marches against Unemployment and Exclusion and the Intergalactic meetings also contributed to transna-tional networking.

A very flexible organizational structure, with heavy use of new communication technologies, characterizes various ad hoc coordination committees as well as more long-lasting transnational social movement organizations. The global justice movement— also defined as a "movement of movements"—adopted a loose organizational structure, which mobilized a plurality of networks active on various issues. Heterogeneous with re-gard to generation, social background, and national belonging, the global justice move-ment aimed at building a flexible organization capable of nurturing a convergence in diversity.

The global justice movement was also very inclusive. The internet had not only steadily reduced the costs of mobilization, allowing for flexible structures, but also facilitated in-teraction among different areas and movements. Organizations from different movements converged in a series of nets and coalitions that were very often not limited to one national state. Various nets, forums, and coordinator committees allowed not for overlapping mem-bership by individual activists, but also for the convergence of collective members. These types of organizational networks emerged in different constellations: loose, rank-and-file movement networks involving mainly grass-roots groups or movement coalitions with a larger influence by more structured associations. Occasionally, however, tensions arose between so-called horizontals and verticals, stressing the respective advantages of their own organizational formulas (Smith et al. 2007).

Cosmopolitan Framing

Social movements construct collective identities through the development of a common interpretation of reality. They construct frames about themselves and their enemies, and provide diagnosing and prognosis for social and political problems and solutions. In global movements, the self and the other are defined at the supranational level. For global movements, the ultimate frame of reference is indeed the world: Although specific actions often have a narrower scope, solutions are sought at the global level, and specific claims are embedded in visions of global change.

In the global justice movement, activists frame their actions around *global concerns*, identifying themselves as part of a "global movement" and targeting "global enemies" at a global level of action. Mainly opposing economic globalization but supporting cosmopolitan values, activists of the global justice movement are in fact defined as alter-globals or globalizers from below. Within these global visions, the main aim of the global justice movement is the struggle for justice—a general term that encompasses more specific domains of intervention, such as human rights, citizens' rights, social rights, peace, the environment, and similar concerns.

Although reference to the global is not new—as indicated by transnational campaigns against slavery and international organizations of the labor movement—this has become increasingly more central for global movements. In fact, whereas in the 1980s, social movements underwent a process of specialization on single issues, research has indicated the multi-issue nature of the global justice movement. Struggles for environmental protection, women's rights, peace, and social inequalities remain as characteristics of subgroups or networks in the mobilization on globalization. The definition of the "movement of movements" stresses the multiplicity of reference bases in terms of class, gender, generation, race, and religion that seem to have developed in the direction of composite identities.

The different concerns of different movements were in fact connected in a long-lasting process. The global justice movement grew during protest campaigns around "broker issues" that bridged the concerns of different movements and organizations. The campaign against the WTO brought together squatters, human rights activists, and labor unionists; the fight against genetically modified food networked peasants and ecologists; and Jubilee 2000 brought development NGOs together with rank-and-file religious groups, critical unionists, and environmentalists. During these protest campaigns, representatives of different cultural traditions—from secular to religious and from radical to reformist—were connected in a broader discourse that targeted social and global injustices. Therefore, at the transnational level, local and global concerns were defined around values such as equality, justice, human rights, and environmental protection.

GLOBAL MOVEMENTS: EXPLAINING AND UNDERSTANDING

The mobilizations for global justice have a marked supranational dimension: They express a conflict defined as "global," allowing cosmopolitan collective identities to emerge; they use protest repertoires in international campaigns; and they build transnational networks. In fact, they have prompted some adaptation in the conceptual toolkit used in social movement studies.

Movements and International Regimes

Global social movements were initially addressed within international relations and international sociology. By examining "transnational relations," Thomas Risse and Kathryn Sikkink (e.g., Risse, Ropp, and Sikkink 1999) highlighted the importance of environmental transnational and human rights campaigns for the establishment of normatively grounded international policy regimes. Research on human rights or peace also analyzed the emergence of international norms that challenged the vision of international politics as an anarchic or exclusively power-oriented system of states. In parallel to the study of IGOs, research began on international non-governmental organizations (INGOs) or, specifically, transnational social movement organizations (Boli and Thomas 1999; Smith, Chatfield, and Pagnucco 1996). In human rights campaigns, national actors suffering from repression in authoritarian regimes found allies abroad in epistemic communities, involving IGOs, national governments, experts, and INGOs. Focusing on the interactions between social movements and IGOs, researchers noted the capacity of transnational social movements to adapt to the IGOs' rules, preferring a diplomatic search for agreement over democratic accountability, discretion over transparency, and persuasion over mobilization in the street.

The Politicization of International Relations

In international relations, a debate on the politicization of international organizations has developed from the observation that, especially in the past several decades, the Westphalian principle of national sovereignty has been challenged (Zürn, Binder, and Ecker-Ehrhard 2010):

> In addition to violations by major powers, international institutions have developed procedures that contradict the consensus principle and the principle of non-intervention. Some international norms and rules create obligations for national governments to take measures even when they have not agreed to do so. Moreover, in some cases, decisions of international institutions even affect individuals directly. (p. 2)

Zürn et al. define *politicization* as the entrance into the political subsystem, which is characterized by the presence of "public communication and by contestation about the common good and collectively binding decisions necessary to advance it. . . . In brief then, politicization means making a matter an object of public discussion about collectively binding decision making" (p. 7). The causes of politicization are therefore related to the increasing power of international institutions. The debate in international relations singled out some structural changes that triggered this politicization—mainly, the increasing power of (especially some of) these organizations. The emergence of a public authority beyond the nation brought about a need for legitimation of international institutions: "The days of permissive consensus for executive multilateralism are over. The procedures for obtaining results in international political processes, their content, and above all the concomitant subsystemic assignment of powers require justification" (p. 3). The politicization of international institutions brings about increasing requests of legitimating their intervention, increasing demands addressed to them, as well as increasing perceived incapacity to address them (Zürn et al. 2010).

These institutional causes have attitudinal and behavioral effects. In the late 1960s, the neofunctional approach had expected a progressive increase in the audience and/or clientele of the European institutions (Schmitter 1969); at the end of the century, opinion polls confirmed that increased interest in transnational issues (Hooghe and Marks 2008). Politicization is therefore viewed as a process that can fundamentally change the visions and practices of international institutions, as increasing requests might expand their range of activities but also increase their need for legitimacy.

Multilevel Political Opportunities

In social movement studies, research tried to adapt concepts and theories that had addressed the domestic political opportunities for social movements. Whereas social movement studies have traditionally focused on the nation-state and representative democracy, global movements challenge IGOs, endowed with low accountability, as well as non-democratic states. In particular, research on the Europeanization of contentious politics has singled out multilevel political opportunities to which social movements tend to strategically adapt through strategies of "crossed influence," with mobilization at the national level to change decisions at the European level as well as the use of the European level as a source of resources for modifying national decisions.

The first path, defined as *domestication* of protests, has been followed by movements that found few opportunities within EU institutions. In addition to the weak electoral accountability of EU representative political institutions, the difficult in building a European public sphere (Gerhards 1993) has been stressed, with institutional actors playing a much more prominent role than civil society actors (Caiani and della Porta 2009). Given limited electoral accountability, movements that seek to pressure the EU tend to put pressure on the national governments, which in turn are expected to negotiate better arrangements at supranational levels. In their analysis of protest in Europe, Doug Imig and Sidney Tarrow (2002) found, in fact, that most EU-related events (406 out of 490) were cases of *domestication*, which characterizes in particular mobilizations of European farmers (Bush and Imi 2001).

Although domestication is a strategy that often allows protestors to overcome the weak democratic accountability of EU institutions, in other cases organized interests view the

EU as an additional arena for the mobilization of resources that may then be used at the national level. This is the case, for instance, with regard to environmental campaigns (Rootes 2002) or the Euro-strike in 1997 (Lefébure and Lagneau 2002). In this case, there is a strategy of *externalization* (Chabanet 2002)—what Keck and Sikkink (1998) term the "boomerang effect"—defined as the mobilization of national bodies targeting the EU in attempts to put pressure on their own governments. This strategy has been used mostly by movements that tend to ally supranationally and have in fact appealed to the kinds of discourse and identity legitimized at the European level. On this, more structured social movement organizations can exploit a search for the legitimization of EU institutions that has pushed, in fact, a consensual model that stresses openness to various societal bodies. In order to obtain some routine access, though usually of an informal nature, to international organizations, transnational social movement organizations tend to adapt to the rules of the game (Guiraudon 2001; Marks and McAdam 1999). Feminists, environmentalists, and unions have also been able to obtain favorable decisions from the Court of Justice, especially with the increasing competence of the EU with regard to environmental and social policies (Balme and Chabanet 2002; Dehousse 1998; Mazey 2002; Rootes 2002). In general, however, some groups—especially business associations and private corporations—are more effective than others in organizing and influencing EU institutions. Moreover, the more important EU institutions become, the more structured and less accessible they seem to be for weakly organized interests (Rootes 2002).

In general, it has been noted that an increasing number of international organizations have triggered global movement campaigns because "international institutions serve as a kind of 'coral reef', helping to form horizontal connections among activists with similar claims across boundaries" (Tarrow 2001: 15). Within international organizations, social movements have found some allies in some sympathetic states, some emerging bureaucracies, or left-wing parties in institutions such as the European Parliament. Support by center-left parties, however, seems more effective on some movement concerns and less so on others: Complex internationalism requires complex strategies (Boli and Thomas 1999; della Porta and Tarrow 2005; Fox and Brown 1998: O'Brien et al. 2000; Sikkink 2005). An important focus of attention has been the types of resources and (effective) strategies that social movements can deploy in the multilevel arenas. Exchange of knowledge, reciprocal potential legitimation, and the impact of "vicarious activism" have been singled out as factors to sensitize public opinion to global problems. At the cognitive level, globalization brought about an intensification of relations across borders. Cross-national diffusion has been noted in movement frames but also in strategies of public order control.

Diverse Opportunities

The development of campaigns addressing diverse IGOs has stimulated further reflections on the range of opportunities that various international institutions offer social movements. Opportunities such as a consensual culture and a reciprocal search for recognition are available for the United Nations but not for the (much more closed and hostile) international finance and trade institutions (WTO, IMF, World Bank, and G7/G8) that became the target of lively protest during campaigns such as "50 Years Is Enough" and "Our World Is Not for Sale." More recent research has indicated, in fact, as many types of institutions at the transnational level as at the national level. Social movements that target international institutions have exploited some specific advantages offered, for example, by the unanimity rules of the WTO, which make alliances with some states particularly relevant, and by access to the international experts and formal channels of consultation with regard to the International Labour Organisation. IGOs emerged in fact as complex and fragmented institutions, composed of different bodies that provide external actors with differentiated opportunities. With regard to the EU, the Council, the Commission, the Parliament, and the European Court of Justice are all targeted by social movements, but protest strategies vary according to the characteristics of these specific bodies (della Porta, Kriesi, and Rucht 1999; Parks 2015). Even when considering only the Commission, it appears that different movements find it more or less difficult to obtain access to or to oppose a specific (sympathetic) General Directorate in the EC (Balme and Chabanet 2008; Ruzza 2004).

Neoliberal Globalization

Attention to transnational contention was also accompanied by a reflection on the specific types or relations between state and market, public institutions and private corporations, that IGOs were promoting. International organizations (especially international financial institutions) have been accused of spreading a specific form of globalization: neoliberal globalization. Against it, social movements have focused on issues of poverty, inequality, and injustice, often mobilizing (at first, especially in the Global South) those who were suffering the most from the retrenchment of social protection in favor of the free market. Wealth distribution re-emerged as central in the political debate. In this sense, the global justice movement presents the challenge to reopen the academic debate on the structural nature of conflicts in capitalism. In discussing the potential for mobilization against neoliberal globalization, research on transnational social movements points at challenges and opportunities.

A main challenge for collective mobilization is in a weakening of traditional collective identities and a fragmentation of their social basis. The deregulation of the labor market, with (especially in the 1990s) the spread of insecure and precarious jobs, has challenged mobilizing capacities. The global movements must therefore manage this challenge by constructing a space for dialogue among and networking of multiple and diverse actors. Autonomy, creativity, spontaneity, and self-realization take on a central role (Bennett 2005; della Porta 2005) and thus characterize the organizational structure, from the choice of flexible forms of coordination to the creation of inclusive forms of participation. The global justice movement must therefore address some of the structural challenges that have developed together with globalization processes at various levels. They react to the effects of the liberalization of markets, framing them as consequences of political decisions dominated by the neoliberal agenda. However, they support cosmopolitan values, suggesting alternative visions of globalization (globalization of rights, globalization from below, etc.). Activists are in fact often characterized as deep-rooted cosmopolitans, embedded in local networks but also often endowed with academic and linguistic skills (Agrikoliansky, Fillieule, and Mayer 2005; della Porta 2005; Tarrow 2005).

WHICH PERSPECTIVE FOR GLOBAL MOVEMENTS?

The global justice movement has been viewed as evidence of a trend toward increasing transnationalization of protest. The wave of anti-austerity protests that started in Europe with the financial crisis of 2008 seems to challenge that expectation. The wave of anti-austerity protests that became visible with the "saucepan" revolt in Iceland in 2008 and then continued with the Arab Spring and the Occupy protests in 2011, Gezi Park in Turkey in 2013, and the Nuit début in France in 2016 has some similarities to but also some differences with the global justice movements, particularly regarding the issues of transnationalization in action, organization, and framing. Those protests have in fact expressed a sense of political dispossession concerning a separation between popular politics and power, with a focus on domestic conditions, even if within a global consciousness.

First, anti-austerity protests emerged and developed mainly at the domestic level, following the different timing and intensity of the financial crisis. While the global justice movement proceeded with a downward scale shift, from the world social forums to the local ones (della Porta and Tarrow 2005), the anti-austerity protests followed instead an opposite mechanism, with upward scale shift from domestic globalization to attempts at transnational coordination (della Porta and Mattoni 2014). An example of this is the Blockupy protests, targeting the European Central Bank, with early marches and action of civil disobedience in Frankfurt.

Organizationally, the anti-austerity protests followed a very horizontal model that found a main expression in the camps in main squares of thousands of cities. Given the extremely low trust in existing representative institutions, anti-austerity protests have addressed requests to the state but also experimented with alternative models of participatory and deliberative democracy. Camps were set in main square as places in which new forms of democracy could be prefigured and experimented with. Those who protested against austerity represented coalitions of various classes and social groups that perceived themselves as the losers of neoliberal development and its crisis. Precariousness was certainly a social and cultural condition for many movement activists. Overwhelmingly present in protests was a generation that characterized by high levels of unemployment and underemployment—that is, employment in positions that are underpaid and unprotected. However, present in camps and marches were also other social groups that had been negatively affected by austerity policies—from public employees to the users of public services, from blue-collar workers in large factories to retired people (della Porta 2015).

Regarding the framing, the need to keep together a heterogeneous social base—as well as the general failures of big ideologies to provide for successful alternative models of social and political organization—fueled the development of pluralist and tolerant identities, praising diversity as an enriching value. This was reflected at the organizational level through the elaboration of a participatory and deliberative model of decision-making (della Porta 2013, 2015).

The neoliberal crisis during the Great Recession also had an impact on progressive politics, with—compared to the first wave of protest against rampant neoliberalism—a change in terms of the social basis of the protest, a focus on the defense of former rights within the national context, as well as an emphasis on the moral protection against an immoral capitalism. Although strongly shaped by the changing culture of neoliberalism, identification processes assume once again a central role. Defining themselves broadly—as citizens, persons, or the 99%—activists of the anti-austerity movement developed a moral discourse that called for the reinstatement of welfare protections, but they also stressed solidarity and the return to the commons.

More central for our argument, referring often to the nation as the basis of reference to a community of solidarity (among others, carrying national flags or appealing to the *patria*, the fatherland), they nevertheless developed a cosmopolitan vision combining inclusive nationalism with recognition of the need to seek global solutions to global problems. Protestors stigmatize the power of large transnational corporations and international organizations, with the related loss of national governments' sovereignty. They claim that representative democracy has been corrupted by the collusion of economic and political elites, calling for participatory democracy and a general return to public concern with common goods. Differently from the global justice movement, which had presented itself as an alliance of minorities in search of a broad constituency (della Porta 2007; della Porta 2009a, 2009b), the anti-austerity movements have constructed a broad definition of the self as a large majority of the citizens (della Porta et al. 2017). Although marked by a focus on national sovereignty against the dispossession of citizens' rights by (electorally unaccountable) global elites, the anti-austerity protests of 2011–2013 have defended civic, political, and social rights as belonging to humanity. While calling for the restoration of citizens' rights, anti-austerity protestors also looked forward, combining concerns for social inequalities with hopes for cultural inclusivity.

Conclusion

The politicization of international organizations brings about conflicts that do not involve only nation-states or just the distribution of competences between different geographical levels of governance but, rather, a complex of different actors (including social and political actors) active at multilevels and using different repertoires of contention.

Social movement studies contribute to this knowledge as they have addressed the complex process of mobilization, examining various levels and steps in the process—even though they have done this by focusing on the local and national levels. As happened during the construction of the nation-state, the territorial shift of power has been followed by a scale shift (McAdam and Tarrow 2005) in protest activities. As in that case, also at the transnational level, social movements seem indeed to move where power is (or at least is perceived to be) in order to influence it on substantive policies, but also to develop institutional political opportunities for themselves (della Porta and Caiani 2009). Politicization of international institutions emerges then as the complex intertwining of contestation of policies and politics, but also legitimation of the emerging polity. Second, however, politicization needs carriers (della Porta and Caiani 2009):

> In fact, there is an increasing politicization of international institutions, and social movements contribute to it by contesting many decisions made by those institutions, as well as lamenting

their lack of democratic accountability. While grievances about the policies and politics at the international level are at the basis of this contentious transnational politics, the organizations and activists of the (progressive) movements I have mentioned show to be "critical cosmopolitans" in that they promote international governance, as indispensable to produce global justice, while at the same time criticizing the existing policies of those organizations. In order to understand this complex development, social movement studies help to specify the types of challenge that politicization by transnational social movements brings about for international organizations. As we have observed, the social movement organizations that gravitate around the Global Justice Movement have very critical views of the policies and politics of some international organizations, and actively try to produce changes. In this sense, they are for sure among the most convinced carriers of the politicization of some international institutions.

The research also confirms that it is especially some international organizations that do attract these criticisms and that these are among the most powerful. At the same time, however, the research allows one to go beyond the analysis of the causes of politicization in terms of the increasing power of international institutions and their (necessarily?) insufficient performances and examining the ways in which opportunities and threats at the international level are perceived by the activists and their organizations, as well as the ways in which resources for transnational contentious politics are mobilized.

International institutions work as targets but also—willy-nilly—as condensers of protest. *In action*, during transnational collective protest, not only are transnational networks created but also critical cosmopolitan identities develop. With some parallel with what happened at the national level, also at the transnational one, new polities are legitimated by contestation (della Porta and Caiani 2009). Global movements—even if active at various territorial levels—also perceive the need to open opportunities at the most distant level of governance. Although social movements have often better chances of success locally, there seems to be widespread agreement that the problems are global and have to be addressed supranationally. In addition, although democracy is easier at the local level, efforts are made to develop models of democratic accountability that could work also for global institutions. In fact, given the difficulty of building representative institutions, participatory and deliberative forms of democracy acquire increasingly more relevance. Given the increasing power of international organizations, the belief seems indeed widespread that democracy either finds a way to be global or is not democracy at all (Marchetti 2008).

In fact, as it happened at the national level, contestation tends to transform the international system as international institutions react to increasing contestation by often opening some (although limited) channels of access for civil society organizations (regarding the United Nations Security Council, see Binder 2008; regarding international financial institutions, see O'Brien et al. 2000) and developing a rhetoric of legitimacy "through" the people (regarding the European Union, see Schmidt 2006). In fact, research seems to confirm that in international institutions, protest has increased access to, as well as control of, international decision-making—the opportunities for participation indeed seem to be linked to "the (varying) strength of politicization" (Binder 2008: 20). International institutions so often become "an opportunity space within which opponents of global capitalism and other claimants can mobilize" (Tarrow 2005: 25–26).

References

Agrikoliansky, Eric, Olivier Fillieule, and Nonna Mayer, eds. 2005. *L'altermondialisme en France: La longue histoire d'une nouvelle cause*. Paris: Flammarion.

Balme, Richard, and Didier Chabanet. 2002. "Introduction: Action collective et gouvernance de l'Union Européenne." In *L'action collective en Europe*, edited by Richard Balme and Didier Chabanet, 21–120. Paris: Presses de Sciences Po.

Balme, Richard, and Didier Chabanet. 2008. *European Governance and Democracy: Power and Protest in the EU*. Lanham, MD: Rowman & Littlefield.

Bennett, Lance. 2005. "Social Movements Beyond Borders: Understanding Two Eras of Transnational Activism." In *Transnational Protest and Global Activism*, edited by Donatella della Porta and Sidney Tarrow, 203–226. Lanham, MD: Rowman & Littlefield.

Binder, Martin. 2008. "The Politicization of International Security Institutions: The UN Security Council and NGOs." Discussion Paper SP IV 2008-305, Wissenschaftszentrum Berlin für Sozialforschung.

Boli, John, and George M. Thomas. 1999. *Constructing the World Culture: International Nongovernmental Organizations Since 1875*. Stanford, CA: Stanford University Press.

Bush, Evelyn, and Pete Imi. 2001. "European Farmers and Their Protests." In *Contentious Europeans: Protest and Politics in an Emerging Polity*, edited by Doug Imig and Sidney Tarrow, 97–121. Lanham, MD: Rowman & Littlefield.

Chabanet, Didier. 2002. "Les marches Européennes contre le chômage, la précarité et les exclusions." In *L'action collective en Europe*, edited by Richard Balme and Didier Chabanet, 461–494. Paris: Presses de Sciences Po.

Cohen, Robin, and Shirin M. Rai, eds. 2000. *Global social movements*. London: Athlone.

Dehousse, Renaud. 1998. *The European Court of Justice*. New York: Macmillan.

della Porta, Donatella. 2005. "Multiple Belongings, Tolerant Identities, and the Construction of 'Another Politics': Between the European Social Forum and the Local Social Fora." In *Transnational Protest and Global Activism*, edited by Donatella della Porta and Sidney Tarrow, 175–202. Lanham, MD: Rowman & Littlefield.

della Porta, Donatella, ed. 2007. *The Global Justice Movement: Cross National and Transnational Perspectives*. Boulder, CO: Paradigm.

della Porta, Donatella, ed. 2009a. *Another Europe*. London: Routledge.

della Porta, Donatella, ed. 2009b. *Democracy in Social Movements*. London: Palgrave.

della Porta, Donatella. 2013. *Can Democracy Be Saved?* Cambridge, UK: Polity.

della Porta, Donatella. 2015. *Social Movements in Times of Austerity*. Cambridge, UK: Polity.

della Porta, Donatella, Massimiliano Andretta, Lorenzo Mosca, and Herbert Reiter. 2006. *Globalization from Below*. Minneapolis: University of Minnesota Press.

della Porta, Donatella, and Manuela Caiani. 2009. *Social Movements and Europeanization*. Oxford, UK: Oxford University Press.

della Porta, Donatella, and Mario Diani. 2006. *Social Movements: An Introduction*. London: Blackwell.

della Porta, Donatella, Hanspeter Kriesi, and Dieter Rucht, eds. 1999. *Social Movements in a Globalizing World*. New York: Macmillan.

della Porta, Donatella, Francis O'Connor, Markos Vogiatzoglou, et al. 2017. *Late Neoliberalism and Its Discontents*. London: Palgrave.

della Porta, Donatella, and Alice Mattoni (eds). 2014. *Spreading Protest: From the Arab Spring to Occupy*. Essex: ECPR Press.

della Porta, Donatella, Abby Peterson, and Herbert Reiter, eds. 2006. *The Policing of Transnational Protest*. Aldershot, UK: Ashgate.

della Porta, Donatella, and Sidney Tarrow, eds. 2005. *Transnational Protest and Global Activism*. Lanham, MD: Rowman & Littlefield.

Diani, Mario. 2005. "Cities in the World: Local Civil Society and Global Issues in Britain." In *Transnational Protest and Global Activism*, edited by Donatella della Porta and Sidney Tarrow, 45–67. Lanham, MD: Rowman & Littlefield.

Edwards, M., and J. Gaventa, eds. 2001. *Global Citizen Action*. Boulder, CO: Rienne.

Fox, Jonathan A., and L. David Brown, eds. 1998. *The Struggle for Accountability: The World Bank, NGOs, and Grassroots Movements*. Cambridge, MA: MIT Press.

Gerhards, Juergen. 1993. "Westeuropäische Integration und die Schwierigkeiten der Entstehung einer Europäischen Öffentlichkeit." *Zeitschrift für Soziologie* 22, 96–110.

Guiraudon, Virginie. 2001. "Weak Weapons of the Weak? Transnational Mobilization Around Migration in the European Union." In *Contentious Europeans: Protest and Politics in an Emerging Polity*, edited by Doug Imig and Sidney Tarrow, 163–183. Lanham, MD: Rowman & Littlefield.

Hooghe, Liesbet, and Gary Marks. 2008. "A Postfunctionalist Theory of European Integration: From Permissive Consensus to Constraining Dissensus." *British Journal of Political Science* 39 (1): 1–23.

Imig, Doug, and Sidney Tarrow, eds. 2002. *Contentious Europeans: Protest and Politics in an Emerging Polity*. Lanham, MD: Rowman & Littlefield.

Keck, Margaret, and Kathryn Sikkink. 1998. *Activists Beyond Borders*. Ithaca, NY: Cornell University Press.

Khagram, Sanjeev, Jamev V. Riker, and Kathryn Sikkink, eds. 2002. *Reconstructing World Politics: Transnational Social Movements, Networks and Norms*. Minneapolis: University of Minnesota Press.

Lefébure, Pierre, and Eric Lagneau. 2002. "Le moment Volvorde: Action protestataire et espace publique Européen." In *L'action collective en Europe*, edited by Richard Balme and Didier Chabanet, 495–529. Paris: Presses de Sciences Po.

Marchetti, Raffaele. 2008. *Global Democracy: For and Against*. London: Routledge.

Marks, Gary, and Doug McAdam. 1999. "On the Relationship of the Political Opportunities to the Form of Collective Action." In *Social Movements in a Globalizing World*, edited by Donatella della Porta, Hanspeter Kriesi, and Dieter Rucht, pp. 97–111. New York: Macmillan.

Mazey, Sonia. 2002. "L'Union Européenne et les droits des femmes: de l'Européanisation des agendas nationaux à la nationalisation d'un agenda Européen?" In *L'action collective en Europe*, edited by Richard Balme and Didier Chabanet, 405–432. Paris: Presses de Sciences Po.

McAdam, Doug, and Sidney Tarrow. 2005. "Scale Shift in Transnational Contention." In *Transnational Protest and Global Activism*, edited by Donatella della Porta and Sidney Tarrow, 121–149. Lanham, MD: Rowman & Littlefield.

Micheletti, Michele. 2003. *Political Virtue and Shopping: Individuals, Consumerism, and Collective Action*. New York: Palgrave Macmillan.

O'Brien, Robert, Anne Marie Goetz, Jaan Aart Scholte, and Marc Williams. 2000. *Contesting Global Governance: Multilateral Economic Institutions and Global Social Movements*. Cambridge, UK: Cambridge University Press.

Parks, Louisa. 2015. *Social Movement Campaigns on EU Policy: In the Corridors and in the Street*. London: Palgrave.

Pianta, Mario. 2002. "Parallel Summits: An Update." In *Global Civil Society*, edited by H. K. Anheier, M. Glasius, and M. Kaldor, 371–377. Oxford, UK: Oxford University Press.

Risse, Thomas, S. Ropp, and K. Sikkink, eds. 1999. *The Power of Human Rights: International Norms and Domestic Change*. New York: Cambridge University Press.

Rootes, Christopher A. 2002. "The Europeanization of Environmentalism." In *L'action collective en Europe*, edited by Richard Balme and Didier Chabanet, 377–404. Paris: Presses de Sciences Po.

Rootes, Christopher A. 2005. "A Limited Transnationalization? The British Environmental Movement." In *Transnational Protest and Global Activism*, edited by Donatella della Porta and Sidney Tarrow, 21–43. Lanham, MD: Rowman & Littlefield.

Rucht, Dieter. 2002. "The EU as a Target of Political Mobilisation: Is There a Europeanisation of Conflict?" In *L'action collective en Europe*, edited by Richard Balme, Didier Chabanet, and Vincent Wright, 163–194. Paris: Presses de Sciences Po.

Rucht, Dieter. 2005. "Un movimento di movimenti? Unità e diversità fra le organizzazioni per una giustizia globale." *Rassegna Italiana di Sociologia* 46: 275–306.

Ruzza, C. 2004. *Europe and Civil Society, Movement Coalitions and European Governance*. Manchester, UK: Manchester University Press.

Schmidt, Vivien. 2006. *Democracy in Europe: The EU and National Politics*. Oxford, UK: Oxford University Press.

Schmitter, Philippe C. 1969. "Three Neo-Functionalist Hypotheses About International Integration." *International Organization* 23 (1): 161–166.

Sikkink, Katryn. 2005. "Patterns of Dynamic Multi-level Governance and the Insider–Outsider Coalition. In *Transnational Protest and Global Activism*, edited by Donatella della Porta and Sidney Tarrow, 151–174. Lanham, MD: Rowman & Littlefield.

Smith, Jackie, Charles Chatfield, and Ron Pagnucco, eds. 1996. *Solidarity Beyond the State: The Dynamics of Transnational Social Movements*. Syracuse, NY: Syracuse University Press.

Smith, Jackie, and Hank Johnston, eds. 2002. *Globalization and Resistance: Transnational Dimensions of Social Movements*. Lanham, MD: Rowman & Littlefield.

Smith, Jackie, Ellen Reese, Scott Byrd, and Elizabeth Smythe. 2007. *The World Social Forum*. Boulder, CO: Paradigm.

Tarrow, Sidney. 2001. "Transnational Politics: Contention and Institutions in International Politics." *Annual Review of Political Science* 4: 1–20.

Tarrow, Sidney. 2005. *The New Transnational Activism*. Cambridge, UK. Cambridge University Press.

Zürn, Michael, Martin Binder, and Matthias Ecker-Ehrhardt. 2010. *International Political Authority and Its Politicization*. Berlin: Social Science Research Center Berlin, Transnational Conflicts and International Institutions.

CHAPTER 43

....

HUMANITARIAN
ORGANIZATIONS

....

KATHERINE MARSHALL

THE term *humanitarian* is broadly linked to efforts to promote human welfare and has
ancient religious and secular roots that highlight an ethic of care. It is associated with compassion and charitable efforts and also with human rights and a respect for human dignity. Histories of humanitarianism thus highlight movements for justice, including the
anti-slavery movement, and campaigns for the rights of vulnerable groups, including—at
different times and in different places—women, children, religious minorities, and the disabled. Some still consider compassionate responses including health care and work for justice
as falling within a rubric of humanitarianism. However, the term in global affairs generally
refers to organized, theoretically short-term emergency efforts to respond to crises and,
most important, to save lives. Core humanitarian work today thus centers on provision of
food, water, shelter, and protection against harm.

Local humanitarian responses are vitally important, but with complex natural and
man-made crises and disasters and in an increasingly interconnected world, transnational
responses have assumed large roles against an expectation of a common human obligation
to help fellow humans even in distant places (Rieff 2015). A complex set of institutions
has emerged that focus on this response, involving international organizations, national
governments, non-governmental actors, and private sector organizations.

Organized humanitarian aid and a set of principles that are still considered core humanitarian principles developed during the nineteenth century. Major catalytic events included
famines in Ireland, Scandinavia, India, and China but especially growing awareness of civilian suffering during wars. The contemporary humanitarian system was deeply marked by
the two World Wars that left millions dead, starving, or displaced and also by the existential
threats of the Holocaust and nuclear weapons.

A critical and quite unique set of institutions that have dominated humanitarian
approaches is the Red Cross. Its conception is traced to Henry Dunant, who was moved
by the 1859 battlefield sufferings at Solferino, where, following clashes between the armies
of imperial Austria and the Franco-Sardinian alliance, thousands of dying and wounded
men were neglected. In 1863, Dunant and colleagues set up the International Committee
for Relief to the Wounded, later to become the International Committee of the Red Cross

(the emblem of a red cross on a white background is the inverse of the Swiss flag). The initial model was national relief societies focused on helping those wounded in war. Adoption of the first Geneva Convention followed a year later, centered on care for the wounded and defining medical services on the battlefield as "neutral." The International Federation of Red Cross and Red Crescent Societies (IFRC) was founded in 1919 in Paris in the aftermath of World War I. During the war, Red Cross Societies, through humanitarian activities on behalf of prisoners of war and combatants, had attracted millions of volunteers and built a large body of expertise. IFRC was a response especially to coordination challenges. The first Nobel Peace Prize was awarded in 1901 to Jean Henry Dunant and Frédéric Passy, reflecting the importance credited to their work.

Humanitarian Principles

Over the decades, a set of principles have evolved that are seen distinctively to guide humanitarian work, and they are associated with a body of international law that includes notably the Geneva Conventions but also various United Nations (UN) conventions and resolutions and, less directly but also significantly, the Responsibility to Protect. Some of these principles have an almost sacrosanct character, but lively debates turn on others.

The first widely accepted and fundamental humanitarian principle is, as the name suggests, humanity, meaning that all humankind is to be treated humanely and equally in all circumstances by saving lives and alleviating suffering while ensuring respect for the individual. Other humanitarian principles were shaped both by ethical debates and by the practical imperatives of working in disaster situations: impartiality (based on need and not on nationality, race, religion, or political viewpoint), independence (humanitarian agencies must formulate and implement their policies independently of government policies or actions), and neutrality (not to take sides in hostilities or engage at any time in controversies of a political, racial, religious, or ideological nature). A central principle is that provision of aid must not exploit the vulnerability of victims or be used to further political or religious creeds.

These principles are formally enshrined in two General Assembly resolutions. The first three principles (humanity, neutrality, and impartiality) are endorsed in UN General Assembly resolution 46/182, which was adopted in 1991. General Assembly resolution 58/114 (2004) added independence as a fourth key principle underlying humanitarian action. The General Assembly has repeatedly reaffirmed the importance of promoting and respecting these principles within the framework of humanitarian assistance. The Code of Conduct for the International Red Cross and Red Crescent Movement and NGOs in Disaster Relief, approved in 1994, defined a humanitarian imperative, meaning the right and obligation to give and the right to receive humanitarian assistance. The code provides a set of common standards for organizations involved in humanitarian activities, including a commitment to adhere to the humanitarian principles. More than 492 organizations have signed the Code of Conduct.

Also of note is the Humanitarian Charter and Minimum Standards in Humanitarian Response elaborated by the Sphere Project. The latter, a voluntary initiative, brings a wide range of humanitarian agencies together around the common aim of improving the quality of humanitarian assistance and the accountability of humanitarian actors to their constituents, donors, and affected populations. The Sphere Handbook, *Humanitarian Charter and Minimum Standards in Humanitarian Response* (Sphere Project 2000), is one of the most widely known and internationally recognized sets of common principles and universal minimum standards in life-saving areas of humanitarian response. Established in 1997, the Sphere Project is a community, not a membership organization. Its governing board is composed of representatives of global networks of humanitarian agencies.

INTERNATIONAL HUMANITARIAN LAW

A major part of international humanitarian law is contained in the four Geneva Conventions of 1949. Nearly every state in the world has agreed to be bound by them. The Conventions have been developed and supplemented by two further agreements: the Additional Protocols of 1977, which relates to the protection of victims of armed conflicts, and Additional Protocol II (also 1977), which covers the protection of victims of non-international armed conflicts. Additional Protocol III (2005) created a new protective emblem, the red crystal, alongside the existing red cross and red crescent.

Other international agreements prohibit the use of certain weapons and military tactics and protect specific categories of people and goods. These agreements include the 1954 Convention for the Protection of Cultural Property in the Event of Armed Conflict, in addition to its two protocols: the 1972 Biological Weapons Convention and the 1980 Conventional Weapons Convention. The latter added the 1993 Chemical Weapons Convention, the 1997 Ottawa Convention on anti-personnel mines, and the 2000 Optional Protocol to the Convention on the Rights of the Child on the involvement of children in armed conflict. Many provisions of international humanitarian law are now accepted as customary law— that is, as general rules by which all states are bound (International Committee of the Red Cross 2010).

Also pertinent for recent consideration of humanitarian intervention is the "Responsibility to Protect." The 2005 World Summit to prevent genocide, war crimes, ethnic cleansing, and crimes against humanity endorsed the principles, and the Secretary-General's 2009 report on its implementation highlighted the following:

1. The State carries the primary responsibility for protecting populations from genocide, war crimes, crimes against humanity and ethnic cleansing, and their incitement.
2. The international community has a responsibility to encourage and assist States in fulfilling this responsibility.
3. The international community has a responsibility to use appropriate diplomatic, humanitarian and other means to protect populations from these crimes. If a State is manifestly failing to protect its populations, the international community must be prepared to take collective action to protect populations, in accordance with the Charter of the United Nations.[1]

THE CONTEMPORARY HUMANITARIAN "SYSTEM"

The 2016 World Humanitarian Summit

The convening in Istanbul, Turkey, in May 2016 of the World Humanitarian Summit (WHS) marked a historic first in the seventy-year history of the UN. Then UN Secretary-General Ban Ki-moon defined its goal as generating commitments to "reduce suffering and deliver better for people around the globe." The summit included 9,000 participants from 173 countries, including approximately 55 heads of state. Intensive reflections and debates about the humanitarian system and principles took place in the lead up to the event and in its wake. Formal discussions centered around what is termed "a Grand Bargain," with numerous commitments by participants and the outlines of future directions. Its main elements are as follows:

- For aid organizations and donors to work more closely together toward
  - more financial transparency;
  - more support and funding tools to national first responders; and
  - scaling up use of cash-based programming and more coordination in its delivery.
- For aid organizations to commit to
  - reducing duplication and management costs;
  - reviewing periodically functional expenditures;
  - assessing needs impartially and jointly; and
  - listening and including beneficiaries in decisions that affect them—"a participation revolution."
- For donors to commit to
  - more multi-year humanitarian funding;
  - fewer earmarks to humanitarian aid organizations; and
  - more harmonized and simplified reporting requirements.

Perhaps the dominant theme to emerge from the summit was the call to "leave no one behind" (Agenda for Humanity 2016).

What Is the Humanitarian System?

Discussions leading up to the WHS shone a spotlight on the complex set of institutions that constitute the so-called humanitarian system—so-called because its continuing, organic evolution and ad hoc features mean that not all view it as meriting the term "system." Each successive jolting world crisis results both in new questions and often in new organizational demands as well as heightened attention to preparedness and risk assessment (Figure 43.1). Observers have variously characterized the humanitarian system as feudal (Barnett 2011), a flotilla, a crisis caravan (Polman 2010), alms dealers (Gourevich 2010), a constellation (Active Learning Network for Accountability and Performance (ALNAP), 2015), and an industry. It includes a number of UN bodies, the Red Cross and Red Crescent

FIGURE 43.1 Haitians stand among the devastation left by a 7.0 magnitude earthquake in 2010.

Source. Photo courtesy of Flickr user RIBI Image Library.

system, many humanitarian agencies of bilateral governments including military services, dedicated international non-governmental organizations (NGOs), local organizations, and private companies. Various mechanisms have evolved to address both advocacy and mobilization of resources and coordination on the ground.

What is included in the "humanitarian system" is affected by understandings of the reach of contemporary humanitarian action. Notably with the 2015 United Nations General Assembly approval of the Sustainable Development Goals (SDGs), and reaffirmed during the WHS, the feasibility and wisdom of drawing sharp boundary lines between humanitarian work and institutions versus social and economic development, peacebuilding, and action on environmental issues is called into question. The complex links between protracted and complex humanitarian crises and development challenges and conflict issues has highlighted the importance of integrating and coordinating action. A thematic network under the UN umbrella focuses on humanitarian–development linkages,[2] attempting to make more operational the commitment to those farthest behind, particularly in the most fragile and conflict-affected states (where support is traditionally classified as "humanitarian" contexts, financed using short-term mechanisms). The network focuses on all SDGs in fragile situations with the aims of giving "clear guidance on how humanitarian considerations can be integrated into SDG national plans and global monitoring processes, particularly in fragile states and conflict-affected countries"[3]; working with partners such as UN agencies, donors, and NGOs to ensure that humanitarian requirements are factored into development planning in fragile states; advocating for a longer term perspective in complex contexts currently considered "humanitarian"; and identifying and tracking SDG indicators related to humanitarian issues.

A result of this ferment about the broadening understanding of global challenges is considerable debate about mandates, the effectiveness of coordination arrangements, and financing mechanisms. In some situations, traditional approaches to humanitarian crises work well, but in protracted crises and in the assessment and management of risk, it is increasingly clear that broader and more integrated approaches are essential.

In summary, defining a humanitarian "system" today is problematic because many relevant institutions are involved in activities beyond those that have traditionally counted as humanitarian (e.g., food distribution and supporting refugees) and the diversity of actors is increasing. A further issue is that important actors are not part of formal humanitarian planning and coordinating mechanisms in meaningful ways ("new actors"). Perhaps most important, there are serious funding shortfalls and questions about the effectiveness of approaches and programs. The question of whether current arrangements are "broken," meaning that there are fundamental flaws and a breakdown of systems, or just "broke," suggesting that the main problem is inadequate funding, is the topic of debate.

HUMANITARIAN ORGANIZATIONS

United Nations Agencies

The UN Office for the Coordination of Humanitarian Affairs (OCHA) is the focal point in the UN system for natural disasters and complex emergencies. Formed in 1991 with the merger of two offices (the Department of Humanitarian Affairs and the United Nations Disaster Relief Coordinator's Office), OCHA is the focal point for international leadership in responding to major disasters, with a mandate that has expanded to include coordination of humanitarian response, policy development, and humanitarian advocacy. Its activities include organization and monitoring of humanitarian funding, information exchange, coordination, and mobilizing rapid response teams for emergency relief. OCHA was responsible for organizing the WHS. OCHA works through an Inter-Agency Standing Committee, whose members include the UN system entities most directly responsible for providing emergency relief. OCHA manages the UN Central Emergency Response Fund that receives voluntary contributions year-round to provide immediate funding for life-saving humanitarian action anywhere in the world.

The three UN agencies with central responsibility for humanitarian response are the UN Refugee Agency (UNHCR; headquartered in Geneva, Switzerland), the World Food Programme (WFP; based in Rome), and the United Nations Children's Fund (UNICEF; headquartered in New York). Other agencies involved include the UN Development Programme and the multilateral development banks; the World Bank and the regional development banks have explicitly eschewed humanitarian action but have long traditions of involvement in reconstruction work and play important roles in most fragile states, especially in mobilizing financing. Also relevant is the International Organization for Migration, established in 1951 and since June 2016 a related organization of the UN; it provides services and advice concerning migration to governments and migrants. Its stated mission is to promote humane and orderly migration.

UNHCR (officially the Office of the United Nations High Commissioner for Refugees or the UN Refugee Agency) has a mandate to protect and support refugees and assist in their voluntary repatriation, local integration, or resettlement in a third country. When the UN was formed after World War II, millions of refugees and internally displaced people presented an acute crisis. The United Nations Relief and Rehabilitation Administration was established in 1944, and then in 1947 the International Refugee Organization, the first international agency to deal comprehensively with all aspects affecting refugees' lives, was established. UNHCR was founded in 1949 as a temporary organization. Later transformed into a permanent body, it was to provide, on a nonpolitical and humanitarian basis, international protection to refugees and to seek permanent solutions for them. UNHCR's mandate was progressively expanded beyond Europe. Decolonization in the 1960s triggered large refugee movements in Africa, and that and other situations resulted in a transformation of UNHCR's mandate and work. By the end of the 1960s, two-thirds of its budget was focused on operations in Africa. Operations expanded, notably with the Pakistan–Bangladesh clash. Superpower rivalries made durable solutions to refugee situations increasingly difficult; thus, UNHCR became more heavily involved with working in refugee camps, often located in hostile environments. The end of the Cold War saw continuing ethnic conflicts and refugee flight. Humanitarian intervention by multinational peacekeeping forces became more frequent, with the media playing a major role. The Rwanda genocide resulted in a massive refugee crisis and further reflection on why such events occurred and how best to address them. The current refugee crisis linked to the civil war in Syria is another goad to deep reflection on the adequacy of existing mechanisms to deal with both refugee and other facets of global migration.

Current refugee flows as well as migration present unprecedented challenges, with broad implications for the humanitarian system. The total number of refugees and internally displaced persons protected or assisted by UNHCR stood at 65.6 million at the end of 2016, compared to 52.6 million at the end of 2015. During 2015, more than 12.4 million individuals were forced to leave their homes and seek protection elsewhere; of this number, approximately 8.6 million remained within their own countries and approximately 1.8 million sought international protection abroad. In addition, 2.0 million new claims for asylum were made within the year (UNHCR 2016). Nearly 6.7 million refugees were considered to be in a protracted displacement situation at the end of 2015; approximately two-thirds of today's refugees are trapped in protracted refugee situations, most in some of the world's poorest and most unstable regions.

The WFP is the world's largest humanitarian agency. Part of the UN system, WFP is voluntarily funded, largely by its member governments, and has a broad mandate to fight hunger. Formed in 1963, it was initially a three-year experiment inspired by a US proposal for a larger, multilateral food assistance organization. Following what was viewed as a successful experience, WFP was expanded after two years into today's form. In 1994, it adopted a mission statement—a first for any UN organization—establishing its focus as using food aid to support economic and social development, meeting refugee and other emergency food needs, and the associated logistics support, in addition to promoting world food security in accordance with the recommendations of the UN and the UN Food and Agriculture Organization (FAO).

Today, WFP plays major roles in getting food to where it is needed, notably to victims of war, civil conflict, and natural disasters. WFP also uses food to help communities rebuild shattered lives. It pursues a vision of the world in which every man, woman, and child has access at all times to the food needed for an active and healthy life; it has a mandate to lead within the UN system on SDG 2, Zero Hunger by 2030. WFP works with the FAO and the International Fund for Agricultural Development, as well as other government, UN, and NGO partners. On average, WFP reaches more than 80 million people with food assistance in eighty-two countries each year. Its staff of close to 14,000 work in remote areas throughout the world. An executive board consisting of representatives from thirty-six member states governs WFP. The executive director is appointed jointly by the UN Secretary General and the Director-General of the FAO for a five-year term.

UNICEF is one of the largest players in international aid and humanitarian work in the world today, and it is widely respected as an effective organization. Founded in 1946, UNICEF began with the specific mission of providing emergency food and health care to children in countries devastated by World War II. Originally called the United Nations International Children's Emergency Fund, the name changed to the United Nation's Children Fund when it was officially adopted as a permanent branch of the UN in 1954. UNICEF operates in more than 190 countries, focusing on the welfare of children in at-risk areas. Since 2006, it has concentrated on several specific areas: child survival and development, basic education and gender equality, mitigating the effects of HIV/AIDS on children, child protection and policy advocacy, and strengthening partnerships. UNICEF operates during emergencies in addition to supporting especially lower income countries to provide children with basic resources and advocate for children's rights.

The International Red Cross and Red Crescent Movement

The Red Cross movement is in many senses a centerpiece of the global humanitarian system. It represents an international movement founded and focused explicitly on a humanitarian mission: to protect human life and health, to ensure respect for all human beings, and to prevent and alleviate human suffering. It counts nearly 100 million volunteers, members, and staff worldwide.

The Red Cross/Red Crescent movement consists of several distinct organizations that are legally independent from each other but united through common basic principles, objectives, symbols, statutes, and governing organizations. The various organizations include the following:

- The International Committee of the Red Cross (ICRC), a private humanitarian institution founded in 1863 in Geneva by Henry Dunant and Gustave Movnier: It is governed by a twenty-five-member committee with a unique authority under international humanitarian law to protect the life and dignity of the victims of international and internal armed conflicts.
- The International Federation of Red Cross and Red Crescent Societies, founded in 1919: Currently, it coordinates activities between the movement's 189 National Red Cross and Red Crescent Societies. At the international level, the IFRC leads and organizes, in close cooperation with the national societies, relief assistance missions

responding to large-scale emergencies. The International Federation Secretariat is based in Geneva.

- National Red Cross and Red Crescent Societies: There are organizations in nearly every country, with 189 national societies currently recognized by ICRC and admitted as full members of the federation. Each entity works in its home country according to the principles of international humanitarian law and the statutes of the international movement. Depending on their specific circumstances and capacities, national societies can take on additional humanitarian tasks that are not directly defined by international humanitarian law or the mandates of the international movement. In many countries, they are tightly linked to the respective national health care system and provide urgent medical services.

During the period of decolonization from 1960 to 1970, there was a large increase in the number of recognized national Red Cross and Red Crescent societies. By the end of the 1960s, there were more than 100 societies throughout the world. In 1983, the league was renamed the League of Red Cross and Red Crescent Societies to reflect the growing number of national societies operating under the Red Crescent symbol. Three years later, the seven basic principles of the movement as adopted in 1965 were incorporated into its statutes.

Every four years, the movement's members hold talks with representatives of the states party to the Geneva Conventions at the International Conference of the Red Cross and Red Crescent. The conference is the movement's highest deliberative body and is the opportunity to examine cross-cutting priorities and challenges. A standing commission serves as the trustee of the conference and offers strategic guidance between meetings. It promotes coordination between movement partners, furthers the implementation of conference resolutions, and examines issues of concern to the movement as a whole.

The ICRC is funded by voluntary contributions from the states party to the Geneva Conventions (governments), national Red Cross and Red Crescent societies, supranational organizations (e.g., the European Commission), and public and private sources. Each year, the ICRC launches appeals to cover its projected costs in the field and at its headquarters. It launches additional appeals if needs in the field increase. The ICRC accounts for its work and expenditure in its annual report.

Government Humanitarian Actors

National governments play central roles in humanitarian response, not least in their critical role in overseeing the work of humanitarian organizations, whether as responders or as financiers. Management arrangements vary by country, but in most instances, bilateral aid agencies have lead roles in coordination and oversight of humanitarian activities across international boundaries. They play major roles in defining policies at different levels (witness roles during the World Humanitarian Summit and at the September 2016 Summit for Refugees and Migrants at the United Nations in New York).

In many disaster situations, as well as in humanitarian crises linked to conflicts, military services play significant roles. Examples include the role of the US military during the West African 2014 Ebola crisis as well as complex activities in Afghanistan and Iraq. In Haiti, protection of civilians in temporary camps is a major issue, and military operations focus on reinforcing those of the police.

Humanitarian crises and especially refugee flight, but also migratory pressures, involve international diplomacy. This includes notably peace negotiations (e.g., in Colombia, the Balkans, and South Sudan) but more broadly international efforts to respond to refugee flows—for example, to Europe or from Central America to the United States. Diplomatic negotiations as well as peacekeeping operations border on humanitarian work and involve the definition and protection of what is known as "humanitarian space." The complex conflicts that characterize the contemporary world, with asymmetrical forces at play and involvement of non-state actors, have spurred the expansion of Track Two or Track One and a Half peace efforts (that involve, for example, NGOs). Humanitarian access and protection of humanitarian workers are commonly an integral part of negotiations.

International Non-Governmental Organizations

Major actors in humanitarian work include prominently a large number of NGOs that work internationally (Figure 43.2). The exact number is difficult to ascertain but counts in the hundreds. However, a relatively small group of organizations tends to dominate both financially and operationally, and thus plays a major role at the level of policy. This group varies in origin, focus, governance structures (notably how national programs relate to the

FIGURE 43.2 Women and children collect water together at Kenya's Dadaab Refugee Camp in August 2011.

Source: Photo courtesy of Flickr user IHH Humanitarian Relief Foundation.

international entity), and mission, although all members of the group profess to adhere to humanitarian principles. Many, although not all, have clear links to religious heritage and bodies (the majority of them Christian). The international NGOs raise funds independently but also rely heavily on financing partnerships with international and national governmental bodies. Some of the larger organizations are closely linked to OCHA.

This section highlights briefly central features of a diverse group (among hundreds) of leading international NGOs active in humanitarian work. Each organization has a distinctive approach, but they all share common principles and challenges. Two organizations, Médecins sans Frontières and the Order of Malta, are treated separately because they fit into a somewhat distinctive category.

Action Against Hunger was established in 1979 by a group of French doctors, scientists, and writers, initially to support Afghan refugees in Pakistan, Ugandan communities, and Cambodian refugees. It has since expanded the scope of its activities but with a primary focus on humanitarian relief.

The Adventist Development and Relief Agency (ADRA), a humanitarian agency operated by the Seventh-Day Adventist Church, works both on disaster relief and on individual and community development. Founded in 1956, its headquarters are in Silver Spring, Maryland. Its staff number more than 4,000 members. ADRA operates in approximately 130 countries.

Aga Khan Development Network coordinates humanitarian assistance activities through the Aga Khan Agency for Habitat, but many network agencies respond to local needs. Focus Humanitarian Assistance (FOCUS), an international group of agencies established in Europe, North America, and South Asia, complements the provision of emergency relief, working to reduce dependence on humanitarian aid and facilitate the transition to sustainable self-reliant, long-term development. It is affiliated with the Aga Khan Development Network. A history of initiatives to assist people affected by natural and man-made disasters in South and Central Asia and Africa was the impetus for the Ismaili Muslim community to establish FOCUS. FOCUS also responds to ongoing natural hazards that cause particular damage and destruction in remote mountain communities, including seasonal events such as spring flash flooding or winter avalanches in northern Afghanistan, Tajikistan, or the Northern Areas of Pakistan.

The Cooperative for Assistance and Relief Everywhere (CARE; formerly the Cooperative for American Remittances to Europe) is a major international provider of emergency relief and long-term development support. It is non-sectarian and non-governmental. Founded in 1945, its work has expanded from emergency support to longer term development. In 2016, CARE worked in eighty-seven countries. It serves as an important advocate for human rights and for policy change in areas such as gender relations and food aid. CARE has invested significant effort into shifting focus from a US agency to an international confederation composed of fourteen CARE national members, each registered as an autonomous NGO.

Caritas Internationalis is a confederation of 165 Catholic relief, development, and social service organizations operating in more than 200 countries and territories worldwide. Catholic social teaching and Vatican moral leadership are significant features. The earliest Caritas organization dates to 1897, but the system expanded rapidly after World War II. Caritas Internationalis serves as an umbrella organization that coordinates and supports member activities. It provides a platform for interaction between the Vatican and member organizations, but individual Caritas members (e.g., Catholic Relief Services, Catholic

Agency For Overseas Development, and Misereor) implement activities in their areas of interest and influence.

Catholic Relief Services (CRS), the international humanitarian agency of the US Catholic community, was founded in 1943 (thus during World War II). It reaches approximately 130 million people in more than ninety countries and territories. CRS provides relief in emergency situations. Since the 1994 Rwanda genocide, CRS has focused on peacebuilding, working to understand and address conflicts at their roots. Assistance is based solely on need, not race, creed, or nationality. CRS has approximately 5,000 employees and is governed by a board of directors consisting of clergy (most of them bishops) and laypeople.

Concern Worldwide, Ireland's largest aid and humanitarian agency, employs 3,200 staff in twenty-five countries throughout the world. Like other organizations with an initial humanitarian focus and ethos, it now engages in long-term development work, in addition to emergency relief. Concern's core work focuses on health, hunger, and humanitarian response in emergencies. It highlights efforts to work in partnership with small community groups as well as governments and large global organizations such as WFP.

Church World Service (CWS) was also born in the wake of World War II, as seventeen protestant denominations came together to reinforce partnerships and make their collective work more effective. CWS has worked on both international emergency response and development, with a focus on working in partnership with other NGOs and with local groups. A measure of success is the formation of various independent organizations, such as the Christian Commission for Development in Bangladesh and CEPAD in Nicaragua. CWS was one of the founding members of a global partnership of faith-based humanitarian agencies, ACT Alliance, which has members in 140 countries and 130 member organizations,

Islamic Relief Worldwide was founded in the United Kingdom in 1984 in response to the drought and security crisis in the Horn of Africa. Today, it is an international humanitarian organization with both emergency relief and development programs in many world regions. It plays a special role as a leading Muslim organization; a large majority of contemporary humanitarian actions are in Muslim majority communities.

The Jesuit Refugee Service (JRS) is an international Catholic organization founded in 1980 (inspired by the Vietnam boat people crisis). Its central mission is to aid refugees, forcibly displaced peoples, and asylum seekers. It operates at national and regional levels. JRS has programs in fifty-one countries, working on education, emergency assistance, health and nutrition, and income-generating activities. More than 1,400 people contribute to the work of JRS, the majority on a voluntary basis, including approximately 78 Jesuit priests, brothers, and scholastics; 66 religious figures from other congregations; and more than 1,000 laypeople. JRS is also involved in advocacy and human rights work.

Lutheran World Relief (LWR), also founded in the post-World War II period (1945), began with a mission to collect and send aid to people in Europe. Today, it is an international NGO focused on both disaster relief and recovery and development more broadly. LWR is a member of the ACT Alliance, the global alliance of churches and related agencies working on development.

Mercy Corps was founded in 1979 as Save the Refugees Fund, renamed in 1982 as Mercy Corps. Its original purpose was to respond to the plight of Cambodian refugees. Today, it is a global humanitarian aid agency focused on environments that have experienced some sort of shock—natural disaster, economic collapse, or conflict—but also long-term hunger and poverty. Revenues for 2016 were reported as $329 million.

Oxfam is an international confederation of charitable organizations that focuses on global poverty, including humanitarian action. Originally established by a group of Quakers, social activists, and academics, it was known in 1942 as the Oxford Committee for Famine Relief, and it advocated with the UK government for famine relief in occupied Greece. Today, it is known for its effective advocacy and for its operations. Since 2000, Oxfam has focused on a rights-based approach as the framework for its work, viewing poverty and powerlessness as avoidable, amenable to human action and political will. The right to a sustainable livelihood and the capacity to participate in societies and make positive changes to people's lives are, Oxfam argues, basic human needs and rights that can be met.

Samaritan's Purse has the explicit objective of supporting people in physical need as part of its evangelical Christian missionary work. The organization operates in more than 100 countries, with a predominantly humanitarian focus.

The Save the Children Fund, commonly known as Save the Children, is an international NGO that focuses on children's rights and provides relief and support to children. Established in the United Kingdom in 1919 with a focus on education, health care, and economic opportunities, it also provides emergency aid in natural disasters, war, and other conflicts. In addition to the UK organization, there are twenty-nine other national Save the Children organizations that are members of Save the Children International, which serves as a global network.

Tzu Chi, the world's largest Buddhist humanitarian organization, is based in Taiwan. Tzu Chi is a faith-based, non-profit, non-governmental humanitarian organization with four major missions: charity, medical care, education, and humanistic culture. "Tzu Chi" in Chinese translates to "compassion and relief" in English. Established in 1966 by the Venerable Dharma Master Cheng Yen, it began with thirty housewives asking people to save two cents from their grocery money each day to help the poor. Tzu Chi is now an organization with 10 million members in more than fifty countries, providing international relief in seventy countries. It is dedicated to relieving all suffering, regardless of nationality, religion, ethnicity, or socioeconomic status.

World Relief was founded in 1944 as the humanitarian arm of the US National Association of Evangelicals. It is supported by churches, foundations, and individual donors, as well as through US government grants from the US Agency for International Development and other agencies. It serves more than 4 million people per year and has more than 100,000 volunteers actively engaged. World Relief's core programs focus on microfinance, AIDS prevention and care, maternal and child health, child development, agricultural training, disaster response, refugee resettlement, and immigrant services. It is a leader in advocating for immigration reform.

World Vision International was founded in 1951 as an evangelical Christian humanitarian aid, development, and advocacy organization. Its religious mission has evolved throughout the years away from deliberate evangelizing. Initially focused on meeting the emergency needs of missionaries and sponsoring children, its mandate and size have expanded so that today it is one of the largest international NGOs, active in more than ninety countries. Total reported 2014 income was $2.8 billion, of which public funding was $394 million. World Vision's government donors include the United Kingdom, the European Union, the United

States, Canada, Australia, and Germany. It also works closely with UN agencies including WFP, UNHCR, and UNICEF.

The Sovereign Order of Malta, one of the oldest institutions of Western and Christian civilization, plays active roles in various humanitarian crises. A lay religious order of the Catholic Church since 1113, it has diplomatic relations with more than 100 states and the European Union, and it has permanent observer status at the UN. It is neutral, impartial, and apolitical. Active in 120 countries, it is especially involved in helping people living in the midst of armed conflicts and natural disasters by providing medical assistance, caring for refugees, and distributing medicines and basic equipment for survival. Its 13,500 members are supported by 80,000 volunteers, with another 25,000 doctors, nurses, and paramedics. The Order manages hospitals, health centers, outpatient units, institutes for the elderly and disabled, terminal patient and palliative care centers, and volunteer corps. Malteser International, the Order of Malta's special relief agency, is on the front line in natural disasters and in alleviating the consequences of armed conflicts. The Order of Malta's Italian Rescue Corps participates in the first-aid operations for boats filled with migrants in the Strait of Sicily, alongside the Italian units.

Médecins sans frontières (MSF) or Doctors Without Borders was founded in France in 1971 by a small group of French doctors and journalists in response to the Biafran War. It is best known for its projects in war-torn regions and in poor countries facing endemic diseases (although it was also centrally involved in the 2014 West African Ebola crisis). In 2015, more than 30,000, mostly local, doctors, nurses, and other medical professionals, logistical experts, water and sanitation engineers, and administrators provided medical aid in more than seventy countries. Private donors provide approximately 90% of MSF's funding, and corporate donations provide the rest, giving MSF an annual budget of approximately $750 million. MSF's ethical code and operating principles are set out in its charter, the Chantilly Principles, and the later La Mancha Agreement. MSF is willing to take on political issues (thus at times challenging the humanitarian principle of neutrality)—for example, in Chechnya, Kosovo, and Rwanda. MSF remains fiercely independent of any political, religious, or economic powers. It is worth noting that it withdrew from participation in the WHS, asserting that the summit was unlikely to achieve significant results.

Local Actors

The major actors, including both formal and informal groups and organizations, in humanitarian response are locally based and almost always act as the "first responders." Many do not have a humanitarian vocation but are mobilized and adapt during a crisis: Churches, mosques, and temples are examples, as are a wide range of community organizations. In some instances (e.g., the Bangladesh Rural Advancement Committee), organizations are comparable in size and capacity to any of the large international players, but in others formal capacities are quite limited. In many situations, disaster preparedness overall is weak, as is the capacity of local entities to manage demanding programs and large financial flows. International actors depend on local organizations for knowledge and access. Their vital role was a source of both inspiration and tension at the WHS—inspiration because their courageous and effective work was acknowledged and lauded, and tension because of concerns and an overall perception that only a small part of the available humanitarian funds are in fact reaching local organizations and that they have little effective say in how the funds are used.

Diaspora communities commonly mobilize support during humanitarian crises; remittances are a major source of funding during crises. These efforts tend to be fragmented and ad hoc, and detailed mapping of flows is limited.

New Actors

The established humanitarian community, centered in the UN and major international NGOs, often tends to exclude a set of important organizations and countries that have potential to contribute. Prominent among this group are the governments and foundations in the Gulf states and China, India, and Brazil (among other emerging powers). The WHS engaged many of these actors, but the disconnects continue to present significant challenges.

Private Sector

Likewise, large transnational companies (as well as smaller and local enterprises) are active in various humanitarian situations, both as suppliers of services and also in every phase of humanitarian response from disaster preparedness to relief follow-up (e.g., through corporate social responsibility programs). Humanitarian actors look especially to private sector actors for innovations in terms of both use of technology (e.g., practical use of geographic information system (GIS) mapping and communications support) and innovative approaches to organization and management. The current focus on cash-based assistance engages banking networks and financial intermediaries, and there is considerable interest in social entrepreneurship and training programs focused on youth in fragile state situations.

Aid Workers

ALNAP, a network of agencies working in the humanitarian system, estimates that there are more than 200,000 people working as full-time aid workers. Approximately 50% work for international NGOs, 25% for the Red Cross/Red Crescent movement, and 25% for UN agencies. Humanitarian work has emerged as a distinct professional category, with university degree programs and a series of informal associations that focus on advocacy to direct attention to humanitarian needs and to important issues such as protection of humanitarian workers (ALNAP 2015).

FINANCIAL AND ORGANIZATIONAL CHALLENGES

The financial and organizational challenges associated with humanitarian aid are many, but three stand out: the amounts available (only a fraction of needs are financed and

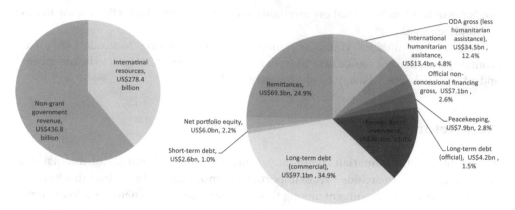

FIGURE 43.3 Resource mix in the twenty countries receiving the most international humanitarian assistance, 2014.

Source: "Global Humanitarian Assistance Report 2016," Global Humanitarian Assistance.

mobilization of funds is complex and often uncertain), the coordination of their use (a common and continuing challenge), and partnership arrangements (with a current focus on expanding direct support to local organizations and on making the links between humanitarian and crisis response, development work, peacebuilding, and environmental protection more meaningful) (Figure 43.3). Total funds going to humanitarian aid are difficult to calculate; most funds are in reality locally raised and managed, supplemented by remittances. Considerable aid goes outside official channels. The humanitarian financing gap and specific issues, including predictability and longer terms of funding (especially for protracted crises), financial controls, crisis financing for middle-income countries in which concessional funds are not readily available, and direct financing to local groups were a major focus of the WHS and the UN September summits (WHS 2016).

Development Initiatives' "Global Humanitarian Assistance Report 2016" estimates that total humanitarian assistance for 2015 was the highest ever at $28 billion, with governments (approximately 126) providing $21.8 million and private donors $6.2 million. The total for the UN coordinated appeals, however, showed a 45% shortfall.[4] Official global humanitarian aid tracked by the Organisation for Economic Co-operation and Development's Development Assistance Committee is estimated at approximately 10% of overall official aid flows.

OCHA has a broad responsibility for mobilization and tracking of funds, for consolidated appeals, and for management of pooled funds designed to allow faster response to humanitarian needs. Humanitarian response plans (HRPs) are designed to ensure coordination of humanitarian action, whereas the tracking of funding facilitates transparency in how humanitarian funding is provided. OCHA works with member states and select private actors to mobilize funds for the pooled funds. Humanitarian programming cycles (HPCs) involve coordinated series of actions to prepare for, manage, and deliver humanitarian response. The HPC process in each country is supposed to be owned and managed by humanitarian actors on the ground. The planning cycle for protracted crises begins with a coordinated needs assessment and analysis, the outcome of which is a humanitarian needs overview. On

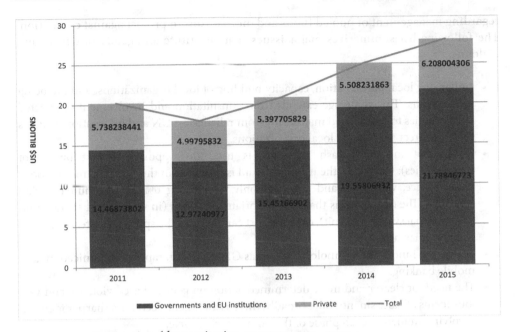

FIGURE 43.4 International humanitarian response, 2011–2015.

Source : "Global Humanitarian Assistance Report 2016," Global Humanitarian Assistance.

this basis, a country team formulates a response analysis with targets and boundaries, sets strategic objectives, and develops cluster plans aimed at meeting those objectives. These strategic country objectives and cluster plans form the HRP, which is the primary planning tool for the humanitarian coordinator and the humanitarian country team. Funding information is recorded in the Financial Tracking Service database, which is managed by OCHA and available to the public.

Two essential elements of the process, which have developed in recent years, are humanitarian needs assessments and a sharpened focus on disaster preparedness and building resilience. These are linked to the systems of international appeals but also to the goal of reducing humanitarian needs by preparing better for disasters, increasing efficiency, and ending conflicts.

Pooled funds are used in emergency situations and, increasingly, in the period that follows to fund reconstruction and development following a conflict or natural disaster. Such funds can help narrow the transitional gap between humanitarian situations and long-term development in many affected countries (Figure 43.4).

DEBATES, ISSUES, AND AGENDAS FOR ACTION

This chapter highlights the active discussions and contestation around humanitarian work and organizations. These extend from fundamental issues about approach, accountability, and ethical responsibilities to practical issues on the ground—for example, regarding management of pooled funds and mechanisms to protect against corruption. The following list summarizes major issues that constitute an agenda of debate and dialogue:

- Enhancing local participation, capacity building of local organizations, and financing mechanisms: This challenge extends from consultation and involvement of affected communities to a proposed major shift from reliance on UN and international NGOs to more direct reliance on local organizations.
- The extent to which cash financing is used (as opposed to distribution of commodities): Currently, the majority of aid is provided in the form of in-kind goods or assistance, with cash and vouchers only comprising 6% of total humanitarian spending. The consensus is that in appropriate situations (in which markets function and financial systems permit), cash support can increase the speed and effectiveness of humanitarian assistance.
- Scaling up innovative technologies, such as GIS mapping, rapid communication, and mobile banking.
- The need for clearer and more determined action on gender-based violence and various forms of harassment: More broadly, there is an urgent need for a sharper focus on involving women in each phase of the humanitarian cycle.
- Debates about the application of the humanitarian principle of neutrality, especially in complex conflict situations.
- Protection of aid workers who are increasingly the targets of violence.
- Involvement of "new actors," including emerging economies and private companies.
- Approaches to protracted crises and to practical implications of linking humanitarian, development, peacebuilding, and environmental strategies, planning, and implementation.
- Addressing the shadow of terrorism and violent extremism, including specific restrictions on financing organizations that may have links to terrorist groups; restrictions can dampen public support and limit activities especially of Muslim aid organizations.
- The overall challenge of shortfalls in meeting financing targets and thus inadequate support for critical humanitarian needs.

WHERE TO GO FROM HERE?

The "broken versus broke" debates that revolve around the humanitarian system pose the continuing question of whether, as some suggest, the existing system has reached its limits. Current organizational arrangements have evolved largely in response to successive crises and a host of local and geopolitical factors. The "system" and individual organizations face numerous challenges. Organizations work together in complex partnership arrangements that, at their best, involve meaningful collaboration and complementarity but also often are undermined by competition with other providers of humanitarian assistance, including affected communities, diaspora groups, religious organizations, national actors, militaries, and the private sector. Both the extensive discussions regarding the SDG framework and the WHS and New York UN summits during 2016 have generated extensive analysis and options for reforms. They are reflected in the 2018 discussions of international compacts on migrants and refugees. The next steps will need to focus on implementation of worthy commitments to reform and to support for a strengthened system positioned to respond to what will certainly be greater humanitarian challenges in the future.

References

Active Learning Network for Accountability and Performance. 2015. *The State of the Humanitarian System*. London: ODI.

Agenda for Humanity. 2016. "Platform for Action, Commitments and Transformation." http://www.agendaforhumanity.org.

Barnett, M. 2011. *Empire of Humanity: A History of Humanitarianism*. Ithaca, NY: Cornell University Press.

Barnett, M., and T. G. Weiss. 2008. "Humanitarianism: A Brief History of the Present." In *Humanitarianism in Question: Politics, Power, Ethics*, edited by M. Barnett and T. G. Weiss, 1–48. Ithaca, NY: Cornell University Press.

Gourevich, P. 2010. "The Moral Hazards of Humanitarian Aid: What Is to Be done?" *New Yorker*, November 3.

International Committee of the Red Cross. 2010. "Treaties and Customary Law." October 29. https://www.icrc.org/en/document/treaties-and-customary-law.

Office for the Coordination of Humanitarian Affairs. 2012. "What Are Humanitarian Principles." June. https://docs.unocha.org/sites/dms/Documents/OOM-humanitarianprinciples_eng_June12.pdf.

Polman, Linda. 2010. *The Crisis Caravan: What's Wrong with Humanitarian Aid?* New York: Picador.

Rieff, David. 2015. *The Reproach of Hunger: Food, Justice, and Money in the Twenty-First Century*. New York: Simon & Schuster.

Sphere Project. 2000. *Humanitarian Charter and Minimum Standards in Humanitarian Response*. Oxford, UK: Oxfam.

United Nations Refugee Agency. 2016. *Global Trends: Forced Displacement in 2015*. http://www.unhcr.org/en-us/statistics/unhcrstats/576408cd7/unhcr-global-trends-2015.html.

World Humanitarian Summit. 2016. "High-Level Panel on Humanitarian Financing Report to the Secretary-General: Too Important to Fail—Addressing the Humanitarian Financing Gap. January. http://reliefweb.int/report/world/high-level-panel-humanitarian-financing-report-secretary-general-too-important-fail.

Notes

1. United Nations Office on Genocide Prevention and the Responsibility to Protect, "Background Information on the Responsibility to Protect," http://www.un.org/en/preventgenocide/rwanda/about/bgresponsibility.shtml.
2. Sustainable Development Solutions Network, "Humanitarian–Development Linkages," http://unsdsn.org/what-we-do/thematic-networks/humanitarian-development-linkages.

3. Sustainable Development Solutions Network, "Humanitarian–Development Linkages," http://unsdsn.org/what-we-do/thematic-networks/humanitarian-development-linkages/
4. Development Initiatives, "Global Humanitarian Assistance Report 2016," http://devinit. org/post/global-humanitarian-assistance-report-2016/#.

FURTHER READING

Ager, Alistair, and Ager, Joey. 2001. "Faith and the Discourse of Secular Humanitarianism." *Journal of Refugee Studies* 24 (3) 456–472:

Barnett, M., and T. G. Weiss. 2011. *Humanitarianism Contested: Where Angels Fear to Tread.* New York: Routledge.

Davey, Eleanor (with John Borton and Matthew Foley). 2013. "A History of the Humanitarian System: Western Origins and Foundations." HPG Working Paper, June. https://www.odi. org/sites/odi.org.uk/files/odi-assets/publications-opinion-files/8439.pdf

Ferris, E. G. 2011. *The Politics of Protection: The Limits of Humanitarian Action.* Washington, DC: Brookings Institution Press.

Hollenbach, D. 2010. *Driven from Home: Protecting the Rights of Forced Migrants.* Washington, DC: Georgetown University Press.

Ignatieff, Michael. 1999. "Human Rights: The Midlife Crisis." *New York Review of Books,* May 20. http://www.nybooks.com/articles/1999/05/20/human-rights-the-midlife-crisis.

Joint Learning Initiative. 2016. "Evidence Brief 1: Engaging Faith Communities to Meet the Needs of People Living in Conflict." http://jliflc.com/wp-content/uploads/2016/05/WHS_JLIFLC_Evidence-Brief_1-ONLINE.pdf.

Juul Petersen, M. 2011. *For Humanity or for the Umma? Ideologies of Aid in Four Transnational Muslim NGOs.* Copenhagen: University of Copenhagen.

Kellett, Jan, and Katie Peters. 2013. Dare to Prepare: Taking Risk Seriously. ODI Research Reports and Studies, December. https://www.odi.org/publications/ 7955-dare-prepare-taking-risk-seriously.

Martin, S. 2014. *International Migration: Evolving Trends from the Early Twentieth Century to the Present.* Cambridge, UK: Cambridge University Press.

Martin, S., S. Weerasinghe, and A. Taylor, eds. 2014. *Humanitarian Crises and Migration: Causes, Consequences and Responses.* New York: Routledge.

Office for the Coordination of Humanitarian Affairs. 2016. "Global Humanitarian Overview 2016." http://www.unocha.org/2016appeal/mid-year/#p=1.

Shaw, D. 2001. *The UN World Food Programme and the Development of Food Aid.* New York: Palgrave Macmillan.

Slim, Hugo. 2015. *Humanitarian Ethics: A Guide to the Morality of Aid in War and Disaster.* New York: Oxford University Press.

Stambach, P. 2015. *The Origins of Global Humanitarianism: Religion, Empires, and Advocacy.* Cambridge, UK: Cambridge University Press.

Weiss, Thomas. 2017. "Humanitarian Action." In *The Oxford Handbook of International Organizations,* edited by Jacob Katz Cogan, Ian Hurd, and Ian Johnstone, 303–322. Oxford, UK: Oxford University Press.

CHAPTER 44

....

GLOBAL LAW

....

RICHARD FALK

As even the strongest federalist states demonstrate, there is a need for overarching legal authority to address common challenges of national scope that cannot be adequately dealt with either through regulatory measures among the component federal states or through cooperative arrangements negotiated by their respective governments. Economic and financial integration, as well as national security, necessitate over time sufficiently strong central governance mechanisms at the level of sovereign states to create and implement common standards and uphold shared values, invigorate national identity, and sustain trust. The specific character of the underlying centralizing political arrangements can be flexible and varied as long as they are effective. In modern times, there are assessments of legitimacy based on the character of the governance arrangement in relation to fundamental human rights, especially the prevention of genocide or the incapacity to govern sovereign territory in ways that uphold transnational security of foreign states.

Turning to international society makes us aware immediately of a basic structural difference. It is a decentralized political system with a minimal capacity to articulate *global* or *human* interests, and it exhibits even less when it comes to implementation. The United Nations (UN), despite its various contributions to relations among sovereign states, is not only lacking in independent and robust capabilities but also its authority is shaped by the interaction of governments representing states whose fundamental vector of influence is premised on the priority of *national* interests. This ingrained decentralization, and subsystem dominance, is further shaped by what might be called "geopolitical exceptionalism"—that is, the role of dominant states to operate without being subject to even weak and irregular procedures of accountability with respect to international law. This feature of international political life has been given a constitutional foundation within the UN System, taking the form of the veto power vested in the five permanent members of the UN Security Council. It is true that the Permanent-5 were given this status in 1945, and this no longer reflects the geopolitical landscape; however, for purposes of understanding the principled weakness of law in the global domain, the idea of exempting certain states helps explain why it is so difficult, while being so necessary, in the context of the twenty-first century to establish a regime of global law that effectively shapes global norms in the human or global interest and is vested with the capabilities to implement and enforce as necessary these norms of all national subsystems.

International society for most of its history has managed to rely on the decentralized regulatory capabilities of territorial sovereign states. This has meant in practice a dependence on norms, procedures, and institutions of national governance, with relevant extraterritorial and interactive concerns dealt with by formal agreement or through consistent patterns of practice, referred to as traditional or customary law. This state-centric legal order was controversially supplemented by the role of dominant states that did use force to manage certain shared interests (e.g., freedom of navigation) or to impose their political will on weaker states (e.g., the protection of foreign investment and nationals living abroad). That is, sovereign states were treated as equal juridical entities but were unequal geopolitically. As a result, there was a tension between the formal legal order based on sovereign equality and the living law of practice and expectations reflecting geopolitical inequality.

Dominant states often succumbed to war in the course of rivalries associated with the pursuit of wealth, influence, and territory. The history of international relations is essentially the narration of major wars and their effects on the distribution of power, authority, and wealth among states. Wars were often devastating for the combatant states and their societies, but warfare did not undermine the stability of the overall system.

In the middle of the twentieth century, this system of law began to break down normatively and substantively for several reasons, three of which seem most significant. First and foremost, the advent of nuclear weapons, and their use in the last stage of World War II, created a challenge of global scope that could not be safely accommodated through reliance on international law.[1] National interests were too diverse, and the stakes too high, if agreements did not work out. It became widely believed that a global approach was needed to uphold the system of sovereign states as a whole, as well as to reliably protect states, strong and weak alike. In other words, nuclear weapons made the outbreak of war among dominant states an unacceptable threat to the stability of the whole that had never been the case in the pre-nuclear world.

The obvious way of managing such a challenge would be a phased and verified process of disarmament that proceeded within a treaty framework of verification and enforcement applicable to every state. As discussed later, this rational and seemingly sensible solution proved to be non-negotiable because several governments of sovereign states believed that their own security and international status depended on the retention of nuclear weapons. These beliefs additionally rationalized the retention and development of the weaponry by adopting a skeptical attitude toward the trustworthiness of any disarming process, fearing the temptations and consequences of cheating (Barnet 1960; Falk 2012; Lifton and Falk 1982; Nye 1986). In effect, entrenched geopolitical interests not only distorted the perception of national interests by dominant states but also subjected the collective destiny of humanity to intolerable risks. There are also innovations in the tactics and weaponry of warfare, especially the use of drones in the setting of transnational mega-terrorism, that radically undermine the traditional approach of international law to the regulation of warfare, but at least in current patterns of usage their impact is to *weaken* but not render it obsolete (Falk 2016).

The second major challenge was directed at the Western domination of state-centric world order, and it assumed historical potency through the anti-colonial movement that arose also in the aftermath of World War II. The further weakening of European colonial powers by this second epic intra-European struggle empowered the peoples of the Global South to rely on various modes of struggle to overcome their subjugation, invoking the emergent legal norm of the right of self-determination and world public opinion. This legal norm would on its own have not produced change, but it was effectively implemented by the political norms associated with nationalism that mobilized people to seek sovereign control over their own territory, governance structures, and resources. The collapse of European colonialism was undoubtedly the most important political transformation of the past 100 years. It did not have the secondary effects of either removing geopolitics from world order or even eliminating the role of Western hegemony, but it altered its characteristic modes of operation in fundamental respects (Bricmont 2006; Kinzer 2003).

Among these respects was the spread of ideas of sovereign rights from the West to the entire world, creating a formal global reality that, as supplemented by technological innovations that facilitated interaction among states, required frameworks of law to enable mutually beneficial interaction. It also gave rise to evasive geopolitical tactics associated with covert operations and humanitarian intervention to uphold Western interests (Bricmont 2006).

The third essentially ecological challenge emerged in two stages. First was a concern in the 1970s about the carrying capacity of the Earth with respect to relevant expansionist trends associated with population, resources, pollution or waste, and the war system (Commoner 1971; Falk 1972; Meadows et al. 1972). It was widely believed that industrial civilization was exceeding the limits of sustainability, but because each country was centered on achieving prosperity based on maximum economic growth, it seemed impossible to plan for the future on the basis of the human interest as distinct from various aggregations of national interest in circumstances of radical inequality with respect to standard of living, resource endowments, population pressures, and industrialization. George H. W. Bush, then the US president, articulated a refusal to address this seeming ecological crisis when he taunted the 1992 Earth Summit in Brazil with the message, "The American way of life is non-negotiable." It turned out that alarmist views of the ecological challenge, although still seemingly accurate over a longer time horizon, were premature, and worries were calmed by some steps toward environmental protection and population control and also by technological developments that revealed the agricultural and energy resources of the planet were far more abundant than had been believed and that global ecosystems were more resilient than feared.

Yet this ecological challenge returned at the start of the twenty-first century in the threatening form of global warming as harmful in many respects to human well-being and the source of systematic worries about the future sustainability of civilizational progress as a result of climate change. As with the earlier manifestation of ecological concerns, there is a furious ongoing debate about the severity of the challenge and what to do about it (Griffin 2015; Hansen 2009; Klein 2014). Unlike the earlier surfacing of ecological worries, this second phase is backed by a strong scientific consensus that has been widely accepted by international public opinion and the overwhelming majority of governments in the world. Yet the capacity to create a globally constituted approach backed by law and responsive to the scientific consensus has so far failed to materialize. What has been agreed upon, although impressive considering the persistence of political decentralization and the inequalities of exposure to global warming and of the ability to mitigate or adapt to its harmful effects, has not come close to meeting standards supported by the recommendations of the scientific community or of imposing enforceable obligations to perform as agreed.

In other words, the absence of a developed system of *global* law is particularly evident in relation to the climate change agenda, especially by its trade-offs between the short-term ambitions of sovereign states associated with economic growth and development and the intermediate- and long-term realization that unchecked global warming will soon cross thresholds of irreversibility, causing catastrophic harm throughout the planet (Griffin 2015; Hamilton 2010; Hansen 2009).

For these reasons, it seems vital to conclude that the world is confronted by a deepening crisis associated with elemental survival and well-being needs due to the absence of *effective and equitable* norms, procedures, and institutions dedicated to upholding the *human interest*—that is, a regime of global law.

The current legal regime remains strongly weighted toward the features of a state-centric world order that has over the course of several centuries evolved to meet many challenges and developed a sophisticated international law regime, although incapable of effectively replacing the war system of dispute settlement and change with peaceful modes of governance. This anarchical regime is able to deal with a range of challenges to national interests and to promote the benefits of international cooperation, but it is not capable of meeting primary challenges of global scope of the sort described previously (McDougal & Associates, 1960; Bull 1977; Suganami and Carr 2017). World order as currently constituted can often deal successfully with secondary challenges of global scope that do not impinge seriously on the relative wealth or geopolitical priorities of dominant states. Among many examples, treaties on the governance of Antarctica or the demilitarization of the moon are protective of the human interest, enabled by enlightened patterns of global leadership (Brzezinski 1997; Kupchan 2012).

Conceptual Perspectives

Global law refers to laws, procedures, and regimes of global scope, applicable to the world as a whole, including the territorial domains governed by sovereign states and the global commons (oceans, atmosphere, outer space, and cyberspace) and oriented around the protection and promotion of human or global interests. It is useful to understand global law as in some ways a complement to and in other ways a sequel to *international* law that developed during the modern period, and as an essential component of the contemporary pedagogic approaches being developed under the rubric of global studies. International law evolved and adapted over the course of recent centuries to become an integral element of the modern system of sovereign states, which initially emerged in Western Europe. Scholars generally regard the state system as originating with the Peace of Westphalia in 1648 but incorporating changes in values, interests, and material changes as world history unfolded, being essentially challenged by and responsive to technological innovation that periodically transformed warfare and the dynamics of interaction. This system was preoccupied with providing order, norms, and procedures to facilitate *horizontal* cooperation among sovereign states in Western Europe, and later North America, and as necessary, regulate international conflict. Beginning in the eighteenth century, this Westphalian framework extended its geographical reach to other areas of the world mainly by way of empire and unequal economic relationships, a *vertical* order that rested on an ideology of Western civilizational superiority and was institutionalized in the form of European colonialism.

International law had the double function of regulating the behavior of states and providing mechanisms that facilitated and stabilized cooperation among states, including the shared use and regulation of the global commons, with particular attention paid to the oceans. It also legitimized the European colonial and hegemonic structures that imposed order and exploited colonies and non-European peoples in many ways, ranging from the appropriation of precious metals and natural resources to the barbarism of the international slave trade. International law upheld this vertical dimension of world order in numerous ways, including the legal protection of foreign investment, the sanctity of unequal treaties, exemption of Western citizens from national criminal accountability, and reliance on superior military force to maintain these unjust relations. In the western hemisphere, this vertical dimension of world order led to the proclamation of the Monroe Doctrine by the United States initially to protect Latin America from European colonial undertakings and later to give a principled foundation to American hegemony.

Because there were no governmental mechanisms for the enforcement of international law, what made *horizontal* international law effective was its valuable instrumental relationship to the pursuit of national interests by states either in the form of providing mutual benefits to one another or by way of the logic of reciprocity. State X generally respects the sovereign rights of State Y and the diplomatic immunity of its ambassadors because it seeks similar respect from State Y and realizes that overall stability is useful for all, strong and weak. This systemic stability is greatly enhanced by the existence and management of a reliable international legal order that covers not only all routine interactions among states but also their shared common interests in such matters as maritime safety, prevention of piracy, the security and sanctity of diplomatic facilities, and frameworks for sustaining scarce renewable resources and endangered species. Such reliability depends on governments complying with most international legal norms almost all of the time. This logic works on the basis of perceived convenience and longer term shared interests in cooperation and stability, and it is only infrequently twisted by disparities in power, values, and interests when dealing with *normal* intercourse among states.

When security and other vital and urgent interests, especially of globally and regionally dominant states, come into play, the *vertical* dimension of international law produces a tendency toward selective compliance with international law, giving rise to well-justified criticisms of "double standards" and "unenforceability." In these domains, the absence of impartial governmental enforcement capabilities exposes a core weakness of international law and prompts cynical questions regarding whether "international law is really law" and whether it is a legal order that primarily serves the interests of rich and powerful states. Such questions are appropriate with respect to war/peace and national security issue areas, as well as in relation to the implementation of human rights and burdensome economic and environmental regulations that touch on the territorial authority of sovereign states. Overall, it is important to acknowledge these limits to the effectiveness of global and international law while nevertheless appreciating its vital contributions to stability, order, and economic development in the welter of routine transactions that constitute the daily experience of international life. In areas of trade, investment, finance, communications, travel, maritime safety, and diplomacy, international law has been overwhelmingly successful in providing practical guidelines and institutional arrangements for most types of transnational intercourse, so much so that the efficient contributions of international law to making many aspects of international life reasonably secure is taken for granted.

As previously noted, the absence of impartial and reliable modes of *comprehensive* enforcement is a definite weakness of Westphalian international law. Another equal, if not greater, weakness that has become more evident in recent decades is the inability of the modalities of international law to address effectively challenges of *global* scope, especially if related to the security of states or in situations that depend on a common approach in the face of radically diverse perceptions of the relative responsibilities and the great disparities of material circumstances among states. It is in such settings that the absence of a robust framework of global law has become deeply troublesome in addressing such leading challenges of the contemporary world as nuclear weaponry, mega-terrorism, climate change, peacemaking, poverty, migration and refugees, disease, and cybersecurity.

Two separate concerns are intertwined. First is an explanation of the flawed and inadequate efforts of international law, understood as law resting on the consent of governments of sovereign states, to respond to twenty-first century challenges of global scope. Second is an argument as to why a system of global law is urgently needed to safeguard the human future and yet has proved so far impossible to bring into being, having no means to overcome the resistances of a state-centric system of world order. Some of these resistances are due to the strength of national sovereignty as a source of human identity and security, whereas others are associated with geopolitical patterns of management and control.

WESTPHALIAN RESPONSES

It is helpful to understand the present world order dilemma. A series of dangerous global challenges exist in an increasingly serious form and would seem to be effectively addressed only within a global law framework. Although rudiments of such a global framework have emerged in recent decades, the framework as a whole is not sufficiently robust to possess the needed level of problem-solving capabilities or to ensure compliance with agreed standards. As a consequence, states continue to rely on international frameworks that incorporate the interplay of horizontal and vertical interactions among states. These frameworks have been pressed to their outer limits by efforts to meet the minimal demands of global/human interests, but results to date have been nevertheless disappointing and have led to widespread pessimism about the human future.

State-centric world order has been under increasing pressure to address these challenges and has relied on three central problem-solving techniques at its disposal: the establishment of the UN as a political actor oriented around the promotion of *global* and *human* interests rather than *national* interests, the systemic extension of international law by means of lawmaking treaties, and reliance on the benign implementation of *geopolitical* priorities through the managerial energies and capabilities of dominant sovereign states that also fill the vacuum associated with protecting global and human interests. Such responses have contributed partial solutions but seem unsatisfactory because they are insufficient in some instances (climate change) and unfair and inequitable in other instances (nuclear weapons). The next section considers these conclusions in relation to the world order approaches that have been relied on in the absence of a viable global law regime.

A Global Law Approach: Aggressive War and Criminal Accountability

After World War II and the sobering short-term effects of the atomic attacks on Hiroshima and Nagasaki, Japan, there was a strong impulse on the part of the victorious governments, led by the United States, to establish a global law regime. Acting on this impulse by extending the earlier global vision embodied in the League of Nations, learning from this world order experiment launched after World War I, there developed widespread support for the establishment of the UN.

In this regard, the Charter of the United Nations sets forth a global law constitutional framework that purports, especially as set forth in the language of its Preamble, to be serving the common interests of humanity. The UN has managed to obtain virtually universal membership of sovereign states, numbering 194. The primary mission of the UN when it came into existence in 1945 was, in the words of the Preamble, "to save succeeding generations from the scourge of war." In the Charter, Articles 2(4) and 51 treat all uses of international force as unlawful except for self-defense against a prior attack. These global norms were reinforced by war crimes trials against surviving German and Japanese leaders that reached judgments declaring that crimes against the peace (i.e., recourse to aggressive war) were the supreme wrong in international political life (Taylor 1992).

Despite this formalization of a global law regime, the actualities of the Charter, and even more so the practice of states over the life of the UN, exhibited deeply embedded ambiguities, contradictions, and, most important between the vertical dimensions of international law, geopolitical patterns of practice, and the aspirations of global law. The privileging of five dominant states by conferring a rights of veto in the Security Council seemed to make compliance with international law or the views of the UN a matter of discretion for the strong and their allies and an obligation for the weak. In effect, whereas the rule of law presupposes an equality of responsibility for compliance, the rule of *global* law as embodied in the UN actually embraced a principled inequality reflecting political hierarchy. In practice, as well as in theory, those who were the most internationally dangerous disruptive actors were formally freed from the shackles of legal constraint. Beyond this, the apparent effort to hold leaders accountable for aggressive war after World War II was tainted from the outset with contentions of "victors' justice," exempting the winners in the war from any accountability for their behavior (Minear 1971).

The practice of the Permanent-5 states has reinforced the weakness of the global law regime by their recourse to aggressive war without being even called to account within the UN (Arend and Beck 1993; Weisbrud 1997). Prominent examples are the use of force by the United States in Vietnam, Afghanistan, and Iraq; France in Indochina and Algeria; China in Tibet, India, and Vietnam; Russia in Afghanistan and Ukraine; and the United Kingdom in Malaysia and Iraq. The United States has been most forthright in its refusal to defer to UN assessments of the right to use force in relation to its vital interests and also in relying on its veto to uphold contested use of force by its close allies, most controversially Israel. The central point here is that despite the many contributions of the UN to a more humane world order, it has notably failed in creating an effective regime of global law pertaining to war/peace and ecological issues. These failures pertain not only to its main pledge to prevent aggressive war internationally but also to its inability to prevent or stop internal wars causing severe and massive human suffering.

Early in its existence, the UN Security Council attempted to fulfill the global law aspirations of the Charter. This effort was mainly due to America's global leadership, which during that period believed that there was no tension between the prohibition of aggressive war and American national and geopolitical interests. In this spirit, the UN Security Council successfully supported the defense of South Korea in the aftermath of the attack by North Korea in 1950. Such a move was only feasible because at the time the Soviet Union was boycotting the Security Council in protest against the failure to allow the Beijing government to represent China in the UN and thus was not present to veto the relevant Security Council resolution, a tactical mistake it never repeated.

The high water mark of the effort to establish a UN global law regime occurred in 1956 when the United States broke with its allies, the United Kingdom, France, and Israel, effectively insisting that these countries withdraw from Egyptian territories occupied in their earlier military operation. The implementation of global law can only occur when its claims are reinforced by a relevant geopolitical will, which was not present in cases occurring after 1956. Arguably, the same kind of possibility existed in the aftermath of Iraqi aggression against Kuwait, which resulted in the restoration of Kuwaiti sovereign rights and punitive sanctions against Iraq.

Compensating for the Weakness of the Global Law Regime

The argument being made up to this point is that international law has not exhibited suitable capabilities to address adequately the most salient *global* challenges to security, sustainability, and survival that have taken shape during the past half century. The word "adequately" requires clarification. It refers both to functionality and effectiveness but also to ethical standards. For instance, it can be argued that deterrence doctrine is an adequate response to the threat of nuclear warfare, but the fact that deterrence rests on an exterminist threat to kill tens of millions and subject the planet to the catastrophic consequences of what has been called a "nuclear famine," disruption of planetary agriculture by at least a decade, makes deterrence ethically unacceptable even if it has demonstrated a certain level of effectiveness (Lifton and Markusen 1990; Thompson 1982). Norms, procedures, and institutional mechanisms have not been developed within the Westphalian framework of international law to remove reliance on nuclear weapons despite many intergovernmental and grass-roots attempts to do so. Furthermore, post-Westphalian globalizing tendencies have not emerged to overcome this and other failures.

The following sections, taking account of this situation, explore what has been and what could be done to mitigate the harm and reduce the risks associated with the current weakness of the global law regime. Currently, it seems that the world is experiencing a statist backlash against all forms of globalization, which is being fueled by a surge of ultra-nationalist political movements throughout the world. As such, poor prospects exist for overcoming major global challenges by either the rise of what could be called *cosmopolitan nationalism* in dominant states or the strengthening of global law capabilities. Yet the dangers of the unmet global challenges make it crucial to pose questions about what can be done in the most imaginative possible terms. We consider three lines of potentially constructive action as second-order solutions in view of the weaknesses of the global law regime: (1) global leadership and expansive multilateralism, (2) voluntary international law, and (3) geopolitics as contingent global law.

Global Leadership and Expansive Multilateralism

In the absence of a globalized lawmaking framework that articulates and debates the content of a collective response to a global challenge, there is a tendency to rely on the interplay of global leadership and multilateralism to engage in a process that is promoted as problem-solving but is viewed by skeptics as problem-deferral (Gill 2012). Such a dynamic can be regarded as either "soft global law" by analogy to the "soft law" component of international law or an attempt to globalize the capabilities of traditional international law. When global challenges do not involve issues that require controversial distributions of burdens and benefits that involve large material allocations of resources and do not affect non-negotiable security policies, then state-centric approaches can be effective.

The most successful instance of this fusion of global leadership and inclusive intergovernmental diplomacy is undoubtedly the Law of the Seas Treaty adopted in 1982. In the course of a negotiation that took a decade to complete, the US government fulfilled its role as global leader, shaping bargains to enlist differently situated states, setting priorities, and providing incentives and applying pressures to secure agreements in relation to specific issues and consensus with respect to the public order of the oceans to be specified in the treaty as a whole. An example of such compromises and trade-offs, indispensable for the purpose of achieving agreement, was the willingness of maritime states and naval powers to agree to broader sovereign control of coastal waters, extending territorial sovereignty from 3 to 12 nautical miles. A related compromise that encouraged participation by less developed countries was the establishment of an exclusive economic zone that extended for 200 miles from the coast in exchange for preserving navigational rights in these waters for commercial activities and naval operations of developed countries. The geopolitical priority attached to freedom of the seas was also upheld, although it exposed weaker countries to possible intervention and intimidation. In other words, the treaty instrument that emerged contained a combination of complex bargains responsive to various categories of national interests and a geopolitically defined ranking of priorities that included some effort to promote the global and human interests in a public order of the oceans that facilitated trade, investment, communications, transportation, and dispute settlement procedures of mutual benefit without diminishing the maritime hegemony of naval powers (McDougal and Burke 1962).

It could be argued that this geopolitically conditioned multilateral agreement was not consistent with the security interests of weaker countries or with aspirations for a more demilitarized world order more in keeping with the provisions of the UN Charter. These criticisms are difficult to refute, but overall, it seems clear that this was a practical adjustment to the complex demands of generating a sustainable framework for achieving stability and mutual benefits with respect to the unregulated global commons—that is, the oceans falling outside the territorial sovereignty of states. Until the degree of interaction and intensity of usage created the need for a regulatory and dispute settlement framework, it was satisfactory to allow all states to use the oceans without restraint, relying on naval powers to address shared concerns and reflect shifting values such as in relation to international piracy, slave trade, and smuggling as they arise.

When we turn to nuclear weapons or climate change, we recognize the shortcomings of global leadership and the constraints that limit even the most expansive forms of multilateralism. In each of these instances, it has proved so far impossible to uphold global interests. In relation to nuclear weapons, the nuclear weapons states have associated their security with the retention of these weapons. Unlike the law of the sea or the prohibition of chlorofluorocarbons damaging to the ozone layer, in the context of nuclear weaponry there is no satisfactory compromise, and the elimination of the weaponry by means of a phased process is the only sustainable solution. For some years, the two dominant nuclear weapons states, the United States and the Soviet Union, gave lip service to negotiating an agreement seeking the phased elimination of the weaponry. Yet the requisite political will needed to reach this outcome was lacking. What has taken the place of disarmament is the non-proliferation agreement, discussed later, which tries to combine geopolitical priorities with an imposed regime of stability. Arguably, it has worked to an extent because no nuclear weapon has been used, but it has failed from the perspective of the ethical exclusion of exterminist weaponry, in relation to the horizontal dimension of world order based on juridical equality, and most of all it is a precarious approach to the avoidance of nuclear war (Schell, 1982, 1998).

Voluntary International Law

Filling the gap created by the absence of institutional capabilities able to protect global and human interests has been facing further difficulties in recent years due to the decline in global leadership, the rise in nativist and chauvinist forms of nationalism, and time pressure associated with climate change as an urgent global challenge that will grow more severe with the passage of time. This weakening of Westphalian potentialities is more concretely associated with problematic developments affecting the main global leader, the United States, epitomized by a nationalist Congress that opposes almost all international legal commitments, including those serving the national interest. In the climate change context, after the failure of the United States to adhere to the 1997 Kyoto Protocol, there has been a concerted effort to frame agreements as pledges rather than as obligations, producing a new phenomenon in state-centric world order, namely "voluntary international law."

Voluntary international law means that there is no formal obligation to comply with the terms of a negotiated agreement, and there are no adverse legal consequences in the event of noncompliance. In some respects, voluntary international law resembles "soft" forms of international law, such as the Declaration on the Right to Development or the Covenant on Economic, Social, and Cultural Rights, in which the obligatory character of the right is affirmed but there is no expectation of enforcement except by grass-roots initiatives of civil society actors such as Amnesty International and Human Rights Watch.

However, these actors focus on civil and political rights, the prohibition on torture, implicitly acknowledging the unenforceability of economic, social, and cultural norms viewed as soft. This distinction between hard and soft law also reflects the vertical dimension of world order, with hard enjoying the backing of geopolitical actors and soft reflecting the hopes and aspirations of the Global South.

Voluntary international law is responsive to a distinct set of circumstances associated with filling the gap arising from the absence of a functionally adequate regime of global law. Its most prominent instances are the 2009 Copenhagen Accord and the 2015 Paris climate agreement. The Paris agreement, in particular, was hailed as a great success because it manifested an acceptance of the imperative goal of keeping global warming below the 2°C ceiling established by the least constraining scientific estimate of what can be tolerated without disaster. Furthermore, there seemed to be an acknowledgment of the reality, indeed the urgency, of the climate change challenge, the necessity of acting expeditiously to limit adaptation and mitigation costs, and the importance of obtaining universal participation of states throughout the world—in some respects, gestures toward global law goals but without making any claim to rely on the obligatory force that is normally expected to follow from the enactment of "law."

At the same time, there were several notable shortcomings, without even touching upon the issues associated with climate justice. First, with deference especially to the expectation that the US Senate would not ratify an agreement if expressed in the form of a treaty, compliance and the definition of pledged reductions of carbon emissions were left to the good faith of the actors. Second, global leadership by the United States was weakened, adopting the restricted form of Barack Obama's presidential enthusiasm, and thus vulnerable to nullification during the presidency of Donald Trump, who has previously referred to climate change as "a hoax." It seems reasonable to believe that the Paris climate agreement could not have happened if Trump had been the US president in 2015, and without the United States there is no prospect of an agreement achieving needed restrictions on emissions or wide enough participation. Without the participation of the United States, the Kyoto Protocol was virtually a dead letter, involving the adherence of states representing less than 12% of global emissions. This situation is accentuated by the absence of alternative global leadership at the present time. Chinese participation is crucial, and China may be able to block agreements it opposes, but its global role up to this point has depended on acting in concert with the United States, as it did in reaching a bilateral agreement on levels of emissions reduction.

Putting aside these structural and procedural issues, it is evident that the expectations of pledged reductions in emissions are highly unlikely to be sufficient to keep global warming below the 2°C level that itself may be too high for prudent management of life on Earth. In other words, the outer limit of negotiability via expanded multilateralism falls substantively short of what must be prudently done to minimize future harm and catastrophic risks. Beyond this, the high levels of carbon emissions from military sources are not regulated at all by the Paris agreement, nor are greenhouse gases other than carbon, which will, if not sufficiently regulated, also cause higher Earth temperatures.

The main conclusion reached is that voluntary international law is a stopgap approach at best and not capable of filling the gap created by the weakness of the global law regime with regard to climate change and other major challenges of global scope.

Geopolitics as Global Law

In some respects, the emergence of the United States as global leader arguably maintained a geopolitical regime of global scope that has performed as a partial guardian of global and human interests. Michael Mandelbaum has elaborately championed this US role as an ideological desirable way to overcome the political fragmentation associated with state-centric world order, and he insists that American leadership is providing international society with a rudimentary form of world government (Mandelbaum 2005; Kupchan 2012). The normative claims on behalf of this role seem less convincing than the problem-deferring contributions. Three domains in which the United States has acted as a global state promoting global policy goals in circumstances in which traditional reliance on multilateralism and international law could not address minimal expectation illustrate Mandelbaum's argument. The failures of international law in these areas were a result of the clash between the horizontal and vertical dimensions of the Westphalian framework and also the primacy of the vertical as expressed via the priorities of the global state—that is, the geopolitically dominant political actor. Illustrative of this pattern are (1) the nuclear non-proliferation treaty and implementing regime, (2) humanitarian intervention, and (3) individual international criminal accountability.

Two general observations seem relevant. First, there are incentives to hide this geopolitical primacy by seeking action via coalition or on the basis of a UN imprimatur. The NATO War of 1999 with respect to Kosovo and the Iraq War of 2003 are both instances in which the iron fist of geopolitics could not be hidden, whereas the first Gulf War of 1991 or the Libyan Intervention of 2011 are examples of UN blue washing for what was in essence geopolitically oriented undertakings of the United States or coercive undertakings carried out with the approval of the US government. Second, although global law goals may be proclaimed as justifications, the implementation of the policies of the global state are often contested from the perspective of international law and international ethics, thereby manifesting the pervasive presence of double standards.

The 1968 Nuclear Non-Proliferation Treaty (NPT) is a classic example of multilateral lawmaking strongly favored by the dominant states. It incorporated what appeared to be a bargain between the nuclear weapons states and the non-nuclear weapons states. The core bargain was that members of the latter much larger group would give up their nuclear weapons option in exchange for promised access to the benefits of so-called peaceful uses of nuclear energy and a commitment by nuclear weapons states to negotiate in good faith a nuclear disarmament agreement as an urgent priority. The non-nuclear states were also given a treaty right of withdrawal after notification in deference to supreme national interests. In effect, the NPT seemed like a sensible stopgap measure that halted the spread of the weaponry while the nuclear weapons states negotiated a prudent and reliable disarmament treaty.

In practice, this formal treaty picture is misleading, and the NPT has been converted from its stopgap pretensions into a quasi-permanent structure of nuclear governance, accentuating the vertical dimension of world order in the domain of war and peace. First, the global leadership role of the United States has been to abandon in practice the disarmament commitment and subtly substitute a managerial approach to risk and cost reduction in the form of "arms control." Beyond this, implementation of the NPT has been taken over by the global state with respect to the selective enforcement of the treaty's provisions giving up rights to acquire the weaponry despite the absence of any mechanism of enforcement in the treaty. The discriminatory pattern of enforcement and tolerance can be viewed by comparing the approach taken toward Iraq and Iran with that taken toward Israel. For the former countries, the geopolitical priority produced aggressive war and its threat, whereas with Israel acquisition of the weaponry was accepted and actually facilitated (Hersh 1991).[2] The argument supportive of this approach is that global interests are best protected if proliferation is prevented in relation to "rogue states," whereas proliferation is tolerated if it occurs in relation to states integral to the grand strategy of the West.

This is a regime of geopolitics, not law. It also indirectly rejects the globally preferred approach of a global law solution. This hierarchical control of nuclear weaponry is currently being challenged by the demand from non-nuclear states that nuclear disarmament be achieved.

Humanitarian intervention has been given a special prominence in the postcolonial era in circumstances in which Western hegemony needs to accommodate respect for the sovereignty of non-Western states. In this regard, moral objectives are substituted for colonial ambitions, with human rights being invoked as a principal justification (Bricmont 2006; Chomsky 1999). There have also been strong discrediting arguments mounted to the effect that humanitarian intervention tends to magnify rather than overcome abuses of human rights and the suffering of the target society (Falk 2015; Menon 2016). The geopolitical nature of the doctrine of humanitarian intervention is confirmed by its irrelevance for any response by way of military force with respect to human rights violations in Western countries, especially the United States, and by its functional inapplicability to larger countries in which one-sided war based on military superiority is not an option.

International criminal accountability discloses a pattern of partial implementation that is similar to claims made under the doctrine of humanitarian intervention. It would certainly be an aspect of a true global law regime that political leaders of states would be held individually accountable for crimes against the peace and crimes against humanity, but as applied geopolitically, procedures of accountability have practical relevance only for the leadership of states that lose wars with the West or are governing subordinate states in sub-Saharan Africa. The withdrawal of several African states from the International Criminal Court (ICC) demonstrates both their vulnerability to this kind of global authority and their self-righteous repudiation of discriminatory enforcement policies. Contrast the African reaction to that of the United States that has entered into as many as 100 bilateral international agreements not to surrender prospective defendants to the ICC, which is backed up by congressional legislation authorizing the use of force to rescue any Americans subjected to the authority of the ICC situated in The Hague.

MEGA-TERRORISM AND DRONE WARFARE

International law allocates legal authority primarily by reference to sovereign states, and this territorial characteristic is especially true of efforts to regulate warfare and violent international conflict. To some formal extent, this horizontal approach is supplemented by

UN authority, exercised by way of the Security Council to grant or withhold permission to use international force.

In the post-September 11, 2001, world, it is no longer feasible to treat large-scale transnational terrorism under the rubric of territorial law. The nature of the threat also cannot be reasonably accommodated by reference to the fundamental prohibition on all nondefensive uses of international force that have not been explicitly authorized by the the UN Security Council. There is almost irresistible pressure to engage in preemptive and even preventive uses of force to uphold the security of states in the face of terrorist threats, especially because retaliatory responses to nonterritorial actors are not viewed as having much deterrent effect. As matters currently stand, the inadequacies of international law combined with the weakness of the UN have led to the menace of mega-terrorism being addressed geopolitically—that is, according to the essentially unregulated discretion of regionally and globally dominant states (Falk 2003).

This situation is aggravated by contemporary technology, as well as by the tactics of non-state extremist groups. There are many high-value soft targets in advanced industrial countries exerting pressure on civil and political rights within states subject to attack. In addition, reliance on attack drones and special forces to address perceived terrorist threats overrides deference to territorial sovereignty, and it raises serious issues of proportionality and discrimination with regard to counterterrorist operations. There are issues of state terror raised by drone warfare, which in addition to targeting specific individual victims also has the effect of terrorizing entire communities, perhaps whole countries.

In these cases, the anachronistic character of international law is evident under circumstances in which the entire world becomes a potential battlefield. It should be clear that a global law regime capable of regulating responses to mega-terrorism would be desirable, but it currently seems unattainable due to the primacy of geopolitical in the spheres of security and war/peace. Given these conditions, the most effective source of regulation is prudent self-restraint by geopolitical actors. President Barack Obama tried to give reassurances along these lines in a widely discussed presentation to the National Defense University (Obama 2013).

Humane Refugee and Migration Policy

Currently, refugee and migrant flows are disrupting the politics of many countries, encouraging anti-immigration and nativist forms of nationalism, as well as causing intense suffering among those who leave their place of residence due to a sense of desperation caused by war-torn conditions, dead-end impoverishment, and environmental collapse induced by global warming. Although international law and international morality counsel humane responses, the regulatory ambitions of international law are very modest, and policy responses are left to the discretion of sovereign states. As recent experience shows, those countries that are more empathetic to these refugee and migrant flows find themselves under increasing internal pressures to build walls, deport those without proper documentation, and take various steps to close borders and impose harsh measures internally. The international law regime that exists is incapable of overcoming such chauvinism, and there is almost no prospect of an effective global regime emerging.

In such circumstances, there is a great dependence on humanitarian initiatives stemming from civil society, which through the relief efforts of NGOs have reduced suffering in a variety of settings. Such an approach is essentially outside the domain of law, although it might be given some indirect grounding in voluntary international law by way of government funding and support.

Recognizing the global scope of these challenges, and the difficulties of overcoming the discretion of territorial states at the receiving end, suggests the self-interested alternative of establishing a global framework that seeks to address the problems that generate migration at their source. This involves major assistance efforts by richer countries to deal with material conditions in poor and environmentally stressed countries, as well as increased recognition of incentives to resolve internal war situations as rapidly as possible. The conflict in Syria that has persisted for six years exemplifies the linkages between violent conflict and civilian desperation generating massive migration and displacement, as well as showcasing geopolitical paralysis within the UN.

The Current Impossibility of Robust Global Law

The previous discussion highlights some of the policy concerns associated with the ineffectiveness of international law approaches and the unavailability of a sufficiently robust global law regime. The severity of these concerns seems to validate referring to this situation as posing a "crisis of global law."

It should not be concluded that international law and state-centric world order are completely outmoded in relation to the contemporary global policy agenda. It would seem, for instance, that state sovereignty is quite capable of building territorial firewalls against cyberhacking but probably not against the potential ravages of cyberwarfare. Because there exists great unevenness with respect to technological capabilities and vulnerabilities, it would be difficult to establish an effective regime of prohibition, and there is likely to be, as with other security-related challenges, a reliance on geopolitical management, with the hope that agreement emerges on informal rules of engagement and prudent patterns of practice. The Russian hacking controversy associated with the 2016 presidential election in the United States is illustrative of the challenge, as well as its vagueness and susceptibility to manipulation by intelligence services and so-called "deep states" following their own agendas.

The macro-trends in world affairs disclose a confusing interplay between centrifugal and centripetal forces. This has produced various types of globalization and several forms of nonterritoriality that generate developments that even the strongest states cannot control. It has also led to resurgent territoriality, seeking to close off sovereign states from unwanted political violence, drugs, migration, hacking, pollution, outsourcing, and ideas. In effect, these issues are being addressed by a combination of geopolitics and territorial sovereignty, but the results are disappointing and dangerous from perspectives of problem-solving and with respect to humane standards of behavior. Overcoming these disappointments and lowering risks could result from the construction of a robust global law regime imbued with a culture of human rights, but under current conditions this is not a feasible political project for reasons outlined previously.

NOTES

1. It should be observed that the terminology of "world war" applied to either the war of 1914–1918 or that of 1939–1945 is suggestive of the geopolitical appropriation of language. These wars were mainly fought to determine and shape political hierarchy in Europe, especially the containment of Germany, and not at all concerned with "the world." Yet given the dominance of the West throughout the world, even the non-West adopted this universalizing language to describe regional struggle centered on the containment of German ambitions.

2. Although Israel was not a party to the NPT, the geopolitical regime does exempt a country such as Iraq, Iran, or North Korea. It treats as irrelevant the right of withdrawal from the treaty.

REFERENCES

Arend, Anthony C., and R. J. Beck. 1993. *International Law and the Use of Force: Beyond the UN Charter Paradigm*. New York: Routledge.

Barnet, Richard J. 1960. *Who Wants Disarmament?* Boston: Beacon.

Bricmont, Jean. 2006. *Humanitarian Imperialism: Using Human Rights to Sell War*. New York: Monthly Review Press.

Brzezinski, Zbigniew. 1997. *Grand Chessboard: American Primacy and Its Geostrategic Implications*. New York: Basic Books.

Bull, Hedley. 1977. *The Anarchical Society: A Study of Order in World Politics*. New York: Columbia University Press.

Chomsky, Noam. 1999. *New Military Humanism: Lessons from Kosovo*. Monroe, ME: Common Courage Press.

Commoner, Barry. 1971. *The Closing Circle: Nature, Man and Technology*. New York: Knopf.

Falk, Richard. 1972. *This Endangered Planet: Prospects and Proposals for Human Survival*. New York: Random House.

Falk, Richard. 2003. *The Great Terror War*. Northampton, MA: Olive Branch.

Falk, Richard. 2012. *The Path to Zero: Dialogues on Nuclear Dangers*. Boulder, CO: Paradigm.

Falk, Richard. 2015. *Humanitarian Intervention and Legitimacy Wars: Seeking Peace in the 21st Century*. London: Routledge.

Falk, Richard. 2016. "Drones are More Dangerous than Nuclear Weapons." Chapter 3 in *Power Shift: On the New Global Order*. London: Zed.

Gill, Stephen, ed. 2012. *Global Crises and the Crisis of Global Leadership*. Cambridge, UK: Cambridge University Press.

Griffin, David Ray. 2015. *Unprecedented: Can Civilization Survive the CO_2 Crisis?* Atlanta: Clarity Press.

Hamilton, Clive. 2010. *Requiem for a Species: Why We Resist the Truth About Climate Change*. London: Earthscan.

Hansen, James. 2009. *Storms of My Grandchildren: The Truth About the Coming Climate Change Catastrophe and Our Last Chance to Save Humanity*. New York: Bloomsbury.

Hersh, Seymour M. 1991. *The Samson Option: Israel's Nuclear Arsenal and American Foreign Policy*. New York: Random House.

Kinzer, Stephen. 2003. *All the Shah's Men: An American Coup and the Roots of Middle East Terror*. Hoboken, NJ: Wiley.

Klein, Naomi. 2014. *This Changes Everything: Capitalism vs. the Climate*. New York: Simon & Schuster.

Kupchan, Charles. 2012. *No One's World: The West, the Rising Rest, and the Coming Global Turn*. New York: Oxford University Press.

Lifton, Robert Jay, and Richard Falk. 1982. *Indefensible Weapons: The Political and Psychological Case Against Nuclearism*. New York: Basic Books.

Lifton, Robert Jay, and Erik Markusen. 1990. *Genocidal Mentality: Nazi Holocaust and Nuclear Threat*. New York: Basic Books.

Mandelbaum, Michael. 2005. *The Case for Goliath: How America Acts as the World's Government for the 21st Century*. New York: Public Books.

McDougal, Myres S., and Associates. 1960. *Studies in World Public Order*. New Haven, CT: Yale University Press.

McDougal, Myres S., and William T. Burke. 1962. *Public Order of the Oceans*. New Haven, CT: Yale University Press.

Meadows, Donella; Club of Rome's Project on the Predicament of Mankind. 1972. *Limits to Growth: Report for the Club of Rome Project on the Predicament of Mankind*. New York: Universe Books.

Menon, Rajan. 2016. *The Conceit of Humanitarian Intervention*. New York: Oxford University Press.

Minear, Richard H. 1971. *Victors' Justice: The Tokyo War Crimes Trial*. Princeton, NJ: Princeton University Press.

Nye, Joseph S. 1986. *Nuclear Ethics*. New York: Free Press.

Obama, Barack. 2013. "Remarks by the President at the National Defense University." May 23. https://obamawhitehouse.archives.gov/the-press-office/2013/05/23/remarks-president-national-defense-university.

Schell, Jonathan. 1982. *The Fate of the Earth*. New York: Knopf.

Schell, Jonathan. 1998. *Gift of Time: The Case for Abolishing Nuclear Weapons Now*. New York: Holt.

Suganami, Hidemi, and Madeline Carr, eds. 2017. *The Anarchical Society at 40: Contemporary Challenges and Prospects*. Oxford, UK: Oxford University Press.

Taylor, Telford. 1992. *Anatomy of the Nuremberg Trials: A Personal Memoir*. New York: Knopf.

Thompson, E. P. 1982. *Beyond the Cold War: A New Approach to the Arms Race and Nuclear Annihilation*. New York: Pantheon.

Weisbrud, A. Mark. 1997. *Use of Force: Practice of States Since World War II*. State Park, PA: Pennsylvania State University Press.

CHAPTER 45

....

GLOBAL GOVERNANCE

....

HELMUT K. ANHEIER

GLOBAL governance is a challenging concept because it combines two contested and ultimately rather imprecise terms: global and governance.[1] *Global* means more than international, and it suggests some degree of transnational, transcontinental, even transcultural reach as well as relevance. At the same time, it factually implies neither an even presence nor the same relevance across all countries and regions. For example, the internet is a global phenomenon, although its reach is far from equal in terms of content and access, and it is likely less relevant for everyday life in rural India than in urban America.[2] Similarly, global financial and trade systems may well impact many areas of Africa and Latin America, but unlike cities such as London, Amsterdam, or Singapore, they could well be sustainable without them. In addition, although some diseases such as malaria affect more people globally than HIV/AIDS, the latter is recognized more as a global threat while the former is primarily regarded as a regional problem.[3]

We could easily add more examples to show that "global" is a rather imprecise term that seems shaped by varying national and local perspectives. As an adjective, it usually refers to phenomena that have worldwide relevance, transcend national boundaries, and could, at least potentially, affect large portions of humankind, countries, and regions. Concepts with essentially global connotations include peace, security, and human rights; environment; trade; economic and social development; health; and refugees. Not surprisingly, the United Nations (UN) and its various specialized agencies and programs correspond to such global issues and concerns, with the Security Council and peacekeeping operations, the UN Environmental Programme (UNEP), the World Trade Organization (WTO), the United Nations Development Programme (UNDP), the World Health Organization (WHO), and the UN High Commission for Refugees (UNHCR), in that order.

Next, governance is a fairly new concept in both the social sciences and policymaking that nonetheless has gained much currency in recent years. It refers to the process whereby actors assume, receive, and wield power and authority, and they influence and enact policies and decisions concerning some aspect of public life, such as security or economic development. Governance is a broader notion than government and its principal elements of legislature, executive, and judiciary.[4] Enderlein, Wälti, and Zürn (2010) suggest a generic definition of governance to "denote the sum of rules and regulations brought about by actors, processes as well as structures and justified with reference to a public problem" (p. 2). In other words, governance is about how we approach and solve a recognized collective issue or problem

Table 45.1 Governance Orders and Dimensions

Governance Order	Dimension	Basic Questions	Main Tasks
First "Politics"	Public Problem	What?	Definition, framing formulation
	Legitimacy	Who?	Power basis, allocation of rights and responsibilities
Second "Policies"	Institutions and organizations	How?	Setting rules, designing, implementing
	Regulation and control	What if?	Monitoring, sanctioning, incentivizing
Outcome	Performance	So what?	Goal attainment, distributional effects

such as public security, poverty, or pollution. Global governance, then, could be defined as the political decisions, policies, institutions, and organizations in place to solve, manage, and address governance problems of international and potentially global relevance.

In this context, Kooiman and Jentoft (2009) distinguish between first- and second-order governance. The first is about deciding who can legitimately address what public problem for whom and how; the second is about the kinds of institutions, organizations, and regulations needed for achieving desired policy outcomes. First-order governance is essentially about power and politics in the large sense as interplay between the exercise of legitimate power and its support enjoyed by stakeholders—that is, the extent to which a distribution of power and its rights and obligations entailed is seen as legitimate (Table 45.1).

First-order governance is about defining and framing of public problems: Should nation-states be the prime actors managing global climate change, or should some form of global government impose and control pollution levels, deal with rising sea levels, or deal with desertification? Should financial markets be allowed to function largely unregulated and rely on public funds to bail them out in times of crisis? Should there be international redistribution systems to serve global equity? Should there be a right to intervene and protect populations at risk when national governments are either unwilling or unable to do so themselves?

Second-order governance includes two dimensions: First, what rules and regulations are needed, and how are we to enact them, and by or through whom? For example, assuming that the global financial system requires tighter regulation, what institutions, organizations, and regulatory measures would be needed and with what capacities? Then, there are issues about the regulations themselves: How can they be monitored? What kind of checks and balances are needed to ensure that rules are observed? And, if violations occur, how to ensure that sanctions can be applied and redress and remedial action sought?

Managing Interdependence

Governance debates often out of necessity assume a high level of abstraction given the sheer complexity of issues and the diversity of phenomena and actors involved. Yet some of the basic issues and indeed dilemmas can be illustrated by way of a hypothetical example. Imagine the following case: A group of approximately 200 cruise ship passengers are stranded on a small, isolated island without means of communication to the outside world. They vary by age, gender, education, occupation, and wealth. Although most are able-bodied adults, there are a few children and frail-elderly among them. They managed to rescue food and medical supplies estimated to last at least three months, and they succeeded in obtaining some basic tools for constructing shelter from the sinking ship. A source of fresh water has been located, although its reliability is unknown. For some reason, and in the fog of frantic rescue efforts, approximately 100 cases of champagne and 10,000 packs of cigarettes were also uploaded and made it to the island's shore.

While exploring the island, they soon encounter a local population that has lived in small communities for time unknown. Their subsistence economy is well adapted to the natural environment but at low levels of economic and technological development. Their customs discourage contacts with outsiders, rare as they are, and communication between the passengers and locals is difficult because no common language can be found. Mutual distrust easily takes hold: Whereas the passengers feel a sense of dependence and expect some form of assistance, the locals view them as unwelcome intruders likely to deplete resources and bring diseases.

The stranded passenger case leads directly to the heart of what governance is about: How to govern what aspects of the situation, for what, by or through whom, and according to what rules? This is the first-order governance problem. How is the power to make decisions to be distributed in terms of rights and obligations among the passengers and with the locals? Should elections be held among the passengers? Should all adults have equal vote, or should those most knowledgeable and able to function have more influence? Should the locals accept such leadership? Who is in charge of cross-group and even cross-border relations?

Then follow second-order issues: Could the locals claim part of the stranded items, and based on what? Should all receive equal portions of food, or should there be separate regimes? Should food be rationed? Who is to oversee the process of dividing and disbursing rations? How to distribute medicines, and on what basis? Should barter be allowed so that vegetarians can exchange meat for nonmeat products? Should trade be allowed so the ample but capped supply of cigarettes could serve as currency? Should those building shelter for others or those helping the injured be rewarded and enjoy privileges such as the conspicuous consumption of champagne?

There are undoubtedly many answers to each of these questions. The crucial point is that first-order governance decisions constrain options for second-order decisions. Had the stranded passengers decided to have a system of direct democracy in seeking their leadership, they would go about establishing market mechanisms or distribution channels in ways and means different from what would happen had some group of strongmen and women taken over by usurping power. Likewise, cross-border relations would be defined and handled differently.

In terms of global governance, the challenges involved are clearly much more complex, but some of the same basic decisions apply. In the absence of some kind of a world government, the first-order decisions are about what actors can make such decisions, for whom, and on what basis of legitimacy. Especially since World War II, the answer of the international community of sovereign nation-states has been the UN system with the Security

Council and the UN specialized agencies, programs, and so on, as well as the Bretton Woods institutions, among others. These institutions and organizations derive their legitimacy from treaties, with nation-states as signatories, ratified by their respective national authorities such as parliaments.

Yet national and international governments are not the only actors in global governance (Table 45.2). Private actors such as transnational business corporations (TNCs) and civil society or non-governmental organizations (NGOs) are prominent, too. Indeed, as Abbott, Green, and Keohane (2016) note, global governance involves an entire organizational ecology. Although many organizations in the ecology command more resources than international organizations such as the UN, they do not have the same kind of legitimacy to act in the public realm as governments do, and their activities are not directly legitimated by international treaties. In contrast, both TNCs and NGOs remain actors of national rather than international jurisdiction. Although many international treaties and the rules and regulations they entail address them, they are subjects rather than objects. For example, the WTO establishes a regulatory framework for trading and tariff regimes, but the signatories are nation-states, not TNCs. Likewise, UNDP or UNHCR work with many NGOs in delivering services and policy advise, but these are based on contracts, not treaty obligations.

The distinction between types of actors is also found in the study of international relations, especially in diplomacy with regard to the differentiation between hard and soft power. Nye (2008) describes *soft power* as the capacity to get the outcomes intended by attracting others rather than through material incentives. Nye (2004) adds, "Soft power uses a different currency (not force, not money) to engender cooperation—an attraction to shared values and the justness and duty of contributing to the achievement of those values" (p. 7).[5] Although hard and soft power are seen primarily in relation to the state, the notion

Table 45.2 Actors in Global Governance

	Track 1 Actors	Track 2 Actors	
Governance Order	State	Business	Civil Society
First "Politics"	International organizations (United Nations) and regional entities (European Union) National, state, and local governments	Transnational business corporations and international and national business groups and networks seeking to influence politics	International and national civil society organizations and advocacy groups, transnational and national social movements seeking to influence politics
Second "Policies"	International, national, regional, and local agencies, ministries, and departments	Businesses and business associations as well as think tanks involved in international or national development and implementation of policies and programs	Civil society groups involved in international or national development and implementation of policies and programs

of Track I actors (e.g., state and public agencies) versus Track II diplomacy (e.g., NGOs and civic leaders) brings in non-state institutions and organizations.

The final dimension is the outcome achieved by first- and second-order governance arrangements (see Table 45.1). It is about performance and achievement, and also the extent to which the governance system in place has brought about solutions, obtained desired levels of goal attainment and intended redistribution outcomes, and, especially, enjoys the legitimacy among key stakeholders. For example, are we making headway in achieving the sustainable development goals? Is the global financial system functioning? Are labor standards observed in global supply chains? Are intellectual property rights honored in cyberspace? Are pandemics avoided and outbreaks of viral and highly contagious deceases soon brought under control? Are environmental aspects such as pollution or loss of habitat well managed?

In a globalizing world, these questions point to interdependencies among nation-states. Financial markets, global supply chains, and the internet are as much indications of interdependencies as are environmental issues, migration, and issues of health and social policies. Such interdependencies have opened up many opportunities, but they also involve risk. They invite competition as well as cooperation—not only among states but also among business corporations, public agencies, and civil society institutions.

The complex, interdependent world is perfectly illustrated by the financial crisis of 2007–2008, especially the tensions between risk and opportunity and between cooperation and conflict among the main actors (see Table 45.2): Weaknesses in national and international financial regulation created short-term opportunities and long-term risks, brought to extremes in the US housing market (Hallerberg 2013). At the height of the crisis, the solution to swap private for public debt pushed sovereign debt to crisis levels for countries such as Greece, putting pressure on interest rates for government bonds and the Euro. Other countries, such as the United States and the United Kingdom, through a policy of quantitative easing opted for higher inflation and loss of purchasing power. Austerity measures enacted by national governments to reduce public debt and ensure liquidity led to economic contraction, increased unemployment, and political instability. Ultimately, political and financial risks increased, as did opportunities and opportunism. Institutions meant to cooperate found themselves in conflict—for example, the European Central Bank and national central banks and also countries until recently on the best of terms suffered from mutual tensions.

Geopolitical dynamics unleashed by the end of the Cold War, the economic globalization spurt that has gathered new momentum with the rise of emerging market economies, and advances in information and communication technologies all appear to threaten the very foundations of many of the successes they themselves helped bring about throughout recent decades. Although achieving good governance may be difficult during the best of times, it is certainly more difficult under conditions of interdependence. Not only are there more "actors" involved—be they governments, regulatory agencies, corporations, political parties, social movements, and civil society—but also there are more high-risk issues at stake, such as climate change, demographic changes, economic development, financial markets, health care costs, research, or the internet.

Interdependence implies constraints as well as opportunities. What corporations have long practiced is being taken up as a seemingly rational choice by nation-states: cooperation when necessary to address matters of common concern, and competition whenever possible in order to secure access to human and natural resources. There are multiple expressions of this emerging trend toward intensifying competitiveness and rivalry among states, often accompanied by corporations: (1) the growing interest in immigration policy regimes aimed at attracting the world's smartest people, (2) the use and abuse of copyright regimes by some countries and firms alike, (3) the purchase of vast tracks of African land by Arab and Asian countries to secure food supply, and (4) the political debates about the routing of oil and gas pipelines.

The interdependencies of today's world go beyond government and corporations to involve religion, politics, and communities. The Danish cartoon crisis in the mid-2000s is a case in point: The public spheres of two regions—that is, Denmark and then the "West," on the one hand, and Iran and Afghanistan, and later the Islamic world, on the other hand—were brought into contact through migrant communities and cyberspace in a conflict over press freedom and religion, causing riots and leaving many dead. The Arab Spring of 2010–2011 revealed how youth activism in several countries in the region, diaspora communities dispersed throughout Europe, the internet, and the international media succeeded in creating a public sphere on Tahrir Square and enacted deliberative politics that proved capable of regime change, even though it later resulted in failure. Finally, the recruitment strategy of the Independent Islamic State, too, shows how connectedness borne out of interdependence due to migration and economic ties creates fertile grounds for converting disenchanted youth to terrorists.

Clearly, interdependencies involve global goods and bads. That air or water pollution does not stop at national borders remains a largely unsolved problem in most countries. That serious environmental pollution levels or poverty impact other policy fields such as food security, health, and migration over time also seems a rather obvious statement, but such interdependencies or spillovers from one policy field to another remain easier stated than addressed and therefore remain frequently unsolved. The 2015 migration crisis in Northern Africa is a case in point, as is the struggle of the European Union and the nations of the Maghreb and the Sahel to find adequate responses.

GOVERNANCE PERFORMANCE, CAPACITIES, AND READINESS

Global governance is rarely some simple command-type structure in which the exercise of power leads to predictable actions to achieve some desired outcome. It is not about some direct input–output relationship addressing well-defined and contained public problems. This may work in limited circumstances, but it is in no way characteristic of contemporary governance challenges. By contrast, as Tables 45.1 and 45.2 illustrate, global governance is a system with multiple actors or stakeholders, multiple levels, and—across policy fields—frequently contested problem frames and definitions. There are spill-ins and spillouts across levels, actors, and fields—the result of the interdependencies characteristic of a globalizing world. Table 45.3 presents the rather inelegant description of global governance as a multi-actor, multilevel system. The global governance of any policy field has to accommodate spill-in and spill-out effects from adjacent fields, from across different levels, and by different actors.

Table 45.3 Global Governance as a System

Policy Level/Actor or Stakeholders	International and Supranational Organizations	National, Regional, and Local Governments and Governmental Agencies	Business Corporations and Associations of Business Interests	Civil Society Organizations, Think Tanks, and Activists	Social Movements and Internet-Based Forms of Organizing
Transnational, international	Other policy field	Other policy field	Focal policy field	Other policy field	Other policy field
	Spill-ins and spill-outs				Spill-ins and spill-outs
National Regional Local	Focal level	Other policy field		Other policy field	Spill-ins and spill-outs
	Spill-ins and spill-outs				Spill-ins and spill-outs

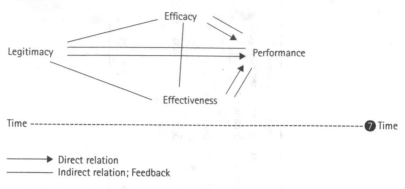

FIGURE 45.1 A Mode of Governance Performance

In summary, global governance is a system of related, nested parts whose interdependence in political, legal, and economic terms implies shared scope of autonomy and responsibility. For some actors, such as governments, this addresses notions of sovereignty; for others, it addresses degrees of independence and hierarchy.

How then are we to understand the performance of such systems in terms of good governance? What first- and second-order arrangement and ways of managing interdependencies bring about the effective, efficient, and reliable set of legitimate institutions and organizations dedicated to dealing with a matter of public concern? For this purpose, this chapter adopts a conceptual model first introduced by Linz and Stepan (1978) to study the performance and stability of political regimes. Whereas they studied regime performance over time, the model, as proposed here, would examine governance systems and distinguish between the following features (Figure 45.1):

> *Legitimacy*, which involves two mutually reinforcing components. First, it requires adherence to the institutional rules and regulations by both the majority of actors and those in position of authority based on first-order allocations of responsibilities, rights, and obligations. Second, it requires trust on the part of those affected to uphold these rules and regulations. For example, we expect the eurozone countries to uphold the Stability Pact and their populations to have confidence in the ability of their governments to do so, just as the legitimacy of the UN depends on its proper discharge of duties and the confidence of member states in the organization.
>
> *Efficacy*, which is the capacity of those in power and leadership positions in relevant organizations and regulatory agencies to find solutions to the public problems identified, both strategically and in the short to medium term. In this sense, we expect the climate treaties and accords to reduce harmful effects of global warming, eurozone governments and central banks to find a solution to the euro crisis, just as the efficacy of the US Congress would rest on finding a proposal for a balanced budget by not raising direct taxes.
>
> *Effectiveness*, which is the capacity of those charged with second-order governance to implement the strategies, policies, and measures formulated, and with the desired results seen as legitimate. For example, even if climate agreements were honored, do they deliver on their promise in efficient and effective ways? Can proposals to reduce

adverse impacts of climate change that most actors regard as efficacious actually be
implemented efficiently to yield effective result?

Performance, which is the "dependent variable" in terms of good governance, defined as
the capacity of the governance system to meet set goals or at least attain a level of performance seen at least satisfactory by key stakeholders to maintain stability over time.
Bad governance, in turn, would be systems that underperform and reveal instabilities.

Thus, the performance of any governance system depends on three crucial aspects and
their interrelationships: legitimacy (Are trusted actors playing by the rules?), efficacy (Do
they know what they are doing?), and effectiveness (Do they achieve results with reasonable
means?). The legitimacy of the global governance system in place becomes a positive and
negative reinforcer that magnifies effects of efficacy and effectiveness. The central role of
legitimacy highlights the precarious role of leadership in governance systems.

Of course, the governance performance model based on Linz and Stepan's (1978) original approach serves as a conceptual framework primarily against which to examine the
role of actors across policy fields and levels (see Figure 45.1). The model incorporates
approaches that distinguish between input legitimacy (modes of political participation by
those affected by certain policies), output legitimacy (problem-solving capacity and impact
of policies), and throughput legitimacy (procedural fairness and accountability). It goes
beyond conventional input–output thinking by emphasizing feedback loops and over-time
performance in achieving results and maintaining stability (Scharpf 1999).

Indeed, any governance system involves trade-offs that can only be solved politically as
first-order decisions, which themselves affect the legitimacy of key actors, their plans, and
performance. To make these trade-offs concrete and to consider their implications for supranational institution-building and cooperation, I present an example to show that at the
global level, "quick fixes" in the form of some "technocratic" solution or another to "solve"
the key problems in global finance are rare—for two reasons.

First, there are no true apolitical technocrats that can perform this function. The
International Monetary Fund, for example, favors the interests of its largest shareholders,
namely the European Union and the United States, and it is not realistic to expect it to propose
policies that somehow maximize economic well-being of others at their detriment. Similarly,
central banks are not politically neutral actors that choose monetary policies that further the
broader economic interest of other countries and regions as their primary concern.

Second, the actors themselves determine which part of a given "trade-off" they prefer—
and any such preferences reveal political preferences and not merely technocratic ones. The
euro crisis of 2011 illustrates this argument and provides a lesson for policymakers regarding
the trade-off between liquidity and moral hazard. To the extent that liquidity support deals
with the main problem of a given member state, the European Central Bank should offer
it. The trade-off, however, is that any such quick and guaranteed support creates a moral
hazard problem: The very knowledge that liquidity support will be provided makes it more
likely that countries will want to access it and that others, as the "insurers," will have to pay.

The relationship between the efficacy and effectiveness of the global governance system
involves four basic capacities:

- Analytical capacities are required to understand how systems are performing, but also
  what kind of future demands and challenges are likely to emerge. Analytical capacity,

therefore, is as much about deciding "whom" to ask as it is about "what" to know. In summary, analytical capacity is about the organization and type of advice that informs governmental policymaking (Lodge and Wegrich 2014: 42–44).

- Most governance action is about coordination: Problem-solving involves the interdependent actions of different, often dispersed actors, and it requires an emphasis on performance-oriented reward systems that focus on results in terms of outputs in particular and that do so across a diverse set of actors that often have divergent agendas (Lodge and Wegrich 2014: 40–41).
- Regulatory capacities are about control and oversight. They entail the presence of regimes that combine standards with an apparatus that detects and enforces compliance. Thus, regulatory capacity is about organizations and strategies that enable the control of particular activities (Lodge and Wegrich 2014).
- Delivery capacity—to "make things happen"—refers to the way in which states execute policy at the street level. In summary, the delivery capacity of "making things happen" relies on a structure that is sufficiently resourced to give life to policy objectives (Lodge and Wegrich 2014: 36–38).

Related to, but distinct from, performance is governance readiness: It is a combination of (1) resilience and preparedness based on the recognition that interdependence requires co-ordination between state and non-state actors and (2) the availability of tools to address policy problems in sustainable ways. Governance readiness is concerned with the creation of conditions in which state and non-state actors achieve active problem-solving—for example, in relation to the achievement of sustainable development goals, global financial market regulation, or the offshore tax treatment of TNCs. Specifically, the notion of governance readiness is about the "fit" between existing governance systems and a set of governance requirements that must be fulfilled in order to address especially the public problems that have arisen alongside globalization. According to Kaul (2013), these include the following:

- Averting the risk of dual—market and state—failure in order to discourage free-riding on the part of various actors in the governance process.
- Correcting fairness deficits to ensure that all parties are genuinely motivated to support, and act on, what was jointly decided. This requires clear rules of participation, which are implemented fairly and transparently.
- Strengthening externality management—that is, addressing spill-ins and spill-outs and recognition of governance actors about the effects that their policy actions and their consumption and production choices have on others.
- Promoting issue focus to ensure that all required inputs fall into place and results orientation.
- Recognizing and promoting synergies among problems and their solutions. This will require strategic leadership that creates and shapes debate.
- Taking account of policy interdependence and promoting positive-sum solutions.

In essence, good governance demands not only performance of a given system to secure legitimacy but also the anticipation of, and reaction to, changing conditions.

As Kaul (2013) demonstrates using her governance readiness framework, most solutions and recent initiatives to address global challenges tend to address the first three governance requirements, especially national-level externality management. Although some do indeed introduce issue focus as an organizational criterion, other requirements for improving the fit between governance systems and global challenges, especially recognition of the global public domain as a new, added policy space and the pursuit of positive-sum strategies, remain wanting. As Kaul summarizes based on her analysis, the global governance system seems to be "gearing up" but hardly ready (p. 52).

INSTITUTIONS, TRANSGRESSIONS, AND VOIDS

Institutions are the backbone on which modern societies in all their complexity and sophistication function.[6] They often go unnoticed; are highly routinized; and mostly enter legislative and public attention when their deficiencies result in systemic interruption, failure, or even collapse. Institutions matter because they act as "the rules of the game," thus establishing stable political, economic, and social interactions within a society (North 1990: 3–6; North, Wallis, and Weingast 2009). They do so by protecting, policing, and enforcing rights and agreements (North 1990: 27) in order to enable cooperation. Because modern societies are highly conflict-prone, they mediate the multiple conflicts that emerge from among diverse segments and interests (Dahrendorf 1961: 223).[7]

However, the way in which economic globalization has progressed in recent decades challenges the institutional capacities to provide and act upon such rules. National governance systems as well as international organizations lack the very institutional capacity needed to legislate, control, and enforce regulations in such transnational spaces (Zürn, Nollkaemper, and Peerenboom 2012). Beck and Lau (2004: 159) point to the underlying pattern of "reflexive modernization," in that more transgression generates more need for decisions. The globalization of finance, for example, would have required a regulatory system of handling more and different kinds of decisions—and not a system of less regulation at the national level. Similarly, migration or cyberspace lack institutional capture to fill such voids created though transgression. Institutional voids result from a systemic under-institutionalization of policy domains—that is, a lack of institutions with a set-up that is adequate to the challenges at hand, be they finance, education, health care, or security.

Following economic institutional theory (North 1990; Williamson 1999) and organizational sociology (Aldrich and Ruef 1999; Perrow 2002; Scott 2014), weaknesses in global governance systems are based on a pattern of double incongruence. Affected fields or domains require a set of institutions, which charge dedicated organizations to regulate and monitor activities. The successful governance of institutions depends on two factors: (1) whether the institutional rules in place—that is, the formal and informal "rules of the game" of an institution—are adequate to the requirements of the policy field that the institution is in charge of regulating and (2) whether the institutional rules are sufficiently implemented by key actors.

Depending on the quality of the institutional rules and of the implementation, one of the four scenarios shown in Table 45.4 may emerge in the context of global governance.

Table 45.4 Requirements, Institutions, and Implementation

Institutions → Implementation	Institutional Framework or Treaties Adequate to Requirements of Field or Policy Domain	Institutional Framework or Treaties Inadequate to Requirements of Field or Policy Domain
Sufficient implementation of institutional rules	Adaptive coping Example: Weapon inspection schemes based on nuclear disarmament treaties	Institutional deficit Example: Cybersecurity policy
Insufficient implementation of institutional rules	Implementation deficit Example: Paris climate change accord	General under-institutionalization/ institutional void Example: Global finance 2010s

Ideal would be a situation of what can be called "adaptive coping." Where institutions provide adequate rules and regulations, and the expectations and specifications set out by the institutional framework are adequately implemented, the interactions are stable and ordered among the actors involved and the system rests in a state of equilibrium. The Paris climate change accord could potentially serve as such a case of adaptive coping, as do weapons inspections programs in non-proliferation regimes such as the Treaty on the Non-Proliferation of Nuclear Weapons.

By contrast, institutional rules can be inadequate for domain-specific requirements, leading to an institutional deficit, or insufficiently implemented by the regulatory organizations in place, bringing about an organizational deficit. When neither adequate institutional rules nor sufficient implementation is in place, there is a severe under-institutionalization that can culminate in institutional voids, where actors are free to engage in self-serving behaviors because rules are either severely limited or unenforced.

Institutions fulfill their requirements by providing formal rules and regulations within a specified polity and policy field (North 1990: Chap. 6). Public agencies have no monopoly in such regulatory frameworks and, depending on the policy field involved, share regulatory tasks with private actors.[8] Important are both the relative presence and the relationship between public and private actors. Fully developed regulations and state agencies may still lead to governance failures when adequate enforcement mechanisms are de facto absent as they would require private actors to comply (Khanna and Palepu 1997; Khanna, Palepu, and Sinha 2005).[9]

Decoupling, on the other hand, creates transgressional spaces in which private operations and interactions have outgrown the regulatory frameworks of individual states, and the shadow of regulation may be too pale. Global rules are lacking, patchy, weak, and contradictory, and governance organizations are either absent or ineffective (Held and McGrew 2007). Such circumstances make institutional voids likely. The global financial crisis is an example of such a general under-institutionalization, caused by the breakdown of "territorial synchrony," where new social spaces outgrow "classical–modernist political institutions" on the state level, thus substantially constraining the latter's effectiveness and legitimacy (Hajer 2003: 182–183). Other examples of such "de-synchronization" between institutions and actors in policy fields are cyberspace, genetic engineering, the "new wars," and failed states.

With formal state structures lacking, the "shadow" of governmental oversight may be sufficient to compel private actors to self-regulate their behavior to avoid stricter regulatory constraints by the state (Héritier and Lehmkuhl 2008). Indeed, in policy fields without immediate threats of government regulation, private actors may choose to impose strict self-regulatory standards and occasionally even press governments to implement and enforce more thorough regulatory systems (Thauer 2010). Voluntary adoptions of greater transparency regimes by TNCs, as pushed by Transparency International and fair trade NGOs, are one example. Voluntary norm and standard setting are another, as illustrated by the International Organization for Standardization (https://www.iso.org), which sets standards for thousands of products and services.

For Börzel et al. (2013), such standards can then be adopted by competitors, leading to a "race to the top." Nationally as well as internationally, business tends to prefer weak regulation over strict regulation, yet under certain conditions it also prefers weak regulation over no regulation. Reputational incentives may lead a firm to self-impose standards that will be marketed, such as the case with "organic" or "fair trade" products. Equally, if the producer of a high-quality product sees its market share threatened by competitors that produce with lower standards, the high-end producer may even pressure for common—usually industry-wide—standards. But for this race to the top to be induced, institutional conditions and incentives must be in place.

The role of international civil society becomes important: It can not only mobilize opinion and bring governments to impose better rules but also play a crucial role in ensuring compliance and implementation by monitoring the behavior of states and economic actors. Civil society is the self-organization of society outside the stricter realms of state power and market interests, and in the words of Gellner (1994), it serves as a countervailing force against the powers of both. The term *civil society* refers to the diverse activities of non-governmental and non-profit organizations, social movements, activists groups, foundations, or think tanks (Anheier, Kaldor, and Glasius 2012). In the present context, civil society can be viewed as a political space where associations, organizations, and movements of many kinds seek deliberately to shape policies, norms, and deeper social structures (Schnabel and Scholte 2002).

Of particular interest is the combination of decoupled, transgressed space with the absence of either public or private actors. In these fields, actors operate without a significant countervailing capacity or at least a potential to act, which leaves the influence of dominating interests on national and international legislation and regulation within a policy domain largely uncontested, and the negatives of institutional voids (e.g., moral hazard, regulatory capture, and profiteering) continue unabated. As a result, institutional voids can widen through contagion effects or deepen by weakening whatever institutions and organization might exist in the field itself.

Institutional void can be accompanied by certain normative weaknesses, even hollowness, as domain actors are alienated from social values and the civic awareness represented by other stakeholders, and increasingly operate under different norms, often rationalized as "logics." For example, in the case of global finance, it is the normative-cultural world of highly specialized professional groups involved—especially corporate lawyers, finance economists, consultants, and accountants. Thus, structural holes (Burt 1995) can emerge in domains in which public and private actors are sealed off from each other. In such cases, neither is able to function as a countervailing force to the behavior of the other nor as a moral corrective and social guide.

What Laumann and Knoke (1987) have shown for the United States applies also to the global level, albeit in an even more challenging context: "Policies are the product of complex interactions among government and non-government organizations, each seeking to influence the collectively binding decisions" (p. 5). Such organizations are "in conflict with one another over the collective allocation of scarce societal resources" and use "power relations within them and inter-organizational networks among them . . . to mobilize political resources that shape public policies beneficial to their organizations" (p. 8). These organizations form issue publics that monitor and react to legislative and regulatory initiatives as well as dynamics within the policy domain, while they simultaneously proactively influence state agencies by mobilizing resources.

Formal regulations are one aspect of governance, and the generation and maintenance of norms and conventions are another (March and Olsen 1989; North 1990: Chap. 5; North et al. 2009). Thus, the institutional–organizational incongruence in global governance represents as much a normative void as it represents a regulatory one. It creates a vacuum where an intersubjective understanding of what is "right" or "appropriate" (and what is not) is lacking, and it invites moral hazard and profiteering.

However, such normative doubtfulness can be mitigated through a guidance of essential institutions (*Basisinstitutionen*) but of socially shared principles (*Basisprinzipien*) (Beck, Bonß, and Lau 2003: 21). In the longer term, institutional under-regulation can cause severe crises for modern liberal–democratic societies as it drastically erodes the legitimacy of the democratic process per se, as also Table 45.5 suggests. It does so because a structural hole (Burt 1995) between a sector or policy field, in this case international finance, and civil society emerges, which deprives the latter to mitigate the normative vacuum.

Table 45.5 exemplifies that where there is congruence between requirements, institutions, and organizations as well as a societal embeddedness of a policy through legitimate processes or social and moral norms, policymakers benefit from a "legitimate dividend" in future actions, while society at large enjoys a comparative adaptive advantage.

Where policies are embedded but there is incongruity, legitimacy is obviously at risk, creating the need for justification, discussion, and revision. This is often the case in large-scale reform projects in the welfare state, be it the labor market or health care reform. The same risk exists in cases in which requirements, institutions, and organizations are in

Table 45.5 Congruency and Incongruity Between Requirements, Institutions, and Organizations: Societal Embeddedness and Transgression

	Congruency Between Requirements, Institutions, and Organizations	Incongruity Between Requirements, Institutions, and Organizations
Societal embeddedness	Legitimacy dividend Example: Environmental policy	Legitimacy risk based on institutional voids Example: Peacekeeping efforts
Transgression	Legitimacy risk based on transgression Example: European Union policy post Maastricht Treaty	Legitimacy depletion Example: Failed states or failed regulatory regimes

congruency but policies are decoupled from the structures, processes, and norms by which a society defines itself. European Union politics are an excellent case in point. Although virtually all European Union states and their respective economies benefit from the Common Market, the euro currency, and free movement across borders, the accompanying policies are often perceived as unwelcome intrusions into domestic affairs, technocratic power grabs, and devoid of a legitimate decision-making process. Finally, where we find both incongruity and decoupling, democracy itself is put at risk—and options for political action are severely limited. As I argue next, the 2009–2011 financial crisis is the most prolific example in this category (Davies 2010).

GLOBAL GOVERNANCE AND INNOVATION

How could global good governance—the effective, efficient, and reliable set of legitimate institutions and organizations dedicated to dealing with a matter of public concern—come about? How could an overall fit between the functioning of governance systems and the governance requirements of policy fields be achieved and maintained? Governance systems are rarely designed from first principles and from some kind of tabula rasa; rather, they evolve from existing systems and through creative tensions between governance requirements, performance, and legitimacy discussed previously (see Figure 45.1).[10]

Assuming that in the foreseeable future, no world government will be able to dictate first- and second-order governance principles and their implementation and operations, and also assuming that no twenty-first-century version of a Bretton Woods conference will likely take place and initiate a new design model for global governance "from scratch," we are left with the improvement of the current system. Innovation research is useful to understand what this could mean for global governance.

There are two perspectives involved, one emphasizing the discontinuous and the other the continuous process of governance innovations—which assumes that governance systems pass through relatively long periods of stability in terms of structure and activity. Governance systems, although aligned with the demands of their policy environments, tend to build up inertia as well as certain "blindness" for small changes especially, thereby reducing their fitness over time. Such stability can be punctuated by seemingly unexpected bursts of fundamental changes, triggered when several key domains are threatened or become critically uncertain, particularly in terms of material resources and legitimacy. In response, some, but not all, institutions and organizations in governance systems seek to adapt by introducing changes in terms of strategy, structure, incentive, and control systems as well as power relations that are more far-reaching than would have been the case without the pressures resulting from the crisis.

Organizational theory (Gersick 1991) suggests that periods of greater uncertainty are also times of greater innovation as organizations break with inertia of embedded routines in order to survive by gaining in performance and, ultimately, legitimacy. Specifically, such periods involve changes in the "deep structure" of institutions and organizations— that is, a set of fundamental, interdependent assumptions and choices about rationales, objectives, and activities. They come about when two types of disruptions occur simultaneously: internal changes such as inertia or bad decisions that create misalignments with the environment; and environmental changes such as new competitors, pronounced free-riding, or spill-ins that threaten the system's overall stability.

It may well be that the current period of crises presents this "rare" combination of external and internal disruptions to the deep structure of existing governance systems. The Westphalian notion of sovereignty—and indeed the very principle that equates sovereignty with the nation-state—as well as the UN system and other international institutions may have come to a point of rapture that requires more fundamental redesign of institutions and corresponding organizations based on some kind of new understanding of assumptions, principles, objectives, and outcomes. If, for example, the current governance of the world's financial system is viewed as seriously deficient *and* essentially broken, what is to take its place?

A second perspective emphasizes the gradual evolution of governance systems. Because governance systems tend to be less complex than the policy fields for which they are designed, they may be unable to manage all demands and contingencies generated. Hence, disruptive changes may be ubiquitous rather than the exception. Organizational theory suggests that two change processes are more or less continuously at work in governance systems: recombination and refunctionality. Together, they shape their evolution, as they improve the efficacy and effectiveness, with positive impacts on performance and legitimacy.

Recombination involves the introduction of new elements into an existing governance system, such as using financial risk management in public sector service delivery (which is the case for the social impact bonds); a shift of competencies from national to supranational jurisdictions (war tribunals lodged with the International Court of Justice rather than victor nations or factions); or, introducing corporate social responsibility programs in mining corporations (as exemplified by the Extractive Industry Transparency Initiative).

Refunctionality is the relocation and expansion into new contexts, policy fields, or jurisdictions. In this case, governance institutions and organization migrate, grow, or are copied and imported. Examples include the adoption of basically US administrative structures into the nascent United Nations or of the French administrative system into the institutions of the European communities in the 1960s; the gradual extension of the European Union from "coal and steel" into a wider range of policy fields at national and regional levels of member states as manifest in the Maastricht, Nice, and Lisbon treaties; the migration of rating agencies to examine an ever broader number of organizations and fields; the introduction of a German system of constitutionally demanded "debt breaks" for public spending in different constituencies throughout Europe and elsewhere; and the use of public budgeting, first pioneered in Brazil, to other countries and budget forms.

Clearly, both perspectives are useful for understanding governance changes, and the processes they imply are rarely mutually exclusive. Punctured equilibriums and more gradual developments can be present at the same time, and indeed the former can create opportunities for the latter: The change in global power relations set in motion after 1989, the rise of the emerging markets, and similar epochal events such as climate change or the internet will take time to sort themselves out, not in the least because they imply serious challenges to conventional notions of national sovereignty. Hence, design innovations and policy reforms are dearly needed.

Inge Kaul (2013) suggests a refunctional innovation: linking a new kind of collective policymaking sovereignty to the established model of collective security (e.g., NATO). In adopting the latter concept, states at that time recognized that if they supported each other in defending any nation against a violation of its territorial integrity, all nations would be more secure. A similar reasoning could apply to national sovereignty if viewed beyond the now limiting notion of non-interference into national affairs or policymaking sovereignty. If nations were to agree that any policy spill-ins, including pressures by non-state actors, constitute a violation of the principle of non-interference and should therefore receive a collective response from all, each nation would be in a stronger position of regaining or retaining its policymaking sovereignty. In other words, if we maintain a world of nation-states, the innovation in terms of refunctionality would be to import the NATO notion of collective security into policy fields characterized by significant spill-ins and spill-outs.

Conclusion: Smart Sovereignty and Global Governance

Adopting a notion of sovereignty implying that states would take the "outside world" of other nations into account in making national policy could also mean that issues more effectively addressed through international cooperation would, by virtue of enlightened national self-interest, move to the level of international cooperation, hence global govern-ance. In addition, nations would have incentives to ensure that such cooperation works. In order to achieve the latter, they would, again in enlightened self-interest, opt for win–win or mutually beneficial bargains so that all concerned parties "crowd in"—rather than do what often happens today, "crowd out."

Some policy domains, such as the environment, are largely outside the full reach of the nation-state, whereas others partially escaped a nation-state frame some time ago—for example, migration and finance (see the previous discussion of transgression). The gov-ernance readiness required for these fields is in stark contrast to the frequently pursued zero-sum strategies or go-alone strategies of many states: pumping money into ever more risky oil exploration; the protection of pipelines for privileged and hence presumably secure gas delivery; expensive new military and political surveillance systems; unilat-eral announcements to switch energy policy, migration rules, or internet regulations; lowering national financial oversight and environmental regulations to lure foreign cap-ital rather than providing level playing fields and sustainable levels; buying up large tracks of land abroad; setting up signposts in the artic regions and on ocean floors; or creating tax havens and privileges for corporations and financiers rather than pushing global eq-uity agendas.

International relations are, in many cases, now composed of three main strands: conven-tional foreign affairs, foreign aid and humanitarian assistance, and provisioning of global public goods. Each of these strands has its own rationale and importance. Each faces its own challenges: Conventional foreign affairs still have to come to terms with a post-Cold War world and the threat of rogue states and terrorism; aid policies are confronting a more self-confident Global South and the emergence of economic powers such as China, India, and Brazil—all developing along their own paths and positioning themselves in the world order; and global public goods policies are generally inhibited by nation-state politics and the underfinanced UN system held hostage to the interests of a few countries.

Global public goods provision continues to suffer not only, as national public goods do, from market failure but also from state failure. Policymakers, civil society, as well as academia have a major responsibility to nudge states into letting go of the conventional notion of sovereignty and their related reluctance to engage in more effective international cooperation. They have to clearly demonstrate that non-cooperation leads to loss of sovereignty and that effective, participatory, and fair international cooperation strengthens national policymaking sovereignty. For example, not designing and enacting policies aimed at governing the world's oceans in effective and sustainable ways will in the longer term lead to a loss of national sovereignty due to inabilities to control the effects of pollution or fish stock depletion. The UN's "2030 Agenda for Sustainable Development" (Berensmann, Berger, and Brandi 2015), while providing targets for member states, remains nonetheless silent on many of the critical institutional and organizations innovations needed for a new global governance that equates sovereignty with responsibility and stewardship—and not with power and protecting the status quo.

Notes

1. This section draws in part on H. Anheier, "Governance: What Are the Issues?" in *The Governance Report 2013*, ed. Hertie School of Governance (Oxford, UK: Oxford University Press, 2013), 11–31.

2. "There remains a major digital divide globally, with 60% of the world offline, the vast majority in Central Africa, Southeast Asia and the Middle East. As a result, a considerable amount of indigenous and traditional knowledge from communities off the grid is not captured in intergovernmental processes" (https://www.una.org.uk/ 6-online-and-ground-connecting-those-most-need-un).

3. There were approximately 36.7 million people living with HIV at the end of 2015. (http:// www.who.int/hiv/en). In 2015, there were approximately 212 million malaria cases and an estimated 429,000 malaria deaths. The sub-Saharan Africa region accounted for 90% of malaria cases and 92% of malaria deaths (http://www.who.int/features/factfiles/malaria/en).

4. The modern term *governance* derives from the world of business. Corporate governance is the system by which firms are directed and controlled by specifying the distribution of rights and responsibilities for boards, managers, shareholders, unions, and other stakeholders, spelling out rules and procedures for making decisions on corporate affairs. In this way, it provides a structure through which business objectives are set, and it also provides means of attaining those objectives and monitoring performance.

    The World Bank (1991) defines governance as the manner in which power is exercised in the management of a country's economic and social resources for development. Note the emphasis on power and management, and the nation-state frame. The corporate governance perspective, in a similar manner, views governance as a way of distributing rights and obligations. The European Union views governance largely as the way in which the European Commission and related institutions function.

    I suggest that neither the power-based nor the rights and obligations approaches, and clearly no longer the nation-state framework alone, are sufficient to capture the complexity and indeed trade-offs involved in modern governance.

5. Note that at a later point in time, Nye transformed the hard–soft power distinction into a trichotomy of soft, hard, and smart power, the latter being the power to effectively

combine hard and soft power and to decide when to use either or both of them (Nye 2008, 2011). This more refined distinction resonates with the notion of smart sovereignty discussed further later.

6. This section draws in part on H. Anheier, "Institutional Voids and the Role of Civil Society: The Case of Global Finance," *Global Policy* 5, no. 1 (2014): 23–35; and on H. Anheier, "Conclusion: How to Rule the Void? Policy Responses to a 'Hollowing Out' of Democracy," *Global Policy* 6 (2015): 127–129, https://doi.org/10.1111/1758-5899.12235.

7. International organizations such as the WTO have dispute settlement mechanisms. Examples at the national level include the institutionalized systems of corporatism in many welfare states (Schmitter 1979) or guaranteed quotas for ethnic minorities in multinational states (Alonso 2011). This insight also applies to institutions designed to "right" past wrongs, such as the institution of Affirmative Action in the United States and the South African Truth Commission.

8. For the United States, Laumann and Knoke (1987) showed that national policy domains are populated by an abundance of private actors that "possess sufficient political clout to ensure that their expressed interests will be taken into account" and significantly influence policy formation by the state (p. 375). Comparatively, Streeck and Schmitter (1985) used the term *private interest government* to stress that regulation involves diverse actors, not state agencies alone.

9. Khanna and Palepu (2000), for example, point to institutional voids of financial markets in emerging economies that are characterized by "a lack of adequate disclosure and weak corporate governance and control. Intermediaries such as financial analysts, mutual funds, investment bankers, venture capitalists and a financial press are either absent or not fully evolved. Securities regulations are generally weak and their enforcement is erratic" (p. 269).

10. H. Anheier and M. Fliegauf, "The Contribution of Innovation Research to Understanding Governance Innovation: A Review," in *Governance Challenges and Innovations: Financial and Fiscal Governance*, ed. H. Anheier (Oxford, UK: Oxford University Press, 2013), 137–169.

References

Abbott, K. W., J. F. Green, and R. O. Keohane. 2016. "Organizational Ecology and Institutional Change in Global Governance." *International Organization* 70 (2): 247–277. https://doi.org/10.1017/S0020818315000338

Aldrich, H. E., and M. Ruef. 1999. *Organizations Evolving*. London: Sage.

Alonso, S. 2011. "Representative Democracy and the Multinational Demos." In *The Future of Representative Democracy*, edited by S. Alonso, J. Keane, and W. Merkel, 169–190. Cambridge, UK: Cambridge University Press.

Anheier, H. 2013. "Governance: What Are the Issues?" In *The Governance Report 2013*, edited by the Hertie School of Governance, 11–31. Oxford, UK: Oxford University Press.

Anheier, H. 2014. "Institutional Voids and the Role of Civil Society: The Case of Global Finance." *Global Policy* 5 (1): 23–35.

Anheier, H. 2015. "Conclusion: How to Rule the Void? Policy Responses to a 'Hollowing Out' of Democracy." *Global Policy* 6: 127–129. https://doi.org/10.1111/1758-5899.12235

Anheier, H., and M. Fliegauf. 2013. "The Contribution of Innovation Research to Understanding Governance Innovation: A Review." In *Governance Challenges and Innovations: Financial and Fiscal Governance*, edited by H. Anheier, 137–169. Oxford, UK: Oxford University Press.

Anheier, H., M. Kaldor, and M. Glasius. 2012. "The Global Civil Society Yearbook: Lessons and Insights 2001–2011." In *Global Civil Society 2012: Ten Years of Critical Reflection*, edited by M. Kaldor, H. L. Moore, and S. Selchow, 2–26. London: Palgrave Macmillan.

Beck, U., W. Bonß, and C. Lau. 2003. "The Theory of Reflexive Modernization: Problematic, Hypotheses and Research Programme." *Theory, Culture & Society* 20 (2): 1–33. https://doi.org/10.1177/0263276403020002001

Beck, U., and C. Lau, eds. 2004. *Entgrenzung und Entscheidung: was ist neu an der Theorie reflexiver Modernisierung?* Frankfurt, Germany: Suhrkamp.

Berensmann, K., A. Berger, and C. Brandi. 2015. "Post 2015: The Need for an Enabling Global Economic Governance Framework." Briefing Paper No. 15/2015. Bonn: Deutsches Institut für Entwicklungspolitik (DIE). http://www.die-gdi.de/uploads/media/BP_15.2015.pdf

Börzel, T., A. Héritier, N. Kranz, and C. Thauer. 2013. "Racing to the Top? Regulatory Competition Among Firms in Areas of Limited Statehood." In *Governance Without a State? Policies and Politics in Areas of Limited Statehood*, edited by T. Risse, 144–170. New York: Columbia University Press.

Burt, R. S. 1995. *Structural Holes: The Social Structure of Competition*. Cambridge, MA: Harvard University Press.

Dahrendorf, R. 1961. *Gesellschaft und Freiheit: Zur soziologischen Analyse der Gegenwart*. Munich, Germany: Piper.

Davies, H. 2010. "Global Financial Regulation After the Credit Crisis: Global Financial Regulation." *Global Policy* i(2): 185–190. https://doi.org/10.1111/j.1758-5899.2010.00025.x

Enderlein, H., S. Wälti, and M. Zürn. 2010. *Handbook on Multi-level Governance*. Cheltenham, UK: Elgar.

Gellner, E. 1994. *Conditions of Liberty: Civil Society and Its Rivals*. London: Hamilton.

Gersick, C. J. G. 1991. "Revolutionary Change Theories: A Multilevel Exploration of the Punctuated Equilibrium Paradigm." *Academy of Management Review* 16 (1): 10–36. https://doi.org/10.5465/AMR.1991.4278988

Hajer, M. 2003. "Policy Without Polity? Policy Analysis and the Institutional Void." *Policy Sciences* 36 (2): 175–195. https://doi.org/10.1023/A:1024834510939

Hallerberg, M. 2013. "Financial and Fiscal Governance: An Introduction." In *Governance Challenges and Innovations*, edited by the Hertie School of Governance, 24–29. Oxford, UK: Oxford University Press.

Held, D., and A. G. McGrew. 2007. *Globalization/Anti-Globalization: Beyond the Great Divide*. 2nd ed. Cambridge, UK: Polity.

Héritier, A., and D. Lehmkuhl. 2008. "The Shadow of Hierarchy and New Modes of Governance." *Journal of Public Policy* 28 (1): 1–17. https://doi.org/10.1017/S0143814X08000755

Kaul, I. 2013. "Meeting Global Challenges: Assessing Governance Readiness." In *The Governance Report 2013*, edited by the Hertie School of Governance, 33–58. Oxford, UK: Oxford University Press.

Khanna, T., and K. G. Palepu. 1997. "Why Focused Strategies May Be Wrong for Emerging Markets." *Harvard Business Review*, July 1. https://hbr.org/1997/07/why-focused-strategies-may-be-wrong-for-emerging-markets. Accessed April 11, 2017.

Khanna, T., and K. G. Palepu. 2000. "The Future of Business Groups in Emerging Markets: Long-Run Evidence from Chile." *The Academy of Management Journal* 43(3): 268–285. http://www.jstor.org/stable/1556395

Khanna, T., K. G. Palepu, and J. Sinha. 2005. "Strategies That Fit Emerging Markets." *Harvard Business Review*, June 1. https://hbr.org/2005/06/strategies-that-fit-emerging-markets. Accessed April 11, 2017.

Kooiman, J., and S. Jentoft. 2009. "Meta-Governance: Values, norms and Principles, and the Making of Hard Choices." *Public Administration* 87: 818–836. doi:10.1111/j.1467-9299.2009.01780.x

Laumann, E. O., and D. Knoke. 1987. *The Organizational State: Social Choice in National Policy Domains*. Madison: University of Wisconsin Press.

Linz, P. J. J., and P. A. Stepan. 1978. *The Breakdown of Democratic Regimes*. Baltimore, MD: Johns Hopkins University Press.

Lodge, M., and K. Wegrich, eds. 2014. *The Problem-Solving Capacity of the Modern State: Governance Challenges and Administrative Capacities*. New York: Oxford University Press.

March, J. G., and J. P. Olsen. 1989. *Rediscovering Institutions: The Organizational Basis of Politics*. New York: Free Press.

North, D. C. 1990. *Institutions, Institutional Change, and Economic Performance*. Cambridge, UK: Cambridge University Press.

North, D. C., J. J. Wallis, and B. R. Weingast. 2009. *Violence and Social Orders: A Conceptual Framework for Interpreting Recorded Human History*. Cambridge, UK: Cambridge University Press.

Nye, J. S. 2004. *Soft Power: The Means to Success in World Politics*. New York: Public Affairs.

Nye, J. S. 2008. "Public Diplomacy and Soft Power." *Annals of the American Academy of Political and Social Science* 616 (1): 94–109. https://doi.org/10.1177/0002716207311699

Nye, J. S. 2011. *The Future of Power*. New York: Public Affairs.

Perrow, C. 2002. *Organizing America Wealth, Power, and the Origins of Corporate Capitalism*. Princeton, NJ: Princeton University Press.

Scharpf, F. 1999. *Governing in Europe: Effective and Democratic?* Oxford, UK: Oxford University Press.

Schmitter, P. C. 1979. "Modes of Interest Intermediation and Models of Societal Change in Western Europe." In *Trends Toward Corporatist Intermediation*, edited by P. C. Schmitter and G. Lehmbruch, 63–94. Beverly Hills, CA: Sage.

Schnabel, A., and J. A. Scholte., eds. 2002. *Civil Society and Global Finance*. London: Routledge.

Scott, W. R. 2014. *Institutions and Organizations: Ideas, Interests, and Identities*. Los Angeles: Sage.

Streeck, W., and P. C. Schmitter, eds. 1985. *Private Interest Government : Beyond Market and State*. Beverly Hills, CA: Sage.

Thauer, C. R. 2010. "Corporate Social Responsibility in the Regulatory Void—Does the Promise Hold? Self-Regulation by Business in South Africa and China." Thesis, European University Institute, Florence, Italy. http://cadmus.eui.eu//handle/1814/14508

Williamson, O. E. 1999. *The Mechanisms of Governance*. Oxford, UK: Oxford University Press.

World Bank. 1991. "Managing Development: The Governance Dimension." SECM91-820, June 26, 1991. Washington, DC: World Bank.

Zürn, M., A. Nollkaemper, and R. Peerenboom, eds. 2012. *Rule of Law Dynamics: In an Era of International and Transnational Governance*. Cambridge, UK: Cambridge University Press.

Index

Tables and figures are indicated by an italic t and f following the page number